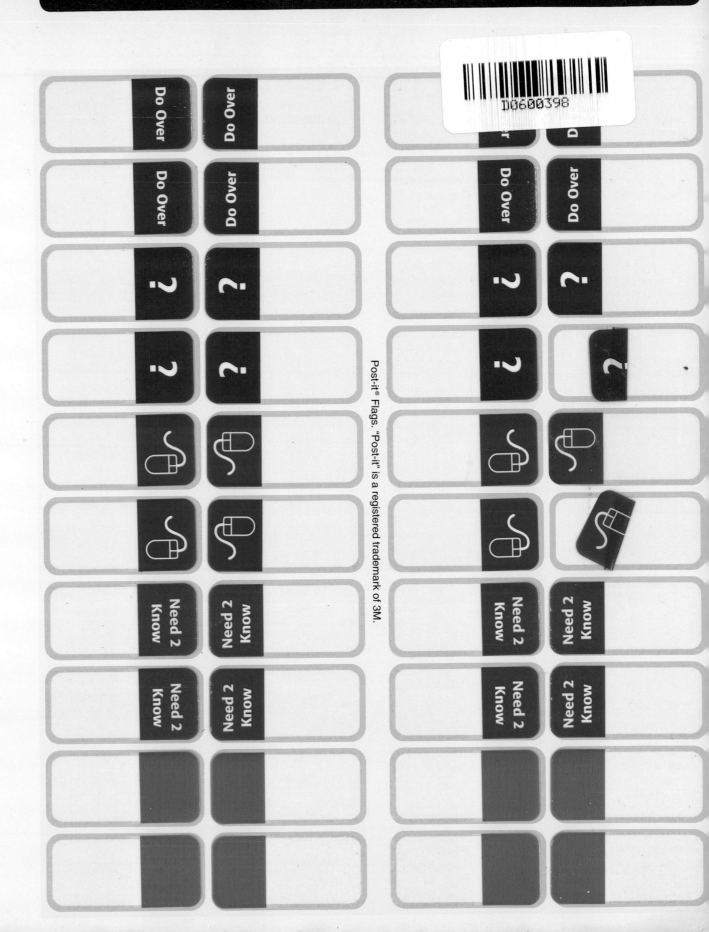

Post-it® Flags. "Post-it" is a registered trademark of 3M.

Do Over
Do Over
Do Over
Do Over
Do Over
Do Over

?
?
?
?
?
?

Need 2 Know
Need 2 Know
Need 2 Know
Need 2 Know
Need 2 Know
Need 2 Know
Need 2 Know
Need 2 Know

Do Over

Do you need to review something? Try again? Work it out on your own after class? Tab it.

?

Got a question for office hours? Do you need to review an example on your own to get a full understanding? Do you need to look something up before moving on? Tab it.

Check out an online source? Complete your online homework? Tab it.

Need 2 Know

Is this going to be on the test? Need to mark a key formula? Do you need to memorize these steps? Tab it.

Do you have your own study system? Do you need to make a note? Do you want to express yourself? Tab it.

Tab it. Do it. Ace it.

ISBN 13: 978-0-495-56095-1
ISBN 10: 0-495-56095-2

		3A (13)	4A (14)	5A (15)	6A (16)	7A (17)	8A (18)
							Helium 2 **He** 4.0026
		Boron 5 **B** 10.811	Carbon 6 **C** 12.011	Nitrogen 7 **N** 14.0067	Oxygen 8 **O** 15.9994	Fluorine 9 **F** 18.9984	Neon 10 **Ne** 20.1797
2B (12)		Aluminum 13 **Al** 26.9815	Silicon 14 **Si** 28.0855	Phosphorus 15 **P** 30.9738	Sulfur 16 **S** 32.066	Chlorine 17 **Cl** 35.4527	Argon 18 **Ar** 39.948
Zinc 30 **Zn** 65.38		Gallium 31 **Ga** 69.723	Germanium 32 **Ge** 72.61	Arsenic 33 **As** 74.9216	Selenium 34 **Se** 78.96	Bromine 35 **Br** 79.904	Krypton 36 **Kr** 83.80
admium 48 **Cd** 12.411		Indium 49 **In** 114.818	Tin 50 **Sn** 118.710	Antimony 51 **Sb** 121.760	Tellurium 52 **Te** 127.60	Iodine 53 **I** 126.9045	Xenon 54 **Xe** 131.29
Mercury 80 **Hg** 200.59		Thallium 81 **Tl** 204.3833	Lead 82 **Pb** 207.2	Bismuth 83 **Bi** 208.9804	Polonium 84 **Po** (208.98)	Astatine 85 **At** (209.99)	Radon 86 **Rn** (222.02)
— 112 — iscovered 1996		— 113 — Discovered 2004	— 114 — Discovered 1999	— 115 — Discovered 2004	— 116 — Discovered 1999		— 118 — Discovered 2002

Terbium 65 **Tb** 58.9254	Dysprosium 66 **Dy** 162.50	Holmium 67 **Ho** 164.9303	Erbium 68 **Er** 167.26	Thulium 69 **Tm** 168.9342	Ytterbium 70 **Yb** 173.054	Lutetium 71 **Lu** 174.9668
erkelium 97 **Bk** 247.07)	Californium 98 **Cf** (251.08)	Einsteinium 99 **Es** (252.08)	Fermium 100 **Fm** (257.10)	Mendelevium 101 **Md** (258.10)	Nobelium 102 **No** (259.10)	Lawrencium 103 **Lr** (262.11)

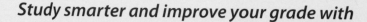

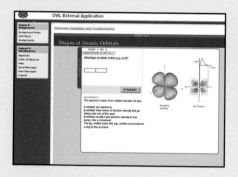 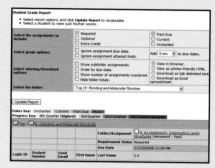 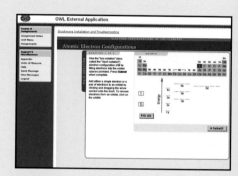

Chemistry & Chemical Reactivity

Enhanced Seventh Edition- Volume One

John C. Kotz | Paul M. Treichel | John R. Townsend

CENGAGE
Learning™

Australia • Brazil • Japan • Korea • Mexico • Singapore • Spain • United Kingdom • United States

CENGAGE
Learning™

Chemistry & Chemical Reactivity:
Enhanced Seventh Edition- Volume One

John C. Kotz | Paul M. Treichel | John R.
Townsend

Executive Editor:
 Maureen Staudt
 Michael Stranz

Senior Project Development Manager:
 Linda de Stefano

Marketing Specialist:
 Sara Mercurio
 Lindsay Shapiro

Production/Manufacturing Manager:
 Donna M. Brown

PreMedia Supervisor:
 Joel Brennecke

Rights & Permissions Specialist:
 Kalina Hintz
 Todd Osborne

Cover Image:
 Getty Images*

For product information and technology assistance, contact us at
Cengage Learning Customer & Sales Support, 1-800-354-9706

For permission to use material from this text or product,
submit all requests online at **cengage.com/permissions**
Further permissions questions can be emailed to
permissionrequest@cengage.com

ISBN-13: 978-1-111-00087-5

ISBN-10: 1-111-00087-5

Cengage Learning
5191 Natorp Boulevard
Mason, Ohio 45040
USA

Cengage Learning is a leading provider of customized learning solutions with office locations around the globe, including Singapore, the United Kingdom, Australia, Mexico, Brazil, and Japan. Locate your local office at:
international.cengage.com/region

Cengage Learning products are represented in Canada by
Nelson Education, Ltd.

For your lifelong learning solutions, visit **www.cengage.com/custom**

Visit our corporate website at **www.cengage.com**

Printed in the United States of America
1 2 3 4 5 6 7 12 11 10 09 08

Contents

The interchapters found in the standard edition are available on this book's companion website at www.cengage.com/chemistry/kotz

This text is available in these student versions:
- Complete text ISBN 978-0-495-38703-9 • Volume 1 (Chapters 1–11) ISBN 978-0-495-38711-4
- Volume 2 (Chapters 11–23) ISBN 978-0-495-38712-1 • Complete Enhanced Edition ISBN 978-0-495-39029-9

Go Chemistry Modules

The new Go Chemistry modules are mini video lectures included in ChemistryNow that are designed for portable use on video iPods, iPhones, MP3 players, and iTunes. Modules are referenced in the text and may include animations, problems, or e-Flashcards for quick review of key concepts. Modules may also be purchased at **www.ichapters.com**.

Preface

The authors of this book have more than 100 years of experience teaching general chemistry and other areas of chemistry at the college level. Although we have been at different institutions during our careers, we share several goals in common. One is to provide a broad overview of the principles of chemistry, the reactivity of the chemical elements and their compounds, and the applications of chemistry. To reach that goal with our students, we have tried to show the close relation between the observations chemists make of chemical and physical changes in the laboratory and in nature and the way these changes are viewed at the atomic and molecular level.

Another of our goals has been to convey a sense of chemistry as a field that not only has a lively history but also one that is currently dynamic, with important new developments occurring every year. Furthermore, we want to provide some insight into the chemical aspects of the world around us. Indeed, a major objective of this book is to provide the tools needed for you to function as a chemically literate citizen. Learning something of the chemical world is just as important as understanding some basic mathematics and biology and as important as having an appreciation for history, music, and literature. For example, you should know what materials are important to our economy, some of the reactions in plants and animals and in our environment, and the role that chemists play in protecting the environment.

These goals and our approach have been translated into *Chemistry & Chemical Reactivity*, a book that has been used by more than 1 million students in its first six editions. We are clearly gratified by this success. But, at the same time, we know that the details of our presentation and organization can always be improved. In addition, there are significant advances in the technology of communicating information, and we want to take advantage of those new approaches. These have been the impetus behind the preparation of this new edition, which incorporates a new organization of material, new ways to describe contemporary uses of chemistry, new technologies, and improved integration with existing technologies.

Enhanced Edition

Why an Enhanced Review Edition?

As authors and publishers we are in constant conversation with instructors and students about their textbooks and courses. To accommodate requests for less costly alternatives to the standard book, we sought a manner in which we could reduce manufacturing costs and pass the savings on to students. Similarly, many users have mentioned a desire for exam preparation materials and study tools in the test itself that better integrate with the book and media. The Enhanced Edition is an attempt to satisfy these requests.

What Is an Enhanced Edition?

The Enhanced Edition of *Chemistry & Chemical Reactivity*, Seventh Edition, is an alternative version that can be used in place of the standard seventh edition. Students and instructors can choose either the standard seventh edition or the Enhanced Edition without loss of continuity between versions. Although we believe the changes for the Enhanced Edition will provide a better learning tool for those who choose it, the new book's alterations are not substantial enough to warrant it being called a new edition because the core chapters and appendices remain unchanged. The standard hardbound seventh edition remains available for purchase and classroom use.

Four new *Let's Review* sections have been added. These cumulative review sections in four of the book parts offer students review aids and questions that bring together material from the several chapters and are similar to those they may see on an exam. The review questions are keyed to text and media material to assist students in preparing for an exam. In order to include these sections, the four supplemental interchapters in the standard seventh edition are available on the book's companion website (**www.cengage.com/chemistry/kotz**) where they are accessible to users of the Enhanced Edition.

What's New in This Edition

1. *New chapter introductions* on topics such as altitude sickness (page 514) and the contribution of ethanol to environmental goals (page 860). Each of these chapter-opening topics has a question or two that is answered in Appendix Q.

2. One or more **Case Studies** are presented in each chapter. These cover practical chemistry and pose questions that can be answered using the concepts of that chapter. Case Studies cover such topics as silver in washing machines (page 148), using isotopes to catch cheaters (page 58), aquarium chemistry (page 992), why garlic stinks (page 541), what is in those French fries (page 96), why Beethoven died at an early age (page 989), and many others.

3. New and completely revised *Interchapters*. John Emsley, a noted science writer, revised the interchapter on the environment (page 949) and wrote a new interchapter on the history of chemistry (page 338).

4. *Reorganization/addition of material:*

   - The first four chapters in particular have been revised and condensed.

   - The "moles of reaction" concept is used in thermodynamics.

   - The material on intermolecular forces (Chapter 12) has been separated from solids (Chapter 13).

   - The chapter on entropy and free energy (Chapter 19) has been thoroughly revised.

   - A brief discussion of modern organometallic chemistry has been added to Chapter 22.

   - Additional challenging questions have been added to each chapter.

   - Additional *Chemical Perspectives* and *Case Studies* boxes have been authored by Jeffrey Kaeffaber (University of Florida) and Eric Scerri (UCLA).

5. **OWL** The *OWL* (Online Web-based Learning) system has been used by over 100,000 students. The contents of OWL are the contents and organization of *Chemistry & Chemical Reactivity*. For the sixth edition, about 20 end-of-chapter questions were assignable in OWL. That number has been approximately doubled for the seventh edition. In addition, the assets of ChemistryNow—Exercises, Tutorials, and Simulations that allow students to practice chemistry—are now fully incorporated in OWL.

6. The new *e-Book in OWL* is a complete electronic version of the text, fully assignable and linked to OWL homework. The e-book can be purchased with the printed book or as an independent text replacement.

7. *Go Chemistry* modules. There are 27 mini-lectures that can be played on an iPod or other personal video player or on a computer. The modules feature narrated examples of the most important material from each chapter and focus on areas in which we know from experience that students may need extra help.

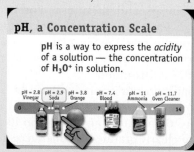

9. *How Do I Solve It?* modules in OWL help students learn how to approach the types of questions asked in each chapter.

8. *In the Laboratory* end-of-chapter Study Questions. These questions pertain directly to situations that the student may confront in a typical laboratory experiment.

The Enhanced Edition is offered with a soft paper binding. The subsequent reduction in manufacturing costs allows us to offer this version at a reduced price compared to the standard edition.

Emerging Developments in Content Usage and Delivery: OWL, the e-Book, and Go Chemistry™

The use of media, presentation tools, and homework management tools has expanded significantly in the last 3 years. More than 10 years ago we incorporated electronic media into this text with the first edition of our interactive CD-ROM, a learning tool used by thousands of students worldwide.

Multimedia technology has evolved over the past 10 years, and so have our students. Our challenge as authors and educators is to use our students' focus on assessment as a way to help them reach a higher level of conceptual understanding. In light of this we have made major changes in our integrated media program. We have redesigned the media so that students now have the opportunity to interact with media based on clearly stated chapter goals that are correlated to end-of-chapter questions. This has been achieved through *OWL (Online Web-based Learning)*, a system developed at the University of Massachusetts and in use by general chemistry students for more than 10 years. In the past few years the system has been used successfully by over 100,000 students.

In addition, as outlined in *What's New in this Edition*, the *electronic book (e-book)* has been enhanced for this edition, and we have developed new *Go Chemistry* modules that consist of mini-lectures of the most important aspect in each chapter.

Audience for *Chemistry & Chemical Reactivity* and OWL

The textbook and OWL are designed for introductory courses in chemistry for students interested in further study in science, whether that science is chemistry, biology, engineering, geology, physics, or related subjects. Our assumption is that students beginning this course have had some preparation in algebra and in general science. Although undeniably helpful, a previous exposure to chemistry is neither assumed nor required.

Philosophy and Approach of the Chemistry & Chemical Reactivity Program

We have had several major, but not independent, objectives since the first edition of the book. The first was to write a book that students would enjoy reading and that would offer, at a reasonable level of rigor, chemistry and chemical principles in a format and organization typical of college and university courses today. Second, we wanted to convey the utility and importance of chemistry by introducing the properties of the elements, their compounds, and their reactions as early as possible and by focusing the discussion as much as possible on these subjects. Finally, with the new *Go Chemistry* modules and even more complete integration of *OWL,* we wanted to give students new and proven tools to bring them to a higher level of conceptual understanding.

The American Chemical Society has been urging educators to put "chemistry" back into introductory chemistry courses. We agree wholeheartedly. Therefore, we have tried to describe the elements, their compounds, and their reactions as early and as often as possible by:

- Using numerous **color photographs** of reactions occurring, of the elements and common compounds, and of common laboratory operations and industrial processes.
- Bringing **material on the properties of elements and compounds** as early as possible into the Exercises and Study Questions and to introduce new principles using realistic chemical situations.
- Introducing each chapter with a **problem in practical chemistry**—a short discussion of the color of an aurora borealis or ethanol in gasoline—that is relevant to the chapter.
- Introducing *Case Studies* on practical chemistry.

General Organization of the Book and Its Features

Chemistry & Chemical Reactivity has two overarching themes: *Chemical Reactivity* and *Bonding and Molecular Structure.* The chapters on *Principles of Reactivity* introduce the factors that lead chemical reactions to be successful in converting reactants to products. Thus, under this topic there is a discussion of common types of reactions, the energy involved in reactions, and the factors that affect the speed of a reaction. One reason for the enormous advances in chemistry and molecular biology in the last several decades has been an understanding of molecular structure. Therefore, sections of the book on *Principles of Bonding and Molecular Structure* lay the groundwork for understanding these developments. Particular attention is paid to an understanding of the structural aspects of such biologically important molecules as DNA.

Flexibility of Chapter Organization

A glance at the introductory chemistry texts currently available shows that there is a generally common order of topics used by educators. With a few minor variations, we have followed that order as well. That is not to say that the chapters in our book cannot be used in some other order. We have written it to be as flexible as possible. The most important example is the chapter on the behavior of gases (Chapter 11), which is placed with chapters on liquids, solids, and solutions (Chapters 12–14) because it logically fits with these topics. It can easily be read and understood, however, after covering only the first four or five chapters of the book.

Similarly, chapters on atomic and molecular structure (Chapters 6–9) could be used before the chapters on stoichiometry and common reactions (Chapters 3 and 4). Also, the chapters on chemical equilibria (Chapters 16–18) can be covered before those on solutions and kinetics (Chapters 14 and 15).

Organic chemistry (Chapter 10) is often left to one of the final chapters in chemistry textbooks. However, we believe the importance of organic compounds in biochemistry and in consumer products means we should present that material earlier in the sequence of chapters. Therefore, it follows the chapters on structure and bonding because organic chemistry nicely illustrates the application of models of chemical bonding and molecular structure. However, one can use the remainder of the book without including this chapter.

The order of topics in the text was also devised to introduce as early as possible the background required for the laboratory experiments usually performed in introductory chemistry courses. For this reason, chapters on chemical and physical properties, common reaction types, and stoichiometry begin the book. In addition, because an understanding of energy is so important

in the study of chemistry, thermochemistry is introduced in Chapter 5.

Interchapters

In addition to the regular chapters, uses and applications of chemistry are described in more detail in supplemental chapters on *The Chemistry of Fuels and Energy Sources; Milestones in the Development of Chemistry and the Modern View of Atoms and Molecules; The Chemistry of Life: Biochemistry; The Chemistry of Modern Materials;* and *The Chemistry of the Environment.*

(The interchapters found in the standard edition are available on this book's companion website accessible from **www.cengage.com/chemistry/kotz.**)

Other Book Sections

As in the sixth edition, we continue with boxed sections titled *Chemical Perspectives, Historical Perspectives, A Closer Look* (for a more in-depth look at relevant material), and *Problem Solving Tips.* As described in "What's New . . ." we have now introduced one or more *Case Studies* in each chapter.

Organization and Purposes of the Sections of the Book

Part 1: The Basic Tools of Chemistry

There are basic ideas and methods that are the basis of all chemistry, and these are introduced in Part 1. Chapter 1 defines important terms, and the accompanying *Let's Review* section reviews units and mathematical methods. Chapter 2 introduces basic ideas of atoms, molecules, and ions, and the most important organizational device in chemistry, the periodic table. In Chapters 3 and 4 we begin to discuss the principles of chemical reactivity and to introduce the numerical methods used by chemists to extract quantitative information from chemical reactions. Chapter 5 is an introduction to the energy involved in chemical processes. The supplemental chapter *The Chemistry of Fuels and Energy Sources,* available on the book's website, uses many of the concepts developed in the preceding chapters.

Part 2: The Structure of Atoms and Molecules

The goal of this section is to outline the current theories of the arrangement of electrons in atoms (Chapters 6 and 7). This discussion is tied closely to the arrangement of elements in the periodic table so that these properties can be recalled and predictions made. In Chapter 8 we discuss for the first time how the electrons of atoms in a molecule lead to chemical bonding and the properties of these bonds. In addition, we show how to derive the three-dimensional structure of simple molecules. Finally, Chapter 9 considers the major theories of chemical bonding in more detail.

This part of the book is completed with a discussion of organic chemistry (Chapter 10), primarily from a structural point of view.

This section includes the interchapter on *Milestones in the Development ...*, and *The Chemistry of Life: Biochemistry* available on the book's website provides an overview of some of the most important aspects of biochemistry.

Part 3: States of Matter

The behavior of the three states of matter—gases, liquids, and solids—is described in that order in Chapters 11–14. The discussion of liquids and solids is tied to gases through the description of intermolecular forces in Chapter 12, with particular attention given to liquid and solid water. In Chapter 14 we describe the properties of solutions, intimate mixtures of gases, liquids, and solids.

The supplemental chapter on *The Chemistry of Modern Materials* is available on the book's website. Designing and making new materials with useful properties is one of the most exciting areas of modern chemistry.

Part 4: The Control of Chemical Reactions

This section is wholly concerned with the *Principles of Reactivity*. Chapter 15 examines the important question of the rates of chemical processes and the factors controlling these rates. With this in mind, we move to Chapters 16-18, chapters that describe chemical reactions at equilibrium. After an introduction to equilibrium in Chapter 16, we highlight the reactions involving acids and bases in water (Chapters 17 and 18) and reactions leading to slightly soluble salts (Chapter 18). To tie together the discussion of chemical equilibria, we again explore thermodynamics in Chapter 19. As a final topic in this section we describe in Chapter 20 a major class of chemical reactions, those involving the transfer of electrons, and the use of these reactions in electrochemical cells.

The Chemistry of the Environment supplemental chapter is available on the book's website. This chapter uses ideas from kinetics and chemical equilibria, in particular, as well as principles described in earlier chapters in the book.

Part 5: The Chemistry of the Elements and Their Compounds

Although the chemistry of the various elements has been described throughout the book to this point, Part 5 considers this topic in a more systematic way. Chapter 21 is devoted to the chemistry of the representative elements, whereas Chapter 22—which has been expanded to include an introduction to organometallic chemistry—is a discussion of the transition elements and their compounds. Finally, Chapter 23 is a brief discussion of nuclear chemistry.

Supporting Materials for the Instructor

Supporting instructor materials are available to qualified adopters. Please consult your local Cengage Learning, Brooks/Cole representative for details. Visit **www.cengage.com/chemistry/kotz** to:

- See samples of materials
- Request a desk copy
- Locate your local representative
- Download electronic files of the *Instructor's Manual*, the *Test Bank*, and other helpful materials for instructors and students

Instructor's Resource Manual
by Susan Young, Hartwick College

ISBN-10: 0-495-38705-3; ISBN-13: 978-0-495-38705-3

Contains worked-out solutions to *all* end-of-chapter Study Questions and features ideas for instructors on how to fully utilize resources and technology in their courses. The *Manual* provides questions for electronic response systems, suggests classroom demonstrations, and emphasizes good and innovative teaching practices. Electronic files of the *Instructor's Resource Manual* are available for download on the PowerLecture DVD-ROM and on the instructor's companion site at **www.cengage.com/chemistry/kotz**.

OWL: Online Web-based Learning
by Roberta Day and Beatrice Botch of the University of Massachusetts, Amherst, and William Vining of the State University of New York at Oneonta

OWL Instant Access (2 Semesters) ISBN-10: 0-495-05099-7; ISBN-13: 978-0-495-05099-5

e-Book in OWL Instant Access (2 Semesters) ISBN-10: 0-495-55499-5; ISBN-13: 978-0-495-55499-8

Used by more than 300 institutions and proven reliable for tens of thousands of students, OWL offers an online homework and quizzing system with unsurpassed ease of use, reliability, and dedicated training and service. OWL makes homework management a breeze and helps students improve their problem-solving skills and visualize concepts, providing instant analysis and feedback on a variety of homework problems, including tutors, simulations, and chemically and/or numerically parameterized short-answer questions. OWL is the only system specifically designed to support mastery learning, where students work as long as they need to master each chemical concept and skill. To view an OWL demo and for more information, visit **www.cengage.com/owl** or contact your Brooks/Cole representative.

New to OWL!

For the seventh edition, approximately 20 new end-of-chapter questions (marked in the text with ■) can be assigned in OWL for a total of approximately 40 end-of-chapter Study Questions for each chapter available in OWL.

The **e-Book in OWL** is a complete electronic version of the text, fully assignable and linked to OWL homework. This exclusive option is available to students with instructor permission. Instructors can consult their Brooks/Cole representative for details and to determine the best option: access to the e-book can be bundled with the text and/or ordered as a text replacement.

Learning Resources allow students to quickly access valuable help to master each homework question with integrated e-book readings, tutors, simulations, and exercises that accompany each question. Learning Resources are configurable by instructors.

More new OWL features:

- New student Learning Resources and Toolbars
- New Answer Input tool for easy subscript and superscript formatting
- Enhanced reports that give instant snapshots of your class progress
- Easier grading access for quick report downloads
- New Survey and Authoring features for creating your own content
- Enhanced security to help you comply with FERPA regulations

A fee-based access code is required for OWL.

Instructor's PowerLecture DVD-ROM with ExamView® and JoinIn™ for *Chemistry & Chemical Reactivity*
ISBN-10: 0-495-38706-1; ISBN-13: 978-0-495-38706-0

PowerLecture is a dual platform, one-stop digital library and presentation tool that includes:

- Prepared Microsoft® PowerPoint® Lecture Slides covering all key points from the text in a convenient format that you can enhance with your own materials or with additional interactive video and animations on the DVD-ROM for personalized, media-enhanced lectures.
- Image Libraries in PowerPoint and in JPEG format that contain electronic files for all text art, most photographs, and all numbered tables in the text. These files can be used to print transparencies or to create your own PowerPoint lectures.
- Electronic files for the complete *Instructor's Resource Manual* and *Test Bank*.
- Sample chapters from the *Student Solutions Manual* and *Study Guide*.
- ExamView testing software, with all the test items from the printed *Test Bank* in electronic format, enables you to create customized tests of up to 250 items in print or online.
- **JoinIn** JoinIn "clicker" questions written specifically for the use of *Chemistry & Chemical Reactivity* with the classroom response system of your choice that allows you to seamlessly display student answers.

Test Bank
by David Treichel, Nebraska Wesleyan University
ISBN-10: 0-495-38709-6; ISBN-13: 978-0-495-38709-1

A printed test bank of more than 1250 questions in a range of difficulty and variety are correlated directly to the chapter sections found in the main text. Numerical, open-ended, or conceptual problems are written in multiple choice, fill-in-the-blank, or short-answer formats. Both single- and multiple-step problems are presented for each chapter. Electronic files of the *Test Bank* are included on the PowerLecture DVD-ROM. WebCT and Blackboard versions of the test bank are available on the instructor's companion site at **www.cengage .com/chemistry/kotz**.

Transparencies
ISBN-10: 0-495-38714-2; ISBN-13: 978-0-495-38714-5

A collection of 150 full-color transparencies of key images selected from the text by the authors. The Power Lecture DVD-ROM includes all text art and many photos to aid in preparing transparencies for material not present in this set.

Supporting Materials for the Student

Visit the student companion website at **www.cengage**
.com/chemistry/kotz to see samples of selected student supplements. Students can purchase any Brooks/
Cole products at your local college store or at our
preferred online store **www.ichapters.com**.

Student Solutions Manual

by Alton J. Banks, North Carolina State University
ISBN-10: 0-495-38707-X; ISBN-13: 978-0-495-38707-7

This manual contains detailed solutions to the text's
blue-numbered end-of-chapter Study Questions that
match the problem-solving strategies from the text. Sample chapters are available for review on the PowerLecture
CD and on the student companion website at **www**
.cengage.com/chemistry/kotz.

Study Guide

by John R. Townsend and Michael J. Moran, West Chester University of Pennsylvania
ISBN-10: 0-495-38708-8; ISBN-13: 978-0-495-38708-4

This study guide contains chapter overviews, key terms
with definitions, and sample tests explicitly linked to the
goals introduced in each chapter. Emphasis is placed on
the text's chapter goals by means of further commen-
tary, study tips, worked examples, and direct references
back to the text. Sample chapters are available for review
on the student companion website at **www.cengage**
.com/chemistry/kotz.

ChemistryNow   Chemistry.·.Now™

ChemistryNow's online self-assessment tools give you the
choices and resources you need to study smarter. You can
explore a variety of tutorials, exercises, and simulations
(cross-referenced throughout the text by margin annota-
tions), view Active Figure interactive versions of key pieces
of art from the text, or take chapter-specific Pre-Tests and
get a Personalized Study Plan that directs you to specific
interactive materials that can help you master the areas
in which you need additional work. Includes access to
one-on-one tutoring and Go Chemistry mini video lectures. Access to ChemistryNow for two semesters may be
included with each new textbook or can be purchased at
www.ichapters.com using ISBN 0-495-39431-9.

Go Chemistry for General Chemistry

27-Module Set ISBN-10: 0-495-38228-0; ISBN-13: 978-0-
495-38228-7

These new mini video lectures, playable on video iPods,
iPhones, and personal video players as well as on

iTunes, include animations and problems for a quick
summary of key concepts. In selected Go Chemistry
modules, e-Flashcards briefly introduce a key concept
and then test student understanding of the basics with
a series of questions. Modules are also available separately. Go Chemistry is included in ChemistryNow and
in OWL. To purchase, enter ISBN 0-495-38228-0 at
www.ichapters.com.

OWL for General Chemistry   ✆WL

See the above description in the instructor support materials section.

Essential Math for Chemistry Students, Second Edition by David W. Ball, Cleveland State University

ISBN-10: 0-495-01327-7; ISBN-13: 978-0-495-01327-3

This short book is intended for students who lack confidence and/or competency in the essential mathematical skills necessary to survive in general chemistry. Each
chapter focuses on a specific type of skill and has worked-
out examples to show how these skills translate to chemical problem solving.

Survival Guide for General Chemistry with Math Review, Second Edition by Charles H. Atwood, Univer-
sity of Georgia

ISBN-10: 0-495-38751-7; ISBN-13: 978-0-495-38751-0

Intended to help you practice for exams, this "survival
guide" shows you how to solve difficult problems by
dissecting them into manageable chunks. The guide
includes three levels of proficiency questions—A, B, and
minimal—to quickly build confidence as you master the
knowledge you need to succeed in your course.

For the Laboratory

Brooks/Cole Lab Manuals

Brooks/Cole offers a variety of printed manuals to meet
all general chemistry laboratory needs. Visit the chemistry site at **www.cengage.com/chemistry** for a full listing
and description of these laboratory manuals and laboratory notebooks. All Brooks/Cole lab manuals can be
customized for your specific needs.

Signature Labs . . . for the customized laboratory

Signature Labs (**www.signaturelabs.com**) combines
the resources of Brooks/Cole, CER, and OuterNet
Publishing to provide you unparalleled service in creating your ideal customized lab program. Select the
experiments and artwork you need from our collection of content and imagery to find the perfect labs

to match your course. Visit **www.signaturelabs.com** or contact your Brooks/Cole representative for more information.

Acknowledgments

Because significant changes have been made from the sixth edition, preparing this new edition of *Chemistry & Chemical Reactivity* took almost 3 years of continuous effort. However, as in our work on the first six editions, we have had the support and encouragement of our families and of some wonderful friends, colleagues, and students.

CENGAGE LEARNING Brooks/Cole

The sixth edition of this book was published by Thomson Brooks/Cole. As often happens in the modern publishing industry, that company was recently acquired by another group and the new name is Cengage Learning Brooks/Cole. In spite of these changes in ownership, we continue with the same excellent team we have had in place for the previous several years.

The sixth edition of the book was very successful, in large part owing to the work of David Harris, our publisher. David again saw us through much of the development of this new edition, but Lisa Lockwood recently assumed his duties as our acquisitions editor; she has considerable experience in textbook publishing and was also responsible for the success of the sixth edition. We will miss David but are looking forward to a close association with Lisa.

Peter McGahey has been our the Development Editor for the fifth and sixth editions and again for this edition. Peter is blessed with energy, creativity, enthusiasm, intelligence, and good humor. He is a trusted friend and confidant and cheerfully answers our many questions during almost-daily phone calls.

No book can be successful without proper marketing. Amee Mosley was a great help in marketing the sixth edition and she is back in that role for this edition. She is knowledgeable about the market and has worked tirelessly to bring the book to everyone's attention.

Our team at Brooks/Cole is completed with Teresa Trego, Production Manager, and Lisa Weber, Technology Project Manager. Schedules are very demanding in textbook publishing, and Teresa has helped to keep us on schedule. We certainly appreciate her organizational skills. Lisa Weber directed the development of the Instructor's PowerLecture DVD-ROM, the *Go Chemistry* modules, and our expanded use of OWL.

People outside of publishing often do not realize the number of people involved in producing a textbook.

Anne Williams of Graphic World Inc. guided the book through its almost year-long production. Marcy Lunetta was the photo researcher for the book and was successful in filling our sometimes offbeat requests for a particular photo.

Photography, Art, and Design

Most of the color photographs for this edition were again beautifully created by Charles D. Winters. He produced several dozen new images for this book, always with a creative eye. Charlie's work gets better and better with each edition. We have worked with Charlie for more than 20 years and have become close friends. We listen to his jokes, both new and old—and always forget them. When we finish the book, we look forward to a kayaking trip.

When the fifth edition was being planned, we brought in Patrick Harman as a member of the team. Pat designed the first edition of the *General ChemistryNow* CD-ROM, and we believe its success is in no small way connected to his design skill. For the fifth edition of the book, Pat went over almost every figure, and almost every word, to bring a fresh perspective to ways to communicate chemistry and he did the same for the sixth edition. Once again he has worked on designing and producing new illustrations for the seventh edition, and his creativity is obvious in their clarity and beauty. Finally, Pat also designed and produced the Go Chemistry modules. As we have worked together so closely for so many years, Pat has become a good friend, as well, and we share interests not only in beautiful books but in interesting music.

Other Collaborators

We have been fortunate to have a number of other colleagues who have played valuable roles in this project.

- Bill Vining (State University of New York, Oneonta), was the lead author of the *General ChemistryNow* CD-ROM and of the media assets in OWL. He has been a friend for many years and recently took the place of one of the authors at SUNY-Oneonta. Bill has again applied his considerable energy and creativity in preparing many more OWL questions with tutorials.
- Susan Young (Hartwick College) has been a good friend and collaborator through five editions and has again prepared the *Instructor's Resource Manual*. She has always been helpful in proofreading, in answering questions on content, and in giving us good advice.
- Alton Banks (North Carolina State University) has also been involved for a number of editions preparing the *Student Solutions Manual*. Both Susan

and Alton have been very helpful in ensuring the accuracy of the Study Question answers in the book, as well as in their respective manuals.

- Michael Moran (West Chester University) has updated and revised the *Study Guide* that was written by John Townsend for the sixth edition. This book has had a history of excellent study guides, and this manual follows that tradition.
- We also wish to acknowledge the support of George Purvis and Fujitsu for use of the CAChe Scientific software for molecular modeling. All the molecular models and the electrostatic potential surfaces in the book were prepared using CAChe software.
- Jay Freedman once again did a masterful job compiling the index/glossary for this edition.

A major task is proofreading the book after it has been set in type. The book is read in its entirety by the authors and accuracy reviewers. After making corrections, the book is read a second time. Any errors remaining at this point are certainly the responsibility of the authors, and students and instructors should contact the authors by email to offer their suggestions. If this is done in a timely manner, corrections can be made when the book is reprinted.

We want to thank the following accuracy reviewers for their invaluable assistance. The book is immeasurably improved by their work.

- William Broderick, Montana State University
- Stephen Z. Goldberg, Adelphi University
- Jeffrey Alan Mack, California State University, Sacramento
- Clyde Metz, College of Charleston
- David Shinn, University of Hawaii, Manoa
- Scott R. White, Southern Arkansas University, Magnolia

Reviewers for the Seventh Edition

- Gerald M. Korenowski, Rensselaer Polytechnic Institute
- Robert L. LaDuca, Michigan State University
- Jeffrey Alan Mack, California State University, Sacramento
- Armando M. Rivera-Figueroa, East Los Angeles College
- Daniel J. Williams, Kennesaw State University
- Steven G. Wood, Brigham Young University
- Roger A. Hinrichs, Weill Cornell Medical College in Qatar (reviewed the Energy interchapter)
- Leonard Fine, Columbia University (reviewed the Materials interchapter)

Advisory Board for the Seventh Edition

As the new edition was being planned, this board listened to some of our ideas and made other suggestions. We hope to continue our association with these energetic and creative chemical educators.

- Donnie Byers, Johnson County Community College
- Sharon Fetzer Gislason, University of Illinois, Chicago
- Adrian George, University of Nebraska
- George Grant, Tidewater Community College, Virginia Beach Campus
- Michael Hampton, University of Central Florida
- Milton Johnston, University of South Florida
- Jeffrey Alan Mack, California State University, Sacramento
- William Broderick, Montana State University
- Shane Street, University of Alabama
- Martin Valla, University of Florida

About the Authors

JOHN C. KOTZ, a State University of New York Distinguished Teaching Professor, Emeritus, at the College at Oneonta, was educated at Washington and Lee University and Cornell University. He held National Institutes of Health postdoctoral appointments at the University of Manchester Institute for Science and Technology in England and at Indiana University.

He has coauthored three textbooks in several editions (*Inorganic Chemistry, Chemistry & Chemical Reactivity,* and *The Chemical World*) and the *General ChemistryNow CD-ROM*. His research in inorganic chemistry and electrochemistry also has been published.

He was a Fulbright Lecturer and Research Scholar in Portugal in 1979 and a Visiting Professor there in 1992. He was also a Visiting Professor at the Institute for Chemical Education (University of Wisconsin, 1991-1992), at Auckland University in New Zealand (1999), and at Potchefstroom University in South Africa in

Left to right: Paul Treichel, John Townsend, and John Kotz.

2006. He has been an invited speaker on chemical education at conferences in South Africa, New Zealand, and Brazil. He also served 3 years as a mentor for the U.S. National Chemistry Olympiad Team.

He has received several awards, among them a State University of New York Chancellor's Award (1979), a National Catalyst Award for Excellence in Teaching (1992), the Estee Lecturership at the University of South Dakota (1998), the Visiting Scientist Award from the Western Connecticut Section of the American Chemical Society (1999), the Distinguished Education Award from the Binghamton (NY) Section of the American Chemical Society (2001), the SUNY Award for Research and Scholarship (2005), and the Squibb Lectureship in Chemistry at the University of North Carolina-Asheville (2007). He may be contacted by email at kotzjc@oneonta.edu.

PAUL M. TREICHEL received his B.S. degree from the University of Wisconsin in 1958 and a Ph.D. from Harvard University in 1962. After a year of postdoctoral study in London, he assumed a faculty position at the University of Wisconsin-Madison. He served as department chair from 1986 through 1995 and was awarded a Helfaer Professorship in 1996. He has held visiting faculty positions in South Africa (1975) and in Japan (1995). Retiring after 44 years as a faculty member in 2007, he is currently Emeritus Professor of Chemistry. During his faculty career he taught courses in general chemistry, inorganic chemistry, organometallic chemistry, and scientific ethics. Professor Treichel's research in organometallic and metal cluster chemistry and in mass spectrometry, aided by 75 graduate and undergraduate students, has led to more than 170 papers in scientific journals. He may be contacted by email at treichel@chem.wisc.edu.

JOHN R. TOWNSEND, Professor of Chemistry at West Chester University of Pennsylvania, completed his B.A. in Chemistry as well as the Approved Program for Teacher Certification in Chemistry at the University of Delaware. After a career teaching high school science and mathematics, he earned his M.S. and Ph.D. in biophysical chemistry at Cornell University. At Cornell he also performed experiments in the origins of life field and received the DuPont Teaching Award. After teaching at Bloomsburg University, Dr. Townsend joined the faculty at West Chester University, where he coordinates the chemistry education program for prospective high school teachers and the general chemistry lecture program for science majors. His research interests are in the fields of chemical education and biochemistry. He may be contacted by email at jtownsend@wcupa.edu.

Contributors

When we designed this edition, we decided to seek chemists outside of our team to author some of the supplemental chapters and other materials.

John Emsley, University of Cambridge

Milestones in the Development of Chemistry and the Modern View of Atoms and Molecules and *The Chemistry of the Environment*

After 22 years as a chemistry lecturer at King's College London, John Emsley became a full-time science writer in 1990. As the Science Writer in Residence at Imperial College London from 1990 to 1997, he wrote the "Molecule of the Month" column for *The Independent* newspaper. Emsley's main activity is writing popular science books that feature chemistry and its role in everyday life. Recent publications include *The Consumer's Good Chemical Guide,* which won the Science Book Prize of 1995; *Molecules at an Exhibition; Was it Something You Ate?; Nature's Building Blocks; The Shocking History of Phosphorus; Vanity, Vitality & Virility;* and *The Elements of Murder.* His most recent book, published in 2007, is *Better Looking, Better Living, Better Loving.*

Jeffrey J. Keaffaber, University of Florida

Case Study: A Healthy Aquarium and the Nitrogen Cycle

Jeffrey J. Keaffaber received his B.S. in biology and chemistry at Manchester College, Indiana, and his Ph.D. in physical organic chemistry at the University of Florida. After finishing his doctoral work, Keaffaber joined the environmental research and development arm of Walt Disney Imagineering. He has worked as a marine environmental consultant and has taught chemistry and oceanography in the California Community College system. His research is in the fields of marine environmental chemistry and engineering, and his contributions have included the design of nitrate reduction and ozone disinfection processes for several large aquarium projects.

Eric Scerri, University of California, Los Angeles

Historical Perspectives: The Story of the Periodic Table

Eric Scerri is a continuing lecturer in the Department of Chemistry and Biochemistry at University of California, Los Angeles. After obtaining an undergraduate degree from the University of London, and a master's degree from the University of Southampton, he obtained his Ph. D. in the history and philosophy of science from King's College, London, focusing on the question of the reduction of chemistry to quantum mechanics. Scerri is the founder and editor of the international journal *Foundations of Chemistry* and recently authored *The Periodic Table: Its Story and Its Significance* (Oxford University Press, 2007), which has been described as the definitive book on the periodic table. He is also the author of more than 100 articles on the history and philosophy of chemistry, as well as chemical education. At UCLA, Scerri regularly teaches general chemistry classes of 350 students and smaller classes in the history and philosophy of science.

Felice Frankel, Harvard University

Cover photograph

As a senior research fellow, Felice Frankel heads the Envisioning Science program at Harvard University's Initiative in Innovative Computing (IIC). Frankel's images have appeared in more than 300 articles and covers in journals and general audience publications. Her awards include the 2007 Lennart Nilsson Award for Scientific Photography, a Guggenheim Fellowship, and grants from the National Science Foundation, the National Endowment for the Arts, the Alfred P. Sloan Foundation, the Graham Foundation for the Advanced Studies in the Fine Arts, and the Camille and Henry Dreyfus Foundation. Frankel's books include *On the Surface of Things, Images of the Extraordinary in Science,* and *Envisioning Science: The Design and Craft of the Science Image,* and she has a regularly appearing column, "Sightings," in *American Scientist* magazine.

About the Cover

© narcisa - floricica buzlea/istockphoto.com

The lotus is the national flower of India and Vietnam. The flowers, seeds, young leaves, and rhizomes of the plant are edible and have been used for centuries in Asia and India. Hindus associate the lotus blossom with the story of creation, and Buddhists believe it represents purity of body, speech, and mind. These ideas have come in part from the fact that the lotus flower grows in a muddy, watery environment, but, when the flower and leaves open, the mud and water are completely shed to leave a clean surface. Chemists recently discovered the underlying reasons for this phenomenon. First, the surface of the leaves is not smooth; it is covered with micro- and nanostructured wax crystals, and these tiny bumps allow only minimal contact between the leaf surface and the water droplet. Thus, only about 2% to 3% of the droplet's surface is actually in contact with the leaf. Second, the surface of the leaf itself is hydrophobic, that is, the forces of attraction between water molecules and the surface of the leaf are relatively weak. Because of strong hydrogen bonding, water molecules within a droplet are strongly attracted to one another instead of the leaf's surface and so form spherical droplets. As these droplets roll off of the surface, any dirt on the surface is swept away. On less hydrophobic surfaces, water molecules interact more strongly with the surface and drops glide off rather than roll off. This self-cleaning property of lotus leaves has been called the "lotus effect," an effect beautifully illustrated by the photograph on the cover of this book. Chemists are now trying to mimic this in new materials that can be incorporated into consumer products such as self-cleaning textiles, paint, and roofing tiles.

1 | Basic Concepts of Chemistry

Charles D. Winters

Sports Drinks

Sports drinks are popular among athletes and nonathletes alike. The original sports drink, Gatorade, contained sucrose, glucose-fructose syrup, citric acid, sodium chloride, sodium citrate, potassium dihydrogen phosphate, and flavoring and coloring agents. This is not unlike the usual soft drink, but the carbohydrates in the sports drink provide only about half of the calories in fruit juice or in an ordinary soda or soft drink. To understand the chemistry behind sports drinks, we have to know the names and composition of the various organic and inorganic compounds in the drink and understand such important areas of chemistry as thermodynamics and colligative properties. As you study chemistry you will learn about these compounds, their structures, and their functions, and you will come to understand more about the ingredients in sports drinks, among other things. For now, think how you would describe a sports drink.

Questions:

1. What are its physical properties? Is it a homogeneous or heterogeneous mixture? Is the density of a sports drink more or less than that of water?
2. What is the volume of a bottle of a typical sports drink in milliliters? In liters? In deciliters?

Answers to these questions are in Appendix Q.

In February 2006 an athlete from the U.S. was sent home from the Winter Olympics Games in Italy because he had used a common treatment for his baldness. The reason was, as the Olympic committee stated, that the remedy can also be used to mask other, illegal drugs. Similarly, athletes were banned from the Summer Olympics Games in Greece in 2004 and the winner of the 2006 Tour de France was stripped of his title for using banned steroids. How can these drugs be detected or identified?

On June 13, 2003, a colorless liquid arrived at the Olympic Analytical Laboratory (OAL) in Los Angeles, California. This laboratory annually tests about 25,000 samples for the presence of illegal drugs. Among its clients are the U.S. Olympic Committee, the National Collegiate Athletic Association, and the National Football League.

About the time of the U.S. Outdoor Track and Field Championships in the summer of 2003, a coach in Colorado tipped off the U.S. Anti-Doping Agency (USADA) that several athletes were using a new steroid. The coach had found a syringe containing an unknown substance and had sent it to the USADA. The USADA chemists dissolved the contents of the syringe in a few milliliters of an alcohol and sent the solution to the OAL. That submission initiated weeks of intense work that led to the identification of a previously unknown steroid that was presumably being used by athletes (Figure 1.1).

Chemistry.⚛.Now™

Throughout the text this icon introduces an opportunity for self-study or to explore interactive tutorials by signing in at **www.cengage.com/login**.

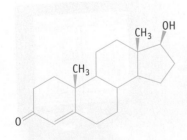

The steroid testosterone. All steroids, including cholesterol, have the same four-ring structure.

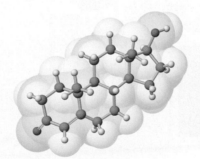

A molecular model of testosterone.

Royalty-free/Photodisc

A photo of crystals of the steroid cholesterol taken with a microscope using polarized light.

FIGURE 1.1 The steroid testosterone. The unknown compound discussed in the text is a steroid closely related to testosterone.

Dr. Donald Catlin, the director of the Olympic Analytical Laboratory in Los Angeles, California.

To identify the unknown substance, chemists at the Olympic Analytical Laboratory used a GC-MS, an instrument widely employed in forensic science work (Figure 1.2). They first passed the sample through a gas chromatograph (GC), an instrument that can separate different chemical compounds in a mixture. A GC has a small-diameter, coiled tube (a typical inside diameter is 0.025 mm) in which the inside surface has been specially treated so that chemicals are attracted to the surface. This tube is placed in an oven and heated to temperatures of 200 °C or higher. The substances in a sample are swept along the tube with a stream of helium gas. Because each component in the sample binds differently to the material on the inside surface of the tube, each component moves through the column at a different rate and exits from the end of the column at a different time. Thus, separation of the components in the mixture is achieved.

After exiting the GC, each compound is routed directly into a mass spectrometer (MS). In a mass spectrometer, the compounds are bombarded with high-energy electrons and each compound is turned into ions, a chemical species with an electric charge. These ions are then passed through a strong magnetic field, causing the ions to be deflected. The path an ion takes in the magnetic field (the extent of deflection) is related to its mass. The masses of the ions are a key piece of information that helps to identify the compound.

Such a straightforward process: separate the compounds in a GC and identify them in an MS. What can go wrong? In fact, many things can go wrong that require ingenuity to overcome. In this case, the unknown steroid did not survive the high temperatures of the GC. It broke apart into pieces, and so it was only possible to study the pieces of the original molecule. However, this gave enough evidence to convince scientists that the compound was indeed a steroid. But what steroid? Dr. Catlin, the director of OAL, said that one hypothesis was that "the new steroid was made by people who knew it was not going to be detectable," that the molecule had been designed in a way that would guarantee that it would not be detected by the standard GC-MS procedure.

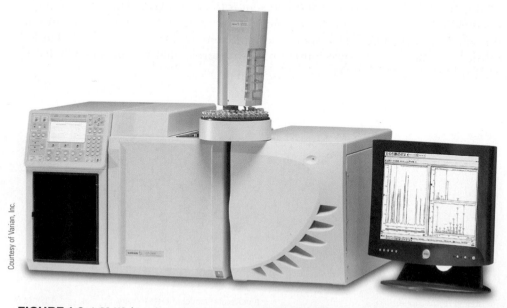

FIGURE 1.2 A GC-MS (gas chromatograph-mass spectrometer). A GC-MS is one of the major tools used in forensic chemistry. The GC portion of the instrument separates the components in a mixture of volatile compounds, and the MS portion then analyzes and identifies them. The GC-MS pictured here has an automated sample changer (carousel, center). An operator will load dozens of samples into the carousel, and the instrument will then process the samples automatically, with the data recorded and stored in a computer.

So, Catlin and his colleagues set out to identify the steroid. The first thing they did was to make the molecule stable during the analysis. This was done by attaching new atoms to the molecule to make what chemists call a *derivative*. A number of approaches to making derivatives were tested, and, within a few weeks, they believed they knew the identity of the unknown steroid.

The final step in solving the mystery was to try to make a sample of the compound in the laboratory and then to use the gas chromatograph and mass spectrometer on this sample. If the material behaved the same way as the unknown sample, then they could be as certain as possible they knew the identify of what they had received from the track coach. These experiments worked, confirming the identity of the compound. It was an entirely new steroid, never seen before in nature or in the laboratory. Its formula is $C_{21}H_{28}O_2$, and its name is tetrahydrogestrinone or THG. It resembled two well-known steroids: gestrinone, used to treat gynecological problems, and trenbolone, a steroid used by ranchers to beef up cattle.

There are two sequels to the story. First, a scientific problem is not solved until it has been verified in another laboratory. Not only was this done, but a test was soon devised to find THG in urine samples. Second, with new analytical procedures, the USADA asked OAL to retest 550 urine samples—and THG was found in several.

Throughout this mystery, chemistry played a critical role, from using the analytical technique of mass spectrometry, to using chemical intuition to determine possible arrangements of the molecular fragments, and finally to synthesizing the derivative and the proposed compound. A knowledge of chemistry is crucial to solving problems not only like this one but many others as well.

■ **Athletes and Steroids** What is the problem with athletes taking steroids? THG is one of a class of steroids called anabolic steroids. They elevate the body's natural testosterone levels and increase body mass, muscle strength, and muscle definition. They can also improve an athlete's capacity to train and compete at the highest levels. Aside from giving steroid users an illegal competitive advantage, the potential side effects of steroids are liver damage, heart disease, anxiety, and rage.

A check of the internet shows that there are hundreds of sources of steroids for athletes. The known performance-enhancing drugs can be detected and their users banned from competitive sports. But what about as-yet unknown steroids? The director of the OAL, Dr. Donald Catlin, believes there are other steroids out in the market, made by secret labs without safety standards, a problem he calls horrifying.

1.1 Chemistry and Its Methods

Chemistry is about change. It was once only about changing one natural substance into another—wood and oil burn; grape juice turns into wine; and cinnabar (Figure 1.3), a red mineral from the earth, changes ultimately into shiny quicksilver (mercury). Chemistry is still about change, but now chemists focus on the change of one pure substance, whether natural or synthetic, into another (Figure 1.4).

(a)

Charles D. Winters

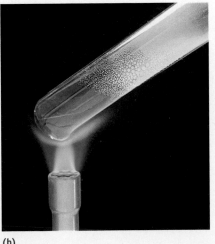

(b)

FIGURE 1.3 Cinnabar and mercury. (a) The red crystals of cinnabar are the chemical compound mercury(II) sulfide. (b) It is heated in air to change it into orange mercury oxide, which, on further heating, is decomposed to the elements oxygen and mercury metal. (The droplets you see on the inside of the test tube wall are mercury.)

Solid sodium, Na

Chlorine gas, Cl_2

Sodium chloride solid, NaCl

FIGURE 1.4 Forming a chemical compound. Sodium chloride, table salt, can be made by combining sodium metal (Na) and yellow chlorine gas (Cl_2). The result is a crystalline solid, common salt. (The tiny spheres show how the atoms are arranged in the substances. In the case of the salt crystal, the spheres represent electrically charged sodium and chlorine ions.)

Although chemistry is endlessly fascinating—at least to chemists—why should you study chemistry? Each person probably has a different answer, but many students take a chemistry course because someone else has decided it is an important part of preparing for a particular career. Chemistry is especially useful because it is central to our understanding of disciplines as diverse as biology, geology, materials science, medicine, physics, and many branches of engineering. In addition, chemistry plays a major role in the economy of developed nations, and chemistry and chemicals affect our daily lives in a wide variety of ways. Furthermore, a course in chemistry can help you see how a scientist thinks about the world and how to solve problems. The knowledge and skills developed in such a course will benefit you in many career paths and will help you become a better-informed citizen in a world that is becoming technologically more complex—and more interesting.

Hypotheses, Laws, and Theories

As scientists, we study questions of our own choosing or ones that someone else poses in the hope of finding an answer or of discovering some useful information. In the story of the banned steroid, THG, the chemists at the Olympic Analytical Laboratory were handed a problem to solve, and they followed the usual methods of science to get to the answer. After some preliminary tests they recognized that the mystery substance was probably a steroid. That is, they formed a **hypothesis**, a tentative explanation or prediction based on experimental observations.

After formulating one or more hypotheses, scientists perform experiments designed to give results that confirm or invalidate these hypotheses. In chemistry this usually requires that both quantitative and qualitative information be collected.

FIGURE 1.5 Qualitative and quantitative observations. A new substance is formed by mixing two known substances in solution. We can make several observations about the substances involved. *Qualitative* observations: The solutions before mixing are colorless and yellow; a yellow, fluffy solid is formed on mixing. *Quantitative* observations: Mixing measured volumes of the solutions produces a measureable mass of solid.

Quantitative information is numerical data, such as the temperature at which a chemical substance melts or its mass (Figure 1.5). **Qualitative** information, in contrast, consists of nonnumerical observations, such as the color of a substance or its physical appearance.

The chemists at the OAL assembled a great deal of qualitative and quantitative information on various drugs. Based on their experience, and on published reports of experiments done in the past by other chemists who study steroids, they became more certain that they knew the identity of the substance. Their preliminary experiments led them to perform still more experiments, such as looking for a way to stabilize the molecule so it would not decompose, and they looked for a way to make the molecule in the laboratory. Final confirmation came when their work was reproduced by scientists in other laboratories.

After scientists have done a number of experiments and the results have been checked to ensure they are reproducible, a pattern of behavior or results may emerge. At this point it may be possible to summarize the observations in the form of a general rule or conclusion. After making a number of experimental observations, the chemists at OAL could conclude, for example, that the unknown substance was a steroid because it had properties characteristic of many other steroids they had observed.

Finally, after numerous experiments by many scientists over an extended period of time, the original hypothesis may become a **law**—a concise verbal or mathematical statement of a behavior or a relation that is consistently observed in nature without contradiction. An example might be the *law of mass conservation* in chemical reactions.

We base much of what we do in science on laws because they help us predict what may occur under a new set of circumstances. For example, we know from experience that if the chemical element sodium comes in contact with water, a violent reaction occurs and new substances are formed (Figure 1.6), and we know that the mass of the substances produced in the reaction is exactly the same as the mass of sodium and water used in the reaction. That is, *mass is always conserved in chemical reactions.* But the result of an experiment might be different from what is expected based on a general rule. When that happens, chemists get excited because experiments that do not follow our expectations are often the most interesting. We know that understanding the exceptions almost invariably gives new insights.

FIGURE 1.6 The metallic element sodium reacts with water.

Once enough reproducible experiments have been conducted, and experimental results have been generalized as a law or general rule, it may be possible to conceive a theory to explain the observations. A **theory** is a well-tested, unifying principle that explains a body of facts and the laws based on them. It is capable of suggesting new hypotheses that can be tested experimentally.

Sometimes nonscientists use the word "theory" to imply that someone has made a guess and that an idea is not yet substantiated. But, to scientists, a theory is based on carefully determined and reproducible evidence. Theories are the cornerstone of our understanding of the natural world at any given time. Remember, though, that theories are inventions of the human mind. Theories can and do change as new facts are uncovered.

Goals of Science

The sciences, including chemistry, have several goals. Two of these are prediction and control. We do experiments and seek generalities because we want to be able to predict what may occur under a given set of circumstances. We also want to know how we might control the outcome of a chemical reaction or process.

A third goal is explanation and understanding. We know, for example, that certain elements such as sodium will react vigorously with water. But why should this be true? To explain and understand this, we turn to theories such as those developed in Chapters 6 and 7.

Dilemmas and Integrity in Science

You may think research in science is straightforward: Do an experiment; draw a conclusion. But, research is seldom that easy. Frustrations and disappointments are common enough, and results can be inconclusive. Experiments sometimes contain some level of uncertainty, and spurious or contradictory data can be collected. For example, suppose you do an experiment expecting to find a direct relation between two experimental quantities. You collect six data sets. When plotted, four of the sets lie on a straight line, but two others lie far away from the line. Should you ignore the last two points? Or should you do more experiments when you know the time they take will mean someone else could publish their results first and thus get the credit for a new scientific principle? Or should you consider that the two points not on the line might indicate that your original hypothesis is wrong, and that you will have to abandon a favorite idea you have worked on for a year? Scientists have a responsibility to remain objective in these situations, but it is sometimes hard to do.

It is important to remember that scientists are human and therefore subject to the same moral pressures and dilemmas as any other person. To help ensure integrity in science, some simple principles have emerged over time that guide scientific practice:

- Experimental results should be reproducible. Furthermore, these results should be reported in the scientific literature in sufficient detail that they can be used or reproduced by others.
- Conclusions should be reasonable and unbiased.
- Credit should be given where it is due.

■ **The Stem Cell Scandal of 2005** In 2004–2005 researchers at Seoul National University in South Korea published several papers in which they claimed to have cloned DNA from human embryonic stem cells. Because it was such an important discovery, scientists around the world examined the data closely. Within months, however, it was discovered that many of the reported results were based on fabricated data, and the results were retracted. Misrepresentation of information does great harm because it misleads scientists into spending time, energy, and funds in trying to replicate the information and using that information in other experiments. The stem cell scandal illustrates, however, the ways in which the scientific community ensures that scientific research is correct and accurate.

Moral and ethical issues frequently arise in science. One of these concerns the use of the pesticide DDT. This is a classic case of the law of "unintended consequences." The pesticide was developed during World War II and promoted as effective in controlling pests but harmless to people. In fact, it was thought to be so effective that it was used in larger and larger quantities around the world. It was especially effective in controlling mosquitoes carrying malaria, although it was soon evident there were consequences. In Borneo, the World Health Organization (WHO) used large quantities of DDT to kill mosquitoes. The mosquito population did indeed decline and so did malaria. Soon, however, the thatch roofs of people's houses fell down because parasitic wasps that ate thatch-eating caterpillars were wiped out by the DDT.

The problem did not end there, however. Small lizards also normally ate the caterpillars and helped to keep that population in check, and the lizard population was controlled by cats. However, DDT was passed up the food chain from caterpillars to lizards to cats, and cats began to die. When the cat population declined, this led to an infestation of rats. Unintended consequences, indeed.

DDT use has been banned in many parts of the world because of its very real, but unforeseen, environmental consequences. The DDT ban began in the United States in 1972 because evidence accumulated that the pesticide affected the reproduction of birds such as the bald eagle.

As expected, the ban on DDT affected the control of malaria-carrying insects. Several million people, primarily children in sub-Saharan Africa, die every year from malaria.

The chairman of the Malaria Foundation International has said that "the malaria epidemic is like loading up seven Boeing 747 airliners each day and crashing them into Mt. Kilimanjaro." Consequently, there has been a movement to return DDT to the arsenal of weapons in fighting the spread of malaria, and in 2006 the WHO approved indoor spraying of DDT in some areas in Africa.

There are many, many moral and ethical issues for chemists. Chemistry has extended and improved lives for millions of people. But just as clearly, chemicals can cause harm, particularly when misused. It is incumbent on all of us to understand enough science to ask pertinent questions and to evaluate sources of information sufficiently to reach reasonable conclusions regarding the health and safety of ourselves and our communities.

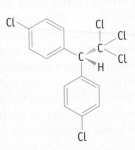

(a) The molecular structure of DDT.

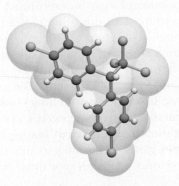

(b) A molecular model of DDT.

(c) DDT can be used to control malaria-carrying insects such as mosquitos.

1.2 Classifying Matter

This chapter begins our discussion of how chemists think about science in general and about matter in particular. After looking at a way to classify matter, we will turn to some basic ideas about elements, atoms, compounds, and molecules and describe how chemists characterize these building blocks of matter.

States of Matter and Kinetic-Molecular Theory

An easily observed property of matter is its **state**—that is, whether a substance is a solid, liquid, or gas (Figure 1.7). You recognize a material as a solid because it has a rigid shape and a fixed volume that changes little as temperature and pressure

Active Figure 1.7 States of matter—solid, liquid, and gas. Elemental bromine exists in all three states near room temperature. The tiny spheres represent bromine (Br) atoms. In elemental bromine, two Br atoms join to form a Br₂ molecule. (See Section 1.3 and Chapter 2.)

Chemistry Now™ Sign in at www.cengage.com/login and go to the Chapter Contents menu to explore an interactive version of this figure accompanied by an exercise.

Photos: Charles D. Winters

Solid   Liquid   Gas

Bromine solid and liquid   Bromine gas and liquid

■ **Water—Changes in Volume on Freezing** Water is an exception to the general statement that a given mass of a substance has a smaller volume as a solid than as a liquid. Water is almost unique in that, for a given mass, the volume *increases* on changing from a liquid to a solid. (That is, its density decreases. See page 15.)

■ **Gases, Liquids, and Solids** Gases and kinetic-molecular theory are discussed in detail in Chapter 11, liquids in Chapter 12, and solids in Chapter 13.

change. Like solids, liquids have a fixed volume, but a liquid is fluid—it takes on the shape of its container and has no definite shape of its own. Gases are fluid as well, but the volume of a gas is determined by the size of its container. The volume of a gas varies more than the volume of a liquid with temperature and pressure.

At low enough temperatures, virtually all matter is found in the solid state. As the temperature is raised, solids usually melt to form liquids. Eventually, if the temperature is high enough, liquids evaporate to form gases. Volume changes typically accompany changes in state. For a given mass of material, there is usually a small increase in volume on melting—water being a significant exception—and then a large increase in volume occurs upon evaporation.

The **kinetic-molecular theory of matter** helps us interpret the properties of solids, liquids, and gases. According to this theory, all matter consists of extremely tiny particles (atoms, molecules, or ions), which are in constant motion.

- In solids these particles are packed closely together, usually in a regular array. The particles vibrate back and forth about their average positions, but seldom does a particle in a solid squeeze past its immediate neighbors to come into contact with a new set of particles.
- The atoms or molecules of liquids are arranged randomly rather than in the regular patterns found in solids. Liquids and gases are fluid because the particles are not confined to specific locations and can move past one another.
- Under normal conditions, the particles in a gas are far apart. Gas molecules move extremely rapidly because they are not constrained by their neighbors. The molecules of a gas fly about, colliding with one another and with the container walls. This random motion allows gas molecules to fill their container, so the volume of the gas sample is the volume of the container.

An important aspect of the kinetic-molecular theory is that the higher the temperature, the faster the particles move. The energy of motion of the particles (their **kinetic energy**) acts to overcome the forces of attraction between particles. A solid melts to form a liquid when the temperature of the solid is raised to the point at which the particles vibrate fast enough and far enough to push one another out of the way and move out of their regularly spaced positions. As the temperature increases even more, the particles move even faster until finally they can escape the clutches of their comrades and enter the gaseous state. *Increasing temperature* *corresponds to faster and faster motions of atoms and molecules*, a general rule you will find useful in many future discussions.

Matter at the Macroscopic and Particulate Levels

The characteristic properties of gases, liquids, and solids are observed by the unaided human senses. They are determined using samples of matter large enough to be seen, measured, and handled. Using such samples, we can also determine, for example, what the color of a substance is, whether it dissolves in water, or whether it conducts electricity or reacts with oxygen. Observations such as these generally take place in the **macroscopic** world of chemistry (Figure 1.8). This is the world of experiments and observations.

Now let us move to the level of atoms, molecules, and ions—a world of chemistry we cannot see. Take a macroscopic sample of material and divide it, again and again, past the point where the amount of sample can be seen by the naked eye, past the point where it can be seen using an optical microscope. Eventually you reach the level of individual particles that make up all matter, a level that chemists refer to as the **submicroscopic** or **particulate** world of atoms and molecules (Figures 1.7 and 1.8).

Chemists are interested in the structure of matter at the particulate level. Atoms, molecules, and ions cannot be "seen" in the same way that one views the macroscopic world, but they are no less real. Chemists imagine what atoms must look like and how they might fit together to form molecules. They create models to represent atoms and molecules (Figures 1.7 and 1.8)—where tiny spheres are used to represent atoms—and then use these models to think about chemistry and to explain the observations they have made about the macroscopic world.

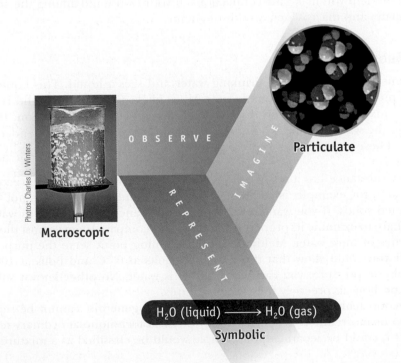

Photos: Charles D. Winters

OBSERVE
IMAGINE
REPRESENT

Particulate

Macroscopic

H₂O (liquid) ⟶ H₂O (gas)
Symbolic

Active Figure 1.8 Levels of matter. We observe chemical and physical processes at the macroscopic level. To understand or illustrate these processes, scientists often try to imagine what has occurred at the particulate atomic and molecular levels and write symbols to represent these observations. A beaker of boiling water can be visualized at the particulate level as rapidly moving H_2O molecules. The process is symbolized by the chemical equation H_2O(liquid) $\longrightarrow$ H_2O(gas).

Chemistry.Now™ Sign in at **www.cengage.com/login** and go to the Chapter Contents menu to explore an interactive version of this figure accompanied by an exercise.

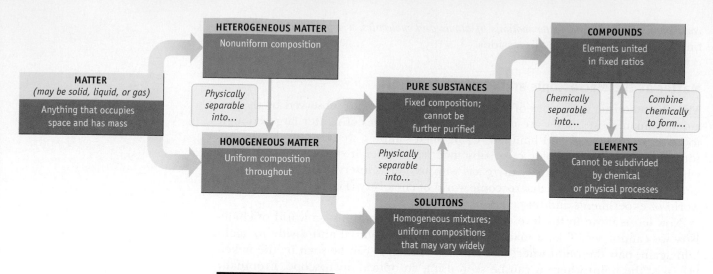

Active Figure 1.9 Classifying Matter.

Chemistry ⊙ Now™ Sign in at www.cengage.com/login and go to the Chapter Contents menu to explore an interactive version of this figure accompanied by an exercise.

It has been said that chemists carry out experiments at the macroscopic level, but they think about chemistry at the particulate level. They then write down their observations as "symbols," the letters (such as H_2O for water or Br_2 for bromine molecules) and drawings that signify the elements and compounds involved. This is a useful perspective that will help you as you study chemistry. Indeed, one of our goals is to help you make the connections in your own mind among the symbolic, particulate, and macroscopic worlds of chemistry.

Pure Substances

A chemist looks at a glass of drinking water and sees a liquid. This liquid could be the pure chemical compound water. More likely, though, the liquid is a *homogeneous* mixture of water and dissolved substances—that is, a **solution.** It is also possible the water sample is a *heterogeneous* mixture, with solids suspended in the liquid. These descriptions represent some of the ways we can classify matter (Figure 1.9).

Every substance has a set of unique properties by which it can be recognized. Pure water, for example, is colorless and odorless and certainly does not contain suspended solids. If you wanted to identify a substance conclusively as water, you would have to examine its properties carefully and compare them against the known properties of pure water. Melting point and boiling point serve the purpose well here. If you could show that the substance melts at 0 °C and boils at 100 °C at atmospheric pressure, you can be certain it is water. No other known substance melts and boils at precisely these temperatures.

A second feature of a pure substance is that it generally cannot be separated into two or more different species by any physical technique at ordinary temperatures. If it could be separated, our sample would be classified as a mixture.

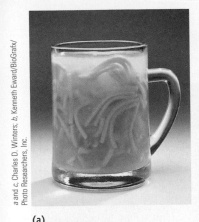
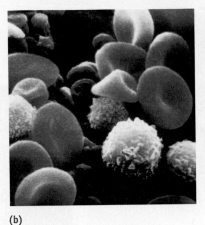

(a)   (b)   (c)

FIGURE 1.10 Mixtures. (a) A cup of noodle soup is a heterogeneous mixture. (b) A sample of blood may look homogeneous, but examination with an optical microscope shows it is, in fact, a heterogeneous mixture of liquids and suspended particles (blood cells). (c) A homogeneous mixture, here consisting of salt in water. The model shows that salt in water consists of separate, electrically charged particles (ions), but the particles cannot be seen with an optical microscope.

Mixtures: Homogeneous and Heterogeneous

A cup of noodle soup is obviously a mixture of solids and liquids (Figure 1.10a). A mixture in which the uneven texture of the material can be detected is called a **heterogeneous** mixture. Heterogeneous mixtures such as blood may appear completely uniform but on closer examination are not (Figure 1.10b). Milk, for example, appears smooth in texture to the unaided eye, but magnification would reveal fat and protein globules within the liquid. In a heterogeneous mixture the properties in one region are different from those in another region.

A **homogeneous** mixture consists of two or more substances in the same phase (Figure 1.10c). No amount of optical magnification will reveal a homogeneous mixture to have different properties in different regions. Homogeneous mixtures are often called **solutions.** Common examples include air (mostly a mixture of nitrogen and oxygen gases), gasoline (a mixture of carbon- and hydrogen-containing compounds called *hydrocarbons*), and an unopened soft drink.

When a mixture is separated into its pure components, the components are said to be **purified.** Efforts at separation are often not complete in a single step, however, and repetition almost always gives an increasingly pure substance. For example, soil particles can be separated from water by filtration (Figure 1.11). When the mixture is passed through a filter, many of the particles are removed. Repeated filtrations will give water a higher and higher state of purity. This purification process uses a property of the mixture, its clarity, to measure the extent of purification. When a perfectly clear sample of water is obtained, all of the soil particles are assumed to have been removed.

Chemistry ⚛ Now™

Sign in at **www.cengage.com/login** and go to Chapter 1 Contents to see:
• Screen 1.5 for an exercise on **identifying pure substances and types of mixtures**
• Screen 1.6 to watch a video on **heterogeneous mixtures**

a, Charles D. Winters; b, Littleton, Massachusetts, Spectacle Pond Iron and Manganese Treatment Facility

(a)

(b)

FIGURE 1.11 Purifying water by filtration. (a) A laboratory setup. A beaker full of muddy water is passed through a paper filter, and the mud and dirt are removed. (b) A water treatment plant uses filtration to remove suspended particles from the water.

 Module 1

1.3 Elements and Atoms

Passing an electric current through water can decompose it to gaseous hydrogen and oxygen (Figure 1.12a). Substances like hydrogen and oxygen that are composed of only one type of atom are classified as **elements.** Currently, 117 elements are known. Of these, only about 90—some of which are illustrated in Figure 1.12— are found in nature. The remainder have been created by scientists. The name and symbol for each element are listed in the tables at the front and back of this book. Carbon (C), sulfur (S), iron (Fe), copper (Cu), silver (Ag), tin (Sn), gold (Au), mercury (Hg), and lead (Pb) were known to the early Greeks and Romans and to the alchemists of ancient China, the Arab world, and medieval Europe. However,

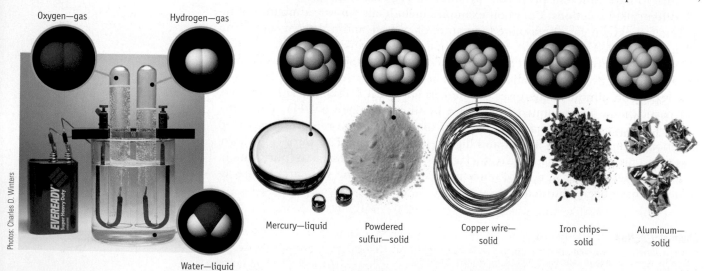

Photos: Charles D. Winters

Oxygen—gas   Hydrogen—gas

Water—liquid

Mercury—liquid   Powdered sulfur—solid   Copper wire—solid   Iron chips—solid   Aluminum—solid

(a)

(b)

FIGURE 1.12 Elements. (a) Passing an electric current through water produces the elements hydrogen (test tube on the right) and oxygen (test tube on the left). (b) Chemical elements can often be distinguished by their color and their state at room temperature.

many other elements—such as aluminum (Al), silicon (Si), iodine (I), and helium (He)—were not discovered until the 18th and 19th centuries. Finally, scientists in the 20th and 21st centuries have made elements that do not exist in nature, such as technetium (Tc), plutonium (Pu), and americium (Am).

The table inside the front cover of this book, in which the symbol and other information for the elements are enclosed in a box, is called the **periodic table.** We will describe this important tool of chemistry in more detail beginning in Chapter 2.

An **atom** is the smallest particle of an element that retains the characteristic chemical properties of that element. Modern chemistry is based on an understanding and exploration of nature at the atomic level (▶ Chapters 6 and 7).

Chemistry.❖.Now™

Sign in at **www.cengage.com/login** and go to Chapter 1 Contents to see Screen 1.7 for a self-study module on **Elements and Atoms,** and the Periodic Table tool on this screen or in the Toolbox.

EXERCISE 1.1 Elements

Using the periodic table inside the front cover of this book:

(a) Find the names of the elements having the symbols Na, Cl, and Cr.

(b) Find the symbols for the elements zinc, nickel, and potassium.

1.4 Compounds and Molecules

A pure substance like sugar, salt, or water, which is composed of two or more different elements held together by **chemical bonds,** is referred to as a **chemical compound.** Even though only 117 elements are known, there appears to be no limit to the number of compounds that can be made from those elements. More than 20 million compounds are now known, with about a half million added to the list each year.

When elements become part of a compound, their original properties, such as their color, hardness, and melting point, are replaced by the characteristic properties of the compound. Consider common table salt (sodium chloride), which is composed of two elements (see Figure 1.4):

- Sodium is a shiny metal that reacts violently with water. Its solid state structure has sodium atoms tightly packed together.
- Chlorine is a light yellow gas that has a distinctive, suffocating odor and is a powerful irritant to lungs and other tissues. The element is composed of Cl_2 units in which two chlorine atoms are tightly bound together.
- Sodium chloride, or common salt, is a colorless, crystalline solid composed of sodium and chloride ions bound tightly together (NaCl). Its properties are completely unlike those of the two elements from which it is made.

It is important to distinguish between a mixture of elements and a chemical compound of two or more elements. Pure metallic iron and yellow, powdered sulfur (Figure 1.13a) can be mixed in varying proportions. In the chemical compound iron pyrite (Figure 1.13b), however, there is no variation in composition. Not only does iron pyrite exhibit properties peculiar to itself and different from those of either iron or sulfur, or a mixture of these two elements, but it also has a definite percentage composition by mass (46.55% Fe and 53.45% S). Thus, two

■ **Writing Element Symbols** Notice that only the first letter of an element's symbol is capitalized. For example, cobalt is Co, not CO. The notation CO represents the chemical compound carbon monoxide. Also note that the element name is not capitalized, except at the beginning of a sentence.

■ **Origin of Element Names and Symbols** Many elements have names and symbols with Latin or Greek origins. Examples include helium (He), from the Greek word *helios* meaning "sun," and lead, whose symbol, Pb, comes from the Latin word for "heavy," *plumbum*. More recently discovered elements have been named for their place of discovery or for a person or place of significance. Examples include americium (Am), californium (Cf), and curium (Cm; for Marie Curie).

■ **Periodic Tables Online** Sign in at **www.cengage.com/login** and go to Chapter 1 Contents to see Screen 1.7 or the Toolbox. See also the extensive information on the periodic table and the elements at the American Chemical Society website:
- acswebcontent.acs.org/games/pt.html

FIGURE 1.13 Mixtures and compounds. (a) The material in the dish is a mixture of iron chips and sulfur. The iron can be removed easily by using a magnet. (b) Iron pyrite is a chemical compound composed of iron and sulfur. It is often found in nature as perfect, golden cubes.

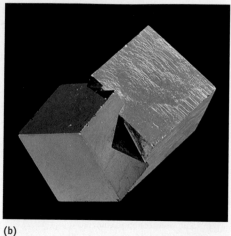

(a)   (b)

Photos: Charles D. Winters

major differences exist between mixtures and pure compounds: Compounds have distinctly different characteristics from their parent elements, and they have a definite percentage composition (by mass) of their combining elements.

Some compounds—such as table salt, NaCl—are composed of **ions,** which are electrically charged atoms or groups of atoms [▶ Chapter 2]. Other compounds—such as water and sugar—consist of **molecules,** the smallest discrete units that retain the composition and chemical characteristics of the compound.

The composition of any compound is represented by its **chemical formula.** In the formula for water, H_2O, for example, the symbol for hydrogen, H, is followed by a subscript "2" indicating that two atoms of hydrogen occur in a single water molecule. The symbol for oxygen appears without a subscript, indicating that one oxygen atom occurs in the molecule.

As you shall see throughout this book, molecules can be represented with models that depict their composition and structure. Figure 1.14 illustrates the names, formulas, and models of the structures of a few common molecules.

1.5 Physical Properties

You recognize your friends by their physical appearance: their height and weight and the color of their eyes and hair. The same is true of chemical substances. You can tell the difference between an ice cube and a cube of lead of the same size not only because of their appearance (one is clear and colorless, and the other is a lustrous metal) (Figure 1.15), but also because one is more dense (lead) than the other (ice). Properties such as these, which can be observed and measured without changing the composition of a substance, are called **physical properties.** The chemical elements in Figure 1.12, for example, clearly differ in terms of their color,

FIGURE 1.14 Names, formulas, and models of some common molecules. Models of molecules appear throughout this book. In such models, C atoms are gray, H atoms are white, N atoms are blue, and O atoms are red.

NAME	Water	Methane	Ammonia	Carbon dioxide
FORMULA	H_2O	CH_4	NH_3	CO_2
MODEL				

TABLE 1.1 Some Physical Properties

Property	Using the Property to Distinguish Substances
Color	Is the substance colored or colorless? What is the color, and what is its intensity?
State of matter	Is it a solid, liquid, or gas? If it is a solid, what is the shape of the particles?
Melting point	At what temperature does a solid melt?
Boiling point	At what temperature does a liquid boil?
Density	What is the substance's density (mass per unit volume)?
Solubility	What mass of substance can dissolve in a given volume of water or other solvent?
Electric conductivity	Does the substance conduct electricity?
Malleability	How easily can a solid be deformed?
Ductility	How easily can a solid be drawn into a wire?
Viscosity	How easily will a liquid flow?

FIGURE 1.15 Physical properties. An ice cube and a piece of lead can be differentiated easily by their physical properties (such as density, color, and melting point).

appearance, and state (solid, liquid, or gas). Physical properties allow us to classify and identify substances. Table 1.1 lists a few physical properties of matter that chemists commonly use.

EXERCISE 1.2 Physical Properties

Identify as many physical properties in Table 1.1 as you can for the following common substances: (a) iron, (b) water, (c) table salt (chemical name is sodium chloride), and (d) oxygen.

Density, the ratio of the mass of an object to its volume, is a physical property useful for identifying substances.

$$\text{Density} = \frac{\text{mass}}{\text{volume}} \qquad (1.1)$$

For example, you can readily tell the difference between an ice cube and a cube of lead of identical size (Figure 1.15). Lead has a high density, 11.35 g/cm^3 (11.35 grams per cubic centimeter), whereas the density of ice is slightly less than 0.917 g/cm^3. An ice cube with a volume of 16.0 cm^3 has a mass of 14.7 g, whereas a cube of lead with the same volume has a mass of 182 g.

The **temperature** of a sample of matter often affects the numerical values of its properties. Density is a particularly important example. Although the change in water density with temperature seems small (Table 1.2), it affects our environment profoundly. For example, as the water in a lake cools, the density of the water increases, and the denser water sinks (Figure 1.16a). This continues until the water temperature reaches 3.98 °C, the point at which water has its maximum density (0.999973 g/cm^3). If the water temperature drops further, the density decreases slightly, and the colder water floats on top of water at 3.98 °C. If water is cooled below about 0 °C, solid ice forms. Water is unique among substances in the universe: Ice is less dense than water, so the solid ice floats on liquid water.

Because the density of liquids changes with temperature, the volume of a given mass of liquid also changes with temperature. This is the reason laboratory glassware used to measure precise volumes of solutions always specifies the temperature at which it was calibrated (Figure 1.16b).

■ **Units of Density** As described on page 25, the SI unit of mass is the kilogram and the SI unit of length is the meter. Therefore, the SI unit of density is kg/m^3. In chemistry, the more commonly used unit is g/cm^3. To convert from kg/m^3 to g/cm^3, divide by 1000.

■ **Calculations Involving Density and Mathematics Review** See *Let's Review* beginning on page 24 for a review of some of the mathematics used in introductory chemistry.

■ **Temperature Scales** Scientists use the Celsius (°C) and Kelvin scales (K) for temperature. See page 26.

TABLE 1.2 Temperature Dependence of Water Density

Temperature (°C)	Density of Water (g/cm³)
0 (ice)	0.917
0 (liq water)	0.99984
2	0.99994
4	0.99997
10	0.99970
25	0.99707
100	0.95836

When you think of chemistry, you probably think of colored liquids bubbling in flasks and maybe a fire or even an explosion. That is not what we usually see in a university laboratory, but pay a visit to Yellowstone National Park in Wyoming (or to areas of the North Island of New Zealand) and you will see just that: bubbling, steaming hot water springs with colorful substances in a natural "laboratory."

Yellowstone Park is unique in having one of the highest concentrations of geysers, hot springs, steam vents, and mudpots on the planet. The reason rests in the geology of the area—the earth's crust is thinner here (about 64 km) compared with the crust covering the rest of the earth (144 km). Hot magma lies not far below Yellowstone's surface (6–16 km), and it heats the rocks above and the reservoirs of water closer to the surface (a physical process). The superheated water dissolves some of the minerals (another physical process), and it is forced upwards through fissures in the rocks and sometimes explodes through the surface as geysers and hot springs.

The hot water shooting to the surface carries with it dissolved minerals such as limestone (calcium carbonate), and they are deposited around the geysers and hot springs as limestone and travertine.

Once the hot water reaches the surface, it can harbor thermophilic or "heat-loving" bacteria. These can grow in enormous colonies

with brilliant colors. Different bacteria grow at different temperatures, usually in the range of 50 °C to 70 °C, and the colors of the pools and streams can change with temperature. In the Grand Prismatic Spring shown in the photo, you can see that bacteria grow in the slightly cooler water around the edge of the spring, but the deep blue, very hot water in

A travertine formation in Yellowstone National Park. The formation consists largely of limestone (calcium carbonate) mixed with silica.

© James Cowlin

the center is devoid of living organisms. The bacteria growing around the hot springs are single-cell organisms ranging in size from 0.2 to 50 μm in diameter. They are often highly colored, owing to pigments such as carotenoids and chlorophylls, and different organisms with different colors grow at different temperatures. Some are anaerobic bacteria and use sulfur instead of oxygen for respiration (a chemical process).

A study of the hot springs of Yellowstone National Park is a good example of the intersection of chemistry, geology, and biology and of all of their subdisciplines (biochemistry, geochemistry, bacteriology, and mineralogy, among others). Our goal in this book is to introduce the chemistry background you will need to study more chemistry or to carve out a career in another field of science.

Stephen Hoerold

Grand Prismatic Spring, Yellowstone National Park.

Extensive and Intensive Properties

Extensive properties depend on the amount of a substance present. The mass and volume of the samples of elements in Figure 1.12, or the amount of heat obtained from burning gasoline, are extensive properties, for example. In contrast, **intensive properties** do *not* depend on the amount of substance. A sample of ice will melt at 0 °C, no matter whether you have an ice cube or an iceberg. Density is also an intensive property. The density of gold, for example, is the same (19.3 g/cm^3 at 20 °C) whether you have a flake of pure gold or a solid gold ring. Intensive properties are often useful in identifying a material. For example, the temperature at which a material melts (its melting point) is often so characteristic that it can be used to identify the solid (Figure 1.17).

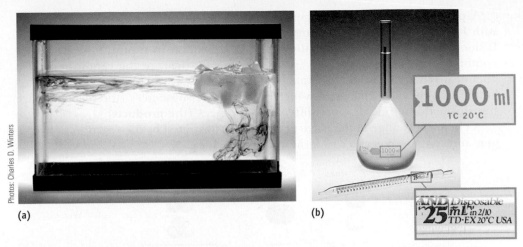

(a)   (b)

FIGURE 1.16 Temperature dependence of physical properties. (a) Change in density with temperature. Ice cubes were placed in the right side of the tank and blue dye in the left side. The water beneath the ice is cooler and denser than the surrounding water, so it sinks. The convection current created by this movement of water is traced by the dye movement as the denser, cooler water sinks. (b) Temperature and calibration. Laboratory glassware is calibrated for specific temperatures. The pipet will deliver and the volumetric flask will contain the specified volume at the indicated temperature.

1.6 Physical and Chemical Changes

Changes in physical properties are called **physical changes.** In a physical change, the identity of a substance is preserved even though it may have changed its physical state or the gross size and shape of its pieces. A physical change does not result in a new chemical substance being produced. The substances (atoms, molecules, or ions) present before and after the change are the same. An example of a physical change is the melting of a solid (Figure 1.17). In the case of ice melting, the molecules present both before and after the change are H_2O molecules. Their chemical identity has not changed; they are now simply able to flow past one another in the liquid state instead of being locked in position in the solid.

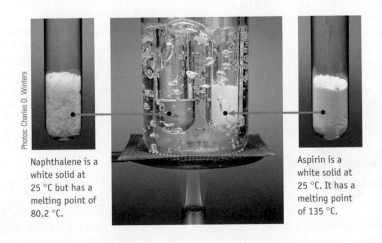

Naphthalene is a white solid at 25 °C but has a melting point of 80.2 °C.

Aspirin is a white solid at 25 °C. It has a melting point of 135 °C.

FIGURE 1.17 A physical property used to distinguish compounds. Aspirin and naphthalene are both white solids at 25 °C. You can tell them apart by, among other things, a difference in physical properties. At the temperature of boiling water, 100 °C, naphthalene is a liquid (left), whereas aspirin is a solid (right).

A physical property of hydrogen gas (H_2) is its low density, so a balloon filled with H_2 floats in air. Suppose, however, that a lighted candle is brought up to the balloon. When the heat causes the skin of the balloon to rupture, the hydrogen combines with the oxygen (O_2) in the air, and the heat of the candle sets off a chemical reaction, producing water, H_2O (Figure 1.18). This reaction is an example of a **chemical change,** in which one or more substances (the **reactants**) are transformed into one or more different substances (the **products**).

A chemical change at the particulate level is illustrated by the reaction of hydrogen and oxygen molecules to form water molecules.

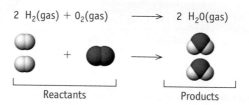

$$2\ H_2(gas) + O_2(gas) \longrightarrow 2\ H_2O(gas)$$

Reactants   Products

Case Study

Ancient and Modern Hair Coloring

Humankind has always been interested in pigments for artistic uses and to decorate their bodies. One of the oldest pigments is galena, PbS (Figure 1), which was first brought from Asia to Egypt thousands of years ago. When powdered, it is black and has been widely used as a cosmetic, particularly for dyeing hair. Some evidence for this is that small piles of galena were found next to the skeleton of a young Egyptian woman whose remains were buried in 3080 BC ± 110 years. Analysis by chemical archeologists found that the galena in this tomb was not from Asia, though. Instead, using modern forensic techniques, they found it came from nearby cities on the Red Sea.

According to recent research, the same effect on hair that galena has could be achieved by applying a mixture of the chemical compounds PbO and Ca(OH)₂. This was originally described by Claudius Galen, a Roman physician who lived between about 130 and 200 AD. Similar formulations have been used through the centuries for dyeing wool, and the present-day hair-coloring product Grecian Formula™ still uses this technique.

In recent research, chemists in France found that only a few hours after applying the PbO and Ca(OH)₂ mixture to hair (Figure 2a), the hair was blackened (Figure 2b), and that the blackening came from tiny particles of PbS (about 5 nanometers in diameter).

But where did the sulfur in PbS come from? The French research found it came from the amino acids in hair. (The amino acids cysteine and methionine both have sulfur as part of their structure.)

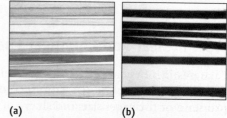

(a)   (b)

FIGURE 2 Photographs of strands of hair before (a) and after (b) treating with a mixture of PbO and Ca(OH)₂. From *C & EN*, Vol. 84, No. 37, p. 12, 2006, "Still Dyeing After 2,000 Years," Dr. B. Halford. Copyright © 2006 American Chemical Society. Used with permission.

Questions:

1. *What is the name of the element Pb? Of Ca?*
2. *What is the density of Pb?*
3. *What is the symbol for the element sulfur?*
4. *Can you find (on the World Wide Web, for example) the common name for the compound Ca(OH)₂?*
5. *A particulate view of galena is illustrated in Figure 1b. Briefly describe the shape of this tiny piece of PbS.*
6. *Compare the particulate view of galena with that of NaCl on page 4. Are there similarities? Any differences?*

Answers to these questions are in Appendix Q.

Charles D. Winters

(a)   (b)

— Pb²⁺ ion

— S²⁻ ion

FIGURE 1 Lead sulfide, galena. (a) Small crystal of the mineral galena, PbS. (b) The particulate view of PbS (where the gray spheres are Pb and the yellow spheres are S).

References: Nano Letters, 2006, p. 2215; J. L. Lambert, *Traces of the Past,* Addison-Wesley, 1997, p. 80.

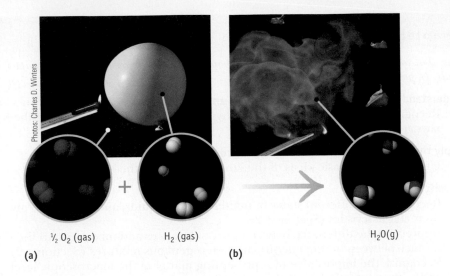

½ O₂ (gas)   H₂ (gas)   H₂O(g)

(a)   (b)

FIGURE 1.18 A chemical change—
the reaction of hydrogen and oxygen.
(a) A balloon filled with molecules of
hydrogen gas and surrounded by molecules of oxygen in the air. (The balloon
floats in air because gaseous hydrogen
is less dense than air.) (b) When ignited
with a burning candle, H₂ and O₂ react to
form water, H₂O.
Chemistry ❄ Now™ Sign in at
www.cengage.com/login and go to
Chapter 1 Contents to see Screen 1.11
Chemical Change, for a video of this
reaction.

The representation of the change using chemical formulas is called a **chemical equation.** It shows that the substances on the left (the reactants) produce the sub-stances on the right (the products). As this equation shows, there are four atoms of H and two atoms of O before *and* after the reaction, but the molecules before the reaction are different from those after the reaction.

A **chemical property** indicates whether and sometimes how readily a material undergoes a chemical change with another material. For example, a chemical property of hydrogen gas is that it reacts vigorously with oxygen gas.

Chemistry ❄ Now™

Sign in at **www.cengage.com/login** and go to Chapter 1 Contents to see:
- Screen 1.12 for an exercise on **identifying physical and chemical changes**
- Screen 1.13 to watch a video and view an animation of the **molecular changes when chlorine gas and solid phosphorus react**

EXERCISE 1.3 Chemical Reactions and Physical Changes

When camping in the mountains, you boil a pot of water on a campfire. What physical and chemical changes take place in this process?

Chemical and physical changes. A pot of water has been put on a campfire. What chemical and physical changes are occur-ring here (Exercise 1.3)?

Chapter Goals Revisited

Now that you have studied this chapter, you should ask whether you have met the chapter goals. In particular, you should be able to:

Understand the nature of hypotheses, laws, and theories
a. Recognize the difference between a hypothesis and a theory and describe how laws are established.

Apply the kinetic-molecular theory to the properties of matter
a. Understand the basic ideas of the kinetic-molecular theory (Section 1.2).

Classify matter
a. Recognize the different states of matter (solids, liquids, and gases) and give their characteristics (Section 1.2).
b. Appreciate the difference between pure substances and mixtures and the difference between homogeneous and heterogeneous mixtures (Section 1.2).
c. Recognize the importance of representing matter at the macroscopic level and at the particulate level (Section 1.2).

Recognize elements, atoms, compounds, and molecules
a. Identify the name or symbol for an element, given its symbol or name (Section 1.3). Study Question(s) assignable in OWL: 2, 4; Go Chemistry Module 1.
b. Use the terms atom, element, molecule, and compound correctly (Sections 1.3 and 1.4).

Identify physical and chemical properties and changes
a. List commonly used physical properties of matter (Section 1.5).
b. Identify several physical and chemical properties of common substances (Sections 1.5 and 1.6). Study Question(s) assignable in OWL: 8, 10, 13, 14, 31, 37.
c. Relate density to the volume and mass of a substance (Section 1.5). Study Question(s) assignable in OWL: 18, 19, 21, 23, 29, 30, 34.
d. Explain the difference between chemical and physical changes (Section 1.6). Study Question(s) assignable in OWL: 8, 13, 33.
e. Understand the difference between extensive and intensive properties and give examples of them (Section 1.5). Study Question(s) assignable in OWL: 11.

KEY EQUATIONS

Equation 1.1 (page 15) Density. In chemistry the common unit of density is g/cm^3, whereas kg/m^3 is common in geology and oceanography.

$$\text{Density} = \frac{\text{mass}}{\text{volume}}$$

STUDY QUESTIONS

◉WL Online homework for this chapter may be assigned in OWL.

▲ denotes challenging questions.

■ denotes questions assignable in OWL.

Blue-numbered questions have answers in Appendix O and fully-worked solutions in the *Student Solutions Manual.*

Practicing Skills

Matter: Elements and Atoms, Compounds, and Molecules
(See Exercise 1.1)

1. Give the name of each of the following elements:
   (a) C   (c) Cl   (e) Mg
   (b) K   (d) P   (f) Ni

2. ■ Give the name of each of the following elements:
   (a) Mn   (c) Na   (e) Xe
   (a) Cu   (d) Br   (f) Fe

3. Give the symbol for each of the following elements:
   (a) barium   (c) chromium   (e) arsenic
   (b) titanium   (d) lead   (f) zinc

4. ■ Give the symbol for each of the following elements:
   (a) silver   (c) plutonium   (e) technetium
   (b) aluminum   (d) tin   (f) krypton

5. In each of the following pairs, decide which is an element and which is a compound.
   (a) Na and NaCl
   (b) Sugar and carbon
   (c) Gold and gold chloride

6. ■ In each of the following pairs, decide which is an element and which is a compound.
   (a) $Pt(NH_3)_2Cl_2$ and Pt
   (b) Copper or copper(II) oxide
   (c) Silicon or sand

Physical and Chemical Properties
(See Exercises 1.2 and 1.3)

7. In each case, decide if the underlined property is a physical or chemical property.
   (a) The color of elemental bromine is <u>orange-red</u>.
   (b) Iron <u>turns to rust</u> in the presence of air and water.
   (c) Hydrogen can <u>explode</u> when ignited in air (Figure 1.18).
   (d) The <u>density</u> of titanium metal is 4.5 g/cm³.
   (e) Tin metal <u>melts</u> at 505 K.
   (f) Chlorophyll, a plant pigment, is <u>green</u>.

8. ■ In each case, decide if the change is a chemical or physical change.
   (a) A cup of household bleach changes the color of your favorite T-shirt from purple to pink.
   (a) Water vapor in your exhaled breath condenses in the air on a cold day.
   (b) Plants use carbon dioxide from the air to make sugar.
   (c) Butter melts when placed in the sun.

9. Which part of the description of a compound or element refers to its physical properties and which to its chemical properties?
   (a) The colorless liquid ethanol burns in air.
   (b) The shiny metal aluminum reacts readily with orange-red bromine.

10. ■ Which part of the description of a compound or element refers to its physical properties and which to its chemical properties?
    (a) Calcium carbonate is a white solid with a density of 2.71 g/cm³. It reacts readily with an acid to produce gaseous carbon dioxide.
    (b) Gray, powdered zinc metal reacts with purple iodine to give a white compound.

General Questions
These questions are not designated as to type or location in the chapter. They may combine several concepts.

11. ■ A piece of turquoise is a blue-green solid; it has a density of 2.65 g/cm³ and a mass of 2.5 g.
    (a) Which of these observations are qualitative and which are quantitative?
    (b) Which of the observations are extensive and which are intensive?
    (c) What is the volume of the piece of turquoise?

12. Give a physical property and a chemical property for the elements hydrogen, oxygen, iron, and sodium. (The elements listed are selected from examples given in Chapter 1.)

13. ■ Eight observations are listed below. What observations identify chemical properties?
    (a) Sugar is soluble in water.
    (b) Water boils at 100 °C.
    (c) Ultraviolet light converts O_3 (ozone) to O_2 (oxygen).
    (d) Ice is less dense than water.
    (e) Sodium metal reacts violently with water.
    (f) CO_2 does not support combustion.
    (g) Chlorine is a green gas.
    (i) Heat is required to melt ice.

14. ■ Azurite, a blue, crystalline mineral, is composed of copper, carbon, and oxygen.

Charles D. Winters

Azurite is a deep blue crystalline mineral. It is surrounded by copper pellets and powdered carbon (in the dish).

   (a) What are the symbols of the three elements that combine to make the mineral azurite?
   (b) Based on the photo, describe some of the physical properties of the elements and the mineral. Are any the same? Are any properties different?

15. The mineral fluorite contains the elements calcium and fluorine and has colors that range from blue, to violet, to green and yellow.

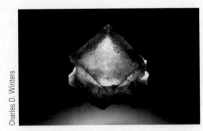

Charles D. Winters

The mineral fluorite, calcium fluoride.

What are the symbols of these elements? How would you describe the shape of the fluorite crystals in the photo? What can this tell us about the arrangement of the particles (ions) inside the crystal?

16. Small chips of iron are mixed with sand (see the following photo). Is this a homogeneous or heterogeneous mixture? Suggest a way to separate the iron from the sand.

Chips of iron mixed with sand.

17. In Figure 1.4 you see a piece of salt and a representation of its internal structure. Which is the macroscopic view and which is the particulate view? How are the macroscopic and particulate views related?

18. ■ The following photo shows copper balls, immersed in water, floating on top of mercury. What are the liquids and solids in this photo? Which substance is most dense? Which is least dense?

Water, copper, and mercury.

19. ■ Carbon tetrachloride, CCl_4, a common liquid compound, has a density of 1.58 g/cm^3. If you place a piece of a plastic soda bottle ($d = 1.37 \text{ g/cm}^3$) and a piece of aluminum ($d = 2.70 \text{ g/cm}^3$) in liquid CCl_4, will the plastic and aluminum float or sink?

20. ▲ You have a sample of a white crystalline substance from your kitchen. You know that it is either salt or sugar. Although you could decide by taste, suggest another property that you could use to decide. (Hint: You may use the World Wide Web or a handbook of chemistry in the library to find some information.)

21. ■ Hexane (C_6H_{14}, density = 0.766 g/cm^3), perfluorohexane (C_6F_{14}, density = 1.669 g/cm^3), and water are immiscible liquids; that is, they do not dissolve in one another. You place 10 mL of each in a graduated cylinder, along with pieces of high-density polyethylene (HDPE, density 0.97 g/cm^3), polyvinyl chloride (PVC, density = 1.36 g/cm^3), and Teflon (density = 2.3 g/cm^3). None of these common plastics dissolves in these liquids. Describe what you expect to see.

22. Milk in a glass bottle was placed in the freezing compartment of a refrigerator overnight. By morning, a column of frozen milk emerged from the bottle. Explain this observation.

Frozen milk in a glass bottle.

23. ■ You can figure out whether a substance floats or sinks if you know its density and the density of the liquid. In which of the liquids listed below will high-density polyethylene (HDPE) float. (HDPE, a common plastic, has a density of 0.97 g/cm^3. It does not dissolve in any of these liquids.)

Substance	Density (g/cm³)	Properties, Uses
Ethylene glycol	1.1088	Toxic; the major component of automobile antifreeze
Water	0.9997	
Ethanol	0.7893	The alcohol in alcoholic beverages
Methanol	0.7914	Toxic; gasoline additive to prevent gas line freezing
Acetic acid	1.0492	Component of vinegar
Glycerol	1.2613	Solvent used in home care products

24. Describe an experimental method that can be used to determine the density of an irregularly shaped piece of metal.

25. ▲ Make a drawing, based on the kinetic-molecular theory and the ideas about atoms and molecules presented in this chapter, of the arrangement of particles in each of the cases listed here. For each case, draw 10 particles of each substance. It is acceptable for your diagram to be two dimensional. Represent each atom as a circle, and distinguish each different kind of atom by shading.
(a) A sample of solid iron (which consists of iron atoms)
(b) A sample of *liquid* water (which consists of H_2O molecules)
(c) A sample of water *vapor*

▲ more challenging ■ in OWL Blue-numbered questions answered in Appendix O

26. ▲ Make a drawing, based on the kinetic-molecular theory and the ideas about atoms and molecules presented in this chapter, of the arrangement of particles in each of the cases listed here. For each case, draw 10 particles of each substance. It is acceptable for your diagram to be two dimensional. Represent each atom as a circle, and distinguish each different kind of atom by shading.
    (a) A homogeneous mixture of water vapor and helium gas (which consists of helium atoms)
    (b) A heterogeneous mixture consisting of liquid water and solid aluminum; show a region of the sample that includes both substances
    (c) A sample of brass (which is a homogeneous solid mixture of copper and zinc)

27. You are given a sample of a silvery metal. What information would you seek to prove that the metal is silver?

28. Suggest a way to determine if the colorless liquid in a beaker is water. If it is water, does it contain dissolved salt? How could you discover if there is salt dissolved in the water?

29. ■ Diabetes can alter the density of urine, and so urine density can be used as a diagnostic tool. Diabetics can excrete too much sugar or excrete too much water. What do you predict will happen to the density of urine under each of these conditions? (*Hint*: Water containing dissolved sugar is more dense than pure water.)

30. ■ Three liquids of different densities are mixed. Because they are not miscible (do not form a homogeneous solution with one another), they form discrete layers, one on top of the other. Sketch the result of mixing carbon tetrachloride (CCl_4, $d = 1.58$ g/cm^3), mercury ($d = 13.546$ g/cm^3), and water ($d = 1.00$ g/cm^3).

31. ■ The following photo shows the element potassium reacting with water to form the element hydrogen, a gas, and a solution of the compound potassium hydroxide.

Charles D. Winters

Potassium reacting with water to produce hydrogen gas and potassium hydroxide.

    (a) What states of matter are involved in the reaction?
    (b) Is the observed change chemical or physical?
    (c) What are the reactants in this reaction, and what are the products?
    (d) What qualitative observations can be made concerning this reaction?

32. A copper-colored metal is found to conduct an electric current. Can you say with certainty that it is copper? Why or why not? Suggest additional information that could provide unequivocal confirmation that the metal is copper.

33. ■ What experiment can you use to:
    (a) Separate salt from water?
    (b) Separate iron filings from small pieces of lead?
    (c) Separate elemental sulfur from sugar?

34. ■ Four balloons are each filled with a different gas of varying density:

    Helium, $d = 0.164$ g/L

    Neon, $d = 0.825$ g/L

    Argon, $d = 1.633$ g/L

    Krypton, $d = 4.425$ g/L

    If the density of dry air is 1.12 g/L, which balloon or balloons float in air?

35. Many foods are fortified with vitamins and minerals. Some breakfast cereals have elemental iron added. Iron chips are used instead of iron compounds because the compounds can be converted by the oxygen in air to a form of iron that is not biochemically useful. Iron chips, on the other hand, are converted to useful iron compounds in the gut, and the iron can then be absorbed. Outline a method by which you could remove the iron (as iron chips) from a box of cereal and determine the mass of iron in a given mass of cereal. (*See ChemistryNow Screens 1.1 and 1.18, Chemical Puzzler.*)

36. Study the animation of the conversion of P_4 and Cl_2 molecules to PCl_3 molecules in *ChemistryNow, Screen 1.12 (Chemical Change on the Molecular Scale)*.
    (a) What are the reactants in this chemical change? What are the products?
    (b) Describe how the structures of the reactant molecules differ from the structures of the product molecules.

37. ■ The photo below shows elemental iodine dissolving in ethanol to give a solution. Is this a physical or chemical change?

Charles D. Winters

Elemental iodine dissolving in ethanol.

(See also the ChemistryNow Screen 1.12, Exercise, Physical Properties of Matter)

Let's Review | The Tools of Quantitative Chemistry

John Kotz

Copper

Copper (Cu) is the 26th element in abundance in the Earth's crust (not too different from its near neighbors nickel and zinc in the periodic table), but it and its minerals are widely distributed, and it is relatively easy to obtain the metal from its ores. As a result, elemental copper is used around the world for many useful items, from cooking pots to electric wires. The photo at the left above shows large copper pots on sale in a market in southwestern China.

Pure copper (often called *native copper*) is found in nature, but more commonly it is found combined with other elements in minerals such as cuprite, azurite, or malachite. Copper metal is relatively soft but, when combined in a ratio of about 2 to 1 with tin, it forms bronze. Bronze was important in early civilizations and gave its name to an epoch of human development, the Bronze Age, which started around 3000 BC and lasted until about 1000 BC. The development of bronze was significant because bronze is stronger than copper and can be shaped into a sharper edge. This improved the cutting edges

of plows and weapons, thus giving cultures that possessed bronze advantages over those that did not.

Copper is now used in wiring because it conducts electricity well, and it is used in cooking pots because it conducts heat well. It is also described as one of the "coinage metals" (along with silver and gold) because it has been used in coins for centuries.

Compounds of copper are common, and copper is one of the eight essential metals in our bodies, where it is needed for some enzymes to use oxygen more effectively. Fortunately, it is found in common foods (in meats such as lamb, duck, pork, and beef, and in almonds and walnuts). The average person has about 72 mg of copper in his or her body.

The figure above also shows what happens as we zoom into copper at the particulate level. We begin to see atoms arranged in a regular array, or *lattice*, as chemists call it. Zooming in even closer, we see the smallest repeating unit of the crystal.

You can learn more about copper and its properties by answering the Study Questions 56 and 57 at the end of this *Let's Review* section.

At its core, chemistry is a quantitative science. Chemists make measurements of, among other things, size, mass, volume, time, and temperature. Scientists then manipulate that information to search for relationships among properties and to provide insight into the molecular basis of matter.

This section reviews the units used in chemistry, briefly describes the proper treatment of numerical data, and reviews some mathematical skills you will need in chemical calculations. After studying this section you should be able to:

- use the common units for measurements in chemistry and make unit conversions (such as liters to milliliters).
- express and use numbers in exponential or scientific notation.
- express quantitative information in an algebraic expression and solve that expression.
- read information from graphs.
- prepare a graph of numerical information. If the graph produces a straight line, find the slope and equation of the line.
- recognize and express uncertainties in measurements.

1 Units of Measurement

Doing chemistry requires observing chemical reactions and physical changes. We make qualitative observations—such as changes in color or the evolution of heat—and quantitative measurements of temperature, time, volume, mass, and length or size. To record and report measurements, the scientific community has chosen a modified version of the **metric system.** This decimal system, used internationally in science, is called the Système International d'Unités (International System of Units), abbreviated **SI.**

All SI units are derived from base units, some of which are listed in Table 1. Larger and smaller quantities are expressed by using appropriate prefixes with the base unit (Table 2). The nanometer (nm), for example, is 1 billionth of a meter. That is, it is equivalent to 1×10^{-9} m (meter). Dimensions on the nanometer scale are common in chemistry and biology because a typical molecule is about 1 nm across and a bacterium is about 1000 nm in length. The prefix *nano-* is also used in the name for a new area of science, *nanotechnology* (▶ *Materials Chemistry,* pages 656–669) which involves the synthesis and study of materials around this tiny size.

TABLE 1   Some SI Base Units

Measured Property	Name of Unit	Abbreviation
Mass	kilogram	kg
Length	meter	m
Time	second	s
Temperature	kelvin	K
Amount of substance	mole	mol
Electric current	ampere	A

1000 g = 1 kg
1×10^9 nm = 1 m
10 mm = 1 cm
100 cm = 10 dm = 1 m
1000 m = 1 km

Conversion factors for SI units are given in Appendix C and inside the back cover of this book.

TABLE 2 Selected Prefixes Used in the Metric System

Prefix	Abbreviation	Meaning	Example
giga-	G	10^9 (billion)	1 gigahertz = 1×10^9 Hz
mega-	M	10^6 (million)	1 megaton = 1×10^6 tons
kilo-	k	10^3 (thousand)	1 kilogram (kg) = 1×10^3 g
deci-	d	10^{-1} (tenth)	1 decimeter (dm) = 1×10^{-1} m
centi-	c	10^{-2} (one hundredth)	1 centimeter (cm) = 1×10^{-2} m
milli-	m	10^{-3} (one thousandth)	1 millimeter (mm) = 1×10^{-3} m
micro-	μ	10^{-6} (one millionth)	1 micrometer (μm) = 1×10^{-6} m
nano-	n	10^{-9} (one billionth)	1 nanometer (nm) = 1×10^{-9} m
pico-	p	10^{-12}	1 picometer (pm) = 1×10^{-12} m
femto-	f	10^{-15}	1 femtometer (fm) = 1×10^{-15} m

Temperature Scales

Two temperature scales are commonly used in scientific work: Celsius and Kelvin (Figure 1). The Celsius scale is generally used worldwide for measurements in the laboratory. When calculations incorporate temperature data, however, the Kelvin scale must be used.

The Celsius Temperature Scale

The size of the Celsius degree is defined by assigning zero as the freezing point of pure water (0 °C) and 100 as its boiling point (100 °C). You may recognize that a comfortable room temperature is around 20 °C and your normal body temperature is 37 °C. And we find that the warmest water we can stand to immerse a finger in is about 60 °C.

Active Figure 1 A comparison of Fahrenheit, Celsius, and Kelvin scales. The reference, or starting point, for the Kelvin scale is absolute zero (0 K = −273.15 °C), which has been shown theoretically and experimentally to be the lowest possible temperature.

Chemistry ⚛ Now™ Sign in at www.cengage.com/login and go to the Chapter Contents menu to explore an interactive version of this figure accompanied by an exercise.

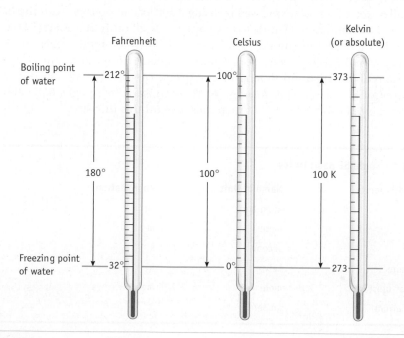

The Kelvin Temperature Scale

William Thomson, known as Lord Kelvin (1824–1907), first suggested the temperature scale that now bears his name. The Kelvin scale uses the same size unit as the Celsius scale, but it assigns zero as the lowest temperature that can be achieved, a point called **absolute zero.** Many experiments have found that this limiting temperature is -273.15 °C (-459.67 °F). *Kelvin units and Celsius degrees are the same size.* Thus, the freezing point of water is reached at 273.15 K; that is, 0 °C = 273.15 K. The boiling point of pure water is 373.15 K. Temperatures in Celsius degrees are readily converted to kelvins, and vice versa, using the relation

$$T \text{ (K)} = \frac{1 \text{ K}}{1 \text{ °C}} (T \text{ °C} + 273.15 \text{ °C}) \qquad \text{(1)}$$

Thus, a common room temperature of 23.5 °C is

$$T \text{ (K)} = \frac{1 \text{ K}}{1 \text{ °C}} (23.5 \text{ °C} + 273.15 \text{ °C}) = 296.7 \text{ K}$$

Finally, notice that the degree symbol (°) is not used with Kelvin temperatures. The name of the unit on this scale is the *kelvin* (not capitalized), and such temperatures are designated with a capital K.

EXERCISE 1 Temperature Scales

Liquid nitrogen boils at 77 K. What is this temperature in Celsius degrees?

■ **Temperature Conversions** When converting 23.5 °C to kelvins, adding 273.15 gives 296.65. However, the rules of "significant figures" (page 35) tell us that the sum or difference of two numbers can have no more decimal places than the number with the fewest decimal places. Thus, we round the answer to 296.7 K, a number with one decimal place.

Length, Volume, and Mass

The meter is the standard unit of *length*, but objects observed in chemistry are frequently smaller than 1 meter. Measurements are often reported in units of centimeters (cm), millimeters (mm), or micrometers (μm) (Figure 2), and objects on the atomic and molecular scale have dimensions of nanometers (nm; 1 nm = 1×10^{-9} m) or picometers (pm; 1 pm = 1×10^{-12} m) (Figure 3).

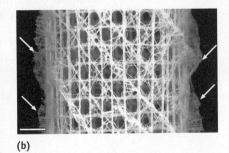

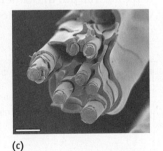

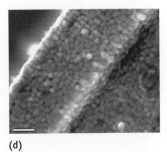

(a)

(b)

(c)

(d)

FIGURE 2 Dimensions in chemistry and biology. (a) Photograph of the glassy skeleton of a sea sponge, *Euplectella*. Scale bar = 5 cm. (b) Fragment of the structure showing the square grid of the lattice with diagonal supports. Scale bar = 1 mm. (c) Scanning electron microscope (SEM) image of a single strand showing its ceramic-composite structure. Scale bar = 20 μm. (d) SEM image of the surface of a strand showing that is it composed of nanoscale spheres of hydrated silica. Scale bar = 500 nm.

FIGURE 3 Dimensions in the molecular world. Dimensions on the molecular scale are often given in terms of nanometers (1 nm = 1 × 10⁻⁹ m) or picometers (1 pm = 1 × 10⁻¹² m). Here, the distance between C atoms in diamond is 0.154 nm or 154 pm. An older, but often-used non-SI unit is the Ångstrom unit (Å), where 1 Å = 1.0 × 10⁻¹⁰ m. The C–C distance in diamond would be 1.54 A.

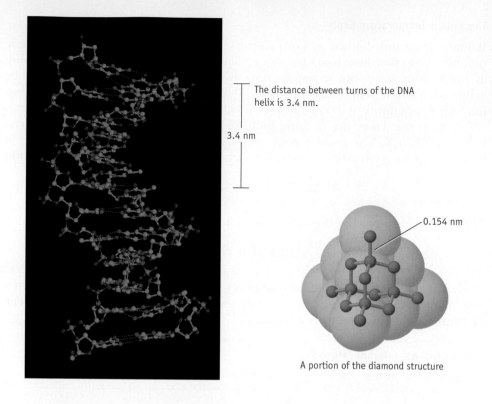

The distance between turns of the DNA helix is 3.4 nm.

3.4 nm

0.154 nm

A portion of the diamond structure

To illustrate the range of dimensions used in science, let us look at a recent study of the glassy skeleton of a sea sponge. The sea sponge in Figure 2a is about 20 cm long and a few centimeters in diameter. A closer look (Figure 2b) shows more detail of the lattice-like structure. Scientists at Bell Laboratories found that each strand of the lattice is a ceramic-fiber composite of silica (SiO_2) and protein less than 100 μm in diameter (Figure 2c). These strands are composed of "spicules," which, at the nanoscale level, consist of silica nanoparticles just a few nanometers in diameter (Figure 2d).

■ **EXAMPLE 1 Distances on the Molecular Scale**

Problem The distance between an O atom and an H atom in a water molecule is 95.8 pm. What is this distance in meters (m)? In nanometers (nm)?

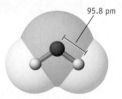

95.8 pm

Strategy You can solve this problem by knowing the relationship or conversion factor between the units in the information you are given (picometers) and the desired units (meters or nanometers). (For more about conversion factors and their use in problem solving, see page 38.) There is no conversion factor given in Table 2 to change nanometers to picometers directly, but relationships are listed between meters and picometers and between meters and nanometers. Therefore, we first convert picometers to meters, and then we convert meters to nanometers.

$$\text{Picometers} \xrightarrow{\times \, ^m/_{pm}} \text{Meters} \xrightarrow{\times \, ^{nm}/_m} \text{Nanometers}$$

Solution Using the appropriate conversion factors (1 pm = 1 × 10⁻¹² m and 1 nm = 1 × 10⁻⁹ m), we have

$$95.8 \text{ pm} \times \frac{1 \times 10^{-12} \text{ m}}{1 \text{ pm}} = 9.58 \times 10^{-11} \text{ m}$$

$$9.58 \times 10^{-11} \text{ m} \times \frac{1 \text{ nm}}{1 \times 10^{-9} \text{ m}} = 9.58 \times 10^{-2} \text{ nm} \text{ or } 0.0958 \text{ nm}$$

Comment Notice how the units cancel to leave an answer whose unit is that of the numerator of the conversion factor. The process of using units to guide a calculation is called *dimensional analysis*. It is explored further on pages 38–39.

EXERCISE 2 Using Units of Length

A platinum sheet is 2.50 cm square and has a thickness of 0.25 mm. What is the volume of the platinum sheet (in cm³)?

FIGURE 4 Some common laboratory glassware. Volumes are marked in units of milliliters (mL). Remember that 1 mL is equivalent to 1 cm³.

Chemists often use glassware such as beakers, flasks, pipets, graduated cylinders, and burets, which are marked in volume units (Figure 4). The SI unit of volume is the cubic meter (m³), which is too large for everyday laboratory use. Chemists usually use the liter, symbolized by L, for volume measurements. One liter is equivalent to the volume of a cube with sides equal to 10 cm [= (0.1 m)³ = 0.001 m³].

$$1 \text{ liter (L)} = 1000 \text{ cm}^3 = 1000 \text{ mL} = 0.001 \text{ m}^3$$

The liter is a convenient unit to use in the laboratory, as is the milliliter (mL). Because there are exactly 1000 mL (= 1000 cm³) in a liter, this means that

$$1 \text{ mL} = 0.001 \text{ L} = 1 \text{ cm}^3$$

The units *milliliter and cubic centimeter* (or "cc") *are interchangeable.* Therefore, a flask that contains exactly 125 mL has a volume of 125 cm³.

Although not widely used in the United States, the cubic decimeter (dm³) is a common unit in the rest of the world. A length of 10 cm is called a decimeter (dm). Because a cube 10 cm on a side defines a volume of 1 liter, *a liter is equivalent to a cubic decimeter*: 1 L = 1 dm³. Products in Europe, Africa, and other parts of the world are often sold by the cubic decimeter.

The *deciliter, dL,* which is exactly equivalent to 0.100 L or 100 mL, is widely used in medicine. For example, standards for concentrations of environmental contaminants are often set as a certain mass per deciliter. The state of Massachusetts recommends that children with more than 10 micrograms (10 × 10⁻⁶ g) of lead per deciliter of blood undergo further testing for lead poisoning.

EXERCISE 3 Volume

(a) A standard wine bottle has a volume of 750 mL. What volume, in liters, does this represent? How many deciliters?

(b) One U.S. gallon is equivalent to 3.7865 L. What is the volume in liters of a 2.0-quart carton of milk? (There are 4 quarts in a gallon.) How many cubic decimeters?

Finally, when chemists prepare chemicals for reactions, they often take given quantities or masses of materials. The *mass* of a body is the fundamental measure of the quantity of matter, and the SI unit of mass is the kilogram (kg). Smaller masses are expressed in grams (g) or milligrams (mg).

$$1 \text{ kg} = 1000 \text{ g} \text{ and } 1 \text{ g} = 1000 \text{ mg}$$

2 Making Measurements: Precision, Accuracy, Experimental Error, and Standard Deviation

The **precision** of a measurement indicates how well several determinations of the same quantity agree. This is illustrated by the results of throwing darts at a target. In Figure 5a, the dart thrower was apparently not skillful, and the precision of the dart's placement on the target is low. In Figures 5b and 5c, the darts are clustered together, indicating much better consistency on the part of the thrower—that is, greater precision.

Accuracy is the agreement of a measurement with the accepted value of the quantity. Figure 5c shows that our thrower was accurate as well as precise—the average of all shots is close to the targeted position, the bull's eye.

Figure 5b shows it is possible to be precise without being accurate—the thrower has consistently missed the bull's eye, although all the darts are clustered precisely around one point on the target. This is analogous to an experiment with some flaw (either in design or in a measuring device) that causes all results to differ from the correct value by the same amount.

The accuracy of a result in the laboratory is often expressed in terms of percent error, whereas the precision is expressed as a standard deviation.

■ **Accuracy and NIST** The National Institute for Standards and Technology (NIST) is an important resource for the standards used in science. Comparison with NIST data is a test of the accuracy of the measurement. See www.nist.gov.

Experimental Error

If you measure a quantity in the laboratory, you may be required to report the error in the result, the difference between your result and the accepted value,

$$\text{Error} = \text{experimentally determined value} - \text{accepted value}$$

(a) Poor precision and poor accuracy   (b) Good precision and poor accuracy   (c) Good precision and good accuracy

FIGURE 5 Precision and accuracy.

Charles D. Winters

or the **percent error.**

$$\text{Percent error} = \frac{\text{error in measurement}}{\text{accepted value}} \times 100\%$$

■ **Percent Error** Percent error can be positive or negative, indicating whether the experimental value is too high or too low compared to the accepted value. In Example 2, Student B's error is −0.2%, indicating it is 0.2% lower than the accepted value.

■ **EXAMPLE 2** **Precision, Accuracy, and Error**

Problem A coin has an "accepted" diameter of 28.054 mm. In an experiment, two students measure this diameter. Student A makes four measurements of the diameter of the coin using a precision tool called a micrometer. Student B measures the same coin using a simple plastic ruler. The two students report the following results:

Student A	Student B
28.246 mm	27.9 mm
28.244	28.0
28.246	27.8
28.248	28.1

What is the average diameter and percent error obtained in each case? Which student's data are more accurate?

Strategy For each set of values, we calculate the average of the results and then compare this average with 28.054 mm.

Solution The average for each set of data is obtained by summing the four values and dividing by 4.

Average value for Student A = 28.246 mm
Average value for Student B = 28.0 mm

Although Student A has four results very close to one another (and so of high precision), student A's result is less accurate than that of Student B. The average diameter for Student A differs from the "accepted" value by 0.192 mm and has a percent error of 0.684%:

$$\text{Percent error} = \frac{28.246 \text{ mm} - 28.054 \text{ mm}}{28.054 \text{ mm}} \times 100\% = 0.684\%$$

Student B's measurement has a percent error of only about −0.2%.

Comment We noted that Student A had precise results; the standard deviation calculated as described below is 2×10^{-3}. In contrast, Student B had less precise results (standard deviation = 0.14). Possible reasons for the error in Students A's result are incorrect use of the micrometer or a flaw in the instrument.

Standard Deviation

Laboratory measurements can be in error for two basic reasons. First, there may be "determinate" errors caused by faulty instruments or human errors such as incorrect record keeping. So-called "indeterminate" errors arise from uncertainties in a measurement where the cause is not known and cannot be controlled by the lab worker. One way to judge the indeterminate error in a result is to calculate the standard deviation.

The **standard deviation** of a series of measurements is equal to the square root of the sum of the squares of the deviations for each measurement from the average divided by one less than the number of measurements. It has a precise statistical significance: assuming a large number of measurements is used to calculate the average, 68% of the values collected are expected to be within one standard deviation of the value determined, and 95% are within two standard deviations.

Suppose you carefully measured the mass of water delivered by a 10-mL pipet. (A pipet containing a green solution is shown in Figure 4.) For five attempts at the measurement (shown in column 2 of the table below), the standard deviation is found as follows: First, the average of the measurements is calculated (here, 9.984). Next, the deviation of each individual measurement from this value is determined (column 3). These values are squared, giving the values in column 4, and the sum of these values is determined. The standard deviation is then calculated by dividing this sum by 4 (the number of determinations minus 1) and taking the square root of the result.

Determination	Measured Mass (g)	Difference between Average and Measurement (g)	Square of Difference
1	9.990	−0.006	4×10^{-5}
2	9.993	−0.009	8×10^{-5}
3	9.973	0.011	12×10^{-5}
4	9.980	0.004	2×10^{-5}
5	9.982	0.002	0.4×10^{-5}

Average mass = 9.984 g

Sum of squares of differences = 26×10^{-5}

$$\text{Standard deviation} = \sqrt{\frac{26 \times 10^{-5}}{4}} = \pm 0.008$$

Based on this calculation, it would be appropriate to represent the measured mass as 9.984 ± 0.008 g. This would tell a reader that if this experiment were repeated, a majority of the values would fall in the range of 9.976 g to 9.992 g.

FIGURE 6 Lake Otsego. This lake, with a surface area of 2.33×10^7 m², is located in northern New York State. Cooperstown is a village at the base of the lake where the Susquehanna River originates. To learn more about the environmental biology and chemistry of the lake, go to **www.oneonta.edu/academics/biofld**

EXERCISE 5 Accuracy, Error, and Standard Deviation

Two students measured the freezing point of an unknown liquid. Student A used an ordinary laboratory thermometer calibrated in 0.1 °C units. Student B used a thermometer certified by NIST (National Institute for Standards and Technology) and calibrated in 0.01 °C units. Their results were as follows:

Student A: −0.3 °C; 0.2 °C; 0.0 °C; and −0.3 °C

Student B: −0.02 °C, +0.02 °C, 0.00 °C, and +0.04 °C

Calculate the average value, and, knowing that the liquid was water, calculate the percent error and standard deviation for each student. Which student has the more precise values? Which has the smaller error?

---

3 Mathematics of Chemistry

Exponential or Scientific Notation

Lake Otsego in northern New York is also called *Glimmerglass*, a name suggested by James Fenimore Cooper (1789–1851), the great American author and an early resident of the village now known as Cooperstown. Extensive environmental studies have been done along this lake (Figure 6), and some quantitative information useful to chemists, biologists, and geologists is given in the following table:

Lake Otsego Characteristics	Quantitative Information
Area	2.33×10^7 m^2
Maximum depth	505 m
Dissolved solids in lake water	2×10^2 mg/L
Average rainfall in the lake basin	1.02×10^2 cm/year
Average snowfall in the lake basin	198 cm/year

FIGURE 7 **Exponential numbers in astronomy.** The spiral galaxy M-83 is 3.0×10^6 parsecs away from Earth and has a diameter of 9.0×10^3 parsecs. The unit used in astronomy, the parsec (pc), is equivalent to 206265 AU (astronomical units) where 1 AU is 1.496×10^8 km. What is the distance between Earth and M-83 in km?

All of the data collected are in metric units. However, some data are expressed in **fixed notation** (505 m, 198 cm/year), whereas other data are expressed in **exponential,** or **scientific, notation** (2.33×10^7 m^2). Scientific notation is a way of presenting very large or very small numbers in a compact and consistent form that simplifies calculations. Because of its convenience, scientific notation is widely used in sciences such as chemistry, physics, engineering, and astronomy (Figure 7).

In scientific notation a number is expressed as a product of two numbers: $N \times 10^n$. N is the digit term and is a number between 1 and 9.9999. . . . The second number, 10^n, the exponential term, is some integer power of 10. For example, 1234 is written in scientific notation as 1.234×10^3, or 1.234 multiplied by 10 three times:

$$1234 = 1.234 \times 10^1 \times 10^1 \times 10^1 = 1.234 \times 10^3$$

Conversely, a number less than 1, such as 0.01234, is written as 1.234×10^{-2}. This notation tells us that 1.234 should be divided twice by 10 to obtain 0.01234:

$$0.01234 = \frac{1.234}{10^1 \times 10^1} = 1.234 \times 10^{-1} \times 10^{-1} = 1.234 \times 10^{-2}$$

When converting a number to scientific notation, notice that the exponent n is positive if the number is greater than 1 and negative if the number is less than 1. The value of n is the number of places by which the decimal is shifted to obtain the number in scientific notation:

$$1\,2\,3\,4\,5. = 1.2345 \times 10^4$$

(a) Decimal shifted four places to the left. Therefore, n is positive and equal to 4.

$$0.0\,0\,0\,1\,2 = 1.2 \times 10^{-3}$$

(b) Decimal shifted three places to the right. Therefore, n is negative and equal to 3.

If you wish to convert a number in scientific notation to one using fixed notation (that is, not using powers of 10), the procedure is reversed:

$$6\,.\,2\,7\,3 \times 10^2 = 627.3$$

(a) Decimal point moved two places to the right because n is positive and equal to 2.

$$0\,0\,6.273 \times 10^{-3} = 0.006273$$

(b) Decimal point shifted three places to the left because n is negative and equal to 3.

Two final points should be made concerning scientific notation. First, be aware that calculators and computers often express a number such as 1.23×10^3 as 1.23E3

Using Your Calculator

You will be performing a number of calculations in general chemistry, most of them using a calculator. Many different types of calculators are available, but this problem-solving tip describes several of the kinds of operations you will need to perform on a typical calculator. Be sure to consult your calculator manual for specific instructions to enter scientific notation and to find powers and roots of numbers.

1. Scientific Notation

When entering a number such as 1.23×10^{-4} into your calculator, you first enter 1.23 and then press a key marked EE or EXP (or something similar). This enters the "$\times 10$" portion of the notation for you. You then complete the entry by keying in the exponent of the number, -4. (To change the exponent from $+4$ to -4, press the "$+/-$" key.)

A common error made by students is to enter 1.23, press the multiply key ($\times$), and then key in 10 before finishing by pressing EE or EXP followed by -4. This gives you an entry that is 10 times too large.

2. Powers of Numbers

Electronic calculators often offer two methods of raising a number to a power. To square a number, enter the number and then press the x^2 key. To raise a number to any power, use the y^x (or similar key such as ^). For example, to raise 1.42×10^2 to the fourth power:

1. Enter 1.42×10^2.
2. Press y^x.
3. Enter 4 (this should appear on the display).
4. Press $=$, and 4.0659×10^8 appears on the display.

3. Roots of Numbers

A general procedure for finding any root is to use the y^x key. For a square root, x is 0.5 (or 1/2), whereas it is 0.3333 (or 1/3) for a cube root, 0.25 (or 1/4) for a fourth root, and so on. For example, to find the fourth root of 5.6×10^{-10}:

1. Enter the number.
2. Press the y^x key.
3. Enter the desired root. Because we want the fourth root, enter 0.25.
4. Press $=$. The answer here is 4.9×10^{-3}.

To make sure you are using your calculator correctly, try these sample calculations:

1. $(6.02 \times 10^{23})(2.26 \times 10^{-5})/367$
   (Answer $= 3.71 \times 10^{16}$)
2. $(4.32 \times 10^{-3})^3$
   (Answer $= 8.06 \times 10^{-8}$)
3. $(4.32 \times 10^{-3})^{1/3}$
   (Answer $= 0.163$)

---

or 6.45×10^{-5} as 6.45E-5. Second, some electronic calculators can readily convert numbers in fixed notation to scientific notation. If you have such a calculator, you may be able to do this by pressing the EE or EXP key and then the "$=$" key (but check your calculator manual to learn how your device operates).

In chemistry, you will often have to use numbers in exponential notation in mathematical operations. The following five operations are important:

- *Adding and Subtracting Numbers Expressed in Scientific Notation*
  When adding or subtracting two numbers, first convert them to the same powers of 10. The digit terms are then added or subtracted as appropriate:

$$(1.234 \times 10^{-3}) + (5.623 \times 10^{-2}) = (0.1234 \times 10^{-2}) + (5.623 \times 10^{-2})$$
$$= 5.746 \times 10^{-2}$$

- *Multiplication of Numbers Expressed in Scientific Notation*
  The digit terms are multiplied in the usual manner, and the exponents are added algebraically. The result is expressed with a digit term with only one nonzero digit to the left of the decimal:

$$(6.0 \times 10^{23}) \times (2.0 \times 10^{-2}) = (6.0)(2.0 \times 10^{23-2}) = 12 \times 10^{21} = 1.2 \times 10^{22}$$

- *Division of Numbers Expressed in Scientific Notation*
  The digit terms are divided in the usual manner, and the exponents are subtracted algebraically. The quotient is written with one nonzero digit to the left of the decimal in the digit term:

$$\frac{7.60 \times 10^3}{1.23 \times 10^2} = \frac{7.60}{1.23} \times 10^{3-2} = 6.18 \times 10^1$$

■ **Comparing the Earth and a Plant Cell—Powers of Ten**

Earth = 12,760,000 meters wide
    = 12.76 million meters
    = 1.276×10^7 meters
Plant cell = 0.00001276 meter wide
    = 12.76 millionths of a meter
    = 1.276×10^{-5} meters

- *Powers of Numbers Expressed in Scientific Notation*
  When raising a number in exponential notation to a power, treat the digit term in the usual manner. The exponent is then multiplied by the number indicating the power:

$$(5.28 \times 10^3)^2 = (5.28)^2 \times 10^{3 \times 2} = 27.9 \times 10^6 = 2.79 \times 10^7$$

- *Roots of Numbers Expressed in Scientific Notation*
  Unless you use an electronic calculator, the number must first be put into a form in which the exponent is exactly divisible by the root. For example, for a square root, the exponent should be divisible by 2. The root of the digit term is found in the usual way, and the exponent is divided by the desired root:

$$\sqrt{3.6 \times 10^7} = \sqrt{36 \times 10^6} = \sqrt{36} \times \sqrt{10^6} = 6.0 \times 10^3$$

Significant Figures

In most experiments, several kinds of measurements must be made, and some can be made more precisely than others. It is common sense that a result calculated from experimental data can be no more precise than the least precise piece of information that went into the calculation. This is where the rules for significant figures come in. **Significant figures** are the digits in a measured quantity that were observed with the measuring device.

Determining Significant Figures

Suppose we place a U.S. dime on the pan of a standard laboratory balance such as the one pictured in Figure 8 and observe a mass of 2.265 g. This number has four significant figures or digits because all four numbers are observed. However, you will learn from experience that the final digit (5) is somewhat uncertain because you may notice the balance readings can change slightly and give masses of 2.264, 2.265, and 2.266, with the mass of 2.265 observed most of the time. Thus, of the four significant digits (2.265) the last (5) is uncertain. In general, *in a number representing a scientific measurement, the last digit to the right is taken to be inexact.* Unless stated otherwise, it is common practice to assign an uncertainty of ±1 to the last significant digit.

Suppose you want to calculate the density of a piece of metal (Figure 9). The mass and dimensions were determined by standard laboratory techniques. Most of these data have two digits to the right of the decimal, but they have different numbers of significant figures.

Measurement	Data Collected	Significant Figures
Mass of metal	13.56 g	4
Length	6.45 cm	3
Width	2.50 cm	3
Thickness	3.1 mm = 0.31 cm	2

The quantity 0.31 cm has two significant figures. That is, the 3 in 0.31 is exactly known, but the 1 is uncertain. This means the thickness of the metal piece may have been as small as 0.30 cm or as large as 0.32 cm, but it is most likely 0.31 cm.

Charles D. Winters

FIGURE 8 Standard laboratory balance and significant figures. Such balances can determine the mass of an object to the nearest milligram. Thus, an object may have a mass of 13.456 g (13456 mg, five significant figures), 0.123 g (123 mg, three significant figures), or 0.072 g (72 mg, two significant figures).

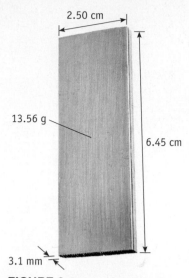

2.50 cm

13.56 g

6.45 cm

3.1 mm

FIGURE 9 Data used to determine the density of a metal.

■ **Zeroes and Common Laboratory Mistakes** We often see students find the mass of a chemical on a balance and fail to write down trailing zeroes. For example, if you find the mass is 2.340 g, the final zero is significant and must be reported as part of the measured value. The number 2.34 g has only three significant figures and implies the 4 is uncertain, when in fact the balance reading indicated the 4 is certain.

In the case of the width of the piece, you found it to be 2.50 cm, where 2.5 is known with certainty, but the final 0 is uncertain. There are three significant figures in 2.50.

When you first read a number in a problem, or collect data in the laboratory, how do you determine how many significant figures it contains?

First, is the number an exact number or a measured quantity? If it is an exact number, you don't have to worry about the number of significant figures. For example, there are exactly 100 cm in 1 m. We could add as many zeros after the decimal place, and the expression would still be true. Using this number in a calculation will not affect how many significant figures you can report in your answer.

If, however, the number is a measured value, you must take into account significant figures. The number of significant figures in our data above is clear, with the possible exception of 0.31 and 2.50. Are the zeroes significant?

1. *Zeroes between two other significant digits are significant.* For example, the zero in 103 is significant.
2. *Zeroes to the right of a nonzero number and also to the right of a decimal place are significant.* For example, in the number 2.50 cm, the zero is significant.
3. *Zeroes that are placeholders are not significant.* There are two types of numbers that fall under this rule.
   a) The first are decimal numbers with zeroes that occur *before* the first nonzero digit. For example, in 0.0013, only the 1 and the 3 are significant; the zeroes are not. This number has two significant figures.
   b) The second are *numbers with trailing zeroes* that must be there to indicate the magnitude of the number. For example, the zeroes in the number 13,000 may or may not be significant; it depends on whether they were measured or not. To avoid confusion with regard to such numbers, we *shall assume in this book that trailing zeroes are significant when there is a decimal point to the right of the last zero.* Thus, we would say that 13,000 has only two significant figures but that 13,000. has five. We suggest that the best way to be unambiguous when writing numbers with trailing zeroes is to use scientific notation. For example 1.300×10^4 clearly indicates four significant figures, whereas 1.3×10^4 indicates two and 1.3000×10^4 indicates five.

Using Significant Figures in Calculations

When doing calculations using measured quantities, we follow some basic rules so that the results reflect the precision of all the measurements that go into the calculations. *The rules used for significant figures in this book are as follows:*

Rule 1. When adding or subtracting numbers, the number of decimal places in the answer is equal to the number of decimal places in the number with the fewest digits after the decimal.

0.12	2 decimal places	2 significant figures
+ 1.9	1 decimal place	2 significant figures
+10.925	3 decimal places	5 significant figures
12.945	3 decimal places	

The sum should be reported as 12.9, a number with one decimal place, because 1.9 has only one decimal place.

Rule 2. In multiplication or division, the number of significant figures in the answer is determined by the quantity with the fewest significant figures.

$$\frac{0.01208}{0.0236} = 0.512, \text{ or in scientific notation, } 5.12 \times 10^{-1}$$

Because 0.0236 has only three significant digits, while 0.01208 has four, the answer should have three significant digits.

Rule 3. When a number is rounded off, the last digit to be retained is increased by one only if the following digit is 5 or greater.

Full Number	Number Rounded to Three Significant Digits
12.696	12.7
16.349	16.3
18.35	18.4
18.351	18.4

Now let us apply these rules to calculate the density of the piece of metal in Figure 9.

$$\text{Length} \times \text{width} \times \text{thickness} = \text{volume}$$

$$6.45 \text{ cm} \times 2.50 \text{ cm} \times 0.31 \text{ cm} = 5.0 \text{ cm}^3$$

$$\text{Density} = \frac{\text{mass (g)}}{\text{volume (cm}^3)} = \frac{13.56 \text{ g}}{5.0 \text{ cm}^3} = 2.7 \text{ g/cm}^3$$

The calculated density has two significant figures because *a calculated result can be no more precise than the least precise data used*, and here the thickness has only two significant figures.

One last word on significant figures and calculations: When working problems, you should do the calculation with all the digits allowed by your calculator and round off only at the end of the calculation. *Rounding off in the middle of a calculation can introduce errors.*

Chemistry ❍ Now™

Sign in at **www.cengage.com/login** and go to Screen 1.17 for a self-study module on **using numerical information**.

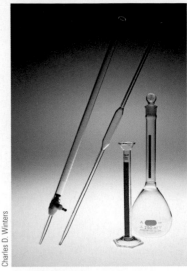

Glassware and significant figures. The 10-mL graduated cylinder is marked in 0.1-mL increments. Graduated cylinders are not considered precision glassware, so, at best, you can expect no more than two significant figures when reading a volume. Conversely, a 50-mL buret is marked in 0.10-mL increments, so it can be read to the nearest 0.01 mL. A volumetric flask is meant to be filled to the mark on the neck. When you have this volume, it is known to the nearest 0.01 mL, so a 250-mL volumetric flask contains 250.00 mL when full to the mark (or five significant figures). Finally, a pipet is like a volumetric flask in that the volume is known to the nearest 0.01 mL.

■ **To Multiply or to Add?** Take the number 4.68.
(a) Take the sum of 4.68 + 4.68 + 4.68. The answer is 14.04, a number with four significant figures.
(b) Multiply 4.68 times 3. The answer can have only three significant figures (14.0). You should recognize that different outcomes are possible, depending on the type of mathematical operation.

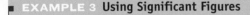

■ **EXAMPLE 3 Using Significant Figures**

Problem An example of a calculation you will do later in the book (Chapter 11) is

$$\text{Volume of gas (L)} = \frac{(0.120)(0.08206)(273.15 + 23)}{(230/760.0)}$$

Calculate the final answer to the correct number of significant figures.

Strategy Let us first decide on the number of significant figures represented by each number and then apply Rules 1–3.

Solution

Number	Number of Significant Figures	Comments
0.120	3	The trailing 0 is significant.
0.08206	4	The first 0 to the immediate right of the decimal is not significant.
$273.15 + 23 = 296$	3	23 has no decimal places, so the sum can have none.
$230/760.0 = 0.30$	2	230 has two significant figures because the last zero is not significant. In contrast, there is a decimal point in 760.0, so there are four significant digits. The quotient may have only two significant digits.

Analysis shows that one of the pieces of information is known to only two significant figures. Therefore, the volume of gas is 9.6 L, a number with two significant figures.

EXERCISE 6 Using Significant Figures

(a) How many significant figures are indicated by 2.33×10^7, by 50.5, and by 200?

(b) What are the sum and the product of 10.26 and 0.063?

(c) What is the result of the following calculation?

$$x = \frac{(110.7 - 64)}{(0.056)(0.00216)}$$

Problem Solving by Dimensional Analysis

Figure 9 illustrated the data that were collected to determine the density of a piece of metal. The thickness was measured in millimeters, whereas the length and width were measured in centimeters. To find the volume of the sample in cubic centimeters, we first had to have the length, width, and thickness in the same units and so converted the thickness to centimeters.

$$3.1 \; \cancel{mm} \times \frac{1 \; cm}{10 \; \cancel{mm}} = 0.31 \; cm$$

Here, we multiplied the number we wished to convert (3.1 mm) by a *conversion factor* (1 cm/10 mm) to produce the result in the desired unit (0.31 cm). Notice that units are treated like numbers. Because the unit "mm" was in both the numerator and the denominator, dividing one by the other leaves a quotient of 1. The units are said to "cancel out." Here, this leaves the answer in centimeters, the desired unit.

This approach to problem solving is often called **dimensional analysis** (or sometimes the **factor-label method**). It is a general problem-solving approach that uses the dimensions or units of each value to guide us through calculations. And, it is often the case that conversion factors are used to change measured quantities to chemically useful information.

A **conversion factor** expresses the equivalence of a measurement in two different units (1 cm ≡ 10 mm; 1 g ≡ 1000 mg; 12 eggs ≡ 1 dozen; 12 inches ≡ 1 foot). Because the numerator and the denominator describe the same quantity, the conversion factor is equivalent to the number 1. Therefore, multiplication by this factor does not change the measured quantity, only its units. A conversion factor is always written so that it has the form "new units divided by units of original number."

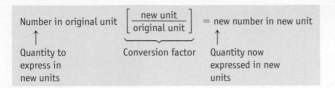

$$\underset{\substack{\uparrow \\ \text{Quantity to} \\ \text{express in} \\ \text{new units}}}{\text{Number in original unit}} \underbrace{\left[\frac{\text{new unit}}{\text{original unit}} \right]}_{\text{Conversion factor}} = \underset{\substack{\uparrow \\ \text{Quantity now} \\ \text{expressed in new} \\ \text{units}}}{\text{new number in new unit}}$$

Chemistry ⟨⟩ Now™

Sign in at **www.cengage.com/login** and go to Screen 1.17 for a self-study module on **dimensional analysis and using numerical information.**

■ **Using Conversion Factors and Doing Calculations** As you work problems in this book and read Example problems, notice that proceeding from given information to an answer very often involves a series of multiplications. That is, we multiply the given data by a conversion factor, multiply that answer of that step by another factor, and so on to the answer.

■ **EXAMPLE 4 Using Conversion Factors and Dimensional Analysis**

Problem Oceanographers often express the density of sea water in units of kilograms per cubic meter. If the density of sea water is 1.025 g/cm^3 at 15 °C, what is its density in kilograms per cubic meter?

Strategy To simplify this problem, break it into three steps. First, change the mass in grams to kilograms. Next, convert the volume in cubic centimeters to cubic meters. Finally, calculate the density by dividing the mass in kilograms by the volume in cubic meters.

Solution First convert the mass in grams to a mass in kilograms.

$$1.025 \text{ g} \times \frac{1 \text{ kg}}{1000 \text{ g}} = 1.025 \times 10^{-3} \text{ kg}$$

No conversion factor is available in one of our tables to directly change units of cubic centimeters to cubic meters. You can find one, however, by cubing (raising to the third power) the relation between the meter and the centimeter:

$$1 \text{ cm}^3 \times \left(\frac{1 \text{ m}}{100 \text{ cm}} \right)^3 = 1 \text{ cm}^3 \times \left(\frac{1 \text{ m}^3}{1 \times 10^6 \text{ cm}^3} \right) = 1 \times 10^{-6} \text{ m}^3$$

Therefore, the density of sea water is

$$\text{Density} = \frac{1.025 \times 10^{-3} \text{ kg}}{1 \times 10^{-6} \text{ m}^3} = \boxed{1.025 \times 10^3} \text{ kg/m}^3$$

EXERCISE 7 Using Dimensional Analysis

(a) The annual snowfall at Lake Otsego is 198 cm each year. What is this depth in meters? In feet (where 1 foot = 30.48 cm)?

(b) The area of Lake Otsego is 2.33 × 10^7 m^2. What is this area in square kilometers?

(c) The density of gold is 19,320 kg/m^3. What is this density in g/cm^3?

(d) See Figure 7. Show that 9.0 × 10^3 pc is 2.8 × 10^{17} km.

Graphing

In a number of instances in this text, graphs are used when analyzing experimental data with a goal of obtaining a mathematical equation that may help us predict new results. The procedure used will often result in a straight line, which has the equation

$$y = mx + b$$

■ **Who Is Right—You or the Book?** If your answer to a problem in this book does not quite agree with the answers in Appendix N through Q, the discrepancy may be the result of rounding the answer after each step and then using that rounded answer in the next step. This book follows these conventions:
(a) Final answers to numerical problems in this book result from retaining four or more digits past the decimal place throughout the calculation and rounding only at the end.
(b) In Example problems, the answer to each step is given to the correct number of significant figures for that step, but a number of digits are carried to the next step. The number of significant figures in the final answer is dictated by the number of significant figures in the original data.

FIGURE 10 Plotting data. Data for the variable x are plotted on the horizontal axis (abscissa), and data for y are plotted on the vertical axis (ordinate). The slope of the line, m in the equation $y = mx + b$, is given by $\Delta y/\Delta x$. The intercept of the line with the y-axis (when $x = 0$) is b in the equation.

Using Microsoft Excel with these data, and doing a linear regression analysis, we find $y = -0.525x + 1.87$.

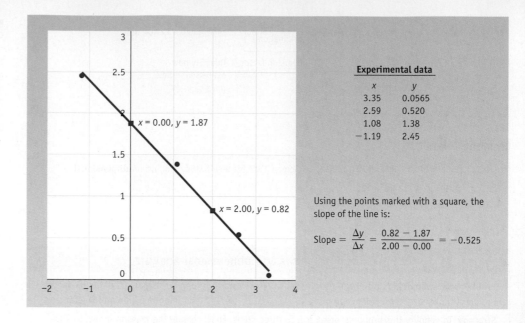

Experimental data

x	y
3.35	0.0565
2.59	0.520
1.08	1.38
−1.19	2.45

Using the points marked with a square, the slope of the line is:

$$\text{Slope} = \frac{\Delta y}{\Delta x} = \frac{0.82 - 1.87}{2.00 - 0.00} = -0.525$$

■ **Determining the Slope with a Computer Program—Least-Squares Analysis** Generally, the easiest method of determining the slope and intercept of a straight line (and thus the line's equation) is to use a program such as Microsoft Excel. These programs perform a "least squares" or "linear regression" analysis and give the best straight line based on the data. (This line is referred to in Excel as a trendline.)

In this equation, y is usually referred to as the dependent variable; its value is determined from (that is, is dependent on) the values of x, m, and b. In this equation, x is called the independent variable, and m is the slope of the line. The parameter b is the y-intercept—that is, the value of y when $x = 0$. Let us use an example to investigate two things: (a) how to construct a graph from a set of data points, and (b) how to derive an equation for the line generated by the data.

A set of data points to be graphed is presented in Figure 10. We first mark off each axis in increments of the values of x and y. Here, our x-data are within the range from −2 to 4, so the x-axis is marked off in increments of 1 unit. The y-data falls within the range from 0 to 2.5, so we mark off the y-axis in increments of 0.5. Each data point is marked as a circle on the graph.

After plotting the points on the graph (round circles), we draw a straight line that comes as close as possible to representing the trend in the data. (Do not connect the dots!) Because there is always some inaccuracy in experimental data, this line will not pass exactly through every point.

To identify the specific equation corresponding to our data, we must determine the y-intercept (b) and slope (m) for the equation $y = mx + b$. The y-intercept is the point at which $x = 0$. (In Figure 10, $y = 1.87$ when $x = 0$). The slope is determined by selecting two points *on the line* (marked with squares in Figure 10) and calculating the difference in values of y ($\Delta y = y_2 - y_1$) and x ($\Delta x = x_2 - x_1$). The slope of the line is then the ratio of these differences, $m = \Delta y/\Delta x$. Here, the slope has the value −0.525. With the slope and intercept now known, we can write the equation for the line

$$y = -0.525x + 1.87$$

and we can use this equation to calculate y-values for points that are not part of our original set of x–y data. For example, when $x = 1.50$, we find $y = 1.08$.

Case Study

Out of Gas!

On July 23, 1983, a new Boeing 767 jet aircraft was flying at 26,000 ft from Montreal to Edmonton as Air Canada Flight 143. Warning buzzers sounded in the cockpit. One of the world's largest planes was now a glider—the plane had run out of fuel!

How did this modern airplane, having the latest technology, run out of fuel? A simple mistake had been made in calculating the amount of fuel required for the flight!

Like all Boeing 767s, this plane had a sophisticated fuel gauge, but it was not working properly. The plane was still allowed to fly, however, because there is an alternative method of determining the quantity of fuel in the tanks. Mechanics can use a stick, much like the oil dipstick in an automobile engine, to measure the fuel level in each of the three tanks. The mechanics in Montreal read the dipsticks, which were calibrated in centimeters, and translated those readings to a volume in liters. According to this, the plane had a total of 7682 L of fuel.

Pilots always calculate fuel quantities in units of mass because they need to know the total mass of the plane before take-off. Air Canada pilots had always calculated the quantity of fuel in pounds, but the new 767's fuel consumption was given in kilograms. The pilots knew that 22,300 kg of fuel was required for the trip. If 7682 L of fuel remained in the tanks, how much had to be added? This involved using the fuel's density to convert 7682 L to a mass in kilograms. The mass of fuel to be added could then be calcu-

lated, and that mass converted to a volume of fuel to be added.

The First Officer of the plane asked a mechanic for the conversion factor to do the volume-to-mass conversion, and the mechanic replied "1.77." Using that number, the First Officer and the mechanics calculated that 4917 L of fuel should be added. But later calculations showed that this is only about one fourth of the required amount of fuel! Why? Because no one thought about the units of the number 1.77. They realized later that 1.77 has units of pounds per liter and not kilograms per liter.

Out of fuel, the plane could not make it to Winnipeg, so controllers directed them to the town of Gimli and to a small airport abandoned by the Royal Canadian Air Force. After gliding for almost 30 minutes, the plane approached the

Gimli runway. The runway, however, had been converted to a race course for cars, and a race was underway. Furthermore, a steel barrier had been erected across the runway. Nonetheless, the pilot managed to touch down very near the end of the runway. The plane sped down the concrete strip; the nose wheel collapsed; several tires blew—and the plane skidded safely to a stop just before the barrier. The Gimli glider had made it! And somewhere an aircraft mechanic is paying more attention to units on numbers.

Question:
1. *What is the fuel density in units of kg/L?*
2. *What mass and what volume of fuel should have been loaded? (1 lb = 453.6 g) (See Study Question 58, page 48.)*

Answers to these questions are in Appendix Q.

© Wayne Glowacki/Winnipeg Free Press, July 23, 1987, reproduced with permission.

The Gimli glider. After running out of fuel, Air Canada Flight 143 glided 29 minutes before landing on an abandoned airstrip at Gimli, Manitoba, near Winnipeg.

Problem Solving and Chemical Arithmetic

Problem-Solving Strategy

Some of the calculations in chemistry can be complex. Students frequently find it is helpful to follow a definite plan of attack as illustrated in examples throughout this book.

Step 1: Problem. State the problem. Read it carefully—and then read it again.

Step 2: Strategy. What key principles are involved? What information is known or not known? What information might be there just to place the question in the context of chemistry? Organize the information to see what is required and to discover the relationships among the data given. Try writing the information down in table form. If it is numerical information, be sure to include units.

One of the greatest difficulties for a student in introductory chemistry is picturing what is being asked for. Try sketching a picture of the situation involved. For example, we sketched a picture of the piece of metal whose density we wanted to calculate, and put the dimensions on the drawing (page 36).

Develop a plan. Have you done a problem of this type before? If not, perhaps the problem is really just a combination of several simpler ones you have seen before. Break it down into those simpler components. Try reasoning backward from the units of the answer. What data do you need to find an answer in those units?

Step 3: Solution. Execute the plan. Carefully write down each step of the problem, being sure to keep track of the units on numbers. (Do the units cancel to give you the answer in the desired units?) Don't skip steps. Don't do anything except the simplest steps in your head. Students often say they got a problem wrong because they "made a stupid mistake." Your instructor—and book authors—make them, too, and it is usually because they don't take the time to write down the steps of the problem clearly.

Step 4: Comment and Check Answer. As a final check, ask yourself whether the answer is reasonable.

■ EXAMPLE 5 Problem Solving

Problem A mineral oil has a density of 0.875 g/cm^3. Suppose you spread 0.75 g of this oil over the surface of water in a large dish with an inner diameter of 21.6 cm. How thick is the oil layer? Express the thickness in centimeters.

Strategy It is often useful to begin solving such problems by sketching a picture of the situation.

This helps recognize that the solution to the problem is to find the volume of the oil on the water. If we know the volume, then we can find the thickness because

Volume of oil layer = (thickness of layer) × (area of oil layer)

So, we need two things: (a) the volume of the oil layer and (b) the area of the layer.

Solution First, calculate the volume of oil. The mass of the oil layer is known, so combining the mass of oil with its density gives the volume of the oil used:

$$0.75 \text{ g} \times \frac{1 \text{ cm}^3}{0.875 \text{ g}} = 0.86 \text{ cm}^3$$

Next, calculate the area of the oil layer. The oil is spread over a circular surface, whose area is given by

$$\text{Area} = \pi \times (\text{radius})^2$$

The radius of the oil layer is half its diameter (= 21.6 cm) or 10.8 cm, so

$$\text{Area of oil layer} = (3.142)(10.8 \text{ cm})^2 = 366 \text{ cm}^2$$

With the volume and the area of the oil layer known, the thickness can be calculated.

$$\text{Thickness} = \frac{\text{Volume}}{\text{Area}} = \frac{0.86 \text{ cm}^3}{366 \text{ cm}^2} = \boxed{0.0023 \text{ cm}}$$

Comment In the volume calculation, the calculator shows 0.857143. . . . The quotient should have two significant figures because 0.75 has two significant figures, so the result of this step is 0.86 cm³. In the area calculation, the calculator shows 366.435. . . . The answer to this step should have three significant figures because 10.8 has three. When these interim results are combined in calculating thickness, however, the final result can have only two significant figures. Premature rounding can lead to errors.

EXERCISE 9 Problem Solving

A particular paint has a density of 0.914 g/cm³. You need to cover a wall that is 7.6 m long and 2.74 m high with a paint layer 0.13 mm thick. What volume of paint (in liters) is required? What is the mass (in grams) of the paint layer?

STUDY QUESTIONS

OWL Online homework for this chapter may be assigned in OWL.

▲ denotes challenging questions.

■ denotes questions assignable in OWL.

Blue-numbered questions have answers in Appendix O and fully-worked solutions in the *Student Solutions Manual.*

Practicing Skills
Temperature Scales
(Exercise 1)

1. Many laboratories use 25 °C as a standard temperature. What is this temperature in kelvins?

2. The temperature on the surface of the sun is 5.5×10^3 °C. What is this temperature in kelvins?

3. ■ Make the following temperature conversions:

	°C	K
(a)	16	
(b)		370
(c)	40	

4. Make the following temperature conversions:

	°C	K
(a)		77
(b)	63	
(c)		1450

Length, Volume, Mass, and Density
(See Example 1 and Exercises 2–4)

5. A marathon distance race covers a distance of 42.195 km. What is this distance in meters? In miles?

6. ■ The average lead pencil, new and unused, is 19 cm long. What is its length in millimeters? In meters?

7. A standard U.S. postage stamp is 2.5 cm long and 2.1 cm wide. What is the area of the stamp in square centimeters? In square meters?

8. ■ A compact disc has a diameter of 11.8 cm. What is the surface area of the disc in square centimeters? In square meters? [Area of a circle = $(\pi)(\text{radius})^2$.]

9. A typical laboratory beaker has a volume of 250. mL. What is its volume in cubic centimeters? In liters? In cubic meters? In cubic decimeters?

10. ■ Some soft drinks are sold in bottles with a volume of 1.5 L. What is this volume in milliliters? In cubic centimeters? In cubic decimeters?

11. A book has a mass of 2.52 kg. What is this mass in grams?

12. A new U.S. dime has a mass of 2.265 g. What is its mass in kilograms? In milligrams?

13. ■ Ethylene glycol, $C_2H_6O_2$, is an ingredient of automobile antifreeze. Its density is 1.11 g/cm^3 at 20 °C. If you need 500. mL of this liquid, what mass of the compound, in grams, is required?

14. ■ A piece of silver metal has a mass of 2.365 g. If the density of silver is 10.5 g/cm^3, what is the volume of the silver?

15. ■ You can identify a metal by carefully determining its density (d). An unknown piece of metal, with a mass of 2.361 g, is 2.35 cm long, 1.34 cm wide, and 1.05 mm thick. Which of the following is the element?
    (a) Nickel, $d = 8.91$ g/cm^3
    (b) Titanium, $d = 4.50$ g/cm^3
    (c) Zinc, $d = 7.14$ g/cm^3
    (d) Tin, $d = 7.23$ g/cm^3

16. ■ Which occupies a larger volume, 600 g of water (with a density of 0.995 g/cm^3) or 600 g of lead (with a density of 11.35 g/cm^3)?

Accuracy, Precision, Error, and Standard Deviation
(See Example 2 and Exercise 5)

17. You and your lab partner are asked to determine the density of an aluminum bar. The mass is known accurately (to four significant figures). You use a simple metric ruler to measure its dimensions and find the results in A. Your partner uses a precision micrometer, and obtains the results in B.

Method A (g/cm^3)	Method B (g/cm^3)
2.2	2.703
2.3	2.701
2.7	2.705
2.4	5.811

The accepted density of aluminum is 2.702 g/cm^3.
    (a) Calculate the average density for each method. Should all the experimental results be included in your calculations? If not, justify any omissions.
    (b) Calculate the percent error for each method's average value.
    (c) Calculate the standard deviation for each set of data.
    (d) Which method's average value is more precise? Which method is more accurate?

18. ■ The accepted value of the melting point of pure aspirin is 135 °C. Trying to verify that value, you obtain 134 °C, 136 °C, 133 °C, and 138 °C in four separate trials. Your partner finds 138 °C, 137 °C, 138 °C, and 138 °C.
    (a) Calculate the average value and percent error for you and your partner.
    (b) Which of you is more precise? More accurate?

Exponential Notation and Significant Figures
(See Example 3)

19. ■ Express the following numbers in exponential or scientific notation, and give the number of significant figures in each.
    (a) 0.054 g   (c) 0.000792 g
    (b) 5462 g   (d) 1600 mL

20. ■ Express the following numbers in fixed notation (e.g., $1.23 \times 10^2 = 123$), and give the number of significant figures in each.
    (a) 1.623×10^3 (c) 6.32×10^{-2}
    (b) 2.57×10^{-4} (d) 3.404×10^3

21. ■ Carry out the following operations. Provide the answer with the correct number of significant figures.
    (a) $(1.52)(6.21 \times 10^{-3})$
    (b) $(6.217 \times 10^3) - (5.23 \times 10^2)$
    (c) $(6.217 \times 10^3) \div (5.23 \times 10^2)$
    (d) $(0.0546)(16.0000)\left[\dfrac{7.779}{55.85}\right]$

22. Carry out the following operations. Provide the answer with the correct number of significant figures.
    (a) $(6.25 \times 10^2)^3$
    (b) $\sqrt{2.35 \times 10^{-3}}$
    (c) $(2.35 \times 10^{-3})^{1/3}$
    (d) $(1.68)\left[\dfrac{23.56 - 2.3}{1.248 \times 10^3}\right]$

Graphing
(See Exercise 8)

23. To determine the average mass of a popcorn kernel, you collect the following data:

Number of kernels	Mass (g)
5	0.836
12	2.162
35	5.801

Plot the data with number of kernels on the x-axis and mass on the y-axis. Draw the best straight line using the points on the graph (or do a least-squares or linear regression analysis using a computer program), and then write the equation for the resulting straight line. What is the slope of the line? What does the slope of the line signify about the mass of a popcorn kernel? What is the mass of 20 popcorn kernels? How many kernels are there in a handful of popcorn with a mass of 20.88 g?

▲ more challenging   ■ in OWL   Blue-numbered questions answered in Appendix O

24. Using the graph below:
(a) What is the value of x when $y = 4.0$?
(b) What is the value of y when $x = 0.30$?
(c) ■ What are the slope and the y-intercept of the line?
(d) What is the value of y when $x = 1.0$?

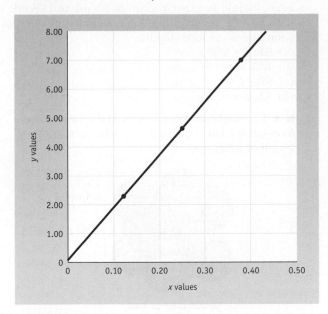

25. ■ Use the graph below to answer the following questions.
(a) Derive the equation for the straight line, $y = mx + b$.
(b) What is the value of y when $x = 6.0$?

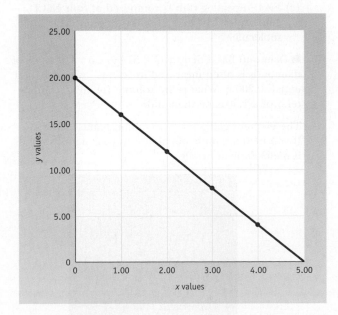

26. The following data were collected in an experiment to determine how an enzyme works in a biochemical reaction.

Amount of H_2O_2	Reaction Speed (amount/second)
1.96	4.75×10^{-5}
1.31	4.03×10^{-5}
0.98	3.51×10^{-5}
0.65	2.52×10^{-5}
0.33	1.44×10^{-5}
0.16	0.585×10^{-5}

(a) Plot these data as 1/amount on the y-axis and 1/speed on the x-axis.
(b) Determine the equation for the data, and give the values of the y-intercept of the slope. (*Note: in biochemistry this is known as a Lineweaver-Burk plot, and the y-intercept is related to the maximum speed of the reaction.*)

Solving Equations

27. Solve the following equation for the unknown value, C.
$$(0.502)(123) = (750.)C$$

28. Solve the following equation for the unknown value, n.
$$(2.34)(15.6) = n(0.0821)(273)$$

29. Solve the following equation for the unknown value, T.
$$(4.184)(244)(T - 292.0) + (0.449)(88.5)(T - 369.0) = 0$$

30. Solve the following equation for the unknown value, n.
$$-246.0 = 1312\left[\frac{1}{2^2} - \frac{1}{n^2}\right]$$

General Questions
These questions are not designated as to type or location in the chapter. They may combine several concepts.

31. Molecular distances are usually given in nanometers (1 nm = 1×10^{-9} m) or in picometers (1 pm = 1×10^{-12} m). However, the angstrom (Å) unit is sometimes used, where 1 Å = 1×10^{-10} m. (The angstrom unit is not an SI unit.) If the distance between the Pt atom and the N atom in the cancer chemotherapy drug cisplatin is 1.97 Å, what is this distance in nanometers? In picometers?

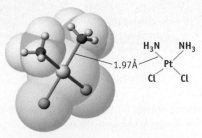

Cisplatin.

32. ■ The separation between carbon atoms in diamond is 0.154 nm. What is their separation in meters? In picometers (pm)? In Angstroms (Å)? (See Study Question 31.)

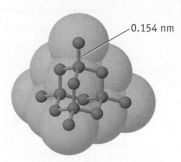

0.154 nm

A portion of the diamond structure.

33. ■ A red blood cell has a diameter of 7.5 μm (micrometers). What is this dimension in (a) meters, (b) nanometers, and (c) picometers?

34. ■ The platinum-containing cancer drug *cisplatin* (Study Question 31) contains 65.0 mass-percent of the metal. If you have 1.53 g of the compound, what mass of platinum (in grams) is contained in this sample?

35. ■ The anesthetic procaine hydrochloride is often used to deaden pain during dental surgery. The compound is packaged as a 10.% solution (by mass; $d = 1.0$ g/mL) in water. If your dentist injects 0.50 mL of the solution, what mass of procaine hydrochloride (in milligrams) is injected?

36. ■ You need a cube of aluminum with a mass of 7.6 g. What must be the length of the cube's edge (in cm)? (The density of aluminum is 2.698 g/cm³.)

37. ■ You have a 250.0-mL graduated cylinder containing some water. You drop 3 marbles with a total mass of 95.2 g into the water. What is the average density of a marble?

(a)   **(b)**

Determining density. (a) A graduated cylinder with 61 mL of water. (b) Three marbles are added to the cylinder.

Charles D. Winters

38. ■ You have a white crystalline solid, known to be one of the potassium compounds listed below. To determine which, you measure its density. You measure out 18.82 g and transfer it to a graduated cylinder containing kerosene (in which salts will not dissolve). The level of liquid kerosene rises from 8.5 mL to 15.3 mL. Calculate the density of the solid, and identify the compound from the following list.
(a) KF, $d = 2.48$ g/cm³
(b) KCl, $d = 1.98$ g/cm³
(c) KBr, $d = 2.75$ g/cm³
(d) KI, $d = 3.13$ g/cm³

39. ■ ▲ The smallest repeating unit of a crystal of common salt is a cube (called a unit cell) with an edge length of 0.563 nm.

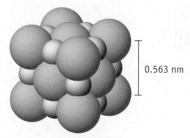

0.563 nm

Sodium chloride, NaCl.

(a) What is the volume of this cube in cubic nanometers? In cubic centimeters?
(b) The density of NaCl is 2.17 g/cm³. What is the mass of this smallest repeating unit ("unit cell")?
(c) Each repeating unit is composed of four NaCl "molecules." What is the mass of one NaCl molecule?

40. ■ Diamond has a density of 3.513 g/cm³. The mass of diamonds is often measured in "carats," where 1 carat equals 0.200 g. What is the volume (in cubic centimeters) of a 1.50-carat diamond?

41. The element gallium has a melting point of 29.8 °C. If you held a sample of gallium in your hand, should it melt? Explain briefly.

Charles D. Winters

Gallium metal.

▲ more challenging   ■ in OWL   Blue-numbered questions answered in Appendix O

42. ■ ▲ The density of pure water is given at various temperatures.

t (°C)	d (g/cm³)
4	0.99997
15	0.99913
25	0.99707
35	0.99406

Suppose your laboratory partner tells you the density of water at 20 °C is 0.99910 g/cm³. Is this a reasonable number? Why or why not?

43. When you heat popcorn, it pops because it loses water explosively. Assume a kernel of corn, with a mass of 0.125 g, has a mass of only 0.106 g after popping.
(a) What percentage of its mass did the kernel lose on popping?
(b) ■ Popcorn is sold by the pound in the United States. Using 0.125 g as the average mass of a popcorn kernel, how many kernels are there in a pound of popcorn? (1 lb = 453.6 g)

44. ■ ▲ The aluminum in a package containing 75 ft² of kitchen foil weighs approximately 12 ounces. Aluminum has a density of 2.70 g/cm³. What is the approximate thickness of the aluminum foil in millimeters? (1 oz = 28.4 g)

45. ■ ▲ The fluoridation of city water supplies has been practiced in the United States for several decades. It is done by continuously adding sodium fluoride to water as it comes from a reservoir. Assume you live in a medium-sized city of 150,000 people and that 660 L (170 gal) of water is consumed per person per day. What mass of sodium fluoride (in kilograms) must be added to the water supply each year (365 days) to have the required fluoride concentration of 1 ppm (part per million)—that is, 1 kilogram of fluoride per 1 million kilograms of water? (Sodium fluoride is 45.0% fluoride, and water has a density of 1.00 g/cm³.)

46. ■ ▲ About two centuries ago, Benjamin Franklin showed that 1 teaspoon of oil would cover about 0.5 acre of still water. If you know that 1.0×10^4 m² = 2.47 acres, and that there is approximately 5 cm³ in a teaspoon, what is the thickness of the layer of oil? How might this thickness be related to the sizes of molecules?

47. ■ ▲ Automobile batteries are filled with an aqueous solution of sulfuric acid. What is the mass of the acid (in grams) in 500. mL of the battery acid solution if the density of the solution is 1.285 g/cm³ and if the solution is 38.08% sulfuric acid by mass?

48. ■ A 26-meter-tall statue of Buddha in Tibet is covered with 279 kg of gold. If the gold was applied to a thickness of 0.0015 mm, what surface area is covered (in square meters)? (Gold density = 19.3 g/cm³)

49. At 25 °C, the density of water is 0.997 g/cm³, whereas the density of ice at −10 °C is 0.917 g/cm³.
(a) If a soft-drink can (volume = 250. mL) is filled completely with pure water at 25 °C and then frozen at −10 °C, what volume does the solid occupy?
(b) Can the ice be contained within the can?

50. ■ Suppose your bedroom is 18 ft long, 15 ft wide, and the distance from floor to ceiling is 8 ft, 6 in. You need to know the volume of the room in metric units for some scientific calculations.
(a) What is the room's volume in cubic meters? In liters?
(b) What is the mass of air in the room in kilograms? In pounds? (Assume the density of air is 1.2 g/L and that the room is empty of furniture.)

51. ■ A spherical steel ball has a mass of 3.475 g and a diameter of 9.40 mm. What is the density of the steel? [The volume of a sphere = $(4/3)\pi r^3$ where r = radius.]

52. ■ ▲ The substances listed below are clear liquids. You are asked to identify an unknown liquid that is known to be one of these liquids. You pipet a 3.50-mL sample into a beaker. The empty beaker had a mass of 12.20 g, and the beaker plus the liquid weighed 16.08 g.

Substance	Density at 25 °C (g/cm³)
Ethylene glycol	1.1088 (the major component of antifreeze)
Water	0.9971
Ethanol	0.7893 (the alcohol in alcoholic beverages)
Acetic acid	1.0492 (the active component of vinegar)
Glycerol	1.2613 (a solvent, used in home care products)

(a) Calculate the density and identify the unknown.
(b) If you were able to measure the volume to only two significant figures (that is, 3.5 mL, not 3.50 mL), will the results be sufficiently accurate to identify the unknown? Explain.

53. ■ ▲ You have an irregularly shaped piece of an unknown metal. To identify it, you determine its density and then compare this value with known values that you look up in the chemistry library. The mass of the metal is 74.122 g. Because of the irregular shape, you measure the volume by submerging the metal in water in a graduated cylinder. When you do this, the water level in the cylinder rises from 28.2 mL to 36.7 mL.
(a) What is the density of the metal? (Use the correct number of significant figures in your answer.)
(b) The unknown is one of the seven metals listed below. Is it possible to identify the metal based on the density you have calculated? Explain.

Metal	Density (g/cm³)	Metal	Density (g/cm³)
zinc	7.13	nickel	8.90
iron	7.87	copper	8.96
cadmium	8.65	silver	10.50
cobalt	8.90		

54. ■ ▲ There are 5 hydrocarbon compounds (compounds of C and H) that have the formula C_6H_{14}. (These are isomers; they differ in the way that C and H atoms are attached. See Chapters 8 and 10.) All are liquids at room temperature but have slightly different densities.

Hydrocarbon	Density (g/mL)
hexane	0.6600
2,3-dimethylbutane	0.6616
1-methylpentane	0.6532
2,2-dimethylbutane	0.6485
2-methylpentane	0.6645

(a) You have a pure sample of one of these hydrocarbons, and to identify it you decide to measure its density. You determine that a 5.0-mL sample (measured in a graduated cylinder) has a mass of 3.2745 g (measured on an analytical balance.) Assume that the accuracy of the values for mass and volume is expressed by the number of significant figures, that is, plus or minus one (± 1) in the last significant figure. What is the density of the liquid?

(b) Express the estimated uncertainty of your value in two other ways:
  i) The value you have calculated for the density is uncertain to ____ g/mL.
  ii) The value calculated for density is between x g/mL and y g/mL.

(c) Can you identify the unknown hydrocarbon based on your experiment?

(d) Can you eliminate any of the five possibilities based on the data? If so, which one(s)?

(e) You need a more accurate volume measurement to solve this problem, and you redetermine the volume to be 4.93 mL. Based on these new data, what is the unknown compound?

55. ■ ▲ Suppose you have a cylindrical glass tube with a thin capillary opening, and you wish to determine the diameter of the capillary. You can do this experimentally by weighing a piece of the tubing before and after filling a portion of the capillary with mercury. Using the following information, calculate the diameter of the capillary.

Mass of tube before adding mercury = 3.263 g

Mass of tube after adding mercury = 3.416 g

Length of capillary filled with mercury = 16.75 mm

Density of mercury = 13.546 g/cm³

Volume of cylindrical capillary filled with mercury = $(\pi)(\text{radius})^2(\text{length})$

56. ■ **COPPER**: Copper has a density of 8.96 g/cm³. An ingot of copper with a mass of 57 kg (126 lb) is drawn into wire with a diameter of 9.50 mm. What length of wire (in meters) can be produced? [Volume of wire = $(\pi)(\text{radius})^2(\text{length})$]

57. ▲ COPPER: See the illustration of the copper lattice on page 24.

(a) Suppose you have a cube of copper metal that is 0.236 cm on a side with a mass of 0.1206 g. If you know that each copper atom (radius = 128 pm) has a mass of 1.055×10^{-22} g (you will learn in Chapter 2 how to find the mass of one atom), how many atoms are there in this cube? What fraction of the cube is filled with atoms? (Or conversely, how much of the lattice is empty space?) Why is there "empty" space in the lattice?

(b) Now look at the smallest, repeating unit of the crystal lattice of copper. Knowing that an edge of this cube is 361.47 pm and the density of copper is 8.960 g/cm³, estimate the number of copper atoms in this smallest, repeating unit.

58. ■ ▲ CASE STUDY: In July 1983, an Air Canada Boeing 767 ran out of fuel over central Canada on a trip from Montreal to Edmonton. (The plane glided safely to a landing at an abandoned airstrip.) The pilots knew that 22,300 kg of fuel were required for the trip, and they knew that 7682 L of fuel were already in the tank. The ground crew added 4916 L of fuel, which was only about one fifth of what was required. The crew members used a factor of 1.77 for the fuel density—the problem is that 1.77 has units of pounds per liter and not kilograms per liter! What is the fuel density in units of kg/L? What mass and what volume of fuel should have been loaded? (1 lb = 453.6 g)

In the Laboratory

59. ■ A sample of unknown metal is placed in a graduated cylinder containing water. The mass of the sample is 37.5 g, and the water levels before and after adding the sample to the cylinder are as shown in the figure. Which metal in the following list is most likely the sample? (d is the density of the metal.)
(a) Mg, d = 1.74 g/cm³   (d) Al, d = 2.70 g/cm³
(b) Fe, d = 7.87 g/cm³   (e) Cu, d = 8.96 g/cm³
(c) Ag, d = 10.5 g/cm³   (f) Pb, d = 11.3 g/cm³

Graduated cylinders with unknown metal (right).

▲ more challenging   ■ in OWL   Blue-numbered questions answered in Appendix O

60. ■ Iron pyrite is often called "fool's gold" because it looks like gold (see page 14). Suppose you have a solid that looks like gold, but you believe it to be fool's gold. The sample has a mass of 23.5 g. When the sample is lowered into the water in a graduated cylinder (see Study Question 37), the water level rises from 47.5 mL to 52.2 mL. Is the sample fool's gold ($d = 5.00$ g/cm^3) or "real" gold ($d = 19.3$ g/cm^3)?

61. You can analyze for a copper compound in water using an instrument called a spectrophotometer. In this technique, the light passing through an aqueous solution of a compound can be absorbed, and the amount of light absorbed (at a given wavelength of light) depends directly on the amount of compound per liter of solution. To calibrate the spectrophotometer, you collect the following data:

Absorbance (A)	Concentration of Copper Compound (g/L)
0.000	0.000
0.257	1.029×10^{-3}
0.518	2.058×10^{-3}
0.771	3.087×10^{-3}
1.021	4.116×10^{-3}

Plot the absorbance (A) against the mass of copper compound per liter (g/L), and find the slope (m) and intercept (b) (assuming that A is y and the amount in solution is x in the equation for a straight line, $y = mx + b$). What is the amount of copper compound in the solution in g/L and mg/mL when the absorbance is 0.635?

62. A gas chromatograph (page 2) is calibrated for the analysis of isooctane (a major gasoline component) using the following data:

Percent Isooctane (x-data)	Instrument Response (y-data)
0.352	1.09
0.803	1.78
1.08	2.60
1.38	3.03
1.75	4.01

If the instrument response is 2.75, what percentage of isooctane is present? (Data are taken from *Analytical Chemistry, An Introduction,* by D.A. Skoog, D.M. West, F. J. Holler, and S. R. Crouch, Thomson-Brooks/Cole, Belmont, CA, 7th Edition, 2000.)

2 | Atoms, Molecules, and Ions

The Periodic Table, the Central Icon of Chemistry

Nineteenth-century chemists such as Newlands, Chancourtois, Mayer, and others devised ways to organize the chemistry of the elements with varying degrees of success. However, it was Dmitri Mendeleev in 1870 who first truly recognized the periodicity of the chem-

Charles D. Winters

TABELLE II.

REIHEN	GRUPPE I. — R^2O	GRUPPE II. — RO	GRUPPE III. — R^2O^3	GRUPPE IV. RH^4 RO^2	GRUPPE V. RH^3 R^2O^5	GRUPPE VI. RH^2 RO^3	GRUPPE VII. RH R^2O^7	GRUPPE VIII. — RO^4
1	H=1							
2	Li=7	Be=9,4	B=11	C=12	N=14	O=16	F=19	
3	Na=23	Mg=24	Al=27,3	Si=28	P=31	S=32	Cl=35,5	
4	K=39	Ca=40	—=44	Ti=48	V=51	Cr=52	Mn=55	Fe=56, Co=59,
								Ni=59, Cu=63
5	(Cu=63)	Zn=65	—=68	—=72	As=75	Se=78	Br=80	
6	Rb=85	Sr=87	?Yt=88	Zr=90	Nb=94	Mo=96	—=100	Ru=104, Rh=104,
								Pd=106, Ag=108
7	(Ag=108)	Cd=112	In=113	Sn=118	Sb=122	Te=125	J=127	
8	Cs=133	Ba=137	?Di=138	?Ce=140	—	—	—	— — — —
9	(—)	—	—	—		—	—	
10	—	—	?Er=178	?La=180	Ta=182	W=184	—	Os=195, Ir=197,
								Pt=198, Au=199
11	(Au=199)	Hg=200	Tl=204	Pb=207	Bi=208	—	—	
12	—	—	—	Th=231	—	U=240	—	— — — —

istry of the elements, who proposed the first periodic table, and who used this to predict the existence of yet-unknown elements.

Mendeleev placed the elements in a table in order of increasing atomic weight. In doing so Li, Be, B, C, N, O, and F became the first row of the table. The next element then known, sodium (Na), had properties quite similar to those of lithium (Li), so Na began the next row of the table. As additional elements were added in order of increasing atomic weight, elements with similar properties fell in columns or groups.

If you compare the periodic table published by Mendeleev in 1871 (shown here) with the table in the front of this book, you will see that many elements are missing in the 1871 table. Mendeleev's genius was that he recognized there must be yet-undiscovered elements, and so

he left a place for them in the table (marking the empty places with a —). For example, Mendeleev concluded that "Gruppe IV" was missing an element between silicon (Si) and tin (Sn) and marked its position as "— = 72." He called the missing element *eka-silicon* and predicted the element would have, for example, an atomic weight of 72 and a density of 5.5 g/cm^3. Based on this and other predictions, chemists knew what to look for in mineral samples, and soon many of the missing elements were discovered.

Questions:
1. What is eka-silicon, and how close were Mendeleev's predictions to the actual values for this element?
2. How many of the missing elements can you identify?

Answers to these questions are in Appendix Q.

The chemical elements are forged in stars, and from these elements molecules such as water and ammonia are made in outer space. These simple molecules and much more complex ones such as DNA and hemoglobin are found on earth. To comprehend the burgeoning fields of molecular biology, as well as all modern chemistry, we have to understand the nature of the chemical elements and the properties and structures of molecules. This chapter begins our exploration of the chemistry of the elements, the building blocks of chemistry, and of the compounds they form.

Chemistry₊ₒ₊Now™

Throughout the text this icon introduces an opportunity for self-study or to explore interactive tutorials by signing in at **www.cengage.com/login**.

2.1 Atomic Structure—Protons, Electrons, and Neutrons

Around 1900, a series of experiments done by scientists such as Sir John Joseph Thomson (1856–1940) and Ernest Rutherford (1871–1937) in England established a model of the atom that is still the basis of modern atomic theory. Three subatomic particles make up all atoms: electrically positive protons, electrically neutral neutrons, and electrically negative electrons. The model places the more massive protons and neutrons in a very small nucleus (Figure 2.1), which contains all the positive charge and almost all the mass of an atom. Electrons, with a much smaller mass than protons or neutrons, surround the nucleus and occupy most of the volume.

The chemical properties of elements and molecules depend largely on the electrons of the atoms involved. We shall look more carefully at their arrangement and how they influence the properties of atoms in Chapters 6 and 7. In this chapter, however, we first want to describe how the composition of the atom relates to its mass and then to the mass of molecules. This is crucial information when we consider the quantitative aspects of chemical reactions in later chapters.

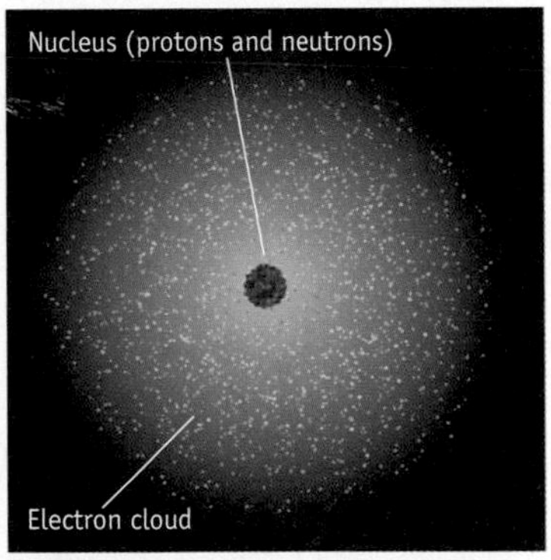

2.2 Atomic Number and Atomic Mass

Atomic Number

All atoms of a given element have the same number of protons in the nucleus. Hydrogen is the simplest element, with one nuclear proton. All helium atoms have two protons, all lithium atoms have three protons, and all beryllium atoms have four protons.

Nucleus (protons and neutrons)

Electron cloud

FIGURE 2.1 The structure of the atom. All atoms contain a nucleus with one or more protons (positive electric charge) and, except for H atoms, neutrons (no charge). Electrons (negative electric charge) are found in space as a "cloud" around the nucleus. In an electrically neutral atom, the number of electrons equals the number of protons. Note that this figure is not drawn to scale. If the nucleus were really the size depicted here, the electron cloud would extend over 200 m. The atom is mostly empty space!

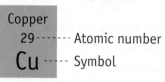
The number of protons in the nucleus of an element is its **atomic number**, which is generally given the symbol **Z**.

Currently known elements are listed in the periodic table inside the front cover of this book and on the list inside the back cover. The integer number at the top of the box for each element in the periodic table is its atomic number. A sodium atom (Na), for example, has an atomic number of 11, so its nucleus contains 11 protons. A uranium atom (U) has 92 nuclear protons and $Z = 92$.

Atomic Weight and the Atomic Mass Unit

With the quantitative work of the great French chemist Antoine Laurent Lavoisier (1743–1794), chemistry began to change from medieval alchemy to a modern field of study. As 18th- and 19th-century chemists tried to understand how the elements combined, they carried out increasingly quantitative studies aimed at learning, for example, how much of one element would combine with another. Based on this work, they learned that the substances they produced had a constant composition, and so they could define the relative masses of elements that would combine to produce a new substance. At the beginning of the 19th century, John Dalton (1766–1844) suggested that the combinations of elements involve atoms, and so he proposed a relative scale of atom masses. Apparently for simplicity, Dalton chose a mass of 1 for hydrogen on which to base his scale.

The atomic weight scale has changed since 1800, but like the 19th-century chemists, we still use *relative* masses. Our standard today, however, is carbon-12. A carbon atom having six protons and six neutrons in the nucleus is assigned a mass value of exactly 12. From chemical experiments and physical measurements, we know an oxygen atom having eight protons and eight neutrons has 1.3329 times the mass of carbon, so it has a relative mass of 15.9949. Masses of atoms of other elements have been assigned in a similar manner.

Masses of fundamental atomic particles are often expressed in **atomic mass units (u).** *One atomic mass unit, 1 u, is one twelfth of the mass of an atom of carbon with six protons and six neutrons.* Thus, such a carbon atom has a mass of 12.000 u. The atomic mass unit can be related to other units of mass using the conversion factor $1 \text{ u} = 1.66054 \times 10^{-24}$ g.

Mass Number

Protons and neutrons have masses very close to 1 u (Table 2.1). The mass of an electron, in contrast, is only about 1/2000 of this value. Because proton and neutron masses are so close to 1 u, the approximate mass of an atom can be estimated if the

TABLE 2.1 Properties of Subatomic Particles*

| Particle | Mass | | Charge | Symbol |
	Grams	*Atomic Mass Units*		
Electron	9.109383×10^{-28}	0.0005485799	1−	$_{-1}^{0}e$ or e^-
Proton	1.672622×10^{-24}	1.007276	1+	$_{1}^{1}p$ or p^+
Neutron	1.674927×10^{-24}	1.008665	0	$_{0}^{1}n$ or n

* These values and others in the book are taken from the National Institute of Standards and Technology website at http://physics.nist.gov/cuu/Constants/index.html

number of neutrons and protons is known. The sum of the number of protons and neutrons for an atom is called its **mass number** and is given the symbol *A*.

$$A = \text{mass number} = \text{number of protons} + \text{number of neutrons}$$

For example, a sodium atom, which has 11 protons and 12 neutrons in its nucleus, has a mass number of $A = 23$. The most common atom of uranium has 92 protons and 146 neutrons, and a mass number of $A = 238$. Using this information, we often symbolize atoms with the notation

$$\text{Mass number} \rightarrow {}^{A}_{Z}X \leftarrow \text{Element symbol}$$
$$\text{Atomic number} \rightarrow$$

The subscript *Z* is optional because the element's symbol tells us what the atomic number must be. For example, the atoms described previously have the symbols ${}^{23}_{11}\text{Na}$ or ${}^{238}_{92}\text{U}$, or just ${}^{23}\text{Na}$ or ${}^{238}\text{U}$. In words, we say "sodium-23" or "uranium-238."

Chemistry ⚛ Now™

Sign in at **www.cengage.com/login** and go to Chapter 2 Contents to see Screen 2.11 for a tutorial on **the notation for symbolizing atoms.**

■ EXAMPLE 2.1 Atomic Composition

Problem What is the composition of an atom of phosphorus with 16 neutrons? What is its mass number? What is the symbol for such an atom? If the atom has an actual mass of 30.9738 u, what is its mass in grams? Finally, what is the mass of this phosphorus atom relative to the mass of a carbon atom with a mass number of 12?

Strategy All P atoms have the same number of protons, 15, which is given by the atomic number. The mass number is the sum of the number of protons and neutrons. The mass of the atom in grams can be obtained from the mass in atomic mass units using the conversion factor $1\ \text{u} = 1.66054 \times 10^{-24}\ \text{g}$.

Solution A phosphorus atom has 15 protons and, because it is electrically neutral, also has 15 electrons. A P atom with 16 neutrons has a mass number of 31.

Mass number = number of protons + number of neutrons = 15 + 16 = $\boxed{31}$

The atom's complete symbol is ${}^{31}_{15}\text{P}$.

Mass of one ${}^{31}\text{P}$ atom = $(30.9738\ \text{u}) \times (1.66054 \times 10^{-24}\ \text{g/u}) = \boxed{5.14332 \times 10^{-23}\ \text{g}}$

An atom of $\boxed{{}^{31}\text{P} \text{ is } 2.58115}$ times heavier than an atom of ${}^{12}\text{C}$: $30.9738/12.0000 = 2.58115$

EXERCISE 2.1 Atomic Composition

(a) What is the mass number of an iron atom with 30 neutrons?

(b) A nickel atom with 32 neutrons has a mass of 59.930788 u. What is its mass in grams?

(c) How many protons, neutrons, and electrons are in a ${}^{64}\text{Zn}$ atom?

(d) What is the mass of ${}^{64}\text{Zn}$ (63.929 u) relative to ${}^{12}\text{C}$?

2.3 Isotopes

In only a few instances (for example, aluminum, fluorine, and phosphorus) do all atoms in a naturally occurring sample of a given element have the same mass. Most elements consist of atoms having several different mass numbers. For example, there are two kinds of boron atoms, one with a mass of about 10 u (${}^{10}\text{B}$) and a second with a mass of about 11 u (${}^{11}\text{B}$). Atoms of tin can have any of 10 different masses. Atoms with the same atomic number but different mass numbers are called **isotopes**.

■ **Atomic Masses of Some Isotopes**

Atom	Relative Mass
${}^{4}\text{He}$	4.0092603
${}^{13}\text{C}$	13.003355
${}^{16}\text{O}$	15.994915
${}^{58}\text{Ni}$	57.935346
${}^{60}\text{Ni}$	59.930788
${}^{79}\text{Br}$	78.918336
${}^{81}\text{Br}$	80.916289
${}^{197}\text{Au}$	196.966543
${}^{238}\text{U}$	238.050784

FIGURE 2.2 Ice made from "heavy water." Water containing ordinary hydrogen ($^1_1$H, protium) forms a solid that is less dense ($d = 0.917$ g/cm³ at 0 °C) than liquid H_2O ($d = 0.997$ g/cm³ at 25 °C) and so floats in the liquid. (Water is unique in this regard. The solid phase of virtually all other substances sinks in the liquid phase of that substance.) Similarly, "heavy ice" (D_2O, deuterium oxide) floats in "heavy water." D_2O-ice is denser than liquid H_2O, however, so cubes made of D_2O sink in liquid H_2O.

Solid H_2O

Liquid H_2O

Solid D_2O

Charles D. Winters

All atoms of an element have the same number of protons—five in the case of boron. To have different masses, isotopes must have different numbers of neutrons. The nucleus of a ^{10}B atom ($Z = 5$) contains five protons and five neutrons, whereas the nucleus of a ^{11}B atom contains five protons and six neutrons.

Scientists often refer to a particular isotope by giving its mass number (for example, uranium-238, ^{238}U), but the isotopes of hydrogen are so important that they have special names and symbols. All hydrogen atoms have one proton. When that is the only nuclear particle, the isotope is called *protium*, or just "hydrogen." The isotope of hydrogen with one neutron, $^2_1$H, is called *deuterium*, or "heavy hydrogen" (symbol = D). The nucleus of radioactive hydrogen-3, $^3_1$H, or *tritium* (symbol = T), contains one proton and two neutrons.

The substitution of one isotope of an element for another isotope of the same element in a compound sometimes can have an interesting effect (Figure 2.2). This is especially true when deuterium is substituted for hydrogen because the mass of deuterium is double that of hydrogen.

Isotope Abundance

A sample of water from a stream or lake will consist almost entirely of H_2O where the H atoms are the ^{1}H isotope. A few molecules, however, will have deuterium (^{2}H) substituted for ^{1}H. We can predict this outcome because we know that 99.985% of all hydrogen atoms on earth are ^{1}H atoms. That is, the **percent abundance** of ^{1}H atoms is 99.985%.

$$\text{Percent abundance} = \frac{\text{number of atoms of a given isotope}}{\text{total number of atoms of all isotopes of that element}} \times 100\% \quad \textbf{(2.1)}$$

The remainder of naturally occurring hydrogen is deuterium, whose abundance is only 0.015% of the total hydrogen atoms. Tritium, the radioactive ^{3}H isotope, occurs naturally in only trace amounts.

Consider again the two isotopes of boron. The boron-10 isotope has an abundance of 19.91%; the abundance of boron-11 is 80.09%. Thus, if you could count out 10,000 boron atoms from an "average" natural sample, 1991 of them would be boron-10 atoms, and 8009 of them would be boron-11 atoms.

Chemistry ⚛ Now™

Sign in at **www.cengage.com/login** and go to Chapter 2 Contents to see Screen 2.12, **Isotopes.**

EXERCISE 2.2 Isotopes

Silver has two isotopes, one with 60 neutrons (percent abundance = 51.839%) and the other with 62 neutrons. What is the mass number and symbol of the isotope with 62 neutrons, and what is its percent abundance?

Determining Atomic Mass and Isotope Abundance

The masses of isotopes and their percent abundances are determined experimentally using a mass spectrometer (Figure 2.3). A gaseous sample of an element is introduced into the evacuated chamber of the spectrometer, and the atoms or

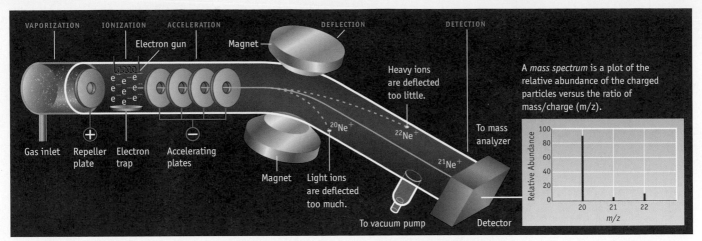

1. A sample is introduced as a vapor into the ionization chamber.

There it is bombarded with high-energy electrons that strip electrons from the atoms or molecules of the sample.

2. The resulting positive particles are accelerated by a series of negatively charged accelerator plates into an analyzing chamber.

3. This chamber is in a magnetic field, which is perpendicular to the direction of the beam of charged particles.

The magnetic field causes the beam to curve. The radius of curvature depends on the mass and charge of the particles (as well as the accelerating voltage and strength of the magnetic field).

4. Here, particles of $^{21}Ne^+$ are focused on the detector, whereas beams of ions of $^{20}Ne^+$ and $^{22}Ne^+$ (of lighter or heavier mass) experience greater and lesser curvature, respectively, and so fail to be detected.

By changing the magnetic field, charged particles of different masses can be focused on the detector to generate the observed spectrum.

Active Figure 2.3 Mass spectrometer.

Chemistry ⚛ Now™ Sign in at **www.cengage.com/login** and go to the Chapter Contents menu to explore an interactive version of this figure accompanied by an exercise.

molecules of the sample are converted to positively charged particles (called *ions*). A beam of these ions is injected into a magnetic field, which causes the paths of the ions to be deflected. The extent of deflection depends on particle mass: The less massive ions are deflected more, and the more massive ions are deflected less. The ions, now separated by mass, are detected at the end of the chamber. Chemists using modern instruments (Figure 1.2) can measure isotopic masses to as many as nine significant figures.

Except for carbon-12, whose mass is defined to be exactly 12 u, isotopic masses do not have integer values. However, the isotopic masses are always very close to the mass numbers for the isotope. For example, the mass of an atom of boron-11 (^{11}B, 5 protons and 6 neutrons) is 11.0093 u, and the mass of an atom of iron-58 (^{58}Fe, 26 protons and 32 neutrons) is 57.9333 u.

■ **Isotopic Masses and the Mass Defect** Actual masses of atoms are always less than the sum of the masses of subatomic particles composing that atom. This is called the *mass defect,* and the reason for it is discussed in Chapter 23.

2.4 Atomic Weight

Because every sample of boron has some atoms with a mass of 10.0129 u and others with a mass of 11.0093 u, the average atomic mass must be somewhere between these values. The **atomic weight** of an element is the average mass of a representa-

TABLE 2.2   Isotope Abundance and Atomic Weight

Element	Symbol	Atomic Weight	Mass Number	Isotopic Mass	Natural Abundance (%)
Hydrogen	H	1.00794	1	1.0078	99.985
	D*		2	2.0141	0.015
	T†		3	3.0161	0
Boron	B	10.811	10	10.0129	19.91
			11	11.0093	80.09
Neon	Ne	20.1797	20	19.9924	90.48
			21	20.9938	0.27
			22	21.9914	9.25
Magnesium	Mg	24.3050	24	23.9850	78.99
			25	24.9858	10.00
			26	25.9826	11.01

*D = deuterium; †T = tritium, radioactive.

■ **Atomic Mass, Relative Atomic Mass, and Atomic Weight** The atomic mass is the mass of an atom at rest. The relative atomic mass, also known as the atomic weight or the average atomic weight, is the average of the atomic masses of all of the element's isotopes. The term "atomic weight" is slowly being phased out in favor of "relative atomic mass."

tive sample of atoms. For boron, for example, the atomic weight is 10.811. If isotope masses and abundances are known, the atomic mass of an element can be calculated using Equation 2.2.

$$\text{Atomic weight} = \left(\frac{\%\ \text{abundance isotope 1}}{100} \right)(\text{mass of isotope 1})$$
$$+ \left(\frac{\%\ \text{abundance isotope 2}}{100} \right)(\text{mass of isotope 2}) + \ldots$$

(2.2)

For boron with two isotopes (^{10}B, 19.91% abundant; ^{11}B, 80.09% abundant), we find

$$\text{Atomic weight} = \left(\frac{19.91}{100} \right) \times 10.0129 + \left(\frac{80.09}{100} \right) \times 11.0093 = 10.81$$

Equation 2.2 gives an average mass, weighted in terms of the abundance of each isotope for the element. As illustrated by the data in Table 2.2, *the atomic mass of an element is usually closer to the mass of the most abundant isotope or isotopes.*

The atomic weight of each stable element has been determined experimentally, and these numbers appear in the periodic table inside the front cover of this book. In the periodic table, each element's box contains the atomic number, the element symbol, and the atomic weight. For unstable (radioactive) elements, the atomic weight or mass number of the most stable isotope is given in parentheses.

Chemistry.ᐤ.Now™

Sign in at **www.cengage.com/login** and go to Chapter 2 Contents to see Screen 2.13 for an exercise and a tutorial on **mass spectrometers and on calculating atomic mass.**

EXAMPLE 2.2 Calculating Atomic Weight from Isotope Abundance

Problem Bromine has two naturally occurring isotopes. One has a mass of 78.918338 and an abundance of 50.69%. The other isotope, of mass 80.916291, has an abundance of 49.31%. Calculate the atomic weight of bromine.

Strategy The atomic weight of any element is the weighted average of the masses of the isotopes in a representative sample. To calculate the atomic weight, multiply the mass of each isotope by its percent abundance divided by 100 (Equation 2.2).

Solution

$$\text{Atomic weight of bromine} = (50.69/100)(78.918338) + (49.31/100)(80.916291)$$
$$= 79.90$$

EXAMPLE 2.3 Calculating Isotopic Abundances

Problem Antimony, Sb, has two stable isotopes: ^{121}Sb, 120.904 u, and ^{123}Sb, 122.904 u. What are the relative abundances of these isotopes?

Strategy The atomic mass of antimony is 121.760 u (see the periodic table). Before we do the calculation we can infer that the lighter isotope (^{121}Sb) must be the more abundant because the atomic weight is closer to 121 than to 123. Next, to calculate the abundances we recognize there are two unknown but related quantities, and we can write the following expression (where the fractional abundance of an isotope is the percent abundance of the isotope divided by 100):

$$\text{Atomic weight} = 121.760$$
$$= (\text{fractional abundance of } ^{121}\text{Sb})(120.904) + (\text{fractional abundance of } ^{123}\text{Sb})(122.904)$$

or

$$121.760 = x(120.904) + y(122.904)$$

where x = fractional abundance of ^{121}Sb and y = fractional abundance of ^{123}Sb. Because we know that the sum of the fractional abundances of the isotopes must equal 1, $x + y = 1$, and we can solve the simultaneous equations for x and y.

Solution

Because y = fractional abundance of ^{123}Sb = $1 - x$, we can make a substitution for y.

$$121.760 = x(120.904) + (1 - x)(122.904)$$

Expanding this equation, we have

$$121.760 = 120.904x + 122.904 - 122.904x$$

Finally, solving for x, we find

$$121.760 - 122.904 = (120.904 - 122.904)x$$
$$x = 0.5720$$

The fractional abundance of ^{121}Sb is 0.5720, and its percent abundance is 57.20%. This means that the percent abundance of ^{123}Sb must be 42.80%. The result confirms our initial inference that the lighter isotope is the more abundant of the two.

Charles D. Winters

Elemental bromine. Bromine is a deep orange, volatile liquid at room temperature. It consists of Br_2 molecules in which two bromine atoms are chemically bonded together. There are two, stable, naturally-occurring isotopes of bromine atoms: ^{79}Br (50.69% abundant) and ^{81}Br (49.31% abundant).

EXERCISE 2.3 Calculating Atomic Weight

Verify that the atomic weight of chlorine is 35.45, given the following information:

^{35}Cl mass = 34.96885; percent abundance = 75.77%

^{37}Cl mass = 36.96590; percent abundance = 24.23%

The U.S. Anti-Doping Agency is responsible for testing for performance-enhancing drugs such as synthetic testosterone that has been used by athletes (page 1). But, if an athlete were to take this synthetic steroid, how can chemists tell the difference between that and the testosterone normally occurring in a male athlete's body?

Testosterone (T) and epitestosterone (E) are closely related steroids, and both are produced naturally. (The latter is an *isomer* of testosterone, a compound with an identical formula to testosterone but with a difference in the way the molecule fills space.) In most adult men the compounds are found in about equal amounts, although the natural T/E ratio can be as high as 4/1. To allow for elevated natural testosterone levels, the Anti-Doping Agency considers that a ratio of 6/1 is an indication an athlete must be using synthetic testosterone. This situation arose when the winner of the 2006 Tour de France bicycle race, Floyd Landis, was found to have a ratio of T/E = 11/1 based on a urine test after one stage of the race.

When the race was over, and the drug-testing results were announced, Landis strongly denied taking testosterone. He

© Robert Houser/Index Stock Imagery

argued that his body may have produced more testosterone than normal because of the rigors of the race. This prompted the doping-control laboratory for the Tour to seek additional evidence. They used a technique developed by the U.S. Anti-Doping Agency called "isotope ratio mass spectrometry," which measures the ratio of carbon isotopes, ^{12}C and ^{13}C, in compounds.

Carbon-13 is a naturally occurring isotope of carbon. When most plants grow using CO_2 from the atmosphere, about 1% of the C atoms incorporated in the plant are ^{13}C. The ^{13}C is ingested either directly by humans when eating plants or indirectly when eating meat

from grazing animals, and it is then incorporated into the carbon-containing molecules, including testosterone, that our bodies build.

Synthetic testosterone is made from wild yams and soy, plants that are so-called warm climate "C3 plants" that take up atmospheric CO_2 differently than temperate-zone "C4 plants." One important result of this difference is that C3 plants have a lower $^{13}C/^{12}C$ ratio than C4 plants. Because diets in most industrialized countries derive from a mixture of C3 and C4 plants, the natural testosterone in male athletes in most countries will have a different $^{13}C/^{12}C$ ratio than synthetic testosterone. A skilled scientist with a mass spectrometer (Figure 2.3), can relatively easily detect the difference. In the Tour de France case, the $^{13}C/^{12}C$ ratio added further evidence to the case that illegal steroid use had occurred.

Questions:

1. *How many neutrons are there in atoms of ^{13}C?*
2. *^{14}C is a radioactive isotope of carbon that occurs in trace amounts in all living materials. How many neutrons are in a ^{14}C atom?*
3. *Use your library or the World Wide Web to find the source of ^{14}C in living materials.*

Answers to these questions are in Appendix Q.

 Module 1

2.5 The Periodic Table

The periodic table of elements is one of the most useful tools in chemistry. Not only does it contain a wealth of information, but it can also be used to organize many of the ideas of chemistry. It is important to become familiar with its main features and terminology.

Developing the Periodic Table

■ **About the Periodic Table**
For more information on the periodic table, we recommend the following:
• The American Chemical Society has a description of every element on its website (http://pubs.acs.org/cen/80th/elements.html).
• J. Emsley: *Nature's Building Blocks—An A–Z Guide to the Elements*, New York, Oxford University Press, 2001.
• O. Sacks: *Uncle Tungsten—Memories of a Chemical Boyhood*, New York, Alfred A. Knopf, 2001.

Although the arrangement of elements in the periodic table is now understood on the basis of atomic structure (▶ Chapters 6 and 7), the table was originally developed from many experimental observations of the chemical and physical properties of elements and is the result of the ideas of a number of chemists in the 18th and 19th centuries.

In 1869, at the University of St. Petersburg in Russia, Dmitri Ivanovitch Mendeleev (1834–1907) was pondering the properties of the elements as he wrote a textbook on chemistry. On studying the chemical and physical properties of the elements, he realized that, if the elements were arranged in order of increasing atomic weight, elements with similar properties appeared in a regular pattern. That is, he saw a **periodicity** or periodic repetition of the properties of elements. Mendeleev organized the known elements into a table by lining them up in a horizontal row in

by Eric R. Scerri, UCLA

Dimitri Mendeleev was probably the greatest scientist produced by Russia. The youngest of 14 children, he was taken by his mother on a long journey, on foot, in order to enroll him into a university. However, several attempts initially proved futile because, as a Siberian, Mendeleev was barred from attending certain institutions. His mother did succeed in enrolling him in a teacher training college, thus giving Mendeleev a lasting interest in science education, which contributed to his eventual discovery of the periodic system that essentially simplified the subject of inorganic chemistry.

After completing a doctorate, Mendeleev headed to Germany for a postdoctoral fellowship and then returned to Russia, where he set about writing a book aimed at summarizing all of inorganic chemistry. It was while writing this book that he identified the organizing principle with which he is now invariably connected—the periodic system of the elements.

More correctly, though, the periodic system was developed by Mendeleev, as well as five other scientists, over a period of about 10 years, after the Italian chemist Cannizzaro had published a consistent set of atomic weights in 1860. It appears that Mendeleev was unaware of the work of several of his co-discoverers, however.

In essence, the periodic table groups together sets of elements with similar properties into vertical columns. The underlying idea is that if the elements are arranged in order of increasing atomic weights, there are approximate repetitions in their chemical properties after certain intervals. As a result of the existence of the periodic table, students and even professors of chemistry were no longer obliged to learn the properties of all the elements in a disorganized fashion. Instead, they could concentrate on the properties of representative members of the eight columns or groups in the early short-form periodic table, from which they could predict properties of other group members.

Mendeleev is justly regarded as the leading discoverer of the periodic table since he continued to champion the finding and drew out its consequences to a far greater extent than any of his contemporaries. First, he accommodated the 65 or so elements that were known at the time into a coherent scheme based on ascending order of atomic weight while also reflecting chemical and physical similarities. Next, he noticed gaps in his system, which he reasoned would eventually be filled by elements that had not yet been discovered. In addition, by judicious interpolation between the properties of known elements, Mendeleev predicted the

Statue of Dmitri Mendeleev and a periodic table mural. This statue and mural are at the Institute for Metrology in St. Petersburg, Russia.

nature of a number of completely new elements. Within a period of about 20 years, three of these elements—subsequently called gallium, scandium, and germanium—were isolated and found to have almost the exact properties that Mendeleev had predicted.

What is not well known is that about half of the elements that Mendeleev predicted were never found. But given the dramatic success of his early predictions, these later lapses have largely been forgotten.

Eric Scerri, *The Periodic Table: Its Story and Its Significance,* Oxford University Press, New York, 2007.

order of increasing atomic weight (page 50). Every time he came to an element with properties similar to one already in the row, he started a new row. For example, the elements Li, Be, B, C, N, O, and F were in a row. Sodium was the next element then known; because its properties closely resembled those of Li, Mendeleev started a new row. As more and more elements were added to the table, new rows were added, and elements with similar properties (such as Li, Na, and K) were found in the same vertical column.

An important feature of Mendeleev's table—and a mark of his genius—was that he left an empty space in a column when an element was not known but should exist and have properties similar to the element above it in his table. He deduced that these spaces would be filled by undiscovered elements. For example, he left a space between Si (silicon) and Sn (tin) in Group 4A for an element he called *ekasilicon.* Based on the progression of properties in this group, Mendeleev was able to predict the properties of this missing element. With the discovery of germanium (Ge) in 1886, Mendeleev's prediction was confirmed.

■ **Mendeleev and Atomic Numbers**
Mendeleev developed the periodic table based on atomic weights because the concept of atomic numbers was not known until after the development of the structure of the atom in the early 20th century.

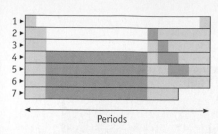

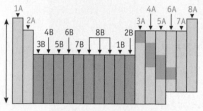

Periods

Groups or Families

Periods and groups in the periodic table. One way to designate periodic groups is to number them 1 through 18 from left to right. This method is generally used outside the United States. The system predominant in the United States labels main group elements as Groups 1A–8A and transition elements as Groups 1B–8B. This book uses the A/B system.

In Mendeleev's table, the elements were ordered by increasing mass. A glance at a modern table, however, shows that, if some elements (such as Ni and Co, Ar and K, and Te and I) were ordered by mass and not chemical and physical properties, they would be reversed in their order of appearance. Mendeleev recognized these discrepancies and simply assumed the atomic weights known at that time were inaccurate—not a bad assumption based on the analytical methods then in use. In fact, his order is correct, and what was wrong was his assumption that element properties were a function of their mass.

In 1913, H. G. J. Moseley (1887–1915), a young English scientist working with Ernest Rutherford (1871–1937), corrected Mendeleev's assumption. Moseley was doing experiments in which he bombarded many different metals with electrons in a cathode-ray tube (page 343) and examined the x-rays emitted in the process. In seeking some order in his data, he realized that the wavelength of the x-rays emitted by a given element was related in a precise manner to the atomic number of the element. Indeed, once the concept of an atomic number was recognized early in the 20th century, chemists realized that organizing the elements in a table by increasing atomic number corrected the inconsistencies in the Mendeleev table. The **law of chemical periodicity** is now stated as *the properties of the elements are periodic functions of atomic number.*

Features of the Periodic Table

The main organizational features of the periodic table are the following:

- Elements are arranged so those with similar chemical and physical properties lie in vertical columns called **groups** or **families**. The periodic table commonly used in the United States has groups numbered 1 through 8, with each number followed by a letter: A or B. The A groups are often called the **main group elements,** and the B groups are the **transition elements**.
- The horizontal rows of the table are called **periods**, and they are numbered beginning with 1 for the period containing only H and He. For example, sodium, Na, in Group 1A, is the first element in the third period. Mercury, Hg, in Group 2B, is in the sixth period (or sixth row).

The periodic table can be divided into several regions according to the properties of the elements. On the table inside the front cover of this book, elements that behave as *metals* are indicated in purple, those that are *nonmetals* are indicated in yellow, and elements called *metalloids* appear in green. Elements gradually become less metallic as one moves from left to right across a period, and the metalloids lie along the metal–nonmetal boundary. Some elements are shown in Figure 2.4.

You are probably familiar with many properties of **metals** from everyday experience (Figure 2.5a). Metals are solids (except for mercury), can conduct electricity, are usually ductile (can be drawn into wires) and malleable (can be rolled into sheets), and can form alloys (solutions of one or more metals in another metal). Iron (Fe) and aluminum (Al) are used in automobile parts because of their ductility, malleability, and low cost relative to other metals. Copper (Cu) is used in electric wiring because it conducts electricity better than most other metals.

The **nonmetals** lie to the right of a diagonal line that stretches from B to Te in the periodic table and have a wide variety of properties. Some are solids (carbon, sulfur, phosphorus, and iodine). Five elements are gases at room temperature (hydrogen, oxygen, nitrogen, fluorine, and chlorine). One nonmetal, bromine, is a liquid at room temperature (Figure 2.5b). With the exception of carbon in the form of graphite, nonmetals do not conduct electricity, which is one of the main features that distinguishes them from metals.

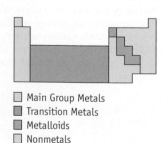

- ☐ Main Group Metals
- ☐ Transition Metals
- ☐ Metalloids
- ☐ Nonmetals

Active Figure 2.4 Some of the known 117 elements.

Chemistry ⚛ Now™ Sign in at www.cengage.com/login and go to the Chapter Contents menu to explore an interactive version of this figure accompanied by an exercise.

Group 1A
Lithium—Li (top)
Potassium—K (bottom)

Group 2A
Magnesium—Mg

Transition Metals
Titanium—Ti, Vanadium—V, Chromium—Cr, Manganese—Mn, Iron—Fe, Cobalt—Co, Nickel—Ni, Copper—Cu

Group 2B
Zinc—Zn (top)
Mercury—Hg (bottom)

	1A												3A	4A	5A	6A	7A	8A
1		2A																
2	Li												B	C	N			Ne
3		Mg	3B	4B	5B	6B	7B		8B		1B	2B	Al	Si	P	S		
4	K			Ti	V	Cr	Mn	Fe	Co	Ni	Cu	Zn				Se	Br	
5														Sn				
6													Hg	Pb				
7															(6A)	(7A)		

(3A) (4A) (5A)

Group 8A, Noble Gases
Neon—Ne

Photos: Charles D. Winters

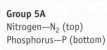

Group 3A
Boron—B (top)
Aluminum—Al (bottom)

Group 4A
Carbon—C (top)
Lead—Pb (left)
Silicon—Si (right)
Tin—Sn (bottom)

Group 5A
Nitrogen—N₂ (top)
Phosphorus—P (bottom)

Group 6A
Sulfur—S (top)
Selenium—Se (bottom)

Group 7A
Bromine—Br

(a) Metals

Bromine, Br₂   Iodine, I₂

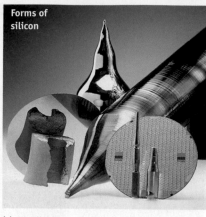
Forms of silicon

(b) Nonmetals

(c) Metalloids

FIGURE 2.5 Metals, nonmetals, and metalloids. (a) Molybdenum (Mo, wire), bismuth (Bi, center object), and copper (Cu) are metals. Metals can generally be drawn into wires, and they conduct electricity. (b) Only 15 or so elements can be classified as nonmetals. Here are orange liquid bromine and purple solid iodine. (c) Only six elements are generally classified as metalloids or semimetals. This photograph shows solid silicon in various forms, including a wafer that holds printed electronic circuits.

The elements next to the diagonal line from boron (B) to tellurium (Te) have properties that make them difficult to classify as metals or nonmetals. Chemists call them **metalloids** or, sometimes, **semimetals** (Figure 2.5c). You should know, however, that chemists often disagree about which elements fit into this category. We will define a metalloid as an element that has some of the physical characteristics of a metal but some of the chemical characteristics of a nonmetal; we include only B, Si, Ge, As, Sb, and Te in this category. This definition reflects the ambiguity in the behavior of these elements. Antimony (Sb), for example, conducts electricity as well as many elements that are true metals. Its chemistry, however, resembles that of the nonmetal phosphorus.

A Brief Overview of the Periodic Table and the Chemical Elements

The metals in the leftmost column, **Group 1A**, are known as the **alkali metals**. All are metals and are solids at room temperature. They are all very reactive. For example, they react with water to produce hydrogen and alkaline solutions (Figure 2.6). Because of their reactivity, these metals are only found in nature combined in compounds (such as NaCl) (Figure 1.4), never as the free element.

The second group in the periodic table, **Group 2A**, is also composed entirely of metals that occur naturally only in compounds. Except for beryllium (Be), these elements react with water to produce alkaline solutions, and most of their oxides (such as lime, CaO) form alkaline solutions; hence, they are known as the **alkaline earth metals**. Magnesium (Mg) and calcium (Ca) are the seventh and fifth most abundant elements in the earth's crust, respectively (Table 2.3). Calcium is one of the important elements in teeth and bones, and it occurs naturally in vast limestone deposits. Calcium carbonate ($CaCO_3$) is the chief constituent of limestone and of corals, sea shells, marble, and chalk. Radium (Ra), the heaviest alkaline earth element, is radioactive and is used to treat some cancers by radiation.

■ **Alkali and Alkaline** The word "alkali" comes from the Arabic language; ancient Arabian chemists discovered that ashes of certain plants, which they called al-qali, gave water solutions that felt slippery and burned the skin. These ashes contain compounds of Group 1A elements that produce alkaline (basic) solutions.

Charles D. Winters

(a) Cutting sodium.

(b) Potassium reacts with water.

FIGURE 2.6 Alkali metals. (a) Cutting a bar of sodium with a knife is about like cutting a stick of cold butter. (b) When an alkali metal such as potassium is treated with water, a vigorous reaction occurs, giving an alkaline solution and hydrogen gas, which burns in air.

TABLE 2.3 **The 10 Most Abundant Elements in the Earth's Crust**

Rank	Element	Abundance (ppm)*
1	Oxygen	474,000
2	Silicon	277,000
3	Aluminum	82,000
4	Iron	41,000
5	Calcium	41,000
6	Sodium	23,000
7	Magnesium	23,000
8	Potassium	21,000
9	Titanium	5,600
10	Hydrogen	1,520

*ppm = g per 1000 kg.

Group 3A contains one element of great importance, aluminum (see Figure 2.4). This element and three others (gallium, indium, and thallium) are metals, whereas boron (B) is a metalloid. Aluminum (Al) is the most abundant metal in the earth's crust at 8.2% by mass. It is exceeded in abundance only by the nonmetal oxygen and metalloid silicon. These three elements are found combined in clays and other common minerals. Boron occurs in the mineral borax, a compound used as a cleaning agent, antiseptic, and flux for metal work.

As a metalloid, boron has a different chemistry than the other elements of the group, all of which are metals. Nonetheless, all form compounds with analogous formulas such as BCl_3 and $AlCl_3$, and this similarity marks them as members of the same periodic group.

Thus far, all the elements we have described, except boron, have been metals. Beginning with **Group 4A**, however, the groups contain more and more nonmetals. In Group 4A, there are a nonmetal, carbon (C), two metalloids, silicon (Si) and germanium (Ge), and two metals, tin (Sn) and lead (Pb) (Figure 2.4). Because of the change from nonmetallic to metallic character, more variation occurs in the properties of the elements of this group than in most others. Nonetheless, there are similarities. For example, these elements form compounds with analogous formulas such as CO_2, SiO_2, GeO_2, and PbO_2.

Carbon is the basis for the great variety of chemical compounds that make up living things. It is found in Earth's atmosphere as CO_2, on the surface of the earth in carbonates like limestone and coral (calcium carbonate, $CaCO_3$), and in coal, petroleum, and natural gas—the fossil fuels.

One interesting aspect of the chemistry of the nonmetals is that a particular element can often exist in several different and distinct forms, called **allotropes**, each having its own properties. Carbon has a number of allotropes, the best known of which are graphite and diamond. Graphite consists of flat sheets in which each carbon atom is connected to three others (Figure 2.7a). Because the sheets of carbon atoms cling only weakly to one another, one layer can slip easily over another. This explains why graphite is soft, is a good lubricant, and is used in pencil lead. (Pencil "lead" is not the element lead (Pb) but a composite of clay and graphite that leaves a trail of graphite on the page as you write.)

Charles D. Winters

Liquid gallium. Bromine and mercury are the only elements that are liquids under ambient conditions. Gallium (29.8 °C) and cesium (28.4 °C) melt slightly above room temperature. Here gallium melts when held in the hand.

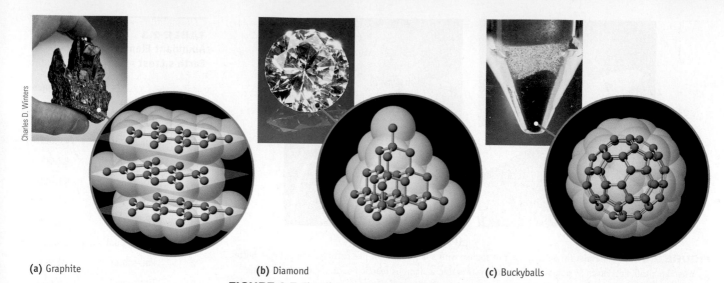

(a) Graphite   **(b)** Diamond   **(c)** Buckyballs

FIGURE 2.7 The allotropes of carbon. (a) Graphite consists of layers of carbon atoms. Each carbon atom is linked to three others to form a sheet of six-member, hexagonal rings. (b) In diamond, the carbon atoms are also arranged in six-member rings, but the rings are not planar because each C atom is connected tetrahedrally by four other C atoms. (c) Buckyballs. A member of the family called buckminsterfullerenes, C_{60} is an allotrope of carbon. Sixty carbon atoms are arranged in a spherical cage that resembles a hollow soccer ball. Notice that each six-member ring shares an edge with three other six-member rings and three five-member rings. Chemists call this molecule a "buckyball." C_{60} is a black powder; it is shown here in the tip of a pointed glass tube.

■ **Special Group Names** Some groups have common and widely used names. (See Figure 2.4)
Group 1A: Alkali metals
Group 2A: Alkaline earth metals
Group 7A: Halogens
Group 8A: Noble gases

In diamond, each carbon atom is connected to four others at the corners of a tetrahedron, and this extends throughout the solid (see Figure 2.7b). This structure causes diamonds to be extremely hard, denser than graphite ($d = 3.51$ g/cm^3 for diamond and $d = 2.22$ g/cm^3 for graphite), and chemically less reactive. Because diamonds are not only hard but are excellent conductors of heat, they are used on the tips of metal- and rock-cutting tools.

In the late 1980s, another form of carbon was identified as a component of black soot, the stuff that collects when carbon-containing materials are burned in a deficiency of oxygen. This substance is made up of molecules with 60 carbon atoms arranged as a spherical "cage" (Figure 2.7c). You may recognize that the surface is made up of five- and six-member rings and resembles a hollow soccer ball. The shape also reminded its discoverers of an architectural dome conceived several decades ago by the American philosopher and engineer, R. Buckminster Fuller. This led to the official name of the allotrope, buckminsterfullerene, although chemists often simply call these C_{60} molecules "buckyballs."

Oxides of silicon are the basis of many minerals such as clay, quartz, and beautiful gemstones like amethyst (Figure 2.8). Tin and lead have been known for centuries because they are easily obtained from their ores. Tin alloyed with copper makes bronze, which was used in ancient times in utensils and weapons. Lead has been used in water pipes and paint, even though the element is toxic to humans.

Nitrogen in **Group 5A** occurs naturally in the form of the diatomic molecule N_2 (Figure 2.9) and makes up about three fourths of Earth's atmosphere. It is also incorporated in biochemically important substances such as chlorophyll, proteins, and DNA. Therefore, scientists have long sought ways to make compounds from atmospheric nitrogen, a process referred to as "nitrogen fixation." Nature accomplishes this easily in some prokaryotic organisms, but severe conditions (high temperatures, for example) must be used in the laboratory and in industry to cause N_2 to react with other elements (such as H_2 to make ammonia, NH_3, which is widely used as a fertilizer).

FIGURE 2.8 Compounds containing silicon. Ordinary clay, sand, and many gemstones are based on compounds of silicon and oxygen. Here, clear, colorless quartz and dark purple amethyst lie in a bed of sand. All are silicon dioxide, SiO_2. The different colors are due to impurities.

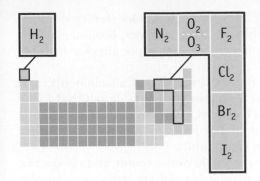

FIGURE 2.9 Elements that exist as diatomic or triatomic molecules. Seven of the elements in the periodic table exist as diatomic, or two-atom, molecules. Oxygen has an additional allotrope, ozone, with three O atoms in each molecule. See also ChemistryNow Screen 2.16, Elements that Exist as Molecules.

■ **Placing H in the Periodic Table** Where to place H? Tables often show it in Group 1A even though it is clearly not an alkali metal. However, in its reactions it forms a 1+ ion just like the alkali metals. For this reason, H is often placed in Group 1A.

Phosphorus is also essential to life. It is an important constituent in bones, teeth, and DNA. The element glows in the dark if it is exposed to air (owing to its reaction with O_2), and its name, based on Greek words meaning "light-bearing," reflects this. This element also has several allotropes, the most important being white (Figure 2.4) and red phosphorus. Both forms of phosphorus are used commercially. White phosphorus ignites spontaneously in air and so is normally stored under water. When it does react with air, it forms P_4O_{10}, which can react with water to form phosphoric acid (H_3PO_4), a compound used in food products such as soft drinks. Red phosphorus is used in the striking strips on match books. When a match is struck, potassium chlorate in the match head mixes with some red phosphorus on the striking strip, and the friction is enough to ignite this mixture.

As with Group 4A, we again see nonmetals (N and P), metalloids (As and Sb), and a metal (Bi, Figure 2.5a) in Group 5A. In spite of these variations, they also form analogous compounds such as the oxides N_2O_5, P_2O_5 and As_2O_5.

Oxygen, which constitutes about 20% of Earth's atmosphere and which combines readily with most other elements, is at the top of **Group 6A**. Most of the energy that powers life on Earth is derived from reactions in which oxygen combines with other substances.

Sulfur has been known in elemental form since ancient times as brimstone or "burning stone" (Figure 2.10). Sulfur, selenium, and tellurium are often referred to collectively as **chalcogens** (from the Greek word, *khalkos*, for copper) because most copper ores contain these elements. Their compounds can be foul smelling and poisonous; nevertheless, sulfur and selenium are essential components of the human diet. By far the most important compound of sulfur is sulfuric acid (H_2SO_4), which is manufactured in larger amounts than any other compound.

As in Group 5A, the second- and third-period elements of Group 6A have different structures. Like nitrogen, oxygen is also a diatomic molecule (see Figure 2.9). Unlike nitrogen, however, oxygen has an allotrope, the triatomic molecule ozone, O_3. Sulfur, which can be found in nature as a yellow solid, has many allotropes. The most common allotrope consists of eight-member, crown-shaped rings of sulfur atoms (see Figure 2.10).

Polonium, a radioactive element in Group 6A, was isolated in 1898 by Marie and Pierre Curie, who separated it from tons of a uranium-containing ore and named it for Madame Curie's native country, Poland.

In Group 6A, we once again observe a variation of properties. Oxygen, sulfur, and selenium are nonmetals; tellurium is a metalloid; and polonium is a metal. Nonetheless, there is a family resemblance in their chemistries. All form oxygen-containing compounds such as SO_2, SeO_2, and TeO_2 and sodium-containing compounds (Na_2O, Na_2S, Na_2Se, and Na_2Te).

At the far right of the periodic table are two groups composed entirely of nonmetals. The **Group 7A** elements—fluorine, chlorine, bromine, iodine, and radioac-

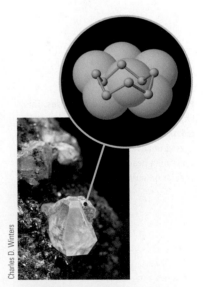

Charles D. Winters

FIGURE 2.10 Sulfur. The most common allotrope of sulfur consists of S atoms arranged in eight-member, crown-shaped rings.

tive astatine—are nonmetals, and all exist as diatomic molecules (see Figure 2.9). At room temperature, fluorine (F_2) and chlorine (Cl_2) are gases. Bromine (Br_2) is a liquid, and iodine (I_2) is a solid, but bromine and iodine vapor are clearly visible over the liquid or solid (see Figure 2.5b).

The Group 7A elements are among the most reactive of all elements, and all combine violently with alkali metals to form salts such as table salt, NaCl (see Figure 1.4). The name for this group, the **halogens**, comes from the Greek words *hals*, meaning "salt," and *genes*, for "forming." The halogens also react with other metals and with most nonmetals to form compounds.

The **Group 8A** elements—helium, neon, argon, krypton, xenon, and radioactive radon—are the least reactive elements (Figure 2.11). All are gases, and none is abundant on Earth or in Earth's atmosphere. Because of this, they were not discovered until the end of the 19th century. Helium, the second most abundant element in the universe after hydrogen, was detected in the sun in 1868 by analysis of the solar spectrum. (The name of the element comes from the Greek word for the sun, *helios*.) It was not found on Earth until 1895, however. Until 1962, when a compound of xenon was first prepared, it was believed that none of these elements would combine chemically with any other element. The name **noble gases** for this group, a term meant to denote their general lack of reactivity, derives from this fact. For the same reason, they are sometimes called the *inert gases* or, because of their low abundance, the *rare gases*.

Stretching between Groups 2A and 3A is a series of elements called the **transition elements.** These fill the B-groups (1B through 8B) in the fourth through the seventh periods in the center of the periodic table. All are metals (see Figure 2.4), and 13 of them are in the top 30 elements in terms of abundance in the earth's crust. Some, like iron (Fe), are abundant in nature (Table 2.3). Most occur naturally in combination with other elements, but a few—copper (Cu), silver (Ag), gold (Au), and platinum (Pt)—are much less reactive and so can be found in nature as pure elements.

Virtually all of the transition elements have commercial uses. They are used as structural materials (iron, titanium, chromium, copper); in paints (titanium, chromium); in the catalytic converters in automobile exhaust systems (platinum and rhodium); in coins (copper, nickel, zinc); and in batteries (manganese, nickel, cadmium, mercury).

A number of the transition elements play important biological roles. For example, iron, a relatively abundant element (see Table 2.3), is the central element in the chemistry of hemoglobin, the oxygen-carrying component of blood.

FIGURE 2.11 The noble gases. This kit is sold for detecting the presence of radioactive radon in the home. Neon gas is used in advertising signs, and xenon-containing headlights are increasingly popular on automobiles.

Charles D. Winters

Two rows at the bottom of the table accommodate the **lanthanides** [the series of elements between the elements lanthanum ($Z = 57$) and hafnium ($Z = 72$)] and the **actinides** [the series of elements between actinium ($Z = 89$) and rutherfordium ($Z = 104$)]. Some lanthanide compounds are used in color television picture tubes; uranium ($Z = 92$) is the fuel for atomic power plants, and americium ($Z = 95$) is used in smoke detectors.

Chemistry.☐.Now™

Sign in at **www.cengage.com/login** and go to Chapter 2 Contents to see:
- Screen 2.14 for an exercise on **periodic table organization**
- Screen 2.15 for an exercise on **chemical periodicity**

EXERCISE 2.4 The Periodic Table

How many elements are in the third period of the periodic table? Give the name and symbol of each. Tell whether each element in the period is a metal, metalloid, or nonmetal.

Charles D. Winters

Lanthanides. If you use a Bunsen burner in the lab, you may light it with a "flint" lighter. The flints are composed of iron and "mischmetal," a mixture of lanthanide elements, chiefly Ce, La, Pr, and Nd with traces of other lanthanides. (The word "mischmetal" comes from the German for "mixed metals.") It is produced by the electrolysis of a mixture of lanthanide oxides.

2.6 Molecules, Compounds, and Formulas

A molecule is the smallest identifiable unit into which a pure substance like sugar or water can be divided and still retain the composition and chemical properties of the substance. Such substances are composed of identical molecules consisting of atoms of two or more elements bound firmly together. For example, atoms of the element aluminum, Al, combine with molecules of the element bromine, Br_2, to produce the compound aluminum bromide, Al_2Br_6 (Figure 2.12).

$$2 \, Al(s) + 3 \, Br_2(\ell) \rightarrow Al_2Br_6(s)$$
$$\text{aluminum} + \text{bromine} \rightarrow \text{aluminum bromide}$$

Photos: Charles D. Winters

(a)   (b)   (c)

Active Figure 2.12 Reaction of the elements aluminum and bromine. (a) Solid aluminum and (in the beaker) liquid bromine. (b) When the aluminum is added to the bromine, a vigorous chemical reaction produces white, solid aluminum bromide, Al_2Br_6 (c).

Chemistry.☐.Now™ Sign in at www.cengage.com/login and go to the Chapter Contents menu to explore an interactive version of this figure accompanied by an exercise.

To describe this chemical change (or chemical reaction) on paper, the composition of each element and compound is represented by a symbol or formula. Here, one molecule of Al_2Br_6 is composed of two Al atoms and six Br atoms.

How do compounds differ from elements? When a compound is produced from its elements, the characteristics of the constituent elements are lost. Solid, metallic aluminum and red-orange liquid bromine, for example, react to form Al_2Br_6, a white solid.

Formulas

For molecules more complicated than water, there is often more than one way to write the formula. For example, the formula of ethanol (also called ethyl alcohol) can be represented as C_2H_6O (Figure 2.13). This **molecular formula** describes the composition of ethanol molecules—two carbon atoms, six hydrogen atoms, and one atom of oxygen occur per molecule—but it gives us no structural information. Structural information—how the atoms are connected and how the molecule fills space—is important, however, because it helps us understand how a molecule can interact with other molecules, which is the essence of chemistry.

To provide some structural information, it is useful to write a **condensed formula**, which indicates how certain atoms are grouped together. For example, the condensed formula of ethanol, CH_3CH_2OH (see Figure 2.13), informs us that the molecule consists of three "groups": a CH_3 group, a CH_2 group, and an OH group. Writing the formula as CH_3CH_2OH also shows that the compound is not dimethyl ether, CH_3OCH_3, a compound with the same molecular formula but with a different structure and distinctly different properties.

That ethanol and dimethyl ether are different molecules is further apparent from their **structural formulas** (Figure 2.13). This type of formula gives us an even higher level of structural detail, showing how all of the atoms are attached within a molecule. The lines between atoms represent the chemical bonds that hold atoms together in this molecule (▶ Chapter 8).

■ **Writing Formulas** When writing molecular formulas of organic compounds (compounds with C, H, and other elements), the convention is to write C first, then H, and finally other elements in alphabetical order. For example, acrylonitrile, a compound used to make consumer plastics, has the condensed formula CH_2CHCN. Its molecular formula is C_3H_3N.

■ **Ethanol and Dimethyl Ether Are Isomers** Compounds having the same molecular formula but different structures are called isomers. (See Chapter 10, and sign in to ChemistryNow and see Screen 2.17, Representing Compounds.)

Chemistry ⚛ Now™

Sign in at **www.cengage.com/login** and go to Chapter 2 Contents to see Screen 2.17 for an exercise and tutorial on **representations of molecules.**

NAME	MOLECULAR FORMULA	CONDENSED FORMULA	STRUCTURAL FORMULA	MOLECULAR MODEL
Ethanol	C_2H_6O	CH_3CH_2OH		
Dimethyl ether	C_2H_6O	CH_3OCH_3		

FIGURE 2.13 Four approaches to showing molecular formulas. Here, the two molecules have the same molecular formula. Condensed or structural formulas, and a molecular model, show that these molecules are different.

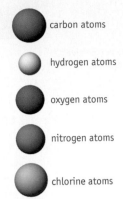

carbon atoms

hydrogen atoms

oxygen atoms

nitrogen atoms

chlorine atoms

EXERCISE 2.5 Molecular Formulas

Cysteine, whose molecular model and structural formula are illustrated here, is an important amino acid and a constituent of many living things. What is its molecular formula?

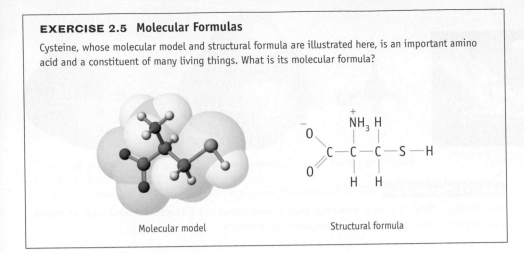

Molecular model   Structural formula

Molecular Models

Molecular structures are often beautiful in the same sense that art is beautiful, and there is something intrinsically beautiful about the pattern created by water molecules assembled in ice (Figure 2.14).

More important, however, is the fact that the physical and chemical properties of a molecular compound are often closely related to its structure. For example, two well-known features of ice are related to its structure. The first is the shape of ice crystals: The sixfold symmetry of macroscopic ice crystals also appears at the particulate level in the form of six-sided rings of hydrogen and oxygen atoms. The second is water's unique property of being less dense when solid than it is when liquid. The lower density of ice, which has enormous consequences for Earth's climate, results from the fact that molecules of water are not packed together tightly.

Because molecules are three-dimensional, it is often difficult to represent their shapes on paper. Certain conventions have been developed, however, that help represent three-dimensional structures on two-dimensional surfaces. Simple perspective drawings are often used (Figure 2.15).

Mehau Kulyk/Science Photo Library/Photo Researchers, Inc.; model by S.M. Young

FIGURE 2.14 Ice. Snowflakes are six-sided structures, reflecting the underlying structure of ice. Ice consists of six-sided rings formed by water molecules, in which each side of a ring consists of two O atoms and an H atom.

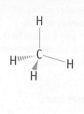

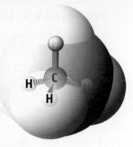

Charles D. Winters

Simple perspective
drawing

Plastic model

Ball-and-stick model

Space-filling model

All visualizing techniques
represent the same molecule.

Active Figure 2.15 Ways of depicting a molecule, here the methane (CH_4) molecule.

Chemistry⚛Now™ Sign in at www.cengage.com/login and go to the Chapter Contents menu to explore an interactive version of this figure accompanied by an exercise.

Several kinds of molecular models exist. In the **ball-and-stick model**, spheres, usually in different colors, represent the atoms, and sticks represent the bonds holding them together. These models make it easy to see how atoms are attached to one another. Molecules can also be represented using **space-filling models**. These models are more realistic because they offer a better representation of relative sizes of atoms and their proximity to each other when in a molecule. A disadvantage of pictures of space-filling models is that atoms can often be hidden from view.

Module 2
Module 3

2.7 Ionic Compounds: Formulas, Names, and Properties

The compounds you have encountered so far in this chapter are **molecular compounds**—that is, compounds that consist of discrete molecules at the particulate level. **Ionic compounds** constitute another major class of compounds. They consist of **ions**, atoms or groups of atoms that bear a positive or negative electric charge. Many familiar compounds are composed of ions (Figure 2.16). Table salt, or sodium chloride ($NaCl$), and lime (CaO) are just two. To recognize ionic compounds, and to be able to write formulas for these compounds, it is important to know the formulas and charges of common ions. You also need to know the names of ions and be able to name the compounds they form.

FIGURE 2.16 Some common ionic compounds.

Common Name	Name	Formula	Ions Involved
Calcite	Calcium carbonate	$CaCO_3$	Ca^{2+}, CO_3^{2-}
Fluorite	Calcium fluoride	CaF_2	Ca^{2+}, F^-
Gypsum	Calcium sulfate dihydrate	$CaSO_4 \cdot 2\,H_2O$	Ca^{2+}, SO_4^{2-}
Hematite	Iron(III) oxide	Fe_2O_3	Fe^{3+}, O^{2-}
Orpiment	Arsenic sulfide	As_2S_3	As^{3+}, S^{2-}

Hematite, Fe_2O_3

Calcite, $CaCO_3$

Gypsum, $CaSO_4 \cdot 2\,H_2O$

Fluorite, CaF_2

Orpiment, As_2S_3

Charles D. Winters

Ions

Atoms of many elements can gain or lose electrons in the course of a chemical reaction. To be able to predict the outcome of chemical reactions (▶ Sections 3.1–3.9), you need to know whether an element will likely gain or lose electrons and, if so, how many.

Cations

If an atom loses an electron (which is transferred to an atom of another element in the course of a reaction), the atom now has one fewer negative electrons than it has positive protons in the nucleus. The result is a positively charged ion called a **cation** (Figure 2.17). (The name is pronounced "cat'-ion.") Because it has an excess of one positive charge, we write the cation's symbol as, for example, Li^+:

$$Li\ atom \rightarrow e + Li^+\ cation$$
(3 protons and 3 electrons)   (3 protons and 2 electrons)

Anions

Conversely, if an atom gains one or more electrons, there is now a greater number of negatively charged electrons than protons. The result is an **anion** (Figure 2.17). (The name is pronounced "ann'-ion.")

$$O\ atom + 2\ e^- \rightarrow O^{2-}\ anion$$
(8 protons and 8 electrons)   (8 protons and 10 electrons)

Here, the O atom has gained two electrons, so we write the anion's symbol as O^{2-}.

How do you know whether an atom is likely to form a cation or an anion? It depends on whether the element is a metal or a nonmetal.

- Metals generally lose electrons in the course of their reactions to form cations.
- Nonmetals frequently gain one or more electrons to form anions in the course of their reactions.

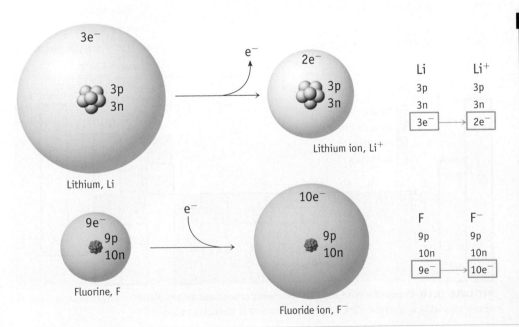

Lithium, Li
Lithium ion, Li$^+$
Fluorine, F
Fluoride ion, F$^-$

Monatomic Ions

Monatomic ions are single atoms that have lost or gained electrons. As indicated in Figure 2.18, metals typically lose electrons to form monatomic cations, and nonmetals typically gain electrons to form monatomic anions.

How can you predict the number of electrons gained or lost? Like lithium in Figure 2.17, *metals of Groups 1A–3A form positive ions having a charge equal to the group number of the metal.*

■ **Writing Ion Formulas** When writing the formula of an ion, the charge on the ion must be included.

Group	Metal Atom	Electron Change		Resulting Metal Cation
1A	Na (11 protons, 11 electrons)	−1	→	Na^+ (11 protons, 10 electrons)
2A	Ca (20 protons, 20 electrons)	−2	→	Ca^{2+} (20 protons, 18 electrons)
3A	Al (13 protons, 13 electrons)	−3	→	Al^{3+} (13 protons, 10 electrons)

Transition metals (B-group elements) also form cations. Unlike the A-group metals, however, no easily predictable pattern of behavior occurs for transition metal cations. In addition, transition metals often form several different ions. An iron-containing compound, for example, may contain either Fe^{2+} or Fe^{3+} ions. Indeed, 2+ and 3+ ions are typical of many transition metals (see Figure 2.18).

Group	Metal Atom	Electron Change		Resulting Metal Cation
7B	Mn (25 protons, 25 electrons)	−2	→	Mn^{2+} (25 protons, 23 electrons)
8B	Fe (26 protons, 26 electrons)	−2	→	Fe^{2+} (26 protons, 24 electrons)
8B	Fe (26 protons, 26 electrons)	−3	→	Fe^{3+} (26 protons, 23 electrons)

Nonmetals often form ions having a negative charge equal to the group number of the element minus 8. For example, nitrogen is in Group 5A, so it forms an ion having a 3− charge because a nitrogen atom can gain three electrons.

Group	Nonmetal Atom	Electron Change		Resulting Nonmetal Anion
5A	N (7 protons, 7 electrons)	+3	→	N^{3-} (7 protons, 10 electrons)
				Charge = 5 − 8
6A	S (16 protons, 16 electrons)	+2	→	S^{2-} (16 protons, 18 electrons)
				Charge = 6 − 8
7A	Br (35 protons, 35 electrons)	+1	→	Br^- (35 protons, 36 electrons)
				Charge = 7 − 8

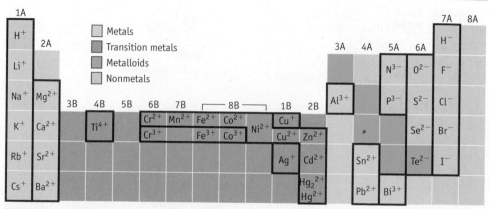

FIGURE 2.18 Charges on some common monatomic cations and anions. Metals usually form cations, and nonmetals usually form anions. (The boxed areas show ions of identical charge.)

Notice that hydrogen appears at two locations in Figure 2.18. The H atom can either lose or gain electrons, depending on the other atoms it encounters.

Electron lost: H (1 proton, 1 electron) $\rightarrow$ H$^+$ (1 proton, 0 electrons) + e$^-$

Electron gained: H (1 proton, 1 electron) + e$^-$ $\rightarrow$ H$^-$ (1 proton, 2 electrons)

Finally, the noble gases *very* rarely form monatomic cations or anions in chemical reactions.

Ion Charges and the Periodic Table

The metals of Groups 1A, 2A, and 3A form ions having 1+, 2+, and 3+ charges (Figure 2.18); that is, their atoms lose one, two, or three electrons, respectively. *For Group 1A and 2A metals and aluminum, the number of electrons remaining on the cation is the same as the number of electrons in an atom of the noble gas that precedes it in the periodic table.* For example, Mg^{2+} has 10 electrons, the same number as in an atom of the noble gas neon (atomic number 10).

An atom of a nonmetal near the right side of the periodic table would have to lose a great many electrons to achieve the same number as a noble gas atom of lower atomic number. (For instance, Cl, whose atomic number is 17, would have to lose seven electrons to have the same number of electrons as Ne.) If a nonmetal atom were to gain just a few electrons, however, it would have the same number as a noble gas atom of higher atomic number. For example, an oxygen atom has eight electrons. By gaining two electrons per atom, it forms O^{2-}, which has ten electrons, the same number as neon. *Anions having the same number of electrons as the noble gas atom succeeding it in the periodic table are commonly observed in chemical compounds.*

Cation charges and the periodic table

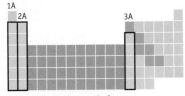

Group 1A, 2A, 3A metals form M^{n+} cations where n = group number.

Chemistry⊙Now™

Sign in at **www.cengage.com/login** and go to Chapter 2 Contents to see Screen 2.18 for an exercise and tutorial on **ion charge**.

EXERCISE 2.6 Predicting Ion Charges

Predict formulas for monatomic ions formed from **(a)** K, **(b)** Se, **(c)** Ba, and **(d)** Cs. In each case, indicate the number of electrons gained or lost by an atom of the element in forming the anion or cation, respectively. For each ion, indicate the noble gas atom having the same total number of electrons.

Polyatomic Ions

Polyatomic ions are made up of two or more atoms, and the collection has an electric charge (Figure 2.19 and Table 2.4). For example, carbonate ion, CO$_3{}^{2-}$, a common polyatomic anion, consists of one C atom and three O atoms. The ion has two units of negative charge because there are two more electrons (a total of 32) in the ion than there are protons (a total of 30) in the nuclei of one C atom and three O atoms.

The ammonium ion, NH$_4{}^+$, is a common polyatomic cation. In this case, four H atoms surround an N atom, and the ion has a 1+ electric charge. This ion has 10 electrons, but there are 11 positively charged protons in the nuclei of the N and H atoms (seven and one each, respectively).

Chemistry⊙Now™

Sign in at **www.cengage.com/login** and go to Chapter 2 Contents to see Screen 2.19 for a tutorial on **polyatomic ions**.

Calcite, CaCO₃
Calcium carbonate

CO_3^{2-}

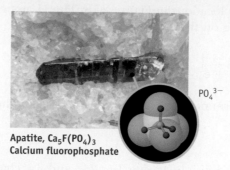

Apatite, Ca₅F(PO₄)₃
Calcium fluorophosphate

PO_4^{3-}

Celestite, SrSO₄
Strontium sulfate

SO_4^{2-}

Active Figure 2.19 Common ionic compounds based on polyatomic ions.

Chemistry ⚛ Now™ Sign in at www.cengage.com/login and go to the Chapter Contents menu to explore an interactive version of this figure accompanied by an exercise.

Formulas of Ionic Compounds

Compounds are electrically neutral; that is, they have no net electric charge. Thus, in an ionic compound, the numbers of positive and negative ions must be such that the positive and negative charges balance. In sodium chloride, the sodium ion has a 1+ charge (Na^+), and the chloride ion has a 1− charge (Cl^-). These ions must be present in a 1 : 1 ratio, and the formula is NaCl.

TABLE 2.4   Formulas and Names of Some Common Polyatomic Ions

Formula	Name	Formula	Name
CATION: Positive Ion			
NH_4^+	ammonium ion		
ANIONS: Negative Ions			
Based on a Group 4A element		**Based on a Group 7A element**	
CN^-	cyanide ion	ClO^-	hypochlorite ion
$CH_3CO_2^-$	acetate ion	ClO_2^-	chlorite ion
CO_3^{2-}	carbonate ion	ClO_3^-	chlorate ion
HCO_3^-	hydrogen carbonate ion (or bicarbonate ion)	ClO_4^-	perchlorate ion
Based on a Group 5A element		**Based on a transition metal**	
NO_2^-	nitrite ion	CrO_4^{2-}	chromate ion
NO_3^-	nitrate ion	$Cr_2O_7^{2-}$	dichromate ion
PO_4^{3-}	phosphate ion	MnO_4^-	permanganate ion
HPO_4^{2-}	hydrogen phosphate ion		
$H_2PO_4^-$	dihydrogen phosphate ion		
Based on a Group 6A element			
OH^-	hydroxide ion		
SO_3^{2-}	sulfite ion		
SO_4^{2-}	sulfate ion		
HSO_4^-	hydrogen sulfate ion (or bisulfate ion)		

The gemstone ruby is largely the compound formed from aluminum ions (Al^{3+}) and oxide ions (O^{2-}) (but the color comes from a trace of Cr^{3+} ions.) Here, the ions have positive and negative charges that are of different absolute value. To have a compound with the same number of positive and negative charges, two Al^{3+} ions [total charge = $2 \times (3+) = 6+$] must combine with three O^{2-} ions [total charge = $3 \times (2-) = 6-$] to give a formula of Al_2O_3.

Calcium is a Group 2A metal, and it forms a cation having a 2+ charge. It can combine with a variety of anions to form ionic compounds such as those in the following table:

Compound	Ion Combination	Overall Charge on Compound
$CaCl_2$	$Ca^{2+} + 2\ Cl^-$	$(2+) + 2 \times (1-) = 0$
$CaCO_3$	$Ca^{2+} + CO_3^{2-}$	$(2+) + (2-) = 0$
$Ca_3(PO_4)_2$	$3\ Ca^{2+} + 2\ PO_4^{3-}$	$3 \times (2+) + 2 \times (3-) = 0$

In writing formulas of ionic compounds, the convention is that *the symbol of the cation is given first, followed by the anion symbol.* Also notice the use of parentheses when more than one of a given polyatomic ion is present.

Chemistry.⚛.Now™

Sign in at **www.cengage.com/login** and go to Chapter 2 Contents to see Screen 2.20 for a video of the **sodium and chlorine reaction** and for a simulation on the **relationship between cations and anions in ionic compounds.**

■ EXAMPLE 2.4 Ionic Compound Formulas

Problem For each of the following ionic compounds, write the symbols for the ions present, and give the number of each: (a) Li_2CO_3, and (b) $Fe_2(SO_4)_3$.

Strategy Divide the formula of the compound into the cation and the anion. To accomplish this, you will have to recognize, and remember, the composition and charges of common ions.

Solution

(a) Li_2CO_3 is composed of two lithium ions, Li^+, and one carbonate ion, CO_3^{2-}. Li is a Group 1A element and always has a 1+ charge in its compounds. Because the two 1+ charges balance the negative charge of the carbonate ion, the latter must be 2−.

(b) $Fe_2(SO_4)_3$ contains two iron ions, Fe^{3+}, and three sulfate ions, SO_4^{2-}. The way to recognize this is to recall that sulfate has a 2− charge. Because three sulfate ions are present (with a total charge of 6−), the two iron cations must have a total charge of 6+. This is possible only if each iron cation has a charge of 3+.

Comment Remember that the formula for an ion must include its composition and its charge. Formulas for ionic compounds are always written with the cation first and then the anion, but ion charges are not included.

■ EXAMPLE 2.5 Ionic Compound Formulas

Problem Write formulas for ionic compounds composed of aluminum cations and each of the following anions: (a) fluoride ion, (b) sulfide ion, and (c) nitrate ion.

Strategy First decide on the formula of the Al cation and the formula of each anion. Combine the Al cation with each type of anion to form an electrically neutral compound.

Solution An aluminum cation is predicted to have a charge of 3+ because Al is a metal in Group 3A.

(a) Fluorine is a Group 7A element. The charge of the fluoride ion is predicted to be 1− (from $7 - 8 = -1$). Therefore, we need 3 F^- ions to combine with one Al^{3+}. The formula of the compound is AlF_3.

(b) Sulfur is a nonmetal in Group 6A, so it forms a 2− anion. Thus, we need to combine two Al^{3+} ions [total charge is $6+ = 2 \times (3+)$] with three S^{2-} ions [total charge is $6- = 3 \times (2-)$]. The compound has the formula Al_2S_3.

■ **Balancing Ion Charges in Formulas**
Aluminum, a metal in Group 3A, loses three electrons to form the Al^{3+} cation. Oxygen, a nonmetal in Group 6A, gains two electrons to form an O^{2-} anion. Notice that in the compound formed from these ions, the charge on the cation is the subscript on the anion, and vice versa.

$$2\ Al^{3+} + 3\ O^{2-} \rightarrow Al_2O_3$$

This often works well, but there are exceptions. For example, the formula of titanium (IV) oxide is TiO_2, the simplest ratio, and not Ti_2O_4.

$$Ti^{4+} + 2\ O^{2-} \rightarrow TiO_2$$

(c) The nitrate ion has the formula NO_3^- (see Table 2.4). The answer here is therefore similar to the AlF_3 case, and the compound has the formula $Al(NO_3)_3$. Here, we place parentheses around NO_3 to show that three polyatomic NO_3^- ions are involved.

Comment The most common error students make is not knowing the correct charge on an ion.

EXERCISE 2.7 Formulas of Ionic Compounds

(a) Give the number and identity of the constituent ions in each of the following ionic compounds: NaF, $Cu(NO_3)_2$, and $NaCH_3CO_2$.

(b) Iron, a transition metal, forms ions having at least two different charges. Write the formulas of the compounds formed between chloride ions and the two different iron cations.

(c) Write the formulas of all neutral ionic compounds that can be formed by combining the cations Na^+ and Ba^{2+} with the anions S^{2-} and PO_4^{3-}.

Names of Ions

Naming Positive Ions (Cations)

With a few exceptions (such as NH_4^+), the positive ions described in this text are metal ions. Positive ions are named by the following rules:

1. For a monatomic positive ion (that is, a metal cation) the name is that of the metal plus the word "cation." For example, we have already referred to Al^{3+} as the aluminum cation.

2. Some cases occur, especially in the transition series, in which a metal can form more than one type of positive ion. In these cases, the charge of the ion is indicated by a Roman numeral in parentheses immediately following the ion name. For example, Co^{2+} is the cobalt(II) cation, and Co^{3+} is the cobalt(III) cation.

Finally, you will encounter the ammonium cation, NH_4^+, many times in this book and in the laboratory. Do not confuse the ammonium cation with the ammonia molecule, NH_3, which has no electric charge and one less H atom.

Naming Negative Ions (Anions)

There are two types of negative ions: those having only one atom (*monatomic*) and those having several atoms (*polyatomic*).

1. A monatomic negative ion is named by adding *-ide* to the stem of the name of the nonmetal element from which the ion is derived (Figure 2.20). The anions of the Group 7A elements, the halogens, are known as the fluoride, chloride, bromide, and iodide ions and as a group are called **halide ions**.

2. Polyatomic negative ions are common, especially those containing oxygen (called **oxoanions**). The names of some of the most common oxoanions are given in Table 2.4. Although most of these names must simply be learned, some guidelines can help. For example, consider the following pairs of ions:

   NO_3^- is the nitrate ion, whereas NO_2^- is the nitrite ion
   SO_4^{2-} is the sulfate ion, whereas SO_3^{2-} is the sulfite ion

The oxoanion having the greater number of oxygen atoms is given the suffix -ate, and the oxoanion having the smaller number of oxygen atoms has the suffix -ite. For a series of oxoanions having more than two members, the ion with the largest number of oxygen atoms has the prefix *per-* and the suffix *-ate*. The ion

■ **"-ous" and "-ic" Endings** An older naming system for metal ions uses the ending -ous for the ion of lower charge and -ic for the ion of higher charge. For example, there are cobaltous (Co^{2+}) and cobaltic (Co^{3+}) ions, and ferrous (Fe^{2+}) and ferric (Fe^{3+}) ions. We do not use this system in this book, but some chemical manufacturers continue to use it.

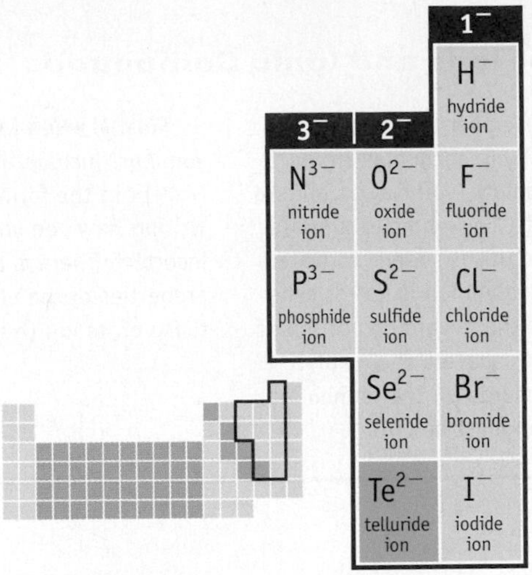

FIGURE 2.20 Names and charges of some common monatomic anions.

	1⁻
	H^- hydride ion

3⁻	2⁻	
N^{3-} nitride ion	O^{2-} oxide ion	F^- fluoride ion
P^{3-} phosphide ion	S^{2-} sulfide ion	Cl^- chloride ion
	Se^{2-} selenide ion	Br^- bromide ion
	Te^{2-} telluride ion	I^- iodide ion

having the smallest number of oxygen atoms has the prefix *hypo-* and the suffix *-ite.* The chlorine oxoanions are the most commonly encountered example.

ClO_4^- *perchlorate* ion
ClO_3^- *chlorate* ion
ClO_2^- *chlorite* ion
ClO^- *hypochlorite* ion

■ **Naming Oxoanions**

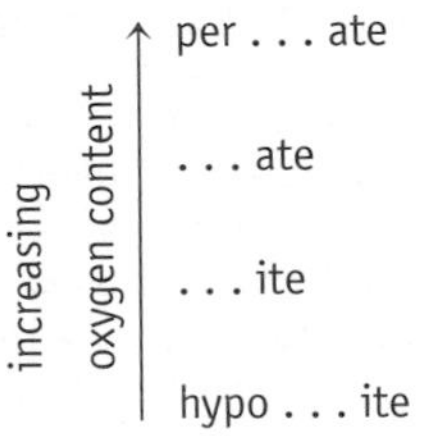

increasing oxygen content ↑
per . . . ate
. . . ate
. . . ite
hypo . . . ite

Oxoanions that contain hydrogen are named by adding the word "hydrogen" before the name of the oxoanion. If two hydrogens are in the anion, we say "dihydrogen." Many hydrogen-containing oxoanions have common names that are used as well. For example, the hydrogen carbonate ion, HCO_3^-, is called the bicarbonate ion.

Ion	Systematic Name	Common Name
HPO_4^{2-}	hydrogen phosphate ion	
$H_2PO_4^-$	dihydrogen phosphate ion	
HCO_3^-	hydrogen carbonate ion	bicarbonate ion
HSO_4^-	hydrogen sulfate ion	bisulfate ion
HSO_3^-	hydrogen sulfite ion	bisulfite ion

Names of Ionic Compounds

The name of an ionic compound is built from the names of the positive and negative ions in the compound. The name of the positive cation is given first, followed by the name of the negative anion. Examples of ionic compound names are given below.

Ionic Compound	Ions Involved	Name
$CaBr_2$	Ca^{2+} and 2 Br^-	calcium bromide
$NaHSO_4$	Na^+ and HSO_4^-	sodium hydrogen sulfate
$(NH_4)_2CO_3$	2 NH_4^+ and CO_3^{2-}	ammonium carbonate
$Mg(OH)_2$	Mg^{2+} and 2 OH^-	magnesium hydroxide
$TiCl_2$	Ti^{2+} and 2 Cl^-	titanium(II) chloride
Co_2O_3	2 Co^{3+} and 3 O^{2-}	cobalt(III) oxide

■ **Names of Compounds Containing Transition Metal Cations** Be sure to notice that the charge on a transition metal cation is indicated by a Roman numeral and is included in the name.

Problem Solving Tip 2.1

Formulas for Ions and Ionic Compounds

Writing formulas for ionic compounds takes practice, and it requires that you know the formulas and charges of the most common ions. The charges on monatomic ions are often evident from the position of the element in the periodic table, but you simply have to remember the formula and charges of polyatomic ions—especially the most common ones such as nitrate, sulfate, carbonate, phosphate, and acetate.

If you cannot remember the formula of a polyatomic ion, or if you encounter an ion you have not seen before, you may be able to figure out its formula. For example, suppose you are told that $NaCHO_2$ is sodium formate. You know that the sodium ion is Na^+, so the formate ion must be the remaining portion of the compound; it must have a charge of 1− to balance the 1+ charge on the sodium ion. Thus, the formate ion must be CHO_2^-.

Finally, when writing the formulas of ions, you *must* include the charge on the ion (except in the formula of an ionic compound). Writing Na when you mean sodium ion is incorrect. There is a vast difference in the properties of the element sodium (Na) and those of its ion (Na^+).

Chemistry Now™

Sign in at **www.cengage.com/login** and go to Chapter 2 Contents to see Screens 2.20 and 2.21 for a tutorial, an exercise, and a simulation on **ionic compounds.**

EXERCISE 2.8 Names of Ionic Compounds

1. Give the formula for each of the following ionic compounds. Use Table 2.4 and Figure 2.20.
   - **(a)** ammonium nitrate
   - **(b)** cobalt(II) sulfate
   - **(c)** nickel(II) cyanide
   - **(d)** vanadium(III) oxide
   - **(e)** barium acetate
   - **(f)** calcium hypochlorite
2. Name the following ionic compounds:
   - **(a)** $MgBr_2$
   - **(b)** Li_2CO_3
   - **(c)** $KHSO_3$
   - **(d)** $KMnO_4$
   - **(e)** $(NH_4)_2S$
   - **(f)** CuCl and $CuCl_2$

Properties of Ionic Compounds

When a substance having a negative electric charge is brought near a substance having a positive electric charge, there is a force of attraction between them (Figure 2.21). In contrast, there is a repulsive force when two substances with the same charge—both positive or both negative—are brought together. These forces are called **electrostatic** forces, and the force of attraction between ions is given by **Coulomb's law** (Equation 2.3)

$$\text{Force of attraction} = k\frac{(n^+e)(n^-e)}{d^2} \quad (2.3)$$

charge on + and − ions; charge on electron; proportionality constant; distance between ions

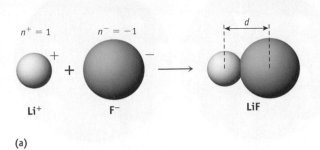

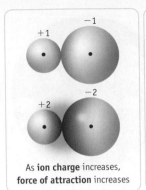

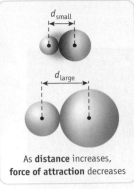

As **ion charge** increases, **force of attraction** increases

As **distance** increases, **force of attraction** decreases

(a)

(b)

Active Figure 2.21 **Coulomb's law and electrostatic forces.** (a) Ions such as Li^+ and F^- are held together by an electrostatic force. Here, a lithium ion is attracted to a fluoride ion, and the distance between the nuclei of the two ions is d. (b) Forces of attraction between ions of opposite charge increase with increasing ion charge and decrease with increasing distance (d).

Chemistry.○.Now™ Sign in at www.cengage.com/login and go to the Chapter Contents menu to explore an interactive version of this figure accompanied by an exercise.

where, for example, n^+ is 3 for Al^{3+} and n^- is -2 for O^{2-}. Based on Coulomb's law, the force of attraction between oppositely charged ions increases:

- As the ion charges (n^+ and n^-) increase. Thus, the attraction between ions having charges of 2+ and 2− is greater than that between ions having 1+ and 1− charges (Figure 2.21).
- As the distance between the ions becomes smaller (Figure 2.21).

Ionic compounds do not consist of simple pairs or small groups of positive and negative ions. The simplest ratio of cations to anions in an ionic compound is represented by its formula, but an ionic solid consists of millions upon millions of ions arranged in an extended three-dimensional network called a **crystal lattice.** A portion of the lattice for NaCl, illustrated in Figure 2.22, illustrates a common way of arranging ions for compounds that have a 1:1 ratio of cations to anions.

Ionic compounds have characteristic properties that can be understood in terms of the charges of the ions and their arrangement in the lattice. Because each ion is surrounded by oppositely charged nearest neighbors, it is held tightly in its allotted location. At room temperature, each ion can move just a bit around its average position, but considerable energy must be added before an ion can escape the attraction of its neighboring ions. Only if enough energy is added will the lattice structure collapse and the substance melt. Greater attractive forces mean that ever more energy—higher and higher temperatures—is required to cause melting. Thus, Al_2O_3, a solid composed of Al^{3+} and O^{2-} ions, melts at a much higher temperature (2072 °C) than NaCl (801 °C), a solid composed of Na^+ and Cl^- ions.

Most ionic compounds are "hard" solids. That is, the solids are not pliable or soft. The reason for this characteristic is again related to the lattice of ions. The nearest neighbors of a cation in a lattice are anions, and the force of attraction makes the lattice rigid. However, a blow with a hammer can cause the lattice to break cleanly along a sharp boundary. The hammer blow displaces layers of ions just enough to cause ions of like charge to become nearest neighbors, and the repulsion between these like-charged ions forces the lattice apart (Figure 2.23).

Photo: Charles D. Winters; model, S. M. Young

FIGURE 2.22 **Sodium chloride.** A crystal of NaCl consists of an extended lattice of sodium ions and chloride ions in a 1 : 1 ratio. (Sign in to ChemistryNow, and see Screen 2.20, Ionic Compounds, to view an animation on the formation of a sodium chloride crystal lattice.)

Charles D. Winters

(a)

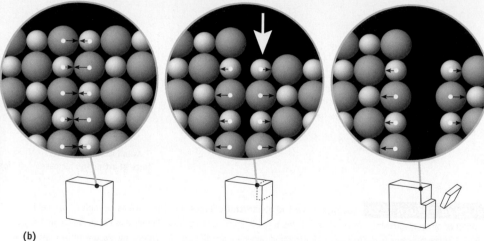

(b)

FIGURE 2.23 Ionic solids. (a) An ionic solid is normally rigid, owing to the forces of attraction between oppositely charged ions. When struck sharply, however, the crystal can cleave cleanly. (b) When a crystal is struck, layers of ions move slightly, and ions of like charge become nearest neighbors. Repulsions between ions of similar charge cause the crystal to cleave. (Sign in to ChemistryNow, and see Screen 2.23, Properties of Ionic Compounds, to watch a video of cleaving a crystal.)

Chemistry.·Now™

Sign in at **www.cengage.com/login** and go to Chapter 2 Contents to see:
• Screen 2.22 for a simulation on **Coulomb's Law**
• Screen 2.23 for an exercise and a simulation on **properties of ionic compounds**

EXERCISE 2.9 Coulomb's Law

Explain why the melting point of MgO (2830 °C) is much higher than the melting point of NaCl (801 °C).

2.8 Molecular Compounds: Formulas and Names

Many familiar compounds are not ionic; they are molecular: the water you drink, the sugar in your coffee or tea, or the aspirin you take for a headache.

Problem Solving Tip 2.2

Is a Compound Ionic?

Students often ask how to know whether a compound is ionic. Here are some useful guidelines.

1. Most metal-containing compounds are ionic. So, if a metal atom appears in the formula of a compound, a good first guess is that it is ionic. (There are interesting exceptions, but few come up in introductory chemistry.) It is helpful in this regard to recall trends in metallic behavior: All

elements to the left of a diagonal line running from boron to tellurium in the periodic table are metallic.

2. If there is no metal in the formula, it is likely that the compound is not ionic. The exceptions here are compounds composed of polyatomic ions based on nonmetals (e.g., NH_4Cl or NH_4NO_3).

3. Learn to recognize the formulas of polyatomic ions (see Table 2.4). Chemists write

the formula of ammonium nitrate as NH_4NO_3 (not as $N_2H_4O_3$) to alert others to the fact that it is an ionic compound composed of the common polyatomic ions NH_4^+ and NO_3^-.

As an example of these guidelines, you can be sure that $MgBr_2$ (Mg^{2+} with Br^-) and K_2S (K^+ with S^{2-}) are ionic compounds. On the other hand, the compound CCl_4, formed from two nonmetals, C and Cl, is not ionic.

Charles D. Winters

FIGURE 2.24 Molecular compounds.
Ionic compounds are generally solids at
room temperature. In contrast, molecular
compounds can be gases, liquids, or
solids. The molecular models are of
caffeine (in coffee), water, and citric
acid (in lemons).

Ionic compounds are generally solids, whereas molecular compounds can range
from gases to liquids to solids at ordinary temperatures (see Figure 2.24). As size and
molecular complexity increase, compounds generally exist as solids. We will explore
some of the underlying causes of these general observations in Chapter 12.

Some molecular compounds have complicated formulas that you cannot, at this
stage, predict or even decide if they are correct. However, there are many simple
compounds you will encounter often, and you should understand how to name
them and, in many cases, know their formulas.

Let us look first at molecules formed from combinations of two nonmetals. These
"two-element" compounds of nonmetals, often called **binary compounds**, can be
named in a systematic way.

Hydrogen forms binary compounds with all of the nonmetals except the noble
gases. For compounds of oxygen, sulfur, and the halogens, the H atom is generally
written first in the formula and is named first. The other nonmetal is named as if
it were a negative ion.

Compound	Name
HF	hydrogen fluoride
HCl	hydrogen chloride
H_2S	hydrogen sulfide

■ **Formulas of Binary Nonmetal
Compounds Containing Hydrogen** Simple
hydrocarbons (compounds of C and H)
such as methane (CH_4) and ethane (C_2H_6)
have formulas written with H following C,
and the formulas of ammonia and hydrazine have H following N. Water and the
hydrogen halides, however, have the
H atom preceding O or the halogen atom.
Tradition is the only explanation for such
irregularities in writing formulas.

Although there are exceptions, *most binary molecular compounds are a combination
of nonmetallic elements from Groups 4A–7A with one another or with hydrogen.* The formula
is generally written by putting the elements in order of increasing group number.
When naming the compound, the number of atoms of a given type in the compound
is designated with a prefix, such as "di-," "tri-," "tetra-," "penta-," and so on.

Compound	Systematic Name
NF_3	nitrogen trifluoride
NO	nitrogen monoxide
NO_2	nitrogen dioxide
N_2O	dinitrogen monoxide
N_2O_4	dinitrogen tetraoxide
PCl_3	phosphorus trichloride
PCl_5	phosphorus pentachloride
SF_6	sulfur hexafluoride
S_2F_{10}	disulfur decafluoride

■ **Hydrocarbons** Compounds such as methane, ethane, propane, and butane belong to a class of hydrocarbons called alkanes. (Sign in to ChemistryNow, and see Screen 2.24, Alkanes.).

methane, CH_4

propane, C_3H_8

ethane, C_2H_6

butane, C_4H_{10}

Finally, many of the binary compounds of nonmetals were discovered years ago and have common names.

Compound	Common Name	Compound	Common Name
CH_4	methane	N_2H_4	hydrazine
C_2H_6	ethane	PH_3	phosphine
C_3H_8	propane	NO	nitric oxide
C_4H_{10}	butane	N_2O	nitrous oxide ("laughing gas")
NH_3	ammonia	H_2O	water

Chemistry ⚬ Now™

Sign in at **www.cengage.com/login** and go to Chapter 2 Contents to see:
• Screen 2.25 for a tutorial on **naming compounds of the nonmetals**
• Screen 2.26 for an exercise on **naming alkanes**

EXERCISE 2.10 Naming Compounds of the Nonmetals

1. Give the formula for each of the following binary, nonmetal compounds:

(a) carbon dioxide   (d) boron trifluoride

(b) phosphorus triiodide   (e) dioxygen difluoride

(c) sulfur dichloride   (f) xenon trioxide

2. Name the following binary, nonmetal compounds:

(a) N_2F_4 (c) SF_4 (e) P_4O_{10}

(b) HBr   (d) BCl_3 (f) ClF_3

 Module 4

2.9 Atoms, Molecules, and the Mole

One of the most exciting aspects of chemical research is the discovery of some new substance, and part of this process of discovery involves quantitative experiments. When two chemicals react with each other, we want to know how many atoms or molecules of each are used so that formulas can be established for the reaction products. To do so, we need some method of counting atoms and molecules. That is, we must discover a way of connecting the macroscopic world, the world we can see, with the particulate world of atoms, molecules, and ions. The solution to this problem is to define a unit of matter that contains a known number of particles. That chemical unit is the mole.

The **mole** (abbreviated mol) is the SI base unit for measuring an *amount of a substance* and is defined as follows:

> A mole is the amount of a substance that contains as many elementary entities (atoms, molecules, or other particles) as there are atoms in exactly 12 g of the carbon-12 isotope.

■ **An Important Difference between the Terms "Amount" and "Quantity"** The terms "amount" and "quantity" are used in a specific sense by chemists. The amount of a substance is the number of moles of that substance. Quantity refers, for example, to the mass or volume of the substance. (See W. G. Davies and J. W. Moore. *Journal of Chemical Education*, Vol. 57, p. 303, 1980.)

The key to understanding the concept of the mole is recognizing that *one mole always contains the same number of particles, no matter what the substance.* One mole of sodium contains the same number of atoms as one mole of iron or as the number of molecules in one mole of water. How many particles? Many, many experiments over the years have established that number as

$$1 \text{ mole} = 6.0221415 \times 10^{23} \text{ particles}$$

This value is known as **Avogadro's number** in honor of Amedeo Avogadro, an Italian lawyer and physicist (1776–1856) who conceived the basic idea (but never determined the number).

■ **The "Mole"** The term "mole" was introduced about 1895 by Wilhelm Ostwald (1853–1932), who derived the term from the Latin word *moles*, meaning a "heap" or a "pile."

Atoms and Molar Mass

The mass in grams of one mole of any element (6.0221415×10^{23} atoms of that element) is the **molar mass** of that element. Molar mass is conventionally abbreviated with a capital italicized *M*, and it has units of grams per mole (g/mol). *An element's molar mass is the quantity in grams numerically equal to its atomic weight.* Using sodium and lead as examples,

Molar mass of sodium (Na) = mass of 1.000 mol of Na atoms
                           = 22.99 g/mol
                           = mass of 6.022×10^{23} Na atoms
Molar mass of lead (Pb)   = mass of 1.000 mol of Pb atoms
                           = 207.2 g/mol
                           = mass of 6.022×10^{23} Pb atoms

Figure 2.25 shows the relative sizes of a mole of some common elements. Although each of these "piles of atoms" has a different volume and different mass, each contains 6.022×10^{23} atoms.

The mole concept is the cornerstone of quantitative chemistry. It is essential to be able to convert from moles to mass and from mass to moles. Dimensional analysis, which is described in *Let's Review*, page 38, shows that this can be done in the following way:

MASS ⟷ MOLES CONVERSION	
Moles to Mass	*Mass to Moles*
$\text{Moles} \times \dfrac{\text{grams}}{1 \text{ mol}} = \text{grams}$	$\text{Grams} \times \dfrac{1 \text{ mol}}{\text{grams}} = \text{moles}$
↑ molar mass	↑ 1/molar mass

FIGURE 2.25 One-mole of common elements. *(left to right)* Sulfur powder, magnesium chips, tin, and silicon. *(Above)* Copper beads.

Copper
63.546 g

Sulfur
32.066 g

Magnesium
24.305 g

Tin
118.71 g

Silicon
28.086 g

Charles D. Winters

For example, what mass, in grams, is represented by 0.35 mol of aluminum? Using the molar mass of aluminum (27.0 g/mol), you can determine that 0.35 mol of Al has a mass of 9.5 g.

$$0.35 \text{ mol Al} \times \frac{27.0 \text{ g Al}}{1 \text{ mol Al}} = 9.5 \text{ g Al}$$

Molar masses are generally known to at least four significant figures. The convention followed in calculations in this book is to use a value of the molar mass with one more significant figure than in any other number in the problem. For example, if you weigh out 16.5 g of carbon, you use 12.01 g/mol for the molar mass of C to find the amount of carbon present.

$$16.5 \text{ g C} \times \frac{1 \text{ mol C}}{12.01 \text{ g C}} = 1.37 \text{ mol C}$$
$\uparrow$
Note that four significant figures are used in the molar mass, but there are three in the sample mass.

Using one more significant figure for the molar mass means the precision of this value will not affect the precision of the result.

Chemistry ○ Now™

Sign in at **www.cengage.com/login** and go to Chapter 2 Contents to see:
• Screen 2.25 for a tutorial on **moles and atoms conversion**
• Screen 2.26 for two tutorials on **molar mass conversion**

EXAMPLE 2.6 Mass, Moles, and Atoms

Problem Consider two elements in the same vertical column of the periodic table, lead and tin.

(a) What mass of lead, in grams, is equivalent to 2.50 mol of lead (Pb, atomic number = 82)?

(b) What amount of tin, in moles, is represented by 36.6 g of tin (Sn, atomic number = 50)? How many atoms of tin are in the sample?

Strategy The molar masses of lead (207.2 g/mol) and tin (118.7 g/mol) are required and can be found in the periodic table inside the front cover of this book. Avogadro's number is needed to convert the amount of each element to number of atoms.

Solution

(a) Convert the amount of lead in moles to mass in grams.

$$2.50 \text{ mol Pb} \times \frac{207.2 \text{ g}}{1 \text{ mol Pb}} = 518 \text{ g Pb}$$

(b) First convert the mass of tin to the amount in moles.

$$36.6 \text{ g Sn} \times \frac{1 \text{ mol Sn}}{118.7 \text{ g Sn}} = 0.308 \text{ mol Sn}$$

Finally, use Avogadro's number to find the number of atoms in the sample.

$$0.308 \text{ mol Sn} \times \frac{6.022 \times 10^{23} \text{ atoms Sn}}{1 \text{ mol Sn}} = 1.85 \times 10^{23} \text{ atoms Sn}$$

Charles D. Winters

Lead. A 150-mL beaker containing 2.50 mol or 518 g of lead.

Charles D. Winters

Tin. A sample of tin having a mass of 36.6 g (or 1.85×10^{23} atoms).

EXERCISE 2.11 Mass/Mole Conversions

(a) What is the mass, in grams, of 1.5 mol of silicon?

(b) What amount (moles) of sulfur is represented by 454 g? How many atoms?

EXERCISE 2.12 Atoms

The density of gold, Au, is 19.32 g/cm³. What is the volume (in cubic centimeters) of a piece of gold that contains 2.6×10^{24} atoms? If the piece of metal is a square with a thickness of 0.10 cm, what is the length (in centimeters) of one side of the piece?

Molecules, Compounds, and Molar Mass

The formula of a compound tells you the type of atoms or ions in the compound and the relative number of each. For example, one molecule of methane, CH_4, is made up of one atom of C and four atoms of H. But suppose you have Avogadro's number of C atoms (6.022×10^{23}) combined with the proper number of H atoms. The compound's formula tells us that four times as many H atoms are required ($4 \times 6.022 \times 10^{23}$ H atoms). What masses of atoms are combined, and what is the mass of this many CH_4 molecules?

C	+	4 H	→	CH_4
6.022×10^{23} C atoms		$4 \times 6.022 \times 10^{23}$ H atoms		6.022×10^{23} CH_4 molecules
= 1.000 mol of C		= 4.000 mol of H atoms		= 1.000 mol of CH_4 molecules
= 12.01 g of C atoms		= 4.032 g of H atoms		= 16.04 g of CH_4 molecules

■ **Molar Mass or Molecular Weight**
Although chemists often use the term "molecular weight," the more correct term is molar mass. The SI unit of molar mass is kg/mol, but chemists worldwide usually express it in units of g/mol. See "NIST Guide to SI Units" at www.NIST.gov

Because we know the number of moles of C and H atoms, we know the masses of carbon and hydrogen that combine to form CH_4. It follows that the mass of CH_4 is the sum of these masses. That is, 1 mol of CH_4 has a mass equivalent to the mass of 1 mol of C atoms (12.01 g) plus 4 mol of H atoms (4.032 g). Thus, the *molar mass*, M, of CH_4 is 16.04 g/mol. The molar masses of some substances are:

Molar and Molecular Masses

Element or Compound	Molar Mass, M (g/mol)	Average Mass of One Molecule (g/molecule)
O_2	32.00	5.314×10^{-23}
NH_3	17.03	2.828×10^{-23}
H_2O	18.02	2.992×10^{-23}
$NH_2CH_2CO_2H$ (glycine)	75.07	1.247×10^{-22}

Ionic compounds such as NaCl do not exist as individual molecules. Thus, we write the simplest formula that shows the relative number of each kind of atom in a "formula unit" of the compound, and the molar mass is calculated from this formula (M for NaCl = 58.44 g/mol). To differentiate substances like NaCl that do not contain molecules, chemists sometimes refer to their *formula weight* instead of their molecular weight.

Figure 2.26 illustrates 1-mole quantities of several common compounds. To find the molar mass of any compound, you need only to add up the atomic masses for each element in one formula unit. As an example, let us find the molar mass of aspirin, $C_9H_8O_4$. In 1 mole of aspirin, there are 9 mol of carbon atoms, 8 mol of

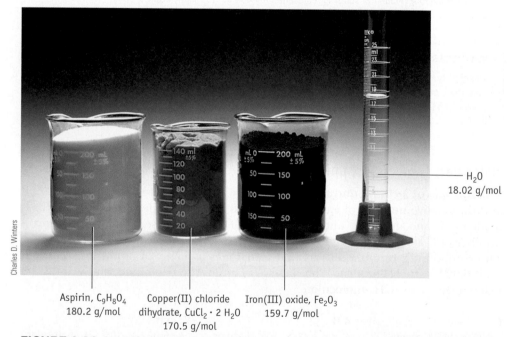

Aspirin, $C_9H_8O_4$
180.2 g/mol

Copper(II) chloride dihydrate, $CuCl_2 \cdot 2\,H_2O$
170.5 g/mol

Iron(III) oxide, Fe_2O_3
159.7 g/mol

H_2O
18.02 g/mol

FIGURE 2.26 One-mole quantities of some compounds. Notice the molar mass for $CuCl_2 \cdot 2H_2O$. This is called a *hydrated compound* because water is associated with the $CuCl_2$ (see page 96). Thus, one "formula unit" consists of one Cu^{2+} ion, two Cl^- ions, and two water molecules. The molar masses are the sum of the mass of 1 mol of Cu, 2 mol of Cl, and 2 mol of H_2O.

Charles D. Winters

hydrogen atoms, and 4 mol of oxygen atoms, which add up to 180.2 g/mol of aspirin:

$$\text{Mass of C in 1 mol } C_9H_8O_4 = 9 \text{ mol C} \times \frac{12.01 \text{ g C}}{1 \text{ mol C}} = 108.1 \text{ g C}$$

$$\text{Mass of H in 1 mol } C_9H_8O_4 = 8 \text{ mol H} \times \frac{1.008 \text{ g H}}{1 \text{ mol H}} = 8.064 \text{ g H}$$

$$\text{Mass of O in 1 mol } C_9H_8O_4 = 4 \text{ mol O} \times \frac{16.00 \text{ g O}}{1 \text{ mol O}} = 64.00 \text{ g O}$$

$$\text{Total mass of 1 mol of } C_9H_8O_4 = \text{molar mass of } C_9H_8O_4 = 180.2 \text{ g}$$

As was the case with elements, it is important to be able to convert between amounts (moles) and mass (grams). For example, if you take 325 mg (0.325 g) of aspirin in one tablet, what amount of the compound have you ingested? Based on a molar mass of 180.2 g/mol, there are 0.00180 mol of aspirin per tablet.

$$0.325 \text{ g aspirin} \times \frac{1 \text{ mol aspirin}}{180.2 \text{ g aspirin}} = 0.00180 \text{ mol aspirin}$$

Using the molar mass of a compound, it is possible to determine the number of molecules in any sample from the sample mass and to determine the mass of one molecule. For example, the number of aspirin molecules in one tablet is

$$0.00180 \text{ mol aspirin} \times \frac{6.022 \times 10^{23} \text{ molecules}}{1 \text{ mol aspirin}} = 1.08 \times 10^{21} \text{ molecules}$$

and the mass of one molecule is

$$\frac{180.2 \text{ g aspirin}}{1 \text{ mol aspirin}} \times \frac{1 \text{ mol aspirin}}{6.022 \times 10^{23} \text{ molecules}} = 2.99 \times 10^{-22} \text{ g/molecule}$$

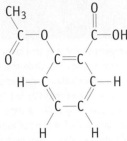

Aspirin formula. Aspirin has the molecular formula $C_9H_8O_4$ and a molar mass of 180.2 g/mol. Aspirin is the common name of the compound acetylsalicylic acid.

Chemistry⚛Now™

Sign in at **www.cengage.com/login** and go to Chapter 2 Contents to see:
• Screen 2.27 for a simulation on **compounds and moles** and a tutorial on **determining molar mass**
• Screen 2.28 for tutorials on **using molar mass**

■ EXAMPLE 2.7 Molar Mass and Moles

Problem You have 16.5 g of oxalic acid, $H_2C_2O_4$.

(a) What amount (moles) is represented by 16.5 g of oxalic acid?

(b) How many molecules of oxalic acid are in 16.5 g?

(c) How many atoms of carbon are in 16.5 g of oxalic acid?

(d) What is the mass of one molecule of oxalic acid?

Strategy The first step in any problem involving the conversion of mass and moles is to find the molar mass of the compound in question. Then you can perform the other calculations as outlined by the scheme shown here to find the number of molecules from the amount of substance and the number of atoms of a particular kind:

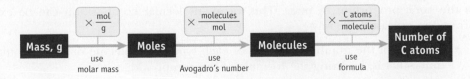

Kenneth G. Libbrecht

What amount of water is in a snow-flake? According to K. G. Libbrecht, there are about a billion billion water molecules in a snowflake. Given that this is 1×10^{18} molecules, how many moles of water are in a snowflake and what mass of water? Libbrecht also calculates that "each of us on Earth has contributed by exhalation and evaporation about 1,000 of the molecules in each snowflake." (D. Overbye, *New York Times*, December 23, 2003, page F3. See also K. G. Libbrecht, *American Scientist*, Vol. 95, pages 52–59, January-February 2007.)

Solution

(a) *Moles represented by 16.5 g*

Let us first calculate the molar mass of oxalic acid:

$$2 \text{ mol C per mol } H_2C_2O_4 \times \frac{12.01 \text{ g C}}{1 \text{ mol C}} = 24.02 \text{ g C per mol } H_2C_2O_4$$

$$2 \text{ mol H per mol } H_2C_2O_4 \times \frac{1.008 \text{ g H}}{1 \text{ mol H}} = 2.016 \text{ g H per mol } H_2C_2O_4$$

$$4 \text{ mol O per mol } H_2C_2O_4 \times \frac{16.00 \text{ g O}}{1 \text{ mol O}} = 64.00 \text{ g O per mol } H_2C_2O_4$$

Molar mass of $H_2C_2O_4$ = 90.04 g per mol $H_2C_2O_4$

Now calculate the amount in moles. The molar mass (expressed in units of 1 mol/90.04 g) is the conversion factor in all mass-to-mole conversions.

$$16.5 \text{ g } H_2C_2O_4 \times \frac{1 \text{ mol}}{90.04 \text{ g } H_2C_2O_4} = 0.183 \text{ mol } H_2C_2O_4$$

(b) *Number of molecules*

Use Avogadro's number to find the number of oxalic acid molecules in 0.183 mol of $H_2C_2O_4$.

$$0.183 \text{ mol} \times \frac{6.022 \times 10^{23} \text{ molecules}}{1 \text{ mol}} = 1.10 \times 10^{23} \text{ molecules}$$

(c) *Number of C atoms*

Because each molecule contains two carbon atoms, the number of carbon atoms in 16.5 g of the acid is

$$1.10 \times 10^{23} \text{ molecules} \times \frac{2 \text{ C atoms}}{1 \text{ molecule}} = 2.20 \times 10^{23} \text{ C atoms}$$

(d) *Mass of one molecule*

Use the molar mass and Avogadro's number to carry out this calculation.

$$\frac{90.04 \text{ g}}{1 \text{ mol}} \times \frac{1 \text{ mol}}{6.0221 \times 10^{23} \text{ molecules}} = 1.495 \times 10^{-22} \text{ g/molecule}$$

EXERCISE 2.13 Molar Mass and Moles-to-Mass Conversions

(a) Calculate the molar masses of citric acid ($H_3C_6H_5O_7$) and $MgCO_3$.

(b) If you have 454 g of citric acid, what amount (moles) does this represent?

(c) To have 0.125 mol of $MgCO_3$, what mass (g) must you have?

2.10 Describing Compound Formulas

Given a sample of an unknown compound, how can its formula be determined? The answer lies in *chemical analysis,* a major branch of chemistry that deals with the determination of formulas and structures.

Percent Composition

Any sample of a pure compound always consists of the same elements combined in the same proportion by mass. This means molecular composition can be expressed in at least three ways:

- In terms of the number of atoms of each type per molecule or per formula unit—that is, by giving the formula of the compound

- In terms of the mass of each element per mole of compound
- In terms of the mass of each element in the compound relative to the total mass of the compound—that is, as a mass percent

Suppose you have 1.0000 mol of NH_3 or 17.031 g. This mass of NH_3 is composed of 14.007 g of N (1.0000 mol) and 3.0237 g of H (3.0000 mol). If you compare the mass of N to the total mass of compound, 82.244% of the total mass is N (and 17.755% is H).

■ **Molecular Composition** Molecular composition can be expressed as a percent (mass of an element in a 100-g sample). For example, NH_3 is 82.244% N. Therefore, it has 82.244 g of N in 100.000 g of compound.

$$\text{Mass of N per mole of } NH_3 \; = \; \frac{1 \text{ mol N}}{1 \text{ mol } NH_3} \times \frac{14.007 \text{ g N}}{1 \text{ mol N}} \; = \; 14.007 \text{ g N/1 mol } NH_3$$

82.244% of NH_3 mass is **nitrogen**.

$$\text{Mass percent N in } NH_3 \; = \; \frac{\text{mass of N in 1 mol } NH_3}{\text{mass of 1 mol } NH_3}$$

17.755% of NH_3 mass is **hydrogen**.

$$= \; \frac{14.007 \text{ g N}}{17.031 \text{ g } NH_3} \times 100\%$$

$$= \; 82.244\% \text{ (or 82.244 g N in 100.000 g } NH_3)$$

$$\text{Mass of H per mole of } NH_3 \; = \; \frac{3 \text{ mol H}}{1 \text{ mol } NH_3} \times \frac{1.0079 \text{ g H}}{1 \text{ mol H}}$$

$$= \; 3.0237 \text{ g H/1 mol } NH_3$$

$$\text{Mass percent H in } NH_3 \; = \; \frac{\text{mass of H in 1 mol } NH_3}{\text{mass of 1 mol } NH_3} \times 100\%$$

$$= \; \frac{3.0237 \text{ g H}}{17.031 \text{ g } NH_3} \times 100\%$$

$$= \; 17.755\% \text{ (or 17.755 g H in 100.000 g } NH_3)$$

These values represent the mass percent of each element, or percent composition by mass. They tell you that in a 100.000-g sample there are 82.244 g of N and 17.755 g of H.

Chemistry ⚗ Now™

Sign in at **www.cengage.com/login** and go to Chapter 2 Contents to see Screen 2.29 for a tutorial on **using percent composition.**

■ **EXAMPLE 2.8 Using Percent Composition**

Problem What is the mass percent of each element in propane, C_3H_8? What mass of carbon is contained in 454 g of propane?

Strategy First, find the molar mass of C_3H_8, and then calculate the mass percent of C and H per mole of C_3H_8. Using the mass percent of C, calculate the mass of carbon in 454 g of C_3H_8.

Solution

(a) The molar mass of C_3H_8 is 44.097 g/mol (= 3 mol C + 8 mol H = 36.03 g + 8.064 g).

(b) Mass percent of C and H in C_3H_8:

$$\frac{3 \text{ mol C}}{1 \text{ mol } C_3H_8} \times \frac{12.01 \text{ g C}}{1 \text{ mol C}} = 36.03 \text{ g C/1 mol } C_3H_8$$

$$\text{Mass percent of C in } C_3H_8 \; = \; \frac{36.03 \text{ g C}}{44.097 \text{ g } C_3H_8} \times 100\% = \boxed{81.71\% \text{ C}}$$

$$\frac{8 \text{ mol H}}{1 \text{ mol } C_3H_8} \times \frac{1.008 \text{ g H}}{1 \text{ mol H}} = 8.064 \text{ g H/1 mol } C_3H_8$$

$$\text{Mass percent of H in } C_3H_8 \; = \; \frac{8.064 \text{ g H}}{44.097 \text{ g } C_3H_8} \times 100\% = \boxed{18.29\% \text{ H}}$$

(c) Mass of C in 454 g of C_3H_8:

$$454 \text{ g } C_3H_8 \times \frac{81.71 \text{ g C}}{100.0 \text{ g } C_3H_8} = \boxed{371 \text{ g C}}$$

EXERCISE 2.14 Percent Composition

(a) Express the composition of ammonium carbonate, $(NH_4)_2CO_3$, in terms of the mass of each element in 1.00 mol of compound and the mass percent of each element.

(b) What is the mass of carbon in 454 g of octane, C_8H_{18}?

Empirical and Molecular Formulas from Percent Composition

Now let us consider the reverse of the procedure just described: using relative mass or percent composition data to find a molecular formula. Suppose you know the identity of the elements in a sample and have determined the mass of each element in a given mass of compound by chemical analysis (▶ Section 4.4). You can then calculate the relative amount (moles) of each element and from this the relative number of atoms of each element in the compound. For example, for a compound composed of atoms of A and B, the steps from percent composition to a formula are

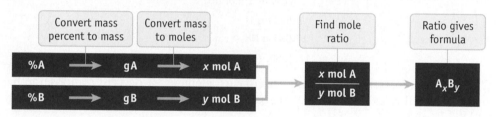

■ **Deriving a Formula** Percent composition gives the mass of an element in 100 g of sample. However, in deriving a formula, any amount of sample is appropriate if you know the mass of each element in that sample mass.

Let us derive the formula for hydrazine, a compound used to remove oxygen from water in heating and cooling systems. It is composed of 87.42% N and 12.58% H and is a close relative of ammonia.

Step 1: *Convert mass percent to mass.* The mass percentages of N and H in hydrazine tell us there are 87.42 g of N and 12.58 g of H in a 100.00 g sample.

Step 2: *Convert the mass of each element to moles.* The amount of each element in the 100.00-g sample is

$$87.42 \text{ g N} \times \frac{1 \text{ mol N}}{14.007 \text{ g N}} = 6.241 \text{ mol N}$$

$$12.58 \text{ g H} \times \frac{1 \text{ mol H}}{1.0079 \text{ g H}} = 12.48 \text{ mol H}$$

■ **Deriving a Formula—Mole Ratios** When finding the ratio of moles of one element relative to another, *always* divide the larger number by the smaller one.

Step 3: *Find the mole ratio of elements.* Use the amount (moles) of each element in the 100.00 g of sample to find the amount of one element relative to the other. For hydrazine, this ratio is 2 mol of H to 1 mol of N,

$$\frac{12.48 \text{ mol H}}{6.241 \text{ mol N}} = \frac{2.00 \text{ mol H}}{1.00 \text{ mol N}} \longrightarrow NH_2$$

showing that there are 2 mol of H atoms for every 1 mol of N atoms in hydrazine. Thus, in one molecule, two atoms of H occur for every atom of N; that is, the formula is NH_2. This simplest, whole-number ratio of atoms in a formula is called the **empirical formula**.

Percent composition data allow us to calculate the atom ratios in a compound. A *molecular formula*, however, must convey two pieces of information: (1) the relative numbers of atoms of each element in a molecule (the atom ratios) and (2) the total number of atoms in the molecule. For hydrazine, there are twice as many H atoms as N atoms, so the molecular formula could be NH_2. Recognize, however, that percent composition data give only the simplest possible ratio of atoms in a molecule. The empirical formula of hydrazine is NH_2, but the true molecular formula could be NH_2, N_2H_4, N_3H_6, N_4H_8, or any other formula having a 1:2 ratio of N to H.

To determine the molecular formula from the empirical formula, the molar mass must be obtained from experiment. For example, experiments show that the molar mass of hydrazine is 32.0 g/mol, twice the formula mass of NH_2, which is 16.0 g/mol. Thus, the molecular formula of hydrazine is two times the empirical formula of NH_2, that is, N_2H_4.

Chemistry ○ Now™

Sign in at **www.cengage.com/login** and go to Chapter 2 Contents to see:
- Screen 2.30 for a tutorial on **determining empirical formulas**
- Screen 2.31 for a tutorial on **determining molecular formulas**

■ **EXAMPLE 2.9 Calculating a Formula from Percent Composition**

Problem Eugenol is the major component in oil of cloves. It has a molar mass of 164.2 g/mol and is 73.14% C and 7.37% H; the remainder is oxygen. What are the empirical and molecular formulas of eugenol?

Strategy To derive a formula, we need to know the mass percent of each element. Because the mass percents of all elements must add up to 100.0%, we find the mass percent of O from the difference between 100.0% and the mass percents of C and H. Next, we assume that the mass percent of each element is equivalent to its mass in grams, and convert each mass to moles. Finally, the ratio of moles gives the empirical formula. The mass of a mole of compound having the calculated empirical formula is compared with the actual, experimental molar mass to find the true molecular formula.

Problem Solving Tip 2.3   Finding Empirical and Molecular Formulas

- The experimental data available to find a formula may be in the form of percent composition or the masses of elements combined in some mass of compound. No matter what the starting point, the first step is always to convert masses of elements to moles.
- Be sure to use *at least* three significant figures when calculating empirical

formulas. Using fewer significant figures can give a misleading result.
- When finding mole ratios, always divide the larger number of moles by the smaller one.
- Empirical and molecular formulas can differ for molecular compounds. In contrast, the formula of an ionic compound is generally the same as its empirical formula.

- Determining the molecular formula of a compound after calculating the empirical formula requires knowing the molar mass.
- When *both* the percent composition and the molar mass are known for a compound, the alternative method mentioned in the comment to Example 2.9 could be used.

Eugenol, $C_{10}H_{12}O_2$, is an important component in oil of cloves.

Solution The mass of oxygen in a 100.00 g sample of eugenol is

$$100.00 \text{ g} = 73.14 \text{ g C} + 7.37 \text{ g H} + \text{mass of O}$$
$$\text{Mass of O} = 19.49 \text{ g}$$

The amount of each element is

$$73.14 \text{ g C} \times \frac{1 \text{ mol C}}{12.011 \text{ g C}} = 6.089 \text{ mol C}$$

$$7.37 \text{ g H} \times \frac{1 \text{ mol H}}{1.008 \text{ g H}} = 7.31 \text{ mol H}$$

$$19.49 \text{ g O} \times \frac{1 \text{ mol O}}{15.999 \text{ g O}} = 1.218 \text{ mol O}$$

To find the mole ratio, the best approach is to base the ratios on the smallest number of moles present—in this case, oxygen.

$$\frac{\text{mol C}}{\text{mol O}} = \frac{6.089 \text{ mol C}}{1.218 \text{ mol O}} = \frac{4.999 \text{ mol C}}{1.000 \text{ mol O}} = \frac{5 \text{ mol C}}{1 \text{ mol O}}$$

$$\frac{\text{mol H}}{\text{mol O}} = \frac{7.31 \text{ mol H}}{1.218 \text{ mol O}} = \frac{6.00 \text{ mol H}}{1.000 \text{ mol O}} = \frac{6 \text{ mol H}}{1 \text{ mol O}}$$

Now we know there are 5 mol of C and 6 mol of H per 1 mol of O. Thus, the empirical formula is C_5H_6O.

The experimentally determined molar mass of eugenol is 164.2 g/mol. This is twice the molar mass of C_5H_6O (82.1 g/mol).

$$\frac{164.2 \text{ g/mol of eugenol}}{82.10 \text{ g/mol of } C_5H_6O} = 2.000 \text{ mol } C_5H_6O \text{ per mol of eugenol}$$

The molecular formula is $C_{10}H_{12}O_2$.

Comment There is another approach to finding the molecular formula here. Knowing the percent composition of eugenol and its molar mass, we could calculate that in 164.2 g of eugenol there are 120.1 g of C (10 mol of C), 12.1 g of H (12 mol of H), and 32.00 g of O (2 mol of O). This gives us a molecular formula of $C_{10}H_{12}O_2$. However, you must recognize that *this approach can only be used when you know both the percent composition and the molar mass.*

EXERCISE 2.15 Empirical and Molecular Formulas

(a) What is the empirical formula of naphthalene, $C_{10}H_8$?

(b) The empirical formula of acetic acid is CH_2O. If its molar mass is 60.05 g/mol, what is the molecular formula of acetic acid?

EXERCISE 2.16 Calculating a Formula from Percent Composition

Isoprene is a liquid compound that can be polymerized to form synthetic rubber. It is composed of 88.17% carbon and 11.83% hydrogen. Its molar mass is 68.11 g/mol. What are its empirical and molecular formulas?

EXERCISE 2.17 Calculating a Formula from Percent Composition

Camphor is found in "camphor wood," much prized for its wonderful odor. It is composed of 78.90% carbon and 10.59% hydrogen. The remainder is oxygen. What is its empirical formula?

Determining a Formula from Mass Data

The composition of a compound in terms of mass percent gives us the mass of each element in a 100.0-g sample. In the laboratory, we often collect information on the composition of compounds slightly differently. We can:

1. Combine known masses of elements to give a sample of the compound of known mass. Element masses can be converted to moles, and the ratio of moles gives the combining ratio of atoms—that is, the empirical formula. This approach is described in Example 2.10.

2. Decompose a known mass of an unknown compound into "pieces" of known composition. If the masses of the "pieces" can be determined, the ratio of moles of the "pieces" gives the formula. An example is a decomposition such as

$$Ni(CO)_4(\ell) \rightarrow Ni(s) + 4\ CO(g)$$

The masses of Ni and CO can be converted to moles, whose 1 : 4 ratio would reveal the formula of the compound. We will describe this approach in Chapter 4 (▶ Section 4.4).

EXAMPLE 2.10 Formula of a Compound from Combining Masses

Problem Gallium oxide, Ga_xO_y, forms when gallium is combined with oxygen. Suppose you allow 1.25 g of gallium (Ga) to react with oxygen and obtain 1.68 g of Ga_xO_y. What is the formula of the product?

Strategy Calculate the mass of oxygen in 1.68 g of product (which you already know contains 1.25 g of Ga). Next, calculate the amounts of Ga and O (in moles), and find their ratio.

Solution The masses of Ga and O combined in 1.68 g of product are

$$1.68\ g\ product - 1.25\ g\ Ga = 0.43\ g\ O$$

Next, calculate the amount of each reactant:

$$1.25\ g\ Ga \times \frac{1\ mol\ Ga}{69.72\ g\ Ga} = 0.0179\ mol\ Ga$$

$$0.43\ g\ O \times \frac{1\ mol\ O}{16.0\ g\ O} = 0.027\ mol\ O$$

Find the ratio of moles of O to moles of Ga:

$$Mole\ ratio = \frac{0.027\ mol\ O}{0.0179\ mol\ Ga} = \frac{1.5\ mol\ O}{1.0\ mol\ Ga}$$

It is 1.5 mol O/1.0 mol Ga, or 3 mol O to 2 mol Ga. Thus, the product is gallium oxide, Ga_2O_3.

EXAMPLE 2.11 Determining a Formula from Mass Data

Problem Tin metal (Sn) and purple iodine (I_2) combine to form orange, solid tin iodide with an unknown formula.

$$Sn\ metal + solid\ I_2 \rightarrow solid\ Sn_xI_y$$

Weighed quantities of Sn and I_2 are combined, where the quantity of Sn is more than is needed to react with all of the iodine. After Sn_xI_y has been formed, it is isolated by filtration. The mass of excess tin is also determined. The following data were collected:

Mass of tin (Sn) in the original mixture	1.056 g
Mass of iodine (I_2) in the original mixture	1.947 g
Mass of tin (Sn) recovered after reaction	0.601 g

Strategy The first step is to find the masses of Sn and I that are combined in Sn_xI_y. The masses are then converted to moles, and the ratio of moles reveals the compound's empirical formula.

(a) Weighed samples of tin (left) and iodine (right).

(b) The tin and iodine are heated in a solvent.

(c) The hot reaction mixture is filtered to recover unreacted tin.

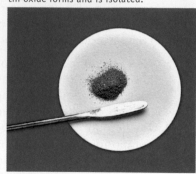
(d) When the solvent cools, solid, orange tin oxide forms and is isolated.

Charles D. Winters

The formula of a compound of tin and iodine can be found by determining the mass of iodine that combines with a given mass of tin.

Solution First, let us find the mass of tin that combined with iodine

Mass of Sn in original mixture	1.056 g
Mass of Sn recovered	− 0.601 g
Mass of Sn combined with 1.947 g I_2	0.455 g

Now convert the mass of tin to the amount of tin.

$$0.455 \text{ g Sn} \times \frac{1 \text{ mol Sn}}{118.7 \text{ g Sn}} = 0.00383 \text{ mol Sn}$$

No I_2 was recovered; it all reacted with Sn. Therefore, 0.00383 mol of Sn combined with 1.947 g of I_2. Because we want to know the amount of I that combined with 0.00383 mol of Sn, we calculate the amount of I from the mass of I_2.

$$1.947 \text{ g } I_2 \times \frac{1 \text{ mol } I_2}{253.81 \text{ g } I_2} \times \frac{2 \text{ mol I}}{1 \text{ mol } I_2} = 0.01534 \text{ mol I}$$

Finally, we find the ratio of moles.

$$\frac{\text{mol I}}{\text{mol Sn}} = \frac{0.01534 \text{ mol I}}{0.00383 \text{ mol Sn}} = \frac{4.01 \text{ mol I}}{1.00 \text{ mol Sn}} = \frac{4 \text{ mol I}}{1 \text{ mol Sn}}$$

There are four times as many moles of I as moles of Sn in the sample. Therefore, there are four times as many atoms of I as atoms of Sn per formula unit. The empirical formula is SnI_4.

EXERCISE 2.18 Determining a Formula from Combining Masses

Analysis shows that 0.586 g of potassium metal combines with 0.480 g of O_2 gas to give a white solid having a formula of K_xO_y. What is the empirical formula of the compound?

Determining a Formula by Mass Spectrometry

We have described chemical methods of determining a molecular formula, but there are many instrumental methods as well. One of them is *mass spectrometry* (Figure 2.27). We introduced this technique where it was used to describe the existence of isotopes and to measure their relative abundance (Figure 2.3). If a compound can be turned into a vapor, the vapor can be passed through an electron beam in a mass spectrometer where high energy electrons collide with the gas phase molecules. These high energy collisions cause the molecule to lose electrons and turn the molecules into positive ions. These ions usually break apart or fragment into smaller pieces. As illustrated in Figure 2.27, the cation created from

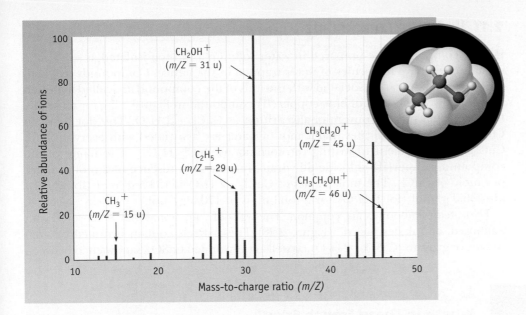

FIGURE 2.27 Mass spectrum of ethanol, CH₃CH₂OH. A prominent peak or line in the spectrum is the "parent" ion ($CH_3CH_2OH^+$) at mass 46. (The "parent" ion is the heaviest ion observed.) The mass designated by the peak for the "parent" ion confirms the formula of the molecule. Other peaks are for "fragment" ions. This pattern of lines can provide further, unambiguous evidence of the formula of the compound. (The horizontal axis is the mass-to-charge ratio of a given ion. Because almost all observed ions have a charge of $Z = +1$, the value observed is the mass of the ion.) (See *A Closer Look: Mass Spectrometry, Molar Mass, and Isotopes.*)

ethanol ($CH_3CH_2OH^+$) fragments (losing an H atom) to give another cation ($CH_3CH_2O^+$), which further fragments. A mass spectrometer detects and records the masses of the different particles. Analysis of the spectrum can help identify a compound and can give an accurate molar mass.

A Closer Look

Mass Spectrometry, Molar Mass, and Isotopes

Bromobenzene, C_6H_5Br, has a molar mass of 157.010 g/mol. Why, then, are there two prominent lines at a mass-to-charge ratio (*m/Z*) 156 and 158 in the mass spectrum of the compound (when $Z = 1$)? The answer shows us the influence of isotopes on molar mass.

Bromine has two naturally occurring isotopes, ^{79}Br and ^{81}Br. They are 50.7% and 49.3% abundant, respectively. What is the mass of C_6H_5Br based on each isotope? If we use the most abundant isotopes of C and H (^{12}C and ^1H), the mass of the molecule having only the ^{79}Br isotope, $C_6H_5{}^{79}Br$, is 156. The mass of the molecule containing only the ^{81}Br isotope, $C_6H_5{}^{81}Br$, is 158.

The calculated molar mass of bromobenzene is 157.010, a value derived from the atomic masses of the elements. Atomic masses reflect the abundances of all of the isotopes. In contrast, the mass spectrum has a line for each possible combination of isotopes. This explains why there are small lines at the mass-to-charge ratios of 157 and 159. They arise from various combinations of ^1H, ^{12}C, ^{13}C, ^{79}Br, and ^{81}Br atoms. In fact, careful analysis of such patterns can identify a molecule unambiguously.

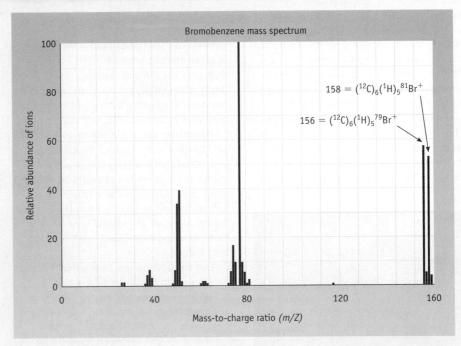

Bromobenzene mass spectrum

$158 = (^{12}C)_6(^1H)_5{}^{81}Br^+$

$156 = (^{12}C)_6(^1H)_5{}^{79}Br^+$

2.11 Hydrated Compounds

FIGURE 2.28 Gypsum wallboard.
Gypsum is hydrated calcium sulfate,
$CaSO_4 \cdot 2H_2O$.

If ionic compounds are prepared in water solution and then isolated as solids, the crystals often have molecules of water trapped in the lattice. Compounds in which molecules of water are associated with the ions of the compound are called **hydrated compounds.** The beautiful blue copper(II) compound in Figure 2.26, for example, has a formula that is conventionally written as $CuCl_2 \cdot 2 H_2O$. The dot between $CuCl_2$ and $2 H_2O$ indicates that 2 mol of water are associated with every mole of $CuCl_2$; it is equivalent to writing the formula as $CuCl_2(H_2O)_2$. The name of the compound, copper(II) chloride dihydrate, reflects the presence of 2 mol of water per mole of $CuCl_2$. The molar mass of $CuCl_2 \cdot 2 H_2O$ is 134.5 g/mol (for $CuCl_2$) plus 36.0 g/mol (for $2 H_2O$) for a total mass of 170.5 g/mol.

Hydrated compounds are common. The walls of your home may be covered with wallboard, or "plaster board" (Figure 2.28) These sheets contain hydrated calcium sulfate, or gypsum ($CaSO_4 \cdot 2 H_2O$), as well as unhydrated $CaSO_4$, sandwiched between

Case Study

What's in Those French Fries?

The U.S. Environmental Protection Agency (EPA) maintains a database of toxicities of chemicals. One compound on that list is acrylamide, $CH_2=CHCONH_2$, which is listed as a possible human carcinogen (cancer-causing substance). Although not confirmed by human data, carcinogenicity has been observed in rats. Based on the animal studies, the EPA suggests that the "Reference Dose" (RfD) of acrylamide should be 0.0002 mg per kilogram of body weight per day. (The RfD is a numerical estimate of a daily oral exposure to the human population, including sensitive subgroups such as children, that is not likely to cause harmful effects during a lifetime.)

In 2002, Swedish chemists announced that they had found previously undetected acrylamide in foods that many find appealing: french fries and potato chips (or chips and crisps as they are called in other countries).

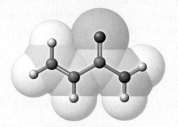

Acrylamide

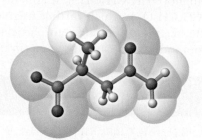

Asparagine, an amino acid

Not only was acrylamide present, but it was in concentrations hundreds of times higher than what the EPA and the World Health Organization (WHO) consider safe. And soon thereafter it was also found in coffee, pastries, cookies, cereals, rolls, and toasted bread.

Where does the acrylamide come from, and can the amount be reduced? Chemists soon understood that the likely source was an interaction between the naturally occurring amino acid asparagine and a simple sugar such as fructose or glucose when the food was cooked. However, the level of acrylamide in food can vary widely with cooking time and temperature.

Can acrylamide levels be reduced in foods? Recent work in England indicates that if 0.39% by weight each of glycine (an amino acid) and citric acid are added before cooking, acrylamide levels can be reduced by 40%.

Should we give up french fries? Before acting precipitously, a closer look is called for. Even the report from the Swedish government's National Food Administration counseled that "...there is not sufficient data to

warrant changing the current dietary recommendation." Other scientists who study carcinogenic compounds point out that acrylamide is not a proven human carcinogen and that the dose of acrylamide from fried foods is 700 times less that the dose that causes cancer in rodents. Furthermore, many common foods that we eat regularly—among them cantaloupe, carrots, cauliflower, cherries, chocolate, and coffee—have substances that have been proven to cause cancer in rodents.

Nonetheless, the warning is there. Clearly, more information is needed, and chemists are the ones with the background to do such studies.

Questions:

1. *Which has the higher mass percent of nitrogen, acrylamide or asparagine?*
2. *If you weigh 150 pounds (1 pound = 453.6 g), how many molecules of acrylamide are you consuming per day if you consume 0.0002 mg per kilogram?*

Answers to these questions are in Appendix Q.

Active Figure 2.29
Dehydrating hydrated cobalt(II) chloride, CoCl$_2$ · 6 H$_2$O. *(left)* Cobalt (II) chloride hexahydrate [CoCl$_2$ · 6 H$_2$O] is a deep red compound. *(left and center)* When it is heated, the compound loses the water of hydration and forms the deep blue compound CoCl$_2$.

Chemistry⚗Now™ Sign in at www.cengage.com/login and go to the Chapter Contents menu to explore an interactive version of this figure accompanied by an exercise.

paper. Gypsum is a mineral that can be mined. Now, however, it is usually obtained as a byproduct in the manufacture of hydrofluoric acid and phosphoric acid.

If gypsum is heated between 120 and 180 °C, the water is partly driven off to give CaSO$_4$ · $\frac{1}{2}$ H$_2$O, a compound commonly called "plaster of Paris." If you have ever broken an arm or leg and had to have a cast, the cast may have been made of this compound. It is an effective casting material because, when added to water, it forms a thick slurry that can be poured into a mold or spread out over a part of the body. As it takes on more water, the material increases in volume and forms a hard, inflexible solid. These properties also make plaster of Paris a useful material for artists, because the expanding compound fills a mold completely and makes a high-quality reproduction.

Hydrated cobalt(II) chloride is the red solid in Figure 2.29. When heated, it turns purple and then deep blue as it loses water to form anhydrous CoCl$_2$; "anhydrous" means a substance without water. On exposure to moist air, anhydrous CoCl$_2$ takes up water and is converted back into the red hydrated compound. It is this property that allows crystals of the blue compound to be used as a humidity indicator. You may have seen them in a small bag packed with a piece of electronic equipment.

There is no simple way to predict how much water will be present in a hydrated compound, so it must be determined experimentally. Such an experiment may involve heating the hydrated material so that all the water is released from the solid and evaporated. Only the anhydrous compound is left. The formula of hydrated copper(II) sulfate, commonly known as "blue vitriol," is determined in this manner in Example 2.12.

■ **Invisible Ink** CoCl$_2$ · 6 H$_2$O also makes a good "invisible ink." A solution of cobalt(II) chloride in water is red, but if you write on paper with the solution, it cannot be seen. When the paper is warmed, however, the cobalt compound dehydrates to give the deep blue anhydrous compound, and the writing becomes visible.

— White CuSO$_4$

— Blue CuSO$_4$ · 5 H$_2$O

Heating a hydrated compound. The formula of a hydrated compound can be determined by heating a weighed sample enough to cause the compound to release its water of hydration. Knowing the mass of the hydrated compound before heating and the mass of the anhydrous compound after heating, we can determine the mass of water in the original sample.

■ **EXAMPLE 2.12 Determining the Formula of a Hydrated Compound**

Problem You want to know the value of *x* in blue, hydrated copper(II) sulfate, CuSO$_4$ · *x* H$_2$O; that is, the number of water molecules for each unit of CuSO$_4$. In the laboratory, you weigh out 1.023 g of the solid. After heating the solid thoroughly in a porcelain crucible (see Figure), 0.654 g of nearly white, anhydrous copper(II) sulfate, CuSO$_4$, remains.

$$1.023 \text{ g CuSO}_4 \cdot x \text{ H}_2\text{O} + \text{heat} \rightarrow 0.654 \text{ g CuSO}_4 + ? \text{ g H}_2\text{O}$$

Strategy To find *x*, we need to know the amount of H$_2$O per mole CuSO$_4$. Therefore, first find the mass of water lost by the sample from the difference between the mass of hydrated compound and the anhydrous form. Finally, find the ratio of the amount of water lost (moles) to the amount of anhydrous CuSO$_4$.

Solution Find the mass of water.

Mass of hydrated compound	1.023 g
— Mass of anhydrous compound, CuSO$_4$	−0.654
Mass of water	0.369 g

Next, convert the masses of $CuSO_4$ and H_2O to moles.

$$0.369 \text{ g } H_2O \times \frac{1 \text{ mol } H_2O}{18.02 \text{ g } H_2O} = 0.0205 \text{ mol } H_2O$$

$$0.654 \text{ g } CuSO_4 \times \frac{1 \text{ mol } CuSO_4}{159.6 \text{ g } CuSO_4} = 0.00410 \text{ mol } CuSO_4$$

The value of x is determined from the mole ratio.

$$\frac{0.0205 \text{ mol } H_2O}{0.00410 \text{ mol } CuSO_4} = \frac{5.00 \text{ mol } H_2O}{1.00 \text{ mol } CuSO_4}$$

The water-to-$CuSO_4$ ratio is 5-to-1, so the formula of the hydrated compound is $CuSO_4 \cdot 5\,H_2O$. Its name is copper(II) sulfate pentahydrate.

EXERCISE 2.19 Determining the Formula of a Hydrated Compound

Hydrated nickel(II) chloride is a beautiful, green, crystalline compound. When heated strongly, the compound is dehydrated. If 0.235 g of $NiCl_2 \cdot x\,H_2O$ gives 0.128 g of $NiCl_2$ on heating, what is the value of x?

Chapter Goals Revisited

Now that you have studied this chapter, you should ask whether you have met the chapter goals. In particular, you should be able to:

Describe atomic structure, and define atomic number and mass number

a. Describe electrons, protons, and neutrons, and the general structure of the atom (Section 2.1). Study Question(s) assignable in OWL: 2.

b. Understand the relative atomic weight scale and the atomic mass unit (Section 2.2).

Understand the nature of isotopes, and calculate atomic weight from isotopic abundances and isotopic masses

a. Define isotope and give the mass number and number of neutrons for a specific isotope (Sections 2.2 and 2.3). Study Question(s) assignable in OWL: 4, 5, 8.

b. Do calculations that relate the atomic weight of an element and isotopic abundances and masses (Section 2.4). Study Question(s) assignable in OWL: 10, 12, 15, 86, 88.

Know the terminology of the periodic table

a. Identify the periodic table locations of groups, periods, metals, metalloids, nonmetals, alkali metals, alkaline earth metals, halogens, noble gases, and the transition elements (Section 2.5). Study Question(s) assignable in OWL: 20, 21, 23, 92; Go Chemistry Module 1.

b. Recognize similarities and differences in properties of some of the common elements of a group.

Interpret, predict, and write formulas for ionic and molecular compounds

a. Recognize and interpret molecular formulas, condensed formulas, and structural formulas (Section 2.6).

b. Recognize that metal atoms commonly lose one or more electrons to form positive ions, called cations, and nonmetal atoms often gain electrons to form negative ions, called anions (see Figure 2.7).

c. Recognize that the charge on a metal cation in Groups 1A, 2A, and 3A is equal to the group number in which the element is found in the periodic table (M^{n+}, n = Group number) (Section 2.7). Charges on transition metal cations are often 2+ or 3+, but other charges are observed. Study Question(s) assignable in OWL: 29, 33, 35; Go Chemistry Module 2.

d. Recognize that the negative charge on a single-atom or monatomic anion, X^{n-}, is given by n = Group number − 8 (Section 2.7).

e. Write formulas for ionic compounds by combining ions in the proper ratio to give no overall charge (Section 2.7).

Name ionic and molecular compounds

a. Give the names or formulas of polyatomic ions, knowing their formulas or names, respectively (Table 2.4 and Section 2.7).

b. Name ionic compounds and simple binary compounds of the nonmetals (Sections 2.7 and 2.8). Study Question(s) assignable in OWL: 41, 43, 49, 51; Go Chemistry Module 3.

Understand some properties of ionic compounds

a. Understand the importance of Coulomb's law (Equation 2.3), which describes the electrostatic forces of attraction and repulsion of ions. Coulomb's law states that the force of attraction between oppositely charged species increases with electric charge and with decreasing distance between the species (Section 2.7). Study Question(s) assignable in OWL: 48.

Explain the concept of the mole, and use molar mass in calculations

a. Understand that the molar mass of an element is the mass in grams of Avogadro's number of atoms of that element (Section 2.9). Study Question(s) assignable in OWL: 53, 55, 57, 89, 93, 96.

b. Know how to use the molar mass of an element and Avogadro's number in calculations (Section 2.9). Study Question(s) assignable in OWL: 55, 57, 93, 98.

c. Understand that the molar mass of a compound (often called the molecular weight) is the mass in grams of Avogadro's number of molecules (or formula units) of a compound (Section 2.9). For ionic compounds, which do not consist of individual molecules, the sum of atomic masses is often called the formula mass (or formula weight).

d. Calculate the molar mass of a compound from its formula and a table of atomic masses (Section 2.9). Study Question(s) assignable in OWL: 59, 61, 105.

e. Calculate the number of moles of a compound that is represented by a given mass, and vice versa (Section 2.9). Study Question(s) assignable in OWL: 63; Go Chemistry Module 4.

Derive compound formulas from experimental data

a. Express the composition of a compound in terms of percent composition (Section 2.10). Study Question(s) assignable in OWL: 67, 69.

b. Use percent composition or other experimental data to determine the empirical formula of a compound (Section 2.10). Study Question(s) assignable in OWL: 71, 76, 77, 79, 81, 120.

c. Understand how mass spectrometry can be used to find a molar mass (Section 2.10).

d. Use experimental data to find the number of water molecules in a hydrated compound (Section 2.11) Study Question(s) assignable in OWL: 141.

KEY EQUATIONS

Equation 2.1 (page 54) Percent abundance of an isotope

$$\text{Percent abundance} = \frac{\text{number of atoms of a given isotope}}{\text{total number of atoms of all isotopes of that element}} \times 100\%$$

Equation 2.2 (page 56) Calculate the average atomic mass (atomic weight) from isotope abundances and the exact atomic mass of each isotope of an element.

$$\text{Atomic weight} = \left(\frac{\% \text{ abundance isotope 1}}{100} \right)(\text{mass of isotope 1})$$
$$+ \left(\frac{\% \text{ abundance isotope 2}}{100} \right)(\text{mass of isotope 2}) + \ldots$$

Equation 2.3 (page 78) **Coulomb's Law,** the force of attraction between oppositely charged ions.

$$\text{Force of attraction} = k \frac{(n^+\text{e})(n^-\text{e})}{d^2}$$

charge on + and − ions   charge on electron
proportionality constant   distance between ions

STUDY QUESTIONS

OWL Online homework for this chapter may be assigned in OWL.

▲ denotes challenging questions.

■ denotes questions assignable in OWL.

Blue-numbered questions have answers in Appendix O and fully-worked solutions in the *Student Solutions Manual*.

Practicing Skills

Atoms: Their Composition and Structure
(See ChemistryNow Screen 2.11.)

1. What are the three fundamental particles from which atoms are built? What are their electric charges? Which of these particles constitute the nucleus of an atom? Which is the least massive particle of the three?

2. ■ If a gold atom has a radius of 145 pm and you could string gold atoms like beads on a thread, how many atoms would you need to have a necklace 36 cm long?

3. Give the complete symbol ($_Z^A X$), including atomic number and mass number, for each of the following atoms: (a) magnesium with 15 neutrons, (b) titanium with 26 neutrons, and (c) zinc with 32 neutrons.

4. ■ Give the complete symbol ($_Z^A X$), including atomic number and mass number, of (a) a nickel atom with 31 neutrons, (b) a plutonium atom with 150 neutrons, and (c) a tungsten atom with 110 neutrons.

5. ■ How many electrons, protons, and neutrons are there in each of the following atoms?
   (a) magnesium-24, ^{24}Mg
   (b) tin-119, ^{119}Sn
   (c) thorium-232, ^{232}Th
   (d) carbon-13, ^{13}C;
   (e) copper-63, ^{63}Cu
   (f) bismuth-205, ^{205}Bi

6. Atomic Structure

(a) The synthetic radioactive element technetium is used in many medical studies. Give the number of electrons, protons, and neutrons in an atom of technetium-99.

(b) Radioactive americium-241 is used in household smoke detectors and in bone mineral analysis. Give the number of electrons, protons, and neutrons in an atom of americium-241.

Isotopes
(See ChemistryNow Screen 2.12.)

7. Cobalt has three radioactive isotopes used in medical studies. Atoms of these isotopes have 30, 31, and 33 neutrons, respectively. Give the symbol for each of these isotopes.

8. ■ Which of the following are isotopes of element X, the atomic number for which is 9: $^{19}_{9}X$, $^{20}_{9}X$, $^{9}_{18}X$ and $^{21}_{9}X$?

Isotope Abundance and Atomic Weight
(See Examples 2.2 and 2.3, Exercises 2.2 and 2.3, and ChemistryNow Screens 2.12 and 2.13.)

9. Thallium has two stable isotopes, ^{203}Tl and ^{205}Tl. Knowing that the atomic weight of thallium is 204.4, which isotope is the more abundant of the two?

10. ■ Strontium has four stable isotopes. Strontium-84 has a very low natural abundance, but ^{86}Sr, ^{87}Sr, and ^{88}Sr are all reasonably abundant. Knowing that the atomic weight of strontium is 87.62, which of the more abundant isotopes predominates?

11. Verify that the atomic weight of lithium is 6.94, given the following information:
^{6}Li, mass = 6.015121 u; percent abundance = 7.50%
^{7}Li, mass = 7.016003 u; percent abundance = 92.50%

12. ■ Verify that the atomic weight of magnesium is 24.31, given the following information:
^{24}Mg, mass = 23.985042 u; percent abundance = 78.99%
^{25}Mg, mass = 24.985837 u; percent abundance = 10.00%
^{26}Mg, mass = 25.982593 u; percent abundance = 11.01%

13. Silver (Ag) has two stable isotopes, ^{107}Ag and ^{109}Ag. The isotopic weight of ^{107}Ag is 106.9051, and the isotopic mass of ^{109}Ag is 108.9047. The atomic weight of Ag, from the periodic table, is 107.868. Estimate the percent of ^{107}Ag in a sample of the element.
(a) 0%   (b) 25%   (c) 50%   (d) 75%

14. Copper exists as two isotopes: ^{63}Cu (62.9298 u) and ^{65}Cu (64.9278 u). What is the approximate percent of ^{63}Cu in samples of this element?
(a) 10%   (c) 50%   (e) 90%
(b) 30%   (d) 70%

15. ■ Gallium has two naturally occurring isotopes, ^{69}Ga and ^{71}Ga, with masses of 68.9257 u and 70.9249 u, respectively. Calculate the percent abundances of these isotopes of gallium.

16. Europium has two stable isotopes, ^{151}Eu and ^{153}Eu, with masses of 150.9197 u and 152.9212 u, respectively. Calculate the percent abundances of these isotopes of europium.

The Periodic Table
(See Section 2.5 and Exercise 2.4. See also the Periodic Table Tool on the ChemistryNow website.)

17. Titanium and thallium have symbols that are easily confused with each other. Give the symbol, atomic number, atomic weight, and group and period number of each element. Are they metals, metalloids, or nonmetals?

18. In Groups 4A–6A, there are several elements whose symbols begin with S. Name these elements, and for each one give its symbol, atomic number, Group number, and period. Describe each as a metal, metalloid, or nonmetal.

19. How many periods of the periodic table have 8 elements; how many have 18 elements, and how many have 32 elements?

20. ■ How many elements occur in the seventh period? What is the name given to the majority of these elements, and what well-known property characterizes them?

21. ■ Select answers to the questions listed below from the following list of elements whose symbols start with the letter C: C, Ca, Cr, Co, Cd, Cl, Cs, Ce, Cm, Cu, and Cf. (You should expect to use some symbols more than once.)
(a) Which are nonmetals?
(b) Which are main group elements?
(c) Which are lanthanides?
(d) Which are transition elements?
(e) Which are actinides?
(f) Which are gases?

22. Give the name and chemical symbol for the following.
(a) a nonmetal in the second period
(b) an alkali metal in the fifth period
(c) the third-period halogen
(d) an element that is a gas at 20°C and 1 atmosphere pressure

23. ■ Classify the following elements as metals, metalloids, or nonmetals: N, Na, Ni, Ne, and Np.

24. Here are symbols for five of the seven elements whose names begin with the letter B: B, Ba, Bk, Bi, and Br. Match each symbol with one of the descriptions below.
(a) a radioactive element
(b) a liquid at room temperature
(c) a metalloid
(d) an alkaline earth element
(e) a Group 5A element

Molecular Formulas and Models
(See Exercise 2.5.)

25. A model of sulfuric acid is illustrated here. Write the molecular formula for sulfuric acid, and draw the structural formula. Describe the structure of the molecule. Is it flat? That is, are all the atoms in the plane of the paper? (Color code: sulfur atoms are yellow; oxygen atoms are red; and hydrogen atoms are white.)

26. A model of the platinum-based chemotherapy agent cisplatin is given here. Write the molecular formula for the compound, and draw its structural formula.

Ions and Ion Charges
(See Exercise 2.6, Figure 2.18, Table 2.4, and ChemistryNow Screens 2.18 and 2.19.)

27. What charges are most commonly observed for monatomic ions of the following elements?
    (a) magnesium   (c) nickel
    (b) zinc   (d) gallium

28. What charges are most commonly observed for monatomic ions of the following elements?
    (a) selenium   (c) iron
    (b) fluorine   (d) nitrogen

29. ■ Give the symbol, including the correct charge, for each of the following ions:
    (a) barium ion   (e) sulfide ion
    (b) titanium(IV) ion   (f) perchlorate ion
    (c) phosphate ion   (g) cobalt(II) ion
    (d) hydrogen carbonate ion   (h) sulfate ion

30. Give the symbol, including the correct charge, for each of the following ions:
    (a) permanganate ion   (d) ammonium ion
    (b) nitrite ion   (e) phosphate ion
    (c) dihydrogen phosphate ion   (f) sulfite ion

31. When a potassium atom becomes a monatomic ion, how many electrons does it lose or gain? What noble gas atom has the same number of electrons as a potassium ion?

32. When oxygen and sulfur atoms become monatomic ions, how many electrons does each lose or gain? Which noble gas atom has the same number of electrons as an oxide ion? Which noble gas atom has the same number of electrons as a sulfide ion?

Ionic Compounds
(See Examples 2.4 and 2.5 and ChemistryNow Screen 2.20.)

33. ■ Predict the charges of the ions in an ionic compound containing the elements barium and bromine. Write the formula for the compound.

34. What are the charges of the ions in an ionic compound containing cobalt(III) and fluoride ions? Write the formula for the compound.

35. ■ For each of the following compounds, give the formula, charge, and the number of each ion that makes up the compound:
    (a) K_2S (d) $(NH_4)_3PO_4$
    (b) $CoSO_4$ (e) $Ca(ClO)_2$
    (c) $KMnO_4$ (f) $NaCH_3CO_2$

36. For each of the following compounds, give the formula, charge, and the number of each ion that makes up the compound:
    (a) $Mg(CH_3CO_2)_2$ (d) $Ti(SO_4)_2$
    (b) $Al(OH)_3$ (e) KH_2PO_4
    (c) $CuCO_3$ (f) $CaHPO_4$

37. Cobalt forms Co^{2+} and Co^{3+} ions. Write the formulas for the two cobalt oxides formed by these transition metal ions.

38. Platinum is a transition element and forms Pt^{2+} and Pt^{4+} ions. Write the formulas for the compounds of each of these ions with (a) chloride ions and (b) sulfide ions.

39. Which of the following are correct formulas for ionic compounds? For those that are not, give the correct formula.
    (a) $AlCl_2$ (c) Ga_2O_3
    (b) KF_2 (d) MgS

40. Which of the following are correct formulas for ionic compounds? For those that are not, give the correct formula.
    (a) Ca_2O (c) Fe_2O_5
    (b) $SrBr_2$ (d) Li_2O

▲ more challenging   ■ in OWL   Blue-numbered questions answered in Appendix O

Naming Ionic Compounds
(See Exercise 2.8 and ChemistryNow Screen 2.21.)

41. ■ Name each of the following ionic compounds:
    (a) K_2S (c) $(NH_4)_3PO_4$
    (b) $CoSO_4$ (d) $Ca(ClO)_2$

42. Name each of the following ionic compounds:
    (a) $Ca(CH_3CO_2)_2$ (c) $Al(OH)_3$
    (b) $Ni_3(PO_4)_2$ (d) KH_2PO_4

43. ■ Give the formula for each of the following ionic compounds:
    (a) ammonium carbonate   (d) aluminum phosphate
    (b) calcium iodide   (e) silver(I) acetate
    (c) copper(II) bromide

44. Give the formula for each of the following ionic compounds:
    (a) calcium hydrogen carbonate
    (b) potassium permanganate
    (c) magnesium perchlorate
    (d) potassium hydrogen phosphate
    (e) sodium sulfite

45. Write the formulas for the four ionic compounds that can be made by combining each of the cations Na^+ and Ba^{2+} with the anions CO_3^{2-} and I^-. Name each of the compounds.

46. Write the formulas for the four ionic compounds that can be made by combining the cations Mg^{2+} and Fe^{3+} with the anions PO_4^{3-} and NO_3^-. Name each compound formed.

Coulomb's Law
(See Equation 2.3, Figure 2.21, and ChemistryNow Screen 2.22.)

47. Sodium ions, Na^+, form ionic compounds with fluoride ions, F^-, and iodide ions, I^-. The radii of these ions are as follows: $Na^+ = 116$ pm; $F^- = 119$ pm; and $I^- = 206$ pm. In which ionic compound, NaF or NaI, are the forces of attraction between cation and anion stronger? Explain your answer.

48. ■ Consider the two ionic compounds NaCl and CaO. In which compound are the cation–anion attractive forces stronger? Explain your answer.

Naming Binary, Nonmetal Compounds
(See Exercise 2.10 and ChemistryNow Screens 2.24 and 2.25.)

49. ■ Name each of the following binary, nonionic compounds:
    (a) NF_3 (b) HI (c) BI_3 (d) PF_5

50. Name each of the following binary, nonionic compounds:
    (a) N_2O_5 (b) P_4S_3 (c) OF_2 (d) XeF_4

51. ■ Give the formula for each of the following compounds:
    (a) sulfur dichloride
    (b) dinitrogen pentaoxide
    (c) silicon tetrachloride
    (d) diboron trioxide (commonly called boric oxide)

52. Give the formula for each of the following compounds:
    (a) bromine trifluoride
    (b) xenon difluoride
    (c) hydrazine
    (d) diphosphorus tetrafluoride
    (e) butane

Atoms and the Mole
(See Example 2.6, Exercises 2.11 and 2.12, and ChemistryNow Screens 2.25 and 2.26.)

53. ■ Calculate the mass, in grams, of each the following:
    (a) 2.5 mol of aluminum   (c) 0.015 mol of calcium
    (b) 1.25×10^{-3} mol of iron   (d) 653 mol of neon

54. Calculate the mass, in grams, of each of the following:
    (a) 4.24 mol of gold   (c) 0.063 mol of platinum
    (b) 15.6 mol of He   (d) 3.63×10^{-4} mol of Pu

55. ■ Calculate the amount (moles) represented by each of the following:
    (a) 127.08 g of Cu   (c) 5.0 mg of americium
    (b) 0.012 g of lithium   (d) 6.75 g of Al

56. Calculate the amount (moles) represented by each of the following:
    (a) 16.0 g of Na   (c) 0.0034 g of platinum
    (b) 0.876 g of tin   (d) 0.983 g of Xe

57. ■ You are given 1.0 g samples of He, Fe, Li, Si, and C. Which sample contains the largest number of atoms? Which contains the smallest?

58. A semiconducting material is composed of 52 g of Ga, 9.5 g of Al, and 112 g of As. Which element has the largest number of atoms in the final mixture?

Molecules, Compounds, and the Mole
(See Example 2.7 and ChemistryNow Screens 2.27 and 2.28.)

59. ■ Calculate the molar mass of each of the following compounds:
    (a) Fe_2O_3, iron(III) oxide
    (b) BCl_3, boron trichloride
    (c) $C_6H_8O_6$, ascorbic acid (vitamin C)

60. Calculate the molar mass of each of the following compounds:
    (a) $Fe(C_6H_{11}O_7)_2$, iron(II) gluconate, a dietary supplement
    (b) $CH_3CH_2CH_2CH_2SH$, butanethiol, has a skunk-like odor
    (c) $C_{20}H_{24}N_2O_2$, quinine, used as an antimalarial drug

61. ■ Calculate the molar mass of each hydrated compound. Note that the water of hydration is included in the molar mass. (See Section 2.11.)
(a) $Ni(NO_3)_2 \cdot 6\ H_2O$
(b) $CuSO_4 \cdot 5\ H_2O$

62. Calculate the molar mass of each hydrated compound. Note that the water of hydration is included in the molar mass. (See Section 2.11.)
(a) $H_2C_2O_4 \cdot 2\ H_2O$
(b) $MgSO_4 \cdot 7\ H_2O$, Epsom salts

63. ■ What mass is represented by 0.0255 mol of each of the following compounds?
(a) C_3H_7OH, propanol, rubbing alcohol
(b) $C_{11}H_{16}O_2$, an antioxidant in foods, also known as BHA (butylated hydroxyanisole)
(c) $C_9H_8O_4$, aspirin
(d) $(CH_3)_2CO$, acetone, an important industrial solvent

64. Assume you have 0.123 mol of each of the following compounds. What mass of each is present?
(a) $C_{14}H_{10}O_4$, benzoyl peroxide, used in acne medications
(b) Dimethylglyoxime, used in the laboratory to test for nickel(II) ions

$$
\begin{array}{c}
CH_3 \\
| \\
C{=}N{-}OH \\
| \\
C{=}N{-}OH \\
| \\
CH_3
\end{array}
$$

(c) The compound below is responsible for the "skunky" taste in poorly made beer.

$$
\begin{array}{c}
CH_3 \quad H \quad\ H \\
|\qquad\ |\quad\ | \\
C{=}C{-}C{-}S{-}H \\
|\qquad\ |\quad\ | \\
CH_3 \qquad H
\end{array}
$$

(d) DEET, a mosquito repellent

$$
\begin{array}{c}
H \qquad O \quad CH_2{-}CH_3 \\
C \qquad \| \\
HC \qquad C{-}C{-}N \\
\| \qquad\qquad CH_2{-}CH_3 \\
HC \quad CH \\
C \\
| \\
CH_3
\end{array}
$$

65. Sulfur trioxide, SO_3, is made industrially in enormous quantities by combining oxygen and sulfur dioxide, SO_2. What amount (moles) of SO_3 is represented by 1.00 kg of sulfur trioxide? How many molecules? How many sulfur atoms? How many oxygen atoms?

66. An Alka-Seltzer tablet contains 324 mg of aspirin ($C_9H_8O_4$), 1904 mg of $NaHCO_3$, and 1000. mg of citric acid ($H_3C_6H_5O_7$). (The last two compounds react with each other to provide the "fizz," bubbles of CO_2, when the tablet is put into water.)
(a) Calculate the amount (moles) of each substance in the tablet.
(b) If you take one tablet, how many molecules of aspirin are you consuming?

Percent Composition
(See Example 2.8 and ChemistryNow Screen 2.29.)

67. ■ Calculate the mass percent of each element in the following compounds:
(a) PbS, lead(II) sulfide, galena
(b) C_3H_8, propane
(c) $C_{10}H_{14}O$, carvone, found in caraway seed oil

68. Calculate the mass percent of each element in the following compounds:
(a) $C_8H_{10}N_2O_2$, caffeine
(b) $C_{10}H_{20}O$, menthol
(c) $CoCl_2 \cdot 6\ H_2O$

69. ■ Calculate the mass percent of copper in CuS, copper(II) sulfide. If you wish to obtain 10.0 g of copper metal from copper(II) sulfide, what mass of CuS (in grams) must you use?

70. Calculate the mass percent of titanium in the mineral ilmenite, $FeTiO_3$. What mass of ilmenite (in grams) is required if you wish to obtain 750 g of titanium?

Empirical and Molecular Formulas
(See Example 2.9 and ChemistryNow Screens 2.31 and 2.32.)

71. ■ Succinic acid occurs in fungi and lichens. Its empirical formula is $C_2H_3O_2$, and its molar mass is 118.1 g/mol. What is its molecular formula?

72. An organic compound has the empirical formula C_2H_4NO. If its molar mass is 116.1 g/mol, what is the molecular formula of the compound?

73. Complete the following table:

Empirical Formula	Molar Mass (g/mol)	Molecular Formula
(a) CH	26.0	_____
(b) CHO	116.1	_____
(c) _____	_____	C_8H_{16}

74. Complete the following table:

Empirical Formula	Molar Mass (g/mol)	Molecular Formula
(a) $C_2H_3O_3$	150.0	_____
(b) C_3H_8	44.1	_____
(c) _____	_____	B_4H_{10}

75. Acetylene is a colorless gas used as a fuel in welding torches, among other things. It is 92.26% C and 7.74% H. Its molar mass is 26.02 g/mol. What are the empirical and molecular formulas of acetylene?

76. ■ A large family of boron-hydrogen compounds has the general formula B_xH_y. One member of this family contains 88.5% B; the remainder is hydrogen. What is its empirical formula?

77. ■ Cumene is a hydrocarbon, a compound composed only of C and H. It is 89.94% carbon, and its molar mass is 120.2 g/mol. What are the empirical and molecular formulas of cumene?

78. In 2006, a Russian team discovered an interesting molecule they called "sulflower" because of its shape and because it was based on sulfur. It is composed of 57.17% S and 42.83% C and has a molar mass of 448.70 g/mol. Determine the empirical and molecular formulas of "sulflower."

79. ■ Mandelic acid is an organic acid composed of carbon (63.15%), hydrogen (5.30%), and oxygen (31.55%). Its molar mass is 152.14 g/mol. Determine the empirical and molecular formulas of the acid.

80. Nicotine, a poisonous compound found in tobacco leaves, is 74.0% C, 8.65% H, and 17.35% N. Its molar mass is 162 g/mol. What are the empirical and molecular formulas of nicotine?

Determining Formulas from Mass Data
(See Examples 2.10 and 2.11 and ChemistryNow Screens 2.30 and 2.31.)

81. ■ A new compound containing xenon and fluorine was isolated by shining sunlight on a mixture of Xe (0.526 g) and excess F_2 gas. If you isolate 0.678 g of the new compound, what is its empirical formula?

82. Elemental sulfur (1.256 g) is combined with fluorine, F_2, to give a compound with the formula SF_x, a very stable, colorless gas. If you have isolated 5.722 g of SF_x, what is the value of x?

83. Zinc metal (2.50 g) combines with 9.70 g of iodine to produce zinc iodide, Zn_xI_y. What is the formula of this ionic compound?

84. You combine 1.25 g of germanium, Ge, with excess chlorine, Cl_2. The mass of product, Ge_xCl_y, is 3.69 g. What is the formula of the product, Ge_xCl_y?

General Questions

These questions are not designed as to type or location in the chapter. They may combine several concepts.

85. Fill in the blanks in the table (one column per element).

Symbol	^{58}Ni	^{33}S	____	____
Number of protons	____	____	10	____
Number of neutrons	____	____	10	30
Number of electrons in the neutral atom	____	____	____	25
Name of element	____	____	____	____

86. ■ Potassium has three naturally occurring isotopes (^{39}K, ^{40}K, and ^{41}K), but ^{40}K has a very low natural abundance. Which of the other two isotopes is the more abundant? Briefly explain your answer.

87. Crossword Puzzle: In the 2 × 2 box shown here, each answer must be correct four ways: horizontally, vertically, diagonally, and by itself. Instead of words, use symbols of elements. When the puzzle is complete, the four spaces will contain the overlapping symbols of 10 elements. There is only one correct solution.

1	2
3	4

Horizontal
1–2: Two-letter symbol for a metal used in ancient times
3–4: Two-letter symbol for a metal that burns in air and is found in Group 5A

Vertical
1–3: Two-letter symbol for a metalloid
2–4: Two-letter symbol for a metal used in U.S. coins

Single squares: All one-letter symbols
1: A colorful nonmetal
2: Colorless, gaseous nonmetal
3: An element that makes fireworks green
4: An element that has medicinal uses

Diagonal
1–4: Two-letter symbol for an element used in electronics
2–3: Two-letter symbol for a metal used with Zr to make wires for superconducting magnets

This puzzle first appeared in *Chemical & Engineering News*, p. 86, December 14, 1987 (submitted by S. J. Cyvin) and in *Chem Matters*, October 1988.

88. ■ *The abundance of the elements in the solar system from H to Zn.* The chart shows a general decline in abundance with increasing mass among the first 30 elements. The decline continues beyond zinc. (Notice that the scale on the vertical axis is logarithmic, that is, it progresses in powers of 10. The abundance of nitrogen, for example, is $1/10,000$ ($1/10^4$) of the abundance of hydrogen. All abundances are plotted as the number of atoms per 10^{12} atoms of H. (The fact that the abundances of Li, Be, and B, as well as those of the elements near Fe, do not follow the general decline is a consequence of the way that elements are synthesized in stars.)

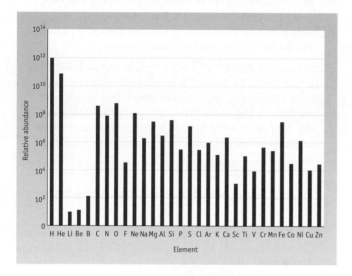

(a) What is the most abundant main group metal?
(b) What is the most abundant nonmetal?
(c) What is the most abundant metalloid?
(d) Which of the transition elements is most abundant?
(e) Which halogens are included on this plot, and which is the most abundant?

89. Copper atoms
(a) ■ What is the average mass of one copper atom?
(b) Students in a college computer science class once sued the college because they were asked to calculate the cost of one atom and could not do it. But you are in a chemistry course, and you can do this. (See E. Felsenthal, *Wall Street Journal,* May 9, 1995.) If the cost of 2.0 mm diameter copper wire (99.999% pure) is currently $41.70 for 7.0 g, what is the cost of one copper atom?

90. Which of the following is impossible?
(a) silver foil that is 1.2×10^{-4} m thick
(b) a sample of potassium that contains 1.784×10^{24} atoms
(c) a gold coin of mass 1.23×10^{-3} kg
(d) 3.43×10^{-27} mol of S_8 molecules

91. Reviewing the periodic table.
(a) Name the element in Group 2A and the fifth period.
(b) Name the element in the fifth period and Group 4B.
(c) Which element is in the second period in Group 4A?
(d) Which element is in the fourth period in Group 5A?
(e) Which halogen is in the fifth period?
(f) Which alkaline earth element is in the third period?
(g) Which noble gas element is in the fourth period?
(h) Name the nonmetal in Group 6A and the third period.
(i) Name a metalloid in the fourth period.

92. ■ Give two examples of nonmetallic elements that have allotropes. Name those elements, and describe the allotropes of each.

93. ■ In each case, decide which represents more mass:
(a) 0.5 mol of Na, 0.5 mol of Si, or 0.25 mol of U
(b) 9.0 g of Na, 0.50 mol of Na, or 1.2×10^{22} atoms of Na
(c) 10 atoms of Fe or 10 atoms of K

94. The recommended daily allowance (RDA) of iron in your diet is 15 mg. How many moles is this? How many atoms?

95. Put the following elements in order from smallest to largest mass:
(a) 3.79×10^{24} atoms Fe   (e) 9.221 mol Na
(b) 19.921 mol H_2 (f) 4.07×10^{24} atoms Al
(c) 8.576 mol C   (g) 9.2 mol Cl_2
(d) 7.4 mol Si

96. ■ ▲ When a sample of phosphorus burns in air, the compound P_4O_{10} forms. One experiment showed that 0.744 g of phosphorus formed 1.704 g of P_4O_{10}. Use this information to determine the ratio of the atomic weights of phosphorus and oxygen (mass P/mass O). If the atomic weight of oxygen is assumed to be 16.000 u, calculate the atomic weight of phosphorus.

97. ▲ Although carbon-12 is now used as the standard for atomic weights, this has not always been the case. Early attempts at classification used hydrogen as the standard, with the weight of hydrogen being set equal to 1.0000 u. Later attempts defined atomic weights using oxygen (with a weight of 16.0000). In each instance, the atomic weights of the other elements were defined relative to these masses. (To answer this question, you need more precise data on current atomic weights: H, 1.00794 u; O, 15.9994 u.)
(a) If H = 1.0000 u was used as a standard for atomic weights, what would the atomic weight of oxygen be? What would be the value of Avogadro's number under these circumstances?
(b) Assuming the standard is O = 16.0000, determine the value for the atomic weight of hydrogen and the value of Avogadro's number.

▲ more challenging   ■ in OWL   Blue-numbered questions answered in Appendix O

98. ■ A reagent occasionally used in chemical synthesis is sodium–potassium alloy. (Alloys are mixtures of metals, and Na-K has the interesting property that it is a liquid.) One formulation of the alloy (the one that melts at the lowest temperature) contains 68 atom percent K; that is, out of every 100 atoms, 68 are K and 32 are Na. What is the mass percent of potassium in sodium–potassium alloy?

99. Write formulas for all of the compounds that can be made by combining the cations NH_4^+ and Ni^{2+} with the anions CO_3^{2-} and SO_4^{2-}.

100. How many electrons are in a strontium atom (Sr)? Does an atom of Sr gain or lose electrons when forming an ion? How many electrons are gained or lost by the atom? When Sr forms an ion, the ion has the same number of electrons as which one of the noble gases?

101. Which of the following compounds has the highest mass percent of chlorine?
  (a) BCl_3 (d) $AlCl_3$
  (b) $AsCl_3$ (e) PCl_3
  (c) $GaCl_3$

102. Which of the following samples has the largest number of ions?
  (a) 1.0 g of $BeCl_2$ (d) 1.0 g of $SrCO_3$
  (b) 1.0 g of $MgCl_2$ (e) 1.0 g of $BaSO_4$
  (c) 1.0 g of CaS

103. The structure of one of the bases in DNA, adenine, is shown here. Which represents the greater mass: 40.0 g of adenine or 3.0×10^{23} molecules of the compound?

104. Ionic and molecular compounds of the halogens.
  (a) What are the names of BaF_2, $SiCl_4$, and $NiBr_2$?
  (b) Which of the compounds in part (a) are ionic, and which are molecular?
  (c) Which has the larger mass, 0.50 mol of BaF_2, 0.50 mol of $SiCl_4$, or 1.0 mol of $NiBr_2$?

105. ■ A drop of water has a volume of about 0.050 mL. How many molecules of water are in a drop of water? (Assume water has a density of 1.00 g/cm³.)

106. Capsaicin, the compound that gives the hot taste to chili peppers, has the formula $C_{18}H_{27}NO_3$.
  (a) Calculate its molar mass.
  (b) If you eat 55 mg of capsaicin, what amount (moles) have you consumed?
  (c) Calculate the mass percent of each element in the compound.
  (d) What mass of carbon (in milligrams) is there in 55 mg of capsaicin?

107. Calculate the molar mass and the mass percent of each element in the blue solid compound $Cu(NH_3)_4SO_4 \cdot H_2O$. What is the mass of copper and the mass of water in 10.5 g of the compound?

108. Write the molecular formula, and calculate the molar mass for each of the molecules shown here. Which has the larger percentage of carbon? Of oxygen?
  (a) Ethylene glycol (used in antifreeze)

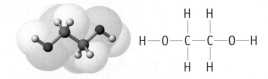

  (b) Dihydroxyacetone (used in artificial tanning lotions)

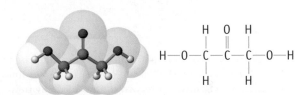

  (c) Ascorbic acid, commonly known as vitamin C

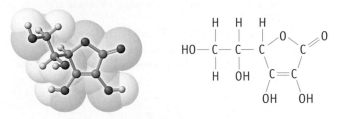

109. Malic acid, an organic acid found in apples, contains C, H, and O in the following ratios: $C_1H_{1.50}O_{1.25}$. What is the empirical formula of malic acid?

110. Your doctor has diagnosed you as being anemic—that is, as having too little iron in your blood. At the drugstore, you find two iron-containing dietary supplements: one with iron(II) sulfate, $FeSO_4$, and the other with iron(II) gluconate, $Fe(C_6H_{11}O_7)_2$. If you take 100. mg of each compound, which will deliver more atoms of iron?

111. A compound composed of iron and carbon monoxide, $Fe_x(CO)_y$, is 30.70% iron. What is the empirical formula for the compound?

112. Ma huang, an extract from the ephedra species of plants, contains ephedrine. The Chinese have used this herb for more than 5000 years to treat asthma. More recently, the substance has been used in diet pills that can be purchased over the counter in herbal medicine shops. However, very serious concerns have been raised regarding these pills following reports that their use led to serious heart problems.
(a) Write the molecular formula for ephedrine, and calculate its molar mass.
(b) What is the weight percent of carbon in ephedrine?
(c) Calculate the amount (moles) of ephedrine in a 0.125 g sample.
(d) How many molecules of ephedrine are there in 0.125 g? How many C atoms?

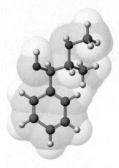

113. Saccharin is more than 300 times sweeter than sugar. It was first made in 1897, a time when it was common practice for chemists to record the taste of any new substances they synthesized.
(a) Write the molecular formula for the compound, and draw its structural formula. (S atoms are yellow.)
(b) If you ingest 125 mg of saccharin, what amount (moles) of saccharin have you ingested?
(c) What mass of sulfur is contained in 125 mg of saccharin?

114. Name each of the following compounds, and tell which ones are best described as ionic:
(a) ClF_3 (f) OF_2
(b) NCl_3 (g) KI
(c) $SrSO_4$ (h) Al_2S_3
(d) $Ca(NO_3)_2$ (i) PCl_3
(e) XeF_4 (j) K_3PO_4

115. Write the formula for each of the following compounds, and tell which ones are best described as ionic:
(a) sodium hypochlorite
(b) boron triiodide
(c) aluminum perchlorate
(d) calcium acetate
(e) potassium permanganate
(f) ammonium sulfite
(g) potassium dihydrogen phosphate
(h) disulfur dichloride
(i) chlorine trifluoride
(j) phosphorus trifluoride

116. Complete the table by placing symbols, formulas, and names in the blanks.

Cation	Anion	Name	Formula
_____	_____	ammonium bromide	_____
Ba^{2+}	_____	_____	BaS
_____	Cl^-	iron(II) chloride	_____
_____	F^-	_____	PbF_2
Al^{3+}	CO_3^{2-}	_____	_____
_____	_____	iron(III) oxide	_____

117. Empirical and molecular formulas.
(a) Fluorocarbonyl hypofluorite is composed of 14.6% C, 39.0% O, and 46.3% F. If the molar mass of the compound is 82 g/mol, determine the empirical and molecular formulas of the compound.
(b) Azulene, a beautiful blue hydrocarbon, is 93.71% C and has a molar mass of 128.16 g/mol. What are the empirical and molecular formulas of azulene?

118. Cacodyl, a compound containing arsenic, was reported in 1842 by the German chemist Robert Wilhelm Bunsen. It has an almost intolerable garlic-like odor. Its molar mass is 210 g/mol, and it is 22.88% C, 5.76% H, and 71.36% As. Determine its empirical and molecular formulas.

119. The action of bacteria on meat and fish produces a compound called cadaverine. As its name and origin imply, it stinks! (It is also present in bad breath and adds to the odor of urine.) It is 58.77% C, 13.81% H, and 27.40% N. Its molar mass is 102.2 g/mol. Determine the molecular formula of cadaverine.

120. ■ ▲ Transition metals can combine with carbon monoxide (CO) to form compounds such as $Fe_x(CO)_y$ (Study Question 2.111). Assume that you combine 0.125 g of nickel with CO and isolate 0.364 g of $Ni(CO)_x$. What is the value of x?

121. ▲ A major oil company has used a gasoline additive called MMT to boost the octane rating of its gasoline. What is the empirical formula of MMT if it is 49.5% C, 3.2% H, 22.0% O, and 25.2% Mn?

122. ▲ Elemental phosphorus is made by heating calcium phosphate with carbon and sand in an electric furnace. What is the mass percent of phosphorus in calcium phosphate? Use this value to calculate the mass of calcium phosphate (in kilograms) that must be used to produce 15.0 kg of phosphorus.

123. ▲ Chromium is obtained by heating chromium(III) oxide with carbon. Calculate the mass percent of chromium in the oxide, and then use this value to calculate the quantity of Cr_2O_3 required to produce 850 kg of chromium metal.

124. ▲ Stibnite, Sb_2S_3, is a dark gray mineral from which antimony metal is obtained. What is the mass percent of antimony in the sulfide? If you have 1.00 kg of an ore that contains 10.6% antimony, what mass of Sb_2S_3 (in grams) is in the ore?

125. ▲ Direct reaction of iodine (I_2) and chlorine (Cl_2) produces an iodine chloride, I_xCl_y, a bright yellow solid. If you completely consume 0.678 g of I_2 (when reacted with excess Cl_2) and produce 1.246 g of I_xCl_y, what is the empirical formula of the compound? A later experiment showed that the molar mass of I_xCl_y was 467 g/mol. What is the molecular formula of the compound?

126. ▲ In a reaction, 2.04 g of vanadium combined with 1.93 g of sulfur to give a pure compound. What is the empirical formula of the product?

127. ▲ Iron pyrite, often called "fool's gold," has the formula FeS_2. If you could convert 15.8 kg of iron pyrite to iron metal, what mass of the metal would you obtain?

128. Which of the following statements about 57.1 g of octane, C_8H_{18}, is (are) *not* true?
(a) 57.1 g is 0.500 mol of octane.
(b) The compound is 84.1% C by weight.
(c) The empirical formula of the compound is C_4H_9.
(d) 57.1 g of octane contains 28.0 g of hydrogen atoms.

129. The formula of barium molybdate is $BaMoO_4$. Which of the following is the formula of sodium molybdate?
(a) Na_4MoO (c) Na_2MoO_3 (e) Na_4MoO_4
(b) $NaMoO$ (d) Na_2MoO_4

130. ▲ A metal M forms a compound with the formula MCl_4. If the compound is 74.75% chlorine, what is the identity of M?

131. Pepto-Bismol, which helps provide soothing relief for an upset stomach, contains 300. mg of bismuth subsalicylate, $C_{21}H_{15}Bi_3O_{12}$, per tablet. If you take two tablets for your stomach distress, what amount (in moles) of the "active ingredient" are you taking? What mass of Bi are you consuming in two tablets?

132. ▲ The weight percent of oxygen in an oxide that has the formula MO_2 is 15.2%. What is the molar mass of this compound? What element or elements are possible for M?

133. The mass of 2.50 mol of a compound with the formula ECl_4, in which E is a nonmetallic element, is 385 g. What is the molar mass of ECl_4? What is the identity of E?

134. ▲ The elements A and Z combine to produce two different compounds: A_2Z_3 and AZ_2. If 0.15 mol of A_2Z_3 has a mass of 15.9 g and 0.15 mol of AZ_2 has a mass of 9.3 g, what are the atomic masses of A and Z?

135. ▲ Polystyrene can be prepared by heating styrene with tribromobenzoyl peroxide in the absence of air. A sample prepared by this method has the empirical formula $Br_3C_6H_3(C_8H_8)_r$, where the value of n can vary from sample to sample. If one sample has 10.46% Br, what is the value of n?

136. A sample of hemoglobin is found to be 0.335% iron. If hemoglobin contains one iron atom per molecule, what is the molar mass of hemoglobin? What is the molar mass if there are four iron atoms per molecule?

137. ▲ Consider an atom of ^{64}Zn.
(a) Calculate the density of the nucleus in grams per cubic centimeter, knowing that the nuclear radius is 4.8×10^{-6} nm and the mass of the ^{64}Zn atom is 1.06×10^{-22} g. (Recall that the volume of a sphere is $[4/3]\pi r^3$.)
(b) Calculate the density of the space occupied by the electrons in the zinc atom, given that the atomic radius is 0.125 nm and the electron mass is 9.11×10^{-28} g.
(c) Having calculated these densities, what statement can you make about the relative densities of the parts of the atom?

138. ▲ Estimating the radius of a lead atom.
(a) You are given a cube of lead that is 1.000 cm on each side. The density of lead is 11.35 g/cm³. How many atoms of lead are in the sample?
(b) Atoms are spherical; therefore, the lead atoms in this sample cannot fill all the available space. As an approximation, assume that 60% of the space of the cube is filled with spherical lead atoms. Calculate the volume of one lead atom from this information. From the calculated volume (V) and the formula $(4/3)\pi r^3$ for the volume of a sphere, estimate the radius (r) of a lead atom.

139. A piece of nickel foil, 0.550 mm thick and 1.25 cm square, is allowed to react with fluorine, F_2, to give a nickel fluoride.
(a) How many moles of nickel foil were used? (The density of nickel is 8.902 g/cm³.)
(b) If you isolate 1.261 g of the nickel fluoride, what is its formula?
(c) What is its complete name?

140. ▲ Uranium is used as a fuel, primarily in the form of uranium(IV) oxide, in nuclear power plants. This question considers some uranium chemistry.

(a) A small sample of uranium metal (0.169 g) is heated to between 800 and 900°C in air to give 0.199 g of a dark green oxide, U_xO_y. How many moles of uranium metal were used? What is the empirical formula of the oxide, U_xO_y? What is the name of the oxide? How many moles of U_xO_y must have been obtained?

(b) The naturally occurring isotopes of uranium are ^{234}U, ^{235}U, and ^{238}U. Knowing that uranium's atomic weight is 238.02 g/mol, which isotope must be the most abundant?

(c) If the hydrated compound $UO_2(NO_3)_2 \cdot z\ H_2O$ is heated gently, the water of hydration is lost. If you have 0.865 g of the hydrated compound and obtain 0.679 g of $UO_2(NO_3)_2$ on heating, how many waters of hydration are in each formula unit of the original compound? (The oxide U_xO_y is obtained if the hydrate is heated to temperatures over 800°C in the air.)

In the Laboratory

141. ■ If Epsom salt, $MgSO_4 \cdot x\ H_2O$, is heated to 250°C, all the water of hydration is lost. On heating a 1.687-g sample of the hydrate, 0.824 g of $MgSO_4$ remains. How many molecules of water occur per formula unit of $MgSO_4$?

142. The "alum" used in cooking is potassium aluminum sulfate hydrate, $KAl(SO_4)_2 \cdot x\ H_2O$. To find the value of x, you can heat a sample of the compound to drive off all of the water and leave only $KAl(SO_4)_2$. Assume you heat 4.74 g of the hydrated compound and that the sample loses 2.16 g of water. What is the value of x?

143. ■ In an experiment, you need 0.125 mol of sodium metal. Sodium can be cut easily with a knife (Figure 2.6), so if you cut out a block of sodium, what should the volume of the block be in cubic centimeters? If you cut a perfect cube, what is the length of the edge of the cube? (The density of sodium is 0.97 g/cm³.)

144. Mass spectrometric analysis showed that there are four isotopes of an unknown element having the following masses and abundances:

Isotope	Mass Number	Isotope Mass	Abundance (%)
1	136	135.9090	0.193
2	138	137.9057	0.250
3	140	139.9053	88.48
4	142	141.9090	11.07

Three elements in the periodic table that have atomic weights near these values are lanthanum (La), atomic number 57, atomic weight 139.9055; cerium (Ce), atomic number 58, atomic weight 140.115; and praeseodymium (Pr), atomic number 59, atomic weight 140.9076. Using the data above, calculate the atomic weight, and identify the element if possible.

145. ▲ Most standard analytical balances can measure accurately to the nearest 0.0001 g. Assume you have weighed out a 2.0000-g sample of carbon. How many atoms are in this sample? Assuming the indicated accuracy of the measurement, what is the largest number of atoms that can be present in the sample?

146. ▲ When analyzed, an unknown compound gave these experimental results: C, 54.0%; H, 6.00%; and O, 40.0%. Four different students used these values to calculate the empirical formulas shown here. Which answer is correct? Why did some students not get the correct answer?

(a) $C_4H_5O_2$ (c) $C_7H_{10}O_4$

(b) $C_5H_7O_3$ (d) $C_9H_{12}O_5$

147. ▲ Two general chemistry students working together in the lab weigh out 0.832 g of $CaCl_2 \cdot 2\ H_2O$ into a crucible. After heating the sample for a short time and allowing the crucible to cool, the students determine that the sample has a mass of 0.739 g. They then do a quick calculation. On the basis of this calculation, what should they do next?

(a) Congratulate themselves on a job well done.

(b) Assume the bottle of $CaCl_2 \cdot 2\ H_2O$ was mislabeled; it actually contained something different.

(c) Heat the crucible again, and then reweigh it.

148. The mass spectrum of CH_3Cl is illustrated here. You know that carbon has two stable isotopes, ^{12}C and ^{13}C with relative abundances of 98.9% and 1.1%, respectively, and chlorine has two isotopes, ^{35}Cl and ^{37}Cl with abundances of 75.77% and 24.23%, respectively.

(a) What molecular species gives rise to the lines at m/Z of 50 and 52? Why is the line at 52 about 1/3 the height of the line at 50?

(b) What species might be responsible for the line at $m/Z = 51$?

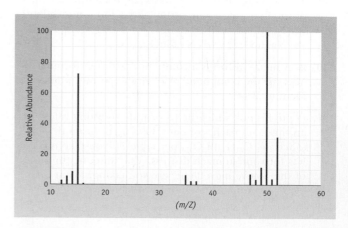

▲ more challenging   ■ in OWL   Blue-numbered questions answered in Appendix O

Summary and Conceptual Questions

The following questions may use concepts from this and the previous chapter.

149. ▲ Identify, from the list below, the information needed to calculate the number of atoms in 1.00 cm³ of iron. Outline the procedure used in this calculation.
    (a) the structure of solid iron
    (b) the molar mass of iron
    (c) Avogadro's number
    (d) the density of iron
    (e) the temperature
    (f) iron's atomic number
    (g) the number of iron isotopes

150. Consider the plot of relative element abundances on page 106. Is there a relationship between abundance and atomic number? Is there any difference between the relative abundance of an element of even atomic number and the relative abundance of an element of odd atomic number?

151. The photo here depicts what happens when a coil of magnesium ribbon and a few calcium chips are placed in water.
    (a) Based on their relative reactivities, what might you expect to see when barium, another Group 2A element, is placed in water?
    (b) Give the period in which each element (Mg, Ca, and Ba) is found; what correlation do you think you might find between the reactivity of these elements and their positions in the periodic table?

Magnesium *(left)* and calcium *(right)* in water.

152. A jar contains some number of jelly beans. To find out precisely how many are in the jar, you could dump them out and count them. How could you estimate their number without counting each one? (Chemists need to do just this kind of "bean counting" when they work with atoms and molecules. They are too small to count one by one, so they have worked out other methods to "count atoms.")

How many jelly beans are in the jar?

153. Cobalt(II) chloride hexahydrate, dissolves readily in water to give a red solution. If we use this solution as an "ink," we can write secret messages on paper. The writing is not visible when the water evaporates from the paper. When the paper is heated, however, the message can be read. Explain the chemistry behind this observation.

A solution of CoCl₂ · 6 H₂O.

Using the secret ink to write on paper.

Heating the paper reveals the writing.

3 | Chemical Reactions

A "black smoker" deep in the Pacific Ocean along the East Pacific Rise.

National Oceanic and Atmospheric Adminstration/Department of Commerce

Black Smokers

In 1977, scientists were exploring the junction of two of the tectonic plates that form the floor of the Pacific Ocean. There they found thermal springs gushing a hot, black soup of minerals. Seawater seeps into cracks in the ocean floor, and, as it sinks deeper into the earth's crust, the water is superheated to between 300 and 400 °C by the magma of the earth's core. This superhot water dissolves minerals in the crust and is pushed back to the surface. When this hot water, now laden with dissolved metal cations and rich in anions such as sulfide and sulfate, gushes through the surface, it cools, and metal sulfates, such as calcium sulfate, and sulfides—such as those of copper, manganese, iron, zinc, and nickel—precipitate. Many metal sulfides are black, and the plume of material coming from the sea bottom looks like black "smoke"; thus, the vents have been called "black smokers." The solid sulfides and other minerals settle around the edges of the vent on the sea floor and eventually form a "chimney" of precipitated minerals.

Question:

1. Write balanced, net ionic equations for the reactions of Fe^{2+} and Bi^{3+} with H_2S and for Ca^{2+} with sulfate ions.

Answer to this question is in Appendix Q.

Chemical reactions are the heart of chemistry. We begin a chemical reaction with one set of materials and end up with different materials. Just reading this sentence involves an untold number of chemical reactions in your body. Indeed, every activity of living things depends on carefully regulated chemical reactions. Our objective in this chapter is to introduce you to the symbolism used to represent chemical reactions and to describe various types of common chemical reactions.

Chemistry.ₒ.Now™

Throughout the text this icon introduces an opportunity for self-study or to explore interactive tutorials by signing in at **www.cengage.com/login**.

3.1 Introduction to Chemical Equations

When a stream of chlorine gas, Cl_2, is directed onto solid phosphorus, P_4, the mixture bursts into flame, and a chemical reaction produces liquid phosphorus trichloride, PCl_3 (Figure 3.1). We can depict this reaction using a **balanced chemical equation**.

$$P_4(s) + 6\ Cl_2(g) \longrightarrow 4\ PCl_3(\ell)$$

Reactants   Product

$$P_4(s) + 6\ Cl_2(g) \longrightarrow 4\ PCl_3(\ell)$$

REACTANTS   PRODUCT

FIGURE 3.1 Reaction of solid white phosphorus with chlorine gas. The product is liquid phosphorus trichloride.

On Monday, August 7, 1774, the Englishman Joseph Priestley (1733–1804) isolated oxygen. (The Swedish chemist Carl Scheele [1742–1786] also discovered the element, perhaps in 1773 or earlier.) Priestley heated solid mercury(II) oxide, HgO, causing the oxide to decompose to mercury and oxygen.

$$2 \; HgO(s) \longrightarrow 2 \; Hg(\ell) + O_2(g)$$

He did not immediately understand the significance of the discovery, but he mentioned it to the French chemist Antoine Lavoisier in October, 1774. One of Lavoisier's contributions to science was his recognition of the importance of exact scientific measure-

The decomposition of red mercury(II) oxide. The decomposition reaction gives mercury metal and oxygen gas. The mercury is seen as a film on the surface of the test tube.

Charles D. Winters

ments and of carefully planned experiments, and he applied these methods to the study of oxygen. From this work, Lavoisier proposed that oxygen was an element, that it was one of the constituents of the compound water, and that burning involved a reaction with oxygen. He also mistakenly came to believe Priestley's gas was present in all acids, and so he named it "oxygen," from the Greek words meaning "to form an acid."

In other experiments, Lavoisier observed that the heat produced by a guinea pig when exhaling a given amount of carbon dioxide is similar to the quantity of heat produced by burning carbon to give the same amount of carbon dioxide. From these and other experiments he concluded that, "Respiration is a combustion, slow it is true, but otherwise perfectly similar to that of charcoal." Although he did not understand the details of the process, this was an important step in the development of biochemistry.

Lavoisier was a prodigious scientist, and the principles of naming chemical substances that he introduced are still in use today. Further, he wrote a textbook in which he applied the principles of the conservation of matter to chemistry, and he used the idea to write early versions of chemical equations.

Because Lavoisier was an aristocrat, he came under suspicion during the Reign of Terror of the French Revolution. He was an investor in the Ferme Générale, the infamous

tax-collecting organization in 18th-century France. Tobacco was a monopoly product of the Ferme Générale, and it was common to cheat the purchaser by adding water to the tobacco, a practice that Lavoisier opposed. Nonetheless, because of his involvement with the Ferme, his career was cut short by the guillotine on May 8, 1794, on the charge of "adding water to the people's tobacco."

Lavoisier and his wife, as painted in 1788 by Jacques-Louis David. Lavoisier was then 45, and his wife, Marie Anne Pierrette Paulze, was 30. (The Metropolitan Museum of Art, Purchase, Mr. and Mrs. Charles Wrightsman gift, in honor of Everett Fahy, 1997. Photograph © 1989 The Metropolitan Museum of Art.)

■ **Information from Chemical Equations**
The same number of atoms must exist after a reaction as before it takes place. However, these atoms are arranged differently. In the phosphorus/chlorine reaction, for example, the P atoms were in the form of P_4 molecules before reaction but appear in the PCl_3 molecules after reaction.

In a chemical equation, the formulas for the **reactants** (the substances combined in the reaction) are written to the left of the arrow, and the formulas of the **products** (the substances produced) are written to the right of the arrow. The physical states of reactants and products can also be indicated. The symbol (s) indicates a solid, (g) a gas, and (ℓ) a liquid. A substance dissolved in water, that is, an *aqueous* solution of a substance, is indicated by (aq).

In the 18th century, the French scientist Antoine Lavoisier (1743–1794) introduced the **law of conservation of matter**, which states that *matter can neither be created nor destroyed*. This means that if the total mass of reactants is 10 g, and if the reaction completely converts reactants to products, you must end up with 10 g of products. This also means that if 1000 atoms of a particular element are contained in the reactants, then those 1000 atoms must appear in the products in some fashion.

When applied to the reaction of phosphorus and chlorine, the law of conservation of matter tells us that 1 molecule of phosphorus, P_4 (with 4 phosphorus atoms) and 6 diatomic molecules of Cl_2 (with 12 atoms of Cl) are required to produce

2 Fe(s) + 3 Cl$_2$(g) $\longrightarrow$ 2 FeCl$_3$(s)

REACTANTS   PRODUCT

FIGURE 3.2 The reaction of iron and chlorine. Here, hot iron gauze is inserted into a flask containing chlorine gas. The heat from the reaction causes the iron gauze to glow, and brown iron(III) chloride forms.

four molecules of PCl$_3$. Because each PCl$_3$ molecule contains 1 P atom and 3 Cl atoms, the four PCl$_3$ molecules are needed to account for 4 P atoms and 12 Cl atoms in the product.

$$
\begin{array}{cc}
6 \times 2 = & 4 \times 3 = \\
12 \text{ Cl atoms} & 12 \text{ Cl atoms}
\end{array}
$$

$$\text{P}_4(s) + 6 \text{ Cl}_2(g) \longrightarrow 4 \text{ PCl}_3(\ell)$$

4 P atoms   4 P atoms

Next, consider the balanced equation for the reaction of iron and and chlorine (Figure 3.2). In this case, there are two iron atoms and six chlorine atoms on both sides of the equation.

$$2 \text{ Fe}(s) + 3 \text{ Cl}_2(g) \longrightarrow 2 \text{ FeCl}_3(s)$$

stoichiometric coefficients

The numbers in front of formulas in balanced chemical equations are required by the law of conservation of matter. They can be read as a number of atoms (2 atoms of Fe), molecules (3 molecules of Cl$_2$), or formula units (2 formula units of the ionic compound FeCl$_3$). They can refer equally well to amounts of reactants and products: 2 moles of solid iron combine with 3 moles of chlorine gas to produce 2 moles of solid FeCl$_3$. The relationship between the quantities of chemical reactants and products is called **stoichiometry** (pronounced "stoy-key-AHM-uh-tree") (▶ Chapter 4), and the coefficients in a balanced equation are the **stoichiometric coefficients**.

Chemistry..Now™

Sign in at **www.cengage.com/login** and go to Chapter 3 Contents to see Screens 3.2 and 3.3 for exercises on **the conservation of mass in reactions.**

EXERCISE 3.1 Chemical Reactions

The reaction of aluminum with bromine is shown on page 67. The equation for the reaction is

$$2 \text{ Al(s)} + 3 \text{ Br}_2(\ell) \rightarrow \text{Al}_2\text{Br}_6(\text{s})$$

(a) What are the stoichiometric coefficients in this equation?

(b) If you were to use 8000 atoms of Al, how many molecules of Br_2 are required to consume the Al completely?

3.2 Balancing Chemical Equations

Balancing a chemical equation ensures that the same number of atoms of each element appears on both sides of the equation. Many chemical equations can be balanced by trial and error, although some will involve more trial than others.

One general class of chemical reactions is the reaction of metals or nonmetals with oxygen to give oxides of the general formula M_xO_y. For example, iron reacts with oxygen to give iron(III) oxide (Figure 3.3a).

$$4 \text{ Fe(s)} + 3 \text{ O}_2(\text{g}) \rightarrow 2 \text{ Fe}_2\text{O}_3(\text{s})$$

The nonmetals sulfur and oxygen react to form sulfur dioxide (Figure 3.3b),

$$\text{S(s)} + \text{O}_2(\text{g}) \rightarrow \text{SO}_2(\text{g})$$

and phosphorus, P_4, reacts vigorously with oxygen to give tetraphosphorus decaoxide, P_4O_{10} (Figure 3.3c).

$$\text{P}_4(\text{s}) + 5 \text{ O}_2(\text{g}) \rightarrow \text{P}_4\text{O}_{10}(\text{s})$$

The equations written above are balanced. The same number of iron, sulfur, or phosphorus atoms and oxygen atoms occurs on each side of these equations.

The **combustion**, or burning, of a fuel in oxygen is accompanied by the evolution of energy. You are familiar with combustion reactions such as the burning of octane, C_8H_{18}, a component of gasoline, in an automobile engine:

$$2 \text{ C}_8\text{H}_{18}(\ell) + 25 \text{ O}_2(\text{g}) \rightarrow 16 \text{ CO}_2(\text{g}) + 18 \text{ H}_2\text{O(g)}$$

FIGURE 3.3 Reactions of a metal and two nonmetals with oxygen. (See ChemistryNow, Screen 3.4, Balancing Chemical Equations, for a video of the phosphorus and oxygen reaction.)

Charles D. Winters

(a) Reaction of iron and oxygen to give iron(III) oxide, Fe_2O_3.

(b) Reaction of sulfur (in the spoon) with oxygen.

(c) Reaction of phosphorus and oxygen to give tetraphosphorus decaoxide, P_4O_{10}.

In all combustion reactions, some or all the elements in the reactants end up as oxides, compounds containing oxygen. When the reactant is a hydrocarbon (a compound such as gasoline, natural gas, or propane that contains only C and H), the products of complete combustion are always just carbon dioxide and water.

When balancing chemical equations, there are two important things to remember.

- Formulas for reactants and products must be correct, or the equation is meaningless.
- Subscripts in the formulas of reactants and products cannot be changed to balance equations. Changing the subscripts changes the identity of the substance. For example, you cannot change CO_2 to CO to balance an equation; carbon monoxide, CO, and carbon dioxide, CO_2, are different compounds.

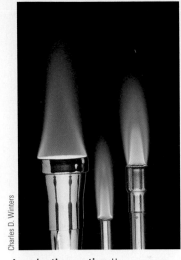

A combustion reaction. Here, propane, C_3H_8, burns to give CO_2 and H_2O. These simple oxides are always the products of the complete combustion of a hydrocarbon.

As an example of equation balancing, let us write the balanced equation for the complete combustion of propane, C_3H_8.

Step 1. *Write correct formulas for the reactants and products.*

$$C_3H_8(g) + O_2(g) \xrightarrow{\text{unbalanced equation}} CO_2(g) + H_2O(\ell)$$

Here, propane and oxygen are the reactants, and carbon dioxide and water are the products.

Step 2. *Balance the C atoms.* In combustion reactions such as this, it is usually best to balance the carbon atoms first and leave the oxygen atoms until the end (because the oxygen atoms are often found in more than one product). In this case, three carbon atoms are in the reactants, so three must occur in the products. Three CO_2 molecules are therefore required on the right side:

$$C_3H_8(g) + O_2(g) \xrightarrow{\text{unbalanced equation}} 3\ CO_2(g) + H_2O(\ell)$$

Step 3. *Balance the H atoms.* Propane, the reactant, contains 8 H atoms. Each molecule of water has two hydrogen atoms, so four molecules of water account for the required eight hydrogen atoms on the right side:

$$C_3H_8(g) + O_2(g) \xrightarrow{\text{unbalanced equation}} 3\ CO_2(g) + 4\ H_2O(\ell)$$

Step 4. *Balance the O atoms.* Ten oxygen atoms are on the right side ($3 \times 2 = 6$ in CO_2 plus $4 \times 1 = 4$ in H_2O). Therefore, five O_2 molecules are needed to supply the required 10 oxygen atoms:

$$C_3H_8(g) + 5\ O_2(g) \rightarrow 3\ CO_2(g) + 4\ H_2O(\ell)$$

Step 5. *Verify that the number of atoms of each element is balanced.* The equation shows three carbon atoms, eight hydrogen atoms, and ten oxygen atoms on each side.

Chemistry．Now™

Sign in at **www.cengage.com/login** and go to Chapter 3 Contents to see Screen 3.4 for an exercise and a tutorial on **balancing the chemical equations for a series of combustion reactions.**

Problem Write the balanced equation for the combustion of ammonia ($NH_3 + O_2$) to give NO and H_2O.

Strategy First, write the unbalanced equation. Next, balance the N atoms, then the H atoms, and finally, balance the O atoms.

Solution

Step 1. Write correct formulas for the reactants and products. The unbalanced equation for the combustion is

$$NH_3(g) + O_2(g) \xrightarrow{\text{unbalanced equation}} NO(g) + H_2O(\ell)$$

Step 2. *Balance the N atoms.* There is one N atom on each side of the equation. The N atoms are in balance, at least for the moment.

$$NH_3(g) + O_2(g) \xrightarrow{\text{unbalanced equation}} NO(g) + H_2O(\ell)$$

Step 3. *Balance the H atoms.* There are three H atoms on the left and two on the right. To have the same number on each side, let us use two molecules of NH_3 on the left and three molecules of H_2O on the right (which gives us six H atoms on each side).

$$2\ NH_3(g) + O_2(g) \xrightarrow{\text{unbalanced equation}} NO(g) + 3\ H_2O(\ell)$$

Notice that when we balance the H atoms, the N atoms are no longer balanced. To bring them into balance, let us use 2 NO molecules on the right.

$$2\ NH_3(g) + O_2(g) \xrightarrow{\text{unbalanced equation}} 2\ NO(g) + 3\ H_2O(\ell)$$

Step 4. *Balance the O atoms.* After Step 3, there are two O atoms on the left side and five on the right. That is, there are an even number of O atoms on the left and an odd number on the right. Because there cannot be an odd number of O atoms on the left (O atoms are paired in O_2 molecules), multiply each coefficient on both sides of the equation by 2 so that an even number of oxygen atoms (10) can now occur on the right side:

$$4\ NH_3(g) + O_2(g) \xrightarrow{\text{unbalanced equation}} 4\ NO(g) + 6\ H_2O(\ell)$$

Now the oxygen atoms can be balanced by having five O_2 molecules on the left side of the equation:

$$4\ NH_3(g) + 5\ O_2(g) \xrightarrow{\text{balanced equation}} 4\ NO(g) + 6\ H_2O(\ell)$$

Step 5. *Verify the result.* Four N atoms, 12 H atoms, and 10 O atoms occur on each side of the equation.

Comment An alternative way to write this equation is

$$2\ NH_3(g) + \tfrac{5}{2}\ O_2(g) \rightarrow 2\ NO(g) + 3\ H_2O(\ell)$$

where a fractional coefficient has been used. This equation is correctly balanced and will be useful under some circumstances. In general, however, we balance equations with whole-number coefficients.

EXERCISE 3.2 Balancing the Equation for a Combustion Reaction

(a) Butane gas, C_4H_{10}, can burn completely in air [use $O_2(g)$ as the other reactant] to give carbon dioxide gas and water vapor. Write a balanced equation for this combustion reaction.

(b) Write a balanced chemical equation for the complete combustion of liquid tetraethyllead, $Pb(C_2H_5)_4$ (which was used until the 1970s as a gasoline additive). The products of combustion are $PbO(s)$, $H_2O(\ell)$, and $CO_2(g)$.

3.3 Introduction to Chemical Equilibrium

To this point, we have treated chemical reactions as proceeding in one direction only, with reactants being converted completely to products. Nature, however, is more complex than this. Chemical reactions are reversible, and many reactions lead to incomplete conversion of reactants to products.

A good example of a reversible reaction that does not proceed completely to products is the reaction of nitrogen with hydrogen to form ammonia gas, a

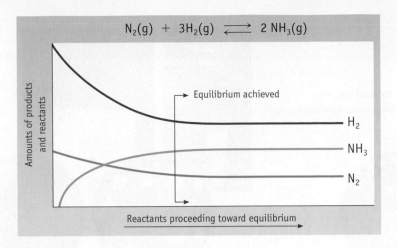

$$N_2(g) \ + \ 3H_2(g) \ \rightleftharpoons \ 2\,NH_3(g)$$

Equilibrium achieved

H₂

NH₃

N₂

Amounts of products and reactants

Reactants proceeding toward equilibrium

FIGURE 3.4 The reaction of N₂ and H₂ to produce NH₃. N₂ and H₂ in a 1:3 mixture react to produce some NH₃. As the reaction proceeds, the rate or speed of NH₃ production slows, as does the rate of consumption of N₂ and H₂. Eventually, the amounts of N₂ and H₂, and NH₃ no longer change. At this point, the reaction has reached equilibrium. Nonetheless, the forward reaction to produce NH₃ continues, as does the reverse reaction (the decomposition of NH₃).

compound used extensively both as a fertilizer and in the production of other fertilizers.

$$N_2(g) \ + \ 3\ H_2(g) \ \rightarrow \ 2\,NH_3(g)$$

Nitrogen and hydrogen react to form ammonia, but, under the conditions of the reaction, the product ammonia also breaks down into nitrogen and hydrogen in the reverse reaction.

$$2\,NH_3(g) \ \rightarrow \ N_2(g) \ + \ 3\ H_2(g)$$

Let us consider what would happen if we mixed nitrogen and hydrogen in a closed container under the proper conditions for the reaction to occur. At first, N_2 and H_2 react to produce some ammonia. As the ammonia is produced, however, some NH_3 molecules decompose to re-form nitrogen and hydrogen in the reverse reaction. At the beginning of the process, the forward reaction to give NH_3 predominates, but, as the reactants are consumed, the rate of the forward reaction is progressively slower. At the same time, the reverse reaction speeds up as the amount of ammonia increases. Eventually, the rate or speed of the forward reaction will equal the rate of the reverse reaction. Once this occurs, no further *macroscopic* change is observed; the amounts of nitrogen, hydrogen, and ammonia in the container stop changing (Figure 3.4). We say the system has reached **chemical equilibrium**. The reaction vessel will contain all three substances: nitrogen, hydrogen, and ammonia. Because both the forward and reverse processes are still occurring (but at equal rates), we refer to this state as a **dynamic equilibrium**. We represent a system at dynamic equilibrium by writing a double arrow symbol ($\rightleftharpoons$) connecting the reactants and products.

$$N_2(g) \ + \ 3\ H_2(g) \ \rightleftharpoons \ 2\,NH_3(g)$$

The formation of stalactites and stalagmites in a limestone cave is another example of a system that depends on the reversibility of a chemical reaction (Figure 3.5). Stalactites and stalagmites are made chiefly of calcium carbonate, a mineral found in underground deposits in the form of limestone, a leftover from ancient oceans. If water seeping through the limestone contains dissolved CO_2, a reaction occurs in which the mineral dissolves, giving an aqueous solution of $Ca(HCO_3)_2$.

$$CaCO_3(s) \ + \ CO_2(aq) \ + \ H_2O(\ell) \ \rightarrow \ Ca(HCO_3)_2(aq)$$

■ **Progression Toward Equilibrium**
Reactions always proceed spontaneously toward equilibrium. A reaction will never proceed on its own in a direction that takes a system further from equilibrium.

Dr. Arthor N. Palmer

FIGURE 3.5 Cave chemistry. Calcium carbonate stalactites cling to the roof of a cave, and stalagmites grow up from the cave floor. The chemistry producing these formations is a good example of the reversibility of chemical reactions.

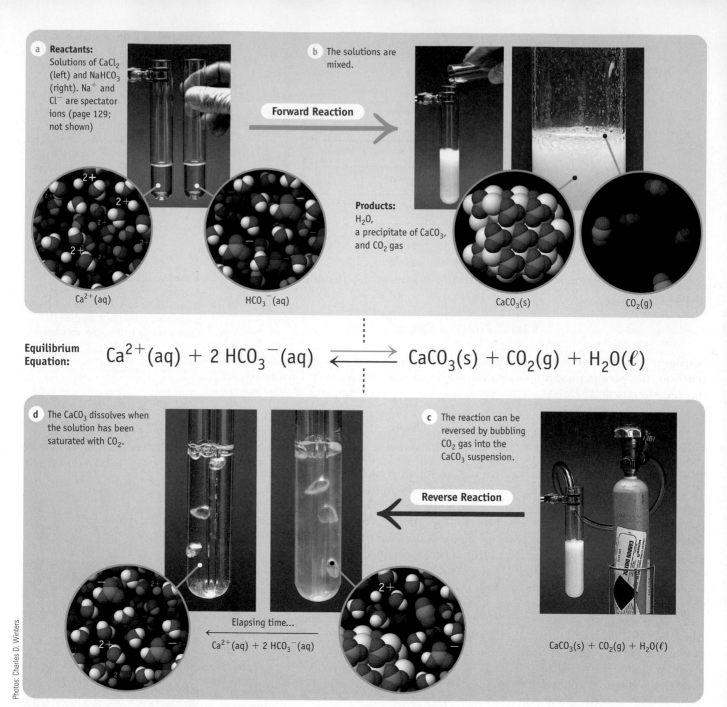

Equilibrium Equation:
$$Ca^{2+}(aq) + 2\,HCO_3^-(aq) \rightleftharpoons CaCO_3(s) + CO_2(g) + H_2O(\ell)$$

a **Reactants:** Solutions of $CaCl_2$ (left) and $NaHCO_3$ (right). Na^+ and Cl^- are spectator ions (page 129; not shown)

$Ca^{2+}(aq)$

$HCO_3^-(aq)$

b The solutions are mixed.

Forward Reaction

Products: H_2O, a precipitate of $CaCO_3$, and CO_2 gas

$CaCO_3(s)$

$CO_2(g)$

d The $CaCO_3$ dissolves when the solution has been saturated with CO_2.

Elapsing time...
$Ca^{2+}(aq) + 2\,HCO_3^-(aq)$

Reverse Reaction

c The reaction can be reversed by bubbling CO_2 gas into the $CaCO_3$ suspension.

$CaCO_3(s) + CO_2(g) + H_2O(\ell)$

FIGURE 3.6 The nature of chemical equilibrium. The experiments here demonstrate the reversibility of chemical reactions. (*top*) Solutions of $CaCl_2$ (a source of Ca^{2+} ions) and $NaHCO_3$ (a source of HCO_3^- ions) are mixed (a) and produce a precipitate of $CaCO_3$ and CO_2 gas (b). (*bottom*) If CO_2 gas is bubbled into a suspension of $CaCO_3$ (c), the reverse of the reaction displayed in the top panel occurs. That is, solid $CaCO_3$ and gaseous CO_2 produce Ca^{2+} and HCO_3^- ions (d).

When the mineral-laden water reaches a cave, the reverse reaction occurs, with CO_2 being evolved into the cave and solid $CaCO_3$ being deposited as stalagmites and stalactites.

$$Ca(HCO_3)_2(aq) \rightarrow CaCO_3(s) + CO_2(g) + H_2O(\ell)$$

Cave chemistry can be done in a laboratory (Figure 3.6) using reactions that further demonstrate the reversiblity of the reactions involved.

A key question that arises is, "When a reaction reaches equilibrium, will the reactants be converted largely to products, or will most of the reactants still be present?" The answer will depend on the nature of the compounds involved, the temperature, and other factors, and that is the subject of later chapters (▶ Chapters 16–18). For the present, though, it is useful to define **product-favored reactions** as *reactions in which reactants are completely or largely converted to products at equilibrium*. The combustion reactions we have been studying are examples of reactions that are product-favored at equilibrium, in contrast to the N_2/H_2 reaction in Figure 3.4. In fact, most of the reactions that we shall study in the rest of this chapter are product-favored reactions at equilibrium. We usually write the equations for reactions that are very product-favored using only the single arrows we have been using up to this point.

The opposite of a product-favored reaction is one that is **reactant-favored** at equilibrium. Such reactions lead to the conversion of only a small amount of the reactants to products. An example of such a reaction is the ionization of acetic acid in water, in which only a tiny fraction of the acid reacts to produce ions.

$$CH_3CO_2H(aq) + H_2O(\ell) \rightleftharpoons H_3O^+(aq) + CH_3CO_2^-(aq)$$

3.4 Chemical Reactions in Aqueous Solution

Many of the reactions you will study in your chemistry course and the reactions that occur in living systems are carried out in aqueous solution. Because reactions in aqueous solution are so important, the remainder of this chapter is an introduction to the behavior of compounds in solution and to some of the types of reactions you will observe.

A **solution** is a homogeneous mixture of two or more substances. One substance is generally considered the **solvent**, the medium in which another substance—the **solute**—is dissolved. In the human body, the solvent for chemical reactions is usually water. Water assists in transporting nutrients and waste products in and out of cells and is necessary for digestive, absorption, circulatory, and excretory functions. In fact, the human body is two-thirds water. Water is an excellent solvent to use for biochemical reactions and also for many other chemical reactions. For the next several sections of this chapter, we shall study chemical reactions that occur in **aqueous solutions** where water is the solvent.

So that you are familiar with types of reactions as you work through the book, we also want to introduce you to four major categories of reactions in aqueous solution: precipitation, acid-base, gas-forming, and oxidation-reduction reactions. As you learn about these reactions, it will be useful to look for patterns that allow you to predict the reaction products. You will notice that many of the reactions are **exchange reactions** in which *the ions of the reactants change partners*.

$$A^+B^- + C^+D^- \longrightarrow A^+D^- + C^+B^-$$

■ **Quantitative Description of Chemical Equilibrium** As you shall see in Chapters 16–18, the extent to which a reaction is product-favored can be described by a simple mathematical expression, called the equilibrium constant expression. Each chemical reaction has a numerical value for the equilibrium constant, symbolized by K. Product-favored reactions have large values of K; small K values indicate reactant-favored reactions. For the ionization of acetic acid in water, $K = 1.8 \times 10^{-5}$.

■ **Acetic Acid, a Weak Acid** Acetic acid is an example of a large number of acids called "weak acids" because only a few percent of the molecules ionize to form ionic products.

FIGURE 3.7 Precipitation of silver chloride. (a) Mixing aqueous solutions of silver nitrate and potassium chloride produces white, insoluble silver chloride, AgCl. In (b) through (d), you see a model of the process at the molecular and ionic level.

(a)

Photo, a, Charles D. Winters; b–d, model from an animation by Roy Tasker, University of Western Sydney, Australia

(b) Initially, the Ag^+ ions (silver color) and Cl^- ions (green) are widely separated.

(c) Ag^+ and Cl^- ions approach and form ion pairs.

(d) As more and more Ag^+ and Cl^- ions come together, a precipitate of solid AgCl forms.

For example, aqueous solutions of silver nitrate and potassium chloride react to produce solid silver chloride and aqueous potassium nitrate. (Figure 3.7a)

$$AgNO_3(aq) + KCl(aq) \rightarrow AgCl(s) + KNO_3(aq)$$

Recognizing that cations exchange anions in many chemical reactions gives us a good way to predict the products of precipitation, acid-base, and many gas-forming reactions.

 Module 5

3.5 Ions and Molecules in Aqueous Solution

To understand reactions occurring in aqueous solution, it is important first to understand something about the behavior of compounds in water. The water you drink every day, the oceans, and the aqueous solutions in your body contain many ions, most of which result from dissolving solid materials present in the environment (Table 3.1).

TABLE 3.1 Concentrations of Some Cations and Anions in the Environment and in Living Cells

Element	Dissolved Species	Sea Water	*Valonia*[†]	Red Blood Cells	Blood Plasma
Chlorine	Cl^-	550	50	50	100
Sodium	Na^+	460	80	11	160
Magnesium	Mg^{2+}	52	50	2.5	2
Calcium	Ca^{2+}	10	1.5	10^{-4}	2
Potassium	K^+	10	400	92	10
Carbon	HCO_3^-, CO_3^{2-}	30	<10	<10	30
Phosphorus	$H_2PO_4^-$, HPO_4^{2-}	<1	5	3	<3

*Data are taken from J. J. R. Fraústo da Silva and R. J. P. Williams: *The Biological Chemistry of the Elements,* Oxford, England, Clarendon Press, 1991. Concentrations are given in millimoles per liter. (A millimole is 1/1000 of a mole.)
[†]*Valonia* are single-celled algae that live in sea water.

Sign in at **www.cengage.com/login** to download the Go Chemistry module for this section or go to **www.ichapters.com** to purchase modules.

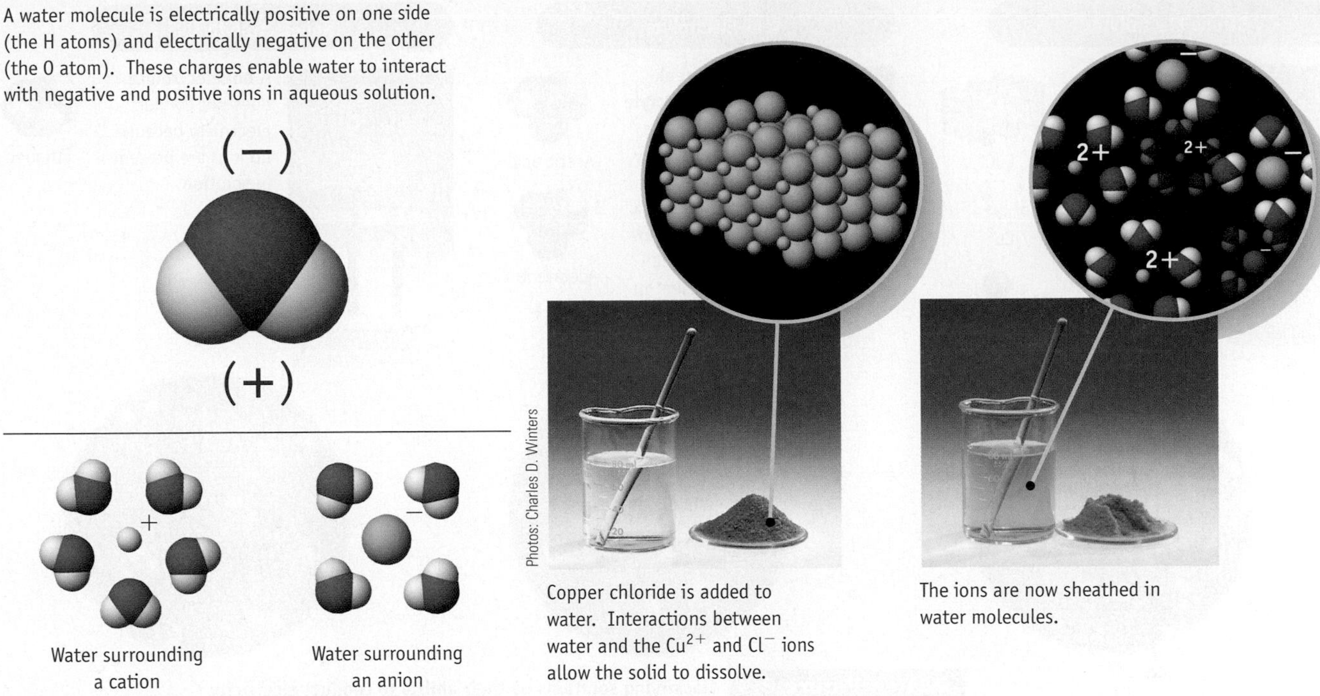

A water molecule is electrically positive on one side (the H atoms) and electrically negative on the other (the O atom). These charges enable water to interact with negative and positive ions in aqueous solution.

$(-)$

$(+)$

Water surrounding a cation

Water surrounding an anion

Photos: Charles D. Winters

Copper chloride is added to water. Interactions between water and the Cu^{2+} and Cl^- ions allow the solid to dissolve.

The ions are now sheathed in water molecules.

FIGURE 3.8 Water as a solvent for ionic substances. (a) Water molecules are attracted to both positive cations and negative anions in aqueous solution. (b) When an ionic substance dissolves in water, each ion is surrounded by water molecules. (The number of water molecules around an ion is often 6.)

Dissolving an ionic solid requires separating each ion from the oppositely charged ions that surround it in the solid state. Water is especially good at dissolving ionic compounds because each water molecule has a positively charged end and a negatively charged end (Figure 3.8). When an ionic compound dissolves in water, each negative ion becomes surrounded by water molecules with the positive end of water molecules pointing toward it, and each positive ion becomes surrounded by the negative ends of several water molecules.

The water-encased ions produced by dissolving an ionic compound are free to move about in solution. Under normal conditions, the movement of ions is random, and the cations and anions from a dissolved ionic compound are dispersed uniformly throughout the solution. However, if two **electrodes** (conductors of electricity such as copper wire) are placed in the solution and connected to a battery, ion movement is no longer random. Positive cations move through the solution to the negative electrode, and negative anions move to the positive electrode (Figure 3.9). If a light bulb is inserted into the circuit, the bulb lights, showing that ions are available to conduct charge in the solution just as electrons conduct charge in the wire part of the circuit. Compounds whose aqueous solutions conduct electricity are called **electrolytes**. *All ionic compounds that are soluble in water are electrolytes.*

For every mole of NaCl that dissolves, 1 mol of Na^+ and 1 mol of Cl^- ions enter the solution.

$$NaCl(s) \rightarrow Na^+(aq) + Cl^-(aq)$$

100% Dissociation $\equiv$ strong electrolyte

Because the solute has dissociated (broken apart) completely into ions, the solution will be a good conductor of electricity. Substances whose solutions are good

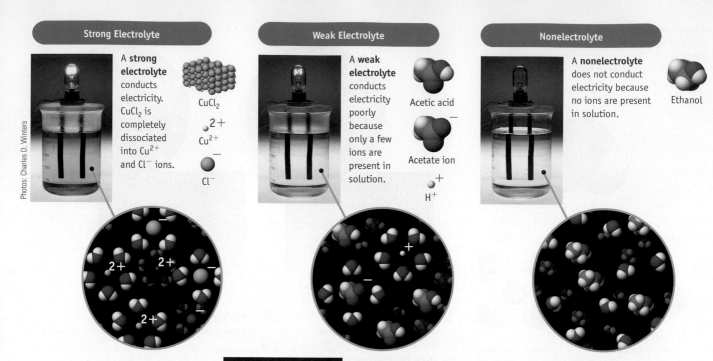

Strong Electrolyte	Weak Electrolyte	Nonelectrolyte

A **strong electrolyte** conducts electricity. $CuCl_2$ is completely dissociated into Cu^{2+} and Cl^- ions.

$CuCl_2$

Cu^{2+} 2+

Cl^- −

A **weak electrolyte** conducts electricity poorly because only a few ions are present in solution.

Acetic acid

Acetate ion   −

H^+ +

A **nonelectrolyte** does not conduct electricity because no ions are present in solution.

Ethanol

Photos: Charles D. Winters

Active Figure 3.9   Classifying solutions by their ability to conduct electricity.

Chemistry ⚛ Now™ Sign in at www.cengage.com/login and go to the Chapter Contents menu to explore an interactive version of this figure accompanied by an exercise.

electrical conductors owing to the presence of ions are **strong electrolytes** (see Figure 3.9). The ions into which an ionic compound will dissociate are given by the compound's name, and the relative amounts of these ions are given by its formula. For example, as we have seen, sodium chloride yields sodium ions (Na^+) and chloride ions (Cl^-) in solution in a 1:1 ratio. The ionic compound barium chloride, $BaCl_2$, is also a strong electrolyte. In this case, there are two chloride ions for each barium ion in solution.

$$BaCl_2(s) \rightarrow Ba^{2+}(aq) + 2\ Cl^-(aq)$$

Notice also that the chloride ions do not stay together as one unit but separate from each other into two separate chloride ions. In yet another example, the ionic compound barium nitrate yields barium ions and nitrate ions in solution. For each Ba^{2+} ion in solution, there are two NO_3^- ions.

$$Ba(NO_3)_2(s) \rightarrow Ba^{2+}(aq) + 2\ NO_3^-(aq)$$

Notice that the polyatomic ion stays together as one unit, NO_3^-, and that the two nitrate ions separate from each other.

Compounds whose aqueous solutions do not conduct electricity are called **nonelectrolytes**. The solute particles present in these aqueous solutions are molecules, not ions. *Most molecular compounds that dissolve in water are nonelectrolytes.* For example, when the molecular compound ethanol (C_2H_5OH) dissolves in water, each molecule of ethanol stays together as a single unit. We do not get ions in the solution.

$$C_2H_5OH(\ell) \rightarrow C_2H_5OH(aq)$$

■ **Dissolving Halides** When an ionic compound with halide ions dissolves in water, the halide ions are released into aqueous solution. Thus, $BaCl_2$ produces two Cl^- ions for each Ba^{2+} ion (and not Cl_2 or Cl_2^{2-} ions).

Other examples of nonelectrolytes are sucrose ($C_{12}H_{22}O_{11}$) and antifreeze (ethylene glycol, $HOCH_2CH_2OH$).

Some molecular compounds (strong acids, weak acids, and weak bases) (▶ Section 3.7), however, react with water to form ions and are thus electrolytes. Hydrogen chloride is a molecular compound, but it reacts with water to form ions, and the solution is referred to as *hydrochloric acid.*

$$HCl(g) + H_2O(\ell) \rightarrow H_3O^+(aq) + Cl^-(aq)$$

This reaction is very product-favored. Each molecule of HCl produces ions in solution so hydrochloric acid is a strong electrolyte.

A **weak electrolyte** is a molecular substance in whose aqueous solutions some of the molecules react with water to form ions but where some of the molecules (usually most) remain as molecules. Their aqueous solutions are poor conductors of electricity (see Figure 3.9). As described on page 135, the interaction of acetic acid with water is very reactant-favored. In vinegar, an aqueous solution of acetic acid, fewer than 100 molecules in every 10,000 molecules of acetic acid are ionized to form acetate and hydronium ions. Thus, aqueous acetic acid is a weak electrolyte.

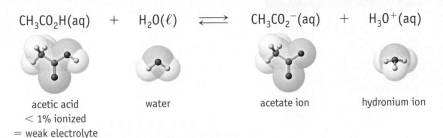

$$CH_3CO_2H(aq) \quad + \quad H_2O(\ell) \quad \rightleftharpoons \quad CH_3CO_2^-(aq) \quad + \quad H_3O^+(aq)$$

acetic acid   water   acetate ion   hydronium ion

< 1% ionized
= weak electrolyte

■ **H^+ Ions in Water** As illustrated for acetic acid in Figure 3.9, the H^+ ions from the acid are surrounded by water molecules. When writing an equation for acid ionization, we symbolize this with the H_3O^+ or hydronium ion. For more on this, see page 134.

Chemistry. Now™

Sign in at **www.cengage.com/login** and go to Chapter 3 Contents to see:
- Screen 3.5 for exercises on **the dissolving of an ionic compound**
- Screen 3.6 for information on **the types of electrolytes**

EXERCISE 3.3 Electrolytes

Epsom salt, $MgSO_4 \cdot 7\ H_2O$, is sold in drugstores and, as a solution in water, is used for various medical purposes. Methanol, CH_3OH, is dissolved in gasoline in the winter in colder climates to prevent the formation of ice in automobile fuel lines. Which of these compounds is an electrolyte, and which is a nonelectrolyte?

Solubility of Ionic Compounds in Water

Many ionic compounds dissolve completely in water, but some dissolve only to a small extent, and still others are essentially insoluble. Fortunately, we can make some general statements about which ionic compounds are water soluble. In this chapter, we consider solubility as an "either–or" question, referring to those materials that are soluble beyond a certain extent as "soluble" and to those that do not dissolve to that extent as "insoluble." To get a better idea of the amounts that will actually dissolve in a given quantity of water, we could do an experiment or perform a calculation that uses the concept of equilibrium (▶ Chapter 18).

Figure 3.10 lists broad guidelines that help predict whether a particular ionic compound is soluble in water. For example, sodium nitrate, $NaNO_3$, contains both an alkali metal cation, Na^+, and the nitrate anion, NO_3^-. The presence of either of these ions ensures that the compound is soluble in water. By contrast, calcium hydroxide is poorly soluble in water. If a spoonful of solid $Ca(OH)_2$ is added to 100 mL of water, only 0.17 g, or 0.0023 mol, will dissolve at 10 °C. Nearly all of the $Ca(OH)_2$ remains as a solid (Figure 3.10c).

Chemistry ⚛ Now™

Sign in at **www.cengage.com/login** and go to Chapter 3 Contents to see Screen 3.7 for a tutorial and simulation on **the solubility of ionic compounds in water.**

SILVER COMPOUNDS

AgNO₃   AgCl   AgOH

(a) Nitrates are generally soluble, as are chlorides (except AgCl). Hydroxides are generally not soluble.

SULFIDES

(NH₄)₂S   CdS   Sb₂S₃   PbS

(b) Sulfides are generally not soluble (exceptions include salts with NH_4^+ and Na^+).

HYDROXIDES

Photos: Charles D. Winters

NaOH   Ca(OH)₂   Fe(OH)₃   Ni(OH)₂

(c) Hydroxides are generally not soluble, except when the cation is a Group 1A metal.

SOLUBLE COMPOUNDS

Almost all salts of Na^+, K^+, NH_4^+

Salts of nitrate, NO_3^-
            chlorate, ClO_3^-
            perchlorate, ClO_4^-
            acetate, $CH_3CO_2^-$

	EXCEPTIONS
Almost all salts of Cl^-, Br^-, I^-	Halides of Ag^+, Hg_2^{2+}, Pb^{2+}
Salts containing F^-	Fluorides of Mg^{2+}, Ca^{2+}, Sr^{2+}, Ba^{2+}, Pb^{2+}
Salts of sulfate, SO_4^{2-}	Sulfates of Ca^{2+}, Sr^{2+}, Ba^{2+}, Pb^{2+}

INSOLUBLE COMPOUNDS

EXCEPTIONS

Most salts of carbonate, CO_3^{2-}
            phosphate, PO_4^{3-}
            oxalate, $C_2O_4^{2-}$
            chromate, CrO_4^{2-}
            sulfide, S^{2-}

Salts of NH_4^+ and the alkali metal cations

Most metal hydroxides and oxides   Alkali metal hydroxides and $Ba(OH)_2$

Active Figure 3.10 **Guidelines to predict the solubility of ionic compounds.** If a compound contains one of the ions in the column on the left in the top chart, it is predicted to be at least moderately soluble in water. There are exceptions, which are noted at the right. Most ionic compounds formed by the anions listed at the bottom of the chart are poorly soluble (with the exception on compounds with NH_4^+ and the alkali metal cations).

Chemistry ⚛ Now™ Sign in at www.cengage.com/login and go to the Chapter Contents menu to explore an interactive version of this figure accompanied by an exercise.

EXAMPLE 3.2 Solubility Guidelines

Problem Predict whether the following ionic compounds are likely to be water-soluble. List the ions present in solution for soluble compounds.

(a) KCl

(b) $MgCO_3$

(c) Fe_2O_3

(d) $Cu(NO_3)_2$

Strategy You must first recognize the cation and anion involved and then decide the probable water solubility based on the guidelines outlined in Figure 3.10.

Solution

(a) KCl is composed of K^+ and Cl^- ions. The presence of *either* of these ions means that the compound is likely to be soluble in water. The solution contains K^+ and Cl^- ions dissolved in water.

$$KCl(s) \rightarrow K^+(aq) + Cl^-(aq)$$

(The solubility of KCl is about 35 g in 100 mL of water at 20 °C.)

(b) Magnesium carbonate is composed of Mg^{2+} and CO_3^{2-} ions. Salts containing the carbonate ion are usually insoluble, unless combined with an ion like Na^+ or NH_4^+. Therefore, $MgCO_3$ is predicted to be insoluble in water. (The solubility of $MgCO_3$ is less than 0.2 g/100 mL of water.)

(c) Iron(III) oxide is composed of Fe^{3+} and O^{2-} ions. Oxides are soluble only when O^{2-} is combined with an alkali metal ion; Fe^{3+} is a transition metal ion, so Fe_2O_3 is insoluble.

(d) Copper(II) nitrate is composed of $Cu^{2+}(aq)$ and $NO_3^-(aq)$ ions. Nitrate salts are soluble, so this compound dissolves in water, giving ions in solution as shown in the equation below

$$Cu(NO_3)_2(s) \rightarrow Cu^{2+}(aq) + 2 NO_3^-(aq)$$

EXERCISE 3.4 Solubility of Ionic Compounds

Predict whether each of the following ionic compounds is likely to be soluble in water. If it is soluble, write the formulas of the ions present in aqueous solution.

(a) $LiNO_3$

(b) $CaCl_2$

(c) CuO

(d) $NaCH_3CO_2$

3.6 Precipitation Reactions

Module 6

A **precipitation reaction** produces a water-insoluble solid product, known as a **precipitate**. The reactants in such reactions are generally water-soluble ionic compounds. When these substances dissolve in water, they dissociate to give the appropriate cations and anions. If the cation from one compound can form an insoluble compound with the anion from the other compound in the solution, precipitation occurs. As described earlier, both silver nitrate and potassium chloride are water-soluble ionic compounds. When combined in water, they undergo an *exchange reaction* to produce insoluble silver chloride and soluble potassium nitrate (Figure 3.7).

$$AgNO_3(aq) + KCl(aq) \rightarrow AgCl(s) + KNO_3(aq)$$

Reactants	Products
$Ag^+(aq) + NO_3^-(aq)$	Insoluble AgCl(s)
$K^+(aq) + Cl^-(aq)$	$K^+(aq) + NO_3^-(aq)$

Predicting the Outcome of a Precipitation Reaction

Many combinations of positive and negative ions give insoluble substances (see Figure 3.10). For example, the solubility guidelines indicate that most compounds containing the chromate ion are not soluble (alkali metal chromates and ammonium chromate are exceptions). Thus, we can predict that yellow, solid lead(II)

FIGURE 3.11 Precipitation reactions. Many ionic compounds are insoluble in water. Guidelines for predicting the solubilities of ionic compounds are given in Figure 3.10.

(a) $Pb(NO_3)_2$ and K_2CrO_4 produce yellow, insoluble $PbCrO_4$ and soluble KNO_3.

(b) $Pb(NO_3)_2$ and $(NH_4)_2S$ produce black, insoluble PbS and soluble NH_4NO_3.

(c) $FeCl_3$ and $NaOH$ produce red, insoluble $Fe(OH)_3$ and soluble $NaCl$.

(d) $AgNO_3$ and K_2CrO_4 produce red, insoluble Ag_2CrO_4 and soluble KNO_3. See Example 3.3.

chromate will precipitate when a water-soluble lead(II) compound is combined with a water-soluble chromate compound (Figure 3.11a).

$$Pb(NO_3)_2(aq) + K_2CrO_4(aq) \rightarrow PbCrO_4(s) + 2\ KNO_3(aq)$$

Reactants	Products
$Pb^{2+}(aq) + 2\ NO_3^-(aq)$	Insoluble $PbCrO_4(s)$
$2\ K^+(aq) + CrO_4^{2-}(aq)$	$2\ K^+(aq) + 2\ NO_3^-(aq)$

Similarly, we know from the solubility guidelines that almost all metal sulfides are insoluble in water (Figure 3.11b). If a solution of a soluble metal compound comes in contact with a source of sulfide ions, the metal sulfide precipitates.

$$Pb(NO_3)_2(aq) + (NH_4)_2S(aq) \rightarrow PbS(s) + 2\ NH_4NO_3(aq)$$

Reactants	Products
$Pb^{2+}(aq) + 2\ NO_3^-(aq)$	Insoluble $PbS(s)$
$2\ NH_4^+(aq) + S^{2-}(aq)$	$2\ NH_4^+(aq) + 2\ NO_3^-(aq)$

In still another example, the solubility guidelines indicate that with the exception of the alkali metal cations (and Ba^{2+}), all metal cations form insoluble hydroxides. Thus, water-soluble iron(III) chloride and sodium hydroxide react to give insoluble iron(III) hydroxide (Figures 3.10c and 3.11c).

$$FeCl_3(aq) + 3\ NaOH(aq) \rightarrow Fe(OH)_3(s) + 3\ NaCl(aq)$$

Reactants	Products
$Fe^{3+}(aq) + 3\ Cl^-(aq)$	Insoluble $Fe(OH)_3(s)$
$3\ Na^+(aq) + 3\ OH^-(aq)$	$3\ Na^+(aq) + 3\ Cl^-(aq)$

Black tongue. Pepto-Bismol™ has anti-diarrheal, antibacterial, and antacid effects in the digestive tract, and has been used for over 100 years as an effective remedy. However, some people find their tongues blackened after taking this over-the-counter medicine. The active ingredient in Pepto-Bismol is bismuth subsalicylate. (It also contains pepsin, zinc salts, oil of wintergreen, and salol, a compound related to aspirin.) The tongue blackening comes from the reaction of bismuth ions with traces of sulfide ions found in saliva to form black Bi_2S_3. The discoloration is harmless and lasts only a few days.

Chemistry ⚛ Now™

Sign in at **www.cengage.com/login** and go to Chapter 3 Contents to see:
- Screen 3.8 for a self-study module on **types of reactions in aqueous solutions**
- Screen 3.9 for a tutorial and simulation on **precipitation reactions**

Problem Is an insoluble product formed when aqueous solutions of potassium chromate and silver nitrate are mixed? If so, write the balanced equation.

Strategy First, decide what ions are formed in solution when the reactants dissolve. Then use information in Figure 3.10 to determine whether a cation from one reactant will combine with an anion from the other reactant to form an insoluble compound.

Solution Both reactants—$AgNO_3$ and K_2CrO_4—are water-soluble. The ions Ag^+, NO_3^-, K^+, and CrO_4^{2-} are released into solution when the compounds are dissolved.

$$AgNO_3(s) \rightarrow Ag^+(aq) + NO_3^-(aq)$$

$$K_2CrO_4(s) \rightarrow 2\ K^+(aq) + CrO_4^{2-}(aq)$$

Here, Ag^+ could combine with CrO_4^{2-}, and K^+ could combine with NO_3^-. Based on the solubility guidelines, we know that the former combination, Ag_2CrO_4, is an insoluble compound, whereas KNO_3 is soluble in water. Thus, the balanced equation for the reaction of silver nitrate and potassium chromate is

$$2\ AgNO_3(aq) + K_2CrO_4(aq) \rightarrow Ag_2CrO_4(s)\ +\ 2\ KNO_3(aq)$$

Comment This reaction is illustrated in Figure 3.11d.

EXERCISE 3.5 Precipitation Reactions

In each of the following cases, does a precipitation reaction occur when solutions of the two water-soluble reactants are mixed? Give the formula of any precipitate that forms, and write a balanced chemical equation for the precipitation reactions that occur.

(a) Sodium carbonate and copper(II) chloride

(b) Potassium carbonate and sodium nitrate

(c) Nickel(II) chloride and potassium hydroxide

■ **Hair Coloring and Black Smokers** The hair-darkening reaction described on page 18 is a precipitation reaction and is much like that in "black smokers" and in the formation of Bi_2S_3 with Pepto-Bismol.

Net Ionic Equations

We have seen that when aqueous solutions of silver nitrate and potassium chloride are mixed, insoluble silver chloride forms, leaving potassium nitrate in solution (see Figure 3.7). The balanced chemical equation for this process is

$$AgNO_3(aq) + KCl(aq) \rightarrow AgCl(s) + KNO_3(aq)$$

We can represent this reaction in another way by writing an equation in which we show that the soluble ionic compounds are present in solution as dissociated ions. An aqueous solution of silver nitrate contains Ag^+ and NO_3^- ions, and an aqueous solution of potassium chloride contains K^+ and Cl^- ions. In the products, the potassium nitrate is present in solution as K^+ and NO_3^- ions. The silver chloride, however, is insoluble and thus is not present in the solution as dissociated ions. It is shown in the equation by its entire formula, AgCl.

$$\underset{\text{before reaction}}{Ag^+(aq) + NO_3^-(aq) + K^+(aq) + Cl^-(aq)} \rightarrow \underset{\text{after reaction}}{AgCl(s) + K^+(aq) + NO_3^-(aq)}$$

This type of equation is called a **complete ionic equation**.

The K^+ and NO_3^- ions are present in solution before and after reaction and so appear on both the reactant and product sides of the complete ionic equation. Such ions are often called **spectator ions** because they do not participate in the net reaction; they only "look on" from the sidelines. Little chemical information is lost if the equation is written without them, and so we can simplify the equation to

$$Ag^+(aq) + Cl^-(aq) \rightarrow AgCl(s)$$

Writing Net Ionic Equations

Net ionic equations are commonly written for chemical reactions in aqueous solution because they describe the actual chemical species involved in a reaction. To write net ionic equations, we must know which compounds exist as ions in solution.

1. Strong acids, strong bases, and soluble salts exist as ions in solution. Examples include the acids HCl and HNO_3, a base such as NaOH, and salts such as NaCl and $CuCl_2$.
2. All other species should be represented by their complete formulas. Weak acids such as acetic acid (CH_3CO_2H) exist in solutions

primarily as molecules. (See Section 3.7.) Insoluble salts such as $CaCO_3(s)$ or insoluble bases such as $Mg(OH)_2(s)$ should not be written in ionic form, even though they are ionic compounds.

The best way to approach writing net ionic equations is to follow precisely a set of steps:

1. Write a complete, balanced equation. Indicate the state of each substance (aq, s, ℓ, g).
2. Next, rewrite the whole equation, writing all strong acids, strong bases, and soluble

salts as ions. (Consider only species labeled with an "(aq)" suffix in this step.)
3. Some ions may remain unchanged in the reaction (the ions that appear in the equation both as reactants or products). These "spectator ions" are not part of the chemistry that is going on. You can cancel them from each side of the equation.
4. Like molecular equations, net ionic equations must be balanced. The same number of atoms must appear on each side of the arrow, and the sum of the ion charges on the two sides must also be equal.

■ **Net Ionic Equations** All chemical equations, including net ionic equations, must be balanced. The same number of atoms of each kind must appear on both the product and reactant sides. In addition, the sum of positive and negative charges must be the same on both sides of the equation.

The balanced equation that results from leaving out the spectator ions is the **net ionic equation** for the reaction. *Only the aqueous ions, insoluble compounds, and weak- or nonelectrolytes* (which can be soluble molecular compounds such as sugar, weak acids, weak bases, or gases) *that participate in a chemical reaction are included in the net ionic equation.*

Leaving out the spectator ions does not imply that K^+ and NO_3^- ions are unimportant in the $AgNO_3$ + KCl reaction. Indeed, Ag^+ ions cannot exist alone in solution; a negative ion, in this case NO_3^-, must be present to balance the positive charge of Ag^+. Any anion will do, however, as long as it forms a water-soluble compound with Ag^+. Thus, we could have used $AgClO_4$ instead of $AgNO_3$. Similarly, there must be a positive ion present to balance the negative charge of Cl^-. In this case, the positive ion present is K^+ in KCl, but we could have used NaCl instead of KCl. The net ionic equation would have been the same.

Finally, notice that there must always be a *charge balance* as well as a mass balance in a balanced chemical equation. Thus, in the Ag^+ + Cl^- net ionic equation, the cation and anion charges on the left add together to give a net charge of zero, the same as the zero charge on AgCl(s) on the right.

Chemistry  Now™

Sign in at **www.cengage.com/login** and go to Chapter 3 Contents to see Screen 3.10 for a tutorial on **writing net ionic equations.**

Charles D. Winters

Precipitation reaction. The reaction of barium chloride and sodium sulfate produces insoluble barium sulfate and water-soluble sodium chloride.

■ EXAMPLE 3.4 Writing and Balancing Net Ionic Equations

Problem Write a balanced, net ionic equation for the reaction of aqueous solutions of $BaCl_2$ and Na_2SO_4.

Strategy Follow the strategy outlined in Problem Solving Tip 3.1.

Solution

Step 1. First, notice that this is an *exchange reaction*. That is, the Ba^{2+} and Na^+ cations exchange anions (Cl^- and SO_4^{2-}) to give $BaSO_4$ and NaCl. Now that the reactants and products are known, we can write an equation for the reaction. To balance the equation, we place a 2 in front of the NaCl.

$$BaCl_2 + Na_2SO_4 \rightarrow BaSO_4 + 2\ NaCl$$

Step 2. Decide on the solubility of each compound (Figure 3.10). Compounds containing sodium ions are always water-soluble, and those containing chloride ions are almost always soluble. Sulfate salts are also usually soluble, one important exception being $BaSO_4$. We can therefore write

$$BaCl_2(aq) + Na_2SO_4(aq) \rightarrow BaSO_4(s) + 2\ NaCl(aq)$$

Step 3. Identify the ions in solution. All soluble ionic compounds dissociate to form ions in aqueous solution.

$$BaCl_2(s) \rightarrow Ba^{2+}(aq) + 2\ Cl^-(aq)$$

$$Na_2SO_4(s) \rightarrow 2\ Na^+(aq) + SO_4^{2-}(aq)$$

$$NaCl(s) \rightarrow Na^+(aq) + Cl^-(aq)$$

This results in the following complete ionic equation:

$$Ba^{2+}(aq) + 2\ Cl^-(aq) + 2\ Na^+(aq) + SO_4^{2-}(aq) \rightarrow BaSO_4(s) + 2\ Na^+(aq) + 2\ Cl^-(aq)$$

Step 4. Identify and eliminate the spectator ions (Na^+ and Cl^-) to give the net ionic equation.

$$Ba^{2+}(aq) + SO_4^{2-}(aq) \rightarrow BaSO_4(s)$$

Comment Notice that the sum of ion charges is the same on both sides of the equation. On the left, 2+ and 2− give zero; on the right, the charge on $BaSO_4$ is also zero.

EXERCISE 3.6 Net Ionic Equations

Write a balanced net ionic equation for each of the following reactions:

(a) $AlCl_3 + Na_3PO_4 \rightarrow AlPO_4 + NaCl$ (not balanced)

(b) Solutions of iron(III) chloride and potassium hydroxide give iron(III) hydroxide and potassium chloride when combined. See Figure 3.10c.

(c) Solutions of lead(II) nitrate and potassium chloride give lead(II) chloride and potassium nitrate when combined.

3.7 Acids and Bases

Acids and bases are two important classes of compounds. You may already be familiar with some common properties of acids. They produce bubbles of CO_2 gas when added to a metal carbonate such as $CaCO_3$ (Figure 3.12a), and they react with many metals to produce hydrogen gas (H_2) (Figure 3.12b). Although tasting substances is *never* done in a chemistry laboratory, you have probably experienced the sour taste of acids such as acetic acid in vinegar and citric acid (commonly found in fruits and added to candies and soft drinks). Acids and bases have some related properties. Solutions of acids or bases, for example, can change the colors of vegetable pigments (Figure 3.12c). You may have seen acids change the color of litmus, a dye derived from certain lichens, from blue to red. If an acid has made blue litmus paper turn red, adding a base reverses the effect, making the litmus blue again. Thus, acids and bases seem to be opposites. A base can neutralize the effect of an acid, and an acid can neutralize the effect of a base. See Table 3.2 for a list of common acids and bases.

Over the years, chemists have examined the properties, chemical structures, and reactions of acids and bases and have proposed different definitions of the terms "acid" and "base." In this section, we shall examine the two most commonly used definitions, one proposed by Svante Arrhenius (1859–1927) and another proposed by Johannes N. Brønsted (1879–1947) and Thomas M. Lowry (1874–1936).

More acidic   More basic

(a) A piece of coral (mostly $CaCO_3$) dissolves in acid to give CO_2 gas.

(b) Zinc reacts with hydrochloric acid to produce zinc chloride and hydrogen gas.

(c) The juice of a red cabbage is normally blue-purple. On adding acid, the juice becomes more red. Adding base produces a yellow color.

FIGURE 3.12 Some properties of acids and bases. (a) Acids react readily with coral ($CaCO_3$) and other metal carbonates to produce gaseous CO_2 (and a salt). (b) Acids react with many metals to produce hydrogen gas (and a metal salt). (c) The colors of natural dyes, such as the juice from a red cabbage, are affected by acids and bases.

Acids and Bases: The Arrhenius Definition

The Swedish chemist Svante Arrhenius made a number of important contributions to chemistry, but he is perhaps best known for his studies of the properties of solutions of salts, acids, and bases. In the late 1800s, Arrhenius proposed that these compounds dissolve in water and ultimately form ions. This theory of electrolytes

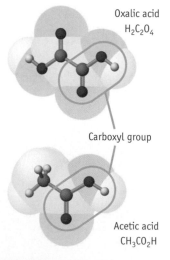

Oxalic acid
$H_2C_2O_4$

Carboxyl group

Acetic acid
CH_3CO_2H

■ **Weak Acids** Common acids and bases are listed in Table 3.2. There are numerous other weak acids and bases, and many of these are natural substances. Oxalic and acetic acid are among them. Many of these natural acids contain CO_2H groups. (The H of this group is lost as H^+.)

TABLE 3.2 Common Acids and Bases in Aqueous Solution

Strong Acids (Strong Electrolytes)		Soluble Strong Bases	
HCl (aq)	Hydrochloric acid	LiOH	Lithium hydroxide
HBr (aq)	Hydrobromic acid	NaOH	Sodium hydroxide
HI (aq)	Hydroiodic acid	KOH	Potassium hydroxide
HNO_3	Nitric acid	$Ba(OH)_2$	Barium hydroxide
$HClO_4$	Perchloric acid		
H_2SO_4	Sulfuric acid		
Weak Acids (Weak Electrolytes)*		**Weak Base (Weak Electrolyte)**	
H_3PO_4	Phosphoric acid	NH_3	Ammonia
H_2CO_3	Carbonic acid		
CH_3CO_2H	Acetic acid		
$H_2C_2O_4$	Oxalic acid		
$H_2C_4H_4O_6$	Tartaric acid		
$H_3C_6H_5O_7$	Citric acid		
$HC_9H_7O_4$	Aspirin		

* These are representative of hundreds of weak acids.

predated any knowledge of the composition and structure of atoms and was not well accepted initially. With a knowledge of atomic structure, however, we now take it for granted.

The Arrhenius definitions for acids and bases derives from his theory of electrolytes and focuses on formation of H^+ and OH^- ions in aqueous solutions.

- An acid is a substance that, when dissolved in water, increases the concentration of hydrogen ions, H^+ in solution.

$$HCl(g) \rightarrow H^+(aq) + Cl^-(aq)$$

- A base is a substance that, when dissolved in water, increases the concentration of hydroxide ions, OH^-, in the solution.

$$NaOH(s) \rightarrow Na^+(aq) + OH^-(aq)$$

- The reaction of an acid and a base produces a salt and water. Because the characteristic properties of an acid are lost when a base is added, and vice versa, acid–base reactions were logically described as resulting from the combination of H^+ and OH^- to form water.

$$HCl(aq) + NaOH(aq) \rightarrow NaCl(aq) + H_2O(\ell)$$

Arrhenius further proposed that acid strength was related to the extent to which the acid ionized. Some acids such as hydrochloric acid (HCl) and nitric acid (HNO_3) ionize completely in water; they are strong electrolytes, and we now call them **strong acids**. Other acids such as acetic acid and hydrofluoric acid are incompletely ionized; they are weak electrolytes and are **weak acids**. Weak acids exist in solution primarily as acid molecules, and only a fraction of these molecules ionize to produce $H^+(aq)$ ions along with the appropriate anion in solution.

Water-soluble compounds that contain hydroxide ions, such as sodium hydroxide (NaOH) or potassium hydroxide (KOH), are strong electrolytes and strong bases.

Aqueous ammonia, $NH_3(aq)$, is a weak electrolyte. Even though it does not have an OH^- ion as part of its formula, it does produce ammonium ions and hydroxide ions from its reaction with water and so is a base (Figure 3.13). The fact that this is a weak electrolyte indicates that only a fraction of ammonia molecules react with water to form ions; most of the base remains in solution in molecular form.

Although the Arrhenius theory is still used to some extent and is interesting in an historical context, modern concepts of acid–base chemistry such as the Brønsted–Lowry theory have gained preference among chemists.

Charles D. Winters

FIGURE 3.13 Ammonia, a weak electrolyte. Ammonia, NH_3, interacts with water to produce a very small number of NH_4^+ and OH^- ions per mole of ammonia molecules. (The name on the bottle, ammonium hydroxide, is misleading. The solution consists almost entirely of NH_3 molecules dissolved in water. It is better referred to as "aqueous ammonia.")

EXERCISE 3.7 Acids and Bases

(a) What ions are produced when nitric acid dissolves in water?

(b) Barium hydroxide is moderately soluble in water. What ions are produced when it dissolves in water?

Acids and Bases: The Brønsted-Lowry Definition

In 1923, Brønsted in Copenhagen (Denmark) and Lowry in Cambridge (England) independently suggested a new concept of acid and base behavior. They viewed acids and bases in terms of the transfer of a proton (H^+) from one species to an-

The Hydronium Ion—The H⁺ Ion in Water

The H^+ ion is a hydrogen atom that has lost its electron. Only the nucleus, a proton, remains. Because a proton is only about 1/100,000 as large as the average atom or ion, water molecules can approach closely, and the proton and water molecules are strongly attracted. In fact, the H^+ ion in water is better represented as H_3O^+, called the **hydronium ion**. This ion is formed by combining H^+ and H_2O. Experiments also show that other forms of the ion exist in water, one example being $[H_3O(H_2O)_3]^+$.

There will be instances when, for simplicity, we will use $H^+(aq)$. However, we will usually use the H_3O^+ symbol to represent the hydrogen ion in water in this book. Thus, hydrochloric acid is better represented as a solution of H_3O^+ and Cl^-.

hydronium ion
$H_3O^+(aq)$

chloride ion
$Cl^-(aq)$

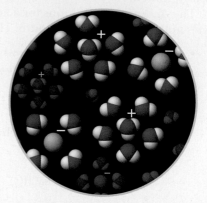

When HCl ionizes in aqueous solution, it produces the hydronium ion, H_3O^+, and the chloride ion, Cl^-.

other, and they described all acid–base reactions in terms of equilibria. The Brønsted–Lowry theory expanded the scope of the definition of acids and bases and helped chemists make predictions of product or reactant favorability based on acid and base strength. We will describe this theory here qualitatively; a more complete discussion will be given in Chapter 17.

The main concepts of the Brønsted-Lowry theory are the following:

- *An acid is a proton donor.* This is similar to the Arrhenius definition.
- *A base is a proton acceptor.* This definition includes the OH^- ion, but it also broadens the number and type of bases.
- *An acid–base reaction involves the transfer of a proton from an acid to a base to form a new acid and a new base. The reaction is written as an equilibrium reaction, and the equilibrium favors the weaker acid and base.* This allows the prediction of product- or reactant-favored reactions based on acid and base strength.

From the point of view of the Brønsted–Lowry theory, the behavior of acids such as HCl or CH_3CO_2H in water is seen to involve an acid–base reaction. Both species (both Brønsted acids) donate a proton to water (a Brønsted base), forming $H_3O^+(aq)$. Hydrochloric acid, HCl(aq), is a strong electrolyte because it ionizes completely in aqueous solution; it is thus classified as a strong acid.

Hydrogen chloride, a strong acid. 100% ionized. Equilibrium strongly favors products.

$$HCl(aq) \quad + \quad H_2O(\ell) \quad \rightleftharpoons \quad H_3O^+(aq) \quad + \quad Cl^-(aq)$$

hydrochloric acid
strong electrolyte
= 100% ionized

water

hydronium ion

chloride ion

For many years, sulfuric acid has been the chemical produced in the largest quantity in the United States (and in many other industrialized countries). About 40–50 billion kilograms (40–50 million metric tons) are made annually in the United States. The acid is so important to the economy of industrialized nations that some economists have said sulfuric acid production is a measure of a nation's industrial strength.

Sulfuric acid is a colorless, syrupy liquid with a density of 1.84 g/mL and a boiling point of 337 °C. It has several desirable properties that have led to its widespread use: it is generally less expensive to produce than other acids, is a strong acid, can be handled in steel containers, reacts readily with many organic compounds to produce useful prod-

Sulfur. Much of the sulfur used in the U.S. is produced by the Frasch process. This works by injecting superheated water into pockets of the element deep in the earth. The sulfur is forced to the surface in the molten state by compressed air.

ucts, and reacts readily with lime (CaO), the least expensive and most readily available base, to give calcium sulfate, a compound used to make wall board for the construction industry.

The first step in the industrial preparation of sulfuric acid is combustion of sulfur in air to give sulfur dioxide.

$$S(s) + O_2(g) \rightarrow SO_2(g)$$

This gas is then combined with more oxygen, in the presence of a catalyst (a substance that speeds up a reaction), to give sulfur trioxide,

$$2\ SO_2(g) + O_2(g) \rightarrow 2\ SO_3(g)$$

which can give sulfuric acid when absorbed in water.

$$SO_3(g) + H_2O(\ell) \rightarrow H_2SO_4(aq)$$

Currently, over two thirds of the production is used in the fertilizer industry. The remainder is used to make pigments, explosives, alcohol, pulp and paper, and detergents, and is employed as a component in storage batteries.

Some products that require sulfuric acid for their manufacture or use.

A sulfuric acid plant.

In contrast, CH_3CO_2H is a weak electrolyte, evidence that it is ionized to a small extent in water and therefore is a weak acid.

Acetic acid, a weak acid, << 100% ionized. Equilibrium favors reactants.

$$CH_3CO_2H(aq) + H_2O(\ell) \rightleftharpoons H_3O^+(aq) + CH_3CO_2^-(aq)$$
Weak Brønsted acid   Brønsted base

The different extent of ionization for these two acids relates to their acid strengths. Hydrochloric acid is a strong acid, and the equilibrium strongly favors the products. In contrast, acetic acid is a weak acid, and equilibrium for its reaction with water is reactant-favored.

Sulfuric acid, a *diprotic acid* (an acid capable of transferring two H⁺ ions), reacts with water in two steps. The first step strongly favors products, whereas the second step is reactant-favored.

■ **Acetic Acid** Acetic acid, CH_3CO_2H, is the substance that gives the taste and odor to vinegar. Fermentation of carbohydrates such as sugar produces ethanol (CH_3CH_2OH), and the action of bacteria on the alcohol results in acetic acid. Even a trace of acetic acid will ruin the taste of wine. This is the source of the name vinegar, which comes from the French *vin egar* meaning "sour wine." In addition to its use in food products such as salad dressings, mayonnaise, and pickles, acetic acid is used in hair-coloring products and in the manufacture of cellulose acetate, a commonly used synthetic fiber.

Strong Acid: $H_2SO_4(aq) + H_2O(\ell) \rightleftharpoons H_3O^+(aq) + HSO_4^-(aq)$
                    sulfuric acid   hydronium ion   hydrogen
                    100% ionized   sulfate ion

Weak Acid: $HSO_4^-(aq) + H_2O(\ell) \rightleftharpoons H_3O^+(aq) + SO_4^{2-}(aq)$
                    hydrogen sulfate ion   hydronium ion   sulfate ion
                    <100% ionized

Ammonia, a weak base, reacts with water to produce $OH^-(aq)$ ions. The reaction is reactant-favored at equilibrium.

Ammonia, a weak base, < 100% ionized. Equilibrium favors reactants.

$$NH_3(aq) + H_2O(\ell) \rightleftharpoons NH_4^+(aq) + OH^-(aq)$$

ammonia, base   water   ammonium   hydroxide ion
weak electrolyte   ion
< 100% ionized

Some species are described as **amphiprotic**, that is, they can function either as acids or as bases depending on the reaction. In the examples above, water functions as a base in reactions with acids (it accepts a proton) and as an acid in its reaction with ammonia (where it donates a proton to ammonia forming the ammonium ion.)

Chemistry. Now™

Sign in at **www.cengage.com/login** and go to Chapter 3 Contents to see:
- Screen 3.11 for a simulation on **acid ionization**
- Screen 3.12 for a self-study module on **weak and strong bases**

EXERCISE 3.8 Brønsted Acids and Bases

(a) Write a balanced equation for the reaction that occurs when H_3PO_4, phosphoric acid, donates a proton to water to form the dihydrogen phosphate ion.

(b) Write a net ionic equation showing the dihydrogen phosphate ion acting as a Brønsted acid in a reaction with water. Write another net ionic equation showing the dihydrogen phosphate ion acting as a Brønsted base in a reaction with water. What term is used to describe a species such as dihydrogen phosphate that can act either as an acid or as a base?

(c) Write a balanced net ionic equation for the reaction that occurs when the cyanide ion, CN^-, accepts a proton from water to form HCN. Is CN^- a Brønsted acid or base?

Reactions of Acids and Bases

Acids and bases in aqueous solution react to produce a salt and water. For example (Figure 3.14),

$$HCl(aq) + NaOH(aq) \longrightarrow H_2O(\ell) + NaCl(aq)$$

hydrochloric acid   sodium hydroxide   water   sodium chloride

The word "salt" has come into the language of chemistry to describe any ionic compound whose cation comes from a base (here Na^+ from NaOH) and whose anion comes from an acid (here Cl^- from HCl). The reaction of any of the acids listed in Table 3.2 with any of the hydroxide-containing bases listed there produces a salt and water.

Hydrochloric acid and sodium hydroxide are strong electrolytes in water (see Figure 3.14 and Table 3.2), so the complete ionic equation for the reaction of HCl(aq) and NaOH(aq) should be written as

$$\underbrace{H_3O^+(aq) + Cl^-(aq)}_{\text{from HCl(aq)}} + \underbrace{Na^+(aq) + OH^-(aq)}_{\text{from NaOH(aq)}} \longrightarrow 2\,H_2O(\ell) + \underbrace{Na^+(aq) + Cl^-(aq)}_{\text{from salt}}$$

water

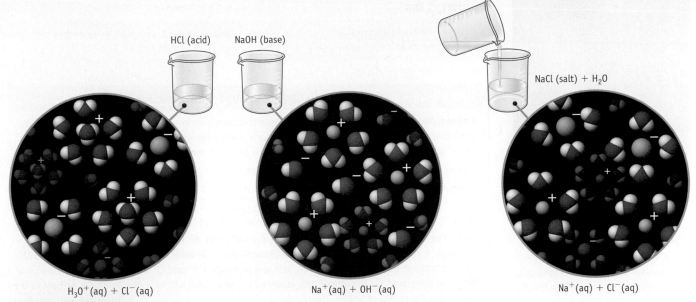

HCl (acid)   NaOH (base)

NaCl (salt) + H₂O

$H_3O^+(aq) + Cl^-(aq)$ $Na^+(aq) + OH^-(aq)$ $Na^+(aq) + Cl^-(aq)$

Active Figure 3.14 An acid–base reaction, HCl and NaOH. On mixing, the H_3O^+ and OH^- ions combine to produce H_2O, whereas the ions Na^+ and Cl^- remain in solution.

Chemistry.ᐤNow™ Sign in at www.cengage.com/login and go to the Chapter Contents menu to explore an interactive version of this figure accompanied by an exercise.

Because Na^+ and Cl^- ions appear on both sides of the equation, the *net ionic equation* is just the combination of the ions H_3O^+ and OH^- to give water.

$$H_3O^+(aq) + OH^-(aq) \rightarrow 2\ H_2O(\ell)$$

This is always the net ionic equation when a strong acid reacts with a strong base.

Reactions between *strong acids* and *strong bases* are called **neutralization reactions** because, on completion of the reaction, the solution is neutral if exactly the same amounts (number of moles) of the acid and base are mixed; that is, it is neither acidic nor basic. The other ions (the cation of the base and the anion of the acid) remain unchanged. If the water is evaporated, however, the cation and anion form a solid salt. In the example above, NaCl can be obtained. If nitric acid, HNO_3, and NaOH were allowed to react, the salt sodium nitrate, $NaNO_3$ (and water) would be obtained.

$$HNO_3(aq) + NaOH(aq) \rightarrow H_2O(\ell) + NaNO_3(aq)$$

If acetic acid and sodium hydroxide are mixed, the following reaction will take place.

$$CH_3CO_2H(aq) + NaOH(aq) \rightarrow H_2O(\ell) + NaCH_3CO_2(aq)$$

Because acetic acid is a weak acid and ionizes to such a small extent (Figure 3.9), the molecular species is the predominant form in aqueous solutions. In ionic equations, therefore, acetic acid is shown as molecular $CH_3CO_2H(aq)$. The *complete ionic equation* for this reaction is

$$CH_3CO_2H(aq) + Na^+(aq) + OH^-(aq) \rightarrow H_2O(\ell) + Na^+(aq) + CH_3CO_2^-(aq)$$

The only spectator ions in this equation are the sodium ions, so the *net ionic equation* is

$$CH_3CO_2H(aq) + OH^-(aq) \rightarrow H_2O(\ell) + CH_3CO_2^-(aq)$$

Reaction of gaseous HCl and NH₃. Open dishes of aqueous ammonia and hydrochloric acid were placed side by side. When gas molecules of NH_3 and HCl escape from solution to the atmosphere and encounter one another, we observe a cloud of solid ammonium chloride, NH_4Cl.

Chemistry ⚛ Now™

Sign in at **www.cengage.com/login** and go to Chapter 3 Contents to see Screen 3.13 for an exercise on **acid–base reactions**.

■ **EXAMPLE 3.5** **Net Ionic Equation for an Acid–Base Reaction**

Problem Ammonia, NH_3, is one of the most important chemicals in industrial economies. Not only is it used directly as a fertilizer but it is the raw material for the manufacture of nitric acid. As a base, it reacts with acids such as hydrochloric acid. Write a balanced, net ionic equation for this reaction.

Strategy Follow the general strategy outlined in Problem Solving Tip 3.1.

Solution The complete balanced equation is

$$NH_3(aq) + HCl(aq) \rightarrow NH_4Cl(aq)$$
$$\text{ammonia} \qquad \text{hydrochloric acid} \quad \text{ammonium chloride}$$

Notice that the reaction produces a salt, NH_4Cl, but not water. An H^+ ion from the acid transfers to ammonia, a weak Brønsted base, to give the ammonium ion. To write the net ionic equation, start with the fact that hydrochloric acid is a strong acid and produces H_3O^+ and Cl^- ions and that NH_4Cl is a soluble, ionic compound. On the other hand, ammonia is a weak base and so is predominantly present in the solution as the molecular species, NH_3.

$$NH_3(aq) + H_3O^+(aq) + Cl^-(aq) \rightarrow NH_4^+(aq) + Cl^-(aq) + H_2O(\ell)$$

Eliminating the spectator ion, Cl^-, we have

$$NH_3(aq) + H_3O^+(aq) \rightarrow NH_4^+(aq) + H_2O(\ell)$$

Comment The net ionic equation shows that the important aspect of the reaction between the weak base ammonia and the strong acid HCl is the transfer of an H^+ ion from the acid to the NH_3. Any strong acid could be used here (HBr, HNO_3, $HClO_4$, H_2SO_4) and the net ionic equation would be the same.

EXERCISE 3.9 **Acid–Base Reactions**

Write the balanced, overall equation and the net ionic equation for the reaction of magnesium hydroxide with hydrochloric acid. *(Hint: Think about the solubility guidelines.)*

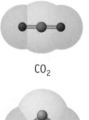

CO_2

SO_2

SO_3

NO_2

Some common nonmetal oxides that form acids in water.

Oxides of Nonmetals and Metals

Each acid shown in Table 3.2 has one or more H atoms in the molecular formula that dissociate in water to form H_3O^+ ions. There are, however, less obvious compounds that form acidic solutions. Oxides of nonmetals, such as carbon dioxide and sulfur trioxide, have no H atoms but react with water to produce H_3O^+ ions. Carbon dioxide, for example, dissolves in water to a small extent, and some of the dissolved molecules react with water to form the weak acid, carbonic acid. This acid then ionizes to a small extent to form the hydronium ion, H_3O^+, and the hydrogen carbonate (bicarbonate) ion, HCO_3^-.

$$CO_2(g) + H_2O(\ell) \rightleftharpoons H_2CO_3(aq)$$

$$H_2CO_3(aq) + H_2O(\ell) \rightleftharpoons HCO_3^-(aq) + H_3O^+(aq)$$

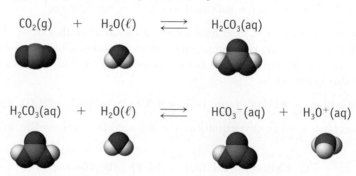

The HCO_3^- ion can also function as an acid, ionizing to produce H_3O^+ and the carbonate ion, CO_3^{2-}.

$$HCO_3^-(aq) \; + \; H_2O(\ell) \; \rightleftharpoons \; CO_3^{2-}(aq) \; + \; H_3O^+(aq)$$

These reactions are important in our environment and in the human body. Carbon dioxide is normally found in small amounts in the atmosphere, so rainwater is always slightly acidic. In the human body, carbon dioxide is dissolved in body fluids, where the HCO_3^- and CO_3^{2-} ions perform an important "buffering" action (▶ Chapter 18).

Oxides like CO_2 that can react with water to produce H_3O^+ ions are known as **acidic oxides.** Other acidic oxides include those of sulfur and nitrogen. For example, sulfur dioxide, SO_2, from human and natural sources, can react with oxygen to give sulfur trioxide, SO_3, which then reacts with water to form sulfuric acid.

$$2 \; SO_2(g) + O_2(g) \rightarrow 2 \; SO_3(g)$$

$$SO_3(g) \; + \; H_2O(\ell) \rightarrow H_2SO_4(aq)$$

Nitrogen dioxide, NO_2, reacts with water to give nitric and nitrous acids.

$$2 \; NO_2(g) + H_2O(\ell) \rightarrow HNO_3(aq) + HNO_2(aq)$$
$$\text{nitric acid} \qquad \text{nitrous acid}$$

Oxides of metals are called **basic oxides** because they give basic solutions if they dissolve appreciably in water. Perhaps the best example is calcium oxide, CaO, often called *lime*, or *quicklime*. Almost 20 billion kg of lime is produced annually in the United States for use in the metals and construction industries, in sewage and pollution control, in water treatment, and in agriculture. This metal oxide reacts with water to give calcium hydroxide, commonly called *slaked lime*. Although only slightly soluble in water (about 0.2 g/100 g H_2O at 10 °C), $Ca(OH)_2$ is widely used in industry as a base because it is inexpensive.

$$CaO(s) + H_2O(\ell) \rightarrow Ca(OH)_2(s)$$
$$\text{lime} \qquad\qquad \text{slaked lime}$$

EXERCISE 3.10 Acidic and Basic Oxides

For each of the following, indicate whether you expect an acidic or basic solution when the compound dissolves in water. Remember that compounds based on elements in the same group usually behave similarly.

(a) SeO_2 **(b)** BaO **(c)** P_4O_{10}

■ **Acid Rain** Oxides of sulfur and nitrogen are the major source of the acid in what is called *acid rain*. These acidic oxides arise from the burning of fossil fuels such as coal and gasoline. The gaseous oxides mix with water and other chemicals in the troposphere, and the rain that falls is more acidic than if it contained only dissolved CO_2. When the rain falls on areas that cannot easily tolerate this greater-than-normal acidity, serious environmental problems can occur.

3.8 Gas-Forming Reactions

Several different chemical reactions lead to gas formation (Table 3.3), but the most common are those leading to CO_2 formation. All metal carbonates (and bicarbonates) react with acids to produce carbonic acid, H_2CO_3, which in turn decomposes

FIGURE 3.15 Dissolving limestone (calcium carbonate, CaCO₃) in vinegar. Notice the bubbles of CO₂ rising from the surface of the limestone. This reaction shows why vinegar can be used as a household cleaning agent. It can be used, for example, to clean the calcium carbonate deposited from hard water.

TABLE 3.3 Gas-Forming Reactions

Metal carbonate or bicarbonate + acid → metal salt + $CO_2(g)$ + $H_2O(\ell)$

$Na_2CO_3(aq) + 2\ HCl(aq) \rightarrow 2\ NaCl(aq) + CO_2(g) + H_2O(\ell)$

$NaHCO_3(aq) + HCl(aq) \rightarrow NaCl(aq) + CO_2(g) + H_2O(\ell)$

Metal sulfide + acid → metal salt + $H_2S(g)$

$Na_2S(aq) + 2\ HCl(aq) \rightarrow 2\ NaCl(aq) + H_2S(g)$

Metal sulfite + acid → metal salt + $SO_2(g)$ + $H_2O(\ell)$

$Na_2SO_3(aq) + 2\ HCl(aq) \rightarrow 2\ NaCl(aq) + SO_2(g) + H_2O(\ell)$

Ammonium salt + strong base → metal salt + $NH_3(g)$ + $H_2O(\ell)$

$NH_4Cl(aq) + NaOH(aq) \rightarrow NaCl(aq) + NH_3(g) + H_2O(\ell)$

rapidly to carbon dioxide and water. For example, the reaction of calcium carbonate and hydrochloric acid is:

$$CaCO_3(s) + 2\ HCl(aq) \rightarrow CaCl_2(aq) + H_2CO_3(aq)$$

$$H_2CO_3(aq) \rightarrow H_2O(\ell) + CO_2(g)$$

Overall reaction: $CaCO_3(s) + 2\ HCl(aq) \rightarrow CaCl_2(aq) + H_2O(\ell) + CO_2(g)$

If the reaction is done in an open beaker, most of the CO₂ gas bubbles out of the solution.

Calcium carbonate is a common residue from hard water in home heating systems and cooking utensils. Washing with vinegar is a good way to clean the system or utensils because the insoluble calcium carbonate is turned into water-soluble calcium acetate in the following gas-forming reaction (Figure 3.15).

$$2\ CH_3CO_2H(aq) + CaCO_3(s) \rightarrow Ca(CH_3CO_2)_2(aq) + H_2O(\ell) + CO_2(g)$$

What is the net ionic equation for this reaction? Acetic acid is a weak acid. Calcium carbonate is insoluble in water. Therefore, the reactants are simply $CH_3CO_2H(aq)$ and $CaCO_3(s)$. On the products side, calcium acetate is water-soluble and forms aqueous calcium and acetate ions. Water and carbon dioxide are molecular compounds, so the net ionic equation is

$$2\ CH_3CO_2H(aq) + CaCO_3(s) \rightarrow Ca^{2+}(aq) + 2\ CH_3CO_2^{-}(aq) + H_2O(\ell) + CO_2(g)$$

There are no spectator ions in this reaction.

Have you ever made biscuits or muffins? As you bake the dough, it rises in the oven (Figure 3.16). But what makes it rise? A gas-forming reaction occurs between an acid and baking soda, sodium hydrogen carbonate (bicarbonate of soda, NaHCO₃). One acid used for this purpose is tartaric acid, a weak acid found in many foods. The net ionic equation for a typical reaction would be

$$\underset{\text{tartaric acid}}{H_2C_4H_4O_6(aq)} + \underset{\text{hydrogen carbonate ion}}{HCO_3^{-}(aq)} \rightarrow \underset{\substack{\text{hydrogen} \\ \text{tartrate ion}}}{HC_4H_4O_6^{-}(aq)} + H_2O(\ell) + CO_2(g)$$

FIGURE 3.16 Muffins rise because of a gas-forming reaction. The acid and sodium bicarbonate in baking powder produce carbon dioxide gas. The acid used in many baking powders is Ca(H₂PO₄)₂, but tartaric acid and NaAl(SO₄)₂ are also common. (Aqueous solutions containing the aluminum ion are acidic.)

In dry baking powder, the acid and $NaHCO_3$ are kept apart by using starch as a filler. When mixed into the moist batter, however, the acid and sodium hydrogen carbonate dissolve and come into contact. Now they can react to produce CO_2, causing the dough to rise.

Chemistry Now™

Sign in at **www.cengage.com/login** and go to Chapter 3 Contents to see Screen 3.14 for a tutorial identifying **the type of reaction that will result from the mixing of solutions** and to watch videos about **four of the most important gases produced in reactions.**

EXAMPLE 3.6 Gas-Forming Reactions

Problem Write a balanced equation for the reaction that occurs when nickel(II) carbonate is treated with sulfuric acid.

Strategy First, identify the reactants and write their formulas (here $NiCO_3$ and H_2SO_4). Next, recognize this as a typical gas-forming reaction (Table 3.3) between a metal carbonate and an acid. The products are water, CO_2, and a salt. The anion of the salt is the anion from the acid (SO_4^{2-}), and the cation is from the metal carbonate (Ni^{2+}).

Solution The complete, balanced equation is

$$NiCO_3(s) + H_2SO_4(aq) \longrightarrow NiSO_4(aq) + H_2O(\ell) + CO_2(g)$$

EXERCISE 3.11 Gas-Forming Reactions

(a) Barium carbonate, $BaCO_3$, is used in the brick, ceramic, glass, and chemical manufacturing industries. Write a balanced equation that shows what happens when barium carbonate is treated with nitric acid. Give the name of each of the reaction products.

(b) Write a balanced equation for the reaction of ammonium sulfate with sodium hydroxide.

3.9 Oxidation-Reduction Reactions

The terms "oxidation" and "reduction" come from reactions that have been known for centuries. Ancient civilizations learned how to change metal oxides and sulfides into the metal, that is, how to "reduce" ore to the metal. A modern example is the reduction of iron(III) oxide with carbon monoxide to give iron metal (Figure 3.17a).

Fe_2O_3 loses oxygen and is reduced.

$$Fe_2O_3(s) + 3\ CO(g) \longrightarrow 2\ Fe(s) + 3\ CO_2(g)$$

CO is the reducing agent. It gains oxygen and is oxidized.

In this reaction, carbon monoxide is the agent that brings about the reduction of iron ore to iron metal, so carbon monoxide is called the **reducing agent.**

When Fe_2O_3 is reduced by carbon monoxide, oxygen is removed from the iron ore and added to the carbon monoxide. The carbon monoxide, therefore, is "oxidized" by the addition of oxygen to give carbon dioxide. *Any process in which oxygen is added to another substance is an oxidation.* In the reaction of oxygen with magnesium,

FIGURE 3.17 Oxidation-reduction.
(a) Iron ore, which is largely Fe_2O_3, is reduced to metallic iron with carbon or carbon monoxide in a blast furnace, a process done on a massive scale.
(b) Burning magnesium metal in air produces magnesium oxide.

a, Jan Halaska/Photo Researchers, Inc.; b, Charles D. Winters

(a)   (b)

for example (see Figure 3.17b), oxygen is the **oxidizing agent** because it is the agent responsible for the oxidation of magnesium.

Mg combines with
oxygen and is oxidized.

$$2 \text{ Mg(s)} + \text{O}_2\text{(g)} \longrightarrow 2 \text{ MgO(s)}$$

O_2 is the oxidizing agent

Oxidation-Reduction Reactions and Electron Transfer

Not all redox reactions involve oxygen, but *all oxidation and reduction reactions can be accounted for by considering them to occur by means of a transfer of electrons between substances.* When a substance accepts electrons, it is said to be **reduced** because there is a reduction in the numerical value of the charge on an atom of the substance. In the net ionic equation for the reaction of a silver salt with copper metal, positively charged Ag^+ ions accept electrons from copper metal and are reduced to uncharged silver atoms (Figure 3.18).

Ag^+ ions accept electrons from Cu and are
reduced to Ag. Ag^+ is the oxidizing agent.
$$Ag^+(aq) + e^- \rightarrow Ag(s)$$

$$2 \text{ Ag}^+(aq) + \text{Cu(s)} \longrightarrow 2 \text{ Ag(s)} + \text{Cu}^{2+}(aq)$$

Cu donates electrons to Ag^+ and is oxidized to Cu^{2+}.
Cu is the reducing agent.
$$Cu(s) \rightarrow Cu^{2+}(aq) + 2 \text{ e}^-$$

Because copper metal supplies the electrons and causes Ag^+ ions to be reduced, Cu is the reducing agent.

When a substance *loses electrons*, the numerical value of the charge on an atom of the substance increases. The substance is said to have been **oxidized**. In our example, copper metal releases electrons on going to Cu^{2+}, so the metal is oxidized. For this to happen, something must be available to accept the electrons from cop-

Pure copper wire

Copper wire in dilute AgNO₃ solution; after several hours

Blue color due to Cu²⁺ ions formed in redox reaction

Silver crystals formed after several weeks

Charles D. Winters

FIGURE 3.18 The oxidation of copper metal by silver ions. A clean piece of copper wire is placed in a solution of silver nitrate, $AgNO_3$. Over time, the copper reduces Ag^+ ions, forming silver crystals, and the copper metal is oxidized to copper ions, Cu^{2+}. The blue color of the solution is due to the presence of aqueous copper(II) ions. (Sign in to ChemistryNow and Screen 3.15, Redox Reactions and Electron Transfer, to watch a video of the reaction.)

per. In this case, Ag^+ is the electron acceptor, and its charge is reduced to zero in silver metal. Therefore, Ag^+ is the "agent" that causes Cu metal to be oxidized; that is, Ag^+ is the *oxidizing agent*.

In every oxidation-reduction reaction, one reactant is reduced (and is therefore the oxidizing agent) and one reactant is oxidized (and is therefore the reducing agent). We can show this by dividing the general redox reaction $X + Y \rightarrow X^{n+} + Y^{n-}$ into two parts or *half-reactions*:

Half Reaction	Electron Transfer	Result
$X \rightarrow X^{n+} + n\,e^-$	X transfers electrons to Y	X is oxidized to X^{n+}. X is the reducing agent
$Y + n\,e^- \rightarrow Y^{n-}$	Y accepts electron from X	Y is reduced to Y^{n-}. Y is the oxidizing agent

In the reaction of magnesium and oxygen, O_2 is reduced because it gains electrons (four electrons per molecule) on going to two oxide ions. Thus, O_2 is the oxidizing agent.

Mg releases 2 e⁻ per atom. Mg is oxidized to Mg^{2+} and is the reducing agent.

$$2\,Mg(s) + O_2(g) \longrightarrow 2\,MgO(s)$$

O_2 gains 4 e⁻ per molecule to form $2\,O^{2-}$. O_2 is reduced and is the oxidizing agent.

In the same reaction, magnesium is the reducing agent because it releases two electrons per atom on being oxidized to the Mg^{2+} ion (and so two Mg atoms are required to supply the four electrons required by one O_2 molecule). All redox reactions can be analyzed in a similar manner.

■ **Balancing Equations for Redox Reactions** The notion that a redox reaction can be divided into an oxidizing portion and a reducing portion will lead us to a method of balancing more complex equations for redox reactions described in Chapter 20.

■ **Chemical Safety and Redox Reactions** A strong oxidizing agent and a strong reducing agent may react violently. For this reason, it would not be a good idea to store a strong oxidizing agent next to a strong reducing agent. Certain chemicals are often stored separately from the bulk of the other chemicals. Examples of chemicals that might be stored in their own separate areas are strong oxidizing agents, acids, water-reactive chemicals, and highly flammable materials.

The observations outlined so far lead to several important conclusions:

- If one substance is oxidized, another substance in the same reaction must be reduced. For this reason, such reactions are called oxidation-reduction reactions, or **redox reactions** for short.
- The reducing agent is itself oxidized, and the oxidizing agent is reduced.
- Oxidation is the opposite of reduction. For example, the removal of oxygen is reduction, and the addition of oxygen is oxidation. The gain of electrons is reduction, and the loss of electrons is oxidation.

Oxidation Numbers

How can you tell an oxidation-reduction reaction when you see one? How can you tell which substance has gained or lost electrons and so decide which substance is the oxidizing (or reducing) agent? Sometimes it is obvious. For example, if an uncombined element becomes part of a compound (Mg becomes part of MgO, for example), the reaction is definitely a redox process. If it's not obvious, then the answer is to *look for a change in the oxidation number of an element in the course of the reaction.* The **oxidation number** of an atom in a molecule or ion is defined as the charge an atom has, *or appears to have*, as determined by the following guidelines for assigning oxidation numbers.

1. **Each atom in a pure element has an oxidation number of zero.** The oxidation number of Cu in metallic copper is 0, and it is 0 for each atom in I_2 and S_8.
2. **For monatomic ions, the oxidation number is equal to the charge on the ion.** You know that magnesium forms ions with a 2+ charge (Mg^{2+}); the oxidation number of magnesium in this ion is therefore +2.
3. **When combined with another element, fluorine always has an oxidation number of −1.**
4. **The oxidation number of O is −2 in most compounds.** The exceptions to this rule occur
   a) when oxygen is combined with fluorine (where oxygen takes on a positive oxidation number)
   b) in compounds called peroxides (such as Na_2O_2) and superoxides (such as KO_2) in which oxygen has an oxidation number of −1 and −1/2, respectively
5. **Cl, Br, and I have oxidation numbers of −1 in compounds, except when combined with oxygen and fluorine.** This means that Cl has an oxidation

■ **Writing Charges on Ions** Conventionally, charges on ions are written as (number, sign), whereas oxidation numbers are written as (sign, number). For example, the oxidation number of the Cu^{2+} ion is +2 and its charge is 2+.

■ **Peroxides** In peroxides, the oxidation number of oxygen is −1. For example, in hydrogen peroxide (H_2O_2), each hydrogen atom has an oxidation number of +1. To balance this, each oxygen must have an oxidation number of −1. A 3% aqueous solution of H_2O_2 is sometimes used as an antiseptic.

A Closer Look

Are Oxidation Numbers "Real"?

Do oxidation numbers reflect the actual electric charge on an atom in a molecule or ion? With the exception of monatomic ions such as Cl^- or Na^+, the answer is no.

Oxidation numbers assume that the atoms in a molecule are positive or negative ions, which is not true. For example, in H_2O, the H atoms are not H^+ ions, and the O atoms are not O^{2-} ions. This is not to say, however, that atoms in molecules do not bear an electric charge of any kind. Calculations on water

indicate the O atom has a charge of about −0.4 (or 40% of the electron charge) and the H atoms are each about +0.2.

So why use oxidation numbers? Oxidation numbers provide a way of dividing up the electrons among the atoms in a molecule or polyatomic ion. Because the distribution of electrons changes in a redox reaction, we use this method as a way to decide whether a redox reaction has occurred and to distinguish the oxidizing and reducing agents.

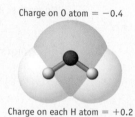

Charge on O atom = −0.4

Charge on each H atom = +0.2

number of -1 in NaCl (in which Na is $+1$, as predicted by the fact that it is an element of Group 1A). In the ion ClO^-, however, the Cl atom has an oxidation number of $+1$ (and O has an oxidation number of -2; see guideline 4).

6. **The oxidation number of H is $+1$ in most compounds.** The key exception to this guideline occurs when H forms a binary compound with a metal. In such cases, the metal forms a positive ion, and H becomes a hydride ion, H^-. Thus, in CaH_2 the oxidation number of Ca is $+2$ (equal to the group number), and that of H is -1.

7. **The algebraic sum of the oxidation numbers for the atoms in a neutral compound must be zero; in a polyatomic ion, the sum must be equal to the ion charge.** For example, in $HClO_4$ the H atom is assigned $+1$, and each O atom is assigned -2. This means the Cl atom must be $+7$.

■ **Why Use Oxidation Numbers?** The reason for learning about oxidation numbers at this point is to be able to identify which reactions are oxidation-reduction processes and to identify the oxidizing agent and the reducing agent in a reaction. We return to a more detailed discussion of redox reactions in Chapter 20.

Chemistry ⚛ Now™

Sign in at **www.cengage.com/login** and go to Chapter 3 Contents to see Screen 3.16 for exercises and a tutorial on **oxidation numbers**.

■ **EXAMPLE 3.7 Determining Oxidation Numbers**

Problem Determine the oxidation number of the indicated element in each of the following compounds or ions:

(a) aluminum in aluminum oxide, Al_2O_3

(b) phosphorus in phosphoric acid, H_3PO_4

(c) sulfur in the sulfate ion, SO_4^{2-}

(d) each Cr atom in the dichromate ion, $Cr_2O_7^{2-}$

Strategy Follow the guidelines in the text, paying particular attention to guidelines 4, 6, and 7.

Solution

(a) Al_2O_3 is a neutral compound. Assuming that O has its usual oxidation number of -2, we can solve the following algebraic equation for the oxidation number of aluminum.

Net charge on Al_2O_3 = sum of oxidation numbers for two Al atoms + three O atoms

$0 = 2(x) + 3(-2)$

$0 = 2x + (-6)$

$+6 = 2x$

$x = +3$

The oxidation number of Al must be $+3$, in agreement with its position in the periodic table.

(b) H_3PO_4 has an overall charge of 0. If each of the oxygen atoms has an oxidation number of -2 and each of the H atoms is $+1$, then we can determine the oxidation number of phosphorus as follows:

Net charge on H_3PO_4 = sum of oxidation numbers for three H atoms + one P atom + four O atoms

$0 = 3(+1) + (x) + 4(-2)$

$x = +5$

The oxidation number of phosphorus in this compound is therefore $+5$.

(c) The sulfate ion, SO_4^{2-}, has an overall charge of $2-$. Oxygen is assigned its usual oxidation number of -2.

Net charge on SO_4^{2-} = sum of oxidation numbers of one S atom + 4 O atoms

$2- = (x) + 4(-2)$

$x = +6$

The sulfur in this ion has an oxidation number of $+6$.

(d) The net charge on the $Cr_2O_7^{2-}$ ion is 2−. Oxygen is assigned its usual oxidation number of −2.

Net charge on $Cr_2O_7^{2-}$ = sum of oxidation numbers for two Cr atoms + seven O atoms

$$2- = 2(x) + 7(-2)$$
$$2- = 2x + (-14)$$
$$12 = 2x$$
$$x = +6$$

The oxidation number of each chromium in this polyatomic ion is +6.

EXERCISE 3.12 Determining Oxidation Numbers

Assign an oxidation number to the underlined atom in each ion or molecule.

(a) $\underline{Fe}_2O_3$ **(b)** $H_2\underline{S}O_4$ **(c)** $\underline{C}O_3^{2-}$ **(d)** $\underline{N}O_2^+$

Recognizing Oxidation-Reduction Reactions

You can always tell if a reaction involves oxidation and reduction by assessing the oxidation number of each element and noting whether any of these numbers change in the course of the reaction. In many cases, however, this will not be necessary. For example, it will be obvious that a redox reaction has occurred if an uncombined element is converted to a compound or if a well-known oxidizing or reducing agent is involved (Table 3.4).

Like oxygen (O_2), the halogens (F_2, Cl_2, Br_2, and I_2) are oxidizing agents in their reactions with metals and nonmetals. An example is the reaction of chlorine with sodium metal (see Figure 1.4).

Na releases 1 e⁻ per atom.
Oxidation number increases.
Na is oxidized to Na⁺ and is the reducing agent.

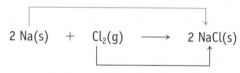

$$2 \, Na(s) \;+\; Cl_2(g) \longrightarrow 2 \, NaCl(s)$$

Cl_2 gains 2 e⁻ per molecule.
Oxidation number decreases by 1 per Cl.
Cl_2 is reduced to Cl⁻ and is the oxidizing agent.

NO₂ gas

Charles D. Winters

Copper metal oxidized to green $Cu(NO_3)_2$

Active Figure 3.19 The reaction of copper with nitric acid. Copper (a reducing agent) reacts vigorously with concentrated nitric acid (an oxidizing agent) to give the brown gas NO_2 and a deep green solution of copper(II) nitrate.

Chemistry Now™ Sign in at www.cengage.com/login and go to the Chapter Contents menu to explore an interactive version of this figure accompanied by an exercise.

TABLE 3.4 Common Oxidizing and Reducing Agents

Oxidizing Agent	Reaction Product	Reducing Agent	Reaction Product
O_2, oxygen	O^{2-}, oxide ion or O combined in H_2O	H_2, hydrogen	$H^+(aq)$, hydrogen ion or H combined in H_2O or other molecule
Halogen, F_2, Cl_2, Br_2, or I_2	Halide ion, F^-, Cl^-, Br^-, or I^-	M, metals such as Na, K, Fe, and Al	M^{n+}, metal ions such as Na^+, K^+, Fe^{2+} or Fe^{3+}, and Al^{3+}
HNO_3, nitric acid	Nitrogen oxides* such as NO and NO_2	C, carbon (used to reduce metal oxides)	CO and CO_2
$Cr_2O_7^{2-}$, dichromate ion	Cr^{3+}, chromium(III) ion (in acid solution)		
MnO_4^-, permanganate ion	Mn^{2+}, manganese(II) ion (in acid solution)		

* NO is produced with dilute HNO_3, whereas NO_2 is a product of concentrated acid.

A chlorine molecule ends up as two Cl⁻ ions, having acquired two electrons (from two Na atoms). Thus, the oxidation number of each Cl atom has decreased from 0 to −1. This means Cl_2 has been reduced, and therefore it is the oxidizing agent.

Figure 3.19 illustrates the chemistry of another excellent oxidizing agent, nitric acid, HNO_3. Here, copper metal is oxidized to give copper(II) nitrate, and the nitrate ion is reduced to the brown gas NO_2. The net ionic equation for the reaction is

Oxidation number of Cu changes from 0 to +2. Cu is oxidized to Cu^{2+} and is the reducing agent.

$$Cu(s) + 2\ NO_3^-(aq) + 4\ H_3O^+(aq) \longrightarrow Cu^{2+}(aq) + 2\ NO_2(g) + 6\ H_2O(\ell)$$

N in NO_3^- changes from +5 to +4 in NO_2. NO_3^- is reduced to NO_2 and is the oxidizing agent.

Nitrogen has been reduced from +5 (in the NO_3^- ion) to +4 (in NO_2); therefore, the nitrate ion in acid solution is the oxidizing agent. Copper metal is the reducing agent; each metal atom has given up two electrons to produce the Cu^{2+} ion.

In the reactions of sodium with chlorine and copper with nitric acid, the metals are oxidized. This is typical of metals. In yet another example of this, aluminum metal, a good reducing agent, is capable of reducing iron(III) oxide to iron metal in a reaction called the *thermite reaction* (Figure 3.20).

$$Fe_2O_3(s) + 2\ Al(s) \rightarrow 2\ Fe(\ell) + Al_2O_3(s)$$
$$\underset{\text{oxidizing agent}}{Fe_2O_3(s)} + \underset{\text{reducing agent}}{2\ Al(s)}$$

Such a large quantity of energy is evolved as heat in the reaction that the iron is produced in the molten state.

Tables 3.4 and 3.5 may help you organize your thinking as you look for oxidation-reduction reactions and use their terminology.

Chemistry ⚛ Now™

Sign in at **www.cengage.com/login** and go to Chapter 3 Contents to see Screen 3.17 for an exercise on **redox reaction.**

■ **EXAMPLE 3.8 Oxidation-Reduction Reaction**

Problem For the reaction of iron(II) ion with permanganate ion in aqueous acid,

$$5\ Fe^{2+}(aq) + MnO_4^-(aq) + 8\ H_3O^+(aq) \rightarrow 5\ Fe^{3+}(aq) + Mn^{2+}(aq) + 12\ H_2O(\ell)$$

decide which atoms are undergoing a change in oxidation number, and identify the oxidizing and reducing agents.

TABLE 3.5 Recognizing Oxidation-Reduction Reactions

	Oxidation	Reduction
In terms of oxidation number	Increase in oxidation number of an atom	Decrease in oxidation number of an atom
In terms of electrons	Loss of electrons by an atom	Gain of electrons by an atom
In terms of oxygen	Gain of one or more O atoms	Loss of one or more O atoms

Charles D. Winters

FIGURE 3.20 Thermite reaction. Here, Fe_2O_3 is reduced by aluminum metal to produce iron metal and aluminum oxide.

Charles D. Winters

$KMnO_4(aq)$ oxidizing agent

$Fe^{2+}(aq)$ reducing agent

The reaction of iron(II) ion and permanganate ion. The reaction of purple permanganate ion (MnO_4^-, the oxidizing agent) with the iron(II) ion (Fe^{2+}, the reducing agent) in acidified aqueous solution gives the nearly colorless manganese(II) ion (Mn^{2+}) and the iron(III) ion (Fe^{3+}).

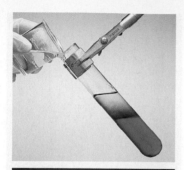

Charles D. Winters

FIGURE 3.21 The redox reaction of ethanol and dichromate ion is the basis of the test used in a Breathalyzer. When ethanol, an alcohol, is poured into a solution of orange-red dichromate ion, it reduces the dichromate ion to green chromium(III) ion. The bottom photo is a breath tester that can be purchased in grocery or drug stores. See Exercise 3.13.

Strategy Determine the oxidation numbers of the atoms in each ion or molecule involved in the reaction. Decide which atoms have increased in oxidation number (oxidation) and which have decreased in oxidation number (reduction).

Solution The Mn oxidation number in MnO_4^- is $+7$, and it decreases to $+2$ in the product, the Mn^{2+} ion. Thus, the MnO_4^- ion has been reduced and is the oxidizing agent (see Table 3.4).

$$5\ Fe^{2+}(aq) + MnO_4^-(aq) + 8\ H_3O^+(aq) \rightarrow 5\ Fe^{3+}(aq) + Mn^{2+}(aq) + 12\ H_2O(\ell)$$
$$+2 \phantom{Fe^{2+}(aq)}\ +7, -2 +1, -2 +3 \phantom{Fe^{3+}(aq)}+2 \phantom{Mn^{2+}(aq) }+1, -2$$

The oxidation number of iron has increased from $+2$ to $+3$, so each Fe^{2+} ion has lost one electron upon being oxidized to Fe^{3+} (see Table 3.5). This means the Fe^{2+} ion is the reducing agent.

Comment If one of the reactants in a redox reaction is a simple substance (here Fe^{2+}), it is usually obvious whether its oxidation number has increased or decreased. Once a species has been established as having been reduced (or oxidized), you know another species has been oxidized (or reduced). It is also helpful to recognize common oxidizing and reducing agents (Table 3.4).

EXERCISE 3.13 Oxidation-Reduction Reactions

The following reaction occurs in a device for testing the breath for the presence of ethanol. Identify the oxidizing and reducing agents, the substance oxidized, and the substance reduced (Figure 3.21).

$$3\ CH_3CH_2OH(aq) + 2\ Cr_2O_7^{2-}(aq) + 16\ H_3O^+(aq) \longrightarrow$$

$$\text{ethanol} \text{dichromate ion;}$$
$$\text{orange-red}$$

$$3\ CH_3CO_2H(aq) + 4\ Cr^{3+}(aq) + 27\ H_2O(\ell)$$

$$\text{acetic acid} \text{chromium(III)}$$
$$\text{ion; green}$$

Case Study

Killing Bacteria with Silver

We recently read about a new washing machine that injects silver ions into the wash water, the purpose being to kill bacteria in the wash water. The advertisement told us that 100 quadrillion silver ions are injected. How does this machine work? Is 100 quadrillion silver ions a lot? Does the silver kill bacteria?

The washing machine works by using electrical energy to oxidize silver metal to give silver ions.

$$Ag(s) \rightarrow Ag^+(aq) + e^-$$

This is a simple electrolysis procedure. (More about that in Chapter 20.) And 100 quadrillion silver ions? This is 100×10^{15} ions.

Do silver ions act as a bacteriocide? There is plenty of medical evidence for this property. In fact, when you were born, the physician or nurse may have put drops of a very dilute silver nitrate solution in your eyes to treat neonatal conjunctivitis. And severely burned patients are treated with silver sulfadiazine ($C_{10}H_9AgN_4O_2S$) to prevent bacterial or fungal infections.

Charles D. Winters

Silver ions as a bacteriocide in dental floss.

The use of silver to prevent infections has a long history. Phoenicians kept wine, water, and vinegar in silver vessels. Early settlers in America put silver coins into water barrels. And you might have been born with a "silver spoon in your mouth." Babies in wealthier

homes, who were fed from silver spoons and used a silver pacifier, were found to be healthier.

The historical uses of silver carry over to modern society. One can buy many different kinds of silver-containing water purifiers for the home, and dental floss coated with silver nitrate is available.

Although silver does have health benefits, beware of fraudulent claims. For example, consuming large amounts of "colloidal silver" (nanosized particles of silver suspended in water) is claimed to have health-giving properties. One person who tried this, Stan Jones, ran for the U.S. Congress in 2002 and 2006. From consuming silver, he acquired argyria, a medically irreversible condition in which the skin turns a gray-blue color.

Questions:

1. *How many moles of silver are used in a wash cycle?*
2. *What mass of silver is used?*

Answers to these questions are in Appendix Q.

FIGURE 3.22 A gas-forming reaction. An Alka-Seltzer tablet contains an acid (citric acid) and sodium hydrogen carbonate ($NaHCO_3$), the reactants in a gas-forming reaction.

EXERCISE 3.14 Recognizing Oxidation-Reduction Reactions

Decide which of the following reactions are oxidation-reduction reactions. In each case, explain your choice, and identify the oxidizing and reducing agents.

(a) $NaOH(aq) + HNO_3(aq) \rightarrow NaNO_3(aq) + H_2O(\ell)$

(b) $Cu(s) + Cl_2(g) \rightarrow CuCl_2(s)$

(c) $Na_2CO_3(aq) + 2\ HClO_4(aq) \rightarrow CO_2(g) + H_2O(\ell) + 2\ NaClO_4(aq)$

(d) $2\ S_2O_3{}^{2-}(aq) + I_2(aq) \rightarrow S_4O_6{}^{2-}(aq) + 2\ I^-(aq)$

3.10 Classifying Reactions in Aqueous Solution

One goal of this chapter has been to explore the most common types of reactions that can occur in aqueous solution. This helps you decide, for example, that a gas-forming reaction occurs when an Alka-Seltzer tablet (containing citric acid and $NaHCO_3$) is dropped into water (Figure 3.22).

$$\underset{\text{citric acid}}{H_3C_6H_5O_7(aq)} + \underset{\text{hydrogen carbonate ion}}{HCO_3{}^-(aq)} \longrightarrow$$

$$\underset{\text{dihydrogen citrate ion}}{H_2C_6H_5O_7{}^-(aq)} + H_2O(\ell) + CO_2(g)$$

We have examined four types of reactions in aqueous solution: precipitation reactions, acid-base reactions, gas-forming reactions, and oxidation-reduction reactions. Three of these four (precipitation, acid-base, and gas-forming) fall into the category of exchange reactions.

Precipitation Reactions (see Figure 3.11): Ions combine in solution to form an insoluble reaction product.
Overall Equation

$$Pb(NO_3)_2(aq) + 2\ KI(aq) \rightarrow PbI_2(s) + 2\ KNO_3(aq)$$

Net Ionic Equation

$$Pb^{2+}(aq) + 2\ I^-(aq) \rightarrow PbI_2(s)$$

Acid–Base Reactions (see Figures 3.12 and 3.14): Water is a product of many acid–base reactions, and the cation of the base and the anion of the acid form a salt.
Overall Equation for the Reaction of a Strong Acid and a Strong Base

$$HNO_3(aq) + KOH(aq) \rightarrow HOH(\ell) + KNO_3(aq)$$

Net Ionic Equation for the Reaction of a Strong Acid and a Strong Base

$$H_3O^+(aq) + OH^-(aq) \rightarrow 2\ H_2O(\ell)$$

Overall Equation for the Reaction of a Weak Acid and a Strong Base

$$CH_3CO_2H(aq) + NaOH(aq) \rightarrow NaCH_3CO_2(aq) + HOH(\ell)$$

Net Ionic Equation for the Reaction of a Weak Acid and a Strong Base

$$CH_3CO_2H(aq) + OH^-(aq) \rightarrow CH_3CO_2^-(aq) + H_2O(\ell)$$

Gas-Forming Reactions (see Figures 3.15 and 3.22): The most common examples involve metal carbonates and acids, but others exist (see Table 3.3). One product with a metal carbonate is always carbonic acid, H_2CO_3, most of which decomposes to H_2O and CO_2. Carbon dioxide is the gas in the bubbles you see during these reactions.

Overall Equation:

$$CuCO_3(s) + 2\ HNO_3(aq) \rightarrow Cu(NO_3)_2(aq) + CO_2(g) + H_2O(\ell)$$

Net Ionic Equation

$$CuCO_3(s) + 2\ H_3O^+(aq) \rightarrow Cu^{2+}(aq) + CO_2(g) + 3\ H_2O(\ell)$$

Oxidation-Reduction Reactions (see Figure 3.18): These reactions are *not* ion exchange reactions. Rather, electrons are transferred from one material to another.

Overall Equation

$$Cu(s) + 2\ AgNO_3(aq) \rightarrow Cu(NO_3)_2(aq) + 2\ Ag(s)$$

Net Ionic Equation

$$Cu(s) + 2\ Ag^+(aq) \rightarrow Cu^{2+}(aq) + 2\ Ag(s)$$

These four types of reactions are usually easy to recognize, but keep in mind that a reaction may fall into more than one category. For example, barium hydroxide reacts readily with sulfuric acid to give barium sulfate and water, a reaction that is both a precipitation and an acid–base reaction.

$$Ba(OH)_2(aq) + H_2SO_4(aq) \rightarrow BaSO_4(s) + 2\ H_2O(\ell)$$

Chemistry.⚛.Now™

Sign in at **www.cengage.com/login** and go to Chapter 3 Contents to see Screen 3.8 for a self-study module on the **four reaction types**.

■ **EXAMPLE 3.9** **Types of Reactions**

Problem Classify each of the following reactions as precipitation, acid–base, gas-forming, or oxidation-reduction.

(a) $2\ HNO_3(aq) + Ca(OH)_2(s) \rightarrow Ca(NO_3)_2(aq) + 2\ H_2O(\ell)$

(b) $2\ MnO_4^-(aq) + 5\ HSO_3^-(aq) + H_3O^+(aq) \rightarrow 2\ Mn^{2+}(aq) + 5\ SO_4^{2-}(aq) + 4\ H_2O(\ell)$

Strategy An acid–base reaction is usually easy to identify. Next, check the oxidation numbers of each element. If they change, then it is a redox reaction. If there is no change, then check to see if it is a simple precipitation or gas-forming process.

Solution Reaction (a) involves a common acid (nitric acid, HNO_3) and a common base [calcium hydroxide, $Ca(OH)_2$]; it produces a salt, calcium nitrate, and water. It is an acid–base reaction. Reaction (b) is a redox reaction because the oxidation numbers of S and Mn change.

$$2\ MnO_4^-(aq) + 5\ HSO_3^-(aq) + H_3O^+(aq) \rightarrow 2\ Mn^{2+}(aq) + 5\ SO_4^{2-}(aq) + 4\ H_2O(\ell)$$

$\quad\quad +7, -2 \quad\quad +1, +4, -2 \quad +1, -2 \quad\quad +2 \quad\quad\quad +6, -2 \quad\quad +1, -2$

The oxidation number of S changes from $+4$ to $+6$, and that of Mn changes from $+7$ to $+2$. Therefore, permanganate ion, MnO_4^-, has been reduced (and is the oxidizing agent), and HSO_3^- has been oxidized (and is the reducing agent).

Comment Note that no changes occur in the oxidation numbers of the elements in reaction (a).

$$HNO_3(aq) \quad + \quad Ca(OH)_2(s) \quad \rightarrow \quad Ca(NO_3)_2(aq) \quad + \quad 2\ H_2O(\ell)$$

$$+1,\ +5,\ -2 \qquad +2,\ -2,\ +1 \qquad\ +2,\ +5,\ -2 \qquad\ +1,\ -2$$

EXERCISE 3.15 Classifying and Predicting Reactions

Classify each of the following reactions as a precipitation, acid–base, gas-forming reaction, or oxidation-reduction reaction. Predict the products of the reaction, and then balance the completed equation. Write the net ionic equation for each.

(a) $CuCO_3(s) + H_2SO_4(aq) \rightarrow$

(b) $Ga(s) + O_2(g) \rightarrow$

(c) $Ba(OH)_2(s) + HNO_3(aq) \rightarrow$

(d) $CuCl_2(aq) + (NH_4)_2S(aq) \rightarrow$

Chapter Goals Revisited

Now that you have studied this chapter, you should ask if you have met the chapter goals. In particular, you should be able to:

Balance equations for simple chemical reactions.
a. Understand the information conveyed by a balanced chemical equation (Section 3.1).
b. Balance simple chemical equations (Section 3.2). Study Question(s) assignable in OWL: 2, 4, 47, 54.

Understand the nature and characteristics of chemical equilibria.
a. Recognize that chemical reactions are reversible (Section 3.3).
b. Describe what is meant by the term dynamic equilibrium.
c. Recognize the difference between reactant-favored and product-favored reactions.

Understand the nature of ionic substances dissolved in water.
a. Explain the difference between electrolytes and nonelectrolytes, and recognize examples of each (Section 3.5 and Figure 3.9).
b. Predict the solubility of ionic compounds in water (Section 3.5 and Figure 3.10). Study Question(s) assignable in OWL: 9, 11, 13, 15, 55, 57, 60, 65, 67; Go Chemistry Module 5.
c. Recognize what ions are formed when an ionic compound or acid or base dissolves in water (Sections 3.5–3.7). Study Question(s) assignable in OWL: 13, 15, 60.

Recognize common acids and bases, and understand their behavior in aqueous solution.
a. Know the names and formulas of common acids and bases (Section 3.7 and Table 3.2). Study Question(s) assignable in OWL: 21, 26, 27.
b. Categorize acids and bases as strong or weak.
c. Define and use the Arrhenius concept of acids and bases.
d. Define and use the Brønsted–Lowry concept of acids and bases.
e. Appreciate when a substance can be amphiprotic.
f. Recognize the Brønsted acid and base in a reaction. Study Question(s) assignable in OWL: 21, 27, 28.

Chemistry ⬡ Now™ Sign in at **www.cengage.com/login** to:
- Assess your understanding with Study Questions in OWL keyed to each goal in the Goals and Homework menu for this chapter
- For quick review, download Go Chemistry mini-lecture flashcard modules (or purchase them at **www.ichapters.com**)
- Check your readiness for an exam by taking the Pre-Test and exploring the modules recommended in your Personalized Study plan.

❓ Access **How Do I Solve It?** tutorials on how to approach problem solving using concepts in this chapter.

For additional preparation for an examination on this chapter see the *Let's Review* section on pages 254–267.

Recognize the common types of reactions in aqueous solution.

a. Recognize the key characteristics of four types of reactions in aqueous solution.

Reaction Type	Key Characteristic
Precipitation	Formation of an insoluble compound
Acid–strong base	Formation of a salt and water; H^+ ion transfer
Gas-forming	Evolution of a water-insoluble gas such as CO_2
Oxidation-reduction	Transfer of electrons (with changes in oxidation numbers)

Study Question(s) assignable in OWL: 47, 48, 51, 52, 70, 76–78.

b. Predict the products of precipitation reactions (Section 3.6), acid–base reactions (Section 3.7), and gas-forming reactions (Section 3.8). These are all examples of exchange reactions, which involve the exchange of anions between the cations involved in the reaction. Study Question(s) assignable in OWL: 17, 19, 21, 27, 37–39, 71.

Write chemical equations for the common types of reactions in aqueous solution.

a. Write overall balanced equations for precipitation, acid–base, and gas-forming reactions.

b. Write net ionic equations (Sections 3.6–3.8). Study Question(s) assignable in OWL: 17, 19, 33, 63, 67, 68; Go Chemistry Module 6.

c. Understand that the net ionic equation for the reaction of a strong acid with a strong base is $H_3O^+(aq) + OH^-(aq) \rightarrow 2\,H_2O(\ell)$ (Section 3.7).

Recognize common oxidizing and reducing agents, and identify oxidation-reduction reactions.

a. Determine oxidation numbers of elements in a compound and understand that these numbers represent the charge an atom has, or appears to have, when the electrons of the compound are counted according to a set of guidelines (Section 3.9). Study Question(s) assignable in OWL: 41, 42, 69.

b. Identify oxidation-reduction reactions (often called redox reactions), and identify the oxidizing and reducing agents and substances oxidized and reduced in the reaction (Section 3.9 and Tables 3.4 and 3.5). Study Question(s) assignable in OWL: 44–46, 61, 73.

STUDY QUESTIONS

OWL Online homework for this chapter may be assigned in OWL.

▲ denotes challenging questions.

■ denotes questions assignable in OWL.

Blue-numbered questions have answers in Appendix O and fully-worked solutions in the *Student Solutions Manual*.

Practicing Skills

Balancing Equations

(See Example 3.1 and ChemistryNow Screen 3.4.)

1. Write a balanced chemical equation for the combustion of liquid pentane, C_5H_{12}.

2. ■ Write balanced chemical equations for the following reactions:
   (a) production of ammonia, $NH_3(g)$, by combining $N_2(g)$ and $H_2(g)$
   (b) production of methanol, $CH_3OH(\ell)$ by combining $H_2(g)$ and $CO(g)$
   (c) production of sulfuric acid by combining sulfur, oxygen, and water

3. Balance the following equations:
   (a) $Cr(s) + O_2(g) \rightarrow Cr_2O_3(s)$
   (b) $Cu_2S(s) + O_2(g) \rightarrow Cu(s) + SO_2(g)$
   (c) $C_6H_5CH_3(\ell) + O_2(g) \rightarrow H_2O(\ell) + CO_2(g)$

4. ■ Balance the following equations:
   (a) $Cr(s) + Cl_2(g) \rightarrow CrCl_3(s)$
   (b) $SiO_2(s) + C(s) \rightarrow Si(s) + CO(g)$
   (c) $Fe(s) + H_2O(g) \rightarrow Fe_3O_4(s) + H_2(g)$

5. Balance the following equations, and name each reactant and product:
   (a) $Fe_2O_3(s) + Mg(s) \rightarrow MgO(s) + Fe(s)$
   (b) $AlCl_3(s) + NaOH(aq) \rightarrow Al(OH)_3(s) + NaCl(aq)$
   (c) $NaNO_3(s) + H_2SO_4(\ell) \rightarrow Na_2SO_4(s) + HNO_3(\ell)$
   (d) $NiCO_3(s) + HNO_3(aq) \rightarrow$
   $$Ni(NO_3)_2(aq) + CO_2(g) + H_2O(\ell)$$

6. Balance the following equations, and name each reactant and product:
   (a) $SF_4(g) + H_2O(\ell) \rightarrow SO_2(g) + HF(\ell)$
   (b) $NH_3(aq) + O_2(aq) \rightarrow NO(g) + H_2O(\ell)$
   (c) $BF_3(g) + H_2O(\ell) \rightarrow HF(aq) + H_3BO_3(aq)$

Chemical Equilibrium
(See Sections 3.3 and 3.5.)

7. Equal amounts of two acids—HCl and HCO₂H (formic acid)—are placed in solution. When equilibrium has been achieved, the HCl solution has a much greater electrical conductivity than the HCO₂H solution. Which reaction is more product favored at equilibrium?

   $$HCl(aq) + H_2O(\ell) \rightleftarrows H_3O^+(aq) + Cl^-(aq)$$

   $$HCO_2H(aq) + H_2O(\ell) \rightleftarrows H_3O^+(aq) + HCO_2^-(aq)$$

8. Equal amounts of two compounds, AgBr and H₃PO₄, are placed in solution. When equilibrium has been achieved, the H₃PO₄ solution has a greater electrical conductivity than the AgBr solution (which is almost a nonelectrolyte). Which reaction is more product favored at equilibrium?

   $$AgBr(s) \rightleftarrows Ag^+(aq) + Br^-(aq)$$

   $$H_3PO_4(aq) + H_2O(\ell) \rightleftarrows H_3O^+(aq) + H_2PO_4^-(aq)$$

Ions and Molecules in Aqueous Solution
(See Exercise 3.3, Example 3.2, and ChemistryNow Screens 3.5–3.7.)

9. ■ What is an electrolyte? How can you differentiate experimentally between a weak electrolyte and a strong electrolyte? Give an example of each.

10. Name two acids that are strong electrolytes and one acid that is a weak electrolyte. Name two bases that are strong electrolytes and one base that is a weak electrolyte.

11. ■ Which compound or compounds in each of the following groups is (are) expected to be soluble in water?
    (a) CuO, $CuCl_2$, $FeCO_3$
    (b) AgI, Ag_3PO_4, $AgNO_3$
    (c) K_2CO_3, KI, $KMnO_4$

12. Which compound or compounds in each of the following groups is (are) expected to be soluble in water?
    (a) $BaSO_4$, $Ba(NO_3)_2$, $BaCO_3$
    (b) Na_2SO_4, $NaClO_4$, $NaCH_3CO_2$
    (c) $AgBr$, KBr, Al_2Br_6

13. ■ The following compounds are water-soluble. What ions are produced by each compound in aqueous solution?
    (a) KOH (c) $LiNO_3$
    (b) K_2SO_4 (d) $(NH_4)_2SO_4$

14. The following compounds are water-soluble. What ions are produced by each compound in aqueous solution?
    (a) KI (c) K_2HPO_4
    (b) $Mg(CH_3CO_2)_2$ (d) $NaCN$

15. ■ Decide whether each of the following is water-soluble. If soluble, tell what ions are produced.
    (a) Na_2CO_3 (c) NiS
    (b) $CuSO_4$ (d) $BaBr_2$

16. Decide whether each of the following is water-soluble. If soluble, tell what ions are produced.
    (a) $NiCl_2$ (c) $Pb(NO_3)_2$
    (b) $Cr(NO_3)_3$ (d) $BaSO_4$

Precipitation Reactions and Net Ionic Equations
(See Examples 3.3 and 3.4 and ChemistryNow Screens 3.9 and 3.10.)

17. ■ Balance the equation for the following precipitation reaction, and then write the net ionic equation. Indicate the state of each species (s, ℓ, aq, or g).

    $$CdCl_2 + NaOH \rightarrow Cd(OH)_2 + NaCl$$

18. Balance the equation for the following precipitation reaction, and then write the net ionic equation. Indicate the state of each species (s, ℓ, aq, or g).

    $$Ni(NO_3)_2 + Na_2CO_3 \rightarrow NiCO_3 + NaNO_3$$

19. ■ Predict the products of each precipitation reaction. Balance the completed equation, and then write the net ionic equation.
    (a) $NiCl_2(aq) + (NH_4)_2S(aq) \rightarrow ?$
    (b) $Mn(NO_3)_2(aq) + Na_3PO_4(aq) \rightarrow ?$

20. Predict the products of each precipitation reaction. Balance the completed equation, and then write the net ionic equation.
    (a) $Pb(NO_3)_2(aq) + KBr(aq) \rightarrow ?$
    (b) $Ca(NO_3)_2(aq) + KF(aq) \rightarrow ?$
    (c) $Ca(NO_3)_2(aq) + Na_2C_2O_4(aq) \rightarrow ?$

Acids and Bases and Their Reactions
(See Exercise 3.8, Example 3.5, Exercise 3.10, and ChemistryNow Screens 3.11–3.13.)

21. ■ Write a balanced equation for the ionization of nitric acid in water.

22. Write a balanced equation for the ionization of perchloric acid in water.

23. Oxalic acid, $H_2C_2O_4$, which is found in certain plants, can provide two hydronium ions in water. Write balanced equations (like those for sulfuric acid on page 135) to show how oxalic acid can supply one and then a second H_3O^+ ion.

24. Phosphoric acid can supply one, two, or three H_3O^+ ions in aqueous solution. Write balanced equations (like those for sulfuric acid on page 135) to show this successive loss of hydrogen ions.

25. Write a balanced equation for reaction of the basic oxide, magnesium oxide, with water.

26. ■ Write a balanced equation for the reaction of sulfur trioxide with water.

27. ■ Complete and balance the following acid–base equations. Name the reactants and products. Decide which is the Brønsted acid and which is the Brønsted base.
    (a) $CH_3CO_2H(aq) + Mg(OH)_2(s) \rightarrow$
    (b) $HClO_4(aq) + NH_3(aq) \rightarrow$

28. ■ Complete and balance the following acid–base equations. Name the reactants and products. Decide which is the Brønsted acid and which is the Brønsted base.
(a) $H_3PO_4(aq) + KOH(aq) \rightarrow$
(b) $H_2C_2O_4(aq) + Ca(OH)_2(s) \rightarrow$
($H_2C_2O_4$ is oxalic acid, an acid capable of donating two H^+ ions.)

29. Write a balanced equation for the reaction of barium hydroxide with nitric acid.

30. Write a balanced equation for the reaction of aluminum hydroxide with sulfuric acid.

31. Name two strong Brønsted acids and one strong Brønsted base.

32. Name three weak Brønsted acids and one weak Brønsted base.

Writing Net Ionic Equations
(See Examples 3.4 and 3.5 and ChemistryNow Screen 3.10.)

33. ■ Balance the following equations, and then write the net ionic equation.
(a) $(NH_4)_2CO_3(aq) + Cu(NO_3)_2(aq) \rightarrow$
$\qquad\qquad\qquad CuCO_3(s) + NH_4NO_3(aq)$
(b) $Pb(OH)_2(s) + HCl(aq) \rightarrow PbCl_2(s) + H_2O(\ell)$
(c) $BaCO_3(s) + HCl(aq) \rightarrow$
$\qquad\qquad BaCl_2(aq) + H_2O(\ell) + CO_2(g)$
(d) $CH_3CO_2H(aq) + Ni(OH)_2(s) \rightarrow$
$\qquad\qquad Ni(CH_3CO_2)_2(aq) + H_2O(\ell)$

34. ■ Balance the following equations, and then write the net ionic equation:
(a) $Zn(s) + HCl(aq) \rightarrow H_2(g) + ZnCl_2(aq)$
(b) $Mg(OH)_2(s) + HCl(aq) \rightarrow MgCl_2(aq) + H_2O(\ell)$
(c) $HNO_3(aq) + CaCO_3(s) \rightarrow$
$\qquad\qquad Ca(NO_3)_2(aq) + H_2O(\ell) + CO_2(g)$
(d) $(NH_4)_2S(aq) + FeCl_3(aq) \rightarrow NH_4Cl(aq) + Fe_2S_3(s)$

35. Balance the following equations, and then write the net ionic equation. Show states for all reactants and products (s, ℓ, g, aq).
(a) the reaction of silver nitrate and potassium iodide to give silver iodide and potassium nitrate
(b) the reaction of barium hydroxide and nitric acid to give barium nitrate and water
(c) the reaction of sodium phosphate and nickel(II) nitrate to give nickel(II) phosphate and sodium nitrate

36. Balance each of the following equations, and then write the net ionic equation. Show states for all reactants and products (s, ℓ, g, aq).
(a) the reaction of sodium hydroxide and iron(II) chloride to give iron(II) hydroxide and sodium chloride
(b) the reaction of barium chloride with sodium carbonate to give barium carbonate and sodium chloride
(c) the reaction of ammonia with phosphoric acid

Gas-Forming Reactions
(See Example 3.6 and ChemistryNow Screen 3.14.)

37. ■ Siderite is a mineral consisting largely of iron(II) carbonate. Write an overall, balanced equation for its reaction with nitric acid, and name the products.

38. ■ The beautiful red mineral rhodochrosite is manganese(II) carbonate. Write an overall, balanced equation for the reaction of the mineral with hydrochloric acid, and name the products.

Charles D. Winters

Rhodochrosite, a mineral consisting largely of MnCO₃.

39. ■ Write an overall, balanced equation for the reaction of $(NH_4)_2S$ with HBr, and name the reactants and products.

40. Write an overall, balanced equation for the reaction of Na_2SO_3 with CH_3CO_2H, and name the reactants and products.

Oxidation Numbers
(See Example 3.7 and ChemistryNow Screens 3.15 and 3.16.)

41. ■ Determine the oxidation number of each element in the following ions or compounds.
(a) BrO_3^- (d) CaH_2
(b) $C_2O_4^{2-}$ (e) H_4SiO_4
(c) F^- (f) HSO_4^-

42. ■ Determine the oxidation number of each element in the following ions or compounds.
(a) PF_6^- (d) N_2O_5
(b) $H_2AsO_4^-$ (e) $POCl_3$
(c) UO^{2+} (f) XeO_4^{2-}

Oxidation–Reduction Reactions
(See Example 3.8 and ChemistryNow Screen 3.17.)

43. Which two of the following reactions are oxidation–reduction reactions? Explain your answer in each case. Classify the remaining reaction.
(a) $Zn(s) + 2 NO_3^-(aq) + 4 H_3O^+(aq) \rightarrow$
$\qquad\qquad Zn^{2+}(aq) + 2 NO_2(g) + 6 H_2O(\ell)$
(b) $Zn(OH)_2(s) + H_2SO_4(aq) \rightarrow$
$\qquad\qquad ZnSO_4(aq) + 2 H_2O(\ell)$
(c) $Ca(s) + 2 H_2O(\ell) \rightarrow Ca(OH)_2(s) + H_2(g)$

44. ■ Which two of the following reactions are oxidation–reduction reactions? Explain your answer briefly. Classify the remaining reaction.
(a) $CdCl_2(aq) + Na_2S(aq) \rightarrow CdS(s) + 2 NaCl(aq)$
(b) $2 Ca(s) + O_2(g) \rightarrow 2 CaO(s)$
(c) $4 Fe(OH)_2(s) + 2 H_2O(\ell) + O_2(g) \rightarrow$
$\qquad\qquad\qquad 4 Fe(OH)_3(aq)$

45. ■ In the following reactions, decide which reactant is oxidized and which is reduced. Designate the oxidizing agent and the reducing agent.
(a) $C_2H_4(g) + 3 O_2(g) \rightarrow 2 CO_2(g) + 2 H_2O(\ell)$
(b) $Si(s) + 2 Cl_2(g) \rightarrow SiCl_4(\ell)$

46. ■ In the following reactions, decide which reactant is oxidized and which is reduced. Designate the oxidizing agent and the reducing agent.

(a) $Cr_2O_7^{2-}$ (aq) + 3 Sn^{2+}(aq) + 14 H_3O^+(aq) →
$\qquad$ 2 Cr^{3+}(aq) + 3 Sn^{4+}(aq) + 21 $H_2O(\ell)$

(b) FeS(s) + 3 NO_3^-(aq) + 4 H_3O^+(aq) →
$\qquad$ 3 NO(g) + SO_4^{2-}(aq) + Fe^{3+}(aq) + 6 $H_2O(\ell)$

Types of Reactions in Aqueous Solution
(See Example 3.9 and ChemistryNow Screen 3.8.)

47. ■ Balance the following equations, and then classify each as a precipitation, an acid–base, or a gas-forming reaction.

(a) $Ba(OH)_2$(aq) + HCl(aq) → $BaCl_2$(aq) + $H_2O(\ell)$

(b) HNO_3(aq) + $CoCO_3$(s) →
$\qquad$ $Co(NO_3)_2$(aq) + $H_2O(\ell)$ + CO_2(g)

(c) Na_3PO_4(aq) + $Cu(NO_3)_2$(aq) →
$\qquad$ $Cu_3(PO_4)_2$(s) + $NaNO_3$(aq)

48. ■ Balance the following equations, and then classify each as a precipitation, an acid–base, or a gas-forming reaction.

(a) K_2CO_3(aq) + $Cu(NO_3)_2$(aq) →
$\qquad$ $CuCO_3$(s) + KNO_3(aq)

(b) $Pb(NO_3)_2$(aq) + HCl(aq) →
$\qquad$ $PbCl_2$(s) + HNO_3(aq)

(c) $MgCO_3$(s) + HCl(aq) →
$\qquad$ $MgCl_2$(aq) + $H_2O(\ell)$ + CO_2(g)

49. Balance the following equations, and then classify each as a precipitation, an acid–base, or a gas-forming reaction. Show states for the products (s, ℓ, g, aq), and then balance the completed equation. Write the net ionic equation.

(a) $MnCl_2$(aq) + Na_2S(aq) → MnS + NaCl

(b) K_2CO_3(aq) + $ZnCl_2$(aq) → $ZnCO_3$ + KCl

50. Balance the following equations, and then classify each as a precipitation, an acid–base, or a gas-forming reaction. Write the net ionic equation.

(a) $Fe(OH)_3$(s) + HNO_3(aq) → $Fe(NO_3)_3$ + H_2O

(b) $FeCO_3$(s) + HNO_3(aq) → $Fe(NO_3)_2$ + CO_2 + H_2O

51. ■ Balance each of the following equations, and classify them as precipitation, acid–base, gas-forming, or oxidation-reduction reactions.

(a) $CuCl_2$ + H_2S → CuS + HCl

(b) H_3PO_4 + KOH → H_2O + K_3PO_4

(c) Ca + HBr → H_2 + $CaBr_2$

(d) $MgCl_2$ + H_2O → $Mg(OH)_2$ + HCl

52. ■ ▲ Complete and balance the equations below, and classify them as precipitation, acid–base, gas-forming, or oxidation-reduction reactions.

(a) $NiCO_3$ + H_2SO_4 → ?

(b) $Co(OH)_2$ + HBr → ?

(c) $AgCH_3CO_2$ + NaCl → ?

(d) NiO + CO → ?

General Questions
These questions are not designated as to type or location in the chapter. They may combine concepts from several chapters.

53. Balance the following equations:

(a) the synthesis of urea, a common fertilizer

$\qquad$ CO_2(g) + NH_3(g) → NH_2CONH_2(s) + $H_2O(\ell)$

(b) reactions used to make uranium(VI) fluoride for the enrichment of natural uranium

UO_2(s) + HF(aq) → UF_4(s) + $H_2O(\ell)$
UF_4(s) + F_2(g) → UF_6(s)

(c) the reaction to make titanium(IV) chloride, which is then converted to titanium metal

TiO_2(s) + Cl_2(g) + C(s) → $TiCl_4(\ell)$ + CO(g)
$TiCl_4(\ell)$ + Mg(s) → Ti(s) + $MgCl_2$(s)

54. ■ Balance the following equations:

(a) reaction to produce "superphosphate" fertilizer

$Ca_3(PO_4)_2$(s) + H_2SO_4(aq) →
$\qquad$ $Ca(H_2PO_4)_2$(aq) + $CaSO_4$(s)

(b) reaction to produce diborane, B_2H_6

$NaBH_4$(s) + H_2SO_4(aq) →
$\qquad$ B_2H_6(g) + H_2(g) + Na_2SO_4(aq)

(c) reaction to produce tungsten metal from tungsten(VI) oxide

$\qquad$ WO_3(s) + H_2(g) → W(s) + $H_2O(\ell)$

(d) decomposition of ammonium dichromate

$\qquad$ $(NH_4)_2Cr_2O_7$(s) → N_2(g) + $H_2O(\ell)$ + Cr_2O_3(s)

55. ■ Give a formula for each of the following:

(a) a soluble compound containing the bromide ion

(b) an insoluble hydroxide

(c) an insoluble carbonate

(d) a soluble nitrate-containing compound

(e) a weak Brønsted acid

56. Give the formula for the following compounds:

(a) a soluble compound containing the acetate ion

(b) an insoluble sulfide

(c) a soluble hydroxide

(d) an insoluble chloride

(e) a strong Brønsted base

57. ■ Which of the following copper(II) salts are soluble in water and which are insoluble: $Cu(NO_3)_2$, $CuCO_3$, $Cu_3(PO_4)_2$, $CuCl_2$?

58. Name two anions that combine with Al^{3+} ion to produce water-soluble compounds.

59. Identify the spectator ion or ions in the reaction of nitric acid and magnesium hydroxide, and write the net ionic equation. What type of reaction is this?

2 H_3O^+(aq) + 2 NO_3^-(aq) + $Mg(OH)_2$(s) →
$\qquad$ 4 $H_2O(\ell)$ + Mg^{2+}(aq) + 2 NO_3^-(aq)

60. ■ Identify and name the water-insoluble product in each reaction and write the net ionic equation:

(a) $CuCl_2$(aq) + H_2S(aq) → CuS + 2 HCl

(b) $CaCl_2$(aq) + K_2CO_3(aq) → 2 KCl + $CaCO_3$

(c) $AgNO_3$(aq) + NaI(aq) → AgI + $NaNO_3$

▲ more challenging ■ in OWL Blue-numbered questions answered in Appendix O

61. ■ Bromine is obtained from sea water by the following reaction:

$$Cl_2(g) + 2\ NaBr(aq) \rightarrow 2\ NaCl(aq) + Br_2(\ell)$$

(a) What has been oxidized? What has been reduced?
(b) Identify the oxidizing and reducing agents.

62. Identify each of the following substances as a likely oxidizing or reducing agent: HNO_3, Na, Cl_2, O_2, $KMnO_4$.

63. ■ The mineral dolomite contains magnesium carbonate. This reacts with hydrochloric acid.

$$MgCO_3(s) + 2\ HCl(aq) \rightarrow$$
$$CO_2(g) + MgCl_2(aq) + H_2O(\ell)$$

(a) Write the net ionic equation for the reaction of magnesium carbonate and hydrochloric acid, and name the spectator ions.
(b) What type of reaction is this?

64. Ammonium sulfide, $(NH_4)_2S$, reacts with $Hg(NO_3)_2$ to produce HgS and NH_4NO_3.
(a) Write the overall balanced equation for the reaction. Indicate the state (s, aq) for each compound.
(b) Name each compound.
(c) What type of reaction is this?

65. ■ What species (atoms, molecules, or ions) are present in an aqueous solution of each of the following compounds? Decide which are Brønsted acids or bases and whether they are strong or weak.
(a) NH_3 (b) CH_3CO_2H (c) NaOH   (d) HBr

66. (a) Name two water-soluble compounds containing the Cu^{2+} ion. Name two water-insoluble compounds based on the Cu^{2+} ion.
(b) Name two water-soluble compounds containing the Ba^{2+} ion. Name two water-insoluble compounds based on the Ba^{2+} ion.

67. ■ Balance equations for these reactions that occur in aqueous solution, and then classify each one as a precipitation, acid–base, or gas-forming reaction. Show states for the products (s, ℓ, g, aq), give their names, and write the net ionic equation.
(a) $K_2CO_3 + HClO_4 \rightarrow KClO_4 + CO_2 + H_2O$
(b) $FeCl_2 + (NH_4)_2S \rightarrow FeS + NH_4Cl$
(c) $Fe(NO_3)_2 + Na_2CO_3(aq) \rightarrow FeCO_3 + NaNO_3$
(d) $NaOH + FeCl_3 \rightarrow NaCl + Fe(OH)_3$

68. ■ For each reaction, write an overall, balanced equation and the net ionic equation.
(a) the reaction of aqueous lead(II) nitrate and aqueous potassium hydroxide
(b) the reaction of aqueous copper(II) nitrate and aqueous sodium carbonate

In the Laboratory

69. ■ The following reaction can be used to prepare iodine in the laboratory.

$$2\ NaI(s) + 2\ H_2SO_4(aq) + MnO_2(s) \rightarrow$$
$$Na_2SO_4(aq) + MnSO_4(aq) + I_2(g) + 2\ H_2O(\ell)$$

(a) Determine the oxidation number of each atom in the equation.
(b) What is the oxidizing agent, and what has been oxidized? What is the reducing agent, and what has been reduced?

(c) Is the reaction observed product-favored or reactant-favored?
(d) Name the reactants and products.

Charles D. Winters

Preparation of iodine. A mixture of NaI and MnO_2 was placed in a flask in a hood *(left)*. On adding concentrated H_2SO_4 *(right)*, brown gaseous I_2 was evolved.

70. ■ ▲ If you have "silverware" in your home, you know it tarnishes easily. Tarnish is from the oxidation of silver in the presence of sulfur-containing compounds (in the atmosphere or in your food) to give black Ag_2S. To remove the tarnish, you can warm the tarnished object with some aluminum foil (in water with a small amount of baking soda). The silver sulfide reacts with aluminum to produce silver as well as aluminum oxide and hydrogen sulfide.

$$3\ Ag_2S(s) + 2\ Al(s) + 3\ H_2O(\ell) \rightarrow$$
$$6\ Ag(s) + Al_2O_3(s) + 3\ H_2S(aq)$$

Hydrogen sulfide is foul smelling, but it is removed by reaction with the baking soda.

$$NaHCO_3(aq) + H_2S(aq) \rightarrow$$
$$NaHS(aq) + H_2O(\ell) + CO_2(g)$$

Classify the two reactions, and identify any acids, bases, oxidizing agents, or reducing agents.

Charles D. Winters

(a)   **(b)**

Removing silver tarnish. A badly tarnished piece of silver (a) is placed in a dish with aluminum foil and aqueous sodium hydrogen carbonate. The portion of the silver in contact with the solution is now free of tarnish (b).

▲ more challenging   ■ in OWL   Blue-numbered questions answered in Appendix O

71. ■ ▲ Suppose you wish to prepare a sample of magnesium chloride. One way to do this is to use an acid–base reaction, the reaction of magnesium hydroxide with hydrochloric acid.

$$Mg(OH)_2(s) + 2 HCl(aq) \rightarrow MgCl_2(aq) + 2 H_2O(\ell)$$

When the reaction is complete, evaporating the water will give solid magnesium chloride. Can you suggest at least one other way to prepare $MgCl_2$?

72. ▲ Suggest a laboratory method for preparing barium phosphate. (See Question 71 for a way to approach this question.)

73. ■ One way to test for the presence of sugars (say in a urine sample) is to treat the sample with silver ions in aqueous ammonia. (This is called the Tollen's test.) Using glucose, $C_6H_{12}O_6$ to illustrate this test, the oxidation-reduction reaction occurring is

$$C_6H_{12}O_6\ (aq) + 2\ Ag^+(aq) + 2\ OH^-(aq) \rightarrow$$
$$C_6H_{12}O_7(aq) + 2\ Ag(s) + H_2O(\ell)$$

What has been oxidized, and what has been reduced? What is the oxidizing agent, and what is the reducing agent?

(a)   (b)

Tollen's test. The reaction of silver ions with a sugar such as glucose produces metallic silver. (a) The set up for the reaction. (b) The silvered testtube

Summary and Conceptual Questions

The following questions may use concepts from this and previous chapters.

74. There are many ionic compounds that dissolve in water to a very small extent. One example is lead(II) chloride. Suppose you stir some solid $PbCl_2$ into water. Explain how you would prove that the compound dissolves but to a small extent? Is the dissolving process product-favored or reactant-favored?

$$PbCl_2(s) \rightleftharpoons Pb^{2+}(aq) + 2\ Cl^-(aq)$$

75. ▲ Most naturally occurring acids are weak acids. Lactic acid is one example.

$$CH_3CH(OH)CO_2H(s) + H_2O(\ell) \rightleftharpoons$$
$$H_3O^+(aq) + CH_3CH(OH)CO_2^-(aq)$$

If you place some lactic acid in water, it will ionize to a small extent, and an equilibrium will be established eventually. Suggest some experiments to prove that this is a weak acid and that the establishment of equilibrium is a reversible process.

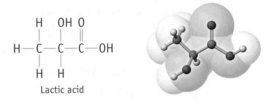

Lactic acid

76. ■ ▲ You want to prepare barium chloride, $BaCl_2$, using an exchange reaction of some type. To do so, you have the following reagents from which to select the reactants: $BaSO_4$, $BaBr_2$, $BaCO_3$, $Ba(OH)_2$, HCl, $HgSO_4$, $AgNO_3$, and HNO_3. Write a complete, balanced equation for the reaction chosen. *(Note: There are several possibilities.)*

77. ■ Describe how to prepare $BaSO_4$, barium sulfate, by (a) a precipitation reaction and (b) a gas-forming reaction. To do so, you have the following reagents from which to select the reactants: $BaCl_2$, $BaCO_3$, $Ba(OH)_2$, H_2SO_4, and Na_2SO_4. Write complete, balanced equations for the reactions chosen. (See page 130 for an illustration of the preparation of a compound.)

78. ■ Describe how to prepare zinc chloride by (a) an acid–base reaction, (b) a gas-forming reaction, and (c) an oxidation-reduction reaction. The available starting materials are $ZnCO_3$, HCl, Cl_2, HNO_3, $Zn(OH)_2$, $NaCl$, $Zn(NO_3)_2$, and Zn. Write complete, balanced equations for the reactions chosen.

4 | Stoichiometry: Quantitative Information About Chemical Reactions

The Chemistry of a Sparkler

This "sparkler," like many forms of fireworks, depends on some very straightforward chemistry. It consists of a mixture of finely powdered metals, such as Al and Fe, other substances such as $KClO_3$, KNO_3, and a binder that holds the mixture onto a wire handle. When ignited, the powdered metal reacts with oxygen in the air (or extracted from $KClO_3$), and the sparks fly!

Questions:

1. What kind of chemical reaction is occurring here?
2. What are the likely products from the reaction of aluminum metal or iron with oxygen in the air or with $KClO_3$?
3. If the sparkler contains 1.0 g of Al, what is the mass of the product of the reaction of aluminum with oxygen?

Answers to these questions are in Appendix Q.

Charles D. Winters

Chapter Goals

Chapter Outline

The objective of this chapter is to introduce the quantitative study of chemical reactions. Quantitative studies are needed to determine, for example, how much oxygen is required for the complete combustion of a given quantity of gasoline and what masses of carbon dioxide and water can be obtained. This part of chemistry is fundamental to much of what chemists, chemical engineers, biochemists, molecular biologists, geochemists, and many others do.

Chemistry.☼.Now™

Throughout the text this icon introduces an opportunity for self-study or to explore interactive tutorials by signing in at **www.cengage.com/login**.

4.1 Mass Relationships in Chemical Reactions: Stoichiometry

 Module 7

A balanced chemical equation shows the quantitative relationship between reactants and products in a chemical reaction. Let us apply this concept to the reaction of phosphorus and chlorine (◄ Figure 3.1).

$$P_4(s) + 6\ Cl_2(g) \longrightarrow 4\ PCl_3(\ell)$$

Suppose you use 1.00 mol of phosphorus (P_4, 124 g/mol) in this reaction. The balanced equation shows that 6.00 mol (= 425 g) of Cl_2 must be used for complete reaction with 1.00 mol of P_4 and that 4.00 mol (= 549 g) of PCl_3 can be produced. The mole and mass relationships of reactants and products in a reaction can be summarized in an *amounts table*. You will find such tables helpful in identifying the amounts of reactants and products and the changes that occur upon reaction.

Equation	$P_4(s)$ +	$6\ Cl_2(g)$ →	$4\ PCl_3(\ell)$
Initial amount (mol)	1.00 mol (124 g)	6.00 mol (425 g)	0 mol (0 g)
Change in amount upon reaction (mol)	−1.00 mol	−6.00 mol	+4.00 mol
Amount after complete reaction (mol)	0 mol (0 g)	0 mol (0 g)	4.00 mol [549 g = 124 g + 425 g]

The balanced equation for a reaction tells us the correct *mole ratios* of reactants and products. Here, 6 mol of Cl_2 should be used per mole of P_4. Now, what if only 0.0100 mol of P_4 (1.24 g) is available? Six times as many moles of Cl_2 are still required (0.0600 mol of Cl_2; 4.25 g), and 0.0400 mol of PCl_3 (5.49 g) will be formed. The only requirement is that there should be a ratio of 6 to 1 for the amount of Cl_2 relative to the amount of P_4.

■ **Amounts Tables** Amounts tables are useful not only here but will also be used extensively when you study chemical equilibria more thoroughly in Chapters 16–18.

■ **Stoichiometry and Reaction Completeness** *Stoichiometry calculations assume reactions are complete.* That is, *all* of at least one of the reactants has been converted to the product or products. Recall from the discussion of chemical equilibrium in Chapter 3 that some reactions do not reach completion, however.

■ **Amount** The amount of a substance is the number of moles of that substance.

Following this line of reasoning, let us determine (a) what mass of Cl_2 is required to react completely with 1.45 g of phosphorus and (b) what mass of PCl_3 can be produced.

Part (a): Mass of Cl_2 Required

Step 1. *Write the balanced equation* (using correct formulas for reactants and products). This is always the first step when dealing with chemical reactions.

$$P_4(s) + 6\ Cl_2(g) \longrightarrow 4\ PCl_3(\ell)$$

Step 2. *Calculate amount (moles) from mass (grams).* From the mass of P_4, calculate the amount of P_4 available.

$$1.45\ \cancel{g\ P_4} \times \frac{1\ mol\ P_4}{123.9\ \cancel{g\ P_4}} = 0.0117\ mol\ P_4$$

1/molar mass of P_4

Step 3. *Use a stoichiometric factor.* The amount of Cl_2 required is related by the balanced equation to the amount of the other reactant (P_4) available.

$$0.0117\ \cancel{mol\ P_4} \times \frac{6\ mol\ Cl_2\ required}{1\ \cancel{mol\ P_4}\ required} = 0.0702\ mol\ Cl_2\ required$$

stoichiometric factor from balanced equation

To perform this calculation the amount of phosphorus available has been multiplied by a **stoichiometric factor**, a mole ratio based on the coefficients for the two chemicals in the balanced equation. Here, the balanced equation specifies that 6 mol of Cl_2 is required for each mole of P_4, so the stoichiometric factor is (6 mol Cl_2/1 mol P_4). Calculation shows that 0.0702 mol of Cl_2 is required to react with all the available phosphorus (1.45 g, 0.0117 mol).

Problem Solving Tip 4.1 Stoichiometry Calculations

You are asked to determine what mass of product can be formed from a given mass of reactant. It is not possible to calculate the mass of product in a single step. Instead, you must follow a route such as that illustrated here for the reaction of a reactant A to give the product B according to an equation such as $x\ A \longrightarrow y\ B$.

- The mass (g) of reactant A is converted to the amount (moles) of A.
- Next, using the stoichiometric factor, find the amount (moles) of B.
- Finally, the mass (g) of B is obtained by multiplying amount of B by its molar mass.

When solving a stoichiometry problem, remember that you will always use a stoichiometric factor at some point.

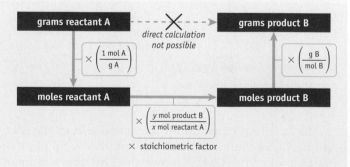

Step 4. *Calculate mass from amount.* Convert the amount (moles) of Cl_2 calculated in Step 3 to mass (in grams) of Cl_2 required.

$$0.0702 \ \text{mol } Cl_2 \times \frac{70.91 \ \text{g } Cl_2}{1 \ \text{mol } Cl_2} = 4.98 \ \text{g } Cl_2$$

Part (b) Mass of PCl_3 Produced from P_4 and Cl_2

What mass of PCl_3 can be produced from the reaction of 1.45 g of phosphorus with 4.98 g of Cl_2? From part (a), we know that these masses are the correct quantities needed for complete reaction. Because matter is conserved, the answer can be obtained by adding the masses of P_4 and Cl_2 used (giving 1.45 g + 4.98 g = 6.43 g of PCl_3 produced). Alternatively, Steps 3 and 4 can be repeated, but with the appropriate stoichiometric factor and molar mass.

Step 3b. *Use a stoichiometric factor. Convert the amount of available P_4 to the amount of PCl_3 produced.* Here, the balanced equation specifies that 4 mol PCl_3 is produced for each mole of P_4 used, so the stoichiometric factor is (4 mol PCl_3/1 mol P_4)

$$0.0117 \ \text{mol } P_4 \times \frac{4 \ \text{mol } PCl_3 \ \text{produced}}{1 \ \text{mol } P_4 \ \text{available}} = 0.0468 \ \text{mol } PCl_3 \ \text{produced}$$

↑

stoichiometric factor from balanced equation

Step 4b. *Calculate the mass of product from its amount.* Convert the amount of PCl_3 produced to a mass in grams.

$$0.0468 \ \text{mol } PCl_3 \times \frac{137.3 \ \text{g } PCl_3}{1 \ \text{mol } PCl_3} = 6.43 \ \text{g } PCl_3$$

Chemistry ⚛ Now™

Sign in at **www.cengage.com/login** and go to Chapter 4 Contents to see:
- Screen 4.2 for (a) a video and animation of **the phosphorus and chlorine reaction discussed in this section,** and (b) an exercise that examines **the reaction between chlorine and elemental phosphorus**
- Screen 4.3 for a tutorial on **yield**

■ **EXAMPLE 4.1 Mass Relations in Chemical Reactions**

Problem Glucose, $C_6H_{12}O_6$, reacts with oxygen to give CO_2 and H_2O. What mass of oxygen (in grams) is required for complete reaction of 25.0 g of glucose? What masses of carbon dioxide and water (in grams) are formed?

Strategy After writing a balanced equation, you can perform the stoichiometric calculations using the scheme in Problem Solving Tip 4.1.

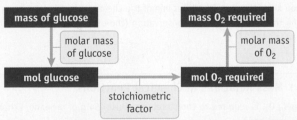

First, find the amount of glucose available; then relate it to the amount of O_2 required using the stoichiometric factor based on the coefficients in the balanced equation. Finally, find the mass of O_2 required from the amount of O_2. Follow the same procedure to calculate the masses of carbon dioxide and water.

■ **Mass Balance and Moles of Reactants and Products** Mass is always conserved in chemical reactions. The total mass of the reactants is always the same as the products. This does not mean, however, that the total amount (moles) of reactants is the same as that of the products. Atoms are rearranged into different "units" (molecules) in the course of a reaction. In the $P_4 + Cl_2$ reaction, 7 mol of reactants gives 4 mol of product.

Solution

Step 1. Write a balanced equation.

$$C_6H_{12}O_6(s) + 6\ O_2(g) \rightarrow 6\ CO_2(g) + 6\ H_2O(\ell)$$

Step 2. Convert the mass of glucose to amount.

$$25.0\ g\ glucose \times \frac{1\ mol}{180.2\ g} = 0.139\ mol\ glucose$$

Step 3. Use the stoichiometric factor. Here we calculate the amount of O_2 required.

$$0.139\ mol\ glucose \times \frac{6\ mol\ O_2}{1\ mol\ glucose} = 0.832\ mol\ O_2$$

Step 4. Calculate mass from amount. Convert the required amount of O_2 to a mass in grams.

$$0.832\ mol\ O_2 \times \frac{32.00\ g}{1\ mol\ O_2} = 26.6\ g\ O_2$$

Repeat Steps 3 and 4 to find the mass of CO_2 produced in the combustion. First, relate the amount (moles) of glucose available to the amount of CO_2 produced using a stoichiometric factor. Then convert the amount of CO_2 to its mass in grams.

$$0.139\ mol\ glucose \times \frac{6\ mol\ CO_2}{1\ mol\ glucose} \times \frac{44.01\ g\ CO_2}{1\ mol\ CO_2} = \boxed{36.6\ g\ CO_2}$$

Now, how can you find the mass of H_2O produced? You could go through Steps 3 and 4 again. However, recognize that the total mass of reactants

$$25.0\ g\ C_6H_{12}O_6 + 26.6\ g\ O_2 = 51.6\ g\ reactants$$

must be the same as the total mass of products. The mass of water that can be produced is therefore

$$\text{Total mass of products} = 51.6\ g = 36.6\ g\ CO_2\ produced + ?\ g\ H_2O$$

$$\text{Mass of } H_2O \text{ produced} = \boxed{15.0\ g}$$

The results of this calculation can be summarized in an amounts table.

Equation	$C_6H_{12}O_6(s)$	+ 6 $O_2(g)$	→ 6 $CO_2(g)$	+ 6 $H_2O(\ell)$
Initial amount (mol)	0.139 mol	6(0.139 mol) = 0.832 mol	0	0
Change (mol)	−0.139 mol	−0.832 mol	+0.832 mol	+0.832 mol
Amount after reaction (mol)	0	0	0.832 mol	0.832 mol

Comment When you know the mass of all but one of the chemicals in a reaction, you can find the unknown mass using the principle of mass conservation (the total mass of reactants must equal the total mass of products; page 114).

EXERCISE 4.1 Mass Relations in Chemical Reactions

What mass of oxygen, O_2, is required to completely combust 454 g of propane, C_3H_8? What masses of CO_2 and H_2O are produced?

4.2 Reactions in Which One Reactant Is Present in Limited Supply

Reactions are often carried out with an excess of one reactant over that required by stoichiometry. This is usually done to ensure that one of the reactants in the reaction is consumed completely, even though some of another reactant remains unused.

Suppose you burn a toy "sparkler," a wire coated with a mixture of aluminum or iron powder and potassium nitrate or chlorate (Figure 4.1 and page 158). The aluminum or iron burns, consuming oxygen from the air or from the potassium salt and producing a metal oxide.

$$4\ Al(s) + 3\ O_2(g) \rightarrow 2\ Al_2O_3(s)$$

The sparkler burns until the metal powder is consumed completely. What about the oxygen? Four moles of aluminum require three moles of oxygen, but there is much, much more O_2 available in the air than is needed to consume the metal in a sparkler. How much metal oxide is produced? That depends on the quantity of metal powder in the sparkler, not on the quantity of O_2 in the atmosphere. The metal powder in this example is called the **limiting reactant** because its amount determines, or limits, the amount of product formed.

Let us look at an example of a limiting reactant situation using the reaction of oxygen and carbon monoxide to give carbon dioxide. The balanced equation for the reaction is

$$2\ CO(g) + O_2(g) \rightarrow 2\ CO_2(g)$$

Suppose you have a mixture of four CO molecules and three O_2 molecules. The four CO molecules require only two O_2 molecules (and produce four CO_2 molecules). This means that one O_2 molecule remains after reaction is complete.

FIGURE 4.1 Burning aluminum and iron powder. A toy sparkler contains a metal powder such as Al or Fe and other chemicals such as KNO_3 or $KClO_3$. When ignited, the metal burns with a brilliant white light.

Reactants: 4 **CO** and 3 **O_2** ⟶ Products: 4 **CO_2** and 1 **O_2**

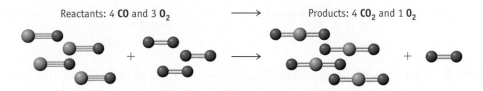

Because more O_2 molecules are available than are required, the number of CO_2 molecules produced is determined by the number of CO molecules available. Carbon monoxide, CO, is therefore the limiting reactant in this case.

A Stoichiometry Calculation with a Limiting Reactant

The first step in the manufacture of nitric acid is the oxidation of ammonia to NO over a platinum-wire gauze (Figure 4.2).

$$4\ NH_3(g) + 5\ O_2(g) \rightarrow 4\ NO(g) + 6\ H_2O(\ell)$$

Suppose that equal masses of NH_3 and O_2 are mixed (750. g of each). Are these reactants mixed in the correct stoichiometric ratio, or is one of them in short supply? That is, will one of them limit the quantity of NO that can be produced? How much NO can be formed if the reaction using this reactant mixture goes to completion? And how much of the excess reactant is left over when the maximum amount of NO has been formed?

■ **Comparing Reactant Ratios** For the CO/O_2 reaction, the stoichiometric ratio of reactants should be (2 mol CO/1 mol O_2). However, the ratio of amounts of reactants available in the text example is (4 mol CO/3 mol O_2) or (1.33 mol CO/1 mol O_2). The fact that the CO/O_2 ratio is not large enough tells us that there is not enough CO to react with all of the available O_2. Carbon monoxide is the limiting reactant, and some O_2 will be left over when all of the CO is consumed.

Charles D. Winters

(a)

(b)

Active Figure 4.2 **Oxidation of ammonia.** (a) Burning ammonia on the surface of a platinum wire produces so much heat that the wire glows bright red. (b) Billions of kilograms of HNO_3 are made annually starting with the oxidation of ammonia over a wire gauze containing platinum.

Chemistry ⬡ Now™ Sign in at www.cengage.com/login and go to the Chapter Contents menu to explore an interactive version of this figure accompanied by an exercise.

Step 1. Find the amount of each reactant.

$$750. \text{ g NH}_3 \times \frac{1 \text{ mol NH}_3}{17.03 \text{ g NH}_3} = 44.0 \text{ mol NH}_3 \text{ available}$$

$$750. \text{ g O}_2 \times \frac{1 \text{ mol O}_2}{32.00 \text{ g O}_2} = 23.4 \text{ mol O}_2 \text{ available}$$

Step 2. What is the limiting reactant? Examine the ratio of amounts of reactants. Are the reactants present in the correct stoichiometric ratio as given by the balanced equation?

$$\text{Stoichiometric ratio of reactants required by balanced equation} = \frac{5 \text{ mol O}_2}{4 \text{ mol NH}_3} = \frac{1.25 \text{ mol O}_2}{1 \text{ mol NH}_3}$$

$$\text{Ratio of reactants } actually \text{ } available = \frac{23.4 \text{ mol O}_2}{44.0 \text{ mol NH}_3} = \frac{0.532 \text{ mol O}_2}{1 \text{ mol NH}_3}$$

Dividing moles of O_2 available by moles of NH_3 available shows that the ratio of available reactants is much smaller than the 5 mol O_2/4 mol NH_3 ratio required by the balanced equation. Thus, there is not sufficient O_2 available to react with all of the NH_3. In this case, oxygen, O_2, is the limiting reactant. That is, 1 mol of NH_3 requires 1.25 mol of O_2, but we have only 0.532 mol of O_2 available.

Step 3. Calculate the mass of product. We can now calculate the expected mass of product, NO, based on the amount of the limiting reactant, O_2.

$$23.4 \text{ mol O}_2 \times \frac{4 \text{ mol NO}}{5 \text{ mol O}_2} \times \frac{30.01 \text{ g NO}}{1 \text{ mol NO}} = 562 \text{ g NO}$$

Step 4. Calculate the mass of excess reactant. Ammonia is the "excess reactant" in this NH_3/O_2 reaction because more than enough NH_3 is available to react with 23.4 mol of O_2. Let us calculate the quantity of NH_3 remaining after all the O_2 has been used. To do so, we first need to know the amount of NH_3 required to consume all the limiting reactant, O_2.

$$23.4 \text{ mol } O_2 \text{ available} \times \frac{4 \text{ mol } NH_3 \text{ required}}{5 \text{ mol } O_2} = 18.8 \text{ mol } NH_3 \text{ required}$$

Because 44.0 mol of NH_3 is available, the amount of excess NH_3 can be calculated,

$$\text{Excess } NH_3 = 44.0 \text{ mol } NH_3 \text{ available} - 18.8 \text{ mol } NH_3 \text{ required}$$
$$= 25.2 \text{ mol } NH_3 \text{ remaining}$$

and then converted to a mass.

$$25.2 \text{ mol } NH_3 \times \frac{17.03 \text{ g } NH_3}{1 \text{ mol } NH_3} = 429 \text{ g } NH_3 \text{ in excess of that required}$$

Finally, because 429 g of NH_3 is left over, this means that 321 g of NH_3 has been consumed ($= 750. \text{ g} - 429 \text{ g}$).

In limiting reactant problems, it is helpful to summarize your results in an amounts table.

Equation	$4 NH_3(g)$	$+$	$5 O_2(g)$	$\rightarrow$	$4 NO(g)$	$+$	$6 H_2O(\ell)$
Initial amount (mol)	44.0		23.4		0		0
Change in amount (mol)	$-(4/5)(23.4)$ $= -18.8$		-23.4		$+(4/5)(23.4)$ $= +18.8$		$+(6/5)(23.4)$ $= +28.1$
After complete reaction (mol)	25.2		0		18.8		28.1

All of the limiting reactant, O_2, is consumed. Of the original 44.0 mol of NH_3, 18.8 mol is consumed and 25.2 mol remains. The balanced equation indicates that the amount of NO produced is equal to the amount of NH_3 consumed, so 18.8 mol of NO is produced from 18.8 mol of NH_3. In addition, 28.1 mol of H_2O is produced.

■ **Conservation of Mass** Mass is conserved in the $NH_3 + O_2$ reaction. The total mass present before reaction (1500. g) is the same as the total mass produced in the reaction plus the mass of NH_3 remaining. That is, 562 g of NO (18.8 mol) and 506 g of H_2O (28.1 mol) are produced. Because 429 g of NH_3 (25.2 mol) remains, the total mass after reaction (562 g + 506 g + 429 g) is the same as the total mass before reaction.

Chemistry ⚛ Now™

Sign in at **www.cengage.com/login** and go to Chapter 4 Contents menu to see:
- Screen 4.4 for a video and animation of **the limiting reactant in the methanol and oxygen reaction**
- Screen 4.5 for (a) an exercise on **zinc and hydrochloric acid in aqueous solution** and (b) a simulation **using limiting reactants**

■ **EXAMPLE 4.2 A Reaction with a Limiting Reactant**

Problem Methanol, CH_3OH, which is used as a fuel, can be made by the reaction of carbon monoxide and hydrogen.

$$CO(g) + 2 H_2(g) \rightarrow CH_3OH(\ell)$$
$$\text{methanol}$$

Suppose 356 g of CO and 65.0 g of H_2 are mixed and allowed to react.

(a) Which is the limiting reactant?

(b) What mass of methanol can be produced?

(c) What mass of the excess reactant remains after the limiting reactant has been consumed?

A car that uses methanol as a fuel. In this car, methanol is converted to hydrogen, which is then combined with oxygen in a fuel cell. The fuel cell generates electric energy to run the car (see Chapter 20). See Example 4.2.

Strategy There are usually two steps to a limiting reactant problem:

(a) After calculating the amount of each reactant, compare the ratio of reactant amounts to the required stoichiometric ratio, here 2 mol H_2/1 mol CO.

- If [mol H_2 available/mol CO available] > 2/1, then CO is the limiting reactant.
- If [mol H_2 available/mol CO available] < 2/1, then H_2 is the limiting reactant.

(b) Use the amount of limiting reactant to find the masses of product and excess reactant.

Solution

(a) *What is the limiting reactant?* The amount of each reactant is

$$\text{Amount of CO} = 356 \text{ g CO} \times \frac{1 \text{ mol CO}}{28.01 \text{ g CO}} = 12.7 \text{ mol CO}$$

$$\text{Amount of H}_2 = 65.0 \text{ g H}_2 \times \frac{1 \text{ mol H}_2}{2.016 \text{ g H}_2} = 32.2 \text{ mol H}_2$$

Are these reactants present in a perfect stoichiometric ratio?

$$\frac{\text{Mol H}_2 \text{ available}}{\text{Mol CO available}} = \frac{32.2 \text{ mol H}_2}{12.7 \text{ mol CO}} = \frac{2.54 \text{ mol H}_2}{1.00 \text{ mol CO}}$$

The required mole ratio is 2 mol of H_2 to 1 mol of CO. Here, we see that more hydrogen is available than is required to consume all the CO. It follows that not enough CO is present to use up all of the hydrogen. CO is the limiting reactant.

(b) *What is the maximum mass of CH_3OH that can be formed?* This calculation must be based on the amount of limiting reactant.

$$12.7 \text{ mol CO} \times \frac{1 \text{ mol CH}_3\text{OH formed}}{1 \text{ mol CO available}} \times \frac{32.04 \text{ g CH}_3\text{OH}}{1 \text{ mol CH}_3\text{OH}} = \boxed{407 \text{ g CH}_3\text{OH}}$$

(c) *What mass of H_2 remains when all the CO has been converted to product?* First, we must find the amount of H_2 required to react with all the CO, then calculate the mass from the amount.

$$12.7 \text{ mol CO} \times \frac{2 \text{ mol H}_2}{1 \text{ mol CO}} = 25.4 \text{ mol H}_2 \text{ required}$$

Because 32.2 mol of H_2 is available, but only 25.4 mol is required by the limiting reactant, 32.2 mol − 25.4 mol = 6.8 mol of H_2 is in excess. This is equivalent to 14 g of H_2.

Comment The amounts table for this reaction is

Equation	CO(g)	+	2 H₂(g)	→	CH₃OH(ℓ)
Initial amount (mol)	12.7		32.2		0
Change (mol)	−12.7		−2(12.7)		+12.7
After complete reaction (mol)	0		6.8		12.7

The mass of product formed plus the mass of H_2 remaining after reaction (407 g CH_3OH produced + 14 g H_2 remaining = 421 g) is equal to the mass of reactants present before reaction (356 g CO + 65.0 g H_2 = 421 g).

Charles D. Winters

Thermite reaction. Iron(III) oxide reacts with aluminum metal to produce aluminum oxide and iron metal. The reaction produces so much heat that the iron melts and spews out of the reaction vessel. See Exercise 4.2.

EXERCISE 4.2 A Reaction with a Limiting Reactant

The thermite reaction produces iron metal and aluminum oxide from a mixture of powdered aluminum metal and iron(III) oxide.

$$\text{Fe}_2\text{O}_3(s) + 2 \text{ Al}(s) \longrightarrow 2 \text{ Fe}(\ell) + \text{Al}_2\text{O}_3(s)$$

A mixture of 50.0 g each of Fe_2O_3 and Al is used.

(a) Which is the limiting reactant?

(b) What mass of iron metal can be produced?

Problem Solving Tip 4.2 Moles of Reaction and Limiting Reactants

There is another method of solving stoichiometry problems that applies especially well to limiting reactant problems. This involves the useful concept of "moles of reaction."

One "mole of reaction" is said to have occurred when the reaction has taken place according to the number of moles given by the coefficients in the equation. For example, for the reaction of CO and O_2,

$$2\ CO(g) + O_2(g) \longrightarrow 2\ CO_2(g)$$

one mol of reaction occurs when 2 mol of CO and 1 mol of O_2 produce 2 mol of CO_2. If the reaction mixture consists of only 1 mol of CO and 0.5 mol of O_2, then only 1 mol of CO_2 is produced, and 0.5 mol of reaction has occurred according to this balanced equation.

To pursue this example further, suppose 9.5 g of CO and excess O_2 are combined. What amount of CO_2 (moles) can be produced?

$$9.5\ g\ CO \times \frac{1\ mol\ CO}{28.0\ g\ CO} \times \frac{1\ mol\text{-}rxn}{2\ mol\ CO}$$
$$= 0.34\ mol\text{-}rxn$$

$$0.34\ mol\text{-}rxn \times \frac{2\ mol\ CO_2}{1\ mol\text{-}rxn} = 0.68\ mol\ CO_2$$

You can see in this example that the number of moles of reaction that occurred is calculated by multiplying the amount (moles) of the reactant CO by the factor, 1 mol-rxn/2 mol CO (which amounts to dividing the amount of CO by its stoichiometric coefficient).

All reactants and products involved in a chemical reaction undergo the same number of moles of reaction because the reaction can only occur a certain number of times before the reactants are consumed and the reaction reaches completion.

If one of the reactants is in short supply, the actual number of times a reaction can be carried out—the number of "moles of reaction"—will be determined by the limiting reactant. To use this approach, we first calculate the amount of each reactant initially present and then calculate the **moles of reaction** that could occur with each amount of reactant. (This is equivalent to dividing amount [moles] of each reactant by its stoichiometric coefficient.) The reactant producing the smallest number of moles of reaction is the limiting reactant. Once the limiting reactant is known, we proceed as before.

Consider again the NH_3/O_2 reaction on page 163:

1. *Calculate the moles of reaction predicted for each reactant, and decide on the limiting reactant.*

   In the case of the NH_3/O_2 reaction,

   $$4\ NH_3(g) + 5\ O_2(g) \longrightarrow 4\ NO(g) + 6\ H_2O(\ell)$$

   1 "mole of reaction" uses 4 mol of NH_3 and 5 mol of O_2 and produces 4 mol of NO and 6 mol of H_2O. In the example on page 163, we started with 44.0 mol of NH_3, so 11.0 mol of reaction can result.

   $$44.0\ mol\ NH_3 \times \frac{1\ mol\text{-}rxn}{4\ mol\ NH_3} = 11.0\ mol\text{-}rxn$$

   Based on the amount of O_2 available, 4.68 mol of reaction can occur.

   $$23.4\ mol\ O_2 \times \frac{1\ mol\text{-}rxn}{5\ mol\ O_2} = 4.68\ mol\text{-}rxn$$

   Fewer moles of reaction can occur with the amount of O_2 available, so O_2 is the limiting reactant.

2. *Calculate the change in amount and the amount upon completion of the reaction, for each reactant and product.* The number of moles of reaction predicted by the limiting reactant corresponds to the number of moles of reaction that can *actually* occur. Each reactant and product will undergo this number of moles of reaction, 4.68 mol-rxn in this case. To calculate the *change* in amount for a given reactant or product, multiply this number of moles of reaction by the stoichiometric coefficient of the reactant or product. To illustrate this step, for NH_3 this corresponds to the following calculation:

$$4.68\ mol\text{-}rxn \times \left(\frac{4\ mole\ NH_3}{1\ mol\text{-}rxn}\right) =$$
$$18.8\ mol\ NH_3.$$

The amount of each reactant and product after reaction is calculated as usual.

Equation $4\ NH_3(g) + 5\ O_2(g) \longrightarrow 4\ NO(g) + 6\ H_2O(g)$			
Initial amount (mol)			
44.0	23.4	0	0
Moles of reaction based on limiting reactant (mol)			
4.68	4.68	4.68	4.68
Change in amount (mol)			
−4.68(4)	−4.68(5)	+4.68(4)	+4.68(6)
= −18.8	= −23.4	= +18.8	= +28.1
Amount remaining after complete reaction (mol)			
25.2	0	18.8	28.1

Finally, from the amounts present after completion, we can calculate the masses of the products and of any reactant remaining.

You may find this approach easier to use particularly when there are more than two reactants, each present initially in some designated quantity.

A final note: the concept of "moles of reaction" will be applied in this text in the discussion of thermochemistry in Chapters 5 and 19.

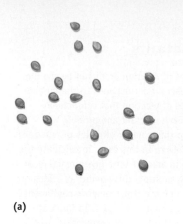

(a)

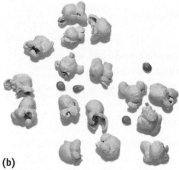

(b)

FIGURE 4.3 Percent yield. Although not a chemical reaction, popping corn is a good analogy to the difference between a theoretical yield and an actual yield. Here, we began with 20 popcorn kernels and found that only 16 of them popped. The percent yield from our "reaction" was (16/20) x 100%, or 80%.

4.3 Percent Yield

The maximum mass of product that can be obtained from a chemical reaction is the **theoretical yield**. Frequently, however, the **actual yield** of the product—the mass of material that is actually obtained in the laboratory or a chemical plant—is less than the theoretical yield. Loss of product often occurs during the isolation and purification steps. In addition, some reactions do not go completely to products, and reactions are sometimes complicated by giving more than one set of products. For all these reasons, the actual yield is almost always less than the theoretical yield (Figure 4.3).

To provide information to other chemists who might want to carry out a reaction, it is customary to report a percent yield. **Percent yield**, which specifies how much of the theoretical yield was obtained, is defined as

$$\text{Percent yield} = \frac{\text{actual yield}}{\text{theoretical yield}} \times 100\% \qquad (4.1)$$

Suppose you made aspirin in the laboratory by the following reaction:

$$C_7H_6O_3(s) \quad + \quad C_4H_6O_3(\ell) \quad \longrightarrow \quad C_9H_8O_4(s) \quad + \quad CH_3CO_2H(\ell)$$

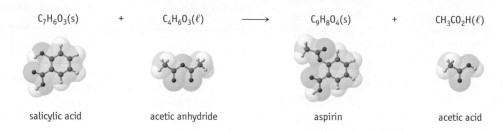

salicylic acid   acetic anhydride   aspirin   acetic acid

and that you began with 14.4 g of salicylic acid and an excess of acetic anhydride. That is, salicylic acid is the limiting reactant. If you obtain 6.26 g of aspirin, what is the percent yield of this product? The first step is to find the amount of the limiting reactant, salicylic acid ($C_6H_4(OH)CO_2H$).

$$14.4 \text{ g } C_6H_4(OH)CO_2H \times \frac{1 \text{ mol } C_6H_4(OH)CO_2H}{138.1 \text{g } C_6H_4(OH)CO_2H} = 0.104 \text{ mol } C_6H_4(OH)CO_2H$$

Next, use the stoichiometric factor from the balanced equation to find the amount of aspirin expected based on the limiting reactant, $C_6H_4(OH)CO_2H$.

$$0.104 \text{ mol } C_6H_4(OH)CO_2H \times \frac{1 \text{ mol aspirin}}{1 \text{ mol } C_6H_4(OH)CO_2H} = 0.104 \text{ mol aspirin}$$

The maximum amount of aspirin that can be produced—the theoretical yield—is 0.104 mol. Because the quantity you measure in the laboratory is the mass of the product, it is customary to express the theoretical yield as a mass in grams.

$$0.104 \text{ mol aspirin} \times \frac{180.2 \text{ g aspirin}}{1 \text{ mol aspirin}} = 18.7 \text{ g aspirin}$$

Finally, with the actual yield known to be only 6.26 g, the percent yield of aspirin can be calculated.

$$\text{Percent yield} = \frac{6.26 \text{ g aspirin obtained (actual yield)}}{18.7 \text{ g aspirin expected (theoretical yield)}} \times 100\% = 33.5\% \text{ yield}$$

> **EXERCISE 4.3 Percent Yield**
>
> Aluminum carbide, Al_4C_3, reacts with water to produce methane.
>
> $$Al_4C_3(s) + 12\ H_2O(\ell) \longrightarrow 4\ Al(OH)_3(s) + 3\ CH_4(g)$$
>
> If 125 g of aluminum carbide is decomposed, what is the theoretical yield of methane? If only 13.6 g of methane is obtained, what is the percent yield of this gas?

FIGURE 4.4 A modern analytical instrument. This nuclear magnetic resonance (NMR) spectrometer is closely related to a magnetic resonance imaging (MRI) instrument found in a hospital. NMR is used to analyze compounds and to decipher their structure. (The instrument is controlled by a computer and console not seen in this photo.)

4.4 Chemical Equations and Chemical Analysis

Analytical chemists use a variety of approaches to identify substances as well as to measure the quantities of components of mixtures. Analytical chemistry is often done now using instrumental methods (Figure 4.4), but classical chemical reactions and stoichiometry still play a central role.

Quantitative Analysis of a Mixture

Quantitative chemical analysis generally depends on one of the following basic ideas:

- A substance, present in unknown amount, can be allowed to react with a known quantity of another substance. If the stoichiometric ratio for their reaction is known, the unknown amount can be determined.
- A material of unknown composition can be converted to one or more substances of known composition. Those substances can be identified, their amounts determined, and these amounts related to the amount of the original, unknown substance.

An example of the first type of analysis is the analysis of a sample of vinegar containing an unknown amount of acetic acid, the ingredient that makes vinegar acidic. The acid reacts readily and completely with sodium hydroxide.

$$\underset{\text{acetic acid}}{CH_3CO_2H(aq)} + NaOH(aq) \longrightarrow CH_3CO_2Na(aq) + H_2O(\ell)$$

If the exact amount of sodium hydroxide used in the reaction can be measured, the amount of acetic acid present can be calculated. This type of analysis is the subject of a later section in this chapter (▶ Section 4.7).

The second type of analysis is exemplified by the analysis of a sample of a mineral, thenardite, which is largely sodium sulfate, Na_2SO_4 (Figure 4.5). Sodium sulfate is soluble in water. Therefore, to find the quantity of Na_2SO_4 in an impure mineral sample, we would crush the rock and then wash the powdered sample thoroughly with water to dissolve the sodium sulfate. Next, we would treat this solution of sodium sulfate with barium chloride to precipitate the water-insoluble compound barium sulfate. The barium sulfate is collected on a filter and weighed (Figure 4.6).

$$Na_2SO_4(aq) + BaCl_2(aq) \longrightarrow BaSO_4(s) + 2\ NaCl(aq)$$

FIGURE 4.5 Thenardite. The mineral thenardite is sodium sulfate, Na_2SO_4. It is named after the French chemist Louis Thenard (1777–1857), a co-discoverer (with J. L. Gay-Lussac and Humphry Davy) of boron. Sodium sulfate is used in making detergents, glass, and paper.

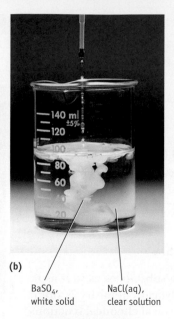

(a)

$Na_2SO_4(aq)$, clear solution

$BaCl_2(aq)$, clear solution

(b)

$BaSO_4$, white solid

$NaCl(aq)$, clear solution

(c)

$NaCl(aq)$, clear solution

$BaSO_4$, white solid caught in filter

(d)

Mass of dry $BaSO_4$ determined

Active Figure 4.6 Analysis for the sulfate content of a sample. The sulfate ions in a solution of Na_2SO_4 react with barium ions (Ba^{2+}) to form $BaSO_4$. The white, solid precipitate, barium sulfate ($BaSO_4$), is collected on a filter and weighed. The amount of $BaSO_4$ obtained can be related to the amount of Na_2SO_4 in the sample.

Chemistry Now™ Sign in at www.cengage.com/login and go to the Chapter Contents menu to explore an interactive version of this figure accompanied by an exercise.

■ **Analysis and 100% Yield** Quantitative analysis requires reactions in which the yield is 100%.

We can then find the amount of sodium sulfate in the mineral sample because it is directly related to the amount of $BaSO_4$.

$$1 \text{ mol } Na_2SO_4(aq) \longrightarrow 1 \text{ mol } BaSO_4(s)$$

Example 4.3 illustrates another instance of the analysis of a mineral in this way.

Chemistry Now™

Sign in at **www.cengage.com/login** and go to Chapter 4 Contents to see Screen 4.7 for a tutorial on **chemical analysis**.

A precipitate of nickel with dimethyl-glyoxime. Red, insoluble $Ni(C_4H_7N_2O_2)_2$ precipitates when dimethylglyoxime ($C_4H_8N_2O_2$) is added to an aqueous solution of nickel(II) ions. (See Example 4.3.)

■ **EXAMPLE 4.3 Mineral Analysis**

Problem Nickel(II) sulfide, NiS, occurs naturally as the relatively rare mineral millerite. One of its occurrences is in meteorites. To analyze a mineral sample for the quantity of NiS, the sample is dissolved in nitric acid to form a solution of $Ni(NO_3)_2$.

$$NiS(s) + 4 \text{ } HNO_3(aq) \longrightarrow Ni(NO_3)_2(aq) + S(s) + 2 \text{ } NO_2(g) + 2 \text{ } H_2O(\ell)$$

The aqueous solution of $Ni(NO_3)_2$ is then treated with the organic compound dimethylglyoxime ($C_4H_8N_2O_2$, DMG) to give the red solid $Ni(C_4H_7N_2O_2)_2$.

$$Ni(NO_3)_2(aq) + 2 \text{ } C_4H_8N_2O_2(aq) \longrightarrow Ni(C_4H_7N_2O_2)_2(s) + 2 \text{ } HNO_3(aq)$$

Suppose a 0.468-g sample containing millerite produces 0.206 g of red, solid $Ni(C_4H_7N_2O_2)_2$. What is the mass percent of NiS in the sample?

Strategy The balanced equations for the reactions show the following "road map":

$$1 \text{ mol NiS} \longrightarrow 1 \text{ mol } Ni(NO_3)_2 \longrightarrow 1 \text{ mol } Ni(C_4H_7N_2O_2)_2$$

If we know the mass of $Ni(C_4H_7N_2O_2)_2$, we can calculate its amount and thus the amount of NiS. The amount of NiS allows us to calculate the mass and mass percent of NiS in the sample.

Solution The molar mass of $Ni(C_4H_7N_2O_2)_2$ is 288.9 g/mol. The amount of this red solid is

$$0.206 \text{ g } Ni(C_4H_7N_2O_2)_2 \times \frac{1 \text{ mol } Ni(C_4H_7N_2O_2)_2}{288.9 \text{ g } Ni(C_4H_7N_2O_2)_2} = 7.13 \times 10^{-4} \text{ mol } Ni(C_4H_7N_2O_2)_2$$

Because 1 mol of $Ni(C_4H_7N_2O_2)_2$ is ultimately produced from 1 mol of NiS, the amount of NiS in the sample must have been 7.13×10^{-4} mol.

With the amount of NiS known, we calculate the mass of NiS.

$$7.13 \times 10^{-4} \text{ mol NiS} \times \frac{90.76 \text{ g NiS}}{1 \text{ mol NiS}} = 0.0647 \text{ g NiS}$$

Finally, the mass percent of NiS in the 0.468-g sample is

$$\text{Mass percent NiS} = \frac{0.0647 \text{ g NiS}}{0.468 \text{ g sample}} \times 100\% = \boxed{13.8\% \text{ NiS}}$$

EXERCISE 4.4 Analysis of a Mixture

One method for determining the purity of a sample of titanium(IV) oxide, TiO_2, an important industrial chemical, is to react the sample with bromine trifluoride.

$$3 \text{ TiO}_2(s) + 4 \text{ BrF}_3(\ell) \longrightarrow 3 \text{ TiF}_4(s) + 2 \text{ Br}_2(\ell) + 3 \text{ O}_2(g)$$

This reaction is known to occur completely and quantitatively. That is, all of the oxygen in TiO_2 is evolved as O_2. Suppose 2.367 g of a TiO_2-containing sample evolves 0.143 g of O_2. What is the mass percent of TiO_2 in the sample?

Determining the Formula of a Compound by Combustion

The empirical formula of a compound can be determined if the percent composition of the compound is known (◄ Section 2.10). But where do the percent composition data come from? One chemical method that works well for compounds that burn in oxygen is analysis by combustion. In this technique, each element in the compound combines with oxygen to produce the appropriate oxide.

Consider an analysis of the hydrocarbon methane, CH_4. A balanced equation for the combustion of methane shows that every atom of C in the original compound appears as CO_2 and every atom of H appears in the form of water. In other words, for every mole of CO_2 observed, there must have been one mole of carbon in the unknown compound. Similarly, for every mole of H_2O observed from combustion, there must have been two moles of H atoms in the unknown carbon-hydrogen compound.

$$CH_4(g) + 2 O_2(g) \longrightarrow CO_2(g) + 2 H_2O(\ell)$$

In the combustion experiment, gaseous carbon dioxide and water are separated (as illustrated in Figure 4.7) and their masses determined. From these masses, it is possible to calculate the amounts of C and H in CO_2 and H_2O, respectively, and

■ **Finding an Empirical Formula by Chemical Analysis** Finding the empirical formula of a compound by chemical analysis always uses the following procedure:
1. The unknown but pure compound is converted in a chemical reaction into known products.
2. The reaction products are isolated, and the amount of each is determined.
3. The amount of each product is related to the amount of each element in the original compound.
4. The empirical formula is determined from the relative amounts of elements in the original compound.

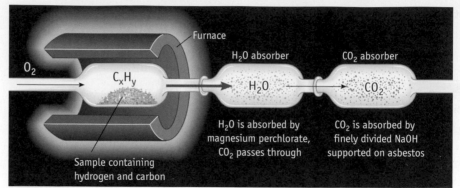

Furnace

O_2

C_xH_y

Sample containing hydrogen and carbon

H_2O absorber

H_2O

H_2O is absorbed by magnesium perchlorate, CO_2 passes through

CO_2 absorber

CO_2

CO_2 is absorbed by finely divided NaOH supported on asbestos

Active Figure 4.7   **Combustion analysis of a hydrocarbon.** If a compound containing C and H is burned in oxygen, CO_2 and H_2O are formed, and the mass of each can be determined. The H_2O is absorbed by magnesium perchlorate, and the CO_2 is absorbed by finely divided NaOH supported on asbestos. The mass of each absorbent before and after combustion gives the masses of CO_2 and H_2O. Only a few milligrams of a combustible compound are needed for analysis.

Chemistry ₒ Now™ Sign in at www.cengage.com/login and go to the Chapter Contents menu to explore an interactive version of this figure accompanied by an exercise.

the ratio of amounts of C and H in a sample of the original compound can then be found. This ratio gives the empirical formula.

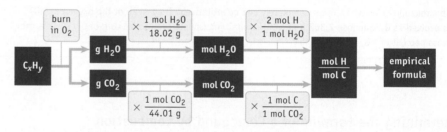

■ **EXAMPLE 4.4 Using Combustion Analysis to Determine the Formula of a Hydrocarbon**

Problem When 1.125 g of a liquid hydrocarbon, C_xH_y, was burned in an apparatus like that shown in Figure 4.7, 3.447 g of CO_2 and 1.647 g of H_2O were produced. The molar mass of the compound was found to be 86.2 g/mol in a separate experiment. Determine the empirical and molecular formulas for the unknown hydrocarbon, C_xH_y.

Strategy As outlined in the preceding diagram, we first calculate the amounts of CO_2 and H_2O. These are then converted to amounts of C and H. The ratio (mol H/mol C) is used to determine the empirical formula of the compound. The molar mass of the compound and the molar mass of the empirical formula are then used to determine the molecular formula.

Solution The amounts of CO_2 and H_2O isolated from the combustion are

$$3.447 \text{ g } CO_2 \times \frac{1 \text{ mol } CO_2}{44.010 \text{ g } CO_2} = 0.07832 \text{ mol } CO_2$$

$$1.647 \text{ g } H_2O \times \frac{1 \text{ mol } H_2O}{18.015 \text{ g } H_2O} = 0.09142 \text{ mol } H_2O$$

For every mole of CO_2 isolated, 1 mol of C must have been present in the unknown compound.

$$0.07832 \text{ mol } CO_2 \times \frac{1 \text{ mol C in unknown}}{1 \text{ mol } CO_2} = 0.07832 \text{ mol C}$$

For every mole of H_2O isolated, 2 mol of H must have been present in the unknown.

$$0.09142 \text{ mol } H_2O \times \frac{2 \text{ mol H in unknown}}{1 \text{ mol } H_2O} = 0.1828 \text{ mol H}$$

The original 1.125 g sample of compound therefore contained 0.07832 mol of C and 0.1828 mol of H. To determine the empirical formula of the unknown, we find the ratio of moles of H to moles of C (◄ Section 2.10).

$$\frac{0.1828 \text{ mol H}}{0.07832 \text{ mol C}} = \frac{2.335 \text{ mol H}}{1.000 \text{ mol C}}$$

Atoms combine to form molecules in whole-number ratios. The translation of this ratio (2.335/1) to a whole-number ratio can usually be done quickly by trial and error. Multiplying the numerator and denominator by 3 gives 7/3. So, we know the ratio is 7 mol H to 3 mol C, which means the empirical formula of the hydrocarbon is C_3H_7.

Comparing the experimental molar mass with the molar mass calculated for the empirical formula,

$$\frac{\text{Experimental molar mass}}{\text{Molar mass of } C_3H_7} = \frac{86.2 \text{ g/mol}}{43.1 \text{ g/mol}} = \frac{2}{1}$$

we find that the molecular formula is twice the empirical formula. That is, the molecular formula is $(C_3H_7)_2$, or C_6H_{14}.

Comment As noted in Problem Solving Tip 2.3 (page 91), for problems of this type be sure to use data with enough significant figures to give accurate atom ratios. Finally, note that the determination of the molecular formula does not end the problem for a chemist. In this case, the formula C_6H_{14} is appropriate for several distinctly different compounds. Two of the five compounds having this formula are shown here:

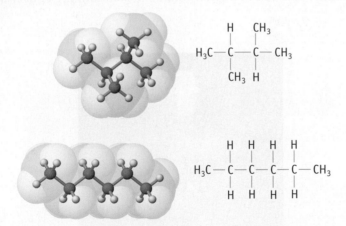

To determine the identity of the unknown compound, more laboratory experiments have to be done. One option is to use an NMR spectrometer such as is pictured in Figure 4.4 or to compare the properties of the unknown with values listed in the chemical literature.

EXERCISE 4.5 Determining the Empirical and Molecular Formulas for a Hydrocarbon

A 0.523-g sample of the unknown compound C_xH_y was burned in air to give 1.612 g of CO_2 and 0.7425 g of H_2O. A separate experiment gave a molar mass for C_xH_y of 114 g/mol. Determine the empirical and molecular formulas for the hydrocarbon.

4.5 Measuring Concentrations of Compounds in Solution

■ **Molar and Molarity** Chemists use "molar" as an adjective to describe a solution. We use "molarity" as a noun. For example, we refer to a 0.1 molar solution or say the solution has a molarity of 0.1 mole per liter.

Most chemical studies require quantitative measurements, including experiments involving aqueous solutions. When doing such experiments, we continue to use balanced equations and moles, but we measure volumes of solution rather than masses of solids, liquids, or gases. Solution concentration expressed as molarity relates the volume of solution in liters to the amount of substance in moles.

Solution Concentration: Molarity

The concept of concentration is useful in many contexts. For example, about 5,500,000 people live in Wisconsin, and the state has a land area of roughly 56,000 square miles; therefore, the average concentration of people is about (5.5×10^6 people/5.6×10^4 square miles) or 98 people per square mile. In chemistry, the amount of solute dissolved in a given volume of solution, the concentration of the

FIGURE 4.8 Volume of solution versus volume of solvent. To make a 0.100 M solution of $CuSO_4$, 25.0 g or 0.100 mol of $CuSO_4 \cdot 5\ H_2O$ (the blue crystalline solid) was placed in a 1.00-L volumetric flask.

For this photo, we measured out exactly 1.00 L of water, which was slowly added to the volumetric flask containing $CuSO_4 \cdot 5\ H_2O$. When enough water had been added so that the solution volume was exactly 1.00 L, approximately 8 mL (the quantity in the small graduated cylinder) was left over from the original 1.00 L of water. This emphasizes that molar concentrations are defined as moles of solute per liter of solution and not per liter of water or other solvent.

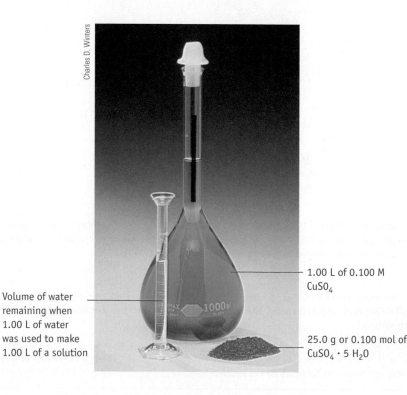

Charles D. Winters

Volume of water remaining when 1.00 L of water was used to make 1.00 L of a solution

1.00 L of 0.100 M $CuSO_4$

25.0 g or 0.100 mol of $CuSO_4 \cdot 5\ H_2O$

solution, can be found in the same way. A useful unit of solute concentration, c, is **molarity**, which is defined as amount of solute per liter of solution.

$$\text{Molarity of } x \ (c_x) = \frac{\text{amount of solute } x \ (\text{mol})}{\text{volume of solution (L)}} \qquad (4.2)$$

For example, if 58.4 g (1.00 mol) of NaCl is dissolved in enough water to give a total solution volume of 1.00 L, the concentration, c, is 1.00 mol/L. This is often abbreviated as 1.00 M, where the capital "M" stands for "moles per liter." Another common notation is to place the formula of the compound in square brackets (for example, [NaCl]); this implies that the concentration of the solute in moles of compound per liter of solution is being specified.

$$c_{NaCl} = [NaCl] = 1.00 \text{ mol/L} = 1.00 \text{ M}$$

It is important to notice that molarity refers to the amount of solute per liter of solution and not per liter of solvent. If one liter of water is added to one mole of a solid compound, the final volume will not be exactly one liter, and the final concentration will not be exactly one mol/L (Figure 4.8). When making solutions of a given molarity, it is always the case that we dissolve the solute in a volume of solvent smaller than the desired volume of solution, then add solvent until the final solution volume is reached.

Potassium permanganate, $KMnO_4$, which was used at one time as a germicide in the treatment of burns, is a shiny, purple-black solid that dissolves readily in water to give a deep purple solution. Suppose 0.435 g of $KMnO_4$ has been dissolved in enough water to give 250. mL of solution (Figure 4.9). What is the concentration

■ **Volumetric Flask** A volumetric flask is a special flask with a line marked on its neck (see Figures 4.8 and 4.9). If the flask is filled with a solution to this line (at a given temperature), it contains precisely the volume of solution specified.

■ **NIST and Solution Concentration** The guidelines from NIST specify that the term "molarity" with its symbol M are obsolete and should no longer be used. Instead, the preferred name is "amount of substance concentration of X" or "amount concentration of X." The numerical value should be followed by the units mol/L. Thus, a solution of salt would be described as having a concentration of $c_{NaCl} = 1.00$ mol/L. Nonetheless, the use of the symbol M, of square brackets, and of the term molarity is so widespread that we shall continue to use them in this edition of the text. See http://physics.nist.gov/Pubs/SP811/sec08.html

Distilled water

250 mL
volumetric flask

0.435 g KMnO₄

The KMnO₄ is first dissolved in a small amount of water.

Distilled water is added to fill the flask with solution just to the mark on the flask.

A mark on the neck of a volumetric flask indicates a volume of exactly 250. mL at 25 °C.

Charles D. Winters

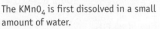

Active Figure 4.9 **Making a solution.** A 0.0110 M solution of KMnO₄ is made by adding enough water to 0.435 g of KMnO₄ to make 0.250 L of solution.

Chemistry **Now**™ Sign in at www.cengage.com/login and go to the Chapter Contents menu to explore an interactive version of this figure accompanied by an exercise.

of $KMnO_4$? The first step is to convert the mass of $KMnO_4$ to an amount (moles) of solute.

$$0.435 \text{ g } KMnO_4 \times \frac{1 \text{ mol } KMnO_4}{158.0 \text{ g } KMnO_4} = 0.00275 \text{ mol } KMnO_4$$

Now that the amount of $KMnO_4$ is known, this information can be combined with the volume of solution—which must be in liters—to give the concentration. Because 250. mL is equivalent to 0.250 L,

$$\text{Concentration of } KMnO_4 = c_{KMnO_4} = [KMnO_4] = \frac{0.00275 \text{ mol } KMnO_4}{0.250 \text{ L}} = 0.0110 \text{ M}$$

The $KMnO_4$ concentration is 0.0110 mol/L, or 0.0110 M. This is useful information, but it is often equally useful to know the concentration of each type of ion in a solution. Like all soluble ionic compounds, $KMnO_4$ dissociates completely into its ions, K^+ and MnO_4^-, when dissolved in water.

$$KMnO_4(aq) \longrightarrow K^+(aq) + MnO_4^-(aq)$$
100% dissociation

One mole of $KMnO_4$ provides 1 mol of K^+ ions and 1 mol of MnO_4^- ions. Accordingly, 0.0110 M $KMnO_4$ gives a concentration of K^+ in the solution of 0.0110 M; similarly, the concentration of MnO_4^- is also 0.0110 M.

Another example of ion concentrations is provided by the dissociation of $CuCl_2$.

$$CuCl_2(aq) \longrightarrow Cu^{2+}(aq) + 2 Cl^-(aq)$$
100% dissociation

If 0.10 mol of $CuCl_2$ is dissolved in enough water to make 1.0 L of solution, the concentration of the copper(II) ion is $[Cu^{2+}] = 0.10$ M. However, the concentration of chloride ions, $[Cl^-]$, is 0.20 M because the compound dissociates in water to provide 2 mol of Cl^- ions for each mole of $CuCl_2$.

Photo: Charles D. Winters

Ion concentrations for a soluble ionic compound. Here, 1 mol of $CuCl_2$ dissociates to 1 mol of Cu^{2+} ions and 2 mol of Cl^- ions. Therefore, the Cl^- concentration is twice the concentration calculated for $CuCl_2$.

Chemistry Now™

Sign in at **www.cengage.com/login** and go to Chapter 4 Contents to see Screen 4.9 for a tutorial on determining **solution concentration** and for a tutorial on **determining ion concentration**.

■ **EXAMPLE 4.5 Concentration**

Problem If 25.3 g of sodium carbonate, Na_2CO_3, is dissolved in enough water to make 250. mL of solution, what is the concentration of Na_2CO_3? What are the concentrations of the Na^+ and CO_3^{2-} ions?

Strategy The concentration of Na_2CO_3 is defined as the amount of Na_2CO_3 per liter of solution. We know the volume of solution (0.250 L). We need the amount of Na_2CO_3. To find the concentrations of the individual ions, recognize that the dissolved salt dissociates completely.

$$Na_2CO_3(s) \longrightarrow 2 Na^+(aq) + CO_3^{2-}(aq)$$

Solution Let us first find the amount of Na_2CO_3.

$$25.3 \text{ g } Na_2CO_3 \times \frac{1 \text{ mol } Na_2CO_3}{106.0 \text{ g } Na_2CO_3} = 0.239 \text{ mol } Na_2CO_3$$

and then the concentration of Na_2CO_3,

$$\text{Concentration of } Na_2CO_3 = \frac{0.239 \text{ mol } Na_2CO_3}{0.250 \text{ L}} = \boxed{0.955 \text{ mol/L}}$$

The ion concentrations follow from the concentration of Na_2CO_3 and the knowledge that each mole of Na_2CO_3 produces 2 mol of Na^+ ions and 1 mol of CO_3^{2-} ions.

$$0.955 \text{ M } Na_2CO_3(aq) \equiv 2 \times 0.955 \text{ M } Na^+(aq) + 0.955 \text{ M } CO_3^{2-}(aq)$$

That is, $[Na^+] = 1.91$ M and $[CO_3^{2-}] = 0.955$ M.

EXERCISE 4.7 Concentration

Sodium bicarbonate, $NaHCO_3$, is used in baking powder formulations and in the manufacture of plastics and ceramics, among other things. If 26.3 g of the compound is dissolved in enough water to make 200. mL of solution, what is the concentration of $NaHCO_3$? What are the concentrations of the ions in solution?

Preparing Solutions of Known Concentration

Chemists often have to prepare a given volume of solution of known concentration. There are two common ways to do this.

Combining a Weighed Solute with the Solvent

Suppose you wish to prepare 2.00 L of a 1.50 M solution of Na_2CO_3. You have some solid Na_2CO_3 and distilled water. You also have a 2.00-L volumetric flask (see Figures 4.8 and 4.9). To make the solution, you must weigh the necessary quantity of Na_2CO_3 as accurately as possible, carefully place all the solid in the volumetric flask, and then add some water to dissolve the solid. After the solid has dissolved completely, more water is added to bring the solution volume to 2.00 L. The solution then has the desired concentration and the volume specified.

But what mass of Na_2CO_3 is required to make 2.00 L of 1.50 M Na_2CO_3? First, calculate the amount of Na_2CO_3 required,

$$2.00 \text{ L} \times \frac{1.50 \text{ mol } Na_2CO_3}{1.00 \text{ L solution}} = 3.00 \text{ mol } Na_2CO_3 \text{ required}$$

and then the mass in grams.

$$3.00 \text{ mol } Na_2CO_3 \times \frac{106.0 \text{ g } Na_2CO_3}{1 \text{ mol } Na_2CO_3} = 318 \text{ g } Na_2CO_3$$

Thus, to prepare the desired solution, you should dissolve 318 g of Na_2CO_3 in enough water to make 2.00 L of solution.

EXERCISE 4.8 Preparing Solutions of Known Concentration

An experiment in your laboratory requires 250. mL of a 0.0200 M solution of $AgNO_3$. You are given solid $AgNO_3$, distilled water, and a 250.-mL volumetric flask. Describe how to make up the required solution.

Diluting a More Concentrated Solution

Another method of making a solution of a given concentration is to begin with a concentrated solution and add water until the desired, lower concentration is reached (Figure 4.10). Many of the solutions prepared for your laboratory course are probably made by this dilution method. It is more efficient to store a small volume of a concentrated solution and then, when needed, add water to make a much larger volume of a dilute solution.

Suppose you need 500. mL of 0.0010 M potassium dichromate, $K_2Cr_2O_7$, for use in chemical analysis. You have some 0.100 M $K_2Cr_2O_7$ solution available. To make

5.00-mL pipet

500-mL volumetric flask

WATER

Charles D. Winters

0.100 M K₂Cr₂O₇

Use a 5.00-mL pipet to withdraw 5.00 mL of 0.100 M K₂Cr₂O₇ solution.

Add the 5.00-mL sample of 0.100 M K₂Cr₂O₇ solution to a 500-mL volumetric flask.

Fill the flask to the mark with distilled water to give 0.00100 M K₂Cr₂O₇ solution.

FIGURE 4.10 Making a solution by dilution. Here, 5.00 mL of a K₂Cr₂O₇ solution is diluted to 500. mL. This means the solution is diluted by a factor of 100, from 0.100 M to 0.00100 M.

■ **Diluting Concentrated Sulfuric Acid** The instruction that one prepares a solution by adding water to a more concentrated solution is correct, except for sulfuric acid solutions. When mixing water and sulfuric acid, the resulting solution becomes quite warm. If water is added to concentrated sulfuric acid, so much heat is evolved that the solution may boil over or splash and burn someone nearby. To avoid this problem, chemists always add concentrated sulfuric acid to water to make a dilute solution.

the required 0.0010 M solution, place a measured volume of the more concentrated K₂Cr₂O₇ solution in a flask, and then add water until the K₂Cr₂O₇ is contained in the appropriate larger volume of water (Figure 4.10).

What volume of a 0.100 M K₂Cr₂O₇ solution must be diluted to make the 0.0010 M solution? If the volume and concentration of a solution are known, the amount of solute is also known. Therefore, the amount of K₂Cr₂O₇ that must be in the final dilute solution is

$$\text{Amount of K}_2\text{Cr}_2\text{O}_7 \text{ in dilute solution} = c_{K_2Cr_2O_7} \times V_{K_2Cr_2O_7} = \left(\frac{0.0010 \text{ mol}}{\text{L}}\right) \times (0.500 \text{ L})$$
$$= 0.00050 \text{ mol K}_2\text{Cr}_2\text{O}_7$$

A more concentrated solution containing this amount of K₂Cr₂O₇ must be placed in a 500.-mL flask and then be diluted to the final volume. The volume of 0.100 M K₂Cr₂O₇ that must be transferred and diluted is 5.0 mL.

$$0.00050 \text{ mol K}_2\text{Cr}_2\text{O}_7 \times \frac{1.00 \text{ L}}{0.100 \text{ mol K}_2\text{Cr}_2\text{O}_7} = 0.0050 \text{ L or 5.0 mL}$$

Thus, to prepare 500. mL of 0.0010 M K₂Cr₂O₇, place 5.0 mL of 0.100 M K₂Cr₂O₇ in a 500.-mL flask and add water until a volume of 500. mL is reached (see Figure 4.10).

Chemistry ⚛ Now™

Sign in at **www.cengage.com/login** and go to Chapter 4 Contents to see Screen 4.11 for an exercise and a tutorial on **the direct addition method of preparing a solution** and for an exercise and tutorial on **the dilution method of preparing a solution**.

EXAMPLE 4.6 Preparing a Solution by Dilution

Problem What is the concentration of iron(III) ion in a solution prepared by diluting 1.00 mL of a 0.236 M solution of iron(III) nitrate to a volume of 100.0 mL?

Strategy First, calculate the amount of iron(III) ion in the 1.00-mL sample. The concentration of the ion in the final, dilute solution is equal to this amount of iron(III) divided by the new volume.

Solution The amount of iron(III) ion in the 1.00 mL sample is

$$\text{Amount of } Fe^{3+} = c_{Fe^{3+}} V_{Fe^{3+}} = \frac{0.236 \text{ mol } Fe^{3+}}{L} \times 1.00 \times 10^{-3} L = 2.36 \times 10^{-4} \text{ mol } Fe^{3+}$$

This amount of iron(III) ion is distributed in the new volume of 100.0 mL, so the final concentration of the diluted solution is

$$c_{Fe^{3+}} = [Fe^{3+}] = \frac{2.36 \times 10^{-4} \text{ mol } Fe^{3+}}{0.100 \text{ L}} = \boxed{2.36 \times 10^{-3} \text{ M}}$$

EXERCISE 4.9 Preparing a Solution by Dilution

An experiment calls for you to use 250. mL of 1.00 M NaOH, but you are given a large bottle of 2.00 M NaOH. Describe how to make desired volume of 1.00 M NaOH.

4.6 pH, a Concentration Scale for Acids and Bases

 Module 9

Vinegar, which contains the weak acid, acetic acid, has a hydronium ion concentration of only 1.2×10^{-3} M, and "pure" rainwater has $[H_3O^+] = 2.5 \times 10^{-6}$ M. These small values can be expressed using scientific notation, but a more convenient way to express such numbers is the logarithmic pH scale.

The pH of a solution is the negative of the base-10 logarithm of the hydronium ion concentration.

$$pH = -\log[H_3O^+] \tag{4.3}$$

Taking vinegar, pure water, blood, and ammonia as examples,

pH of vinegar $= -\log(1.2 \times 10^{-3} \text{ M}) = -(-2.92) = 2.92$
pH of pure water (at 25 °C) $= -\log(1.0 \times 10^{-7} \text{ M}) = -(-7.00) = 7.00$
pH of blood $= -\log(4.0 \times 10^{-8} \text{ M}) = -(-7.40) = 7.40$
pH of household ammonia $= -\log(4.3 \times 10^{-12} \text{ M}) = -(-11.37) = 11.37$

you see that something you recognize as acidic has a relatively low pH, whereas ammonia, a common base, has a very low hydronium ion concentration and a high

■ **pH of Pure Water** Highly purified water, which is said to be "neutral," has a pH of exactly 7 at 25 °C. This is the "dividing line" between acidic substances (pH < 7) and basic substances (pH > 7) at 25 °C.

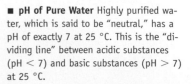

A Closer Look

We often find in the laboratory that a solution is too concentrated for the analytical technique we want to use. You might want to analyze a seawater sample for its chloride ion content, for instance. To obtain a solution with a chloride concentration of the proper magnitude for analysis by the Mohr method (Case Study, page 186), for example, you might want to dilute the sample, not once but several times.

Suppose you have 100.0 mL of a seawater sample that has a NaCl concentration of 0.550 mol/L. You transfer 10.0 mL of that sample to a 100.0-mL volumetric flask and fill to the mark with distilled water. You then transfer 5.00 mL of that diluted sample to another 100.0 mL flask and fill to the mark with distilled water. What is the NaCl concentration in the final 100.0-mL sample?

The original solution contains 0.550 mol/L of NaCl. If you remove 10.00 mL, you have removed

$$0.01000 \text{ L} \times 0.550 \text{ mol/L}$$
$$= 5.50 \times 10^{-3} \text{ mol NaCl}$$

and the concentration in 100.0 mL of the diluted solution is

$$c_{NaCl} = 5.50 \times 10^{-3} \text{ mol/0.100 L}$$
$$= 5.50 \times 10^{-2} \text{ M}$$

Serial Dilutions

or 1/10 of the concentration of the original solution (because we diluted the sample by a factor of 10).

Now we take 5.0 mL of the diluted solution and dilute that once again to 100.0 mL. The final concentration is

$$0.00500 \text{ L} \times 5.50 \times 10^{-2} \text{ mol/L}$$
$$= 2.75 \times 10^{-4} \text{ mol NaCl}$$

$$c_{NaCl} = 2.75 \times 10^{-4} \text{ mol/0.1000 L}$$
$$= 2.75 \times 10^{-3} \text{ M}$$

This is 1/200 of the concentration of the original solution.

A fair question at this point is why we did not just take 1 mL of the original solution and dilute to 200 mL. The answer is that there is less error in using larger pipets such as 5.00- or 10.00-mL pipets rather than a 1.00-mL pipet. And then there is a limitation in available glassware. A 200.00-mL volumetric flask is not often available.

Question: *You have a 100.0-mL sample of a blue dye having a concentration of 0.36 M. You dilute a 10.0-mL sample of this to 100.0 mL and then a 2.00-mL sample of that solution to 100.0 mL. What is the final dye concentration? (Answer: 7.2×10^{-4} M)*

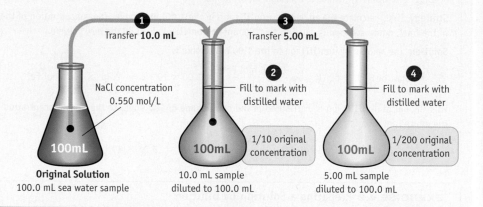

Transfer **10.0 mL**   Transfer **5.00 mL**

NaCl concentration 0.550 mol/L

Fill to mark with distilled water

Fill to mark with distilled water

1/10 original concentration

1/200 original concentration

100mL   **100mL**   **100mL**

Original Solution
100.0 mL sea water sample

10.0 mL sample diluted to 100.0 mL

5.00 mL sample diluted to 100.0 mL

---

pH. Blood, which your common sense tells you is likely to be neither acidic nor basic, has a pH near 7. Indeed, for aqueous solutions at 25 °C, we can say that acids will have pH values less than 7, bases will have values greater than 7, and a pH of 7 represents a neutral solution (Figure 4.11).

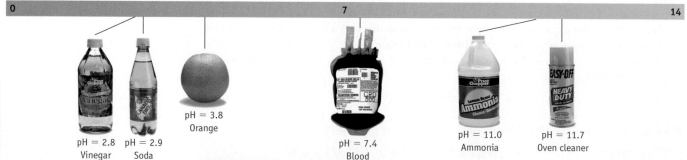

0   7   14

pH = 2.8   pH = 2.9
Vinegar   Soda

pH = 3.8
Orange

pH = 7.4
Blood

pH = 11.0
Ammonia

pH = 11.7
Oven cleaner

Active Figure 4.11   **pH values of some common substances.** Here, the "bar" is colored red at one end and blue at the other. These are the colors of litmus paper, commonly used in the laboratory to decide whether a solution is acidic (litmus is red) or basic (litmus is blue).

Chemistry ⚛ Now™ Sign in at www.cengage.com/login and go to the Chapter Contents menu to explore an interactive version of this figure accompanied by an exercise.

Charles D. Winters

(a)

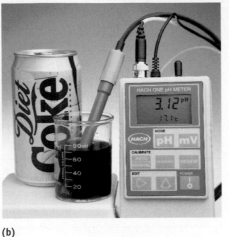

(b)

FIGURE 4.12 **Determining pH.**
(a) Some household products. Each solution contains a few drops of a universal indicator, a mixture of several acid–base indicators. A color of yellow or red indicates a pH less than 7. A green to purple color indicates a pH greater than 7. (b) The pH of a soda is measured with a modern pH meter. Soft drinks are often quite acidic, owing to the dissolved CO_2 and other ingredients.

Suppose you know the pH of a solution. To find the hydronium ion concentration, you take the antilog of the pH. That is,

$$[H_3O^+] = 10^{-pH} \qquad (4.4)$$

For example, the pH of a diet soda is 3.12, and the hydronium ion concentration of the solution is

$$[H_3O^+] = 10^{-3.12} = 7.6 \times 10^{-4} \text{ M}$$

The approximate pH of a solution may be determined using any of a variety of dyes. Litmus paper contains a dye extracted from a type of lichen, but many other dyes are also available (Figure 4.12a). A more accurate measurement of pH is done with a pH meter such as that shown in Figure 4.12b. Here, a pH electrode is immersed in the solution to be tested, and the pH is read from the instrument.

Chemistry ⚛ Now™

Sign in at **www.cengage.com/login** and go to Chapter 4 Contents to see Screen 4.11 for a tutorial on **determining the pH of a solution.**

■ **Logarithms** Numbers less than 1 have negative logs. Defining pH as $-\log[H^+]$ produces a positive number. See Appendix A for a discussion of logs.

■ **Logs and Your Calculator** All scientific calculators have a key marked "log." To find an antilog, use the key marked "10^x" or the inverse log. In determining $[H_3O^+]$ from a pH, when you enter the value of x for 10^x, make sure it has a negative sign.

■ **pH-Indicating Dyes** Many natural substances change color in solution as pH changes. See the extract of red cabbage in Figure 3.12. Tea changes color when acidic lemon juice is added.

■ **EXAMPLE 4.7 pH of Solutions**

Problem

(a) Lemon juice has $[H_3O^+] = 0.0032$ M. What is its pH?

(b) Sea water has a pH of 8.30. What is the hydronium ion concentration of this solution?

(c) A solution of nitric acid has a concentration of 0.0056 mol/L. What is the pH of this solution?

Strategy Use Equation 4.3 to calculate pH from the H_3O^+ concentration. Use Equation 4.4 to find $[H_3O^+]$ from the pH.

Solution

(a) Lemon juice: Because the hydronium ion concentration is known, the pH is found using Equation 4.3.

$$pH = -\log[H_3O^+] = -\log(3.2 \times 10^{-3}) = -(-2.49) = 2.49$$

(b) Sea water: Here, pH = 8.30. Therefore,

$$[H_3O^+] = 10^{-pH} = 10^{-8.30} = 5.0 \times 10^{-9} \text{ M}$$

(c) Nitric acid: Nitric acid, a strong acid (Table 3.2, page 132), is completely ionized in aqueous solution. Because the concentration of HNO_3 is 0.0056 mol/L, the ion concentrations are

$$[H_3O^+] = [NO_3^-] = 0.0056 \text{ M}$$

$$pH = -\log[H_3O^+] = -\log(0.0056 \text{ M}) = \boxed{2.25}$$

Comment A comment on logarithms and significant figures (Appendix A) is useful. The number to the left of the decimal point in a logarithm is called the *characteristic*, and the number to the right is the *mantissa*. The mantissa has as many significant figures as the number whose log was found. For example, the logarithm of 3.2×10^{-3} (two significant figures) is 2.49 (two numbers to the right of the decimal point).

EXERCISE 4.10 pH of Solutions

(a) What is the pH of a solution of HCl in which $[HCl] = 2.6 \times 10^{-2}$ M?

(b) What is the hydronium ion concentration in orange juice with a pH of 3.80?

4.7 Stoichiometry of Reactions in Aqueous Solution

Solution Stoichiometry

Suppose we want to know what mass of $CaCO_3$ is required to react completely with 25 mL of 0.750 M HCl. The first step in finding the answer is to write a balanced equation. In this case, we have a gas-forming exchange reaction involving a metal carbonate and an aqueous acid (Figure 4.13).

$$CaCO_3(s) + 2 HCl(aq) \longrightarrow CaCl_2(aq) + H_2O(\ell) + CO_2(g)$$

metal carbonate +   acid $\longrightarrow$ salt   + water + carbon dioxide

This problem can be solved in the same way as all the stoichiometry problems you have seen so far, except that the quantity of one reactant is given as a volume of a solution of known concentration instead of as a mass in grams. The first step is to find the amount of HCl.

$$\text{Amount of HCl} = c_{HCl}V_{HCl} = \frac{0.750 \text{ mol HCl}}{1 \text{ L HCl}} \times 0.025 \text{ L HCl} = 0.019 \text{ mol HCl}$$

This is then related to the amount of $CaCO_3$ required.

$$0.019 \text{ mol HCl} \times \frac{1 \text{ mol CaCO}_3}{2 \text{ mol HCl}} = 0.0094 \text{ mol CaCO}_3$$

Finally, the amount of $CaCO_3$ is converted to a mass in grams.

$$0.0094 \text{ mol CaCO}_3 \times \frac{100. \text{ g CaCO}_3}{1 \text{ mol CaCO}_3} = 0.94 \text{ g CaCO}_3$$

Chemists are likely to do such calculations many times in the course of their work. If you follow the general scheme outlined in Problem Solving Tip 4.4 and pay attention to the units on the numbers, you can successfully carry out any kind of stoichiometry calculations involving concentrations.

Chemistry ⚛ Now™

Sign in at **www.cengage.com/login** and go to Chapter 4 Contents to see Screen 4.12 for an exercise on **solution stoichiometry,** for a tutorial on **determining the mass of a product,** and for a tutorial on **determining the volume of a reactant.**

Charles D. Winters

FIGURE 4.13 A commercial remedy for excess stomach acid. The tablet contains calcium carbonate, which reacts with hydrochloric acid, the acid present in the digestive system. The most obvious product is CO_2 gas.

Stoichiometry Calculations Involving Solutions

In Problem Solving Tip 4.1, you learned about a general approach to stoichiometry problems. We can now modify that scheme for a reaction involving solutions such as $x\,A(aq) + y\,B(aq) \longrightarrow$ products.

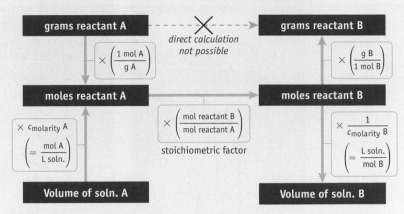

■ **EXAMPLE 4.8** **Stoichiometry of a Reaction in Solution**

Problem Metallic zinc reacts with aqueous HCl.

$$Zn(s) + 2\,HCl(aq) \longrightarrow ZnCl_2(aq) + H_2(g)$$

What volume of 2.50 M HCl, in milliliters, is required to convert 11.8 g of Zn completely to products?

Strategy Here, the mass of zinc is known, so you first calculate the amount of zinc. Next, use a stoichiometric factor (= 2 mol HCl/1 mol Zn) to relate amount of HCl required to amount of Zn available. Finally, calculate the volume of HCl from the amount of HCl and its concentration.

Solution Begin by calculating the amount of Zn.

$$11.8 \text{ g Zn} \times \frac{1 \text{ mol Zn}}{65.39 \text{ g Zn}} = 0.180 \text{ mol Zn}$$

Use the stoichiometric factor to calculate the amount of HCl required.

$$0.180 \text{ mol Zn} \times \frac{2 \text{ mol HCl}}{1 \text{ mol Zn}} = 0.360 \text{ mol HCl}$$

Use the amount of HCl and the solution concentration to calculate the volume.

$$0.360 \text{ mol HCl} \times \frac{1.00 \text{ L solution}}{2.50 \text{ mol HCl}} = \boxed{0.144 \text{ L HCl}}$$

The answer is requested in units of milliliters, so we convert the volume to milliliters and find that 144 mL of 2.50 M HCl is required to convert 11.8 g of Zn completely to products.

EXERCISE 4.11 **Solution Stoichiometry**

If you combine 75.0 mL of 0.350 M HCl and an excess of Na_2CO_3, what mass of CO_2, in grams, is produced?

$$Na_2CO_3(s) + 2\,HCl(aq) \longrightarrow 2\,NaCl(aq) + H_2O(\ell) + CO_2(g)$$

Titration: A Method of Chemical Analysis

Oxalic acid, $H_2C_2O_4$, is a naturally occurring acid. Suppose you are asked to determine the mass of this acid in an impure sample. Because the compound is an acid, it reacts with a base such as sodium hydroxide.

■ **Titrations** Acid–base titrations are discussed in more detail in Chapter 18.

$$H_2C_2O_4(aq) + 2\,NaOH(aq) \longrightarrow Na_2C_2O_4(aq) + 2\,H_2O(\ell)$$

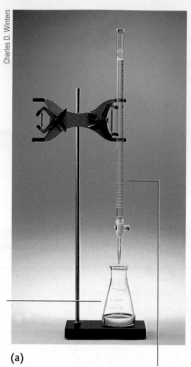

(a)

Flask containing aqueous solution of sample being analyzed

Buret containing aqueous NaOH of accurately known concentration.

(b)

A solution of NaOH is added slowly to the sample being analyzed.

(c)

When the amount of NaOH added from the buret equals the amount of H_3O^+ supplied by the acid being analyzed, the dye (indicator) changes color.

Active Figure 4.14 **Titration of an acid in aqueous solution with a base.** (a) A buret, a volumetric measuring device calibrated in divisions of 0.1 mL, is filled with an aqueous solution of a base of known concentration. (b) Base is added slowly from the buret to the solution containing the acid being analyzed and an indicator. (c) A change in the color of the indicator signals the equivalence point. (The indicator used here is phenolphthalein.)

Chemistry ⚗ Now™ Sign in at www.cengage.com/login and go to the Chapter Contents menu to explore an interactive version of this figure accompanied by an exercise.

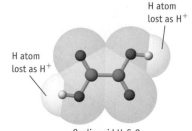

H atom lost as H^+

H atom lost as H^+

Oxalic acid $H_2C_2O_4$

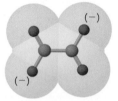

$(-)$

$(-)$

Oxalate anion $C_2O_4{}^{2-}$

Oxalic acid. Oxalic acid has two groups that can supply an H^+ ion to solution. Hence, 1 mol of the acid requires 2 mol of NaOH for complete reaction.

You can use this reaction to determine the quantity of oxalic acid present in a given mass of sample if the following conditions are met:

- You can determine when the amount of sodium hydroxide added is just enough to react with all the oxalic acid present in solution.
- You know the concentration of the sodium hydroxide solution and the volume that has been added at the point of complete reaction.

These conditions are fulfilled in a titration, a procedure illustrated in Figure 4.14. The solution containing oxalic acid is placed in a flask along with an acid–base indicator, a dye that changes color when the pH of the reaction solution reaches a certain value. Aqueous sodium hydroxide of accurately known concentration is placed in a buret. The sodium hydroxide in the buret is added slowly to the acid solution in the flask. As long as some acid is present in solution, all the base supplied from the buret is consumed, the solution remains acidic, and the indicator color is unchanged. At some point, however, the amount of OH^- added exactly equals the amount of H_3O^+

that can be supplied by the acid. This is called the **equivalence point**. As soon as the slightest excess of base has been added beyond the equivalence point, the solution becomes basic, and the indicator changes color (see Figure 4.14). The example that follows shows how to use the equivalence point and the other information to determine the percentage of oxalic acid in a mixture.

Chemistry‿Now™

Sign in at **www.cengage.com/login** and go to Chapter 4 Contents to see Screen 4.13 for a tutorial on the **volume of titrant used**, for a tutorial on **determining the concentration of acid solution**, and for a tutorial on **determining the concentration of an unknown acid.**

■ EXAMPLE 4.9 Acid–Base Titration

Problem A 1.034-g sample of impure oxalic acid is dissolved in water and an acid–base indicator added. The sample requires 34.47 mL of 0.485 M NaOH to reach the equivalence point. What is the mass of oxalic acid, and what is its mass percent in the sample?

Strategy The balanced equation for the reaction of NaOH and $H_2C_2O_4$ is

$$H_2C_2O_4(aq) + 2\ NaOH(aq) \longrightarrow Na_2C_2O_4(aq) + 2\ H_2O(\ell)$$

The concentration and volume of NaOH delivered in the titration are used to determine the amount of NaOH. A stoichiometric factor is used to relate the amount of NaOH to the amount of $H_2C_2O_4$, and the amount of $H_2C_2O_4$ is converted to a mass. The mass percent of acid in the sample is then calculated. See Problem Solving Tip 4.4.

Solution The amount of NaOH is given by

$$\text{Amount of NaOH} = c_{NaOH} \times V_{NaOH} = \frac{0.485\ \text{mol NaOH}}{\cancel{L}} \times 0.03447\ \cancel{L} = 0.0167\ \text{mol NaOH}$$

The balanced equation for the reaction shows that 1 mol of oxalic acid requires 2 mol of sodium hydroxide. This is the required stoichiometric factor to obtain the amount of oxalic acid present.

$$0.0167\ \cancel{\text{mol NaOH}} \times \frac{1\ \text{mol}\ H_2C_2O_4}{2\ \cancel{\text{mol NaOH}}} = 0.00836\ \text{mol}\ H_2C_2O_4$$

The mass of oxalic acid is found from the amount of the acid.

$$0.00836\ \cancel{\text{mol}\ H_2C_2O_4} \times \frac{90.04\ \text{g}\ H_2C_2O_4}{1\ \cancel{\text{mol}\ H_2C_2O_4}} = \boxed{0.753\ \text{g}\ H_2C_2O_4}$$

This mass of oxalic acid represents 72.8% of the total sample mass.

$$\frac{0.753\ \text{g}\ H_2C_2O_4}{1.034\ \text{g sample}} \times 100\% = \boxed{72.8\%\ H_2C_2O_4}$$

EXERCISE 4.12 Acid–Base Titration

A 25.0-mL sample of vinegar (which contains the weak acid, acetic acid, CH_3CO_2H) requires 28.33 mL of a 0.953 M solution of NaOH for titration to the equivalence point. What mass of acetic acid, in grams, is in the vinegar sample, and what is the concentration of acetic acid in the vinegar?

$$CH_3CO_2H(aq) + NaOH(aq) \longrightarrow NaCH_3CO_2(aq) + H_2O(\ell)$$

There is a French legend about a princess who told her father, the king, that she loved him as much as she loved salt. Thinking that this was not a great measure of love, he banished her from the kingdom. Only later did he realize how much he needed, and valued, salt.

Salt has played a key role in history. The earliest written record of salt production dates from around 800 BC, but the sea has always been a source of salt, and there is evidence of the Chinese harvesting salt from seawater by 6000 BC.

The average human body contains about 50 g of salt. Because we continually lose salt in urine, sweat, and other excretions, salt must be a part of our diet. Early humans recognized that salt deficiency causes headaches, cramps, loss of appetite, and, in extreme cases, death. Consuming meat provides salt, but consuming vegetables does not. This is the reason herbivorous animals seek out salt.

Saltiness is one of the basic taste sensations, and a taste of seawater quickly reveals it is salty. How did the oceans become salty? And why is chloride ion the most abundant ion?

A result of the interaction of atmospheric CO_2 and water is hydronium ions and bicarbonate ions.

$$CO_2(g) + H_2O(\ell) \longrightarrow H_2CO_3(aq)$$

$$H_2CO_3(aq) + H_2O(\ell) \rightleftharpoons H_3O^+(aq) + HCO_3^-(aq)$$

Indeed, this is the reason rain is normally acidic, and this slightly acidic rainwater can then cause substances such as limestone or corals to dissolve, producing calcium ions and more bicarbonate ions.

$$CaCO_3(s) + CO_2(g) + H_2O(\ell) \longrightarrow$$
$$Ca^{2+}(aq) + 2\,HCO_3^-(aq)$$

Seawater contains many dissolved salts. Among the ions in seawater are halide anions, alkali metal cations, and anions such as carbonate and hydrogen phosphate. See Table 3.1, page 122.

Sodium ions arrive in the oceans by a similar reaction with sodium-bearing minerals such as albite, $NaAlSi_3O_6$. Acidic rain falling on the land extracts sodium ions that are then carried by rivers to the ocean.

The average chloride content of rocks in the earth's crust is only 0.01%, so only a minute proportion of the chloride ion in the oceans can come from the weathering of rocks and minerals. What then is the origin of the chloride ions in seawater? The answer is volcanoes. Hydrogen chloride gas, HCl, is a constituent of volcanic gases. Early in Earth's history, the planet was much hotter, and volcanoes were much more widespread. The HCl gas emitted from these volcanoes is very soluble in water and is quickly dissolved to give a dilute solution of hydrochloric acid. The chloride ions from dissolved HCl gas and sodium ions from weathered rocks are the source of the salt in the sea.

Suppose you are an oceanographer, and you want to determine the concentration of chloride ions in a sample of seawater. How can you do this? And what results might you find?

There are several ways to analyze a solution for its chloride ion content, among them the classic "Mohr method." Here, a solution containing chloride ions is titrated with standardized silver nitrate. You know that the following reaction should occur,

$$Ag^+(aq) + Cl^-(aq) \longrightarrow AgCl(s)$$

and will continue until the chloride ions have been precipitated completely. To detect the equivalence point of the titration of Cl^- with Ag^+, the Mohr method specifies the addition of a few drops of a solution of potassium chromate. This "indicator" works because silver chromate is slightly more soluble than AgCl, so the red Ag_2CrO_4 precipitates only after all of the AgCl is precipitated.

$$2\,Ag^+(aq) + CrO_4^{2-}(aq) \longrightarrow Ag_2CrO_4(s)$$

The appearance of the red color of Ag_2CrO_4 (see Figure 3.11d) signals the equivalence point.

Question:

1. *Using the following information, calculate the chloride ion concentration in a sample of seawater.*
   a. *Volume of original seawater sample = 100.0 mL.*
   b. *A 10.00 mL sample of the seawater was diluted to 100.0 mL with distilled water.*
   c. *10.00 mL of the diluted sample was again diluted to 100.0 mL.*
   d. *A Mohr titration was done on 50.00 mL of the diluted sample (from step 3) and required 26.25 mL of 0.100 M $AgNO_3$. What was the chloride ion concentration in the original seawater sample?*

Answer to this question is in Appendix Q.

Standardizing an Acid or Base

In Example 4.9, the concentration of the base used in the titration was given. In actual practice, this usually has to be found by a prior measurement. The procedure by which the concentration of an analytical reagent is determined accurately is called **standardization**, and there are two general approaches.

One approach is to weigh accurately a sample of a pure, solid acid or base (known as a *primary standard*) and then titrate this sample with a solution of the base or acid to be standardized (Example 4.10). An alternative approach to standardizing a solution is to titrate it with another solution that is already standardized (Exercise 4.13). This is often done using standard solutions purchased from chemical supply companies.

Problem Sodium carbonate, Na_2CO_3, is a base, and an accurately weighed sample can be used to standardize an acid. A sample of sodium carbonate (0.263 g) requires 28.35 mL of aqueous HCl for titration to the equivalence point. What is the concentration of the HCl?

Strategy The balanced equation for the reaction is written first.

$$Na_2CO_3(aq) + 2\ HCl(aq) \longrightarrow 2\ NaCl(aq) + H_2O(\ell) + CO_2(g)$$

The amount of Na_2CO_3 can be calculated from its mass, and then, using the stoichiometric factor, the amount of HCl in 28.35 mL can be calculated. The amount of HCl divided by the volume of solution (in liters) gives its concentration (mol/L).

Solution Convert the mass of Na_2CO_3 used as the standard to amount.

$$0.263\ \text{g Na}_2\text{CO}_3 \times \frac{1\ \text{mol Na}_2\text{CO}_3}{106.0\ \text{g Na}_2\text{CO}_3} = 0.00248\ \text{mol Na}_2\text{CO}_3$$

Use the stoichiometric factor to calculate the amount of HCl in 28.35 mL.

$$0.00248\ \text{mol Na}_2\text{CO}_3 \times \frac{2\ \text{mol HCl required}}{1\ \text{mol Na}_2\text{CO}_3\ \text{available}} = 0.00496\ \text{mol HCl}$$

The 28.35-mL (0.02835-L) sample of aqueous HCl contains 0.00496 mol of HCl, so the concentration of the HCl solution is 0.175 M.

$$[HCl] = \frac{0.00496\ \text{mol HCl}}{0.02835\ \text{L}} = \boxed{0.175\ \text{M}}$$

Comment In this example, Na_2CO_3 is a primary standard. Sodium carbonate can be obtained in pure form, can be weighed accurately, and reacts completely with a strong acid.

EXERCISE 4.13 **Standardization of a Base**

Hydrochloric acid, HCl, can be purchased from chemical supply houses with a concentration of 0.100 M, and this solution can be used to standardize the solution of a base. If titrating 25.00 mL of a sodium hydroxide solution to the equivalence point requires 29.67 mL of 0.100 M HCl, what is the concentration of the base?

Determining Molar Mass by Titration

In Chapter 2 and this chapter, we used analytical data to determine the empirical formula of a compound. The molecular formula could then be derived if the molar mass were known. If the unknown substance is an acid or a base, it is possible to determine the molar mass by titration.

■ **EXAMPLE 4.11** **Determining the Molar Mass of an Acid by Titration**

Problem To determine the molar mass of an organic acid, HA, we titrate 1.056 g of HA with standardized NaOH. Calculate the molar mass of HA assuming the acid reacts with 33.78 mL of 0.256 M NaOH according to the equation

$$HA(aq) + OH^-(aq) \longrightarrow A^-(aq) + H_2O(\ell)$$

Strategy The key to this problem is to recognize that the molar mass of a substance is the ratio of the mass of a sample (g) to the amount of substance (mol) in the sample. Here, molar mass of HA = 1.056 g HA/x mol HA. Because 1 mol of HA reacts with 1 mol of NaOH in this case, the amount of acid (x mol) is equal to the amount of NaOH used in the titration, which is determined by its concentration and volume.

Solution Let us first calculate the amount of NaOH used in the titration.

$$\text{Amount of NaOH} = c_{\text{NaOH}}V_{\text{NaOH}} = \frac{0.256\ \text{mol}}{\text{L}} \times 0.03378\ \text{L} = 8.65 \times 10^{-3}\ \text{mol NaOH}$$

Next, recognize that the amount of NaOH used in the titration is the same as the amount of acid titrated. That is,

$$8.65 \times 10^{-3} \text{ mol NaOH} \times \frac{1 \text{ mol HA}}{1 \text{ mol NaOH}} = 8.65 \times 10^{-3} \text{ mol HA}$$

Finally, calculate the molar mass of HA.

$$\text{Molar mass of acid} = \frac{1.056 \text{ g HA}}{8.65 \times 10^{-3} \text{ mol HA}} = \boxed{122 \text{ g/mol}}$$

EXERCISE 4.14 Determining the Molar Mass of an Acid by Titration

An acid reacts with NaOH according to the net ionic equation

$$HA(aq) + OH^-(aq) \longrightarrow A^-(aq) + H_2O(\ell)$$

Calculate the molar mass of HA if 0.856 g of the acid requires 30.08 mL of 0.323 M NaOH.

Titrations Using Oxidation-Reduction Reactions

Analysis by titration is not limited to acid–base chemistry. Many oxidation-reduction reactions go rapidly to completion in aqueous solution, and methods exist to determine their equivalence point.

■ EXAMPLE 4.12 Using an Oxidation-Reduction Reaction in a Titration

Problem The iron in a sample of an iron ore can be converted quantitatively to the iron(II) ion, Fe^{2+}, in aqueous solution, and this solution can then be titrated with aqueous potassium permanganate, $KMnO_4$. The balanced, net ionic equation for the reaction occurring in the course of this titration is

$$MnO_4^-(aq) + 5 Fe^{2+}(aq) + 8 H_3O^+(aq) \longrightarrow Mn^{2+}(aq) + 5 Fe^{3+}(aq) + 12 H_2O(\ell)$$
$$\text{purple} \quad\quad \text{colorless} \quad\quad\quad\quad \text{colorless} \quad \text{pale yellow}$$

Case Study

Forensic Chemistry: Titrations and Food Tampering

The U.S. Food and Drug Administration (FDA) has recently discovered cases of product tampering involving the addition of bleach to products such as soup, infant formula, and soft drinks. Household bleach is a dilute solution of sodium hypochlorite (NaClO), a compound that is an oxidizing agent and is dangerous if swallowed.

One method of detecting bleach uses starch-iodide paper. The bleach oxidizes the iodide ion to iodine in an acid solution,

$$2 I^-(aq) + HClO(aq) + H_3O^+(aq) \longrightarrow$$
$$I_2(aq) + 2 H_2O(\ell) + Cl^-(aq)$$

and the I_2 is then detected by a deep blue color in the presence of starch.

This reaction is also used in the quantitative analysis of solutions containing bleach. Excess iodide ion (in the form of KI) is added to the sample. The bleach in the sample (which forms HClO in acid solution) oxidizes

I^- in a ratio of 1 mol HClO to 2 mol I^-. The iodine formed in the reaction is then titrated with sodium thiosulfate, $Na_2S_2O_3$ in another oxidation-reduction reaction (as in Exercise 4.15).

$$I_2(aq) + 2 S_2O_3^{2-}(aq) \longrightarrow$$
$$2 I^-(aq) + S_4O_6^{2-}(aq)$$

The amount of $Na_2S_2O_3$ used in the titration can then be used to determine the amount of NaClO in the sample.

Question:
Excess KI is added to a 100.0 mL sample of a soft drink that had been contaminated with bleach, NaClO. The iodine (I_2) generated in the solution was then titrated with 0.0425 M $Na_2S_2O_3$ and required 25.3 mL to reach the equivalence point. What mass of NaClO was contained in the 100.0-mL sample of adulterated soft drink?

Answer to this question is in Appendix Q.

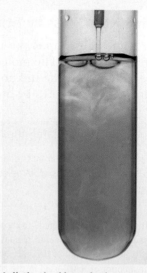

Charles D. Winters

A distinctive blue color is generated when iodine reacts with water-soluble starch.

A 1.026-g sample of iron-containing ore requires 24.35 mL of 0.0195 M $KMnO_4$ to reach the equivalence point. What is the mass percent of iron in the ore?

Strategy Because the volume and concentration of the $KMnO_4$ solution are known, the amount of $KMnO_4$ used in the titration can be calculated. Using the stoichiometric factor, the amount of $KMnO_4$ is related to the amount of iron(II) ion. The amount of iron(II) is converted to its mass, and the mass percent of iron in the sample is determined.

Solution First, calculate the amount of $KMnO_4$.

$$\text{Amount of } KMnO_4 = c_{KMnO_4} \times V_{KMnO_4} = \frac{0.0195 \text{ mol } KMnO_4}{\text{L}} \times 0.02435 \text{ L} = 0.000475 \text{ mol}$$

Use the stoichiometric factor to calculate the amount of iron(II) ion.

$$0.000475 \text{ mol } KMnO_4 \times \frac{5 \text{ mol Fe}^{2+}}{1 \text{ mol } KMnO_4} = 0.00237 \text{ mol Fe}^{2+}$$

The mass of iron can now be calculated,

$$0.00237 \text{ mol Fe}^{2+} \times \frac{55.85 \text{ g Fe}^{2+}}{1 \text{ mol Fe}^{2+}} = 0.133 \text{ g Fe}^{2+}$$

Finally, the mass percent can be determined.

$$\frac{0.133 \text{ g Fe}^{2+}}{1.026 \text{ g sample}} \times 100\% = 12.9\% \text{ iron}$$

Comment This is a useful analytical reaction because it is easy to detect when all the iron(II) ion has reacted. The MnO_4^- ion is a deep purple color, but when it reacts with Fe^{2+}, the color disappears because the reaction product, Mn^{2+}, is colorless. Therefore, $KMnO_4$ solution is added from a buret until the initially colorless, Fe^{2+}-containing solution just turns a faint purple color (due to unreacted $KMnO_4$), the signal that the equivalence point has been reached.

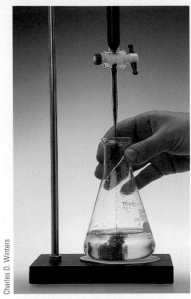

Charles D. Winters

Using an oxidation-reduction reaction for analysis by titration. Purple, aqueous $KMnO_4$ is added to a solution containing Fe^{2+}. As $KMnO_4$ drops into the solution, colorless Mn^{2+} and pale yellow Fe^{3+} form. Here, an area of the solution containing unreacted $KMnO_4$ is seen. As the solution is mixed, this disappears until the equivalence point is reached.

EXERCISE 4.15 Using an Oxidation-Reduction Reaction in a Titration

Vitamin C, ascorbic acid ($C_6H_8O_6$), is a reducing agent. One way to determine the ascorbic acid content of a sample is to mix the acid with an excess of iodine,

$$C_6H_8O_6(aq) + I_2(aq) + 2 H_2O(\ell) \longrightarrow C_6H_6O_6(aq) + 2 H_3O^+(aq) + 2 I^-(aq)$$

and then titrate the iodine that did not react with the ascorbic acid with sodium thiosulfate. The balanced, net ionic equation for the reaction occurring in this titration is

$$I_2(aq) + 2 S_2O_3^{2-}(aq) \longrightarrow 2 I^-(aq) + S_4O_6^{2-}(aq)$$

Suppose 50.00 mL of 0.0520 M I_2 was added to the sample containing ascorbic acid. After the ascorbic acid/I_2 reaction was complete, the I_2 not used in this reaction required 20.30 mL of 0.196 M $Na_2S_2O_3$ for titration to the equivalence point. Calculate the mass of ascorbic acid in the unknown sample.

4.8 Spectrophotometry, Another Method of Analysis

Solutions of many compounds are colored, a consequence of the absorption of light (Figure 4.15). It is possible to measure, quantitatively, the extent of light absorption and to relate this to the concentration of the dissolved solute. This kind of experiment, called **spectrophotometry**, is an important analytical method.

Every substance absorbs or transmits certain wavelengths of radiant energy but not others (Figures 4.15 and 4.16). For example, nickel(II) ions (and chlorophyll) absorb red and blue/violet light, while transmitting or reflecting green light. Your eyes "see" the transmitted or reflected wavelengths, those not absorbed, as the color

FIGURE 4.15 Light absorption and color. A beam of white light shines on a solution of nickel(II) ions in water, and the light that emerges is green. The color of a solution is due to the color of the light *not* absorbed by the solution. Here, red and blue/violet light was absorbed, and green light is transmitted.

Charles D. Winters

FIGURE 4.16 An absorption spectrophotometer. A beam of white light passes through a prism or diffraction grating, which splits the light into its component wavelengths. After passing through the sample, the light reaches a detector. The spectrophotometer "scans" all wavelengths of light and determines the amount of light absorbed at each wavelength. The output is a *spectrum*, a plot of the amount of light absorbed as a function of the wavelength or frequency of the incoming or incident light. Here, the sample absorbs light in the green-blue part of the spectrum and transmits light in the remaining wavelengths. The sample would appear red to orange to your eye.

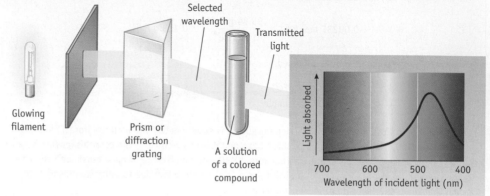

green. Furthermore, the specific wavelengths absorbed and transmitted are characteristic for a substance, and so a spectrum serves as a "fingerprint" of the substance that can help identify an unknown.

Now suppose you look at two solutions of the same substance, one a deeper color than the other. Your common sense tells you that the intensely colored one is the more concentrated (Figure 4.17a). This is true, and the intensity of the color is a measure of the concentration of the material in the solution.

In recent years, spectrophotometry has become one of the most frequently used methods of quantitative analysis. It is applicable to many industrial and clinical problems involving the quantitative determination of compounds that are colored or that react to form a colored product.

Transmittance, Absorbance, and the Beer–Lambert Law

To understand the exact relationship of light absorption and solution concentration, we need to define several terms. **Transmittance** (T) is the ratio of the amount of light transmitted by or passing through the sample relative to the amount of light that initially fell on the sample (the incident light).

$$\text{Transmittance } (T) = \frac{P}{P_0} = \frac{\text{intensity of transmitted light}}{\text{intensity of incident light}}$$

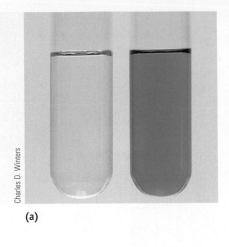 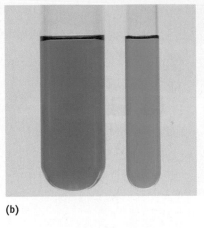

(a)   (b)

FIGURE 4.17 **Light absorption, concentration, and path length.**
(a) The test tube on the left has a solution of copper(II) sulfate with a concentration of 0.05 M. On the right, the concentration is 1.0 M in copper(II) sulfate. More light is absorbed by the more concentrated sample, and it appears more blue.
(b) The amount of light absorbed by a solution depends on the path length. Here, both solutions have the same concentration, but the distance the light travels is longer in one than the other.

Absorbance is defined as the negative logarithm of the transmittance, and you will note that absorbance and transmittance bear an inverse relationship. That is, as the absorbance of a solution increases, the transmittance decreases

$$\text{Absorbance} = -\log T = -\log P/P_0$$

Going back to our example of an aqueous solution of copper(II) ions in Figure 4.17, if you have two colored solutions, you may deduce that the bluer solution appears more blue because it absorbs more of the light falling on it. That is, the *absorbance, A, of a sample increases as the concentration increases.*

Next, suppose that there are two test tubes, both containing the same solution at the same concentration. The only difference is that one of the test tubes has a smaller diameter than the other (Figure 4.17b). We shine light of the same intensity (P_0) on both test tubes. In the first case, the light has to travel only a short distance through the sample, whereas in the second case it has to pass through more of the sample. In the second case more of the light will be absorbed because the path length is longer. In other words, *absorbance increases as path length increases.*

The two observations described above constitute the **Beer–Lambert law.**

■ **Beer–Lambert Law** The Beer–Lambert law applies strictly to relatively dilute solutions. At higher solute concentrations, the dependence of absorbance on concentration may not be linear.

$$\text{Absorbance } (A) \propto \text{path length } (\ell) \times \text{concentration } (c)$$
$$A = \varepsilon \times \ell \times c \tag{4.5}$$

where

- A, the absorbance of the sample, is a dimensionless number.
- ε, proportionality constant, is called the *molar absorptivity*. It is a constant for a given substance, provided the temperature and wavelength are constant. It has units of L/mol·cm.
- ℓ and c have the units of length (cm) and concentration (mol/L), respectively.

The Beer–Lambert law shows that *there is a linear relationship between a sample's absorbance and its concentration for a given path length.*

Charles D. Winters

Spectrophotometric Analysis

There are usually four steps in carrying out a spectrophotometric analysis.

- **Record the absorption spectrum of the substance to be analyzed.** In introductory chemistry laboratories, this is often done using an instrument such as the ones shown in Figure 4.18. The result is a spectrum such as that for aqueous permanganate ions (MnO_4^-) in Figure 4.19. The spectrum is a plot of the absorbance of the sample versus the wavelength of incident light. Here, the maximum in absorbance is at about 525 nm.

- **Choose the wavelength for the measurement.** According to the Beer–Lambert Law, the absorbance at each wavelength is proportional to concentration. Therefore, in theory we could choose any wavelength for quantitative estimations of concentration. However, the magnitude of the absorbance is important, especially when you are trying to detect very small amounts of material. In the spectra of permanganate ions in Figure 4.19, note that the difference in absorbance between curves 1 and 2 is at a maximum at about 525 nm, and at this wavelength the change in absorbance is greatest for a given change in concentration. That is, the measurement of concentration as a function of concentration is most sensitive at this wavelength. For this reason, *we generally select the wavelength of maximum absorbance for our measurements.*

- **Prepare a calibration plot.** Once we have chosen the wavelength, the next step is to construct a **calibration curve** or **calibration plot.** This consists of a plot of absorbance versus concentration for a series of standard solutions whose concentrations are accurately known. Because of the linear relation between concentration and absorbance (at a given wavelength and pathlength), this plot is a straight line with a positive slope. Once the plot has been made, and the equation for the line is known, you can find the concentration of an unknown sample from its absorbance.

Example 4.13 illustrates the preparation of a calibration curve and its use in determining the concentration of a species in solution.

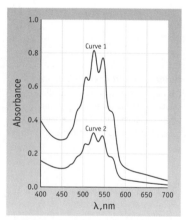

FIGURE 4.19 The absorption spectrum of solutions of potassium permanganate (KMnO₄) at different concentrations. The solution for curve 1 has a higher concentration than that for curve 2.

Problem A solution of $KMnO_4$ has an absorbance of 0.539 when measured at 540 nm in a 1.0-cm cell. What is the concentration of the $KMnO_4$?

Prior to determining the absorbance for the unknown solution, the following calibration data were collected for the spectrophotometer.

Concentration of $KMnO_4$ (M)	Absorbance
0.0300	0.162
0.0600	0.330
0.0900	0.499
0.120	0.670
0.150	0.840

Strategy The first step is to prepare a calibration plot from the data above. You can then use the plot to estimate the unknown concentration from the measured absorbance or, better, find the equation for the straight line in the calibration plot (see pages 39 and 40) and calculate the unknown concentration. We shall do the latter.

Solution Using Excel or a calculator, prepare a calibration plot from the experimental data. The equation for the straight line (as determined using Excel) is

$$y = 5.633x - 0.009$$

$$\text{Absorbance} = 5.633 \ (\text{Conc}) - 0.009$$

If we put in the absorbance for the unknown solution,

$$0.539 = 5.633 \ (\text{Conc}) - 0.009$$

$$\text{Unknown concentration} = 0.0973$$

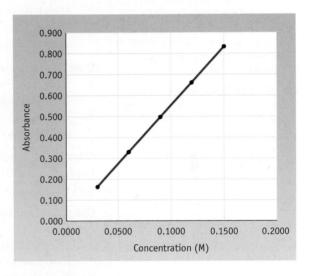

EXERCISE 4.16 Analysis Using Spectrophotometry

Using the following data, calculate the concentration of copper(II) ions in the unknown solution. (The cell pathlength is 1.00 cm in all cases, and the wavelength used in the determination was 645 nm.)

Calibration data

Concentration of Cu^{2+} (M)	Absorbance
0.0562	0.720
0.0337	0.434
0.0281	0.332
0.0169	0.219

Absorbance of unknown solution containing Cu^{2+} ions = 0.418

Chapter Goals Revisited

Now that you have studied this chapter, you should ask whether you have met the chapter goals. In particular, you should be able to:

Perform stoichiometry calculations using balanced chemical equations

a. Understand the principle of the conservation of matter, which forms the basis of chemical stoichiometry.

b. Calculate the mass of one reactant or product from the mass of another reactant or product by using the balanced chemical equation (Section 4.1). Study Question(s) assignable in OWL: 2, 5, 8, 77, 81, 93, 95, 97, 99, 100; Go Chemistry Module 7.

c. Use amounts tables to organize stoichiometric information. Study Question(s) assignable in OWL: 8.

Understand the meaning of a limiting reactant in a chemical reaction

a. Determine which of two reactants is the limiting reactant (Section 4.2). Study Question(s) assignable in OWL: 12, 14, 96, 132; Go Chemistry Module 8.

b. Determine the yield of a product based on the limiting reactant. Study Question(s) assignable in OWL: 12, 14, 16, 18.

Calculate the theoretical and percent yields of a chemical reaction

Explain the differences among actual yield, theoretical yield, and percent yield, and calculate percent yield (Section 4.3). Study Question(s) assignable in OWL: 19.

Use stoichiometry to analyze a mixture of compounds or to determine the formula of a compound

a. Use stoichiometry principles to analyze a mixture (Section 4.4). Study Question(s) assignable in OWL: 23, 123, 125, 127.

b. Find the empirical formula of an unknown compound using chemical stoichiometry (Section 4.4). Study Question(s) assignable in OWL: 29, 34.

Define and use concentrations in solution stoichiometry

a. Calculate the concentration of a solute in a solution in units of moles per liter (molarity), and use concentrations in calculations (Section 4.5). Study Question(s) assignable in OWL: 37, 39, 41.

b. Describe how to prepare a solution of a given concentration from the solute and a solvent or by dilution from a more concentrated solution (Section 4.5). Study Question(s) assignable in OWL: 46, 47, 51.

c. Calculate the pH of a solution from the concentration of hydronium ion in the solution. Calculate the hydronium ion concentration of a solution from the pH (Section 4.6). Study Question(s) assignable in OWL: 54, 55; Go Chemistry Module 9.

d. Solve stoichiometry problems using solution concentrations (Section 4.7). Study Question(s) assignable in OWL: 59, 62, 106, 107.

e. Explain how a titration is carried out, explain the procedure of standardization, and calculate concentrations or amounts of reactants from titration data (Section 4.7). Study Question(s) assignable in OWL: 67, 71.

f. Understand and use the principles of spectrophotometry to determine the concentration of a species in solution. (Secton 4.8). Study Question(s) assignable in OWL: 75.

KEY EQUATIONS

Equation 4.1 (page 168) Percent yield

$$\text{Percent yield} = \frac{\text{actual yield}}{\text{theoretical yield}} \times 100\%$$

Equation 4.2 (page 175) Definition of molarity, a measure of the concentration of a solute in a solution.

$$\text{Molarity of } x \ (c_x) = \frac{\text{amount of solute} \times \text{(mol)}}{\text{volume of solution (L)}}$$

A useful form of this equation is

$$\text{Amount of solute } x \text{ (mol)} = c_x \text{ (mol/L)} \times \text{volume of solution (L)}$$

Dilution Equation (page 179) This is a shortcut to find, for example, the concentration of a solution (c_d) after diluting some volume (V_c) of a more concentrated solution (c_c) to a new volume (V_d).

$$c_c \times V_c = c_d \times V_d$$

Equation 4.3 (page 179) pH. The pH of a solution is the negative logarithm of the hydronium ion concentration.

$$pH = -\log[H_3O^+]$$

Equation 4.4 (page 181) Calculating $[H_3O^+]$ from pH. The equation for calculating the hydronium ion concentration of a solution from the pH of the solution.

$$[H_3O^+] = 10^{-pH}$$

Equation 4.5 (page 192) Beer–Lambert Law. The absorbance of light (A) by a substance in solution is equal to the molar absorptivity of the substance (ε), the pathlength of the cell (ℓ), and the concentration of the solute (c).

$$\text{Absorbance } (A) \propto \text{path length } (\ell) \times \text{concentration } (c)$$
$$A = \varepsilon \times \ell \times c$$

STUDY QUESTIONS

ʊWL Online homework for this chapter may be assigned in OWL.

▲ denotes challenging questions.

■ denotes questions assignable in OWL.

Blue-numbered questions have answers in Appendix O and fully-worked solutions in the *Student Solutions Manual*.

Practicing Skills

Mass Relationships in Chemical Reactions: Basic Stoichiometry
(See Example 4.1 and ChemistryNow Screens 4.2 and 4.3.)

1. Aluminum reacts with oxygen to give aluminum oxide.

$$4 \text{ Al(s)} + 3 \text{ O}_2(g) \rightarrow 2 \text{ Al}_2\text{O}_3(s)$$

What amount of O_2, in moles, is needed for complete reaction with 6.0 mol of Al? What mass of Al_2O_3, in grams, can be produced?

2. ■ What mass of HCl, in grams, is required to react with 0.750 g of $Al(OH)_3$? What mass of water, in grams, is produced?

$$Al(OH)_3(s) + 3 \text{ HCl(aq)} \rightarrow AlCl_3(aq) + 3 \text{ H}_2O(\ell)$$

3. Like many metals, aluminum reacts with a halogen to give a metal halide (see Figure 2.12).

$$2\ Al(s) + 3\ Br_2(\ell) \rightarrow Al_2Br_6(s)$$

What mass of Br_2, in grams, is required for complete reaction with 2.56 g of Al? What mass of white, solid Al_2Br_6 is expected?

4. The balanced equation for a reaction in the process of the reduction of iron ore to the metal is

$$Fe_2O_3(s) + 3\ CO(g) \rightarrow 2\ Fe(s) + 3\ CO_2(g)$$

(a) What is the maximum mass of iron, in grams, that can be obtained from 454 g (1.00 lb) of iron(III) oxide?
(b) What mass of CO is required to react with 454 g of Fe_2O_3?

5. ■ Methane, CH_4, burns in oxygen.
(a) What are the products of the reaction?
(b) Write the balanced equation for the reaction.
(c) What mass of O_2, in grams, is required for complete combustion of 25.5 g of methane?
(d) What is the total mass of products expected from the combustion of 25.5 g of methane?

6. The formation of water-insoluble silver chloride is useful in the analysis of chloride-containing substances. Consider the following *unbalanced* equation:

$$BaCl_2(aq) + AgNO_3(aq) \rightarrow AgCl(s) + Ba(NO_3)_2(aq)$$

(a) Write the balanced equation.
(b) What mass of $AgNO_3$, in grams, is required for complete reaction with 0.156 g of $BaCl_2$? What mass of AgCl is produced?

Amounts Tables and Chemical Stoichiometry

For each question below, set up an amounts table that lists the initial amount or amounts of reactants, the changes in amounts of reactants and products, and the amounts of reactants and products after reaction. See page 159 and Example 4.1.

7. A major source of air pollution years ago was the metals industry. One common process involved "roasting" metal sulfides in the air:

$$2\ PbS(s) + 3\ O_2(g) \rightarrow 2\ PbO(s) + 2\ SO_2(g)$$

If you heat 2.50 mol of PbS in the air, what amount of O_2 is required for complete reaction? What amounts of PbO and SO_2 are expected?

8. ■ Iron ore is converted to iron metal in a reaction with carbon.

$$2\ Fe_2O_3(s) + 3\ C(s) \rightarrow 4\ Fe(s) + 3\ CO_2(g)$$

If 6.2 mol of $Fe_2O_3(s)$ is used, what amount of C(s) is needed, and what amounts of Fe and CO_2 are produced?

9. Chromium metal reacts with oxygen to give chromium(III) oxide, Cr_2O_3.
(a) Write a balanced equation for the reaction.
(b) If a piece of chromium has a mass of 0.175 g, what mass (in grams) of Cr_2O_3 is produced if the metal is converted completely to the oxide?
(c) What mass of O_2 (in grams) is required for the reaction?

10. Ethane, C_2H_6, burns in oxygen.
(a) What are the products of the reaction?
(b) Write the balanced equation for the reaction.
(c) What mass of O_2, in grams, is required for complete combustion of 13.6 of ethane?
(d) What is the total mass of products expected from the combustion of 13.6 g of ethane?

Limiting Reactants
(See Example 4.2 and Exercise 4.2. See also ChemistryNow Screens 4.4 and 4.5.)

11. Sodium sulfide, Na_2S, is used in the leather industry to remove hair from hides. The Na_2S is made by the reaction

$$Na_2SO_4(s) + 4\ C(s) \rightarrow Na_2S(s) + 4\ CO(g)$$

Suppose you mix 15 g of Na_2SO_4 and 7.5 g of C. Which is the limiting reactant? What mass of Na_2S is produced?

12. ■ Ammonia gas can be prepared by the reaction of a metal oxide such as calcium oxide with ammonium chloride.

$$CaO(s) + 2\ NH_4Cl(s) \rightarrow$$
$$2\ NH_3(g) + H_2O(g) + CaCl_2(s)$$

If 112 g of CaO and 224 g of NH_4Cl are mixed, what is the limiting reactant, and what mass of NH_3 can be produced?

13. The compound SF_6 is made by burning sulfur in an atmosphere of fluorine. The balanced equation is

$$S_8(s) + 24\ F_2(g) \rightarrow 8\ SF_6(g)$$

If you begin with 1.6 mol of sulfur, S_8, and 35 mol of F_2, which is the limiting reagent?

14. ■ Disulfur dichloride, S_2Cl_2, is used to vulcanize rubber. It can be made by treating molten sulfur with gaseous chlorine:

$$S_8(\ell) + 4\ Cl_2(g) \rightarrow 4\ S_2Cl_2(\ell)$$

Starting with a mixture of 32.0 g of sulfur and 71.0 g of Cl_2,
(a) Which is the limiting reactant?
(b) What is the theoretical yield of S_2Cl_2?
(c) What mass of the excess reactant remains when the reaction is completed?

▲ more challenging   ■ in OWL   Blue-numbered questions answered in Appendix 0

15. The reaction of methane and water is one way to prepare hydrogen for use as a fuel:

$$CH_4(g) + H_2O(g) \rightarrow CO(g) + 3\ H_2(g)$$

If you begin with 995 g of CH_4 and 2510 g of water,
(a) Which reactant is the limiting reactant?
(b) What is the maximum mass of H_2 that can be prepared?
(c) What mass of the excess reactant remains when the reaction is completed?

16. ■ Aluminum chloride, $AlCl_3$, is made by treating scrap aluminum with chlorine.

$$2\ Al(s) + 3\ Cl_2(g) \rightarrow 2\ AlCl_3(s)$$

If you begin with 2.70 g of Al and 4.05 g of Cl_2,
(a) Which reactant is limiting?
(b) What mass of $AlCl_3$ can be produced?
(c) What mass of the excess reactant remains when the reaction is completed?
(d) Set up an amounts table for this problem.

17. Hexane (C_6H_{14}) burns in air (O_2) to give CO_2 and H_2O.
(a) Write a balanced equation for the reaction.
(b) If 215 g of C_6H_{14} is mixed with 215 g of O_2, what masses of CO_2 and H_2O are produced in the reaction?
(c) What mass of the excess reactant remains after the hexane has been burned?
(d) Set up an amounts table for this problem.

18. ■ Aspirin, $C_6H_4(OCOCH_3)CO_2H$, is produced by the reaction of salicylic acid, $C_6H_4(OH)CO_2H$, and acetic anhydride, $(CH_3CO)_2O$ (page 168).

$$C_6H_4(OH)CO_2H(s) + (CH_3CO)_2O(\ell) \rightarrow$$
$$C_6H_4(OCOCH_3)CO_2H(s) + CH_3CO_2H(\ell)$$

If you mix 100. g of each of the reactants, what is the maximum mass of aspirin that can be obtained?

Percent Yield
(See Exercise 4.3 and ChemistryNow Screen 4.3.)

19. ■ In Example 4.2, you found that a particular mixture of CO and H_2 could produce 407 g CH_3OH.

$$CO(g) + 2\ H_2(g) \rightarrow CH_3OH(\ell)$$

If only 332 g of CH_3OH is actually produced, what is the percent yield of the compound?

20. Ammonia gas can be prepared by the following reaction:

$$CaO(s) + 2\ NH_4Cl(s) \rightarrow$$
$$2\ NH_3(g) + H_2O(g) + CaCl_2(s)$$

If 112 g of CaO and 224 g of NH_4Cl are mixed, the theoretical yield of NH_3 is 68.0 g (Study Question 12). If only 16.3 g of NH_3 is actually obtained, what is its percent yield?

21. The deep blue compound $Cu(NH_3)_4SO_4$ is made by the reaction of copper(II) sulfate and ammonia.

$$CuSO_4(aq) + 4\ NH_3(aq) \rightarrow Cu(NH_3)_4SO_4(aq)$$

(a) If you use 10.0 g of $CuSO_4$ and excess NH_3, what is the theoretical yield of $Cu(NH_3)_4SO_4$?
(b) If you isolate 12.6 g of $Cu(NH_3)_4SO_4$, what is the percent yield of $Cu(NH_3)_4SO_4$?

22. Black smokers are found in the depths of the oceans (page 112). Thinking that the conditions in these smokers might be conducive to the formation of organic compounds, two chemists in Germany found the following reaction could occur in similar conditions.

$$2\ CH_3SH + CO \rightarrow CH_3COSCH_3 + H_2S$$

If you begin with 10.0 g of CH_3SH and excess CO,
(a) What is the theoretical yield of CH_3COSCH_3?
(b) If 8.65 g of CH_3COSCH_3 is isolated, what is its percent yield?

Analysis of Mixtures
(See Example 4.3 and ChemistryNow Screen 4.7.)

23. ■ A mixture of $CuSO_4$ and $CuSO_4 \cdot 5\ H_2O$ has a mass of 1.245 g. After heating to drive off all the water, the mass is only 0.832 g. What is the mass percent of $CuSO_4 \cdot 5\ H_2O$ in the mixture? (See page 97.)

24. A 2.634-g sample containing impure $CuCl_2 \cdot 2H_2O$ was heated. The sample mass after heating to drive off the water was 2.125 g. What was the mass percent of $CuCl_2 \cdot 2\ H_2O$ in the original sample?

25. A sample of limestone and other soil materials was heated, and the limestone decomposed to give calcium oxide and carbon dioxide.

$$CaCO_3(s) \rightarrow CaO(s) + CO_2(g)$$

A 1.506-g sample of limestone-containing material gave 0.558 g of CO_2, in addition to CaO, after being heated at a high temperature. What is the mass percent of $CaCO_3$ in the original sample?

26. At higher temperatures, $NaHCO_3$ is converted quantitatively to Na_2CO_3.

$$2\ NaHCO_3(s) \rightarrow Na_2CO_3(s) + CO_2(g) + H_2O(g)$$

Heating a 1.7184-g sample of impure $NaHCO_3$ gives 0.196 g of CO_2. What was the mass percent of $NaHCO_3$ in the original 1.7184-g sample?

27. A pesticide contains thallium(I) sulfate, Tl_2SO_4. Dissolving a 10.20-g sample of impure pesticide in water and adding sodium iodide precipitates 0.1964 g of thallium(I) iodide, TlI.

$$Tl_2SO_4(aq) + 2\ NaI(aq) \rightarrow 2\ TlI(s) + Na_2SO_4(aq)$$

What is the mass percent of Tl_2SO_4 in the original 10.20-g sample?

28. ▲ The aluminum in a 0.764-g sample of an unknown material was precipitated as aluminum hydroxide, $Al(OH)_3$, which was then converted to Al_2O_3 by heating strongly. If 0.127 g of Al_2O_3 is obtained from the 0.764-g sample, what is the mass percent of aluminum in the sample?

Using Stoichiometry to Determine Empirical and Molecular Formulas
(See Example 4.4, Exercise 4.6, and ChemistryNow Screen 4.8.)

29. ■ Styrene, the building block of polystyrene, consists of only C and H. If 0.438 g of styrene is burned in oxygen and produces 1.481 g of CO_2 and 0.303 g of H_2O, what is the empirical formula of styrene?

30. Mesitylene is a liquid hydrocarbon. Burning 0.115 g of the compound in oxygen gives 0.379 g of CO_2 and 0.1035 g of H_2O. What is the empirical formula of mesitylene?

31. Cyclopentane is a simple hydrocarbon. If 0.0956 g of the compound is burned in oxygen, 0.300 g of CO_2 and 0.123 g of H_2O are isolated.
(a) What is the empirical formula of cyclopentane?
(b) If a separate experiment gave 70.1 g/mol as the molar mass of the compound, what is its molecular formula?

32. Azulene is a beautiful blue hydrocarbon. If 0.106 g of the compound is burned in oxygen, 0.364 g of CO_2 and 0.0596 g of H_2O are isolated.
(a) What is the empirical formula of azulene?
(b) If a separate experiment gave 128.2 g/mol as the molar mass of the compound, what is its molecular formula?

33. An unknown compound has the formula $C_xH_yO_z$. You burn 0.0956 g of the compound and isolate 0.1356 g of CO_2 and 0.0833 g of H_2O. What is the empirical formula of the compound? If the molar mass is 62.1 g/mol, what is the molecular formula? (See Exercise 4.6.)

34. ■ An unknown compound has the formula $C_xH_yO_z$. You burn 0.1523 g of the compound and isolate 0.3718 g of CO_2 and 0.1522 g of H_2O. What is the empirical formula of the compound? If the molar mass is 72.1 g/mol, what is the molecular formula? (See Exercise 4.6.)

35. Nickel forms a compound with carbon monoxide, $Ni_x(CO)_y$. To determine its formula, you carefully heat a 0.0973-g sample in air to convert the nickel to 0.0426 g of NiO and the CO to 0.100 g of CO_2. What is the empirical formula of $Ni_x(CO)_y$?

36. To find the formula of a compound composed of iron and carbon monoxide, $Fe_x(CO)_y$, the compound is burned in pure oxygen to give Fe_2O_3 and CO_2. If you burn 1.959 g of $Fe_x(CO)_y$ and obtain 0.799 g of Fe_2O_3 and 2.200 g of CO_2, what is the empirical formula of $Fe_x(CO)_y$?

Solution Concentration
(See Example 4.5 and ChemistryNow Screen 4.9.)

37. ■ If 6.73 g of Na_2CO_3 is dissolved in enough water to make 250. mL of solution, what is the molar concentration of the sodium carbonate? What are the molar concentrations of the Na^+ and CO_3^{2-} ions?

38. Some potassium dichromate ($K_2Cr_2O_7$), 2.335 g, is dissolved in enough water to make exactly 500. mL of solution. What is the molar concentration of the potassium dichromate? What are the molar concentrations of the K^+ and $Cr_2O_7^{2-}$ ions?

39. ■ What is the mass of solute, in grams, in 250. mL of a 0.0125 M solution of $KMnO_4$?

40. What is the mass of solute, in grams, in 125 mL of a 1.023×10^{-3} M solution of Na_3PO_4? What is the molar concentration of the Na^+ and PO_4^{3-} ion?

41. ■ What volume of 0.123 M NaOH, in milliliters, contains 25.0 g of NaOH?

42. What volume of 2.06 M $KMnO_4$, in liters, contains 322 g of solute?

43. For each solution, identify the ions that exist in aqueous solution, and specify the concentration of each ion.
(a) 0.25 M $(NH_4)_2SO_4$
(b) 0.123 M Na_2CO_3
(c) 0.056 M HNO_3

44. For each solution, identify the ions that exist in aqueous solution, and specify the concentration of each ion.
(a) 0.12 M $BaCl_2$
(b) 0.0125 M $CuSO_4$
(c) 0.500 M $K_2Cr_2O_7$

Preparing Solutions
(See Exercises 4.7–4.9, Example 4.6, and ChemistryNow Screen 4.10.)

45. An experiment in your laboratory requires 500. mL of a 0.0200 M solution of Na_2CO_3. You are given solid Na_2CO_3, distilled water, and a 500.-mL volumetric flask. Describe how to prepare the required solution.

46. ■ What mass of oxalic acid, $H_2C_2O_4$, is required to prepare 250. mL of a solution that has a concentration of 0.15 M $H_2C_2O_4$?

47. ■ If you dilute 25.0 mL of 1.50 M hydrochloric acid to 500. mL, what is the molar concentration of the dilute acid?

48. If 4.00 mL of 0.0250 M $CuSO_4$ is diluted to 10.0 mL with pure water, what is the molar concentration of copper(II) sulfate in the diluted solution?

49. Which of the following methods would you use to prepare 1.00 L of 0.125 M H_2SO_4?
(a) Dilute 20.8 mL of 6.00 M H_2SO_4 to a volume of 1.00 L.
(b) Add 950. mL of water to 50.0 mL of 3.00 M H_2SO_4.

▲ more challenging ■ in OWL Blue-numbered questions answered in Appendix O

50. Which of the following methods would you use to prepare 300. mL of 0.500 M $K_2Cr_2O_7$?
(a) Add 30.0 mL of 1.50 M $K_2Cr_2O_7$ to 270. mL of water.
(b) Dilute 250. mL of 0.600 M $K_2Cr_2O_7$ to a volume of 300. mL.

Serial Dilutions
(See A Closer Look: Serial Dilutions, page 180.)

51. ■ You have 250. mL of 0.136 M HCl. Using a volumetric pipet, you take 25.00 mL of that solution and dilute it to 100.00 mL in a volumetric flask. Now you take 10.00 mL of that solution, using a volumetric pipet, and dilute it to 100.00 mL in a volumetric flask. What is the concentration of hydrochloric acid in the final solution?

52. ▲ Suppose you have 100.00 mL a solution of a dye and transfer 2.00 mL of the solution to a 100.00-mL volumetric flask. After adding water to the 100.00 mL mark, you take 5.00 mL of that solution and again dilute to 100.00 mL. If you find the dye concentration in the final diluted sample is 0.000158 M, what was the dye concentration in the original solution?

Calculating and Using pH
(See Example 4.7 and ChemistryNow Screen 4.11.)

53. A table wine has a pH of 3.40. What is the hydronium ion concentration of the wine? Is it acidic or basic?

54. ■ A saturated solution of milk of magnesia, $Mg(OH)_2$, has a pH of 10.5. What is the hydronium ion concentration of the solution? Is the solution acidic or basic?

55. ■ What is the hydronium ion concentration of a 0.0013 M solution of HNO_3? What is its pH?

56. What is the hydronium ion concentration of a 1.2×10^{-4} M solution of $HClO_4$? What is its pH?

57. Make the following conversions. In each case, tell whether the solution is acidic or basic.

pH	$[H_3O^+]$
(a) 1.00	_____
(b) 10.50	_____
(c) _____	1.3×10^{-5} M
(d) _____	2.3×10^{-8} M

58. Make the following conversions. In each case, tell whether the solution is acidic or basic.

pH	$[H_3O^+]$
(a) _____	6.7×10^{-10} M
(b) _____	2.2×10^{-6} M
(c) 5.25	_____
(d) _____	2.5×10^{-2} M

Stoichiometry of Reactions in Solution
(See Example 4.8 and ChemistryNow Screen 4.12.)

59. ■ What volume of 0.109 M HNO_3, in milliliters, is required to react completely with 2.50 g of $Ba(OH)_2$?

$$2\ HNO_3(aq) + Ba(OH)_2(s) \rightarrow$$
$$2\ H_2O(\ell) + Ba(NO_3)_2(aq)$$

60. What mass of Na_2CO_3, in grams, is required for complete reaction with 50.0 mL of 0.125 M HNO_3?

$$Na_2CO_3(aq) + 2\ HNO_3(aq) \rightarrow$$
$$2\ NaNO_3(aq) + CO_2(g) + H_2O(\ell)$$

61. When an electric current is passed through an aqueous solution of NaCl, the valuable industrial chemicals $H_2(g)$, $Cl_2(g)$, and NaOH are produced.

$$2\ NaCl(aq) + 2\ H_2O(\ell) \rightarrow$$
$$H_2(g) + Cl_2(g) + 2\ NaOH(aq)$$

What mass of NaOH can be formed from 15.0 L of 0.35 M NaCl? What mass of chlorine is obtained?

62. ■ Hydrazine, N_2H_4, a base-like ammonia, can react with sulfuric acid.

$$2\ N_2H_4(aq) + H_2SO_4(aq) \rightarrow 2\ N_2H_5^+(aq) + SO_4^{2-}(aq)$$

What mass of hydrazine reacts with 250. mL of 0.146 M H_2SO_4?

63. In the photographic developing process, silver bromide is dissolved by adding sodium thiosulfate.

$$AgBr(s) + 2\ Na_2S_2O_3(aq) \rightarrow$$
$$Na_3Ag(S_2O_3)_2(aq) + NaBr(aq)$$

If you want to dissolve 0.225 g of AgBr, what volume of 0.0138 M $Na_2S_2O_3$, in milliliters, should be used?

Charles D. Winters

(a)   **(b)**

Silver chemistry. (a) A precipitate of AgBr formed by adding $AgNO_3(aq)$ to KBr(aq). (b) On adding $Na_2S_2O_3(aq)$, sodium thiosulfate, the solid AgBr dissolves.

64. You can dissolve an aluminum soft-drink can in an aqueous base such as potassium hydroxide.

$$2 \text{ Al(s)} + 2 \text{ KOH(aq)} + 6 \text{ H}_2\text{O}(\ell) \rightarrow$$
$$2 \text{ KAl(OH)}_4(\text{aq}) + 3 \text{ H}_2(\text{g})$$

If you place 2.05 g of aluminum in a beaker with 185 mL of 1.35 M KOH, will any aluminum remain? What mass of $KAl(OH)_4$ is produced?

65. What volume of 0.750 M $Pb(NO_3)_2$, in milliliters, is required to react completely with 1.00 L of 2.25 M NaCl solution? The balanced equation is

$$Pb(NO_3)_2(\text{aq}) + 2 \text{ NaCl(aq)} \rightarrow$$
$$PbCl_2(\text{s}) + 2 \text{ NaNO}_3(\text{aq})$$

66. What volume of 0.125 M oxalic acid, $H_2C_2O_4$ is required to react with 35.2 mL of 0.546 M NaOH?

$$H_2C_2O_4(\text{aq}) + 2 \text{ NaOH(aq)} \rightarrow$$
$$Na_2C_2O_4(\text{aq}) + 2 \text{ H}_2\text{O}(\ell)$$

Titrations

(See Examples 4.9–4.12 and ChemistryNow Screen 4.13.)

67. ■ What volume of 0.812 M HCl, in milliliters, is required to titrate 1.45 g of NaOH to the equivalence point?

$$\text{NaOH(aq)} + \text{HCl(aq)} \rightarrow \text{H}_2\text{O}(\ell) + \text{NaCl(aq)}$$

68. What volume of 0.955 M HCl, in milliliters, is required to titrate 2.152 g of Na_2CO_3 to the equivalence point?

$$Na_2CO_3(\text{aq}) + 2 \text{ HCl(aq)} \rightarrow$$
$$\text{H}_2\text{O}(\ell) + \text{CO}_2(\text{g}) + 2 \text{ NaCl(aq)}$$

69. If 38.55 mL of HCl is required to titrate 2.150 g of Na_2CO_3 according to the following equation, what is the concentration (mol/L) of the HCl solution?

$$Na_2CO_3(\text{aq}) + 2 \text{ HCl(aq)} \rightarrow$$
$$2 \text{ NaCl(aq)} + \text{CO}_2(\text{g}) + \text{H}_2\text{O}(\ell)$$

70. Potassium hydrogen phthalate, $KHC_8H_4O_4$, is used to standardize solutions of bases. The acidic anion reacts with strong bases according to the following net ionic equation:

$$HC_8H_4O_4^-(\text{aq}) + OH^-(\text{aq}) \rightarrow$$
$$C_8H_4O_4^{2-}(\text{aq}) + \text{H}_2\text{O}(\ell)$$

If a 0.902-g sample of potassium hydrogen phthalate is dissolved in water and titrated to the equivalence point with 26.45 mL of NaOH, what is the molar concentration of the NaOH?

71. ■ You have 0.954 g of an unknown acid, H_2A, which reacts with NaOH according to the balanced equation

$$H_2A(\text{aq}) + 2 \text{ NaOH(aq)} \rightarrow Na_2A(\text{aq}) + 2 \text{ H}_2\text{O}(\ell)$$

If 36.04 mL of 0.509 M NaOH is required to titrate the acid to the second equivalence point, what is the molar mass of the acid?

72. An unknown solid acid is either citric acid or tartaric acid. To determine which acid you have, you titrate a sample of the solid with aqueous NaOH and from this determine the molar mass of the unknown acid. The appropriate equations are as follows:

Citric acid:

$$H_3C_6H_5O_7(\text{aq}) + 3 \text{ NaOH(aq)} \rightarrow$$
$$3 \text{ H}_2\text{O}(\ell) + Na_3C_6H_5O_7(\text{aq})$$

Tartaric acid:

$$H_2C_4H_4O_6(\text{aq}) + 2 \text{ NaOH(aq)} \rightarrow$$
$$2 \text{ H}_2\text{O}(\ell) + Na_2C_4H_4O_6(\text{aq})$$

A 0.956-g sample requires 29.1 mL of 0.513 M NaOH to consume the acid completely. What is the unknown acid?

73. To analyze an iron-containing compound, you convert all the iron to Fe^{2+} in aqueous solution and then titrate the solution with standardized $KMnO_4$. The balanced, net ionic equation is

$$MnO_4^-(\text{aq}) + 5 \text{ Fe}^{2+}(\text{aq}) + 8 \text{ H}_3\text{O}^+(\text{aq}) \rightarrow$$
$$Mn^{2+}(\text{aq}) + 5 \text{ Fe}^{3+}(\text{aq}) + 12 \text{ H}_2\text{O}(\ell)$$

A 0.598-g sample of the iron-containing compound requires 22.25 mL of 0.0123 M $KMnO_4$ for titration to the equivalence point. What is the mass percent of iron in the sample?

74. Vitamin C has the formula $C_6H_8O_6$. Besides being an acid, it is a reducing agent. One method for determining the amount of vitamin C in a sample is therefore to titrate it with a solution of bromine, Br_2, an oxidizing agent.

$$C_6H_8O_6(\text{aq}) + Br_2(\text{aq}) \rightarrow 2 \text{ HBr(aq)} + C_6H_6O_6(\text{aq})$$

A 1.00-g "chewable" vitamin C tablet requires 27.85 mL of 0.102 M Br_2 for titration to the equivalence point. What is the mass of vitamin C in the tablet?

Spectrophotometry

(See Section 4.8. The problems below are adapted from Fundamentals of Analytical Chemistry, 8th ed., by D. A. Skoog, D. M. West, F. J. Holler, and S. R. Crouch, Thomson/Brooks-Cole, Belmont, CA 2004.)

75. ■ A solution of a dye was analyzed by spectrophotometry, and the following calibration data were collected.

Dye Concentration	Absorbance at 475 nm
0.50×10^{-6} M	0.24
1.5×10^{-6} M	0.36
2.5×10^{-6} M	0.44
3.5×10^{-6} M	0.59
4.5×10^{-6} M	0.70

(a) Construct a calibration plot, and determine the slope and intercept.
(b) What is the dye concentration in a solution with $A = 0.52$?

76. The nitrite ion is involved in the biochemical nitrogen cycle. You can analyze for the nitrite ion content of a sample using spectrophotometry by first using several organic compounds to create a colored compound from the ion. The following data were collected.

NO_2^- Ion Concentration	Absorbance at 550 nm of Nitrite-Ion Containing Solution
2.00×10^{-6} M	0.065
6.00×10^{-6} M	0.205
10.00×10^{-6} M	0.338
14.00×10^{-6} M	0.474
18.00×10^{-6} M	0.598
Unknown solution	0.402

(a) Construct a calibration plot, and determine the slope and intercept.
(b) What is the nitrite ion concentration in the unknown solution?

General Questions on Stoichiometry

These questions are not designated as to type or location in the chapter. They may combine several concepts from the chapter.

77. ■ Suppose 16.04 g of benzene, C_6H_6, is burned in oxygen.
(a) What are the products of the reaction?
(b) What is the balanced equation for the reaction?
(c) What mass of O_2, in grams, is required for complete combustion of benzene?
(d) What is the total mass of products expected from 16.04 g of benzene?

78. The metabolic disorder diabetes causes a buildup of acetone, CH_3COCH_3, in the blood. Acetone, a volatile compound, is exhaled, giving the breath of untreated diabetics a distinctive odor. The acetone is produced by a breakdown of fats in a series of reactions. The equation for the last step, the breakdown of acetoacetic acid to give acetone and CO_2, is

$$CH_3COCH_2CO_2H \rightarrow CH_3COCH_3 + CO_2$$

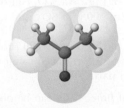

acetone, CH_3COCH_3

What mass of acetone can be produced from 125 mg of acetoacetic acid?

79. Your body deals with excess nitrogen by excreting it in the form of urea, NH_2CONH_2. The reaction producing it is the combination of arginine ($C_6H_{14}N_4O_2$) with water to give urea and ornithine ($C_5H_{12}N_2O_2$).

$$C_6H_{14}N_4O_2 + H_2O \rightarrow NH_2CONH_2 + C_5H_{12}N_2O_2$$
Arginine   Urea   Ornithine

If you excrete 95 mg of urea, what mass of arginine must have been used? What mass of ornithine must have been produced?

80. The reaction of iron metal and chlorine gas to give iron(III) chloride is illustrated in Figure 3.2.
(a) Write the balanced chemical equation for the reaction.
(b) Beginning with 10.0 g of iron, what mass of Cl_2, in grams, is required for complete reaction? What mass of $FeCl_3$ can be produced?
(c) If only 18.5 g of $FeCl_3$ is obtained from 10.0 g of iron and excess Cl_2, what is the percent yield?
(d) If 10.0 g each of iron and chlorine are combined, what is the theoretical yield of iron(III) chloride?

81. ■ Some metal halides react with water to produce the metal oxide and the appropriate hydrogen halide (see photo). For example,

$$TiCl_4(\ell) + 2\ H_2O(\ell) \rightarrow TiO_2(s) + 4\ HCl(g)$$

Charles D. Winters

The reaction of $TiCl_4$ with the water in moist air.

(a) Name the four compounds involved in this reaction.
(b) If you begin with 14.0 mL of $TiCl_4$ ($d = 1.73$ g/mL), what mass of water, in grams, is required for complete reaction?
(c) What mass of each product is expected?

82. The reaction of 750. g each of NH_3 and O_2 was found to produce 562 g of NO (see pages 163–165).

$$4\ NH_3(g) + 5\ O_2(g) \rightarrow 4\ NO(g) + 6\ H_2O(\ell)$$
(a) What mass of water is produced by this reaction?
(b) What mass of O_2 is required to consume 750. g of NH_3?

83. Sodium azide, the explosive chemical used in automobile airbags, is made by the following reaction:

$$NaNO_3 + 3\ NaNH_2 \rightarrow NaN_3 + 3\ NaOH + NH_3$$

If you combine 15.0 g of $NaNO_3$ (85.0 g/mol) with 15.0 g of $NaNH_2$, what mass of NaN_3 is produced?

84. Iodine is made by the following reaction

$$2\ NaIO_3(aq) + 5\ NaHSO_3(aq) \rightarrow$$
$$3\ NaHSO_4(aq) + 2\ Na_2SO_4(aq) + H_2O(\ell) + I_2(aq)$$

   (a) Name the two reactants.
   (b) If you wish to prepare 1.00 kg of I_2, what mass of $NaIO_3$ is required? What mass of $NaHSO_3$?
   (c) What is the theoretical yield of I_2 if you mixed 15.0 g of $NaIO_3$ with 125 mL of 0.853 M $NaHSO_3$?

85. Saccharin, an artificial sweetener, has the formula $C_7H_5NO_3S$. Suppose you have a sample of a saccharin-containing sweetener with a mass of 0.2140 g. After decomposition to free the sulfur and convert it to the SO_4^{2-} ion, the sulfate ion is trapped as water-insoluble $BaSO_4$ (see Figure 4.6). The quantity of $BaSO_4$ obtained is 0.2070 g. What is the mass percent of saccharin in the sample of sweetener?

86. ■▲ Boron forms an extensive series of compounds with hydrogen, all with the general formula B_xH_y.

$$B_xH_y(s) + \text{excess } O_2(g) \rightarrow \frac{x}{2}\ B_2O_3(s) + \frac{y}{2}\ H_2O(g)$$

If 0.148 g of B_xH_y gives 0.422 g of B_2O_3 when burned in excess O_2, what is the empirical formula of B_xH_y?

87. ▲ Silicon and hydrogen form a series of compounds with the general formula Si_xH_y. To find the formula of one of them, a 6.22-g sample of the compound is burned in oxygen. All of the Si is converted to 11.64 g of SiO_2, and all of the H is converted to 6.980 g of H_2O. What is the empirical formula of the silicon compound?

88. ▲ Menthol, from oil of mint, has a characteristic odor. The compound contains only C, H, and O. If 95.6 mg of menthol burns completely in O_2, and gives 269 mg of CO_2 and 110 mg of H_2O, what is the empirical formula of menthol?

89. ▲ Quinone, a chemical used in the dye industry and in photography, is an organic compound containing only C, H, and O. What is the empirical formula of the compound if 0.105 g of the compound gives 0.257 g of CO_2 and 0.0350 g of H_2O when burned completely in oxygen?

90. ▲ Iron(II) chloride and sodium sulfide react to form iron(II)sulfide and sodium chloride (ChemistryNow Screen 4.8.)
   (a) Write the balanced equation for the reaction.
   (b) If you combine 40 g each of Na_2S and $FeCl_2$, what is the limiting reactant?
   (c) What mass of FeS is produced?
   (d) What mass of Na_2S or $FeCl_2$ remains after the reaction?
   (e) What mass of $FeCl_2$ is required to react completely with 40 g of Na_2S?

91. Sulfuric acid can be prepared starting with the sulfide ore, cuprite (Cu_2S). If each S atom in Cu_2S leads to one molecule of H_2SO_4, what is the theoretical yield of H_2SO_4 from 3.00 kg of Cu_2S?

92. ▲ In an experiment, 1.056 g of a metal carbonate, containing an unknown metal M, is heated to give the metal oxide and 0.376 g CO_2.

$$MCO_3(s) + \text{heat} \rightarrow MO(s) + CO_2(g)$$

   What is the identity of the metal M?
   (a) M = Ni   (c) M = Zn
   (b) M = Cu   (d) M = Ba

93. ■▲ An unknown metal reacts with oxygen to give the metal oxide, MO_2. Identify the metal based on the following information:

   Mass of metal = 0.356 g

   Mass of sample after converting metal completely to oxide = 0.452 g

94. ▲ Titanium(IV) oxide, TiO_2, is heated in hydrogen gas to give water and a new titanium oxide, Ti_xO_y. If 1.598 g of TiO_2 produces 1.438 g of Ti_xO_y, what is the empirical formula of the new oxide?

95. ■▲ Potassium perchlorate is prepared by the following sequence of reactions:

$$Cl_2(g) + 2\ KOH(aq) \rightarrow KCl(aq) + KClO(aq) + H_2O(\ell)$$

$$3\ KClO(aq) \rightarrow 2\ KCl(aq) + KClO_3(aq)$$

$$4\ KClO_3(aq) \rightarrow 3\ KClO_4(aq) + KCl(aq)$$

   What mass of $Cl_2(g)$ is required to produce 234 kg of $KClO_4$?

96. ■▲ Commercial sodium "hydrosulfite" is 90.1% $Na_2S_2O_4$. The sequence of reactions used to prepare the compound is

$$Zn(s) + 2\ SO_2(g) \rightarrow ZnS_2O_4(s)$$

$$ZnS_2O_4(s) + Na_2CO_3(aq) \rightarrow ZnCO_3(s) + Na_2S_2O_4(aq)$$

   (a) What mass of pure $Na_2S_2O_4$ can be prepared from 125 kg of Zn, 500 g of SO_2, and an excess of Na_2CO_3?
   (b) What mass of the commercial product would contain the $Na_2S_2O_4$ produced using the amounts of reactants in part (a)?

97. ■ What mass of lime, CaO, can be obtained by heating 125 kg of limestone that is 95.0% by mass $CaCO_3$?

$$CaCO_3(s) \rightarrow CaO(s) + CO_2(g)$$

98. ▲ The elements silver, molybdenum, and sulfur combine to form Ag_2MoS_4. What is the maximum mass of Ag_2MoS_4 that can be obtained if 8.63 g of silver, 3.36 g of molybdenum, and 4.81 g of sulfur are combined?

▲ more challenging ■ in OWL Blue-numbered questions answered in Appendix 0

99. ■▲ A mixture of butene, C_4H_8, and butane, C_4H_{10}, is burned in air to give CO_2 and water. Suppose you burn 2.86 g of the mixture and obtain 8.80 g of CO_2 and 4.14 g of H_2O. What are the mass percentages of butene and butane in the mixture?

100. ■▲ Cloth can be waterproofed by coating it with a silicone layer. This is done by exposing the cloth to $(CH_3)_2SiCl_2$ vapor. The silicon compound reacts with OH groups on the cloth to form a waterproofing film (density = 1.0 g/cm³) of $[(CH_3)_2SiO]_n$, where n is a large integer number.

$$n\,(CH_3)_2SiCl_2 + 2n\,OH^- \rightarrow$$
$$2n\,Cl^- + n\,H_2O + [(CH_3)_2SiO]_n$$

The coating is added layer by layer, each layer of $[(CH_3)_2SiO]_n$ being 0.60 nm thick. Suppose you want to waterproof a piece of cloth that is 3.00 m square, and you want 250 layers of waterproofing compound on the cloth. What mass of $(CH_3)_2SiCl_2$ do you need?

101. ■▲ Copper metal can be prepared by roasting copper ore, which can contain cuprite (Cu_2S) and copper(II) sulfide.

$$Cu_2S(s) + O_2(g) \rightarrow 2\,Cu(s) + SO_2(g)$$
$$CuS(s) + O_2(g) \rightarrow Cu(s) + SO_2(g)$$

Suppose an ore sample contains 11.0% impurity in addition to a mixture of CuS and Cu_2S. Heating 100.0 g of the mixture produces 75.4 g of copper metal with a purity of 89.5%. What is the weight percent of CuS in the ore? The weight percent of Cu_2S?

102. Which has the larger concentration of hydronium ions, 0.015 M HCl or aqueous HCl with a pH of 1.2?

103. The mineral dolomite contains magnesium carbonate.

$$MgCO_3(s) + 2\,HCl(aq) \rightarrow$$
$$CO_2(g) + MgCl_2(aq) + H_2O(\ell)$$

(a) Write the net ionic equation for the reaction of $MgCO_3$ and HCl(aq).
(b) What type of reaction is this?
(c) What mass of $MgCO_3$ will react with 125 mL of HCl(aq) with a pH of 1.56?

104. An Alka-Seltzer tablet contains exactly 100. mg of citric acid, $H_3C_6H_5O_7$, plus some sodium bicarbonate. If the following reaction occurs, what mass of sodium bicarbonate must the tablet also contain if citric acid is completely consumed by the following reaction?

$$H_3C_6H_5O_7(aq) + 3\,NaHCO_3(aq) \rightarrow$$
$$3\,H_2O(\ell) + 3\,CO_2(g) + Na_3C_6H_5O_7(aq)$$

105. ▲ Sodium bicarbonate and acetic acid react according to the equation

$$NaHCO_3(aq) + CH_3CO_2H(aq) \rightarrow$$
$$NaCH_3CO_2(aq) + CO_2(g) + H_2O(\ell)$$

What mass of sodium acetate can be obtained from mixing 15.0 g of $NaHCO_3$ with 125 mL of 0.15 M acetic acid?

106. ■ A noncarbonated soft drink contains an unknown amount of citric acid, $H_3C_6H_5O_7$. If 100. mL of the soft drink requires 33.51 mL of 0.0102 M NaOH to neutralize the citric acid completely, what mass of citric acid does the soft drink contain per 100. mL? The reaction of citric acid and NaOH is

$$H_3C_6H_5O_7(aq) + 3\,NaOH(aq) \rightarrow$$
$$Na_3C_6H_5O_7(aq) + 3\,H_2O(\ell)$$

107. Sodium thiosulfate, $Na_2S_2O_3$, is used as a "fixer" in black-and-white photography. Suppose you have a bottle of sodium thiosulfate and want to determine its purity. The thiosulfate ion can be oxidized with I_2 according to the balanced, net ionic equation

$$I_2(aq) + 2\,S_2O_3{}^{2-}(aq) \rightarrow 2\,I^-(aq) + S_4O_6{}^{2-}(aq)$$

If you use 40.21 mL of 0.246 M I_2 in a titration, what is the weight percent of $Na_2S_2O_3$ in a 3.232-g sample of impure material?

108. You have a mixture of oxalic acid, $H_2C_2O_4$, and another solid that does not react with sodium hydroxide. If 29.58 mL of 0.550 M NaOH is required to titrate the oxalic acid in the 4.554-g sample to the second equivalence point, what is the mass percent of oxalic acid in the mixture? Oxalic acid and NaOH react according to the equation

$$H_2C_2O_4(aq) + 2\,NaOH(aq) \rightarrow$$
$$Na_2C_2O_4(aq) + 2\,H_2O(\ell)$$

109. (a) What is the pH of a 0.105 M HCl solution?
(b) What is the hydronium ion concentration in a solution with a pH of 2.56? Is the solution acidic or basic?
(c) A solution has a pH of 9.67. What is the hydronium ion concentration in the solution? Is the solution acidic or basic?
(d) A 10.0-mL sample of 2.56 M HCl is diluted with water to 250. mL. What is the pH of the dilute solution?

110. A solution of hydrochloric acid has a volume of 125 mL and a pH of 2.56. What mass of $NaHCO_3$ must be added to completely consume the HCl?

111. ▲ One half liter (500. mL) of 2.50 M HCl is mixed with 250. mL of 3.75 M HCl. Assuming the total solution volume after mixing is 750. mL, what is the concentration of hydrochloric acid in the resulting solution? What is its pH?

112. A solution of hydrochloric acid has a volume of 250. mL and a pH of 1.92. Exactly 250. mL of 0.0105 M NaOH is added. What is the pH of the resulting solution?

113. ▲ You place 2.56 g of $CaCO_3$ in a beaker containing 250. mL of 0.125 M HCl. When the reaction has ceased, does any calcium carbonate remain? What mass of $CaCl_2$ can be produced?

$$CaCO_3(s) + 2\,HCl(aq) \rightarrow$$
$$CaCl_2(aq) + CO_2(g) + H_2O(\ell)$$

114. The cancer chemotherapy drug cisplatin, $Pt(NH_3)_2Cl_2$, can be made by reacting $(NH_4)_2PtCl_4$ with ammonia in aqueous solution. Besides cisplatin, the other product is NH_4Cl.

(a) Write a balanced equation for this reaction.

(b) To obtain 12.50 g of cisplatin, what mass of $(NH_4)_2PtCl_4$ is required? What volume of 0.125 M NH_3 is required?

(c) ▲ Cisplatin can react with the organic compound pyridine, C_5H_5N, to form a new compound.

$$Pt(NH_3)_2Cl_2(aq) + x\,C_5H_5N(aq) \rightarrow$$
$$Pt(NH_3)_2Cl_2(C_5H_5N)_x(s)$$

Suppose you treat 0.150 g of cisplatin with what you believe is an excess of liquid pyridine (1.50 mL; $d = 0.979$ g/mL). When the reaction is complete, you can find out how much pyridine was not used by titrating the solution with standardized HCl. If 37.0 mL of 0.475 M HCl is required to titrate the excess pyridine,

$$C_5H_5N(aq) + HCl(aq) \rightarrow C_5H_5NH^+(aq) + Cl^-(aq)$$

what is the formula of the unknown compound $Pt(NH_3)_2Cl_2(C_5H_5N)_x$?

115. ▲ You need to know the volume of water in a small swimming pool, but, owing to the pool's irregular shape, it is not a simple matter to determine its dimensions and calculate the volume. To solve the problem, you stir in a solution of a dye (1.0 g of methylene blue, $C_{16}H_{18}ClN_3S$, in 50.0 mL of water). After the dye has mixed with the water in the pool, you take a sample of the water. Using a spectrophotometer, you determine that the concentration of the dye in the pool is 4.1×10^{-8} M. What is the volume of water in the pool?

116. ▲ Calcium and magnesium carbonates occur together in the mineral dolomite. Suppose you heat a sample of the mineral to obtain the oxides, CaO and MgO, and then treat the oxide sample with hydrochloric acid. If 7.695 g of the oxide sample requires 125 mL of 2.55 M HCl,

$$CaO(s) + 2\,HCl(aq) \rightarrow CaCl_2(aq) + H_2O(\ell)$$

$$MgO(s) + 2\,HCl(aq) \rightarrow MgCl_2(aq) + H_2O(\ell)$$

What is the weight percent of each oxide (CaO and MgO) in the sample?

117. ■ Gold can be dissolved from gold-bearing rock by treating the rock with sodium cyanide in the presence of oxygen.

$$4\,Au(s) + 8\,NaCN(aq) + O_2(g) + 2\,H_2O(\ell) \rightarrow$$
$$4\,NaAu(CN)_2(aq) + 4\,NaOH(aq)$$

(a) Name the oxidizing and reducing agents in this reaction. What has been oxidized, and what has been reduced?

(b) If you have exactly one metric ton (1 metric ton = 1000 kg) of gold-bearing rock, what volume of 0.075 M NaCN, in liters, do you need to extract the gold if the rock is 0.019% gold?

118. ▲ You mix 25.0 mL of 0.234 M $FeCl_3$ with 42.5 mL of 0.453 M NaOH.

(a) What mass of $Fe(OH)_3$ (in grams) will precipitate from this reaction mixture?

(b) One of the reactants ($FeCl_3$ or NaOH) is present in a stoichiometric excess. What is the molar concentration of the excess reactant remaining in solution after $Fe(OH)_3$ has been precipitated?

In the Laboratory

119. ■ Suppose you dilute 25.0 mL of a 0.110 M solution of Na_2CO_3 to exactly 100.0 mL. You then take exactly 10.0 mL of this diluted solution and add it to a 250-mL volumetric flask. After filling the volumetric flask to the mark with distilled water (indicating the volume of the new solution is 250. mL), what is the concentration of the diluted Na_2CO_3 solution?

120. ▲ In some laboratory analyses, the preferred technique is to dissolve a sample in an excess of acid or base and then "back-titrate" the excess with a standard base or acid. This technique is used to assess the purity of a sample of $(NH_4)_2SO_4$. Suppose you dissolve a 0.475-g sample of impure $(NH_4)_2SO_4$ in aqueous KOH.

$$(NH_4)_2SO_4(aq) + 2\,KOH(aq) \rightarrow$$
$$2\,NH_3(aq) + 2\,K_2SO_4(aq) + 2\,H_2O(\ell)$$

The NH_3 liberated in the reaction is distilled from the solution into a flask containing 50.0 mL of 0.100 M HCl. The ammonia reacts with the acid to produce NH_4Cl, but not all of the HCl is used in this reaction. The amount of excess acid is determined by titrating the solution with standardized NaOH. This titration consumes 11.1 mL of 0.121 M NaOH. What is the weight percent of $(NH_4)_2SO_4$ in the 0.475-g sample?

121. You wish to determine the weight percent of copper in a copper-containing alloy. After dissolving a 0.251-g sample of the alloy in acid, an excess of KI is added, and the Cu^{2+} and I^- ions undergo the reaction

$$2\,Cu^{2+}(aq) + 5\,I^-(aq) \rightarrow 2\,CuI(s) + I_3^-(aq)$$

The liberated I_3^- is titrated with sodium thiosulfate according to the equation

$$I_3^-(aq) + 2\,S_2O_3^{2-}(aq) \rightarrow S_4O_6^{2-}(aq) + 3\,I^-(aq)$$

(a) Designate the oxidizing and reducing agents in the two reactions above.

(b) If 26.32 mL of 0.101 M $Na_2S_2O_3$ is required for titration to the equivalence point, what is the weight percent of Cu in the alloy?

122. ▲ A compound has been isolated that can have either of two possible formulas: (a) $K[Fe(C_2O_4)_2(H_2O)_2]$ or (b) $K_3[Fe(C_2O_4)_3]$. To find which is correct, you dissolve a weighed sample of the compound in acid and then titrate the oxalate ion ($C_2O_4^{2-}$, which in acid becomes $H_2C_2O_4$) with potassium permanganate, $KMnO_4$ (the source of the MnO_4^- ion). The balanced, net ionic equation for the titration is

$$5\ H_2C_2O_4(aq) + 2\ MnO_4^-(aq) + 6\ H_3O^+(aq) \rightarrow$$
$$2\ Mn^{2+}(aq) + 10\ CO_2(g) + 14\ H_2O(\ell)$$

Titration of 1.356 g of the compound requires 34.50 mL of 0.108 M $KMnO_4$. Which is the correct formula of the iron-containing compound: (a) or (b)?

123. ▲ Chromium(III) ion forms many compounds with ammonia. To find the formula of one of these compounds, you titrate the NH_3 in the compound with standardized acid.

$$Cr(NH_3)_xCl_3(aq) + x\ HCl(aq) \rightarrow$$
$$x\ NH_4^+(aq) + Cr^{3+}(aq) + (x + 3)\ Cl^-(aq)$$

Assume that 24.26 mL of 1.500 M HCl is used to titrate 1.580 g of $Cr(NH_3)_xCl_3$. What is the value of x?

124. ▲ Thioridazine, $C_{21}H_{26}N_2S_2$, is a pharmaceutical agent used to regulate dopamine. (Dopamine, a neurotransmitter, affects brain processes that control movement, emotional response, and ability to experience pleasure and pain.) A chemist can analyze a sample of the pharmaceutical for the thioridazine content by decomposing it to convert the sulfur in the compound to sulfate ion. This is then "trapped" as water-insoluble barium sulfate (see Figure 4.6).

$$SO_4^{2-}(aq, \text{from thioridazine}) + BaCl_2(aq) \rightarrow$$
$$BaSO_4(s) + 2\ Cl^-(aq)$$

Suppose a 12-tablet sample of the drug yielded 0.301 g of $BaSO_4$. What is the thioridazine content, in milligrams, of each tablet?

125. ■▲ A herbicide contains 2,4-D (2,4-dichlorophenoxyacetic acid), $C_8H_6Cl_2O_3$. A 1.236-g sample of the herbicide was decomposed to liberate the chlorine as Cl^- ion. This was precipitated as AgCl, with a mass of 0.1840 g. What is the mass percent of 2,4-D in the sample?

126. ▲ Sulfuric acid is listed in a catalog with a concentration of 95–98%. A bottle of the acid in the stockroom states that 1.00 L has a mass of 1.84 kg. To determine the concentration of sulfuric acid in the stockroom bottle, a student dilutes 5.00 mL to 500. mL. She then takes four 10.00-mL samples and titrates each with standardized sodium hydroxide ($c = 0.1760$ mol/L).

Sample	1	2	3	4
Volume NaOH (mL)	20.15	21.30	20.40	20.35

(a) What is the average concentration of the diluted sulfuric acid sample?

(b) What is the mass percent of H_2SO_4 in the original bottle of the acid?

127. ▲ Anhydrous calcium chloride is a good drying agent as it will rapidly pick up water. Suppose you have stored some carefully dried $CaCl_2$ in a dessicator. Unfortunately, someone did not close the top of the dessicator tightly, and the $CaCl_2$ became partially hydrated. A 150-g sample of this partially hydrated material was dissolved in 80 g of hot water. When the solution was cooled to 20 °C, 74.9 g of $CaCl_2 \cdot 6\ H_2O$ precipitated. Knowing the solubility of calcium chloride in water at 20 °C is 74.5 g $CaCl_2$/100 g water, determine the water content of the 150-g sample of partially hydrated calcium chloride (in moles of water per mole of $CaCl_2$).

128. ▲ A sample consisting of a mixture of iron and iron(III) oxide was dissolved completely in acid (which converted the iron to iron(III) ions.) After adding a reducing agent to ensure that all of the iron was in the form of iron(II) ions, the solution was titrated with the standardized $KMnO_4$ (0.04240 M); 37.50 mL of the $KMnO_4$ solution was required. Calculate the mass percent of Fe and Fe_2O_3 in the 0.5510-g sample. (See Example 4.12 for the reaction of iron(II) and $KMnO_4$.)

129. ▲ Phosphate in urine can be determined by spectrophotometry. After removing protein from the sample, it is treated with a molybdenum compound to give, ultimately, a deep blue polymolybdate. The absorbance of the blue polymolybdate can be measured at 650 nm and is directly related to the urine phosphate concentration. A 24-hour urine sample was collected from a patient; the volume of urine was 1122 mL. The phosphate in a 1.00 mL portion of the urine sample was converted to the blue polymolybdate (P) and diluted to 50.00 mL. A calibration curve was prepared using phosphate-containing solutions.

Solution (mass P/L)	Absorbance at 650 nm in a 1.0 cm cell
1.00×10^{-6} g	0.230
2.00×10^{-6} g	0.436
3.00×10^{-6} g	0.638
4.00×10^{-6} g	0.848
Urine sample	0.518

(a) What are the slope and intercept of the calibration curve?

(b) What is the mass of phosphorus per liter of urine?

(c) What mass of phosphate did the patient excrete per day?

130. ▲ A 4.000-g sample containing KCl and KClO$_4$ was dissolved in sufficient water to give 250.00 mL of solution. A 50.00-mL portion of the solution required 41.00 mL of 0.0750 M AgNO$_3$ in a Mohr titration (page 186). Next, a 25.00-mL portion of the original solution was treated with V$_2$(SO$_4$)$_3$ to reduce the perchlorate ion to chloride,

$$8 \, V^{3+}(aq) + ClO_4^-(aq) + 12 \, H_2O(\ell) \rightarrow$$
$$Cl^-(aq) + 8 \, VO^{2+}(aq) + 8 \, H_3O^+(aq)$$

and the resulting solution was titrated with AgNO$_3$. This titration required 38.12 mL of 0.0750 M AgNO$_3$. What is the mass percent of KCl and KClO$_4$ in the mixture?

Summary and Conceptual Questions

The following questions may use concepts from this and preceding chapters.

131. Two beakers sit on a balance; the total mass is 167.170 g. One beaker contains a solution of KI; the other contains a solution of Pb(NO$_3$)$_2$. When the solution in one beaker is poured completely into the other, the following reaction occurs:

$$2 \, KI(aq) + Pb(NO_3)_2(aq) \rightarrow 2 \, KNO_3(aq) + PbI_2(s)$$

Charles D. Winters

Solutions of KI and Pb(NO$_3$)$_2$ before reaction.

Solutions after reaction.

What is the total mass of the beakers and solutions after reaction? Explain completely.

132. ▲ A weighed sample of iron (Fe) is added to liquid bromine (Br$_2$) and allowed to react completely. The reaction produces a single product, which can be isolated and weighed. The experiment was repeated a number of times with different masses of iron but with the same mass of bromine. (See the graph below.)

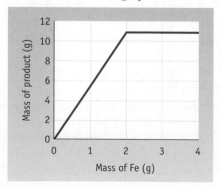

(a) What mass of Br$_2$ is used when the reaction consumes 2.0 g of Fe?
(b) What is the mole ratio of Br$_2$ to Fe in the reaction?
(c) What is the empirical formula of the product?
(d) Write the balanced chemical equation for the reaction of iron and bromine.
(e) What is the name of the reaction product?
(f) Which statement or statements best describe the experiments summarized by the graph?
   (i)   When 1.00 g of Fe is added to the Br$_2$, Fe is the limiting reagent.
   (ii) When 3.50 g of Fe is added to the Br$_2$, there is an excess of Br$_2$.
   (iii) When 2.50 g of Fe is added to the Br$_2$, both reactants are used up completely.
   (iv) When 2.00 g of Fe is added to the Br$_2$, 10.0 g of product is formed. The percent yield must therefore be 20.0%.

133. Let us explore a reaction with a limiting reactant. (See ChemistryNow Screens 4.4 and 4.5.) Here, zinc metal is added to a flask containing aqueous HCl, and H$_2$ gas is a product.

$$Zn(s) + 2 \, HCl(aq) \rightarrow ZnCl_2(aq) + H_2(g)$$

The three flasks each contain 0.100 mol of HCl. Zinc is added to each flask in the following quantities.

Flask 1: 7.00 g Zn
Flask 2: 3.27 g Zn
Flask 3: 1.31 g Zn

Charles D. Winters

When the reactants are combined, the H$_2$ inflates the balloon attached to the flask. The results are as follows:

Flask 1: Balloon inflates completely, but some Zn remains when inflation ceases.
Flask 2: Balloon inflates completely. No Zn remains.
Flask 3: Balloon does not inflate completely. No Zn remains.

Explain these results. Perform calculations that support your explanation.

▲ more challenging ■ in OWL Blue-numbered questions answered in Appendix O

134. The reaction of aluminum and bromine is pictured in Figure 2.12 and below. The white solid on the lip of the beaker at the end of the reaction is Al_2Br_6. In the reaction pictured below, which was the limiting reactant, Al or Br_2? (See ChemistryNow Screen 4.2.)

Charles D. Winters

Before reaction.

Charles D. Winters

After reaction.

135. ▲ Two students titrate different samples of the same solution of HCl using 0.100 M NaOH solution and phenolphthalein indicator (see Figure 4.14). The first student pipets 20.0 mL of the HCl solution into a flask, adds 20 mL of distilled water and a few drops of phenolphthalein solution, and titrates until a lasting pink color appears. The second student pipets 20.0 mL of the HCl solution into a flask, adds 60 mL of distilled water and a few drops of phenolphthalein solution, and titrates to the first lasting pink color. Each student correctly calculates the molarity of an HCl solution. What will the second student's result be?
(a) four times less than the first student's result
(b) four times greater than the first student's result
(c) two times less than the first student's result
(d) two times greater than the first student's result
(e) the same as the first student's result

136. A video on Screen 4.12 of ChemistryNow shows the reaction of Fe^{2+} with MnO_4^- in aqueous solution.
(a) What is the balanced equation for the reaction that occurred?
(b) What is the oxidizing agent, and what is the reducing agent?
(c) Equal volumes of Fe^{2+}-containing solution and MnO_4^--containing solution were mixed. The amount of Fe^{2+} was just sufficient to consume all of the MnO_4^-. Which ion (Fe^{2+} or MnO_4^-) was initially present in larger concentration?

137. In some states, a person will receive a "driving while intoxicated" (DWI) ticket if the blood alcohol level (BAL) is 100 mg per deciliter (dL) of blood or higher. Suppose a person is found to have a BAL of 0.033 mol of ethanol (C_2H_5OH) per liter of blood. Will the person receive a DWI ticket?

5 | Principles of Chemical Reactivity: Energy and Chemical Reactions

©Nicolas Raymond

A Hot Air Balloon

These colorful balloons usually consist of a gas bag or envelope of nylon with a basket suspended below for passengers. A propane burner sits on top of the basket and below the gas envelope. When the air inside the envelope is heated by burning propane, the balloon can ascend (because the density of heated air in the bag is less than that of the cooler surrounding air). Under normal conditions, about 3 m³ of envelope volume is required to lift 1 kg of mass. Thus, to carry one person and the needed equipment, most balloons have a volume of about 1000 m³.

Question:

You have a balloon with a volume of 1100 m³ and want to heat the air inside of the envelope from 22 °C to 110 °C. What mass of propane must you burn to accomplish this? (The specific heat capacity of air is 1.01 J/g · K, and the density of dry air [at sea level] is about 1.2 kg/m³. Other information you need is in this chapter or Appendix L.)

Answer to this question is in Appendix Q.

Chapter Goals

- Assess the transfer of energy as heat associated with changes in temperature and changes of state.
- Understand and apply the first law of thermodynamics.
- Define and understand state functions (enthalpy, internal energy).
- Learn how energy changes are measured.
- Calculate the energy evolved or required for physical changes and chemical reactions using tables of thermodynamic data.

Chapter Outline

The importance of energy is evident in our daily lives—in heating and cooling our homes, in powering our appliances, and in propelling our vehicles, among other things. Most of the energy we use for these purposes is obtained by carrying out chemical reactions, mostly by burning fossil fuels. We use natural gas for heating, coal and natural gas to generate most of our electric power, and fuels derived from petroleum for automobiles and for heat. In addition, energy is required for all life processes. Chemical reactions in our bodies provide the energy for all body functions, for movement, and to maintain body temperature. It is not surprising that the topic of energy is a prominent part of our discussion of chemistry.

To scientists, however, energy has significance that goes well beyond these many practical uses. In this chapter, we will begin the discussion of **thermodynamics**, the science of heat and work. This subject will provide important insights on the following questions:

- How do we measure and calculate the energy changes that are associated with physical changes and chemical reactions?
- What is the relationship between energy changes, heat, and work?
- How can we determine whether a chemical reaction is product-favored or reactant-favored at equilibrium?
- How can we determine whether a chemical reaction or physical process will occur spontaneously, that is, without outside intervention?

We will concentrate attention on the first two questions in this chapter and address the last two questions in Chapter 19.

Chemistry⋅Now™

Throughout the text this icon introduces an opportunity for self-study or to explore interactive tutorials by signing in at www.cengage.com/login.

■ **World Energy Consumption** Burning fossil fuels provides about 85% of the total energy used by people on our planet. Nuclear and hydroelectric power each contribute about 6%. The remaining 3% is provided from biomass, solar, wind, and geothermal sources.

5.1 Energy: Some Basic Principles

Energy is defined as the capacity to do work. You do work against the force of gravity when carrying yourself and hiking equipment up a mountain. The energy to do this is provided by the food you have eaten. Food is a source of chemical energy—energy stored in chemical compounds and released when the compounds undergo the chemical reactions of metabolism in your body.

(a) Gravitational energy   (b) Chemical potential energy   (c) Electrostatic energy

Active Figure 5.1   **Energy and its conversion.** (a) Water at the top of a waterfall represents stored, or potential, energy. As water falls, its potential energy is converted to mechanical energy. (b) Chemical potential energy of the fuel and oxygen is converted to thermal and mechanical energy. (c) Lightning converts electrostatic energy into radiant and thermal energy.

Chemistry.Now™ Sign in at www.cengage.com/login and go to the Chapter Contents menu to explore an interactive version of this figure accompanied by an exercise.

Energy can be classified as kinetic or potential. **Kinetic energy** is energy associated with motion, such as:

- The motion of atoms, molecules, or ions at the submicroscopic (particulate) level (*thermal energy*). All matter has thermal energy.
- The motion of macroscopic objects like a moving tennis ball or automobile (*mechanical energy*).
- The movement of electrons through a conductor (*electrical energy*).
- The compression and expansion of the spaces between molecules in the transmission of sound (*acoustic energy*).

Potential energy results from an object's position and includes:

- Energy possessed by a ball held above the floor and by water at the top of a waterfall (*gravitational energy*) (Figure 5.1a).
- Energy stored in fuels (*chemical energy*) (Figure 5.1b). All chemical reactions involve a change in chemical energy.
- The energy associated with the separation of two electrical charges (*electrostatic energy*) (Figure 5.1c).

Potential energy and kinetic energy can be interconverted. For example, as water falls over a waterfall, its potential energy is converted into kinetic energy. Similarly, kinetic energy can be converted into potential energy: The kinetic energy of falling water can turn a turbine to produce electricity, which can then be used to convert water into H_2 and O_2 by electrolysis. Hydrogen gas contains stored chemical potential energy because it can be burned to produce heat and light or electricity.

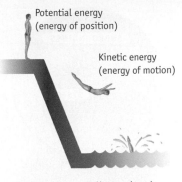

FIGURE 5.2 The law of energy conservation. The diver's potential energy is converted to kinetic energy, and this is then transferred to the water, illustrating the law of conservation of energy. See ChemistryNow Screen 5.2 Energy, to view an animation of this figure.

Conservation of Energy

Standing on a diving board, you have considerable potential energy because of your position above the water. Once you jump off the board, some of that potential energy is converted into kinetic energy (Figure 5.2). During the dive, the force of gravity accelerates your body so that it moves faster and faster. Your kinetic energy increases, and your potential energy decreases. At the moment you hit the water, your velocity is abruptly reduced, and much of your kinetic energy is transferred to the water as your body moves it aside. Eventually, you float to the surface, and the water becomes still again. If you could see them, however, you would find that the water molecules are moving a little faster in the vicinity of your entry into the water; that is, the kinetic energy of the water molecules is slightly higher.

This series of energy conversions illustrates the **law of conservation of energy**, which states that *energy can neither be created nor destroyed.* Or, to state this law differently, *the total energy of the universe is constant.* The law of conservation of energy summarizes the results of a great many experiments in which the amounts of energy transferred have been measured and in which the total energy content has been found to be the same before and after an event.

Temperature and Heat

The temperature of an object is a measure of its ability to transfer energy as heat. When two objects at different temperatures are brought into contact, energy will be transferred as heat from the one at the higher temperature to the one at the lower temperature. One way to measure temperature is with a thermometer containing mercury or some other liquid (Figure 5.3). When the thermometer is placed

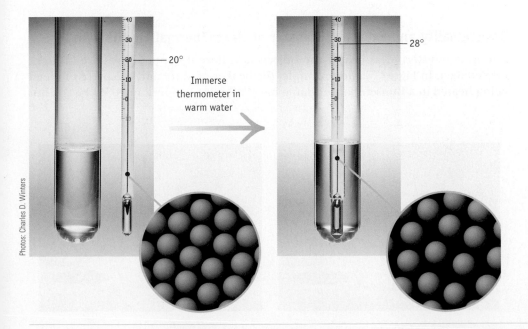

FIGURE 5.3 Measuring temperature. The volume of liquid mercury in a thermometer increases slightly when immersed in warm water. The volume increase causes the mercury to rise in the thermometer, which is calibrated to give the temperature.

FIGURE 5.4 Systems and their surroundings. Earth can be considered a thermodynamic system, with the rest of the universe as its surroundings. A chemical reaction occurring in a laboratory is also a system, with the laboratory its surroundings.

in hot water, thermal energy is transferred from the water to the thermometer (heating the thermometer and cooling the water). This causes the atoms of liquid mercury to move more rapidly (increasing their kinetic energy) and the space between them to increase slightly. The resulting increase in volume causes the column of liquid to rise higher in the thermometer tube.

Several important aspects of thermal energy and temperature should be recognized:

- Temperature determines the direction of thermal energy transfer.
- The higher the temperature of a given object, the greater the thermal energy (energy associated with molecular motion) of its atoms, ions, or molecules.
- Heating and cooling are processes by which energy is transferred as heat from an object at a higher temperature to one at a lower temperature. Heat is not a substance. (See *A Closer Look: What Is Heat?*)

Systems and Surroundings

In thermodynamics, the terms "system" and "surroundings" have precise and important scientific meanings. A **system** is defined as an object, or collection of objects, being studied (Figure 5.4). The **surroundings** include everything outside the system that can exchange energy and/or matter with the system. In the discussion that follows, we will need to define systems precisely. If we are studying the energy evolved in a chemical reaction carried out in solution, for example, the system might be defined as the reactants, products, and solvent. The surroundings would be the reaction vessel and the air in the room and anything else in contact with the vessel that might exchange energy or matter. At the atomic level, the system could be a single atom or molecule, and the surroundings would be the atoms or molecules in its vicinity. How we choose to define the system and its surroundings for each situation depends on the information we are trying to obtain or convey.

This concept of a system and its surroundings applies to nonchemical situations as well. If we want to study the energy balance on this planet, we might choose to define Earth as the system and outer space as the surroundings. On a cosmic level, the solar system might be defined as the system being studied, and the rest of the galaxy would be the surroundings.

Directionality and Extent of Transfer of Heat: Thermal Equilibrium

Energy is transferred as heat if two objects at different temperatures are brought into contact. In Figure 5.5, for example, the beaker of water and the piece of metal being heated in a Bunsen burner flame have different temperatures. When the hot

FIGURE 5.5 Energy transfer. Energy transfer as heat occurs from the hotter metal bar to the cooler water. Eventually, the water and metal reach the same temperature and are said to be in thermal equilibrium.

See ChemistryNow Screen 5.4, Energy Transfer Between Substances, for a simulation and tutorial.

What Is Heat?

Two hundred years ago, scientists characterized heat as a real substance called a caloric fluid. The caloric hypothesis supposed that when a fuel burned and a pot of water was heated, for example, caloric fluid was transferred from the fuel to the water. Burning the fuel released caloric fluid, and the temperature of the water increased as the caloric fluid was absorbed.

Over the next 50 years, however, the caloric hypothesis lost favor, and we now know it is incorrect. Experiments by James Joule (1818–1889) and Benjamin Thompson (1753–1814) that showed the interrelationship between heat and other forms of energy such as mechanical energy provided the key to dispelling this idea. Even so, some of our everyday language retains the influence of this early theory. For example, we often speak of heat flowing as if it were a fluid.

From our discussion so far, we know one thing that "heat" is not—but what is it? Heat is said to be a "process quantity" as opposed to a "state quantity." That is, heating is a *process* that changes the internal energy of a system. It is the process by which energy is transferred across the boundary of a system owing to a difference in temperature between the two sides of the boundary. In this process, the energy of one object increases, and the energy of another object decreases.

Heating is not the only way to transfer energy. Work is another process by which energy can be transferred between objects.

The idea of energy transfer by the processes of heat and work is embodied in the definition of thermodynamics: the science of heat and work.

Richard Howard

Work and heat. A classic experiment that showed the relationship between work and heat was performed by Benjamin Thompson (also known as Count Rumford) (1753–1814) using an apparatus similar to that shown here. Thompson measured the rise in temperature of water (in the vessel mostly hidden at the back of the apparatus) that resulted from the energy expended to turn the crank.

metal is plunged into the cold water, energy is transferred as heat from the metal to the water. The thermal energy (molecular motion) of the water molecules increases; the thermal energy of the metal atoms decreases. Eventually, the two objects reach the same temperature. At that point, the system has reached **thermal equilibrium**. The distinguishing feature of thermal equilibrium is that, on the macroscopic scale, no further temperature change occurs; both the metal and water are at the same temperature.

Putting a hot metal bar into a beaker of water and following the temperature change may seem like a rather simple experiment with an obvious outcome. Illustrated in the experiment, however, are three principles that are important in our further discussion:

- Energy transfer as heat will occur spontaneously from an object at a higher temperature to an object at a lower temperature.
- Transfer of energy as heat continues until both objects are at the same temperature and thermal equilibrium is achieved.
- After thermal equilibrium is attained, the object whose temperature increased has gained thermal energy, and the object whose temperature decreased has lost thermal energy.

For the specific case where energy is transferred as heat within an isolated system (that is, a system that cannot transfer either energy or matter with its surroundings), we can also say that the quantity of thermal energy lost by a hotter object and the quantity of thermal energy gained by a cooler object are numerically equal. (This is required by the law of conservation of energy.) When energy is transferred as

■ **Thermal Equilibrium** Although no change is evident at the macroscopic level when thermal equilibrium is reached, on the molecular level transfer of energy between individual molecules will continue to occur. A general feature of systems at equilibrium is that there is no change on a macroscopic level but that processes still occur at the particulate level. (See Section 3.3, page 118.)

Exothermic
$q_{sys} < 0$

SYSTEM

SURROUNDINGS

Exothermic: energy transferred
from system to surroundings

Endothermic
$q_{sys} > 0$

SYSTEM

SURROUNDINGS

Endothermic: energy transferred
from surroundings to system

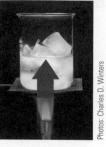

Photos: Charles D. Winters

Active Figure 5.6 **Exothermic and endothermic processes.** The symbol q represents the energy transferred as heat, and the subscript sys refers to the system.

Chemistry ☼ Now™ Sign in at www.cengage.com/login and go to the Chapter Contents menu to explore an interactive version of this figure accompanied by an exercise.

■ **Exothermic and Endothermic** The terms "endothermic" and "exothermic" apply specifically to energy transfer as heat. The more general terms "endoergic" and "exoergic" are sometimes used, encompassing any type of energy transfer between system and surroundings.

heat between a system and its surroundings, we describe the directionality of this transfer as exothermic or endothermic (Figure 5.6).

- In an **exothermic process**, energy is transferred as heat from a system to its surroundings. The energy of the system decreases, and the energy of the surroundings increases.
- An **endothermic process** is the opposite of an exothermic process. Energy is transferred as heat from the surroundings to the system, increasing the energy of the system, decreasing the energy of the surroundings.

Energy Units

■ **James Joule** The joule is named for James P. Joule (1818–1889), the son of a wealthy brewer in Manchester, England. The family wealth and a workshop in the brewery gave Joule the opportunity to pursue scientific studies. Among the topics that Joule studied was the issue of whether heat was a massless fluid. Scientists at that time referred to this idea as the caloric hypothesis. Joule's careful experiments showed that heat and mechanical work are related, providing evidence that heat is not a fluid. (See *A Closer Look: What Is Heat?*)

Oesper Collection in the History of Chemistry/University of Cincinnati

When expressing energy quantities, most chemists (and much of the world outside the United States) use the **joule** (J), the SI unit. The joule is related directly to the units used for mechanical energy: 1 J equals 1 kg · m²/s². Because the joule is inconveniently small for most uses in chemistry, the kilojoule (kJ), equivalent to 1000 joules, is often the unit of choice.

To give you some feeling for joules, suppose you drop a six-pack of soft-drink cans, each full of liquid, on your foot. Although you probably will not take time to calculate the kinetic energy at the moment of impact, it is between 4 J and 10 J.

The calorie (cal) is an older energy unit. It is defined as the energy transferred as heat that is required to raise the temperature of 1.00 g of pure liquid water from 14.5 °C to 15.5 °C. A kilocalorie (kcal) is equivalent to 1000 calories. The conversion factor relating joules and calories is

> **1 calorie (cal) = 4.184 joules (J)**

The dietary Calorie (with a capital C) is often used in the United States to represent the energy content of foods. The dietary Calorie (Cal) is equivalent to the kilocalorie or 1000 calories. Thus, a breakfast cereal that gives you 100.0 Calories of nutritional energy per serving provides 100.0 kcal or 418.4 kJ.

Chemistry ☼ Now™

Sign in at **www.cengage.com/login** and go to Chapter 5 Contents to see Screen 5.4 to view an animation on **endothermic and exothermic systems** and Screen 5.5 for a tutorial on **converting between different energy units.**

Chemical Perspectives

Food and Calories

The U.S. Food and Drug Administration (FDA) mandates that nutritional data, including energy content, be included on almost all packaged food. The Nutrition Labeling and Education Act of 1990 requires that the total energy from protein, carbohydrates, fat, and alcohol be specified. How is this determined? Initially, the method used was calorimetry. In this method, which is described in Section 5.6, a food product is burned, and the energy transferred as heat in the combustion is measured. Now, however, energy contents are estimated using the Atwater system. This specifies the following average values for energy sources in foods:

    1 g protein = 4 kcal (17 kJ)
    1 g carbohydrate = 4 kcal (17 kJ)
    1 g fat = 9 kcal (38 kJ)
    1 g alcohol = 7 kcal (29 kJ)

Because carbohydrates may contain some indigestible fiber, the mass of fiber is subtracted from the mass of carbohydrate when calculating the energy from carbohydrates.

As an example, one serving of cashew nuts (about 28 g) has

    14 g fat = 126 kcal
    6 g protein = 24 kcal
    7 g carbohydrates − 1 g fiber = 24 kcal
    Total = 174 kcal (728 kJ)

A value of 170 kcal is reported on the package.

You can find data on more than 6000 foods at the Nutrient Data Laboratory website (www.ars.usda.gov/ba/bhnrc/ndl).

Nutrition Facts

Serving Size 1 cup (30g)
    Children Under 4 - ¾ cup (20g)
Servings Per Container About 19
    Children Under 4 - About 28

Amount Per Serving	Cheerios	with ½ cup skim milk	Cereal for Children Under 4
Calories	110	150	70
Calories from Fat	15	20	10
	% Daily Value**		
Total Fat 2g*	3%	3%	1g
Saturated Fat 0g	0%	3%	0g
Polyunsaturated Fat 0.5g			0g
Monounsaturated Fat 0.5g			0g
Cholesterol 0mg	0%	1%	0mg
Sodium 210mg	9%	12%	140mg
Potassium 200mg	6%	12%	130mg

Charles D. Winters

Energy and food labels. All packaged foods must have labels specifying nutritional values, with energy given in Calories (where 1 Cal = 1 kilocalorie).

EXERCISE 5.1 Energy Units

(a) In an old textbook, you read that the burning 1.00 g of hydrogen to form liquid water produces 3800 calories. What is this energy in units of joules?

(b) The label on a cereal box indicates that one serving (with skim milk) provides 250 Cal. What is this energy in kilojoules (kJ)?

■ **Kinetic Energy** Kinetic energy is calculated by the equation KE = $1/2\, mv^2$. One joule is the kinetic energy of a 2.0 kg mass (m) moving at 1.0 m/s (v).
KE = $(1/2)(2.0\text{ kg})(1.0\text{ m/s})^2$
   = 1.0 kg · m²/s² = 1.0 J

5.2 Specific Heat Capacity: Heating and Cooling

When an object is heated or cooled, the quantity of energy transferred depends on three things:

- The quantity of material
- The magnitude of the temperature change
- The identity of the material gaining or losing energy

Specific heat capacity (*C*) is defined as *the energy transferred as heat that is required to raise the temperature of 1 gram of a substance by one kelvin.* It has units of joules per gram per kelvin (J/g · K). A few specific heat capacities are listed in Figure 5.7, and a longer list of specific heat capacities is given in Appendix D (Table 11).

    The energy gained or lost as heat when a given mass of a substance is warmed or cooled can be calculated using Equation 5.1.

$$q = C \times m \times \Delta T \qquad (5.1)$$

Here, q is the energy gained or lost as heat by a given mass of substance (m); C is the specific heat capacity, and ΔT is the change in temperature. The change in temperature, ΔT, is calculated as the final temperature minus the initial temperature.

$$\Delta T = T_{final} - T_{initial} \qquad (5.2)$$

■ **Change in Temperature, ΔT**

Sign of ΔT	Meaning
Positive	$T_{final} > T_{initial}$, so T has increased, and q will be positive. Energy has been transferred to the object under study.
Negative	$T_{initial} > T_{final}$, so T has decreased, and q will be negative. Energy has been transferred out of the object under study.

Specific Heat Capacities of Some Elements, Compounds, and Substances

Substances	Specific Heat Capacity (J/g · K)	Molar Heat Capacity (J/mol · K)
Al, aluminum	0.897	24.2
Fe, iron	0.449	25.1
Cu, copper	0.385	24.5
Water (liquid)	4.184	75.4
Water (ice)	2.06	37.1
$HOCH_2CH_2OH(\ell)$, ethylene glycol (antifreeze)	2.39	14.8
Wood	1.8	—
Glass	0.8	—

Charles D. Winters

FIGURE 5.7 Specific heat capacity. Metals have different values of specific heat capacity on a per-gram basis. However, their molar heat capacities are all in the range of 25 J/mol · K. Among common substances, liquid water has the highest specific heat capacity on a per-gram or per-mole basis (except for liquid ammonia), a fact that plays a significant role in Earth's weather and climate.

■ **Molar Heat Capacity** Heat capacities can be expressed on a per-mole basis. The amount of energy that is transferred as heat in raising the temperature of one mole of a substance by one Kelvin is the molar heat capacity. For water, the molar heat capacity is 75.4 J/mol · K. The molar heat capacity of metals at room temperature is always near 25 kJ/mol · K.

Calculating a change in temperature using Equation 5.2 will give a result with an algebraic sign that indicates the direction of energy transfer. For example, we can use the specific heat capacity of copper, 0.385 J/g · K, to calculate the energy that must be transferred as heat to a 10.0-g sample of copper if its temperature is raised from 298 K (25 °C) to 598 K (325 °C).

$$q = \left(0.385 \ \frac{J}{g \cdot K}\right)(10.0 \ g)(598 \ K \ - \ 298 \ K) = \ +1160 \ J$$

T_{final}
Final temp.

$T_{initial}$
Initial temp.

Notice that the answer has a positive sign. This indicates that the thermal energy of the sample of copper has increased by 1160 J, which is in accord with energy being transferred as heat to the copper from the water.

The relationship between energy, mass, and specific heat capacity has numerous implications. The high specific heat capacity of liquid water, 4.184 J/g · K, is a major reason why large bodies of water have a profound influence on weather. In spring, lakes warm up more slowly than the air. In autumn, the energy given off by a large lake as it cools moderates the drop in air temperature. The relevance of specific heat capacity is also illustrated when bread is wrapped in aluminum foil (specific heat capacity 0.897 J/g · K) and heated in an oven. You can remove the foil with your fingers after taking the bread from the oven. The bread and the aluminum foil are very hot, but the small mass of aluminum foil used and its low specific heat capacity result in only a small quantity of energy being transferred to your fingers (which have a larger mass and a higher specific heat capacity) when you touch the hot foil. This is also the reason why a chain of fast-food restaurants warns you that the filling of an apple pie can be much warmer than the paper wrapper or the pie crust. Although the wrapper, pie crust, and filling are at the same temperature, the quantity of energy transferred to your fingers (or your mouth!) from the filling is greater than that transferred from the wrapper and crust.

Charles D. Winters

A practical example of specific heat capacity. The filling of the apple pie has a higher specific heat (and higher mass) than the pie crust and wrapper. Notice the warning on the wrapper.

Chemistry ⚗ Now™

Sign in at **www.cengage.com/login** and go to Chapter 5 Contents to see Screen 5.7 for a simulation and exercise on **energy transfer as heat.**

■ **EXAMPLE 5.1** **Specific Heat Capacity**

Problem How much energy must be transferred to raise the temperature of a cup of coffee (250 mL) from 20.5 °C (293.7 K) to 95.6 °C (368.8 K)? Assume that water and coffee have the same density (1.00 g/mL), and specific heat capacity (4.184 J/g · K).

Strategy Use Equation 5.1. For the calculation, you will need the specific heat capacity for H_2O, the mass of the coffee (calculated from its density and volume), and the change in temperature ($T_{final} - T_{initial}$).

Solution

$$\text{Mass of coffee} = (250 \text{ mL})(1.00 \text{ g/mL}) = 250 \text{ g}$$

$$\Delta T = T_{final} - T_{initial} = 368.8 \text{ K} - 293.7 \text{ K} = 75.1 \text{ K}$$

$$q = C \times m \times \Delta T$$

$$q = (4.184 \text{ J/g} \cdot \text{K})(250 \text{ g})(75.1 \text{ K})$$

$$\boxed{q = 79,000 \text{ J (or 79 kJ)}}$$

Comment The positive sign in the answer indicates that thermal energy has been transferred to the coffee as heat. The thermal energy of the coffee is now higher.

EXERCISE 5.2 **Specific Heat Capacity**

In an experiment, it was determined that 59.8 J was required to raise the temperature of 25.0 g of ethylene glycol (a compound used as antifreeze in automobile engines) by 1.00 K. Calculate the specific heat capacity of ethylene glycol from these data.

Quantitative Aspects of Energy Transferred as Heat

Like melting point, boiling point, and density, specific heat capacity is a characteristic intensive property of a pure substance. The specific heat capacity of a substance can be determined experimentally by accurately measuring temperature changes that occur when energy is transferred as heat from the substance to a known quantity of water (whose specific heat capacity is known).

Suppose a 55.0-g piece of metal is heated in boiling water to 99.8 °C and then dropped into cool water in an insulated beaker (Figure 5.8). Assume the beaker contains 225 g of water and its initial temperature (before the metal was dropped in) was 21.0 °C. The final temperature of the metal and water is 23.1 °C. What is the specific heat capacity of the metal? Here are the important aspects of this experiment.

- Let us define the metal and the water as the system and the beaker and environment as the surroundings. We will assume that energy is transferred only within the system and not between the system and the surroundings. (This assumption is good, but not perfect; for a more accurate result, we would also want to account for any energy transfer to the surroundings.)
- The water and the metal bar end up at the same temperature. (T_{final} is the same for both.)
- We will also assume energy is transferred *only as heat* within the system.
- The energy transferred as heat from the metal to the water, q_{metal}, has a negative value because the temperature of the metal drops. Conversely, q_{water} has a positive value because its temperature increases.
- The values of q_{water} and q_{metal} are numerically equal but of opposite sign.

Because of the law of conservation of energy, *in an isolated system the sum of the energy changes within the system must be zero*. If energy is transferred only as heat, then

$$q_1 + q_2 + q_3 + \ldots = 0 \qquad (5.3)$$

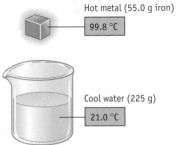

Hot metal (55.0 g iron)

99.8 °C

Cool water (225 g)

21.0 °C

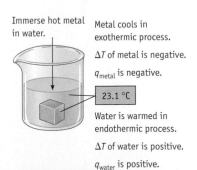

Immerse hot metal in water.

Metal cools in exothermic process.

ΔT of metal is negative.

q_{metal} is negative.

23.1 °C

Water is warmed in endothermic process.

ΔT of water is positive.

q_{water} is positive.

Active Figure 5.8 **Transfer of energy as heat.** When energy is transferred as heat from a hot metal to cool water, the thermal energy of the metal decreases, and that of the water increases. The value of q_{metal} is thus negative, and that of q_{water} is positive.

Chemistry ·ᴏ· Now™ Sign in at www.cengage.com/login and go to the Chapter Contents menu to explore an interactive version of this figure accompanied by an exercise.

Specific heat capacity values are given in units of joules per gram per kelvin (J/g · K). Virtually all calculations that involve temperature in chemistry are expressed in kelvins. In calculat-ing ΔT, however, we can use Celsius tempera-tures because a kelvin and a Celsius degree are the same size. That is, the difference between two temperatures is the same on both scales.

For example, the difference between the boil-ing and freezing points of water is

$$\Delta T, \text{Celsius} = 100\ °C - 0\ °C = 100\ °C$$
$$\Delta T, \text{kelvin} = 373\ K - 273\ K = 100\ K$$

where the quantities q_1, q_2, and so on represent the energies transferred as heat for the individual parts of the system. For this specific problem, there are thermal energy changes associated with water and metal, q_{water} and q_{metal}, the two compo-nents of the system; thus

$$q_{\text{water}} + q_{\text{metal}} = 0$$

Each of these quantities is related individually to specific heat capacities, mass, and change of temperature, as defined by Equation 5.1. Thus

$$[C_{\text{water}} \times m_{\text{water}} \times (T_{\text{final}} - T_{\text{initial, water}})] + [C_{\text{metal}} \times m_{\text{metal}} \times (T_{\text{final}} - T_{\text{initial, metal}})] = 0$$

The specific heat capacity of the metal, C_{metal}, is the unknown in this problem. Using the specific heat capacity of water (4.184 J/g · K) and converting Celsius to kelvin temperature gives

$$[(4.184\ \text{J/g · K})(225\ g)(296.3\ K - 294.2\ K)] + [(C_{\text{metal}})(55.0\ g)(296.3\ K - 373.0\ K)] = 0$$
$$C_{\text{metal}} = 0.469\ \text{J/g · K}$$

Chemistry ⚛ Now™

Sign in at **www.cengage.com/login** and go to Chapter 5 Contents to see Screens 5.8 and 5.10 for exercises, tutorials, and simulations on **energy transfers as heat between substances** and **calculating energy transfer.**

■ **EXAMPLE 5.2 Using Specific Heat Capacity**

Problem An 88.5-g piece of iron whose temperature is 78.8 °C (352.0 K) is placed in a beaker contain-ing 244 g of water at 18.8 °C (292.0 K). When thermal equilibrium is reached, what is the final tempera-ture? (Assume no energy is lost to warm the beaker and its surroundings.)

Strategy First, define the system as consisting of the iron and water. Within the system, energy is trans-ferred as heat from the metal to the water; the metal thus loses thermal energy, and the water gains thermal energy. The sum of these energy changes must equal zero. Each of these energy changes is related to the specific heat capacity, mass, and temperature change of the substance (Equation 5.1). The specific heat capacities of iron and water are given in Appendix D, and the final temperature is unknown. The change in temperature, ΔT, may be in °C or K (see Problem Solving Tip 5.1).

Solution

$$q_{\text{metal}} + q_{\text{water}} = 0$$
$$[C_{\text{water}} \times m_{\text{water}} \times (T_{\text{final}} - T_{\text{initial, water}})] + [C_{Fe} \times m_{Fe} \times (T_{\text{final}} - T_{\text{initial, Fe}})] = 0$$
$$[(4.184\ \text{J/g · K})(244\ g)(T_{\text{final}} - 292.0\ K)] + [(0.449\ \text{J/g · K})(88.5\ g)(T_{\text{final}} - 352.0\ K)] = 0$$
$$T_{\text{final}} = 295\ K\ (22\ °C)$$

Comment Be sure to notice that T_{initial} for the metal and T_{initial} for the water in this problem have differ-ent values. Also, the low specific heat capacity and smaller quantity of iron result in the temperature of iron being reduced by about 60 degrees; in contrast, the temperature of the water has been raised by only a few degrees.

5.3 Energy and Changes of State

A *change of state* is a change, for example, between solid and liquid or between liquid and gas. When a solid melts, its atoms, molecules, or ions move about vigorously enough to break free of the attractive forces holding them in rigid positions in the solid lattice. When a liquid boils, particles move much farther apart from one another, to distances at which attractive forces are minimal. In both cases, energy must be furnished to overcome attractive forces among the particles.

The energy transferred as heat that is required to convert a substance from a solid at its melting point to a liquid is called the **heat of fusion.** The energy transferred as heat to convert a liquid at its boiling point to a vapor is called the **heat of vaporization.** Heats of fusion and vaporization for many substances are provided along with other physical properties in reference books. Values for a few common substances are given in Appendix D (Table 12).

It is important to recognize that *temperature is constant throughout a change of state* (Figure 5.9). During a change of state, the added energy is used to overcome the forces holding one molecule to another, not to increase the temperature (Figures 5.9 and 5.10).

For water, the heat of fusion at 0 °C is 333 J/g, and the heat of vaporization at 100 °C is 2256 J/g. These values are used to calculate the heat required for a given mass of water to melt or boil, respectively. For example, the energy required to convert 500. g of water from the liquid to gaseous state at 100 °C is

$$(2256 \text{ J/g})(500. \text{ g}) = 1.13 \times 10^6 \text{ J } (= 1130 \text{ kJ})$$

In contrast, to melt the same mass of ice to form liquid water at 0 °C requires only 167 kJ.

$$(333 \text{ J/g})(500. \text{ g}) = 1.67 \times 10^5 \text{ J } (= 167 \text{ kJ})$$

■ **Heats of Fusion and Vaporization for H₂O at the Normal Melting and Boiling Points**

Heat of fusion = 333 J/g
              = 6.00 kJ/mol
Heat of vaporization = 2256 J/g
                    = 40.65 kJ/mol

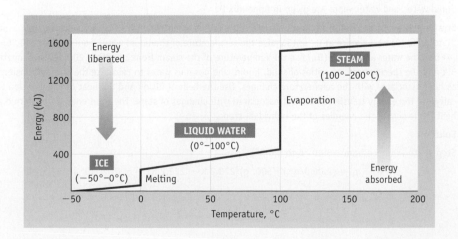

FIGURE 5.9 Energy transfer as heat and the temperature change for water. This graph shows the energy transferred as heat to 500. g of water and the consequent temperature change as the water warms from − 50 °C to 200 °C (at 1 atm).

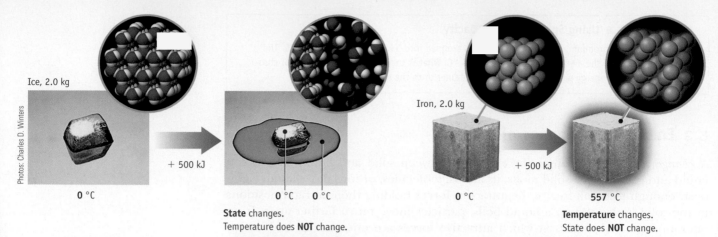

Ice, 2.0 kg

0 °C

+ 500 kJ

0 °C   0 °C

State changes.
Temperature does **NOT** change.

Iron, 2.0 kg

0 °C

+ 500 kJ

557 °C

Temperature changes.
State does **NOT** change.

Photos: Charles D. Winters

Active Figure 5.10 **Changes of state.** (*left*) Transferring 500 kJ of energy as heat to 2.0 kg of ice at 0 °C will cause 1.5 kg of ice to melt to water at 0 °C (and 0.5 kg of ice will remain). No temperature change occurs. (*right*) In contrast, transferring 500 kJ of energy as heat to 2.0 kg of iron at 0 °C will cause the temperature to increase to 557 °C (and the metal to expand slightly).

Chemistry.Now™ Sign in at www.cengage.com/login and go to the Chapter Contents menu to explore an interactive version of this figure accompanied by an exercise.

Figure 5.9 gives a profile of a process in which 500. g of ice at − 50 °C is converted to water vapor at 200 °C . This process involves a series of steps: (1) warming ice to 0 °C, (2) conversion to liquid water at 0 °C, (3) warming liquid water to 100 °C, (4) evaporation at 100 °C, and (5) warming the water vapor to 200 °C. Each step requires the input of additional energy. The energy transferred as heat to raise the temperature of solid, liquid, and vapor can be calculated with Equation 5.1, using the specific heat capacities of ice, liquid water, and water vapor (which are different), and the energies transferred as heat for the changes of state can be calculated using heats of fusion and vaporization. These calculations are carried out in Example 5.3.

■ **EXAMPLE 5.3 Energy and Changes of State**

Problem Calculate the energy that is transferred as heat to convert 500. g of ice at −50.0 °C to steam at 200.0 °C. (The temperature change occurring in each step is illustrated in Figure 5.9.) The heat of fusion of water is 333 J/g, and the heat of vaporization is 2256 J/g. The specific heat capacities of ice, liquid water, and water vapor are given in Appendix D.

Strategy The problem is broken down into a series of steps as noted above: (1) warm the ice from −50 °C to 0 °C; (2) melt the ice at 0 °C; (3) raise the temperature of the liquid water from 0 °C to 100 °C; (4) boil the water at 100 °C; (5) raise the temperature of the steam from 100 °C to 200 °C. Use Equation 5.1 and the specific heat capacities of solid, liquid, and gaseous water to calculate the energy transferred as heat associated with the temperature changes. Use the heat of fusion and the heat of vaporization to calculate the energy transferred as heat associated with changes of state. The total energy transferred as heat is the sum of the energies of the individual steps.

Solution

Step 1. (to warm ice from −50.0 °C to 0.0 °C)

$$q_1 = (2.06 \text{ J/g} \cdot \text{K})(500. \text{ g})(273.2 \text{ K} - 223.2 \text{ K}) = 5.15 \times 10^4 \text{ J}$$

Step 2. (to melt ice at 0.0 °C)

$$q_2 = (500. \text{ g})(333 \text{ J/g}) = 1.67 \times 10^5 \text{ J}$$

Step 3. (to raise temperature of liquid water from 0.0 °C to 100.0 °C)

$$q_3 = (4.184 \text{ J/g} \cdot \text{K})(500. \text{ g})(373.2 \text{ K} - 273.2 \text{ K}) = 2.09 \times 10^5 \text{ J}$$

Step 4. (to evaporate water at 100.0 °C)

$$q_4 = (2256 \text{ J/g})(500. \text{ g}) = 1.13 \times 10^6 \text{ J}$$

Step 5. (to raise temperature of water vapor from 100.0 °C to 200.0 °C)

$$q_5 = (1.86 \text{ J/g} \cdot \text{K})(500. \text{ g})(473.2 \text{ K} - 373.2 \text{ K}) = 9.30 \times 10^4 \text{ J}$$

The total energy transferred as heat is the sum of the energies of the individual steps.

$$q_{total} = q_1 + q_2 + q_3 + q_4 + q_5$$

$$q_{total} = 1.65 \times 10^6 \text{ J (or 1650 kJ)}$$

Comment The conversion of liquid water to steam is the largest increment of energy added by a considerable margin. (You may have noticed that it does not take much time to heat water to boiling on a stove, but to boil off the water takes a much greater time.)

■ **EXAMPLE 5.4 Change of State**

Problem What is the minimum amount of ice at 0 °C that must be added to the contents of a can of diet cola (340. mL) to cool the cola from 20.5 °C to 0.0 °C? Assume that the specific heat capacity and density of diet cola are the same as for water.

Strategy It is easiest to define the system as the ice and cola; the calculation will then involve energy transfers between the two components in the system. We need to assume that, within the system, energy transfers only as heat and that there is no transfer of energy between the surroundings and the system. The law of conservation of energy then dictates that $q_{ice} + q_{cola} = 0$. The value of q_{cola} can be calculated using the specific heat capacity of the cola and Equation 5.1, and the energy transferred as heat required to melt ice can be calculated using the heat of fusion for water.

Solution The mass of cola is 340. g [(340. mL)(1.00 g/mL) = 340. g], and its temperature changes from 293.7 K to 273.2 K. The heat of fusion of water is 333 J/g, and the mass of ice is the unknown.

$$q_{cola} + q_{ice} = 0$$

$$C_{cola} \times m \times (T_{final} - T_{initial}) + q_{ice} = 0$$

$$[(4.184 \text{ J/g} \cdot \text{K})(340. \text{ g})(273.2 \text{ K} - 293.7 \text{ K})] + [(333 \text{ J/g})(m_{ice})] = 0$$

$$m_{ice} = 87.6 \text{ g}$$

Comment This quantity of ice is just sufficient to cool the cola to 0 °C. If more than 87.6 g of ice is added, then the final temperature will still be 0 °C when thermal equilibrium is reached, and some ice will remain (see Exercise 5.4). If less than 87.6 g of ice is added, the final temperature will be greater than 0 °C. In this case, all the ice will melt, and the liquid water formed by melting the ice will absorb additional energy to warm up to the final temperature (an example is given in Study Question 71, page 248).

EXERCISE 5.4 Changes of State

To make a glass of iced tea, you pour 250 mL of tea, whose temperature is 18.2 °C, into a glass containing five ice cubes. Each cube has a mass of 15 g. What quantity of ice will melt, and how much ice will remain to float at the surface in this beverage? Assume that iced tea has a density of 1.0 g/mL and a specific heat capacity of 4.2 J/g · K, that energy is transferred only as heat within the system, that ice is at 0.0 °C, and that no energy is transferred between system and surroundings.

If you put a pot of water on a kitchen stove or a campfire, or if you put the pot in the sun, the water will evaporate. You must supply energy in some form because evaporation requires the input of energy. This well-known principle was applied in a novel way by a young African teacher, Mohammed Bah Abba in Nigeria, to improve the life of his people.

Life is hard in northern Nigerian communities. In this rural semi-desert area, most people eke out a living by subsistence farming. Without modern refrigeration, food spoilage is a major problem. Using a simple thermodynamic principle, Abba developed a refrigerator that cost about 30 cents to make and does not use electricity.

Abba's refrigerator is made of two earthen pots, one inside the other, separated by a layer of sand. The pots are covered with damp cloth and placed in a well-ventilated area. Water seeps through the pot's outer wall and rapidly evaporates in the dry desert air. The water remaining in

Mohammed Bah Abba. Abba earned a college degree in business, and while still in his 20s, became an instructor in a college of business in Jigwa, Nigeria, and a consultant to the United Nations Development Program. That brought him into close contact with rural communities in Northern Nigeria and made him aware of the hardships of the families there.

the pot and its contents drop in temperature, so much so that food in the inner pot can stay cool for days and not spoil.

In the 1990s, at his own expense, Abba made and distributed almost 10,000 pots in the villages of northern Nigeria. He estimates that about 75% of the families in this area are now using his refrigerator. The impact of this simple device has implications not only for the health of his people but also for their economy and their social structure. Prior to the development of the pot-in-pot device for food storage, it was necessary to sell produce immediately upon harvesting. The young girls in the family who sold food on the street daily could now be released from this chore to attend school and improve their lives.

Every two years, the Rolex Company, the Swiss maker of timepieces, gives a series of awards for enterprise. For his pot-in-pot refrigerator, Abba was one of the five recipients of a Rolex Award in 2000.

Questions:
1. *What quantity of energy must be transferred as heat to evaporate 95 g of water at 25°C? (The heat of vaporization at 25 °C is 44.0 kJ/mol.)*
2. *If this quantity of energy is transferred as heat out of 750 g of water, what is the temperature change of the water?*

Answers to these questions are in Appendix Q.

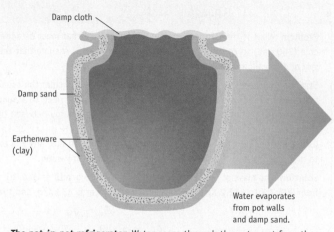

The Rolex Awards for Enterprise/Tomas Bertelsen/Scientific American, Nov. 2000, p. 26

The pot-in-pot refrigerator. Water seeps through the outer pot from the damp sand layer separating the pots, or from food stored in the inner pot. As the water evaporates from the surface of the outer pot, the food inside the pot is cooled.

Labels on figure: Damp cloth, Damp sand, Earthenware (clay), Water evaporates from pot walls and damp sand.

5.4 The First Law of Thermodynamics

To this point, we have only considered energy transfers as heat. Now we need to broaden the discussion. Recall the definition of thermodynamics as *the science of heat and work.* Work is done whenever a mass is moved against an opposing force; some form of energy is required for work to be done.

As described earlier, energy transferred as heat between a system and its surroundings changes the energy of the system. Work done by a system or on a system will also affect the energy in the system. If a system does work on its surroundings, energy must be expended by the system, and the system's energy will decrease. Conversely, if work is done by the surroundings on a system, the energy of the system increases.

A system doing work on its surroundings is illustrated in Figure 5.11. A small quantity of dry ice, solid CO_2, is sealed inside a plastic bag, and a weight (a book) is placed on top of the bag. When energy is transferred as heat from the surround-

(a) Pieces of dry ice [CO_2(s), −78 °C] are placed in a plastic bag. The dry ice will sublime (change directly from a solid to a gas) upon the input of energy.

(b) Energy is absorbed by CO_2(s) when it sublimes, and the system (the contents of the bag) does work on its surroundings by lifting the book against the force of gravity.

Charles D. Winters

Active Figure 5.11 **Energy changes in a physical process.**

Chemistry .Now™ Sign in at www.cengage.com/login and go to the Chapter Contents menu to explore an interactive version of this figure accompanied by an exercise.

ings to the dry ice, the dry ice changes directly from solid to gas at −78 °C, in a process called **sublimation:**

$$CO_2(s, \; -78 \; °C) \longrightarrow CO_2(g, \; -78 \; °C)$$

As sublimation proceeds, gaseous CO_2 expands within the plastic bag, lifting the book against the force of gravity. The system (the CO_2 inside the bag) is expending energy to do this work.

Even if the book had not been on top of the plastic bag, work would have been done by the expanding gas because the gas must push back the atmosphere when it expands. Instead of raising a book, the expanding gas moves a part of the atmosphere.

Now let us restate this example in terms of thermodynamics. First, we must identify the system and the surroundings. The system is the CO_2, initially a solid and later a gas. The surroundings consist of the objects that exchange energy with the system. This includes the plastic bag, the book, the table-top, and the surrounding air. Thermodynamics focuses on energy transfer. Sublimation of CO_2 requires energy, which is transferred as heat to the system (the CO_2) from the surroundings. At the same time, the system does work on the surroundings by lifting the book. An energy balance for the system will include both quantities, heat and work.

This example can be generalized. For any system, we can identify energy transfers both as heat and as work between system and surroundings. We can express the change of energy in a system explicitly as an equation:

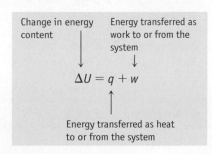

Change in energy content

Energy transferred as work to or from the system

$$\Delta U = q + w \qquad\qquad (5.4)$$

Energy transferred as heat to or from the system

■ **More on Heat and Work** To better understand the nature of heat and work, consider this passage from a classic book on chemical thermodynamics:

"Heat and work are birds of passage—never found as such in residence. Quantities of heat and work are perfectly determinate as they are transferred across the boundary that delimits the system. But after completion of the transfers we cannot speak of the system (or of its surroundings) as having some new heat content or some new work content."

L. K. Nash, *Elements of Chemical Thermodynamics*, Addison-Wesley, 1962.

■ **Heat and Work** For an in-depth look at heat and work in thermodynamics, see E. A. Gislason and N. C. Craig, *Journal of Chemical Education*, Vol. 64, No. 8, pages 660–668, 1987.

Equation 5.4 is a mathematical statement of the **first law of thermodynamics:** The energy change for a system (ΔU) is the sum of the energy transferred as heat between the system and its surroundings (q) and the energy transferred as work between the system and its surroundings (w).

The equation defining the first law of thermodynamics can be thought of as a version of the general principle of conservation of energy. Because energy is conserved, we must be able to account for any change in the energy of the system. All energy transfers between a system and the surroundings occur by the processes of heat and work. Equation 5.4 thus states that the change in the energy of the system is exactly equal to the sum of all of the energy transfers (heat or work) between the system and its surroundings.

The quantity U in Equation 5.4 has a formal name—**internal energy**—and a precise meaning in thermodynamics. The internal energy in a chemical system is the sum of the potential and kinetic energies of the atoms, molecules, or ions in the system. The potential energy here is the energy associated with the attractive and repulsive forces between all the nuclei and electrons in the system. It includes the energy associated with bonds in molecules, forces between ions, and forces between molecules. The kinetic energy is the energy of motion of the atoms, ions, and molecules in the system. Actual values of internal energy are rarely determined or needed. In most instances, we are interested in the *change* in internal energy, and this is a measurable quantity. In fact, Equation 5.4 tells us how to determine ΔU: *Measure the energy transferred as heat and work to or from the system.*

The sign conventions for Equation 5.4 are important. The following table summarizes how the internal energy of a system is affected by energy transferred as heat and work.

Sign Conventions for q and w of the System

Change	Sign Convention	Effect on U_{system}
Energy transferred as heat to the system (endothermic)	$q > 0$ (+)	U increases
Energy transferred as heat from the system (exothermic)	$q < 0$ (−)	U decreases
Energy transferred as work done on system	$w > 0$ (+)	U increases
Energy transferred as work done by system	$w < 0$ (−)	U decreases

The work in the example involving the sublimation of CO_2 (Figure 5.11) is of a specific type, called *P–V* (pressure–volume) work. It is the work (w) associated with a change in volume (ΔV) that occurs against a resisting external pressure (P). For a system in which the external pressure is constant, the value of *P–V* work can be calculated using Equation 5.5:

Work (at constant pressure) Change in volume

$$w = -P \times \Delta V$$ (5.5)

Pressure

Chemistry.๐.Now™

Sign in at **www.cengage.com/login** and go to Chapter 5 Contents to see Screen 5.11 for a self-study module on **energy changes in a physical process.**

Enthalpy

Most experiments in a chemical laboratory are carried out in beakers or flasks open to the atmosphere, where the external pressure is constant. Similarly, chemical processes that occur in living systems are open to the atmosphere. Because many processes in chemistry and biology are carried out under conditions of constant pressure, it is useful to have a specific measure of the energy transferred as heat under these conditions.

Let us first examine ΔU under conditions of constant pressure:

$$\Delta U = q_p + w_p$$

where the subscript p indicates conditions of constant pressure. If the only type of work that occurs is P–V work, then

$$\Delta U = q_p - P\Delta V$$

Rearranging this gives

$$q_p = \Delta U + P\Delta V$$

We now introduce a new thermodynamic function called the **enthalpy, H**, which is defined as

$$H = U + PV$$

■ **Energy Transfer Under Conditions of Constant Volume** Under conditions of constant volume, $\Delta V = 0$. If energy is transferred as heat under these conditions and if the only type of work possible is P–V work, the equation for the first law of thermodynamics simplifies to $\Delta U = q_v$. The subscript v indicates conditions of constant volume. In this case, the energy transferred as heat is equal to ΔU.

A Closer Look

P–V Work

Work is done when an object of some mass is moved against an external resisting force. We know this from common experience, such as when we use a pump to blow up a bicycle tire.

To evaluate the work done when a gas is compressed, we can use, for example, a cylinder with a movable piston, as would occur in a bicycle pump (see figure). The drawing on the left shows the initial position of the piston, and the one on the right shows its final position. To depress the piston, we would have to expend some energy (the energy of this process comes from the energy obtained by food metabolism in our body). The work required to depress the piston is calculated from a law of physics, $w = F \times d$, or work equals the magnitude of the force (F) applied times the distance (d) over which the force is applied.

Pressure is defined as a force divided by the area over which the force is applied: $P = F/A$. In this example, the force is

being applied to a piston with an area A. Substituting $P \times A$ for F in the equation gives $w = (P \times A) \times d$. The product of $A \times d$ is equivalent to the change in the volume of the gas in the pump, and, because $\Delta V = V_{final} - V_{initial}$, this change in volume is negative. Finally, because work done on a system is defined as positive, this means that $w = -P\Delta V$.

Pushing down on the piston means we have done work on the system, the gas contained within the cylinder. The gas is now compressed to a smaller volume and has attained a higher energy as a consequence. The additional energy is equal to $-P\Delta V$.

Notice how energy has been converted from one form to another—from chemical energy in food to mechanical energy used to depress the piston, to potential energy stored in a system of a gas at a higher pressure. In each step, energy was conserved, and the total energy of the universe remained constant.

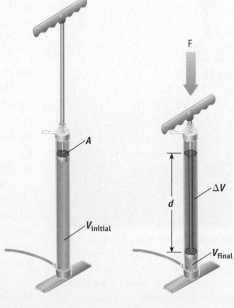

Changes in enthalpy for a system at constant pressure would be calculated from the following equation:

$$\Delta H = \Delta U + P\Delta V$$

Thus,

$$\Delta H = q_p$$

Now we see that, for a system where the only type of work possible is P–V work, the change in enthalpy, ΔH, is equal to the energy transferred as heat at constant pressure, often symbolized by q_p.

Under conditions of constant pressure and where the only type of work possible is P–V work, ΔU ($= q_p - P\Delta V$) and ΔH ($= q_p$) differ by $P\Delta V$ (the energy transferred to or from the system as work). We observe that in many processes—such as the melting of ice—the volume change, ΔV, is small, and hence the amount of work is small. Under these circumstances, ΔU and ΔH have almost the same value. The amount of work will be significant, however, in processes in which the volume change is large. This usually occurs when gases are formed or consumed. In the evaporation or condensation of water, the sublimation of CO_2, and chemical reactions in which the number of moles of gas changes, ΔU and ΔH have significantly different values.

Similar sign and symbol conventions apply to both ΔU and ΔH.

- Negative values of ΔH specify that energy is transferred as heat from the system to the surroundings.
- Positive values of ΔH specify that energy is transferred as heat from the surroundings to the system.

State Functions

Internal energy and enthalpy share a significant characteristic—namely, changes in these quantities that accompany chemical or physical processes depend only on the initial and final states. They do not depend on the path taken to go from the initial state to the final state. No matter how you go from reactants to products in a reaction, for example, the value of ΔH and ΔU for the reaction is always the same. A quantity that has this property is called a **state function**.

Many commonly measured quantities, such as the pressure of a gas, the volume of a gas or liquid, the temperature of a substance, and the size of your bank account, are state functions. You could have arrived at a current bank balance of $25 by having deposited $25 or you could have deposited $100 and then withdrawn $75. You can blow up a balloon to a large volume and then let some air out to arrive at the desired volume. Alternatively, you can blow up the balloon in stages, adding tiny amounts of air at each stage. The change in your bank balance or change in volume of the balloon does not depend on how you got there.

Not all quantities are state functions. For instance, distance traveled is not a state function (Figure 5.12). The travel distance from New York City to Denver depends on the route taken. Nor is the elapsed time of travel between these two locations a state function. In contrast, the altitude above sea level is a state function; in going from New York City (at sea level) to Denver (1600 m above sea level), there is an altitude change of 1600 m, regardless of the route followed.

Significantly, neither the energy transferred as heat nor the energy transferred as work individually is a state function but their sum, the change in internal energy,

FIGURE 5.12 State functions. There are many ways to climb a mountain, but the change in altitude from the base of the mountain to its summit is the same. The change in altitude is a state function. The distance traveled to reach the summit is not.

ΔU, is. The value of ΔU is fixed by $U_{initial}$ and U_{final}. A transition between the initial and final states can be accomplished by different routes having different values of q and w, but the sum of q and w for each path must always give the same ΔU.

Enthalpy is also a state function. The enthalpy change occurring when 1.0 g of water is heated from 20 °C to 50 °C is independent of how the process is carried out.

5.5 Enthalpy Changes for Chemical Reactions

Enthalpy changes accompany chemical reactions. In this book, we shall follow the conventions used by physical chemists and report the **standard reaction enthalpy,** $\Delta_r H°$ for reactions. For example, for the decomposition of water vapor to hydrogen and oxygen, with the reactant and products all in their standard states at 25 °C, the standard reaction enthalpy is +241.8 kJ/mol-rxn.

$$H_2O(g) \rightarrow H_2(g) + \tfrac{1}{2} O_2(g) \qquad \Delta_r H° = +241.8 \text{ kJ/mol-rxn}$$

The positive sign of $\Delta_r H°$ in this case indicates that the decomposition is an endothermic process.

There are several important things to know about $\Delta_r H°$.

- The designation of $\Delta_r H°$ as a "standard enthalpy change" means that the pure, unmixed reactants in their standard states have formed pure, unmixed products in their standard states (where the superscript ° indicates standard conditions). The **standard state** of an element or a compound is defined as the most stable form of the substance in the physical state that exists at a pressure of 1 bar and at a specified temperature. [Most sources report standard reaction enthalpies at 25 °C (298 K).]

- The "per mol-rxn" designation in the units for $\Delta_r H°$ means this is the enthalpy change for a "mole of reaction" (where *rxn* is an abbreviation for reaction). For example, for the reaction $H_2O(g) \rightarrow H_2(g) + 1/2\,O_2(g)$, a mole of reaction has occurred when 1 mol of water vapor has been converted completely to 1 mol of H_2 and 1/2 mol of O_2.

Now consider the opposite reaction, the combination of hydrogen and oxygen to form 1 mol of water. The magnitude of the enthalpy change for this reaction is the same as that for the decomposition reaction, but the sign of $\Delta_r H°$ is reversed. The exothermic formation of 1 mol of water vapor from 1 mol of H_2 and 1/2 mol of O_2 transfers 241.8 kJ to the surroundings (Figure 5.13).

$$H_2(g) + \tfrac{1}{2} O_2(g) \rightarrow H_2O(g) \qquad \Delta_r H° = -241.8 \text{ kJ/mol-rxn}$$

The value of $\Delta_r H°$ depends on the chemical equation used. For example, $\Delta_r H°$ for 1 mole of the reaction

$$2\,H_2(g) + O_2(g) \rightarrow 2\,H_2O(g) \qquad \Delta_r H° = -483.6 \text{ kJ/mol-rxn}$$

will be twice that of $\Delta_r H°$ for the reaction

$$H_2(g) + \tfrac{1}{2} O_2(g) \rightarrow H_2O(g) \qquad \Delta_r H° = -241.8 \text{ kJ/mol-rxn}$$

This happens because 1 mole of reaction for the first equation uses twice the amount of reactants and produces twice the amount of product as the second equation.

■ **Notation for Thermodynamic Parameters** NIST and IUPAC (International Union of Pure and Applied Chemistry) specify that parameters such as ΔH should have a subscript, between Δ and the thermodynamic parameter, that specifies the type of process. Among the subscripts you will see are: a lower case r for "reaction," f for "formation," c for "combustion," fus for "fusion," and vap for "vaporization."

■ **Moles of Reaction, Mol-rxn** One "mole of reaction" is said to have occurred when the reaction has occurred according to the number of moles given by the coefficients in the balanced equation. (This concept was described as a way to solve limiting reactant problems on page 167.)

■ **Fractional Stoichiometric Coefficients** When writing balanced equations to define thermodynamic quantities, chemists often use fractional stoichiometric coefficients. For example, to define $\Delta_r H$ for the decomposition or formation of 1 mol of H_2O, the coefficient for O_2 must be 1/2.

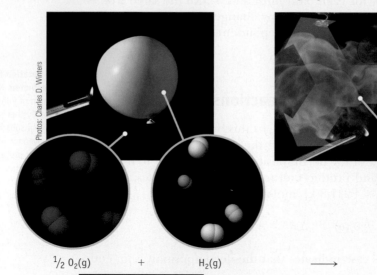

(a) A lighted candle is brought up to a balloon filled with hydrogen gas.

(b) When the balloon breaks, the candle flame ignites the hydrogen.

$\Delta_r H^0 = -241.8$ kJ/mol-rxn

Photos: Charles D. Winters

$\frac{1}{2}$ O$_2$(g) + H$_2$(g) $\longrightarrow$ H$_2$O(g)

Active Figure 5.13 **The exothermic combustion of hydrogen in air.** The reaction transfers energy to the surroundings in the form of heat, work, and light.

Chemistry Now™ Sign in at www.cengage.com/login and go to the Chapter Contents menu to explore an interactive version of this figure accompanied by an exercise.

■ **Standard Conditions** The superscript ° indicates standard conditions. It is applied to any type of thermodynamic data, such as enthalpy of fusion and vaporization ($\Delta_{fus}H°$ and $\Delta_{vap}H°$) and enthalpy of a reaction ($\Delta_r H°$). Standard conditions refers to reactants and products in their standard states at a pressure of 1 bar. One bar is approximately one atmosphere (1 atm = 1.013 bar; see Appendix B).

It is important to identify the states of reactants and products in a reaction because the magnitude of $\Delta_r H°$ depends on whether they are solids, liquids, or gases. For the formation of 1 mol of *liquid water* from the elements, the enthalpy change is −285.8 kJ.

$$H_2(g) + \tfrac{1}{2}\,O_2(g) \longrightarrow H_2O(\ell) \qquad \Delta_r H° = -285.8 \text{ kJ/mol-rxn}$$

Notice that this value is not the same as $\Delta_r H°$ for the formation of *water vapor* from hydrogen and oxygen. The difference between the two values is equal to the enthalpy change for the condensation of 1 mol of water vapor to 1 mol of liquid water.

These examples illustrate several general features of the enthalpy changes for chemical reactions.

- Enthalpy changes are specific to the reaction being carried out. The identities of reactants and products and their states (s, ℓ, g) are important, as are the amounts of reactants and products.
- The enthalpy change depends on the number of moles of reaction; that is, the number of times the reaction *as written* is carried out.
- $\Delta_r H°$ has a negative value for an exothermic reaction. It has a positive value for an endothermic reaction.
- Values of $\Delta_r H°$ are numerically the same, but opposite in sign, for chemical reactions that are the reverse of each other.

■ **Enthalpy of Fusion and Enthalpy of Vaporization** Previously, we called $\Delta_{fus}H°$ and $\Delta_{vap}H°$ the heat of fusion and heat of vaporization, respectively. You can see now that, based on the way that the process is carried out (at constant pressure) and by the use of *H* in their symbols, these are more properly referred to as the enthalpy of fusion and the enthalpy of vaporization. From this point on, we will refer to them by these designations.

Standard reaction enthalpies can be used to calculate the quantity of energy transferred as heat under conditions of constant pressure by any given mass of a reactant or product. Suppose you want to know the energy transferred to the surroundings as heat if 454 g of propane, C$_3$H$_8$, is burned (at constant pressure), given the equation for the exothermic combustion and the enthalpy change for the reaction.

$$C_3H_8(g) + 5\,O_2(g) \longrightarrow 3\,CO_2(g) + 4\,H_2O(\ell) \qquad \Delta_r H° = -2220 \text{ kJ/mol-rxn}$$

Two steps are needed. First, find the amount of propane present in the sample:

$$454 \text{ g } C_3H_8 \left(\frac{1 \text{ mol } C_3H_8}{44.10 \text{ g } C_3H_8} \right) = 10.3 \text{ mol } C_3H_8$$

Second, multiply $\Delta_r H°$ by the amount of propane:

$$\Delta_r H° = 10.3 \text{ mol } C_3H_8 \left(\frac{1 \text{ mol-rxn}}{1 \text{ mol } C_3H_8} \right)\left(\frac{-2220 \text{ kJ}}{1 \text{ mol-rxn}} \right) = -22,900 \text{ kJ}$$

Chemistry. Now™

Sign in at **www.cengage.com/login** and go to Chapter 5 Contents to see Screens 5.12 and 5.13 for self-study modules and a tutorial on **enthalpy changes.**

EXAMPLE 5.5 **Calculating the Enthalpy Change for a Reaction**

Problem Sucrose (sugar, $C_{12}H_{22}O_{11}$) can be oxidized to CO_2 and H_2O and the enthalpy change for the reaction can be measured (under conditions of constant pressure).

$$C_{12}H_{22}O_{11}(s) + 12 \text{ } O_2(g) \longrightarrow 12 \text{ } CO_2(g) + 11 \text{ } H_2O(\ell) \qquad \Delta_r H° = -5645 \text{ kJ/mol-rxn}$$

What is the energy transferred as heat by burning 5.00 g of sugar?

Strategy We will first determine the amount (mol) of sucrose in 5.00 g, then use this with the value given for the enthalpy change for the oxidation of 1 mol of sucrose.

Solution

$$5.00 \text{ g sucrose} \times \frac{1 \text{ mol sucrose}}{342.3 \text{ g sucrose}} = 1.46 \times 10^{-2} \text{ mol sucrose}$$

$$\Delta_r H° = 1.46 \times 10^{-2} \text{ mol sucrose} \left(\frac{1 \text{ mol-rxn}}{1 \text{ mol sucrose}} \right)\left(\frac{-5645 \text{ kJ}}{1 \text{ mol-rxn}} \right)$$

$$\Delta_r H° = -82.5 \text{ kJ}$$

Comment A person on a diet might note that a (level) teaspoonful of sugar (about 3.5 g) supplies about 15 Calories (dietary Calories; the conversion is 4.184 kJ = 1 Cal). As diets go, a single spoonful of sugar doesn't have a large caloric content. But will you use just one level teaspoonful?

EXERCISE 5.5 **Enthalpy Calculation**

The combustion of ethane, C_2H_6, has an enthalpy change of -2857.3 kJ for the reaction as written below. Calculate the value of energy transferred as heat when 15.0 g of C_2H_6 is burned.

$$2 \text{ } C_2H_6(g) + 7 \text{ } O_2(g) \longrightarrow 4 \text{ } CO_2(g) + 6 \text{ } H_2O(g) \qquad \Delta_r H° = -2857.3 \text{ kJ/mol-rxn}$$

■ Chemical Potential Energy Gummi Bears are mostly sugar. See Example 5.5 for a calculation of the energy in a spoonful of sugar, and see ChemistryNow Screen 5.2 for a video of a Gummi bear consumed by an oxidizing agent.

Charles D. Winters

5.6 Calorimetry

The energy evolved or required as heat in a chemical or physical process can be measured by **calorimetry**. The apparatus used in this kind of experiment is a *calorimeter*.

Constant Pressure Calorimetry, Measuring ΔH

A constant pressure calorimeter can be used to measure the energy change for a chemical reaction as energy is transferred as heat under constant pressure conditions, that is, it measures the enthalpy change.

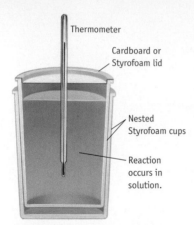

Thermometer

Cardboard or
Styrofoam lid

Nested
Styrofoam cups

Reaction
occurs in
solution.

**FIGURE 5.14 A coffee-cup calo-
rimeter.** A chemical reaction produces a
change in temperature of the solution in
the calorimeter. The Styrofoam container
is fairly effective in preventing the transfer of energy as heat between the solution and its surroundings. Because the
cup is open to the atmosphere, this is a
constant pressure measurement.

In general chemistry laboratories, a "coffee-cup calorimeter" is often used to estimate enthalpy changes for chemical reactions. This inexpensive device consists of two nested Styrofoam coffee cups with a loose-fitting lid and a temperature-measuring device such as a thermometer (Figure 5.14) or thermocouple. Styrofoam, a fairly good insulator, minimizes energy transfer as heat between the system and the surroundings. The reaction is carried out in solution in the cup. If the reaction is exothermic, it releases energy as heat to the solution, and the temperature of the solution rises. If the reaction is endothermic, energy is absorbed as heat from the solution, and a decrease in the temperature of the solution will be seen. The change in temperature of the solution is measured. Knowing the mass and specific heat capacity of the solution and the temperature change, the enthalpy change for the reaction can be calculated.

In this calorimetry experiment, it will be convenient to define the chemicals and the solution as the system. The surroundings are the cup and everything beyond the cup. As noted above, we assume that there is no energy transfer to the cup or beyond and that energy is transferred only as heat within the system. Two energy changes occur within the system. One is the change that takes place as the chemical reaction occurs, either releasing the potential energy stored in the reactants or absorbing energy and converting it to potential energy stored in the products. We label this energy as q_r. The other energy change is the energy gained or lost as heat by the solution ($q_{solution}$). Based on the law of conservation of energy,

$$q_r + q_{solution} = 0$$

The value of $q_{solution}$ can be calculated from the specific heat capacity, mass, and change in temperature of the solution. The quantity of energy evolved or absorbed as heat for the reaction (q_r) is the unknown in the equation.

The accuracy of a calorimetry experiment depends on the accuracy of the measured quantities (temperature, mass, specific heat capacity). In addition, it depends on how closely the assumption is followed that there is no energy transfer beyond the solution. A coffee-cup calorimeter is an unsophisticated apparatus, and the results obtained with it are not highly accurate, largely because this assumption is poorly met. In research laboratories, calorimeters are used that more effectively limit the energy transfer between system and surroundings. In addition, it is also possible to estimate and correct for the minimal energy transfer that occurs between the system and the surroundings.

■ **EXAMPLE 5.6 Using a Coffee-Cup Calorimeter**

Problem Suppose you place 0.0500 g of magnesium chips in a coffee-cup calorimeter and then add 100.0 mL of 1.00 M HCl. The reaction that occurs is

$$Mg(s) + 2 HCl(aq) \longrightarrow H_2(g) + MgCl_2(aq)$$

The temperature of the solution increases from 22.21 °C (295.36 K) to 24.46 °C (297.61 K). What is the enthalpy change for the reaction per mole of Mg? Assume that the specific heat capacity of the solution is 4.20 J/g · K and the density of the HCl solution is 1.00 g/mL.

Strategy The energy evolved in the reaction is absorbed by the solution. Solving the problem has three steps. First, calculate $q_{solution}$ from the values of the mass, specific heat capacity, and ΔT using Equation 5.1. Second, calculate q_r, assuming no energy transfer as heat occurs beyond the solution, that is, $q_r + q_{solution} = 0$. Third, use the value of q_r and the amount of Mg to calculate the enthalpy change per mole of Mg.

Solution

Step 1. Calculate $q_{solution}$. The mass of the solution is the mass of the 100.0 mL of HCl plus the mass of magnesium.

$$q_{solution} = (100.0 \text{ g HCl solution} + 0.0500 \text{ g Mg})(4.20 \text{ J/g K})(297.61 \text{ K} - 295.36 \text{ K})$$
$$= 9.45 \times 10^2 \text{ J}$$

Step 2. Calculate q_r.

$$q_r + q_{solution} = 0$$
$$q_r + 9.45 \times 10^2 \text{ J} = 0$$
$$q_r = -9.45 \times 10^2 \text{ J}$$

Step 3. Calculate the value of ΔH per mole of Mg. Note that q_r found in Step 2 resulted from the reaction of 0.0500 g of Mg. The enthalpy change per mole of Mg is therefore

$$\Delta_r H = (-9.45 \times 10^2 \text{ J}/0.0500 \text{ g Mg})(24.31 \text{ g Mg}/1 \text{ mol Mg})$$
$$= -4.60 \times 10^5 \text{ J/mol Mg} \ (= -460. \text{ kJ/mol-rxn Mg})$$

Comment The calculation gives the correct sign of q_r and $\Delta_r H$. The negative sign indicates that this is an exothermic reaction.

EXERCISE 5.6 Using a Coffee-Cup Calorimeter

Assume 200. mL of 0.400 M HCl are mixed with 200. mL of 0.400 M NaOH in a coffee-cup calorimeter. The temperature of the solutions before mixing was 25.10 °C; after mixing and allowing the reaction to occur, the temperature is 27.78 °C. What is the enthalpy change when one mole of acid is neutralized? (Assume that the densities of all solutions are 1.00 g/mL and their specific heat capacities are 4.20 J/g · K.)

Constant Volume Calorimetry: Measuring ΔU

Constant volume calorimetry is often used to evaluate heats of combustion of fuels and the caloric value of foods. A weighed sample of a combustible solid or liquid is placed inside a "bomb," often a cylinder about the size of a large fruit juice can with thick steel walls and ends (Figure 5.15). The bomb is placed in a water-filled container with well-insulated walls. After filling the bomb with pure oxygen, the sample is ignited, usually by an electric spark. The heat generated by the combustion reaction warms the bomb and the water around it. The bomb, its contents, and the water are defined as the system. Assessment of energy transfers as heat within the system shows that

$$q_r + q_{bomb} + q_{water} = 0$$

where q_r is the energy produced by the reaction, q_{bomb} is the energy involved in heating the calorimeter bomb, and q_{water} is the energy involved in heating the water in the calorimeter. Because the volume does not change in a constant volume calorimeter, energy transfer as work cannot occur. Therefore, the energy transferred as heat at constant volume (q_v) is the change in internal energy, ΔU.

■ **Calorimetry, ΔU, and ΔH** The two types of calorimetry (constant volume and constant pressure) highlight the differences between enthalpy and internal energy. The energy transferred as heat at constant pressure, q_p, is, by definition, ΔH, whereas the energy transferred as heat at constant volume, q_v, is ΔU.

Chemistry ☌ Now™

Sign in at **www.cengage.com/login** and go to Chapter 5 Contents to see Screen 5.14 for a simulation and exercise exploring **reactions in a constant volume calorimeter** and for a tutorial on **calculating the enthalpy change for a reaction from a calorimetry experiment.**

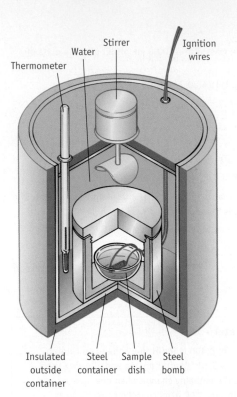

Thermometer
Water
Stirrer
Ignition wires

Insulated outside container
Steel container
Sample dish
Steel bomb

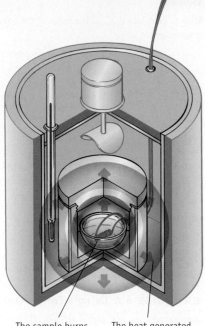

The sample burns in pure oxygen, warming the bomb.

The heat generated warms the water, and ΔT is measured by the thermometer.

EXAMPLE 5.7 Constant Volume Calorimetry

Problem Octane, C_8H_{18}, a primary constituent of gasoline, burns in air:

$$C_8H_{18}(\ell) + 25/2\ O_2(g) \longrightarrow 8\ CO_2(g) + 9\ H_2O(\ell)$$

A 1.00-g sample of octane is burned in a constant volume calorimeter similar to that shown in Figure 5.15. The calorimeter is in an insulated container with 1.20 kg of water. The temperature of the water and the bomb rises from 25.00 °C (298.15 K) to 33.20 °C (306.35 K). The heat capacity of the bomb, C_{bomb}, is 837 J/K. (a) What is the heat of combustion per gram of octane? (b) What is the heat of combustion per mole of octane?

Strategy (a) The sum of all the energies transferred as heat in the system will be zero; that is, $q_r + q_{bomb} + q_{water} = 0$. The first term, q_r, is the unknown. The second and third terms in the equation can be calculated from the data given: q_{bomb} is calculated from the bomb's heat capacity and ΔT, and q_{water} is determined from the specific heat capacity, mass, and ΔT for water. (b) The value of q_r calculated in part (a) is the energy evolved in the combustion of 1.00 g of octane. Use this and the molar mass of octane (114.2 g/mol) to calculate the energy evolved as heat per mole of octane.

Solution

(a)
$$q_{water} = C_{water} \times m_{water} \times \Delta T$$
$$= (4.184\ \text{J/g} \cdot \text{K})(1.20 \times 10^3\ \text{g})(306.35\ \text{K} - 298.15\ \text{K}) = +41.2 \times 10^3\ \text{J}$$
$$q_{bomb} = (C_{bomb})(\Delta T) = (837\ \text{J/K})(306.35\ \text{K} - 298.15\ \text{K}) = 6.86 \times 10^3\ \text{J}$$
$$q_r + q_{water} + q_{bomb} = 0$$
$$q_r + 41.2 \times 10^3\ \text{J} + 6.86 \times 10^3\ \text{J} = 0$$
$$q_r = -48.1 \times 10^3\ \text{J (or } -48.1\ \text{kJ)}$$

Heat of combustion per gram $= -48.1$ kJ

(b) Heat of combustion per mol of octane $= (-48.1\ \text{kJ/g})(114.2\ \text{g/mol}) = \boxed{-5.49 \times 10^3\ \text{kJ/mol}}$

Comment Because the volume does not change, no energy transfer in the form of work occurs. The change of internal energy, ΔU, for the combustion of $C_8H_{18}(\ell)$ is -5.49×10^3 kJ/mol. Also note that C_{bomb} has no mass units. It is the heat required to warm the whole object by 1 kelvin.

EXERCISE 5.7 Constant Volume Calorimetry

A 1.00-g sample of ordinary table sugar (sucrose, $C_{12}H_{22}O_{11}$) is burned in a bomb calorimeter. The temperature of 1.50×10^3 g of water in the calorimeter rises from 25.00 °C to 27.32 °C. The heat capacity of the bomb is 837 J/K, and the specific heat capacity of the water is 4.20 J/g · K. Calculate (a) the heat evolved per gram of sucrose and (b) the heat evolved per mole of sucrose.

5.7 Enthalpy Calculations

Module 10

Enthalpy changes for an enormous number of chemical and physical processes are available on the World Wide Web and in reference books. These data have been collected by scientists over a number of years from many experiments and are used to calculate enthalpy changes for chemical processes. Now we want to discuss how to use such data.

Hess's Law

The enthalpy change can be measured by calorimetry for many, but not all, chemical processes. Consider, for example, the oxidation of carbon to form carbon monoxide.

$$C(graphite) + \tfrac{1}{2} O_2(g) \longrightarrow CO(g)$$

Even if a deficiency of oxygen is used, the primary product of the reaction of carbon and oxygen is CO_2. As soon as CO is formed, it reacts with O_2 to form CO_2. Because the reaction cannot be carried out in a way that allows CO to be the sole product, it is not possible to measure the change in enthalpy for this reaction by calorimetry.

The enthalpy change for the reaction forming CO(g) from C(s) and O_2(g) can be determined indirectly, however, from enthalpy changes for other reactions that can be measured. The calculation is based on **Hess's law**, which states that if a reaction is the sum of two or more other reactions, $\Delta_r H°$ for the overall process is the sum of the $\Delta_r H°$ values of those reactions.

The oxidation of C(s) to CO_2(g) can be viewed as occurring in two steps: first the oxidation of C(s) to CO(g) (Equation 1), and then the oxidation of CO(g) to CO_2(g) (Equation 2). Adding these two equations gives the equation for the oxidation of C(s) to CO_2(g) (Equation 3).

Equation 1:	$C(graphite) + \tfrac{1}{2} O_2(g) \longrightarrow CO(g)$	$\Delta_r H_1° = ?$
Equation 2:	$CO(g) + \tfrac{1}{2} O_2(g) \longrightarrow CO_2(g)$	$\Delta_r H_2° = -283.0$ kJ/mol-rxn
Equation 3:	$C(graphite) + O_2(g) \longrightarrow CO_2(g)$	$\Delta_r H_3° = -393.5$ kJ/mol-rxn

Hess's law tells us that the enthalpy change for the overall reaction ($\Delta_r H_3°$) will equal the sum of the enthalpy changes for reactions 1 and 2 ($\Delta_r H_1° + \Delta_r H_2°$). Both $\Delta_r H_2°$ and $\Delta_r H_3°$ can be measured, and these values are then used to calculate the enthalpy change for reaction 1.

$$\Delta_r H_3° = \Delta_r H_1° + \Delta_r H_2°$$
$$-393.5 \text{ kJ/mol-rxn} = \Delta_r H_1° + (-283.0 \text{ kJ/mol-rxn})$$
$$\Delta_r H_1° = -110.5 \text{ kJ/mol-rxn}$$

Hess's law also applies to physical processes. The enthalpy change for the reaction of H_2(g) and O_2(g) to form 1 mol of H_2O vapor is different from the enthalpy change to form 1 mol of liquid H_2O. The difference is the negative of the *enthalpy of vaporization* of water, $\Delta_r H°_2 \; (= -\Delta_{vap}H°)$ as shown in the following analysis

Equation 1:	$H_2(g) + \frac{1}{2} O_2(g) \longrightarrow H_2O(g)$	$\Delta_r H_1° = -241.8$ kJ/mol-rxn
Equation 2:	$H_2O(g) \longrightarrow H_2O(\ell)$	$\Delta_r H_2° = -44.0$ kJ/mol-rxn
Equation 3:	$H_2(g) + \frac{1}{2} O_2(g) \longrightarrow H_2O(\ell)$	$\Delta_r H_3° = -285.8$ kJ/mol-rxn

Energy Level Diagrams

When using Hess's law, it is often helpful to represent enthalpy data schematically in an energy level diagram. In such drawings, the various substances being studied—the reactants and products in a chemical reaction, for example—are placed on an arbitrary energy scale. The relative enthalpy of each substance is given by its position on the vertical axis, and numerical differences in enthalpy between them are shown by the vertical arrows. Such diagrams provide a visual perspective on the magnitude and direction of enthalpy changes and show how enthalpy changes of the substances are related.

Energy level diagrams that summarize the two examples of Hess's law discussed earlier are shown in Figure 5.16. In Figure 5.16a, the elements, C(s) and $O_2(g)$ are at the highest enthalpy. The reaction of carbon and oxygen to form $CO_2(g)$ lowers the enthalpy by 393.5 kJ. This can occur either in a single step, shown on the left in Figure 5.16a, or in two steps via initial formation of CO(g), as shown on the right. Similarly, in Figure 5.16b, the mixture of $H_2(g)$ and $O_2(g)$ is at the highest enthalpy. Both liquid and gaseous water have lower enthalpies, with the difference between the two being the enthalpy of vaporization.

Chemistry‿Now™

Sign in at **www.cengage.com/login** and go to Chapter 5 Contents to see Screen 5.15 for a simulation and exercise on **Hess's law.**

Active Figure 5.16 Energy level diagrams. (a) Relating enthalpy changes in the formation of $CO_2(g)$. (b) Relating enthalpy changes in the formation of $H_2O(\ell)$. Enthalpy changes associated with changes between energy levels are given alongside the vertical arrows.

Chemistry‿Now™ Sign in at **www.cengage.com/login** and go to the Chapter Contents menu to explore an interactive version of this figure accompanied by an exercise.

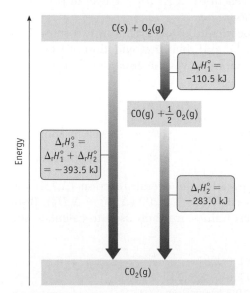

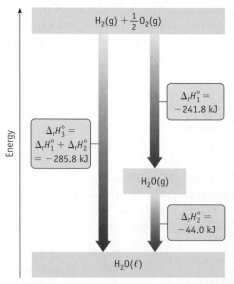

(a) The formation of CO_2 can occur in a single step or in a succession of steps. $\Delta_r H°$ for the overall process is -393.5 kJ, no matter which path is followed.

(b) The formation of $H_2O(\ell)$ can occur in a single step or in a succession of steps. $\Delta_r H°$ for the overall process is -285.8 kJ, no matter which path is followed.

EXAMPLE 5.8	**Using Hess's Law**

Problem Suppose you want to know the enthalpy change for the formation of methane, CH_4, from solid carbon (as graphite) and hydrogen gas:

$$C(s) + 2 H_2(g) \longrightarrow CH_4(g) \qquad \Delta_r H° = ?$$

The enthalpy change for this reaction cannot be measured in the laboratory because the reaction is very slow. We can, however, measure enthalpy changes for the combustion of carbon, hydrogen, and methane.

Equation 1:	$C(s) + O_2(g) \longrightarrow CO_2(g)$	$\Delta_r H_1° = -393.5$ kJ/mol-rxn
Equation 2:	$H_2(g) + \frac{1}{2} O_2(g) \longrightarrow H_2O(\ell)$	$\Delta_r H_2° = -285.8$ kJ/mol-rxn
Equation 3:	$CH_4(g) + 2 O_2(g) \longrightarrow CO_2(g) + 2 H_2O(\ell)$	$\Delta_r H_3° = -890.3$ kJ/mol-rxn

Use this information to calculate $\Delta_r H°$ for the formation of methane from its elements.

Strategy The three reactions (1, 2, and 3), as they are written, cannot be added together to obtain the equation for the formation of CH_4 from its elements. Methane, CH_4, is a product in the reaction for which we wish to calculate $\Delta_r H°$, but it is a reactant in Equation 3. Water appears in two of these equations although it is not a component of the reaction forming CH_4 from carbon and hydrogen. To use Hess's law to solve this problem, we will first have to manipulate the equations and adjust the $\Delta_r H°$ values accordingly before adding equations together. Recall, from Section 5.5, that writing an equation in the reverse direction changes the sign of $\Delta_r H°$ and that doubling the amount of reactants and products doubles the value of $\Delta_r H°$. Adjustments to Equations 2 and 3 will produce new equations that, along with Equation 1, can be combined to give the desired net reaction.

Solution To have CH_4 appear as a product in the overall reaction, we reverse Equation 3, which changes the sign of $\Delta_r H°$.

Equation 3': $\qquad CO_2(g) + 2 H_2O(\ell) \longrightarrow CH_4(g) + 2 O_2(g)$

$\qquad\qquad \Delta_r H_3°' = -\Delta_r H_3° = +890.3$ kJ/mol-rxn

Next, we see that 2 mol of $H_2(g)$ is on the reactant side in our desired equation. Equation 2 is written for only 1 mol of $H_2(g)$ as a reactant. Therefore we multiply the stoichiometric coefficients in Equation 2 by 2 and multiply the value of $\Delta_r H°$ by 2.

Equation 2': $\qquad 2 H_2(g) + O_2(g) \longrightarrow 2 H_2O(\ell)$

$\qquad\qquad \Delta_r H_2°' = 2 \Delta_r H_2° = 2 (-285.8$ kJ/mol-rxn$) = -571.6$ kJ/mol-rxn

We now have three equations that, when added together, will give the targeted equation for the formation of methane from carbon and hydrogen. In this summation process, $O_2(g)$, $H_2O(\ell)$, and $CO_2(g)$ all cancel.

Equation 1:	$C(s) + O_2(g) \longrightarrow CO_2(g)$	$\Delta_r H_1° = -393.5$ kJ/mol-rxn
Equation 2':	$2 H_2(g) + O_2(g) \longrightarrow 2 H_2O(\ell)$	$\Delta_r H_2°' = 2 \Delta_r H_2° = -571.6$ kJ/mol-rxn
Equation 3':	$CO_2(g) + 2 H_2O(\ell) \longrightarrow CH_4(g) + 2 O_2 (g)$	$\Delta_r H_3°' = -\Delta_r H_3° = +890.3$ kJ/mol-rxn

Net Equation:	$C(s) + 2 H_2(g) \longrightarrow CH_4(g)$	$\Delta_r H_{net}° = \Delta_r H_1° + 2 \Delta_r H_2° + (-\Delta_r H_3°)$

$\qquad\qquad \Delta_r H_{net}° = (-393.5$ kJ/mol-rxn$) + (-571.6$ kJ/mol-rxn$) + (+890.3$ kJ/mol-rxn$)$

$\qquad\qquad\qquad = -74.8$ kJ/mol-rxn

Thus, for the formation of 1 mol of $CH_4(g)$ from the elements, we find $\boxed{\Delta_r H° = -74.8 \text{ kJ/mol-rxn.}}$

EXERCISE 5.8 Using Hess's Law

Use Hess's law to calculate the enthalpy change for the formation of $CS_2(\ell)$ from $C(s)$ and $S(s)$ $[C(s) + 2 S(s) \longrightarrow CS_2(\ell)]$ from the following enthalpy values.

$C(s) + O_2(g) \longrightarrow CO_2(g)$	$\Delta_r H° = -393.5$ kJ/mol-rxn
$S(s) + O_2(g) \longrightarrow SO_2(g)$	$\Delta_r H° = -295.8$ kJ/mol-rxn
$CS_2(\ell) + 3 O_2(g) \longrightarrow CO_2(g) + 2 SO_2(g)$	$\Delta_r H° = -1103.9$ kJ/mol-rxn

How did we know how the three equations should be adjusted in Example 5.8? Here is a general strategy for solving this type of problem.

Step 1. Inspect the equation whose $\Delta_r H°$ you wish to calculate, identifying the reactants and products, and locate those substances in the equations available to be added. In Example 5.8, the reactants, C(s) and $H_2(g)$,

are reactants in Equations 1 and 2, and the product, $CH_4(g)$, is a reactant in Equation 3. Equation 3 was reversed to get CH_4 on the product side.

Step 2. Get the correct amount of the substances on each side. In Example 5.8, only one adjustment was needed. There was 1 mol of H_2 on the left (reactant side) in Equation 2. We needed 2 mol of H_2 in the overall equa-

tion; this required doubling the quantities in Equation 2.

Step 3. Make sure other substances in the equations cancel when the equations are added. In Example 5.8, equal amounts of O_2 and H_2O appeared on the left and right sides in the three equations, and so they canceled when the equations were added together.

Standard Enthalpies of Formation

■ **$\Delta_f H°$ Values** Consult the National Institute for Standards and Technology website (webbook.nist.gov/chemistry) for an extensive compilation of enthalpies of formation.

Calorimetry and the application of Hess's law have made available a great many $\Delta_r H°$ values for chemical reactions. Often, these values are assembled into tables. The table in Appendix L, for example, lists **standard molar enthalpies of formation, $\Delta_f H°$.** *The standard molar enthalpy of formation is the enthalpy change for the formation of 1 mol of a compound directly from its component elements in their standard states.*

Several examples of standard molar enthalpies of formation will be helpful to illustrate this definition.

$\Delta_f H°$ **for NaCl(s):** At 25 °C and a pressure of 1 bar, Na is a solid, and Cl_2 is a gas. The standard enthalpy of formation of NaCl(s) is defined as the enthalpy change that occurs when 1 mol of NaCl(s) is formed from 1 mol of Na(s) and ½ mol of $Cl_2(g)$.

$$\text{Na(s)} + \text{½ Cl}_2\text{(g)} \longrightarrow \text{NaCl(s)} \qquad \Delta_f H° = -411.12 \text{ kJ/mol}$$

$\Delta_f H°$ **for NaCl(aq):** The enthalpy of formation for an aqueous solution of a compound refers to the enthalpy change for the formation of a 1 mol/L solution of the compound starting with the elements making up the compound. It is thus the enthalpy of formation of the compound plus the enthalpy change that occurs when the substance dissolves in water.

$$\text{Na(s)} + \text{½ Cl}_2\text{(g)} \longrightarrow \text{NaCl(aq)} \qquad \Delta_f H° = -407.27 \text{ kJ/mol}$$

■ **Units for Enthalpy of Formation** The units for values of $\Delta_f H°$ are usually given simply as kJ/mol where the denominator is really mol-rxn. However, because an enthalpy of formation is defined as the change in enthalpy for the formation of 1 mol of compound, it is understood that "per mol" means "per mol of compound," which, in this case, is the same thing as "per mol-rxn."

$\Delta_f H°$ **for $C_2H_5OH(\ell)$:** At 25 °C and 1 bar, the standard states of the elements are C(s, graphite), $H_2(g)$, and $O_2(g)$. The standard enthalpy of formation of $C_2H_5OH(\ell)$ is defined as the enthalpy change that occurs when 1 mol of $C_2H_5OH(\ell)$ is formed from 2 mol of C(s), 3 mol of $H_2(g)$, and 1/2 mol of $O_2(g)$.

$$\text{2 C(s)} + \text{3 H}_2\text{(g)} + \text{½ O}_2\text{(g)} \longrightarrow \text{C}_2\text{H}_5\text{OH}(\ell) \qquad \Delta_f H° = -277.0 \text{ kJ/mol}$$

Notice that the reaction defining the enthalpy of formation for liquid ethanol is not a reaction that a chemist can carry out in the laboratory. This illustrates an important point: *the enthalpy of formation of a compound does not necessarily correspond to a reaction that can be carried out.*

Appendix L lists values of $\Delta_f H°$ for some common substances, and a review of these values leads to some important observations.

- *The standard enthalpy of formation for an element in its standard state is zero.*
- Most $\Delta_f H°$ values are negative, indicating that formation of most compounds from the elements is exothermic. A very few values are positive, and these

represent compounds that are unstable with respect to decomposition to the elements. (One example is NO(g) with $\Delta_f H° = +90.29$ kJ/mol.)

- Values of $\Delta_f H°$ can often be used to compare the stabilities of related compounds. Consider the values of $\Delta_f H°$ for the hydrogen halides. Hydrogen fluoride is the most stable of these compounds with respect to decomposition to the elements, whereas HI is the least stable (as indicated by $\Delta_f H°$ of HF being the most negative value and that of HI being the most positive).

■ **$\Delta_f H°$ Values of Hydrogen Halides**

Compound	$\Delta_f H°$ (kJ/mol)
HF(g)	−273.3
HCl(g)	−92.31
HBr(g)	−35.29
HI(g)	+25.36

EXERCISE 5.9 Standard Enthalpies of Formation

Write equations for the reactions that define the standard enthalpy of formation of $FeCl_3$(s) and of solid sucrose (sugar, $C_{12}H_{22}O_{11}$).

Enthalpy Change for a Reaction

Using standard molar enthalpies of formation and Equation 5.6, it is possible to calculate the enthalpy change for a reaction under standard conditions.

$$\Delta_r H° = \Sigma\Delta_f H°\text{(products)} - \Sigma\Delta_f H°\text{(reactants)} \qquad (5.6)$$

In this equation, the symbol Σ (the Greek capital letter sigma) means "take the sum." To find $\Delta_r H°$, add up the molar enthalpies of formation of the products, each multiplied by its stoichiometric coefficient, and subtract from this the sum of the molar enthalpies of formation of the reactants, each multiplied by its stoichiometric coefficient. This equation is a logical consequence of the definition of $\Delta_f H°$ and Hess's law (see *A Closer Look: Hess's Law and Equation 5.6*).

Suppose you want to know how much heat is required to decompose 1 mol of calcium carbonate (limestone) to calcium oxide (lime) and carbon dioxide under standard conditions:

$$CaCO_3(s) \longrightarrow CaO(s) + CO_2(g) \qquad \Delta_r H° = ?$$

You would use the following enthalpies of formation (from Appendix L):

Compound	$\Delta_f H°$ (kJ/mol)
$CaCO_3$(s)	−1207.6
CaO(s)	−635.1
CO_2(g)	−393.5

and then use Equation 5.6 to find the standard enthalpy change for the reaction, $\Delta_r H°$.

$$\Delta_r H° = \left[\left(\frac{1\ \text{mol CaO}}{1\ \text{mol-rxn}}\right)\left(\frac{-635.1\ \text{kJ}}{\text{mol CaO}}\right) + \left(\frac{1\ \text{mol CO}_2}{1\ \text{mol-rxn}}\right)\left(\frac{-393.5\ \text{kJ}}{1\ \text{mol CO}_2}\right)\right]$$
$$- \left[\left(\frac{1\ \text{mol CaCO}_3}{1\ \text{mol-rxn}}\right)\left(\frac{-1207.6\ \text{kJ}}{1\ \text{mol CaCO}_3}\right)\right]$$
$$= +179.0\ \text{kJ/mol-rxn}$$

The decomposition of limestone to lime and CO_2 is endothermic. That is, energy (179.0 kJ) must be supplied to decompose 1 mol of $CaCO_3$(s) to CaO(s) and CO_2(g).

■ **Δ = Final − Initial** Equation 5.6 is another example of the convention that a change (Δ) is always calculated by subtracting the value for the initial state (the reactants) from the value for the final state (the products).

Chemistry.❀.Now™

Sign in at **www.cengage.com/login** and go to Chapter 5 Contents to see Screen 5.16 for a tutorial on **calculating the standard enthalpy change for a reaction.**

Equation 5.6 is an application of Hess's law. To illustrate this, let us look further at the decomposition of calcium carbonate.

$$CaCO_3(s) \longrightarrow CaO(s) + CO_2(g) \qquad \Delta_r H^\circ = ?$$

Because enthalpy is a state function, the change in enthalpy for this reaction is independent of the route from reactants to products. We can imagine an alternate route from reactant to products that involves first converting the reactant to elements in their standard states, then recombining these elements to give the reaction products. Notice that the enthalpy changes for these processes are the enthalpies of formation of the reactants and products in the equation above:

$CaCO_3(s) \longrightarrow Ca(s) + C(s) + 3/2\ O_2(g)$ $-\Delta_f H^\circ[CaCO_3(s)] = \Delta_r H_1^\circ$

$C(s) + O_2(g) \longrightarrow CO_2(g)$ $\Delta_f H^\circ[CO_2(g)] = \Delta_r H_2^\circ$

$Ca(s) + \frac{1}{2}\ O_2(g) \longrightarrow CaO(s)$ $\Delta_f H^\circ[CaO(s)] = \Delta_r H_3^\circ$

$CaCO_3(s) \longrightarrow CaO(s) + CO_2(g)$ $\Delta_r H_{net}^\circ$

$\Delta_r H_{net}^\circ = \Delta_r H_1^\circ + \Delta_r H_2^\circ + \Delta_r H_3^\circ$

$\Delta_r H^\circ = \Delta_f H^\circ[CaO(s)] + \Delta_f H^\circ[CO_2(g)] - \Delta_f H^\circ[CaCO_3(s)]$

That is, the change in enthalpy for the reaction is equal to the enthalpies of formation of products (CO_2 and CaO) minus the enthalpy of formation of the reactant ($CaCO_3$), which is, of course, what one does when using Equation 5.6 for this calculation. The relationship among these enthalpy quantities is illustrated in the energy-level diagram.

Energy level diagram for the decomposition of $CaCO_3(s)$

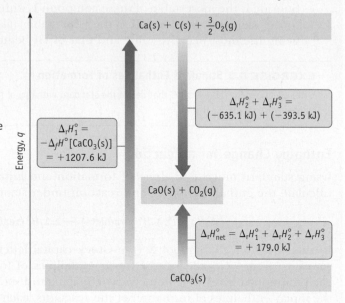

■ **EXAMPLE 5.9** **Using Enthalpies of Formation**

Problem Nitroglycerin is a powerful explosive that forms four different gases when detonated:

$$2\ C_3H_5(NO_3)_3(\ell) \longrightarrow 3\ N_2(g) + \frac{1}{2}\ O_2(g) + 6\ CO_2(g) + 5\ H_2O(g)$$

Calculate the enthalpy change that occurs when 10.0 g of nitroglycerin is detonated. The standard enthalpy of formation of nitroglycerin, $\Delta_f H^\circ$, is −364 kJ/mol. Use Appendix L to find other $\Delta_f H^\circ$ values that are needed.

Strategy Use values of $\Delta_f H^\circ$ for the reactants and products in Equation 5.6 to calculate the enthalpy change produced by one mole of reaction ($\Delta_r H^\circ$). From Appendix L, $\Delta_f H^\circ[CO_2(g)] = -393.5$ kJ/mol, $\Delta_f H^\circ[H_2O(g)] = -241.8$ kJ/mol, and $\Delta_f H^\circ = 0$ for $N_2(g)$ and $O_2(g)$. Determine the amount (mol) represented by 10.0 g of nitroglycerin; then use this value with $\Delta_r H^\circ$ and the balanced chemical equation to obtain the answer.

Solution Using Equation 5.6, we find the enthalpy change for the explosion of 2 mol of nitroglycerin is

$$\Delta_r H^\circ = \left(\frac{6\ \text{mol}\ CO_2}{1\ \text{mol-rxn}}\right)\Delta_f H^\circ[CO_2(g)] + \left(\frac{5\ \text{mol}\ H_2O}{1\ \text{mol-rxn}}\right)\Delta_f H^\circ[H_2O(g)]$$
$$- \left(\frac{2\ \text{mol}\ C_3H_5(NO_3)_3}{1\ \text{mol-rxn}}\right)\Delta_f H^\circ[C_3H_5(NO_3)_3(\ell)]$$

$$\Delta_r H^\circ = \left(\frac{6\ \text{mol}\ CO_2}{1\ \text{mol-rxn}}\right)\left(\frac{-393.5\ \text{kJ}}{1\ \text{mol}\ CO_2}\right) + \left(\frac{5\ \text{mol}\ H_2O}{1\ \text{mol-rxn}}\right)\left(\frac{-241.8\ \text{kJ}}{1\ \text{mol}\ H_2O}\right)$$
$$- \left(\frac{2\ \text{mol}\ C_3H_5(NO_3)_3}{1\ \text{mol-rxn}}\right)\left(\frac{-364\ \text{kJ}}{1\ \text{mol}\ C_3H_5(NO_3)_3}\right) = -2842\ \text{kJ/mol-rxn}$$

The problem asks for the enthalpy change using 10.0 g of nitroglycerin. We next need to determine the amount of nitroglycerin in 10.0 g.

$$10.0 \text{ g nitroglycerin} \left(\frac{1 \text{ mol nitroglycerin}}{227.1 \text{ g nitroglycerin}} \right) = 0.0440 \text{ mol nitroglycerin}$$

The enthalpy change for the detonation of 0.0440 mol of nitroglycerin is

$$\Delta H^\circ = 0.0440 \text{ mol nitroglycerin} \left(\frac{1 \text{ mol-rxn}}{2 \text{ mol nitroglycerin}} \right) \left(\frac{-2842 \text{ kJ}}{1 \text{ mol-rxn}} \right)$$

$$= -62.6 \text{ kJ}$$

Comment The large value of ΔH° is in accord with the fact that this reaction is highly energetic.

EXERCISE 5.10 Using Enthalpies of Formation

Calculate the standard enthalpy of combustion for benzene, C_6H_6.

$$C_6H_6(\ell) + 15/2\ O_2(g) \longrightarrow 6\ CO_2(g) + 3\ H_2O(\ell) \qquad \Delta_rH^\circ = ?$$

$$\Delta_fH^\circ[C_6H_6(\ell)] = +49.0 \text{ kJ/mol}.$$

Other values needed can be found in Appendix L.

5.8 Product- or Reactant-Favored Reactions and Thermodynamics

At the beginning of this chapter, we noted that thermodynamics would provide answers to four questions. How much energy is evolved or required in physical changes and in chemical reactions, and the relationship of heat and work have been the primary topics of this chapter. The first two questions were addressed in this chapter, but there are two other important questions: How can we determine whether a reaction is product-favored or reactant-favored at equilibrium? And what determines whether a chemical reaction will occur spontaneously; that is, without outside intervention?

In Chapter 3, we learned that chemical reactions proceed toward equilibrium, and spontaneous changes occur in a way that allows a system to approach equilibrium. Reactions in which reactants are largely converted to products when equilibrium is reached are said to be *product-favored*. Reactions in which only a small amount of products are present at equilibrium are called *reactant-favored* (◄ page 121).

Let us look back at the many chemical reactions that we have seen. For example, all combustion reactions are exothermic, and the oxidation of iron (Figure 5.17) is clearly exothermic.

$$4\ Fe(s) + 3\ O_2(g) \longrightarrow 2\ Fe_2O_3(s)$$

$$\Delta_rH^\circ = 2\ \Delta_fH^\circ[Fe_2O_3(s)] = \left(\frac{2 \text{ mol } Fe_2O_3}{1 \text{ mol-rxn}} \right) \left(\frac{-825.5 \text{ kJ}}{1 \text{ mol } Fe_2O_3} \right) = -1651.0 \text{ kJ/mol-rxn}$$

The reaction has a negative value for Δ_rH°, and it is also spontaneous and product-favored.

Conversely, the decomposition of calcium carbonate is endothermic.

$$CaCO_3(s) \longrightarrow CaO(s) + CO_2(g) \qquad \Delta_rH^\circ = +179.0 \text{ kJ/mol-rxn}$$

Charles D. Winters

FIGURE 5.17 The product-favored oxidation of iron. Iron powder, sprayed into a bunsen burner flame, is rapidly oxidized. The reaction is exothermic and is product-favored.

It is clear that supplies of fossil fuels are declining, and their price is increasing, just as the nations of the earth have ever greater energy needs. We will have more to say about this in the Interchapter (Energy) that follows. Here, however, let's analyze the debate about replacing gasoline with ethanol (C_2H_5OH).

As Matthew Wald says in the article "Is Ethanol in for the Long Haul?" (*Scientific American*, January 2007), "The U.S. has gone on an ethanol binge." In 2005, the U.S. Congress passed an energy bill stating that ethanol production should be 7.5 billion gallons a year by 2012, up from about 5 billion gallons a year presently. The goal is to at least partially replace gasoline with ethanol.

Is the goal of replacing gasoline with ethanol reasonable? This is a lofty goal, given that present gasoline consumption in the U.S. is about 140 billion gallons annually. Again, according to Matthew Wald, "Even if 100 percent of the U.S. corn supply was distilled into ethanol, it would supply only a small fraction of the fuel consumed by the nation's vehicles." Wald's thesis in his article, which is supported by numerous scientific studies, is that if ethanol is to be pursued as an alternative to gasoline, more emphasis should be placed on deriving ethanol from sources other than corn, such as cellulose from cornstalks and various grasses.

Ethanol available at a service station. E85 fuel is a blend of 85% ethanol and 15% gasoline. Be aware that you can only use E85 in vehicles designed for the fuel. In an ordinary vehicle, the ethanol leads to deterioration of seals in the engine and fuel system.

© Stephen Lunetta Photography, 2007

Beyond this, there are other problems associated with ethanol. One is that it cannot be distributed through a pipeline system as gasoline can. Any water in the pipeline is miscible with ethanol, which causes the fuel value to decline. Instead, ethanol must be trucked to service stations.

Finally, E85 fuel—a blend of 85% ethanol and 15% gasoline—cannot be used in most current vehicles because relatively few vehicles as yet have engines designed for fuels with a high ethanol content (so-called "flexible fuel" engines). The number of these vehicles would need to be increased in order for E85 to have a significant effect on our gasoline usage.

For more information, see the references in Wald's *Scientific American* article.

Questions:
For the purposes of this analysis, let us use octane (C_8H_{18}) as a substitute for the complex mixture of hydrocarbons in gasoline. Data you will need for this question (in addition to Appendix L) are:

$$\Delta_f H° \ [C_8H_{18}(\ell)] = -250.1 \text{ kJ/mol}$$
Density of ethanol = 0.785 g/mL
Density of octane = 0.699 g/mL

1. *Calculate $\Delta_r H°$ for the combustion of ethanol and octane, and compare the values per mol and per gram. Which provides more energy per gram?*

2. *Compare the energy produced per liter of the two fuels. Which produces more energy for a given volume (something useful to know when filling your gas tank)?*

3. *What mass of CO_2, a greenhouse gas, is produced per liter of fuel (assuming complete combustion)?*

4. *Now compare the fuels on an energy-equivalent basis. What volume of ethanol would have to be burned to get the same energy as 1.00 L of octane? When you burn enough ethanol to have the same energy as a liter of octane, which fuel produces more CO_2?*

5. *On the basis of this analysis and assuming the same price per liter, which fuel will propel your car further? Which will produce less greenhouse gas?*

Answers to these questions are in Appendix Q.

■ **Reactant-Favored or Product-Favored?** In most—but not all—cases exothermic reactions are product-favored at equilibrium and endothermic reactions are reactant-favored at equilibrium.

The decomposition of $CaCO_3$ proceeds spontaneously to an equilibrium that favors the reactants; that is, it is reactant-favored.

Are all exothermic reactions product-favored and all endothermic reactions reactant-favored? From these examples, we might formulate that idea as a hypothesis that can be tested by experiment and by examination of other examples. We would find that *in most cases, product-favored reactions have negative values of $\Delta_r H°$, and reactant-favored reactions have positive values of $\Delta_r H°$*. But this is not *always* true; there are exceptions.

Clearly, a further discussion of thermodynamics must be tied to the concept of equilibrium. This relationship, and the complete discussion of the third and fourth questions, will be presented in Chapter 19.

Chemistry ⚛ Now™

Sign in at **www.cengage.com/login** and go to Chapter 5 Contents to see Screen 5.17 Product-Favored Systems, for an exercise on **the reaction when a Gummi Bear is placed in molten potassium chlorate.**

Chapter Goals Revisited

Now that you have studied this chapter, you should ask whether you have met the chapter goals. In particular, you should be able to:

Assess the transfer of energy as heat associated with changes in temperature and changes of state

a. Describe various forms of energy and the nature of energy transfers as heat (Section 5.1).

b. Use the most common energy unit, the joule, and convert between other energy units and joules (Section 5.1). Study Question(s) assignable in OWL: 5.

c. Recognize and use the language of thermodynamics: the system and its surroundings; exothermic and endothermic reactions (Section 5.1). Study Question(s) assignable in OWL: 61, 92.

d. Use specific heat capacity in calculations of energy transfer as heat and of temperature changes (Section 5.2). Study Question(s) assignable in OWL: 8, 10, 12, 13, 16, 18, 83.

e. Understand the sign conventions in thermodynamics.

f. Use enthalpy (heat) of fusion and enthalpy (heat) of vaporization to find the quantity of energy transferred as heat that is involved in changes of state (Section 5.3). Study Question(s) assignable in OWL: 20, 22, 23, 24, 28, 68, 70, 71, 88, 93, 97.

Understand and apply the first law of thermodynamics

a. Understand the basis of the first law of thermodynamics (Section 5.4).

b. Recognize how energy transferred as heat and work done on or by a system contribute to changes in the internal energy of a system (Section 5.4).

Define and understand state functions (enthalpy, internal energy)

a. Recognize state functions whose values are determined only by the state of the system and not by the pathway by which that state was achieved (Section 5.4).

Learn how energy changes are measured

a. Recognize that when a process is carried out under constant pressure conditions, the energy transferred as heat is the enthalpy change, ΔH (Section 5.5). Study Question(s) assignable in OWL: 28, 29, 30, 52, 54.

b. Describe how to measure the quantity of energy transferred as heat in a reaction by calorimetry (Section 5.6). Study Question(s) assignable in OWL: 32, 33, 34, 36, 38, 40, 42.

Calculate the energy evolved or required for physical changes and chemical reactions using tables of thermodynamic data.

a. Apply Hess's law to find the enthalpy change for a reaction (Section 5.7). Study Question(s) assignable in OWL: 44, 73, 74, 79; Go Chemistry Module 10.

b. Know how to draw and interpret energy level diagrams (Section 5.7).

c. Use standard molar enthalpies of formation, $\Delta_f H°$, to calculate the enthalpy change for a reaction $\Delta_r H°$ (Section 5.7). Study Question(s) assignable in OWL: 49, 53, 58.

Chemistry‿Now™ Sign in at www. cengage.com/login to:

- Assess your understanding with Study Questions in OWL keyed to each goal in the Goals and Homework menu for this chapter

- For quick review, download Go Chemistry mini-lecture flashcard modules (or purchase them at **www.ichapters.com**)

- Check your readiness for an exam by taking the Pre-Test and exploring the modules recommended in your Personalized Study plan.

Access **How Do I Solve It?** tutorials on how to approach problem solving using concepts in this chapter.

For additional preparation for an examination on this chapter see the *Let's Review* section on pages 254–267.

KEY EQUATIONS

Equation 5.1 (page 215)   The energy transferred as heat when the temperature of a substance changes. Calculated from the specific heat capacity (C), mass (m), and change in temperature (ΔT).

$$q(J) = C(J/g \cdot K) \times m(g) \times \Delta T(K)$$

Equation 5.2 (page 215) Temperature changes are always calculated as final temperature minus initial temperature.

$$\Delta T = T_{final} - T_{initial}$$

Equation 5.3 (page 217) If no energy is transferred between a system and its surroundings and if energy is transferred within the system only as heat, the sum of the thermal energy changes within the system equals zero.

$$q_1 + q_2 + q_3 + \ldots = 0$$

Equation 5.4 (page 223) The first law of thermodynamics: The change in internal energy (ΔU) in a system is the sum of the energy transferred as heat (q) and the energy transferred as work (w).

$$\Delta U = q + w$$

Equation 5.5 (page 224) Work (w) at constant pressure is the product of pressure (P) and change in volume (ΔV)

$$w = -P(\Delta V)$$

Equation 5.6 (page 237) This equation is used to calculate the standard enthalpy change of a reaction ($\Delta_r H°$) when the enthalpies of formation ($\Delta_f H°$) of all of the reactants and products are known.

$$\Delta_r H° = \Sigma \Delta_f H°(\text{products}) - \Sigma \Delta_f H°(\text{reactants})$$

STUDY QUESTIONS

OWL Online homework for this chapter may be assigned in OWL.

▲ denotes challenging questions.

■ denotes questions assignable in OWL.

Blue-numbered questions have answers in Appendix O and fully-worked solutions in the *Student Solutions Manual*.

Practicing Skills

Energy
(See Section 5.1 and ChemistryNow Screen 5.2.)

1. The flashlight in the photo does not use batteries. Instead, you move a lever, which turns a geared mechanism and results finally in light from the bulb. What type of energy is used to move the lever? What type or types of energy are produced?

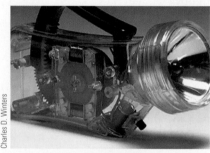

Charles D. Winters

A hand-operated flashlight.

2. A solar panel is pictured in the photo. When light shines on the panel, it generates an electric current that is used by a small electric motor to propel the car. What types of energy are involved in this setup?

Charles D. Winters

A solar panel operates a toy car.

Energy Units
(See Exercise 5.1 and ChemistryNow Screen 5.5.)

3. You are on a diet that calls for eating no more than 1200 Cal/day. What is this energy in joules?

4. A 2-in. piece of chocolate cake with frosting provides 1670 kJ of energy. What is this in dietary Calories (Cal)?

5. ■ One food product has an energy content of 170 kcal per serving, and another has 280 kJ per serving. Which food provides the greater energy per serving?

6. Which provides the greater energy per serving, a raw apple or a raw apricot? Go to the USDA Nutrient Database on the World Wide Web for the information: http://www.ars.usda.gov/main/site_main. htm?modecode=12354500. Report the energy content of the fruit in kcal and kJ.

Specific Heat Capacity
(See Examples 5.1 and 5.2 and ChemistryNow Screens 5.6–5.10.)

7. The molar heat capacity of mercury is 28.1 J/mol · K. What is the specific heat capacity of this metal in J/g · K?

8. ■ The specific heat capacity of benzene (C_6H_6) is 1.74 J/g · K. What is its molar heat capacity (in J/mol · K)?

9. The specific heat capacity of copper is 0.385 J/g · K. How much energy is required to heat 168 g of copper from -12.2 °C to $+25.6$ °C?

10. ■ How much energy is required to raise the temperature of 50.00 mL of water from 25.52 °C to 28.75 °C? (The density of water at this temperature is 0.997 g/mL.)

11. The initial temperature of a 344-g sample of iron is 18.2 °C. If the sample absorbs 2.25 kJ of energy as heat, what is its final temperature?

12. ■ After absorbing 1.850 kJ of energy as heat, the temperature of a 0.500-kg block of copper is 37 °C. What was its initial temperature?

13. ■ A 45.5-g sample of copper at 99.8 °C is dropped into a beaker containing 152 g of water at 18.5 °C. What is the final temperature when thermal equilibrium is reached?

14. A 182-g sample of gold at some temperature is added to 22.1 g of water. The initial water temperature is 25.0 °C, and the final temperature is 27.5 °C. If the specific heat capacity of gold is 0.128 J/g · K, what was the initial temperature of the gold?

15. One beaker contains 156 g of water at 22 °C, and a second beaker contains 85.2 g of water at 95 °C. The water in the two beakers is mixed. What is the final water temperature?

16. ■ When 108 g of water at a temperature of 22.5 °C is mixed with 65.1 g of water at an unknown temperature, the final temperature of the resulting mixture is 47.9 °C. What was the initial temperature of the second sample of water?

17. A 13.8-g piece of zinc was heated to 98.8 °C in boiling water and then dropped into a beaker containing 45.0 g of water at 25.0 °C. When the water and metal come to thermal equilibrium, the temperature is 27.1 °C. What is the specific heat capacity of zinc?

18. ■ A 237-g piece of molybdenum, initially at 100.0 °C, is dropped into 244 g of water at 10.0 °C. When the system comes to thermal equilibrium, the temperature is 15.3 °C. What is the specific heat capacity of molybdenum?

Changes of State
(See Examples 5.3 and 5.4 and ChemistryNow Screen 5.8.)

19. How much energy is evolved when 1.0 L of water at 0 °C solidifies to ice? (The heat of fusion of water is 333 J/g.)

20. ■ The energy required to melt 1.00 g of ice at 0 °C is 333 J. If one ice cube has a mass of 62.0 g and a tray contains 16 ice cubes, what quantity of energy is required to melt a tray of ice cubes to form liquid water at 0 °C?

21. ■ How much energy is required to vaporize 125 g of benzene, C_6H_6, at its boiling point, 80.1 °C? (The heat of vaporization of benzene is 30.8 kJ/mol.)

22. ■ Chloromethane, CH_3Cl, arises from microbial fermentation and is found throughout the environment. It is also produced industrially and is used in the manufacture of various chemicals and has been used as a topical anesthetic. How much energy is required to convert 92.5 g of liquid to a vapor at its boiling point, -24.09 °C? (The heat of vaporization of CH_3Cl is 21.40 kJ/mol.)

23. The freezing point of mercury is -38.8 °C. What quantity of energy, in joules, is released to the surroundings if 1.00 mL of mercury is cooled from 23.0 °C to -38.8 °C and then frozen to a solid? (The density of liquid mercury is 13.6 g/cm³. Its specific heat capacity is 0.140 J/g · K and its heat of fusion is 11.4 J/g.)

24. ■ What quantity of energy, in joules, is required to raise the temperature of 454 g of tin from room temperature, 25.0 °C, to its melting point, 231.9 °C, and then melt the tin at that temperature? (The specific heat capacity of tin is 0.227 J/g · K, and the heat of fusion of this metal is 59.2 J/g.)

25. Ethanol, C_2H_5OH, boils at 78.29 °C. How much energy, in joules, is required to raise the temperature of 1.00 kg of ethanol from 20.0 °C to the boiling point and then to change the liquid to vapor at that temperature? (The specific heat capacity of liquid ethanol is 2.44 J/g · K, and its enthalpy of vaporization is 855 J/g.)

26. ■ A 25.0-mL sample of benzene at 19.9 °C was cooled to its melting point, 5.5 °C, and then frozen. How much energy as heat was given off in this process? (The density of benzene is 0.80 g/mL; its specific heat capacity is 1.74 J/g · K, and its heat of fusion is 127 J/g.)

Enthalpy Changes

(See Example 5.5 and ChemistryNow Screens 5.12 and 5.13.)

27. Nitrogen monoxide, a gas recently found to be involved in a wide range of biological processes, reacts with oxygen to give brown NO_2 gas.

$$2\ NO(g) + O_2(g) \rightarrow 2\ NO_2(g)$$
$$\Delta_r H° = -114.1\ kJ/mol\text{-}rxn$$

Is this reaction endothermic or exothermic? What is the enthalpy change if 1.25 g of NO is converted completely to NO_2?

28. ■ Calcium carbide, CaC_2, is manufactured by the reaction of CaO with carbon at a high temperature. (Calcium carbide is then used to make acetylene.)

$$CaO(s) + 3\ C(s) \rightarrow CaC_2(s) + CO(g)$$
$$\Delta_r H° = +464.8\ kJ/mol\text{-}rxn$$

Is this reaction endothermic or exothermic? What is the enthalpy change if 10.0 g of CaO is allowed to react with an excess of carbon?

29. ■ Isooctane (2,2,4-trimethylpentane), one of the many hydrocarbons that make up gasoline, burns in air to give water and carbon dioxide.

$$2\ C_8H_{18}(\ell) + 25\ O_2(g) \rightarrow 16\ CO_2(g) + 18\ H_2O(\ell)$$
$$\Delta_r H° = -10{,}922\ kJ/mol\text{-}rxn$$

What is the enthalpy change if you burn 1.00 L of isooctane (density = 0.69 g/mL)?

30. ■ Acetic acid, CH_3CO_2H, is made industrially by the reaction of methanol and carbon monoxide.

$$CH_3OH(\ell) + CO(g) \rightarrow CH_3CO_2H(\ell)$$
$$\Delta_r H° = -355.9\ kJ/mol\text{-}rxn$$

If you produce 1.00 L of acetic acid (*d* = 1.044 g/mL) by this reaction, how much energy as heat is evolved?

Calorimetry

(See Examples 5.6 and 5.7 and ChemistryNow Screens 5.8, 5.9, and 5.14.)

31. Assume you mix 100.0 mL of 0.200 M CsOH with 50.0 mL of 0.400 M HCl in a coffee-cup calorimeter. The following reaction occurs:

$$CsOH(aq) + HCl(aq) \rightarrow CsCl(aq) + H_2O(\ell)$$

The temperature of both solutions before mixing was 22.50 °C, and it rises to 24.28 °C after the acid–base reaction. What is the enthalpy change for the reaction per mole of CsOH? Assume the densities of the solutions are all 1.00 g/mL and the specific heat capacities of the solutions are 4.2 J/g · K.

32. ■ You mix 125 mL of 0.250 M CsOH with 50.0 mL of 0.625 M HF in a coffee-cup calorimeter, and the temperature of both solutions rises from 21.50 °C before mixing to 24.40 °C after the reaction.

$$CsOH(aq) + HF(aq) \rightarrow CsF(aq) + H_2O(\ell)$$

What is the enthalpy of reaction per mole of CsOH? Assume the densities of the solutions are all 1.00 g/mL and the specific heats of the solutions are 4.2 J/g · K.

33. ■ A piece of titanium metal with a mass of 20.8 g is heated in boiling water to 99.5 °C and then dropped into a coffee-cup calorimeter containing 75.0 g of water at 21.7 °C. When thermal equilibrium is reached, the final temperature is 24.3 °C. Calculate the specific heat capacity of titanium.

34. ■ A piece of chromium metal with a mass of 24.26 g is heated in boiling water to 98.3 °C and then dropped into a coffee-cup calorimeter containing 82.3 g of water at 23.3 °C. When thermal equilibrium is reached, the final temperature is 25.6 °C. Calculate the specific heat capacity of chromium.

35. Adding 5.44 g of $NH_4NO_3(s)$ to 150.0 g of water in a coffee-cup calorimeter (with stirring to dissolve the salt) resulted in a decrease in temperature from 18.6 °C to 16.2 °C. Calculate the enthalpy change for dissolving $NH_4NO_3(s)$ in water, in kJ/mol. Assume that the solution (whose mass is 155.4 g) has a specific heat capacity of 4.2 J/g · K. (Cold packs take advantage of the fact that dissolving ammonium nitrate in water is an endothermic process.)

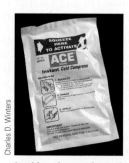

Charles D. Winters

A cold pack uses the endothermic enthalpy of solution of ammonium nitrate.

36. ■ You should use care when dissolving H_2SO_4 in water because the process is highly exothermic. To measure the enthalpy change, 5.2 g $H_2SO_4(\ell)$ was added (with stirring) to 135 g of water in a coffee-cup calorimeter. This resulted in an increase in temperature from 20.2 °C to 28.8 °C. Calculate the enthalpy change for the process $H_2SO_4(\ell) \rightarrow H_2SO_4(aq)$, in kJ/mol.

▲ more challenging ■ in OWL   Blue-numbered questions answered in Appendix O

37. Sulfur (2.56 g) is burned in a constant volume calorimeter with excess $O_2(g)$. The temperature increases from 21.25 °C to 26.72 °C. The bomb has a heat capacity of 923 J/K, and the calorimeter contains 815 g of water. Calculate ΔU per mole of SO_2 formed, for the reaction

$$S_8(s) + 8\ O_2(g) \rightarrow 8\ SO_2(g)$$

Sulfur burns in oxygen with a bright blue flame to give $SO_2(g)$.

38. ■ Suppose you burn 0.300 g of C(graphite) in an excess of $O_2(g)$ in a constant volume calorimeter to give $CO_2(g)$.

$$C(\text{graphite}) + O_2(g) \rightarrow CO_2(g)$$

The temperature of the calorimeter, which contains 775 g of water, increases from 25.00 °C to 27.38 °C. The heat capacity of the bomb is 893 J/K. Calculate ΔU per mole of carbon.

39. Suppose you burn 1.500 g of benzoic acid, $C_6H_5CO_2H$, in a constant volume calorimeter and find that the temperature increases from 22.50 °C to 31.69 °C. The calorimeter contains 775 g of water, and the bomb has a heat capacity of 893 J/K. Calculate ΔU per mole of benzoic acid.

Benzoic acid, $C_6H_5CO_2H$, occurs naturally in many berries. Its heat of combustion is well known, so it is used as a standard to calibrate calorimeters.

40. ■ A 0.692-g sample of glucose, $C_6H_{12}O_6$, is burned in a constant volume calorimeter. The temperature rises from 21.70 °C to 25.22 °C. The calorimeter contains 575 g of water, and the bomb has a heat capacity of 650 J/K. What is ΔU per mole of glucose?

41. An "ice calorimeter" can be used to determine the specific heat capacity of a metal. A piece of hot metal is dropped onto a weighed quantity of ice. The energy transferred from the metal to the ice can be determined from the amount of ice melted. Suppose you heat a 50.0-g piece of silver to 99.8 °C and then drop it onto ice. When the metal's temperature has dropped to 0.0 °C, it is found that 3.54 g of ice has melted. What is the specific heat capacity of silver?

42. ■ A 9.36-g piece of platinum is heated to 98.6 °C in a boiling water bath and then dropped onto ice. (See Study Question 41.) When the metal's temperature has dropped to 0.0 °C, it is found that 0.37 g of ice has melted. What is the specific heat capacity of platinum?

Hess's Law
(See Example 5.8 and ChemistryNow Screen 5.15.)

43. The enthalpy changes for the following reactions can be measured:

$$CH_4(g) + 2\ O_2(g) \rightarrow CO_2(g) + 2\ H_2O(g)$$
$$\Delta_r H° = -802.4 \text{ kJ/mol-rxn}$$

$$CH_3OH(g) + \tfrac{3}{2}\ O_2(g) \rightarrow CO_2(g) + 2\ H_2O(g)$$
$$\Delta_r H° = -676 \text{ kJ/mol-rxn}$$

(a) Use these values and Hess's law to determine the enthalpy change for the reaction

$$CH_4(g) + \tfrac{1}{2}\ O_2(g) \rightarrow CH_3OH(g)$$

(b) Draw an energy-level diagram that shows the relationship between the energy quantities involved in this problem.

44. ■ The enthalpy changes of the following reactions can be measured:

$$C_2H_4(g) + 3\ O_2(g) \rightarrow 2\ CO_2(g) + 2\ H_2O(\ell)$$
$$\Delta_r H° = -1411.1 \text{ kJ/mol-rxn}$$

$$C_2H_5OH(\ell) + 3\ O_2(g) \rightarrow 2\ CO_2(g) + 3\ H_2O(\ell)$$
$$\Delta_r H° = -1367.5 \text{ kJ/mol-rxn}$$

(a) ■ Use these values and Hess's law to determine the enthalpy change for the reaction

$$C_2H_4(g) + H_2O(\ell) \rightarrow C_2H_5OH(\ell)$$

(b) Draw an energy-level diagram that shows the relationship between the energy quantities involved in this problem.

45. Enthalpy changes for the following reactions can be determined experimentally:

$$N_2(g) + 3 H_2(g) \rightarrow 2 NH_3(g)$$
$$\Delta_r H° = -91.8 \text{ kJ/mol-rxn}$$

$$4 NH_3(g) + 5 O_2(g) \rightarrow 4 NO(g) + 6 H_2O(g)$$
$$\Delta_r H° = -906.2 \text{ kJ/mol-rxn}$$

$$H_2(g) + \tfrac{1}{2} O_2(g) \rightarrow H_2O(g)$$
$$\Delta_r H° = -241.8 \text{ kJ/mol-rxn}$$

Use these values to determine the enthalpy change for the formation of NO(g) from the elements (an enthalpy change that cannot be measured directly because the reaction is reactant-favored).

$$\tfrac{1}{2} N_2(g) + \tfrac{1}{2} O_2(g) \rightarrow NO(g) \qquad \Delta_r H° = ?$$

46. You wish to know the enthalpy change for the formation of liquid PCl_3 from the elements.

$$P_4(s) + 6 Cl_2(g) \rightarrow 4 PCl_3(\ell) \qquad \Delta_r H° = ?$$

The enthalpy change for the formation of PCl_5 from the elements can be determined experimentally, as can the enthalpy change for the reaction of $PCl_3(\ell)$ with more chlorine to give $PCl_5(s)$:

$$P_4(s) + 10 Cl_2(g) \rightarrow 4 PCl_5(s)$$
$$\Delta_r H° = -1774.0 \text{ kJ/mol-rxn}$$

$$PCl_3(\ell) + Cl_2(g) \rightarrow PCl_5(s)$$
$$\Delta_r H° = -123.8 \text{ kJ/mol-rxn}$$

Use these data to calculate the enthalpy change for the formation of 1.00 mol of $PCl_3(\ell)$ from phosphorus and chlorine.

Standard Enthalpies of Formation
(See Example 5.9 and ChemistryNow Screen 5.16.)

47. Write a balanced chemical equation for the formation of $CH_3OH(\ell)$ from the elements in their standard states. Find the value for $\Delta_f H°$ for $CH_3OH(\ell)$ in Appendix L.

48. Write a balanced chemical equation for the formation of $CaCO_3(s)$ from the elements in their standard states. Find the value for $\Delta_f H°$ for $CaCO_3(s)$ in Appendix L.

49. (a) Write a balanced chemical equation for the formation of 1 mol of $Cr_2O_3(s)$ from Cr and O_2 in their standard states. Find the value for $\Delta_f H°$ for $Cr_2O_3(s)$ in Appendix L.
(b) ■ What is the standard enthalpy change if 2.4 g of chromium is oxidized to $Cr_2O_3(s)$?

50. (a) Write a balanced chemical equation for the formation of 1 mol of MgO(s) from the elements in their standard states. Find the value for $\Delta_f H°$ for MgO(s) in Appendix L.
(b) What is the standard enthalpy change for the reaction of 2.5 mol of Mg with oxygen?

51. Use standard enthalpies of formation in Appendix L to calculate enthalpy changes for the following:
(a) 1.0 g of white phosphorus burns, forming $P_4O_{10}(s)$
(b) 0.20 mol of NO(g) decomposes to $N_2(g)$ and $O_2(g)$
(c) 2.40 g of NaCl(s) is formed from Na(s) and excess $Cl_2(g)$
(d) 250 g of iron is oxidized with oxygen to $Fe_2O_3(s)$

52. ■ Use standard enthalpies of formation in Appendix L to calculate enthalpy changes for the following:
(a) 0.054 g of sulfur burns, forming $SO_2(g)$
(b) 0.20 mol of HgO(s) decomposes to $Hg(\ell)$ and $O_2(g)$
(c) 2.40 g of $NH_3(g)$ is formed from $N_2(g)$ and excess $H_2(g)$
(d) 1.05×10^{-2} mol of carbon is oxidized to $CO_2(g)$

53. The first step in the production of nitric acid from ammonia involves the oxidation of NH_3.

$$4 NH_3(g) + 5 O_2(g) \rightarrow 4 NO(g) + 6 H_2O(g)$$

(a) Use standard enthalpies of formation to calculate the standard enthalpy change for this reaction.
(b) ■ How much energy as heat is evolved or absorbed in the oxidation of 10.0 g of NH_3?

54. ■ The Romans used calcium oxide, CaO, to produce a strong mortar to build stone structures. The CaO was mixed with water to give $Ca(OH)_2$, which reacted slowly with CO_2 in the air to give $CaCO_3$.

$$Ca(OH)_2(s) + CO_2(g) \rightarrow CaCO_3(s) + H_2O(g)$$

(a) Calculate the standard enthalpy change for this reaction.
(b) How much energy as heat is evolved or absorbed if 1.00 kg of $Ca(OH)_2$ reacts with a stoichiometric amount of CO_2?

55. The standard enthalpy of formation of solid barium oxide, BaO, is -553.5 kJ/mol, and the standard enthalpy of formation of barium peroxide, BaO_2, is -634.3 kJ/mol.
(a) Calculate the standard enthalpy change for the following reaction. Is the reaction exothermic or endothermic?

$$2 BaO_2(s) \rightarrow 2 BaO(s) + O_2(g)$$

(b) Draw an energy-level diagram that shows the relationship between the enthalpy change of the decomposition of BaO_2 to BaO and O_2 and the enthalpies of formation of BaO(s) and $BaO_2(s)$.

▲ more challenging   ■ in OWL   Blue-numbered questions answered in Appendix O

56. An important step in the production of sulfuric acid is the oxidation of SO_2 to SO_3.

$$SO_2(g) + ½ O_2(g) \rightarrow SO_3(g)$$

Formation of SO_3 from the air pollutant SO_2 is also a key step in the formation of acid rain.

(a) Use standard enthalpies of formation to calculate the enthalpy change for the reaction. Is the reaction exothermic or endothermic?

(b) Draw an energy-level diagram that shows the relationship between the enthalpy change for the oxidation of SO_2 to SO_3 and the enthalpies of formation of $SO_2(g)$ and $SO_3(g)$.

57. The enthalpy change for the oxidation of naphthalene, $C_{10}H_8$, is measured by calorimetry.

$$C_{10}H_8(s) + 12 O_2(g) \rightarrow 10 CO_2(g) + 4 H_2O(\ell)$$
$$\Delta_r H° = -5156.1 \text{ kJ/mol-rxn}$$

Use this value, along with the standard enthalpies of formation of $CO_2(g)$ and $H_2O(\ell)$, to calculate the enthalpy of formation of naphthalene, in kJ/mol.

58. ■ The enthalpy change for the oxidation of styrene, C_8H_8, is measured by calorimetry.

$$C_8H_8(\ell) + 10 O_2(g) \rightarrow 8 CO_2(g) + 4 H_2O(\ell)$$
$$\Delta_r H° = -4395.0 \text{ kJ/mol-rxn}$$

Use this value, along with the standard enthalpies of formation of $CO_2(g)$ and $H_2O(\ell)$, to calculate the enthalpy of formation of styrene, in kJ/mol.

General Questions on Thermochemistry

These questions are not designated as to type or location in the chapter. They may combine several concepts.

59. The following terms are used extensively in thermodynamics. Define each and give an example.

(a) exothermic and endothermic
(b) system and surroundings
(c) specific heat capacity
(d) state function
(e) standard state
(f) enthalpy change, ΔH
(g) standard enthalpy of formation

60. For each of the following, tell whether the process is exothermic or endothermic. (No calculations are required.)

(a) $H_2O(\ell) \rightarrow H_2O(s)$
(b) $2 H_2(g) + O_2(g) \rightarrow 2 H_2O(g)$
(c) $H_2O(\ell, 25 °C) \rightarrow H_2O(\ell, 15 °C)$
(d) $H_2O(\ell) \rightarrow H_2O(g)$

61. ■ For each of the following, define a system and its surroundings, and give the direction of energy transfer between system and surroundings.

(a) Methane is burning in a gas furnace in your home.
(b) Water drops, sitting on your skin after a dip in a swimming pool, evaporate.
(c) Water, at 25 °C, is placed in the freezing compartment of a refrigerator, where it cools and eventually solidifies.
(d) Aluminum and $Fe_2O_3(s)$ are mixed in a flask sitting on a laboratory bench. A reaction occurs, and a large quantity of energy is evolved as heat.

62. What does the term "standard state" mean? What are the standard states of the following substances at 298 K: H_2O, NaCl, Hg, CH_4?

63. Use Appendix L to find the standard enthalpies of formation of oxygen atoms, oxygen molecules (O_2), and ozone (O_3). What is the standard state of oxygen? Is the formation of oxygen atoms from O_2 exothermic? What is the enthalpy change for the formation of 1 mol of O_3 from O_2?

64. See the ChemistryNow website, Screen 5.9, Heat Transfer Between Substances. Use the Simulation section of this screen to do the following experiment: Add 10.0 g of Al at 80 °C to 10.0 g of water at 20 °C. What is the final temperature when equilibrium is achieved? Use this value to estimate the specific heat capacity of aluminum.

65. See the ChemistryNow website, Screen 5.15, Hess's Law. Use the Simulation section of this screen to find the value of $\Delta_r H°$ for

$$SnBr_2(s) + TiCl_4(\ell) \rightarrow SnCl_4(\ell) + TiBr_2(s)$$

66. Which gives up more energy on cooling from 50 °C to 10 °C, 50.0 g of water or 100. g of ethanol (specific heat capacity of ethanol = 2.46 J/g · K)?

67. You determine that 187 J of heat is required to raise the temperature of 93.45 g of silver from 18.5 °C to 27.0 °C. What is the specific heat capacity of silver?

68. ■ Calculate the quantity of energy required to convert 60.1 g of $H_2O(s)$ at 0.0 °C to $H_2O(g)$ at 100.0 °C. The heat of fusion of ice at 0 °C is 333 J/g; the heat of vaporization of liquid water at 100 °C is 2260 J/g.

69. ■ You add 100.0 g of water at 60.0 °C to 100.0 g of ice at 0.00 °C. Some of the ice melts and cools the water to 0.00 °C. When the ice and water mixture has come to a uniform temperature of 0 °C, how much ice has melted?

70. ▲ ■ Three 45-g ice cubes at 0 °C are dropped into 5.00×10^2 mL of tea to make iced tea. The tea was initially at 20.0 °C; when thermal equilibrium was reached, the final temperature was 0 °C. How much of the ice melted, and how much remained floating in the beverage? Assume the specific heat capacity of tea is the same as that of pure water.

71. ▲ ■ Suppose that only two 45-g ice cubes had been added to your glass containing 5.00×10^2 mL of tea (see Study Question 70). When thermal equilibrium is reached, all of the ice will have melted, and the temperature of the mixture will be somewhere between 20.0 °C and 0 °C. Calculate the final temperature of the beverage. (Note: The 90 g of water formed when the ice melts must be warmed from 0 °C to the final temperature.)

72. You take a diet cola from the refrigerator and pour 240 mL of it into a glass. The temperature of the beverage is 10.5 °C. You then add one ice cube (45 g). Which of the following describes the system when thermal equilibrium is reached?
(a) The temperature is 0 °C, and some ice remains.
(b) The temperature is 0 °C, and no ice remains.
(c) The temperature is higher than 0 °C, and no ice remains.

Determine the final temperature and the amount of ice remaining, if any.

73. ▲ ■ The standard molar enthalpy of formation of diborane, $B_2H_6(g)$, cannot be determined directly because the compound cannot be prepared by the reaction of boron and hydrogen. It can be calculated from other enthalpy changes, however. The following enthalpy changes can be measured.

$4 B(s) + 3 O_2(g) \rightarrow 2 B_2O_3(s)$
$$\Delta_rH° = -2543.8 \text{ kJ/mol-rxn}$$

$H_2(g) + \frac{1}{2} O_2(g) \rightarrow H_2O(g) \quad \Delta_rH° = -241.8 \text{ kJ/mol-rxn}$

$B_2H_6(g) + 3 O_2(g) \rightarrow B_2O_3(s) + 3 H_2O(g)$
$$\Delta_rH° = -2032.9 \text{ kJ/mol-rxn}$$

(a) Show how these equations can be added together to give the equation for the formation of $B_2H_6(g)$ from $B(s)$ and $H_2(g)$ in their standard states. Assign enthalpy changes to each reaction.
(b) Calculate $\Delta_fH°$ for $B_2H_6(g)$.
(c) Draw an energy-level diagram that shows how the various enthalpies in this problem are related.
(d) Is the formation of $B_2H_6(g)$ from its elements product-favored or reactant-favored?

74. Chloromethane, CH_3Cl, a compound found ubiquitously in the environment, is formed in the reaction of chlorine atoms with methane.

$$CH_4(g) + 2 Cl(g) \rightarrow CH_3Cl(g) + HCl(g)$$

(a) ■ Calculate the enthalpy change for the reaction of $CH_4(g)$ and Cl atoms to give $CH_3Cl(g)$ and $HCl(g)$. Is the reaction product-favored or reactant-favored?
(b) Draw an energy-level diagram that shows how the various enthalpies in this problem are related.

75. When heated to a high temperature, coke (mainly carbon, obtained by heating coal in the absence of air) and steam produce a mixture called water gas, which can be used as a fuel or as a chemical feedstock for other reactions. The equation for the production of water gas is

$$C(s) + H_2O(g) \rightarrow CO(g) + H_2(g)$$

(a) Use standard enthalpies of formation to determine the enthalpy change for this reaction.
(b) Is the reaction product-favored or reactant-favored?
(c) What is the enthalpy change if 1.0 metric ton (1000.0 kg) of carbon is converted to water gas?

76. Camping stoves are fueled by propane (C_3H_8), butane [$C_4H_{10}(g)$, $\Delta_fH° = -127.1$ kJ/mol], gasoline, or ethanol (C_2H_5OH). Calculate the enthalpy of combustion per gram of each of these fuels. [Assume that gasoline is represented by isooctane, $C_8H_{18}(\ell)$, with $\Delta_fH° = -259.2$ kJ/mol.] Do you notice any great differences among these fuels? Are these differences related to their composition?

A camping stove that uses butane as a fuel.

77. Methanol, CH_3OH, a compound that can be made relatively inexpensively from coal, is a promising substitute for gasoline. The alcohol has a smaller energy content than gasoline, but, with its higher octane rating, it burns more efficiently than gasoline in combustion engines. (It has the added advantage of contributing to a lesser degree to some air pollutants.) Compare the enthalpy of combustion per gram of CH_3OH and C_8H_{18} (isooctane), the latter being representative of the compounds in gasoline. ($\Delta_fH° = -259.2$ kJ/mol for isooctane.)

78. Hydrazine and 1,1-dimethylhydrazine both react spontaneously with O_2 and can be used as rocket fuels.

$$N_2H_4(\ell) + O_2(g) \rightarrow N_2(g) + 2\ H_2O(g)$$
hydrazine

$$N_2H_2(CH_3)_2(\ell) + 4\ O_2(g) \rightarrow$$
1,1-dimethylhydrazine $\quad 2\ CO_2(g) + 4\ H_2O(g) + N_2(g)$

The molar enthalpy of formation of $N_2H_4(\ell)$ is +50.6 kJ/mol, and that of $N_2H_2(CH_3)_2(\ell)$ is +48.9 kJ/mol. Use these values, with other $\Delta_fH°$ values, to decide whether the reaction of hydrazine or 1,1-dimethylhydrazine with oxygen provides more energy per gram.

NASA

A control rocket in the Space Shuttle uses hydrazine as the fuel.

79. ■ (a) Calculate the enthalpy change, $\Delta_rH°$, for the formation of 1.00 mol of strontium carbonate (the material that gives the red color in fireworks) from its elements.

$$Sr(s) + C(graphite) + \tfrac{3}{2}\ O_2(g) \rightarrow SrCO_3(s)$$

The experimental information available is

$Sr(s) + \tfrac{1}{2}\ O_2(g) \rightarrow SrO(s) \quad \Delta_fH° = -592$ kJ/mol-rxn

$SrO(s) + CO_2(g) \rightarrow SrCO_3(s) \quad \Delta_rH° = -234$ kJ/mol-rxn

$C(graphite) + O_2(g) \rightarrow CO_2(g) \quad \Delta_fH° = -394$ kJ/mol-rxn

(b) Draw an energy-level diagram relating the energy quantities in this problem.

80. You drink 350 mL of diet soda that is at a temperature of 5 °C.
(a) How much energy will your body expend to raise the temperature of this liquid to body temperature (37 °C)? Assume that the density and specific heat capacity of diet soda are the same as for water.
(b) Compare the value in part (a) with the caloric content of the beverage. (The label says that it has a caloric content of 1 Calorie.) What is the net energy change in your body resulting from drinking this beverage?

(c) Carry out a comparison similar to that in part (b) for a nondiet beverage whose label indicates a caloric content of 240 Calories.

81. ▲ Chloroform, $CHCl_3$, is formed from methane and chlorine in the following reaction.

$$CH_4(g) + 3\ Cl_2(g) \rightarrow 3\ HCl(g) + CHCl_3(g)$$

Calculate $\Delta_rH°$, the enthalpy change for this reaction, using the enthalpies of formation of $CO_2(g)$, $H_2O(\ell)$, and $CHCl_3(g)$ ($\Delta_fH° = -103.1$ kJ/mol), and the enthalpy changes for the following reactions:

$$CH_4(g) + 2\ O_2(g) \rightarrow 2\ H_2O(\ell) + CO_2(g)$$
$$\Delta_rH° = -890.4\ \text{kJ/mol-rxn}$$

$$2\ HCl(g) \rightarrow H_2(g) + Cl_2(g)$$
$$\Delta_rH° = +184.6\ \text{kJ/mol-rxn}$$

82. Water gas, a mixture of carbon monoxide and hydrogen, is produced by treating carbon (in the form of coke or coal) with steam at high temperatures. (See Question 75.)

$$C(s) + H_2O(g) \rightarrow CO(g) + H_2(g)$$

Not all of the carbon available is converted to water gas since some is burned to provide the heat for the endothermic reaction of carbon and water. What mass of carbon must be burned (to CO_2 gas) to provide the energy to convert 1.00 kg of carbon to water gas?

In the Laboratory

83. ■ A piece of lead with a mass of 27.3 g was heated to 98.90 °C and then dropped into 15.0 g of water at 22.50 °C. The final temperature was 26.32 °C. Calculate the specific heat capacity of lead from these data.

84. A 192-g piece of copper is heated to 100.0 °C in a boiling water bath and then dropped into a beaker containing 751 g of water (density = 1.00 g/cm³) at 4.0 °C. What is the final temperature of the copper and water after thermal equilibrium is reached? (The specific heat capacity of copper is 0.385 J/g · K.)

85. Insoluble $AgCl(s)$ precipitates when solutions of $AgNO_3(aq)$ and $NaCl(aq)$ are mixed.

$$AgNO_3(aq) + NaCl(aq) \rightarrow AgCl(s) + NaNO_3(aq)$$
$$\Delta_rH° = ?$$

To measure the energy evolved in this reaction, 250. mL of 0.16 M $AgNO_3(aq)$ and 125 mL of 0.32 M $NaCl(aq)$ are mixed in a coffee-cup calorimeter. The temperature of the mixture rises from 21.15 °C to 22.90 °C. Calculate the enthalpy change for the precipitation of $AgCl(s)$, in kJ/mol. (Assume the density of the solution is 1.0 g/mL and its specific heat capacity is 4.2 J/g · K.)

86. Insoluble $PbBr_2(s)$ precipitates when solutions of $Pb(NO_3)_2(aq)$ and $NaBr(aq)$ are mixed.

$$Pb(NO_3)_2(aq) + 2\ NaBr(aq) \rightarrow PbBr_2(s) + 2\ NaNO_3(aq)$$
$$\Delta_r H° = ?$$

To measure the enthalpy change, 200. mL of 0.75 M $Pb(NO_3)_2(aq)$ and 200. mL of 1.5 M $NaBr(aq)$ are mixed in a coffee-cup calorimeter. The temperature of the mixture rises by 2.44 °C. Calculate the enthalpy change for the precipitation of $PbBr_2(s)$, in kJ/mol. (Assume the density of the solution is 1.0 g/mL and its specific heat capacity is 4.2 J/g · K.)

87. The value of ΔU in the decomposition of 7.647 g of ammonium nitrate can be measured in a bomb calorimeter. The reaction that occurs is

$$NH_4NO_3(s) \rightarrow N_2O(g) + 2\ H_2O(g)$$

The temperature of the calorimeter, which contains 415 g of water, increases from 18.90 °C to 20.72 °C. The heat capacity of the bomb is 155 J/K. What is the value of ΔU for this reaction, in kJ/mol?

The decomposition of ammonium nitrate is clearly exothermic.

88. ■ A bomb calorimetric experiment was run to determine the heat of combustion of ethanol (a common fuel additive). The reaction is

$$C_2H_5OH(\ell) + 3\ O_2(g) \rightarrow 2\ CO_2(g) + 3\ H_2O(\ell)$$

The bomb had a heat capacity of 550 J/K, and the calorimeter contained 650 g of water. Burning 4.20 g of ethanol, $C_2H_5OH(\ell)$ resulted in a rise in temperature from 18.5 °C to 22.3 °C. Calculate the enthalpy of combustion of ethanol, in kJ/mol.

89. The meals-ready-to-eat (MREs) in the military can be heated on a flameless heater. You can purchase a similar product called "Heater Meals." Just pour water into the heater unit, wait a few minutes, and you have a hot meal. The source of energy in the heater is

$$Mg(s) + 2\ H_2O(\ell) \rightarrow Mg(OH)_2(s) + H_2(g)$$

The "heater meal" uses the reaction of magnesium with water as a source of energy as heat.

Calculate the enthalpy change under standard conditions, in joules, for this reaction. What quantity of magnesium is needed to supply the energy required to warm 25 mL of water ($d = 1.00$ g/mL) from 25 °C to 85 °C? (See W. Jensen: *Journal of Chemical Education*, Vol. 77, pp. 713–717, 2000.)

90. On a cold day, you can warm your hands with a "heat pad," a device that uses the oxidation of iron to produce energy as heat.

$$4\ Fe(s) + 3\ O_2(g) \rightarrow 2\ Fe_2O_3(s)$$

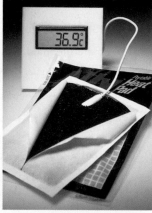

A hand warmer uses the oxidation of iron as a source of thermal energy.

What mass of iron is needed to supply the energy required to warm 15 mL of water ($d = 1.00$ g/mL) from 23 °C to 37 °C?

Summary and Conceptual Questions

The following questions may use concepts from this and previous chapters.

91. Without doing calculations, decide whether each of the following is product-favored or reactant-favored.
(a) the combustion of natural gas
(b) the decomposition of glucose, $C_6H_{12}O_6$, to carbon and water

92. ■ Which of the following are state functions?
(a) the volume of a balloon
(b) the time it takes to drive from your home to your college or university
(c) the temperature of the water in a coffee cup
(d) the potential energy of a ball held in your hand

93. ▲ ■ You want to determine the value for the enthalpy of formation of $CaSO_4(s)$.

$$Ca(s) + S(s) + 2\ O_2(g) \rightarrow CaSO_4(s)$$

This reaction cannot be done directly. You know, however, that both calcium and sulfur react with oxygen to produce oxides in reactions that can be studied calorimetrically. You also know that the basic oxide CaO reacts with the acidic oxide $SO_3(g)$ to produce $CaSO_4(s)$ with $\Delta_r H° = -402.7$ kJ. Outline a method for determining $\Delta_f H°$ for $CaSO_4(s)$, and identify the information that must be collected by experiment. Using information in Appendix L, confirm that $\Delta_f H°$ for $CaSO_4(s) = -1433.5$ kJ/mol.

94. Prepare a graph of specific heat capacities for metals versus their atomic weights. Combine the data in Figure 5.7 and the values in the following table. What is the relationship between specific heat capacity and atomic weight? Use this relationship to predict the specific heat capacity of platinum. The specific heat capacity for platinum is given in the literature as 0.133 J/g · K. How good is the agreement between the predicted and actual values?

Metal	Specific Heat Capacity (J/g · K)
Chromium	0.450
Lead	0.127
Silver	0.236
Tin	0.227
Titanium	0.522

95. Observe the molar heat capacity values for the metals in Figure 5.7. What observation can you make about these values—specifically, are they widely different or very similar? Using this information, estimate the specific heat capacity for silver. Compare this estimate with the correct value for silver, 0.236 J/g · K.

96. ▲ Suppose you are attending summer school and are living in a very old dormitory. The day is oppressively hot. There is no air-conditioner, and you can't open the windows of your room because they are stuck shut from layers of paint. There is a refrigerator in the room, however. In a stroke of genius, you open the door of the refrigerator, and cool air cascades out. The relief does not last long, though. Soon the refrigerator motor and condenser begin to run, and not long thereafter the room is hotter than it was before. Why did the room warm up?

97. ■ You want to heat the air in your house with natural gas (CH_4). Assume your house has 275 m² (about 2800 ft²) of floor area and that the ceilings are 2.50 m from the floors. The air in the house has a molar heat capacity of 29.1 J/mol · K. (The number of moles of air in the house can be found by assuming that the average molar mass of air is 28.9 g/mol and that the density of air at these temperatures is 1.22 g/L.) What mass of methane do you have to burn to heat the air from 15.0 °C to 22.0 °C?

98. Water can be decomposed to its elements, H_2 and O_2, using electrical energy or in a series of chemical reactions. The following sequence of reactions is one possibility:

$$CaBr_2(s) + H_2O(g) \rightarrow CaO(s) + 2\ HBr(g)$$
$$Hg(\ell) + 2\ HBr(g) \rightarrow HgBr_2(s) + H_2(g)$$
$$HgBr_2(s) + CaO(s) \rightarrow HgO(s) + CaBr_2(s)$$
$$HgO(s) \rightarrow Hg(\ell) + \tfrac{1}{2}\ O_2(g)$$

(a) Show that the net result of this series of reactions is the decomposition of water to its elements.
(b) If you use 1000. kg of water, what mass of H_2 can be produced?
(c) Calculate the value of $\Delta_r H°$ for each step in the series. Are the reactions predicted to be product-favored or reactant-favored?

$$\Delta_f H° \ [CaBr_2(s)] = -683.2\ \text{kJ/mol}$$
$$\Delta_f H° \ [HgBr_2(s)] = -169.5\ \text{kJ/mol}$$

(e) Comment on the commercial feasibility of using this series of reactions to produce $H_2(g)$ from water.

99. Suppose that an inch of rain falls over a square mile of ground. (Density of water is 1.0 g/cm³.) The enthalpy of vaporization of water at 25 °C is 44.0 kJ/mol. How much energy as heat is transferred to the surroundings from the condensation of water vapor in forming this quantity of liquid water? (The huge number tells you how much energy is "stored" in water vapor and why we think of storms as such great forces of energy in nature. It is interesting to compare this result with the energy given off, 4.2×10^6 kJ, when a ton of dynamite explodes.)

100. ▲ Peanuts and peanut oil are organic materials and burn in air. How many burning peanuts does it take to provide the energy to boil a cup of water (250 mL of water)? To solve this problem, we assume each peanut, with an average mass of 0.73 g, is 49% peanut oil and 21% starch; the remainder is non-combustible. We further assume peanut oil is palmitic acid, $C_{16}H_{32}O_2$, with an enthalpy of formation of -848.4 kJ/mol. Starch is a long chain of $C_6H_{10}O_5$ units, each unit having an enthalpy of formation of -960 kJ. (*See ChemistryNow Screens 5.1 and 5.19: Chemical Puzzler.*)

How many burning peanuts are required to provide the energy to boil 250 mL of water?

101. ▲ Isomers are molecules with the same elemental composition but a different atomic arrangement. Three isomers with the formula C_4H_8 are shown in the models below. The enthalpy of combustion ($\Delta_c H°$) of each isomer, determined using a calorimeter, is:

Compound	$\Delta_{com}H°$ (kJ/mol-rxn)
cis-2 butene	-2687.5
trans-2-butene	-2684.2
1-butene	-2696.7

(a) Draw an energy level diagram relating the energy content of the three isomers to the energy content of the combustion products, $CO_2(g)$ and $H_2O(g)$.

(b) Use the $\Delta_c H°$ data in part (a), along with the enthalpies of formation of $CO_2(g)$ and $H_2O(g)$ from Appendix L, to calculate the enthalpy of formation for each of the isomers.

(c) Draw an energy level diagram that relates the enthalpies of formation of the three isomers to the energy of the elements in their standard states.

(d) What is the enthalpy change for the conversion of *cis*-2-butene to *trans*-2-butene?

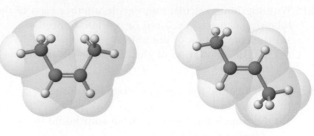

cis-2-butene   trans-2-butene

1-butene

102. Several standard enthalpies of formation (from Appendix L) are given below. Use these data to calculate:

(a) The standard enthalpy of vaporization of bromine.

(b) The energy required for the reaction $Br_2(g) \rightarrow 2\ Br(g)$. (This is the Br—Br bond energy.)

Species	$\Delta_f H°$ (kJ/mol)
Br(g)	111.9
$Br_2(\ell)$	0
$Br_2(g)$	30.9

103. When 0.850 g of Mg is burned in oxygen in a constant volume calorimeter, 25.4 kJ of energy as heat is evolved. The calorimeter is in an insulated container with 750. g of water at an initial temperature of 18.6 °C. The heat capacity of the calorimeter is 820. J/K.

(a) Calculate ΔU for the oxidation of Mg (in kJ/mol Mg).

(b) What will be the final temperature of the water and the bomb calorimeter in this experiment?

104. A piece of gold (10.0 g, $C = 0.129$ J/g · K) is heated to 100.0 °C. A piece of copper (also 10.0 g, $C = 0.385$ J/g · K) is chilled in an ice bath to 0 °C. Both pieces of metal are placed in a beaker containing 150. g H_2O at 20 °C. Will the temperature of the water be greater than or less than 20 °C when thermal equilibrium is reached? Calculate the final temperature.

▲ more challenging ■ in OWL Blue-numbered questions answered in Appendix O

105. Methane, CH_4, can be converted to methanol which, like ethanol, can be used as a fuel. The energy level diagram shown here presents relationships between energies of the fuels and their oxidation products. Use the information in the diagram to answer the following questions. (The energy terms are per mol-rxn.)

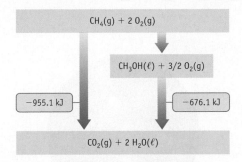

(a) Which fuel, methanol or methane, yields the most energy per mole when burned?

(b) Which fuel yields the most energy per gram when burned?

(c) What is the enthalpy change for the conversion of methane to methanol?

(d) Each arrow on the diagram represents a chemical reaction. Write the equation for the reaction that converts methane to methanol.

106. Calculate $\Delta_r H°$ for the reaction

$2\ C(s) + 3\ H_2(g) + \frac{1}{2}\ O_2(g) \rightarrow C_2H_5OH(\ell)$
given the information below.

$C(s) + O_2(g) \rightarrow CO_2(g) \quad \Delta_r H° = -393.5\ \text{kJ/mol-rxn}$

$2\ H_2(g) + O_2(g) \rightarrow 2\ H_2O(\ell)$
$\Delta_r H° = -571.6\ \text{kJ/mol-rxn}$

$C_2H_5OH(\ell) + 3\ O_2(g) \rightarrow 2\ CO_2(g) + 3\ H_2O(\ell)$
$\Delta_r H° = -1367.5\ \text{kJ/mol-rxn}$

107. You have the six pieces of metal listed below, plus a beaker of water containing 3.00×10^2 g of water. The water temperature is 21.00 °C.

Metals	Specific Heat (J/g K)	Mass (g)
1. Al	0.9002	100.0
2. Al	0.9002	50.0
3. Au	0.1289	100.0
4. Au	0.1289	50.0
5. Zn	0.3860	100.0
6. Zn	0.3860	50.0

(a) In your first experiment you select one piece of metal and heat it to 100 °C, and then select a second piece of metal and cool it to −10 °C. Both pieces of metal are then placed in the beaker of water and the temperatures equilibrated. You want to select two pieces of metal to use, such that the final temperature of the water is as high as possible. What piece of metal will you heat? What piece of metal will you cool? What is the final temperature of the water?

(b) The second experiment is done in the same way as the first. However, your goal now is to cause the temperature to change the least, that is, the final temperature should be be as near to 21.00 °C as possible. What piece of metal will you heat? What piece of metal will you cool? What is the final temperature of the water?

108. In lab, you plan to carry out a calorimetry experiment to determine the $\Delta_r H$ for the exothermic reaction of $Ca(OH)_2(s)$ and $HCl(aq)$. Predict how each of the following will affect the calculated value of $\Delta_r H$. (The value calculated for $\Delta_r H$ for this reaction is a negative value so choose your answer from the following: $\Delta_r H$ will be too low [that is, a larger negative value], $\Delta_r H$ will be unaffected, $\Delta_r H$ will be too high [that is, a smaller negative value.])

(a) You spill a little bit of the $Ca(OH)_2$ on the benchtop before adding it to the calorimeter.

(b) Because of a miscalculation, you add an excess of HCl to the measured amount of $Ca(OH)_2$ in the calorimeter.

(b) $Ca(OH)_2$ readily absorbs water from the air. The $Ca(OH)_2$ sample you weighed had been exposed to the air prior to weighing and had absorbed some water.

(c) After weighing out $Ca(OH)_2$, the sample sat in an open beaker and absorbed water.

(d) You delay too long in recording the final temperature.

(e) The insulation in your coffee cup calorimeter was poor and so some energy as heat was lost to the surroundings during the experiment.

(e) You have ignored the fact that energy as heat also raised the temperature of the stirrer and the thermometer in your system.

Photo source: Charles D. Winters

When solid NH_4Cl is heated it is converted to gaseous NH_3 and HCl. The white "smoke" you see consists of tiny particles of solid NH_4Cl formed by the recombination of gaseous NH_3 and HCl. At this point in your study of chemistry you should be able to:

a) write a balanced chemical equation for the decomposition of NH_4Cl,
b) name each of the compounds involved,
c) calculate the enthalpy change to decompose the NH_4Cl,
d) and determine the mass of product expected if you know the masses of the reactants.

This section, called *Let's Review*, will explore questions about this and other reactions.

THE PURPOSE OF *LET'S REVIEW*

- *Let's Review* provides additional questions for Chapters 1 through 5. Routine questions covering the concepts in a chapter are in the Study Questions at the end of that chapter and are usually identified by topic. In contrast, *Let's Review* questions combine several concepts from one or more chapters. Many come from the examinations given by the authors and others are based on actual experiments or processes in chemical research or in the chemical industries.

- *Let's Review* provides guidance for Chapters 1 through 5 as you prepare for an exam on these chapters. Although this is designated for Chapters 1 through 5, you may choose only material appropriate to the exam in your course.

- To direct your review, **Comprehensive Questions** are correlated with relevant chapter sections and with the OWL online homework system to which you may have purchased access. Some questions

may include a screen shot from one of these tools so you see what resources are available to help you review.

PREPARING FOR AN EXAMINATION ON CHAPTERS 1–5

1.   Review **Go Chemistry** modules for these chapters. Go Chemistry modules are available at **www.cengage.com/chemistry/kotz** or **www.ichapters.com**.

2. Take the ChemistryNow **Pre-Test** and work through your **Personalized Learning Plan.** Work through ChemistryNow **Exercises, Guided Simulations,** and **Intelligent Tutors.**

3. **OWL** If you subscribe to OWL, use the **Tutorials** in that system.

4. Work on the questions below that are relevant to a particular chapter or chapters. See the solutions to those questions at the end of this section.

5. For background and help answering a question, use the Go Chemistry and OWL questions correlated with it.

KEY POINTS TO KNOW FOR CHAPTERS 1–5

Here are some of the key points you must know to be successful in Chapters 1–5.

- Identify chemical and physical properties.
- Use temperature in kelvins and other units of measurement in chemistry.
- Give the names and symbols of the chemical elements, and understand basic atomic structure and the arrangement of the periodic table.
- Carry out mass to amount (moles) and amount (moles) to mass conversions.
- Calculate the molar mass of a chemical compound.
- Gives names and formulas of chemical compounds.
- Identify empirical and molecular formulas.
- Balance chemical equations.
- Understand and use chemical stoichiometry.
- Know the names and formulas of common cations and anions and of acids and bases.
- Write chemical equations for precipitation, acid-base, and gas-forming reactions.
- Calculate and use solution concentrations.
- Know the terminology of thermochemistry.
- Relate heat, mass, temperature, and specific heat capacity.
- Calculate the enthalpy change for a chemical reaction ($\Delta_r H°$).

EXAMINATION PREPARATION QUESTIONS

▲ denotes more challenging questions.

Important information about the questions that follow:

- See the Study Questions in each chapter for questions on basic concepts.
- Some of these questions arise from recent research in chemistry and the other sciences. They often involve concepts from more than one chapter and may be more challenging than those in earlier chapters. Not all chapter goals or concepts are necessarily addressed in these questions.
- **Assessing Key Points** are short-answer questions covering the Key Points to Know on this page.

- **Comprehensive Questions** bring together concepts from multiple chapters and are correlated with text sections covering that topic, with Go Chemistry modules, and with questions in OWL that may provide additional background.
- The screen shots are largely taken from Go Chemistry modules available at **www.cengage.com/chemistry/kotz** or **www.ichapters.com.**

Assessing Key Points

1. Sulfur is a *(metal)(nonmetal)(metalloid)* _____ and its symbol is _____. The element has _____ protons in the nucleus. Sulfur-32 and sulfur-34 account for 99.2% of all S atoms; _____ is the more abundant of the two. In the sulfur-34 isotope there are _____ neutrons in the nucleus. Sulfur forms a common monatomic ion whose symbol is _____.

2. A flask having 0.0123 g of Ar contains _____ mol and _____ atoms.

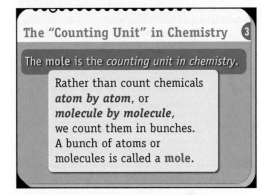

Screen from Go Chemistry module 4 on moles.

3. Fill in the table with the correct formula or name.

Cation	Anion	Name	Formula
NH_4^+		ammonium bromide	
		iron(II) sulfate	
			$Mg(CH_3CO_2)_2$
Al^{3+}	NO_3^-		

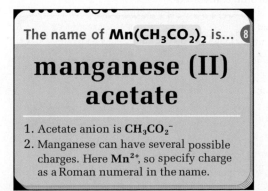

Screen from Go Chemistry module 3 on naming ionic compounds.

4. Which has the greater mass, 0.50 mol of silicon dioxide or 0.50 mol of iron?

5. What is the molar mass of Epsom salt, $MgSO_4\cdot7H_2O$?

6. Which formula below is NOT correct?
   (a) $Ba(NO_3)_2$
   (b) $KClO_4$
   (c) Na_3N
   (d) $Al_2(SO_4)_3$
   (e) Ca_2HPO_4

7. Sodium oxalate has the formula $Na_2C_2O_4$. Based on this information, the formula for iron(III) oxalate is
   (a) FeC_2O_4
   (b) $Fe(C_2O_4)_2$
   (c) $Fe(C_2O_4)_3$
   (d) $Fe_2(C_2O_4)_3$
   (e) $Fe_3(C_2O_4)_2$

8. Which of the following series contains only *known non-metal anions*?
   (a) S^{2-}, Br^-, Al^{3+}
   (b) N^{2-}, I^-, O^{2-}
   (c) P^{3-}, F^-, Se^{2-}
   (d) Cl^-, Fe^{3+}, S^{2-}
   (e) In^+, Br^{2-}, Te^{2-}

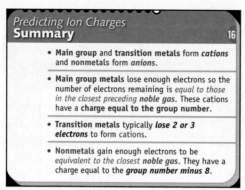

Screen from Go Chemistry module 2 on ion charges.

9. Balance the following chemical equations.
   (a) $Fe_2O_3(s) + Mg(s) \rightarrow MgO(s) + Fe(s)$
   (b) $C_6H_5CH_3(\ell) + O_2(g) \rightarrow H_2O(\ell) + CO_2(g)$

10. The reaction of iron with oxygen produces iron(III) oxide.

    $$4\,Fe(s) + 3\,O_2(g) \rightarrow 2\,Fe_2O_3(s)$$

    If you have 1.6 mol of Fe, what amount of O_2 is needed for complete reaction and what amount of Fe_2O_3 is produced? What are the masses of the reactants and products involved?

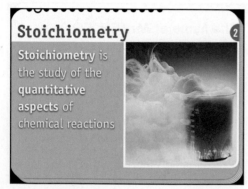

Screen from Go Chemistry module 7 on stoichiometry.

11. Give the oxidation number of each underlined atom:
    (a) $\underline{Br}O_3^-$
    (b) $H_2\underline{C}_2O_4$
    (c) $\underline{S}O_4^{2-}$

12. Zinc reacts readily with nitric acid to give the metal ion and other products such as NO_2.

    $Zn(s) + 2\,NO_3^-(aq) + 4\,H_3O^+(aq)$
    $\qquad \rightarrow Zn^{2+}(aq) + 2\,NO_2(g) + 6\,H_2O(\ell)$

    The oxidation number of N in NO_3^- is _____. The substance oxidized is _____ and the oxidizing agent is _____.

13. What mass of Na_2CO_3 (molar mass = 106 g/mol) must be used to make 250. mL of a 0.100 M solution of sodium carbonate? What is the concentration of Na^+ ions in this solution?

14. In the laboratory you added water to 125 mL of 0.160 M H_2SO_4. If the final volume of the diluted solution is 1.00 L, what is the concentration of the acid in the diluted solution?

15. Which of the following ionic compounds are water-soluble?

    $BaSO_4$ $Ba(NO_3)_2$ $BaCO_3$ Na_2SO_4
    $AgBr$ KCl $Mg(CH_3CO_2)_2$

Screen from Go Chemistry module 5 on solubility guidelines.

16. Complete and balance the equation for the following reaction. Describe the reaction as an acid-base, precipitation, gas-forming, or redox reaction:

    $$Na_2CO_3(aq) + HNO_3(aq) \rightarrow$$

17. Vinegar has a pH of 4.52. What is the hydronium ion concentration in the vinegar?

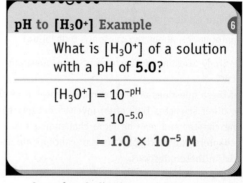

Screen from Go Chemistry module 9b on pH.

18. A sample of Na_2CO_3 (0.412 g) is titrated to the equivalence point with 35.63 mL of HNO_3. What is the concentration of the HNO_3 solution?

19. Write the net ionic equation for the reaction of aqueous solutions of sodium hydroxide and iron(II) chloride.

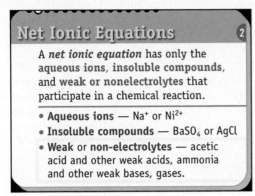

Net Ionic Equations ②

A *net ionic equation* has only the aqueous ions, insoluble compounds, and weak or nonelectrolytes that participate in a chemical reaction.

• **Aqueous ions** — Na^+ or Ni^{2+}
• **Insoluble compounds** — $BaSO_4$ or $AgCl$
• **Weak or non-electrolytes** — acetic acid and other weak acids, ammonia and other weak bases, gases.

Screen from Go Chemistry module 6 on writing net ionic equations.

20. What quantity of energy as heat must be transferred to warm 225 g of water from room temperature (25 °C) to 93 °C?

21. What is the enthalpy change for the combustion of exactly one mole of gaseous propane at 25 °C? Is the reaction exo- or endothermic?

$$C_3H_8(g) + 5\ O_2(g) \rightarrow 3\ CO_2(g) + 4\ H_2O(g)$$

Comprehensive Questions

22. (Chapters 1 and 2) Nanotechnology is a rapidly growing field of chemistry, and much research is being done to discover ways of making particles that have dimensions of only a few nanometers.
    (a) Gold has only one naturally occurring isotope. How many neutrons are there in an atom of gold?
    (b) Gold's density is 19.3 g/cm^3. If you have 0.0125 mol of gold, what is the volume of the piece? How many atoms are contained in the piece?
    (c) ▲ A spherical gold nanoparticle has a diameter of 3.00 nm. If the radius of a gold atom is 0.144 nm, estimate the number of gold atoms in the nanoparticle. [Assume the gold atoms are tiny spheres and that they occupy 74.0% of the available space in the spherical nanoparticle. Volume of a sphere = $(4/3)\pi r^3$]
    Text Sections: Tools of Quantiative Chemistry, 2.1 and 2.3
    OWL Questions: 1.5c, 2.2c

23. (Chapters 1 and 2) Copper is commonly used, in spite of the fact that its abundance on Earth is only 50 parts per million.
    (a) Copper has two isotopes: ^{63}Cu (62.930 u) and ^{65}Cu (64.928 u). Which is more abundant?
    (b) ▲ What are the relative abundances of the two isotopes?

(c) Two copper-containing compounds are $CuCO_3$ and Cu_2S. Name each compound and give the charge on the copper ion in each.
(d) What amount of copper (mol) is in a piece of copper wire with a diameter of 2.50 mm and 16.0 cm long? How many copper atoms are contained in the wire? (The density of copper metal is 8.96 g/cm^3.) [Volume of a cylinder = πr^2(length)]
Text Sections: 2.3, 2.4, and 2.9
OWL Questions: 1,5c, 2.3a, 2.4b, 2.9b, 2.9g, 2.9h

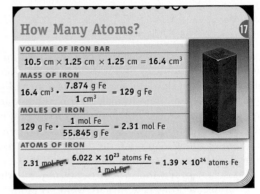

How Many Atoms? ⑰

VOLUME OF IRON BAR
10.5 cm × 1.25 cm × 1.25 cm = 16.4 cm^3

MASS OF IRON
$16.4\ cm^3 \cdot \dfrac{7.874\ g\ Fe}{1\ cm^3} = 129\ g\ Fe$

MOLES OF IRON
$129\ g\ Fe \cdot \dfrac{1\ mol\ Fe}{55.845\ g\ Fe} = 2.31\ mol\ Fe$

ATOMS OF IRON
$2.31\ mol\ Fe \cdot \dfrac{6.022 \times 10^{23}\ atoms\ Fe}{1\ mol\ Fe} = 1.39 \times 10^{24}\ atoms\ Fe$

Screen from Go Chemistry module 4 on moles.

24. (Chapter 2) Nuclear power plants are relatively common in much of the world and most use uranium.
    (a) Natural uranium exists mostly as the ^{238}U isotope, but fissionable uranium is the ^{235}U isotope. Give the number of protons and neutrons in each of these isotopes.
    (b) Several common uranium-containing compounds are (i) UO_2, (ii) $U(SO_4)_2$, and (iii) UF_6. Name each compound, calculate its molar mass, and give the oxydation number of uranium in each.
    Text Sections 2.3, 2.7, 2.9, and 3.9
    OWL Questions: 2.2c, 2.7k, 2.9d

25. (Chapter 2) Silver, a Group 1B element, has two stable isotopes. If one of the silver isotopes has a mass of 106.905 u and an abundance of 51.839%, what is the mass of the other silver isotope? What is its mass number?
    Text Section 2.4
    OWL Questions: 2.4b

26. (Chapters 2–4) The common mineral fluorite has the formula CaF_2.

Violet crystals of the mineral fluorite, CaF_2.

(a) What is the proper chemical name of the mineral?

(b) How many electrons do the ions Ca^{2+} and F^- have? Do these have the same number of electrons as a noble gas? Which of the gases?

(c) Fluorite is the commercial source of hydrogen fluoride. Balance the equation for the reaction of sulfuric acid, H_2SO_4, with CaF_2 to give calcium sulfate and hydrogen fluoride.

(d) If you combine 1.0 kg of CaF_2 with excess sulfuric acid, what mass of hydrogen fluoride can be produced?

Text Sections 2.7, 3.2, and 4.1

OWL Questions: 2.7d, 2.7k, 3.2d, 4.1c

27. (Chapter 2) "Green chemistry" is a movement within the chemistry community to find ways to produce chemicals in a way that does not lead to environmental problems. Caprolactam, used to make nylon, is made in large quantities. One problem is that production of each kilogram of caprolactam results in 4 kilograms of ammonium sulfate. Ammonium sulfate has few commercial uses, so it is often deposited in landfills.

(a) Caprolactam has the structure shown here (where C atoms are gray, H atoms are white, N atoms are blue, and O atoms are red). What is the formula of caprolactam?

Structure of a molecule of caprolactam

(b) What is the molar mass of caprolactam?

(c) What is the weight percent of each element in caprolactam?

(d) What volume of landfill (in m^3) is required for the ammonium sulfate that is the by-product of the production of 1.00 metric ton (1.00×10^3 kg) of caprolactam? (Density of ammonium sulfate is 1.77 g/cm^3.)

Text Sections 2.9 and 2.10

OWL: 1.5c, 2.6, 2.9d, 2.10b

28. (Chapters 2 and 3) An article by C. M. Johnson and B. L. Beard (*Science*, Vol. 309, page 1025, 2005) described the biogeochemical cycling of iron isotopes. The authors stated that "In terms of isotopic studies of the transition elements, iron has received the most attention because of its high abundance on Earth and its prominent role in biogeochemical processes."

(a) Give the number of electrons and protons in an atom of Fe and in ions Fe^{2+} and Fe^{3+}. Which is the most oxidized form?

(b) Name the following iron compounds:
$Fe(CH_3CO_2)_2$, $FePO_4$, $Fe(ClO_4)_3$.

Text Sections 2.7 and 3.9

OWL: 2.2c, 2.7d, 2.7k, 3.9b

29. (Chapter 2) Inorganic nanotubes have been prepared based on tungsten and sulfur. The tungsten content of one such nanotube is 74.14%. What is the empirical formula of these nanotubes?

Text Section 2.10

OWL: 2.10f

30. (Chapter 2) Nepetalactone is the chemical name for catnip. It is one of a family of compounds that sets many cats into a frenzy. It is 72.26% carbon, 8.49% hydrogen, and the remainder is oxygen. It has a molar mass of 166.21 g/mol. What are the empirical and molecular formulas of catnip?

Text Section 2.10

OWL: 2.10f

31. (Chapter 4) There is great interest in finding inexpensive ways to produce hydrogen gas, which can be used as a fuel in homes and cars and trucks. A recently discovered method uses a catalyst to promote the reaction of ethanol, water, and oxygen.

$$2\ C_2H_5OH(g)\ +\ 4\ H_2O(g)\ +\ O_2(g)$$
$$\rightarrow 4\ CO_2(g)\ +\ 10\ H_2(g)$$

(a) What mass of H_2 can be produced from 1.00 kg of ethanol and unlimited amounts of water and oxygen?

(b) What masses of H_2O and O_2 are required to react with 1.00 kg of ethanol?

Text Section 4.1

OWL: 4.1c

32. (Chapters 4 and 5) Methane, CH_4, can be converted to gaseous CH_3OH under special circumstances.

(a) Write a balanced equation for the conversion of O_2 and CH_4 to gaseous CH_3OH.

(b) If you combine 125 g of CH_4 with 145 g of O_2 what mass of CH_3OH would be obtained in theory?

(c) Is the conversion of CH_4 to CH_3OH with O_2 exothermic or endothermic? What is the enthalpy change for the conversion of 1.00 kg of CH_4 to $CH_3OH(g)$?

Text Sections 3.2, 4.1, 4.2, 5.1, and 5.7

OWL: 3.2d, 4.2d, 4.2f, 5.5c, 5.7d

Example of a reaction with a limiting reactant 3

REACTANTS   PRODUCTS
$2\ CH_3OH(\ell) + 3\ O_2(g) \longrightarrow 4\ H_2O(g) + 2\ CO_2(g)$
METHANOL   OXYGEN

Screen from Go Chemistry module 8a on limiting reactants.

33. (Chapters 2–4) Gold is an important commodity in our economy. Gold (in rocks) dissolves in the presence of CN^- ion (from KCN) and oxygen to form the stable anion $[Au(CN)_2]^-$.

$$4 \, Au(s) + 8 \, CN^-(aq) + O_2(g) + 2 \, H_2O(\ell)$$
$$\rightarrow 4 \, [Au(CN)_2]^-(aq) + 4 \, OH^-(aq)$$

(a) What is the name of the CN^- ion and of KCN?

(b) This is an oxidation-reduction reaction. Describe how you would reach that conclusion and then identify the substance oxidized, the substance reduced, and the oxidizing and reducing agents.

(c) What mass of KCN would be needed to dissolve 1.00 kg of gold?

(d) If the KCN is used as a 0.15 M solution, what volume of solution is required to dissolve 1.00 kg of gold?

Text Sections 2.7, 3.9, 4.1, and 4.5

OWL: 2.7f, 2.7k, 3.9b, 4.1c, 4.5e

34. (Chapters 2 and 4) Linoleic acid is an essential fatty acid and a component of many vegetable oils such as peanut, corn, safflower, and soybean oils.

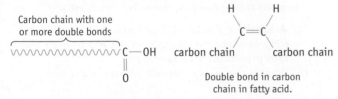

All fatty acids have a long hydrocarbon chain with an acid group ($-CO_2H$) at one end. The chain consists of carbon atoms bonded mostly by single C—C bonds, but there can be one or more C=C double bonds.

(a) Analysis of linoleic acid indicates it is 77.09% carbon and 11.50% H; the remainder is oxygen. What is the empirical formula of linoleic acid?

(b) A 1.234-g sample is titrated with 0.113 M NaOH. The volume of base required is 38.94 mL. What is the molar mass of the acid? What is its molecular formula?

(c) One can determine the number of double bonds in a fatty acid by reacting it with iodine, I_2. Each double bond reacts with one I_2 molecule. If 0.351 g of linoleic acid requires 0.636 g of I_2, how many double bonds does the fatty acid contain?

Text Sections 2.10, 4.1, 4.5, and 4.7

OWL: 2.10f, 4.7g, 4.7h

35. (Chapter 3 and 4) Oyster beds in the oceans require chloride ions for growth. The minimum concentration is 8 mg/L (8 parts per million). To analyze for the amount of chloride ion in a 50.0-mL sample of water, you add a few drops of aqueous potassium chromate and then titrate the sample with 25.60 mL of 0.001036 M silver nitrate. The silver nitrate reacts with chloride ion, and, when the chloride ion is completely removed, the silver nitrate reacts with potassium chromate to give a red precipitate.

(a) Write a balanced net ionic equation for the reaction of silver nitrate with chloride ions.

(b) Write a complete balanced equation and a net ionic equation for the reaction of silver nitrate with potassium chromate, indicating whether each compound is water-soluble or not.

(c) What is the concentration of chloride ions in the sample? Is it sufficient to promote oyster growth?

Text Sections 3.5, 3.6, 4.4, 4.5, and 4.7

OWL: 3.5f, 3.6b, 3.6g, 4.7g, 4.7h

36. ▲ (Chapters 2 and 4) A 0.463-g sample of a compound composed of Ti, Cl, C, and H was burned in air to produce 0.818 g of CO_2 and 0.168 g of H_2O. Aqueous silver nitrate was added to the residue from the combustion and produced 0.533 g of AgCl. What is the empirical formula of the compound?

Text Sections 2.10 and 4.7

OWL: 4.4c

37. (Chapter 3) You have a bottle of solid barium hydroxide and some dilute sulfuric acid. You then dissolve some of the barium hydroxide in water and slowly add sulfuric acid to the mixture. While adding the sulfuric acid, you measure the electrical conductivity of the mixture (as in Active Figure 3.9, page 124).

(a) Write the complete, balanced equation for the reaction occurring when barium hydroxide and sulfuric acid are mixed.

(b) Write the net ionic equation for the barium hydroxide and sulfuric acid reaction.

(c) Which diagram below represents the change in conductivity as the acid is added to the aqueous barium hydroxide? Explain briefly.

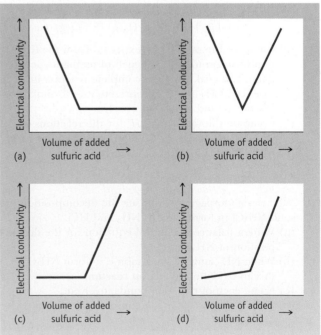

Text Sections 3.2, 3.5, 3.6, and 3.7

OWL: 3.5c, 3.7e

38. (Chapter 5) A 9.40-g sample of KBr was dissolved in 105 g of water at 23.6 °C in a coffee cup calorimeter. After mixing, the temperature of the solution was 20.3 °C. Assume no energy as heat is transferred to the cup or the surroundings. Find the enthalpy of solution, $\Delta_{soln}H$, of KBr. (The specific heat capacity of the solution is assumed to be 4.184 J/g·K.)
Text Section 5.6
OWL: 5.6b

39. (Chapter 5) The enthalpy of combustion of isooctane (C_8H_{18}) is 5.45×10^3 kJ/mol. Calculate the energy transferred as heat per gram of isooctane and per liter of isooctane ($d = 0.688$ g/mL). (Isooctane is one of many hydrocarbons in gasoline, and its enthalpy of combustion will approximate the energy obtained when gasoline burns.)

Isooctane
C_8H_{18}

Text Section 5.5
OWL: 1.5c, 2.9g, 2.9h, 3.2d

40. (Chapters 4 and 5) Hydrogen can be produced (along with CO) using the reaction of steam (H_2O) with carbon (as coal), methane, and other hydrocarbons. For example,

$$C(s) + H_2O(g) \rightarrow H_2(g) + CO(g)$$

(a) Compare the mass of H_2 expected from the reaction of steam with 100. g each of methane, petroleum, and coal. (Assume complete reaction in each case. Use CH_2 and C as representative formulas for petroleum and coal, respectively.)
(b) Compare the values of $\Delta_rH°$ for the reactions of 1.00 mol of carbon and 1.00 mol of methane with steam. Which involves more energy?
Text Sections 4.1 and 5.7
OWL: 4.1c, 5.7d

41. (All chapters) On page 254 you see the decomposition of solid NH_4Cl to form gaseous NH_3 and HCl.
(a) Write a balanced chemical equation for the decomposition of NH_4Cl.
(b) When NH_3 and HCl recombine to form NH_4Cl, is this an oxidation-reduction reaction?
(c) Name each of the compounds involved.
(d) Calculate $\Delta_rH°$ for the decomposition of 1.00 mol of NH_4Cl.
(e) Determine the mass of NH_3 expected if you decompose 1.00 g of NH_4Cl.

(f) If the HCl from the decomposition (part e) is absorbed by 126 mL of water, what is the pH of the solution?
Text Sections 3.2, 3.7, 3.9, 4.1, and 5.7
OWL: 2.7k, 3.2d, 3.7a, 3.7e, 3.9b, 4.1c, 4.7g, 4.7h, and 5.7d

42. (Chapter 2) Prussian blue was first made by a German artist in 1704, but the nature of the compound was not understood until well into the 20th century. The formula for Prussian blue is $Fe_4[Fe(CN)_6]_3$.

Preparing Prussian blue from aqueous $FeCl_3$ and $K_4[Fe(CN)_6]$.

(a) ▲ Knowing that the CN group is the cyanide ion, CN^-, what are the charges on the two types of iron ions present in Prussian blue?
(b) What is the weight percent of iron in Prussian blue?
Text Sections 2.7 and 2.10
OWL: 2.7d, 2.10b

43. (Chapter 2) The structures of alanine and phenylalanine are illustrated here.

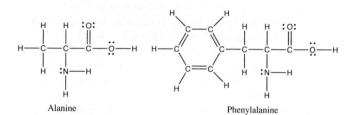

Alanine   Phenylalanine

(a) What is the molecular formula and molar mass of each of these amino acids?
(b) What structural elements do these molecules have in common?
(c) Which molecule has the greater mass percent of N?
(d) If you have 5.12 g of each, which sample has more molecules?
Text Sections 2.6, 2.9, and 2.10
OWL: 2.6, 2.9b, 2.9d, 2.10b

44. (Chapters 3–5) Titanium compounds, especially TiO_2 and $TiCl_4$, are important in industry. The chloride, $TiCl_4$, can be prepared by the reaction of white, solid TiO_2 with chlorine gas and carbon to give liquid $TiCl_4$ and carbon dioxide gas.

(a) Write a balanced chemical equation for this reaction.

(b) Name the compounds TiO_2 and $TiCl_4$.

(c) Calculate the enthalpy change for the reaction. Is the reaction exo- or endothermic?

(d) If 1.000 kg of TiO_2 is treated with 1.000 kg of chlorine gas, what mass of $TiCl_4$ can be produced? If 893 g of $TiCl_4$ are produced, what is the percent yield?

Text Sections 2.7, 3.2, 4.1, 4.2, and 5.7

OWL: 3.2d, 3.9b, 4.2f, 5.7d

45. (Chapter 5) ▲ Calculate the enthalpy change for the reaction

$$CaC_2(s) + 2 H_2O(\ell) \rightarrow Ca(OH)_2(s) + C_2H_2(g)$$

based on the enthalpy changes for the following reactions:

$$H_2(g) + 1/2 O_2(g) \rightarrow H_2O(\ell)$$
$$\Delta_r H° = -285.83 \text{ kJ/mol-rxn}$$

$$C(s) + 1/2 O_2(g) \rightarrow CO(g)$$
$$\Delta_r H° = -110.525 \text{ kJ/mol-rxn}$$

$$2 C(s) + H_2(g) \rightarrow C_2H_2(g) \quad \Delta_r H° = 226.73 \text{ kJ/mol-rxn}$$

$$CaO(s) + H_2O(\ell) \rightarrow Ca(OH)_2(s)$$
$$\Delta_r H° = -65.17 \text{ kJ/mol-rxn}$$

$$CaO(s) + 3 C(s) \rightarrow CaC_2(s) + CO(g)$$
$$\Delta_r H° = 464.77 \text{ kJ/mol-rxn}$$

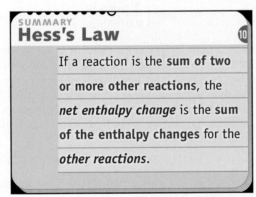

SUMMARY

Hess's Law   10

If a reaction is the **sum of two or more other reactions**, the **net enthalpy change** is the **sum of the enthalpy changes** for the **other reactions**.

Screen from Go Chemistry module 10 on Hess's law.

Text Section 5.7

OWL: 5.7b

Answers to Assessing Key Points Questions

1. The nonmetal, sulfur (S), has 16 protons. The ^{32}S isotope, with 16 neutrons, is more abundant because the atomic weight is very close to 32. ^{34}S has 18 neutrons. A common ion is S^{2-}.

2. 3.08×10^{-4} mol Ar and 1.85×10^{20} atoms

3. NH_4^+, Br^-, ammonium bromide, NH_4Br

   Fe^{2+}, SO_4^{2-}, iron(II) sulfate, $FeSO_4$

   Mg^{2+}, $CH_3CO_2^-$, magnesium acetate, $Mg(CH_3CO_2)_2$

   Al^{3+}, NO_3^-, aluminum nitrate, $Al(NO_3)_3$

4. 0.50 mol of SiO_2 (with a molar mass of 60.1 g/mol) has more mass (30. g) than 0.50 mol of Fe (55.85 g/mol) (28 g).

5. 246.5 g/mol. **Comment:** Make sure to add in 7 mol of H_2O.

6. (e) The calcium ion is always Ca^{2+}, and the hydrogen phosphate ion is HPO_4^{2-}. The correct formula is $CaHPO_4$.

7. Based on the formula of $Na_2C_2O_4$ you know the oxalate ion has a 2− charge, $C_2O_4^{2-}$. Thus, the correct formula is (d).

8. (c) Answers (a) and (d) also have correct ions, but two of the ions (Al^{3+} and Fe^{3+}) are based on metals.

9. (a) $Fe_2O_3(s) + 3 Mg(s) \rightarrow 3 MgO(s) + 2 Fe(s)$
   (b) $C_6H_5CH_3(\ell) + 9 O_2(g) \rightarrow 4 H_2O(\ell) + 7 CO_2(g)$

10. Stoichiometry

$$1.6 \text{ mol Fe} \left(\frac{3 \text{ mol } O_2}{4 \text{ mol Fe}} \right) = 1.2 \text{ mol } O_2 \text{ required}$$

$$1.6 \text{ mol Fe} \left(\frac{2 \text{ mol } Fe_2O_3}{4 \text{ mol Fe}} \right) = 0.80 \text{ mol } Fe_2O_3 \text{ produced}$$

$$1.6 \text{ mol Fe} \left(\frac{55.85 \text{ g Fe}}{\text{mol Fe}} \right) = 89 \text{ g Fe}$$

$$1.2 \text{ mol } O_2 \left(\frac{32.0 \text{ g } O_2}{\text{mol } O_2} \right) = 38 \text{ g } O_2$$

$$0.80 \text{ mol } Fe_2O_3 \left(\frac{159.7 \text{ g } Fe_2O_3}{\text{mol } Fe_2O_3} \right) = 130 \text{ g } Fe_2O_3$$

11. Br = +5; C = +3; S = +6

12. N in NO_3^- is +5. Zn is oxidized (oxidation number goes from 0 to +2) and the oxidizing agent is NO_3^-. (Note that the oxidation number of N goes from +5 to +4.)

13.

$$0.250 \text{ L} \left(\frac{0.100 \text{ mol}}{\text{L}} \right) \left(\frac{106.0 \text{ g } Na_2CO_3}{1 \text{ mol } Na_2CO_3} \right) = 2.65 \text{ g } Na_2CO_3$$

The Na^+ concentration is $2 \times 0.100 \text{ M} = 0.200 \text{ M}$

14. Here we can use the shortcut equation $c_c \cdot V_c = c_d \cdot V_d$. See Problem-Solving Tip 4.3, page 179.

$$\left(\frac{0.160 \text{ mol } H_2SO_4}{\text{L}} \right)(0.125 \text{ L}) = \left(c_{\text{dilute}} \right)(1.00 \text{ L})$$

$$c_{\text{dilute}} = \frac{0.0200 \text{ mol } H_2SO_4}{\text{L}} = 0.0200 \text{ M}$$

15. $Ba(NO_3)_2$, Na_2SO_4, KCl, $Mg(CH_3CO_2)_2$. Nitrates, sodium salts, potassium salts, and acetates are almost always soluble in water.

16. $Na_2CO_3(aq) + 2 HNO_3(aq)$
$$\rightarrow 2 NaNO_3(aq) + CO_2(g) + H_2O(\ell)$$

This is a gas-forming reaction.

17. $pH = -\log [H_3O^+]$ or $[H_3O^+] = 10^{-pH}$. See page 179, Equation 4.3 and page 181, Equation 4.4.

$$[H_3O^+] = 1 \times 10^{-4.52} = 3.0 \times 10^{-5} \text{ M}$$

Comment: Don't forget that the power of 10 is a negative number when using the equation $[H_3O^+] = 10^{-pH}$.

18. The first step is to write a balanced equation for the reaction. See the answer to 16 above.

$$0.412 \text{ g Na}_2CO_3 \left(\frac{1 \text{ mol Na}_2CO_3}{106.0 \text{ g Na}_2CO_3} \right)$$
$$= 3.89 \times 10^{-3} \text{ mol Na}_2CO_3$$

$$3.89 \times 10^{-3} \text{ mol Na}_2CO_3 \left(\frac{2 \text{ mol HNO}_3}{1 \text{ mol Na}_2CO_3} \right)$$
$$= 7.77 \times 10^{-3} \text{ mol HNO}_3$$

$$\frac{7.77 \times 10^{-3} \text{ mol HNO}_3}{0.03563 \text{ L}} = 0.218 \text{ M HNO}_3$$

19. Complete balanced equation:

$$2 NaOH(aq) + FeCl_2(aq) \rightarrow 2 NaCl(aq) + Fe(OH)_2(s)$$

Net ionic equation:

$$2 OH^-(aq) + Fe^{2+}(aq) \rightarrow Fe(OH)_2(s)$$

20. Use Equation 5.1 on page 215.

$$q = (225 \text{ g})(4.184 \text{ J/g·K})(366 \text{ K} - 298 \text{ K}) = 6.40 \times 10^4 \text{ J}$$

21. Use Equation 5.6 on page 237.

$$\Delta_r H° = 3 \Delta_f H°[CO_2(g)] + 4 \Delta_f H°[H_2O(g)]$$
$$- \{\Delta_f H°[C_3H_8(g)] + 5 \Delta_f H°[O_2(g)]\}$$
$$= (3 \text{ mol CO}_2/1 \text{ mol-rxn})(-393.5 \text{ kJ/mol CO}_2)$$
$$+ (4 \text{ mol H}_2O/1 \text{ mol-rxn})(-241.8 \text{ kJ/mol H}_2O)$$
$$- [(1 \text{ mol C}_3H_8/1 \text{ mol-rxn})(-104.7 \text{ kJ/mol C}_3H_8)$$
$$+ (5 \text{ mol O}_2/1 \text{ mol-rxn})(0 \text{ kJ/mol O}_2)]$$
$$= -2043.0 \text{ kJ/mol-rxn}$$

Reaction is exothermic. The energy transferred as heat per mole of C_3H_8 is 2043.0 kJ.

Solutions to Comprehensive Questions

22. (a) The atomic weight of gold is 196.967, so the mass number of the single gold isotope is 197 ($^{197}_{79}Au$).

Mass number = 197 = No. of protons + no. of neutrons

No. of neutrons = 118

(b) Calculate the volume of the piece of gold. Let us first convert amount of gold (mol) to mass (g) using the atomic weight and then convert the mass to a volume using the density.

$$0.0125 \text{ mol} \left(\frac{196.967 \text{ g}}{1 \text{ mol}} \right) = 2.46 \text{ g}$$

$$2.46 \text{ g} \left(\frac{1 \text{ cm}^3}{19.3 \text{ g}} \right) = 0.128 \text{ cm}^3$$

Calculate the number of atoms of gold from the amount of gold using Avogadro's number.

$$0.0125 \text{ mol Au} \left(\frac{6.022 \times 10^{23} \text{ atoms Au}}{1 \text{ mol Au}} \right)$$
$$= 7.53 \times 10^{21} \text{ atoms Au}$$

(c) The strategy here is first to calculate the volume of the nanoparticle. Next, we find the volume occupied by gold atoms. The third step is to calculate the volume of one gold atom. Finally, we divide the volume occupied by gold atoms by the volume of one gold atom.

$$\text{Volume of gold nanoparticle} = \frac{4}{3}\pi r^3$$
$$= \frac{4}{3}\pi(1.50 \text{ nm})^3 = 14.1 \text{ nm}^3$$

Volume of particle occupied by gold atoms
$$= 14.1 \text{ nm}^3 (0.740) = 10.5 \text{ nm}^3$$

$$\text{Volume of one gold atom} = \frac{4}{3}\pi r^3$$
$$= \frac{4}{3}\pi(0.144 \text{ nm})^3 = 0.0125 \text{ nm}^3 \text{ per atom}$$

Number of atoms in the nanoparticle
$$= 10.5 \text{ nm}^3 \left(\frac{1 \text{ atom Au}}{0.0125 \text{ nm}^3} \right) = 836 \text{ Au atoms}$$

23. (a) The atomic weight of an element is the weighted average of the isotopic weights and their abundances. The atomic weight of copper is closer to 63 than to 65 so ^{63}Cu is more abundant than ^{65}Cu.

(b) To calculate the isotopes abundances begin by assuming the percent abundance of ^{63}Cu is X and that of ^{65}Cu is Y. Therefore,

$$63.546 \text{ u} = (X/100)(62.930 \text{ u}) + (Y/100)(64.928 \text{ u})$$

Because X + Y must equal 100, this means that Y = 100 − X, and so

$$63.546 \text{ u} = (X/100)(62.930 \text{ u}) + [(100 - X)/100](64.928 \text{ u})$$

Solving for X, we find a percent abundance of 69.17%. This means Y is 30.83%.

(c) $CuCO_3$, copper(II) carbonate, Cu^{2+}
Cu_2S, copper(I) sulfide, Cu^+

(d) The strategy here is to find the volume of the wire (cm^3), convert that volume to a mass (g) using the density, and then find the amount of copper using the molar mass.

$$\text{Volume of wire} = \pi r^2(\text{length})$$
$$= \pi(0.125 \text{ cm})^2(16.0 \text{ cm})$$
$$= 0.785 \text{ cm}^3$$

$$\text{Mass of copper} = 0.785 \text{ cm}^3 \left(\frac{8.96 \text{ g Cu}}{1 \text{ cm}^3} \right)$$
$$= 7.04 \text{ g Cu}$$
$$\text{Amount of copper} = 7.04 \text{ g Cu} \left(\frac{1 \text{ mol Cu}}{63.55 \text{ g Cu}} \right)$$
$$= 0.111 \text{ mol Cu}$$

The number of atoms can be found from the amount and Avogadro's number.

Number of atoms in the wire
$$= 0.111 \text{ mol Cu} \left(\frac{6.022 \times 10^{23} \text{ atoms Cu}}{1 \text{ mol Cu}} \right)$$
$$= 6.67 \times 10^{22} \text{ atoms Cu}$$

24. (a) ^{238}U has 92 proton and 146 neutrons. ^{235}U has 92 protons and 143 neutrons.
    (b) Formulas

Formula	Name	Molar Mass (g/mol)	Charge on U
UO_2	uranium(IV) oxide	270.0	+4
$U(SO_4)_2$	uranium(IV) sulfate	430.2	+4
UF_6	uranium(VI) fluoride	352.0	+6

25. This question is similar to question 23b above. Here we want to find the mass of one isotope knowing the mass of the other isotope and the percent abundance of each.

Atomic mass of silver = 107.868 u
= (51.839/100)(106.905 u) + [(100 − 51.839)/100] X

where X = mass of other silver isotope = 108.905 u. The mass number of the isotope is 109 (^{109}Ag).

26. (a) The name of the mineral is calcium fluoride
    (b) Ca^{2+} ions have 18 electrons, the same as the number of electrons in argon, Ar. F^- ions have 10 electrons, the same as the number of electrons in Ne.
    (c) $CaF_2 + H_2SO_4 \rightarrow CaSO_4 + 2 HF$
    (d) See Problem-Solving Tip 4.1 on page 160. First convert the mass of CaF_2 to amount (mol). Next, use the stoichiometric factor to calculate the amount of HF expected (the theoretical yield). Finally, convert this amount to mass.

$$1.0 \times 10^3 \text{ g CaF}_2 \left(\frac{1 \text{ mol}}{78.07 \text{ g CaF}_2} \right) = 13 \text{ mol CaF}_2$$
$$13 \text{ ml CaF}_2 \left(\frac{2 \text{ mol HF}}{1 \text{ mol CaF}_2} \right) = 26 \text{ mol HF}$$
$$26 \text{ mol HF} \left(\frac{20.0 \text{ g}}{1 \text{ mol HF}} \right) = 5.1 \times 10^2 \text{ g HF}$$

27. (a) Molecular formula: $C_6H_{11}NO$
    Comment: Note that it is usual to write formulas of compounds having C and H with those elements first. Any other elements follow in alphabetical order.
    (b) Molar mass: 113.2 g/mol
    (c) The mass percent is calculated as on page 89.

    Mass percent of carbon
    $$= \frac{6 \text{ mol C } (12.011 \text{ g/mol C})}{113.2 \text{ g/mol caprolactam}} \times 100\% = 63.66\%$$

    In the same manner, we find 9.80% for H, 12.38% for N, and 14.14% for O.
    (d) The first step is to convert the mass of ammonium sulfate to grams and then use the density to calculate the volume in cubic centimeters. This is used to calculate the volume in units of cubic meters.

    Volume occupied by $(NH_4)_2SO_4$
    $$= 4.00 \times 10^3 \text{ kg} \left(\frac{1 \times 10^3 \text{ g}}{\text{kg}} \right) \left(\frac{1 \text{ cm}^3}{1.77 \text{ g}} \right)$$
    $$= 2.26 \times 10^6 \text{ cm}^3$$
    Volume in cubic meters
    $$= 2.26 \times 10^6 \text{ cm}^3 \left(\frac{1 \text{ m}}{100 \text{ cm}} \right)^3 = 2.26 \text{ m}^3$$

28. (a)

Atom/Ion	Protons	Electrons
Fe	26	26
Fe^{2+}	26	24
Fe^{3+}	26	23

The most oxidized form is Fe^{3+}.
Comment: Students occasionally and incorrectly add electrons to make a positive ion and subtract them to make a negative, the opposite of the correct procedure. Remember that the plus or minus sign on the ion indicates its electric charge. Positive ions occur when there are fewer electrons than protons, and negative ions result when there are more electrons than protons.

(b)

Formula	Name
$Fe(CH_3CO_2)_2$	Iron(II) acetate
$FePO_4$	Iron(III) phosphate
$Fe(ClO_4)_3$	Iron(III) perchlorate

29. We assume that the weight percent of an element is the mass of the element in a 100-g sample. To find the empirical formula, you first find the amount (mol) of each element in the 100-g sample, then compare the amounts of all elements in the 100-g sample. These amounts are in the same ratio as the number of atoms in one molecule or formula unit.

$$74.14 \text{ g W} \left(\frac{1 \text{ mol W}}{183.84 \text{ g}} \right) = 0.4033 \text{ mol W}$$

$$25.86 \text{ g S} \left(\frac{1 \text{ mol S}}{32.066 \text{ g}} \right) = 0.8065 \text{ mol S}$$

$$\frac{0.8065 \text{ mol S}}{0.4033 \text{ mol W}} = \frac{2 \text{ mol S}}{1 \text{ mol W}}$$

The formula of the compound is WS_2.

Comment: When finding a formula from weight percent data, always use as many significant figures as possible (usually at least 3). See Problem-Solving Tip 2.3 on page 91.

30. This follows the same procedure as in question 29.

$$72.26 \text{ g C} \left(\frac{1 \text{ mol C}}{12.011 \text{ g}} \right) = 6.016 \text{ mol C}$$

$$8.49 \text{ g H} \left(\frac{1 \text{ mol H}}{1.008 \text{ g}} \right) = 8.423 \text{ mol H}$$

$$19.25 \text{ g O} \left(\frac{1 \text{ mol O}}{15.999 \text{ g}} \right) = 1.203 \text{ mol O}$$

With the amount of each element in a 100-g sample known, we divide each amount by the amount of the element present in the smallest amount (here oxygen).

$$\frac{6.016 \text{ mol C}}{1.203 \text{ mol O}} = 5 \text{ C to } 1 \text{ O} \qquad \frac{8.423 \text{ mol H}}{1.203 \text{ mol O}} = 7 \text{ H to } 1 \text{ O}$$

This leads to an empirical formula of C_5H_7O. Because the experimental molar mass (166.21 g/mol) is twice the empirical formula mass, the molecular formula is $C_{10}H_{14}O_2$. The structure of the active ingredient in catnip is illustrated here.

Nepetalactone, catnip

31. (a) After calculating the amount of C_2H_5OH, we use a stoichiometric factor to relate the amount of H_2 produced to the amount of C_2H_5OH available.

$$1.00 \times 10^3 \text{ g } C_2H_5OH \left(\frac{1 \text{ mol } C_2H_5OH}{46.07 \text{ g}} \right)$$
$$= 21.7 \text{ mol } C_2H_5OH$$

$$21.7 \text{ mol } C_2H_5OH \left(\frac{10 \text{ mol } H_2}{2 \text{ mol } C_2H_5OH} \right) = 109 \text{ mol } H_2$$

$$109 \text{ mol } H_2 \left(\frac{2.016 \text{ g}}{1 \text{ mol } H_2} \right) = 219 \text{ g } H_2$$

(b) The amount of C_2H_5OH is known from part (a), and this can be related to the amount and mass of H_2O and O_2 required, again using the appropriate stoichiometric factors.

$$21.7 \text{ mol } C_2H_5OH \left(\frac{1 \text{ mol } O_2 \text{ required}}{2 \text{ mol } C_2H_5OH \text{ available}} \right)$$
$$= 10.9 \text{ mol } O_2 \text{ required}$$

$$10.9 \text{ mol } O_2 \left(\frac{32.0 \text{ g } O_2}{1 \text{ mol } O_2} \right) = 347 \text{ g } O_2 \text{ required}$$

$$21.7 \text{ mol } C_2H_5OH \left(\frac{4 \text{ mol } H_2O \text{ required}}{2 \text{ mol } C_2H_5OH \text{ available}} \right)$$
$$= 43.4 \text{ mol } H_2O \text{ required}$$

$$43.4 \text{ mol } H_2O \left(\frac{18.02 \text{ g } H_2O}{1 \text{ mol } H_2O} \right) = 782 \text{ g } H_2O \text{ required}$$

32. Stoichiometry and thermochemistry of methanol production

(a) $2 CH_4(g) + O_2(g) \rightarrow 2 CH_3OH(g)$

(b) This is a limiting reactant problem, so we first calculate the amounts of each reactant and then determine if they are in the correct stoichiometric ratio or if one is in limited supply.

$$125 \text{ g } CH_4 \left(\frac{1 \text{ mol } CH_4}{16.04 \text{ g } CH_4} \right) = 7.79 \text{ mol } CH_4$$

$$145 \text{ g } O_2 \left(\frac{1 \text{ mol } O_2}{31.999 \text{ g } O_2} \right) = 4.53 \text{ mol } O_2$$

$$\text{Ratio of amounts} = \frac{7.79 \text{ mol } CH_4}{4.53 \text{ mol } O_2} = \frac{1.72 \text{ mol } CH_4}{1.00 \text{ mol } O_2}$$

The balanced equation specifies there should be twice as much CH_4 as O_2. The ratio of amounts available (1.72 mol CH_4 to 1.00 mol O_2) is less than the required 2 to 1, so CH_4 is the limiting reactant and is used in the stoichiometric calculation.

$$7.79 \text{ mol } CH_4 \left(\frac{2 \text{ mol } CH_3OH}{2 \text{ mol } CH_4} \right) = 7.79 \text{ mol } CH_3OH$$

$$7.79 \text{ mol } CH_3OH \left(\frac{32.04 \text{ g } CH_3OH}{1 \text{ mol } CH_3OH} \right)$$
$$= 250. \text{ g } CH_3OH$$

(c) See Equation 5.6 on page 237 for the way to calculate the enthalpy change for a reaction from enthalpies of formation.

$$\Delta_r H° = 2 \Delta_f H°[CH_3OH(g)]$$
$$- \{2 \Delta_f H°[CH_4(g)] + \Delta_f H°[O_2(g)]\}$$
$$\Delta_r H° = (2 \text{ mol } CH_3OH/1 \text{ mol-rxn})(-201.0 \text{ kJ/mol } CH_3OH)$$
$$- (2 \text{ mol } CH_4/1 \text{ mol-rxn})(-74.87 \text{ kJ/mol } CH_4)$$
$$\Delta_r H° = -252.3 \text{ kJ/mol-rxn}$$

The reaction is exothermic.

$$1.00 \times 10^3 \text{ g CH}_4 \left(\frac{1 \text{ mol CH}_4}{16.04 \text{ g CH}_4} \right) = 62.3 \text{ mol CH}_4$$

$$62.3 \text{ mol CH}_4 \left(\frac{1 \text{ mol-rxn}}{2 \text{ mol CH}_4} \right) \left(\frac{-252.3 \text{ kJ}}{1 \text{ mol-rxn}} \right)$$
$$= -7860 \text{ kJ for } 1.00 \text{ kg of CH}_4$$

33. (a) CN^- is the cyanide ion and KCN is potassium cyanide.

(b) Oxygen begins with an oxidation number of 0 in O_2 and appears as an O atom with an oxidation number of -2 in H_2O. Thus, the oxygen is reduced and is the oxidizing agent. Gold begins as gold(0), whereas it is the Au^+ ion in the anion $[Au(CN)_2]^-$. This means the gold has been oxidized and is the reducing agent.

(c) Mass of KCN required by 1.00 kg of gold

$$1.00 \times 10^3 \text{ g Au} \left(\frac{1 \text{ mol Au}}{196.97 \text{ g Au}} \right) = 5.08 \text{ mol Au}$$

$$5.08 \text{ mol Au} \left(\frac{8 \text{ mol KCN required}}{4 \text{ mol Au available}} \right)$$
$$= 10.2 \text{ mol KCN required}$$

$$10.2 \text{ mol KCN} \left(\frac{65.12 \text{ g KCN}}{1 \text{ mol KCN}} \right) = 661 \text{ g KCN}$$

(d) Volume of 0.15 M KCN solution required by 1.00 kg of gold

$$10.2 \text{ mol KCN} \left(\frac{1 \text{ L}}{0.15 \text{ mol KCN}} \right) = 68 \text{ L KCN solution}$$

34. (a) Use the percent composition to determine the empirical formula.

$$77.09 \text{ g C} \left(\frac{1 \text{ mol C}}{12.011 \text{ g C}} \right) = 6.418 \text{ mol C}$$

$$11.50 \text{ g H} \left(\frac{1 \text{ mol H}}{1.008 \text{ g H}} \right) = 11.41 \text{ mol H}$$

$$11.41 \text{ g O} \left(\frac{1 \text{ mol O}}{15.999 \text{ g O}} \right) = 0.7132 \text{ mol O}$$

To find the empirical formula, find the ratio of amounts of the elements.

$$\frac{6.418 \text{ mol C}}{0.7132 \text{ mol O}} = \frac{9 \text{ mol C}}{1 \text{ mol O}} \qquad \frac{11.41 \text{ mol H}}{0.7132 \text{ mol O}} = \frac{16 \text{ mol H}}{1 \text{ mol O}}$$

The empirical formula is $C_9H_{16}O$.

(b) Use titration data to determine the molar mass and thus the molecular formula.

$$0.03894 \text{ L NaOH soln} \left(\frac{0.113 \text{ mol NaOH}}{1 \text{ L NaOH}} \right)$$
$$= 4.40 \times 10^{-3} \text{ mol NaOH}$$

Because each molecule of fatty acid has only one acid group to react with a base, the amount of acid in the sample is 4.40×10^{-3} mol. The molar mass is

$$\text{Molar mass} = \frac{\text{sample mass}}{\text{amount of acid in sample}}$$
$$= \frac{1.234 \text{ g}}{4.40 \times 10^{-3} \text{ mol}} = 2.80 \times 10^2 \text{ g/mol}$$

This is twice the molar mass of the empirical formula, so the molecular formula is therefore $C_{18}H_{32}O_2$.

(c) Number of double bonds in the carbon chain.

$$0.636 \text{ g I}_2 \left(\frac{1 \text{ mol I}_2}{253.8 \text{ g I}_2} \right)$$
$$= 2.51 \times 10^{-3} \text{ mol I}_2 \text{ and mol of}$$
$$\text{double bonds in carbon chain}$$

$$0.351 \text{ g fatty acid} \left(\frac{1 \text{ mol fatty acid}}{280.4 \text{ g fatty acid}} \right)$$
$$= 1.25 \times 10^{-3} \text{ mol fatty acid}$$
$$\frac{2.51 \times 10^{-3} \text{ mol double bonds}}{1.25 \times 10^{-3} \text{ mol fatty acid}}$$
$$= 2 \text{ mol double bonds per mol of fatty acid}$$

35. (a) $Ag^+(aq) + Cl^-(aq) \rightarrow AgCl(s)$

(b) Complete equation:

$$2 \text{ AgNO}_3(aq) + K_2CrO_4(aq)$$
$$\rightarrow Ag_2CrO_4(s) + 2 \text{ KNO}_3(aq)$$

Net ionic equation:

$$2 \text{ Ag}^+(aq) + CrO_4{}^{2-}(aq) \rightarrow Ag_2CrO_4(s)$$

(c) Concentration of chloride ions: From the volume and concentration of silver ions used in the titration, we know the amount of silver used.

$$0.02560 \text{ L AgNO}_3 \left(\frac{1.036 \times 10^{-3} \text{ mol Ag}^+}{1 \text{ L AgNO}_3} \right)$$
$$= 2.652 \times 10^{-5} \text{ mol Ag}^+$$

Because each silver ion reacts with one Cl^- ion, the 50.0-mL sample contained 2.652×10^{-5} mol Cl^-.

$$2.652 \times 10^{-5} \text{ mol Cl}^- \left(\frac{35.453 \text{ g Cl}^-}{1 \text{ mol Cl}} \right) \left(\frac{1000 \text{ mg}}{1 \text{ g}} \right)$$
$$= 0.9403 \text{ mg Cl}^-$$

$$Cl^- \text{ concentration in the water} = \frac{\text{mass of Cl}^-}{\text{sample volume}}$$
$$= \left(\frac{0.9403 \text{ mg Cl}^-}{50.0 \text{ mL}} \right) \left(\frac{1000 \text{ mL}}{\text{L}} \right) = 18.8 \text{ mg/L}$$

The Cl^- concentration is sufficient.

36. From the combustion of the compound we can find the amount and mass of C and H in the 0.463-g sample.

$$0.818 \text{ g CO}_2 \left(\frac{1 \text{ mol CO}_2}{44.01 \text{ g CO}_2} \right) \left(\frac{1 \text{ mol C}}{1 \text{ mol CO}_2} \right)$$
$$= 0.0186 \text{ mol C}$$

$$0.0186 \text{ mol C} \left(\frac{12.011 \text{ g C}}{1 \text{ mol C}} \right) = 0.223 \text{ g C}$$

$$0.168 \text{ g H}_2\text{O} \left(\frac{1 \text{ mol H}_2\text{O}}{18.02 \text{ g H}_2\text{O}} \right) \left(\frac{2 \text{ mol H}}{1 \text{ mol H}_2\text{O}} \right)$$
$$= 0.0186 \text{ mol H}$$

$$0.0186 \text{ mol H} \left(\frac{1.008 \text{ g H}}{1 \text{ mol H}} \right) = 0.0188 \text{ g H}$$

By precipitating the Cl as AgCl, we find the amount and mass of Cl in the sample.

$$0.533 \text{ g AgCl} \left(\frac{1 \text{ mol AgCl}}{143.3 \text{ g AgCl}} \right) \left(\frac{1 \text{ mol Cl}}{1 \text{ mol AgCl}} \right)$$
$$= 0.00372 \text{ mol Cl}$$

$$0.00372 \text{ mol Cl} \left(\frac{35.45 \text{ g Cl}}{1 \text{ mol Cl}} \right) = 0.132 \text{ g Cl}$$

The total mass of C, H, and Cl in the 0.463-g sample is 0.374 g. Thus, the mass of Ti is 0.089 g or 1.9×10^{-3} mol.

$$0.089 \text{ g Ti} \left(\frac{1 \text{ mol Ti}}{47.9 \text{ g Ti}} \right) = 0.0019 \text{ mol Ti}$$

Ratio of amounts:

$$\frac{0.0186 \text{ mol C}}{0.0019 \text{ mol Ti}} = 10 \text{ C to 1 Ti}$$

$$\frac{0.0186 \text{ mol H}}{0.0019 \text{ mol Ti}} = 10 \text{ H to 1 Ti}$$

$$\frac{0.00372 \text{ mol Cl}}{0.0019 \text{ mol Ti}} = 2 \text{ Cl to 1 Ti}$$

The empirical formula of the compound is $C_{10}H_{10}TiCl_2$.

37. (a) $Ba(OH)_2(aq) + H_2SO_4(aq) \rightarrow BaSO_4(s) + 2 H_2O(\ell)$
    (b) $Ba^{2+}(aq) + 2 OH^-(aq) + 2 H_3O^+(aq) + SO_4^{2-}(aq)$
    $\rightarrow BaSO_4(s) + 4 H_2O(\ell)$
    (c) Plot (b). As H_2SO_4 is added to the $Ba(OH)_2$ solution, both are consumed, and the reaction products are both nonconducting. The number of ions in solution declines and so does the conductivity. At some point both of the reactants are completely consumed, so the conductivity drops to a minimum. If addition of H_2SO_4 continues, the conductivity increases due to excess H_2SO_4.

38. Calculate the energy as heat involved in the solution process.

$$q_{solution} = (105 \text{ g water} + 9.40 \text{ g KBr})(4.184 \text{ J/g·K})(-3.3 \text{ K})$$
$$= -1600 \text{ J}$$

The sign of the energy transferred as heat in the solution process is negative, indicating that the water has given energy as heat to the KBr.

Now we recognize that

$$q_{solution} + q_{KBr} = 0 \text{ and so } q_{KBr} = +1600 \text{ J}$$

Calculate the amount of KBr.

$$9.40 \text{ g KBr} \left(\frac{1 \text{ mol KBr}}{119.0 \text{ g KBr}} \right) = 0.0790 \text{ mol KBr}$$

Calculate the energy involved per mole.

$$\text{Enthalpy of solution per mol} = \frac{+1600 \text{ J}}{0.0790 \text{ mol KBr}}$$
$$= 2.0 \times 10^4 \text{ J/mol or 20. kJ/mol}$$

Comment: The solution process is endothermic, so the temperature drops when KBr dissolves, and q for the solution ($q_{solution}$) is a negative quantity. This means the heat of solution of KBr is a positive quantity. This can be verified using the enthalpies of formation.

$$\Delta_{soln}H° = \Delta_fH°[KBr(aq)] - \Delta_fH°[KBr(s)]$$
$$= (1 \text{ mol KBr(aq)}/1 \text{ mol-rxn})[-373.9 \text{ kJ/mol KBr(aq)}]$$
$$- (1 \text{ mol KBr(s)}/1 \text{ mol-rxn})[-393.8 \text{ kJ/mol KBr(s)}]$$
$$= +19.9 \text{ kJ/mol-rxn}$$

39. Burning isooctane.

$$\left(\frac{5.45 \times 10^3 \text{ kJ}}{1 \text{ mol isooctane}} \right) \left(\frac{1 \text{ mol isooctane}}{114.2 \text{ g}} \right) = 47.7 \text{ kJ/g}$$
$$\left(\frac{47.7 \text{ kJ}}{1 \text{ g isooctane}} \right) \left(\frac{0.688 \text{ g isooctane}}{\text{mL}} \right) \left(\frac{1000 \text{ mL}}{\text{L}} \right)$$
$$= 3.28 \times 10^4 \text{ kJ/L}$$

40. (a) Compare the mass of hydrogen obtained from methane, petroleum, and coal.

Methane: $CH_4(g) + H_2O(g) \rightarrow 3 H_2(g) + CO(g)$

$$100. \text{ g} \left(\frac{1 \text{ mol CH}_4}{16.04 \text{ g}} \right) \left(\frac{3 \text{ mol H}_2}{1 \text{ mol CH}_4} \right) \left(\frac{2.016 \text{ g H}_2}{1 \text{ mol H}_2} \right) = 37.7 \text{ g H}_2$$

Petroleum: $CH_2(g) + H_2O(g) \rightarrow 2 H_2(g) + CO(g)$

$$100. \text{ g} \left(\frac{1 \text{ mol CH}_2}{14.03 \text{ g}} \right) \left(\frac{2 \text{ mol H}_2}{1 \text{ mol CH}_2} \right) \left(\frac{2.016 \text{ g H}_2}{1 \text{ mol H}_2} \right) = 28.7 \text{ g H}_2$$

Coal: $C(s) + H_2O(g) \rightarrow H_2(g) + CO(g)$

$$100. \text{ g} \left(\frac{1 \text{ mol C}}{12.01 \text{ g}} \right) \left(\frac{1 \text{ mol H}_2}{1 \text{ mol C}} \right) \left(\frac{2.016 \text{ g H}_2}{1 \text{ mol H}_2} \right) = 16.8 \text{ g H}_2$$

(b) Enthapy changes for the reaction of steam with methane and coal.

Methane:

$$\Delta_rH° = \Delta_fH°[CO(g)] + 3 \Delta_fH°[H_2(g)]$$
$$- \{\Delta_fH°[CH_4(g)] + \Delta_fH°[H_2O(g)]\}$$
$$= (1 \text{ mol CO}_2/1 \text{ mol-rxn}) (-110.525 \text{ kJ/mol CO}_2)$$
$$+ (3 \text{ mol H}_2/1 \text{ mol-rxn}) (0 \text{ kJ/mol H}_2)$$
$$- [(1 \text{ mol CH}_4/1 \text{ mol-rxn}) (-74.87 \text{ kJ/mol CH}_4)$$
$$- (1 \text{ mol H}_2O/1 \text{ mol-rxn}) (-241.83 \text{ kJ/mol H}_2O)]$$
$$- +206.18 \text{ kJ/mol-rxn}$$

Coal:

$\Delta_r H^\circ = \Delta_f H^\circ \,[\mathrm{CO(g)}] + \Delta_f H^\circ \,[\mathrm{H_2(g)}]$
$\qquad - \{\Delta_f H^\circ \,[\mathrm{C(s)}] + \Delta_f H^\circ \,[\mathrm{H_2O(g)}]\}$
$= (1 \text{ mol CO}_2/1 \text{ mol-rxn})(-110.525 \text{ kJ/mol})$
$\qquad + (1 \text{ mol H}_2/1 \text{ mol-rxn})(0 \text{ kJ/mol})$
$\qquad - \left[\begin{array}{l} (1 \text{ mol C}/1 \text{ mol-rxn})(0 \text{ kJ/mol}) \\ + (1 \text{ mol H}_2\text{O}/1 \text{ mol-rxn})(-241.83 \text{ kJ/mol}) \end{array} \right]$
$= +131.31 \text{ kJ/mol-rxn}$

Methane requires more energy than coal per mol.

41. (a) $\mathrm{NH_4Cl(s)} \rightarrow \mathrm{NH_3(g)} + \mathrm{HCl(g)}$

    (b) The combination of $\mathrm{NH_3}$ and HCl is an acid-base reaction.

    (c) Ammonium chloride, ammonia, and hydrogen chloride

    (d) $\Delta_r H^\circ = \Delta_f H^\circ [\mathrm{NH_3(g)}] + \Delta_f H^\circ \,[\mathrm{HCl(g)}]$
$\qquad - \Delta_f H^\circ \,[\mathrm{NH_4Cl(s)}]$
$= (1 \text{ mol NH}_3/1 \text{ mol-rxn})(-45.90 \text{ kJ/mol})$
$\quad + (1 \text{ mol HCl}/1 \text{ mol-rxn})(-92.31 \text{ kJ/mol HCl})$
$\quad - (1 \text{ mol NH}_4\text{Cl}/1 \text{ mol-rxn})$
$\qquad\qquad (-314.55 \text{ kJ/mol NH}_4\text{Cl})$
$= +176.34 \text{ kJ/mol-rxn}$

    (e) Mass of ammonia expected from 1.0 g $\mathrm{NH_4Cl}$

$1.00 \text{ g NH}_4\text{Cl} \left(\dfrac{1 \text{ mol NH}_4\text{Cl}}{53.49 \text{ g}} \right) \left(\dfrac{1 \text{ mol NH}_3}{1 \text{ mol NH}_4\text{Cl}} \right) \left(\dfrac{17.03 \text{ g NH}_3}{1 \text{ mol NH}_3} \right)$
$= 0.318 \text{ g NH}_3$

    (f) pH of solution

$1.00 \text{ g NH}_4\text{Cl} \left(\dfrac{1 \text{ mol NH}_4\text{Cl}}{53.49 \text{ g}} \right) \left(\dfrac{1 \text{ mol HCl}}{1 \text{ mol NH}_4\text{Cl}} \right)$
$= 0.0187 \text{ mol HCl}$

Concentration of HCl solution $= \dfrac{0.0187 \text{ mol HCl}}{0.126 \text{ L}}$
$= 0.148 \text{ M}$

Hydrochloric acid is a strong acid, so the concentration of $\mathrm{H_3O^+}$ ion in solution is also 0.148 M. This gives a pH of 0.830.

$\mathrm{pH} = -\log [\mathrm{H_3O^+}] = -\log (0.148) = -(-0.830) = 0.830$

42. (a) $\mathrm{Fe_4[Fe(CN)_6]_3}$ is composed of four $\mathrm{Fe^{3+}}$ ions and, attached to the $\mathrm{CN^-}$ ions, a total of three $\mathrm{Fe^{2+}}$ ions. (There is one $\mathrm{Fe^{2+}}$ ion for each 6 $\mathrm{CN^-}$ ions.) That is, the ions are $(\mathrm{Fe^{3+}})_4[\mathrm{Fe^{2+}(CN)_6}]_3$.

    (b) Weight percent iron
$= \dfrac{7 \text{ mol Fe (55.845 g/mol Fe)}}{859.2 \text{ g of Prussian blue}} \times 100\% = 45.50\% \text{ Fe}$

43. (a) Alanine, $\mathrm{C_3H_7NO_2}$, 89.09 g/mol; phenylalanine, $\mathrm{C_9H_{11}NO_2}$, 165.19 g/mol.

    (b) Both molecules have the structural element $\mathrm{H_2N-CH-CO_2H}$. This is common to all of the α-amino acids that are found in proteins.

    (c) Both have 1 N atom per molecule. Because alanine has a lower molar mass, it has a greater weight percent of N (15.72%) than phenylalanine (8.48%).

    (d) Because alanine has a lower molar mass than phenylalanine, there are more molecules in a given mass of alanine (5.12 g or 0.0575 mol) than in the same mass of phenylalanine (0.0310 mol).

44. (a) $\mathrm{TiO_2(s)} + 2 \,\mathrm{Cl_2(g)} + \mathrm{C(s)} \rightarrow \mathrm{TiCl_4(\ell)} + \mathrm{CO_2(g)}$

    (b) $\mathrm{TiO_2}$ = titanium(IV) oxide; $\mathrm{TiCl_4}$ = titanium(IV) chloride

    (c) $\Delta_r H^\circ = \Delta_f H^\circ [\mathrm{TiCl_4(\ell)}] + \Delta_f H^\circ [\mathrm{CO_2(g)}]$
$\quad - \{\Delta_f H^\circ [\mathrm{TiO_2(s)}] + 2 \,\Delta_f H^\circ [\mathrm{Cl_2(g)}] +$
$\qquad\qquad\qquad\qquad\qquad \Delta_f H^\circ (\mathrm{C})\}$

    (c) $\Delta_r H^\circ = (1 \text{ mol TiCl}_4(\ell)/1 \text{ mol-rxn})$
$\qquad\qquad\qquad\qquad (-804.2 \text{ kJ/mol-rxn})$
$\quad + (1 \text{ mol CO}_2(\mathrm{g})/1 \text{ mol-rxn})$
$\qquad\qquad\qquad\qquad (-393.5 \text{ kJ/mol-rxn})$
$\quad - (1 \text{ mol TiO}_2(\mathrm{s})/1 \text{ mol-rxn})$
$\qquad\qquad\qquad\qquad (-939.7 \text{ kJ/mol-rxn})$
$= -258.0 \text{ kJ/mol-rxn}$
The reaction is exothermic.

    (d) First, decide on the limiting reactant

$1.000 \times 10^3 \text{ g TiO}_2 = 12.52 \text{ mol}$
$1.000 \times 10^3 \text{ g Cl}_2 = 14.10 \text{ mol}$

Now compare the amounts available:

$\dfrac{\text{mol Cl}_2}{\text{mol TiO}_2} = \dfrac{14.10 \text{ mol Cl}_2}{12.52 \text{ mol TiO}_2} = \dfrac{1.126 \text{ mol Cl}_2}{1 \text{ mol TiO}_2}$

This is less than the 2 to 1 ratio defined by the balanced equation, so $\mathrm{Cl_2}$ is the limiting reactant. Now calculate the theoretical yield of $\mathrm{TiCl_4}$.

$(14.10 \text{ mol Cl}_2)\left(\dfrac{1 \text{ mol TiCl}_4}{2 \text{ mol Cl}_2} \right)\left(\dfrac{189.68 \text{ g}}{1 \text{ mol TiCl}_4} \right)$
$= 1337 \text{ g TiCl}_4$

Percent yield $\mathrm{TiCl_4} = \left(\dfrac{893 \text{ g}}{1337 \text{ g}} \right)100\% = 66.8\%$

45. $\mathrm{H_2O(\ell)} \rightarrow \mathrm{H_2(g)} + 1/2 \,\mathrm{O_2(g)}$
$\qquad\qquad\qquad \Delta_r H^\circ = +285.83 \text{ kJ/mol-rxn}$

$\mathrm{C(s)} + 1/2 \,\mathrm{O_2(g)} \rightarrow \mathrm{CO(g)}$
$\qquad\qquad\qquad \Delta_r H^\circ = -110.525 \text{ kJ/mol-rxn}$

$2 \,\mathrm{C(s)} + \mathrm{H_2(g)} \rightarrow \mathrm{C_2H_2(g)} \qquad \Delta_r H^\circ = 226.73 \text{ kJ/mol-rxn}$

$\mathrm{CaC_2(s)} + \mathrm{CO(g)} \rightarrow \mathrm{CaO(s)} + 3 \,\mathrm{C(s)}$
$\qquad\qquad\qquad \Delta_r H^\circ = -464.77 \text{ kJ/mol-rxn}$

$\mathrm{CaO(s)} + \mathrm{H_2O(\ell)} \rightarrow \mathrm{Ca(OH)_2(s)}$
$\qquad\qquad\qquad \Delta_r H^\circ = -65.17 \text{ kJ/mol-rxn}$

$\rule{6cm}{0.4pt}$

$\mathrm{CaC_2(s)} + 2 \,\mathrm{H_2O(\ell)} \rightarrow \mathrm{Ca(OH)_2(s)} + \mathrm{C_2H_2(g)}$
$\qquad\qquad\qquad \Delta_r H^\circ = -127.91 \text{ kJ/mol-rxn}$

6 | The Structure of Atoms

©Arctic-Images/Corbis

Aurora Borealis

The beautiful display of "northern lights" can light up the night sky in the Northern Hemisphere. Colors can range from white to red, green, orange, and others. The display comes from the collision of electrons in the solar wind with atoms and molecules in the upper atmosphere near Earth's poles. This excites the atoms or molecules energetically, and they emit light.

Questions:

This photo shows an aurora with green light.
1. Which has the longer wavelength, red light or green light?
2. Which has the greater energy?
3. How do the colors of light emitted by excited atoms contribute to our understanding of electronic structure?

Answer to these questions are in Appendix Q.

OWL *See Chapter Goals Revisited (page 295) for Study Questions keyed to these goals and assignable in OWL.*

- Describe the properties of electromagnetic radiation.
- Understand the origin of light emitted by excited atoms and its relationship to atomic structure.
- Describe the experimental evidence for particle–wave duality.
- Describe the basic ideas of quantum mechanics.
- Define the four quantum numbers (n, ℓ, m_ℓ, and m_s) and recognize their relationship to electronic structure.

The work of the Curies, Rutherford, and other scientists early in the 20th century (Chapter 2 and pages 338–347) led to a model for an atom with a small nucleus of neutrons and protons containing most of the mass and with electrons surrounding the nucleus and filling most of the volume. This is still the basic model of the atom. But, at the beginning of the 21st century, is there a more useful model? Will a more complete model help us understand why atoms of different elements have different properties and help us predict properties of an element? To answer these and other questions, we want to probe more deeply into atomic structure in this and the next chapter.

Much of our understanding of atomic structure comes from a knowledge of how atoms interact with light and how excited atoms emit light. The first three sections of this chapter, therefore, describe radiation and its relation to our modern view of the atom.

Chemistry.Now™

Throughout the text this icon introduces an opportunity for self-study or to explore interactive tutorials by signing in at **www.cengage.com/login**.

6.1 Electromagnetic Radiation

In 1864, James Clerk Maxwell (1831–1879) developed a mathematical theory to describe all forms of radiation in terms of oscillating, or wave-like, electric and magnetic fields (Figure 6.1). Thus, light, microwaves, television and radio signals, x-rays, and other forms of radiation are now called **electromagnetic radiation**.

Electromagnetic radiation is characterized by its wavelength and frequency.

- **Wavelength**, symbolized by the Greek letter *lambda* (λ), is defined as the distance between successive crests or high points of a wave (or between successive troughs or low points). This distance can be given in meters, nanometers, or whatever unit of length is convenient.
- **Frequency**, symbolized by the Greek letter *nu* (ν), refers to the number of waves that pass a given point in some unit of time, usually per second. The unit for frequency, written either as s^{-1} or $1/s$ and standing for 1 per second, is now called a **hertz**.

Wavelength and frequency are related to the speed (c) at which a wave is propagated (Equation 6.1).

$$c \ (m/s) = \lambda \ (m) \times \nu \ (1/s) \tag{6.1}$$

■ **Heinrich Hertz** Heinrich Hertz (1857–1894) was the first person to send and receive radio waves. He showed that they could be reflected and refracted the same as light, confirming that different forms of radiation such as radio and light waves are related. Scientists now use "hertz" as the unit of frequency.

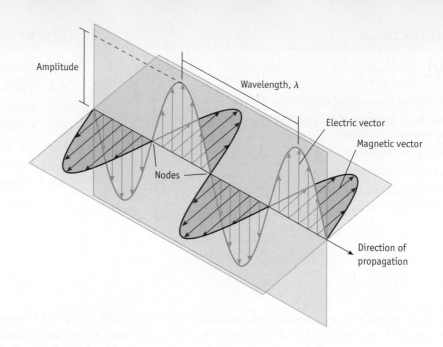

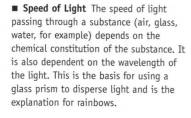

■ **Speed of Light** The speed of light
passing through a substance (air, glass,
water, for example) depends on the
chemical constitution of the substance. It
is also dependent on the wavelength of
the light. This is the basis for using a
glass prism to disperse light and is the
explanation for rainbows.

The speed of visible light and all other forms of electromagnetic radiation in a
vacuum is a constant, c (= 2.99792458×10^8 m/s; approximately 186,000 miles/s
or 1.079×10^9 km/h). For calculations, we will generally use the value of c with
four or fewer significant figures.

Different types of electromagnetic radiation are related, as shown in Figure 6.2.
Notice that visible light is only a very small portion of the total spectrum of electromagnetic radiation. Ultraviolet (UV) radiation, the radiation that can lead to
sunburn, has wavelengths shorter than those of visible light. X-rays and γ-rays, the
latter emitted in the process of radioactive disintegration of some atoms, have even
shorter wavelengths. At wavelengths longer than those of visible light, we first encounter infrared radiation (IR). At even longer wavelengths is the radiation used
in microwave ovens and in television and radio transmissions.

Chemistry‗ॐ‗Now™

Sign in at **www.cengage.com/login** and go to Chapter 6 Contents to see:
• Screen 6.3 for a tutorial on **calculating the frequency of ultraviolet light** and for a tutorial on **calculating
the wavelength of visible light**
• Screen 6.4 for a simulation exploring **the wavelength and frequency of visible light**

■ **EXAMPLE 6.1** **Wavelength–Frequency Conversions**

Problem The frequency of the radiation used in microwave ovens sold in the United States is 2.45 GHz.
(GHz stands for "gigahertz"; 1 GHz = 10^9 1/s.) What is the wavelength of this radiation in meters?

Strategy Rearrange Equation 6.1 to solve for λ, and then substitute the appropriate values into this
equation.

Solution

$$\lambda = \frac{c}{\nu} = \frac{2.998 \times 10^8 \text{ m/s}}{2.45 \times 10^9 \text{ 1/s}} = \boxed{0.122 \text{ m}}$$

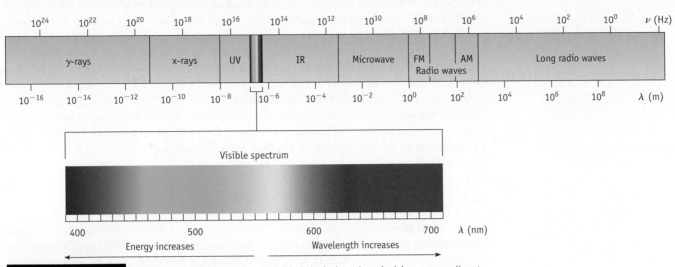

Active Figure 6.2 **The electromagnetic spectrum.** Visible light (enlarged portion) is a very small part of the entire spectrum. The radiation's energy increases from the radio-wave end of the spectrum (low frequency, ν, and long wavelength, λ) to the γ-ray end (high frequency and short wavelength).

Chemistry.Now™ Sign in at www.cengage.com/login and go to the Chapter Contents menu to explore an interactive version of this figure accompanied by an exercise.

EXERCISE 6.1 Radiation, Wavelength, and Frequency

(a) Which color in the visible spectrum has the highest frequency? Which has the lowest frequency?

(b) Is the frequency of the radiation used in a microwave oven higher or lower than that from your favorite FM radio station (for example, 91.7 MHz), where 1 MHz (megahertz) = 10^6 1/s?

(c) Is the wavelength of x-rays longer or shorter than that of ultraviolet light?

6.2 Quantization: Planck, Einstein, Energy, and Photons

Planck's Equation

If you heat a piece of metal to a high temperature, electromagnetic radiation is emitted with wavelengths that depend on temperature. At lower temperatures, the color is a dull red (Figure 6.3a). As the temperature increases, the red color brightens, and at even higher temperatures a brilliant white light is emitted.

Your eyes detect the radiation that occurs in the visible region of the electromagnetic spectrum. However, radiation with wavelengths both shorter (in the ultraviolet region) and longer (in the infrared region) than those of visible light is also given off by the hot metal (Figure 6.3b). In addition, it is observed that the wavelength of the most intense radiation is related to temperature: as the temperature of the metal is raised, the maximum intensity shifts toward shorter wavelengths (Figure 6.3b). This corresponds to the change in color observed as the temperature is raised.

At the end of the 19th century, scientists were not able to explain the relationship between the intensity and the wavelength for radiation given off by a heated object (often called *blackbody radiation*, Figure 6.3c). Theories available at the time predicted that the intensity should increase continuously with decreasing wavelength, instead of reaching a maximum and then declining as is actually observed. This perplexing situation became known as the *ultraviolet catastrophe* because predictions failed in the ultraviolet region.

In 1900, a German physicist, Max Planck (1858–1947), offered an explanation. Planck assumed that the electromagnetic radiation emitted was caused by vibrating atoms (called *oscillators*) in the heated object. He proposed that each oscillator had a fundamental frequency (ν) of oscillation and that the emitted radiation could have only certain energies, given by the equation

$$E = nh\nu$$

where n is a positive integer. That is, Planck proposed that the energy is *quantized*. **Quantization** means that only certain energies are allowed. The proportionality constant h in the equation is now called **Planck's constant** and its experimental

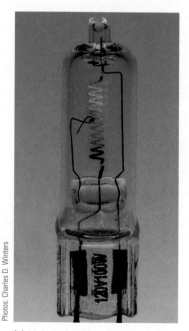

(a) Light emitted by a heated metal.

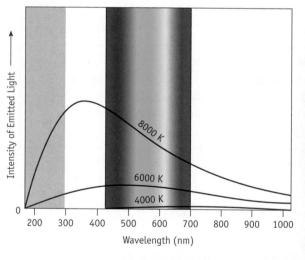

(b) The spectrum of light emitted by a heated metal at different temperatures.

(c) Blackbody radiation from burning charcoal.

FIGURE 6.3 The radiation given off by a heated body. (a) The heated filament of an incandescent bulb emits radiation at the long wavelength or red end of the visible spectrum. (b) When an object is heated, it emits radiation covering a spectrum of wavelengths. For a given temperature, some of the radiation is emitted at long wavelengths and some at short wavelengths. Most, however, is emitted at some intermediate wavelength, the maximum in the curve. As the temperature of the object increases, the maximum moves from the red end of the spectrum to the violet end. At still higher temperatures, intense light is emitted at all wavelengths in the visible region, and the maximum in the curve is in the ultraviolet region. The object is described as "white hot." (Stars are often referred to as "red giants" or "white dwarfs," a reference to their temperatures and relative sizes.) (c) In physics a blackbody is a theoretical concept in which a body absorbs all radiation that falls on it. However, it will emit energy with a temperature-dependent wavelength. The light emanating from the spaces between the burning charcoal briquets in this photo is a close approximation to blackbody radiation. The color of the light depends on the temperature of the briquets.

value is $6.6260693 \times 10^{-34}$ J · s. The unit of frequency is $1/s$, so the energy calculated using this equation is in joules (J). If an oscillator changes from a higher energy to a lower one, energy is emitted as electromagnetic radiation, where the difference in energy between the higher and lower energy states is

$$\Delta E = E_{higher\ n} - E_{lower\ n} = \Delta n h \nu$$

If the value of Δn is 1, which corresponds to changing from one energy level to the next lower one for that oscillator, then the energy change for the oscillator and the electromagnetic radiation emitted would have an energy equal to

$$E = h\nu \qquad \qquad \textbf{(6.2)}$$

This equation is called **Planck's equation.**

Now, assume as Planck did that there must be a *distribution* of vibrations of atoms in an object—some atoms are vibrating at a high frequency; some are vibrating at a low frequency, but most have some intermediate frequency. The few atoms with high-frequency vibrations are responsible for some of the light, as are those few with low-frequency vibrations. However, most of the light must come from the majority of the atoms that have intermediate vibrational frequencies. That is, a spectrum of light is emitted with a maximum intensity at some intermediate wavelength, in accord with experiment. The intensity should not become greater and greater on approaching the ultraviolet region. With this realization, the ultraviolet catastrophe was solved.

Einstein and the Photoelectric Effect

As often happens, the explanation of one fundamental phenomenon leads to other important discoveries. A few years after Planck's work, Albert Einstein (1879–1955) incorporated Planck's ideas into an explanation of the photoelectric effect and in doing so changed the model that described electromagnetic radiation.

In the photoelectric effect, electrons are ejected when light strikes the surface of a metal (Figure 6.4), but only if the frequency of the light is high enough. If light with a lower frequency is used, no electrons are ejected, regardless of the light's intensity (its brightness). If the frequency is at or above a minimum, critical frequency, increasing the light intensity causes more electrons to be ejected.

Einstein decided the experimental observations could be explained by combining Planck's equation ($E = h\nu$) with a new idea, that light has particle-like properties. Einstein characterized these massless particles, now called **photons,** as packets of energy, and stated that the energy of each photon is proportional to the frequency of the radiation as defined by Planck's equation. In the photoelectric effect, photons striking atoms on a metal surface will cause electrons to be ejected only if the photons have high enough energy. The greater the number of photons that strike the surface at or above the threshold energy, the greater the number of electrons dislodged. The metal atoms will not lose electrons, however, if no individual photon has enough energy to dislodge an electron from an atom.

Energy and Chemistry: Using Planck's Equation

Compact disc players use lasers that emit red light with a wavelength of 685 nm. What is the energy of one photon of this light? What is the energy of 1 mole of photons of red light? To answer these questions, first convert the wavelength to the frequency of the radiation, and then use the frequency to calculate the energy per

■ **The Photoelectric Effect** The photoelectric effect is put to use in photoelectric cells, light-operated switches that are commonly used in automatic door openers in stores and elevators.

■ **The Relationship of Energy, Wavelength, and Frequency**

As frequency (ν) increases, energy (E) increases

$$\uparrow$$
$$E = h\nu = \frac{hc}{\lambda}$$
$$\downarrow$$

As wavelength (λ) decreases, energy (E) increases

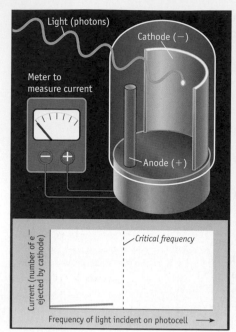

(a) A photocell operates by the photoelectric effect. The main part of the cell is a light-sensitive cathode. This is a material, usually a metal, that ejects electrons if struck by photons of light of sufficient energy. No current is observed until the critical frequency is reached.

FIGURE 6.4 A photoelectric cell.

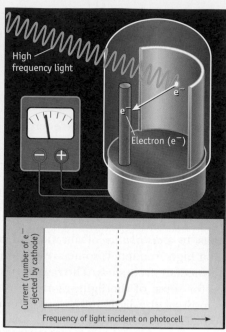

(b) When light of higher frequency than the minimum is used, the excess energy of the photon allows the electron to escape the atom with greater velocity. The ejected electrons move to the anode, and a current flows in the cell. Such a device can be used as a switch in electric circuits.

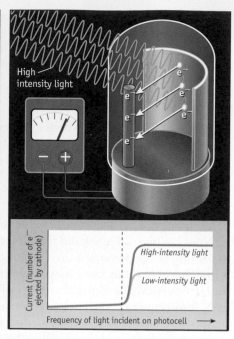

(c) If higher intensity light is used, the only effect is to cause more electrons to be released from the surface. The onset of current is observed at the same frequency as with lower intensity light, but more current flows.

photon. Finally, calculate the energy of a mole of photons by multiplying the energy per photon by Avogadro's number:

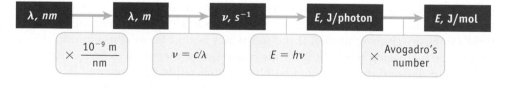

For $\lambda = 685$ nm, $\nu = 4.38 \times 10^{14}$ 1/s (Calculated using Equation 6.1)

E per photon $= h\nu = (6.626 \times 10^{-34}$ J $\cdot$ s/photon$) \times (4.38 \times 10^{14}$ 1/s$)$

$\qquad = 2.90 \times 10^{-19}$ J/photon

E per mole $= (2.90 \times 10^{-19}$ J/photon$) \times (6.022 \times 10^{23}$ photons/mol$)$

$\qquad = 1.75 \times 10^{5}$ J/mol (or 175 kJ/mol)

The energy of red light photons with a wavelength of 685 nm is 175 kJ/mol, whereas the energy of blue light photons ($\lambda = 400$ nm) is about 300 kJ/mol. The energy of the blue light photons, and of ultraviolet light photons in particular, is in the range of the energies necessary to break the chemical bonds in proteins. This is what happens if you spend too much time unprotected in the sun (Figure 6.5). In contrast, the energy of light at the red end of the spectrum and infrared radiation has a lower energy and, although it is generally not energetic enough to break chemical bonds, it can affect the vibrations of molecules. We sense infrared radiation as heat, such as the heat given off by a glowing burner on an electric stove.

EXERCISE 6.2 Photon Energies

Compare the energy of a mole of photons of orange light (625 nm) with the energy of a mole of photons of microwave radiation having a frequency of 2.45 GHz (1 GHz = 10^9 s^{-1}). Which has the greater energy?

FIGURE 6.5 Damage from radiation. Various manufacturers have developed mixtures of compounds that protect skin from UVA and UVB radiation. These sunscreens are given "sun protection factor" (SPF) labels that indicate how long the user can stay in the sun without burning. Sunscreens produced by Coppertone, for example, contain the organic compounds 2-ethylhexyl-p-methoxycinnamate and oxybenzene. These molecules absorb UV radiation, preventing it from reaching your skin.

6.3 Atomic Line Spectra and Niels Bohr

If a high voltage is applied to atoms of an element in the gas phase at low pressure, the atoms absorb energy and are said to be "excited." The excited atoms can then emit light, and a familiar example is the colored light from neon advertising signs.

The light falling on Earth from the Sun, or the light emitted by a very hot object, consists of a continuous spectrum of wavelengths (Figures 6.2 and 6.3b). In contrast, the light from excited atoms consists of only a few different wavelengths of light (Figure 6.6). We can demonstrate this by passing a beam of light from excited neon or hydrogen through a prism; only a few colored lines are seen. The spectrum obtained in this manner, such as that for excited H atoms (Figure 6.6), is called a **line emission spectrum.**

The line emission spectra of hydrogen, mercury, and neon are shown in Figure 6.7, and you can see that every element has a unique spectrum. Indeed, the characteristic lines in the emission spectrum of an element can be used in chemical analysis, both to identify the element and to determine how much of it is present.

Neon sign. If a high voltage is applied to a tube containing a gas like neon, light is emitted. Different colors result if different gases are used.

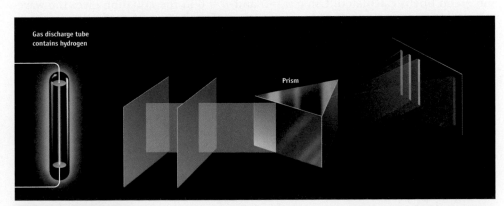

Active Figure 6.6 **The line emission spectrum of hydrogen.** The emitted light is passed through a series of slits to create a narrow beam of light, which is then separated into its component wavelengths by a prism. A photographic plate or photocell can be used to detect the separate wavelengths as individual lines. Hence, the name "line spectrum" for the light emitted by a glowing gas.

Chemistry.·.Now™ Sign in at **www.cengage.com/login** and go to the Chapter Contents menu to explore an interactive version of this figure accompanied by an exercise.

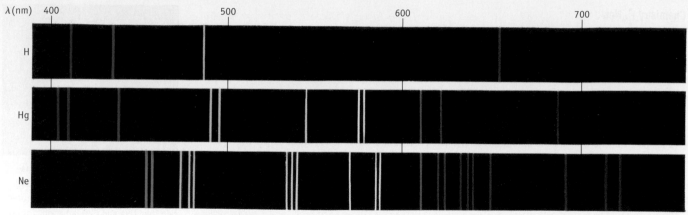

FIGURE 6.7 Line emission spectra of hydrogen, mercury, and neon. Excited gaseous elements produce characteristic spectra that can be used to identify the elements as well as to determine how much of each element is present in a sample.

A goal of scientists in the late 19th century was to explain why excited gaseous atoms emitted light of only certain frequencies. One approach was to look for a mathematical relationship among the observed frequencies because a regular pattern of information implies a logical explanation. The first steps in this direction were taken by Johann Balmer (1825–1898) and later by Johannes Rydberg (1854–1919). From these studies, an equation—now called the **Balmer equation** (Equation 6.3)— was found that could be used to calculate the wavelength of the red, green, and blue lines in the visible emission spectrum of hydrogen (Figure 6.7).

$$\frac{1}{\lambda} = R\left(\frac{1}{2^2} - \frac{1}{n^2}\right) \qquad \text{when } n > 2 \tag{6.3}$$

In this equation n is an integer, and R, now called the **Rydberg constant,** has the value 1.0974×10^7 m^{-1}. If $n = 3$, the wavelength of the red line in the hydrogen spectrum is obtained (6.563×10^{-7} m, or 656.3 nm). If $n = 4$, the wavelength for the green line is calculated. Using $n = 5$ and $n = 6$ in the equation gives the wavelengths of the blue lines. The four visible lines in the spectrum of hydrogen atoms are now known as the **Balmer series**.

The Bohr Model of the Hydrogen Atom

Early in the 20th century, the Danish physicist Niels Bohr (1885–1962) proposed a model for the electronic structure of atoms and with it an explanation for the emission spectra of excited atoms. Bohr proposed a planetary structure for the hydrogen atom in which the electron moved in a circular orbit around the nucleus, similar to a planet revolving about the sun. In proposing this model, however, he had to contradict the laws of classical physics. According to classical theories, a charged electron moving in the positive electric field of the nucleus should lose energy, and, eventually, the electron should crash into the nucleus. This is clearly not the case; if it were so, matter would eventually self-destruct. To solve this contradiction, Bohr postulated that there are certain orbits corresponding to particular energy levels where this would not occur. As long as an electron is in one of these energy levels, the system is stable. That is, Bohr introduced *quantization* into the description of electronic structure. By combining this quantization postulate with the laws of motion from classical physics, Bohr derived an equation for the energy possessed by the single electron in the nth orbit (energy level) of the H atom.

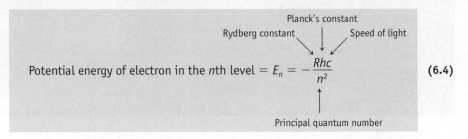

Potential energy of electron in the nth level $= E_n = -\dfrac{Rhc}{n^2}$ **(6.4)**

Here, E_n is the energy of the electron (in J/atom); and R, h, and c are constants (the Rydberg constant, Planck's constant, and the speed of light, respectively). The symbol n is a positive, unitless integer called the **principal quantum number**. It can have integral values of 1, 2, 3, and so on.

Equation 6.4 has several important features (which are illustrated in Figure 6.8).

- The quantum number n defines the energies of the allowed orbits in the H atom.
- The energy of an electron in an orbit has a negative value. (Because the negative electron is attracted to the positive nucleus, the energy of attraction is a negative value).
- An atom with its electrons in the lowest possible energy levels is said to be in its **ground state**; for the hydrogen atom, this is the level defined by the quantum number $n = 1$. States for the H atom with higher energies (and $n > 1$) are called **excited states**, and, as the value of n increases, states have less negative energy values.

Bohr also showed that, as the value of n increases, the distance of the electron from the nucleus increases. An electron in the $n = 1$ orbit is closest to the nucleus and has the lowest (most negative) energy. For higher integer values of n, the electron is further from the nucleus and has a higher (less negative) energy.

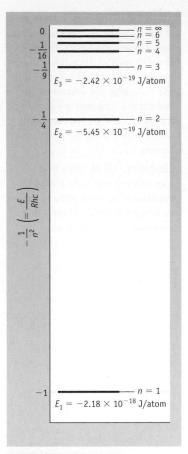

Active Figure 6.8 Energy levels for the H atom in the Bohr model. The energies of the electron in the hydrogen atom depend on the value of the principal quantum number n ($E_n = -Rhc/n^2$). The larger the value of n, the larger the Bohr radius and the less negative the value of the energy. Energies are given in joules per atom (J/atom). Notice that the difference between successive energy levels becomes smaller as n becomes larger.

Chemistry ⚛ Now™ Sign in at **www.cengage.com/login** and go to the Chapter Contents menu to explore an interactive version of this figure accompanied by an exercise.

■ **EXAMPLE 6.2** **Energies of the Ground and Excited States of the H Atom**

Problem Calculate the energies of the $n = 1$ and $n = 2$ states of the hydrogen atom in joules per atom and in kilojoules per mole. What is the difference in energy of these two states in kJ/mol?

Strategy Use Equation 6.4 with the following constants: $R = 1.097 \times 10^7$ m^{-1}, $h = 6.626 \times 10^{-34}$ J · s, and $c = 2.998 \times 10^8$ m/s.

Solution When $n = 1$, the energy of an electron in a single H atom is

$E_1 = -Rhc$
$E_1 = -(1.097 \times 10^7 \text{ m}^{-1})(6.626 \times 10^{-34} \text{ J} \cdot \text{s})(2.998 \times 10^8 \text{ m/s})$
$\quad = -2.179 \times 10^{-18} \text{ J/atom}$

In units of kJ/mol,

$E_1 = \dfrac{-2.179 \times 10^{-18} \text{ J}}{\text{atom}} \times \dfrac{6.022 \times 10^{23} \text{ atoms}}{\text{mol}} \times \dfrac{1 \text{ kJ}}{1000 \text{ J}}$
$\quad = -1312 \text{ kJ/mol}$

When $n = 2$, the energy is

$E_2 = -\dfrac{Rhc}{2^2} = -\dfrac{E_1}{4} = -\dfrac{2.179 \times 10^{-18} \text{ J/atom}}{4}$
$\quad = -5.448 \times 10^{-19} \text{ J/atom}$

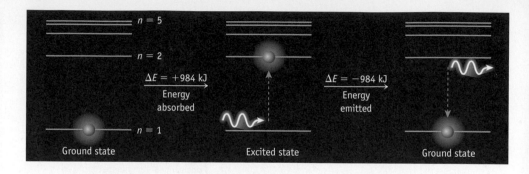

Active Figure 6.9 Absorption of energy by the atom as the electron moves to an excited state. Energy is absorbed when an electron moves from the $n = 1$ state to the $n = 2$ state ($\Delta E > 0$). When the electron returns to the $n = 1$ state from $n = 2$, energy is evolved ($\Delta E < 0$). The change in energy is 984 kJ/mol, as calculated in Example 6.2.

Chemistry ⚗ Now™ Sign in at www.cengage.com/login and go to the Chapter Contents menu to explore an interactive version of this figure accompanied by an exercise.

In units of kJ/mol,

$$E_1 = \frac{-5.448 \times 10^{-19} \text{ J}}{\text{atom}} \times \frac{6.022 \times 10^{23} \text{ atoms}}{\text{mol}} \times \frac{1 \text{ kJ}}{1000 \text{ J}}$$

$$= -328.1 \text{ kJ/mol}$$

The difference in energy, ΔE, between the first two energy states of the H atom is

$$\Delta E = E_2 - E_1 = (-328.1 \text{ kJ/mol}) - (-1312 \text{ kJ/mol}) = \boxed{984 \text{ kJ/mol}}$$

Comment The calculated energies are negative, with E_1 more negative than E_2. The $n = 2$ state is higher in energy than the $n = 1$ state by 984 kJ/mol. Also, be sure to notice that 1312 kJ/mol is the value of Rhc multiplied by Avogadro's number N_A (i.e., $N_A Rhc$). This will be useful in future calculations.

EXERCISE 6.3 Electron Energies

Calculate the energy of the $n = 3$ state of the H atom in **(a)** joules per atom and **(b)** kilojoules per mole.

The Bohr Theory and the Spectra of Excited Atoms

Bohr's theory describes electrons as having only specific orbits and energies. If an electron moves from one energy level to another, then energy must be absorbed or evolved. This idea allowed Bohr to relate energies of electrons and the emission spectra of hydrogen atoms.

To move an electron from the $n = 1$ state to an excited state, such as the $n = 2$ state, the atom must absorb energy. When E_{final} has $n = 2$ and E_{initial} has $n = 1$, then 984 kJ of energy must be absorbed (Figure 6.9). This is the difference in energy between final and initial states:

$$\Delta E = E_{\text{final state}} - E_{\text{initial state}} = (-N_A Rhc/2^2) - (-N_A Rhc/1^2) = (0.75)N_A Rhc = 984 \text{ kJ/mol}$$

(where $N_A Rhc/1^2$ is the energy in kJ/mol calculated in Example 6.2 for an electron in the $n = 1$ energy level in the H atom). Moving an electron from the first to the second energy state requires input of 984 kJ/mol of atoms—no more and no less. If $0.7N_A Rhc$ or $0.8N_A Rhc$ is provided, a transition between states is not possible. Requiring a specific and precise amount of energy is a consequence of quantization.

Moving an electron from a state of low n to one of higher n requires that energy be absorbed. The opposite process, in which an electron "falls" from a level of higher n to one of lower n, leads to emission of energy (Figure 6.9). For example, for a transition from the $n = 2$ level to $n = 1$ level,

$$\Delta E = E_{\text{final state}} - E_{\text{initial state}} = -984 \text{ kJ/mol}$$

The negative sign indicates energy is evolved; 984 kJ must be *emitted* per mole of H atoms.

We can now visualize the mechanism by which the characteristic line emission spectrum of hydrogen originates according to the Bohr model. Energy is provided to the atoms from an electric discharge or by heating. Depending on how much energy is added, some atoms have their electrons excited from the $n = 1$ state to the $n = 2$, 3, or even higher states. After absorbing energy, these electrons can return to any lower level (either directly or in a series of steps), releasing energy. We observe this released energy as photons of electromagnetic radiation, and, because only certain energy levels are possible, only photons with particular energies and wavelengths are observed. A line spectrum is thus predicted for the emission spectrum of H atoms, which is exactly what is observed.

The energy of any emission line (in kJ/mol) for excited hydrogen atoms can be calculated using Equation 6.5.

$$\Delta E = E_{\text{final}} - E_{\text{initial}} = -N_A Rhc \left(\frac{1}{n_{\text{final}}^2} - \frac{1}{n_{\text{initial}}^2} \right) \qquad (6.5)$$

For hydrogen, a series of emission lines having energies in the ultraviolet region (called the **Lyman series**; Figure 6.10) arises from electrons moving from states with $n > 1$ to the $n = 1$ state. The series of lines that have energies in the visible region—the **Balmer series**—arises from electrons moving from states with $n > 2$ to the $n = 2$ state. There are also series of lines in the infrared spectral region, arising from transitions from higher levels to the $n = 3$, 4 or 5 levels.

Bohr's model, introducing quantization into a description of the atom, tied the unseen (the structure of the atom) to the seen (the observable lines in the hydrogen spectrum). Agreement between theory and experiment is taken as evidence

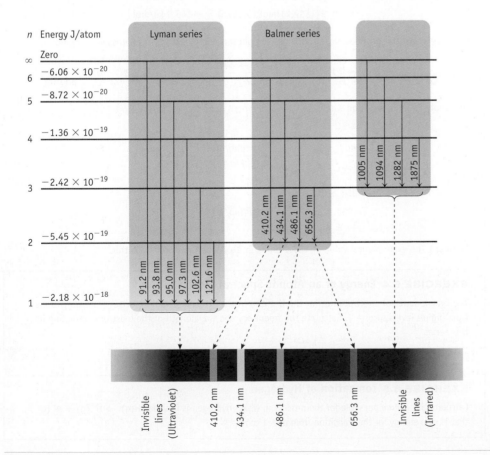

Active Figure 6.10 Some of the electronic transitions that can occur in an excited H atom. The Lyman series of lines in the ultraviolet region results from transitions to the $n = 1$ level. Transitions from levels with values of n greater than 2 to $n = 2$ occur in the visible region (Balmer series; see Figures 6.6 and 6.7). Lines in the infrared region result from transitions from levels with n greater than 3 or 4 to the $n = 3$ or 4 levels. (Only the series ending at $n = 3$ is illustrated.)

Chemistry ⚬ Now™ Sign in at www.cengage.com/login and go to the Chapter Contents menu to explore an interactive version of this figure accompanied by an exercise.

that the theoretical model is valid. It was apparent, however, that Bohr's theory was inadequate. This model of the atom explained only the spectrum of hydrogen atoms and of other systems having one electron (such as He^+), but failed for all other systems. A better model of electronic structure was needed.

Chemistry ⊙ Now™

Sign in at **www.cengage.com/login** and go to Chapter 6 Contents to see Screen 6.6 for a simulation and exercise exploring **the radiation emitted when electrons of excited hydrogen atoms return to the ground state,** and for a tutorial on **calculating the wavelength of radiation emitted when electrons change energy levels.**

■ EXAMPLE 6.3 Energies of Emission Lines for Excited Atoms

Problem Calculate the wavelength of the green line in the visible spectrum of excited H atoms.

Strategy First, locate the green line in Figure 6.10 and determine $n_{initial}$ and n_{final}. Then use Equation 6.5 to calculate the difference in energy, ΔE, between these states. Finally, calculate the wavelength from the value of ΔE.

Solution The green line arises from electrons moving from $n = 4$ to $n = 2$. Using Equation 6.5 where $n_{final} = 2$ and $n_{initial} = 4$, and the value of $N_A Rhc$ (1312 kJ/mol), we have

$$\Delta E = E_{final} - E_{initial} = \left(-\frac{N_A Rhc}{2^2}\right) - \left(-\frac{N_A Rhc}{4^2}\right)$$

$$\Delta E = -N_A Rhc \left(\frac{1}{4} - \frac{1}{16}\right) = -N_A Rhc(0.1875)$$

$$\Delta E = -(1312 \text{ kJ/mol})(0.1875) = -246.0 \text{ kJ/mol}$$

The wavelength can now be calculated. First, the photon energy, E_{photon}, is expressed as J/photon.

$$E_{photon} = \left(246.0 \ \frac{kJ}{mol}\right)\left(1 \times 10^3 \ \frac{J}{kJ}\right)\left(\frac{1 \text{ mol}}{6.022 \times 10^{23} \text{ photons}}\right) = 4.085 \times 10^{-19} \ \frac{J}{photon}$$

Now apply Planck's equation where $E_{photon} = h\nu = hc/\lambda$, and so $\lambda = hc/E_{photon}$.

$$\lambda = \frac{hc}{E_{photon}} = \frac{\left(6.626 \times 10^{-34} \ \frac{J \cdot s}{photon}\right)\left(2.998 \times 10^8 \ m \cdot s^{-1}\right)}{4.085 \times 10^{-19} \ J/photon}$$

$$= 4.863 \times 10^{-7} \ m$$

$$= (4.863 \times 10^{-7} \ m)(1 \times 10^9 \ nm/m)$$

$$= \boxed{486.3 \ nm}$$

Comment The experimental value of 486.1 nm is in excellent agreement with this.

EXERCISE 6.4 Energy of an Atomic Spectral Line

The Lyman series of spectral lines for the H atom, in the ultraviolet region, arises from transitions from higher levels to $n = 1$. Calculate the frequency and wavelength of the least energetic line in this series.

EXERCISE 6.5 Ionization of Hydrogen

Calculate the energy per mole for the process in which hydrogen is ionized [$H(g) \rightarrow H^+(g) + e^-(g)$]; that is, the energy for the transition from $n = 1$ to $n = \infty$.

What Makes the Colors in Fireworks?

The colors of the beautiful fireworks displays you see on holidays such as July 4 in the U.S. are just the emission spectra of excited atoms. But what is their chemistry? What elements are involved?

Typical fireworks have several important chemical components. For example, there must be an oxidizer. Today, this is usually potassium perchlorate ($KClO_4$), potassium chlorate ($KClO_3$), or potassium nitrate (KNO_3). Potassium salts are used instead of sodium salts because the latter have two important drawbacks. They are hygroscopic—they absorb water from the air—and so do not remain dry on storage. Also, when heated, sodium salts give off an intense, yellow light that is so bright it can mask other colors.

The parts of any fireworks display we remember best are the vivid colors and brilliant flashes. White light can be produced by oxidizing magnesium or aluminum metal at high temperatures. The flashes you see at rock concerts or similar events, for example, are typically $Mg/KClO_4$ mixtures.

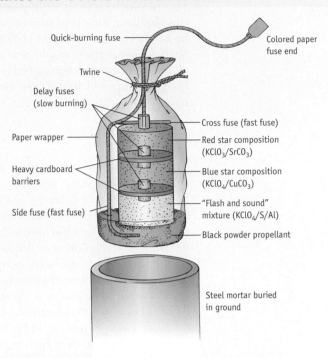

Quick-burning fuse
Colored paper fuse end
Twine
Delay fuses (slow burning)
Cross fuse (fast fuse)
Paper wrapper
Red star composition ($KClO_3/SrCO_3$)
Heavy cardboard barriers
Blue star composition ($KClO_4/CuCO_3$)
"Flash and sound" mixture ($KClO_4/S/Al$)
Side fuse (fast fuse)
Black powder propellant
Steel mortar buried in ground

The design of an aerial rocket for a fireworks display. When the fuse is ignited, it burns quickly to the delay fuses at the top of the red star mixture as well as to the black powder propellant at the bottom. The propellant ignites, sending the shell into the air. Meanwhile, the delay fuses burn. If the timing is correct, the shell bursts high in the sky into a red star. This is followed by a blue burst and then a flash and sound.

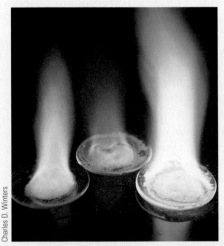

Charles D. Winters

Emission of light by excited atoms. Flame tests are often used to identify elements in a chemical sample. Shown here are the colors produced in a flame (burning methanol) by NaCl (yellow), $SrCl_2$ (red), and boric acid (green). (See ChemistryNow Screen 6.1, Chemical Puzzler, for a description of colors in fireworks.)

Yellow light is easiest to produce because sodium salts give an intense light with a wavelength of 589 nm. Fireworks mixtures usually contain sodium in the form of non-hygroscopic compounds such as cryolite, Na_3AlF_6. Strontium salts are most often used to produce a red light, and green is produced by barium salts such as $Ba(NO_3)_2$.

The next time you see a fireworks display, watch for the ones that are blue. Blue has always been the most difficult color to produce. Recently, however, fireworks designers have learned that the best way to get a really good "blue" is to decompose copper(I) chloride at low temperatures. To achieve this effect, CuCl is mixed with $KClO_4$, copper powder, and the organic chlorine-containing compound hexachloroethane, C_2Cl_6.

Questions:

1. The main lines in the emission spectrum of sodium are at wavelengths (nm) of 313.5, 589, 590, 818, and 819. Which one or ones are most responsible for the characteristic yellow color of excited sodium atoms?
2. Does the main emission line for $SrCl_2$ (in the photo) have a higher or lower wavelength than that of the yellow line from NaCl?
3. Mg is oxidized by $KClO_4$ to make white flashes. One product of the reaction is KCl. Write a balanced equation for the reaction.

Answers to these questions are in Appendix Q.

6.4 Particle–Wave Duality: Prelude to Quantum Mechanics

The photoelectric effect demonstrated that light, usually considered to be a wave, can also have the properties of particles, albeit without mass. This fact was pondered by Louis Victor de Broglie (1892–1987), who asked if light can have both wave and particle properties, would matter behave similarly? Could an object such as an electron, normally considered a particle, also exhibit wave properties? In 1925, de Broglie proposed that a free electron of mass m moving with a velocity v should have an associated wavelength λ, calculated by the equation

$$\lambda = \frac{h}{mv} \tag{6.6}$$

This revolutionary idea linked the particle properties of the electron (mass and velocity) with a wave property (wavelength). Experimental proof was soon produced. In 1927, C. J. Davisson (1881–1958) and L. H. Germer (1896–1971), working at the Bell Telephone Laboratories in New Jersey, found that a beam of electrons was diffracted like light waves by the atoms of a thin sheet of metal foil and that de Broglie's relation was followed quantitatively. Because diffraction is best explained based on the wave properties of radiation (Figure 6.11), it follows that electrons can be described as having wave properties in certain situations.

De Broglie's equation suggests that any moving particle has an associated wavelength. For λ to be measurable, however, the product of m and v must be very small because h is so small. A 114-g baseball, traveling at 110 mph, for example, has a large mv product (5.6 kg · m/s) and therefore an incredibly small wavelength, 1.2×10^{-34} m! Such a small value cannot be measured with any instrument now available, nor is such a value meaningful. As a consequence, wave properties are never assigned to a baseball or any other massive object. It is possible to observe wave-like properties only for particles of extremely small mass, such as protons, electrons, and neutrons.

Cathode ray tubes, such as were found in television sets before the advent of LCD and plasma TVs, generate a beam of electrons. When the electrons impact the screen, the beam gives rise to tiny flashes of colored light. In contrast to this effect, best explained by assuming electrons are particles, diffraction experiments suggest that electrons are waves. But, how can an electron be both a particle and a wave? In part, we are facing limitations in language; the words "particle" and "wave" accurately describe things encountered on a macroscopic scale. However, they apply less well on the submicroscopic scale associated with subatomic particles.

■ **Cathode Rays** Experiments with cathode rays led to the discovery and understanding of electrons. See the interchapter on *Milestones in the Development of the Modern View of Atoms and Molecules*.

FIGURE 6.11 Diffraction. (a) When two water waves come together, constructive and destructive interference occurs. Similar interference patterns are observed when electrons, which have wave properties, encounter atoms in the gas or solid phase. (b) The pattern observed when a thin film of magnesium oxide diffracts a beam of electrons.

Charles D. Winters

(a) Constructive/destructive interference in water waves.

R. K. Bohn, Department of Chemistry, University of Connecticut

(b) Diffraction of an electron beam by a thin film of magnesium oxide.

In some experiments, electrons behave like particles. In other experiments, we find that they behave like waves. No single experiment can be done to show the electron behaving *simultaneously* as a wave and a particle. Scientists now accept this **wave–particle duality**—that is, the idea that the electron has the properties of both a wave and a particle. Which is observed depends on the experiment.

Chemistry.Now™

Sign in at **www.cengage.com/login** and go to Chapter 6 Contents to see Screen 6.8 for a tutorial on **calculating the wavelength of a moving electron.**

■ **EXAMPLE 6.4 Using de Broglie's Equation**

Problem Calculate the wavelength associated with an electron of mass $m = 9.109 \times 10^{-28}$ g that travels at 40.0% of the speed of light.

Strategy First, consider the units involved. Wavelength is calculated from h/mv, where h is Planck's constant expressed in units of joule seconds (J · s). As discussed in Chapter 5 (page 214), $1\,J = 1\,kg \cdot m^2/s^2$. Therefore, the mass must be in kilograms and speed in meters per second.

Solution

Electron mass $= 9.109 \times 10^{-31}$ kg

Electron speed (40.0% of light speed) $= (0.400)(2.998 \times 10^8\ m \cdot s^{-1}) = 1.20 \times 10^8\ m \cdot s^{-1}$

Substituting these values into de Broglie's equation, we have

$$\lambda = \frac{h}{mv} = \frac{6.626 \times 10^{-34}\ (kg \cdot m^2/s^2)(s)}{(9.109 \times 10^{-31}\ kg)(1.20 \times 10^8\ m/s)} = 6.07 \times 10^{-12}\ m$$

In nanometers, the wavelength is

$$\lambda = (6.07 \times 10^{-12}\ m)(1.00 \times 10^9\ nm/m) = 6.07 \times 10^{-3}\ nm$$

Comment The calculated wavelength is about 1/12 of the diameter of the H atom.

EXERCISE 6.6 De Broglie's Equation

Calculate the wavelength associated with a neutron having a mass of 1.675×10^{-24} g and a kinetic energy of 6.21×10^{-21} J. (Recall that the kinetic energy of a moving particle is $E = \frac{1}{2}mv^2$.)

6.5 The Modern View of Electronic Structure: Wave or Quantum Mechanics

How does wave–particle duality affect our model of the arrangement of electrons in atoms? Following World War I, German scientists Erwin Schrödinger (1887–1961), Werner Heisenberg (1901–1976), and Max Born (1882–1970) provided the answer.

In Bohr's model of the atom, both the energy and location (the orbit) for the electron in the hydrogen atom can be described accurately. However, Heisenberg determined that, for a tiny object such as an electron in an atom, it is impossible to determine accurately *both* its position and its energy. That is, any attempt to determine accurately either the location or the energy will leave the other uncertain. This is now known as Heisenberg's **uncertainty principle.**

Born proposed the following application of Heisenberg's idea to understand the arrangement of electrons in atoms: *If we choose to know the energy of an electron in an atom with only a small uncertainty, then we must accept a correspondingly large uncertainty*

■ **History of the Modern View of Structure** For the historical background to efforts to understand atomic structure see the interchapter *Milestones in the Development of the Modern View of Atoms and Molecules* (pages 338–347).

in its position. The importance of this idea is that we can assess only the likelihood, or *probability*, of finding an electron with a given energy within a given region of space. Because electron energy is the key to understanding the chemistry of an atom, chemists accept the notion of knowing only the approximate location of the electron.

Erwin Schrödinger (1887–1961) worked on a comprehensive theory of the behavior of electrons in atoms. Starting with de Broglie's hypothesis that an electron could be described as a wave, Schrödinger developed a model for electrons in atoms that has come to be called **quantum mechanics** or **wave mechanics.** This model used the mathematical equations of wave motion to generate a series of equations called wave equations or **wave functions,** which are designated by the Greek letter ψ (psi).

Unlike Bohr's model, Schrödinger's model can be difficult to visualize, and the mathematical approach is complex. Nonetheless, the consequences of the model are important, and understanding its implications is essential to understanding the modern view of the atom. The following points summarize the important issues concerning wave mechanics:

1. An electron in the atom is described as a **standing wave.** If you tie down a string at both ends, as you would the string of a guitar, and then pluck it, the string vibrates as a standing wave (Figure 6.12). A two-dimensional standing wave such as a vibrating string must have two or more points of zero amplitude (called **nodes**), and only certain vibrations are possible. These allowed vibrations have wavelengths of $n(\lambda/2)$, where n is an integer ($n = 1$, 2, 3, ...). In the first vibration illustrated in Figure 6.12, the distance between the ends of the string is half a wavelength, or $\lambda/2$. In the second, the string's length equals one complete wavelength, or $2(\lambda/2)$. In the third vibration, the string's length is $3(\lambda/2)$. That is, for standing waves, vibrations are quantized, and the integer n is a **quantum number.**

2. By defining the electron as a standing wave, quantization is introduced into the description of electronic structure. The mathematics describing a one-dimensional vibrating string requires one "quantum number" (n). Schrödinger's equations for an electron in three-dimensional space requires three quantum numbers: n, ℓ, and m_ℓ, all integers. Only certain combinations of their values are possible as outlined below.

■ **Wave Functions and Energy** In Bohr's theory, the electron energy for the H atom is given by $E_n = -Rhc/n^2$. Schrödinger's electron wave model gives the same result.

FIGURE 6.12 Standing waves. In the first wave, the end-to-end distance is $(1/2)\lambda$; in the second wave, it is λ, and in the third wave, it is $(3/2)\lambda$. (In addition to the nodes marked, there are nodes at the ends of the string.)

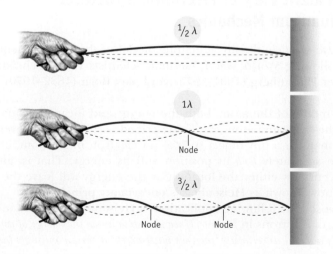

$^{1}/_{2}\lambda$

1λ

Node

$^{3}/_{2}\lambda$

Node   Node

3. Each wave function is associated with an allowed energy value. That is, the energy is quantized because only certain values of energy are possible for the electron.

4. The value of the wave function ψ at a given point in space is the amplitude (height) of the wave. This value has both a magnitude and a sign that can be either positive or negative. (Visualize a vibrating string in a guitar or piano, for example. Points of positive amplitude are above the axis of propagation, and points of negative amplitude are below it.)

5. At any point in space, the square of the value of the wave function (ψ^2) defines the *probability* of finding the electron. Scientists refer to this probability as the **electron density.**

6. Schrödinger's theory defines the energy of the electron precisely. The uncertainty principle, however, tells us there must be uncertainty in the electron's position. Thus, we describe the **probability** of the electron being within a certain region in space when in a given energy state. **Orbitals** define the region of space within which an electron of a given energy is most likely to be located.

Quantum Numbers and Orbitals

Quantum numbers are used to identify the energy states and orbitals available to electrons. We will first describe the quantum numbers and the information they provide and then turn to the connection between quantum numbers and the energies and shapes of atomic orbitals.

n, the Principal Quantum Number ($n = 1, 2, 3, \ldots$)

The principal quantum number n can have any integer value from 1 to infinity. The value of n is the primary factor in determining the *energy* of an orbital. It also defines the *size* of an orbital: for a given atom, the greater the value of n, the greater the size of the orbital.

In atoms having more than one electron, two or more electrons may have the same n value. These electrons are then said to be in the same **electron shell.**

■ **Electron Energy and Quantum Numbers** The electron energy in the H atom depends only on the value of n. In atoms with more electrons, the energy depends on both n and ℓ.

ℓ, the Azimuthal Quantum Number ($\ell = 0, 1, 2, 3, \ldots, n - 1$)

Orbitals of a given shell can be grouped into **subshells**, where each subshell is characterized by a different value of the quantum number ℓ. The quantum number ℓ can have any integer value from 0 to a maximum of $n - 1$. This quantum number defines the *characteristic shape of an orbital*; different ℓ values correspond to different orbital shapes.

Because ℓ can be no larger than $n - 1$, the value of n limits the number of subshells possible for each shell. For the shell with $n = 1$, ℓ must equal 0; thus, only one subshell is possible. When $n = 2$, ℓ can be either 0 or 1. Because two values of ℓ are now possible, there are two subshells in the $n = 2$ electron shell.

Subshells are usually identified by letters. For example, an $\ell = 1$ subshell is called a "*p* subshell," and an orbital in that subshell is called a "*p* orbital."

■ **Orbital Symbols** Early studies of the emission spectra of elements classified lines into four groups on the basis of their appearance. These groups were labeled sharp, principal, diffuse, and fundamental. From these names came the labels we now apply to orbitals: *s*, *p*, *d*, and *f*.

Subshell labels

Value of ℓ	Subshell Label
0	*s*
1	*p*
2	*d*
3	*f*

Subshell	Number of Orbitals in Subshell (= 2ℓ + 1)
s	1
p	3
d	5
f	7

m_ℓ, the Magnetic Quantum Number ($m_\ell = 0, \pm 1, \pm 2, \pm 3, \ldots, \pm \ell$)

The magnetic quantum number, m_ℓ, is related to the *orientation in space of the orbitals within a subshell*. Orbitals in a given subshell differ in their orientation in space, not in their energy.

The value of m_ℓ can range from $+\ell$ to $-\ell$, with 0 included. For example, when $\ell = 2$, m_ℓ can have five values: $+2, +1, 0, -1,$ and -2. The number of values of m_ℓ for a given subshell ($= 2\ell + 1$) specifies the number of orbitals in the subshell.

Shells and Subshells

Allowed values of the three quantum numbers are summarized in Table 6.1. By analyzing the sets of quantum numbers in this table, you will discover the following:

- n = the number of subshells in a shell.
- $2\ell + 1$ = the number of orbitals in a subshell = the number of values of m_ℓ
- n^2 = the number of orbitals in a shell.

The First Electron Shell, $n = 1$

When $n = 1$, the value of ℓ can only be 0, and so m_ℓ must also have a value of 0. This means that, in the shell closest to the nucleus, only one subshell exists, and that subshell consists of only a single orbital, the $1s$ orbital.

The Second Electron Shell, $n = 2$

When $n = 2$, ℓ can have two values (0 and 1), so there are two subshells in the second shell. One of these is the $2s$ subshell ($n = 2$ and $\ell = 0$), and the other is the $2p$ subshell ($n = 2$ and $\ell = 1$). Because the values of m_ℓ can be $-1, 0,$ and $+1$ when $\ell = 1$, three $2p$ orbitals exist. All three orbitals have the same shape. However, because each has a different m_ℓ value, the three orbitals differ in their orientation in space.

TABLE 6.1 Summary of the Quantum Numbers, Their Interrelationships, and the Orbital Information Conveyed

Principal Quantum Number	Azimuthal Quantum Number	Magnetic Quantum Number	Number and Type of Orbitals in the Subshell
Symbol = n Values = 1, 2, 3, . . . n = number of subshells	Symbol = ℓ Values = 0 . . . $n - 1$	Symbol = m_ℓ Values = $+\ell$ . . . 0 . . . $-\ell$	Number of orbitals in shell = n^2 and number of orbitals in subshell = $2\ell + 1$
1	0	0	one $1s$ orbital (one orbital of one type in the $n = 1$ shell)
2	0 1	0 +1, 0, −1	one $2s$ orbital three $2p$ orbitals (four orbitals of two types in the $n = 2$ shell)
3	0 1 2	0 +1, 0, −1 +2, +1, 0, −1, −2	one $3s$ orbital three $3p$ orbitals five $3d$ orbitals (nine orbitals of three types in the $n = 3$ shell)
4	0 1 2 3	0 +1, 0, −1 +2, +1, 0, −1, −2 +3, +2, +1, 0, −1, −2, −3	one $4s$ orbital three $4p$ orbitals five $4d$ orbitals seven $4f$ orbitals (16 orbitals of four types in the $n = 4$ shell)

The Third Electron Shell, $n = 3$

When $n = 3$, three subshells are possible for an electron because ℓ has the values 0, 1, and 2. The first two subshells within the $n = 3$ shell are the $3s$ ($\ell = 0$, one orbital) and $3p$ ($\ell = 1$, three orbitals) subshells. The third subshell is labeled $3d$ ($n = 3$, $\ell = 2$). Because m_ℓ can have five values (-2, -1, 0, $+1$, and $+2$) for $\ell = 2$, there are five d orbitals in this d subshell.

The Fourth Electron Shell, $n = 4$, and Beyond

There are four subshells in the $n = 4$ shell. In addition to $4s$, $4p$, and $4d$ subshells, there is the $4f$ subshell for which $\ell = 3$. Seven such orbitals exist because there are seven values of m_ℓ when $\ell = 3$ (-3, -2, -1, 0, $+1$, $+2$, and $+3$).

Chemistry⚛Now™

Sign in at **www.cengage.com/login** and go to Chapter 6 Contents to see:
- Screen 6.9 to view an animation on **the quantum mechanical view of the atom**
- Screen 6.12 for a tutorial on **determining values for the quantum numbers for an orbital**

■ Shells, Subshells, and Orbitals— A Summary Electrons in atoms are arranged in shells. Within each shell, there can be one or more electron subshells, each comprised of one or more orbitals.

Electron Location	Quantum Number
Shell	n
Subshell	ℓ
Orbital	m_ℓ

> **EXERCISE 6.7 Using Quantum Numbers**
>
> Complete the following statements:
>
> **(a)** When $n = 2$, the values of ℓ can be _____ and _____.
>
> **(b)** When $\ell = 1$, the values of m_ℓ can be _____ , _____ , and _____ , and the subshell has the letter label _____.
>
> **(c)** The subshell with $\ell = 2$ is called a _____ subshell.
>
> **(d)** When a subshell is labeled s, the value of ℓ is _____, and m_ℓ has the value _____.
>
> **(e)** There are _____ orbitals in the p subshell.
>
> **(f)** When a subshell is labeled f, there are _____ values of m_ℓ, corresponding to _____ orbitals.

6.6 The Shapes of Atomic Orbitals

We often say the electron is assigned to, or "occupies," an orbital. But what does this mean? What is an orbital? What does it look like? To answer these questions, we must examine the wave functions for the orbitals.

s Orbitals

A $1s$ orbital is associated with the quantum numbers $n = 1$ and $\ell = 0$. If we could photograph a $1s$ electron at one-second intervals for a few thousand seconds, the composite picture would look like the drawing in Figure 6.13a. This resembles a cloud of dots, and chemists often refer to such representations of electron orbitals as *electron cloud pictures*. In Figure 6.13a, the density of dots is greater close to the nucleus, that is, the electron cloud is denser close to the nucleus. This indicates that the $1s$ electron is most likely to be found near the nucleus. However, the density of dots declines on moving away from the nucleus and so, therefore, does the probability of finding the electron.

The thinning of the electron cloud at increasing distance is illustrated in a different way in Figure 6.13b. Here we have plotted the square of the wave function for the electron in a $1s$ orbital (ψ^2), times 4π and the distance squared ($4\pi r^2$), as a function of the distance of the electron from the nucleus. This plot represents

■ Atomic Orbitals for the H Atom Orbitals and their shapes discussed here are for the H atom, that is, for a one-electron atom. Orbitals for multielectron atoms are approximated by assuming they are hydrogen-like. For most purposes this is a reasonable assumption.

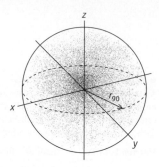

(a) Dot picture of an electron in a 1s orbital. Each dot represents the position of the electron at a different instant in time. Note that the dots cluster closest to the nucleus. r_{90} is the radius of a sphere within which the electron is found 90% of the time.

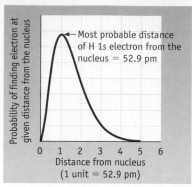

Most probable distance of H 1s electron from the nucleus = 52.9 pm

Probability of finding electron at given distance from the nucleus

Distance from nucleus
(1 unit = 52.9 pm)

(b) A plot of the surface density ($4\pi r^2 \psi^2$) as a function of distance for a hydrogen atom 1s orbital. This gives the probability of finding the electron at a given distance from the nucleus.

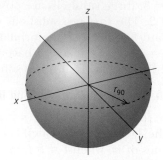

(c) The surface of the sphere within which the electron is found 90% of the time for a 1s orbital. This surface is often called a "boundary surface." (A 90% surface was chosen arbitrarily. If the choice was the surface within which the electron is found 50% of the time, the sphere would be considerably smaller.)

Active Figure 6.13 Different views of a 1s ($n = 1$, $\ell = 0$) orbital.

Chemistry.Now™ Sign in at www.cengage.com/login and go to the Chapter Contents menu to explore an interactive version of this figure accompanied by an exercise.

■ **Surface Density Plot for 1s** The maximum value of the radial distribution plot for a 1s electron in a hydrogen atom occurs at 52.9 pm. It is interesting to note that this maximum is at exactly the same distance from the nucleus that Niels Bohr calculated for the radius of the orbit occupied by the $n = 1$ electron.

the probability of finding the electron in a thin spherical shell at a distance r from the nucleus. For this reason, the plot of $4\pi r^2 \psi^2$ vs. r is sometimes called a **surface density plot** or a **radial distribution plot.** For the 1s orbital, $4\pi r^2 \psi^2$ is zero at the nucleus—there is no probability the electron will be exactly at the nucleus—but the probability rises rapidly on moving away from the nucleus, reaches a maximum a short distance from the nucleus (at 52.9 pm), and then decreases rapidly as the distance from the nucleus increases. Notice that the probability of finding the electron approaches but never quite reaches zero, even at very large distances.

Figure 6.13a shows that, for the 1s orbital, the probability of finding an electron is the same at a given distance from the nucleus, no matter in which direction you proceed from the nucleus. Consequently, the *1s orbital is spherical in shape.*

Because the probability of finding the electron approaches but never quite reaches zero, there is no sharp boundary beyond which the electron is never found (although the probability can be incalculably small). Nonetheless, the *s* orbital (and other types of orbitals as well) is often depicted as having a **boundary surface** (Figure 6.13c), largely because it is easier to draw such pictures. To create Figure 6.13c, we drew a sphere about the nucleus in such a way that the probability of finding the electron somewhere inside the sphere is 90%. The choice of 90% is arbitrary—we could have chosen a different value—and if we do, the shape would be the same, but the size of the sphere would be different.

There are misconceptions about pictures of orbitals. First, there is not an impenetrable surface within which the electron is "contained." Second, the probability of finding the electron is not the same throughout the volume enclosed by the surface. (An electron in the 1s orbital of a H atom has a greater probability of being 52.9 pm from the nucleus than of being closer or farther away.) Third, the terms "electron cloud" and "electron distribution" imply that the electron is a particle, but the basic premise in quantum mechanics is that the electron is treated as a wave, not a particle.

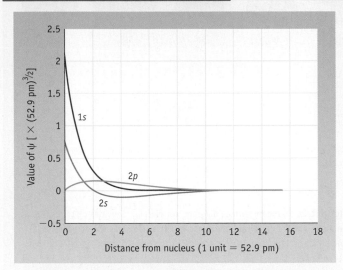

FIGURE A Plot of the wave functions for 1*s*, 2*s*, and 2*p* orbitals versus distance from the nucleus.

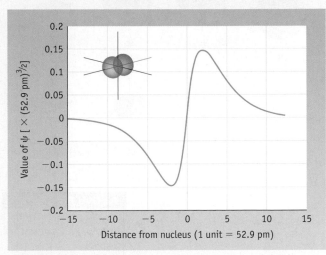

FIGURE B Wave functions for a 2*p* orbital. The sign of ψ for a 2*p* orbital is positive on one side of the nucleus and negative on the other (but it has a 0 value at the nucleus). A nodal plane separates the two lobes of this "dumbbell-shaped" orbital. (The vertical axis is the value of ψ, and the horizontal axis is the distance from the nucleus, where 1 unit = 52.9 pm.)

Waves have crests, troughs, and nodes, and these terms can be applied to the description of an electron as a wave. For a 1*s* orbital of the H atom, the wave function ψ approaches a maximum at the nucleus, but the wave's amplitude declines rapidly at points farther removed from the nucleus (Figure A). The sign of ψ is positive at all points in space.

For a 2*s* orbital, there is a different profile; the sign of ψ is positive near the nucleus, drops to zero (there is a node at 2 × 52.9 pm), and then becomes negative before approaching zero at greater distances.

For the 2*p* orbital, the value of ψ is zero at the nucleus because there is a nodal surface passing through the nucleus. Moving away from the nucleus in one direction, say along the *x*-axis, we see the value of ψ rises to a maximum around 106 pm before falling off at greater distances. Moving away along

the −*x* direction, the value of ψ is the same but opposite in sign (Figure B). The 2*p* electron is a wave with a node at the nucleus. (In drawing orbitals, we indicate this with + or − signs or with two different colors as in Figure 6.14 or Figure B.)

For the 2*s* orbital, there is a node at 105.8 pm when plotting the wave function. However, because ψ has the same value in all directions, this means there is a *spherical nodal surface* surrounding the nucleus as illustrated in Figure C.

As noted on page 290, the number of nodal surfaces passing through the nucleus for any orbital is equal to ℓ. The number of spherical nodes is $n - \ell - 1$. Thus, for a 2*s* orbital, $2 - 0 - 1 = 1$ spherical nodes, as we have seen. In general, the consequence of this is that electron density in all *s* orbitals (except 1*s*) occurs as a series of nested shells.

A possible analogy to this picture is that an *s* orbital resembles an onion with layers of electron density, the number of layers increasing with *n*.

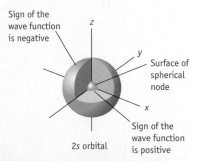

FIGURE C Wave functions for a 2*s* orbital. A 2*s* orbital for the H atom showing the spherical node (at 105.8 pm) around the nucleus.

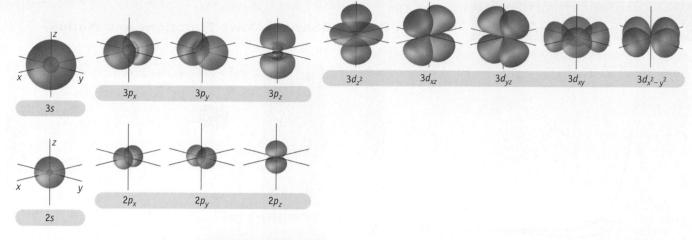

Active Figure 6.14 Atomic orbitals. Boundary surface diagrams for electron densities of 1s, 2s, 2p, 3s, 3p, and 3d orbitals for the hydrogen atom. For the p orbitals, the subscript letter indicates the cartesian axis along which the orbital lies. For more about orbitals, see *A Closer Look: H Atom Orbital Shapes—Wave Functions and Nodes*.

Chemistry.Now™ Sign in at www.cengage.com/login and go to the Chapter Contents menu to explore an interactive version of this figure accompanied by an exercise.

All *s* orbitals (1s, 2s, 3s ...) are spherical in shape. However, for any atom, the size of *s* orbitals increases as *n* increases (Figure 6.14). For a given atom, the 1s orbital is more compact than the 2s orbital, which is in turn more compact than the 3s orbital.

p Orbitals

All atomic orbitals for which $\ell = 1$ (*p* orbitals) have the same basic shape. If you enclose 90% of the electron density in a *p* orbital within a surface, the electron cloud has a shape that resembles a weight lifter's "dumbbell," and chemists describe *p* orbitals as having dumbbell shapes (Figures 6.14 and 6.15) because there is a **nodal surface**—a surface on which the electron has no probability—that passes through the nucleus. (The nodal surface is a consequence of the wave function for *p* orbitals,

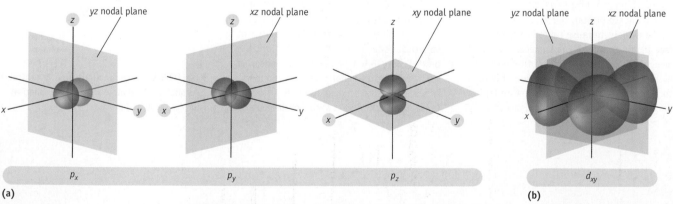

FIGURE 6.15 Nodal surfaces of *p* and *d* orbitals. A plane passing through the nucleus (perpendicular to the axis) is called a nodal surface. (a) The three *p* orbitals each have one nodal surface ($\ell = 1$). (b) The d_{xy} orbital. All five *d* orbitals have two nodal surfaces ($\ell = 2$) through the nucleus. Here, the nodal surfaces are the *xz*- and *yz*-planes, so the regions of electron density lie in the *xy*-plane and between the *x*- and *y*-axes.

which has no value at the nucleus but which rises rapidly in value on moving way from the nucleus. See *A Closer Look: H Atom Orbital Shapes—Wave Functions and Nodes.*)

There are three *p* orbitals in a subshell, and all have the same basic shape with one planar node through the nucleus. Usually, *p* orbitals are drawn along the *x*-, *y*-, and *z*-axes and labeled according to the axis along which they lie (p_x, p_y, or p_z).

d Orbitals

Orbitals with $\ell = 0$, *s* orbitals, have no nodal surfaces through the nucleus, and *p* orbitals, for which $\ell = 1$, have one nodal surface through the nucleus. *The value of ℓ is equal to the number of nodal surfaces slicing through the nucleus.* It follows that the five *d* orbitals, for which $\ell = 2$, have two nodal surfaces through the nucleus, resulting in four regions of electron density. The d_{xy} orbital, for example, lies in the *xy*-plane, and the two nodal surfaces are the *xz*- and *yz*-planes (Figure 6.15). Two other orbitals, d_{xz} and d_{yz}, lie in planes defined by the *xz*- and *yz*-axes, respectively; they also have two, mutually perpendicular nodal surfaces (Figure 6.14).

Of the two remaining *d* orbitals, the $d_{x^2-y^2}$ orbital is easier to visualize. In the $d_{x^2-y^2}$ orbital, the nodal planes bisect the *x*- and *y*-axes, so the regions of electron density lie along the *x*- and *y*-axes. The d_{z^2} orbital has two main regions of electron density along the *z*-axis, and a "doughnut" of electron density also occurs in the *xy*-plane. This orbital has two cone-shaped nodal surfaces.

f Orbitals

Seven *f* orbitals arise with $\ell = 3$. Three nodal surfaces through the nucleus cause the electron density to lie in eight regions of space. One of the *f* orbitals is illustrated in Figure 6.16.

Chemistry ⚛ Now™

Sign in at **www.cengage.com/login** and go to Chapter 6 Contents to see Screen 6.13 for exercises on **orbital shapes, quantum numbers, and nodes.**

EXERCISE 6.8 Orbital Shapes

(a) What are the *n* and ℓ values for each of the following orbitals: *6s*, *4p*, *5d*, and *4f*?

(b) How many nodal planes exist for a *4p* orbital? For a *6d* orbital?

FIGURE 6.16 One of the seven possible *f* orbitals. Notice the presence of three nodal planes as required by an orbital with $\ell = 3$.

Charles D. Winters

■ **Nodal Surfaces** Nodal surfaces through the nucleus occur for all *p, d,* and *f* orbitals. These surfaces are usually flat, so they are referred to as nodal planes. In some cases (for example, d_{z^2}), however, the "plane" is not flat and so is better referred to as a "surface."

■ **ℓ and Nodal Surfaces** The number of nodal surfaces passing through the nucleus for an orbital = ℓ.

Orbital	ℓ	Number of Nodal Surfaces through the Nucleus
s	0	0
p	1	1
d	2	2
f	3	3

6.7 One More Electron Property: Electron Spin

There is one more property of the electron that plays an important role in the arrangement of electrons in atoms and gives rise to properties of elements you observe every day: electron spin.

The Electron Spin Quantum Number, m_s

In 1921 Otto Stern and Walther Gerlach performed an experiment that probed the magnetic behavior of atoms by passing a beam of silver atoms in the gas phase through a magnetic field. Although the results were complex, they were best interpreted by imagining the electron has a spin and behaves as a tiny magnet that can be attracted or repelled by another magnet (Figure 6.17). If atoms with a single unpaired electron are placed in a magnetic field, the Stern-Gerlach ex-

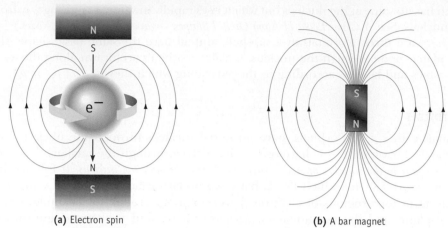

(a) Electron spin   **(b)** A bar magnet

FIGURE 6.17 Magnetic fields—a bar magnet and an electron. The electron, with its spin and negative electric charge, can be thought of as a small bar magnet. Relative to a magnetic field, only two spin directions are possible for the electron, clockwise or counterclockwise. The north pole of the spinning electron can therefore be either aligned with an external magnetic field or opposed to that field.

A Closer Look

Paramagnetism and Ferromagnetism

Magnetic materials are relatively common, and many are important in our economy. For example, a large magnet is at the heart of the magnetic resonance imaging (MRI) used in medicine, and tiny magnets are found in stereo speakers and in telephone handsets. Magnetic oxides are used in recording tapes and computer disks.

The magnetic materials we use are **ferromagnetic**. The magnetic effect of ferromagnetic materials is much larger than that of paramagnetic ones. Ferromagnetism occurs when the spins of unpaired electrons in a cluster of atoms (called a *domain*) in the solid align themselves in the same direction. Only the metals of the iron, cobalt, and nickel subgroups, as well as a few other metals such as neodymium, exhibit this property. They are also unique in that, once the domains are aligned in a magnetic field, the metal is permanently magnetized.

Many alloys exhibit greater ferromagnetism than do the pure metals themselves. One example of such a material is Alnico, which is composed of aluminum, nickel, and cobalt as well as copper and iron.

Audio and video tapes are plastics coated with crystals of ferromagnetic oxides such as Fe_2O_3 or CrO_2. The recording head uses an electromagnetic field to create a varying magnetic field based on signals from a microphone. This magnetizes the tape as it passes through the head, with the strength and direction of magnetization varying with the frequency of the sound to be recorded. When the tape is played back, the magnetic field of the moving tape induces a current, which is amplified and sent to the speakers.

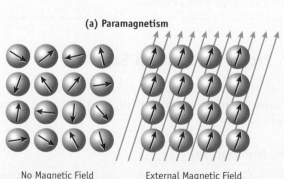

(a) Paramagnetism   **(b) Ferromagnetism**

No Magnetic Field   External Magnetic Field

The spins of unpaired electrons
align themselves in the same direction

Magnetism. (a) Paramagnetism: In the absence of an external magnetic field, the unpaired electrons in the atoms or ions of the substance are randomly oriented. If a magnetic field is imposed, however, these spins will tend to become aligned with the field. (b) Ferromagnetism: The spins of the unpaired electrons in a cluster of atoms or ions align themselves in the same direction in the absence of a magnetic field.

Magnets. Many common consumer products such as loud speakers contain permanent magnets.

Charles D. Winters

periment showed there are two orientations for the atoms: with the electron spin aligned with the field or opposed to the field. That is, *the electron spin is quantized,* which introduces another quantum number, the **electron spin quantum number,** m_s. One orientation is associated with a value of m_s of $+\frac{1}{2}$ and the other with m_s of $-\frac{1}{2}$.

When it was recognized that electron spin is quantized, scientists realized that a complete description of an electron in any atom requires four quantum numbers, n, ℓ, m_ℓ, and m_s. The important consequences of this fact are explored in Chapter 7.

Diamagnetism and Paramagnetism

A hydrogen atom has a single electron. If a hydrogen atom is placed in a magnetic field, the magnetic field of the single electron will tend to align with the external field like the needle of a compass. There is an attractive force. Helium atoms, each with two electrons, are not attracted to a magnet, however. In fact, they are slightly repelled by the magnet. To account for this observation, we assume the two electrons of helium have opposite spin orientations. We say their spins are *paired,* and the result is that the magnetic field of one electron can be canceled out by the magnetic field of the second electron with opposite spin. To account for this, the two electrons are assigned different values of m_s.

It is important to understand the relationship between electron spin and magnetism. *Elements and compounds that have unpaired electrons are attracted to a magnet.* These species are referred to as **paramagnetic.** The effect can be quite weak, but, by placing a sample of an element or compound in a magnetic field, it can be observed (Figure 6.18). For example, the oxygen you breathe, is paramagnetic. You can observe this experimentally because liquid oxygen sticks to a magnet of the kind you may have in the speakers of a music player (Figure 6.18b).

Substances in which all electrons are paired (with the two electrons of each pair having opposite spins) experience a slight repulsion when subjected to a magnetic

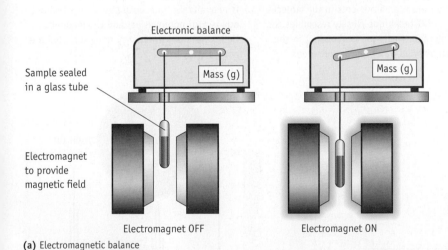

(a) Electromagnetic balance

(b) Liquid oxygen clings to a magnet.

Active Figure 6.18 **Observing and measuring paramagnetism.** (a) A magnetic balance is used to measure the magnetism of a sample. The sample is first weighed with the electromagnet turned off. The magnet is then turned on and the sample reweighed. If the substance is paramagnetic, the sample is drawn into the magnetic field, and the apparent weight increases. (b) Liquid oxygen (boiling point 90.2 K) clings to a strong magnet. Elemental oxygen is paramagnetic because it has unpaired electrons. (See Chapter 9.)

Chemistry⚛Now™ Sign in at www.cengage.com/login and go to the Chapter Contents menu to explore an interactive version of this figure accompanied by an exercise.

Just as electrons have a spin, so do atomic nuclei. In the hydrogen atom, the single proton of the nucleus spins on its axis. For most heavier atoms, the atomic nucleus includes both protons and neutrons, and the entire entity has a spin. This property is important, because nuclear spin allows scientists to detect these atoms in molecules and to learn something about their chemical environments.

The technique used to detect the spins of atomic nuclei is *nuclear magnetic resonance* (NMR). It is one of the most powerful methods currently available to determine molecular structures. About 20 years ago, it was adapted as a diagnostic technique in medicine, where it is known as *magnetic resonance imaging* (MRI).

Just as electron spin is quantized, so too is nuclear spin. The H atom nucleus can spin in either of two directions. If the H atom is placed in a strong, external magnetic field, however, the spinning nuclear magnet can align itself with or against the external field. If a sample of ethanol (CH_3CH_2OH), for example, is placed in a strong magnetic field, a slight excess of the H atom nuclei (and ^{13}C atom nuclei) is aligned with the lines of force of the field.

The nuclei aligned with the field have a slightly lower energy than when aligned against the field. The NMR and MRI technologies depend on the fact that energy in the radio-frequency region can be absorbed by the sample and can cause the nuclear spins switch alignments—that is, to move to a

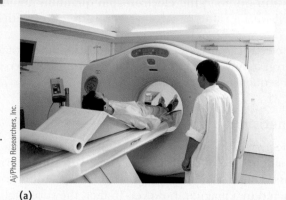

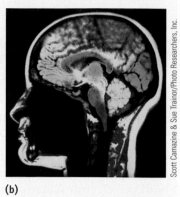

(a)   **(b)**

Magnetic resonance imaging. (a) MRI instrument. The patient is placed inside a large magnet, and the tissues to be examined are irradiated with radio-frequency radiation. (b) An MRI image of the human brain.

higher energy state. This absorption of energy is detected by the instrument.

The most important aspect of the magnetic resonance technique is that the difference in energy between two different spin states depends on the electronic environment of atoms in the molecule. In the case of ethanol, the three CH_3 protons are different from the two CH_2 protons, and both sets are different from the OH proton. These three different sets of H atoms absorb radiation of slightly different energies. The instrument measures the frequencies absorbed, and a scientist familiar with the technique can quickly distinguish the three different environments in the molecule.

The MRI technique closely resembles the NMR method. Hydrogen is abundant in the human body as water and in numerous

organic molecules. In the MRI device, the patient is placed in a strong magnetic field, and the tissues being examined are irradiated with pulses of radio-frequency radiation.

The MRI image is produced by detecting how fast the excited nuclei "relax"; that is, how fast they return to the lower energy state from the higher energy state. The "relaxation time" depends on the type of tissue. When the tissue is scanned, the H atoms in different regions of the body show different relaxation times, and an accurate "image" is built up.

MRI gives information on soft tissue—muscle, cartilage, and internal organs—which is unavailable from x-ray scans. This technology is also noninvasive, and the magnetic fields and radio-frequency radiation used are not harmful to the body.

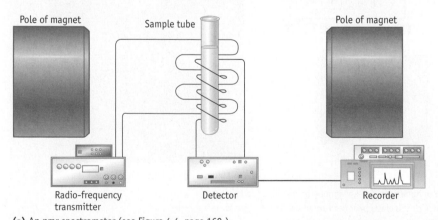

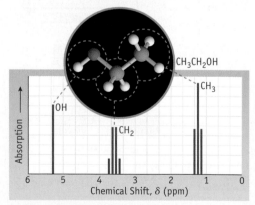

(a) An nmr spectrometer (see Figure 4.4, page 169.)   **(b)** The nmr spectrum of ethanol

Nuclear magnetic resonance. (a) A schematic diagram of an NMR spectrometer. (b) The NMR spectrum of ethanol, showing that the three different types of protons appear in distinctly different regions of the spectrum. The pattern observed for the CH_2 and CH_3 protons is characteristic of these groups of atoms and signals the chemist that they are present in the molecule.

field; they are called **diamagnetic**. Therefore, by determining the magnetic behavior of a substance (see Figure 16.8) we can gain information on the electronic structure.

In summary, *paramagnetism is the attraction to a magnetic field of substances in which the constituent ions or atoms contain unpaired electrons.* Substances in which all electrons are paired with partners of opposite spin are diamagnetic. This explanation opens the way to understanding the arrangement of electrons in atoms with more than one electron.

Chemistry‚Now™

Sign in at **www.cengage.com/login** and go to Chapter 6 Contents to see:
• Screen 6.15 for a self-study module on **electron spin**
• Screen 6.16 for an exercise on **spinning electrons and magnetism**

Chapter Goals Revisited

Now that you have studied this chapter, you should ask whether you have met the chapter goals. In particular, you should be able to:

Describe the properties of electromagnetic radiation
a. Use the terms wavelength, frequency, amplitude, and node (Section 6.1). Study Question(s) assignable in OWL: 3.
b. Use Equation 6.1 ($c = \lambda \nu$), relating wavelength (λ) and frequency (ν) of electromagnetic radiation and the speed of light (c).
c. Recognize the relative wavelength (or frequency) of the various types of electromagnetic radiation (Figure 6.2). Study Question(s) assignable in OWL: 1.
d. Understand that the energy of a photon, a massless particle of radiation, is proportional to its frequency (Planck's equation, Equation 6.2) (Section 6.2). Study Question(s) assignable in OWL: 5, 8, 9, 12, 14, 56, 57, 58, 63, 64, 66, 72, 73, 78, 83.

Understand the origin of light from excited atoms and its relationship to atomic structure
a. Describe the Bohr model of the atom, its ability to account for the emission line spectra of excited hydrogen atoms, and the limitations of the model (Section 6.3).
b. Understand that, in the Bohr model of the H atom, the electron can occupy only certain energy states, each with an energy proportional to $1/n^2$ ($E_n = -Rhc/n^2$), where n is the principal quantum number (Equation 6.4, Section 6.3). If an electron moves from one energy state to another, the amount of energy absorbed or emitted in the process is equal to the difference in energy between the two states (Equation 6.5, Section 6.3). Study Question(s) assignable in OWL: 16, 18, 22, 60.

Describe the experimental evidence for particle-wave duality
a. Understand that in the modern view of the atom, electrons can be described either as particles or as waves (Section 6.4). The wavelength of an electron or any subatomic particle is given by de Broglie's equation (Equation 6.6). Study Question(s) assignable in OWL: 24, 26, 47.

Chemistry‚Now™ Sign in at **www. cengage.com/login** to:
• Assess your understanding with Study Questions in OWL keyed to each goal in the Goals and Homework menu for this chapter
• For quick review, download Go Chemistry mini-lecture flashcard modules (or purchase them at **www.ichapters.com**)
• Check your readiness for an exam by taking the Pre-Test and exploring the modules recommended in your Personalized Study plan.

❓ Access **How Do I Solve It?** tutorials on how to approach problem solving using concepts in this chapter.

For additional preparation for an examination on this chapter see the *Let's Review* section on pages 496–513.

Describe the basic ideas of quantum mechanics

a. Recognize the significance of quantum mechanics in describing atomic structure (Section 6.5).

b. Understand that an orbital for an electron in an atom corresponds to the allowed energy of that electron.

c. Understand that the position of the electron is not known with certainty; only the probability of the electron being at a given point of space can be calculated. This is a consequence of the Heisenberg uncertainty principle.

Define the four quantum numbers (n, ℓ, m_ℓ, and m_s), and recognize their relationship to electronic structure

a. Describe the allowed energy states of the orbitals in an atom using three quantum numbers n, ℓ, and m_ℓ (Section 6.5). Study Question(s) assignable in OWL: 28, 30, 32, 34, 36, 37, 38, 40, 43, 44, 80, 83.

b. Describe the shapes of the orbitals (Section 6.6). Study Question(s) assignable in OWL: 46, 51, 53, 67f.

c. Recognize the spin quantum number, m_s, which has values of $\pm\frac{1}{2}$. Classify substances as paramagnetic (attracted to a magnetic field; characterized by unpaired electron spins) or diamagnetic (repelled by a magnetic field, all electrons paired) (Section 6.7).

KEY EQUATIONS

Equation 6.1 (page 269)   The product of the wavelength (λ) and frequency (ν) of electromagnetic radiation is equal to the speed of light (c).

$$c = \lambda \times \nu$$

Equation 6.2 (page 273)   Planck's equation: the energy of a photon, a massless particle of radiation, is proportional to its frequency (ν). The proportionality constant, h, is called Planck's constant (6.626×10^{-34} J · s).

$$E = h\nu$$

Equation 6.4 (page 277)   In Bohr's theory, the potential energy of the electron, E_n, in the nth quantum level of the H atom is proportional to $1/n^2$, where n is a positive integer (the principal quantum number and $Rhc = 2.179 \times 10^{-18}$ J/atom or $N_A Rhc = 1312$ kJ/mol).

$$E_n = -\frac{Rhc}{n^2}$$

Equation 6.5 (page 279)   The energy change for an electron moving between two quantum levels (n_{final} and $n_{initial}$) in the H atom.

$$\Delta E = E_{final} - E_{initial} = -Rhc \left(\frac{1}{n_{final}^2} - \frac{1}{n_{initial}^2} \right)$$

Equation 6.6 (page 282)   De Broglie's equation: the wavelength of a particle (λ) is related to its mass (m) and speed (v) and to Planck's constant (h).

$$\lambda = \frac{h}{mv}$$

STUDY QUESTIONS

OWL Online homework for this chapter may be assigned in OWL.

▲ denotes challenging questions.

■ denotes questions assignable in OWL.

Blue-numbered questions have answers in Appendix O and fully-worked solutions in the *Student Solutions Manual*.

Practicing Skills

Electromagnetic Radiation

(See Example 6.1, Exercise 6.1, Figure 6.2, and ChemistryNow Screen 6.3.)

1. ■ Answer the following questions based on Figure 6.2:
   (a) Which type of radiation involves less energy, x-rays or microwaves?
   (b) Which radiation has the higher frequency, radar or red light?
   (c) Which radiation has the longer wavelength, ultraviolet or infrared light?

2. Consider the colors of the visible spectrum.
   (a) Which colors of light involve less energy than green light?
   (b) Which color of light has photons of greater energy, yellow or blue?
   (c) Which color of light has the greater frequency, blue or green?

3. ■ Traffic signals are often now made of LEDs (light-emitting diodes). Amber and green ones are pictured here.
   (a) The light from an amber signal has a wavelength of 595 nm, and that from a green signal has wavelength of 500 nm. Which has the higher frequency?
   (b) Calculate the frequency of amber light.

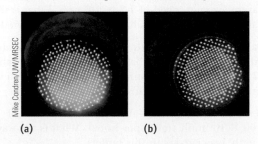

Mike Condren/UW/MRSEC

(a)　　　　　(b)

4. Suppose you are standing 225 m from a radio transmitter. What is your distance from the transmitter in terms of the number of wavelengths if:
   (a) the station is broadcasting at 1150 kHz (on the AM radio band)? (1 kHz = 1 × 10³ Hz.)
   (b) the station is broadcasting at 98.1 MHz (on the FM radio band)? (1 MHz = 10⁶ Hz.)

Electromagnetic Radiation and Planck's Equation

(See page 274, Exercise 6.2, and ChemistryNow Screens 6.4 and 6.5.)

5. ■ Green light has a wavelength of 5.0×10^2 nm. What is the energy, in joules, of one photon of green light? What is the energy, in joules, of 1.0 mol of photons of green light?

6. Violet light has a wavelength of about 410 nm. What is its frequency? Calculate the energy of one photon of violet light. What is the energy of 1.0 mol of violet photons? Compare the energy of photons of violet light with those of red light. Which is more energetic?

7. The most prominent line in the spectrum of aluminum is at 396.15 nm. What is the frequency of this line? What is the energy of one photon with this wavelength? Of 1.00 mol of these photons?

8. ■ The most prominent line in the spectrum of magnesium is 285.2 nm. Other lines are found at 383.8 and 518.4 nm. In what region of the electromagnetic spectrum are these lines found? Which is the most energetic line? What is the energy of 1.00 mol of photons with the wavelength of the most energetic line?

9. ■ Place the following types of radiation in order of increasing energy per photon:
   (a) yellow light from a sodium lamp
   (b) x-rays from an instrument in a dentist's office
   (c) microwaves in a microwave oven
   (d) your favorite FM music station at 91.7 MHz

10. Place the following types of radiation in order of increasing energy per photon:
    (a) radiation within a microwave oven
    (b) your favorite radio station
    (c) gamma rays from a nuclear reaction
    (d) red light from a neon sign
    (e) ultraviolet radiation from a sun lamp

Photoelectric Effect

(See page 274 and Figure 6.4.)

11. An energy of 2.0×10^2 kJ/mol is required to cause a cesium atom on a metal surface to lose an electron. Calculate the longest possible wavelength of light that can ionize a cesium atom. In what region of the electromagnetic spectrum is this radiation found?

12. ■ You are an engineer designing a switch that works by the photoelectric effect. The metal you wish to use in your device requires 6.7×10^{-19} J/atom to remove an electron. Will the switch work if the light falling on the metal has a wavelength of 540 nm or greater? Why or why not?

Atomic Spectra and the Bohr Atom
(See Examples 6.2 and 6.3, Figures 6.6–6.10, and ChemistryNow Screens 6.6 and 6.7.)

13. The most prominent line in the spectrum of mercury is at 253.652 nm. Other lines are located at 365.015 nm, 404.656 nm, 435.833 nm, and 1013.975 nm.
    (a) Which of these lines represents the most energetic light?
    (b) What is the frequency of the most prominent line? What is the energy of one photon with this wavelength?
    (c) Are any of these lines found in the spectrum of mercury shown in Figure 6.7? What color or colors are these lines?

14. ■ The most prominent line in the spectrum of neon is found at 865.438 nm. Other lines are located at 837.761 nm, 878.062 nm, 878.375 nm, and 1885.387 nm.
    (a) In what region of the electromagnetic spectrum are these lines found?
    (b) Are any of these lines found in the spectrum of neon shown in Figure 6.7?
    (c) Which of these lines represents the most energetic radiation?
    (d) What is the frequency of the most prominent line? What is the energy of one photon with this wavelength?

15. A line in the Balmer series of emission lines of excited H atoms has a wavelength of 410.2 nm (Figure 6.10). What color is the light emitted in this transition? What quantum levels are involved in this emission line? That is, what are the values of $n_{initial}$ and n_{final}?

16. ■ What are the wavelength and frequency of the radiation involved in the least energetic emission line in the Lyman series? What are the values of $n_{initial}$ and n_{final}?

17. Consider only transitions involving the $n = 1$ through $n = 5$ energy levels for the H atom (See Figures 6.8 and 6.10).
    (a) How many emission lines are possible, considering only the five quantum levels?
    (b) Photons of the highest frequency are emitted in a transition from the level with $n =$ _____ to a level with $n =$ _____.
    (c) The emission line having the longest wavelength corresponds to a transition from the level with $n =$ _____ to the level with $n =$ _____.

18. ■ Consider only transitions involving the $n = 1$ through $n = 4$ energy levels for the hydrogen atom (See Figures 6.8 and 6.10).
    (a) How many emission lines are possible, considering only the four quantum levels?
    (b) Photons of the lowest energy are emitted in a transition from the level with $n =$ _____ to a level with $n =$ _____.

(c) The emission line having the shortest wavelength corresponds to a transition from the level with $n =$ _____ to the level with $n =$ _____.

19. The energy emitted when an electron moves from a higher energy state to a lower energy state in any atom can be observed as electromagnetic radiation.
    (a) Which involves the emission of less energy in the H atom, an electron moving from $n = 4$ to $n = 2$ or an electron moving from $n = 3$ to $n = 2$?
    (b) Which involves the emission of more energy in the H atom, an electron moving from $n = 4$ to $n = 1$ or an electron moving from $n = 5$ to $n = 2$? Explain fully.

20. If energy is absorbed by a hydrogen atom in its ground state, the atom is excited to a higher energy state. For example, the excitation of an electron from the level with $n = 1$ to the level with $n = 3$ requires radiation with a wavelength of 102.6 nm. Which of the following transitions would require radiation of *longer wavelength* than this?
    (a) $n = 2$ to $n = 4$ (c) $n = 1$ to $n = 5$
    (b) $n = 1$ to $n = 4$ (d) $n = 3$ to $n = 5$

21. Calculate the wavelength and frequency of light emitted when an electron changes from $n = 3$ to $n = 1$ in the H atom. In what region of the spectrum is this radiation found?

22. ■ Calculate the wavelength and frequency of light emitted when an electron changes from $n = 4$ to $n = 3$ in the H atom. In what region of the spectrum is this radiation found?

DeBroglie and Matter Waves
(See Example 6.4 and ChemistryNow Screen 6.8.)

23. An electron moves with a velocity of 2.5×10^8 cm/s. What is its wavelength?

24. ■ A beam of electrons ($m = 9.11 \times 10^{-31}$ kg/electron) has an average speed of 1.3×10^8 m/s. What is the wavelength of electrons having this average speed?

25. Calculate the wavelength, in nanometers, associated with a 1.0×10^2-g golf ball moving at 30. m/s (about 67 mph). How fast must the ball travel to have a wavelength of 5.6×10^{-3} nm?

26. ■ A rifle bullet (mass = 1.50 g) has a velocity of 7.00×10^2 mph (miles per hour). What is the wavelength associated with this bullet?

Quantum Mechanics
(See Sections 6.5–6.7 and ChemistryNow Screens 6.9–6.14.)

27. (a) When $n = 4$, what are the possible values of ℓ?
    (b) When ℓ is 2, what are the possible values of m_ℓ?
    (c) For a 4s orbital, what are the possible values of n, ℓ, and m_ℓ?
    (d) For a 4f orbital, what are the possible values of n, ℓ, and m_ℓ?

28. ■ (a) When $n = 4$, $\ell = 2$, and $m_\ell = -1$, to what orbital type does this refer? (Give the orbital label, such as $1s$.)

(b) How many orbitals occur in the $n = 5$ electron shell? How many subshells? What are the letter labels of the subshells?

(c) If a subshell is labeled f, how many orbitals occur in the subshell? What are the values of m_ℓ?

29. A possible excited state of the H atom has the electron in a $4p$ orbital. List all possible sets of quantum numbers n, ℓ, and m_ℓ for this electron.

30. ■ A possible excited state for the H atom has an electron in a $5d$ orbital. List all possible sets of quantum numbers n, ℓ, and m_ℓ for this electron.

31. How many subshells occur in the electron shell with the principal quantum number $n = 4$?

32. ■ How many subshells occur in the electron shell with the principal quantum number $n = 5$?

33. Explain briefly why each of the following is not a possible set of quantum numbers for an electron in an atom.
(a) $n = 2$, $\ell = 2$, $m_\ell = 0$
(b) $n = 3$, $\ell = 0$, $m_\ell = -2$
(c) $n = 6$, $\ell = 0$, $m_\ell = 1$

34. ■ Which of the following represent valid sets of quantum numbers? For a set that is invalid, explain briefly why it is not correct.
(a) $n = 3$, $\ell = 3$, $m_\ell = 0$ (c) $n = 6$, $\ell = 5$, $m_\ell = -1$
(b) $n = 2$, $\ell = 1$, $m_\ell = 0$ (d) $n = 4$, $\ell = 3$, $m_\ell = -4$

35. ■ What is the maximum number of orbitals that can be identified by each of the following sets of quantum numbers? When "none" is the correct answer, explain your reasoning.
(a) $n = 3$, $\ell = 0$, $m_\ell = +1$ (c) $n = 7$, $\ell = 5$
(b) $n = 5$, $\ell = 1$ (d) $n = 4$, $\ell = 2$, $m_\ell = -2$

36. ■ What is the maximum number of orbitals that can be identified by each of the following sets of quantum numbers? When "none" is the correct answer, explain your reasoning.
(a) $n = 4$, $\ell = 3$ (c) $n = 2$, $\ell = 2$
(b) $n = 5$ (d) $n = 3$, $\ell = 1$, $m_\ell = -1$

37. ■ Explain briefly why each of the following is not a possible set of quantum numbers for an electron in an atom. In each case, change the incorrect value (or values) to make the set valid.
(a) $n = 4$, $\ell = 2$, $m_\ell = 0$, $m_s = 0$
(b) $n = 3$, $\ell = 1$, $m_\ell = -3$, $m_s = -\frac{1}{2}$
(c) $n = 3$, $\ell = 3$, $m_\ell = -1$, $m_s = +\frac{1}{2}$

38. Explain briefly why each of the following is not a possible set of quantum numbers for an electron in an atom. In each case, change the incorrect value (or values) to make the set valid.
(a) $n = 2$, $\ell = 2$, $m_\ell = 0$, $m_s = +\frac{1}{2}$
(b) $n = 2$, $\ell = 1$, $m_\ell = -1$, $m_s = 0$
(c) $n = 3$, $\ell = 1$, $m_\ell = +2$, $m_s = +\frac{1}{2}$

39. State which of the following orbitals cannot exist according to the quantum theory: $2s$, $2d$, $3p$, $3f$, $4f$, and $5s$. Briefly explain your answers.

40. ■ State which of the following are incorrect designations for orbitals according to the quantum theory: $3p$, $4s$, $2f$, and $1p$. Briefly explain your answers.

41. Write a complete set of quantum numbers (n, ℓ, and m_ℓ) that quantum theory allows for each of the following orbitals: (a) $2p$, (b) $3d$, and (c) $4f$.

42. ■ Write a complete set of quantum numbers (n, ℓ, and m_ℓ) for each of the following orbitals: (a) $5f$, (b) $4d$, and (c) $2s$.

43. ■ A particular orbital has $n = 4$ and $\ell = 2$. What must this orbital be: (a) $3p$, (b) $4p$, (c) $5d$, or (d) $4d$?

44. ■ A given orbital has a magnetic quantum number of $m_\ell = -1$. This could *not* be a (an)
(a) f orbital (c) p orbital
(b) d orbital (d) s orbital

45. How many planar nodes are associated with each of the following orbitals?
(a) $2s$ (b) $5d$ (c) $5f$

46. ■ How many planar nodes are associated with each of the following atomic orbitals?
(a) $4f$ (b) $2p$ (c) $6s$

General Questions on Atomic Structure
These questions are not designated as to type or location in the chapter. They may combine several concepts.

47. ■ Which of the following are applicable when explaining the photoelectric effect? Correct any statements that are wrong.
(a) Light is electromagnetic radiation.
(b) The intensity of a light beam is related to its frequency.
(c) Light can be thought of as consisting of massless particles whose energy is given by Planck's equation, $E = h\nu$

48. In what region of the electromagnetic spectrum for hydrogen is the Lyman series of lines found? The Balmer series?

49. Give the number of nodal surfaces through the nucleus (planar nodes) for each orbital type: s, p, d, and f.

50. What is the maximum number of s orbitals found in a given electron shell? The maximum number of p orbitals? Of d orbitals? Of f orbitals?

51. ■ Match the values of ℓ shown in the table with orbital type (s, p, d, or f).

ℓ Value	Orbital Type
3	_____
0	_____
1	_____
2	_____

52. Sketch a picture of the 90% boundary surface of an s orbital and the p_x orbital. Be sure the latter drawing shows why the p orbital is labeled p_x and not p_y, for example.

53. ■ Complete the following table.

Orbital Type	Number of Orbitals in a Given Subshell	Number of Nodal Surfaces through the Nucleus
s	_____	_____
p	_____	_____
d	_____	_____
f	_____	_____

54. Excited H atoms have many emission lines. One series of lines, called the Pfund series, occurs in the infrared region. It results when an electron changes from higher energy levels to a level with $n = 5$. Calculate the wavelength and frequency of the lowest energy line of this series.

55. An advertising sign gives off red light and green light.
    (a) Which light has the higher-energy photons?
    (b) One of the colors has a wavelength of 680 nm, and the other has a wavelength of 500 nm. Which color has which wavelength?
    (c) Which light has the higher frequency?

56. ■ Radiation in the ultraviolet region of the electromagnetic spectrum is quite energetic. It is this radiation that causes dyes to fade and your skin to develop a sunburn. If you are bombarded with 1.00 mol of photons with a wavelength of 375 nm, what amount of energy, in kilojoules per mole of photons, are you being subjected to?

57. ■ A cell phone sends signals at about 850 MHz ($1 \text{ MHz} = 1 \times 10^6 \text{ Hz}$ or cycles per second).
    (a) What is the wavelength of this radiation?
    (b) What is the energy of 1.0 mol of photons with a frequency of 850 MHz?
    (c) Compare the energy in part (b) with the energy of a mole of photons of blue light (420 nm).
    (d) Comment on the difference in energy between 850 MHz radiation and blue light.

58. ■ Assume your eyes receive a signal consisting of blue light, $\lambda = 470$ nm. The energy of the signal is 2.50×10^{-14} J. How many photons reach your eyes?

59. If sufficient energy is absorbed by an atom, an electron can be lost by the atom and a positive ion formed. The amount of energy required is called the ionization energy. In the H atom, the ionization energy is that required to change the electron from $n = 1$ to $n = $ infinity. (See Exercise 6.5, page 280.) Calculate the ionization energy for the He$^+$ ion. Is the ionization energy of the He$^+$ more or less than that of H? (Bohr's theory applies to He$^+$ because it, like the H atom, has a single electron. The electron energy, however, is now given by $E = -Z^2 Rhc/n^2$, where Z is the atomic number of helium.)

60. ■ Suppose hydrogen atoms absorb energy so that electrons are excited to the $n = 7$ energy level. Electrons then undergo these transitions, among others: (a) $n = 7 \rightarrow n = 1$; (b) $n = 7 \rightarrow n = 6$; and (c) $n = 2 \rightarrow n = 1$. Which transition produces a photon with (i) the smallest energy, (ii) the highest frequency, and (iii) the shortest wavelength?

61. Rank the following orbitals in the H atom in order of increasing energy: $3s$, $2s$, $2p$, $4s$, $3p$, $1s$, and $3d$.

62. ■ How many orbitals correspond to each of the following designations?
    (a) $3p$ (d) $6d$ (g) $n = 5$
    (b) $4p$ (e) $5d$ (h) $7s$
    (c) $4p_x$ (f) $5f$

63. ■ Cobalt-60 is a radioactive isotope used in medicine for the treatment of certain cancers. It produces β particles and γ rays, the latter having energies of 1.173 and 1.332 MeV. ($1 \text{ MeV} = 10^6$ electron-volts and $1 \text{ eV} = 9.6485 \times 10^4$ J/mol.) What are the wavelength and frequency of a γ-ray photon with an energy of 1.173 MeV?

64. ▲ ■ Exposure to high doses of microwaves can cause tissue damage. Estimate how many photons, with $\lambda = 12$ cm, must be absorbed to raise the temperature of your eye by 3.0 °C. Assume the mass of an eye is 11 g and its specific heat capacity is 4.0 J/g · K.

65. When the Sojourner spacecraft landed on Mars in 1997, the planet was approximately 7.8×10^7 km from Earth. How long did it take for the television picture signal to reach Earth from Mars?

66. ■ The most prominent line in the emission spectrum of chromium is found at 425.4 nm. Other lines in the chromium spectrum are found at 357.9 nm, 359.3 nm, 360.5 nm, 427.5 nm, 429.0 nm, and 520.8 nm.
    (a) Which of these lines represents the most energetic light?
    (b) What color is light of wavelength 425.4 nm?

▲ more challenging   ■ in OWL   Blue-numbered questions answered in Appendix O

67. Answer the following questions as a summary quiz on the chapter.

(a) The quantum number n describes the _____ of an atomic orbital.

(b) The shape of an atomic orbital is given by the quantum number _____.

(c) A photon of green light has _____ (less or more) energy than a photon of orange light.

(d) The maximum number of orbitals that may be associated with the set of quantum numbers $n = 4$ and $\ell = 3$ is _____.

(e) The maximum number of orbitals that may be associated with the quantum number set $n = 3$, $\ell = 2$, and $m_\ell = -2$ is _____.

(f) ■ Label each of the following orbital pictures with the appropriate letter:

(g) When $n = 5$, the possible values of ℓ are _____.

(h) The number of orbitals in the $n = 4$ shell is _____.

(i) A Co^{2+} ion has three unpaired electrons. A sample of $CoCl_2$ is (paramagnetic) (diamagnetic).

68. Answer the following questions as a summary quiz on this chapter.

(a) The quantum number n describes the _____ of an atomic orbital, and the quantum number ℓ describes its _____.

(b) When $n = 3$, the possible values of ℓ are _____.

(c) What type of orbital corresponds to $\ell = 3$? _____

(d) For a $4d$ orbital, the value of n is _____, the value of ℓ is _____, and a possible value of m_ℓ is _____.

(e) Each of the following drawings represents a type of atomic orbital. Give the letter designation for the orbital; give its value of ℓ, and specify the number of nodal surfaces.

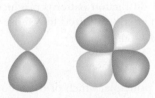

Letter = _____   _____
ℓ value = _____   _____
Planar nodes = _____   _____

(f) An atomic orbital with three nodal surfaces through the nucleus is _____.

(g) Which of the following orbitals cannot exist according to modern quantum theory: $2s$, $3p$, $2d$, $3f$, $5p$, $6p$?

(h) Which of the following is not a valid set of quantum numbers?

n	ℓ	m_ℓ	m_s
3	2	1	$-\frac{1}{2}$
2	1	2	$+\frac{1}{2}$
4	3	0	0

(i) What is the maximum number of orbitals that can be associated with each of the following sets of quantum numbers? (One possible answer is "none.")

(i) $n = 2$ and $\ell = 1$

(ii) $n = 3$

(iii) $n = 3$ and $\ell = 3$

(iv) $n = 2$, $\ell = 1$, and $m_\ell = 0$

(j) A Cu^{2+} ion has one unpaired electron. Is a sample of $CuBr_2$ paramagnetic or diamagnetic?

69. The diagrams below represent a small section of a solid. Each circle represents an atom, and an arrow represents an electron.

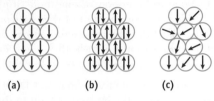

(a)   (b)   (c)

(a) Which represents a diamagnetic solid, which a paramagnetic solid, and which a ferromagnetic solid?

(b) Which is most strongly attracted to a magnetic field? Which is least strongly attracted?

In the Laboratory

70. A solution of $KMnO_4$ absorbs light at 540 nm (page 192). What is the frequency of the light absorbed? What is the energy of one mole of photons with $\lambda = 540$ nm?

71. A large pickle is attached to two electrodes, which are then attached to a 110-V power supply (see the problem on Screen 6.7 of ChemistryNow). As the voltage is increased across the pickle, it begins to glow with a yellow color. Knowing that pickles are made by soaking the vegetable in a concentrated salt solution, describe why the pickle might emit light when electrical energy is added.

The "electric pickle."

72. ■ The spectrum shown here is for aspirin. The vertical axis is the amount of light absorbed, and the horizontal axis is the wavelength of incident light (in nm).

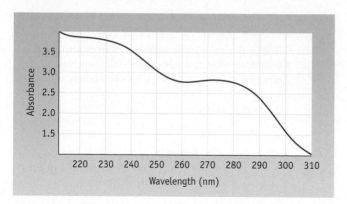

What is the frequency of light with a wavelength of 278 nm? What is the energy of one mole of photons with $\lambda = 278$ nm? What region of the electromagnetic spectrum is covered by the spectrum above? Knowing that aspirin only absorbs light in the region depicted by this spectrum, what is the color of aspirin?

73. ■ The infrared spectrum for methanol, CH_3OH, is illustrated below. It shows the amount of light in the infrared region that methanol transmits as a function of wavelength. The vertical axis is the amount of light transmitted. At points near the top of the graph, most of the incident light is being transmitted by the sample (or, conversely, little light is absorbed.) Therefore, the "peaks" or "bands" that descend from the top indicate light absorbed; the longer the band, the more light is being absorbed (or, conversely, the less is being transmitted). The horizontal scale is in units of "wavenumbers," abbreviated cm^{-1}. The energy of light is given by Planck's law as $E = hc/\lambda$; that is, E is proportional to $1/\lambda$. Therefore, the horizontal scale is in units of $1/\lambda$ and reflects the energy of the light incident on the sample.

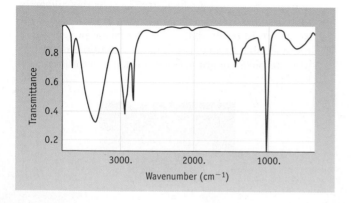

(a) One point on the horizontal axis is marked as 2000 cm^{-1}. What is the wavelength of light at this point?
(b) Which is the low energy end of this spectrum (left or right), and which is the high energy end?
(c) The broad absorption at about 3300–3400 cm^{-1} indicates that infrared radiation is interacting with the OH group of the methanol molecule. The narrower absorptions around 2800–3000 cm^{-1} are for interactions with C—H bonds. Which interaction requires more energy, with O—H or with C—H?

Summary and Conceptual Questions
The following questions use concepts from this and previous chapters.

74. Bohr pictured the electrons of the atom as being located in definite orbits about the nucleus, just as the planets orbit the sun. Criticize this model.

75. Light is given off by a sodium- or mercury-containing streetlight when the atoms are excited. The light you see arises for which of the following reasons?
(a) Electrons are moving from a given energy level to one of higher energy.
(b) Electrons are being removed from the atom, thereby creating a metal cation.
(c) Electrons are moving from a given energy level to one of lower energy.

76. How do we interpret the physical meaning of the square of the wave function? What are the units of $4\pi r^2 \psi^2$?

77. What does "wave–particle duality" mean? What are its implications in our modern view of atomic structure?

78. ■ Which of these are observable?
(a) position of an electron in an H atom
(b) frequency of radiation emitted by H atoms
(c) path of an electron in an H atom
(d) wave motion of electrons
(e) diffraction patterns produced by electrons
(f) diffraction patterns produced by light
(g) energy required to remove electrons from H atoms
(h) an atom
(i) a molecule
(j) a water wave

79. In principle, which of the following can be determined?
(a) the energy of an electron in the H atom with high precision and accuracy
(b) the position of a high-speed electron with high precision and accuracy
(c) at the same time, both the position and the energy of a high-speed electron with high precision and accuracy

80. ▲ ■ Suppose you live in a different universe where a different set of quantum numbers is required to describe the atoms of that universe. These quantum numbers have the following rules:

N, principal	$1, 2, 3, \ldots, \infty$
L, orbital	$= N$
M, magnetic	$-1, 0, +1$

How many orbitals are there altogether in the first three electron shells?

81. A photon with a wavelength of 93.8 nm strikes a hydrogen atom, and light is emitted by the atom. How many emission lines would be observed? At what wavelengths? Explain briefly (see Figure 6.10).

82. Explain why you could or could not measure the wavelength of a golf ball in flight.

83. ■ The radioactive element technetium is not found naturally on earth; it must be synthesized in the laboratory. It is a valuable element, however, because it has medical uses. For example, the element in the form of sodium pertechnetate ($NaTcO_4$) is used in imaging studies of the brain, thyroid, and salivary glands and in renal blood flow studies, among other things.
    (a) In what group and period of the periodic table is the element found?
    (b) The valence electrons of technetium are found in the $5s$ and $4d$ subshells. What is a set of quantum numbers (n, ℓ, and m_ℓ) for one of the electrons of the $5s$ subshell?
    (c) ■ Technetium emits a γ-ray with an energy of 0.141 MeV. (1 MeV = 10^6 electron-volts, where 1 eV = 9.6485×10^4 J/mol.) What are the wavelength and frequency of a γ-ray photon with an energy of 0.141 MeV?

    (d) To make $NaTcO_4$, the metal is dissolved in nitric acid.

    $$7 HNO_3(aq) + Tc(s) \rightarrow$$
    $$HTcO_4(aq) + 7 NO_2(g) + 3 H_2O(\ell)$$

    and the product, $HTcO_4$, is treated with NaOH to make $NaTcO_4$.
    (i) Write a balanced equation for the reaction of $HTcO_4$ with NaOH.
    (ii) If you begin with 4.5 mg of Tc metal, how much $NaTcO_4$ can be made? What mass of NaOH, in grams, is required to convert all of the $HTcO_4$ into $NaTcO_4$?
    (e) If you synthesize 1.5 micromoles of $NaTcO_4$, what mass of compound do you have? If the compound is dissolved in 10.0 mL of solution, what is the concentration?

84. See ChemistryNow Screen 6.1, Chemical Puzzler. This screen shows that light of different colors can come from a "neon" sign or from certain salts when they are placed in a burning organic liquid. ("Neon" signs are glass tubes filled with neon, argon, and other gases, and the gases are excited by an electric current.) What do these two sources of light have in common? How is the light generated in each case?

85. See ChemistryNow Screen 6.7, Bohr's Model of the Hydrogen Atom, Simulation. A photon with a wavelength of 97.3 nm is fired at a hydrogen atom and leads to the emission of light. How many emission lines are emitted? Explain why more than one line is emitted.

7 | The Structure of Atoms and Periodic Trends

Charles D. Winters

The Chromium-Bearing Mineral Crocoite, PbCrO₄

Minerals containing the chromate ion are extremely rare. The best example is crocoite, lead(II) chromate, which is found almost exclusively in Tasmania. Although it is nearly insoluble in water, traces will nonetheless dissolve and contaminate groundwater with Pb^{2+} and CrO_4^{2-} ions.

Chromium compounds in groundwater can be a problem. In the United States, 56% of the population relies on groundwater for drinking water, and the shallow aquifers from which the water is often obtained are susceptible to contamination. One such contaminant is chromium in its various ionic forms (Cr^{3+}, CrO_4^{2-}, and $Cr_2O_7^{2-}$). The source of such ions can be mineral deposits, but more significant sources are industries involved in leather tanning [which uses $Cr(OH)SO_4$] or electroplating of chromium for corrosion protection. In a case depicted in the movie *Erin Brockovich*, a gas and electric utility was found to have contaminated groundwater in southern California with chromates that had been used in water-cooling towers to prevent rust.

Chromium compounds can also be biochemically active, although they are not implicated in as many important processes as another element in Group 6B, molybdenum. There is some evidence that chromium is one of the essential elements, and it is implicated in insulin regulation. In fact, the recommended daily dose of chromium is 5–200 μg. A compound called chromium(III) picolinate is marketed as a "nutritional" supplement and is widely used as a weight-loss aid. The majority of research has found, however, that it is neither helpful nor beneficial in weight-loss programs.

Questions:
1. What is the electron configuration for the Cr atom, for the Cr^{3+} ion, and for the chromium in the CrO_4^{2-} ion?
2. Is chromium in any of the ionic forms paramagnetic?
3. What is the electron configuration for the lead ions in PbCrO₄?

Answers to these questions are in Appendix Q.

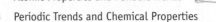
The wave mechanical model of the atom has spinning electrons assigned to orbitals that are best described as matter waves. The orbitals are arranged in subshells that are in turn part of electron shells. One objective of this chapter is to apply this model to the electronic structure of all of the elements.

A second objective is to explore some of the physical properties of elements, among them the ease with which atoms lose or gain electrons to form ions and the sizes of atoms and ions. These properties are directly related to the arrangement of electrons in atoms and thus to the chemistry of the elements and their compounds.

Chemistry.Now™

Throughout the text this icon introduces an opportunity for self-study or to explore interactive tutorials by signing in at **www.cengage.com/login**.

7.1 The Pauli Exclusion Principle

To make the quantum theory consistent with experiment, the Austrian physicist Wolfgang Pauli (1900–1958) stated in 1925 his **exclusion principle:** no two electrons in an atom can have the same set of four quantum numbers (n, ℓ, m_ℓ, and m_s). The consequence of this is that *no atomic orbital can be assigned more than two electrons,* and the two electrons assigned to an orbital must have different values of m_s.

An electron assigned to the $1s$ orbital of the H atom may have the set of quantum numbers $n = 1$, $\ell = 0$, and $m_\ell = 0$, and $m_s = +\frac{1}{2}$. Let us represent an orbital by a box and the electron spin by an arrow ($\uparrow$ or $\downarrow$). A representation of the hydrogen atom is then:

Electrons in $1s$ orbital: $\boxed{\uparrow}$ Quantum number set
$1s$ $n = 1$, $\ell = 0$, $m_\ell = 0$, $m_s = +\frac{1}{2}$

The choice of m_s (either $+\frac{1}{2}$ or $-\frac{1}{2}$) and the direction of the electron spin arrow are arbitrary; that is, we could choose either value, and the arrow may point in either direction. Diagrams such as these are called **orbital box diagrams.**

A *helium* atom has two electrons, both assigned to the $1s$ orbital. The Pauli exclusion principle requires that each electron must have a different set of quantum numbers, so the orbital box diagram now is:

$1s$

Two electrons in $1s$ orbital: $\boxed{\uparrow\downarrow}$ ◄──── This electron has $n = 1$, $\ell = 0$, $m_\ell = 0$, $m_s = -\frac{1}{2}$

──── This electron has $n = 1$, $\ell = 0$, $m_\ell = 0$, $m_s = +\frac{1}{2}$

By having opposite spins, the two electrons in the $1s$ orbital of an He atom have different sets of the four quantum numbers.

■ **Orbitals Are Not Boxes** Orbitals are not boxes in which electrons are placed. Thus, it is not conceptually correct to talk about electrons being in orbitals or occupying orbitals, although this is commonly done for the sake of simplicity.

TABLE 7.1 Number of Electrons Accommodated in Electron Shells and Subshells with $n = 1$ to 6

Electron Shell (n)	Subshells Available	Orbitals Available ($2\ell + 1$)	Number of Electrons Possible in Subshell [$2(2\ell + 1)$]	Maximum Electrons Possible for nth Shell ($2n^2$)
1	s	1	2	2
2	s	1	2	8
	p	3	6	
3	s	1	2	18
	p	3	6	
	d	5	10	
4	s	1	2	32
	p	3	6	
	d	5	10	
	f	7	14	
5	s	1	2	50
	p	3	6	
	d	5	10	
	f	7	14	
	$g*$	9	18	
6	s	1	2	72
	p	3	6	
	d	5	10	
	$f*$	7	14	
	$g*$	9	18	
	$h*$	11	22	

*These orbitals are not occupied in the ground state of any known element.

■ **Spin Quantum Number and Arrows**
In this book, we arbitrarily use an arrow pointing up (↑) to represent $m_s = +\frac{1}{2}$ and an arrow pointing down (↓) to represent $m_s = -\frac{1}{2}$. We will usually designate the first electron assigned to an orbital as having $m_s = +\frac{1}{2}$ though it could just as readily have $m_s = -\frac{1}{2}$.

Our understanding of orbitals and the knowledge that an orbital can accommodate no more than two electrons tell us the maximum number of electrons that can occupy each electron shell or subshell. For example, because each of the three orbitals in a p subshell can hold two electrons, p subshells can hold a maximum of six electrons. By the same reasoning, the five orbitals of a d subshell can accommodate a total of 10 electrons, and the seven f orbitals can accommodate 14 electrons. Recall that there are n subshells in the nth shell, and that there are n^2 orbitals in that shell (◀ Table 6.1, page 286). Thus, *the maximum number of electrons in any shell is $2n^2$*. The relationship among the quantum numbers and the numbers of electrons is shown in Table 7.1.

7.2 Atomic Subshell Energies and Electron Assignments

Our goal in this section is to understand and predict the orbital distribution of electrons in atoms with many electrons. The procedure by which electrons are assigned to orbitals is known as the *aufbau* principle (aufbau means "building up").

Electrons in an atom are assigned to shells (defined by the quantum number n) and subshells (defined by the quantum number ℓ) in order of increasingly higher energy. In this way, the total energy of the atom is as low as possible.

Order of Subshell Energies and Assignments

Quantum theory and the Bohr model state that the energy of the H atom, with a single electron, depends only on the value of n ($E_n = -Rhc/n^2$). For atoms with more than one electron, however, the situation is more complex. The order of subshell energies for $n = 1$, 2, and 3 in Figure 7.1 shows that subshell energies in multielectron atoms depend on *both n and ℓ*.

Based on theoretical and experimental studies of orbital electron distributions in atoms, chemists have found that there are two general rules that help predict these arrangements:

- Electrons are assigned to subshells in order of increasing "$n + \ell$" value.
- For two subshells with the same value of "$n + \ell$," electrons are assigned first to the subshell of lower n.

The following are examples of these rules:

- Electrons are assigned to the 2s subshell ($n + \ell = 2 + 0 = 2$) before the 2p subshell ($n + \ell = 2 + 1 = 3$).
- Electrons are assigned to 2p orbitals ($n + \ell = 2 + 1 = 3$) before the 3s subshell ($n + \ell = 3 + 0 = 3$) because n for the 2p electrons is less than for the 3s electrons.
- Electrons are assigned to 4s orbitals ($n + \ell = 4 + 0 = 4$) before the 3d subshell ($n + \ell = 3 + 2 = 5$) because $n + \ell$ is less for 4s than for 3d.

Figure 7.2 summarizes the assignment of electrons according to increasing $n + \ell$ values, and the discussion that follows explores the underlying causes and their consequences and connects atomic electron configurations to the periodic table.

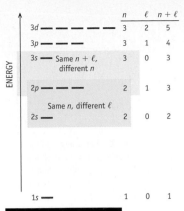

Active Figure 7.1 **Order of subshell energies.** Energies of electron shells increase with increasing n, and, within a shell, subshell energies increase with increasing ℓ. (The energy axis is not to scale.) The energy gaps between subshells of a given shell become smaller as n increases.

Chemistry Now™ Sign in at www.cengage.com/login and go to the Chapter Contents menu to explore an interactive version of this figure accompanied by an exercise.

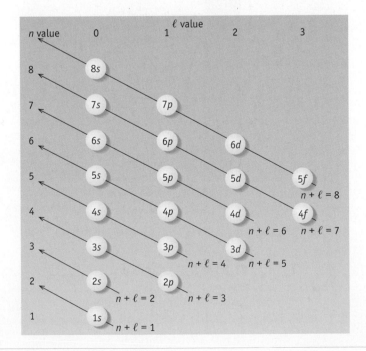

FIGURE 7.2 Subshell filling order. Subshells in atoms are filled in order of increasing $n + \ell$. When two subshells have the same $n + \ell$ value, the subshell of lower n is filled first. To use the diagram, begin at 1s and follow the arrows of increasing $n + \ell$. (Thus, the order of filling is 1s ⟹ 2s ⟹ 2p ⟹ 3s ⟹ 3p ⟹ 4s ⟹ 3d and so on.)

EXERCISE 7.1 Order of Subshell Assignments

To which of the following subshells should an electron be assigned first?

(a) 4s or 4p   **(b)** 5d or 6s   **(c)** 4f or 5s

Effective Nuclear Charge, Z*

■ **More About Z*** For a more complete discussion of effective nuclear charge, see D. M. P. Mingos: *Essential Trends in Inorganic Chemistry*, New York, Oxford University Press, 1998.

The order in which electrons are assigned to subshells in an atom, and many atomic properties, can be rationalized by introducing the concept of **effective nuclear charge** *(Z*)*. This is the net charge experienced by a particular electron in a multielectron atom resulting from the nucleus and the other electrons. Knowing Z^* provides a convenient way to assess the attractive and repulsive forces on that electron by the nucleus and the other electrons and to assess the energy of that electron.

The surface density plot $(4\pi r^2 \psi^2)$ for a 2s electron for lithium in plotted in Figure 7.3. (Lithium has three protons in the nucleus, two 1s electrons in the first shell, and a 2s electron in the second shell.) The probability of finding the 2s electron (recorded on the vertical axis) changes as one moves away from the nucleus (horizontal axis). Lightly shaded on this figure is the region in which the two 1s electrons have their highest probability. Observe that the 2s electron wave occurs partly within the region of space occupied by 1s electrons. Chemists say that the 2s orbital *penetrates* the region defining the 1s orbital.

At a large distance from the nucleus, the lithium 2s electron will experience a +1 charge, the net effect of the two 1s electrons (total charge = −2) and the nucleus (+3 charge.) The 1s electrons are said to *screen* the 2s electron from experiencing the full nuclear charge. However, this screening of the nuclear charge varies with the distance of the 2s electron from the nucleus. As the 2s electron wave penetrates the 1s electron region, it experiences an increasingly higher net positive charge. Very near the nucleus, the 1s electrons do not effectively screen the electron from the nucleus, and the 2s electron experiences a charge close to +3. Figure 7.3 shows that a 2s electron has some probability of being both inside and outside the

FIGURE 7.3 Effective nuclear charge, Z*. The two 1s electrons of lithium have their highest probability in the shaded region, but this region is penetrated by the 2s electron (whose approximate surface density plot is shown here). As the 2s electron penetrates the 1s region, however, the 2s electron experiences a larger and larger positive charge, to a maximum of +3. On average, the 2s electron experiences a charge, called the effective nuclear charge *(Z*)* that is smaller than +3 but greater than +1.

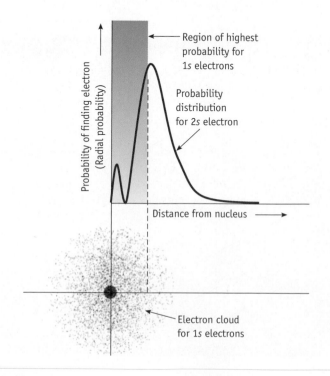

Region of highest probability for 1s electrons

Probability distribution for 2s electron

Distance from nucleus ⟶

Electron cloud for 1s electrons

region occupied by the $1s$ electrons. Thus, on average, a $2s$ electron experiences a positive charge greater than $+1$ but much smaller than $+3$. The *average* charge experienced by the electron is called the *effective nuclear charge* (Z^*).

In the hydrogen atom, with only one electron, the $2s$ and $2p$ subshells have the same energy. However, in atoms with two or more electrons, the energies of the $2s$ and $2p$ subshells are different. Why should this be true? It is observed that the relative extent to which an outer electron penetrates inner orbitals occurs in the order $s > p > d > f$. Thus, the effective nuclear charge experienced by electrons in a multielectron atom is in the order $ns > np > nd > nf$. The values of Z^* for s and p electrons for the second-period elements (Table 7.2) illustrate this. In each case, Z^* is greater for s electrons than for p electrons. In a given shell, s electrons always have a lower energy than p electrons; p electrons have a lower energy than d electrons, and d electrons have a lower energy than f electrons. A consequence of this is that subshells within an electron shell are filled in the order ns before np before nd before nf.

Table 7.2 also shows that for the second-period elements the value of Z^* for the higher energy electrons increases across the period. As you will see in Section 7.5, this effect is important in understanding trends in properties of elements across a period.

What emerges from this analysis is the order of shell and subshell energies for any given atom and the filling order in Figure 7.2. With this as background, we turn to the periodic table and use it as a guide to electron arrangements in atoms.

Chemistry．Now™

Sign in at **www.cengage.com/login** and go to Chapter 7 Contents to see Screen 7.2 and Screen 7.3, as well as Screen 7.4, which has a simulation and exercise exploring **effective nuclear charge and shielding value.**

7.3 Electron Configurations of Atoms

Arrangements of electrons in the elements up to 109—their **electron configurations**—are given in Table 7.3. Specifically, these are the ground state electron configurations, where electrons are found in the shells, subshells, and orbitals that result in the lowest energy for the atom. In general, electrons are assigned to orbitals in order of increasing $n + \ell$. The emphasis here, however, will be to connect the configurations of the elements with their positions in the periodic table (Figure 7.4).

Electron Configurations of the Main Group Elements

Hydrogen, the first element in the periodic table, has one electron in a $1s$ orbital. One way to depict its electron configuration is with the orbital box diagram used earlier, but an alternative and more frequently used method is the *spdf* notation. Using this method, the electron configuration of H is $1s^1$, read "one s one." This indicates that there is one electron (indicated by the superscript) in the $1s$ orbital.

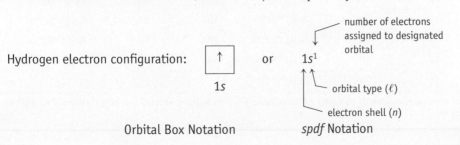

Hydrogen electron configuration:

Orbital Box Notation   *spdf* Notation

number of electrons assigned to designated orbital

orbital type (ℓ)

electron shell (n)

■ **Z^* for s and p Subshells** Z^* is greater for s electrons than for p electrons in the same shell. This difference becomes larger as n becomes larger. For example, compare the Group 4A elements.

Atom	$Z^*(ns)$	$Z^*(np)$	Value of n
C	3.22	3.14	2
Si	4.90	4.29	3
Ge	8.04	6.78	4

TABLE 7.2 Effective Nuclear Charges, Z^*, for $n = 2$ Elements

Atom	$Z^*(2s)$	$Z^*(2p)$
Li	1.28	
B	2.58	2.42
C	3.22	3.14
N	3.85	3.83
O	4.49	4.45
F	5.13	5.10

TABLE 7.3 Ground State Electron Configurations

Z	Element	Configuration	Z	Element	Configuration	Z	Element	Configuration
1	H	$1s^1$	37	Rb	$[Kr]5s^1$	74	W	$[Xe]4f^{14}5d^46s^2$
2	He	$1s^2$	38	Sr	$[Kr]5s^2$	75	Re	$[Xe]4f^{14}5d^56s^2$
3	Li	$[He]2s^1$	39	Y	$[Kr]4d^15s^2$	76	Os	$[Xe]4f^{14}5d^66s^2$
4	Be	$[He]2s^2$	40	Zr	$[Kr]4d^25s^2$	77	Ir	$[Xe]4f^{14}5d^76s^2$
5	B	$[He]2s^22p^1$	41	Nb	$[Kr]4d^45s^1$	78	Pt	$[Xe]4f^{14}5d^96s^1$
6	C	$[He]2s^22p^2$	42	Mo	$[Kr]4d^55s^1$	79	Au	$[Xe]4f^{14}5d^{10}6s^1$
7	N	$[He]2s^22p^3$	43	Tc	$[Kr]4d^55s^2$	80	Hg	$[Xe]4f^{14}5d^{10}6s^2$
8	O	$[He]2s^22p^4$	44	Ru	$[Kr]4d^75s^1$	81	Tl	$[Xe]4f^{14}5d^{10}6s^26p^1$
9	F	$[He]2s^22p^5$	45	Rh	$[Kr]4d^85s^1$	82	Pb	$[Xe]4f^{14}5d^{10}6s^26p^2$
10	Ne	$[He]2s^22p^6$	46	Pd	$[Kr]4d^{10}$	83	Bi	$[Xe]4f^{14}5d^{10}6s^26p^3$
11	Na	$[Ne]3s^1$	47	Ag	$[Kr]4d^{10}5s^1$	84	Po	$[Xe]4f^{14}5d^{10}6s^26p^4$
12	Mg	$[Ne]3s^2$	48	Cd	$[Kr]4d^{10}5s^2$	85	At	$[Xe]4f^{14}5d^{10}6s^26p^5$
13	Al	$[Ne]3s^23p^1$	49	In	$[Kr]4d^{10}5s^25p^1$	86	Rn	$[Xe]4f^{14}5d^{10}6s^26p^6$
14	Si	$[Ne]3s^23p^2$	50	Sn	$[Kr]4d^{10}5s^25p^2$	87	Fr	$[Rn]7s^1$
15	P	$[Ne]3s^23p^3$	51	Sb	$[Kr]4d^{10}5s^25p^3$	88	Ra	$[Rn]7s^2$
16	S	$[Ne]3s^23p^4$	52	Te	$[Kr]4d^{10}5s^25p^4$	89	Ac	$[Rn]6d^17s^2$
17	Cl	$[Ne]3s^23p^5$	53	I	$[Kr]4d^{10}5s^25p^5$	90	Th	$[Rn]6d^27s^2$
18	Ar	$[Ne]3s^23p^6$	54	Xe	$[Kr]4d^{10}5s^25p^6$	91	Pa	$[Rn]5f^26d^17s^2$
19	K	$[Ar]4s^1$	55	Cs	$[Xe]6s^1$	92	U	$[Rn]5f^36d^17s^2$
20	Ca	$[Ar]4s^2$	56	Ba	$[Xe]6s^2$	93	Np	$[Rn]5f^46d^17s^2$
21	Sc	$[Ar]3d^14s^2$	57	La	$[Xe]5d^16s^2$	94	Pu	$[Rn]5f^67s^2$
22	Ti	$[Ar]3d^24s^2$	58	Ce	$[Xe]4f^15d^16s^2$	95	Am	$[Rn]5f^77s^2$
23	V	$[Ar]3d^34s^2$	59	Pr	$[Xe]4f^36s^2$	96	Cm	$[Rn]5f^76d^17s^2$
24	Cr	$[Ar]3d^54s^1$	60	Nd	$[Xe]4f^46s^2$	97	Bk	$[Rn]5f^97s^2$
25	Mn	$[Ar]3d^54s^2$	61	Pm	$[Xe]4f^56s^2$	98	Cf	$[Rn]5f^{10}7s^2$
26	Fe	$[Ar]3d^64s^2$	62	Sm	$[Xe]4f^66s^2$	99	Es	$[Rn]5f^{11}7s^2$
27	Co	$[Ar]3d^74s^2$	63	Eu	$[Xe]4f^76s^2$	100	Fm	$[Rn]5f^{12}7s^2$
28	Ni	$[Ar]3d^84s^2$	64	Gd	$[Xe]4f^75d^16s^2$	101	Md	$[Rn]5f^{13}7s^2$
29	Cu	$[Ar]3d^{10}4s^1$	65	Tb	$[Xe]4f^96s^2$	102	No	$[Rn]5f^{14}7s^2$
30	Zn	$[Ar]3d^{10}4s^2$	66	Dy	$[Xe]4f^{10}6s^2$	103	Lr	$[Rn]5f^{14}6d^17s^2$
31	Ga	$[Ar]3d^{10}4s^24p^1$	67	Ho	$[Xe]4f^{11}6s^2$	104	Rf	$[Rn]5f^{14}6d^27s^2$
32	Ge	$[Ar]3d^{10}4s^24p^2$	68	Er	$[Xe]4f^{12}6s^2$	105	Db	$[Rn]5f^{14}6d^37s^2$
33	As	$[Ar]3d^{10}4s^24p^3$	69	Tm	$[Xe]4f^{13}6s^2$	106	Sg	$[Rn]5f^{14}6d^47s^2$
34	Se	$[Ar]3d^{10}4s^24p^4$	70	Yb	$[Xe]4f^{14}6s^2$	107	Bh	$[Rn]5f^{14}6d^57s^2$
35	Br	$[Ar]3d^{10}4s^24p^5$	71	Lu	$[Xe]4f^{14}5d^16s^2$	108	Hs	$[Rn]5f^{14}6d^67s^2$
36	Kr	$[Ar]3d^{10}4s^24p^6$	72	Hf	$[Xe]4f^{14}5d^26s^2$	109	Mt	$[Rn]5f^{14}6d^77s^2$
			73	Ta	$[Xe]4f^{14}5d^36s^2$			

*This table follows the general convention of writing the orbitals in order of increasing n when writing electron configurations. For a given n, the subshells are listed in order of increasing ℓ.

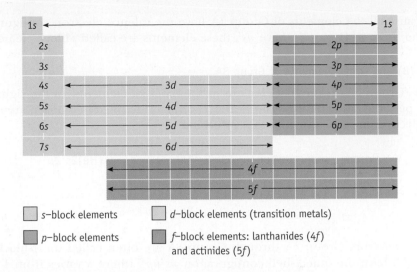

Active Figure 7.4 Electron configurations and the periodic table. The periodic table can serve as a guide in determining the order of filling of atomic orbitals. As one moves from left to right in a period, electrons are assigned to the indicated orbitals. See Table 7.3.

Chemistry. Now™ Sign in at www.thomsonedu.com/login and go to the Chapter Contents menu to explore an interactive version of this figure accompanied by an exercise.

- s–block elements
- p–block elements
- d–block elements (transition metals)
- f–block elements: lanthanides ($4f$) and actinides ($5f$)

Lithium (Li) and Other Elements of Group 1A

Lithium, with three electrons, is the first element in the second period of the periodic table. The first two electrons are in the $1s$ subshell, and the third electron must be in the $2s$ subshell of the $n = 2$ shell. The *spdf* notation, $1s^2 2s^1$, is read "one *s* two, two *s* one."

Lithium: *spdf* notation $1s^2 2s^1$

Box notation

| $1s$ | $2s$ | $2p$ |

Electron configurations are often written in abbreviated form by writing in brackets the symbol for the noble gas preceding the element (called the **noble gas notation**) and then indicating any electrons beyond those in the noble gas by using *spdf* or orbital box notation. In lithium, the arrangement preceding the $2s$ electron is the electron configuration of the noble gas helium, so, instead of writing out $1s^2 2s^1$, using this shorthand lithium's configuration would be written as $[\text{He}]2s^1$.

The electrons included in the noble gas notation are often referred to as the **core electrons** of the atom. The core electrons can generally be ignored when considering the chemistry of an element. The electrons beyond the core electrons—the $2s^1$ electron in the case of lithium—are called **valence electrons**; these are the electrons that determine the chemical properties of an element.

All the elements of Group 1A have one electron assigned to an *s* orbital of the *n*th shell, for which *n* is the number of the period in which the element is found (Figure 7.4). For example, potassium is the first element in the $n = 4$ row (the fourth period), so potassium has the electron configuration of the element preceding it in the table (Ar) plus a final electron assigned to the $4s$ orbital: $[\text{Ar}]4s^1$.

Beryllium (Be) and Other Elements of Group 2A

All elements of Group 2A have electron configurations of [electrons of preceding noble gas] ns^2, where *n* is the period in which the element is found in the periodic table. Beryllium, for example, has two electrons in the $1s$ orbital plus two additional electrons.

Beryllium: *spdf* notation $1s^2 2s^2$ or $[\text{He}]2s^2$

Box notation

| $1s$ | $2s$ | $2p$ |

Because all the elements of Group 1A have the valence electron configuration ns^1, and those in Group 2A have ns^2, these elements are called *s*-block elements.

Boron (B) and Other Elements of Group 3A

Boron (Group 3A) is the first element in the block of elements on the right side of the periodic table. Because the $1s$ and $2s$ orbitals are filled in a boron atom, the fifth electron must be assigned to a $2p$ orbital.

Boron: *spdf* notation $1s^2 2s^2 2p^1$ or $[He]2s^2 2p^1$

Box notation

1s   2s   2p

Elements from Group 3A through Group 8A are often called the *p*-block elements. All have the outer shell configuration $ns^2 np^x$, where x varies from 1 to 6. The elements in Group 3A, for example, have two s electrons and one p electron ($ns^2 np^1$) in their outer shells.

Carbon (C) and Other Elements of Group 4A

Carbon (Group 4A) is the second element in the *p*-block, with two electrons assigned to the $2p$ orbitals. You can write the electron configuration of carbon by referring to the periodic table: Starting at H and moving from left to right across the successive periods, you write $1s^2$ to reach the end of period 1 and then $2s^2$ and finally $2p^2$ to bring the electron count to six. For carbon to be in its lowest energy (ground) state, these electrons must be assigned to different p orbitals, and both will have the same spin direction.

Carbon: *spdf* notation $1s^2 2s^2 2p^2$ or $[He]2s^2 2p^2$

Box notation

1s   2s   2p

When assigning electrons to p, d, or f orbitals, each successive electron is assigned to a different orbital of the subshell, and each electron has the same spin as the previous one, until the subshell is half full. Additional electrons must then be assigned to half-filled orbitals. This procedure follows **Hund's rule,** which states that *the most stable arrangement of electrons is that with the maximum number of unpaired electrons, all with the same spin direction.*

All elements in Group 4A have similar outer shell configurations, $ns^2 np^2$, where n is the period in which the element is located in the periodic table.

Nitrogen (N) and Oxygen (O) and Elements of Groups 5A and 6A

Nitrogen (Group 5A) has five valence electrons. Besides the two $2s$ electrons, it has three electrons, all with the same spin, in three different $2p$ orbitals.

Nitrogen: *spdf* notation $1s^2 2s^2 2p^3$ or $[He]2s^2 2p^3$

Box notation

1s   2s   2p

Oxygen (Group 6A) has six valence electrons. Two of these six electrons are assigned to the $2s$ orbital, and the other four electrons are assigned to $2p$ orbitals.

Oxygen: *spdf* notation $1s^2 2s^2 2p^4$ or $[\text{He}]2s^2 2p^4$

Box notation   ⊡ ⊡ ⊡⊡⊡

                           1s   2s   2p

The fourth $2p$ electron must pair up with one already present. It makes no difference to which orbital this electron is assigned (the $2p$ orbitals all have the same energy), but it must have a spin opposite to the other electron already assigned to that orbital so that each electron has a different set of quantum numbers.

All elements in Group 5A have an outer shell configuration of $ns^2 np^3$, and all elements in Group 6A have an outer shell configuration of $ns^2 np^4$, where n is the period in which the element is located in the periodic table.

Fluorine (F) and Neon (Ne) and Elements of Groups 7A and 8A

Fluorine (Group 7A) has seven electrons in the $n = 2$ shell. Two of these electrons occupy the $2s$ subshell, and the remaining five electrons occupy the $2p$ subshell.

Fluorine: *spdf* notation $1s^2 2s^2 2p^5$ or $[\text{He}]2s^2 2p^5$

Box notation   ⊡ ⊡ ⊡⊡⊡

                           1s   2s   2p

All halogen atoms have similar outer shell configurations, $ns^2 np^5$, where n is the period in which the element is located.

Like all the elements in Group 8A, neon is a noble gas. The Group 8A elements (except helium) have eight electrons in the shell of highest n value, so all have the outer shell configuration $ns^2 np^6$, where n is the period in which the element is found. That is, all the noble gases have filled ns and np subshells. The nearly complete chemical inertness of the noble gases is associated with this electron configuration.

Neon: *spdf* notation $1s^2 2s^2 2p^6$ or $[\text{He}]2s^2 2p^6$

Box notation   ⊡ ⊡ ⊡⊡⊡

                           1s   2s   2p

Elements of Period 3

The elements of the third period have valence electron configurations similar to those of the second period, except that the preceding noble gas is neon and the valence shell is the third energy level. For example, silicon has four electrons and a neon core. Because it is the second element in the p block, it has two electrons in $3p$ orbitals. Thus, its electron configuration is

Silicon: *spdf* notation $1s^2 2s^2 2p^6 3s^2 3p^2$ or $[\text{Ne}]3s^2 3p^2$

Box notation   ⊡ ⊡ ⊡⊡⊡ ⊡ ⊡⊡⬚

                           1s   2s   2p   3s   3p

EXAMPLE 7.1 Electron Configurations

Problem Give the electron configuration of sulfur, using the *spdf*, noble gas, and orbital box notations.

Strategy Sulfur, atomic number 16, is the sixth element in the third period ($n = 3$) and is in the *p*-block. The last six electrons assigned to the atom, therefore, have the configuration $3s^2 3p^4$. These are preceded by the completed shells $n = 1$ and $n = 2$, the electron arrangement for Ne.

Solution The electron configuration of sulfur is

Complete *spdf* notation: $\qquad 1s^2 2s^2 2p^6 3s^2 3p^4$

spdf with noble gas notation: $\qquad [Ne]3s^2 3p^4$

Orbital box notation: $\qquad$ [Ne] ⇅ ⇅ ↑ ↑

$\qquad\qquad\qquad\qquad\qquad\qquad$ 3s $\quad$ 3p

EXAMPLE 7.2 Electron Configurations and Quantum Numbers

Problem Write the electron configuration for Al using the noble gas notation, and give a set of quantum numbers for each of the electrons with $n = 3$ (the valence electrons).

Strategy Aluminum is the third element in the third period. It therefore has three electrons with $n = 3$. Because Al is in the *p*-block of elements, two of the electrons are assigned to 3s, and the remaining electron is assigned to 3p.

Solution The element is preceded by the noble gas neon, so the electron configuration is $[Ne]3s^2 3p^1$. Using box notation, the configuration is

Aluminum configuration: $\qquad$ [Ne] ⇅ ↑ ☐ ☐

$\qquad\qquad\qquad\qquad\qquad\qquad$ 3s $\quad$ 3p

The possible sets of quantum numbers for the two 3s electrons are

	n	ℓ	m_ℓ	m_s
For ↑	3	0	0	$+\frac{1}{2}$
For ↓	3	0	0	$-\frac{1}{2}$

For the single 3p electron, one of six possible sets is $n = 3$, $\ell = 1$, $m_\ell = 11$, and $m_s = 1\frac{1}{2}$.

EXERCISE 7.2 *spdf* Notation, Orbital Box Diagrams, and Quantum Numbers

(a) Which element has the configuration $1s^2 2s^2 2p^6 3s^2 3p^5$?

(b) Using *spdf* notation and a box diagram, show the electron configuration of phosphorus.

(c) Write one possible set of quantum numbers for the valence electrons of calcium.

Electron Configurations of the Transition Elements

The elements of the fourth through the seventh periods use d and f subshells, in addition to s and p subshells, to accommodate electrons (see Figure 7.4 and Tables 7.3 and 7.4). Elements whose atoms are filling d subshells are called **transition elements.** Those elements for which atoms are filling f subshells are sometimes called the **inner transition elements** or, more usually, the **lanthanides** (filling $4f$ orbitals) and **actinides** (filling $5f$ orbitals).

In a given period in the periodic table, the transition elements are always preceded by two s-block elements. After filling the ns orbital in the period, we begin filling the $(n-1)d$ orbitals. Scandium, the first transition element, has the configuration $[\text{Ar}]3d^14s^2$, and titanium follows with $[\text{Ar}]3d^24s^2$ (Table 7.4).

The general procedure for assigning electrons would suggest that the configuration of a chromium atom is $[\text{Ar}]3d^44s^2$. The actual configuration, however, has one electron assigned to each of the six available $3d$ and $4s$ orbitals: $[\text{Ar}]3d^54s^1$. This apparently anomalous configuration is explained by assuming that the $4s$ and $3d$ orbitals have approximately the same energy in Cr, and each of the six valence electrons of chromium is assigned to one of these orbitals.

Following chromium, atoms of manganese, iron, and nickel have the configurations that would be expected from the order of orbital filling in Figure 7.2. Copper ($[\text{Ar}]3d^{10}4s^1$) is the second exception in this series; it has a single electron in the $4s$ orbital, and the remaining 10 electrons beyond the argon core are assigned to the $3d$ orbitals. Zinc, with the configuration $[\text{Ar}]3d^{10}4s^2$, ends the first transition series.

The fifth period transition elements follow the pattern of the fourth period with minor variations.

■ **Writing Configurations for Transition Metals** We follow the convention of writing configurations with shells listed in order of increasing n and, within a given shell, writing subshells in order of increasing ℓ. Many educators write them as, for example, $[\text{Ar}]4s^23d^2$ to reflect the order of orbital filling. In fact, either notation is correct.

TABLE 7.4 Orbital Box Diagrams for the Elements Ca Through Zn

		3d	4s
Ca	$[\text{Ar}]4s^2$	☐ ☐ ☐ ☐ ☐	↑↓
Sc	$[\text{Ar}]3d^14s^2$	↑ ☐ ☐ ☐ ☐	↑↓
Ti	$[\text{Ar}]3d^24s^2$	↑ ↑ ☐ ☐ ☐	↑↓
V	$[\text{Ar}]3d^34s^2$	↑ ↑ ↑ ☐ ☐	↑↓
Cr*	$[\text{Ar}]3d^54s^1$	↑ ↑ ↑ ↑ ↑	↑
Mn	$[\text{Ar}]3d^54s^2$	↑ ↑ ↑ ↑ ↑	↑↓
Fe	$[\text{Ar}]3d^64s^2$	↑↓ ↑ ↑ ↑ ↑	↑↓
Co	$[\text{Ar}]3d^74s^2$	↑↓ ↑↓ ↑ ↑ ↑	↑↓
Ni	$[\text{Ar}]3d^84s^2$	↑↓ ↑↓ ↑↓ ↑ ↑	↑↓
Cu*	$[\text{Ar}]3d^{10}4s^1$	↑↓ ↑↓ ↑↓ ↑↓ ↑↓	↑
Zn	$[\text{Ar}]3d^{10}4s^2$	↑↓ ↑↓ ↑↓ ↑↓ ↑↓	↑↓

*These configurations do not follow the "$n + \ell$" rule.

Lanthanides and Actinides

The sixth period includes the lanthanide series beginning with lanthanum, La. As the first element in the d-block, lanthanum has the configuration $[Xe]5d^16s^2$. The next element, cerium (Ce), is set out in a separate row at the bottom of the periodic table, and it is with the elements in this row (Ce through Lu) that electrons are first assigned to f orbitals. Thus, the configuration of cerium is $[Xe]4f^15d^16s^2$. Moving across the lanthanide series, the pattern continues (although with occasional variations in occupancy of the $5d$ and $4f$ orbitals). The lanthanide series ends with 14 electrons being assigned to the seven $4f$ orbitals in the last element, lutetium (Lu, $[Xe]4f^{14}5d^16s^2$) (see Table 7.3).

The seventh period also includes an extended series of elements utilizing f orbitals, the actinides, which begin with actinium (Ac, $[Rn]6d^17s^2$). The next element is thorium (Th), which is followed by protactinium (Pa) and uranium (U). The electron configuration of uranium is $[Rn]5f^36d^17s^2$.

■ **EXAMPLE 7.3 Electron Configurations of the Transition Elements**

Problem Using the *spdf* and noble gas notations, give electron configurations for (a) technetium, Tc, and (b) osmium, Os.

Strategy Base your answer on the positions of the elements in the periodic table. That is, for each element, find the preceding noble gas, and then note the number of *s, p, d,* and *f* electrons that lead from the noble gas to the element.

Solution

(a) Technetium, Tc: The noble gas that precedes Tc is krypton, Kr, at the end of the $n = 4$ row. After the 36 electrons of Kr are assigned to the Kr core as [Kr], seven electrons remain. Two of these electrons are in the $5s$ orbital, and the remaining five are in $4d$ orbitals. Therefore, the technetium configuration is $[Kr]4d^55s^2$.

(b) Osmium, Os: Osmium is a sixth-period element and the twenty-second element following the noble gas xenon. Of the 22 electrons to be added after the Xe core, two are assigned to the $6s$ orbital and 14 to $4f$ orbitals. The remaining six are assigned to $5d$ orbitals. Thus, the osmium configuration is $[Xe]4f^{14}5d^66s^2$.

EXERCISE 7.3 Electron Configurations

Using the periodic table and without looking at Table 7.3, write electron configurations for the following elements:

(a) P	**(c)** Zr	**(e)** Pb
(b) Zn	**(d)** In	**(f)** U

Use the *spdf* and noble gas notations. When you have finished, check your answers with Table 7.4.

7.4 Electron Configurations of Ions

We can also determine electron configurations for ions. To form a cation from a neutral atom, one or more of the valence electrons is removed. Electrons are always removed from the electron shell of highest n. If several subshells are present within the nth shell, the electron or electrons of maximum ℓ are removed. Thus, a sodium ion is formed by removing the $3s^1$ electron from the Na atom,

$$\text{Na: } [1s^22s^22p^63s^1] \rightarrow \text{Na}^+: [1s^22s^22p^6] + \text{e}^-$$

Questions About Transition Element Electron Configurations

Why don't all of the $n = 3$ subshells fill before beginning to fill the $n = 4$ subshells? Why is scandium's configuration [Ar]$3d^14s^2$ and not [Ar]$3d^3$?

Theoretical chemists have calculated that for the atoms from scandium to zinc the energies of the $3d$ orbitals are always lower than the energy of the $4s$ orbital, so for scandium the configuration [Ar]$3d^3$ would seem to be preferred. One way to understand why it is not is to consider the effect of electron–electron repulsion in $3d$ and $4s$ orbitals. The ground state configuration will be the one that most effectively minimizes electron–electron repulsions and that leads to the lowest total energy.

If we prepare plots for $3d$ and $4s$ orbitals such as that in Figure 7.3, we find that the most probable distance of a $3d$ electron from the nucleus is less than that for a $4s$ electron. Being closer to the nucleus, the $3d$ orbitals are more compact than the $4s$ orbital. This means the $3d$ electrons are closer together, and so two $3d$ electrons would repel each other more strongly than two $4s$ electrons, for example. A consequence is that placing electrons in the slightly higher energy $4s$ orbital lessens the effect of electron–electron repulsions and lowers the overall energy of the atom.

For more on this question, and for insight into an interesting scientific debate, see a series of papers in the *Journal of Chemical Education,* and *The Periodic Table* by E. Scerri, Oxford, 2007. For example,

a) F. L. Pilar, "4s is Always Above 3d," *Journal of Chemical Education*, Vol. 55, pages 1–6, 1978.
b) E. R. Scerri, "Transition Metal Configurations and Limitations of the Orbital Approximation," *Journal of Chemical Education*, Vol. 66, pages 481–483, 1989.
c) L. G. Vanquickenborne, K. Pierloot, and D. Devoghel, "Transition Metals and the Aufbau Principle," *Journal of Chemical Education*, Vol. 71, pages 469–471, 1994.
d) M. P. Melrose and E. R. Scerri, "Why the 4s Orbital is Occupied before the 3d," *Journal of Chemical Education*, Vol. 73, pages 498–503, 1996.

---

and Ge^{2+} is formed by removing two $4p$ electrons from a germanium atom,

$$\text{Ge: [Ar]}3d^{10}4s^24p^2 \longrightarrow \text{Ge}^{2+}\text{: [Ar]}3d^{10}4s^2 + 2\ e^-$$

The same general rule applies to transition metal atoms. This means, for example, that the titanium(II) cation has the configuration [Ar]$3d^2$

$$\text{Ti: [Ar]}3d^24s^2 \longrightarrow \text{Ti}^{2+}\text{: [Ar]}3d^2 + 2\ e^-$$

Iron(II) and iron(III) cations have the configurations [Ar]$3d^6$ and [Ar]$3d^5$, respectively:

$$\text{Fe: [Ar]}3d^64s^2 \longrightarrow \text{Fe}^{2+}\text{: [Ar]}3d^6 + 2\ e^-$$

$$\text{Fe}^{2+}\text{: [Ar]}3d^6 \longrightarrow \text{Fe}^{3+}\text{: [Ar]}3d^5 + e^-$$

Note that in the ionization of transition metals the ns electrons are lost before $(n - 1)d$ electrons. All the common transition metals lose their ns electrons first, and the cations formed have electron configurations of the general type [noble gas core]$(n - 1)d^x$. This point is important to remember because the magnetic properties of transition metal cations are determined by the number of unpaired electrons in d orbitals. For example, the Fe^{3+} ion is paramagnetic to the extent of five unpaired electrons (Figures 6.18, 7.5, and 7.6 and *A Closer Look: Paramagnetism*, page 292). If three $3d$ electrons had been removed instead of two s electrons and one d electron, the Fe^{3+} ion would still be paramagnetic but only to the extent of three unpaired electrons.

Chemistry.⚛.Now™

Sign in at **www.cengage.com/login** and go to Chapter 7 Contents to see Screen 7.6 for a simulation of the changes to an element's electron configuration when it ionizes, a tutorial on **determining an ion's box notation,** and a tutorial on **determining whether an element is diamagnetic or paramagnetic.**

Charles D. Winters

FIGURE 7.5 Formation of iron(III) chloride. Iron reacts with chlorine (Cl$_2$) to produce FeCl$_3$. The paramagnetic Fe^{3+} ion has the configuration [Ar]$3d^5$.

FIGURE 7.6 Paramagnetism of Transition Metals and Their Compounds. (a) A sample of iron(III) oxide is packed into a plastic tube and suspended from a thin nylon filament. (b) When a powerful magnet is brought near, the paramagnetic iron(III) ions in Fe_2O_3 cause the sample to be attracted to the magnet. (The magnet is made of neodymium, iron, and boron [$Nd_2Fe_{14}B$]. These powerful magnets are used in acoustic speakers.)

Charles D. Winters

(a)   (b)

■ **EXAMPLE 7.4 Configurations of Transition Metal Ions**

Problem Give the electron configurations for Cu, Cu^+ and Cu^{2+}. Are either of the ions paramagnetic? How many unpaired electrons does each have?

Strategy Observe the configuration of copper in Table 7.4. Recall that s and then d electrons are removed to form a transition metal ion.

Solution Copper has only one electron in the $4s$ orbital and ten electrons in $3d$ orbitals:

$$Cu: \quad [Ar]3d^{10}4s^1$$

     ⇅ | ⇅ | ⇅ | ⇅ | ⇅   ↑
     $3d$ $4s$

When copper is oxidized to Cu^+, the $4s$ electron is lost.

$$Cu^+: \quad [Ar]3d^{10}$$

     ⇅ | ⇅ | ⇅ | ⇅ | ⇅   ☐
     $3d$ $4s$

The copper(II) ion is formed from copper(I) by removal of one of the $3d$ electrons.

$$Cu^{2+}: \quad [Ar]3d^9$$

     ⇅ | ⇅ | ⇅ | ⇅ | ↑   ☐
     $3d$ $4s$

A copper(II) ion (Cu^{2+}) has one unpaired electron, so it is paramagnetic. In contrast, Cu^+ is diamagnetic.

EXERCISE 7.4 Metal Ion Configurations

Depict the electron configurations for V^{2+}, V^{3+}, and Co^{3+}. Use orbital box diagrams and the noble gas notation. Are any of the ions paramagnetic? If so, give the number of unpaired electrons.

7.5 Atomic Properties and Periodic Trends

Once electron configurations were understood, chemists realized that *similarities in properties of the elements are the result of similar valence shell electron configurations.* An objective of this section is to describe how atomic electron configurations are related to some of the physical and chemical properties of the elements and why those properties change in a reasonably predictable manner when moving down groups and across periods. This background should make the periodic table an even more useful tool in your study of chemistry. With an understanding of electron configurations and their relation to properties, you should be able to organize and predict many chemical and physical properties of the elements and their compounds.

Atomic Size

An orbital has no sharp boundary (◄ Figure 6.13a), so how can we define the size of an atom? There are actually several ways, and they can give slightly different results.

One of the simplest and most useful ways to define atomic size is to relate it to the distance between atoms in a sample of the element. Let us consider a diatomic molecule such as Cl_2 (Figure 7.7a). The radius of a Cl atom is assumed to be half the experimentally determined distance between the centers of the two atoms (198 pm), so the radius of one Cl atom is 99 pm. Similarly, the C—C distance in diamond is 154 pm, so a radius of 77 pm can be assigned to carbon. To test these estimates, we can add them together to estimate the C—Cl distance in CCl_4. The predicted distance of 176 pm agrees with the experimentally measured C—Cl distance of 176 pm. (Radii determined this way are often called "covalent radii.")

This approach to determining atomic radii applies only if molecular compounds of the element exist (and so it is limited to nonmetals and metalloids). For metals, atomic radii are sometimes estimated from measurements of the atom-to-atom distance in a crystal of the element (Figure 7.7b).

Some interesting periodic trends are seen immediately on looking at a table of radii (Figure 7.8). *For the main group elements, atomic radii generally increase going down*

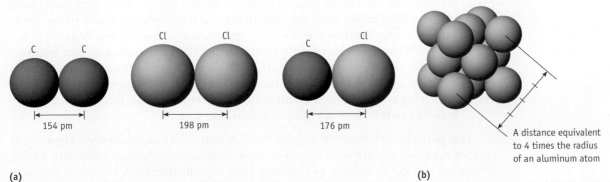

FIGURE 7.7 Determining atomic radii. (a) The sum of the atomic radii of C and Cl provides a good estimate of the C–Cl distance in a molecule having such a bond. (b) Pictured here is a tiny piece of an aluminum crystal. Each sphere represents an aluminum atom. Measuring the distance shown allows a scientist to estimate the radius of an aluminum atom.

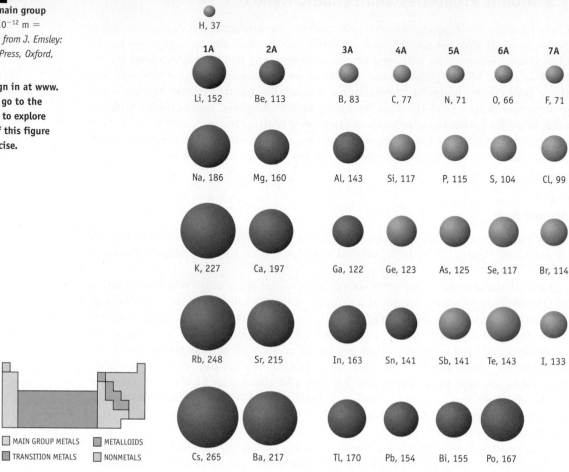

MAIN GROUP METALS METALLOIDS
TRANSITION METALS NONMETALS

a group in the periodic table and decrease going across a period. These trends reflect two important effects:

- The size of an atom is determined by the outermost electrons. In going from the top to the bottom of a group in the periodic table, the outermost electrons are assigned to orbitals with increasingly higher values of the principal quantum number, n. Because the underlying electrons require some space, these higher energy electrons are, on average, further from the nucleus.
- For main group elements of a given period, the principal quantum number, n, of the valence electron orbitals is the same. In going from one element to the next across a period, Z^*, the effective nuclear charge increases (Table 7.2). This results in an increased attraction between the nucleus and the valence electrons, and the atomic radius decreases.

The periodic trend in the atomic radii of transition metal atoms (Figure 7.9) across a period is somewhat different from that for main group elements. Going from left to right in a given period, the radii initially decrease. However, the sizes of the elements in the middle of a transition series change very little, and a small increase in size occurs at the end of the series. The size of transition metal atoms is determined largely by electrons in the outermost shell—that is, by the electrons of the ns subshell—but electrons are being added to the $(n - 1)d$ orbitals across the series. The increased nuclear charge on the atoms as one moves from left to

■ **Atomic Radii—Caution** Numerous tabulations of atomic and covalent radii exist, and the values quoted in them often differ somewhat. The variation comes about because several methods are used to determine the radii of atoms.

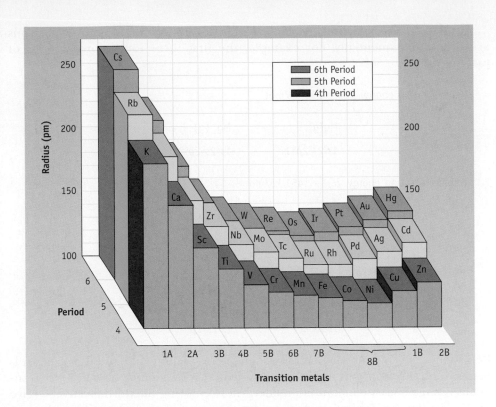

FIGURE 7.9 Trends in atomic radii for the transition elements. Atomic radii of the Group 1A and 2A metals and the transition metals of the fourth, fifth, and sixth periods.

right should cause the radius to decrease. This effect, however, is mostly canceled out by increased electron–electron repulsion. On reaching the Group 1B and 2B elements at the end of the series, the size increases slightly because the *d* subshell is filled and electron–electron repulsions dominate.

■ **Trends in Atomic Radii** General trends in atomic radii of *s*- and *p*-block elements with position in the periodic table.

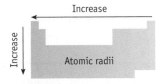

Chemistry.⚛.Now™

Sign in at **www.cengage.com/login** and go to Chapter 7 Contents to see:
- Screen 7.8 for a simulation exploring **the trends in atomic size moving across and down the periodic table**
- Screen 7.9 for a simulation exploring **energy levels of orbitals and the ability to retain electrons**

EXERCISE 7.5 Periodic Trends in Atomic Radii

Place the three elements Al, C, and Si in order of increasing atomic radius.

Ionization Energy

Ionization energy *(IE)* is the energy required to remove an electron from an atom in the gas phase.

$$\text{Atom in ground state(g)} \longrightarrow \text{Atom}^+(g) + e^-$$

$$\Delta U \equiv \text{ionization energy, } IE$$

To separate an electron from an atom, energy must be supplied to overcome the attraction of the nuclear charge. Because energy must be supplied, ionization energies always have positive values.

Atoms other than hydrogen have a series of ionization energies as electrons are removed sequentially. For example, the first three ionization energies of magnesium are

■ **Valence and Core Electrons** Removal of core electrons requires much more energy than removal of a valence electron. Core electrons are not lost in chemical reactions.

■ **Measuring Ionization Energy** Ionization energy values can be measured accurately as compared with the estimations that must be made when measuring atomic radii.

First ionization energy, $IE_1 = 738$ kJ/mol

$$Mg(g) \quad \longrightarrow \quad Mg^+(g) + e^-$$
$$1s^2 2s^2 2p^6 3s^2 \qquad 1s^2 2s^2 2p^6 3s^1$$

Second ionization energy, $IE_2 = 1451$ kJ/mol

$$Mg^+(g) \quad \longrightarrow \quad Mg^{2+}(g) + e^-$$
$$1s^2 2s^2 2p^6 3s^1 \qquad 1s^2 2s^2 2p^6$$

Third ionization energy, $IE_3 = 7732$ kJ/mol

$$Mg^{2+}(g) \quad \longrightarrow \quad Mg^{3+}(g) + e^-$$
$$1s^2 2s^2 2p^6 \qquad 1s^2 2s^2 2p^5$$

Removing each subsequent electron requires more energy because the electron is being removed from an increasingly positive ion (Table 7.5), but there is a particularly large increase in ionization energy for removing the third electron to give Mg^{3+}. The first two ionization steps are for the removal of electrons from the outermost or valence shell of electrons. The third electron, however, must come from the $2p$ subshell, which has a much lower energy than the $3s$ subshell. *This large increase is experimental evidence for the electron shell structure of atoms.*

For main group (s- and p-block) elements, *first ionization energies generally increase across a period and decrease down a group* (Figure 7.10, Table 7.5, and Appendix F). The trend across a period corresponds to the increase in effective nuclear charge, Z^*, with increasing atomic number. As Z^* increases, the energy required to remove an electron increases. The general decrease in ionization energy down a group

TABLE 7.5 First, Second, and Third Ionization Energies for the Main Group Elements in Periods 2–4 (kJ/mol)

2nd Period	Li	Be	B	C	N	O	F	Ne
1st	513	899	801	1086	1402	1314	1681	2080
2nd	7298	1757	2427	2352	2856	3388	3374	3952
3rd	11815	14848	3660	4620	4578	5300	6050	6122

3rd Period	Na	Mg	Al	Si	P	S	Cl	Ar
1st	496	738	577	787	1012	1000	1251	1520
2nd	4562	1451	1817	1577	1903	2251	2297	2665
3rd	6912	7732	2745	3231	2912	3361	3826	3928

4th Period	K	Ca	Ga	Ge	As	Se	Br	Kr
1st	419	590	579	762	947	941	1140	1351
2nd	3051	1145	1979	1537	1798	2044	2104	2350
3rd	4411	4910	2963	3302	2735	2974	3500	3565

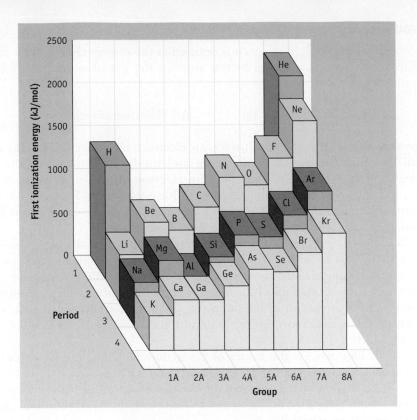

Active Figure 7.10 First ionization energies of the main group elements these first four periods. (For data on these elements see Table 7.5 and Appendix F.)

Chemistry‿♦‿Now™ Sign in at www. cengage.com/login and go to the Chapter Contents menu to explore an interactive version of this figure accompanied by an exercise.

occurs because the electron removed is increasingly farther from the nucleus and thus held less strongly.

Notice that atomic radius and ionization energy are both linked to Z^*. They are inversely related: *as the atomic radius decreases, the ionization energy increases.*

A closer look at ionization energies reveals that there are exceptions to the general trend in a period. One exception occurs on going from s-block to p-block elements—from beryllium to boron, for example. The $2p$ electrons are slightly higher in energy than the $2s$ electrons so the ionization energy for boron is slightly less than that for beryllium. Another dip to lower ionization energy occurs on going from nitrogen to oxygen. No change occurs in either n or ℓ, but electron–electron repulsions increase for the following reason. In Groups 3A–5A, electrons are assigned to separate p orbitals (p_x, p_y, and p_z). Beginning in Group 6A, however, two electrons are assigned to the same p orbital. The fourth p electron shares an orbital with another electron and thus experiences greater repulsion than it would if it had been assigned to an orbital of its own.

$$O \text{ (oxygen atom)} \xrightarrow{+1314 \text{ kJ/mol}} O^+ \text{ (oxygen cation)} + e^-$$

[Ne] ↑↓   ↑↑ ↑ ↑   [Ne] ↑↓   ↑ ↑ ↑
  2s   2p   2s   2p

The greater repulsion experienced by the fourth $2p$ electron makes it easier to remove. The usual trend resumes on going from oxygen to fluorine to neon, however, reflecting the increase in Z^*.

■ **Trends in Ionization Energy** General trends in first ionization energies of s- and p-block elements with position in the periodic table.

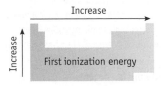

Electron Affinity

■ **Trends in EA** General trends in electron affinities of A-group elements. Exceptions occur at Groups 2A and 5A and in moving from period 2 to period 3 in the *p*-block.

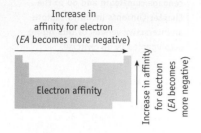

■ **EA and Nonmetals** Nonmetals generally have much more negative values of *EA* than metals. This observation agrees with chemical experience; nonmetals form anions, and metals generally do not.

The electron affinity, *EA*, of an atom is defined as the energy change for a process in which an electron is acquired by the atom in the gas phase (Figure 7.11 and Appendix F).

$$A(g) + e^-(g) \longrightarrow A^-(g) \qquad \Delta U \equiv \text{electron affinity, } EA$$

The greater the affinity an atom has for an electron, the lower the energy of the ion will be compared to that of the atom and the free electron, and the more negative the value of *EA*. For example, the electron affinity of fluorine is −328 kJ/mol, indicating an exothermic reaction to form the anion, F⁻, from a fluorine atom and an electron. Boron has a much lower affinity for an electron, as indicated by a much less negative *EA* value of −26.7 kJ/mol.

Because electron affinity and ionization energy represent the energy involved in the gain or loss of an electron by an atom, it is not surprising that periodic trends in these properties are also related. The increase in effective nuclear charge of atoms across a period (Table 7.2) makes it more difficult to ionize the atom and also increases the attraction of the atom for an additional electron. Thus, an element with a high ionization energy generally has a more negative value for its electron affinity.

As seen in Figure 7.11, the values of *EA* generally become more negative on moving across a period, but the trend is not smooth. The elements in Group 2A and 5A appear as variations to the general trend, corresponding to cases where the added electron would start a *p* subshell or would be paired with another electron in the *p* subshell, respectively.

Active Figure 7.11 **Electron affinity.** The larger the affinity *(EA)* of an atom for an electron, the more negative the value. For numerical values, see Appendix F. (Data were taken from H. Hotop and W. C. Lineberger: "Binding energies of atomic negative ions," *Journal of Physical Chemistry*, Reference Data, Vol. 14, p. 731, 1985.)

Chemistry☼Now™ **Sign in at www. cengage.com/login and go to the Chapter Contents menu to explore an interactive version of this figure accompanied by an exercise.**

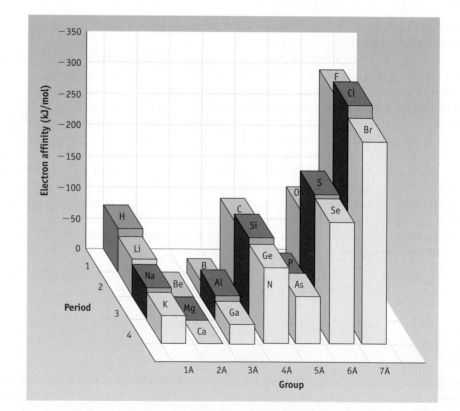

The value of electron affinity usually becomes less negative on descending a group of the periodic table. Electrons are added increasingly farther from the nucleus, so the attractive force between the nucleus and electrons decreases. This general trend does not apply to second period elements, however. For example, the value of the electron affinity of fluorine is higher (less negative) than the *EA* value for chlorine. The same phenomenon is observed in Groups 3A through 6A. One explanation is that significant electron–electron repulsions occur in small anions such as F^-. That is, adding an electron to the seven electrons already present in the $n = 2$ shell of the small F atom leads to considerable repulsion between electrons. Chlorine has a larger atomic volume than fluorine, so adding an electron does not result in such significant electron–electron repulsions.

A few elements, such as nitrogen and the Group 2A elements, have no affinity for electrons and are listed as having an *EA* value of zero. The noble gases are generally not listed in electron affinity tables. They have no affinity for electrons, because any additional electron must be added to the next higher electron shell.

No atom has a negative electron affinity for a second electron. So what accounts for the existence of ions such as O^{2-} that occur in many compounds? The answer is that doubly charged anions can be stabilized in crystalline environments by electrostatic attraction to neighboring positive ions (see Chapters 8 and 13).

■ **Electron Affinity and Sign Conventions** Changes in sign conventions for electron affinities over the years have caused confusion. For a useful discussion of electron affinity, see J. C. Wheeler: "Electron affinities of the alkaline earth metals and the sign convention for electron affinity," *Journal of Chemical Education*, Vol. 74, pp. 123–127, 1997.

Chemistry⸱Now™

Sign in at **www.cengage.com/login** and go to Chapter 7 Contents to see Screens 7.8–7.10 for simulations exploring the **periodic trends in these properties.**

EXAMPLE 7.5 Periodic Trends

Problem Compare the three elements C, O, and Si.

(a) Place them in order of increasing atomic radius.

(b) Which has the largest ionization energy?

(c) Which has the more negative electron affinity, O or C?

Strategy Review the trends in atomic properties in Figures 7.8–7.11, Table 7.5, and Appendix F.

Solution

(a) Atomic size: Atomic radius declines on moving across a period, so oxygen must have a smaller radius than carbon. However, the radius increases on moving down a periodic group. Because C and Si are in the same group (Group 4A), Si must be larger than C. The trend is O < C < Si.

(b) Ionization energy: Ionization energies generally increase across a period and decrease down a group. Thus, the trend in ionization energies is Si (787 kJ/mol) < C (1086 kJ/mol) < O (1314 kJ/mol).

(c) Electron affinity: Electron affinity values generally become less negative down a group (except for the second period elements) and more negative across a period. Therefore, the *EA* for O (= −141.0 kJ/mol) has a more negative *EA* than C (= −121.9 kJ/mol).

EXERCISE 7.6 Periodic Trends

Compare the three elements B, Al, and C.

(a) Place the three elements in order of increasing atomic radius.

(b) Rank the elements in order of increasing ionization energy. (Try to do this without looking at Table 7.5; then compare your prediction with the table.)

(c) Which element, B or C, is expected to have the more negative electron affinity value?

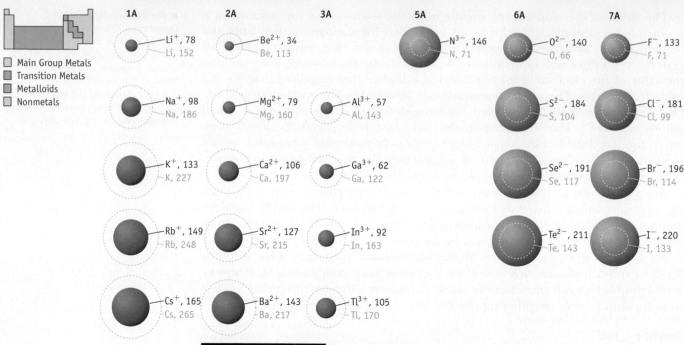

Active Figure 7.12 **Relative sizes of some common ions.** Radii are given in picometers (1 pm = 1 × 10⁻¹² m). (Data taken from J. Emsley, *The Elements*, Clarendon Press, Oxford, 1998, 3rd edition.)

Chemistry.Now™ Sign in at www.cengage.com/login and go to the Chapter Contents menu to explore an interactive version of this figure accompanied by an exercise.

Trends in Ion Sizes

The trend in the sizes of ions down a periodic group are the same as those for neutral atoms: Positive and negative ions increase in size when descending the group (Figure 7.12). Pause for a moment, however, and compare the ionic radii with the atomic radii, as illustrated in Figure 7.12. When an electron is removed from an atom to form a cation, the size shrinks considerably. The radius of a cation is always smaller than that of the atom from which it is derived. For example, the radius of Li is 152 pm, whereas the radius of Li^+ is only 78 pm. When an electron is removed from an Li atom, the attractive force of three protons is now exerted on only two electrons, so the remaining electrons are drawn closer to the nucleus. The decrease in ion size is especially great when the last electron of a particular shell is removed, as is the case for Li. The loss of the $2s$ electron from Li leaves Li^+ with no electrons in the $n = 2$ shell.

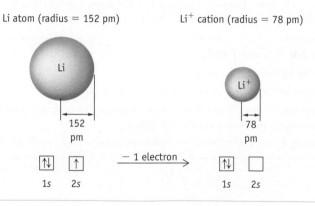

Case Study   Metals in Biochemistry and Medicine

Many main group and transition metals play an important role in biochemistry and in medicine. Your body has low levels of the following metals in the form of various compounds: Ca, 1.5%; Na, 0.1%; Mg, 0.05%, and the metals iron, cobalt zinc, and copper, all less than about 0.05%. (Levels are percentages by mass.)

Much of the 3–4 g of iron in your body is found in hemoglobin, the substance responsible for carrying oxygen to cells. Iron deficiency is marked by fatigue, infections, and mouth inflammations.

Iron in your diet can come from eggs, and brewer's yeast has a very high iron content. In addition, foods such as many breakfast cereals are "fortified" with metallic iron [made by the decomposition of $Fe(CO)_5$]. (In an interesting experiment you can do at home, you can remove the iron by stirring the cereal with a strong magnet.) Vitamin pills often contain iron(II) compounds with anions such as sulfate and succinate $(C_4H_4O_4^{2-})$.

The average person has about 75 mg of copper, about one third of which is found in the muscles. Copper is involved in many biological functions, and a deficiency shows up in many ways: anemia, degeneration of the nervous system, and impaired immunity. Wilson's disease, a genetic disorder, leads to the over-accumulation of copper in the body and results in hepatic and neurological damage.

Like silver ions (page 148), copper ions can also act as a bacteriocide. Scientists

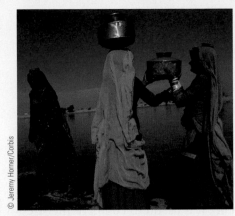

Filling a brass water jug for drinking water in India. Copper ions released in tiny amounts from the brass kill bacteria in contaminated water.

from Britain and India recently investigated a long-held belief among people in India that storing water in brass pitchers can ward off illness. (Brass is an alloy of copper and zinc.) They filled brass pitchers with sterile water inoculated with *E. coli* bacteria and filled other brass pitchers with contaminated river water from India. In both cases, they found that fecal bacteria counts dropped from as high as 1,000,000 bacteria per milliliter to zero in two days. In contrast, bacteria levels stayed high in plastic or earthenware pots. Apparently, just enough copper ions are released by the brass to kill the bacteria but not enough to affect humans.

Questions:

1. Give the electron configurations for iron and the iron(II) and iron(III) ions.
2. In hemoglobin, iron can be in the iron(II) or iron(III) state. Are either of these iron ions paramagnetic?
3. Give the electron configurations for copper and the copper(I) and copper(II) ions. Is copper in any of these forms paramagnetic?
4. Why are copper atoms (radius = 128 pm) slightly larger than iron atoms (radius = 124 pm)?
5. In hemoglobin, the iron is enclosed by the porphyrin group, a flat grouping of carbon, hydrogen, and nitrogen atoms. (This is in turn encased in a protein.) When iron is in the form of the Fe^{3+} ion, it just fits into the space within the four N atoms, and the arrangement is flat. Speculate on what occurs to the structure when iron is reduced to the Fe^{2+} ion.

Answers to these questions are in Appendix Q.

A large decrease in size is also expected if two or more electrons are removed. For example, an aluminum ion, Al^{3+}, has a radius of 57 pm; in contrast, the atomic radius of an aluminum atom is 143 pm.

Al atom (radius = 143 pm) Al^{3+} cation (radius = 57 pm)

$$[Ne]\begin{array}{|c|}\hline \uparrow\downarrow \\ \hline\end{array}\ \begin{array}{|c|c|c|}\hline \uparrow & & \\ \hline\end{array} \xrightarrow{-3\ electrons} [Ne]\begin{array}{|c|}\hline \\ \hline\end{array}\ \begin{array}{|c|c|c|}\hline & & \\ \hline\end{array}$$

3s   3p   3s   3p

You can also see by comparing Figures 7.8 and 7.12 that anions are always larger than the atoms from which they are derived. Here, the argument is the opposite of that used to explain positive ion radii. The F atom, for example, has nine protons and nine electrons. On forming the anion, the nuclear charge is still +9, but the anion has ten electrons. The F⁻ ion is larger than the F atom because of increased electron–electron repulsions.

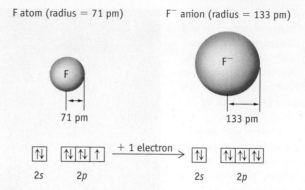

F atom (radius = 71 pm)   F⁻ anion (radius = 133 pm)

Finally, it is useful to compare the sizes of isoelectronic ions across the periodic table. **Isoelectronic** ions have the same number of electrons (but a different number of protons). One such series of ions is N^{3-}, O^{2-}, F^-, Na^+, and Mg^{2+}:

Ion	N^{3-}	O^{2-}	F^-	Na^+	Mg^{2+}
Number of electrons	10	10	10	10	10
Number of nuclear protons	7	8	9	11	12
Ionic radius (pm)	146	140	133	98	79

All these ions have 10 electrons but they differ in the number of protons. As the number of protons increases in a series of isoelectronic ions, the balance between electron–proton attraction and electron–electron repulsion shifts in favor of attraction, and the radius decreases.

Chemistry ⚛ Now™

Sign in at **www.cengage.com/login** and go to Chapter 7 Contents to see Screen 7.12 for simulations on **the relationship between ion formation and orbital energies in main group elements** and on the **relationship between orbital energies and electron configurations on the size of the main group element ions.**

EXERCISE 7.7 Ion Sizes

What is the trend in sizes of the ions K^+, S^{2-}, and Cl^-? Briefly explain why this trend exists.

7.6 Periodic Trends and Chemical Properties

Atomic and ionic radii, ionization energies, and electron affinities are properties associated with atoms and their ions. It is reasonable to expect that knowledge of these properties will be useful as we explore the chemistry involving formation of ionic compounds.

The periodic table was created by grouping together elements having similar chemical properties (Figure 7.13). Alkali metals, for example, characteristically form compounds containing a 1+ ion, such as Li^+, Na^+, or K^+. Thus, the reaction

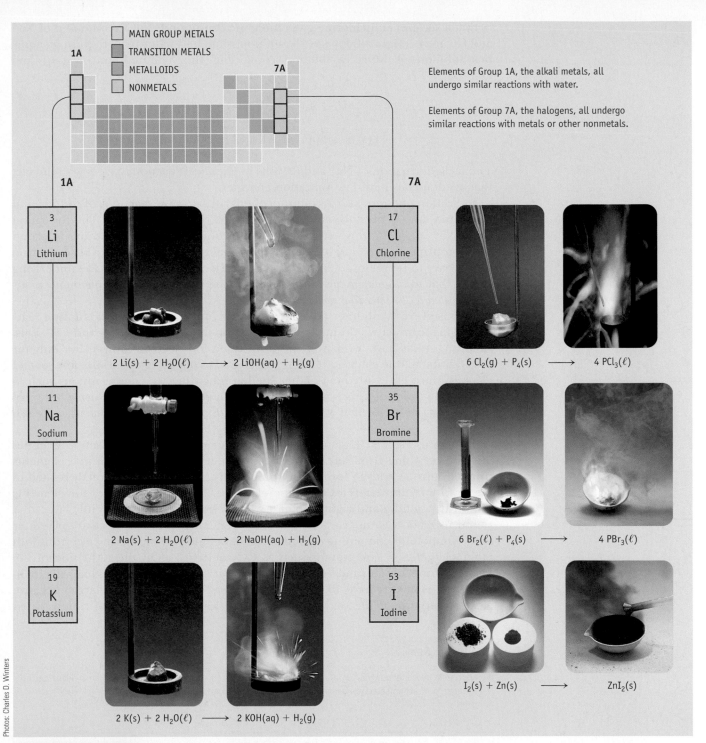

Elements of Group 1A, the alkali metals, all undergo similar reactions with water.

Elements of Group 7A, the halogens, all undergo similar reactions with metals or other nonmetals.

MAIN GROUP METALS
TRANSITION METALS
METALLOIDS
NONMETALS

1A

3
Li
Lithium

$2 Li(s) + 2 H_2O(\ell) \longrightarrow 2 LiOH(aq) + H_2(g)$

11
Na
Sodium

$2 Na(s) + 2 H_2O(\ell) \longrightarrow 2 NaOH(aq) + H_2(g)$

19
K
Potassium

$2 K(s) + 2 H_2O(\ell) \longrightarrow 2 KOH(aq) + H_2(g)$

7A

17
Cl
Chlorine

$6 Cl_2(g) + P_4(s) \longrightarrow 4 PCl_3(\ell)$

35
Br
Bromine

$6 Br_2(\ell) + P_4(s) \longrightarrow 4 PBr_3(\ell)$

53
I
Iodine

$I_2(s) + Zn(s) \longrightarrow ZnI_2(s)$

Photos: Charles D. Winters

Active Figure 7.13 **Examples of the periodicity of Group 1A and Group 7A elements.** Dimitri Mendeleev developed the first periodic table by listing elements in order of increasing atomic weight. Every so often, an element had properties similar to those of a lighter element, and these were placed in vertical columns or groups. We now recognize that the elements should be listed in order of increasing atomic number and that the periodic occurrence of similar properties is related to the electron configurations of the elements.

Chemistry .ᐤ. Now™ Sign in at www.cengage.com/login and go to the Chapter Contents menu to explore an interactive version of this figure accompanied by an exercise.

between sodium and chlorine gives the ionic compound, NaCl (composed of Na^+ and Cl^- ions) [Figure 1.4, page 4], and potassium and water react to form an aqueous solution of KOH, a solution containing the hydrated ions $K^+(aq)$ and $OH^-(aq)$.

$$2\ Na(s) + Cl_2(g) \longrightarrow 2\ NaCl(s)$$

$$2\ K(s) + 2\ H_2O(\ell) \longrightarrow 2\ K^+(aq) + 2\ OH^-(aq) + H_2(g)$$

The facile formation of Na^+ and K^+ ions in chemical reactions agrees with the fact that alkali metals have low ionization energies.

Ionization energies also account for the fact that these reactions of sodium and potassium do not produce compounds such as $NaCl_2$ or $K(OH)_2$. The formation of an Na^{2+} or K^{2+} ion would be a very unfavorable process. Removing a second electron from these metals requires a great deal of energy because a core electron would have to be removed. The energetic barrier to this process is the underlying reason that *main group metals generally form cations with an electron configuration equivalent to that of the preceding noble gas.*

Why isn't Na_2Cl another possible product from the sodium and chlorine reaction? This formula would imply that the compound contains Na^+ and Cl^{2-} ions. Chlorine atoms have a relatively negative value for electron affinity, but only for the addition of one electron. Adding two electrons per atom means that the second electron must enter the next higher shell at much higher energy. Anions such as Cl^{2-} are not known. This example leads us to a general statement: *nonmetals generally acquire enough electrons to form an anion with the electron configuration of the next noble gas.*

We can use similar logic to rationalize other observations. Ionization energies increase on going from left to right across a period. We have seen that elements from Groups 1A and 2A form ionic compounds, an observation directly related to the low ionization energies for these elements. Ionization energies for elements toward the middle and right side of a period, however, are sufficiently large that cation formation is unfavorable. Thus, we generally do not expect to encounter ionic compounds containing carbon; instead, we find carbon sharing electrons with other elements in compounds such as CO_2 and CCl_4. On the right side of the second period, oxygen and fluorine much prefer taking on electrons to giving them up; these elements have high ionization energies and relatively large, negative electron affinities. Thus, oxygen and fluorine form anions and not cations when they react.

Chemistry ⊕ Now™

Sign in at **www.cengage.com/login** and go to Chapter 7 Contents to see Screen 7.13 to watch videos on **the relationship of atomic electron configurations and orbital energies on periodic trends.**

EXERCISE 7.8 Energies and Compound Formation

Give a plausible explanation for the observation that magnesium and chlorine react to form $MgCl_2$ and not $MgCl_3$.

Chapter Goals Revisited

Now that you have studied this chapter, you should ask whether you have met the chapter goals. In particular, you should be able to:

Recognize the relationship of the four quantum numbers (n, ℓ, m_ℓ, and m_s) to atomic structure

a. Recognize that each electron in an atom has a different set of the four quantum numbers, n, ℓ, m_ℓ, and m_s (Sections 6.5–6.7, 7.1, and 7.3). Study Questions assignable in OWL: 11, 13, 35, 37, 52.

b. Understand that the Pauli exclusion principle leads to the conclusion that no atomic orbital can be assigned more than two electrons and that the two electrons in an orbital must have opposite spins (different values of m_s) (Section 7.1).

Write the electron configuration for atoms and monatomic ions

a. Recognize that electrons are assigned to the subshells of an atom in order of increasing subshell energy (Aufbau principle, Section 7.2). In the H atom, the subshell energies increase with increasing n, but, in a many-electron atom, the energies depend on both n and ℓ (see Figure 7.2).

b. Understand effective nuclear charge, Z^*, and its ability to explain why different subshells in the same shell of multielectron atoms have different energies. Also, understand the role of Z^* in determining the properties of atoms (Section 7.2).

c. Using the periodic table as a guide, depict electron configurations of neutral atoms (Section 7.3) and monatomic ions (Section 7.4) using the orbital box or *spdf* notation. In both cases, configurations can be abbreviated with the noble gas notation. Study Question(s) assignable in OWL: 2, 3, 6, 10, 13, 15, 18, 20, 21, 33, 34, 35, 36, 39, 44, 52, 59, 71.

d. When assigning electrons to atomic orbitals, apply the Pauli exclusion principle and Hund's rule (Sections 7.3 and 7.4).

e. Understand the role magnetism plays in revealing atomic structure (Section 7.4). Study Question(s) assignable in OWL: 20, 21, 33, 34, 39, 52.

Rationalize trends in atom and ion sizes, ionization energy, and electron affinity

a. Predict how properties of atoms—size, ionization energy *(IE)*, and electron affinity *(EA)*—change on moving down a group or across a period of the periodic table (Section 7.5). The general periodic trends for these properties are as follows: Study Question(s) assignable in OWL: 24, 26, 28, 30, 32, 40–43, 45–50, 52, 56–58, 64.

  (i) Atomic size decreases across a period and increases down a group.

  (ii) *IE* increases across a period and decreases down a group.

  (iii) The value of *EA* becomes more negative across a period and becomes less negative down a group.

b. Recognize the role that ionization energy and electron affinity play in forming ionic compounds (Section 7.6). Study Question(s) assignable in OWL: 72.

Chemistry ⚛ Now™ Sign in at www.cengage.com/login to:

- Assess your understanding with Study Questions in OWL keyed to each goal in the Goals and Homework menu for this chapter
- For quick review, download Go Chemistry mini-lecture flashcard modules (or purchase them at **www.ichapters.com**)
- Check your readiness for an exam by taking the Pre-Test and exploring the modules recommended in your Personalized Study plan.

❓ Access **How Do I Solve It?** tutorials on how to approach problem solving using concepts in this chapter.

For additional preparation for an examination on this chapter see the *Let's Review* section on pages 496–513.

STUDY QUESTIONS

OWL Online homework for this chapter may be assigned in OWL.

▲ denotes challenging questions.

■ denotes questions assignable in OWL.

Blue-numbered questions have answers in Appendix O and fully-worked solutions in the *Student Solutions Manual*.

Practicing Skills

Writing Electron Configurations of Atoms
(See Examples 7.1–7.3; Tables 7.1, 7.3, and 7.4; and Screen 7.5 and the Toolbox in ChemistryNow.)

1. Write the electron configurations for P and Cl using both *spdf* notation and orbital box diagrams. Describe the relationship between each atom's electron configuration and its position in the periodic table.

2. ■ Write the electron configurations for Mg and Ar using both *spdf* notation and orbital box diagrams. Describe the relationship of the atom's electron configuration to its position in the periodic table.

3. ■ Using *spdf* notation, write the electron configurations for atoms of chromium and iron, two of the major components of stainless steel.

4. Using *spdf* notation, give the electron configuration of vanadium, V, an element found in some brown and red algae and some toadstools.

5. Depict the electron configuration for each of the following atoms using *spdf* and noble gas notations.
   (a) Arsenic, As. A deficiency of As can impair growth in animals even though larger amounts are poisonous.
   (b) Krypton, Kr. It ranks seventh in abundance of the gases in Earth's atmosphere.

6. ■ Using *spdf* and noble gas notations, write electron configurations for atoms of the following elements, and then check your answers with Table 7.3.
   (a) Strontium, Sr. This element is named for a town in Scotland.
   (b) Zirconium, Zr. The metal is exceptionally resistant to corrosion and so has important industrial applications. Moon rocks show a surprisingly high zirconium content compared with rocks on Earth.
   (c) Rhodium, Rh. This metal is used in jewelry and in catalysts in industry.
   (d) Tin, Sn. The metal was used in the ancient world. Alloys of tin (solder, bronze, and pewter) are important.

7. Use noble gas and *spdf* notations to depict electron configurations for the following metals of the third transition series.
   (a) Tantalum, Ta. The metal and its alloys resist corrosion and are often used in surgical and dental tools.
   (b) Platinum, Pt. This metal was used by pre-Columbian Indians in jewelry. It is used now in jewelry and for anticancer drugs and catalysts (such as those in automobile exhaust systems).

8. The lanthanides, once called the rare earth elements, are really only "medium rare." Using noble gas and *spdf* notations, depict reasonable electron configurations for the following elements.
   (a) Samarium, Sm. This lanthanide is used in magnetic materials.
   (b) Ytterbium, Yb. This element was named for the village of Ytterby in Sweden, where a mineral source of the element was found.

9. The actinide americium, Am, is a radioactive element that has found use in home smoke detectors. Depict its electron configuration using noble gas and *spdf* notations.

10. ■ Predict reasonable electron configurations for the following elements of the actinide series of elements. Use noble gas and *spdf* notations.
    (a) Plutonium, Pu. The element is best known as a by-product of nuclear power plant operations.
    (b) Curium, Cm. This actinide was named for Marie Curie (page 342).

Quantum Numbers and Electron Configurations
(See Example 7.2 and ChemistryNow Screens 6.12 and 7.2–7.5.)

11. ■ What is the maximum number of electrons that can be identified with each of the following sets of quantum numbers? In one case, the answer is "none." Explain why this is true.
    (a) $n = 4$, $\ell = 3$, $m_\ell = 1$
    (b) $n = 6$, $\ell = 1$, $m_\ell = -1$, $m_s = -\frac{1}{2}$
    (c) $n = 3$, $\ell = 3$, $m_\ell = -3$

12. What is the maximum number of electrons that can be identified with each of the following sets of quantum numbers? In some cases, the answer may be "none." In such cases, explain why "none" is the correct answer.
    (a) $n = 3$
    (b) $n = 3$ and $\ell = 2$
    (c) $n = 4$, $\ell = 1$, $m_\ell = -1$, and $m_s = +\frac{1}{2}$
    (d) $n = 5$, $\ell = 0$, $m_\ell = -1$, $m_s = +\frac{1}{2}$

13. ■ Depict the electron configuration for magnesium using an orbital box diagram and noble gas notation. Give a complete set of four quantum numbers for each of the electrons beyond those of the preceding noble gas.

14. Depict the electron configuration for phosphorus using an orbital box diagram and noble gas notation. Give one possible set of four quantum numbers for each of the electrons beyond those of the preceding noble gas.

15. ■ Using an orbital box diagram and noble gas notation, show the electron configuration of gallium, Ga. Give a set of quantum numbers for the highest-energy electron.

16. Using an orbital box diagram and noble gas notation, show the electron configuration of titanium. Give one possible set of four quantum numbers for each of the electrons beyond those of the preceding noble gas.

Electron Configurations of Atoms and Ions and Magnetic Behavior
(See Example 7.4, Section 6.7, and ChemistryNow Screens 6.16, 7.5, and 7.6.)

17. Using orbital box diagrams, depict an electron configuration for each of the following ions: (a) Mg^{2+}, (b) K^+, (c) Cl^-, and (d) O^{2-}.

18. ■ Using orbital box diagrams, depict an electron configuration for each of the following ions: (a) Na^+, (b) Al^{3+}, (c) Ge^{2+}, and (d) F^-.

19. Using orbital box diagrams and noble gas notation, depict the electron configurations of (a) V, (b) V^{2+}, and (c) V^{5+}. Are any of the ions paramagnetic?

20. ■ Using orbital box diagrams and noble gas notation, depict the electron configurations of (a) Ti, (b) Ti^{2+}, and (c) Ti^{4+}. Are any of the ions paramagnetic?

21. ■ Manganese is found as MnO_2 in deep ocean deposits.
    (a) Depict the electron configuration of this element using the noble gas notation and an orbital box diagram.
    (b) Using an orbital box diagram, show the electrons beyond those of the preceding noble gas for the 4+ ion.
    (c) Is the 4+ ion paramagnetic?
    (d) How many unpaired electrons does the Mn^{4+} ion have?

22. One compound found in alkaline batteries is NiOOH, a compound containing Ni^{3+} ions. When the battery is discharged, the Ni^{3+} is reduced to Ni^{2+} ions [as in $Ni(OH)_2$]. Using orbital box diagrams and the noble gas notation, show electron configurations of these ions. Are either of these ions paramagnetic?

Periodic Properties
(See Section 7.5, Example 7.5, and ChemistryNow Screens 7.7–7.13.)

23. Arrange the following elements in order of increasing size: Al, B, C, K, and Na. (Try doing it without looking at Figure 7.8, and then check yourself by looking up the necessary atomic radii.)

24. ■ Arrange the following elements in order of increasing size: Ca, Rb, P, Ge, and Sr. (Try doing it without looking at Figure 7.8; then check yourself by looking up the necessary atomic radii.)

25. Select the atom or ion in each pair that has the larger radius.
    (a) Cl or Cl^- (b) Al or O   (c) In or I

26. ■ Select the atom or ion in each pair that has the larger radius.
    (a) Cs or Rb   (b) O^{2-} or O   (c) Br or As

27. Which of the following groups of elements is arranged correctly in order of increasing ionization energy?
    (a) C < Si < Li < Ne   (c) Li < Si < C < Ne
    (b) Ne < Si < C < Li   (d) Ne < C < Si < Li

28. ■ Arrange the following atoms in order of increasing ionization energy: Li, K, C, and N.

29. Compare the elements Na, Mg, O, and P.
    (a) Which has the largest atomic radius?
    (b) Which has the most negative electron affinity?
    (c) Place the elements in order of increasing ionization energy.

30. ■ Compare the elements B, Al, C, and Si.
    (a) Which has the most metallic character?
    (b) Which has the largest atomic radius?
    (c) Which has the most negative electron affinity?
    (d) Place the three elements B, Al, and C in order of increasing first ionization energy.

31. Explain each answer briefly.
    (a) Place the following elements in order of increasing ionization energy: F, O, and S.
    (b) Which has the largest ionization energy: O, S, or Se?
    (c) Which has the most negative electron affinity: Se, Cl, or Br?
    (d) Which has the largest radius: O^{2-}, F^-, or F?

32. ■ Explain each answer briefly.
    (a) Rank the following in order of increasing atomic radius: O, S, and F.
    (b) Which has the largest ionization energy: P, Si, S, or Se?
    (c) Place the following in order of increasing radius: O^{2-}, N^{3-}, and F^-.
    (d) Place the following in order of increasing ionization energy: Cs, Sr, and Ba.

General Questions

These questions are not designated as to type or location in the chapter. They may combine several concepts.

33. ■ Using an orbital box diagram and noble gas notation, show the electron configurations of uranium and of the uranium(IV) ion. Is either of these paramagnetic?

34. ■ The rare earth elements, or lanthanides, commonly exist as 3+ ions. Using an orbital box diagram and noble gas notation, show the electron configurations of the following elements and ions.
    (a) Ce and Ce^{3+} (cerium)
    (b) Ho and Ho^{3+} (holmium)

35. ■ A neutral atom has two electrons with $n = 1$, eight electrons with $n = 2$, eight electrons with $n = 3$, and two electrons with $n = 4$. Assuming this element is in its ground state, supply the following information:
    (a) atomic number
    (b) total number of s electrons
    (c) total number of p electrons
    (d) total number of d electrons
    (e) Is the element a metal, metalloid, or nonmetal?

36. ■ Element 109, now named meitnerium (in honor of the Austrian–Swedish physicist, Lise Meitner [1878–1968]), was produced in August 1982 by a team at Germany's Institute for Heavy Ion Research. Depict its electron configuration using *spdf* and noble gas notations. Name another element found in the same group as meitnerium.

Lise Meitner (1878–1968) and Otto Hahn (1879–1968). Element 109 (Mt) was named after Meitner. She earned her Ph.D. in physics under Ludwig Boltzmann at the University of Vienna, the first woman to do so at that university.

37. Which of the following is *not* an allowable set of quantum numbers? Explain your answer briefly. For those sets that are valid, identify an element in which an outermost valence electron could have that set of quantum numbers.

	n	ℓ	m_ℓ	m_s
(a)	2	0	0	$-\frac{1}{2}$
(b)	1	1	0	$+\frac{1}{2}$
(c)	2	1	-1	$-\frac{1}{2}$
(d)	4	2	$+2$	$-\frac{1}{2}$

38. A possible excited state for the H atom has an electron in a $4p$ orbital. List all possible sets of quantum numbers (n, ℓ, m_ℓ, m_s) for this electron.

39. ■ The magnet in the photo is made from neodymium, iron, and boron.

A magnet made of an alloy containing the elements Nd, Fe, and B.

(a) Write the electron configuration of each of these elements using an orbital box diagram and noble gas notation.

(b) Are these elements paramagnetic or diamagnetic?

(c) Write the electron configurations of Nd^{3+} and Fe^{3+} using orbital box diagrams and noble gas notation. Are these ions paramagnetic or diamagnetic?

40. ■ Name the element corresponding to each characteristic below.

(a) the element with the electron configuration $1s^2 2s^2 2p^6 3s^2 3p^3$

(b) the alkaline earth element with the smallest atomic radius

(c) the element with the largest ionization energy in Group 5A

(d) the element whose 2+ ion has the configuration $[Kr]4d^5$

(e) the element with the most negative electron affinity in Group 7A

(f) the element whose electron configuration is $[Ar]3d^{10}4s^2$

41. ■ Arrange the following atoms in the order of increasing ionization energy: Si, K, P, and Ca.

42. ■ Rank the following in order of increasing ionization energy: Cl, Ca^{2+}, and Cl^-. Briefly explain your answer.

43. ■ Answer the questions below about the elements A and B, which have the electron configurations shown.

$$A = [Kr]5s^1 \quad B = [Ar]3d^{10}4s^2 4p^4$$

(a) Is element A a metal, nonmetal, or metalloid?

(b) Which element has the greater ionization energy?

(c) Which element has the less negative electron affinity?

(d) Which element has the larger atomic radius?

(e) What is the formula for a compound formed between A and B?

44. ■ Answer the following questions about the elements with the electron configurations shown here:

$$A = [Ar]4s^2 \quad B = [Ar]3d^{10}4s^2 4p^5$$

(a) Is element A a metal, metalloid, or nonmetal?

(b) Is element B a metal, metalloid, or nonmetal?

(c) Which element is expected to have the larger ionization energy?

(d) Which element has the smaller atomic radius?

45. ■ Which of the following ions are unlikely to be found in a chemical compound: Cs^+, In^{4+}, Fe^{6+}, Te^{2-}, Sn^{5+}, and I^-? Explain briefly.

46. ■ Place the following ions in order of decreasing size: K^+, Cl^-, S^{2-}, and Ca^{2+}.

47. ■ Answer each of the following questions:

(a) Of the elements S, Se, and Cl, which has the largest atomic radius?

(b) Which has the larger radius, Br or Br^-?

(c) Which should have the largest difference between the first and second ionization energy: Si, Na, P, or Mg?

(d) Which has the largest ionization energy: N, P, or As?

(e) Which of the following has the largest radius: O^{2-}, N^{3-}, or F^-?

48. ■ The following are isoelectronic species: Cl^-, K^+, and Ca^{2+}. Rank them in order of increasing (a) size, (b) ionization energy, and (c) electron affinity.

49. ■ Compare the elements Na, B, Al, and C with regard to the following properties:
(a) Which has the largest atomic radius?
(b) Which has the most negative electron affinity?
(c) Place the elements in order of increasing ionization energy.

50. ■ ▲ Two elements in the second transition series (Y through Cd) have four unpaired electrons in their 3+ ions. What elements fit this description?

51. The configuration for an element is given here.

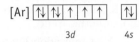

3d   4s

(a) What is the identity of the element with this configuration?
(b) Is a sample of the element paramagnetic or diamagnetic?
(c) How many unpaired electrons does a 3+ ion of this element have?

52. ■ The configuration of an element is given here.

$[Ar]$ ↑ ↑ ↑ □ □   ↑↓

3d   4s

(a) What is the identity of the element?
(b) In what group and period is the element found?
(c) Is the element a nonmetal, a main group element, a transition metal, a lanthanide, or an actinide?
(d) Is the element diamagnetic or paramagnetic? If paramagnetic, how many unpaired electrons are there?
(e) Write a complete set of quantum numbers (n, ℓ, m_ℓ, m_s) for each of the valence electrons.
(f) What is the configuration of the 2+ ion formed from this element? Is the ion diamagnetic or paramagnetic?

In the Laboratory

53. Nickel(II) formate $[Ni(HCO_2)_2]$ is widely used as catalyst precursor and to make metallic nickel. It can be prepared in the general chemistry laboratory by treating readily available nickel(II) acetate with formic acid (HCO_2H).

$$Ni(CH_3CO_2)_2(aq) + 2\ HCO_2H(aq) \rightarrow$$
$$Ni(HCO_2)_2(aq) + 2\ CH_3CO_2H(aq)$$

Green crystalline $Ni(HCO_2)_2$ is precipitated after adding ethanol to the solution.
(a) What is the theoretical yield of nickel(II) formate from 0.500 g of nickel(II) acetate and excess formic acid?
(b) Is nickel(II) formate paramagnetic or diamagnetic? If it is paramagnetic, how many unpaired electrons would you expect?
(c) If nickel(II) formate is heated to 300 °C in the absence of air for 30 minutes, the salt decomposes to form pure nickel powder. What mass of nickel powder should be produced by heating 253 mg of nickel(II) formate? Are nickel atoms paramagnetic?

54. ▲ Spinels are solids with the general formula $M^{2+}(M'^{3+})_2O_4$ (where M^{2+} and M'^{3+} are metal cations of the same or different metals). The best-known example is common magnetite, Fe_3O_4 [which you can formulate as $(Fe^{2+})(Fe^{3+})_2O_4$].

A crystal of a spinel.

(a) Given its name, it is evident that magnetite is ferromagnetic. How many unpaired electrons are there in iron(II) and in iron(III) ions?
(b) Two other spinels are $CoAl_2O_4$ and $SnCo_2O_4$. What metal ions are involved in each? What are their electron configurations? Are the metal ions also paramagnetic, and if so how many unpaired electrons are involved?

Summary and Conceptual Questions

The following questions use concepts from this and previous chapters.

55. Why is the radius of Li^+ so much smaller than the radius of Li? Why is the radius of F^- so much larger than the radius of F?

56. ■ Which ions in the following list are not likely to be found in chemical compounds: K^{2+}, Cs^+, Al^{4+}, F^{2-}, and Se^{2-}? Explain briefly.

57. ■ ▲ Two elements have the following first through fourth ionization energies. Deduce the group in the periodic table to which they probably belong. Explain briefly.

Ionization Energy (kJ/mol)	Element 1	Element 2
1st IE	1086.2	577.4
2nd IE	2352	1816.6
3rd IE	4620	2744.6
4th IE	6222	11575

58. ■ ▲ The ionization of the hydrogen atom can be calculated from Bohr's equation for the electron energy.

$$E = -(N_A Rhc)(Z^2/n^2)$$

where $N_A Rhc = 1312$ kJ/mol and Z is the atomic number. Let us use this approach to calculate a possible ionization energy for helium. First, assume the electrons of the He experience the full 2+ nuclear charge. This gives us the upper limit for the ionization energy. Next, assume one electron of He completely screens the nuclear charge from the other electrons, so $Z = 1$. This gives us a lower limit to the ionization energy. Compare these calculated values for the upper and lower limits to the experimental value of 2372.3 kJ/mol. What does this tell us about the ability of one electron to screen the nuclear charge?

59. ■ Compare the configurations below with two electrons located in *p* orbitals. Which would be the most stable (have the lowest energy)? Which would be the least stable? Explain your answers.

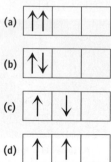

60. The bond lengths in Cl_2, Br_2, and I_2 are 200, 228, and 266 pm, respectively. Knowing that the tin radius is 141 pm, estimate the bond distances in Sn—Cl, Sn—Br, and Sn—I. Compare the estimated values with the experimental values of 233, 250, and 270 pm, respectively.

61. Write electron configurations to show the first two ionization processes for potassium. Explain why the second ionization energy is much greater than the first.

62. Explain how the ionization energy of atoms changes and why the change occurs when proceeding down a group of the periodic table.

63. (a) Explain why the sizes of atoms change when proceeding across a period of the periodic table.
(b) Explain why the sizes of transition metal atoms change very little across a period.

64. ■ Which of the following elements has the greatest difference between its first and second ionization energies: C, Li, N, Be? Explain your answer.

65. ▲ What arguments would you use to convince another student in general chemistry that MgO consists of the ions Mg^{2+} and O^{2-} and not the ions Mg^+ and O^-? What experiments could be done to provide some evidence that the correct formulation of magnesium oxide is $Mg^{2+}O^{2-}$?

66. Explain why the first ionization energy of Ca is greater than that of K, whereas the second ionization energy of Ca is lower than the second ionization energy of K.

67. The energies of the orbitals in many elements have been determined. For the first two periods they have the following values:

Element	1*s* (kJ/mol)	2*s* (kJ/mol)	2*p* (kJ/mol)
H	−1313		
He	−2373		
Li		−520.0	
Be		−899.3	
B		−1356	−800.8
C		−1875	−1029
N		−2466	−1272
O		−3124	−1526
F		−3876	−1799
Ne		−4677	−2083

(a) ▲ Why do the orbital energies generally become more negative on proceeding across the second period?
(b) How are these values related to the ionization energy and electron affinity of the elements?
(c) Use these energy values to explain the observation that the ionization energies of the first four second-period elements are in the order Li < Be > B < C.

Note that these energy values are the basis for the discussion in the Simulation on ChemistryNow Screen 7.8. (Data from J. B. Mann, T. L. Meek, and L. C. Allen: *Journal of the American Chemical Society*, Vol. 122, p. 2780, 2000.)

68. ▲ The ionization energies for the removal of the first electron in Si, P, S, and Cl are as listed in the table below. Briefly rationalize this trend.

Element	First Ionization Energy (kJ/mol)
Si	780
P	1060
S	1005
Cl	1255

69. Using your knowledge of the trends in element sizes on going across the periodic table, explain briefly why the density of the elements increases from K through V.

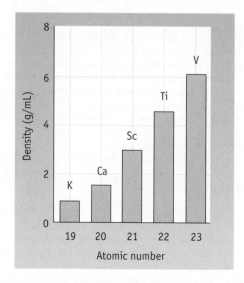

70. The densities (in g/cm³) of elements in Groups 6B, 8B, and 1B are given in the table below.

Period 4	Cr, 7.19	Co, 8.90	Cu, 8.96
Period 5	Mo, 10.22	Rh, 12.41	Ag, 10.50
Period 6	W, 19.30	Ir, 22.56	Au, 19.32

Transition metals in the sixth period all have much greater densities than the elements in the same groups in the fourth and fifth periods. Refer to Figure 7.9, and explain this observation.

71. ■ The discovery of two new elements (atomic numbers 113 and 115) was announced in February 2004.

Some members of the team that discovered elements 113 and 115 at the Lawrence Livermore National Laboratory (left to right): Jerry Landrum, Dawn Shaughnessy, Joshua Patin, Philip Wilk, and Kenton Moody.

(a) Use *spdf* and noble gas notations to give the electron configurations of these two elements.

(b) Name an element in the same periodic group as the two elements.

(c) Element 113 was made by firing a light atom at a heavy americium atom. The two combine to give a nucleus with 113 protons. What light atom was used as a projectile?

72. ■ Explain why the reaction of calcium and fluorine does not form CaF_3.

73. ▲ Thionyl chloride, $SOCl_2$, is an important chlorinating and oxidizing agent in organic chemistry. It is prepared industrially by oxygen atom transfer from SO_3 to SCl_2.

$$SO_3(g) + SCl_2(g) \rightarrow SO_2(g) + SOCl_2(g)$$

(a) Give the electron configuration for an atom of sulfur using an orbital box diagram. Do not use the noble gas notation.

(b) Using the configuration given in part (a), write a set of quantum numbers for the highest-energy electron in a sulfur atom.

(c) What element involved in this reaction (O, S, Cl) should have the smallest ionization energy? The smallest radius?

(d) Which should be smaller: the sulfide ion, S^{2-}, or a sulfur atom, S?

(e) If you want to make 675 g of $SOCl_2$, what mass of SCl_2 is required?

(f) If you use 10.0 g of SO_3 and 10.0 g of SCl_2, what is the theoretical yield of $SOCl_2$?

(g) $\Delta_rH°$ for the reaction of SO_3 and SCl_2 is -96.0 kJ/mol $SOCl_2$ produced. Using data in Appendix L, calculate the standard molar enthalpy of formation of SCl_2.

74. Sodium metal reacts readily with chlorine gas to give sodium chloride. (*See ChemistryNow Screen 7.17 Chemical Puzzler.*)

$$Na(s) + \tfrac{1}{2} Cl_2(g) \rightarrow NaCl(s)$$

(a) What is the reducing agent in this reaction? What property of the element contributes to its ability to act as a reducing agent?

(b) What is the oxidizing agent in this reaction? What property of the element contributes to its ability to act as an oxidizing agent?

(c) Why does the reaction produce NaCl and not a compound such as Na_2Cl or $NaCl_2$?

75. ▲ Slater's rules are a simple way to estimate the effective nuclear charge experienced by an electron. In this approach, the "shielding constant," σ, is calculated. The effective nuclear charge is then the difference between σ and the atomic number, Z. (Note that the results in Table 7.2 were calculated in a slightly different way.)

$$Z^* = Z - \sigma$$

The shielding constant, σ, is calculated using the following rules:

1. The electrons of an atom are grouped as follows: $(1s)$ $(2s, 2p)$ $(3s, 3p)$ $(3d)$ $(4s, 4p)$ $(4d)$, and so on.
2. Electrons in higher groups (to the right) do not shield those in the lower groups.
3. For ns and np valence electrons
   a) Electrons in the same ns, np group contribute 0.35 (for $1s$ 0.30 works better).
   b) Electrons in the $n - 1$ group contribute 0.85.
   c) Electrons in the $n - 2$ group (and lower) contribute 1.00.
4. For nd and nf electrons, electrons in the same nd or nf group contribute 0.35, and those in groups to the left contribute 1.00.

As an example, let us calculate Z^* for the outermost electron of oxygen:

$$\sigma = (2 \times 0.85) + (5 \times 0.35) = 3.45$$
$$Z^* = 8 - 3.45 = 4.55$$

(a) Calculate Z^* for F and Ne. Relate the Z^* values for O, F, and Ne to their relative atomic radii and ionization energies.

(b) Calculate Z^* for one of the $3d$ electrons of Mn, and compare this with Z^* for one of the $4s$ electrons of the element. Do the Z^* values give us some insight into the ionization of Mn to give the cation?

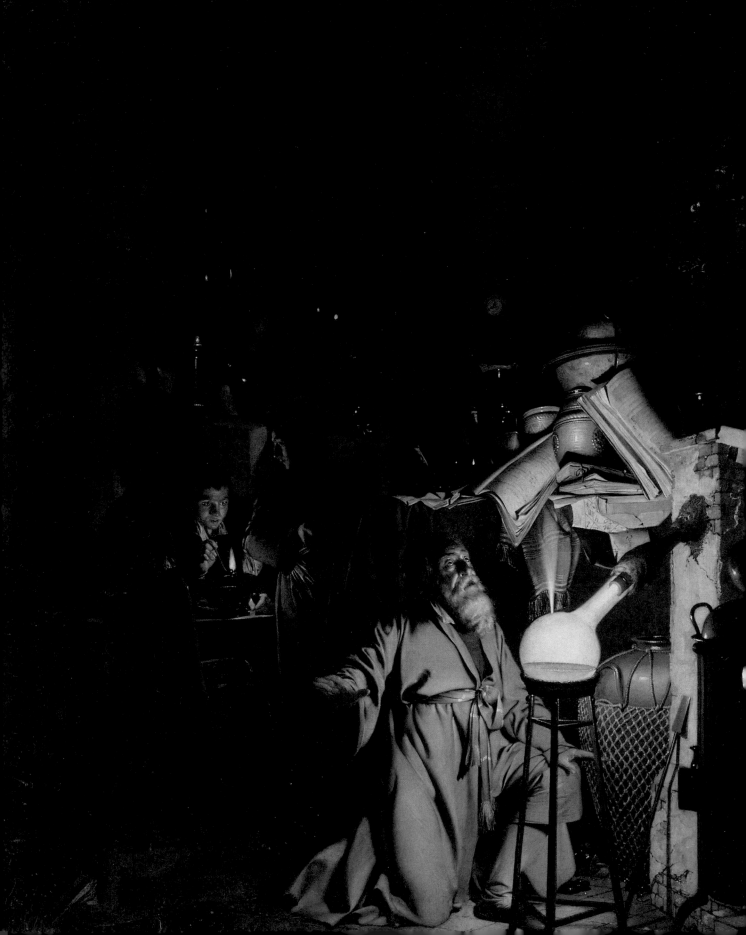

Milestones in the Development of Chemistry and the Modern View of Atoms and Molecules

John Emsley
University of Cambridge

The journey to our understanding of atoms and molecules began 2500 years ago in ancient Greece and continues today with developments in our understanding of chemical bonding and molecular structure. The journey may have started long ago, but it was only when chemistry developed in the 1700s that real progress was made. Today, we have instruments like the scanning tunneling microscope to help us visualize these tiny objects.

But let us start at the beginning and pay a short visit to the Greeks of 450 BC. Their civilization valued learning, and this led to various schools of philosophy. Their teachers did not engage in scientific research as we know it, so their theories were never more than thought experiments. Nevertheless, they correctly deduced that the world was made up of a few basic elements and that these existed as atoms, but they had no way of knowing which elements existed, or how small atoms were. Today, we know of 117 elements—at the last count—and that atoms are so tiny that the dot at the end of this sentence contains billions of them.

Greek Philosophers and Medieval Alchemists

The early Greek philosophers thought that there would be just one element and debated what it might be. Some favored air, some fire, some water, and some said earth. Eventually, Empedocles (who lived from around 490 to 430 BC) argued that all four were elements. This theory was believed for 2000 years—and yet it was wrong.

What form did these elements take? The first person to give an answer was Leucippus, around 450 BC, who said

they must exist as atoms. This idea was developed by his pupil Democritus (460–370 BC), who was the first to use the word "atom," which means un-cut-able or indivisible. Epicurus (341–270 BC) said atoms were spherical, varied in size, and were constantly in motion. This theory remained also unchanged for 2000 years—but it was right.

Alchemy can trace its roots to ancient Egypt. The most famous Egyptian alchemist was Zosimos, who lived around 300 AD. He described such chemical processes as distillation and sublimation, crediting a woman alchemist, Maria the Jewess, with their invention. She lived about 100 AD and experimented with mercury and sulfur, but her best-known invention was the bain-Marie, which is still used in cooking.

Early Muslim rulers encouraged learning, and alchemy flourished. The best-known Arab alchemists were Geber (Jabir ibn Hayyan, 721–815 AD) and Rhazes (Abu Bakr Mohammad ibn Zakariyya al-Razi, 865–925 AD). Geber knew that when mercury and sulfur were combined, the product was a red compound, which we know as mercury(II) sulfide, but he believed that if the recipe were exactly right, then gold would be formed. Rhazes thought that all metals were made from mercury and sulfur, and his influential book, *Secret of Secrets*, contained a long list of chemicals, minerals, and apparatus that a modern chemist would recognize.

In the early Middle Ages, alchemists were at work in Europe, but only a little progress was made. A Spaniard, who also called himself Geber, discovered how to make nitric acid and knew that a mixture of nitric and hydrochloric acids (*aqua regia*) would dissolve gold. The European center for alchemy was Prague, where many alchemists practiced their art while some of their number merely

• **The Alchymist in Search of the Philosophere's Stone, Discovers Phosphorus.** Painted by J. Wright of Derby (1734–1797).

practiced deception, often convincing onlookers that they could turn base metals into gold.

The 1600s saw the gradual emergence of chemistry from alchemy, and in this period we find several men who are now recognized as true scientists but who were also secret alchemists, such as Robert Boyle (1626–1691) and even the great Isaac Newton (1642–1727). Today, Boyle is considered one of the founding fathers of chemistry. His book, *The Sceptical Chymist*, is regarded as the seminal work that broke the link between chemistry and alchemy.

The Philosopher's Stone, a legendary substance that can supposedly turn ordinary substances into gold, was the ultimate prize sought by alchemists. So, when the alchemist Hennig Brandt of Hamburg discovered phosphorus in 1669, he believed it would lead him to the Philosopher's Stone because of the almost miraculous ability of phosphorus to shine in the dark and burst into flames. Some of this new wonder material was shown to Boyle, who eventually was able to make it himself. (It was formed by heating evaporated urine residues to red heat.) What Boyle did next distinguished him as a true chemist: he researched the properties of phosphorus and its reactions with other materials and published his findings, not in the secret language of the alchemists but in plain English, and in a manner that would allow even a modern chemist to repeat what he had done. Phosphorus was a new element although it was not recognized as such for another century.

Boyle too thought about the nature of matter, and he came up with a definition of an element. He wrote:

> "I mean by Elements, as those Chymists that speak plainest do by the Principles, certain Primitive and Simple, or perfectly unmingled bodies; which not being made of any other bodies, or of one another, are the ingredients of which all those call'd perfectly mixt Bodies are immediately compounded, and into which they are ultimately resolved."

We can see that Boyle was struggling with the idea of elements and how these can be compounded together.

Chemists of the 18th–19th Centuries

The theory of four elements was dealt its first body blow by a shy but extremely wealthy Englishman, Henry Cavendish (1731–1810), who had his own laboratory near London. There, he investigated gases. In 1784, he discovered hydrogen and observed that when it burned, water was formed. The French chemist Antoine Lavoisier (1743–1794) (◀ page 114) also studied gases, but he went one step further and noted that when a *mixture* of hydrogen

Henry Cavendish (1731–1810, left) and John Dalton (1766–1844, right).

and another newly discovered gas, oxygen, was sparked, it formed only water. Obviously, water was not an element, but hydrogen and oxygen were.

In 1789, Lavoisier wrote his influential book *Elements of Chemistry*, in which he defined a chemical element as something that could not be further broken down, and he listed 33 of them. Most of these are still considered elements today, but some—such as light, heat, and the earths (later shown to be oxides)—are not. His list is given in Table 1. Lavoisier was the founder of modern chemistry, but, as described on page 114, he fell out of favor with the leaders of the French Revolution and was guillotined.

The next major advance in chemical understanding came from a modest school teacher, John Dalton (1766–1844), who lived in Manchester, England. He knew of the *Law of Fixed Proportions*, which said elements combined in definite ratios by weight, and said it could only be so if they were composed of atoms. The idea of atoms had been revived by scientists like Newton in the 1600s, who said elements would cluster together, but nothing had come of such speculations because chemistry was still little more than mystical alchemy.

In 1803, Dalton gave a talk to the Manchester (England) Literary and Philosophical Society on the way gases dis-

TABLE 1 The Elements According to Lavoisier (1789)

Gases	Nonmetals	Metals		Earths
Light	Sulfur	Antimony	Mercury	Lime
Heat	Phosphorus	Arsenic	Molybdenum	Magnesia
Oxygen	Carbon	Bismuth	Nickel	Barytes
Nitrogen	Chloride	Cobalt	Platinum	Alumina
Hydrogen	Fluoride	Copper	Silver	Silica
	Borate	Gold	Tin	
		Iron	Tungsten	
		Lead	Zinc	
		Manganese		

solved in water, and when his talk was published in the Society's Proceedings he included a table of relative atomic weights, which were based on hydrogen having a value of 1. He listed 20 elements with their weights and said they combined to form "compound atoms," his name for what we now call molecules. At a stroke, Dalton not only revived the idea of atoms, but gave them weight. In his book of 1808, *New System of Chemical Philosophy*, he went further, and he said an atom was a "solid, massy, hard, impenetrable, moveable particle." This description was eventually proved wrong on many counts, but he was right that they existed.

Chemists in the early 1800s were puzzled by the fact that most of the new atomic weights were whole numbers. An explanation was suggested in 1815 by William Prout (1785–1850), who went further than Dalton and reasoned that atoms were not indivisible but were composed of hydrogen. If the atomic weight of hydrogen was taken as 1, then it explained why all the other elements had weights that were whole numbers, or nearly so. In fact, most elements have atomic weights that fall within the limits of ± 0.1 of a whole number, with very few having fractional numbers. Nevertheless, it was the few exceptions that seemed to disprove Prout's theory, which could not explain the atomic weight of chlorine, which was 35.5, or copper, which was 63.5. (The explanation, of course, lies with their isotopic composition, a concept that lay 100 years in the future.)

Prout was almost right. Hydrogen, or at least 99.99% of it, consists of a single proton surrounded by a single electron. The proton is the nucleus, and that accounts for virtually all of the mass. We now classify elements based on how many protons their nuclei contain, with each element on the periodic table differing from the one immediately preceding it by one proton. In some ways, then, they differ according to the nucleus of hydrogen. When the proton was finally identified in 1919, and its importance realized, it took its name from the Greek word *protos* meaning first, although Ernest Rutherford, who made the discovery, also said the name was chosen partly in honor of Prout.

Back in the early 1800s, chemists preferred atomic weights that were calculated relative to that of oxygen because oxygen forms compounds with almost all other elements. (Today, atomic weights are based on the carbon isotope carbon-12, which is taken as exactly 12.) Like Dalton, they believed water consisted of one oxygen and one hydrogen atom, so naturally their scale of atomic weights was of little use.

Inaccurate atomic weights, however, did not hinder the discovery of more and more elements. The 1860s were a particularly fruitful decade with the introduction of the atomic spectroscope, which revealed that each element had a characteristic "fingerprint" pattern of lines in its visible spectrum. As a result, the discoveries of rubidium, cesium, thallium, and indium were announced in the years 1860–1863. The total of known elements was now 65, and chemists were beginning to ask whether there was a limit to their number.

Meanwhile, the Italian chemist Stanislao Cannizzaro (1826–1910) had published a correct list of atomic weights, which he circulated at the First International Chemical Congress, held in Karlsruhe, Germany, in 1860. Dimitri Mendeleev attended the conference and took a copy of Cannizzaro's atomic weights back to St. Petersburg in Russia. What he did with it was to revolutionize chemistry, a story that is told in Chapter 2.

Dalton had suggested ways in which atoms might combine to form larger units. It was clear that the world was composed primarily not of single atoms but of molecules, and chemistry was the science of studying them. The word *molecule* was first given a chemical meaning in 1811; before then, it had simply been a French word for something extremely small. In 1873, its chemical meaning was spelled out by James Clerk Maxwell, who wrote a milestone paper in the journal *Nature* in which he defined a molecule as "the smallest possible portion of a particular substance" beyond which it would no longer have the properties associated with that substance. This is the meaning it still has.

In the 1800s, chemical analysis became quite sophisticated, and the elements in a chemical compound could be identified and expressed as numbers. For example, alcohol was C_2H_6O, but what was it really? And why did dimethyl ether, which was a different substance, have exactly the same formula? The concept of valency could explain how elements combined. Hydrogen had a valency of 1, oxygen of 2 as in H_2O, nitrogen of 3 as in NH_3, and carbon of 4 as in CH_4, but this in itself was not enough to explain what molecules really were. Turning valences into actual molecular arrangements was the next step, and two people were instrumental in doing this: 29-year-old August Kekulé (1829–1896) in 1858, and 22-year-old Jacobus van 't Hoff (1852–1911) in 1878.

Kekulé was one of the great chemists of the second half of the 1800s. He is best known for his theory of molecule structures based on valence and especially of organic molecules in which carbon is four-valent and bonds in various ways to other atoms including car-

August Kekulé (1829–1896).

bon atoms. He published his paper only weeks before one by Archibald Scott Couper (1831–1892), a young Scottish chemist, who was studying in Paris. In fact, Couper had written his paper before Kekulé, but his supervisor took rather a long time to read it, so he lost out. In some ways, Scott Couper's paper was even more advanced than Kekulé's because he drew lines between atoms to indicate actual chemical bonds. (Scott Couper's sad life was to end in an insane asylum.)

Kekulé also claimed some undeserved fame for having deduced that benzene, a molecule whose formula, C_6H_6, seemed to violate the laws of valency, consisted of a ring of six carbon atoms each with hydrogen attached. Late in life, he said it had come to him in a dream while he was working in London in the mid-1850s and fell asleep on the bus taking him home one evening. What he had conveniently forgotten was that Johann Loschmidt (1821–1895), a modest high school teacher from Vienna, had deduced the structure as many as 4 years earlier and published it in an essay that Kekulé had read.

Van't Hoff focused on the problem of how two compounds with exactly the same formula and physical properties could differ in two respects: their crystal shapes could vary but were mirror images of each other and the way they rotated a beam of polarized light, one clockwise, the other counterclockwise. He put forward his theory, in 1874, that this could be explained if carbon formed four bonds arranged tetrahedrally. The idea was ridiculed by older chemists as "fantastic foolishness" and the "shallow speculations" of a youth, yet it could not be ignored because it explained why molecules could be left and right handed (▶ page 446). In any event, he had the laugh on them because he was awarded the first ever Nobel Prize in Chemistry in 1901.

Atomic Structure—Remarkable Discoveries—1890s and Beyond

Like the 1860s, the 1890s was another decade of remarkable chemical discovery, the most surprising being that atoms could spontaneously disintegrate. It began in 1896 when Henri Becquerel (1852–1908) started to investigate the mineral potassium uranyl sulfate [$K_2SO_4 \cdot UO_2(SO_4)_2 \cdot 2\ H_2O$]. He found by chance that it was emitting invisible rays that caused a photographic plate to produce an image. Other uranium compounds also gave off these rays. What was equally intriguing was the observation that the common uranium ore pitchblende contained something that gave off more of this invisible radiation than could be explained by the uranium it contained. The husband and wife team of Pierre Curie (1859–1906) and Marie Curie (1867–1934) worked for weeks in an old shed in Paris to separate this impurity. Eventually, they succeeded, and in 1898 they an-

Marie Curie (1867–1934) and Pierre Curie (1859–1906). Marie Curie is one of very few people and the only woman to have ever received two Nobel Prizes. She was born in Poland but studied and carried out her research in Paris. In 1903, she shared the Nobel Prize in physics with H. Becquerel and her husband Pierre for their discovery of radioactivity. She received a second Nobel Prize in 1911 for chemistry, for the discovery of two new chemical elements, radium and polonium (the latter named from her homeland, Poland). A unit of radioactivity (curie, Ci) and an element (curium, Cm) are named in her honor. Pierre, who died in an accident in 1906, was also well known for his research on magnetism. One of their daughters, Irène, married Frédéric Joliot, and they shared in the 1935 Nobel Prize in chemistry for their discovery of artificial radioactivity.

Emilio Segre Visual Archives

nounced the discovery of two new, intensely radioactive elements: polonium and radium. Radioactivity was the word they invented to describe the new phenomenon of invisible rays (Figure 1), and they called one of the new elements radium because of its intense rays, and the other polonium after Marie's native country Poland.

In 1897, J. J. Thomson (1856–1940) reported his studies of another type of ray, cathode rays. Cathode ray tubes were glass vacuum tubes containing two metal electrodes. When a high voltage is applied to the electrodes, electricity flows from the negative electrode (cathode) to the positive electrode (anode) even though there is nothing there to conduct it. Thomson showed that there was, in fact, a stream of charged particles moving from the cathode to the anode and that these could be deflected by electric and magnetic fields, which showed they were negatively charged (Figure 2). He deduced they were two thousand times lighter than even the lightest element, hydrogen. They became known as *electrons*, a term already invented to describe the smallest particle of electricity.

Sir Joseph John Thomson (1856–1940). Cavendish Professor of Experimental Physics at Cambridge University in England. In 1896, he gave a series of lectures at Princeton University in the U.S. on the discharge of electricity in gases. It was this work on cathode rays that led to his discovery of the electron, which he announced at a lecture on the evening of Friday, April 30, 1897. He later published a number of books on the electron and was awarded the Nobel Prize in physics in 1906.

Oesper Collection in the History of Chemistry/University of Cincinnati

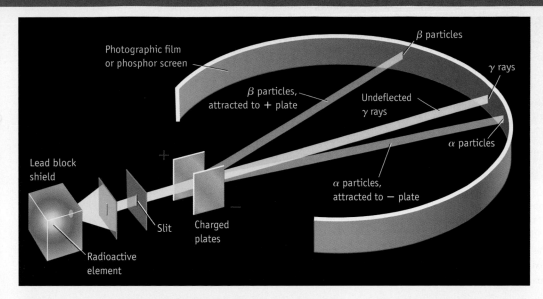

Figure 1 **Radioactivity.** Alpha (α), beta (β), and gamma (γ) rays from a radioactive element are separated by passing them between electrically charged plates. Positively charged α particles are attracted to the negative plate, and negatively charged β particles are attracted to the positive plate. (Note that the heavier α particles are deflected less than the lighter β particles.) Gamma rays have no electric charge and pass undeflected between the charged plates.

(See ChemistryNow Screen 2.5 for an interactive version of this figure.)

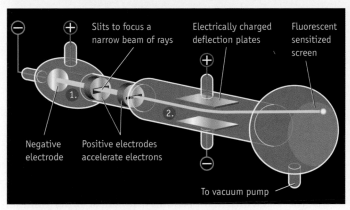

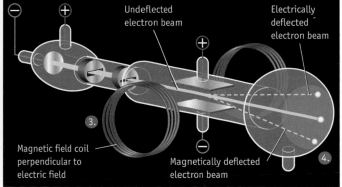

1. A beam of electrons (cathode rays) is accelerated through two focusing slits.

2. When passing through an electric field, the beam of electrons is deflected.

3. The experiment is arranged so that the electric field causes the beam of electrons to be deflected in one direction. The magnetic field deflects the beam in the opposite direction.

4. By balancing the effects of the electrical and magnetic fields, the charge-to-mass ratio of the electron can be determined.

Figure 2 **Thomson's experiment to measure the electron's charge-to-mass ratio.** This experiment was done by J. J. Thomson in 1896–1897. (See ChemistryNow Screen 2.6 for an interactive version of this figure.)

Thomson reasoned that electrons must originate from the atoms of the cathode, and he suggested that an atom was a uniform sphere of positively charged matter in which negative electrons were embedded. That view of an atom was not to persist for long.

In 1886, a few years before Thomson's report, Eugene Goldstein (1850–1930) had also explored cathode rays and had noticed something rather unexpected. Although negatively charged particles were streaming from the cathode to the anode, there were also positively charged particles moving in the opposite direction, and these could be observed if tiny holes were drilled into the cathode plate. These rays, which he called *Kanalstrahlen* from the German word meaning channel rays, became known as canal rays or anode rays (Figure 3). Goldstein thought he had discovered a basic type of atomic particle, the opposite of the

electron, but his positive particles were just traces of residual gas ions in the cathode-ray tube.

The man most associated with discovering the true nature of the atom was Ernest Rutherford (1871–1937), better known as Lord Rutherford. He contributed to the story of atoms in three important ways: he identified the rays that radioactive atoms emitted; he proved that an atom has a tiny nucleus of positively charged protons; and he split the atom; in other words, he converted one element into another. Rutherford, who was born near Nelson on the South Island of New Zealand, went to Cambridge University in England, where he studied under Thomson. He concerned himself with radioactive phenomena and in the years 1898–1900 he identified the various types of radiation: alpha (α), beta (β), and gamma (γ) rays. Alpha and beta rays were particles, the former with an electric charge ($+2$) twice as

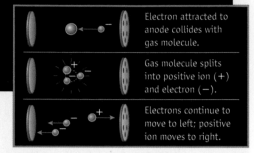

Like cathode rays, positive rays (or "canal rays") are deflected by electric and magnetic fields but much less so than cathode rays for a given value of the field because positive particles are much heavier than electrons.

Electron attracted to anode collides with gas molecule.

Gas molecule splits into positive ion (+) and electron (−).

Electrons continue to move to left; positive ion moves to right.

1. Electrons collide with gas molecules in this cathode-ray tube with a perforated cathode.

2. The molecules become positively charged, and these are attracted to the negatively charged, perforated cathode.

3. Some positive particles pass through the holes and form a beam, or "ray."

Figure 3 Canal rays. In 1886, Eugene Goldstein detected a stream of particles traveling in the direction opposite to that of the negatively charged cathode rays. We now know that these particles are positively charged ions formed by collisions of electrons with gaseous molecules in the cathode-ray tube. (See ChemistryNow Screen 2.8 for an animation of this experiment.)

large as that of the latter, which was negatively charged (−1). We now know that α particles are helium nuclei and that β particles are electrons. Gamma rays are like light rays but with much shorter wavelengths.

Rutherford moved to McGill University in Montreal, Canada, where he collaborated with Frederick Soddy (1877–1956), and together they were able to show that another element, thorium, was radioactive and that it decayed via a series of elements, finally ending up as stable lead. Together, they published their theory of radioactivity in 1908. That same year, Rutherford returned to England to become Professor of Physics at Manchester, where his research was to reveal even more spectacular discoveries about atoms.

Soddy had already returned to England in 1903 and was now working in University College London, where he was able to prove that as radium decayed it formed helium gas. He then moved to Glasgow, Scotland, and there his research showed that atoms of the same element could have more than one atomic mass, and the idea of isotopes was born. These made it possible to explain why an element could have an atomic weight which was not a whole num-

ber. For example, chlorine's was 35.5 because it consisted of 76% the isotope chlorine-35 plus 24% of chlorine-37.

Meanwhile at Manchester, two of Rutherford's students—Hans Geiger (1882–1945) and Ernest Marsden (1889–1970)—bombarded thin gold foil with α particles to test whether Thomson's model of a solid atom with embedded electrons was correct (Figure 4). Almost all the particles passed straight through the gold foil as if there was nothing there. However, they were surprised to find that a few were deflected sideways; some even bounced right back. This experiment proved that an atom of gold is mostly empty space with a tiny nucleus at its center. It was the electrons that accounted for most of its volume. Rutherford calculated that the central nucleus of an atom occupied only 1/10,000th of its volume. He also calculated that a gold nucleus had a positive charge of around 100 units and a radius of about 10^{-12} cm. (The currently accepted values are +79 for atomic charge and 10^{-13} cm for the radius.) Just as Dalton had done more than a century before, Rutherford announced his findings at a meeting of the Manchester Literary and Philosophical Society. The date was March 7, 1911.

In 1908, the American physicist Robert Millikan (1868–1953), based at the California Institute of Technology (Caltech), measured the charge on the electron as 1.592 $\times 10^{-19}$ coulombs, not far from today's accepted value of 1.602 $\times 10^{-19}$ C (Figure 5). Millikan rightly assumed this was the fundamental unit of charge. Knowing this, and the charge-to-mass ratio determined by Thomson, enabled the mass of an electron to be calculated as 9.109 $\times 10^{-28}$ g.

In 1913, Henry G. J. Moseley (1887–1915) realized it was not its atomic weight that defined an element but its atomic number, which he deduced from a study of the wavelengths of lines in x-ray spectra. Moseley was then able to put the periodic table of elements on a more secure footing. (Sadly, his life came to an end when a bullet from a sniper killed him in World War I.) Mendeleev had been

Ernest Rutherford (1871–1937). Rutherford was born in New Zealand in 1871 but went to Cambridge University in England to pursue his Ph.D. in physics in 1895. There, he worked with J. J. Thomson, and it was at Cambridge that he discovered α and β radiation. At McGill University in Canada in 1899, Rutherford did further experiments to prove that α radiation is composed of helium nuclei and that β radiation consists of electrons. He received the Nobel Prize in chemistry for his work in 1908. His research on the structure of the atom was done after he moved to Manchester University in England. In 1919, he returned to Cambridge University, where he took up the position formerly held by Thomson. In his career, Rutherford guided the work of 10 future recipients of the Nobel Prize. Element 104 has been named *rutherfordium* in his honor.

Oesper Collection in the History of Chemistry/University of Cincinnati

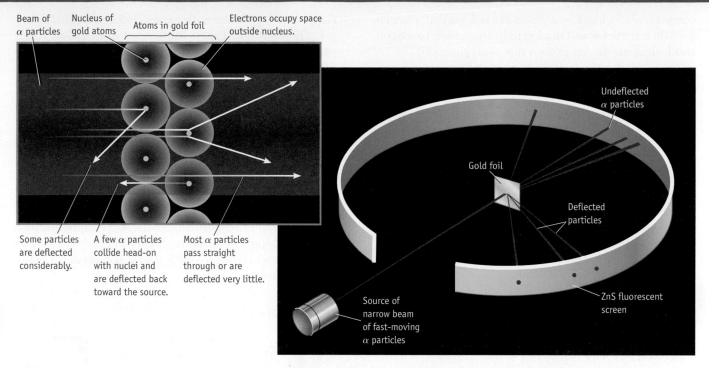

Figure 4 Rutherford's experiment to determine the structure of the atom. A beam of positively charged α particles was directed at a thin gold foil. A fluorescent screen coated with zinc sulfide (ZnS) was used to detect particles passing through or deflected by the foil. (A flash of light is seen when a particle strikes the screen.) Most of the particles passed through the foil, but some were deflected from their path. A few were even deflected backward. (See ChemistryNow Screen 2.10 to explore an interactive version of this figure accompanied by an exercise.)

perplexed by some elements when he arranged them in order of increasing atomic weight. For example, tellurium has an atomic weight of 127.6, and iodine has an atomic weight of 126.9. The problem was that their properties indicated that tellurium should be placed before iodine in the periodic table. Arranging the elements in order of increasing atomic number, however, removed this problem. Tellurium has an atomic number of 52, and iodine has an atomic number of 53, thus justifying placing tellurium before iodine in the table.

Although he was not to know it, Moseley's atomic number corresponded to the number of protons in the nucleus. In 1919, Rutherford proved there were such things as protons, and these were the positive charges located at the center of an atom. Atoms were at last correctly seen as consisting of positive protons balanced by the same number of negative electrons.

In 1919, Rutherford "split the atom" according to the newspapers of the day. What he had performed was the first-ever successful experiment deliberately designed to

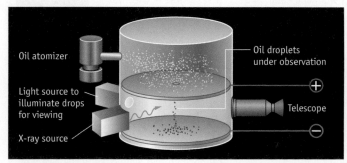

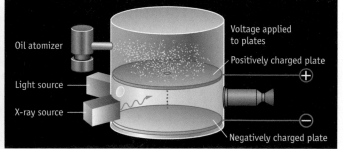

1. A fine mist of oil drops is introduced into one chamber.

2. The droplets fall one by one into the lower chamber under the force of gravity.

3. Gas molecules in the bottom chamber are ionized (split into electrons and a positive fragment) by a beam of x-rays. The electrons adhere to the oil drops, some droplets having one electron, some two, and so on.

These negatively charged droplets continue to fall due to gravity.

4. By carefully adjusting the voltage on the plates, the force of gravity on the droplet is exactly counterbalanced

by the attraction of the negative droplet to the upper, positively charged plate.

Analysis of these forces led to a value for the charge on the electron.

Figure 5 Millikan's experiment to determine the electron charge. The experiment was done by R. A. Millikan in 1909. (See ChemistryNow Screen 2.7 for an interactive exercise on this experiment.)

convert one element into another. He bombarded nitrogen gas with α particles, and this led to its conversion to oxygen and hydrogen. We can express this as an equation:

$$^{14}\text{N (7 protons)} + \alpha \text{ particle (}^{4}\text{He, 2 protons)} \rightarrow$$
$$^{17}\text{O (8 protons)} + {}^{1}\text{H (1 proton)}$$

By about 1920, the image of an atom was that it consisted of a tight nucleus, where all the protons were located, surrounded by a fuzzy cloud of negatively charged electrons, and that these were circling the nucleus rather like planets orbiting the sun. And just as the planets don't move in a random way, so electrons were confined to particular orbits, some nearer the nucleus, some farther away.

The physical nature of atoms was known, but how could the arrangement of electrons be explained? Niels Bohr (1885–1962) was the scientist who helped solve that puzzle.

He lived in Copenhagen, Denmark, and had trained under J. J. Thomson and Ernest Rutherford in England. It was while studying atomic spectra in England that he began to develop his theory of electrons circulating in orbits around the nucleus and with specific quantized energies (◄ page 276). Bohr postulated that the electrons were confined to specific energy levels called orbits. He could then understand the atomic emission spectrum of hydrogen by postulating that the lines it displayed corresponded to discrete quantities of energy (quanta) that an electron emitted as it jumped from one orbit to another.

Bohr's idea of specific energy levels is still retained, but his idea of orbits at specific distances has been revised to be the orbitals of modern atomic theory (Chapter 6). Also involved in applying quantum theory to electron energies were Erwin Schrödinger (1887–1961), who devised a math-

Historical Perspectives   20th-Century Giants of Science

Many of the advances in science occurred during the early part of the 20th century, as the result of theoretical studies by some of the greatest minds in the history of science.

Max Karl Ernst Ludwig Planck (1858–1947) was raised in Germany, where his father was a professor at a university. While still in his teens, Planck decided to become a physicist, against the advice of the head of the physics department at

Max Planck

Munich, who told him, "The important discoveries [in physics] have been made. It is hardly worth entering physics anymore." Fortunately, Planck did not take this advice and went on to study thermodynamics. This interest led him eventually to consider the ultraviolet catastrophe in explanations of blackbody radiation and to develop his revolutionary hypothesis of quantized energy, which was announced 2 weeks before Christmas in 1900. He was awarded the Nobel Prize in physics in 1918 for this work. Einstein later said it was a longing to find harmony and order in nature, a "hunger in his soul," that spurred Planck on.

Erwin Schrödinger (1887–1961) was born in Vienna, Austria. Following his service as an artillery officer in World War I, he became a professor of physics. In 1928, he succeeded Planck as professor of physics at the University of Berlin. He shared the Nobel Prize in physics in 1933.

Erwin Schrödinger

Niels Bohr (1885–1962) was born in Copenhagen, Denmark. He earned a Ph.D. in physics in Copenhagen in 1911 and then went to work first with J. J. Thomson and later with Ernest Rutherford in England. It was there that he began to develop his theory of atomic structure and his explanation of atomic spectra. (He received the Nobel Prize in physics in 1922 for this work.) Bohr returned to Copenhagen, where he eventually became director of the Institute for Theoretical Physics. Many young physicists worked with him at the Institute, seven of whom eventually received Nobel Prizes in chemistry and physics. Among these scientists were Werner Heisenberg, Wolfgang Pauli, and Linus Pauling. Element 107 was recently named bohrium in Bohr's honor.

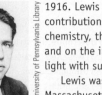

Niels Bohr

Werner Heisenberg (1901–1976) studied with Max Born and later with Bohr. He received the Nobel Prize in physics in 1932. The recent play *Copenhagen*, which has been staged in London and New York, centers on the relationship between Bohr and Heisenberg and their involvement in the development of atomic weapons in World War II.

Gilbert Newton Lewis (1875–1946) introduced the theory of the shared electron-pair chemical bond in a paper published in the *Journal of the American Chemical Society* in

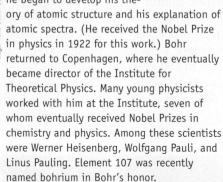

Werner Heisenberg

1916. Lewis also made major contributions in acid–base chemistry, thermodynamics, and on the interaction of light with substances.

Lewis was born in Massachusetts but raised in Nebraska. After earning his B. A. and Ph.D. at Harvard, he began his career in 1912 at the University of California at Berkeley. He was not only a productive researcher, but was also an influential teacher. Among his ideas was the use of problem sets in teaching, an idea still in use today.

Gilbert Newton Lewis

Linus Pauling (1901–1994) was born in Portland, Oregon, earned a B.Sc. degree in chemical engineering from Oregon State College in 1922, and completed his Ph.D. in chemistry at the California Institute of Technology in 1925. In chemistry, he is best known for his book *The Nature of the Chemical Bond*. He also studied protein structure, and, in the words of Francis Crick, was "one of the founders of molecular biology." It was this work and his study of chemical bonding that were cited in the award of the Nobel Prize in chemistry in 1954. Although chemistry was the focus of his life, at the urging of his wife, Ava Helen, he was also involved in nuclear disarmament issues, and he received the Nobel Peace Prize in 1962 for the role he played in advocating for the nuclear test ban treaty.

Linus Pauling

ematical equation that described orbitals, and Werner Heisenberg (1901–1976), whose *Uncertainty Principle* said that we cannot ever know exactly both the position and the energy of an electron.

The nucleus of an atom still presented a problem in 1930. How could a large number of positively charged protons co-exist in a nucleus without their repelling one another so much so that the atom falls apart? Lead, for example, had 82 protons. There had to be something else in the nucleus, and it had to be a heavy particle to account for the atomic weight of an element, which was more than double its atomic number and in the case of lead was 207. In 1932, the British physicist James Chadwick (1891–1974) found the missing particles. He directed the very powerful α rays that were released from radioactive polonium towards a beryllium target. The secondary emanations emitted by the latter metal were strange in that they carried no charge but massive enough to knock protons out of the nuclei of other atoms. These new particles, now known as *neutrons*, had no electric charge and a mass of 1.674927×10^{-24} g, slightly greater than the mass of a proton. (At the same time, Hans Falkenhagen in Germany discovered neutrons also, but he did not publish his results.) Chadwick had found the missing particle. It completed the chemists' picture of an atom. It also made it possible to produce elements heavier than uranium—as well as to create atomic bombs.

The Nature of the Chemical Bond

Molecules presented a more complex problem: how did atoms join together to form them? The first person to provide an answer based on the new view of the atom was the American chemist Gilbert Newton Lewis (1875–1946). In his chemistry lectures at the University of California–Berkeley in the early 1900s, he used dots to symbolize electrons, and he developed this idea so that it became more than just a teaching aid. Lewis said in 1916 that a single chemical bond was the sharing of a pair of electrons between two atoms; a double bond was the sharing of two pairs; and a triple bond the sharing of three pairs. This simple concept explained valency and structure and had enormous influence because it made so much of the chemistry of atoms and molecules understandable.

More sophisticated concepts of bonding were developed based on Max Planck's (1858–1947) theory that energy was quantized. Neils Bohr (1885–1962) and Robert Mulliken (1896–1986) saw that this implied there were only certain energy levels within an atom that its electrons could inhabit. Mulliken proposed a theory of chemical bonding based on combining atomic orbitals into molecular orbitals and showed how the energies of these related to the way the atomic orbitals overlapped. He also developed the theory of electronegativity, which is based on the relative abilities of atoms in molecules to attract electrons, again a concept useful in explaining chemical behavior.

For chemists, the man whose name is most famously linked to bonding was Linus Pauling (1901–1994). He wrote his first paper on the subject when he was only 27 years old, in 1928, and followed it with several more. He brought all his thoughts together in his seminal work *The Nature of the Chemical Bond* in 1939.

Of course, there are still many things to be discovered about atoms and molecules, but as far as chemistry was concerned, the age-old questions of what elements, atoms, and molecules really were had been answered by the mid-twentieth century. The world of the nucleus and of subatomic particles could be left to the physicists to investigate.

SUGGESTED READINGS

1. Eric Scerri, *The Periodic Table: Its Story and Its Significance,* Oxford University Press, New York, 2007.
2. John Emsley, *The 13th Element: The Sordid Tale of Murder, Fire, and Phosphorus,* John Wiley and Sons, New York, 2000.
3. John Emsley, *Nature's Building Blocks,* Oxford University Press, 2002.
4. Arthur Greenberg, *A Chemical History Tour: Picturing Chemistry from Alchemy to Modern Molecular Science,* Wiley-Interscience, New York, 2000.
5. Aaron Ihde, *The Development of Modern Chemistry,* Dover Publications, New York, 1984.
6. L. K. James, ed., *Nobel Laureates in Chemistry, 1901–1992,* American Chemical Society and Chemical Heritage Foundation, 1993.

STUDY QUESTIONS

Blue-numbered questions have answers in Appendix P and fully-worked solutions in the *Student Solutions Manual*.

1. Dalton proposed that an atom was a "solid, massy, hard, impenetrable, moveable particle." Critique this description. How does this description misrepresent atomic structure.

2. Dalton's hypotheses on the structure of atoms was based in part on the observation of a "Law of definite proportions," which said that atoms combined in a definite ratio by weight. Using the formula for water and atomic weights from the current atomic mass scale, calculate the ratio of the mass of hydrogen to the mass of oxygen in water.

3. From cathode ray experiments, J. J. Thomson estimated that the mass of an electron was "about a thousandth" of the mass of a proton. How accurate is that estimate? Calculate the ratio of the mass of an electron to the mass of a hydrogen atom.

4. Goldstein observed positively charged particles moving in the opposite direction to electrons in a cathode ray tube. From their mass, he concluded that these particles were formed from residual gas in the tube. For example, if the cathode ray tube contained helium, the cathode rays consisted of He^+ ions. Describe the process that forms these ions.

8 | Bonding and Molecular Structure

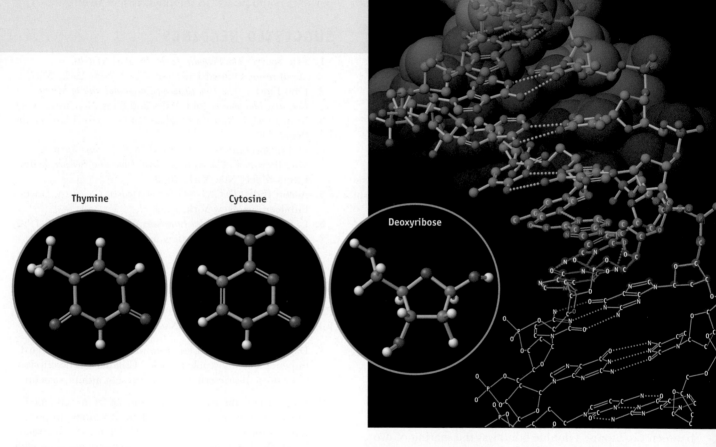

Thymine

Cytosine

Deoxyribose

Chemical Bonding in DNA

The theme of this chapter and the next is molecular bonding and structure, and the subject is well-illustrated by the structure of DNA. This molecule is a helical coil of two chains of tetrahedral phosphate groups and deoxyribose groups. Organic bases (such as thymine and cytosine) on one chain interact with complementary bases on the other chain.

Questions:

Among the many questions you can answer from studying this chapter are the following:

1. Why are there four bonds to carbon and phosphorus?
2. Why are the C atoms and P atoms in the backbone, and the C atoms in deoxyribose, surrounded by other atoms at an angle of 109°?
3. What are the angles in the six-member rings of the bases thymine and cytosine? Why are the six-member rings flat?
4. Are thymine and cytosine polar molecules?

Answers to these questions are in Appendix Q.

Chemistry.⊹.Now™

Throughout the text this icon introduces an opportunity for self-study or to explore interactive tutorials by signing in at **www.cengage.com/login**.

Scientists have long known that the key to interpreting the properties of a chemical substance is first to recognize and understand its structure and bonding. **Structure** refers to the way atoms are arranged in space, and **bonding** describes the forces that hold adjacent atoms together.

Our discussion of structure and bonding begins with small molecules and then progresses to larger molecules. From compound to compound, atoms of the same element participate in bonding and structure in a predictable way. This consistency allows us to develop a group of principles that apply to many different chemical compounds, including such complex molecules as DNA.

8.1 Chemical Bond Formation

When a chemical reaction occurs between two atoms, their valence electrons are reorganized so that a net attractive force—a **chemical bond**—occurs between atoms. There are two general types of bonds, ionic and covalent, and their formation can be depicted using Lewis symbols.

An **ionic bond** forms when *one or more valence electrons is transferred from one atom to another,* creating positive and negative ions. When sodium and chlorine react (Figure 8.1a), an electron is transferred from a sodium atom to a chlorine atom to form Na$^+$ and Cl$^-$.

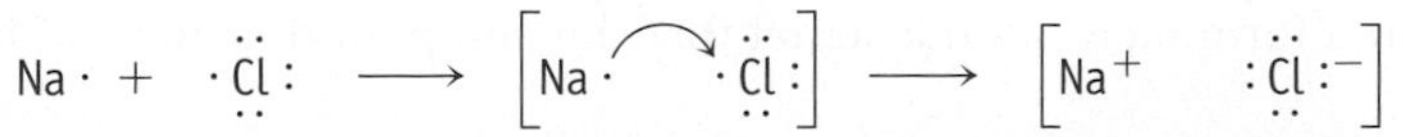

$$\text{Na} \cdot \ + \ \cdot \ddot{\underset{\cdot\cdot}{\text{Cl}}} : \ \longrightarrow \ \left[\text{Na} \cdot \ \overset{\frown}{} \ \ddot{\underset{\cdot\cdot}{\text{Cl}}} : \right] \ \longrightarrow \ \left[\text{Na}^+ \quad : \ddot{\underset{\cdot\cdot}{\text{Cl}}} : ^- \right]$$

Metal atom / Nonmetal atom — Electron transfer from reducing agent to oxidizing agent — Ionic compound. Ions have noble gas electron configurations.

■ **Valence Electron Configurations and Ionic Compound Formation** For the formation of NaCl:

Na changes from $1s^2 2s^2 2p^6 3s^1$ to Na$^+$ with $1s^2 2s^2 2p^6$, equivalent to the Ne configuration.

Cl changes from [Ne]$3s^2 3p^5$ to Cl$^-$ with [Ne]$3s^2 3p^6$, equivalent to the Ar configuration.

The "bond" is the attractive force between the positive and negative ions.

Covalent bonding, in contrast, *involves sharing of valence electrons between atoms.* Two chlorine atoms, for example, share a pair of electrons, one electron from each atom, to form a covalent bond.

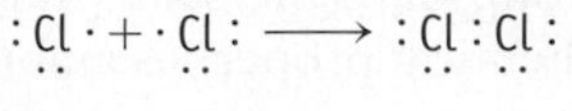

$$: \ddot{\underset{\cdot\cdot}{\text{Cl}}} \cdot \ + \ \cdot \ddot{\underset{\cdot\cdot}{\text{Cl}}} : \ \longrightarrow \ : \ddot{\underset{\cdot\cdot}{\text{Cl}}} : \ddot{\underset{\cdot\cdot}{\text{Cl}}} :$$

(a) The reaction of elemental sodium and chlorine to give sodium chloride.
$\Delta_f H^\circ$ [NaCl(s)] = −411.12 kJ/mol

(b) The reaction of elemental calcium and oxygen to give calcium oxide.
$\Delta_f H^\circ$ [CaO(s)] = −635.09 kJ/mol

As bonding is described in greater detail, you will discover that the two types of bonding—complete electron transfer and the equal sharing of electrons—are extreme cases. In most chemical compounds, electrons are shared unequally, with the extent of sharing varying widely from very little sharing (largely ionic) to considerable sharing (largely covalent).

Ionic bonding will be described in more detail in Chapter 13, while the present chapter focuses on bonding in covalent compounds.

Module 12

8.2 Covalent Bonding and Lewis Structures

There are many examples of compounds having covalent bonds, including the gases in our atmosphere (O_2, N_2, H_2O, and CO_2), common fuels (CH_4), and most of the compounds in your body. Covalent bonding is also responsible for the atom-to-atom connections in common ions such as CO_3^{2-}, CN^-, NH_4^+, NO_3^-, and PO_4^{3-}. We will develop the basic principles of structure and bonding using these and other small molecules and ions, but the same principles apply to larger molecules from aspirin to proteins and DNA with thousands of atoms.

The molecules and ions just mentioned are composed entirely of *nonmetal* atoms. A point that needs special emphasis is that, in molecules or ions made up *only* of nonmetal atoms, the atoms are attached by covalent bonds. Conversely, the presence of a metal in a formula is often a signal that the compound is likely to be ionic.

Valence Electrons and Lewis Symbols for Atoms

The electrons in an atom are of two types: **valence electrons** and **core electrons.** Chemical reactions result in the loss, gain, or rearrangement of valence electrons. The core electrons are not involved in bonding or in chemical reactions.

For main group elements (elements of the A groups in the periodic table), the valence electrons are the *s* and *p* electrons in the outermost shell (Table 8.1). All electrons in inner shells are core electrons. A useful guideline for *main group elements* is that *the number of valence electrons is equal to the group number.* The fact that all elements in a periodic group have the same number of valence electrons accounts for the similarity of chemical properties among members of the group.

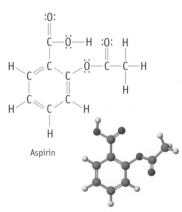

Aspirin

One goal of this chapter is to understand why a molecule such as aspirin has the shape that it exhibits.

TABLE 8.1 Core and Valence Electrons for Several Common Elements

Element	Periodic Group	Core Electrons	Valence Electrons	Total Configuration
Main Group Elements				
Na	1A	$1s^2 2s^2 2p^6 = $ [Ne]	$3s^1$	[Ne]$3s^1$
Si	4A	$1s^2 2s^2 2p^6 = $ [Ne]	$3s^2 3p^2$	[Ne]$3s^2 3p^2$
As	5A	$1s^2 2s^2 2p^6 3s^2 3p^6 3d^{10} = $ [Ar]$3d^{10}$	$4s^2 4p^3$	[Ar]$3d^{10} 4s^2 4p^3$
Transition Elements				
Ti	4B	$1s^2 2s^2 2p^6 3s^2 3p^6 = $ [Ar]	$3d^2 4s^2$	[Ar]$3d^2 4s^2$
Co	8B	[Ar]	$3d^7 4s^2$	[Ar]$3d^7 4s^2$
Mo	6B	[Kr]	$4d^5 5s^1$	[Kr]$4d^5 5s^1$

Valence electrons for transition elements include the electrons in the ns and $(n-1)d$ orbitals (see Table 8.1). The remaining electrons are core electrons. As with main group elements, the valence electrons for transition metals determine the chemical properties of these elements.

The American chemist Gilbert Newton Lewis (1875–1946) introduced a useful way to represent electrons in the valence shell of an atom. The element's symbol represents the atomic nucleus together with the core electrons. Up to four valence electrons, represented by dots, are placed one at a time around the symbol; then, if any valence electrons remain, they are paired with ones already there. Chemists now refer to these pictures as **Lewis electron dot symbols.** Lewis dot symbols for main group elements of the second and third periods are shown in Table 8.2.

Arranging the valence electrons of a main group element around an atom in four groups suggests that the valence shell can accommodate four pairs of electrons. Because this represents eight electrons in all, this is referred to as an **octet** of electrons. An octet of electrons surrounding an atom is regarded as a stable configuration. The noble gases, with the exception of helium, have eight valence electrons and demonstrate a notable lack of reactivity. (Helium, neon, and argon do not undergo any chemical reactions, and the other noble gases have very limited chemical reactivity.) Because chemical reactions involve changes in the valence electron shell, the limited reactivity of the noble gases is taken as evidence of the stability of their noble gas ($ns^2 np^6$) electron configuration. Hydrogen, which in its compounds has two electrons in its valence shell, obeys the spirit of this rule by matching the electron configuration of He.

Chemistry ⚛ **Now**™

Sign in at **www.cengage.com/login** and go to Chapter 8 Contents to see Screen 8.2 for more on **the correlation of the periodic table and valence electrons.**

TABLE 8.2 Lewis Dot Symbols for Main Group Atoms

1A ns^1	2A ns^2	3A ns^2np^1	4A ns^2np^2	5A ns^2np^3	6A ns^2np^4	7A ns^2np^5	8A ns^2np^6
Li·	·Be·	·B·	·C·	·N·	:O·	:F·	:Ne:
Na·	·Mg·	·Al·	·Si·	·P·	:S·	:Cl·	:Ar:

Lewis Electron Dot Structures and the Octet Rule

In a simple description of covalent bonding, a bond results when one or more electron pairs are shared between two atoms. The electron pair bond between the two atoms of an H_2 molecule is represented by a pair of dots or, alternatively, a line.

Electron pair bond

H:H   H—H

The representation of a molecule in this fashion is called a **Lewis electron dot structure** or just a **Lewis structure** in honor of G. N. Lewis.

Simple Lewis structures, such as that for F_2, can be drawn starting with Lewis dot symbols for atoms and arranging the valence electrons to form bonds. Fluorine, an element in Group 7A, has seven valence electrons. The Lewis symbol shows that an F atom has a single unpaired electron along with three electron pairs. In F_2, the single electrons, one on each F atom, pair up in the covalent bond.

Lone pair of electrons

:F· + ·F: ⟶ :F:F: or :F—F:

Shared or bonding electron pair

In the Lewis structure for F_2 the pair of electrons in the F—F bond is the bonding pair, or **bond pair.** The other six pairs reside on single atoms and are called **lone pairs.** Because they are not involved in bonding, they are also called **nonbonding electrons.**

Carbon dioxide, CO_2, and dinitrogen, N_2, are examples of molecules in which two atoms are multiply bonded; that is, they share more than one electron pair.

■ **H Atoms and Electron Octets**
Hydrogen atoms cannot be surrounded by an octet of electrons. An atom of H, which has only a $1s$ valence electron orbital, can accommodate only a pair of electrons.

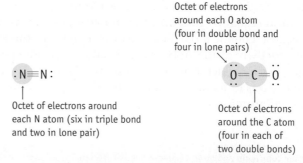

Octet of electrons around each O atom (four in double bond and four in lone pairs)

:N≡N:

Octet of electrons around each N atom (six in triple bond and two in lone pair)

O=C=O

Octet of electrons around the C atom (four in each of two double bonds)

■ **Importance of Lone Pairs** Lone pairs can be important in a structure. Since they are in the same valence electron shell as the bonding electrons, they can influence molecular shape. See Section 8.6.

In carbon dioxide, the carbon atom shares two pairs of electrons with each oxygen and so is linked to each O atom by a double bond. The valence shell of each oxygen atom in CO_2 has two bonding pairs and two lone pairs. In dinitrogen, the two nitrogen atoms share three pairs of electrons, so they are linked by a triple bond. In addition, each N atom has a single lone pair.

An important observation can be made about the molecules you have seen so far: each atom (except H) has a share in four pairs of electrons, so each has achieved a *noble gas configuration. Each atom is surrounded by an octet of eight electrons.* (Hydrogen typically forms a bond to only one other atom, resulting in two electrons in its valence shell.) *The tendency of molecules and polyatomic ions to have structures in which eight electrons surround each atom* is known as the **octet rule.** As an example, a triple bond is necessary in dinitrogen in order to have an octet around each nitrogen atom. The carbon atom and both oxygen atoms in CO_2 achieve the octet configuration by forming double bonds.

The octet rule is extremely useful, but keep in mind that it is more a *guideline* than a rule. Particularly for the second period elements C, N, O, and F, a Lewis structure in which each atom achieves an octet is likely to be correct. Although there are a few exceptions, if an atom such as C, N, O, or F in a Lewis structure does not follow the octet rule, you should question the structure's validity. If a structure obeying the octet rule cannot be written, then it is possible an incorrect formula has been assigned to the compound or the atoms have been assembled in an incorrect way.

■ **Exceptions to the Octet Rule** Although the octet rule is widely applicable, there are exceptions. Fortunately, many will be obvious, such as when there are more than four bonds to an element or when an odd number of electrons occur. See Section 8.5.

Drawing Lewis Electron Dot Structures

There is a systematic approach to constructing Lewis structures of molecules and ions. Let us take formaldehyde, CH_2O, as an example.

1. *Determine the arrangement of atoms within a molecule.* The central atom is *usually* the one with the lowest electron affinity. In CH_2O, the central atom is C. You will come to recognize that certain elements often appear as the central atom, among them C, N, P, and S. Halogens are often terminal atoms forming a single bond to one other atom, but they can be the central atom when combined with O in oxoacids (such as $HClO_4$). Oxygen is the central atom in water, but in conjunction with nitrogen, phosphorus, and the halogens it is usually a terminal atom. Hydrogen is a terminal atom because it typically bonds to only one other atom.

2. *Determine the total number of valence electrons in the molecule or ion.* In a neutral molecule, this number will be the sum of the valence electrons for each atom. For an *anion, add* the number of electrons equal to the negative charge; for a *cation, subtract* the number of electrons equal to the positive charge. The number of valence electron pairs will be half the total number of valence electrons. For CH_2O,

   Valence electrons = 12 electrons (or 6 electron pairs)
   = 4 for C + (2 × 1 for two H atoms) + 6 for O

3. *Place one pair of electrons between each pair of bonded atoms to form a single bond.*

   Here, three electron pairs are used to make three single bonds (which are represented by single lines). Three pairs of electrons remain to be used.

4. *Use any remaining pairs as lone pairs around each terminal atom (except H) so that each terminal atom is surrounded by eight electrons.* If, after this is done, there are electrons left over, assign them to the central atom. (If the central atom is an element in the third or higher period, it can have more than eight electrons. See page 364.)

■ **Choosing the Central Atom**
1. The electronegativities of atoms can also be used to choose the central atom. Electronegativity is discussed in Section 8.7.
2. For simple compounds, the first atom in a formula is often the central atom (e.g., SO_2, NH_4^+, NO_3^-). This is not always a reliable predictor, however. Notable exceptions include water (H_2O) and most common acids (HNO_3, H_2SO_4), in which the acidic hydrogen is usually written first but where another atom (such as N or S) is the central atom.

Here, all six pairs have been assigned, but notice that the C atom has a share in only three pairs.

5. *If the central atom has fewer than eight electrons at this point, change one or more of the lone pairs on the terminal atoms into a bonding pair between the central and terminal atom to form a multiple bond.*

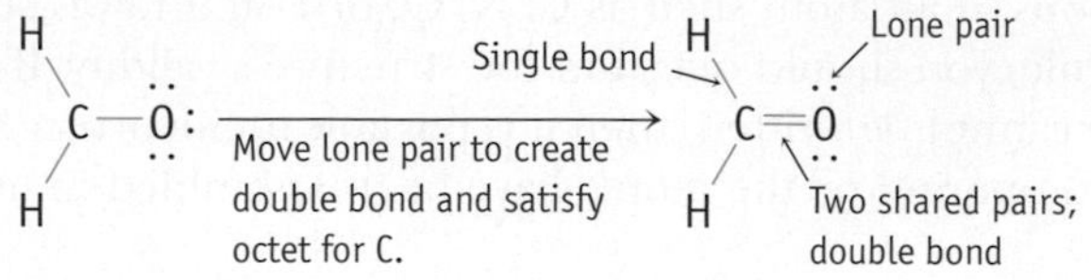

■ **O as a Terminal Atom** Oxygen atoms are usually terminal atoms when combined with many other atoms such as B, C, Si, S, N, P, and the halogens.

As a general rule, double or triple bonds are most often encountered when *both* atoms are from the following list: C, N, or O. That is, bonds such as C═C, C═N, and C═O will be encountered frequently.

ChemistryNow™

Sign in at **www.cengage.com/login** and go to Chapter 8 Contents to see:

- Screen 8.4 for an animation of the **factors influencing bond formation**
- Screen 8.5 for a tutorial on **Lewis structures**
- Screen 8.6 for a tutorial and an exercise on **drawing Lewis structures**

EXAMPLE 8.1 Drawing Lewis Structures

Problem Draw Lewis structures for the chlorate ion (ClO_3^-) and the nitronium ion (NO_2^+).

Strategy Follow the five steps outlined for CH_2O in the preceding text.

Solution for chlorate ion

1. Cl is the central atom, and the O atoms are terminal atoms.
2. Valence electrons = 26 (13 pairs)

   = 7 (for Cl) + 18 (six for each O) + 1 (for the negative charge)
3. Three electron pairs form single bonds from Cl to the O terminal atoms.

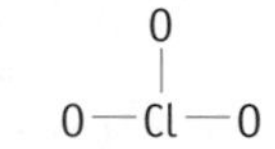

4. Distribute three lone pairs on each of the terminal O atoms to complete the octet of electrons around each of these atoms.

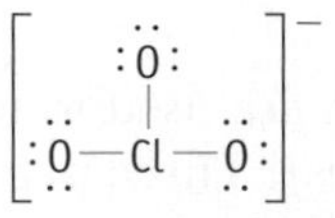

5. One pair of electrons remains, and it is placed on the central Cl atom to complete its octet.

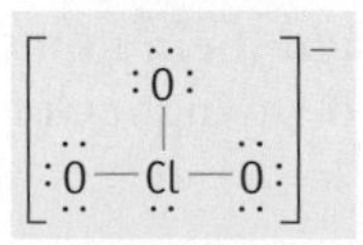

Each atom now has a share in four pairs of electrons, and the Lewis structure is complete.

Solution for nitronium ion

1. Nitrogen is the central atom, because its electron affinity is lower than that of oxygen.

2. Valence electrons = 16 (8 valence pairs)

= 5 (for N) + 12 (six for each O) − 1 (for the positive charge)

3. Two electron pairs form single bonds from the nitrogen to each oxygen:

O—N—O

4. Distribute the remaining six pairs of electrons on the terminal O atoms:

$$\left[:\ddot{\text{O}}\text{—N—}\ddot{\text{O}}: \right]^+$$

5. The central nitrogen atom is two electron pairs short of an octet. Thus, a lone pair of electrons on each oxygen atom is converted to a bonding electron pair to give two N=O double bonds. Each atom in the ion now has four electron pairs. Nitrogen has four bonding pairs, and each oxygen atom has two lone pairs and shares two bond pairs.

Move lone pairs to create double bonds and satisfy the octet for N.

$$\left[:\ddot{\text{O}}\text{—N—}\ddot{\text{O}}: \right]^+ \longrightarrow \left[\ddot{\text{O}}\text{=N=}\ddot{\text{O}} \right]^+$$

Comment Why don't we take two lone pairs from one side and none from the other? We shall discuss that after describing charge distribution in molecules and ions (page 377).

EXERCISE 8.1 Drawing Lewis Structures

Draw Lewis structures for NH_4^+, CO, NO^+, and SO_4^{2-}.

Predicting Lewis Structures

Lewis structures are useful in gaining a perspective on the structure and chemistry of a molecule or ion. The guidelines for drawing Lewis structures are helpful, but chemists also rely on patterns of bonding in related molecules.

Hydrogen Compounds

Some common compounds and ions formed from second-period nonmetal elements and hydrogen are shown in Table 8.3. Their Lewis structures illustrate the fact that the Lewis symbol for an element is a useful guide in determining the number of bonds formed by the element. For example, if there is no charge, nitrogen has five valence electrons. Two electrons occur as a lone pair; the other three occur as unpaired electrons. To reach an octet, it is necessary to pair each of the unpaired electrons with an electron from another atom. Thus, N is predicted

---

Problem Solving Tip 8.1

Useful Ideas to Consider When Drawing Lewis Electron Dot Structures

- The octet rule is a useful guideline when drawing Lewis structures.
- Carbon forms four bonds (four single bonds; two single bonds and one double bond; two double bonds; or one single bond and one triple bond). In uncharged species, nitrogen forms three bonds and oxygen forms two bonds. Hydrogen typically forms only one bond to another atom.

- When multiple bonds are formed, both of the atoms involved are usually one of the following: C, N, and O. Oxygen has the ability to form multiple bonds with a variety of elements. Carbon forms many compounds having multiple bonds to another carbon or to N or O.
- Nonmetals may form single, double, and triple bonds but never quadruple bonds.

- Always account for single bonds and lone pairs before determining whether multiple bonds are present.
- Be alert for the possibility the molecule or ion you are working on is isoelectronic (page 358) with a species you have seen before.

TABLE 8.3 Lewis Structures of Common Hydrogen-Containing Molecules and Ions of Second-Period Elements

Group 4A	Group 5A	Group 6A	Group 7A
CH_4 methane H—C—H with H above and below (4 H's)	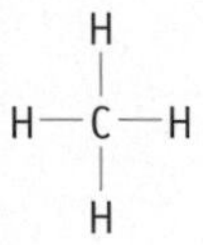 NH_3 ammonia H—N̈—H with H below 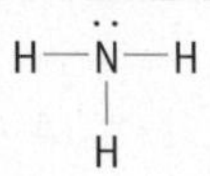	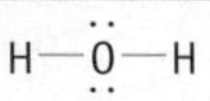 H_2O water H—Ö—H	HF hydrogen fluoride H—F̈: 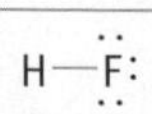
C_2H_6 ethane H—C—C—H (H's above and below each C)	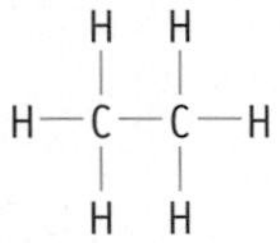 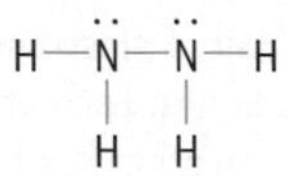 N_2H_4 hydrazine H—N̈—N̈—H with H below each N	H_2O_2 hydrogen peroxide H—Ö—Ö—H	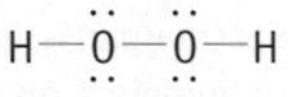
C_2H_4 ethylene H—C=C—H (H below each C)	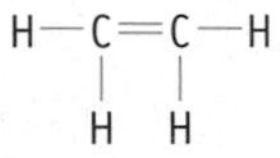 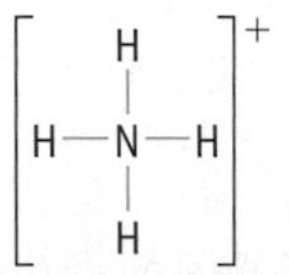 NH_4^+ ammonium ion [H—N—H with H above and below]$^+$	H_3O^+ hydronium ion [H—Ö—H with H below]$^+$	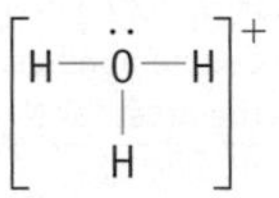
C_2H_2 acetylene H—C≡C—H	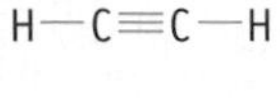 NH_2^- amide ion [H—N̈—H]$^-$	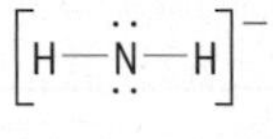 OH^- hydroxide ion [:Ö—H]$^-$	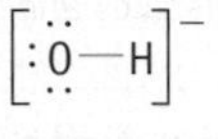

to form three bonds in uncharged molecules, and this is indeed the case. Similarly, carbon is expected to form four bonds, oxygen two, and fluorine one.

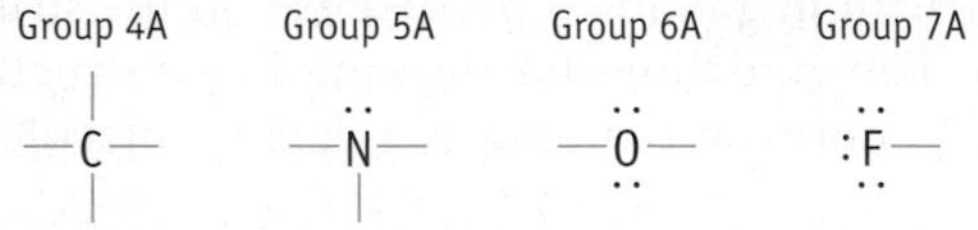

Group 4A	Group 5A	Group 6A	Group 7A
—C̶—	—N̈—	—Ö—	:F̈—

EXAMPLE 8.2 Predicting Lewis Structures

Problem Draw Lewis electron dot structures for CCl_4 and NF_3.

Strategy One way to answer this is to recognize that CCl_4 and NF_3 are similar to CH_4 and NH_3 (in Table 8.3), respectively, except that H atoms have been replaced by halogen atoms.

Solution Recall that carbon is expected to form four bonds and nitrogen three bonds to give an octet of electrons. In addition, halogen atoms have seven valence electrons, so both Cl and F can attain an octet by forming one covalent bond, just as hydrogen does.

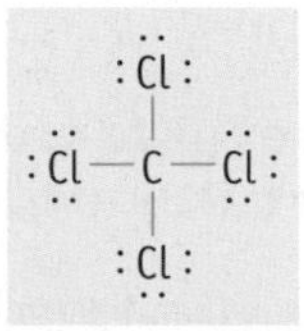

$$:\ddot{C}l:$$
$$:\ddot{C}l—C—\ddot{C}l:$$
$$:\ddot{C}l:$$

$$:\ddot{F}—N—\ddot{F}:$$
$$:\ddot{F}:$$

carbon tetrachloride 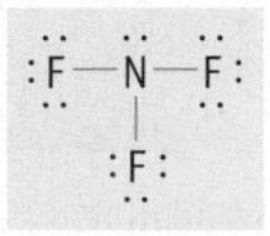   nitrogen trifluoride

As a check, count the number of valence electrons for each molecule, and verify that all are present.

CCl_4: Valence electrons = 4 for C + 4 × 7 (for Cl) = 32 electrons (16 pairs)

The structure shows eight electrons in single bonds and 24 electrons as lone pair electrons, for a total of 32 electrons. The structure is correct.

NF_3: Valence electrons = 5 for N + 3 × 7 (for F) = 26 electrons (13 pairs)

The structure shows six electrons in single bonds and 20 electrons as lone pair electrons, for a total of 26 electrons. The structure is correct.

Oxoacids and Their Anions

Lewis structures of common acids and their anions are illustrated in Table 8.4. In the absence of water, these acids are covalently bonded molecular compounds, a conclusion that we should draw because all elements in the formula are nonmetals. (Nitric acid, for example, has properties that we associate with a covalent compound: it is a colorless liquid with a boiling point of 83 °C.) In aqueous solution, however, HNO_3, H_2SO_4, and $HClO_4$ are ionized to give a hydronium ion and the appropriate anion. A Lewis structure for the nitrate ion, for example, can be created using the guidelines on page 353, and the result is a structure with two N—O single bonds and one N=O double bond. To form nitric acid from the nitrate ion, a hydrogen ion is attached to one of the O atoms that has a single bond to the central N.

nitrate ion   nitric acid

A characteristic property of acids in aqueous solution is their ability to donate a hydrogen ion (H^+, which combines with water to give the hydronium ion). The NO_3^- anion is formed when the acid, HNO_3, loses a hydrogen ion. The H^+ ion

■ **Lewis Structures for Anions of Oxoacids** Stuctures for oxoanions such as PO_4^{3-}, SO_4^{2-}, and ClO_4^- are sometimes drawn with multiple bonds between the central atom and oxygen. Theory suggests that this does not accurately represent the bonding in these species, and that structures obeying the octet rule are more appropriate. See L. Suidan, J. K. Badenhoop, E. D. Glendening, and F. Weinhold, *Journal of Chemical Education*, Vol. 72, pages 583–585, 1995.

TABLE 8.4 Lewis Structures of Common Oxoacids and Their Anions

separates from the acid by breaking the H—O bond, the electrons of the bond staying with the O atom. As a result, HNO_3 and NO_3^- have the same number of electrons, 24, and their structures are closely related.

EXERCISE 8.3 Lewis Structures of Acids and Their Anions

Draw a Lewis structure for the anion $H_2PO_4^-$, derived from phosphoric acid.

Isoelectronic Species

The species NO^+, N_2, CO, and CN^- are similar in that they each have two atoms and the same total number of valence electrons, 10, which leads to the same Lewis structure for each molecule or ion. The two atoms in each are linked with a triple bond. With three bonding pairs and one lone pair, each atom thus has an octet of electrons.

$$[:N{\equiv}O:]^+ \qquad :N{\equiv}N: \qquad :C{\equiv}O: \qquad [:C{\equiv}N:]^-$$

Molecules and ions having the *same number of valence electrons and the same Lewis structures* are said to be **isoelectronic** (Table 8.5). You will find it helpful to recognize isoelectronic molecules and ions because this is another way to see relationships in bonding among common chemical substances.

There are similarities and important differences in chemical properties of isoelectronic species. For example, both carbon monoxide, CO, and cyanide ion, CN^-, are very toxic, which results from the fact that they can bind to the iron of hemoglobin in blood and block the uptake of oxygen. They are different, though, in their acid–base chemistry. In aqueous solution, cyanide ion readily adds H^+ to form hydrogen cyanide, whereas CO does not protonate in water.

EXERCISE 8.4 Identifying Isoelectronic Species

(a) Is the acetylide ion, C_2^{2-}, isoelectronic with N_2?

(b) Identify a common molecular (uncharged) species that is isoelectronic with nitrite ion, NO_2^-. Identify a common ion that is isoelectronic with HF.

TABLE 8.5 Some Common Isoelectronic Molecules and Ions

Formulas	Representative Lewis Structure	Formulas	Representative Lewis Structure
BH_4^-, CH_4, NH_4^+	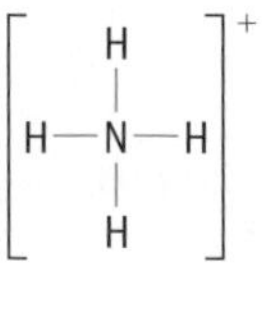 $\begin{bmatrix} & H & \\ H\!-\!N\!-\!H \\ & H & \end{bmatrix}^+$	CO_3^{2-}, NO_3^-	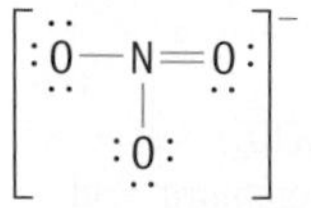 $\begin{bmatrix} :O\!-\!N{=}O: \\ :O: \end{bmatrix}^-$
NH_3, H_3O^+	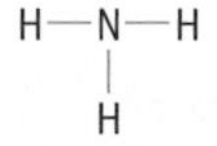 $H\!-\!\overset{..}{N}\!-\!H$ with H below	PO_4^{3-}, SO_4^{2-}, ClO_4^-	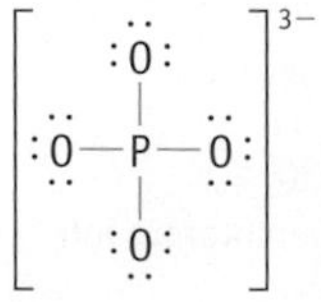 $\begin{bmatrix} :O: \\ :O\!-\!P\!-\!O: \\ :O: \end{bmatrix}^{3-}$
CO_2, OCN^-, SCN^-, N_2O NO_2^+, OCS, CS_2	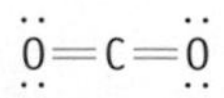 $\overset{..}{O}{=}C{=}\overset{..}{O}$		

8.3 Atom Formal Charges in Covalent Molecules and Ions

You have seen that Lewis structures show how electron pairs are placed in a covalently bonded species, whether it is a neutral molecule or a polyatomic ion. Now we turn to one of the consequences of the placement of electron pairs in this way: individual atoms can be negatively or positively charged or have no electric charge. The location of a positive or negative charge in a molecule or ion will influence, among other things, the atom at which a reaction occurs. For example, does a positive H^+ ion attach itself to the Cl or the O of ClO^-? Is the product HClO or HOCl? It is reasonable to expect H^+ to attach to the more negatively charged atom. We can predict this by evaluating atom formal charges in molecules and ions.

The **formal charge** is the charge on an atom in a molecule or polyatomic ion, and the sum of the formal charges for the atoms in a species equals the overall charge on the ion or is zero (for an uncharged molecule). The formal charge for an atom in a molecule or ion is calculated based on the Lewis structure of the molecule or ion, using Equation 8.1.

> Formal charge of an atom in a molecule or ion =
> group number of the atom − [LPE + ½(BE)] **(8.1)**

In this equation:

- The group number gives the number of valence electrons brought by a particular atom to the molecule or ion.
- LPE = number of lone pair electrons on an atom.
- BE = number of bonding electrons around an atom.

The term in square brackets is the number of electrons assigned by the Lewis structure to an atom in a molecule or ion. The difference between this term and the group number is the formal charge. An atom in a molecule or ion will be positive if it "contributes" more electrons to bonding than it "gets back." The atom's formal charge will be negative if the reverse is true.

There are two important assumptions in Equation 8.1. First, lone pairs are assumed to belong to the atom on which they reside in the Lewis structure. Second, bond pairs are assumed to be divided equally between the bonded atoms. (The factor of ½ divides the bonding electrons equally between the atoms linked by the bond.)

The sum of the formal charges on the atoms in a molecule or ion always equals the net charge on the molecule or ion. Consider the hypochlorite ion. Oxygen is in Group 6A and so has six valence electrons. However, oxygen can lay claim to seven electrons (six lone pair electrons and one bonding electron), and so the atom has a formal charge of −1. The O atom has "formally" gained an electron as part of the ion.

Formal charge $= -1 = 6 - [6 + \frac{1}{2}(2)]$

$$\left[:\overset{..}{\underset{..}{Cl}} - \overset{..}{\underset{..}{O}} : \right]^-$$

Assume a covalent bond, so bonding electrons are divided equally between Cl and O.

Formal charge $= 0 = 7 - [6 + \frac{1}{2}(2)]$

Sum of formal charges $= -1$

The formal charge on the Cl atom in ClO^- is zero. So we have −1 for oxygen and 0 for chlorine, and the sum of these equals the net charge of −1 for the ion. An important conclusion we can draw from the formal charges in ClO^- is that, if an

H^+ ion approaches the ion, it should attach itself to the negatively charged O atom to give hypochlorous acid, HOCl.

Chemistry ⚛ Now™

Sign in at **www.cengage.com/login** and go to Chapter 8 Contents to see Screen 8.11 for practice **determining formal charge.**

■ **HClO_x Acids and Formal Charge** Both ClO^- and ClO_3^- ions attract a proton to give the corresponding acid, HClO and HClO_3. In all of the HClO_x acids, the H^+ ion is attached to an O atom, owing to the negative formal charge on that atom. See Table 8.4.

■ **EXAMPLE 8.3 Calculating Formal Charges**

Problem Calculate formal charges for the atoms of the ClO_3^- ion.

Strategy The first step is always to write the Lewis structure for the molecule or ion. (The Lewis structure for the ClO_3^- ion is in Example 8.1.) Then Equation 8.1 can be used to calculate the formal charges.

Solution

$$\text{Formal charge} = -1 = 6 - [6 + \tfrac{1}{2}(2)]$$

$$\left[\ddot{\underset{..}{O}} - Cl - \ddot{\underset{..}{O}} \right]^-$$

$$\text{Formal charge} = +2 = 7 - [2 + \tfrac{1}{2}(6)]$$

The formal charge on each O atom is −1, whereas for the Cl atom it is +2. The sum of the atom's formal charges is the charge on the ion, which is −1 for ClO_3^-.

EXERCISE 8.5 Calculating Formal Charges

Calculate formal charges on each atom in **(a)** CN^- and **(b)** SO_3^{2-}.

A Closer Look | Comparing Formal Charge and Oxidation Number

In Chapter 3, you learned to calculate the oxidation number of an atom as a way to tell if a reaction involves oxidation and reduction. Are an atom's oxidation number and its formal charge related? To answer this question, let us look at the hydroxide ion. The formal charges are −1 on the O atom and 0 on the H atom. Recall that these formal charges are calculated assuming the O—H bond electrons are shared equally in an O—H covalent bond.

$$\text{Formal charge} = -1 = 6 - [6 + \tfrac{1}{2}(2)]$$

$$\left[\ddot{\underset{..}{O}} - H \right]^- \quad \textit{Sum of formal charges} = -1$$

$$\text{Formal charge} = 0 = 1 - [0 + \tfrac{1}{2}(2)]$$

In contrast, in Chapter 3 (page 144), you learned that O has an oxidation number of −2 and H has a number of +1. Oxidation numbers are determined by assuming that the bond between a pair of atoms is ionic, not covalent. For OH⁻ this means the pair of electrons between O and H is located fully on O. Thus, the O atom now has eight valence electrons instead of six and a charge of −2. The H atom now has no valence electrons and a charge of +1.

$$\text{Oxidation number} = -2$$

$$\left[\ddot{\underset{..}{O}} : H \right]^- \quad \begin{array}{l}\textit{Sum of oxidation} \\ \textit{numbers} = -1\end{array}$$

Assume an ionic bond   Oxidation number = +1

Formal charges and oxidation numbers are calculated using different assumptions. Both are useful, but for different purposes. Oxidation numbers allow us to follow changes in redox reactions. Formal charges provide insight into atom charges in molecules and polyatomic ions.

8.4 Resonance

Ozone, O_3, an unstable, blue, diamagnetic gas with a characteristic pungent odor, protects the earth and its inhabitants from intense ultraviolet radiation from the sun. An important feature of its structure is that the two oxygen–oxygen bonds are the same length, which suggests that the two bonds are equivalent. That is, equal O—O bond lengths imply an equal number of bond pairs in each O—O bond. Using the guidelines for drawing Lewis structures, however, you might come to a different conclusion. There are two possible ways of writing the Lewis structure for the molecule:

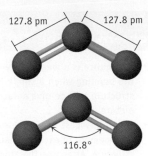

Ozone, O_3, is a bent molecule with oxygen–oxygen bonds of the same length.

Alternative Ways of Drawing the Ozone Structure

Double bond on the left: :O̤=O̤—O̤:

Double bond on the right: :O̤—O̤=O̤:

These structures are equivalent in that each has a double bond on one side of the central oxygen atom and a single bond on the other side. If either were the actual structure of ozone, one bond (O=O) should be shorter than the other (O—O). The actual structure of ozone shows this is not the case. The inescapable conclusion is that these Lewis structures do not correctly represent the bonding in ozone.

Linus Pauling (1901–1994) proposed the theory of **resonance** to solve the problem. *Resonance structures are used to represent bonding in a molecule or ion when a single Lewis structure fails to describe accurately the actual electronic structure.* The alternative structures shown for ozone are called **resonance structures.** They have identical patterns of bonding and equal energy. The actual structure of this molecule is a *composite*, or **resonance hybrid,** of the equivalent resonance structures. In this hybrid, the bonds between the oxygens are between a single bond and a double bond in length, in this case corresponding to one and a half bonds. This is a reasonable conclusion because we see that the O—O bonds both have a length of 127.8 pm, intermediate between the average length of an O=O double bond (121 pm) and an O—O single bond (132 pm). Because we cannot accurately draw fractions of a bond, chemists draw the resonance structures and connect them with double-headed arrows ($\longleftrightarrow$) to indicate that the true structure is somewhere in between these extremes.

Lone pair becomes a bond pair.   Bond pair becomes a lone pair.

:O̤—O̤=O̤: $\longleftrightarrow$:O̤=O̤—O̤:

■ **Depicting Resonance Structures** The use of an arrow ($\longleftrightarrow$) as a symbol to link resonance structures and the name "resonance" are somewhat unfortunate. An arrow might seem to imply that a change is occurring, and the term resonance has the connotation of vibrating or alternating back and forth between different forms. Neither view is correct. Electron pairs are not actually moving from one place to another.

Benzene is the classic example of the use of resonance to represent a structure. The benzene molecule is a six-member ring of carbon atoms with six equivalent carbon–carbon bonds (and a hydrogen atom attached to each carbon atom). The carbon–carbon bonds are 139 pm long, intermediate between the average length of a C=C double bond (134 pm) and a C—C single bond (154 pm).

Resonance structures of benzene, C_6H_6 Abbreviated representation of resonance structures

- Resonance is a means of representing the bonding when a single Lewis structure fails to give an accurate picture.
- The atoms must have the same arrangement in each resonance structure. Attaching the atoms in a different fashion creates a different compound.

- Resonance structures differ only in the assignment of electron-pair positions, never atom positions.
- Resonance structures differ in the number of bond pairs between a given pair of atoms.
- Even though the formal process of converting one resonance structure to another seems to move electrons

about, resonance is not meant to indicate the motion of electrons.
- The actual structure of a molecule is a composite or hybrid of the resonance structures.
- There will always be at least one multiple bond (double or triple) in each resonance structure.

Two resonance structures that differ only in double bond placement can be written for the molecule. A hybrid of these two structures, however, will lead to a molecule with six equivalent carbon–carbon bonds.

Let us apply the concepts of resonance to describe bonding in the carbonate ion, CO_3^{2-}, an anion with 24 valence electrons (12 pairs).

$$\left[\begin{array}{c} :\!O\!\!=\!\!C\!\!-\!\!\ddot{O}\!: \\ | \\ :\!\ddot{O}\!: \end{array}\right]^{2-} \longleftrightarrow \left[\begin{array}{c} :\!\ddot{O}\!\!-\!\!C\!\!-\!\!\ddot{O}\!: \\ \| \\ :\!O\!: \end{array}\right]^{2-} \longleftrightarrow \left[\begin{array}{c} :\!\ddot{O}\!\!-\!\!C\!\!=\!\!O\!: \\ | \\ :\!\ddot{O}\!: \end{array}\right]^{2-}$$

Three equivalent structures can be drawn for this ion, differing only in the location of the C=O double bond. This fits the classical situation for resonance, so it is appropriate to conclude that no single structure correctly describes this ion. Instead, the actual structure is the composite of the three structures, in good agreement with experimental results. In the CO_3^{2-} ion, all three carbon–oxygen bond distances are 129 pm, intermediate between C—O single bond (143 pm) and C=O double bond (122 pm) distances.

Formal charges can be calculated for each atom in the resonance structure for a molecule or ion. For example, using one of the resonance structures for the nitrate ion, we find that the central N atom has a formal charge of +1, and the singly bonded O atoms are both −1. The doubly bonded O atom has no charge. The net charge for the ion is thus −1.

$$\begin{array}{l} \text{Formal charge} = 0 = 6 - [4 + \tfrac{1}{2}(4)] \\ \qquad\qquad | \\ \left[\begin{array}{c} :\!O\!: \\ \| \\ :\!\ddot{O}\!\!-\!\!N\!\!-\!\!\ddot{O}\!: \\ | \end{array}\right]^{-} \\ \qquad\qquad\text{Formal charge} = +1 = 5 - [0 + \tfrac{1}{2}(8)] \\ \text{Formal charge} = -1 = 6 - [6 + \tfrac{1}{2}(2)] \end{array}$$

Sum of formal charges $= -1$

Is this a reasonable charge distribution for the nitrate ion? The answer is no. The actual structure of the nitrate ion is a resonance hybrid of three equivalent resonance structures. Because the three oxygen atoms in NO_3^- are equivalent, the charge on one oxygen atom should not be different from the other two. This can be resolved, however, if the formal charges are averaged to give a formal charge of $-\tfrac{2}{3}$ on the oxygen atoms. Summing the charges on the three oxygen atoms and the +1 charge on the nitrogen atom then gives −1, the charge on the ion.

In the resonance structures for O_3, CO_3^{2-}, and NO_3^-, for example, all the possible resonance structures are equally likely; they are "equivalent" structures. The molecule or ion therefore has a symmetrical distribution of electrons over all the atoms involved—that is, its electronic structure consists of an equal "mixture," or "hybrid," of the resonance structures.

Chemistry.Now™

Sign in at **www.cengage.com/login** and go to Chapter 8 Contents to see Screen 8.7 for a tutorial on **drawing resonance structures.**

EXAMPLE 8.4 Drawing Resonance Structures

Problem Draw resonance structures for the nitrite ion, NO_2^-. Are the N—O bonds single, double, or intermediate in value? What are the formal charges on the N and O atoms?

Strategy Draw the Lewis structure in the usual manner. If multiple bonds are required, resonance structures may exist. This will be the case if the octet of an atom can be completed by using an electron pair from more than one terminal atom to form a multiple bond. Bonds to the central atom cannot then be "pure" single or double bonds but rather are somewhere between the two.

Solution Nitrogen is the central atom in the nitrite ion, which has a total of 18 valence electrons (nine pairs).

Valence electrons = 5 (for the N atom) + 12 (6 for each O atom) + 1 (for negative charge)

After forming N—O single bonds, and distributing lone pairs on the terminal O atoms, a pair remains, which is placed on the central N atom.

$$\left[:\overset{..}{\underset{..}{O}}-\overset{..}{N}-\overset{..}{\underset{..}{O}}: \right]^-$$

To complete the octet of electrons about the N atom, form an N=O double bond.

$$\left[:\overset{..}{O}=\overset{..}{N}-\overset{..}{\underset{..}{O}}: \right]^- \longleftrightarrow \left[:\overset{..}{\underset{..}{O}}-\overset{..}{N}=\overset{..}{O}: \right]^-$$

Because there are two ways to do this, two equivalent structures can be drawn, and the actual structure must be a resonance hybrid of these two structures. The nitrogen–oxygen bonds are neither single nor double bonds but have an intermediate value.

Taking one of the resonance structures, we find the formal charge for the N atom is 0. The charge on one O atom is 0 and −1 for the other O atom. Because the two resonance structures are of equal importance, however, the net formal charge on each O atom is −½.

$$\begin{array}{cc}
\text{Formal charge} = & \text{Formal charge} = \\
0 = 6 - [4 + \tfrac{1}{2}(4)] & -1 = 6 - [6 + \tfrac{1}{2}(2)]
\end{array}$$

$$\left[\overset{..}{O}=N-\overset{..}{\underset{..}{O}}: \right]^-$$

$$\text{Formal charge} = 0 = 5 - [2 + \tfrac{1}{2}(6)]$$

EXERCISE 8.6 Drawing Resonance Structures

Draw resonance structures for the bicarbonate ion, HCO_3^-.

(a) Does HCO_3^- have the same number of resonance structures as the CO_3^{2-} ion?

(b) What are the formal charges on the O and C atoms in HCO_3^-? What is the average formal charge on the O atoms? Compare this with the O atoms in CO_3^{2-}.

(c) What do formal charges predict about the point of attachment of the H atom in HCO_3^-?

8.5 Exceptions to the Octet Rule

Although the vast majority of molecular compounds and ions obey the octet rule, there are exceptions. These include molecules and ions that have fewer than four pairs of electrons on a central atom, those that have more than four pairs, and those that have an odd number of electrons.

Compounds in Which an Atom Has Fewer Than Eight Valence Electrons

Boron, a metalloid in Group 3A, has three valence electrons and so is expected to form three covalent bonds with other nonmetallic elements. This results in a valence shell for boron in its compounds with only six electrons, two short of an octet. Many boron compounds of this type are known, including such common compounds as boric acid ($B(OH)_3$), borax ($Na_2B_4O_5(OH)_4 \cdot 8\ H_2O$) (Figure 8.2), and the boron trihalides (BF_3, BCl_3, BBr_3, and BI_3).

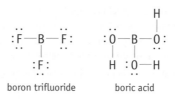

boron trifluoride   boric acid

Boron compounds such as BF_3 that are two electrons short of an octet are quite reactive. The boron atom can accommodate a fourth electron pair when that pair is provided by another atom, and molecules or ions with lone pairs can fulfill this role. Ammonia, for example, reacts with BF_3 to form $H_3N{\rightarrow}BF_3$.

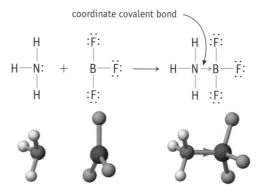

coordinate covalent bond

If a bonding pair of electrons originates on one of the bonded atoms, the bond is called a **coordinate covalent bond.** In Lewis structures, a coordinate covalent bond is often designated by an arrow that points away from the atom donating the electron pair.

Compounds in Which an Atom Has More Than Eight Valence Electrons

Elements in the third or higher periods often form compounds and ions in which the central element is surrounded by more than four valence electron pairs (Table 8.6). With most compounds and ions in this category, the central atom is bonded to fluorine, chlorine, or oxygen.

It is often obvious from the formula of a compound that an octet around an atom has been exceeded. As an example, consider sulfur hexafluoride, SF_6, a gas

B atom surrounded by 4 electron pairs

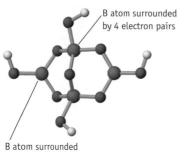

B atom surrounded by 3 electron pairs

FIGURE 8.2 The anion in Borax.
Borax is a common mineral, which is used in soaps and contains an interesting anion, $B_4O_5(OH)_4{}^{2-}$. The anion has two B atoms surrounded by four electron pairs, and two B atoms surrounded by only three pairs.

TABLE 8.6 Lewis Structures in Which the Central Atom Exceeds an Octet

Group 4A	Group 5A	Group 6A	Group 7A	Group 8
SiF_5^-	PF_5	SF_4	ClF_3	XeF_2
SiF_6^{2-}	PF_6^-	SF_6	BrF_5	XeF_4

formed by the reaction of sulfur and excess fluorine. Sulfur is the central atom in this compound, and fluorine typically bonds to only one other atom with a single electron pair bond (as in HF and CF_4). Six S—F bonds are required in SF_6, meaning there will be six electron pairs in the valence shell of the sulfur atom.

If there are more than four groups bonded to a central atom, this is a reliable signal that there are more than eight electrons around a central atom. But be careful—the central atom octet can also be exceeded with four or fewer atoms bonded to the central atom. Consider three examples from Table 8.6: the central atom in SF_4, ClF_3, and XeF_2 has five electron pairs in its valence shell.

A useful observation is that *only elements of the third and higher periods in the periodic table may form compounds and ions in which an octet is exceeded.* Second-period elements (B, C, N, O, F) are restricted to a maximum of eight electrons in their compounds. For example, nitrogen forms compounds and ions such as NH_3, NH_4^+, and NF_3, but NF_5 is unknown. Phosphorus, the third-period element just below nitrogen in the periodic table, forms many compounds similar to nitrogen (PH_3, PH_4^+, PF_3), but it also readily accommodates five or six valence electron pairs in compounds such as PF_5 or in ions such as PF_6^-. Arsenic, antimony, and bismuth, the elements below phosphorus in Group 5A, resemble phosphorus in their behavior.

The usual explanation for the contrasting behavior of second- and third-period elements centers on the number of orbitals in the valence shell of an atom. Second-period elements have four valence orbitals (one 2s and three 2p orbitals). Two electrons per orbital result in a total of eight electrons being accommodated around an atom. For elements in the third and higher periods, the d orbitals in the outer shell are traditionally included among valence orbitals for the elements. Thus, for phosphorus, the 3d orbitals are included with the 3s and 3p orbitals as valence orbitals. The extra orbitals provide the element with an opportunity to accommodate up to 12 electrons.

Chemistry⚗Now™

Sign in at www.cengage.com/login and go to Chapter 8 Contents to see Screen 8.8 for a tutorial on **identifying electron-deficient compounds.**

■ **Xenon Compounds** Compounds of xenon are among the more interesting entries in Table 8.6 because noble gas compounds were not discovered until the early 1960s. One of the more intriguing compounds is XeF_2, in part because of the simplicity of its synthesis. Xenon difluoride can be made by placing a flask containing xenon gas and fluorine gas in the sunlight. After several weeks, crystals of colorless XeF_2 are found in the flask (see page 404).

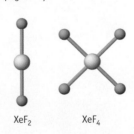

XeF_2 XeF_4

Problem Sketch the Lewis structure of the $[ClF_4]^-$ ion.

Strategy Use the guidelines on page 353.

Solution

1. The Cl atom is the central atom.

2. This ion has 36 valence electrons [$= 7$ (for Cl) $+ 4 \times 7$ (for F) $+ 1$ (for ion charge)] or 18 pairs.

3. Draw the ion with four single covalent Cl–F bonds.

$$
\begin{bmatrix}
 & F & \\
 & | & \\
F & - Cl - & F \\
 & | & \\
 & F &
\end{bmatrix}^-
$$

4. Place lone pairs on the terminal atoms. Because two electron pairs remain after placing lone pairs on the four F atoms, and because we know that Cl can accommodate more than four pairs, these two pairs are placed on the central Cl atom.

$$
\begin{bmatrix}
 & :\ddot{F}: & \\
 & | & \\
:\ddot{F} & - Cl - & \ddot{F}: \\
 & | & \\
 & :\ddot{F}: &
\end{bmatrix}^-
$$

The last two electron pairs are added to the central Cl atom. $\longrightarrow$

$$
\begin{bmatrix}
 & :\ddot{F}: & \\
 & | & \\
:\ddot{F} & - \ddot{Cl} - & \ddot{F}: \\
 & | & \\
 & :\ddot{F}: &
\end{bmatrix}^-
$$

EXERCISE 8.7 Lewis Structures in Which the Central Atom Has More Than Eight Electrons

Sketch the Lewis structures for $[ClF_2]^+$ and $[ClF_2]^-$. How many lone pairs and bond pairs surround the Cl atom in each ion?

Molecules with an Odd Number of Electrons

Two nitrogen oxides—NO, with 11 valence electrons, and NO_2, with 17 valence electrons—are among a very small group of stable molecules with an odd number of electrons. Because they have an odd number of electrons, it is impossible to draw a structure obeying the octet rule; at least one electron must be unpaired.

Even though NO_2 does not obey the octet rule, an electron dot structure can be written that approximates the bonding in the molecule. This Lewis structure places the unpaired electron on nitrogen. Two resonance structures show that the nitrogen–oxygen bonds are expected to be equivalent.

$$
\ddot{O} \diagdown \overset{\cdot}{N} \diagup \ddot{O}: \quad \longleftrightarrow \quad :\ddot{O} \diagup \overset{\cdot}{N} \diagdown \ddot{O}
$$

Experimental evidence for NO indicates that the bonding between N and O is intermediate between a double and a triple bond. It is not possible to write a Lewis structure for NO that is in accord with the properties of this substance, so a different theory is needed to understand bonding in this molecule. We shall return to compounds of this type when molecular orbital theory is introduced in Section 9.3.

The two nitrogen oxides, NO and NO_2, are members of a class of chemical substances called free radicals. **Free radicals** are chemical species—both atomic and molecular—with an unpaired electron. Free radicals are generally quite reac-

The Importance of an Odd-Electron Molecule, NO

Small molecules such as H_2, O_2, H_2O, CO, and CO_2 are among the most important molecules commercially, environmentally, and biologically. Imagine the surprise of chemists and biologists when it was discovered a few years ago that nitrogen monoxide (nitric oxide, NO), which was widely considered toxic, also has an important biological role.

Nitric oxide is a colorless, paramagnetic gas that is moderately soluble in water. In the laboratory, it can be synthesized by the reduction of nitrite ion with iodide ion:

$$KNO_2(aq) + KI(aq) + H_2SO_4(aq) \rightarrow$$
$$NO(g) + K_2SO_4(aq) + H_2O(\ell) + \tfrac{1}{2} I_2(aq)$$

The formation of NO from the elements is an unfavorable, energetically uphill reaction ($\Delta_f H° = 90.2$ kJ/mol). Nevertheless, small quantities of this compound form from nitrogen and oxygen at high temperatures. For example, conditions in an internal combustion engine are favorable for this to happen.

Nitric oxide reacts rapidly with O_2 to form the reddish-brown gas NO_2.

$$2\ NO(\text{colorless, g}) + O_2(g) \rightarrow$$
$$2\ NO_2(\text{brown, g})$$

The result is that compounds such as NO_2 and HNO_3 arising from reactions of NO with O_2 and H_2O are among the air pollutants produced by automobiles.

A few years ago, chemists learned that NO is synthesized in a biological process by animals as diverse as barnacles, fruit flies, horseshoe crabs, chickens, trout, and humans. Even more recently, chemists have found that NO is important in an astonishing range of physiological processes in humans and other animals. These include a role in neurotransmission, blood clotting, and blood pressure control as well as in the immune system's ability to kill tumor cells and intracellular parasites.

Questions: *Oxygen is needed by many living organisms, but some reactions with oxygen can lead to oxidative damage. One species that can produce damage in an organism is the superoxide ion, O_2^-. Fortunately, this ion is removed extremely rapidly by reaction with NO to produce the peroxynitrite ion, $ONOO^-$.*
1. Draw the Lewis structure for the ion.

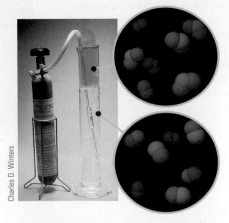

Charles D. Winters

The colorless gas NO is bubbled into water from a high-pressure tank. When the gas emerges into the air, the NO reacts rapidly with O_2 to give brown NO_2 gas.

2. Are there any multiple bonds in the ion?
3. Are there any resonance structures needed?

Answers to these questions are in Appendix Q.

---

tive. Free atoms such as H and Cl, for example, are free radicals and readily combine with each other to give molecules such as H_2, Cl_2, and HCl.

Free radicals are involved in many reactions in the environment. For example, small amounts of NO are released from vehicle exhausts. The NO rapidly forms NO_2, which is even more harmful to human health and to plants. Exposure to NO_2 at concentrations of 50–100 parts per million can lead to significant inflammation of lung tissue. Nitrogen dioxide is also generated by natural processes. For example, when hay, which has a high level of nitrates, is stored in silos on farms, NO_2 can be generated as the hay ferments, and there have been reports of farm workers dying from exposure to this gas in the silo.

The two nitrogen oxides, NO and NO_2, are unique in that they can be isolated and neither has the extreme reactivity of most free radicals. When cooled, however, two NO_2 molecules join or "dimerize" to form colorless N_2O_4; the unpaired electrons combine to form an N—N bond in N_2O_4 (Figure 8.3).

8.6 Molecular Shapes

One reason for drawing Lewis electron dot structures is to be able to predict the three-dimensional geometry of molecules and ions. Because the physical and chemical properties of compounds are tied to their structures, the importance of this subject cannot be overstated.

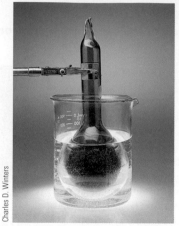

FIGURE 8.3 Free radical chemistry.
When cooled, the brown gas NO_2, a free radical, forms colorless N_2O_4, a molecule with an N—N single bond. The coupling of two free radicals is a common type of chemical reaction. Because identical free radicals come together, the product is called a dimer, and the process is called a dimerization. (Sign in to ChemistryNow, Screen 8.9, to see a video of this reaction.)

Charles D. Winters

When cooled, NO_2 free radicals couple to form N_2O_4 molecules.

N_2O_4 gas is colorless.

A flask of brown NO_2 gas in warm water

Charles D. Winters

A flask of NO_2 gas in ice water

The **valence shell electron-pair repulsion (VSEPR)** model is a reliable method for predicting the shapes of covalent molecules and polyatomic ions. This model is based on the idea that *bond and lone electron pairs in the valence shell of an element repel each other and seek to be as far apart as possible.* The positions assumed by the valence electrons of an atom thus define the angles between bonds to surrounding atoms. VSEPR is remarkably successful in predicting structures of molecules and ions of main group elements. However, it is less effective (and seldom used) to predict structures of compounds containing transition metals.

To have a sense of how valence shell electron pairs repel and determine structure, blow up several balloons to a similar size. Imagine that each balloon represents an electron cloud. When two, three, four, five, or six balloons are tied together at a central point (representing the nucleus and core electrons of a central atom), the balloons naturally form the shapes shown in Figure 8.4. These geometric arrangements minimize interactions between the balloons.

■ **VSEPR Theory** The VSEPR theory was devised by Ronald J. Gillespie (1924–) and Ronald S. Nyholm (1917–1971).

Central Atoms Surrounded Only by Single-Bond Pairs

The simplest application of VSEPR theory is to molecules and ions in which all the electron pairs around the central atom are involved in single covalent bonds. Figure 8.5 illustrates the geometries predicted for molecules or ions with the general formulas AX_n, where A is the central atom and n is the number of X groups bonded to it.

Charles D. Winters

Linear

Trigonal planar

Tetrahedral

Trigonal bipyramidal

Octahedral

FIGURE 8.4 Balloon models of electron-pair geometries for two to six electron pairs. If two to six balloons of similar size and shape are tied together, they will naturally assume the arrangements shown. These pictures illustrate the predictions of VSEPR.

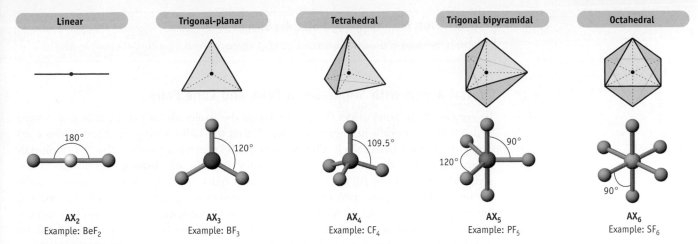

Linear	Trigonal-planar	Tetrahedral	Trigonal bipyramidal	Octahedral
180°	120°	109.5°	120° / 90°	90° / 90°
AX_2	AX_3	AX_4	AX_5	AX_6
Example: BeF_2	Example: BF_3	Example: CF_4	Example: PF_5	Example: SF_6

Active Figure 8.5 **Various geometries predicted by VSEPR.** Geometries predicted by VSEPR for molecules that contain only single covalent bonds around the central atom.

Chemistry⚛Now™ Sign in at www.cengage.com/login and go to the Chapter Contents menu to explore an interactive version of this figure accompanied by an exercise.

The linear geometry for two bond pairs and the trigonal-planar geometry for three bond pairs involve a central atom that does not have an octet of electrons (see Section 8.5). The central atom in a tetrahedral molecule obeys the octet rule with four bond pairs. The central atoms in trigonal-bipyramidal and octahedral molecules have five and six bonding pairs, respectively, and are expected only when the central atom is an element in Period 3 or higher of the periodic table (▶ page 372).

Chemistry⚛Now™

Sign in at **www.cengage.com/login** and go to Chapter 8 Contents to see:
• Screen 8.13 for an animation of **the electron-pair geometries** and on **identifying geometries**
• Screen 8.14 for practice **predicting molecular geometry**

■ EXAMPLE 8.6 Predicting Molecular Shapes

Problem Predict the shape of silicon tetrachloride, $SiCl_4$.

Strategy The first step is to draw the Lewis structure. The Lewis structure does not need to be drawn in any particular way because its purpose is only to describe the number of bonds around an atom and to determine if there are any lone pairs. The number of bond and lone pairs of electrons around the central atom determines the molecular shape (Figure 8.5).

Solution The Lewis structure of $SiCl_4$ has four electron pairs, all of them bond pairs, around the central Si atom. Therefore, a tetrahedral structure is predicted for the $SiCl_4$ molecule, with Cl—Si—Cl bond angles of 109.5°. This agrees with the actual structure for $SiCl_4$.

■ **Lewis Structures and Molecular Shapes** Drawing the Lewis structure is the first step in determining the shape of a molecule or ion.

Lewis structure   Molecular geometry

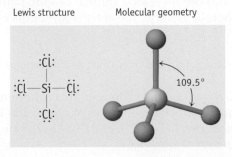

109.5°

Central Atoms with Single-Bond Pairs and Lone Pairs

To see how lone pairs affect the geometry of the molecule or polyatomic ion, return to the balloon models in Figure 8.4. Recall that the balloons represented *all* the electron pairs in the valence shell. The balloon model therefore predicts the "electron-pair geometry" rather than the "molecular geometry." The **electron-pair geometry** is the geometry taken up by *all* the valence electron pairs around a central atom, whereas the **molecular geometry** describes the arrangement in space of the central atom and the atoms directly attached to it. It is important to recognize that *lone pairs of electrons on the central atom occupy spatial positions, even though their location is not included in the verbal description of the shape of the molecule or ion.*

Let us use the VSEPR model to predict the molecular geometry and bond angles in the NH_3 molecule. On drawing the Lewis structure, we see there are four pairs of electrons in the nitrogen valence shell, three bond pairs, and one lone pair. Thus, the predicted *electron-pair geometry* is tetrahedral. The *molecular geometry,* however, is said to be *trigonal pyramidal* because that describes the location of the atoms. The nitrogen atom is at the apex of the pyramid, and the three hydrogen atoms form the trigonal base.

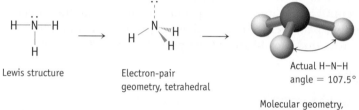

Lewis structure

Electron-pair
geometry, tetrahedral

Actual H–N–H
angle = 107.5°

Molecular geometry,
trigonal pyramidal

Effect of Lone Pairs on Bond Angles

Because the electron-pair geometry in NH_3 is tetrahedral, we would expect the H—N—H bond angle to be 109.5°. However, the experimentally determined bond angles in NH_3 are 107.5°, and the H—O—H angle in water is smaller still (104.5°) (Figure 8.6). These angles are close to the tetrahedral angle but not exactly that value. This highlights the fact that VSEPR is not an accurate model; it can only predict the approximate geometry. Small variations in geometry (e.g., bond angles a few degrees different from predicted) are quite common and often arise because there is a difference between the spatial requirements of lone pairs and bond pairs. Lone pairs of electrons seem to occupy a larger volume than bonding pairs, and the increased volume of lone pairs causes bond pairs to squeeze closer together. In general, the relative strengths of repulsions are in the order

Lone pair–lone pair > lone pair–bond pair > bond pair–bond pair

The different spatial requirements of lone pairs and bond pairs can be used to predict variations in the bond angles in series of molecules. For example, the bond angles decrease in the series CH_4, NH_3, and H_2O as the number of lone pairs on the central atom increases (Figure 8.6).

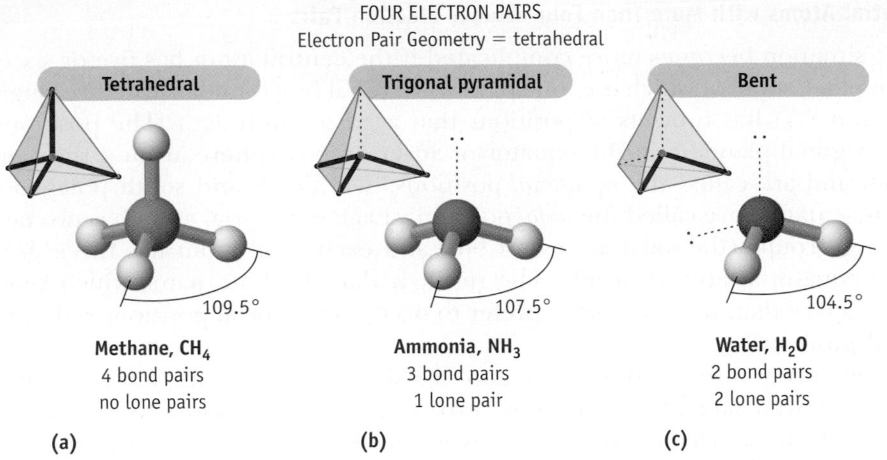

FOUR ELECTRON PAIRS
Electron Pair Geometry = tetrahedral

| Tetrahedral | Trigonal pyramidal | Bent |

109.5°   107.5°   104.5°

Methane, CH$_4$
4 bond pairs
no lone pairs

(a)

Ammonia, NH$_3$
3 bond pairs
1 lone pair

(b)

Water, H$_2$O
2 bond pairs
2 lone pairs

(c)

FIGURE 8.6 The molecular geometries of methane, ammonia, and water. All have four electron pairs around the central atom, so all have a tetrahedral electron-pair geometry. (a) Methane has four bond pairs and so has a tetrahedral molecular shape. (b) Ammonia has three bond pairs and one lone pair, so it has a trigonal-pyramidal molecular shape. (c) Water has two bond pairs and two lone pairs, so it has a bent, or angular, molecular shape. The decrease in bond angles in the series can be explained by the fact that the lone pairs have a larger spatial requirement than the bond pairs.

■ **EXAMPLE 8.7 Finding the Shapes of Molecules**

Problem What are the shapes of the ions H_3O^+ and ClF_2^+?

Strategy Draw the Lewis structures for each ion. Count the number of lone and bond pairs around the central atom. Use Figure 8.5 to decide on the electron-pair geometry. Finally, the location of the atoms in the ion—which is determined by the bond and lone pairs—gives the geometry of the ion.

Solution

(a) The Lewis structure of the hydronium ion, H_3O^+, shows that the oxygen atom is surrounded by four electron pairs, so the electron-pair geometry is tetrahedral.

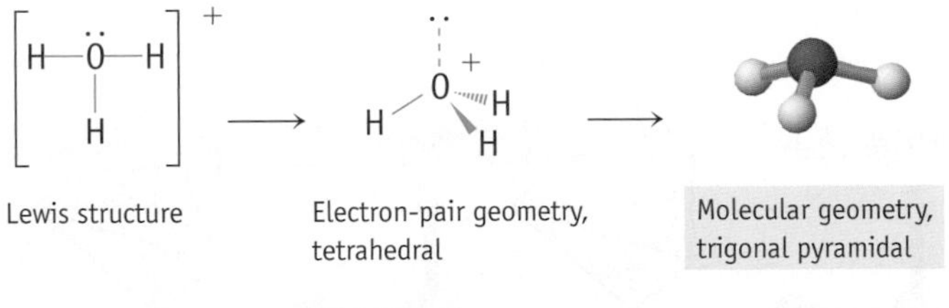

Lewis structure   Electron-pair geometry, tetrahedral   Molecular geometry, trigonal pyramidal

Because three of the four pairs are used to bond terminal atoms, the central O atom and the three H atoms form a trigonal-pyramidal molecular shape like that of NH_3.

(b) Chlorine is the central atom in ClF_2^+. It is surrounded by four electron pairs, so the electron-pair geometry around chlorine is tetrahedral. Because only two of the four pairs are bonding pairs, the ion has a bent geometry.

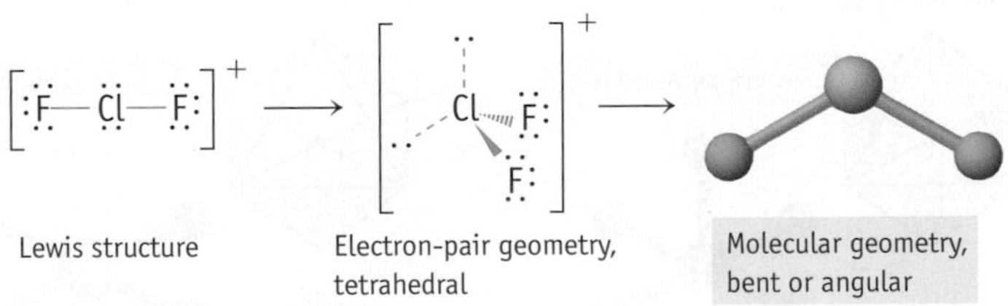

Lewis structure   Electron-pair geometry, tetrahedral   Molecular geometry, bent or angular

■ **"Energized Water" with a Bond Angle of 114°!** There are many dubious products sold over the internet, and one of them claims that water is "energized" by increasing its bond angle. One advertisement said that in the past water had a bond angle of a healthy 110°, but now it is "wimpy" and unhealthy with an angle of only 104°. Further, it is claimed that distilled water only has a bond angle of 101° and is biologically dead. To cure this problem, you can buy a costly machine that "energizes" water and causes a bond angle increase to as much as 114°. Now, it is also claimed, this water has enough energy to destroy pathogens. The old circus master, P. T. Barnum, once said there is a sucker born every minute.

EXERCISE 8.9 VSEPR and Molecular Shape

Give the electron-pair geometry and molecular shape for BF_3 and BF_4^-. What is the effect on the molecular geometry of adding an F^- ion to BF_3 to give BF_4^-?

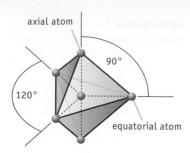

FIGURE 8.7 The trigonal pyramid showing the axial and equatorial atoms. The angles between atoms in the equator are 120°. The angles between equatorial and axial atoms are 90°.

Central Atoms with More Than Four Valence Electron Pairs

The situation becomes more complicated if the central atom has five or six electron pairs, some of which are lone pairs. A trigonal-bipyramidal structure (Figures 8.5 and 8.7) has two sets of positions that are not equivalent. The positions in the trigonal plane lie in the equator of an imaginary sphere around the central atom and are called the *equatorial* positions. The north and south poles in this representation are called the *axial* positions. Each equatorial atom has two neighboring groups (the axial atoms) at 90°, and each axial atom has three groups (the equatorial atoms) at 90°. The result is that the lone pairs, which require more space than bonding pairs, prefer to occupy equatorial positions rather than axial positions.

The entries in the top line of Figure 8.8 show species having a total of five valence electron pairs, with zero, one, two, and three lone pairs. In SF_4, with one lone pair, the molecule assumes a "seesaw" shape with the lone pair in one of the equatorial positions. The ClF_3 molecule has three bond pairs and two lone pairs. The two lone pairs in ClF_3 are in equatorial positions; two bond pairs are axial, and the third is in the equatorial plane, so the molecular geometry is T-shaped. The third molecule shown is XeF_2. Here, all three equatorial positions are occupied by lone pairs so the molecular geometry is linear.

The geometry assumed by six electron pairs is octahedral (see Figure 8.8), and all the angles at adjacent positions are 90°. Unlike the trigonal bipyramid, the octahedron has no distinct axial and equatorial positions; all positions are the same. Therefore, if the molecule has one lone pair, as in BrF_5, it makes no difference which position it occupies. The lone pair is often drawn in the top or bottom posi-

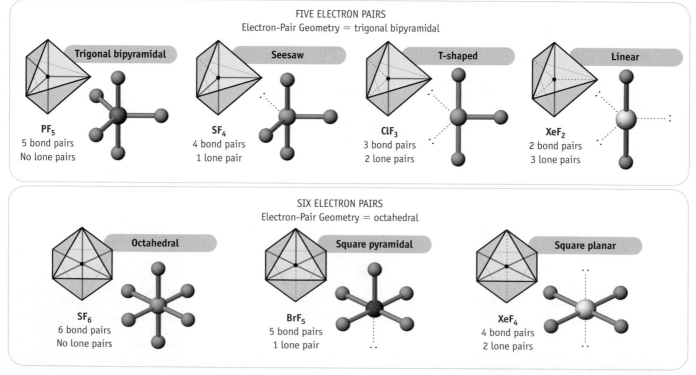

FIGURE 8.8 Electron-pair geometries and molecular shapes for molecules and ions with five or six electron pairs around the central atom.

tion to make it easier to visualize the molecular geometry, which in this case is square-pyramidal. If two pairs of electrons in an octahedral arrangement are lone pairs, they seek to be as far apart as possible. The result is a square-planar molecule, as illustrated by XeF_4.

EXAMPLE 8.8 Predicting Molecular Shape

Problem What is the shape of the ICl_4^- ion?

Strategy Draw the Lewis structure, and then decide on the electron-pair geometry. The position of the atoms gives the molecular geometry of the ion. (See Example 8.7 and Figure 8.8.)

Solution A Lewis structure for the ICl_4^- ion shows that the central iodine atom has six electron pairs in its valence shell. Two of these are lone pairs. Placing the lone pairs on opposite sides leaves the four chlorine atoms in a square-planar geometry.

Electron-pair geometry, octahedral

Molecular geometry, square planar

EXERCISE 8.10 Predicting Molecular Shape

Draw the Lewis structure for ICl_2^-, and then decide on the geometry of the ion.

Multiple Bonds and Molecular Geometry

Double and triple bonds involve more electron pairs than single bonds, but this has little effect on the overall molecular shape. All of the electron pairs in a multiple bond are shared between the same two nuclei and therefore occupy the same region of space. Because they must remain in that region, two electron pairs in a double bond (or three pairs in a triple bond) have the same effect on the structure as one electron pair in a single bond. That is, all electron pairs in a multiple bond count as one bond and contribute to molecular geometry the same as a single bond does. For example, the carbon atom in CO_2 has no lone pairs and participates in two double bonds. Each double bond counts as one for the purpose of predicting geometry, so the structure of CO_2 is linear.

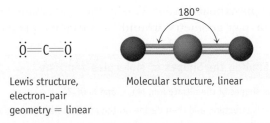

Lewis structure, electron-pair geometry = linear

Molecular structure, linear

When resonance structures are possible, the geometry can be predicted from any of the Lewis resonance structures or from the resonance hybrid structure. For example, the geometry of the CO_3^{2-} ion is predicted to be trigonal planar because the carbon atom has three sets of bonds and no lone pairs.

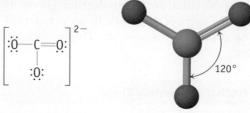

$$\left[\ddot{\text{O}} - \text{C} = \text{O} \right]^{2-}$$
$$\begin{array}{c} | \\ \ddot{\text{O}} \end{array}$$

Lewis structure, one resonance
structure, electron-pair
geometry = trigonal planar

Molecular structure,
trigonal planar

The NO_2^- ion also has a trigonal-planar electron-pair geometry. Because there is a lone pair on the central nitrogen atom, and bonds in the other two positions, the geometry of the ion is angular or bent.

$$\left[\ddot{\text{O}} - \text{N} = \text{O} \right]^-$$

Lewis structure, one
resonance structure,
electron-pair geometry
= trigonal planar

Molecular structure,
angular or bent

115°

The techniques just outlined can be used to find the geometries around the atoms in more complicated molecules. Consider, for example, cysteine, one of the natural amino acids.

Cysteine, $HSCH_2CH(NH_2)CO_2H$

Four pairs of electrons occur around the S, N, C_2, and C_3 atoms, so the electron-pair geometry around each is tetrahedral. Thus, the S—C—H and H—N—H angles are predicted to be approximately 109°. The O atom in the grouping C—O—H and the S atom in the grouping H—S—C are also surrounded by four pairs, and so these angles are likewise approximately 109°. Finally, the angle made by O—C_1—O is 120° because the electron-pair geometry around C_1 is trigonal planar.

■ **EXAMPLE 8.9** **Finding the Shapes of Molecules and Ions**

Problem What are the shapes of the nitrate ion, NO_3^-, and $XeOF_4$?

Strategy Draw the Lewis structure, and then decide on the electron pair geometry. The position of the atoms gives the molecular geometry of the ion. Follow the procedure used in Examples 8.6–8.8.

Solution

(a) The NO_3^- and CO_3^{2-} ions are isoelectronic. Thus, like the carbonate ion described in the text above, the electron-pair geometry and molecular shape of NO_3^- are trigonal planar.

(b) The $XeOF_4$ molecule has a Lewis structure with a total of six electron pairs about the central Xe atom, one of which is a lone pair. It has a square-pyramidal molecular structure. Two structures are possible, based on the position occupied by the oxygen, but there is no way to predict which is correct. The actual structure is the one shown, with the oxygen in the apex of the square pyramid.

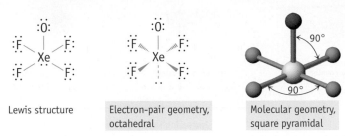

| Lewis structure | Electron-pair geometry, octahedral | Molecular geometry, square pyramidal |

EXERCISE 8.11 Determining Molecular Shapes

Use Lewis structures and the VSEPR model to determine the electron-pair and molecular geometries for **(a)** the phosphate ion, PO_4^{3-}; **(b)** the sulfite ion, SO_3^{2-}; and **(c)** IF_5.

8.7 Bond Polarity and Electronegativity

The models used to represent covalent and ionic bonding are the extreme situations in bonding. Pure covalent bonding, in which atoms share an electron pair equally, occurs *only* when two identical atoms are bonded. When two dissimilar atoms form a covalent bond, the electron pair will be unequally shared. The result is a **polar covalent bond,** a bond in which the two atoms have residual or partial charges (Figure 8.9).

Bonds are polar because not all atoms hold onto their valence electrons with the same force, nor do atoms take on additional electrons with equal ease. Recall from the discussion of atom properties that different elements have different values of ionization energy and electron affinity (Section 7.5). These differences in behavior for free atoms carry over to atoms in molecules.

If a bond pair is not equally shared between atoms, the bonding electrons are on average nearer to one of the atoms. The atom toward which the pair is displaced has a larger share of the electron pair and thus acquires a partial negative charge. At the same time, the atom at the other end of the bond is depleted in electrons and acquires a partial positive charge. The bond between the two atoms has a positive end and a negative end; that is, it has negative and positive poles. The bond is called a **polar bond.**

In ionic compounds, displacement of the bonding pair to one of the two atoms is essentially complete, and + and − symbols are written alongside the atom symbols in the Lewis drawings. For a polar covalent bond, the polarity is indicated by writing the symbols $\delta+$ and $\delta-$ alongside the atom symbols, where δ (the Greek letter "delta") stands for a *partial* charge. Hydrogen fluoride, water, and ammonia are three simple molecules having polar, covalent bonds.

FIGURE 8.9 A polar covalent bond. Iodine has a larger share of the bonding electrons, and hydrogen has a smaller share. The result is that I has a partial negative charge ($\delta-$), and H has a partial positive charge ($\delta+$).

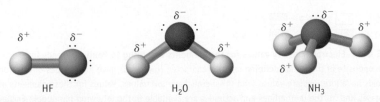

Three simple molecules with polar covalent bonds. In each case, F, O, and N are more electronegative than H.

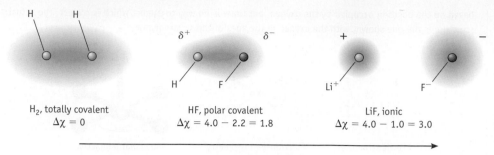

H₂, totally covalent	HF, polar covalent	LiF, ionic
$\Delta\chi = 0$	$\Delta\chi = 4.0 - 2.2 = 1.8$	$\Delta\chi = 4.0 - 1.0 = 3.0$

Increasing ionic character

FIGURE 8.10 Covalent to ionic bonding. As the electronegativity difference increases between the atoms of a bond, the bond becomes increasingly ionic.

With so many atoms to use in covalent bond formation, it is not surprising that bonds between atoms can fall anywhere in a continuum from pure covalent to pure ionic (Figure 8.10). There is no sharp dividing line between an ionic bond and a covalent bond.

In the 1930s, Linus Pauling proposed a parameter called atom electronegativity that allows us to decide if a bond is polar, which atom of the bond is negative and which is positive, and if one bond is more polar than another. The **electronegativity, χ,** of an atom is defined as a measure of *the ability of an atom in a molecule to attract electrons to itself.*

Values of electronegativity are given in Figure 8.11. Several features and periodic trends are apparent. The element with the largest electronegativity is fluorine; it is assigned a value of $\chi = 4.0$. The element with the smallest value is the alkali metal cesium. Electronegativities generally increase from left to right across a period and decrease down a group. This is the opposite of the trend observed for metallic character. Metals typically have low values of electronegativity, ranging from slightly less than 1 to about 2. Electronegativity values for the metalloids are around 2, whereas nonmetals have values greater than 2.

												H 2.2						
1A	**2A**												**3A**	**4A**	**5A**	**6A**	**7A**
Li 1.0	Be 1.6												B 2.0	C 2.5	N 3.0	O 3.5	F 4.0
Na 0.9	Mg 1.3	**3B**	**4B**	**5B**	**6B**	**7B**		**8B**		**1B**	**2B**		Al 1.6	Si 1.9	P 2.2	S 2.6	Cl 3.2
K 0.8	Ca 1.0	Sc 1.4	Ti 1.5	V 1.6	Cr 1.7	Mn 1.5	Fe 1.8	Co 1.9	Ni 1.9	Cu 1.9	Zn 1.6	Ga 1.8	Ge 2.0	As 2.2	Se 2.6	Br 3.0
Rb 0.8	Sr 1.0	Y 1.2	Zr 1.3	Nb 1.6	Mo 2.2	Tc 1.9	Ru 2.2	Rh 2.3	Pd 2.2	Ag 1.9	Cd 1.7	In 1.8	Sn 2.0	Sb 1.9	Te 2.1	I 2.7
Cs 0.8	Ba 0.9	La 1.1	Hf 1.3	Ta 1.5	W 2.4	Re 1.9	Os 2.2	Ir 2.2	Pt 2.3	Au 2.5	Hg 2.0	Tl 1.6	Pb 2.3	Bi 2.0	Po 2.0	At 2.2

- <1.0
- 1.0–1.4
- 1.5–1.9
- 2.0–2.4
- 2.5–2.9
- 3.0–4.0

FIGURE 8.11 Electronegativity values for the elements according to Pauling. Trends for electronegativities are the opposite of the trends defining metallic character. Nonmetals have high values of electronegativity; the metalloids have intermediate values, and the metals have low values. Values for these elements as well as for the noble gases and for the lanthanides and actinides are available in the following handbook: Emsley, J., *The Elements*, 3rd edition, Clarendon Press, Oxford, 1998.

There is a large *difference* in electronegativity for atoms from the left- and right-hand sides of the periodic table. For cesium fluoride, for example, the difference in electronegativity values, $\Delta\chi$, is 3.2 [= 4.0 (for F) − 0.8 (for Cs)]. The bond is decidedly ionic in CsF, therefore, with Cs the cation (Cs^+) and F the anion (F^-). In contrast, the electronegativity difference between H and F in HF is only 1.8 [= 4.0 (for F) − 2.2 (for H)]. We conclude that bonding in HF must be more covalent, as expected for a compound formed from two nonmetals. The H—F bond is polar, however, with hydrogen being the positive end of the molecule and fluorine the negative end ($H^{\delta+}$—$F^{\delta-}$).

Chemistry⚛Now™

Sign in at **www.cengage.com/login** and go to Chapter 8 Contents to see Screen 8.15 for **relative electronegativity values.**

©Ted Streshinsky/Corbis

Linus Pauling (1901–1994). Linus Pauling was born in Portland, Oregon, earned a B.Sc. degree in chemical engineering from Oregon State College in 1922, and completed his Ph.D. in chemistry at the California Institute of Technology in 1925. In chemistry, he is well known for his book *The Nature of the Chemical Bond*. He also studied protein structure and, in the words of Francis Crick, was "one of the founders of molecular biology." It was this work and his study of chemical bonding that were cited in the award of the Nobel Prize in chemistry in 1954. Although chemistry was the focus of his life, at the urging of his wife, Ava Helen, he was also involved in nuclear disarmament issues, and he received the Nobel Peace Prize in 1962 for the role he played in advocating for the nuclear test ban treaty.

■ EXAMPLE 8.10 Estimating Bond Polarities

Problem For each of the following bond pairs, decide which is the more polar and indicate the negative and positive poles.

(a) B–F and B–Cl

(b) Si–O and P–P

Strategy Locate the elements in the periodic table. Recall that electronegativity generally increases across a period and up a group.

Solution

(a) B and F lie relatively far apart in the periodic table. B is a metalloid, and F is a nonmetal. Here, χ for B = 2.0, and χ for F = 4.0. Similarly, B and Cl are relatively far apart in the periodic table, but Cl is below F in the periodic table (χ for Cl = 3.2) and is therefore less electronegative than F. The difference in electronegativity for B—F is 2.0, and for B—Cl it is 1.2. Both bonds are expected to be polar, with B positive and the halide atom negative, but a B—F bond is more polar than a B—Cl bond.

(b) Because the bond is between two atoms of the same kind, the P—P bond is nonpolar. Silicon is in Group 4A and the third period, whereas O is in Group 6A and the second period. Consequently, O has a greater electronegativity (3.5) than Si (1.9), so the bond is highly polar ($\Delta\chi$ = 1.6), with O the more negative atom.

EXERCISE 8.12 Bond Polarity

For each of the following pairs of bonds, decide which is the more polar. For each polar bond, indicate the positive and negative poles. First, make your prediction from the relative atom positions in the periodic table; then check your prediction by calculating $\Delta\chi$.

(a) H—F and H—I   **(b)** B—C and B—F   **(c)** C—Si and C—S

Charge Distribution: Combining Formal Charge and Electronegativity

The way electrons are distributed in a molecule or ion is called its **charge distribution.** The charge distribution can profoundly affect the properties of a molecule. Examples include its physical properties, such as its melting and boiling points, and its chemical properties, such as its susceptibility to attack by an anion or cation or whether it is an acid or a base.

We saw earlier (◀ page 359) that formal charge calculations can locate the site of a charge in a molecule or an ion. However, this can sometimes lead to results that are incorrect because formal charge calculations assume that there is equal sharing of electrons in all bonds. The ion BF_4^- illustrates this point. Boron has a formal charge of −1 in this ion, whereas the formal charge calculated for the fluorine atoms is 0. This is not logical: fluorine is the more electronegative atom so the negative charge should reside on F and not on B.

Electronegativity is a useful, if somewhat vague, concept. It is, however, related to the ionic character of bonds. Chemists have found, as illustrated in the figure, that a correlation exists between the difference in electronegativity of bonded atoms and the degree of ionicity expressed as "% ionic character."

As the difference in electronegativity increases, ionic character increases. Does this trend allow us to say that one compound is ionic and another is covalent? No, we can say only that one bond is more ionic or more covalent than another.

Electron affinity was introduced in Section 7.5. At first glance, it may appear that electronegativity and electron affinity measure the same property, but they do not. Electronegativity is a parameter that applies only to atoms in molecules, whereas electron affinity is a measurable energy quantity for atoms in the gas phase.

Although electron affinity was introduced earlier as a criterion with which to predict the central atom in a molecule, experience indicates that electronegativity is a better choice. That is, *the central atom is generally the atom of lowest electronegativity.*

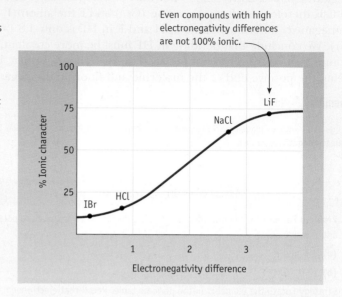

Even compounds with high electronegativity differences are not 100% ionic.

The way to resolve this dilemma is to consider electronegativity in conjunction with formal charge. Based on the electronegativity difference between fluorine and boron ($\Delta\chi = 2.0$), the B—F bonds are expected to be polar, with fluorine being the negative end of the bond, $B^{\delta+}$—$F^{\delta-}$. So, in this instance, predictions based on electronegativity and formal charge work in opposite directions. The formal charge calculation places the negative charge on boron, but the electronegativity difference leads us to say the negative charge on boron is distributed onto the fluorine atoms, effectively spreading it out over the molecule.

Linus Pauling pointed out two basic guidelines to use when describing charge distributions in molecules and ions. The first is the **electroneutrality principle.** This declares that electrons will be distributed in such a way that the charges on all atoms are as close to zero as possible. Second, he noted that if a negative charge is present, it should reside on the most electronegative atoms. Similarly, positive charges are expected on the least electronegative atoms. The effect of these principles is clearly seen in the case of BF_4^-, where the negative charge is distributed over the four fluorine atoms rather than residing on boron.

Considering the concepts of electronegativity and formal charge together can help to decide which of several resonance structures is the more important. For example, Lewis structure A for CO_2 is the logical one to draw. But what is wrong with B, in which each atom also has an octet of electrons?

Formal charge =
$0 = 7 - [6 + \frac{1}{2}(2)]$

$$\left[\begin{array}{c} :\ddot{F}: \\ | \\ :\ddot{F}-B-\ddot{F}: \\ | \\ :\ddot{F}: \end{array} \right]^{-}$$

Formal charge =
$-1 = 3 - [0 + \frac{1}{2}(8)]$

Formal charges for the B and F atoms of the BF_4^- anion.

	Formal charges	0 0 0	+1 0 −1
Resonance structures		$\ddot{O}=C=\ddot{O}$	$:O\equiv C-\ddot{O}:$
		A	B

For structure A, each atom has a formal charge of 0, a favorable situation. In B, however, one oxygen atom has a formal charge of +1, and the other has −1. This is contrary to the principle of electroneutrality. In addition, B places a positive charge on the more electronegative O atom. Thus, we can conclude that structure B is a much less satisfactory structure than A.

Now use the logic applied to CO_2 to decide which of the three possible resonance structures for the OCN^- ion is the most reasonable. Formal charges for each atom are given above the element's symbol.

Formal charges

Resonance structures

$$\begin{bmatrix} \overset{-1}{:\ddot{O}} {-} \overset{0}{C} {\equiv} \overset{0}{N:} \end{bmatrix}^- \longleftrightarrow \begin{bmatrix} \overset{0}{:\ddot{O}} {=} \overset{0}{C} {=} \overset{-1}{\ddot{N}} \end{bmatrix}^- \longleftrightarrow \begin{bmatrix} \overset{+1}{:O} {\equiv} \overset{0}{C} {-} \overset{-2}{\ddot{N}:} \end{bmatrix}^-$$

A   B   C

■ **Formal Charges in OCN⁻**
Example of formal charge calculation: For resonance form C for OCN^-, we have

$O = 6 - [2 + (½)(6)] = +1$
$C = 4 - [0 + (½)(8)] = 0$
$N = 5 - [6 + (½)(2)] = -2$

Sum of formal charges $= -1 =$ charge on the ion.

Structure C will not contribute significantly to the overall electronic structure of the ion. It has a -2 formal charge on the N atom and a $+1$ formal charge on the O atom. Not only is the charge on the N atom high, but O is more electronegative than N and would be expected to take on a negative charge. Structure A is more significant than structure B because the negative charge in A is placed on the most electronegative atom (O). We predict, therefore, that structure A is the best representation for this ion and that the carbon–nitrogen bond will resemble a triple bond. The result for OCN^- also allows us to predict that protonation of the ion will lead to HOCN and not HNCO. That is, an H^+ ion will add to the more negative oxygen atom.

■ **EXAMPLE 8.11 Calculating Formal Charges**

Problem Boron-containing compounds often have a boron atom with only three bonds (and no lone pairs). Why not form a double bond with a terminal atom to complete the boron octet? To answer this, consider possible resonance structures of BF_3, and calculate the atoms' formal charges. Are the bonds polar in BF_3? If so, which is the more negative atom?

Strategy Calculate the formal charges on each atom in the resonance structures. The preferred structure will have atoms with low formal charges. Negative formal charges should be on the most electronegative atoms.

Solution The two possible structures for BF_3 are illustrated here with the calculated formal charges on the B and F atoms.

Formal charge = 0
$= 7 - [6 + \frac{1}{2}(2)]$

Formal charge = +1
$= 7 - [4 + \frac{1}{2}(4)]$

$$:\ddot{F}:$$
$$:\ddot{F}-B-\ddot{F}:$$

$$:\ddot{F}:$$
$$:\ddot{F}-B-\ddot{F}:$$

Formal charge = 0
$= 3 - [0 + \frac{1}{2}(6)]$

Formal charge = −1
$= 3 - [0 + \frac{1}{2}(8)]$

The structure on the left is strongly preferred because all atoms have a zero formal charge and the very electronegative F atom does not have a charge of $+1$.

F $(\chi = 4.0)$ is more electronegative than B $(\chi = 2.0)$, so the B—F bond is highly polar, the F atom being partially negative and the B atom partially positive.

EXERCISE 8.13 Formal Charge, Bond Polarity, and Electronegativity

Consider all possible resonance structures for SO_2. What are the formal charges on each atom in each resonance structure? What are the bond polarities? Do they agree with the formal charges?

8.8 Bond and Molecular Polarity

The term "polar" was used in Section 8.7 to describe a bond in which one atom has a partial positive charge and the other a partial negative charge. Because most molecules have polar bonds, molecules as a whole can also be polar. In a polar molecule, electron density accumulates toward one side of the molecule, giving that side a partial negative charge, $\delta-$, and leaving the other side with a partial positive charge of equal value, $\delta+$ (Figure 8.12a).

Before describing the factors that determine whether a molecule is polar, let us look at the experimental measurement of the polarity of a molecule. When placed in an electric field, polar molecules experience a force that tends to align them with the field (Figure 8.12). When the electric field is created by a pair of oppositely charged plates, the positive end of each molecule is attracted to the negative plate, and the negative end is attracted to the positive plate (Figure 8.12b). The extent to which the molecules line up with the field depends on their **dipole moment, μ,** which is defined as the product of the magnitude of the partial charges ($\delta+$ and $\delta-$) on the molecule and the distance by which they are separated. The SI unit of the dipole moment is the coulomb-meter, but dipole moments have traditionally been given using a derived unit called the *debye* (D; 1 D = 3.34×10^{-30} C · m). Experimental values of some dipole moments are listed in Table 8.7.

To predict if a molecule is polar, we need to consider if the molecule has polar bonds and how these bonds are positioned relative to one another. Diatomic molecules composed of two atoms with different electronegativities are always polar (see Table 8.7); there is one bond, and the molecule has a positive and a negative end. But what happens with a molecule with three or more atoms, in which there are two or more polar bonds?

Consider first a linear triatomic molecule such as carbon dioxide, CO_2 (Figure 8.13). Here, each C=O bond is polar, with the oxygen atom the negative end of the bond dipole. The terminal atoms are at the same distance from the C atom; they both have the same $\delta-$ charge, and they are symmetrically arranged around the central C atom. Therefore, CO_2 has no molecular dipole, even though each

■ **Dipole–Dipole Forces** The force of attraction between the negative end of one polar molecule and the positive end of another (called a dipole–dipole force and discussed in Section 12.2) affects the properties of polar compounds. Intermolecular forces (forces between molecules) influence the temperature at which a liquid freezes or boils, for example.

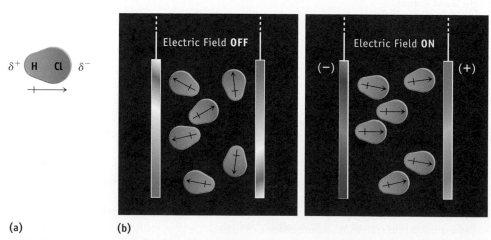

(a)   (b)

FIGURE 8.12 Polar molecules in an electric field. (a) A representation of a polar molecule. To indicate the direction of molecular polarity, an arrow is drawn with the head pointing to the negative side and a plus sign placed at the positive end. (b) When placed in an electric field (between charged plates), polar molecules experience a force that tends to align them with the field. The negative end of the molecules is drawn to the positive plate, and vice versa. The orientation of the polar molecule affects the electrical capacitance of the plates (their ability to hold a charge), and this provides a way to measure experimentally the magnitude of the dipole moment.

TABLE 8.7 Dipole Moments of Selected Molecules

Molecule (AX)	Moment (μ, D)	Geometry	Molecule (AX$_2$)	Moment (μ, D)	Geometry
HF	1.78	linear	H_2O	1.85	bent
HCl	1.07	linear	H_2S	0.95	bent
HBr	0.79	linear	SO_2	1.62	bent
HI	0.38	linear	CO_2	0	linear
H_2	0	linear			

Molecule (AX$_3$)	Moment (μ, D)	Geometry	Molecule (AX$_4$)	Moment (μ, D)	Geometry
NH_3	1.47	trigonal pyramidal	CH_4	0	tetrahedral
NF_3	0.23	trigonal pyramidal	CH_3Cl	1.92	tetrahedral
BF_3	0	trigonal planar	CH_2Cl_2	1.60	tetrahedral
			$CHCl_3$	1.04	tetrahedral
			CCl_4	0	tetrahedral

bond is polar. This is analogous to a tug-of-war in which the people at opposite ends of the rope are pulling with equal force.

In contrast, water is a bent triatomic molecule. Because O has a larger electronegativity ($\chi = 3.5$) than H ($\chi = 2.2$), each of the O—H bonds is polar, with the H atoms having the same $\delta+$ charge and oxygen having a negative charge ($\delta-$) (Figure 8.13). Electron density accumulates on the O side of the molecule, making the molecule electrically "lopsided" and therefore polar ($\mu = 1.85$ D).

In trigonal-planar BF_3, the B—F bonds are highly polar because F is much more electronegative than B (χ of B = 2.0 and χ of F = 4.0) (Figure 8.14). The molecule is nonpolar, however, because the three terminal F atoms have the same $\delta-$ charge, are the same distance from the boron atom, and are arranged symmetrically and in the same plane as the central boron atom. In contrast, the trigonal-planar molecule phosgene is polar (Cl_2CO, $\mu = 1.17$ D) (Figure 8.14). Here, the angles are all about 120°, so the O and Cl atoms are symmetrically arranged around the C atom. The

■ **Peter Debye and Dipoles** The commonly used unit of dipole moments is named in honor of Peter Debye (1884–1966). He was born in The Netherlands, but attended university in Germany and later studied for his Ph.D. in physics in Munich. He developed a theory on the diffraction of x-rays by solids, a new concept for magnetic cooling, and (with E. Hückel) a model for interionic attractions in aqueous solution. As his interests turned more to chemistry, he worked on methods of determining the shapes of polar molecules. Debye received the Nobel Prize in chemistry in 1936.

Peter Debye (1884–1966)

Rare Book & Manuscript Collections/Carl A. Knoch Library/Cornell University

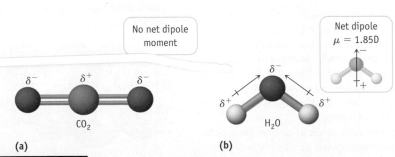

No net dipole moment

Net dipole $\mu = 1.85$D

CO_2 (a)

H_2O (b)

Active Figure 8.13 Polarity of triatomic molecules, AX$_2$. For CO_2, the CO bonds are polar, but the electron density is distributed evenly over the molecule, and the charges of $\delta-$ lie 180° apart. (Charges calculated using advanced molecular modeling software: C = +0.42 and O = −0.21.) The molecule has no net dipole. In the water molecule, the O atom is negative, and the H atoms are positive. (Calculated charges: H = +0.19 and O = −0.38.) However, the positively charged H atoms lie on one side of the molecule, and the negatively charged O atom is on the other side. The molecule is polar. (The calculated dipole of 1.86 D is in good agreement with experiment.)

Chemistry.ᐧ.Now™ Sign in at www.cengage.com/login and go to the Chapter Contents menu to explore an interactive version of this figure accompanied by an exercise.

Visualizing Charge Distributions and Molecular Polarity—Electrostatic Potential Surfaces and Partial Charge

In Chapter 6, you saw atomic orbitals, regions of space within which an electron is most probably found. The boundary surface of these orbitals was created in such a way that the electron wave amplitude at all points of the surface was the same value (◀ page 288). Using advanced molecular modeling software, we can generate the same type of pictures for molecules, and in Figure A you see a surface defining the electron density in the HF molecule. The electron density surface, calculated using software from CAChe, is made up of all of the points in space around the HF molecule where the electron density is at least 0.002 $e^-/Å^3$ (where 1 Å = 0.1 nm). You can see that the surface bulges toward the F end of the molecule, an indication of the larger size of the F atom. The larger size of the F atom here is mainly related to the fact that it has more valence electrons than H, and to a lesser extent to the fact that H—F bond is polar and electron density in that bond is shifted toward the F atom.

We can add another layer of information. The electron density surface can be colored according to the *electrostatic potential*. (Hence, this figure is called an *electrostatic potential surface*.) The computer program calculates the electrostatic potential that would be observed by a proton (H^+) on the surface. This is the sum of the attractive and repulsive forces on that proton due to the nuclei and the electrons in the molecule. Regions of the molecule in which there is an attractive potential are colored red. That is, this is a region of negative charge on the molecule. Repulsive potentials occur in regions where the molecule is positively charged; these regions are colored blue. As might be expected, the net electrostatic potential will change continuously as one moves from a negative portion of a molecule to a positive portion, and this is indicated by a progression of colors from blue to red (from positive to negative).

The electrostatic potential surface for HF shows the H atom is positive (the H atom end of the molecule is blue), and the F atom is

FIGURE A Three views of the electrostatic potential surface for HF.

(*left*) The electron density surface around HF. The F atom is at the left. The surface is made up of all of the points in space around the HF molecule where the electron density is 0.002 $e^-/Å^3$ (where 1 Å = 0.1 nm).

(*middle*) The surface is made more transparent, so you can see the HF atom nuclei inside the surface.

(*right*) The front of the electron density surface has been "peeled away" for a view of the HF molecule inside.

Color scheme: The colors on the electron density surface reflect the charge in the different regions of the molecule ⟶ 384. Colors to the blue end of the spectrum indicate a positive charge, whereas colors to the red end of the spectrum indicate a negative charge.

negative (the F atom end is red). This is, of course, what we would predict based on electronegativity.

Our program also calculated that the F atom has a charge of −0.29 and H has a charge of +0.29. Finally, the calculated dipole moment for the molecule is 1.74 D, in good agreement with the experimental value in Table 8.7.

Other examples of electrostatic potential surfaces illustrate the polarity of water and methylamine, CH_3NH_2.

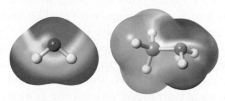

Water   Methylamine

The surface shows the O atom of the water molecule bears a partial negative charge and the H atoms are positive. The surface for the amine clearly shows the molecule is polar and that the region around the N atom is also negative. Indeed, we know from experiment that an H^+ ion will attack the N atom to give the cation $CH_3NH_3^+$.

Electrostatic potential surfaces are becoming more widely used, particularly in organic chemistry and biochemistry, to probe the reactive sites of more and more complex molecules. One example is the dipeptide glycylglycine.

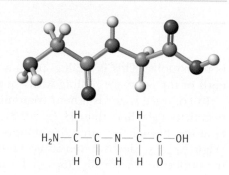

$$H_2N-\overset{\overset{\textstyle H}{|}}{\underset{\underset{\textstyle H}{|}}{C}}-\overset{\overset{\textstyle }{\|}}{\underset{\underset{\textstyle O}{}}{C}}-\overset{\overset{\textstyle H}{|}}{\underset{\underset{\textstyle H}{|}}{N}}-\overset{\overset{\textstyle H}{|}}{\underset{\underset{\textstyle H}{|}}{C}}-\overset{\overset{\textstyle }{\|}}{\underset{\underset{\textstyle O}{}}{C}}-OH$$

The electrostatic surface for the molecule shows that the O atoms of the C=O groups have a partial negative charge as does the N of the NH_2 group. Positive regions of the molecule include the H atom of the C(O)—NH grouping (the amide grouping) and the H atom of the OH group. Such pictures can help you see quickly the regions of a molecule that may be a proton donor (an acid) or a proton acceptor (a base).

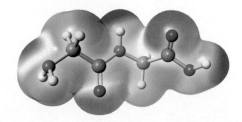

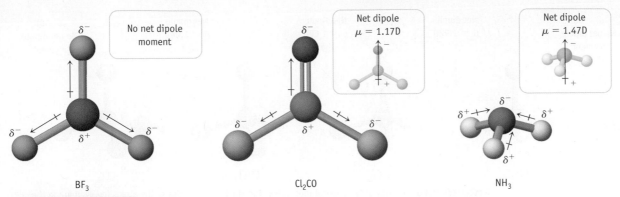

BF₃   Cl₂CO   NH₃

Active Figure 8.14 Polar and nonpolar molecules of the type AX₃. In BF₃, the negative charge on the F atoms is distributed symmetrically, so the molecular dipole is zero. In contrast, in Cl₂CO and NH₃, the negative charge in the molecules is shifted to one side and the positive charge to the other side.

Molecule	Calculated Partial Charges	Calculated dipole
BF₃	B = 0.44, F = −0.15	0
Cl₂CO	O = −0.21, C = 0.23, Cl = −0.01	1.25
NH₃	N = −0.40, H = 0.13	1.58

The calculated dipoles are in reasonable agreement with experimentally measured dipoles. (Calculations were done with molecular modeling software from CAChe.)

Chemistry.⊙.Now™ Sign in at www.cengage.com/login and go to the Chapter Contents menu to explore an interactive version of this figure accompanied by an exercise.

■ **Electrostatic Potential Surfaces for BF₃ and Cl₂CO** Notice that the charge distribution for BF₃ (left) is symmetrical whereas that for Cl₂CO (right) has a partial negative charge on the O atom and much less negative charges on the Cl atoms.

electronegativities of the three atoms in the molecule differ, however: $\chi(O) > \chi(Cl) > \chi(C)$. There is therefore a net displacement of electron density away from the center of the molecule, more toward the O atom than the Cl atoms.

Ammonia, like BF₃, has AX₃ stoichiometry and polar bonds. In contrast to BF₃, however, NH₃ is a trigonal-pyramidal molecule. The positive H atoms are located in the base of the pyramid, and the negative N atom is on the apex of the pyramid. As a consequence, NH₃ is polar (Figure 8.14). Indeed, trigonal-pyramidal molecules are generally polar.

Molecules like carbon tetrachloride, CCl₄, and methane, CH₄, are nonpolar, owing to their symmetrical, tetrahedral structures. The four atoms bonded to C have the same partial charge and are the same distance from the C atom. Tetrahedral molecules with both Cl and H atoms (CHCl₃, CH₂Cl₂, and CH₃Cl) are polar, however (Figure 8.15). The electronegativity for H atoms (2.2) is less than that of Cl atoms (3.2), and the carbon–hydrogen distance is different from the carbon–chlorine distances. Because Cl is more electronegative than H, the Cl atoms are on the more negative side of the molecule. This means the positive end of the molecular dipole is toward the H atom.

To summarize this discussion of molecular polarity, look again at Figure 8.5 (page 369). These are sketches of molecules of the type AX_n where A is the central atom and X is a terminal atom. You can predict that a molecule AX_n will *not* be polar, regardless of whether the A—X bonds are polar, if

- All the terminal atoms (or groups), X, are identical, and
- All the X atoms (or groups) are arranged symmetrically around the central atom, A.

On the other hand, if one of the X atoms (or groups) is different in the structures in Figure 8.5 (as in Figures 8.14 and 8.15), or if one of the X positions is occupied by a lone pair, the molecule will be polar.

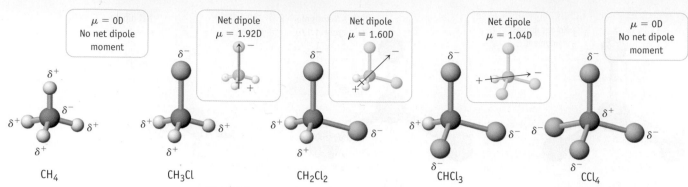

$\mu = 0D$ No net dipole moment	Net dipole $\mu = 1.92D$	Net dipole $\mu = 1.60D$	Net dipole $\mu = 1.04D$	$\mu = 0D$ No net dipole moment
CH_4	CH_3Cl	CH_2Cl_2	$CHCl_3$	CCl_4

FIGURE 8.15 Polarity of tetrahedral molecules. The electronegativities of the atoms involved are in the order Cl (3.2) > C(2.5) > H (2.2). This means the C—H and C—Cl bonds are polar with a net displacement of electron density away from the H atoms and toward the Cl atoms [H $^{\delta+}$–C $^{\delta-}$ and C $^{\delta+}$–Cl $^{\delta-}$]. Although the electron-pair geometry around the C atom in each molecule is tetrahedral, only in CH_4 and CCl_4 are the polar bonds totally symmetrical in their arrangement. Therefore, CH_3Cl, CH_2Cl_2, and $CHCl_3$ are polar molecules, with the negative end toward the Cl atoms and the positive end toward the H atoms.

Chemistry⚛Now™

Sign in at **www.cengage.com/login** and go to Chapter 8 Contents to see Screen 8.16 for practice **determining polarity**.

■ **EXAMPLE 8.12 Molecular Polarity**

Problem Are nitrogen trifluoride (NF_3) and sulfur tetrafluoride (SF_4) polar or nonpolar? If polar, indicate the negative and positive sides of the molecule.

Strategy You cannot decide if a molecule is polar without determining its structure. Therefore, start with the Lewis structure, decide on the electron-pair geometry, and then decide on the molecular geometry. If the molecular geometry is one of the highly symmetrical geometries in Figure 8.5, the molecule is not polar. If it does not fit one of these categories, it will be polar.

Solution

(a) NF_3 has the same trigonal-pyramidal structure as NH_3. Because F is more electronegative than N, each bond is polar, the more negative end being the F atom. Because this molecule contains polar bonds and because the geometry is not symmetrical but has instead three positions of the tetrahedron occupied by bonding groups and one by a lone pair, the NF_3 molecule as a whole is expected to be polar.

You will notice, however, that the dipole moment for NF_3 is quite small (0.23 D in Table 8.7), much smaller than that of NH_3. This illustrates that *lone pairs have an effect on polarity*. For NH_3, the N-atom lone pair adds to the overall polarity of the molecule. (The lone electron pair extends into space beyond the N atom and increases the charge separation in NH_3; this enhances the dipole.) For NF_3, however, the effect of the lone pair on the nitrogen atom of the molecule is counterbalanced by the highly polar N—F bonds on the other side and the magnitude of the dipole pointing toward the side with the F atoms is reduced.

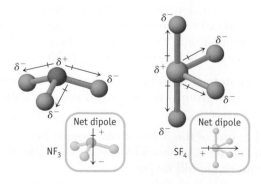

(b) The S—F bonds in sulfur tetrafluoride, SF_4, are highly polar, the bond dipole having F as the negative end (χ for S is 2.6 and χ for F is 4.0). The molecule has an electron-pair geometry of a trigonal bipyramid (see Figure 8.8). Because the lone pair occupies one of the positions, the S—F bonds are not arranged symmetrically. The axial S—F bond dipoles cancel each other because they point in opposite directions. The equatorial S—F bonds, however, both point to one side of the molecule.

Comment In general, we do not consider lone pair effects on molecular dipoles. Nonetheless, they do have an effect, as seen when comparing the dipole moment for NF_3 (0.23 D) with that for NH_3 (1.47 D).

This is a case in which electrostatic potential surfaces and calculated atom charges are useful in showing the difference between these molecules. The N atom in NH_3 is decidedly negative (-0.40), and the H atoms are positive ($+0.13$). In contrast, in NF_3 the N atom is positively charged, and the F atoms are negatively charged (N $= +0.3$ and F $= -0.1$). The difference in charge between N and F is not as great as between N and H in NH_3.

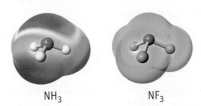

NH₃   NF₃

Electrostatic potential maps.

■ **EXAMPLE 8.13 Molecular Polarity**

Problem 1,2-Dichloroethylene can exist in two forms. Is either of these planar molecules polar?

$$
\begin{array}{cc}
\underset{\text{Cl}}{\overset{\text{H}}{>}}\text{C}=\text{C}\underset{\text{Cl}}{\overset{\text{H}}{<}} & \underset{\text{H}}{\overset{\text{Cl}}{>}}\text{C}=\text{C}\underset{\text{Cl}}{\overset{\text{H}}{<}} \\
A & B
\end{array}
$$

Strategy To decide if a molecule is polar, we first sketch the structure and then, using electronegativity values, decide on the bond polarity. Finally, we decide if the electron density in the bonds is distributed symmetrically or if it is shifted to one side of the molecule.

Solution Here, the H and Cl atoms are arranged around the C=C double bonds with all bond angles 120° (and all the atoms lie in one plane). The electronegativities of the atoms involved are in the order Cl(3.2) $>$ C(2.5) $>$ H (2.2). This means the C—H and C—Cl bonds are polar with a net displacement of electron density away from the H atoms and toward the Cl atoms [$H^{\delta+}$—$C^{\delta-}$ and $C^{\delta+}$—$Cl^{\delta-}$]. In structure A, the Cl atoms are located on one side of the molecule, so electrons in the H—C and C—Cl bonds are displaced toward the side of the molecule with Cl atoms and away from the side with the H atoms. Molecule A is polar. In molecule B, the displacement of electron density toward the Cl atom on one end of the molecule is counterbalanced by an opposing displacement on the other end. Molecule B is not polar.

Overall displacement of bonding electrons

$$
\begin{array}{c}
\overset{\delta+}{\text{H}} \qquad \overset{\delta+}{\text{H}} \\
\searrow \qquad \swarrow \\
\text{C}=\text{C} \\
\swarrow \qquad \searrow \\
\underset{\delta-}{\text{Cl}} \qquad \underset{\delta-}{\text{Cl}}
\end{array}
$$

A, polar, diplacement of bonding electrons to one side of the molecule

Displacement of bonding electrons

$$
\begin{array}{c}
\overset{\delta-}{\text{Cl}} \qquad \overset{\delta+}{\text{H}} \\
\searrow \qquad \swarrow \\
\text{C}=\text{C} \\
\nearrow \qquad \searrow \\
\underset{\delta+}{\text{H}} \qquad \underset{\delta-}{\text{Cl}}
\end{array}
$$

Displacement of bonding electrons

B, not polar, no net displacement of bonding electrons to one side of the molecule

Comment The electrostatic potential surfaces reflect the fact that molecule A is polar because the electron density is shifted to one side of the molecule. Molecule B is not polar because the electron density is distributed symmetrically.

Molecule A

Molecule B

EXERCISE 8.14 Molecular Polarity

For each of the following molecules, decide whether the molecule is polar and which side is positive and which negative: $BFCl_2$, NH_2Cl, and SCl_2.

EXERCISE 8.15 Molecular Polarity

The electrostatic potential surface for $OSCl_2$ is pictured here.

(a) Draw a Lewis electron dot picture for the molecule, and give the formal charge of each atom.

(b) What is the molecular geometry of $OSCl_2$?

(c) Is the molecule polar? If so, locate the positive and negative charges and the direction of the dipole.

8.9 Bond Properties: Order, Length, Energy

Bond Order

The **order of a bond** is the number of bonding electron pairs shared by two atoms in a molecule (Figure 8.16). You will encounter bond orders of 1, 2, and 3, as well as fractional bond orders.

When the bond order is 1, there is only a single covalent bond between a pair of atoms. Examples are the bonds in molecules such as H_2, NH_3, and CH_4. The bond order is 2 when two electron pairs are shared between atoms, such as the C=O bonds in CO_2 and the C=C bond in ethylene, $H_2C=CH_2$. The bond order is 3 when two atoms are connected by three bonds. Examples include the carbon–oxygen bond in carbon monoxide, CO and the nitrogen–nitrogen bond in N_2.

Fractional bond orders occur in molecules and ions having resonance structures. For example, what is the bond order for each oxygen–oxygen bond in O_3? Each resonance structure of O_3 has one O—O single bond and one O=O double bond, for a total of three shared bonding pairs accounting for two oxygen–oxygen links.

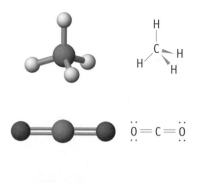

FIGURE 8.16 Bond order. The four C—H bonds in methane each have a bond order of 1. The two C=O bonds of CO_2 each have a bond order of two, whereas the nitrogen–nitrogen bond in N_2 has an order of 3.

Bond order = 1

Bond order = 2

Bond order for each oxygen–oxygen bond = $\frac{3}{2}$, or 1.5

One resonance structure

We can define the bond order between any bonded pair of atoms X and Y as

$$\text{Bond order} = \frac{\text{number of shared pairs in all X—Y bonds}}{\text{number of X—Y links in the molecule or ion}} \tag{8.2}$$

For ozone, there are three bond pairs involved in two oxygen-oxygen links, so the bond order for each oxygen–oxygen bond is $\frac{3}{2}$, or 1.5.

Chemistry ⚗ Now™

Sign in at **www.cengage.com/login** and go to Chapter 8 Contents to see Screen 8.17 to see **how bond order, bond length, and bond energy are related.**

Bond Length

Bond length is the distance between the nuclei of two bonded atoms. Bond lengths are therefore related to the sizes of the atoms (Section 7.5), but, for a given pair of atoms, the order of the bond also plays a role.

Table 8.8 lists average bond lengths for a number of common chemical bonds. It is important to recognize that these are *average* values. Neighboring parts of a molecule can affect the length of a particular bond. For example, Table 8.8 specifies that the average C—H bond has a length of 110 pm. In methane, CH_4, the measured bond length is 109.4 pm, whereas the C—H bond is only 105.9 pm long in acetylene, H—C≡C—H. Variations as great as 10% from the average values listed in Table 8.8 are possible.

TABLE 8.8 Some Average Single- and Multiple-Bond Lengths in Picometers (pm)*

Single Bond Lengths

	1A	4A	5A	6A	7A	4A	5A	6A	7A	7A	7A
	H	C	N	O	F	Si	P	S	Cl	Br	I
H	74	110	98	94	92	145	138	132	127	142	161
C		154	147	143	141	194	187	181	176	191	210
N			140	136	134	187	180	174	169	184	203
O				132	130	183	176	170	165	180	199
F					128	181	174	168	163	178	197
Si						234	227	221	216	231	250
P							220	214	209	224	243
S								208	203	218	237
Cl									200	213	232
Br										228	247
I											266

Multiple Bond Lengths

C=C	134	C≡C	121
C=N	127	C≡N	115
C=O	122	C≡O	113
N=O	115	N≡O	108

*1 pm = 10^{-12} m.

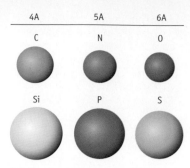

4A	5A	6A
C	N	O

| Si | P | S |

Relative sizes of some atoms of Groups 4A, 5A, and 6A.

Bond lengths are related to atom sizes.

C—H	N—H	O—H
110	98	94 pm
Si—H	P—H	S—H
145	138	132 pm

Because atom sizes vary in a regular fashion with the position of the element in the periodic table (Figure 7.8), predictions of trends in bond length can be made quickly. For example, the H—X distance in the hydrogen halides increases in the order predicted by the relative sizes of the halogens: H—F < H—Cl < H—Br < H—I. Likewise, bonds between carbon and another element in a given period decrease going from left to right, in a predictable fashion; for example, C—C > C—N > C—O > C—F. Trends for multiple bonds are similar. A C=O bond is shorter than a C=S bond, and a C=N bond is shorter than a C=C bond.

The effect of bond order is evident when bonds between the same two atoms are compared. For example, the bonds become shorter as the bond order increases in the series C—O, C=O, and C≡O:

Bond	C—O	C=O	C≡O
Bond Order	1	2	3
Bond Length (pm)	143	122	113

Double bonds are shorter than single bonds between the same set of atoms, and triple bonds between those same atoms are shorter still.

The carbonate ion, CO_3^{2-}, has three equivalent resonance structures. Each CO bond has a bond order of 1.33 (or $\frac{4}{3}$) because four electron pairs are used to form three carbon–oxygen links. The CO bond distance (129 pm) is intermediate between a C—O single bond (143 pm) and a C=O double bond (122 pm).

$$
\begin{bmatrix} :\!O\!: \\ \| \\ C \\ :\!O \quad O\!: \end{bmatrix}^{2-}
$$

Bond order = 2
Bond order = 1
Bond order = 1

Average bond order = $\frac{4}{3}$, or 1.33
Bond length = 129 pm

EXERCISE 8.16 Bond Order and Bond Length

(a) Give the bond order of each of the following bonds, and arrange them in order of decreasing bond distance: C=N, C≡N, and C—N.

(b) Draw resonance structures for NO_2^-. What is the NO bond order in this ion? Consult Table 8.8 for N—O and N=O bond lengths. Compare these with the NO bond length in NO_2^- (124 pm). Account for any differences you observe.

Bond Dissociation Enthalpy

The **bond dissociation enthalpy** is the enthalpy change for breaking a bond in a molecule with the reactants and products in the gas phase.

$$\text{Molecule (g)} \underset{\text{Energy released} = \Delta H < 0}{\overset{\text{Energy supplied} = \Delta H > 0}{\rightleftarrows}} \text{Molecular fragments (g)}$$

Suppose you wish to break the carbon–carbon bonds in ethane (H_3C—CH_3), ethylene (H_2C=CH_2), and acetylene (HC≡CH). The carbon–carbon bond orders in these molecules are 1, 2, and 3, respectively, and these bond orders are reflected in the bond dissociation enthalpies. Carbon–carbon bond breaking in ethane requires the least energy in this group, and acetylene requires the most energy.

$H_3C—CH_3(g) \rightarrow H_3C(g) + CH_3(g)$ $\Delta_rH = +368 \text{ kJ/mol-rxn}$

$H_2C{=}CH_2(g) \rightarrow H_2C(g) + CH_2(g)$ $\Delta_rH = +682 \text{ kJ/mol-rxn}$

$HC{\equiv}CH(g) \rightarrow HC(g) + CH(g)$ $\Delta_rH = +962 \text{ kJ/mol-rxn}$

Because ΔH represents the energy transferred to the molecule from its surroundings, ΔH has a positive value; that is, *the process of breaking bonds in a molecule is always endothermic.*

The energy supplied to break carbon–carbon bonds must be the same as the energy released when the same bonds form. *The formation of bonds from atoms or radicals in the gas phase is always exothermic.* This means, for example, that Δ_rH for the formation of $H_3C—CH_3$ from two $CH_3(g)$ radicals is -368 kJ/mol-rxn.

$H_3C \cdot (g) + \cdot CH_3(g) \rightarrow H_3C–CH_3(g)$ $\Delta_rH = -368 \text{ kJ/mol-rxn}$

Generally, the bond energy for a given type of bond (a C—C bond, for example) varies somewhat, depending on the compound, just as bond lengths vary from one molecule to another. They are sufficiently similar, however, so it is possible to create a table of *average bond dissociation enthalpies* (Table 8.9). The values in such tables may be used to *estimate* the enthalpy change for a reaction, as described below.

■ **Variability in Bond Dissociation Enthalpies** The values of Δ_rH for ethane, ethylene, and acetylene in the text are for those molecules in particular. The bond dissociation enthalpies in Table 8.9 are average values for a range of molecules containing the indicated bond.

TABLE 8.9   Some Average Bond Dissociation Enthalpies (kJ/mol)*

Single Bonds

	H	C	N	O	F	Si	P	S	Cl	Br	I
H	436	413	391	463	565	328	322	347	432	366	299
C		346	305	358	485	—	—	272	339	285	213
N			163	201	283	—	—	—	192	—	—
O				146	—	452	335	—	218	201	201
F					155	565	490	284	253	249	278
Si						222	—	293	381	310	234
P							201	—	326	—	184
S								226	255	—	—
Cl									242	216	208
Br										193	175
I											151

Multiple Bonds

N=N	418	C=C	610
N≡N	945	C≡C	835
C=N	615	C=O	745
C≡N	887	C≡O	1046
O=O (in O_2)	498		

*Sources of dissociation enthalpies: I. Klotz and R. M. Rosenberg: *Chemical Thermodynamics*, 4th Ed., p. 55, New York, John Wiley, 1994; and J. E. Huheey, E. A. Keiter, and R. L. Keiter: *Inorganic Chemistry* 4th Ed., Table E. 1, New York, Harper-Collins, 1993. See also Lange's *Handbook of Chemistry*, J. A. Dean (ed.), McGraw-Hill Inc., New York.

■ **Bond Energy and Electronegativity**
Linus Pauling derived electronegativity
values from a consideration of bond energies. He recognized that the energy required to break a bond between two different atoms is often greater than
expected, based on an assumption that
bond electrons are shared equally. He
postulated that the "extra energy" arises
from the fact that the atoms do not share
electrons equally. One atom is slightly
positive and the other slightly negative.
This means there is a small coulombic
force of attraction involving oppositely
charged ions in addition to the force of
attraction arising from the sharing of
electrons. This coulombic force enhances
the overall force of attraction.

In reactions between molecules, bonds in reactants are broken; new bonds are formed as products form. If the total energy released when new bonds form exceeds the energy required to break the original bonds, the overall reaction is exothermic. If the opposite is true, then the overall reaction is endothermic. Let us see how this works in practice.

Let us use bond dissociation enthalpies to estimate the enthalpy change for the hydrogenation of propene to propane:

The first step is to examine the reactants and product to see what bonds are broken and what bonds are formed. In this case, the C=C bond in propene and the H—H bond in hydrogen are broken. A C—C bond and two C—H bonds are formed.

Bonds broken: 1 mol of C=C bonds and 1 mol of H—H bonds

Energy required = 610 kJ for C=C bonds + 436 kJ for H—H bonds = 1046 kJ/mol-rxn

Bonds formed: 1 mol of C—C bonds and 2 mol of C—H bonds

Energy evolved = 346 kJ for C—C bonds + 2 mol × 413 kJ/mol for C—H bonds =
1172 kJ/mol-rxn

■ **Hydrogenation Reactions** Adding hydrogen to a double (or triple) bond is
called a hydrogenation reaction. It is
commonly done to convert vegetable oils,
whose molecules contain C=C double
bonds, to solid fats.

By combining the energy required to break bonds and the energy evolved in making bonds, we can estimate $\Delta_r H$ for the hydrogenation of propene and see that the reaction is exothermic.

$$\Delta_r H = 1046 \text{ kJ/mol-rxn} - 1172 \text{ kJ/mol-rxn} = -126 \text{ kJ/mol-rxn}$$

The example of the propene–hydrogen reaction illustrates the fact that the enthalpy change for any reaction can be estimated using the equation

■ **$\Delta_r H$ from Enthalpies of**
Formation Using $\Delta_f H°$ values for propane and propene, we calculate $\Delta_r H$ for
the reaction of −125.1 kJ/mol-rxn. The
bond dissociation enthalpy calculation is
in excellent agreement with that from
enthalpies of formation.

$$\Delta_r H = \Sigma \Delta H (\text{bonds broken}) - \Sigma \Delta H (\text{bonds formed}) \tag{8.3}$$

To use this equation, first identify all the bonds in the reactants that are broken, and add up their bond dissociation enthalpies. Then, identify all the new bonds formed in the products, and add up their bond dissociation enthalpies. The difference between the energy required to break bonds [= $\Sigma \Delta H$(bonds broken)] and the energy evolved when bonds are made $[= \Sigma\Delta H(\text{bonds formed})]$ gives the estimated enthalpy change for the reaction. Such calculations can give acceptable results in many cases.

Chemistry.$\dot{\ominus}$.Now™

Sign in at **www.cengage.com/login** and go to Chapter 8 Contents to see Screen 8.18 to explore **how reactant and product bond energies influence the energy of reaction.**

■ **EXAMPLE 8.14** **Using Bond Dissociation Enthalpies**

Problem Acetone, a common industrial solvent, can be converted to isopropanol, rubbing alcohol, by hydrogenation. Calculate the enthalpy change for this reaction using bond energies.

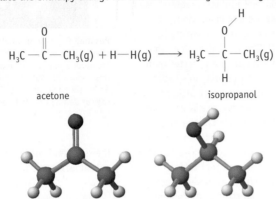

acetone   isopropanol

Strategy Examine the reactants and products to determine which bonds are broken and which are formed. Add up the energies required to break bonds in the reactants and the energy evolved to form bonds in the product. The difference in the sums of bond dissociation enthalpies is an estimate of the enthalpy change of the reaction (Equation 8.3).

Solution

Bonds broken: 1 mol of C=O bonds and 1 mol of H—H bonds

$$H_3C - \overset{\overset{\text{O}}{\|}}{C} - CH_3(g) \ + H\!-\!H(g)$$

$\Sigma\Delta H$(bonds broken) = 745 kJ for C=O bonds + 436 kJ for H—H bonds = 1181 kJ/mol-rxn

Bonds formed: 1 mol of C—H bonds, 1 mol of C—O bonds, and 1 mol of O—H bonds

$$H_3C - \overset{\overset{\text{O} - \text{H}}{|}}{C} - CH_3(g)$$

$\Sigma\Delta H$(bonds formed) = 413 kJ for C—H + 358 kJ for C—O + 463 kJ for O—H = 1234 kJ/mol-rxn

$\Delta_r H = \Sigma\Delta H$(bonds broken) $- \Sigma\Delta H$(bonds formed)

$\Delta_r H = 1181$ kJ $- 1234$ kJ $= \boxed{-53 \text{ kJ/mol-rxn}}$

Comment The overall reaction is predicted to be exothermic by 53 kJ per mol of product formed. This is in good agreement with the value calculated from $\Delta_f H°$ values ($= -55.8$ kJ/mol-rxn).

EXERCISE 8.17 **Using Bond Dissociation Enthalpies**

Using the bond dissociation enthalpies in Table 8.9, estimate the enthalpy of combustion of gaseous methane, CH_4. That is, estimate $\Delta_r H$ for the reaction of methane with O_2 to give water vapor and carbon dioxide gas.

DNA is the substance in every plant and animal that carries the exact blueprint of that plant or animal. The structure of this molecule, the cornerstone of life, was uncovered in 1953, and James D. Watson, Francis Crick, and Maurice Wilkins shared the 1962 Nobel Prize in medicine and physiology for the work. It was one of the most important scientific discoveries of the 20th century, and the story

has been told by Watson in his book *The Double Helix*.

When Watson was a graduate student at Indiana University, he had an interest in the gene and said he hoped that its biological role might be solved "without my learning any chemistry." Later, however, he and Crick found out just how useful chemistry can be when they began to unravel the structure of DNA.

Solving important problems requires teamwork among scientists of many kinds, so Watson went to Cambridge University in England in 1951. There he met Crick, who, Watson said, talked louder and faster than anyone else. Crick shared Watson's belief in the fundamental importance of DNA, and the pair soon learned that Maurice Wilkins and Rosalind Franklin at King's College in London were using a technique called x-ray crystallography to learn more about DNA's structure. Watson and Crick believed that understanding this structure was crucial to understanding genetics. To solve the structural problem, however, they needed experimental data of the type that could come from the experiments at King's College.

The King's College group was initially reluctant to share their data; and, what is more, they did not seem to share Watson and Crick's sense of urgency. There was also an ethical dilemma: Could Watson and Crick work on a problem that others had claimed as

Rosalind Franklin of King's College, London. She died in 1958 at the age of 37. Because Nobel Prizes are never awarded posthumously, she did not share in this honor with Watson, Crick, and Wilkins. For more on Rosalind Franklin, read *Rosalind Franklin: The Dark Lady of DNA* by Brenda Maddox.

theirs? "The English sense of fair play would not allow Francis to move in on Maurice's problem," said Watson.

Watson and Crick approached the problem through a technique chemists now use frequently—model building. They built models of the pieces of the DNA chain, and they tried various chemically reasonable ways of fitting them together. Finally, they discovered that one arrangement was "too pretty not to be true." Ultimately, the experimental evidence of Wilkins and Franklin confirmed the "pretty structure" to be the real DNA structure.

James D. Watson and Francis Crick. In a photo taken in 1953, Watson (left) and Crick (right) stand by their model of the DNA double helix. Together with Maurice Wilkins, Watson and Crick received the Nobel Prize in medicine and physiology in 1962. (A Barrington Brown/Science/Photo Researchers, Inc.)

8.10 DNA, Revisited

This chapter opened with some questions about the structure of DNA, one of the key molecules in all biological systems. The tools are now in place to say more about the structure of this important molecule and why it looks the way it does.

As shown in Figure 8.17, each strand of the double-stranded DNA molecule consists of three units: a phosphate, a deoxyribose molecule (a sugar molecule with a five-member ring), and a nitrogen-containing base. (The bases in DNA can be one of four molecules: adenine, guanine, cytosine, and thymine; in Figure 8.17, the base is adenine.) Two units of the backbone (without the adenine on the deoxyribose ring) are also illustrated in Figure 8.17.

The important point here is that the repeating unit in the backbone of DNA consists of the atoms O—P—O—C—C—C. Each atom has a tetrahedral electron-pair geometry. Therefore, the chain cannot be linear. In fact, the chain twists as one moves along the backbone. This twisting gives DNA its helical shape.

Why are there two strands in DNA with the O—P—O—C—C—C backbone on the outside and the nitrogen-containing bases on the inside? This structure arises from the polarity of the bonds in the base molecules attached to the backbone.

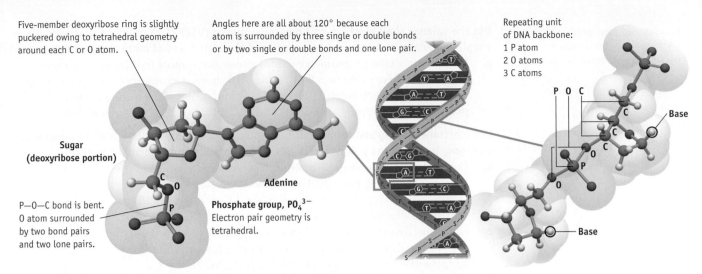

Five-member deoxyribose ring is slightly puckered owing to tetrahedral geometry around each C or O atom.

Angles here are all about 120° because each atom is surrounded by three single or double bonds or by two single or double bonds and one lone pair.

Repeating unit of DNA backbone:
1 P atom
2 O atoms
3 C atoms

Sugar (deoxyribose portion)

P—O—C bond is bent. O atom surrounded by two bond pairs and two lone pairs.

Adenine

Phosphate group, PO_4^{3-}
Electron pair geometry is tetrahedral.

Base

Base

FIGURE 8.17 A portion of the DNA molecule. A repeating unit consists of a phosphate portion, a deoxyribose portion (a sugar molecule with a five-member ring), and a nitrogen-containing base (here adenine) attached to the deoxyribose ring.

For example, the N-H bonds in the adenine molecule are very polar, which leads to a special form of intermolecular forces—hydrogen bonding—to the base molecule in the neighboring chain. More about this in Chapter 12 when we explore intermolecular forces and again in *The Chemistry of Life: Biochemistry* (pages 496–512).

Chapter Goals Revisited

Now that you have studied this chapter, you should ask whether you have met the chapter goals. In particular, you should be able to:

Understand the difference between ionic and covalent bonds

a. Describe the basic forms of chemical bonding—ionic and covalent—and the differences between them, and predict from the formula whether a compound has ionic or covalent bonding, based on whether a metal is part of the formula (Section 8.1).

b. Write Lewis symbols for atoms (Section 8.2).

Draw Lewis electron dot structures for small molecules and ions

a. Draw Lewis structures for molecular compounds and ions (Section 8.2). Study Question(s) assignable in OWL: 6, 8, 10.

b. Understand and apply the octet rule; recognize exceptions to the octet rule (Sections 8.2–8.5). Study Question(s) assignable in OWL: 6, 8, 10, 12, 56.

c. Write resonance structures, understand what resonance means, and how and when to use this means of representing bonding (Section 8.4). Study Question(s) assignable in OWL: 10.

Chemistry ⚛ Now™ Sign in at **www.cengage.com/login** to:

- Assess your understanding with Study Questions in OWL keyed to each goal in the Goals and Homework menu for this chapter
- For quick review, download Go Chemistry mini-lecture flashcard modules (or purchase them at **www.ichapters.com**)
- Check your readiness for an exam by taking the Pre-Test and exploring the modules recommended in your Personalized Study plan.

❓ Access **How Do I Solve It?** tutorials on how to approach problem solving using concepts in this chapter.

For additional preparation for an examination on this chapter see the *Let's Review* section on pages 496–513.

Use the valence shell electron-pair repulsion theory (VSEPR) to predict the shapes of simple molecules and ions and to understand the structures of more complex molecules.

a. Predict the shape or geometry of molecules and ions of main group elements using VSEPR theory (Section 8.6). Table 8.10 shows a summary of the relation between valence electron pairs, electron-pair and molecular geometry, and molecular polarity. Study Question(s) assignable in OWL: 18, 20, 22, 24, 86, 88; Go Chemistry Module 12.

Use electronegativity and formal charge to predict the charge distribution in molecules and ions, to define the polarity of bonds, and to predict the polarity of molecules.

a. Calculate formal charges for atoms in a molecule based on the Lewis structure (Section 8.3). Study Question(s) assignable in OWL: 14, 16, 36.

b. Define electronegativity and understand how it is used to describe the unequal sharing of electrons between atoms in a bond (Section 8.7).

c. Combine formal charge and electronegativity to gain a perspective on the charge distribution in covalent molecules and ions (Section 8.7). Study Question(s) assignable in OWL: 28, 29, 31, 32, 34, 71.

d. Understand why some molecules are polar whereas others are nonpolar (Section 8.8). See Table 8.7. Study Question(s) assignable in OWL: 38.

e. Predict the polarity of a molecule (Section 8.8). Study Question(s) assignable in OWL: 38, 40, 78, 79, 81, 86; Go Chemistry Module 13.

Understand the properties of covalent bonds and their influence on molecular structure

a. Define and predict trends in bond order, bond length, and bond dissociation energy (Section 8.9). Study Question(s) assignable in OWL: 27, 42, 44, 45, 48, 58, 81.

b. Use bond dissociation enthalpies in calculations (Section 8.9 and Example 8.14). Study Question(s) and assignable in OWL: 50, 51, 52, 69.

TABLE 8.10 Summary of Molecular Shapes and Molecular Polarity

Valence Electron Pairs	Electron-Pair Geometry	Number of Bond Pairs	Number of Lone Pairs	Molecular Geometry	Molecular Dipole?*	Examples
2	linear	2	0	linear	no	$BeCl_2$
3	trigonal planar	3	0	trigonal planar	no	BF_3, BCl_3
		2	1	bent	yes	$SnCl_2(g)$
4	tetrahedral	4	0	tetrahedral	no	CH_4, BF_4^-
		3	1	trigonal pyramidal	yes	NH_3, PF_3
		2	2	bent	yes	H_2O, SCl_2
5	trigonal bipyramidal	5	0	trigonal bipyramidal	no	PF_5
		4	1	seesaw	yes	SF_4
		3	2	T-shaped	yes	ClF_3
		2	3	linear	no	XeF_2, I_3^-
6	octahedral	6	0	octahedral	no	SF_6, PF_6^-
		5	1	square pyramidal	yes	ClF_5
		4	2	square planar	no	XeF_4

*For molecules of the AX_n, where the X atoms are identical.

KEY EQUATIONS

Equation 8.1 (page 359) Calculating the formal charge on an atom in a molecule

Formal charge of an atom in a molecule or ion = Group Number − [LPE + ½(BE)]

Equation 8.2 (page 387) Calculating bond order

$$\text{Bond order} = \frac{\text{number of shared pairs in all X—Y bonds}}{\text{number of X—Y links in the molecule or ion}}$$

Equation 8.3 (page 390) Estimating the enthalpy change for a reaction using bond dissociation enthalpies

$$\Delta_r H = \Sigma \Delta H(\text{bonds broken}) - \Sigma \Delta H(\text{bonds formed})$$

STUDY QUESTIONS

OWL Online homework for this chapter may be assigned in OWL.

▲ denotes challenging questions.

■ denotes questions assignable in OWL.

Blue-numbered questions have answers in Appendix O and fully-worked solutions in the *Student Solutions Manual*.

Practicing Skills

Valence Electrons and the Octet Rule
(See Section 8.1 and ChemistryNow Screen 8.2.)

1. Give the periodic group number and number of valence electrons for each of the following atoms.
   (a) O   (d) Mg
   (b) B   (c) F
   (c) Na   (f) S

2. Give the periodic group number and number of valence electrons for each of the following atoms.
   (a) C   (d) Si
   (b) Cl   (e) Se
   (c) Ne   (f) Al

3. For elements in Groups 4A–7A of the periodic table, give the number of bonds an element is expected to form if it obeys the octet rule.

4. Which of the following elements are capable of forming compounds in which the indicated atom has more than four valence electron pairs?
   (a) C   (d) F   (g) Se
   (b) P   (e) Cl   (h) Sn
   (c) O   (f) B

Lewis Electron Dot Structures
(See Examples 8.1, 8.2, 8.4, and 8.5, and ChemistryNow Screens 8.5–8.11.)

5. Draw a Lewis structure for each of the following molecules or ions.
   (a) NF_3 (c) HOBr
   (b) ClO_3^- (d) SO_3^{2-}

6. ■ Draw a Lewis structure for each of the following molecules or ions:
   (a) CS_2
   (b) BF_4^-
   (c) HNO_2 (where the bonding is in the order HONO)
   (d) $OSCl_2$ (where S is the central atom)

7. Draw a Lewis structure for each of the following molecules:
   (a) Chlorodifluoromethane, $CHClF_2$ (C is the central atom)
   (b) Acetic acid, CH_3CO_2H. Its basic structure is pictured.

   ```
       H   O
       |   ‖
   H — C — C — O — H
       |
       H
   ```

   (c) Acetonitrile, CH_3CN (the framework is H_3C—C—N)
   (d) Allene, H_2CCCH_2

8. ■ Draw a Lewis structure for each of the following molecules:
   (a) Methanol, CH_3OH
   (b) Vinyl chloride, $H_2C{=}CHCl$, the molecule from which PVC plastics are made.
   (c) Acrylonitrile, $H_2C{=}CHCN$, the molecule from which materials such as Orlon are made

9. Show all possible resonance structures for each of the following molecules or ions:
   (a) SO_2
   (b) HNO_2
   (c) SCN^-

10. ■ Show all possible resonance structures for each of the following molecules or ions:
    (a) Nitrate ion, NO_3^-
    (b) Nitric acid, HNO_3
    (c) Nitrous oxide (laughing gas), N_2O (where the bonding is in the order N-N-O)

11. Draw a Lewis structure for each of the following molecules or ions:
    (a) BrF_3 (c) XeO_2F_2
    (b) I_3^- (d) XeF_3^+

12. ■ Draw a Lewis structure for each of the following molecules or ions:
    (a) BrF_5 (c) IBr_2^-
    (b) IF_3 (d) BrF_2^+

Formal Charge
(See Example 8.3 and ChemistryNow Screen 8.11.)

13. Determine the formal charge on each atom in the following molecules or ions:
    (a) N_2H_4 (c) BH_4^-
    (b) PO_4^{3-} (d) NH_2OH

14. ■ Determine the formal charge on each atom in the following molecules or ions:
    (a) SCO
    (b) HCO_2^- (formate ion)
    (c) CO_3^{2-}
    (d) HCO_2H (formic acid)

15. Determine the formal charge on each atom in the following molecules and ions:
    (a) NO_2^+ (c) NF_3
    (b) NO_2^- (d) HNO_3

16. ■ Determine the formal charge on each atom in the following molecules and ions:
    (a) SO_2 (c) O_2SCl_2
    (b) $OSCl_2$ (d) FSO_3^-

Molecular Geometry
(See Examples 8.6 and ChemistryNow Screens 8.12–8.14.
Note that many of these molecular structures are available in ChemistryNow.)

17. Draw a Lewis structure for each of the following molecules or ions. Describe the electron-pair geometry and the molecular geometry around the central atom.
    (a) NH_2Cl
    (b) Cl_2O (O is the central atom)
    (c) SCN^-
    (d) HOF

18. ■ Draw a Lewis structure for each of the following molecules or ions. Describe the electron-pair geometry and the molecular geometry around the central atom.
    (a) ClF_2^+ (c) PO_4^{3-}
    (b) $SnCl_3^-$ (d) CS_2

19. The following molecules or ions all have two oxygen atoms attached to a central atom. Draw a Lewis structure for each one, and then describe the electron-pair geometry and the molecular geometry around the central atom. Comment on similarities and differences in the series.
    (a) CO_2 (c) O_3
    (b) NO_2^- (d) ClO_2^-

20. ■ The following molecules or ions all have three oxygen atoms attached to a central atom. Draw a Lewis structure for each one, and then describe the electron-pair geometry and the molecular geometry around the central atom. Comment on similarities and differences in the series.
    (a) CO_3^{2-} (c) SO_3^{2-}
    (b) NO_3^- (d) ClO_3^-

21. Draw a Lewis structure for each of the following molecules or ions. Describe the electron-pair geometry and the molecular geometry around the central atom.
    (a) ClF_2^- (c) ClF_4^-
    (b) ClF_3 (d) ClF_5

22. ■ Draw a Lewis structure of each of the following molecules or ions. Describe the electron-pair geometry and the molecular geometry around the central atom.
    (a) SiF_6^{2-} (c) SF_4
    (b) PF_5 (d) XeF_4

23. Give approximate values for the indicated bond angles.
    (a) O—S—O in SO_2
    (b) F—B—F angle in BF_3
    (c) Cl—C—Cl angle in Cl_2CO
    (d) H—C—H (angle 1) and C—C≡N (angle 2) in acetonitrile

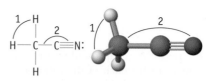

24. ■ Give approximate values for the indicated bond angles.
    (a) Cl—S—Cl in SCl_2
    (b) N—N—O in N_2O
    (c) Bond angles 1, 2, and 3 in vinyl alcohol (a component of polymers and a molecule found in outer space).

▲ more challenging ■ in OWL Blue-numbered questions answered in Appendix O

25. Phenylalanine is one of the natural amino acids and is a "breakdown" product of aspartame. Estimate the values of the indicated angles in the amino acid. Explain why the —CH₂—CH(NH₂)—CO₂H chain is not linear.

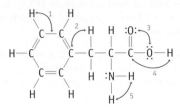

26. ■ Acetylacetone has the structure shown here. Estimate the values of the indicated angles.

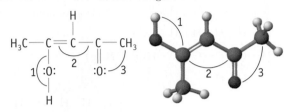

Bond Polarity, Electronegativity, and Formal Charge
(See Examples 8.10 and 8.11 and ChemistryNow Screens 8.11 and 8.15.)

27. ■ For each pair of bonds, indicate the more polar bond, and use an arrow to show the direction of polarity in each bond.
   (a) C—O and C—N   (c) B—O and B—S
   (b) P—Br and P—Cl   (d) B—F and B—I

28. ■ For each of the bonds listed below, tell which atom is the more negatively charged.
   (a) C—N   (c) C—Br
   (b) C—H   (d) S—O

29. ■ Acrolein, C_3H_4O, is the starting material for certain plastics.

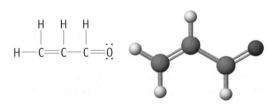

   (a) Which bonds in the molecule are polar, and which are nonpolar?
   (b) Which is the most polar bond in the molecule? Which is the more negative atom of this bond?

30. Urea, $(NH_2)_2CO$, is used in plastics and fertilizers. It is also the primary nitrogen-containing substance excreted by humans.
   (a) Which bonds in the molecule are polar, and which are nonpolar?

(b) Which is the most polar bond in the molecule? Which atom is the negative end of the bond dipole?

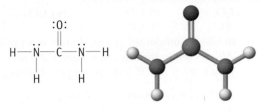

31. ■ Considering both formal charges and bond polarities, predict on which atom or atoms the negative charge resides in the following anions:
   (a) OH^- (b) BH_4^- (c) $CH_3CO_2^-$

32. ■ Considering both formal charge and bond polarities, predict on which atom or atoms the positive charge resides in the following cations.
   (a) H_3O^+ (c) NO_2^+
   (b) NH_4^+ (d) NF_4^+

33. Three resonance structures are possible for dinitrogen monoxide, N_2O.
   (a) Draw the three resonance structures.
   (b) Calculate the formal charge on each atom in each resonance structure.
   (c) Based on formal charges and electronegativity, predict which resonance structure is the most reasonable.

34. ■ Compare the electron dot structures of the carbonate (CO_3^{2-}) and borate (BO_3^{3-}) ions.
   (a) Are these ions isoelectronic?
   (b) How many resonance structures does each ion have?
   (c) What are the formal charges of each atom in these ions?
   (d) If an H^+ ion attaches to CO_3^{2-} to form the bicarbonate ion, HCO_3^-, does it attach to an O atom or to the C atom?

35. The chemistry of the nitrite ion and HNO_2:
   (a) Two resonance structures are possible for NO_2^-. Draw these structures, and then find the formal charge on each atom in each resonance structure.
   (b) If an H^+ ion is attached to NO_2^- (to form the acid HNO_2), it attaches to the O atom and not the N atom. Explain why you would predict this structure.
   (c) Two resonance structures are possible for HNO_2. Draw these structures, and then find the formal charge on each atom in each resonance structure. Is either of these structures strongly preferred over the other?

36. ■ Draw the resonance structures for the formate ion, HCO_2^-, and find the formal charge on each atom. If an H^+ ion is attached to HCO_2^- (to form formic acid), does it attach to C or O?

Molecular Polarity
(See Examples 8.12 and 8.13 and ChemistryNow Screen 8.16.)

37. Consider the following molecules:
    (a) H_2O (c) CO_2 (e) CCl_4
    (b) NH_3 (d) ClF
    (i) In which compound are the bonds most polar?
    (ii) Which compounds in the list are *not* polar?
    (iii) Which atom in ClF is more negatively charged?

38. ■ Consider the following molecules:
    (a) CH_4 (c) BF_3
    (b) NH_2Cl (d) CS_2
    (i) Which compound has the most polar bonds?
    (ii) Which compounds in the list are *not* polar?

39. Which of the following molecules is (are) polar? For each polar molecule, indicate the direction of polarity— that is, which is the negative end, and which is the positive end of the molecule.
    (a) $BeCl_2$ (c) CH_3Cl
    (b) HBF_2 (d) SO_3

40. ■ Which of the following molecules is (are) not polar? Which molecule has bonds with the largest polarity?
    (a) CO   (d) PCl_3
    (b) BCl_3 (e) GeH_4
    (c) CF_4

Bond Order and Bond Length
(See Exercise 8.16 and ChemistryNow Screen 8.17.)

41. Give the bond order for each bond in the following molecules or ions:
    (a) CH_2O (c) NO_2^+
    (b) SO_3^{2-} (d) NOCl

42. ■ Give the bond order for each bond in the following molecules or ions:
    (a) CN^- (c) SO_3
    (b) CH_3CN (d) $CH_3CH{=}CH_2$

43. In each pair of bonds, predict which is shorter.
    (a) B—Cl or Ga—Cl   (c) P—S or P—O
    (b) Sn—O or C—O   (d) C=O or C≡N

44. ■ In each pair of bonds, predict which is shorter.
    (a) Si—N or Si—O
    (b) Si—O or C—O
    (c) C—F or C—Br
    (d) The C—N bond or the C≡N bond in $H_2NCH_2C{\equiv}N$

45. ■ Consider the nitrogen–oxygen bond lengths in NO_2^+, NO_2^-, and NO_3^-. In which ion is the bond predicted to be longest? In which is it predicted to be the shortest? Explain briefly.

46. Compare the carbon–oxygen bond lengths in the formate ion (HCO_2^-), in methanol (CH_3OH), and in the carbonate ion (CO_3^{2-}). In which species is the carbon–oxygen bond predicted to be longest? In which is it predicted to be shortest? Explain briefly.

Bond Strength and Bond Dissociation Enthalpy
(See Table 8.9, Example 8.14, and ChemistryNow Screen 8.18.)

47. ■ Consider the carbon–oxygen bond in formaldehyde (CH_2O) and carbon monoxide (CO). In which molecule is the CO bond shorter? In which molecule is the CO bond stronger?

48. ■ Compare the nitrogen–nitrogen bond in hydrazine, H_2NNH_2, with that in "laughing gas," N_2O. In which molecule is the nitrogen–nitrogen bond shorter? In which is the bond stronger?

49. Hydrogenation reactions, which involve the addition of H_2 to a molecule, are widely used in industry to transform one compound into another. For example, 1-butene (C_4H_8) is converted to butane (C_4H_{10}) by addition of H_2.

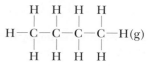

    Use the bond dissociation enthalpies in Table 8.9 to estimate the enthalpy change for this hydrogenation reaction.

50. ■ Phosgene, Cl_2CO, is a highly toxic gas that was used as a weapon in World War I. Using the bond dissociation enthalpies in Table 8.9, estimate the enthalpy change for the reaction of carbon monoxide and chlorine to produce phosgene. (*Hint:* First draw the electron dot structures of the reactants and products so you know the types of bonds involved.)

$$CO(g) + Cl_2(g) \rightarrow Cl_2CO(g)$$

51. ■ The compound oxygen difluoride is quite reactive, giving oxygen and HF when treated with water:

$$OF_2(g) + H_2O(g) \rightarrow O_2(g) + 2\ HF(g)$$

$$\Delta_rH° = -318\ \text{kJ/mol-rxn}$$

    Using bond dissociation enthalpies, calculate the bond dissociation energy of the O—F bond in OF_2.

52. ■ Oxygen atoms can combine with ozone to form oxygen:

$$O_3(g) + O(g) \rightarrow 2\ O_2(g)$$

$$\Delta_rH° = -394\ \text{kJ/mol-rxn}$$

    Using $\Delta_rH°$ and the bond dissociation enthalpy data in Table 8.9, estimate the bond dissociation enthalpy for the oxygen–oxygen bond in ozone, O_3. How does your estimate compare with the energies of an O—O single bond and an O=O double bond? Does the oxygen–oxygen bond dissociation enthalpy in ozone correlate with its bond order?

▲ more challenging ■ in OWL Blue-numbered questions answered in Appendix O

General Questions on Bonding and Molecular Structure

These questions are not designated as to type or location in the chapter. They may combine several concepts.

53. ■ Specify the number of valence electrons for Li, Ti, Zn, Si, and Cl.

54. In boron compounds, the B atom often is not surrounded by four valence electron pairs. Illustrate this with BCl_3. Show how the molecule can achieve an octet configuration by forming a coordinate covalent bond with ammonia (NH_3).

55. Which of the following compounds or ions do not have an octet of electrons surrounding the central atom: BF_4^-, SiF_4, SeF_4, BrF_4^-, XeF_4?

56. ■ In which of the following does the central atom obey the octet rule: NO_2, SF_4, NH_3, SO_3, ClO_2, and ClO_2^-? Are any of these species odd-electron molecules or ions?

57. Draw resonance structures for the formate ion, HCO_2^- and then determine the C—O bond order in the ion.

58. ■ Consider a series of molecules in which carbon is bonded by single bonds to atoms of second-period elements: C—O, C—F, C—N, C—C, and C—B. Place these bonds in order of increasing bond length.

59. To estimate the enthalpy change for the reaction

$$O_2(g) + 2 H_2(g) \rightarrow 2 H_2O(g)$$

what bond dissociation enthalpies do you need? Outline the calculation, being careful to show correct algebraic signs.

60. What is the principle of electroneutrality? Use this rule to exclude a possible resonance structure of CO_2.

61. Draw Lewis structures (and resonance structures where appropriate) for the following molecules and ions. What similarities and differences are there in this series?
    (a) CO_2 (b) N_3^- (c) OCN^-

62. Draw resonance structures for the SO_2 molecule, and indicate the partial charges on the S and O atoms. Are the S—O bonds polar, and is the molecule as a whole polar? If so, what is the direction of the net dipole in SO_2? Is your prediction confirmed by the electrostatic potential surface? Explain briefly.

Electrostatic potential surface for sulfur dioxide.

63. What are the orders of the N—O bonds in NO_2^- and NO_2^+? The nitrogen–oxygen bond length in one of these ions is 110 pm and 124 pm in the other. Which bond length corresponds to which ion? Explain briefly.

64. Which has the greater O—N—O bond angle, NO_2^- or NO_2^+? Explain briefly.

65. Compare the F—Cl—F angles in ClF_2^+ and ClF_2^-. Using Lewis structures, determine the approximate bond angle in each ion. Decide which ion has the greater bond angle, and explain your reasoning.

66. Draw an electron dot structure for the cyanide ion, CN^-. In aqueous solution, this ion interacts with H^+ to form the acid. Should the acid formula be written as HCN or CNH?

67. Draw the electron dot structure for the sulfite ion, SO_3^{2-}. In aqueous solution, the ion interacts with H^+. Predict whether a H^+ ion will attach to the S atom or the O atom of SO_3^{2-}.

68. Dinitrogen monoxide, N_2O, can decompose to nitrogen and oxygen gas:

$$2 N_2O(g) \rightarrow 2 N_2(g) + O_2(g)$$

Use bond dissociation enthalpies to estimate the enthalpy change for this reaction.

69. ▲ ■ The equation for the combustion of gaseous methanol is

$$2 CH_3OH(g) + 3 O_2(g) \rightarrow 2 CO_2(g) + 4 H_2O(g)$$

(a) Using the bond dissociation enthalpies in Table 8.9, estimate the enthalpy change for this reaction. What is the enthalpy of combustion of one mole of gaseous methanol?

(b) Compare your answer in part (a) with a calculation of $\Delta_r H°$ using thermochemical data and the methods of Chapter 5 (see Equation 5.6).

70. ▲ Acrylonitrile, C_3H_3N, is the building block of the synthetic fiber Orlon.

Electrostatic potential surface for acrylonitrile.

(a) Give the approximate values of angles 1, 2, and 3.
(b) Which is the shorter carbon–carbon bond?
(c) Which is the stronger carbon–carbon bond?
(d) Based on the electrostatic potential surface, where are the positive and negative charges located in the molecule?
(e) Which is the most polar bond?
(f) Is the molecule polar?

71. ▲ ■ The cyanate ion, NCO⁻, has the least electronegative atom, C, in the center. The very unstable fulminate ion, CNO⁻, has the same formula, but the N atom is in the center.
   (a) Draw the three possible resonance structures of CNO⁻.
   (b) On the basis of formal charges, decide on the resonance structure with the most reasonable distribution of charge.
   (c) Mercury fulminate is so unstable it is used in blasting caps. Can you offer an explanation for this instability? (*Hint:* Are the formal charges in any resonance structure reasonable in view of the relative electronegativities of the atoms?)

72. Vanillin is the flavoring agent in vanilla extract and in vanilla ice cream. Its structure is shown here:

   (a) Give values for the three bond angles indicated.
   (b) Indicate the shortest carbon–oxygen bond in the molecule.
   (c) Indicate the most polar bond in the molecule.

73. ▲ Given that the spatial requirement of a lone pair is greater than that of a bond pair, explain why
   (a) XeF_2 has a linear molecular structure and not a bent one.
   (b) ClF_3 has a T-shaped structure and not a trigonal-planar one.

74. The formula for nitryl chloride is $ClNO_2$.
   (a) Draw the Lewis structure for the molecule, including all resonance structures.
   (b) What is the N—O bond order?
   (c) Describe the electron-pair and molecular geometries, and give values for all bond angles.
   (d) What is the most polar bond in the molecule? Is the molecule polar?
   (e) ▲ The computer program used to calculate electrostatic potential surfaces gave the following charges on atoms in the molecule: A = −0.03, B = −0.26, and C = +0.56. Identify the atoms A, B, and C. Are these calculated charges in accord with your predictions?

Electrostatic potential surface for $ClNO_2$.

75. Hydroxyproline is a less-common amino acid.

   (a) ■ Give approximate values for the indicated bond angles.
   (b) Which are the most polar bonds in the molecule?

76. Amides are an important class of organic molecules. They are usually drawn as sketched here, but another resonance structure is possible.

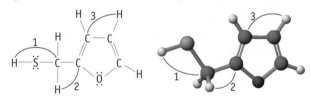

   (a) Draw that structure, and then suggest why it is usually not pictured.
   (b) Suggest a reason for the fact that the H—N—H angle is close to 120°.

77. Use the bond dissociation enthalpies in Table 8.9 to calculate the enthalpy change for the decomposition of urea (Study Question 30) to hydrazine, H_2N—NH_2, and carbon monoxide. (Assume all compounds are in the gas phase.)

78. The molecule shown here, 2-furylmethanethiol, is responsible for the aroma of coffee:

   (a) What are the formal charges on the S and O atoms?
   (b) ■ Give approximate values of angles 1, 2, and 3.
   (c) Which are the shorter carbon–carbon bonds in the molecule?
   (d) Which bond in this molecule is the most polar?
   (e) Is the molecule as a whole polar or nonpolar?
   (f) The molecular model makes it clear that the four C atoms of the ring are all in a plane. Is the O atom in that same plane (making the five-member ring planar), or is the O atom bent above or below the plane?

79. ▲ ■ Dihydroxyacetone is a component of quick-tanning lotions. (It reacts with the amino acids in the upper layer of skin and colors them brown in a reaction similar to that occurring when food is browned as it cooks.)

(a) Supposing you can make this compound by treating acetone with oxygen, use bond dissociation enthalpies to estimate the enthalpy change for the following reaction (which is assumed to occur in the gas phase). Is the reaction exothermic or endothermic?

$$
\underset{\text{acetone}}{\text{H–C–C–C–H}} + O_2 \longrightarrow \underset{\text{dihydroxyacetone}}{\text{H–O–C–C–C–O–H}}
$$

(b) Is acetone polar?

(c) Positive H atoms can sometimes be removed (as H$^+$) from molecules with strong bases (which is in part what happens in the tanning reaction). Which H atoms are the most positive in dihydroxyacetone?

80. Nitric acid, HNO$_3$, has three resonance structures. One of them, however, contributes much less to the resonance hybrid than the other two. Sketch the three resonance structures, and assign a formal charge to each atom. Which one of your structures is the least important?

81. ▲ ■ Acrolein is used to make plastics. Suppose this compound can be prepared by inserting a carbon monoxide molecule into the C—H bond of ethylene.

$$
\underset{\text{ethylene}}{\text{C=C}} + :\text{C}\equiv\text{O}: \longrightarrow \underset{\text{acrolein}}{\text{C=C}}
$$

(a) Which is the stronger carbon–carbon bond in acrolein?

(b) Which is the longer carbon–carbon bond in acrolein?

(c) Is ethylene or acrolein polar?

(d) Is the reaction of CO with C$_2$H$_4$ to give acrolein endothermic or exothermic?

82. Molecules in space:

(a) In addition to molecules such as CO, HCl, H$_2$O, and NH$_3$, glycolaldehyde has been detected in outer space. Is the molecule polar?

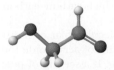

HOCH$_2$CHO, glycolaldehyde.

(b) Where do the positive and negative charges lie in the molecule?

(c) One molecule found in the 1995 Hale-Bopp comet is HC$_3$N. Suggest a structure for this molecule.

83. 1,2-Dichloroethylene can be synthesized by adding Cl$_2$ to the carbon–carbon triple bond of acetylene.

$$
\text{H–C}\equiv\text{C–H} + Cl_2 \longrightarrow \text{C=C}
$$

Using bond dissociation enthalpies, estimate the enthalpy change for this reaction in the gas phase.

84. The molecule pictured below is epinephrine, a compound used as a bronchodilator and antiglaucoma agent.

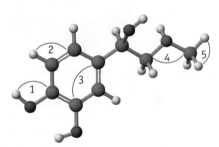

(a) ■ Give a value for each of the indicated bond angles.

(b) What are the most polar bonds in the molecule?

In the Laboratory

85. You are doing an experiment in the laboratory and want to prepare a solution in a polar solvent. Which solvent would you choose, methanol (CH$_3$OH) or toluene (C$_6$H$_5$CH$_3$)? Explain your choice.

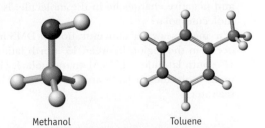

Methanol   Toluene

Methanol (left) and toluene (right).

86. ■ Methylacetamide, $CH_3CONHCH_3$, is a small molecule with an amide link (CO—NH), the group that binds one amino acid to another in proteins.
(a) Is this molecule polar?
(b) Where do you expect the positive and negative charges to lie in this molecule? Does the electrostatic potential surface confirm your predictions?. (Compare this with the dipeptide model in the *A Closer Look* box on page 382.)

Methylacetamide
Ball-and-stick model.

Electrostatic potential surface.

87. ▲ A paper published in the research journal *Science* in 2007 (S. Vallina and R. Simo, *Science*, Vol. 315, page 506, January 26, 2007) reported studies of dimethylsulfide (DMS), an important greenhouse gas that is released by marine phytoplankton. This gas "represents the largest natural source of atmospheric sulfur and a major precursor of hygroscopic (i.e., cloud-forming) particles in clean air over the remote oceans, thereby acting to reduce the amount of solar radiation that crosses the atmosphere and is absorbed by the ocean."
(a) Sketch the Lewis structure of dimethylsulfide, CH_3SCH_3, and give the unique bond angles in the molecule.
(b) Use electronegativities to decide where the positive and negative charges lie in the molecule. Is the molecule polar?
(c) The mean seawater concentration of DMS in the ocean in the region between 15° north latitude and 15° south latitude is 2.7 nM (nanomolar). How many molecules of DMS are present in 1.0 m^3 of seawater?

88. ■ Uracil is one of the bases in DNA.

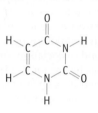

Uracil, $C_4H_4N_2O_2$.

Electrostatic potential surface for uracil.

(a) What are the values of the O—C—N and C—N—H angles?
(b) There are two carbon–carbon bonds in the molecule. Which is predicted to be shorter?
(c) If a proton attacks the molecule, decide on the basis of the electrostatic potential surface to which atom or atoms it could be attached.

Summary and Conceptual Questions

The following questions may use concepts from this and previous chapters.

89. Bromine-containing species play a role in environmental chemistry. For example, they are evolved in volcanic eruptions.
(a) The following molecules are important in bromine environmental chemistry: HBr, BrO, and HOBr. Which are odd-electron molecules?
(b) Use bond dissociation enthalpies to estimate $\Delta_r H$ for three reactions of bromine:

$$Br_2(g) \rightarrow 2\ Br(g)$$

$$2\ Br(g) + O_2(g) \rightarrow 2\ BrO(g)$$

$$BrO(g) + H_2O(g) \rightarrow HOBr(g) + OH(g)$$

(c) Using bond dissociation enthalpies, estimate the standard enthalpy of formation of HOBr(g) from $H_2(g)$, $O_2(g)$, and $Br_2(g)$.
(d) Are the reactions in parts (b) and (c) exothermic or endothermic?

90. Acrylamide, $H_2C{=}CHC({=}O)NH_2$, is a known neurotoxin and possible carcinogen. It was a shock to all consumers of potato chips and french fries a few years ago when it was found to occur in those products (page 90).
(a) Sketch the molecular structure of acrylamide, showing all unique bond angles.
(b) Indicate which carbon–carbon bond is the stronger of the two.
(c) Is the molecule polar or nonpolar?
(d) The amount of acrylamide found in potato chips is 1.7 mg/kg. If a serving of potato chips is 28 g, how many moles of acrylamide are you consuming?

▲ more challenging   ■ in OWL   Blue-numbered questions answered in Appendix 0

91. See ChemistryNow Screen 8.16, Molecular Polarity. Use the Molecular Polarity tool on this screen to explore the polarity of molecules.
    (a) Is BF₃ a polar molecule? Does the molecular polarity change as the F atoms of BF₃ are replaced by H atoms?
    (b) Is BeCl₂ a polar molecule? Does the polarity change when Cl is replaced by Br?

92. Locate the molecules in the table shown here in the Molecular Models available in ChemistryNow. Measure the carbon–carbon bond length in each, and complete the table. (Note that the bond lengths are given in angstrom units, where 1 Å = 0.1 nm.)

Formula	Measured Bond Distance (Å)	Bond Order
ethane, C_2H_6	_____	_____
butane, C_4H_{10}	_____	_____
ethylene, C_2H_4	_____	_____
acetylene, C_2H_2	_____	_____
benzene, C_6H_6	_____	_____

What relationship between bond order and carbon–carbon bond length do you observe?

9 | Bonding and Molecular Structure: Orbital Hybridization and Molecular Orbitals

White crystals of xenon difluoride, XeF₂, form when a mixture of Xe and F₂ gases is irradiated with UV light.

©Gary J. Schrobilgen

The Chemistry of the Noble Gases

It was a shock when, in 1962, we learned that the noble gases were not chemically inert as our chemistry professors had taught us. Xenon at the very least was found to form compounds! The first was an ionic compound, now known to be $XeF^+Pt_2F_{11}^-$. However, this was followed shortly thereafter with the discovery of a large number of covalently bonded compounds, including XeF_4, XeF_6, $XeOF_4$, and XeO_3.

Since 1962, the field of noble gas chemistry has expanded with the discovery of such interesting molecules as FXeOXeF and, at low temperatures, species such as HArF, HXeH, HXeCl, and even HKrF.

Initially, xenon compounds were thought to form only under the most severe conditions. Therefore, it was again a surprise when it was learned that irradiating a mixture of xenon and fluorine gases at room temperature gave crystals of XeF_2 (as seen in the photo).

Questions:

1. What is the most reasonable structure of XeF_2? Does knowing that the molecule has no dipole moment confirm your structural choice? Why or why not?
2. Describe the bonding in XeF_2 using valence bond theory.
3. Predict a structure for FXeOXeF.

Answers to these questions are in Appendix Q.

Chapter Goals

ⓌWL *See Chapter Goals Revisited (page 433) for Study Questions keyed to these goals and assignable in OWL.*

- Understand the differences between valence bond theory and molecular orbital theory.
- Identify the hybridization of an atom in a molecule or ion.
- Understand the differences between bonding and antibonding molecular orbitals and be able to write the molecular orbital configurations for simple diatomic molecules.

Chapter Outline

9.1 Orbitals and Theories of Chemical Bonding

9.2 Valence Bond Theory

9.3 Molecular Orbital Theory

Just how are molecules held together? How can two molecules with distinctly different properties have the same formula? Why is oxygen paramagnetic, and how is this property connected with bonding in the molecule? These are just a few of the fundamental and interesting questions that are raised in this chapter and that require us to take a more advanced look at bonding.

Chemistry.◌.Now™

Throughout the text this icon introduces an opportunity for self-study or to explore interactive tutorials by signing in at **www.cengage.com/login**.

9.1 Orbitals and Theories of Chemical Bonding

From Chapter 6, you know that the location of the valence electrons in atoms is described by an orbital model. It seems reasonable that an orbital model could also be used to describe electrons in molecules.

Two common approaches to rationalizing chemical bonding based on orbitals are **valence bond (VB) theory** and **molecular orbital (MO) theory.** The former was developed largely by Linus Pauling (page 377) and the latter by another American scientist, Robert S. Mulliken (1896–1986). The valence bond approach is closely tied to Lewis's idea of bonding electron pairs between atoms and lone pairs of electrons localized on a particular atom. In contrast, Mulliken's approach was to derive molecular orbitals that are "spread out," or *delocalized*, over the molecule. One way to do this is to combine atomic orbitals to form a set of orbitals that are the property of the molecule, and then distribute the electrons of the molecule within these orbitals.

Why are two theories used? Is one more correct than the other? Actually, both give good descriptions of the bonding in molecules and polyatomic ions, but they are used for different purposes. Valence bond theory is generally the method of choice to provide a qualitative, visual picture of molecular structure and bonding. This theory is particularly useful for molecules made up of many atoms. In contrast, molecular orbital theory is used when a more quantitative picture of bonding is needed. Furthermore, valence bond theory provides a good description of bonding for molecules in their ground, or lowest, energy state. On the other hand, MO theory is essential if we want to describe molecules in higher energy, excited states. Among other things, this is important in explaining the colors of compounds. Finally, for a few molecules such as NO and O_2, MO theory is the only theory that can describe their bonding accurately.

■ **Bonds Are a "Figment of Our Own Imagination"** C. A. Coulson, a prominent theoretical chemist at the University of Oxford, England, has said that "Sometimes it seems to me that a bond between atoms has become so real, so tangible, so friendly, that I can almost see it. Then I awake with a little shock, for a chemical bond is not a real thing. It does not exist. No one has ever seen one. No one ever can. It is a figment of our own imagination" (*Chemical and Engineering News,* January 29, 2007, page 37). Nonetheless, bonds are a useful figment, and this chapter will present some of these useful ideas.

9.2 Valence Bond Theory

The Orbital Overlap Model of Bonding

What happens if two atoms at an infinite distance apart are brought together to form a bond? This process is often illustrated with H_2 because, with two electrons and two nuclei, this is the simplest molecular compound known (Figure 9.1). Initially, when two hydrogen atoms are widely separated, they do not interact. If the atoms move closer together, however, the electron on one atom begins to experience an attraction to the positive charge of the nucleus of the other atom. Because of the attractive forces, the electron clouds on the atoms distort as the electron of one atom is drawn toward the nucleus of the second atom, and the potential energy of the system is lowered. Calculations show that when the distance between the H atoms is 74 pm, the potential energy reaches a minimum and the H_2 molecule is most stable. Significantly, 74 pm corresponds to the experimentally measured bond distance in the H_2 molecule.

Individual hydrogen atoms each have a single electron. In H_2 the two electrons pair up to form the bond. There is a net stabilization, representing the extent to which the energies of the two electrons are lowered from their value in the free atoms. The net stabilization (the extent to which the potential energy is lowered) can be calculated, and the calculated value approximates the experimentally determined bond energy. Agreement between theory and experiment on both bond distance and energy is evidence that this theoretical approach has merit.

Bond formation is depicted in Figures 9.1 and 9.2 as occurring when the electron clouds on the two atoms interpenetrate or overlap. This **orbital overlap** increases the probability of finding the bonding electrons in the region of space between the two nuclei. *The idea that bonds are formed by overlap of atomic orbitals is the basis for valence bond theory.*

■ **Bonds in Valence Bond Theory** In the language of valence bond theory, a pair of electrons of opposite spin located between a pair of atoms constitutes a bond.

Active Figure 9.1 Potential energy change during H—H bond formation from isolated hydrogen atoms. The lowest energy is reached at an H—H separation of 74 pm, where there is overlap of 1s orbitals. At greater distances, the overlap is less, and the bond is weaker. At H—H distances less than 74 pm, repulsions between the nuclei and between the electrons of the two atoms increase rapidly, and the potential energy curve rises steeply.

Chemistry ⚛ Now™ Sign in at www.cengage.com/login and go to the Chapter Contents menu to explore an interactive version of this figure accompanied by an exercise.

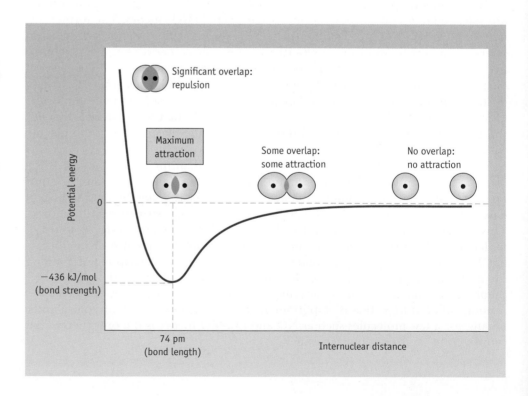

When the single covalent bond is formed in H_2, the $1s$ electron cloud of each atom is distorted in a way that gives the electrons a higher probability of being in the region between the two hydrogen atoms (Figure 9.2a). This makes sense because this distortion results in the electrons being situated so they can be attracted equally to the two positively charged nuclei. Placing the electrons between the nuclei also matches the Lewis electron dot model.

The covalent bond that arises from the overlap of two s orbitals, one from each of two atoms as in H_2, is called a **sigma (σ) bond.** *The electron density of a sigma bond is greatest along the axis of the bond.*

In summary, the main points of the valence bond approach to bonding are:

- Orbitals overlap to form a bond between two atoms.
- Two electrons, *of opposite spin*, can be accommodated in the overlapping orbitals. Usually, one electron is supplied by each of the two bonded atoms.
- Because of orbital overlap, the bonding electrons have a higher probability of being found within a region of space influenced by both nuclei. Both electrons are simultaneously attracted to both nuclei.

What happens for elements beyond hydrogen? In the Lewis structure of HF, for example, a bonding electron pair is placed between H and F, and three lone pairs of electrons are depicted as localized on the F atom (Figure 9.2b). To use an orbital approach, look at the valence shell electrons and orbitals for each atom that can overlap. The hydrogen atom will use its $1s$ orbital in bond formation. The electron configuration of fluorine is $1s^2 2s^2 2p^5$, and the unpaired electron for this atom is assigned to one of the $2p$ orbitals. A sigma bond results from overlap of the hydrogen $1s$ and the fluorine $2p$ orbital.

Formation of the H—F bond is similar to formation of an H—H bond. A hydrogen atom approaches a fluorine atom along the axis containing the $2p$ orbital with

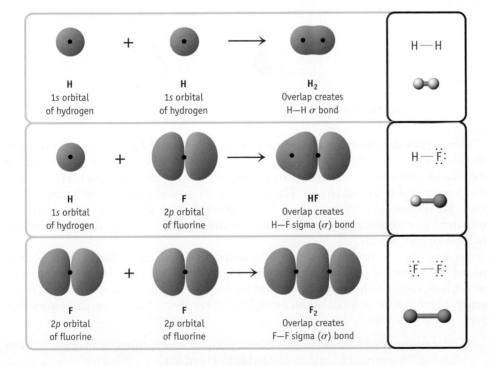

FIGURE 9.2 Covalent bond formation in H_2, HF, and F_2.

(a) Overlap of hydrogen $1s$ orbitals to form the H—H sigma (σ) bond.

(b) Overlap of hydrogen $1s$ and fluorine $2p$ orbitals to form the sigma (σ) bond in HF.

(c) Overlap of $2p$ orbitals on two fluorine atoms forming the sigma (σ) bond in F_2.

H
1s orbital
of hydrogen

H
1s orbital
of hydrogen

H_2
Overlap creates
H—H σ bond

H—H

H
1s orbital
of hydrogen

F
2p orbital
of fluorine

HF
Overlap creates
H—F sigma (σ) bond

H—F̈:

F
2p orbital
of fluorine

F
2p orbital
of fluorine

F_2
Overlap creates
F—F sigma (σ) bond

:F̈—F̈:

a single electron. The orbitals (1*s* on H and 2*p* on F) distort as each atomic nucleus influences the electron and orbital of the other atom. Still closer together, the 1*s* and 2*p* orbitals overlap, and the two electrons, with opposite spins, pair up to give a σ bond (Figure 9.2b). There is an optimum distance (92 pm) at which the energy is lowest, and this corresponds to the bond distance in HF. The net stabilization achieved in this process is the energy for the H—F bond.

The remaining electrons on the fluorine atom (a pair of electrons in the 2*s* orbital and two pairs of electrons in the other two 2*p* orbitals) are not involved in bonding. They are nonbonding electrons, the lone pairs associated with this element in the Lewis structure.

Extension of this model gives a description of bonding in F_2. The 2*p* orbitals on the two atoms overlap, and the single electron from each atom is paired in the resulting σ bond (Figure 9.2c). The 2*s* and the 2*p* electrons not involved in the bond are the lone pairs on each atom.

Chemistry ⚛ Now™

Sign in at **www.cengage.com/login** and go to Chapter 9 Contents to see Screen 9.3 for an exercise on **bond formation.**

Hybridization of Atomic Orbitals

The simple picture using orbital overlap to describe bonding in H_2, HF, and F_2 works well, but we run into difficulty when molecules with more atoms are considered. For example, a Lewis dot structure of methane, CH_4, shows four C—H covalent bonds. VSEPR theory predicts, and experiments confirm, that the electron-pair geometry of the C atom in CH_4 is tetrahedral, with an angle of 109.5° between the bond pairs. The hydrogens are identical in this structure. This means that four equivalent bonding electron pairs occur around the C atom. An orbital picture of the bonds should convey both the geometry and the fact that all C—H bonds are the same.

| Lewis structure | Molecular model | Electron-pair geometry |

If we apply the orbital overlap model used for H_2 and F_2 without modification to describe the bonding in CH_4, a problem arises. The three orbitals for the 2*p* valence electrons of carbon are at right angles, 90° (Figure 9.3), and do not match the tetrahedral angle of 109.5°. The spherical 2*s* orbital could bond in any direction. Furthermore, a carbon atom in its ground state $(1s^2 2s^2 2p^2)$ has only two unpaired electrons (in the 2*p* orbitals), not the four that are needed to allow formation of four bonds.

To describe the bonding in methane and other molecules, Linus Pauling proposed the theory of **orbital hybridization** (Figure 9.4). He suggested that a new set of orbitals, called **hybrid orbitals,** could be created by mixing the *s*, *p*, and (when required) *d* atomic orbitals on an atom. There are three important principles that govern the outcome.

- The number of hybrid orbitals is always equal to the number of atomic orbitals that are mixed to create the hybrid orbital set.

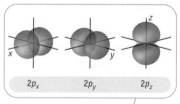
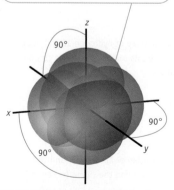

FIGURE 9.3 The 2*p* orbitals of an atom. The $2p_x$, $2p_y$, and $2p_z$ orbitals lie along the *x*-, *y*-, and *z*-axes, 90° to each other.

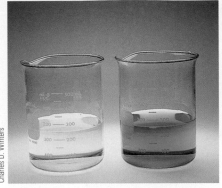

Charles D. Winters

FIGURE 9.4 Hybridization: an analogy. Atomic orbitals can mix, or hybridize, to form hybrid orbitals. When two atomic orbitals on an atom combine, two new orbitals are produced on that atom. The new orbitals have a different direction in space than the original orbitals. An analogy is mixing two different colors (left) to produce a third color, which is a "hybrid" of the original colors (center). After mixing, there are still two beakers (right), each containing the same volume of solution as before, but the color is a "hybrid" color.

- Hybrid orbital sets are always built by combining an *s* orbital with as many *p* orbitals (and *d* orbitals if necessary) to have enough hybrid orbitals to accommodate the bond and lone pairs on the central atom.
- The hybrid orbitals are directed toward the terminal atoms, leading to better orbital overlap and a stronger bond between the central and terminal atoms.

Chemistry ⚛ Now™

Sign in at **www.cengage.com/login** and go to Chapter 9 Contents to see:
- Screen 9.4 for exercises on **hybrid orbitals**
- Screen 9.6 for a tutorial on **determining hybrid orbitals**

The sets of hybrid orbitals that arise from mixing *s*, *p*, and *d* atomic orbitals are illustrated in Figure 9.5. *The hybrid orbitals required by an atom in a molecule or ion are chosen to match the electron pair geometry of the atom* because a hybrid orbital is required for each sigma bond electron pair and each lone pair. The following types of hybridization are important:

- *sp*: If the valence shell *s* orbital on the central atom in a molecule or ion is mixed with a valence shell *p* orbital on that same atom, two *sp* hybrid orbitals are created. They are separated by 180°.
- *sp²*: If an *s* orbital is combined with two *p* orbitals, all in the same valence shell, three *sp²* hybrid orbitals are created. They are in the same plane and are separated by 120°.
- *sp³*: When the *s* orbital in a valence shell is combined with three *p* orbitals, the result is four hybrid orbitals, each labeled *sp³*. The hybrid orbitals are separated by 109.5°, the tetrahedral angle.
- *sp³d* and *sp³d²*: If one or two *d* orbitals are combined with *s* and *p* orbitals in the same valence shell, two other hybrid orbital sets are created. These are utilized by the central atom of a molecule or ion with a trigonal-bipyramidal or octahedral electron-pair geometry, respectively.

Valence Bond Theory for Methane, CH₄

In methane, four orbitals directed to the corners of a tetrahedron are needed to match the electron-pair geometry on the central carbon atom. By mixing the four valence shell orbitals, the 2*s* and all three of the 2*p* orbitals on carbon, a new set of

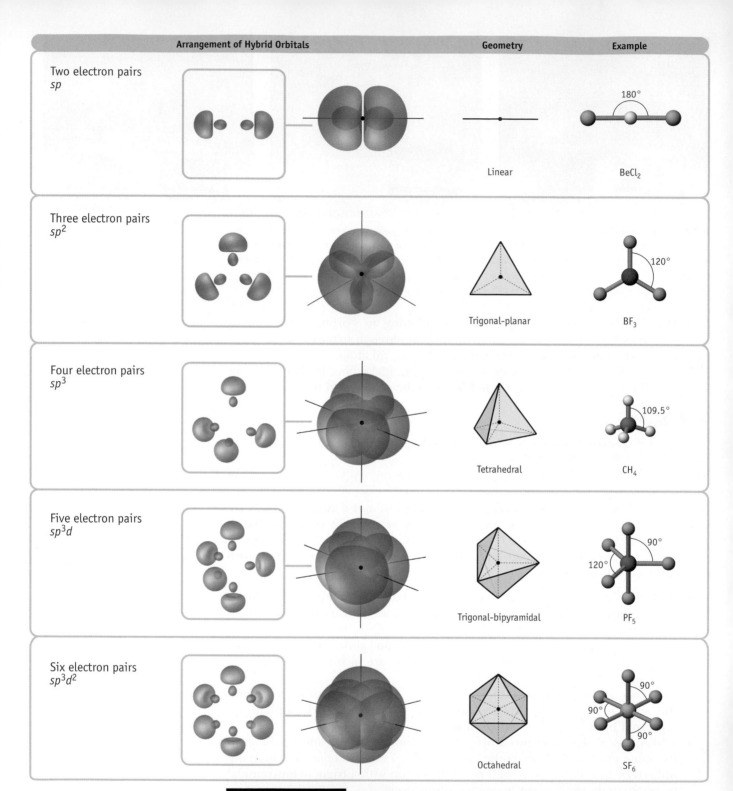

Arrangement of Hybrid Orbitals	Geometry	Example
Two electron pairs *sp*	Linear	$BeCl_2$ 180°
Three electron pairs sp^2	Trigonal-planar	BF_3 120°
Four electron pairs sp^3	Tetrahedral	CH_4 109.5°
Five electron pairs sp^3d	Trigonal-bipyramidal	PF_5 90° 120°
Six electron pairs sp^3d^2	Octahedral	SF_6 90° 90° 90°

Active Figure 9.5 **Hybrid orbitals for two to six electron pairs.** The geometry of the hybrid orbital sets for two to six valence shell electron pairs is given in the right column. In forming a hybrid orbital set, the *s* orbital is always used, plus as many *p* orbitals (and *d* orbitals) as are required to give the necessary number of σ-bonding and lone-pair orbitals.

Chemistry Now™ Sign in at www.cengage.com/login and go to the Chapter Contents menu to explore an interactive version of this figure accompanied by an exercise.

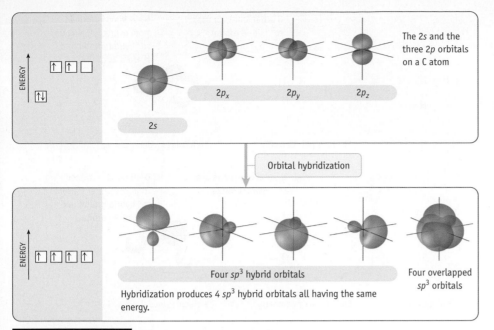

The 2s and the three 2p orbitals on a C atom

2p_x   2p_y   2p_z

2s

Orbital hybridization

Each C—H bond uses one C atom sp^3 hybrid orbital and a H atom 1s orbital

Four sp^3 hybrid orbitals

Four overlapped sp^3 orbitals

Hybridization produces 4 sp^3 hybrid orbitals all having the same energy.

Molecular model, CH_4 Orbital representation

Active Figure 9.6 Bonding in the methane (CH_4) molecule.

Chemistry Now™ Sign in at www.cengage.com/login and go to the Chapter Contents menu to explore an interactive version of this figure accompanied by an exercise.

four hybrid orbitals is created that has tetrahedral geometry (Figures 9.5 and 9.6). Each of the four hybrid orbitals is labeled sp^3 to indicate the atomic orbital combination (an s orbital and three p orbitals) from which they are derived. All four sp^3 orbitals have an identical shape, and the angle between them is 109.5°, the tetrahedral angle. Because the orbitals have the same energy, one electron can be assigned to each according to Hund's rule (see Section 7.3 [page 312]). Then, each C—H bond is formed by overlap of one of the carbon sp^3 hybrid orbitals with the 1s orbital from a hydrogen atom; one electron from the C atom is paired with an electron from an H atom.

■ **Hybrid and Atomic Orbitals** Be sure to notice that *four* atomic orbitals produce *four* hybrid orbitals. The number of hybrid orbitals produced is always the same as the number of atomic orbitals used.

Valence Bond Theory for Ammonia, NH_3

The Lewis structure for ammonia shows there are four electron pairs in the valence shell of nitrogen: three bond pairs and a lone pair (Figure 9.7). VSEPR theory predicts a tetrahedral electron-pair geometry and a trigonal-pyramidal molecular geometry. The actual structure is a close match to the predicted structure; the H—N—H bond angles are 107.5° in this molecule.

Based on the electron-pair geometry of NH_3, we predict sp^3 hybridization to accommodate the four electron pairs on the N atom. The lone pair is assigned to one of the hybrid orbitals, and each of the other three hybrid orbitals is occupied by a single electron. Overlap of each of the singly occupied, sp^3 hybrid orbitals with a 1s orbital from a hydrogen atom, and pairing of the electrons in these orbitals, create the N—H bonds.

Valence Bond Theory for Water, H_2O

The oxygen atom of water has two bonding pairs and two lone pairs in its valence shell, and the H—O—H angle is 104.5° (Figure 9.7). Four sp^3 hybrid orbitals are created from the 2s and 2p atomic orbitals of oxygen. Two of these sp^3 orbitals are

FIGURE 9.7 Bonding in ammonia, NH₃, and water, H₂O.

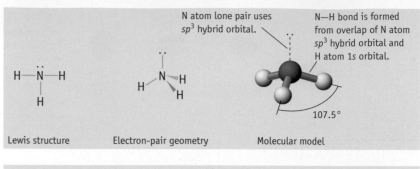

N atom lone pair uses
sp^3 hybrid orbital.

N—H bond is formed
from overlap of N atom
sp^3 hybrid orbital and
H atom 1s orbital.

107.5°

Lewis structure   Electron-pair geometry   Molecular model

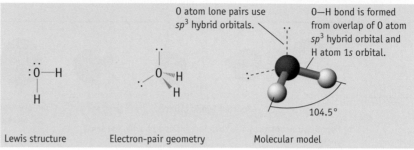

O atom lone pairs use
sp^3 hybrid orbitals.

O—H bond is formed
from overlap of O atom
sp^3 hybrid orbital and
H atom 1s orbital.

104.5°

Lewis structure   Electron-pair geometry   Molecular model

occupied by unpaired electrons and are used to form O—H bonds. Lone pairs occupy the other two hybrid orbitals.

Chemistry ⚛ Now™

Sign in at **www.cengage.com/login** and go to Chapter 9 Contents to see:
• Screen 9.4 for exercises on **hybrid orbitals**
• Screen 9.5 for a tutorial on **sigma bonding**
• Screen 9.6 for a tutorial on **determining hybrid orbitals**

■ **Hybridization and Geometry**
Hybridization reconciles the electron-pair geometry with the orbital overlap criterion of bonding. A statement such as "the atom is tetrahedral because it is sp^3 hybridized" is backward. That the electron-pair geometry around the atom is tetrahedral is a fact. Hybridization is one way to rationalize that fact.

■ **EXAMPLE 9.1 Valence Bond Description of Bonding in Ethane**

Problem Describe the bonding in ethane, C_2H_6, using valence bond theory.

Strategy First, draw the Lewis structure, and predict the electron-pair geometry at both carbon atoms. Next, assign a hybridization to these atoms. Finally, describe covalent bonds that arise based on orbital overlap, and place electron pairs in their proper locations.

Solution Each carbon atom has an octet configuration, sharing electron pairs with three hydrogen atoms and with the other carbon atom. The electron pairs around carbon have tetrahedral geometry, so carbon is assigned sp^3 hybridization. The C—C bond is formed by overlap of sp^3 orbitals on each C atom, and each of the C—H bonds is formed by overlap of an sp^3 orbital on carbon with a hydrogen 1s orbital.

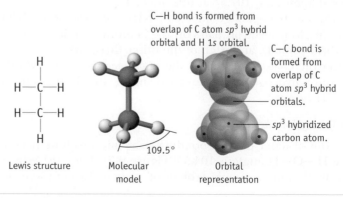

C—H bond is formed from
overlap of C atom sp^3 hybrid
orbital and H 1s orbital.

C—C bond is
formed from
overlap of C
atom sp^3 hybrid
orbitals.

sp^3 hybridized
carbon atom.

109.5°

Lewis structure   Molecular model   Orbital representation

Problem Describe the bonding in the methanol molecule, CH_3OH, using valence bond theory.

Strategy First, construct the Lewis structure for the molecule. The electron pair geometry around each atom determines the hybrid orbital set used by that atom.

Solution The electron-pair geometry around both the C and O atoms in CH_3OH is tetrahedral. Thus, we may assign sp^3 hybridization to each atom, and the C—O bond is formed by overlap of sp^3 orbitals on these atoms. Each C—H bond is formed by overlap of a carbon sp^3 orbital with a hydrogen $1s$ orbital, and the O—H bond is formed by overlap of an oxygen sp^3 orbital with the hydrogen $1s$ orbital. Two lone pairs on oxygen occupy the remaining sp^3 orbitals on the atom.

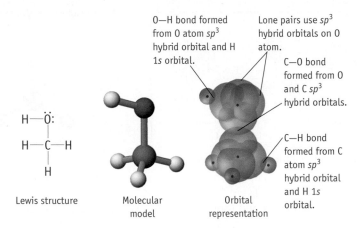

O—H bond formed from O atom sp^3 hybrid orbital and H $1s$ orbital.

Lone pairs use sp^3 hybrid orbitals on O atom.

C—O bond formed from O and C sp^3 hybrid orbitals.

C—H bond formed from C atom sp^3 hybrid orbital and H $1s$ orbital.

Lewis structure   Molecular   Orbital
                          model   representation

Comment Notice that one end of the CH_3OH molecule (the CH_3 or methyl group) is just like the CH_3 group in the methane molecule, and the OH group resembles the OH group in water. It is helpful to recognize pieces of molecules and their bonding descriptions.

This example also shows how to predict the structure and bonding in a complicated molecule by looking at each atom separately. This is an important principle that is essential when dealing with molecules made up of many atoms.

EXERCISE 9.1 Valence Bond Description of Bonding

Use valence bond theory to describe the bonding in the hydronium ion, H_3O^+, and methylamine, CH_3NH_2.

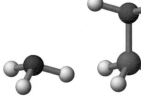

Hydronium ion, H_3O^+ Methylamine, CH_3NH_2

Hybrid Orbitals for Molecules and Ions with Trigonal-Planar Electron Pair Geometries

The central atoms in species such as BF_3, O_3, NO_3^-, and CO_3^{2-} all have a trigonal-planar electron-pair geometry, which requires a central atom with three hybrid orbitals in a plane, 120° apart. Three hybrid orbitals mean three atomic orbitals must be combined, and the combination of an s orbital with two p orbitals is appropriate (Figure 9.8). If p_x and p_y orbitals are used in hybrid orbital formation, the three hybrid sp^2 orbitals will lie in the xy-plane. The p_z orbital not used to form these hybrid orbitals is perpendicular to the plane containing the three sp^2 orbitals (Figure 9.8).

Boron trifluoride has a trigonal-planar electron-pair and molecular geometry. Each boron–fluorine bond in this compound results from overlap of an sp^2 orbital on boron with a p orbital on fluorine. Notice that the p_z orbital on boron, which is not used to form the sp^2 hybrid orbitals, is not occupied by electrons.

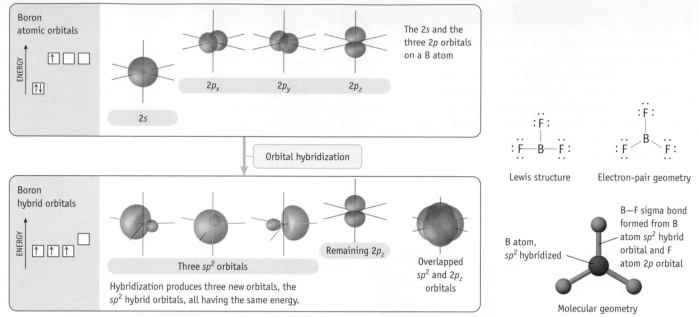

FIGURE 9.8 Bonding in a trigonal-planar molecule.

Hybrid Orbitals for Molecules and Ions with Linear Electron-Pair Geometries

For molecules in which the central atom has a linear electron-pair geometry, two hybrid orbitals, 180° apart, are required. One s and one p orbital can be hybridized to form two sp hybrid orbitals (Figure 9.9). If the p_z orbital is used, then the sp orbitals are oriented along the z-axis. The p_x and p_y orbitals are perpendicular to this axis.

Beryllium dichloride, $BeCl_2$, is a solid under ordinary conditions. When it is heated to over 520 °C, however, it vaporizes to give $BeCl_2$ vapor. In the gas phase, $BeCl_2$ is a linear molecule, so sp hybridization is appropriate for the beryllium atom in this species. Combining beryllium's $2s$ and $2p_z$ orbitals gives the two sp hybrid orbitals that lie along the z-axis. Each Be—Cl bond arises by overlap of an sp hybrid orbital on beryllium with a $3p$ orbital on chlorine. In this molecule, there are only two electron pairs around the beryllium atom, so the p_x and p_y orbitals are not occupied (Figure 9.9).

Hybrid Orbitals for Molecules and Ions with Trigonal-Bipyramidal or Octahedral Electron-Pair Geometries

Bonding in compounds having five or six electron pairs on a central atom (such as PF_5 or SF_6) requires the atom to have five or six hybrid orbitals, which must be created from five or six atomic orbitals. This is possible if additional atomic orbitals from the d subshell are used in hybrid orbital formation. The d orbitals are considered to be valence shell orbitals for main group elements of the third and higher periods.

To accommodate six electron pairs in the valence shell of an element, six sp^3d^2 hybrid orbitals can be created from one s, three p, and two d orbitals. The six sp^3d^2 hybrid orbitals are directed to the corners of an octahedron (Figure 9.5). Thus, they are oriented to accommodate the valence electron pairs for a compound that has an octahedral electron-pair geometry. Five coordination and trigonal-bipyramidal electron-pair geometry are matched to sp^3d hybridization. One s, three p, and one d orbital combine to produce five sp^3d hybrid orbitals.

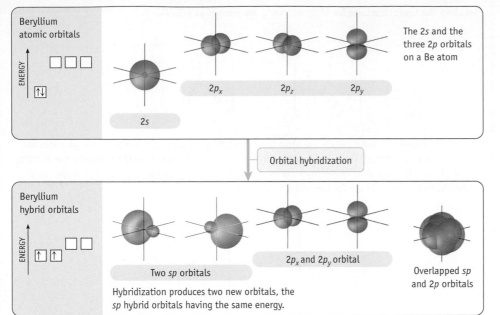

Beryllium atomic orbitals — The 2s and the three 2p orbitals on a Be atom

$2p_x$ $2p_z$ $2p_y$

$2s$

Orbital hybridization

Beryllium hybrid orbitals

Two sp orbitals $2p_x$ and $2p_y$ orbital   Overlapped sp and 2p orbitals

Hybridization produces two new orbitals, the sp hybrid orbitals having the same energy.

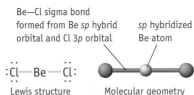

Be—Cl sigma bond formed from Be sp hybrid orbital and Cl 3p orbital

sp hybridized Be atom

Lewis structure   Molecular geometry

FIGURE 9.9 Bonding in a linear molecule. Because only one p orbital is incorporated in the hybrid orbital, two p orbitals remain unhybridized. These orbitals are perpendicular to each other and to the axis along which the two sp hybrid orbital lies.

■ **EXAMPLE 9.3 Hybridization Involving d Orbitals**

Problem Describe the bonding in PF_5 using valence bond theory.

Strategy The first step is to establish the electron-pair and molecular geometry of PF_5. The electron-pair geometry around the P atom gives the number of hybrid orbitals required. If five hybrid orbitals are required, the combination of atomic orbitals is sp^3d.

Solution Here, the P atom is surrounded by five electron pairs, so PF_5 has a trigonal-bipyramidal electron-pair and molecular geometry. The hybridization scheme is therefore sp^3d.

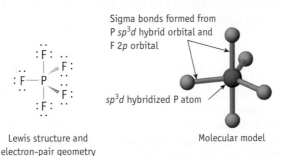

Sigma bonds formed from P sp^3d hybrid orbital and F 2p orbital

sp^3d hybridized P atom

Lewis structure and electron-pair geometry   Molecular model

■ **Do $(n − 1)d$ orbitals participate in bonding?** Because the $(n − 1)d$ orbitals are at a relatively high energy their involvement in bonding is believed to be minimal. Using molecular orbital theory, it is possible to describe the bonding in compounds with expanded octets without using d orbitals to form hybrid orbital sets.

■ **EXAMPLE 9.4 Recognizing Hybridization**

Problem Identify the hybridization of the central atom in the following compounds and ions:

(a) SF_3^+ **(c)** SF_4 **(b)** $SO_4^{2−}$ **(d)** I_3^-

Strategy The hybrid orbitals used by a central atom are determined by the electron-pair geometry (see Figure 9.5). Thus, to answer this question first write the Lewis structure, and then predict the electron-pair geometry.

Solution The Lewis structures for SF_3^+, and SO_4^{2-} are written as follows:

$$\left[\begin{array}{c} \ddot{S}-\ddot{F}: \\ :\ddot{F} \quad \ddot{F}: \end{array}\right]^+ \qquad \left[\begin{array}{c} :\ddot{O}: \\ \ddot{S}-\ddot{O}: \\ :\ddot{O} \quad :\ddot{O}: \end{array}\right]^{2-}$$

Four electron pairs surround the central atom in each of these ions, and the electron-pair geometry for these atoms is tetrahedral. Thus, sp^3 hybridization for the central atom is used to describe the bonding. For SF_4 and I_3^-, five pairs of electrons are in the valence shell of the central atom. For these, sp^3d hybridization is appropriate for the central S or I atom.

$$\begin{array}{c} :\ddot{F}: \\ | \quad \ddot{F}: \\ :-\ddot{S} \ddots \\ | \quad \ddot{F}: \\ :\ddot{F}: \end{array} \qquad \left[\begin{array}{c} :\ddot{I}: \\ | \\ :-\ddot{I} \ddots \\ | \\ :\ddot{I}: \end{array}\right]^-$$

EXERCISE 9.2 Recognizing Hybridization

Identify the hybridization of the underlined central atom in the following compounds and ions:

(a) $\underline{B}H_4^-$ (d) $\underline{Cl}F_3$

(b) $\underline{S}F_5^-$ (e) $\underline{B}Cl_3$

(c) $OS\underline{F}_4$ (f) $\underline{Xe}O_6^{4-}$

■ **Multiple Bonds**

Double bond requires two sets of overlapping orbitals and two pairs of electrons.

C≡C

Triple bond requires three sets of overlapping orbitals and three pairs of electrons.

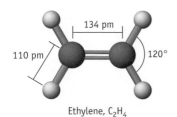

110 pm

134 pm

120°

Ethylene, C_2H_4

Multiple Bonds

According to valence bond theory, bond formation requires that two orbitals on adjacent atoms overlap. Many molecules have two or three bonds between pairs of atoms. Therefore, according to valence bond theory, a double bond requires *two* sets of overlapping orbitals and *two* electron pairs. For a triple bond, *three* sets of atomic orbitals are required, each set accommodating a pair of electrons.

Double Bonds

Consider ethylene, $H_2C{=}CH_2$, a common molecule with a double bond. The molecular structure of ethylene places all six atoms in a plane, with H—C—H and H—C—C angles of approximately 120°. Each carbon atom has trigonal-planar geometry, so sp^2 hybridization is assumed for these atoms. Thus, a description of bonding in ethylene starts with each carbon atom having three sp^2 hybrid orbitals in the molecular plane and an unhybridized p orbital perpendicular to that plane. Because each carbon atom is involved in four bonds, a single unpaired electron is placed in each of these orbitals.

↑   Unhybridized p orbital. Used for π bonding in C_2H_4.

↑↑↑↑   Three sp^2 hybrid orbitals. Used for C—H and C—C σ bonding in C_2H_4.

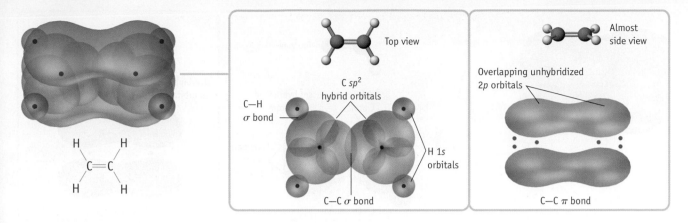

(a) Lewis structure and bonding of ethylene, C_2H_4.

(b) The C—H σ bonds are formed by overlap of C atom sp^2 hybrid orbitals with H atom $1s$ orbitals. The σ bond between C atoms arises from overlap of sp^2 orbitals.

(c) The carbon–carbon π bond is formed by overlap of an unhybridized $2p$ orbital on each atom. Note the lack of electron density along the C—C bond axis from this bond.

Active Figure 9.10 The valence bond model of bonding in ethylene, C_2H_4. Each C atom is assumed to be sp^2 hybridized.

Chemistry ⚬Now™ Sign in at www.cengage.com/login and go to the Chapter Contents menu to explore an interactive version of this figure accompanied by an exercise.

Now we can visualize the C—H bonds, which arise from overlap of sp^2 orbitals on carbon with hydrogen $1s$ orbitals. After accounting for the C—H bonds, one sp^2 orbital on each carbon atom remains. These orbitals point toward each other and overlap to form one of the bonds linking the carbon atoms (Figure 9.10). This leaves only one other orbital unaccounted for on each carbon, an unhybridized p orbital, and it is these orbitals that can be used to create the second bond between carbon atoms in C_2H_4. If they are aligned correctly, the unhybridized p orbitals on the two carbons can overlap, allowing the electrons in these orbitals to be paired. The overlap does not occur directly along the C—C axis, however. Instead, the arrangement compels these orbitals to overlap sideways, and the electron pair occupies an orbital with electron density above and below the plane containing the six atoms.

This description results in two types of bonds in C_2H_4. One type is the C—H and C—C bonds that arise from the overlap of atomic orbitals so that the bonding electrons that lie along the bond axes form sigma (σ) bonds. The other is the bond formed by sideways overlap of p atomic orbitals, called a **pi (π) bond.** In a π bond, the overlap region is above and below the internuclear axis, and the electron density of the π bond is above and below the bond axis.

Be sure to notice that a π bond can form *only* if (a) there are unhybridized p orbitals on adjacent atoms and (b) the p orbitals are perpendicular to the plane of the molecule and parallel to one another. This happens only if the sp^2 orbitals of both carbon atoms are in the same plane. A consequence of this is that both atoms involved in the π bond have trigonal-planar geometry, and the six atoms in and around the π bond (the two atoms involved in the π bond and the four atoms attached to the π-bonded atoms) lie in one plane.

Double bonds between carbon and oxygen, sulfur, or nitrogen are quite common. Consider formaldehyde, CH_2O, in which a carbon–oxygen π bond occurs

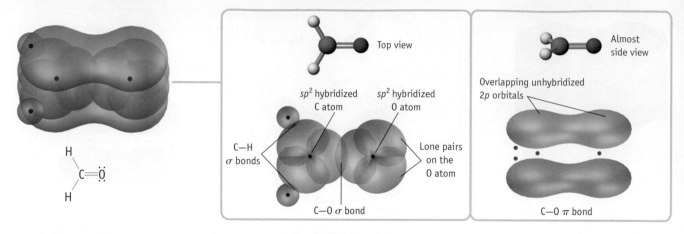

(a) Lewis structure and bonding of formaldehyde, CH_2O.

(b) The C—H σ bonds are formed by overlap of C atom sp^2 hybrid orbitals with H atom $1s$ orbitals. The σ bond between C and O atoms arises from overlap of sp^2 orbitals.

(c) The C—O π bond comes from the side-by-side overlap of p orbitals on the two atoms.

FIGURE 9.11 Valence bond description of bonding in formaldehyde, CH_2O.

■ **Alternative View of the C—O π Bond in CH_2O** An alternative but still satisfactory explanation of the C—O π bond is to assume the O atom is unhybridized and that the π bond is constructed from an unhybridized $2p$ oxygen orbital overlapping with a p orbital on the carbon atom.

(Figure 9.11). A trigonal-planar electron-pair geometry indicates sp^2 hybridization for the C atom. The σ bonds from carbon to the O atom and the two H atoms form by overlap of sp^2 hybrid orbitals with half-filled orbitals from the oxygen and two hydrogen atoms. An unhybridized p orbital on carbon is oriented perpendicular to the molecular plane (just as for the carbon atoms of C_2H_4). This p orbital is available for π bonding, this time with an oxygen orbital.

What orbitals on oxygen are used in this model? The approach in Figure 9.11 assumes sp^2 hybridization for oxygen. This uses one O atom sp^2 orbital in σ bond formation, leaving two sp^2 orbitals to accommodate lone pairs. The remaining p orbital on the O atom participates in the π bond.

Chemistry⚛Now™

Sign in at **www.cengage.com/login** and go to Chapter 9 Contents menu to see Screen 9.7 for exercises and a tutorial on **hybrid orbitals and σ and π bonding.**

■ **EXAMPLE 9.5** **Bonding in Acetic Acid**

Problem Using valence bond theory, describe the bonding in acetic acid, CH_3CO_2H, the important ingredient in vinegar.

Strategy Write a Lewis electron dot structure, and determine the geometry around each atom using VSEPR theory. Use this geometry to decide on the hybrid orbitals used in σ bonding. If unhybridized p orbitals are available on adjacent C and O atoms, then C—O π bonding can occur.

Solution The carbon atom of the CH_3 group has tetrahedral electron-pair geometry, which means it is sp^3 hybridized. Three sp^3 orbitals are used to form the C—H bonds. The fourth sp^3 orbital is used to bond to the adjacent carbon atom. This carbon atom has a trigonal-planar electron-pair geometry; it must be sp^2 hybridized. The C—C bond is formed using one of these hybrid orbitals, and the other two sp^2 orbitals are used to form the σ bonds to the two oxygens. The oxygen of the O—H group has four electron pairs; it must be tetrahedral and sp^3 hybridized. Thus, this O atom uses two sp^3 orbitals to bond to the adjacent carbon and the hydrogen, and two sp^3 orbitals accommodate the two lone pairs.

Finally, the carbon–oxygen double bond can be described by assuming the C and O atoms are both sp^2 hybridized (like the C—O π bond in formaldehyde, Figure 9.11). The unhybridized p orbital remaining on each atom is used to form the carbon–oxygen π bond, and the lone pairs on the O atom are accommodated in sp^2 hybrid orbitals.

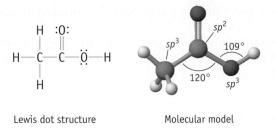

Lewis dot structure   Molecular model

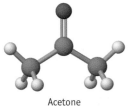

Acetone

EXERCISE 9.3 Bonding in Acetone

Use valence bond theory to describe the bonding in acetone, CH_3COCH_3.

Triple Bonds

Acetylene, H—C≡C—H, is an example of a molecule with a triple bond. VSEPR theory predicts that the four atoms lie in a straight line with H—C—C angles of 180°. This implies that the carbon atom is sp hybridized (Figure 9.12). For each carbon atom, there are two sp orbitals, one directed toward hydrogen and used to create the C—H σ bond, and the second directed toward the other carbon and used to create a σ bond between the two carbon atoms. Two unhybridized p orbitals remain on each carbon, and they are oriented so that it is possible to form *two* π bonds in HC≡CH.

⟦↑│↑⟧ Two unhybridized p orbitals. Used for π bonding in C_2H_2.

⟦↑│↑⟧ Two sp hybrid orbitals. Used for C—H and C—C σ bonding in C_2H_2.

These π bonds are perpendicular to the molecular axis and perpendicular to each other. Three electrons on each carbon atom are paired to form the triple bond consisting of a σ bond and two π bonds (Figure 9.12).

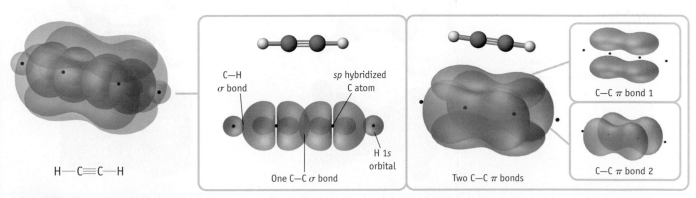

FIGURE 9.12 Bonding in acetylene.

Now that we have examined two cases of multiple bonds, let us summarize several important points:

- In valence bond theory a double bond always consists of a σ bond and a π bond. Similarly, a triple bond always consists of a σ bond and *two* π bonds.
- A π bond may form only if unhybridized p orbitals remain on the bonded atoms.
- If a Lewis structure shows multiple bonds, the atoms involved must therefore be either sp^2 or sp hybridized. Only in this manner will unhybridized p orbitals be available to form a π bond.

EXERCISE 9.4 Triple Bonds Between Atoms

Describe the bonding in a nitrogen molecule, N_2.

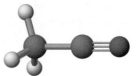

Acetonitrile, CH_3CN

EXERCISE 9.5 Bonding and Hybridization

Estimate values for the H—C—H, H—C—C, and C—C—N angles in acetonitrile, $CH_3C{\equiv}N$. Indicate the hybridization of both carbon atoms and the nitrogen atom, and analyze the bonding using valence bond theory.

Cis-Trans Isomerism: A Consequence of π Bonding

Ethylene, C_2H_4, is a planar molecule, a geometry that allows the unhybridized p orbitals on the two carbon atoms to line up and form a π bond (see Figure 9.13b). Let us speculate on what would happen if one end of the ethylene molecule were twisted relative to the other end. This action would distort the molecule away from planarity, and the p orbitals would rotate out of alignment. Rotation would diminish the extent of overlap of these orbitals, and, if a twist of 90° were achieved, the two p orbitals would no longer overlap at all; the π bond would be broken. However, so much energy is required to break this bond (about 260 kJ/mol) that rotation around a C=C bond is not expected to occur at room temperature.

Active Figure 9.13 Rotation around bonds.

Chemistry Now™ Sign in at www.cengage.com/login and go to the Chapter Contents menu to explore an interactive version of this figure accompanied by an exercise.

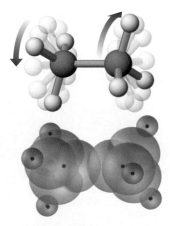

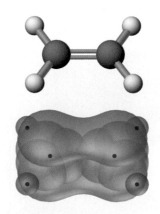

(a) In ethane nearly free rotation can occur around the axis of a single (σ) bond.

(b) Ethylene rotation is severely restricted around double bonds because doing so would break the π bond, a process generally requiring a great deal of energy.

A consequence of restricted rotation is that isomers occur for many compounds containing a C=C bond. **Isomers** are compounds that have the same formula but different structures. In this case, the two isomeric compounds differ with respect to the orientation of the groups attached to the carbons of the double bond. Two isomers of $C_2H_2Cl_2$ are *cis-* and *trans*-1,2-dichloroethylene. Their structures resemble ethylene, except that two hydrogen atoms have been replaced by chlorine atoms. Because a large amount of energy is required to break the π bond, the *cis* compound cannot rearrange to the *trans* compound under ordinary conditions. Each compound can be obtained separately, and each has its own identity. *Cis*-1,2-dichloroethylene boils at 60.3 °C, whereas *trans*-1,2-dichloroethylene boils at 47.5 °C.

cis-1,2-dichloroethylene

trans-1,2-dichloroethylene

■ *Cis* and *Trans* **Isomers** Compounds having the same formula, but different structures, are isomers. *Trans* isomers have distinguishing groups on opposite sides of a double bond. *Cis* isomers have these groups on the same side of the double bond.

Although *cis* and *trans* isomers do not interconvert at ordinary temperatures, they will do so at higher temperatures. If the temperature is sufficiently high, the molecular motions can become sufficiently energetic that rotation around the C=C bond can occur. This may also occur under other special conditions, such as when the molecule absorbs light energy.

Chemistry.◌.Now™

Sign in at **www.cengage.com/login** and go to Chapter 9 Contents to see Screen 9.8 for an exercise on **isomers and multiple bonds.**

Benzene: A Special Case of π Bonding

Benzene, C_6H_6, is the simplest member of a large group of substances known as *aromatic* compounds, a historical reference to their odor. It occupies a pivotal place in the history and practice of chemistry.

To 19th-century chemists, benzene was a perplexing substance with an unknown structure. Based on its chemical reactions, however, August Kekulé (1829–1896) suggested that the molecule has a planar, symmetrical ring structure. We know now he was correct. The ring is flat, and all the carbon–carbon bonds are the same length, 139 pm, a distance intermediate between the average single bond (154 pm) and double bond (134 pm) lengths. Assuming the molecule has two resonance structures with alternating double bonds, the observed structure is rationalized. The C—C bond order in C_6H_6(1.5) is the average of a single and a double bond.

resonance structures   or   resonance hybrid

Benzene, C_6H_6

FIGURE 9.14 Bonding in benzene, C_6H_6. (left) The C atoms of the ring are bonded to each other through σ bonds using C atom sp^2 hybrid orbitals. The C—H bonds also use C atom sp^2 hybrid orbitals. The π framework of the molecule arises from overlap of C atom p orbitals not used in hybrid orbital formation. Because these orbitals are perpendicular to the ring, π electron density is above and below the plane of the ring. (right) A composite of σ and π bonding in benzene.

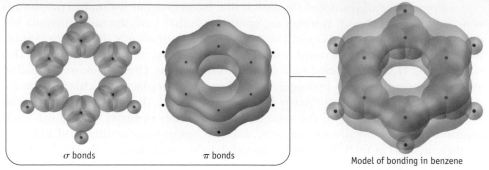

σ bonds π bonds   Model of bonding in benzene

σ and π bonding in benzene

Understanding the bonding in benzene (Figure 9.14) is important because the benzene ring structure occurs in an enormous number of chemical compounds. We assume that the trigonal-planar carbon atoms have sp^2 hybridization. Each C—H bond is formed by overlap of an sp^2 orbital of a carbon atom with a $1s$ orbital of hydrogen, and the C—C σ bonds arise by overlap of sp^2 orbitals on adjacent carbon atoms. After accounting for the σ bonding, an unhybridized p orbital remains on each C atom, and each is occupied by a single electron. These six orbitals and six electrons form π bonds. Because all carbon–carbon bond lengths are the same, each p orbital overlaps equally well with the p orbitals of both adjacent carbons, and the π interaction is unbroken around the six-member ring.

9.3 Molecular Orbital Theory

Molecular orbital (MO) theory is an alternative way to view orbitals in molecules. In contrast to the localized bond and lone pair electrons of valence bond theory, MO theory assumes that pure s and p atomic orbitals of the atoms in the molecule combine to produce orbitals that are spread out, or delocalized, over several atoms or even over an entire molecule. These orbitals are called **molecular orbitals.**

One reason for learning about the MO concept is that it correctly predicts the electronic structures of molecules such as O_2 that do not follow the electron-pairing assumptions of the Lewis approach. The rules of Section 8.2 would guide you to draw the electron dot structure of O_2 with all the electrons paired, which fails to explain its paramagnetism (Figure 9.15). The molecular orbital approach can account for this property, but valence bond theory cannot. To see how MO theory can be used to describe the bonding in O_2 and other diatomic molecules, we shall first describe four principles used to develop the theory.

Principles of Molecular Orbital Theory

In MO theory, we begin with a given arrangement of atoms in the molecule at the known bond distances. We then determine the *sets* of molecular orbitals. One way to do this is to combine available valence orbitals on all the constituent atoms. These molecular orbitals more or less encompass all the atoms of the molecule, and the valence electrons for all the atoms in the molecule are assigned to the molecular orbitals. Just as with orbitals in atoms, electrons are assigned in order of increasing orbital energy and according to the Pauli principle and Hund's rule (see Sections 7.1 and 7.3).

The **first principle of molecular orbital theory** is that *the total number of molecular orbitals is always equal to the total number of atomic orbitals contributed by the atoms that*

(a) Making liquid O_2

(b) Liquid O_2 is a light blue color.

Charles D. Winters

(c) Paramagnetic liquid O_2 clings to a magnet.

(d) Diamagnetic liquid N_2 is not attracted to a magnet.

FIGURE 9.15 The paramagnetism of liquid oxygen. Oxygen gas condenses (a) to a pale blue liquid at $-183\ ^\circ$C (b). Because O_2 molecules have two unpaired electrons, oxygen in the liquid state is paramagnetic and clings a relatively strong neodymium magnet (c). In contrast, liquid N_2 is diamagnetic and does not stick to the magnet (d). It just splashes on the surface when poured onto the magnet.

have combined. To illustrate this orbital conservation principle, let us consider the H_2 molecule.

Molecular Orbitals for H_2

Molecular orbital theory specifies that when the $1s$ orbitals of two hydrogen atoms overlap, *two* molecular orbitals result. One molecular orbital results from *addition* of the $1s$ atomic orbital wave functions, leading to an increased probability that electrons will reside in the bond region between the two nuclei (Figure 9.16). This is called a **bonding molecular orbital.** It is also a σ orbital because the region of electron probability lies directly along the bond axis. This molecular orbital is labeled σ_{1s}, the subscript $1s$ indicating that $1s$ atomic orbitals were used to create the molecular orbital.

The other molecular orbital is constructed by *subtracting* one atomic orbital wave function from the other (see Figure 9.16). When this happens, the probability of finding an electron between the nuclei in the molecular orbital is reduced, and the probability of finding the electron in other regions is higher. Without significant electron density between them, the nuclei repel one another. This type of orbital is called an **antibonding molecular orbital.** Because it is also a σ orbital, it is labeled σ^*_{1s}. The asterisk signifies that it is antibonding. *Antibonding orbitals have no counterpart in valence bond theory.*

A **second principle of molecular orbital theory** is that *the bonding molecular orbital is lower in energy than the parent orbitals, and the antibonding orbital is higher in energy* (Figure 9.16). This means that the energy of a group of atoms is lower than the energy of the separated atoms when electrons are assigned to bonding molecular orbitals. Chemists say the system is "stabilized" by chemical bond formation.

■ **Orbitals and Electron Waves** Orbitals are characterized as electron waves; therefore, a way to view molecular orbital formation is to assume that two electron waves, one from each atom, interfere with each other. The interference can be constructive, giving a bonding MO, or destructive, giving an antibonding MO.

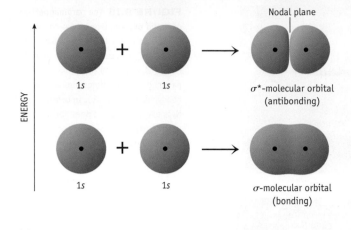

(a)

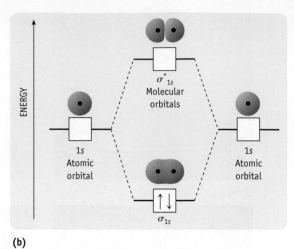

(b)

FIGURE 9.16 Molecular orbitals. (a) Bonding and antibonding σ molecular orbitals are formed from two $1s$ atomic orbitals on adjacent atoms. Notice the presence of a node in the antibonding orbital. (The node is a plane on which there is zero probability of finding an electron.) (b) A molecular orbital diagram for H_2. The two electrons are placed in the σ_{1s} orbital, the molecular orbital lower in energy.

Sign in at **www.cengage.com/login** and go to Chapter 9 Contents to see Screen 9.11 for an animated version of this figure.

Conversely, the system is "destabilized" when electrons are assigned to antibonding orbitals because the energy of the system is higher than that of the atoms themselves.

A **third principle of molecular orbital theory** is that the *electrons of the molecule are assigned to orbitals of successively higher energy* according to the Pauli exclusion principle and Hund's rule. This is analogous to the procedure for building up electronic structures of atoms. Thus, electrons occupy the lowest energy orbitals available, and when two electrons are assigned to an orbital, their spins must be paired. Because the energy of the electrons in the bonding orbital of H_2 is lower than that of either parent $1s$ electron (see Figure 9.16b), the H_2 molecule is more stable than two separate H atoms. We write the electron configuration of H_2 as $(\sigma_{1s})^2$.

What would happen if we tried to combine two helium atoms to form dihelium, He_2? Both He atoms have a $1s$ valence orbital that can produce the same kind of molecular orbitals as in H_2. Unlike H_2, however, four electrons need to be assigned to these orbitals (Figure 9.17). The pair of electrons in the σ_{1s} orbital stabilizes He_2. The two electrons in σ^*_{1s}, however, destabilize the He_2 molecule. The energy decrease from the electrons in the σ_{1s}-bonding molecular orbital is offset by the energy increase due to the electrons in the σ^*_{1s}-antibonding molecular orbital. Thus, molecular orbital theory predicts that He_2 has no net stability; two He atoms have no tendency to combine. This confirms what we already know, that elemental helium exists in the form of single atoms and not as a diatomic molecule.

Bond Order

Bond order was defined in Section 8.9 as the net number of bonding electron pairs linking a pair of atoms. This same concept can be applied directly to molecular orbital theory, but now bond order is defined as

Bond order = 1/2 (number of electrons in bonding MOs −
number of electrons in antibonding MOs)   (9.1)

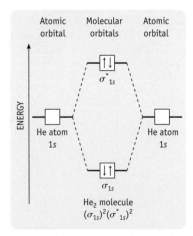

FIGURE 9.17 A molecular orbital energy level diagram for the dihelium molecule, He₂. This diagram provides a rationalization for the nonexistence of the molecule. In He₂, both the bonding (σ_{1s}) and antibonding orbitals (σ^*_{1s}) would be fully occupied.

In the H_2 molecule, there are two electrons in a bonding orbital and none in an antibonding orbital, so H_2 has a bond order of 1. In contrast, in He_2 the stabilizing effect of the σ_{1s} pair is canceled by the destabilizing effect of the σ^*_{1s} pair, and so the bond order is 0.

Fractional bond orders are possible. Consider the ion He_2^+. Its molecular orbital electron configuration is $(\sigma_{1s})^2(\sigma^*_{1s})^1$. In this ion, there are two electrons in a bonding molecular orbital, but only one in an antibonding orbital. MO theory predicts that He_2^+ should have a bond order of 0.5; that is, a weak bond should exist between helium atoms in such a species. Interestingly, this ion has been identified in the gas phase using special experimental techniques.

Chemistry.:. Now™

Sign in at **www.cengage.com/login** and go to Chapter 9 Contents to see:
- Screen 9.9 for exercises on **molecular orbital theory**
- Screen 9.10 for a description of **molecular electron configurations**

■ **EXAMPLE 9.6 Molecular Orbitals and Bond Order**

Problem Write the electron configuration of the H_2^- ion in molecular orbital terms. What is the bond order of the ion?

Strategy Count the number of valence electrons in the ion, and then place those electrons in the MO diagram for the H_2 molecule. Find the bond order from Equation 9.1.

Solution This ion has three electrons (one each from the H atoms plus one for the negative charge). Therefore, its electronic configuration is $(\sigma_{1s})^2(\sigma^*_{1s})^1$, identical with the configuration for He_2^+. This means H_2^- also has a net bond order of 0.5. The H_2^- ion is thus predicted to exist under special circumstances.

EXERCISE 9.6 Molecular Orbitals and Bond Order

What is the electron configuration of the H_2^+ ion? Compare the bond order of this ion with He_2^+ and H_2^-. Do you expect H_2^+ to exist?

Molecular Orbitals of Li_2 and Be_2

A **fourth principle of molecular orbital theory** is that *atomic orbitals combine to form molecular orbitals most effectively when the atomic orbitals are of similar energy.* This principle becomes important when we move past He_2 to Li_2, dilithium, and heavier molecules such as O_2 and N_2.

A lithium atom has electrons in two orbitals of the *s* type (1*s* and 2*s*), so a $1s \pm 2s$ combination is theoretically possible. Because the 1*s* and 2*s* orbitals are quite different in energy, however, this interaction can be disregarded. Thus, the molecular orbitals come only from $1s \pm 1s$ and $2s \pm 2s$ combinations (Figure 9.18). This means the molecular orbital electron configuration of dilithium, Li_2, is

Li_2 MO Configuration: $(\sigma_{1s})^2(\sigma^*_{1s})^2(\sigma_{2s})^2$

The bonding effect of the σ_{1s} electrons is canceled by the antibonding effect of the σ^*_{1s} electrons, so these pairs make no net contribution to bonding in Li_2. Bonding in Li_2 is due to the electron pair assigned to the σ_{2s} orbital, and the bond order is 1.

The fact that the σ_{1s} and σ^*_{1s} electron pairs of Li_2 make no net contribution to bonding is exactly what you observed in drawing electron dot structures in

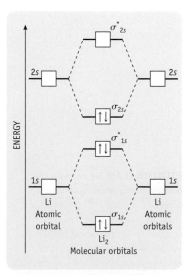

FIGURE 9.18 Energy level diagram for the combination of two Li atoms with 1*s* and 2*s* atomic orbitals. Notice that the molecular orbitals are created by combining orbitals of similar energies. The electron configuration is shown for Li_2.

Section 8.2: *core electrons are ignored*. In molecular orbital terms, core electrons are assigned to bonding and antibonding molecular orbitals that offset one another.

A diberyllium molecule, Be_2, is not expected to exist. Its electron configuration is

$$Be_2 \text{ MO Configuration:} \qquad [\text{core electrons}](\sigma_{2s})^2(\sigma^*_{2s})^2$$

The effects of σ_{2s} and σ^*_{2s} electrons cancel, and there is no net bonding. The bond order is 0, so the molecule does not exist.

■ **EXAMPLE 9.7 Molecular Orbitals in Diatomic Molecules**

Problem Be_2 does not exist. But what about the Be_2^+ ion? Describe its electron configuration in molecular orbital terms, and give the net bond order. Do you expect the ion to exist?

Strategy Count the number of electrons in the ion, and place them in the MO diagram in Figure 9.18. Write the electron configuration, and calculate the bond order from Equation 9.1.

Solution The Be_2^+ ion has only seven electrons (in contrast to eight for Be_2), of which four are core electrons. (The core electrons are assigned to σ_{1s} and σ^*_{1s} molecular orbitals.) The remaining three electrons are assigned to the σ_{2s} and σ^*_{2s} molecular orbitals, so the MO electron configuration is [core electrons]$(\sigma_{2s})^2(\sigma^*_{2s})^1$. This means the net bond order is 0.5, and so Be_2^+ is predicted to exist under special circumstances.

EXERCISE 9.7 Molecular Orbitals in Diatomic Molecules

Could the anion Li_2^- exist? What is the ion's bond order?

Molecular Orbitals from Atomic *p* Orbitals

■ **Diatomic Molecules** Molecules such as H_2, Li_2, and N_2, in which two identical atoms are bonded, are examples of *homonuclear* diatomic molecules.

With the principles of molecular orbital theory in place, we are ready to account for bonding in such important homonuclear diatomic molecules as N_2, O_2, and F_2. To describe the bonding in these molecules, we will have to use both *s* and *p* valence orbitals in forming molecular orbitals.

For *p*-block elements, sigma-bonding and antibonding molecular orbitals are formed by their *s* orbitals interacting as in Figure 9.16. Similarly, it is possible for a *p* orbital on one atom to interact with a *p* orbital on the other atom to produce a pair of σ-bonding and σ*-antibonding molecular orbitals (Figure 9.19).

In addition, each *p*-block atom has *two p* orbitals in planes perpendicular to the σ bond connecting the two atoms. These *p* orbitals can interact sideways to give π-bonding and π-antibonding molecular orbitals (Figure 9.20). Combining these

FIGURE 9.19 Sigma molecular orbitals from *p* atomic orbitals. Sigma-bonding (σ_{2p}) and antibonding (σ^*_{2p}) molecular orbitals arise from overlap of 2*p* orbitals. Each orbital can accommodate two electrons. The *p* orbitals in electron shells of higher *n* give molecular orbitals of the same basic shape.

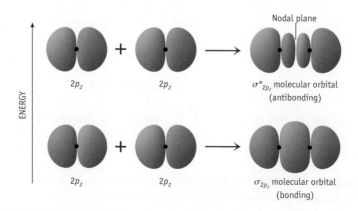

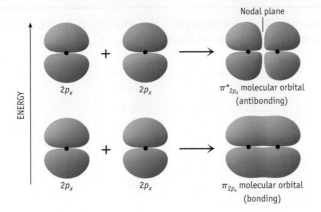

two p orbitals on each atom produces *two* π-bonding molecular orbitals (π_p) and *two* π-antibonding molecular orbitals (π^*_p).

Electron Configurations for Homonuclear Molecules for Boron Through Fluorine

Orbital interactions in a second-period, homonuclear, diatomic molecule lead to the energy level diagram in Figure 9.21. Electron assignments can be made using this diagram, and the results for the diatomic molecules B_2 through F_2 are assembled in Table 9.1, which has two noteworthy features.

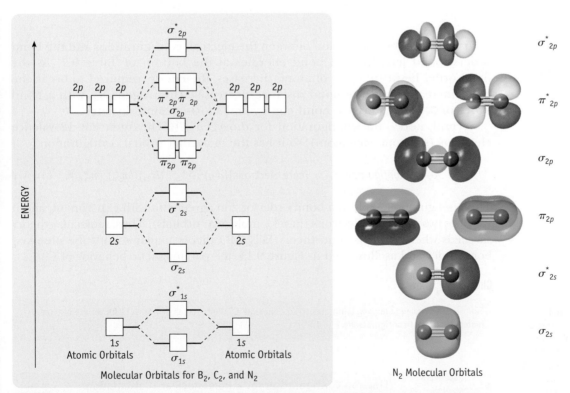

FIGURE 9.21 Molecular orbitals for homonuclear diatomic molecules of second period elements. (left) Energy level diagram. Although the diagram leads to the correct conclusions regarding bond order and magnetic behavior for O_2 and F_2, the energy ordering of the MOs in this figure is correct only for B_2, C_2, and N_2. For O_2 and F_2, the σ_{2p} MO is lower in energy than the π_{2p} MOs. See *A Closer Look,* page 429. (right) Calculated molecular orbitals for N_2. (Color scheme: occupied MOs are blue/green. Unoccupied MOs are red/yellow. The different colors reflect the different phases [positive or negative signs] of the wave functions.)

TABLE 9.1 Molecular Orbital Occupations and Physical Data for Homonuclear Diatomic Molecules of Second-Period Elements

	B_2	C_2	N_2		O_2	F_2
σ^*_{2p}	☐	☐	☐	σ^*_{2p}	☐	☐
π^*_{2p}	☐ ☐	☐ ☐	☐ ☐	π^*_{2p}	↑ ↑	↑↓ ↑↓
σ_{2p}	☐	☐	↑↓	π_{2p}	↑↓ ↑↓	↑↓ ↑↓
π_{2p}	↑ ↑	↑↓ ↑↓	↑↓ ↑↓	σ_{2p}	↑↓	↑↓
σ^*_{2s}	↑↓	↑↓	↑↓	σ^*_{2s}	↑↓	↑↓
σ_{2s}	↑↓	↑↓	↑↓	σ_{2s}	↑↓	↑↓
Bond order	One	Two	Three		Two	One
Bond-dissociation energy (kJ/mol)	290	620	945		498	155
Bond distance (pm)	159	131	110		121	143
Observed magnetic behavior (paramagnetic or diamagnetic)	Para	Dia	Dia		Para	Dia

■ **Highest Occupied Molecular Orbital (HOMO)** Chemists often refer to the highest energy MO that contains electrons as the HOMO. For O_2, this is the π^*_{2p} orbital. Chemists also use the term LUMO for the lowest unoccupied molecular orbital. For O_2, this would be σ^*_{2p}.

First, notice the correlation between the electron configurations and the bond orders, bond lengths, and bond energies at the bottom of Table 9.1. As the bond order between a pair of atoms increases, the energy required to break the bond increases, and the bond distance decreases. Dinitrogen, N_2, with a bond order of 3, has the largest bond energy and shortest bond distance.

Second, notice the configuration for dioxygen, O_2. Dioxygen has 12 valence electrons (six from each atom), so it has the molecular orbital configuration

O_2 MO Configuration: $[\text{core electrons}](\sigma_{2s})^2(\sigma^*_{2s})^2(\sigma_{2p})^2(\pi_{2p})^4(\pi^*_{2p})^2$

This configuration leads to a bond order of 2 in agreement with experiment, and it specifies two unpaired electrons (in π^*_{2p} molecular orbitals). Thus, molecular theory succeeds where valence bond theory fails. MO theory explains both the observed bond order and as illustrated in Figure 9.15, the paramagnetic behavior of O_2.

Chemistry⚛Now™

Sign in at **www.cengage.com/login** and go to Chapter 9 Contents to see Screen 9.11 for an exercise on **molecular orbital configurations.**

■ **Phases of Atomic Orbitals and Molecular Orbitals** Recall from page 289 in Chapter 6 that electron orbitals are electron waves and as such have positive and negative phases. For this reason, the atomic orbitals in Figures 9.19–9.21 are drawn with two different colors. Looking at the p orbitals in Figure 9.19, you see that a bonding MO is formed when p orbitals with the same wave function sign overlap (+ with +). An antibonding orbital arises if they overlap out of phase (+ with −).

■ **EXAMPLE 9.8 Electron Configuration for a Homonuclear Diatomic Ion**

Problem When potassium reacts with O_2, potassium superoxide, KO_2, is one of the products. This is an ionic compound, and the anion is the superoxide ion, O_2^-. Write the molecular orbital electron configuration for the ion. Predict its bond order and magnetic behavior.

Strategy Use the energy level diagram for O_2 in Table 9.1 to generate the electron configuration of this ion, and use Equation 9.1 to determine the bond order.

Several features of the molecular orbital energy level diagram in Figure 9.21 should be described in more detail.

(a) The bonding and antibonding σ orbitals from 2s interactions are lower in energy than the σ and π MOs from 2p interactions. The reason is that 2s orbitals have a lower energy than 2p orbitals in the separated atoms.

(b) The energy separation of the bonding and antibonding orbitals is greater for σ_{2p} than for π_{2p}. This happens because

p orbitals overlap to a greater extent when they are oriented head to head (to give σ_{2p} MOs) than when they are side by side (to give π_{2p} MOs). The greater the orbital overlap, the greater the stabilization of the bonding MO and the greater the destabilization of the antibonding MO. Figure 9.21 shows an energy ordering of molecular orbitals that you might not have expected, but there are reasons for this. A more sophisticated approach takes into

account the "mixing" of s and p atomic orbitals, which have similar energies. This causes the σ_{2s} and σ^{*}_{2s} molecular orbitals to be lower in energy than otherwise expected, and the σ_{2p} and σ^{*}_{2p} orbitals to be higher in energy.

The mixing of s and p orbitals is important for B_2, C_2, and N_2, so Figure 9.21 applies strictly only to these molecules. For O_2 and F_2, σ_{2p} is lower in energy than π_{2p}, and Table 9.1 takes this into account.

Solution The MO electron configuration for O_2^- is

O_2^- MO Configuration: [core electrons]$(\sigma_{2s})^2(\sigma^{*}_{2s})^2(\sigma_{2p})^2(\pi_{2p})^4(\pi^{*}_{2p})^3$

The ion is predicted to be paramagnetic to the extent of one unpaired electron, a prediction confirmed by experiment. The bond order is 1.5, because there are eight bonding electrons and five antibonding electrons. The bond order for O_2^- is lower than O_2 so we predict the O—O bond length in O_2^- should be longer than the oxygen–oxygen bond length in O_2. The superoxide ion in fact has an O—O bond length of 134 pm, whereas the bond length in O_2 is 121 pm.

Comment You should quickly spot the fact that the superoxide ion (O_2^-), contains an odd number of electrons. This is another diatomic species (in addition to NO and O_2) for which it is not possible to write a Lewis structure that accurately represents the bonding.

EXERCISE 9.8 Molecular Electron Configurations

The cations O_2^+ and N_2^+ are important components of Earth's upper atmosphere. Write the electron configuration of O_2^+. Predict its bond order and magnetic behavior.

Electron Configurations for Heteronuclear Diatomic Molecules

The compounds NO, CO, and ClF, molecules containing two different elements, are examples of **heteronuclear diatomic molecules.** MO descriptions for heteronuclear diatomic molecules generally resemble those for homonuclear diatomic molecules. As a consequence, an energy level diagram like Figure 9.21 can be used to judge the bond order and magnetic behavior for heteronuclear diatomics.

Let us do this for nitrogen monoxide, NO. Nitrogen monoxide has 11 valence electrons. If these are assigned to the MOs for a homonuclear diatomic molecule, the molecular electron configuration is

NO MO Configuration: [core electrons]$(\sigma_{2s})^2(\sigma^{*}_{2s})^2(\pi_{2p})^4(\sigma_{2p})^2(\pi^{*}_{2p})^1$

The net bond order is 2.5, in accord with bond length information. The single, unpaired electron is assigned to the π^{*}_{2p} molecular orbital, and the molecule is paramagnetic, as predicted for a molecule with an odd number of electrons.

Nature is based on millions of chemical compounds, and chemists have created thousands more in the laboratory. In general, we understand their structures and bonding reasonably well, but from time to time nature gives us wonderful mysteries to solve.

Some of the mysteries are about the simplest molecules. One is B_2H_6, diborane, the simplest member of a large class of compounds. When it was discovered in the 1930s, chemists thought it must look like ethane, $H_3C–CH_3$. However, by the 1940s it was known that its structure had B—H—B bridges.

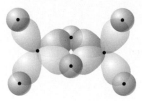

| (a) | (b) |

There are two mysteries. If each line in the structure represents a two-electron bond, you realize the molecule is "electron-deficient"; two B atoms and six H atoms do not contribute enough electrons for eight two-electron bonds. Also, notice that hydrogen is bonded to two different atoms, something we don't expect to happen because H has only one valence electron. One way to approach this problem is to begin by assuming each B atom is sp^3 hybridized. The four outside or terminal H atoms are then bonded to the B atoms by normal, two-electron bonds using two of the sp^3 hybrid orbitals on each B atom. The remaining two sp^3 hybrid orbitals on each B atom point into the bridging region where H atom 1s orbitals overlap with sp^3 orbitals from two different B atoms. Two electrons are assigned to each set of the bridging B—H—B groups, so the bridging bonds are two-electron/three-center bonds.

One can also apply molecular orbital theory to the molecule, and the bonding picture that emerges likewise has stable B—H—B bridges. The lowest energy molecular orbital, shown here, shows that electron density is spread over the B_2H_2 portion of the molecule.

The molecular orbital that accounts for B—H—B bridge bonding.

It turns out that hydrogen bridges are also found in many other boron compounds and in other kinds of molecules. William Lipscomb

received the Nobel Prize in Chemistry in 1976 for "his studies of boranes which have illuminated problems with chemical bonding."

Another bonding mystery involves Zeise's salt, a compound first discovered in the 1820s. However, it was not until the 1950s that three chemists (M. Dewar, J. Chatt, and Duncanson) devised a reasonable bonding model. The salt is based on the anion $[(C_2H_4)PtCl_3]^-$. The most interesting aspect of this ion is that the ethylene molecule, C_2H_4, is bonded sideways to the Pt^{2+} ion. How can this occur? As illustrated in the figure below, the π–bonding electrons of ethylene are donated to Pt^{2+} through overlap of the filled π orbital for C_2H_4 with an empty Pt^{2+} orbital. To account for the stability of the ion, however, there is another important aspect: a filled d-orbital on the Pt^{2+} ion donates electron density to the empty π-antibonding LUMO on the ethylene.

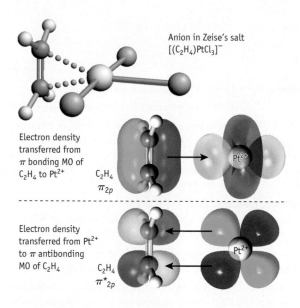

Anion in Zeise's salt
$[(C_2H_4)PtCl_3]^-$

Electron density transferred from π bonding MO of C_2H_4 to Pt^{2+} C_2H_4 π_{2p} Pt^{2+}

Electron density transferred from Pt^{2+} to π antibonding MO of C_2H_4 C_2H_4 π^*_{2p} Pt^{2+}

An understanding of bonding in Zeise's salt was a seminal event in chemistry because the ion is the model for the binding of other molecules like ethylene to transition metal centers.

Questions:

1. *If you treat each line in the B_2H_6 structure above as a two-electron bond, how many electrons are required for bonding in the molecule? How many electrons are actually available?*
2. *Diborane reacts with molecules such as NH_3 to give, for example, $H_3B–NH_3$. Draw a Lewis structure for this compound, estimate bond angles, and indicate the B and N hybridization. Is the molecule polar? What are the formal charges on the atoms?*
3. *Silver(I) ion is known to bond to ethylene, forming an ion of the formula $[Ag(C_2H_4)_x]^+$. When heated, the reaction $[Ag(C_2H_4)_x]BF_4(s) \rightarrow AgBF_4(s) + x\ C_2H_4(g)$ occurs. If 62.1 mg of the silver(I) complex is heated, 54.3 mg of $AgBF_4$ remains. What is the value of x?*

Answers to these questions are in Appendix Q.

Resonance and MO Theory

Ozone, O_3, is a simple triatomic molecule with equal oxygen–oxygen bond lengths. Equal X—O bond lengths are also observed in other molecules and ions, such as SO_2, NO_2^-, and HCO_2^-. Valence bond theory introduced resonance to rationalize the equivalent bonding to the oxygen atoms in these structures, but MO theory provides another view of this problem.

To understand the bonding in ozone, we begin by looking at the valence bond picture. Let us assume that all three O atoms are sp^2 hybridized. The central atom uses its sp^2 hybrid orbitals to form two σ bonds and to accommodate a lone pair. The terminal atoms use their sp^2 hybrid orbitals to form one σ bond and to accommodate two lone pairs. In total, the lone pairs and bonding pairs in the σ framework of O_3 account for seven of the nine valence electron pairs in O_3.

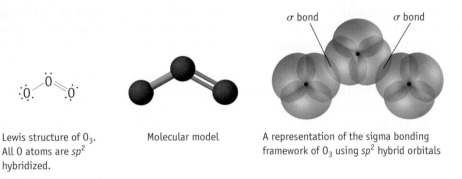

Lewis structure of O_3. All O atoms are sp^2 hybridized.

Molecular model

A representation of the sigma bonding framework of O_3 using sp^2 hybrid orbitals

The π bond in ozone arises from the two remaining pairs (Figure 9.22). Because we have assumed that each oxygen atom in O_3 is sp^2 hybridized, an unhybridized p orbital perpendicular to the O_3 plane remains on each of the three oxygen atoms. The orbitals are in the correct orientation to form π bonds.

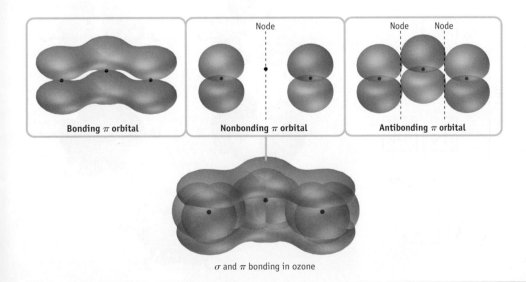

σ and π bonding in ozone

FIGURE 9.22 Pi-bonding in ozone, O_3. Each O atom in O_3 is sp^2 hybridized. The three $2p$ orbitals, one on each atom, are used to create the three π molecular orbitals. Two pairs of electrons are assigned to the orbitals: one pair in the bonding orbital and one pair in the nonbonding orbital. The π bond order is 0.5, as one bonding pair is spread across two bonds.

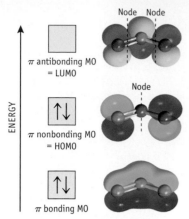

FIGURE 9.23. The π molecular diagram for ozone. Notice that, as in the other MO diagrams illustrated (especially Figure 9.21), the energy of the molecular orbitals increases as the number of nodes increases.

Now let's apply MO theory to the pi bonds. A principle of MO theory is that the number of molecular orbitals must equal the number of atomic orbitals. Thus, the three $2p$ atomic orbitals must be combined in a way that forms three molecular orbitals.

One π_p MO for ozone is a bonding orbital because the three p orbitals are "in phase" across the molecule. Another π_p MO is an antibonding orbital because the atomic orbital on the central atom that is "out of phase" with the terminal atom p orbitals. The third π_p MO is a nonbonding orbital because the middle p orbital does not participate in the MO. The bonding π_p MO is filled by a pair of electrons that is delocalized, or "spread over," the molecule, just as the resonance hybrid implies. The nonbonding orbital is also occupied, but the electrons in this orbital are concentrated near the two terminal oxygens. As the name implies, electrons in this molecular orbital neither help nor hinder the bonding in the molecule. The π bond order of O_3 is 0.5 (Figure 9.23). Because the σ bond order is 1.0 and the π bond order is 0.5, the net oxygen–oxygen bond order is 1.5—the same value given by valence bond theory.

The observation that two of the π molecular orbitals for ozone extend over three atoms illustrates an important point regarding molecular orbital theory: *Orbitals can extend beyond two atoms.* In valence bond theory, in contrast, all representations for bonding are based on being able to localize pairs of electrons in bonds between two atoms. To further illustrate the MO approach, look again at benzene (Figure 9.24). On page 421, we noted that the π electrons in this molecule were spread out over all six carbon atoms. We can now see how the same case can be made with MO theory. Six p orbitals contribute to the π system. Based on the premise that the number of molecular orbitals must equal the number of atomic orbitals, there must be six π molecular orbitals in benzene. An energy level diagram for benzene shows that the six π electrons reside in the three lowest-energy (bonding) molecular orbitals.

FIGURE 9.24 Molecular orbital energy level diagram for benzene. Because there are six unhybridized p orbitals, six π molecular orbitals can be formed—three bonding and three antibonding. The three bonding molecular orbitals accommodate the six π electrons.

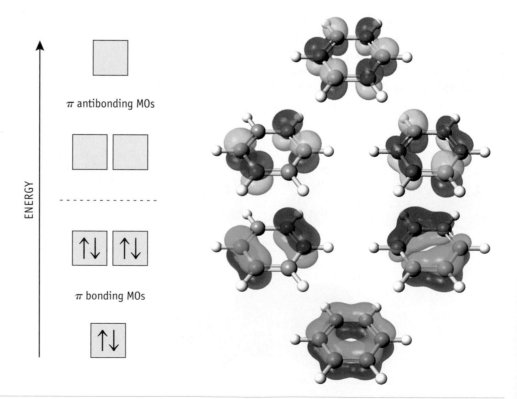

Chapter Goals Revisited

Now that you have studied this chapter, you should ask whether you have met the chapter goals. In particular, you should be able to:

Understand the differences between valence bond theory and molecular orbital theory

a. Describe the main features of valence bond theory and molecular orbital theory, the two commonly used theories for covalent bonding (Section 9.1).

b. Recognize that the premise for valence bond theory is that bonding results from the overlap of atomic orbitals. By virtue of the overlap of orbitals, electrons are concentrated (or localized) between two atoms (Section 9.2).

c. Distinguish how sigma (σ) and pi (π) bonds arise. For σ bonding, orbitals overlap in a head-to-head fashion, concentrating electrons along the bond axis. Sideways overlap of p atomic orbitals results in π bond formation, with electron density above and below the molecular plane (Section 9.2).

d. Understand how molecules having double bonds can have isomeric forms. Study Question(s) assignable in OWL: 14.

Identify the hybridization of an atom in a molecule or ion

a. Use the concept of hybridization to rationalize molecular structure (Section 9.2). Study Question(s) assignable in OWL: 2, 3, 4, 5, 6, 8, 9, 11, 12, 21, 22, 24, 27, 32, 35, 36, 38, 44, 45, 47–50, 51, 52–54; Go Chemistry Module 14.

Hybrid Orbitals	Atomic Orbitals Used	Number of Hybrid Orbitals	Electron-Pair Geometry
sp	$s + p$	2	Linear
sp^2	$s + p + p$	3	Trigonal-planar
sp^3	$s + p + p + p$	4	Tetrahedral
sp^3d	$s + p + p + p + d$	5	Trigonal bipyramidal
sp^3d^2	$s + p + p + p + d + d$	6	Octahedral

Understand the differences between bonding and antibonding molecular orbitals and be able to write the molecular orbital configurations for simple diatomic molecules.

a. Understand molecular orbital theory (Section 9.3), in which atomic orbitals are combined to form bonding orbitals, nonbonding orbitals, or antibonding orbitals that are delocalized over several atoms. In this description, the electrons of the molecule or ion are assigned to the orbitals beginning with the one at lowest energy, according to the Pauli exclusion principle and Hund's rule.

b. Use molecular orbital theory to explain the properties of O_2 and other diatomic molecules. Study Question(s) assignable in OWL: 15–20, 40, 42, 43, 57.

Chemistry⸱Now™ Sign in at **www.cengage.com/login** to:

- Assess your understanding with Study Questions in OWL keyed to each goal in the Goals and Homework menu for this chapter
- For quick review, download Go Chemistry mini-lecture flashcard modules (or purchase them at **www.ichapters.com**)
- Check your readiness for an exam by taking the Pre-Test and exploring the modules recommended in your Personalized Study plan.

❓ Access **How Do I Solve It?** tutorials on how to approach problem solving using concepts in this chapter.

For additional preparation for an examination on this chapter see the *Let's Review* section on pages 496–513.

KEY EQUATIONS

Equation 9.1 (page 424) Calculating the order of a bond from the molecular orbital electron configuration

Bond order = 1/2 (number of electrons in bonding MOs
− number of electrons in antibonding MOs)

STUDY QUESTIONS

$\bigcirc$WL Online homework for this chapter may be
assigned in OWL.

▲ denotes challenging questions.

■ denotes questions assignable in OWL.

Blue-numbered questions have answers in Appendix O and
fully-worked solutions in the *Student Solutions Manual*.

Practicing Skills

Valence Bond Theory
(See Examples 9.1–9.5 and ChemistryNow Screens 9.2–9.7.)

1. Draw the Lewis structure for chloroform, $CHCl_3$. What
   are its electron-pair and molecular geometries? What
   orbitals on C, H, and Cl overlap to form bonds involving these elements?

2. ■ Draw the Lewis structure for NF_3. What are its
   electron-pair and molecular geometries? What is the
   hybridization of the nitrogen atom? What orbitals on
   N and F overlap to form bonds between these elements?

3. ■ Specify the electron-pair and molecular geometry for
   each underlined atom in the following list. Describe
   the hybrid orbital set used by this atom in each molecule or ion.
   (a) $\underline{B}Br_3$ (b) $\underline{C}O_2$ (c) $\underline{C}H_2Cl_2$ (d) $\underline{C}O_3^{2-}$

4. ■ Specify the electron-pair and molecular geometry for
   each underlined atom in the following list. Describe
   the hybrid orbital set used by this atom in each molecule or ion.
   (a) $\underline{C}Se_2$ (b) $\underline{S}O_2$ (c) $\underline{C}H_2O$ (d) $\underline{N}H_4^+$

5. ■ Describe the hybrid orbital set used by each of the
   indicated atoms in the molecules below:
   (a) the carbon atoms and the oxygen atom in dimethyl
       ether, H_3COCH_3
   (b) each carbon atom in propene

$$\begin{array}{c} H \\ | \\ H_3C-C=CH_2 \end{array}$$

   (c) the two carbon atoms and the nitrogen atom in the
       amino acid glycine

$$\begin{array}{ccccc} H & H & :\!O\!: \\ | & | & \| \\ H-N-C-C-\ddot{O}-H \\ \;\;\ddot{}\;\; & | \\ & H \end{array}$$

6. ■ Give the hybrid orbital set used by each of the underlined atoms in the following molecules.

$$\begin{array}{c} H \;\; :\!O\!: \; H \\ | \quad \| \quad | \\ \text{(a) } H-\underline{N}-\underline{C}-\underline{N}-H \\ \;\;\ddot{}\;\; \quad \quad \ddot{}\;\; \\ \\ H \; H \; H \\ | \; | \; | \\ \text{(b) } H_3\underline{C}-\underline{C}=C-\underline{C}=\ddot{O} \\ \quad\quad\quad\quad\quad \ddot{} \end{array}$$

$$\begin{array}{c} H \; H \\ | \; | \\ \text{(c) } H-\underline{C}=\underline{C}-\underline{C}\equiv N\!: \end{array}$$

7. Draw the Lewis structure, and then specify the
   electron-pair and molecular geometries for each
   of the following molecules or ions. Identify the
   hybridization of the central atom.
   (a) SiF_6^{2-} (b) SeF_4 (c) ICl_2^- (d) XeF_4

8. ■ Draw the Lewis structure, and then specify the
   electron-pair and molecular geometries for each of
   the following molecules or ions. Identify the hybridization of the central atom.
   (a) $XeOF_4$ (c) central S in SOF_4
   (b) BrF_5 (d) central Br in Br_3^-

9. ■ Draw the Lewis structures of the acid HPO_2F_2 and its
   anion $PO_2F_2^-$. What is the molecular geometry and hybridization for the phosphorus atom in each species?
   (H is bonded to an O atom in the acid.)

10. Draw the Lewis structures of HSO_3F and SO_3F^-. What
    is the molecular geometry and hybridization for the
    sulfur atom in each species? (H is bonded to an O
    atom in the acid.)

11. ■ What is the hybridization of the carbon atom in
    phosgene, Cl_2CO? Give a complete description of the
    σ and π bonding in this molecule.

12. ■ What is the hybridization of the sulfur atom in sulfu-
    ryl fluoride, SO_2F_2?

13. The arrangement of groups attached to the C atoms
    involved in a $C=C$ double bond leads to *cis* and *trans*
    isomers. For each compound below, draw the other
    isomer.

$$\begin{array}{cc} H_3C \qquad\qquad H & Cl \qquad\qquad CH_3 \\ \diagdown \quad\quad \diagup & \diagdown \quad\quad \diagup \\ C=C & C=C \\ \diagup \quad\quad \diagdown & \diagup \quad\quad \diagdown \\ \text{(a)} \quad H \qquad\qquad CH_3 & \text{(b) } H \qquad\qquad H \end{array}$$

14. ■ For each compound below, decide whether *cis* and
    trans isomers are possible. If isomerism is possible, draw
    the other isomer.

$$\begin{array}{c} H_3C \qquad\qquad H \\ \diagdown \quad\quad \diagup \\ C=C \\ \diagup \quad\quad \diagdown \\ \text{(a)} \quad H \qquad\qquad CH_2CH_3 \end{array}$$

$$\begin{array}{cc} H \qquad\qquad CH_3 & Cl \qquad\qquad CH_2OH \\ \diagdown \quad\quad \diagup & \diagdown \quad\quad \diagup \\ C=C & C=C \\ \diagup \quad\quad \diagdown & \diagup \quad\quad \diagdown \\ \text{(b) } H \qquad\qquad H & \text{(c) } H \qquad\qquad H \end{array}$$

Molecular Orbital Theory
(See Examples 9.6–9.8 and ChemistryNow Screens 9.9–9.12.)

15. ■ The hydrogen molecular ion, H_2^+, can be detected
    spectroscopically. Write the electron configuration of
    the ion in molecular orbital terms. What is the bond
    order of the ion? Is the hydrogen–hydrogen bond
    stronger or weaker in H_2^+ than in H_2?

16. ■ Give the electron configurations for the ions Li_2^+ and Li_2^- in molecular orbital terms. Compare the Li—Li bond order in these ions with the bond order in Li_2.

17. ■ Calcium carbide, CaC_2, contains the acetylide ion, C_2^{2-}. Sketch the molecular orbital energy level diagram for the ion. How many net σ and π bonds does the ion have? What is the carbon–carbon bond order? How has the bond order changed on adding electrons to C_2 to obtain C_2^{2-}? Is the C_2^{2-} ion paramagnetic?

18. ■ Oxygen, O_2, can acquire one or two electrons to give O_2^- (superoxide ion) or O_2^{2-} (peroxide ion). Write the electron configuration for the ions in molecular orbital terms, and then compare them with the O_2 molecule on the following bases.
(a) magnetic character
(b) net number of σ and π bonds
(c) bond order
(d) oxygen–oxygen bond length

19. ■ Assume the energy level diagram for homonuclear diatomic molecules (Figure 9.21) can be applied to heteronuclear diatomics such as CO.
(a) Write the electron configuration for carbon monoxide, CO.
(b) What is the highest-energy, occupied molecular orbital?
(c) Is the molecule diamagnetic or paramagnetic?
(d) What is the net number of σ and π bonds? What is the CO bond order?

20. ■ The nitrosyl ion, NO^+, has an interesting chemistry.
(a) Is NO^+ diamagnetic or paramagnetic? If paramagnetic, how many unpaired electrons does it have?
(b) Assume the molecular orbital diagram for a homonuclear diatomic molecule (Figure 9.21) applies to NO^+. What is the highest-energy molecular orbital occupied by electrons?
(c) What is the nitrogen–oxygen bond order?
(d) Is the N—O bond in NO^+ stronger or weaker than the bond in NO?

General Questions on Valence Bond and Molecular Orbital Theory

These questions are not designated as to type or location in the chapter. They may combine several concepts from this and other chapters.

21. ■ Draw the Lewis structure for AlF_4^-. What are its electron-pair and molecular geometries? What orbitals on Al and F overlap to form bonds between these elements? What are the formal charges on the atoms? Is this a reasonable charge distribution?

22. ■ Draw the Lewis structure for ClF_3. What are its electron-pair and molecular geometries? What is the hybridization of the chlorine atom? What orbitals on Cl and F overlap to form bonds between these elements?

23. ■ Describe the O—S—O angle and the hybrid orbital set used by sulfur in each of the following molecules or ions:
(a) SO_2 (b) SO_3 (c) SO_3^{2-} (d) SO_4^{2-}

Do all have the same value for the O—S—O angle? Does the S atom in all these species use the same hybrid orbitals?

24. ■ Sketch the Lewis structures of ClF_2^+ and ClF_2^-. What are the electron-pair and molecular geometries of each ion? Do both have the same F—Cl—F angle? What hybrid orbital set is used by Cl in each ion?

25. Sketch the resonance structures for the nitrite ion, NO_2^-. Describe the electron-pair and molecular geometries of the ion. From these geometries, decide on the O—N—O bond angle, the average NO bond order, and the N atom hybridization.

26. Sketch the resonance structures for the nitrate ion, NO_3^-. Is the hybridization of the N atom the same or different in each structure? Describe the orbitals involved in bond formation by the central N atom.

27. ■ Sketch the resonance structures for the N_2O molecule. Is the hybridization of the N atoms the same or different in each structure? Describe the orbitals involved in bond formation by the central N atom.

28. Compare the structure and bonding in CO_2 and CO_3^{2-} with regard to the O—C—O bond angles, the CO bond order, and the C atom hybridization.

29. Numerous molecules are detected in deep space. Three of them are illustrated here.

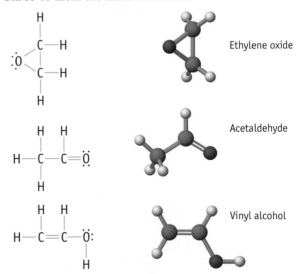

Ethylene oxide

Acetaldehyde

Vinyl alcohol

(a) Comment on the similarities or differences in the formulas of these compounds. Are they isomers?
(b) Indicate the hybridization of each C atom in each molecule.
(c) Indicate the value of the H—C—H angle in each of the three molecules.
(d) Are any of these molecules polar?
(e) Which molecule should have the strongest carbon–carbon bond? The strongest carbon–oxygen bond?

30. Acrolein, a component of photochemical smog, has a pungent odor and irritates eyes and mucous membranes.

H H :O:
A⁀| |‿B‖⁀C
H⁀C=C⁀C⁀H
    1   2

(a) What are the hybridizations of carbon atoms 1 and 2?
(b) What are the approximate values of angles *A*, *B*, and *C*?
(c) Is *cis-trans* isomerism possible here?

31. The organic compound below is a member of a class known as oximes.

H   :O̤—H
| |
H—C—C=N̤:
| |
H   H

(a) What are the hybridizations of the two C atoms and of the N atom?
(b) What is the approximate C—N—O angle?

32. ■ The compound sketched below is acetylsalicylic acid, commonly known as aspirin:

:O:
‖
D⁀C—Ö—H :O: H
           ‖ |₃
H.   C   Ö—C—C—H
 \   /1 \ 2 ‿ | ⁀
  C   C   H   C
 /   B   ⁀
H.   C   C
  \   //   \\
   C   C
  / \ A / \
 H   C   H
        |
        H

(a) What are the approximate values of the angles marked *A*, *B*, *C*, and *D*?
(b) What hybrid orbitals are used by carbon atoms 1, 2, and 3?

33. Phosphoserine is a less-common amino acid.

A   2
:Ö‿⁀Ö—H
    \1 /
     C ‿
     | C
H—N—C—H
3| 4|
B‿H   CH₂
      |
     :O:
      | 5
:Ö—P—Ö:
      |
     :O:‿D
      |
      H

(a) Describe the hybridizations of atoms 1 through 5.
(b) What are the approximate values of the bond angles *A*, *B*, *C*, and *D*?
(c) What are the most polar bonds in the molecule?

34. ■ Lactic acid is a natural compound found in sour milk.

A⁀ H H :O:
| | | ‖
H—C—C—²C—Ö³—H
    1| 2| ⁀
    H :O:‿
         | B
         H

(a) How many π bonds occur in lactic acid? How many σ bonds?
(b) Describe the hybridization of atoms 1, 2, and 3.
(c) Which CO bond is the shortest in the molecule? Which CO bond is the strongest?
(d) What are the approximate values of the bond angles *A*, *B*, and *C*?

35. ■ Cinnamaldehyde occurs naturally in cinnamon oil.

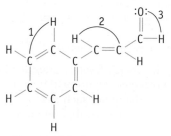

Cinnamaldehyde

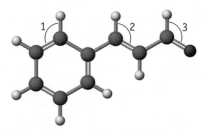

(a) What is the most polar bond in the molecule?
(b) How many sigma (σ) bonds and how many pi (π) bonds are there?
(c) Is *cis-trans* isomerism possible? If so, draw the isomers of the molecule.
(d) Give the hybridization of the C atoms in the molecule.
(e) What are the values of the bond angles 1, 2, and 3?

36. ■ Iodine and oxygen form a complex series of ions, among them IO_4^- and IO_5^{3-}. Draw the Lewis structures for these ions, and specify their electron-pair geometries and the shapes of the ions. What is the hybridization of the I atom in these ions?

37. Antimony pentafluoride reacts with HF according to the equation

$$2\ HF + SbF_5 \rightarrow [H_2F]^+[SbF_6]^-$$

(a) What is the hybridization of the Sb atom in the reactant and product?
(b) Draw a Lewis structure for H_2F^+. What is the geometry of H_2F^+? What is the hybridization of F in H_2F^+?

▲ more challenging   ■ in OWL   Blue-numbered questions answered in Appendix O

38. ■ Xenon forms well-characterized compounds (◄ page 404). Two xenon–oxygen compounds are XeO_3 and XeO_4. Draw the Lewis structures of these compounds, and give their electron-pair and molecular geometries. What are the hybrid orbital sets used by xenon in these two oxides?

39. The simple valence bond picture of O_2 does not agree with the molecular orbital view. Compare these two theories with regard to the peroxide ion, O_2^{2-}.

(a) Draw an electron dot structure for O_2^{2-}. What is the bond order of the ion?

(b) Write the molecular orbital electron configuration for O_2^{2-}. What is the bond order based on this approach?

(c) Do the two theories of bonding lead to the same magnetic character and bond order for O_2^{2-}?

40. ■ Nitrogen, N_2, can ionize to form N_2^+ or add an electron to give N_2^-. Using molecular orbital theory, compare these species with regard to (a) their magnetic character, (b) net number of π bonds, (c) bond order, (d) bond length, and (e) bond strength.

41. Which of the homonuclear, diatomic molecules of the second-period elements (from Li_2 to Ne_2) are paramagnetic? Which have a bond order of 1? Which have a bond order of 2? Which diatomic molecule has the highest bond order?

42. ■ Which of the following molecules or molecule ions should be paramagnetic? What is the highest occupied molecular orbital (HOMO) in each one? Assume the molecular orbital diagram in Figure 9.21 applies to all of them.

(a) NO   (c) O_2^{2-} (e) CN

(b) OF^- (d) Ne_2^+

43. ■ The CN molecule has been found in interstellar space. Assuming the electronic structure of the molecule can be described using the molecular orbital energy level diagram in Figure 9.21, answer the following questions.

(a) What is the highest energy occupied molecular orbital (HOMO) to which an electron (or electrons) is (are) assigned?

(b) What is the bond order of the molecule?

(c) How many net σ bonds are there? How many net π bonds?

(d) Is the molecule paramagnetic or diamagnetic?

44. ■ Amphetamine is a stimulant. Replacing one H atom on the NH_2, or amino, group with CH_3 gives methamphetamine, a particularly dangerous drug commonly known as "speed."

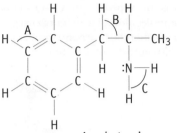

Amphetamine

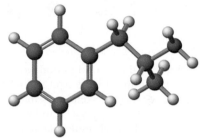

(a) What are the hybrid orbitals used by the C atoms of the C_6 ring, by the C atoms of the side chain, and by the N atom?

(b) Give approximate values for the bond angles A, B, and C.

(c) How many σ bonds and π bonds are in the molecule?

(d) Is the molecule polar or nonpolar?

(e) Amphetamine reacts readily with a proton (H^+) in aqueous solution. Where does this proton attach to the molecule? Does the electrostatic potential map shown above confirm this possibility?

45. ■ Menthol is used in soaps, perfumes, and foods. It is present in the common herb mint, and it can be prepared from turpentine.
(a) What are the hybridizations used by the C atoms in the molecule?
(b) What is the approximate C—O—H bond angle?
(c) Is the molecule polar or nonpolar?
(d) Is the six-member carbon ring planar or nonplanar? Explain why or why not.

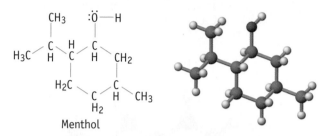

Menthol

46. The elements of the second period from boron to oxygen form compounds of the type $X_nE—EX_n$, where X can be H or a halogen. Sketch possible molecular structures for B_2F_4, C_2H_4, N_2H_4, and O_2H_2. Give the hybridizations of E in each molecule and specify approximate X—E—E bond angles.

In the Laboratory

47. ■ Suppose you carry out the following reaction of ammonia and boron trifluoride in the laboratory.

$$H—N: + B—F \longrightarrow H—N \rightarrow B—F$$

(a) What is the geometry of the boron atom in BF_3? In $H_3N{\rightarrow}BF_3$?
(b) What is the hybridization of the boron atom in the two compounds?
(c) Does the boron atom's hybridization change on formation of the coordinate covalent bond?
(d) Considering atom electronegativities and the bonding in NH_3 and BF_3, why do you expect the nitrogen on NH_3 to donate an electron pair to the B atom of BF_3?
(e) BF_3 also reacts readily with water. Based on the ammonia reaction above, speculate on how water can interact with BF_3.

48. ▲ ■ Ethylene oxide is an intermediate in the manufacture of ethylene glycol (antifreeze) and polyester polymers. More than 4 million tons are produced annually

in the U.S. The molecule has a three-member ring of two C atoms and an O atom.

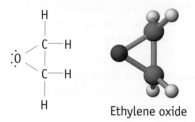

Ethylene oxide

(a) What are the expected bond angles in the ring?
(b) What is the hybridization of each atom in the ring?
(c) Comment on the relation between the bond angles expected based on hybridization and the bond angles expected for a three-member ring.
(d) Is the molecule polar? Based on the electrostatic potential map shown below, where do the negative and positive charges lie in the molecule?

Electrostatic potential map for ethylene oxide.

49. ■ The sulfamate ion, $H_2NSO_3^-$, can be thought of as having been formed from the amide ion, NH_2^-, and sulfur trioxide, SO_3.
(a) What are the geometries of the amide ion and of SO_3? What are the hybridizations of the N and S atoms, respectively?
(b) Sketch a structure for the sulfamate ion, and estimate the bond angles.
(c) What changes in hybridization do you expect for N and S in the course of the reaction

$$NH_2^- + SO_3 \rightarrow H_2N—SO_3^-?$$

(d) Is SO_3 the donor of an electron pair or the acceptor of an electron pair in the reaction with amide ion? Does the electrostatic potential map shown below confirm your prediction?

Electrostatic potential map for sulfur trioxide.

▲ more challenging ■ in OWL Blue-numbered questions answered in Appendix O

50. ▲ ■ The compound whose structure is shown here is acetylacetone. It exists in two forms: the *enol* form and the *keto* form.

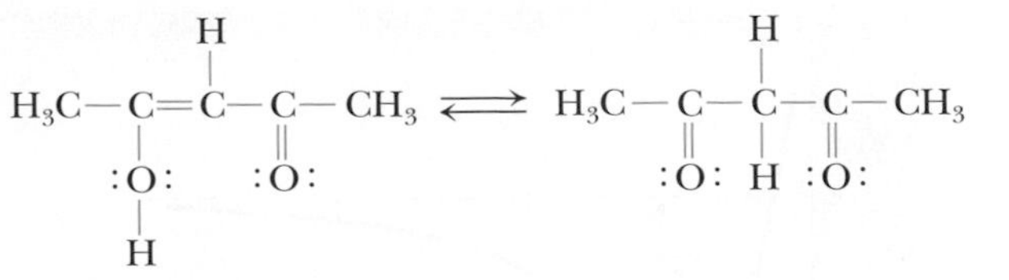

enol form   *keto* form

The molecule reacts with OH⁻ to form an anion, [CH₃COCHCOCH₃]⁻ (often abbreviated acac⁻ for acetylacetonate ion). One of the most interesting aspects of this anion is that one or more of them can react with transition metal cations to give stable, highly colored compounds.

(a) Are the *keto* and *enol* forms of acetylacetone resonance forms? Explain your answer.

(b) What is the hybridization of each atom (except H) in the *enol* form? What changes in hybridization occur when it is transformed into the *keto* form?

(c) What are the electron-pair geometry and molecular geometry around each C atom in the *keto* and *enol* forms? What changes in geometry occur when the *keto* form changes to the *enol* form?

(d) Draw three possible resonance structures for the acac⁻ ion.

(e) Is *cis-trans* isomerism possible in either the *enol* or the *keto* form?

(f) Is the enol form of acetylacetone polar? Where do the positive and negative charges lie in the molecule?

Summary and Conceptual Questions

The following questions may use concepts from this and previous chapters.

51. ■ What is the maximum number of hybrid orbitals that a carbon atom may form? What is the minimum number? Explain briefly.

52. ■ Consider the three fluorides BF_4^-, SiF_4, and SF_4.
(a) Identify a molecule that is isoelectronic with BF_4^-.
(b) Are SiF_4 and SF_4 isoelectronic?
(c) What is the hybridization of the central atom in each of these species?

53. ▲ ■ When two amino acids react with each other, they form a linkage called an amide group, or a peptide link. (If more linkages are added, a protein or polypeptide is formed.)
(a) What are the hybridizations of the C and N atoms in the peptide linkage?

(b) Is the structure illustrated the only resonance structure possible for the peptide linkage? If another resonance structure is possible, compare it with the one shown. Decide which is the more important structure.

(c) The computer-generated structure shown here, which contains a peptide linkage, shows that the linkage is flat. This is an important feature of proteins. Speculate on reasons that the CO—NH linkage is planar. What are the sites of positive and negative charge in this dipeptide?

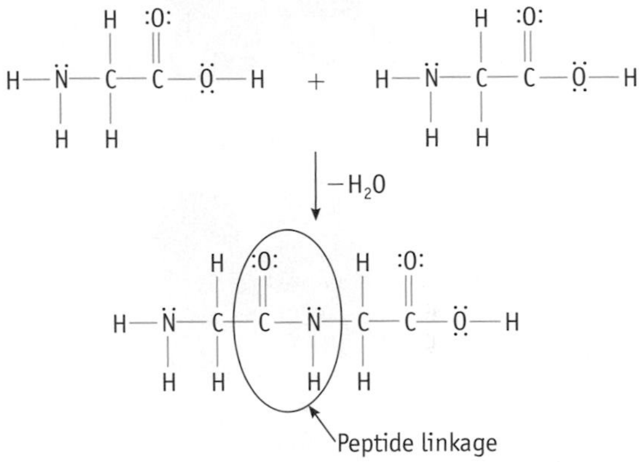

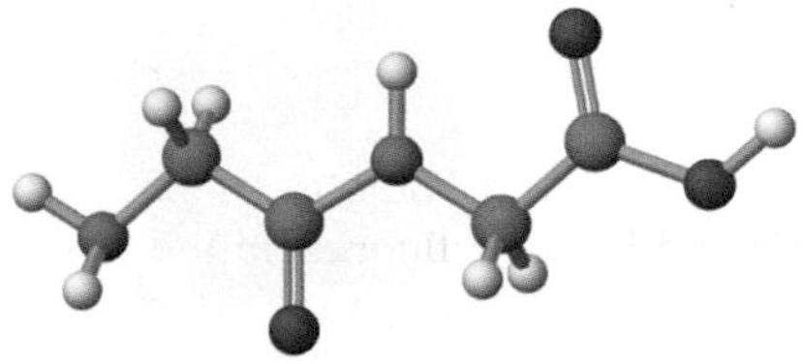

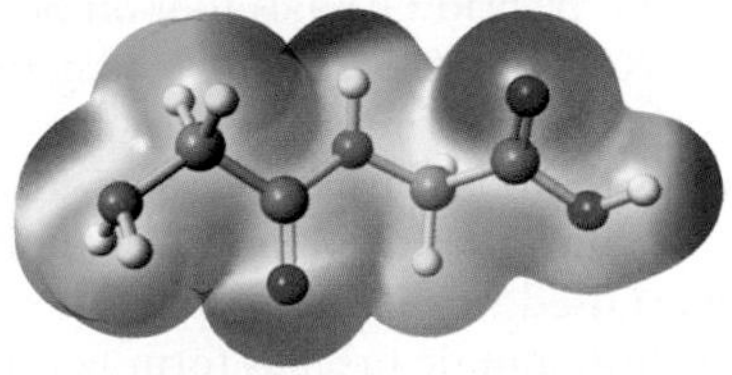

Peptide linkage

54. ■ What is the connection between bond order, bond length, and bond energy? Use ethane (C_2H_6), ethylene (C_2H_4), and acetylene (C_2H_2) as examples.

55. When is it desirable to use MO theory rather than valence bond theory?

56. How do valence bond theory and molecular orbital theory differ in their explanation of the bond order of 1.5 for ozone?

57. ■ Three of the four π molecular orbitals for cyclobutadiene are pictured here. Place them in order of increasing energy. (Remember that orbitals increase in
energy in order of an increasing number of nodes. If a
pair of orbitals have the same number of nodes, they
have the same energy.)

Orbital A

Orbital B

Orbital C

58. Examine the Hybrid Orbitals tool on Screen 9.6 of
ChemistryNow. Use this tool to systematically combine
atomic orbitals to form hybrid atomic orbitals.
   (a) What is the relationship between the number of hy-
       brid orbitals produced and the number of atomic
       orbitals used to create them?
   (b) Do hybrid atomic orbitals form between different p
       orbitals without involving s orbitals?
   (c) What is the relationship between the energy of hy-
       brid atomic orbitals and the atomic orbitals from
       which they are formed?
   (d) Compare the shapes of the hybrid orbitals formed
       from an s orbital and a p_x orbital with the hybrid
       atomic orbitals formed from an s orbital and a p_z
       orbital.
   (e) Compare the shape of the hybrid orbitals formed
       from s, p_x, and p_y orbitals with the hybrid atomic or-
       bitals formed from s, p_x, and p_z orbitals.

59. Screen 9.2 of ChemistryNow shows the change in energy as a function of the H—H distance when H_2 forms
from separated H atoms.

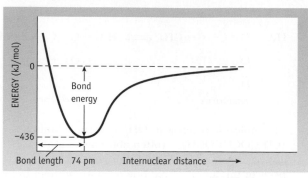

   (a) Screen 9.3 describes the attractive and repulsive
       forces that occur when two atoms approach each
       other. What must be true about the relative
       strengths of those attractive and repulsive forces if
       a covalent bond is to form?
   (b) When two atoms are widely separated, the energy
       of the system is defined as zero. As the atoms ap-
       proach each other, the energy drops, reaches a
       minimum, and then increases as they approach still
       more closely. Explain these observations.
   (c) For a bond to form, orbitals on adjacent atoms
       must overlap, and each pair of overlapping orbitals
       will contain two electrons. Explain why neon does
       not form a diatomic molecule, Ne_2, whereas fluo-
       rine forms F_2.

60. Examine the bonding in ethylene, C_2H_4, on Screen 9.7
of ChemistryNow and then go to the *A Closer Look* aux-
iliary screen.

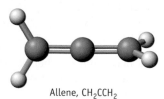

Allene, CH_2CCH_2

   (a) Explain why the allene molecule is not flat. That is,
       explain why the CH_2 groups at opposite ends do
       not lie in the same plane.
   (b) Based on the theory of orbital hybridization, ex-
       plain why benzene is a planar, symmetrical mole-
       cule.
   (c) What are the hybrid orbitals used by the three C at-
       oms of allyl alcohol?

$$\underset{\overset{|}{H}}{\overset{\overset{H}{|}}{C}}=\underset{\overset{|}{H}}{\overset{\overset{H}{|}}{C}}-\underset{\overset{|}{H}}{\overset{\overset{H}{|}}{C}}-\overset{..}{\underset{..}{O}}-H$$

▲ more challenging   ■ in OWL   Blue-numbered questions answered in Appendix O

61. Screen 9.8 of ChemistryNow describes the motions of molecules.

(a) Observe the animations of the rotations of *trans*-2-butene and butane about their carbon–carbon bonds.

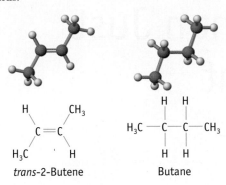

trans-2-Butene   Butane

As one end of *trans*-2-butene rotates relative to the other end, the energy increases about 20-25 kJ/mol and then drops as the rotation produces *cis*-2-butene. In contrast, the rotation of the butane molecule requires much less energy (only 12.5 kJ/mol). When butane has reached the halfway point in its rotation, the energy has reached a maximum. Why does *trans*-2-butene require so much more energy to rotate about the central carbon–carbon bond than does butane?

(b) Can the two CH_2 fragments of allene (see the sidebar of Screen 9.7) rotate with respect to each other? Briefly explain why or why not.

10 | Carbon: More Than Just Another Element

Charles D. Winters

Camphor, an "Aromatic" Molecule

You might know just what this compound smells like! When you were a child and had a cold or cough, your mother might have smeared some Vick's® VapoRub on your chest. This home remedy, now more than 100 years old, contains camphor (5% by weight) as well as eucalyptus oil, turpentine oil, and menthol as active ingredients.

Camphor is said to be the first pure chemical that humans isolated and purified. Beginning in about 3000 BC, it was isolated from the camphor tree (*Cinnamomum camphora*), a native of China, Japan, and Indonesia, by chipping the wood from the tree and then steaming it. Camphor, being quite volatile, readily sublimes, and the solid is collected by cooling the resulting vapor.

An early use for camphor was as a wine additive, but the compound is toxic when taken internally, so this was clearly not a healthy practice. In the Middle Ages, it was said to be an aphrodisiac, but later it was declared an antiaphrodisiac.

Camphor was also used as a treatment during the yellow fever epidemic in 1793 that killed thousands in Philadelphia. Benjamin Rush, a Philadelphia physician, chemist (who published the first American chemistry textbook), and signer of the Declaration of Independence, recommended a mixture of vinegar and camphor to ward off the yellow fever. It did not cure the disease, but it did keep away mosquitoes, the carrier of yellow fever.

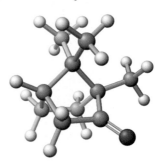

Questions:
1. The structure of camphor is interesting, although it was not known until 1893.
   a) The O atom is attached to a structurally unique C atom. What is the geometry around this atom? What is its hybridization? What are the geometry and hybridization of the other C atoms in the molecule?
   b) The five- and six-carbon rings in the molecule are not flat. Why is this so?
   c) Is there a chiral center in this molecule? (See page 446.)
2. Organic compounds are often classified by their "functional group." To what class does this molecule belong?

Answers to these questions are in Appendix Q.

The vast majority of the millions of chemical compounds currently known are organic; that is, they are compounds built on a carbon framework. Organic compounds vary greatly in size and complexity, from the simplest hydrocarbon, methane, to molecules made up of many thousands of atoms. As you read this chapter, you will see why the range of possible materials is huge.

Chemistry Now™

Throughout the text this icon introduces an opportunity for self-study or to explore interactive tutorials by signing in at **www.cengage.com/login**.

10.1 Why Carbon?

We begin this discussion of organic chemistry with a question: What features of carbon lead to both the abundance and the complexity of organic compounds? Answers fall into two categories: structural diversity and stability.

Structural Diversity

With four electrons in its outer shell, carbon will form four bonds to reach an octet configuration. In contrast, the elements boron and nitrogen form three bonds in molecular compounds; oxygen forms two bonds; and hydrogen and the halogens form one bond. With a larger number of bonds comes the opportunity to create more complex structures. This will become increasingly evident in this brief tour of organic chemistry.

A carbon atom can reach an octet of electrons in various ways (Figure 10.1):

- *By forming four single bonds.* A carbon atom can bond to four other atoms, which can be either atoms of other elements (often H, N, or O) or other carbon atoms.
- *By forming a double bond and two single bonds.* The carbon atoms in ethylene, $H_2C=CH_2$, are linked to other atoms in this way.
- *By forming two double bonds,* as in carbon dioxide ($O=C=O$).
- *By forming a triple bond and a single bond,* an arrangement seen in acetylene, $HC\equiv CH$.

Recognize, with each of these arrangements, the various possible geometries around carbon: tetrahedral, trigonal planar, and linear. Carbon's tetrahedral

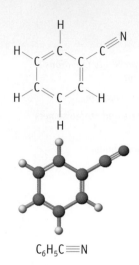

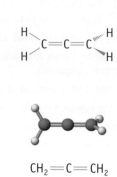

$CH_2\!\!=\!\!C\!\!=\!\!CH_2$

CH_3COH

$C_6H_5C\!\!\equiv\!\!N$

(a) Acetic acid. One carbon atom in this compound is attached to four other atoms by single bonds and has tetrahedral geometry. The second carbon atom, connected by a double bond to one oxygen and by single bonds to the other oxygen and to carbon, has trigonal-planar geometry.

(b) Benzonitrile. Six trigonal-planar carbon atoms make up the benzene ring. The seventh C atom, bonded by a single bond to carbon and a triple bond to nitrogen, has a linear geometry.

(c) Carbon is linked by double bonds to two other carbon atoms in C_3H_4, a linear molecule commonly called allene.

FIGURE 10.1 Ways that carbon atoms bond.

geometry is of special significance because it leads to three-dimensional chains and rings of carbon atoms, as in propane and cyclopentane.

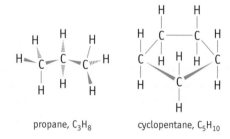

propane, C_3H_8 cyclopentane, C_5H_{10}

The ability to form multiple bonds leads to families of compounds with double and triple bonds.

Isomers

A hallmark of carbon chemistry is the remarkable array of isomers that can exist. **Isomers** are compounds that have identical composition but different structures. Two broad categories of isomers exist: structural isomers and stereoisomers.

Structural isomers are compounds having the same elemental composition, but the atoms are linked together in different ways. Ethanol and dimethyl ether are structural isomers, as are 1-butene and 2-methylpropene.

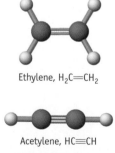

Ethylene, $H_2C\!\!=\!\!CH_2$

Acetylene, $HC\!\!\equiv\!\!CH$

Ethylene and acetylene. These two-carbon hydrocarbons can be the building blocks of more complex molecules. These are their common names, but their systematic names are ethene and ethyne.

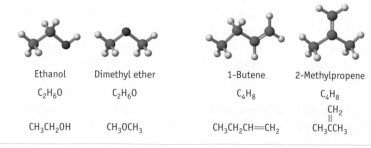

Ethanol	Dimethyl ether	1-Butene	2-Methylpropene
C_2H_6O	C_2H_6O	C_4H_8	C_4H_8
			$\overset{\displaystyle CH_2}{\underset{\displaystyle\parallel}{}}$
CH_3CH_2OH	CH_3OCH_3	$CH_3CH_2CH\!\!=\!\!CH_2$	CH_3CCH_3

Writing Formulas and Drawing Structures

In Chapter 2, you learned that there are various ways of presenting structures (page 68). It is appropriate to return to this topic as we look at organic compounds. Consider methane and ethane, for example. We can represent these molecules in several ways:

1. *Molecular formula:* CH_4 or C_2H_6. This type of formula gives information on composition only.
2. *Condensed formula:* For ethane, this would be written CH_3CH_3 (or as H_3CCH_3). This method of writing the formula gives some information on the way atoms are connected.
3. *Structural formula:* You will recognize this formula as the Lewis structure. An elaboration on the condensed formula in (2), this representation defines more clearly how the atoms are connected,

but it fails to describe the shapes of molecules.

Methane, CH_4 Ethane, C_2H_6

4. *Perspective drawings:* These drawings are used to convey the three-dimensional nature of molecules. Bonds extending out of the plane of the paper are drawn with wedges, and bonds behind the plane of the paper are represented as dashed wedges (page 70). Using these guidelines, the structures of methane and ethane could be drawn as follows:

5. *Computer-drawn ball-and-stick and space-filling models.*

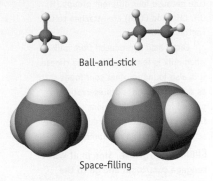

Ball-and-stick

Space-filling

Stereoisomers are compounds with the same formula and in which there is a similar attachment of atoms. However, the atoms have different orientations in space. Two types of stereoisomers exist: geometric isomers and optical isomers.

Cis- and *trans-*2-butene are **geometric isomers.** Geometric isomerism in these compounds occurs as a result of the C=C double bond. Recall that the carbon atom and the attached groups cannot rotate around a double bond (page 420). Thus, the geometry around the C=C double bond is fixed in space. If identical groups occur on the adjacent carbon atoms and on the same side of the double bond, a *cis* isomer is produced. If those groups appear on opposite sides, a *trans* isomer is produced.

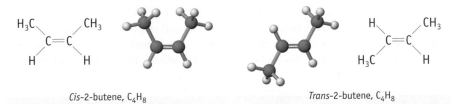

Cis-2-butene, C_4H_8 Trans-2-butene, C_4H_8

Optical isomerism is a second type of stereoisomerism. Optical isomers are molecules that have nonsuperimposable mirror images (Figure 10.2). Molecules (and other objects) that have nonsuperimposable mirror images are termed **chiral.** Pairs of nonsuperimposable molecules are called **enantiomers.**

Pure samples of enantiomers have the same physical properties, such as melting point, boiling point, density, and solubility in common solvents. They differ in one significant way, however: When a beam of plane-polarized light passes through a solution of a pure enantiomer, the plane of polarization rotates. The two enantiomers rotate polarized light to an equal extent, but in opposite directions (Figure 10.3). The term "optical isomerism" is used because this effect involves light.

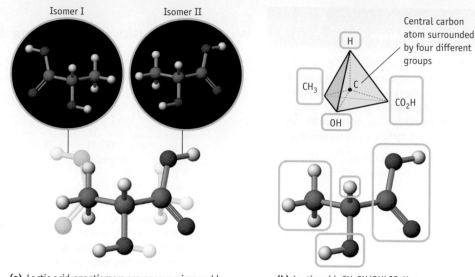

(a) Lactic acid enantiomers are nonsuperimposable

(b) Lactic acid, CH₃CH(OH)CO₂H

The most common examples of chiral compounds are those in which four different atoms (or groups of atoms) are attached to a tetrahedral carbon atom. Lactic acid,
found in milk and a product of normal human metabolism, is an example of one
such chiral compound (Figure 10.2). Optical isomerism is particularly important in
the amino acids (▶ *The Chemistry of Life: Biochemistry*) and other biologically important
molecules. Among the many interesting examples is a compound, frontalin, produced
naturally by male elephants (see "Chemical Perspectives: Chirality and Elephants").

Stability of Carbon Compounds

Carbon compounds are notable for their resistance to chemical change. This resistance is a result of two things: strong bonds and slow reactions.

Strong bonds are needed for molecules to survive in their environment.
Molecular collisions in gases, liquids, and solutions often provide enough energy
to break some chemical bonds, and bonds can be broken if the energy associated
with photons of visible and ultraviolet light exceeds the bond energy. Carbon–
carbon bonds are relatively strong, however, as are the bonds between carbon and
most other atoms. The average C—C bond energy is 346 kJ/mol; the C—H bond
energy is 413 kJ/mol; and carbon–carbon double and triple bond energies are even
higher (◀ Section 8.9). Contrast these values with bond energies for the Si—H
bond (328 kJ/mol) and the Si—Si bond (222 kJ/mol). The consequence of high

FIGURE 10.3 Rotation of plane-
polarized light by an optical isomer.
Monochromatic light (light of only one
wavelength) is produced by a sodium
lamp. After it passes through a polarizing filter, the light vibrates in only one
direction—it is polarized. A solution of an
optical isomer placed between the first
and second polarizing filters causes rotation of the plane of polarized light. The
angle of rotation can be determined by
rotating the second filter until maximum
light transmission occurs. The magnitude
and direction of rotation are unique
physical properties of the optical isomer
being tested.

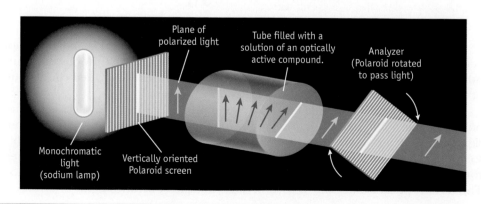

Plane of
polarized light

Tube filled with a
solution of an optically
active compound.

Analyzer
(Polaroid rotated
to pass light)

Monochromatic
light
(sodium lamp)

Vertically oriented
Polaroid screen

During a period known as musth, male elephants undergo a time of heightened sexual activity. They can become more aggressive and can work themselves into a frenzy. Aside from these physical changes, the males also produce chemical signals. A secretion containing the enantiomers of frontalin ($C_8H_{14}O_2$) is emitted from a gland between the eye and the ear. Young males produce mixtures containing more of one enantiomer than the other, whereas older elephants produce a more balanced and more concentrated mixture. When that occurs in older elephants, other males are repelled, but ovulating female elephants are more highly attracted.

Frontalin

John Katz

An African elephant in musth. Fluid containing the enantiomers of frontalin flows from a gland between the elephant's eye and ear.

bond energies for bonds to carbon is that, for the most part, organic compounds do not degrade under normal conditions.

Oxidation of most organic compounds is strongly product-favored, but most organic compounds survive contact with O_2. The reason is that these reactions occur slowly. Most organic compounds burn only if their combustion is initiated by heat or by a spark. As a consequence, oxidative degradation is not a barrier to the existence of organic compounds.

10.2 Hydrocarbons

 Module 15

Hydrocarbons, compounds made of carbon and hydrogen only, are classified into several subgroups: alkanes, cycloalkanes, alkenes, alkynes, and aromatic compounds (Table 10.1). We begin our discussion by considering compounds that have carbon atoms with four single bonds, the alkanes and cycloalkanes.

Chemistry⚛Now™

Sign in at **www.cengage.com/login** and go to Chapter 10 Contents to see Screen 10.3 for a description of the **classes of hydrocarbons.**

TABLE 10.1 Some Types of Hydrocarbons

Type of Hydrocarbon	Characteristic Features	General Formula	Example
alkanes	C—C single bonds and all C atoms have four single bonds	C_nH_{2n+2}	CH_4, methane C_2H_6, ethane
cycloalkanes	C—C single bonds and all C atoms have four single bonds	C_nH_{2n}	C_6H_{12}, cyclohexane
alkenes	C=C double bond	C_nH_{2n}	$H_2C=CH_2$, ethylene
alkynes	C≡C triple bond	C_nH_{2n-2}	HC≡CH, acetylene
aromatics	rings with π bonding extending over several C atoms	—	benzene, C_6H_6

TABLE 10.2 Selected Hydrocarbons of the Alkane Family, C_nH_{2n+2}*

Name	Molecular Formula	State at Room Temperature
methane	CH_4	
ethane	C_2H_6	gas
propane	C_3H_8	
butane	C_4H_{10}	
pentane	C_5H_{12} (pent- = 5)	
hexane	C_6H_{14} (hex- = 6)	
heptane	C_7H_{16} (hept- = 7)	liquid
octane	C_8H_{18} (oct- = 8)	
nonane	C_9H_{20} (non- = 9)	
decane	$C_{10}H_{22}$ (dec- = 10)	
octadecane	$C_{18}H_{38}$ (octadec- = 18)	solid
eicosane	$C_{20}H_{42}$ (eicos- = 20)	

* This table lists only selected alkanes. Liquid compounds with 11 to 16 carbon atoms are also known. Many solid alkanes with more than 20 carbon atoms also exist.

Alkanes

Alkanes have the general formula C_nH_{2n+2}, with n having integer values (Table 10.2). Formulas of specific compounds can be generated from this general formula, the first four of which are CH_4 (methane), C_2H_6 (ethane), C_3H_8 (propane), and C_4H_{10} (butane) (Figure 10.4). Methane has four hydrogen atoms arranged tetrahedrally around a single carbon atom. Replacing a hydrogen atom in methane by a $—CH_3$ group gives ethane. If an H atom of ethane is replaced by yet another $—CH_3$ group, propane results. Butane is derived from propane by replacing an H atom of one of the chain-ending carbon atoms with a $—CH_3$ group. In all of these compounds, each C atom is attached to four other atoms, either C or H, so alkanes are often called **saturated compounds**.

Structural Isomers

Structural isomers are possible for all alkanes larger than propane. For example, there are two structural isomers for C_4H_{10} and three for C_5H_{12}. As the number of carbon atoms in an alkane increases, the number of possible structural isomers

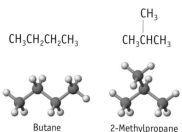

$CH_3CH_2CH_2CH_3$

$$CH_3\overset{\overset{\textstyle CH_3}{|}}{C}HCH_3$$

Butane   2-Methylpropane

Structural isomers of butane, C_4H_{10}.

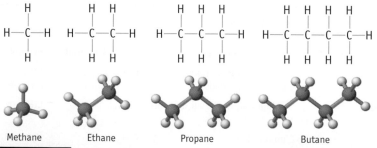

Methane   Ethane   Propane   Butane

Active Figure 10.4 **Alkanes.** The lowest–molar-mass alkanes, all gases under normal conditions, are methane, ethane, propane, and butane.

Chemistry ⚛ Now™ Sign in at www.cengage.com/login and go to the Chapter Contents menu to explore an interactive version of this figure accompanied by an exercise.

greatly increases; there are five isomers possible for C_6H_{14}, nine isomers for C_7H_{16}, 18 for C_8H_{18}, 75 for $C_{10}H_{22}$, and 366,319 for $C_{20}H_{42}$.

To recognize the isomers corresponding to a given formula, keep in mind the following points:

- Each alkane is built upon a framework of tetrahedral carbon atoms, and each carbon must have four single bonds.
- An effective approach is to create a framework of carbon atoms and then fill the remaining positions around carbon with H atoms so that each C atom has four bonds.
- Nearly free rotation occurs around carbon–carbon single bonds. Therefore, when atoms are assembled to form the skeleton of an alkane, the emphasis is on how carbon atoms are attached to one another and not on how they might lie relative to one another in the plane of the paper.

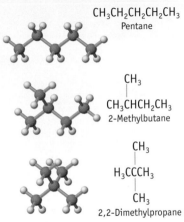

Structural isomers of pentane, C_5H_{12}.

■ **EXAMPLE 10.1 Drawing Structural Isomers of Alkanes**

Problem Draw structures of the five isomers of C_6H_{14}. Are any of these isomers chiral?

Strategy Focus first on the different frameworks that can be built from six carbon atoms. Having created a carbon framework, fill hydrogen atoms into the structure so that each carbon has four bonds.

Solution

Step 1. Placing six carbon atoms in a chain gives the framework for the first isomer. Now fill in hydrogen atoms: three on the carbons on the ends of the chain, two on each of the carbons in the middle. You have created the first isomer, hexane.

carbon framework of hexane → hexane

Step 2. Draw a chain of five carbon atoms; then add the sixth carbon atom to one of the carbons in the middle of this chain. (Adding it to a carbon at the end of the chain gives a six-carbon chain, the same framework drawn in Step 1.) Two different carbon frameworks can be built from the five-carbon chain, depending on whether the sixth carbon is linked to the 2 or 3 position. For each of these frameworks, fill in the hydrogens.

carbon framework of methylpentane isomers → 2-methylpentane

→ 3-methylpentane

■ **Chirality in Alkanes** To be chiral, *a compound must have at least one C atom attached to four different groups.* Thus, the C_7H_{16} isomer here is chiral.

We often designate the center of chirality with an asterisk.

Step 3. Draw a chain of four carbon atoms. Add in the two remaining carbons, again being careful not to extend the chain length. Two different structures are possible: one with the remaining carbon atoms in the 2 and 3 positions, and another with both extra carbon atoms attached at the 2 position. Fill in the 14 hydrogens. You have now drawn the fourth and fifth isomers.

carbon atom frameworks
for dimethylbutane isomers

2,3-dimethylbutane

2,2-dimethylbutane

None of the isomers of C_6H_{14} is chiral. *To be chiral, a compound must have at least one C atom with four different groups attached.* This condition is not met in any of these isomers.

Comment Should we look for structures in which the longest chain is three carbon atoms? Try it, but you will see that it is not possible to add the three remaining carbons to a three-carbon chain without creating one of the carbon chains already drawn in a previous step. Thus, we have completed the analysis, with five isomers of this compound being identified.

Names have been given to each of these compounds. See the text that follows this Example, and see Appendix E for guidelines on nomenclature.

EXERCISE 10.1 Drawing Structural Isomers of Alkanes

(a) Draw the nine isomers having the formula C_7H_{16}. (Hint: There is one structure with a seven-carbon chain, two structures with six-carbon chains, five structures in which the longest chain has five carbons [one is illustrated in the margin], and one structure with a four-carbon chain.)

(b) Identify the isomers of C_7H_{16} that are chiral.

One possible isomer of an alkane with the formula C_7H_{16}.

■ **Naming Guidelines** For more details on naming organic compounds, see Appendix E.

Naming Alkanes

With so many possible isomers for a given alkane, chemists need a systematic way of naming them. The guidelines for naming alkanes and their derivatives follow:

- The names of alkanes end in "-ane."
- The names of alkanes with chains of one to 10 carbon atoms are given in Table 10.2. After the first four compounds, the names are derived from Latin numbers—pentane, hexane, heptane, octane, nonane, decane—and this regular naming continues for higher alkanes.
- When naming a specific alkane, the root of the name corresponds to the longest carbon chain in the compound. One isomer of C_5H_{12} has a three—

An error students sometimes make is to suggest that the three carbon skeletons drawn here are different. They are, in fact, the same. All are five-carbon chains with another C atom in the 2 position.

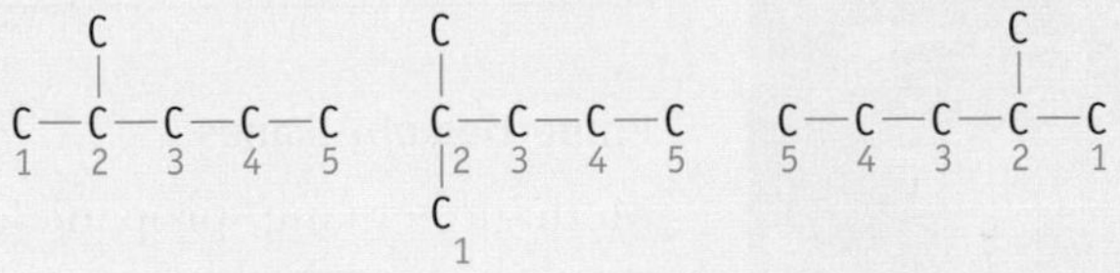

```
        C                    C                        C
        |                    |                        |
C — C — C — C — C    C — C — C — C    C — C — C — C — C
1   2   3   4   5    |2   3   4   5    5   4   3   2   1
                     C
                     1
```

Remember that Lewis structures do not indicate the geometry of molecules.

carbon chain with two —CH_3 groups on the second C atom of the chain. Thus, its name is based on propane.

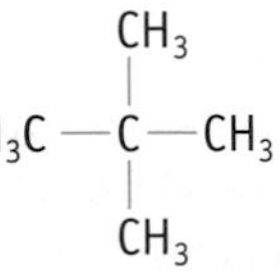

```
        CH_3
        |
H_3C — C — CH_3
        |
        CH_3
```
2,2-dimethylpropane

- Substituent groups on a hydrocarbon chain are identified by a name and the position of substitution in the carbon chain; this information precedes the root of the name. The position is indicated by a number that refers to the carbon atom to which the substituent is attached. (Numbering of the carbon atoms in a chain should begin at the end of the carbon chain that allows the substituent groups to have the lowest numbers.) Both —CH_3 groups in 2,2-dimethylpropane are located at the 2 position.
- Names of hydrocarbon substituents, called **alkyl groups,** are derived from the name of the hydrocarbon. The group —CH_3, derived by taking a hydrogen from methane, is called the methyl group; the C_2H_5 group is the ethyl group.
- If two or more of the same substituent groups occur, the prefixes di-, tri-, and tetra- are added. When different substituent groups are present, they are generally listed in alphabetical order.

■ **Systematic and Common Names** The IUPAC (International Union of Pure and Applied Chemistry) has formulated rules for systematic names, which are generally used in this book. (See Appendix E.) However, many organic compounds are known by common names. For example, 2,2-dimethyl-propane is also called neopentane.

■ **EXAMPLE 10.2 Naming Alkanes**

Problem Give the systematic name for

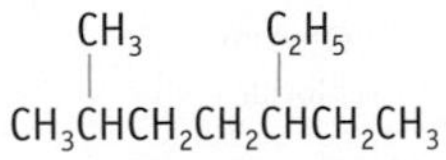

```
        CH_3        C_2H_5
        |           |
CH_3CHCH_2CH_2CHCH_2CH_3
```

Strategy Identify the longest carbon chain and base the name of the compound on that alkane. Identify the substituent groups on the chain and their locations. When there are two or more substituents (the groups attached to the chain), number the parent chain from the end that gives the lower number to the substituent encountered first. If the substituents are different, list them in alphabetical order. (For more on naming compounds, see Appendix E.)

Solution Here, the longest chain has seven C atoms, so the root of the name is *heptane*. There is a methyl group on C-2 and an ethyl group on C-5. Giving the substituents in alphabetic order and numbering the chain from the end having the methyl group, the systematic name is   5-ethyl-2-methylheptane.

Charles D. Winters

FIGURE 10.5 Paraffin wax and mineral oil. These common consumer products are mixtures of alkanes.

Properties of Alkanes

Methane, ethane, propane, and butane are gases at room temperature and pressure, whereas the higher–molar-mass compounds are liquids or solids (Table 10.2). An increase in melting point and boiling point with molar mass is a general phenomenon that reflects the increased forces of attraction between molecules (▶ Section 12.2).

You already know about alkanes in a nonscientific context because several are common fuels. Natural gas, gasoline, kerosene, fuel oils, and lubricating oils are all mixtures of various alkanes. White mineral oil is also a mixture of alkanes, as is paraffin wax (Figure 10.5).

Pure alkanes are colorless. (The colors seen in gasoline and other petroleum products are due to additives.) The gases and liquids have noticeable but not unpleasant odors. All of these substances are insoluble in water, which is typical of compounds that are nonpolar or nearly so. Low polarity is expected for alkanes because the electronegativities of carbon ($\chi = 2.5$) and hydrogen ($\chi = 2.2$) are not greatly different (◀ Section 8.8).

All alkanes burn readily in air to give CO_2 and H_2O in very exothermic reactions. This is, of course, the reason they are widely used as fuels.

$$CH_4(g) + 2\,O_2(g) \rightarrow CO_2(g) + 2\,H_2O(\ell) \qquad \Delta_rH° = -890.3 \text{ kJ/mol-rxn}$$

Other than in combustion reactions, alkanes exhibit relatively low chemical reactivity. One reaction that does occur, however, is the replacement of the hydrogen atoms of an alkane by chlorine atoms on reaction with Cl_2. It is formally an oxidation because Cl_2, like O_2, is a strong oxidizing agent. These reactions, which can be initiated by ultraviolet radiation, are free radical reactions. Highly reactive Cl atoms are formed from Cl_2 under UV radiation. Reaction of methane with Cl_2 under these conditions proceeds in a series of steps, eventually yielding CCl_4, commonly known as carbon tetrachloride. (HCl is the other product of these reactions.)

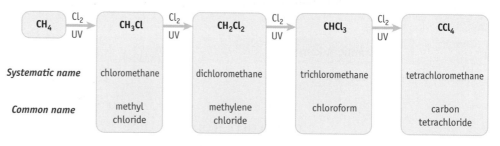

	CH_4	$\xrightarrow[\text{UV}]{Cl_2}$	CH_3Cl	$\xrightarrow[\text{UV}]{Cl_2}$	CH_2Cl_2	$\xrightarrow[\text{UV}]{Cl_2}$	$CHCl_3$	$\xrightarrow[\text{UV}]{Cl_2}$	CCl_4
Systematic name			chloromethane		dichloromethane		trichloromethane		tetrachloromethane
Common name			methyl chloride		methylene chloride		chloroform		carbon tetrachloride

The last three compounds are used as solvents, albeit less frequently today because of their toxicity. Carbon tetrachloride was also once widely used as a dry cleaning fluid and, because it does not burn, in fire extinguishers.

Cycloalkanes, C_nH_{2n}

Cycloalkanes are constructed with tetrahedral carbon atoms joined together to form a ring. For example, cyclopentane, C_5H_{10}, consists of a ring of five carbon atoms. Each carbon atom is bonded to two adjacent carbon atoms and to two hydrogen atoms. Notice that the five carbon atoms fall very nearly in a plane because

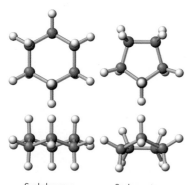

Cyclohexane, top and front views   Cyclopentane, top and front views

The structures of cyclopentane, C_5H_{10}, and cyclohexane, C_6H_{12}. The C_5 ring is nearly planar. In contrast, the tetrahedral geometry around carbon means that the C_6 ring is decidedly puckered.

Flexible Molecules

Most organic molecules are flexible; that is, they can twist and bend in various ways. Few molecules better illustrate this behavior than cyclohexane. Two structures are possible: "chair" and "boat" forms. These forms can interconvert by partial rotation of several bonds.

The more stable structure is the chair form, which allows the hydrogen atoms to remain as far apart as possible. A side view of this form of cyclohexane reveals two sets of hydrogen atoms in this molecule. Six hydrogen atoms, called the equatorial hydrogens,

lie in a plane around the carbon ring. The other six hydrogens are positioned above and below the plane and are called axial hydrogens. Flexing the ring (a rotation around the C—C single bonds) moves the hydrogen atoms between axial and equatorial environments.

chair form   boat form   chair form

the internal angles of a pentagon, 108°, closely match the tetrahedral angle of 109.5°. The small distortion from planarity allows hydrogen atoms on adjacent carbon atoms to be a little farther apart.

Cyclohexane has a nonplanar ring with six —CH_2 groups. If the carbon atoms were in the form of a regular hexagon with all carbon atoms in one plane, the C—C—C bond angles would be 120°. To have tetrahedral bond angles of 109.5° around each C atom, the ring has to pucker. The C_6 ring is flexible, however, and exists in two interconverting forms (see *A Closer Look: Flexible Molecules*).

Interestingly, cyclobutane and cyclopropane are also known, although the bond angles in these species are much less than 109.5°. These compounds are examples of **strained hydrocarbons,** so named because an unfavorable geometry is imposed around carbon. One of the features of strained hydrocarbons is that the C—C bonds are weaker and the molecules readily undergo ring-opening reactions that relieve the bond angle strain.

Alkenes and Alkynes

The diversity seen for alkanes is repeated with **alkenes,** hydrocarbons with one or more C=C double bonds. The presence of the double bond adds two features missing in alkanes: the possibility of geometric isomerism and increased reactivity.

The general formula for alkenes is C_nH_{2n}. The first two members of the series of alkenes are ethene, C_2H_4 (common name, ethylene), and propene, C_3H_6 (common name, propylene). Only a single structure can be drawn for these compounds. As with alkanes, the occurrence of isomers begins with species containing four carbon atoms. Four alkene isomers have the formula C_4H_8, and each has distinct chemical and physical properties (Table 10.3).

Cyclopropane, C_3H_6 Cyclobutane, C_4H_8

Cyclopropane and cyclobutane. Cyclopropane was at one time used as a general anesthetic in surgery. However, its explosive nature when mixed with oxygen soon eliminated this application. The *Columbia Encyclopedia* states that "cyclopropane allowed the transport of more oxygen to the tissues than did other common anesthetics and also produced greater skeletal muscle relaxation. It is not irritating to the respiratory tract. Because of the low solubility of cyclopropane in the blood, postoperative recovery was usually rapid but nausea and vomiting were common."

1-butene   2-methylpropene   *cis*-2-butene   *trans*-2-butene

C_2H_4
Systematic name:
Ethene
Common name:
Ethylene

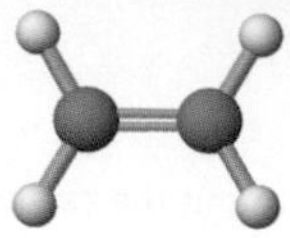

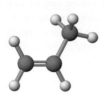

C_3H_6
Systematic name:
Propene
Common name:
Propylene

TABLE 10.3   Properties of Butene Isomers

Name	Boiling Point	Melting Point	Dipole Moment (D)	$\Delta_fH°$ (gas) (kJ/mol)
1-butene	−6.26 °C	−185.4 °C	—	−20.5
2-methylpropene	−6.95 °C	−140.4 °C	0.503	−37.5
cis-2-butene	3.71 °C	−138.9 °C	0.253	−29.7
trans-2-butene	0.88 °C	−105.5 °C	0	−33.0

Alkene names end in "-ene." As with alkanes, the root name for alkenes is that of the longest carbon chain that contains the double bond. The position of the double bond is indicated with a number, and, when appropriate, the prefix *cis* or *trans* is added. Three of the C_4H_8 isomers have four-carbon chains and so are butenes. One has a three-carbon chain and is a propene. Notice that the carbon chain is numbered from the end that gives the double bond the lowest number. In the first isomer at the left, the double bond is between C atoms 1 and 2, so the name is 1-butene and not 3-butene.

■ **EXAMPLE 10.3 Determining Isomers of Alkenes from a Formula**

Problem Draw structures for the six possible alkene isomers with the formula C_5H_{10}. Give the systematic name of each.

Strategy A procedure that involved drawing the carbon skeleton and then adding hydrogen atoms served well when drawing structures of alkanes (Example 10.1), and a similar approach can be used here. It will be necessary to put one double bond into the framework and to be alert for *cis-trans* isomerism.

Solution

1. A five-carbon chain with one double bond can be constructed in two ways. *Cis–trans* isomers are possible for 2-pentene.

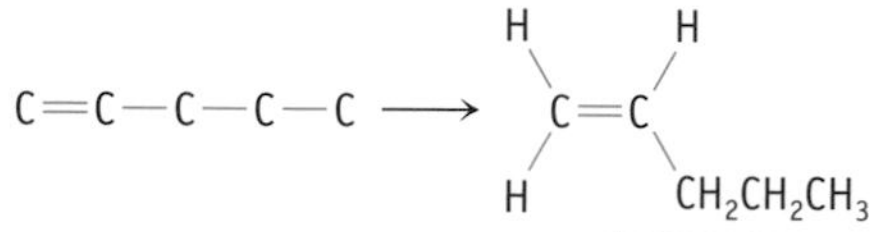

$$C=C-C-C-C \longrightarrow$$

1-pentene

$$C-C=C-C-C$$

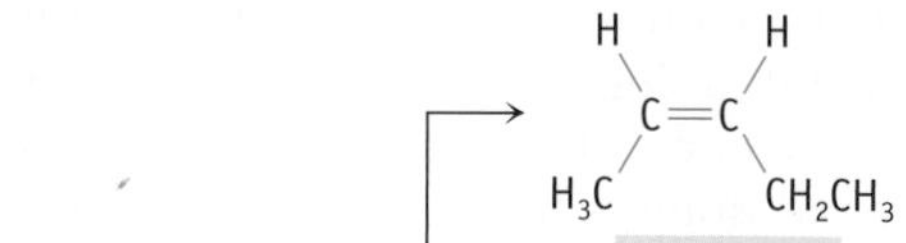

cis-2-pentene

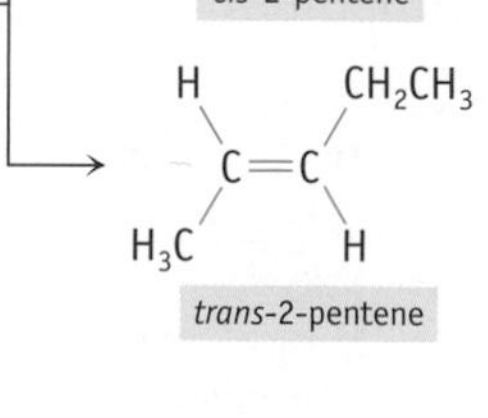

trans-2-pentene

2. Draw the possible four-carbon chains containing a double bond. Add the fifth carbon atom to either the 2 or 3 position. When all three possible combinations are found, fill in the hydrogen atoms. This results in three more structures:

$$\underset{1}{C}=\underset{2}{\overset{\overset{\displaystyle C}{|}}{C}}-\underset{3}{C}-\underset{4}{C} \longrightarrow$$

$$\begin{array}{cc} H & CH_3 \\ \diagdown & \diagup \\ C=C \\ \diagup & \diagdown \\ H & CH_2CH_3 \end{array}$$

2-methyl-1-butene

$$\underset{1}{C}=\underset{2}{C}-\underset{3}{\overset{\overset{\displaystyle C}{|}}{C}}-\underset{4}{C} \longrightarrow$$

$$\begin{array}{cc} H & H \\ \diagdown & \diagup \\ C=C \\ \diagup & \diagdown \\ H & CHCH_3 \\ & | \\ & CH_3 \end{array}$$

3-methyl-1-butene

$$\underset{4}{C}-\underset{3}{C}=\underset{2}{\overset{\overset{\displaystyle C}{|}}{C}}-\underset{1}{C} \longrightarrow$$

$$\begin{array}{cc} H & CH_3 \\ \diagdown & \diagup \\ C=C \\ \diagup & \diagdown \\ H_3C & CH_3 \end{array}$$

2-methyl-2-butene

EXERCISE 10.3 Determining Structural Isomers of Alkenes from a Formula

There are 17 possible alkene isomers with the formula C_6H_{12}. Draw structures of the five isomers in which the longest chain has six carbon atoms, and give the name of each. Which of these isomers is chiral? (There are also eight isomers in which the longest chain has five carbon atoms, and four isomers in which the longest chain has four carbon atoms. How many can you find?)

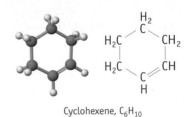

Cyclohexene, C_6H_{10}

$$H_2C=CHCH=CH_2$$

1,3-Butadiene, C_4H_6

Cycloalkenes and dienes. Cyclohexene, C_6H_{10} (*top*), and 1,3-butadiene (C_4H_6) (*bottom*).

More than one double bond can be present in a hydrocarbon. Butadiene, for example, has two double bonds and is known as a *diene*. Many natural products have numerous double bonds (Figure 10.6). There are also cyclic hydrocarbons, such as cyclohexene, with double bonds.

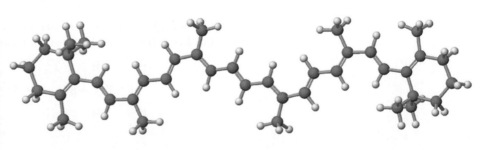

FIGURE 10.6 Carotene, a naturally occurring compound with 11 C=C bonds. The π electrons can be excited by visible light in the blue-violet region of the spectrum. As a result, carotene appears orange-yellow to the observer. Carotene or carotene-like molecules are partnered with chlorophyll in nature in the role of assisting in the harvesting of sunlight. Green leaves have a high concentration of carotene. In autumn, green chlorophyll molecules are destroyed, and the yellows and reds of carotene and related molecules are seen. The red color of tomatoes, for example, comes from a molecule very closely related to carotene. As a tomato ripens, its chlorophyll disintegrates, and the green color is replaced by the red of the carotene-like molecule.

An oxy-acetylene torch. The reaction of ethyne (acetylene) with oxygen produces a very high temperature. Oxy-acetylene torches, used in welding, take advantage of this fact.

TABLE 10.4 Some Simple Alkynes C_nH_{2n-2}

Structure	Systematic Name	Common Name	BP (°C)
HC≡CH	ethyne	acetylene	−85
CH_3C≡CH	propyne	methylacetylene	−23
CH_3CH_2C≡CH	1-butyne	ethylacetylene	9
CH_3C≡CCH_3	2-butyne	dimethylacetylene	27

Alkynes, compounds with a carbon–carbon triple bond, have the general formula (C_nH_{2n-2}). Table 10.4 lists alkynes that have four or fewer carbon atoms. The first member of this family is ethyne (common name, acetylene), a gas used as a fuel in metal cutting torches.

Properties of Alkenes and Alkynes

Like alkanes, alkenes and alkynes are colorless. Low–molar-mass compounds are gases, whereas compounds with higher molecular weights are liquids or solids. Alkanes, alkenes, and alkynes are also oxidized by O_2 to give CO_2 and H_2O.

In contrast to alkanes, alkenes and alkynes have an elaborate chemistry. We gain an insight into their chemical behavior by noting that they are called **unsaturated compounds.** Carbon atoms are capable of bonding to a maximum of four other atoms, and they do so in alkanes and cycloalkanes. In alkenes, however, the carbon atoms linked by a double bond are bonded to only three atoms; in alkynes, they bond to two atoms. It is possible to increase the number of groups attached to carbon by **addition reactions,** in which molecules with the general formula X—Y (such as hydrogen, halogens, hydrogen halides, and water) add across the carbon–carbon double bond (Figure 10.7). The result is a compound with four groups bonded to each carbon.

$$\begin{array}{c} \text{H} \quad \text{H} \\ \text{C}{=}\text{C} \\ \text{H} \quad \text{H} \end{array} + \text{X}{-}\text{Y} \longrightarrow \begin{array}{c} \text{X} \quad \text{Y} \\ \text{H}{-}\text{C}{-}\text{C}{-}\text{H} \\ \text{H} \quad \text{H} \end{array}$$

X—Y = H_2, Cl_2, Br_2; H—Cl, H—Br, H—OH, HO—Cl

The products of addition reactions are often substituted alkanes. For example, the addition of bromine to ethylene forms 1,2-dibromoethane.

$$\begin{array}{c} \text{H} \quad \text{H} \\ \text{C}{=}\text{C} \\ \text{H} \quad \text{H} \end{array} + \text{Br}_2 \longrightarrow \begin{array}{c} \text{Br} \quad \text{Br} \\ \text{H}{-}\text{C}{-}\text{C}{-}\text{H} \\ \text{H} \quad \text{H} \end{array}$$

1,2-dibromoethane

The addition of 2 mol of chlorine to acetylene gives 1,1,2,2-tetrachloroethane.

$$\text{HC}{\equiv}\text{CH} + 2\,\text{Cl}_2 \longrightarrow \begin{array}{c} \text{Cl} \quad \text{Cl} \\ \text{Cl}{-}\text{C}{-}\text{C}{-}\text{Cl} \\ \text{H} \quad \text{H} \end{array}$$

1,1,2,2-tetrachloroethane

During the 1860s, a Russian chemist, Vladimir Markovnikov, examined a large number of alkene addition reactions. In cases in which two isomeric products were

A few minutes →

FIGURE 10.7 Bacon fat and addition reactions. The fat in bacon is partially unsaturated. Like other unsaturated compounds, bacon fat reacts with Br_2 in an addition reaction. Here, you see the color of Br_2 vapor fade when a strip of bacon is introduced.

possible, he found that one was more likely to predominate. Based on these results, Markovnikov formulated a rule (now called *Markovnikov's rule*) stating that, when a reagent HX adds to an unsymmetrical alkene, the hydrogen atom in the reagent becomes attached to the carbon that already has the largest number of hydrogens. An example of Markovnikov's rule is the reaction of 2-methylpropene with HCl that results in formation of 2-chloro-2-methylpropane rather than 1-chloro-2-methylpropane.

■ **Nomenclature of Substituted Alkanes** The substituent groups in substituted alkanes are identified by the name and position of the substituent on the alkane chain.

$$H_3C \atop H_3C} C{=}CH_2 + HCl \longrightarrow H_3C{-}\underset{\underset{CH_3}{|}}{\overset{\overset{Cl}{|}}{C}}{-}CH_3 \quad + \quad H_3C{-}\underset{\underset{CH_3}{|}}{\overset{\overset{H}{|}}{C}}{-}CH_2Cl$$

2-methylpropene   2-chloro-2-methylpropane   1-chloro-2-methylpropane
                Sole product   NOT formed

If the reagent added to a double bond is hydrogen ($X{-}Y = H_2$), the reaction is called **hydrogenation.** Hydrogenation is usually a very slow reaction, but it can be speeded up in the presence of a catalyst, often a specially prepared form of a metal, such as platinum, palladium, and rhodium. You may have heard the term hydrogenation because certain foods contain "hydrogenated" or "partially hydrogenated" ingredients. One brand of crackers has a label that says, "Made with 100% pure vegetable shortening . . . (partially hydrogenated soybean oil with hydrogenated cottonseed oil)." One reason for hydrogenating an oil is to make it less susceptible to spoilage; another is to convert it from a liquid to a solid.

■ **Catalysts** A catalyst is a substance that causes a reaction to occur at a faster rate without itself being permanently changed in the reaction. We will describe catalysts in more detail in Chapter 15.

Chemistry ☼ Now™

Sign in at **www.cengage.com/login** and go to Chapter 10 Contents to see Screen 10.4 for a simulation and tutorial on **alkene addition reactions.**

■ EXAMPLE 10.4 Reaction of an Alkene

Problem Draw the structure of the compound obtained from the reaction of Br_2 with propene, and name the compound.

Strategy Bromine adds across the C=C double bond. The name includes the name of the carbon chain and indicates the positions of the Br atoms.

Solution

$$\underset{H}{\overset{H}{}}\atop} C{=}C \underset{CH_3}{\overset{H}{}} + Br_2 \longrightarrow H{-}\underset{\underset{H}{|}}{\overset{\overset{Br}{|}}{C}}{-}\underset{\underset{H}{|}}{\overset{\overset{Br}{|}}{C}}{-}CH_3$$

propene   1,2-dibromopropane

Aromatic Compounds

Benzene, C_6H_6, is a key molecule in chemistry. It is the simplest **aromatic compound,** a class of compounds so named because they have significant, and usually not unpleasant, odors. Other members of this class, which are all based on benzene, include toluene and naphthalene. A source of many aromatic compounds is coal. These compounds, and many other volatile substances, are released when coal is heated to a high temperature in the absence of air (Table 10.5).

benzene   toluene   naphthalene

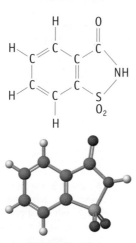

Saccharin ($C_7H_5NO_3S$). This compound, an artificial sweetener, contains an aromatic ring.

Benzene occupies a pivotal place in the history and practice of chemistry. Michael Faraday discovered this compound in 1825 as a by-product of illuminating gas, a fuel produced by heating coal. Today, benzene is an important industrial chemical, usually ranking among the top 25 chemicals in production annually in the United States. It is used as a solvent and is also the starting point for making thousands of different compounds by replacing the H atoms of the ring.

Toluene was originally obtained from tolu balsam, the pleasant-smelling gum of a South American tree, *Toluifera balsamum.* This balsam has been used in cough syrups and perfumes. Naphthalene is an ingredient in "moth balls," although 1,4-dichlorobenzene is now more commonly used. Aspartame and another artificial sweetener, saccharin, are also benzene derivatives.

TABLE 10.5 Some Aromatic Compounds from Coal Tar

Common Name	Formula	Boiling Point (°C)	Melting Point (°C)
benzene	C_6H_6	80	+6
toluene	$C_6H_5CH_3$	111	−95
o-xylene	1,2-$C_6H_4(CH_3)_2$	144	−25
m-xylene	1,3-$C_6H_4(CH_3)_2$	139	−48
p-xylene	1,4-$C_6H_4(CH_3)_2$	138	+13
naphthalene	$C_{10}H_8$	218	+80

The Structure of Benzene

The formula of benzene suggested to 19th-century chemists that this compound should be unsaturated, but, if viewed this way, its chemistry was perplexing. Whereas alkenes readily add Br_2, for example, benzene does not do so under similar conditions. The structural question was finally solved by August Kekulé (1829–1896). We now recognize that benzene's different reactivity relates to its structure and bonding, both of which are quite different from the structure and bonding in alkenes. Benzene has equivalent carbon–carbon bonds, 139 pm in length, intermediate between a C—C single bond (154 pm) and a C=C double bond (134 pm). The π bonds are formed by the continuous overlap of the p orbitals on the six carbon atoms (page 421). Using valence bond terminology, the structure is represented by a hybrid of two resonance structures.

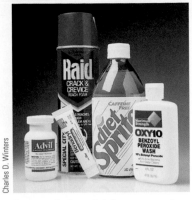

Some products containing compounds based on benzene. Examples include sodium benzoate in soft drinks, ibuprofen in Advil, and benzoyl peroxide in Oxy-10.

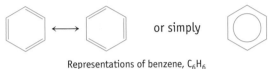

Representations of benzene, C_6H_6

Benzene Derivatives

Toluene, chlorobenzene, benzoic acid, aniline, styrene, and phenol are common examples of benzene derivatives.

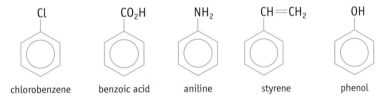

chlorobenzene   benzoic acid   aniline   styrene   phenol

If more than one H atom of benzene is replaced, isomers can arise. Thus, the systematic nomenclature for benzene derivatives involves naming substituent groups and identifying their positions on the ring by numbering the six carbon atoms (▶ Appendix E). Some common names, which are based on an older naming scheme, are also used. This scheme identified isomers of disubstituted benzenes with the prefixes *ortho* (*o-*, substituent groups on adjacent carbons in the benzene ring), *meta* (*m-*, substituents separated by one carbon atom), and *para* (*p-*, substituent groups on carbons on opposite sides of the ring).

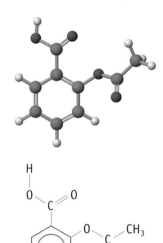

Aspirin, a commonly used analgesic. It is based on benzoic acid with an acetate group, $—O_2CCH_3$, in the *ortho* position.

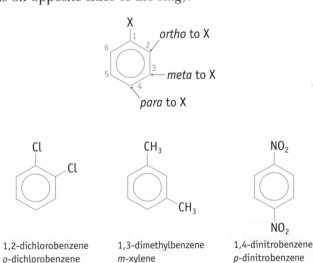

Systematic name:	1,2-dichlorobenzene	1,3-dimethylbenzene	1,4-dinitrobenzene
Common name:	*o*-dichlorobenzene	*m*-xylene	*p*-dinitrobenzene

Problem Draw and name the isomers of $C_6H_3Cl_3$.

Strategy Begin by drawing the structure of C_6H_5Cl. Place a second Cl atom on the ring in the *ortho*, *meta*, and *para* positions. Add the third Cl in one of the remaining positions.

Solution The three isomers of $C_6H_3Cl_3$ are shown here. They are named as derivatives of benzene by specifying the number of substituent groups with the prefix "tri-," the name of the substituent, and the positions of the three groups around the six-member ring.

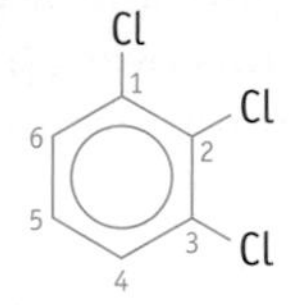

1,2,3-trichlorobenzene

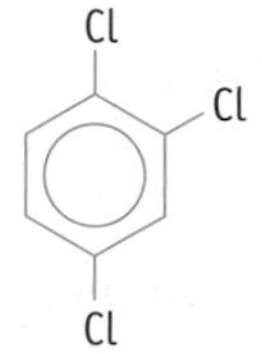

1,2,4-trichlorobenzene

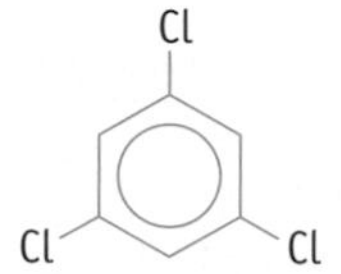

1,3,5-trichlorobenzene

EXERCISE 10.5 Isomers of Substituted Benzenes

Aniline, $C_6H_5NH_2$, is the common name for aminobenzene. Draw a structure for *p*-diaminobenzene, a compound used in dye manufacture. What is the systematic name for *p*-diaminobenzene?

Properties of Aromatic Compounds

Benzene is a colorless liquid, and simple substituted benzenes are liquids or solids under normal conditions. The properties of aromatic hydrocarbons are typical of hydrocarbons in general: They are insoluble in water, soluble in nonpolar solvents, and oxidized by O_2 to form CO_2 and H_2O.

One of the most important properties of benzene and other aromatic compounds is an unusual stability that is associated with the unique π bonding in this molecule. Because the π bonding in benzene is typically described using resonance structures, the extra stability is termed **resonance stabilization.** The extent of resonance stabilization in benzene is evaluated by comparing the energy evolved in the hydrogenation of benzene to form cyclohexane

$$C_6H_6(\ell) + 3\ H_2(g) \xrightarrow{\text{catalyst}} C_6H_{12}(\ell) \qquad \Delta_r H° = -206.7 \text{ kJ/mol-rxn}$$

with the energy evolved in hydrogenation of three isolated double bonds.

$$3\ H_2C{=}CH_2(g) + 3\ H_2(g) \rightarrow 3\ C_2H_6(g) \qquad \Delta_r H° = -410.8 \text{ kJ/mol-rxn}$$

The hydrogenation of benzene is about 200 kJ less exothermic than the hydrogenation of three moles of ethylene. The difference is attributable to the added stability associated with π bonding in benzene.

Much of the world's current technology relies on petroleum. Burning fuels derived from petroleum provides by far the largest amount of energy in the industrial world (see *The Chemistry of Fuels and Energy Sources*, pages 254–267). Petroleum and natural gas are also the chemical raw materials used in the manufacture of plastics, rubber, pharmaceuticals, and a vast array of other compounds.

The petroleum that is pumped out of the ground is a complex mixture whose composition varies greatly, depending on its source. The primary components of petroleum are always alkanes, but, to varying degrees, nitrogen- and sulfur-containing compounds are also present. Aromatic compounds are present as well, but alkenes and alkynes are not.

An early step in the petroleum refining process is distillation, in which the crude mix-

A modern petrochemical plant.

Thomas Kitchin/Tom Stack & Associates

ture is separated into a series of fractions based on boiling point: first a gaseous fraction (mostly alkanes with one to four carbon atoms; this fraction is often burned off), and then gasoline, kerosene, and fuel oils. After distillation, considerable material, in the form of a semi-solid, tar-like residue, remains.

The petrochemical industry seeks to maximize the amounts of the higher-valued fractions of petroleum produced and to make specific compounds for which a particular need exists. This means carrying out chemical reactions involving the raw materials on a huge scale. One process to which petroleum is subjected is known as *cracking*. At very high temperatures, bond breaking or "cracking" can occur, and longer-chain hydrocarbons will fragment into smaller molecular units. These reactions are carried out in the presence of a wide array of catalysts, materials that speed up reactions and direct them toward specific products. Among the important products of cracking are ethylene and other alkenes, which serve as the raw materials for the formation of materials such as polyethylene. Cracking also produces gaseous hydrogen, a widely used raw material in the chemical industry.

Other important reactions involving petroleum are run at elevated temperatures and in the presence of specific catalysts. Such reactions include *isomerization* reactions, in which

the carbon skeleton of an alkane rearranges to form a new isomeric species, and *reformation* processes, in which smaller molecules combine to form new molecules. Each process is directed toward achieving a specific goal, such as increasing the proportion of branched-chain hydrocarbons in gasoline to obtain higher octane ratings. A great amount of chemical research has gone into developing and understanding these highly specialized processes.

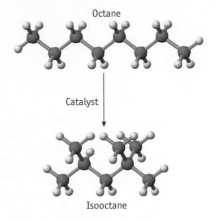

Producing gasoline. Branched hydrocarbons have a higher octane rating in gasoline. Therefore, an important process in producing gasoline is the isomerization of octane to a branched hydrocarbon such as isooctane, 2,2,4-trimethylpentane.

Although aromatic compounds are unsaturated hydrocarbons, they do not undergo the addition reactions typical of alkenes and alkynes. Instead, *substitution reactions* occur, in which one or more hydrogen atoms are replaced by other groups. Such reactions require a strong Brønsted acid such as H_2SO_4 or a Lewis acid such as $AlCl_3$ or $FeBr_3$.

Nitration: $\quad C_6H_6(\ell) + HNO_3(\ell) \xrightarrow{H_2SO_4} C_6H_5NO_2(\ell) + H_2O(\ell)$

Alkylation: $\quad C_6H_6(\ell) + CH_3Cl(\ell) \xrightarrow{AlCl_3} C_6H_5CH_3(\ell) + HCl(g)$

Halogenation: $\quad C_6H_6(\ell) + Br_2(\ell) \xrightarrow{FeBr_3} C_6H_5Br(\ell) + HBr(g)$

10.3 Alcohols, Ethers, and Amines

Other types of organic compounds arise as elements other than carbon and hydrogen are included in the compound. Two elements in particular, oxygen and nitrogen, add a rich dimension to carbon chemistry.

TABLE 10.6 Common Functional Groups and Derivatives of Alkanes

Functional Group*	General Formula*	Class of Compound	Examples
F, Cl, Br, I	RF, RCl, RBr, RI	haloalkane	CH_3CH_2Cl, chloroethane
OH	ROH	alcohol	CH_3CH_2OH, ethanol
OR'	ROR'	ether	$(CH_3CH_2)_2O$, diethyl ether
NH_2†	RNH_2	(primary) amine	$CH_3CH_2NH_2$, ethylamine
$\overset{O}{\overset{\|}{-CH}}$	RCHO	aldehyde	CH_3CHO, ethanal (acetaldehyde)
$\overset{O}{\overset{\|}{-C-R'}}$	RCOR'	ketone	CH_3COCH_3, propanone (acetone)
$\overset{O}{\overset{\|}{-C-OH}}$	RCO_2H	carboxylic acid	CH_3CO_2H, ethanoic acid (acetic acid)
$\overset{O}{\overset{\|}{-C-OR'}}$	RCO_2R'	ester	$CH_3CO_2CH_3$, methyl acetate
$\overset{O}{\overset{\|}{-C-NH_2}}$	$RCONH_2$	amide	CH_3CONH_2, acetamide

* R and R' can be the same or different hydrocarbon groups.
† Secondary amines (R_2NH) and tertiary amines (R_3N) are also possible, see discussion in the text.

Organic chemistry organizes compounds containing elements other than carbon and hydrogen as derivatives of hydrocarbons. Formulas (and structures) are represented by substituting one or more hydrogens in a hydrocarbon molecule by a **functional group.** A functional group is an atom or group of atoms attached to a carbon atom in the hydrocarbon. Formulas of hydrocarbon derivatives are then written as R—X, in which R is a hydrocarbon lacking a hydrogen atom, and X is the functional group that has replaced the hydrogen. The chemical and physical properties of the hydrocarbon derivatives are a blend of the properties associated with hydrocarbons and the group that has been substituted for hydrogen.

Table 10.6 identifies some common functional groups and the families of organic compounds resulting from their attachment to a hydrocarbon.

Chemistry ⚛ Now™

Sign in at **www.cengage.com/login** and go to Chapter 10 Contents to see Screen 10.5 for a description of the **types of organic functional groups** and for tutorials on **their structures, bonding, and chemistry.**

Alcohols and Ethers

If one of the hydrogen atoms of an alkane is replaced by a hydroxyl (—OH) group, the result is an **alcohol,** ROH. Methanol, CH_3OH, and ethanol, CH_3CH_2OH, are the most important alcohols, but others are also commercially important (Table 10.7). Notice that several have more than one OH functional group.

More than 5×10^8 kg of methanol is produced in the United States annually. Most of this production is used to make formaldehyde (CH_2O) and acetic acid

Alcohol racing fuel. Methanol, CH_3OH, is used as the fuel in cars of the type that race in Indianapolis.

TABLE 10.7 **Some Important Alcohols**

Condensed Formula	BP (°C)	Systematic Name	Common Name	Use
CH_3OH	65.0	methanol	methyl alcohol	fuel, gasoline additive, making formaldehyde
CH_3CH_2OH	78.5	ethanol	ethyl alcohol	beverages, gasoline additive, solvent
$CH_3CH_2CH_2OH$	97.4	1-propanol	propyl alcohol	industrial solvent
$CH_3CH(OH)CH_3$	82.4	2-propanol	isopropyl alcohol	rubbing alcohol
$HOCH_2CH_2OH$	198	1,2-ethanediol	ethylene glycol	antifreeze
$HOCH_2CH(OH)CH_2OH$	290	1,2,3-propanetriol	glycerol (glycerin)	moisturizer in consumer products

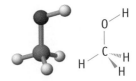

Methanol, CH_3OH, is the simplest alcohol. Methanol is often called "wood alcohol" because it was originally produced by heating wood in the absence of air.

(CH_3CO_2H), both important chemicals in their own right. Methanol is also used as a solvent, as a de-icer in gasoline, and as a fuel in high-powered racing cars. It is found in low concentration in new wine, where it contributes to the odor, or "bouquet." Like ethanol, methanol causes intoxication, but methanol differs in being more poisonous, largely because the human body converts it to formic acid (HCO_2H) and formaldehyde (CH_2O). These compounds attack the cells of the retina in the eye, leading to permanent blindness.

Ethanol is the "alcohol" of alcoholic beverages, in which it is formed by the anaerobic (without air) fermentation of sugar. For many years, industrial alcohol, which is used as a solvent and as a starting material for the synthesis of other compounds, was made by fermentation. In the last several decades, however, it has become cheaper to make ethanol from petroleum by-products—specifically, by the addition of water to ethylene.

■ **Aerobic Fermentation** Aerobic fermentation (in the presence of O_2) of sugar leads to the formation of acetic acid. This is how wine vinegar is made.

$$\underset{\text{ethylene}}{\overset{H}{\underset{H}{>}}C=C\overset{H}{\underset{H}{<}}} \text{ (g)} + H_2O\text{(g)} \xrightarrow{\text{catalyst}} \underset{\text{ethanol}}{H-\overset{\overset{H}{|}}{\underset{\underset{H}{|}}{C}}-\overset{\overset{H}{|}}{\underset{\underset{H}{|}}{C}}-OH(\ell)}$$

Beginning with three-carbon alcohols, structural isomers are possible. For example, 1-propanol and 2-propanol (common name, isopropyl alcohol) are different compounds (Table 10.7).

Ethylene glycol and glycerol are common alcohols having two and three —OH groups, respectively. Ethylene glycol is used as antifreeze in automobiles. Glycerol's most common use is as a softener in soaps and lotions. It is also a raw material for the preparation of nitroglycerin (Figure 10.8).

	$H-\overset{\overset{H}{|}}{\underset{\underset{OH}{|}}{C}}-\overset{\overset{H}{|}}{\underset{\underset{OH}{|}}{C}}-H$	$H-\overset{\overset{H}{|}}{\underset{\underset{OH}{|}}{C}}-\overset{\overset{H}{|}}{\underset{\underset{OH}{|}}{C}}-\overset{\overset{H}{|}}{\underset{\underset{OH}{|}}{C}}-H$
Systematic name:	1,2-ethanediol	1,2,3-propanetriol
Common name:	ethylene glycol	glycerol or glycerin

Charles D. Winters

Rubbing alcohol. Common rubbing alcohol is 2-propanol, also called isopropyl alcohol.

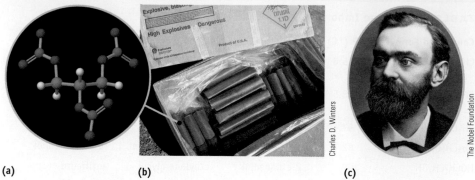

(a)   (b)   (c)

FIGURE 10.8 Nitroglycerin. (a) Concentrated nitric acid and glycerin react to form an oily, highly unstable compound called nitroglycerin, $C_3H_5(ONO_2)_3$. (b) Nitroglycerin is more stable if absorbed onto an inert solid, a combination called dynamite. (c) The fortune of Alfred Nobel (1833–1896), built on the manufacture of dynamite, now funds the Nobel Prizes.

■ EXAMPLE 10.6 Structural Isomers of Alcohols

Problem How many different alcohols are derivatives of pentane? Draw structures, and name each alcohol.

Strategy Pentane, C_5H_{12}, has a five-carbon chain. An —OH group can replace a hydrogen atom on one of the carbon atoms. Alcohols are named as derivatives of the alkane (pentane) by replacing the "-e" at the end with "-ol" and indicating the position of the —OH group by a numerical prefix (Appendix E).

Solution Three different alcohols are possible, depending on whether the —OH group is placed on the first, second, or third carbon atom in the chain. (The fourth and fifth positions are identical to the second and first positions in the chain, respectively.)

1-pentanol

2-pentanol

3-pentanol

Comment Additional structural isomers with the formula $C_5H_{11}OH$ are possible in which the longest carbon chain has three C atoms (one isomer) or four C atoms (four isomers).

EXERCISE 10.6 Structures of Alcohols

Draw the structure of 1-butanol and alcohols that are structural isomers of the compound.

Properties of Alcohols and Ethers

Methane, CH_4, is a gas (boiling point, $-161\ °C$) with low solubility in water. Methanol, CH_3OH, by contrast, is a liquid that is *miscible* with water in all proportions. The boiling point of methanol, 65 °C, is 226 °C higher than the boiling point of methane. What a difference the addition of a single atom into the structure can make in the properties of simple molecules!

Alcohols are related to water, with one of the H atoms of H_2O being replaced by an organic group. If a methyl group is substituted for one of the hydrogens of water, methanol results. Ethanol has a —C_2H_5 (ethyl) group, and propanol has a —C_3H_7 (propyl) group in place of one of the hydrogens of water. Viewing alcohols as related to water also helps in understanding the properties of alcohols.

The two parts of methanol, the —CH_3 group and the —OH group, contribute to its properties. For example, methanol will burn, a property associated with hydrocarbons. On the other hand, its boiling point is more like that of water. The temperature at which a substance boils is related to the forces of attraction between molecules, called *intermolecular forces:* The stronger the attractive, intermolecular forces in a sample, the higher the boiling point (▶ Section 12.4). These forces are particularly strong in water, a result of the polarity of the —OH group in this molecule (◀ Section 8.8). Methanol is also a polar molecule, and it is the polar —OH group that leads to a high boiling point. In contrast, methane is nonpolar and its low boiling point is the result of weak intermolecular forces.

It is also possible to explain the differences in the solubility of methane and methanol in water. The solubility of methanol is conferred by the polar —OH portion of the molecule. Methane, which is nonpolar, has low water-solubility.

■ **Hydrogen Bonding** The intermolecular forces of attraction of compounds with hydrogen attached to a highly electronegative atom, like O, N, or F, are so exceptional that they are accorded a special name: hydrogen bonding. We will discuss hydrogen bonding in Section 12.2.

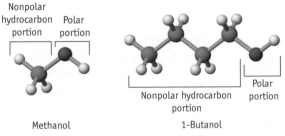

Nonpolar hydrocarbon portion   Polar portion

Methanol

Nonpolar hydrocarbon portion   Polar portion

1-Butanol

As the size of the alkyl group in an alcohol increases, the alcohol boiling point rises, a general trend seen in families of similar compounds and related to molar mass (see Table 10.7). The solubility in water in this series decreases. Methanol and ethanol are completely miscible in water, whereas 1-propanol is moderately water-soluble; 1-butanol is less soluble than 1-propanol. With an increase in the size of the hydrocarbon group, the organic group (the nonpolar part of the molecule) has become a larger fraction of the molecule, and properties associated with nonpolarity begin to dominate. Space-filling models show that in methanol, the polar and nonpolar parts of the molecule are approximately similar in size, but in 1-butanol the —OH group is less than 20% of the molecule. The molecule is less like water and more "organic."

Attaching an additional—OH group to a hydrocarbon framework has an effect on water solubility (Figure 10.9). Two —OH groups on a three-carbon framework, as found in propylene glycol, convey complete miscibility with water, in contrast to the limited solubility of 1-propanol and 2-propanol.

Ethers have the general formula ROR′. The best-known ether is diethyl ether, $CH_3CH_2OCH_2CH_3$. Lacking an —OH group, the properties of ethers are in sharp contrast to those of alcohols. Diethyl ether, for example, has a lower boiling point (34.5 °C) than ethanol, CH_3CH_2OH (78.3 °C), and is only slightly soluble in water.

Chemistry.☼.Now™

Sign in at **www.cengage.com/login** and go to Chapter 10 Contents to see Screen 10.6 for an exercise on **substitution and elimination reactions of alcohols.**

Charles D. Winters

Safe antifreeze—propylene glycol, $CH_3CHOHCH_2OH$. Most antifreeze sold today consists of about 95% ethylene glycol. Cats and dogs are attracted by the smell and taste of the compound, but it is toxic. In fact, only a few milliliters can prove fatal to a small dog or cat. In the first stage of poisoning, an animal may appear drunk, but within 12–36 hours the kidneys stop functioning, and the animal slips into a coma. To avoid accidental poisoning of domestic and wild animals, you can use propylene glycol antifreeze. This compound affords the same antifreeze protection but is much less toxic.

Polar portion   Nonpolar hydrocarbon portion

Polar portion

Methanol is often added to automobile gasoline tanks in the winter to prevent fuel lines from freezing. It is soluble in water and lowers the water's freezing point.

Ethylene glycol is used in automobile radiators. It is soluble in water, and lowers the freezing point and raises the boiling point of the water in the cooling system. (See Section 14.4.)

Ethylene glycol, a major component of automobile antifreeze, is completely miscible with water.

FIGURE 10.9 Properties and uses of methanol and ethylene glycol.

Amines

It is often convenient to think about water and ammonia as being similar molecules: They are the simplest hydrogen compounds of adjacent second-period elements. Both are polar and exhibit some similar chemistry, such as protonation (to give H_3O^+ and NH_4^+) and deprotonation (to give OH^- and NH_2^-).

This comparison of water and ammonia can be extended to alcohols and amines. Alcohols have formulas related to water in which one hydrogen in H_2O is replaced with an organic group (R—OH). In organic **amines,** one or more hydrogen atoms of NH_3 are replaced with an organic group. Amine structures are similar to ammonia's structure; that is, the geometry about the N atom is trigonal pyramidal.

Amines are categorized based on the number of organic substituents as primary (one organic group), secondary (two organic groups), or tertiary (three organic groups). As examples, consider the three amines with methyl groups: CH_3NH_2, $(CH_3)_2NH$, and $(CH_3)_3N$.

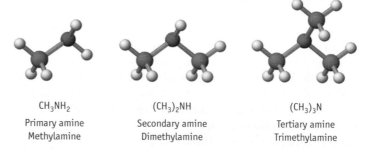

CH_3NH_2
Primary amine
Methylamine

$(CH_3)_2NH$
Secondary amine
Dimethylamine

$(CH_3)_3N$
Tertiary amine
Trimethylamine

Properties of Amines

Amines usually have offensive odors. You know what the odor is if you have ever smelled decaying fish. Two appropriately named amines, putrescine and cadaverine, add to the odor of urine, rotten meat, and bad breath.

$H_2NCH_2CH_2CH_2CH_2NH_2$
putrescine
1,4-butanediamine

$H_2NCH_2CH_2CH_2CH_2CH_2NH_2$
cadaverine
1,5-pentanediamine

The smallest amines are water-soluble, but most amines are not. All amines are bases, however, and they react with acids to give salts, many of which are water-soluble. As with ammonia, the reactions involve adding H^+ to the lone pair of electrons on the N atom. This is illustrated by the reaction of aniline (aminobenzene) with H_2SO_4 to give anilinium sulfate, a compound of some historical interest (see "Historical Perspectives: Mauvine").

$$C_6H_5NH_2(aq) + H_2SO_4(aq) \longrightarrow C_6H_5NH_3^+(aq) + HSO_4^-(aq)$$

Aniline Anilinium ion

Historical Perspectives

Mauveine

Among the roots of modern organic chemistry was the synthesis, in 1856, of the compound mauveine (or mauve) by William Henry Perkin (1838–1907). This discovery led to a flourishing dye industry, one of the first chemical industries.

The discovery of mauve is an interesting tale. At the age of 13, Perkin enrolled at the City of London School. His father paid an

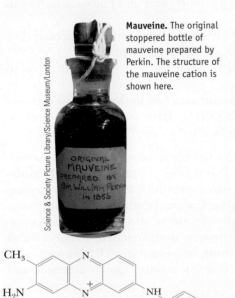

Mauveine. The original stoppered bottle of mauveine prepared by Perkin. The structure of the mauveine cation is shown here.

extra fee for him to attend a lunchtime chemistry course and set up a lab at home for him to do experiments. He began attending the public lectures that Michael Faraday gave on Saturdays at the Royal Institution. At 15, Perkin enrolled in the Royal College of Science in London to study chemistry under the school's Director, August Wilhelm von Hofmann. After he completed his studies at age 17, he took a position at the college as Hofmann's assistant, rather a great honor.

Perkin's first project was to synthesize quinine, an antimalarial drug. The route he proposed involved oxidizing anilinium sulfate. From the reaction, he obtained a black solid that dissolved in a water-ethanol mixture to give a purple solution that stained cloth a beautiful purple color. The color didn't wash out, an essential feature for a dye. Later, it was learned that the anilinium sulfate Perkin used had been impure and that the impurity was essential in the synthesis. Had Perkins used a pure sample or his starting reagent, the discovery of mauve would not have happened. A study in 1994 on samples of mauve preserved in museums determined that Perkin's mauve was actually a mixture of two very similar compounds, along with traces of several others.

At the age of 18, Perkin quit his assistantship and, with financial help from his family, set up a dye factory outside of London. By the age of 36, he was a very wealthy man. He

then retired from the dye business and devoted the rest of his life to chemical research on various topics, including the synthesis of fragrances and a study of optical activity. During his lifetime, he received numerous honors for his research, but one honor came many years after his death. In 1972, when The Chemical Society (in England) renamed its journals after famous society members, it chose Perkin's name for the organic chemistry journals. (See *Mauve,* a book on Perkin's life, by S. Garfield, W. W. Norton Publishers, New York.)

A silk dress dyed with Perkin's original sample of mauve in 1862, at the dawning of the synthetic dye industry. From *Mauve.*

Nicotine

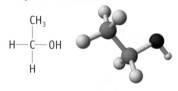
Primary alcohol: ethanol

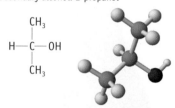
Secondary alcohol: 2-propanol

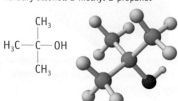
Tertiary alcohol: 2-methyl-2-propanol

Nicotine. Two nitrogen atoms in the nicotine molecule can be protonated, which is the form in which nicotine is normally found. The protons can be removed, however, by treating it with a base. This "free-base" form is much more poisonous and addictive. See J. F. Pankow: *Environmental Science & Technology,* Vol 31, p. 2428, August 1997.

The facts that an amine can be protonated and that the proton can be removed again by treating the compound with a base have practical and physiological importance. Nicotine in cigarettes is normally found in the protonated form. (This water-soluble form is often used in insecticides.) Adding a base such as ammonia removes the H⁺ ion to leave nicotine in its "free-base" form.

$$NicH_2^{2+}(aq) + 2\ NH_3(aq) \rightarrow Nic(aq) + 2\ NH_4^+(aq)$$

In this form, nicotine is much more readily absorbed by the skin and mucous membranes, so the compound is a much more potent poison.

10.4 Compounds with a Carbonyl Group

Formaldehyde, acetic acid, and acetone are among the organic compounds referred to in previous examples. These compounds have a common structural feature: Each contains a trigonal-planar carbon atom doubly bonded to an oxygen. The C=O group is called the **carbonyl group,** and all of these compounds are members of a large class of compounds called **carbonyl compounds.**

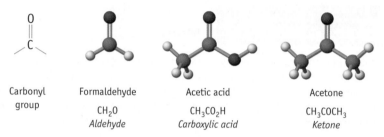

| Carbonyl group | Formaldehyde CH_2O *Aldehyde* | Acetic acid CH_3CO_2H *Carboxylic acid* | Acetone CH_3COCH_3 *Ketone* |

In this section, we will examine five groups of carbonyl compounds (Table 10.6, page 462):

- *Aldehydes* (RCHO) have an organic group (—R) and an H atom attached to a carbonyl group.
- *Ketones* (RCOR′) have two —R groups attached to the carbonyl carbon; they may be the same groups, as in acetone, or different groups.
- *Carboxylic acids* (RCO₂H) have an —R group and an —OH group attached to the carbonyl carbon.
- *Esters* (RCO₂R′) have —R and —OR′ groups attached to the carbonyl carbon.
- *Amides* (RCONR₂′, RCONHR′, and RCONH₂) have an —R group and an amino group (—NH₂, —NHR, —NR₂) bonded to the carbonyl carbon.

Aldehydes, ketones, and carboxylic acids are oxidation products of alcohols and, indeed, are commonly made by this route. The product obtained through oxidation of an alcohol depends on the alcohol's structure, which is classified according to the number of carbon atoms bonded to the C atom bearing the —OH group. *Primary alcohols* have one carbon and two hydrogen atoms attached, whereas *secondary alcohols* have two carbon atoms and one hydrogen atom attached. *Tertiary alcohols* have three carbon atoms attached to the C atom bearing the —OH group.

A *primary alcohol* is oxidized in two steps. It is first oxidized to an aldehyde and then in a second step to a carboxylic acid:

For example, the air oxidation of ethanol in wine produces wine (with excess oxygen) vinegar, the most important ingredient of which is acetic acid.

$$\underset{\text{ethanol}}{\text{H}-\overset{\displaystyle\overset{\text{H}}{|}}{\underset{\displaystyle\underset{\text{H}}{|}}{\text{C}}}-\overset{\displaystyle\overset{\text{H}}{|}}{\underset{\displaystyle\underset{\text{H}}{|}}{\text{C}}}-\text{OH}(\ell)} \xrightarrow{\text{oxidizing agent}} \underset{\text{acetic acid}}{\text{H}-\overset{\displaystyle\overset{\text{H}}{|}}{\underset{\displaystyle\underset{\text{H}}{|}}{\text{C}}}-\overset{\displaystyle\overset{\text{O}}{\|}}{\text{C}}-\text{OH}(\ell)}$$

FIGURE 10.10 Alcohol tester. This device for testing a person's breath for the presence of ethanol relies on the oxidation of the alcohol. If present, ethanol is oxidized by potassium dichromate, $K_2Cr_2O_7$, to acetaldehyde, and then to acetic acid. The yellow-orange dichromate ion is reduced to green $Cr^{3+}(aq)$, the color change indicating that ethanol was present.

Acids have a sour taste. The word "vinegar" (from the French *vin aigre*) means sour wine. A device to test one's breath for alcohol relies on a similar oxidation of ethanol (Figures 3.21 and 10.10).

In contrast to primary alcohols, oxidation of a *secondary alcohol* produces a ketone:

$$\underset{\text{secondary alcohol}}{\text{R}-\overset{\displaystyle\overset{\text{OH}}{|}}{\underset{\displaystyle\underset{\text{H}}{|}}{\text{C}}}-\text{R}'} \xrightarrow[\text{agent}]{\text{oxidizing}} \underset{\text{ketone}}{\text{R}-\overset{\displaystyle\overset{\text{O}}{\|}}{\text{C}}-\text{R}'}$$

(—R and —R′ are organic groups. They may be the same or different.)

Common oxidizing agents used for these reactions are reagents such as $KMnO_4$ and $K_2Cr_2O_7$ (Table 3.4).

Finally, tertiary alcohols do *not* react with the usual oxidizing agents.

$$(CH_3)_3COH \xrightarrow{\text{oxidizing agent}} \text{no reaction}$$

Aldehydes and Ketones

Aldehydes and **ketones** have pleasant odors and are often used in fragrances. Benzaldehyde is responsible for the odor of almonds and cherries; cinnamaldehyde is found in the bark of the cinnamon tree; and the ketone 4-(*p*-hydroxyphenyl) 2-butanone is responsible for the odor of ripe raspberries (a favorite of the authors of this book). Table 10.8 lists several simple aldehydes and ketones.

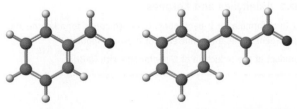

Benzaldehyde, C_6H_5CHO *trans*-Cinnamaldehyde, $C_6H_5CH{=}CHCHO$

Aldehydes and ketones are the oxidation products of primary and secondary alcohols, respectively. The reverse reactions—reduction of aldehydes to primary alcohols and reduction of ketones to secondary alcohols—are also known.

TABLE 10.8 Simple Aldehydes and Ketones

Structure	Common Name	Systematic Name	BP (°C)
$\overset{\text{O}}{\overset{\|}{\text{HCH}}}$	formaldehyde	methanal	−19
$\overset{\text{O}}{\overset{\|}{\text{CH}_3\text{CH}}}$	acetaldehyde	ethanal	20
$\overset{\text{O}}{\overset{\|}{\text{CH}_3\text{CCH}_3}}$	acetone	propanone	56
$\overset{\text{O}}{\overset{\|}{\text{CH}_3\text{CCH}_2\text{CH}_3}}$	methyl ethyl ketone	butanone	80
$\overset{\text{O}}{\overset{\|}{\text{CH}_3\text{CH}_2\text{CCH}_2\text{CH}_3}}$	diethyl ketone	3-pentanone	102

Aldehydes and odors. The odors of almonds and cinnamon are due to aldehydes, but the odor of fresh raspberries comes from a ketone.

Commonly used reagents for such reductions are $NaBH_4$ and $LiAlH_4$, although H_2 is used on an industrial scale.

$$R-\overset{\text{O}}{\overset{\|}{\text{C}}}-H \xrightarrow{\text{NaBH}_4 \text{ or LiAlH}_4} R-\overset{\text{OH}}{\underset{\text{H}}{\overset{\|}{\text{C}}}}-H$$

aldehyde   primary alcohol

$$R-\overset{\text{O}}{\overset{\|}{\text{C}}}-R \xrightarrow{\text{NaBH}_4 \text{ or LiAlH}_4} R-\overset{\text{OH}}{\underset{\text{H}}{\overset{\|}{\text{C}}}}-R$$

ketone   secondary alcohol

EXERCISE 10.7 Aldehydes and Ketones

(a) Draw the structural formula for 2-pentanone. Draw structures for a ketone and two aldehydes that are isomers of 2-pentanone, and name each of these compounds.

(b) What is the product of the reduction of 2-pentanone with $NaBH_4$?

EXERCISE 10.8 Aldehydes and Ketones

Draw the structures, and name the aldehyde or ketone formed upon oxidation of the following alcohols: **(a)** 1-butanol, **(b)** 2-butanol, **(c)** 2-methyl-1-propanol. Are these three alcohols structural isomers? Are the oxidation products structural isomers?

Carboxylic Acids

Acetic acid is the most common and most important **carboxylic acid.** For many years, acetic acid was made by oxidizing ethanol produced by fermentation. Now, however, acetic acid is generally made by combining carbon monoxide and methanol in the presence of a catalyst:

$$CH_3OH(\ell) + CO(g) \xrightarrow{\text{catalyst}} CH_3CO_2H(\ell)$$
$$\text{methanol} \qquad\qquad\qquad \text{acetic acid}$$

About 1 billion kilograms of acetic acid are produced annually in the United States for use in plastics, synthetic fibers, and fungicides.

Many organic acids are found naturally (Table 10.9). Acids are recognizable by their sour taste (Figure 10.11) and are found in common foods: Citric acid in fruits, acetic acid in vinegar, and tartaric acid in grapes are just three examples.

Some carboxylic acids have common names derived from the source of the acid (Table 10.9). Because formic acid is found in ants, its name comes from the Latin word for ant (*formica*). Butyric acid gives rancid butter its unpleasant odor, and the name is related to the Latin word for butter (*butyrum*). The systematic names of acids (Table 10.10) are formed by dropping the "-e" on the name of the corresponding alkane and adding "-oic" (and the word "acid").

Because of the substantial electronegativity of oxygen, the two O atoms of the carboxylic acid group are slightly negatively charged, and the H atom of the —OH group is positively charged. This charge distribution has several important implications:

- The polar acetic acid molecule dissolves readily in water, which you already know because vinegar is an aqueous solution of acetic acid. (Acids with larger organic groups are less soluble, however.)

FIGURE 10.11 Acetic acid in bread. Acetic acid is produced in bread when leavened with the yeast *Saccharomyces exigus*. Another group of bacteria, *Lactobacillus sanfrancisco*, contributes to the flavor of sourdough bread. These bacteria metabolize the sugar maltose, excreting acetic acid and lactic acid, $CH_3CH(OH)CO_2H$, thereby giving the bread its unique sour taste.

TABLE 10.9 Some Naturally Occurring Carboxylic Acids

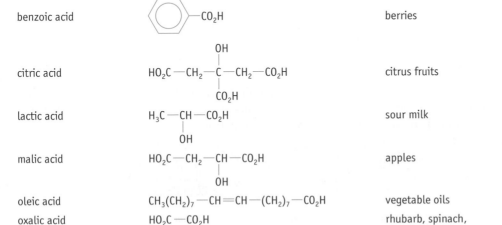

Name	Structure	Natural Source
benzoic acid	⬡—CO₂H	berries
citric acid	HO₂C—CH₂—C(OH)—CH₂—CO₂H (with CO₂H below)	citrus fruits
lactic acid	H₃C—CH(OH)—CO₂H	sour milk
malic acid	HO₂C—CH₂—CH(OH)—CO₂H	apples
oleic acid	CH₃(CH₂)₇—CH=CH—(CH₂)₇—CO₂H	vegetable oils
oxalic acid	HO₂C—CO₂H	rhubarb, spinach, cabbage, tomatoes
stearic acid	CH₃(CH₂)₁₆—CO₂H	animal fats
tartaric acid	HO₂C—CH(OH)—CH(OH)—CO₂H	grape juice, wine

Formic acid, HCO_2H. This acid puts the sting in ant bites.

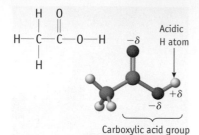

Acetic acid. The H atom of the carboxylic acid group (—CO₂H) is the acidic proton of this and other carboxylic acids.

TABLE 10.10 Some Simple Carboxylic Acids

Structure	Common Name	Systematic Name	BP (°C)
$\underset{\text{HCOH}}{\overset{\displaystyle O \atop \|}{}}$	formic acid	methanoic acid	101
$\underset{CH_3COH}{\overset{\displaystyle O \atop \|}{}}$	acetic acid	ethanoic acid	118
$\underset{CH_3CH_2COH}{\overset{\displaystyle O \atop \|}{}}$	propionic acid	propanoic acid	141
$\underset{CH_3(CH_2)_2COH}{\overset{\displaystyle O \atop \|}{}}$	butyric acid	butanoic acid	163
$\underset{CH_3(CH_2)_3COH}{\overset{\displaystyle O \atop \|}{}}$	valeric acid	pentanoic acid	187

- The hydrogen of the —OH group is the acidic hydrogen. As noted in Chapter 3, acetic acid is a weak acid in water, as are most other organic acids.

Carboxylic acids undergo a number of reactions. Among these is the reduction of the acid (with reagents such as $LiAlH_4$ or $NaBH_4$) first to an aldehyde and then to an alcohol. For example, acetic acid is reduced first to acetaldehyde and then to ethanol.

$$CH_3CO_2H \xrightarrow{\text{LiAlH}_4} CH_3CHO \xrightarrow{\text{LiAlH}_4} CH_3CH_2OH$$
$$\text{acetic acid} \qquad\qquad \text{acetaldehyde} \qquad\qquad \text{ethanol}$$

Yet another important aspect of carboxylic acid chemistry is these acids' reaction with bases to give carboxylate anions. For example, acetic acid reacts with sodium hydroxide to give sodium acetate (sodium ethanoate).

$$CH_3CO_2H(aq) + OH^-(aq) \rightarrow CH_3CO_2^-(aq) + H_2O(\ell)$$

Esters

Carboxylic acids (RCO_2H) react with alcohols ($R'OH$) to form esters (RCO_2R') in an **esterification** reaction. (These reactions are generally run in the presence of strong acids because acids accelerate the reaction.)

$$\underset{\text{carboxylic acid}}{\overset{\displaystyle O \atop \|}{RC}-(O-H)} + \underset{\text{alcohol}}{R'-O-(H)} \xrightarrow{\text{H}_3\text{O}^+} \underset{\text{ester}}{\overset{\displaystyle O \atop \|}{RC}-O-R'} + H_2O$$

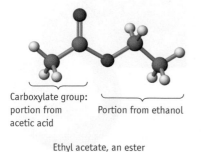

Carboxylate group: portion from acetic acid   Portion from ethanol

Ethyl acetate, an ester
$CH_3CO_2CH_2CH_3$

$$\underset{\text{acetic acid}}{\overset{\displaystyle O \atop \|}{CH_3COH}} + \underset{\text{ethanol}}{CH_3CH_2OH} \xrightarrow{\text{H}_3\text{O}^+} \underset{\text{ethyl acetate}}{\overset{\displaystyle O \atop \|}{CH_3COCH_2CH_3}} + H_2O$$

Glucose and Sugars

Having described alcohols and carbonyl compounds, we now pause to look at glucose, the most common, naturally occurring carbohydrate.

As their name implies, formulas of carbohydrates can be written as though they are a combination of carbon and water, $C_x(H_2O)_y$. Thus, the formula of glucose, $C_6H_{12}O_6$, is equivalent to $C_6(H_2O)_6$. This compound is a sugar, or, more accurately, a **monosaccharide**.

Carbohydrates are polyhydroxy aldehydes or ketones. Glucose is an interesting molecule that exists in three different isomeric forms. Two of the isomers contain six-member rings; the third isomer features a chain structure. In solution, the three forms rapidly interconvert.

Notice that glucose is a chiral molecule. In the chain structure, four of the carbon atoms are bonded to four different groups.

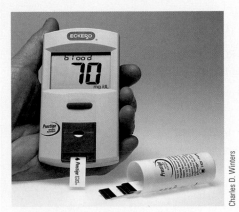

Home test for glucose.

Charles D. Winters

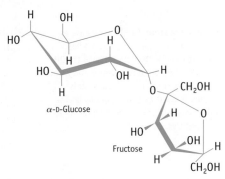

α-D-Glucose   Open-chain form β-D-Glucose

In nature, glucose occurs in just one of its enantiomeric forms; thus, a solution of glucose rotates polarized light.

Knowing glucose's structure allows one to predict some of its properties. With five polar —OH groups in the molecule, glucose is, not surprisingly, soluble in water.

The aldehyde group is susceptible to chemical oxidation to form a carboxylic acid. Detection of glucose (in urine or blood) takes advantage of this fact; diagnostic tests for glucose involve oxidation with subsequent detection of the products.

Glucose is in a class of sugar molecules called hexoses, molecules having six carbon atoms. 2-Deoxyribose, the sugar in the backbone of the DNA molecule, is a pentose, a molecule with five carbon atoms.

deoxyribose, a pentose, part of the DNA backbone

Glucose and other monosaccharides serve as the building blocks for larger carbohydrates. Sucrose, a disaccharide, is formed from a molecule of glucose and a molecule of fructose, another monosaccharide. Starch is a polymer composed of many monosaccharide units.

α-D-Glucose

Fructose

The structure of sucrose. Sucrose is formed from α-D-glucose and fructose. An ether linkage is formed by loss of H_2O from two —OH groups.

When a carboxylic acid and an alcohol react to form an ester, the OR group of the alcohol ends up as part of the ester (as shown above). This fact is known because of isotope labeling experiments. If the reaction is run using an alcohol in which the alcohol oxygen is ^{18}O, all of the ^{18}O ends up in the ester molecule.

Table 10.11 lists a few common esters and the acid and alcohol from which they are formed. The two-part name of an ester is given by (1) the name of the hydrocarbon group from the alcohol and (2) the name of the carboxylate group derived from the acid name by replacing "-ic" with "-ate." For example, ethanol (commonly called ethyl alcohol) and acetic acid combine to give the ester ethyl acetate.

An important reaction of esters is their **hydrolysis** (literally, reaction with water), a reaction that is the reverse of the formation of the ester. The reaction, generally

Charles D. Winters

Esters. Many fruits such as bananas and strawberries as well as consumer products (here, perfume and oil of wintergreen) contain esters.

TABLE 10.11   Some Acids, Alcohols, and Their Esters

Acid	Alcohol	Ester	Odor of Ester
CH_3CO_2H acetic acid	$\overset{\displaystyle CH_3}{\underset{\displaystyle \text{3-methyl-1-butanol}}{CH_3CHCH_2CH_2OH}}$	$\overset{\displaystyle O \quad\quad CH_3}{\underset{\displaystyle \text{3-methylbutyl acetate}}{CH_3COCH_2CH_2CHCH_3}}$	banana
$CH_3CH_2CH_2CO_2H$ butanoic acid	$CH_3CH_2CH_2CH_2OH$ 1-butanol	$\underset{\displaystyle \text{butyl butanoate}}{CH_3CH_2CH_2COCH_2CH_2CH_2CH_3}$	pineapple
$CH_3CH_2CH_2CO_2H$ butanoic acid	benzyl alcohol — CH_2OH	$CH_3CH_2CH_2COCH_2$ — (ring) benzyl butanoate	rose

■ **Saponification** Fats and oils are esters of glycerol and long-chain acids. When reacted with a strong base (NaOH or KOH), they produce glycerol and a salt of the long-chain acid. Because this product is used as soap, the reaction is called *saponification*. See *A Closer Look: Fats and Oils,* page 476.

done in the presence of a base such as NaOH, produces the alcohol and a sodium salt of the carboxylic acid:

$$\underset{\text{ester}}{RCOR'} + NaOH \xrightarrow[\text{in water}]{\text{heat}} \underset{\text{carboxylate salt}}{RCO^-Na^+} + \underset{\text{alcohol}}{R'OH}$$

$$\underset{\text{ethyl acetate}}{CH_3COCH_2CH_3} + NaOH \xrightarrow[\text{in water}]{\text{heat}} \underset{\text{sodium acetate}}{CH_3CO^-Na^+} + \underset{\text{ethanol}}{CH_3CH_2OH}$$

The carboxylic acid can be recovered if the sodium salt is treated with a strong acid such as HCl:

$$\underset{\text{sodium acetate}}{CH_3CO^-Na^+(aq)} + HCl(aq) \longrightarrow \underset{\text{acetic acid}}{CH_3COH(aq)} + NaCl(aq)$$

Unlike the acids from which they are derived, esters often have pleasant odors (see Table 10.11). Typical examples are methyl salicylate, or "oil of wintergreen," and benzyl acetate. Methyl salicylate is derived from salicylic acid, the parent compound of aspirin.

$$\underset{\substack{\text{salicylic acid}}}{\text{(ring)}-COH} + \underset{\text{methanol}}{CH_3OH} \longrightarrow \underset{\substack{\text{methyl salicylate,}\\\text{oil of wintergreen}}}{\text{(ring)}-COCH_3} + H_2O$$

Benzyl acetate, the active component of "oil of jasmine," is formed from benzyl alcohol ($C_6H_5CH_2OH$) and acetic acid. The chemicals are inexpensive, so synthetic jasmine is a common fragrance in less-expensive perfumes and toiletries.

$$CH_3\overset{\overset{\displaystyle O}{\|}}{C}OH + \langle\bigcirc\rangle-CH_2OH \longrightarrow CH_3\overset{\overset{\displaystyle O}{\|}}{C}OCH_2-\langle\bigcirc\rangle + H_2O$$

acetic acid   benzyl alcohol   benzyl acetate
oil of jasmine

EXERCISE 10.9 Esters

Draw the structure, and name the ester formed from each of the following reactions:

(a) propanoic acid and methanol

(b) butanoic acid and 1-butanol

(c) hexanoic acid and ethanol

EXERCISE 10.10 Esters

Draw the structure, and name the acid and alcohol from which the following esters are derived:

(a) propyl acetate

(b) 3-methyl-1-pentyl benzoate

(c) ethyl salicylate

Amides

An acid and an alcohol react by loss of water to form an ester. In a similar manner, another class of organic compounds—amides—form when an acid reacts with an amine, again with loss of water.

$$R-\overset{\overset{\displaystyle O}{\|}}{C}-\overset{}{OH} + \overset{}{H}-\overset{\overset{\displaystyle R'}{|}}{N}-R' \longrightarrow R-\overset{\overset{\displaystyle O}{\|}}{C}-\overset{\overset{\displaystyle R'}{|}}{N}-R' + H_2O$$

Carboxylic acid   Amine   Amide

Amides have an organic group and an amino group ($-NH_2$, $-NHR'$, or $-NR'R$) attached to the carbonyl group.

The C atom involved in the amide bond has three bonded groups and no lone pairs around it. We would predict it should be sp^2 hybridized with trigonal-planar geometry and bond angles of approximately 120°—and this is what is found. However, the structure of the amide group offers a surprise. The N atom is also observed to have trigonal-planar geometry with bonds to three attached atoms at 120°. Because the amide nitrogen is surrounded by four pairs of electrons, we would have predicted the N atom would have sp^3 hybridization and bond angles of about 109°.

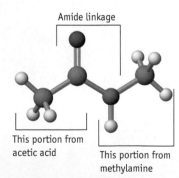

Amide linkage

This portion from acetic acid   This portion from methylamine

An amide, *N*-methylacetamide. The *N*-methyl portion of the name derives from the amine portion of the molecule, where the *N* indicates that the methyl group is attached to the nitrogen atom. The "-acet" portion of the name indicates the acid on which the amide is based.

A Closer Look

Fats and Oils

Fats and oils are among the many compounds found in plants and animal tissues. In the body, these substances serve several functions, a primary one being the storage of energy.

Fats (solids) and oils (liquids) are triesters formed from glycerol (1,2,3-propanetriol) and three carboxylic acids that can be the same or different.

$$
\begin{array}{c}
\text{H}_2\text{C}-\text{O}-\overset{\displaystyle \overset{\text{O}}{\|}}{\text{C}}\text{R} \\
\text{HC}-\text{O}-\overset{\displaystyle \overset{\text{O}}{\|}}{\text{C}}\text{R} \\
\text{H}_2\text{C}-\text{O}-\overset{\displaystyle \overset{\text{O}}{\|}}{\text{C}}\text{R}
\end{array}
$$

The carboxylic acids in fats and oils, known as *fatty acids*, have a lengthy carbon chain, usually containing between 12 and 18 carbon atoms. The hydrocarbon chains can be saturated or may include one or more double bonds. The latter are referred to as monounsaturated or polyunsaturated, depending on the number of double bonds. Saturated compounds are more common in animal products, while unsaturated fats and oils are more common in plants.

About 94% of the fatty acids in olive oil are monounsaturated. The major fatty acid is oleic acid.

Common Fatty Acids

Name	Number of C Atoms	Formula
Saturated Acids		
lauric	C_{12}	$CH_3(CH_2)_{10}CO_2H$
myristic	C_{14}	$CH_3(CH_2)_{12}CO_2H$
palmitic	C_{16}	$CH_3(CH_2)_{14}CO_2H$
stearic	C_{18}	$CH_3(CH_2)_{16}CO_2H$
Unsaturated Acid		
oleic	C_{18}	$CH_3(CH_2)_7CH{=}CH(CH_2)_7CO_2H$

In general, fats containing saturated fatty acids are solids, and those containing unsaturated fatty acids are liquids at room temperature. The difference in melting point relates to the molecular structure. With only single bonds linking carbon atoms in saturated fatty acids, the hydrocarbon group is flexible, allowing the molecules to pack more closely together. The double bonds in unsaturated fats introduce kinks that make the hydrocarbon group less flexible; consequently, the molecules pack less tightly together.

Food companies often hydrogenate vegetable oils to reduce unsaturation. The chemical rationale is that double bonds are reactive and unsaturated compounds are more susceptible to oxidation, which results in unpleasant odors. There are also aesthetic reasons for this practice. Food processors often want solid fats to improve the quality and appearance of the food. If liquid vegetable oil is used in a cake icing, for example, the icing may slide off the cake.

Polar bear fat. Polar bears feed primarily on seal blubber and build up a huge fat reserve during winter. During summer, they maintain normal activity but eat nothing, relying entirely on body fat for sustenance. A polar bear will burn about 1 to 1.5 kg of fat per day.

The conditions under which hydrogenation occurs can also lead to the isomerization of an unsaturated fat to the *trans* configuration. Such "trans-fats" in the diet have been linked to coronary heart disease.

Like other esters, fats and oils can undergo hydrolysis. This process is catalyzed by enzymes in the body. In industry, hydrolysis is carried out using aqueous NaOH or KOH to produce a mixture of glycerol and the sodium salts of the fatty acids. This reaction is called *saponification*, a term meaning "soap making."

Glyceryl stearate, a fat
R = —$(CH_2)_{16}CH_3$

$$
\begin{array}{c}
\text{H}_2\text{C}-\text{O}-\overset{\displaystyle \overset{\text{O}}{\|}}{\text{C}}\text{R} \\
\text{HC}-\text{O}-\overset{\displaystyle \overset{\text{O}}{\|}}{\text{C}}\text{R} + 3\ \text{NaOH} \\
\text{H}_2\text{C}-\text{O}-\overset{\displaystyle \overset{\text{O}}{\|}}{\text{C}}\text{R}
\end{array}
$$

$$\downarrow$$

$$
\begin{array}{c}
\text{H}_2\text{C}-\text{O}-\text{H} \\
\text{HC}-\text{O}-\text{H} + 3\ \text{R}-\overset{\displaystyle \overset{\text{O}}{\|}}{\text{C}}-\text{O}^-\ \text{Na}^+ \\
\text{H}_2\text{C}-\text{O}-\text{H}
\end{array}
$$

glycerol   sodium stearate, a soap

Simple soaps are sodium salts of fatty acids. The anion in these compounds has an ionic end (the carboxylate group) and a nonpolar end (the large hydrocarbon tail). The ionic end allows these molecules to interact with water, and the nonpolar end enables them to mix with oily and greasy substances to form an emulsion that can be washed away with water.

Charles D. Winters

©Randy Green/Taxi/Getty Images

Based on the observed geometry of the amide N atom, the atom is assigned sp^2 hybridization. To explain the observed angle and to rationalize sp^2 hybridization, we can introduce a second resonance form of the amide.

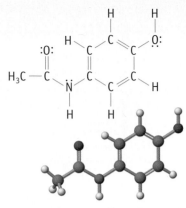

Acetaminophen, *N*-acetyl-*p*-aminophenol. This analgesic is an amide. It is used in over-the-counter painkillers such as Tylenol.

Form B contains a C=N double bond, and the O and N atoms have negative and positive charges, respectively. The N atom can be assigned sp^2 hybridization, and the π bond in B arises from overlap of p orbitals on C and N.

The existence of a second resonance structure for an amide link explains why the carbon–nitrogen bond is relatively short, about 132 pm, a value between that of a C—N single bond (149 pm) and a C=N double bond (127 pm). In addition, restricted rotation occurs around the C=N bond, making it possible for isomeric species to exist if the two groups bonded to N are different.

The amide grouping is particularly important in some synthetic polymers (Section 10.5) and in proteins (pages 496–513), where it is referred to as a *peptide link*. The compound *N*-acetyl-*p*-aminophenol, an analgesic known by the generic name acetaminophen and sold under the brand names Tylenol, Datril, and Momentum, among others, is another amide. Use of this compound as an analgesic was apparently discovered by accident when a common organic compound called acetanilide (like acetaminophen but without the —OH group) was mistakenly put into a prescription for a patient. Acetanilide acts as an analgesic, but it can be toxic. An —OH group *para* to the amide group makes the compound nontoxic, an interesting example of how a seemingly small structural difference affects chemical function.

■ **Amides, Peptides, and Proteins** When amino acids combine, they form amide or peptide links. Polymers of amino acids are proteins. For more on amino acids and proteins, see *The Chemistry of Life: Biochemistry*, pages 496–513.

Chemistry⬡Now™

Sign in at **www.cengage.com/login** and go to Chapter 10 Contents to see Screen 10.5 for a description of the **types of organic functional groups** and for tutorials on **their structures, bonding, and chemistry.**

■ **EXAMPLE 10.7 Functional Group Chemistry**

Problem

(a) Name the product of the reaction between ethylene and HCl.

(b) Draw the structure of the product of the reaction between propanoic acid and 1-propanol. What is the systematic name of the reaction product, and what functional group does it contain?

(c) What is the result of reacting 2-butanol with an oxidizing agent? Give the name, and draw the structure of the reaction product.

Strategy Ethylene is an alkene (page 453); propanoic acid is a carboxylic acid (page 471); and 2-butanol is an alcohol (page 462). Consult the discussion regarding their chemistry.

Solution

(a) HCl will add to the double bond of ethylene to produce chloroethane.

$$H_2C=CH_2 + HCl \longrightarrow H-\overset{\overset{\displaystyle H}{|}}{\underset{\underset{\displaystyle H}{|}}{C}}-\overset{\overset{\displaystyle H}{|}}{\underset{\underset{\displaystyle H}{|}}{C}}-Cl$$

ethylene   chloroethane

(b) Carboxylic acids such as propanoic acid react with alcohols to give esters.

$$CH_3CH_2\overset{\overset{\displaystyle O}{\|}}{C}OH \ + \ CH_3CH_2CH_2OH \ \longrightarrow \ CH_3CH_2\overset{\overset{\displaystyle O}{\|}}{C}OCH_2CH_2CH_3 \ + \ H_2O$$

propanoic acid   1-propanol   propyl propanoate, an ester

(c) 2-Butanol is a secondary alcohol. Such alcohols are oxidized to ketones.

$$CH_3\overset{\overset{\displaystyle OH}{|}}{C}HCH_2CH_3 \ \xrightarrow{\text{oxidizing agent}} \ CH_3\overset{\overset{\displaystyle O}{\|}}{C}CH_2CH_3$$

2-butanol   butanone, a ketone

EXERCISE 10.11 Functional Groups

(a) Name each of the following compounds and its functional group.

1. $CH_3CH_2CH_2OH$ 2. $CH_3\overset{\overset{\displaystyle O}{\|}}{C}OH$ 3. $CH_3CH_2NH_2$

(b) Name the product from the reaction of compounds 1 and 2.

(c) What is the name and structure of the product from the oxidation of 1?

(d) What compound could result from combining compounds 2 and 3?

(e) What is the result of adding an acid (say HCl) to compound 3?

10.5 Polymers

We now turn to the very large molecules known as polymers. These can be either synthetic materials or naturally occurring substances such as proteins or nucleic acids. Although these materials have widely varying compositions, their structures and properties are understandable, based on the principles developed for small molecules.

Classifying Polymers

The word *polymer* means "many parts" (from the Greek, *poly* and *meros*). **Polymers** are giant molecules made by chemically joining many small molecules called **monomers.** Polymer molar masses range from thousands to millions.

Extensive use of synthetic polymers is a fairly recent development. A few synthetic polymers (Bakelite, rayon, and celluloid) were made early in the 20th century, but most of the products with which you are familiar originated in the last 50 years. By 1976, synthetic polymers outstripped steel as the most widely used materials in the United States. The average production of synthetic polymers in the United States is approximately 150 kg per person annually.

The polymer industry classifies polymers in several different ways. One is their response to heating. **Thermoplastics** (such as polyethylene) soften and flow when they are heated and harden when they are cooled. **Thermosetting plastics** (such as Formica) are initially soft but set to a solid when heated and cannot be resoftened. Another classification scheme depends on the end use of the polymer—for example, plastics, fibers, elastomers, coatings, and adhesives.

■ **Biochemical Polymers** Polymer chemistry extends to biochemistry, where chemists study proteins and other large molecules. See *The Chemistry of Life: Biochemistry,* pages 496–513.

Biodiesel, promoted as an alternative to petroleum-based fuels used in diesel engines, is made from plant and animal oils. In the past 7 years, there has been a spectacular increase in its production and use, from under 1 million gallons in 1999 to 75 million gallons in 2005. But what is biodiesel?

© Adrian Dennis/AFP/Getty Images

Biodiesel, a mixture of long-chain esters of fatty acids.

Chemically, biodiesel is a mixture of esters of long-chain fatty acids. It is prepared from plant and animal fats and oils by *trans-esterification*. This is a reaction between an ester and an alcohol in which the —OR″ on the alcohol exchanges with the OR′ group of the ester:

$$RCO_2R' + R''OH \rightarrow RCO_2R'' + R'OH$$

Recall that fats and oils are esters (page 476), derivatives of glycerol and high–molar-mass organic acids (fatty acids). Their reaction with methanol (in the presence of a catalyst to speed up the reaction) produces a mixture of the methyl esters of long chain fatty acids and glycerol.

Glycerol, a by-product of the reaction, is a valuable commodity for the health care products industry, so it is separated and sold. The mixture of esters that remains can be used directly as a fuel in existing diesel engines, or it can be blended with petroleum products. In the latter case, the fuel mixture is identified by a designation such as B20 (B = biodiesel, 20 refers to 20% by volume.) The fuel has the advantage of being clean burning with fewer environmental problems associated with exhaust gases. In particular, there are no SO_2 emissions, one of the common problems associated with petroleum-based diesel fuels.

Proponents of the use of biodiesel note that biodiesel is produced from renewable resources, in contrast to petroleum. Critics point out, however, that growing crops for this purpose brings two problems. The first is that if crops are grown for biodiesel production, this has a negative effect on food supply. The case for biodiesel would be improved significantly, however, if it were possible to convert agricultural waste (corn stalks, for example) into a biofuel. Scientists are now actively trying to do this.

It is also pointed out that it would be impossible to grow enough crops to supply the raw materials to replace all petroleum-based diesel fuel—there isn't enough land available. Economics is also in the picture: Biodiesel is currently more expensive to produce; it is presently competitive only due to government subsidies.

Trans-esterification might seem like another kind of reaction, but it is actually closely related to chemistry we have already seen, the hydrolysis of an ester.

Ester hydrolysis:

Trans-esterification:

In both reactions, the OR′ group on the ester combines with hydrogen of second reagent (water or alcohol) as shown. In drawing this analogy, it is useful to recognize that there are other similarities in the chemistry of alcohols and water. For example, both can be protonated with strong acids (giving H_3O^+ and ROH_2^+) and deprotonated by strong bases (giving OH^- and OR^-).

Questions:

1. *Write a balanced chemical equation for the reaction that occurs when methyl myristate, $C_{13}H_{27}CO_2CH_3(\ell)$, is burned, forming $CO_2(g)$ and $H_2O(g)$.*

2. *Using enthalpy of formation data, calculate the standard enthalpy change per mole in the oxidation of methyl myristate ($\Delta_f H° = -771.0$ kJ/mol).*

3. *Which compound, methyl myristate ($C_{15}H_{30}O_2$) or hexadecane ($C_{16}H_{34}$, one of many hydrocarbons in petroleum based diesel fuel) is predicted to provide the greater energy per mole? Per liter? ($\Delta_f H°$ for $C_{16}H_{34} = -456.1$ kJ/mol) [d(methyl myristate) = 0.86 g/mL, and d($C_{16}H_{34}$) = 0.77 g/mL]*

Answers to these questions are in Appendix Q.

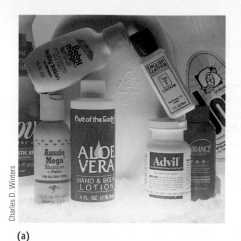
(a)

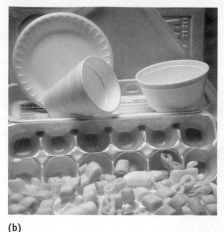
(b)

(c)

FIGURE 10.12 Common polymer-based consumer products. (a) Packaging materials from high-density polyethylene; (b) from polystyrene; and (c) from polyvinyl chloride. Recycling information is provided on most plastics (often molded into the bottom of bottles). High-density polyethylene is designated with a "2" inside a triangular symbol and the letters "HDPE." PVC is designated with a "3" inside a triangular symbol with the letter "V" below.

A more chemically oriented approach to polymer classification is based on the method of synthesis. **Addition polymers** are made by directly adding monomer units together. **Condensation polymers** are made by combining monomer units and splitting out a small molecule, often water.

Addition Polymers

Polyethylene, polystyrene, and polyvinyl chloride (PVC) are common addition polymers (Figure 10.12). They are built by "adding together" simple alkenes such as ethylene ($CH_2\!=\!CH_2$), styrene ($C_6H_5CH\!=\!CH_2$), and vinyl chloride ($CH_2\!=\!CHCl$). These and other addition polymers (Table 10.12), all derived from alkenes, have widely varying properties and uses.

Chemistry ⚛ Now™

Sign in at **www.cengage.com/login** and go to Chapter 10 Contents to see Screen 10.9 for an animation of **addition polymerization.**

Polyethylene and Other Polyolefins

Polyethylene is by far the leader in terms of addition polymer production. Ethylene (C_2H_4), the monomer from which polyethylene is made, is a product of petroleum refining and one of the top five chemicals produced in the United States. When ethylene is heated to between 100 and 250 °C at a pressure of 1000 to 3000 atm in the presence of a catalyst, polymers with molar masses up to several million are formed. The reaction can be expressed as a balanced chemical equation:

$$n\ H_2C\!=\!CH_2\ \longrightarrow\ \left(\!\begin{array}{cc} H & H \\ | & | \\ C\!-\!C \\ | & | \\ H & H \end{array}\!\right)_n$$

ethylene   polyethylene

TABLE 10.12 Ethylene Derivatives That Undergo Addition Polymerization

Formula	Monomer Common Name	Polymer Name (Trade Names)	Uses	U.S. Polymer Production (Metric tons/year) *
$H_2C=CH_2$ (H, H / C=C / H, H)	ethylene	polyethylene (polythene)	squeeze bottles, bags, films, toys and molded objects, electric insulation	7 million
(H, H / C=C / H, CH_3)	propylene	polypropylene (Vectra, Herculon)	bottles, films, indoor-outdoor carpets	1.2 million
(H, H / C=C / H, Cl)	vinyl chloride	polyvinyl chloride (PVC)	floor tile, raincoats, pipe	1.6 million
(H, H / C=C / H, CN)	acrylonitrile	polyacrylonitrile (Orlan, Acrilan)	rugs, fabrics	0.5 million
(H, H / C=C / H, C₆H₅)	styrene	polystyrene (Styrofoam, Styron)	food and drink coolers, building material insulation	0.9 million
(H, H / C=C / H, O—C(=O)—CH₃)	vinyl acetate	polyvinyl acetate (PVA)	latex paint, adhesives, textile coatings	200,000
(H, CH₃ / C=C / H, C(=O)—O—CH₃)	methyl methacrylate	polymethyl methacrylate (Plexiglass, Lucite)	high-quality transparent objects, latex paints, contact lenses	200,000
(F, F / C=C / F, F)	tetrafluoroethylene	polytetrafluoroethylene (Teflon)	gaskets, insulation, bearings, pan coatings	6,000

* One metric ton = 1000 kg.

The abbreviated formula of the reaction product, $\left(\!-CH_2CH_2\!-\right)_n$, shows that polyethylene is a chain of carbon atoms, each bearing two hydrogens. The chain length for polyethylene can be very long. A polymer with a molar mass of 1 million would contain almost 36,000 ethylene molecules linked together.

Polyethylene formed under various pressures and catalytic conditions has different properties, as a result of different molecular structures. For example, when chromium oxide is used as a catalyst, the product is almost exclusively a linear chain (Figure 10.13a). If ethylene is heated to 230 °C at high pressure, however, irregular branching occurs. Still other conditions lead to cross-linked polyethylene, in which different chains are linked together (Figures 10.13b and c).

The high–molar-mass chains of linear polyethylene pack closely together and result in a material with a density of 0.97 g/cm³. This material, referred to as

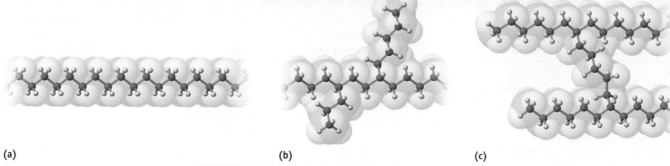

(a)   (b)   (c)

FIGURE 10.13 Polyethylene. (a) The linear form, high-density polyethylene (HDPE). (b) Branched chains occur in low-density polyethylene (LDPE). (c) Cross-linked polyethylene (CLPE).

high-density polyethylene (HDPE), is hard and tough, which makes it suitable for items such as milk bottles. If the polyethylene chain contains branches, however, the chains cannot pack as closely together, and a lower-density material (0.92 g/cm^3) known as low-density polyethylene (LDPE) results. This material is softer and more flexible than HDPE. It is used in plastic wrap and sandwich bags, among other things. Linking up the polymer chains in cross-linked polyethylene (CLPE) causes the material to be even more rigid and inflexible. Plastic bottle caps are often made of CLPE.

Polymers formed from substituted ethylenes (CH_2=CHX) have a range of properties and uses (see Table 10.12). Sometimes, the properties are predictable based on the molecule's structure. Polymers without polar substituent groups, such as polystyrene, often dissolve in organic solvents, a property useful for some types of fabrication (Figure 10.14).

Polymers based on substituted ethylenes, H_2C=CHX

$$\left(CH_2CH\atop OH\right)_n \qquad \left(CH_2CH\atop \underset{O}{\overset{}{OCCH_3}}\right)_n \qquad \left(CH_2CH\atop C_6H_5\right)_n$$

polyvinyl alcohol   polyvinyl acetate   polystyrene

Polyvinyl alcohol is a polymer with little affinity for nonpolar solvents but an affinity for water, which is not surprising, based on the large number of polar OH groups (Figure 10.15). Vinyl alcohol itself is not a stable compound (it isomerizes to acetaldehyde CH_3CHO), so polyvinyl alcohol cannot be made from this compound. Instead, it is made by hydrolyzing the ester groups in polyvinyl acetate.

$$\left(\begin{matrix}H & H\\ | & |\\ C\!-\!C\\ | & |\\ H & OCCH_3\\ & \parallel\\ & O\end{matrix}\right)_n + n\ H_2O \longrightarrow \left(\begin{matrix}H & H\\ | & |\\ C\!-\!C\\ | & |\\ H & OH\end{matrix}\right)_n + n\ CH_3CO_2H$$

Solubility in water or organic solvents can be a liability for polymers. The many uses of polytetrafluoroethylene [Teflon, $(\!-\!CF_2CF_2\!-\!)_n$] stem from the fact that it does not interact with water or organic solvents.

Polystyrene, with $n = 5700$, is a clear, hard, colorless solid that can be molded easily at 250 °C. You are probably more familiar with the very light, foam-like mate-

Polyethylene film. The polymer film is produced by extruding the molten plastic through a ring-like gap and inflating the film like a balloon.

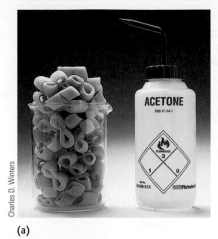
(a)

(b)

FIGURE 10.14 Polystyrene. (a) The polymer is a clear, hard, colorless solid, but it may be more familiar as a light, foam-like material called Styrofoam. (b) Styrofoam has no polar groups and thus dissolves well in organic solvents such as acetone. See also Figure 10.12b.

rial known as Styrofoam that is used widely for food and beverage containers and for home insulation (Figure 10.14). Styrofoam is produced by a process called "expansion molding." Polystyrene beads containing 4% to 7% of a low-boiling liquid like pentane are placed in a mold and heated with steam or hot air. Heat causes the solvent to vaporize, creating a foam in the molten polymer that expands to fill the shape of the mold.

Natural and Synthetic Rubber

Natural rubber was first introduced in Europe in 1740, but it remained a curiosity until 1823, when Charles Macintosh invented a way of using it to waterproof cotton cloth. The mackintosh, as rain coats are still sometimes called, became popular despite major problems: Natural rubber is notably weak and is soft and tacky when warm but brittle at low temperatures. In 1839, after 5 years of research on natural rubber, the American inventor Charles Goodyear (1800–1860) discovered that heating gum rubber with sulfur produces a material that is elastic, water-repellent, resilient, and no longer sticky.

Rubber is a naturally occurring polymer, the monomers of which are molecules of 2-methyl-1,3-butadiene, commonly called *isoprene*. In natural rubber, isoprene monomers are linked together through carbon atoms 1 and 4—that is, through the end carbon atoms of the C_4 chain (Figure 10.16). This leaves a double bond between carbon atoms 2 and 3. In natural rubber, these double bonds have a *cis* configuration.

In vulcanized rubber, the material that Goodyear discovered, the polymer chains of natural rubber are cross-linked by short chains of sulfur atoms. Cross-linking helps to align the polymer chains, so the material does not undergo a permanent change when stretched and it springs back when the stress is removed. Substances that behave this way are called **elastomers**.

With a knowledge of the composition and structure of natural rubber, chemists began searching for ways to make synthetic rubber. When they first tried to make the polymer by linking isoprene monomers together, however, what they made was sticky and useless. The problem was that synthesis procedures gave a mixture of *cis* and *trans* polyisoprene. In 1955, however, chemists at the Goodyear and Firestone companies discovered special catalysts to prepare the all-*cis* polymer. This synthetic material, which was structurally identical to natural rubber, is now manufactured cheaply. In fact, more than 8.0×10^8 kg of synthetic polyisoprene is produced annually in the United States.

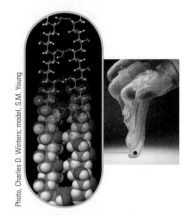

FIGURE 10.15 Slime. When boric acid, $B(OH)_3$, is added to an aqueous suspension of polyvinyl alcohol, $(CH_2CHOH)_n$, the mixture becomes very viscous because boric acid reacts with the —OH groups on the polymer chain, causing cross-linking to occur. (The model shows an idealized structure of a portion of the polymer.)

Isoprene, 2-methyl-1,3-butadiene.

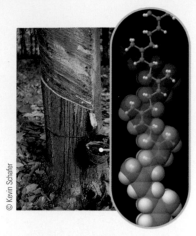

FIGURE 10.16 Natural rubber. The sap that comes from the rubber tree is a natural polymer of isoprene. All the linkages in the carbon chain are *cis*. When natural rubber is heated strongly in the absence of air, it smells of isoprene. This observation provided a clue that rubber is composed of this building block.

Other kinds of polymers have further expanded the repertoire of elastomeric materials now available. Polybutadiene, for example, is currently used in the production of tires, hoses, and belts. Some elastomers, called **copolymers,** are formed by polymerization of two (or more) different monomers. A copolymer of styrene and butadiene, made with a 1:3 ratio of these raw materials, is the most important synthetic rubber now made; more than about 1 billion kg of styrene-butadiene rubber (SBR) is produced each year in the United States for making tires.

$$3n \; \text{HC} - \text{CH} \quad + \quad n \; \text{H}_2\text{C} = \text{C}$$

1,3-butadiene   styrene

styrene-butadiene rubber (SBR)

And a little is left over each year to make bubble gum. The stretchiness of bubble gum once came from natural rubber, but SBR is now used to help you blow bubbles.

Chemistry ⚛ Now™

Sign in at **www.cengage.com/login** and go to Chapter 10 Contents to see Screen 10.11 for a self-study module on **the polymer used in bubble gum.**

Condensation Polymers

A chemical reaction in which two molecules react by splitting out, or eliminating, a small molecule is called a **condensation reaction.** The reaction of an alcohol with a carboxylic acid to give an ester is an example of a condensation reaction. One way to form a condensation polymer uses *two* different reactant molecules, each containing *two* functional groups. Another route uses a single molecule with two different functional groups. Commercial polyesters are made using both types of reactions.

Chemistry ⚛ Now™

Sign in at **www.cengage.com/login** and go to Chapter 10 Contents to see Screen 10.10 to view an animation of **condensation polymerization** and to watch a video of **the synthesis of nylon.**

Polyesters

Terephthalic acid contains two carboxylic acid groups, and ethylene glycol contains two alcohol groups. When mixed, the acid and alcohol functional groups at both ends of these molecules can react to form ester linkages, splitting out water. The

Copolymer of styrene and butadiene, SBR rubber. The elasticity of bubble gum comes from SBR rubber.

result is a polymer called polyethylene terephthalate (PET). The multiple ester linkages make this substance a **polyester.**

$$n \; \text{HOC} \underset{O}{\overset{O}{\|}} \text{—} \bigcirc \text{—} \overset{O}{\underset{\|}{\text{COH}}} + n \; \text{HOCH}_2\text{CH}_2\text{OH} \longrightarrow \left(\overset{O}{\underset{\|}{\text{C}}} \text{—} \bigcirc \text{—} \overset{O}{\underset{\|}{\text{COCH}_2\text{CH}_2\text{O}}} \right)_n + 2n \; \text{H}_2\text{O}$$

terephthalic acid   ethylene glycol   polyethylene terephthalate (PET), a polyester

Polyester textile fibers made from PET are marketed as Dacron and Terylene. The inert, nontoxic, noninflammatory, and non–blood-clotting properties of Dacron polymers make Dacron tubing an excellent substitute for human blood vessels in heart bypass operations, and Dacron sheets are sometimes used as temporary skin for burn victims. A polyester film, Mylar, has unusual strength and can be rolled into sheets one-thirtieth the thickness of a human hair. Magnetically coated Mylar films are used to make audio and video tapes (Figure 10.17).

There is considerable interest in another polyester, polylactic acid (PLA). Lactic acid contains both carboxylic acid and alcohol functional groups, so condensation between molecules of this monomer gives a polymer.

$$n \; \text{HO} \text{—} \overset{\overset{\text{H}}{|}}{\underset{\underset{\text{CH}_3}{|}}{\text{C}}} \text{—} \overset{\overset{O}{\|}}{\text{C}} \text{—OH} \longrightarrow \left(\text{O} \text{—} \overset{\overset{\text{H}}{|}}{\underset{\underset{\text{CH}_3}{|}}{\text{C}}} \text{—} \overset{\overset{O}{\|}}{\text{C}} \text{—O} \right)_n + n \; \text{H}_2\text{O}$$

There is interest in polylactic acid for two reasons. First, the monomer used to make this polymer is obtained by biological fermentation of plant materials. (Most of the chemicals used in the manufacture of other types of polymers are derived from petroleum, and there is increased concern about the availability and cost of raw materials in the future.) Second, this polymer, which is currently being used in packaging material, is biodegradable, which has the potential to alleviate land-fill disposal problems.

Polyamides

In 1928, the DuPont Company embarked on a basic research program headed by Wallace Carothers (1896–1937). Carothers was interested in high–molar-mass compounds, such as rubbers, proteins, and resins. In 1935, his research yielded

FIGURE 10.17 Polyesters. Polyethylene terephthalate is used to make clothing and soda bottles. The two students are wearing jackets made from recycled PET soda bottles. Mylar film, another polyester, is used to make recording tape as well as balloons. Because the film has very tiny pores, Mylar can be used for helium-filled balloons; the atoms of gaseous helium move through the pores in the film very slowly.

Active Figure 10.18 Nylon-6,6. Hexamethylenediamine is dissolved in water (bottom layer), and adipoyl chloride (a derivative of adipic acid) is dissolved in hexane (top layer). The two compounds react at the interface between the layers to form nylon, which is being wound onto a stirring rod.

Chemistry.ₒ.Now™ Sign in at www.cengage.com/login and go to the Chapter Contents menu to explore an interactive version of this figure accompanied by an exercise.

nylon-6,6 (Figure 10.18), a **polyamide** prepared from adipoyl chloride, a derivative of adipic acid, a diacid, and hexamethylenediamine, a diamine:

$$n \ \text{ClC(CH}_2)_4\text{CCl} \ + \ 2n \ \text{H}_2\text{N(CH}_2)_6\text{NH}_2 \longrightarrow \left(\begin{array}{c} \text{C(CH}_2)_4\text{C} - \text{N(CH}_2)_6\text{N} \\ | \quad\quad | \\ \text{H} \quad\quad \text{H} \end{array} \right)_n + \ 2n \ \text{HCl}$$

adipoyl chloride   hexamethylenediamine   amide link in nylon-6,6 a polyamide

Nylon can be extruded easily into fibers that are stronger than natural fibers and chemically more inert. The discovery of nylon jolted the American textile industry at a critical time. Natural fibers were not meeting 20th-century needs. Silk was expensive and not durable; wool was scratchy; linen crushed easily; and cotton did not have a high-fashion image. Perhaps the most identifiable use for the new fiber was in nylon stockings. The first public sale of nylon hosiery took place on October 24, 1939, in Wilmington, Delaware (the site of DuPont's main office). This use of nylon in commercial products ended shortly thereafter, however, with the start of World War II. All nylon was diverted to making parachutes and other military gear. It was not until about 1952 that nylon reappeared in the consumer marketplace.

Figure 10.19 illustrates why nylon makes such a good fiber. To have good tensile strength (the ability to resist tearing), the polymer chains should be able to attract one another, albeit not so strongly that the plastic cannot be initially extended to form fibers. Ordinary covalent bonds between the chains (cross-linking) would be too strong. Instead, cross-linking occurs by a somewhat weaker intermolecular force called *hydrogen bonding* (▶ Section 12.2) between the hydrogens of N—H groups on one chain and the carbonyl oxygens on another chain. The polarities of the $N^{\delta-}$—$H^{\delta+}$ group and the $C^{\delta+}$=$O^{\delta-}$ group lead to attractive forces between the polymer chains of the desired magnitude.

■ **EXAMPLE 10.8 Condensation Polymers**

Problem What is the repeating unit of the condensation polymer obtained by combining $HO_2CCH_2CH_2CO_2H$ (succinic acid) and $H_2NCH_2CH_2NH_2$ (1,2-ethylenediamine)?

Strategy Recognize that the polymer will link the two monomer units through the amide linkage. The smallest repeating unit of the chain will contain two parts, one from the diacid and the other from the diamine.

Solution The repeating unit of this polyamide is

$$\left(\begin{array}{c} \overset{\text{amide linkage}}{} \\ \text{CCH}_2\text{CH}_2\text{C} - \text{NCH}_2\text{CH}_2\text{N} \\ | \quad\quad | \\ \text{H} \quad\quad \text{H} \end{array} \right)_n$$

FIGURE 10.19 Hydrogen bonding between polyamide chains. Carbonyl oxygen atoms with a partial negative charge on one chain interact with an amine hydrogen with a partial positive charge on a neighboring chain. (This form of bonding is described in more detail in Section 12.3.)

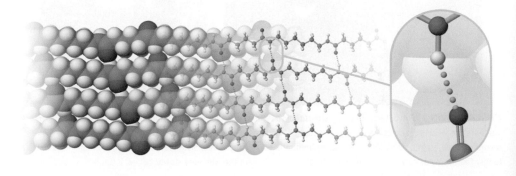

Chemical Perspectives

Super Diapers

Disposable diapers are a miracle of modern chemistry: Most of the materials used are synthetic polymers. The outer layer is mostly microporous polyethylene; it keeps the urine in but remains breathable. The inside layer is polypropylene, a material prized by winter-camping enthusiasts. It stays soft and dry while wicking moisture away from the skin. Sandwiched between these layers is powdered sodium polyacrylate combined with cellulose;

the latter is the only natural part of the materials used. The package is completed with elasticized hydrophobic polypropylene cuffs around the baby's thighs, and Velcro tabs hold the diaper on the baby.

The key ingredient in the diaper is the polyacrylate polymer filling. This substance can absorb up to 800 times its weight in water. When dry, the polymer has a carboxylate group associated with sodium ions. When placed in water, osmotic pressure causes water molecules to enter the polymer (because the ion concentration in the polymer is higher than in water; see Chapter 14). As water enters, the sodium ions dissociate from the polymer, and the polar water molecules are attracted to these positive ions and to the negative carboxylate groups of the polymer. At the same time, the negative carboxylate groups repel one another, forcing them apart and causing the polymer to unwind. Evidence for the unwinding of the polymer is seen as swelling of the diaper. In addition, because it contains so much water, the polymer becomes gel-like.

If the gelled polymer is put into a salt solution, water is attracted to the Na^+ and Cl^- ions and is drawn from the polymer. Thus, the polymer becomes solid once again. The diminished ability of sodium polyacrylate to absorb water in a salt solution is the reason that disposable diapers do not absorb urine as well as pure water.

These kinds of superabsorbent materials—sodium polyacrylate and a related material, polyacrylamide—are useful not only in diapers but also for cleaning up spills in hospitals, for protecting power and optical cables from moisture, for filtering water out of aviation gasoline, and for conditioning garden soil to retain water. You will also find them in the toy store as "gro-creatures."

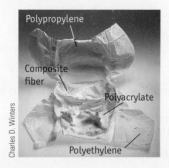

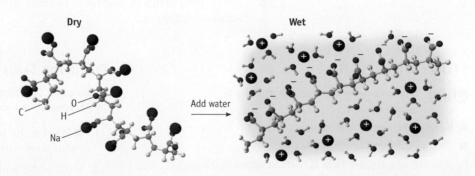

Dry   Wet

Add water

Chapter Goals Revisited

Now that you have studied this chapter, you should ask whether you have met the chapter goals. In particular, you should be able to:

Classify organic compounds based on formula and structure

a. Understand the factors that contribute to the large numbers of organic compounds and the wide array of structures (Section 10.1). Study Question(s) assignable in OWL: 3.

Recognize and draw structures of structural isomers and stereoisomers for carbon compounds

a. Recognize and draw structures of geometric isomers and optical isomers (Section 10.1). Study Question(s) assignable in OWL: 11, 12, 15, 58.

Name and draw structures of common organic compounds

a. Draw structural formulas, and name simple hydrocarbons, including alkanes, alkenes, alkynes, and aromatic compounds (Section 10.2). Study Question(s) assignable in OWL: 1, 5, 7, 28, 67, 69, 70, 96; Go Chemistry Module 15.

b. Identify possible isomers for a given formula (Section 10.2).

c. Name and draw structures of alcohols and amines (Section 10.3). Study Question(s) assignable in OWL: 31, 32, 34.

d. Name and draw structures of carbonyl compounds—aldehydes, ketones, acids, esters, and amides (Section 10.4). Study Question(s) assignable in OWL: 38, 39, 40, 41, 43, 51.

Know the common reactions of organic functional groups

a. This goal applies specifically to the reactions of alkenes, alcohols, amines, aldehydes and ketones, and carboxylic acids. Study Question(s) assignable in OWL: 19, 21, 24, 46, 64, 76, 79, 81, 83–85, 90–92, 97.

Relate properties to molecular structure

a. Describe the physical and chemical properties of the various classes of hydrocarbon compounds (Section 10.2).

b. Recognize the connection between the structures and the properties of alcohols (Section 10.3).

c. Know the structures and properties of several natural products, including carbohydrates (Section 10.4) and fats and oils (Section 10.4). Study Question(s) assignable in OWL: 49, 50.

Identify common polymers

a. Write equations for the formation of addition polymers and condensation polymers, and describe their structures (Section 10.5).

b. Relate properties of polymers to their structures (Section 10.5). Study Question(s) assignable in OWL: 95.

STUDY QUESTIONS

Ⓦ**WL** Online homework for this chapter may be assigned in OWL.

▲ denotes challenging questions.

■ denotes questions assignable in OWL.

Blue-numbered questions have answers in Appendix O and fully-worked solutions in the *Student Solutions Manual*.

Practicing Skills

Alkanes and Cycloalkanes
(See Examples 10.1 and 10.2 and ChemistryNow Screen 10.3.)

1. ■ What is the name of the straight (unbranched) chain alkane with the formula C_7H_{16}?

2. What is the molecular formula for an alkane with 12 carbon atoms?

3. ■ Which of the following is an alkane? Which could be a cycloalkane?
   (a) C_2H_4
   (b) C_5H_{10}
   (c) $C_{14}H_{30}$
   (d) C_7H_8

4. Isooctane, 2,2,4-trimethylpentane, is one of the possible structural isomers with the formula C_8H_{18}. Draw the structure of this isomer, and draw and name structures of two other isomers of C_8H_{18} in which the longest carbon chain is five atoms.

5. ■ Give the systematic name for the following alkane:

$$CH_3$$
$$|$$
$$CH_3CHCHCH_3$$
$$|$$
$$CH_3$$

6. Give the systematic name for the following alkane. Draw a structural isomer of the compound, and give its name.

$$CH_3$$
$$|$$
$$CH_3CHCH_2CH_2CHCH_3$$
$$|$$
$$CH_2CH_3$$

7. ■ Draw the structure of each of the following compounds:
   (a) 2,3-dimethylhexane
   (b) 2,3-dimethyloctane
   (c) 3-ethylheptane
   (d) 3-ethyl-2-methylhexane

8. Draw structures for 3-ethylpentane and 2,3-dimethylpentane.

9. Draw Lewis structures, and name all possible compounds that have a seven-carbon chain with one methyl substituent group. Which of these isomers has a chiral carbon center?

10. Draw a structure for cycloheptane. Is the seven-member ring planar? Explain your answer.

11. ■ There are two ethylheptanes (compounds with a seven-carbon chain and one ethyl substituent). Draw the structures, and name these compounds. Is either isomer chiral?

12. ■ Among the 18 structural isomers with the formula C_8H_{18} are two with a five-carbon chain having one ethyl and one methyl substituent group. Draw their structures, and name these two isomers.

13. List several typical physical properties of C_4H_{10}. Predict the following physical properties of dodecane, $C_{12}H_{26}$: color, state (s, ℓ, g), solubility in water, solubility in a nonpolar solvent.

14. Write balanced equations for the following reactions of alkanes.
    (a) The reaction of methane with excess chlorine.
    (b) Complete combustion of cyclohexane, C_6H_{12}, with excess oxygen.

Alkenes and Alkynes
(See Examples 10.3 and 10.4 and ChemistryNow Screens 10.3 and 10.4.)

15. ■ Draw structures for the *cis* and *trans* isomers of 4-methyl-2-hexene.

16. What structural requirement is necessary for an alkene to have *cis* and *trans* isomers? Can *cis* and *trans* isomers exist for an alkane? For an alkyne?

17. A hydrocarbon with the formula C_5H_{10} can be either an alkene or a cycloalkane.
    (a) Draw a structure for each of the isomers possible for C_5H_{10}, assuming it is an alkene. Six isomers are possible. Give the systematic name of each isomer you have drawn.
    (b) Draw a structure for a cycloalkane having the formula C_5H_{10}.

18. Five alkenes have the formula C_7H_{14} and a seven-carbon chain. Draw their structures, and name them.

19. ■ Draw the structure, and give the systematic name for the products of the following reactions:
    (a) $CH_3CH{=}CH_2 + Br_2 \rightarrow$
    (b) $CH_3CH_2CH{=}CHCH_3 + H_2 \rightarrow$

20. Draw the structure, and give the systematic name for the products of the following reactions:

    (a)
$$\begin{array}{ccc} H_3C & & CH_2CH_3 \\ & \diagdown \ \ / & \\ & C{=}C & \ \ \ \ + \ H_2 \longrightarrow \\ & / \ \ \diagdown & \\ H_3C & & H \end{array}$$

    (b) $CH_3C{\equiv}CCH_2CH_3 + 2\,Br_2 \longrightarrow$

21. ■ The compound 2-bromobutane is a product of addition of HBr to an alkene. Identify the alkene and give its name.

22. The compound 2,3-dibromo-2-methylhexane is formed by addition of Br_2 to an alkene. Identify the alkene, and write an equation for this reaction.

23. Draw structures for alkenes that have the formula C_3H_5Cl, and name each compound. (These are derivatives of propene in which a chlorine atom replaces one hydrogen atom.)

24. ■ Elemental analysis of a colorless liquid has given its formula as C_5H_{10}. You recognize that this could be either a cycloalkane or an alkene. A chemical test to determine the class to which this compound belongs involves adding bromine. Explain how this would allow you to distinguish between the two classes.

▲ more challenging ■ in OWL Blue-numbered questions answered in Appendix O

Aromatic Compounds
(See Example 10.5, Exercise 10.5, and ChemistryNow Screen 10.3.)

25. Draw structural formulas for the following compounds:
(a) 1,3-dichlorobenzene (alternatively called *m*-dichlorobenzene)
(b) 1-bromo-4-methylbenzene (alternatively called *p*-bromotoluene)

26. Give the systematic name for each of the following compounds:

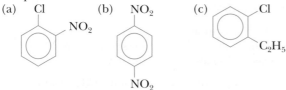

27. Write an equation for the preparation of ethylbenzene from benzene and an appropriate compound containing an ethyl group.

28. ■ Write an equation for the preparation of hexylbenzene from benzene and other appropriate reagents.

29. A single compound is formed by alkylation of 1,4-dimethylbenzene. Write the equation for the reaction of this compound with CH_3Cl and $AlCl_3$. What is the structure and name of the product?

30. Nitration of toluene gives a mixture of two products, one with the nitro group ($-NO_2$) in the *ortho* position and one with the nitro group in the *para* position. Draw structures of the two products.

Alcohols, Ethers, and Amines
(See Example 10.6 and ChemistryNow Screen 10.5.)

31. ■ Give the systematic name for each of the following alcohols, and tell if each is a primary, secondary, or tertiary alcohol:
(a) $CH_3CH_2CH_2OH$
(b) $CH_3CH_2CH_2CH_2OH$
(c)

$$H_3C-\underset{\underset{CH_3}{|}}{\overset{\overset{CH_3}{|}}{C}}-OH$$

(d)

$$H_3C-\underset{\underset{OH}{|}}{\overset{\overset{CH_3}{|}}{C}}-CH_2CH_3$$

32. ■ Draw structural formulas for the following alcohols, and tell if each is primary, secondary, or tertiary:
(a) 1-butanol
(b) 2-butanol
(c) 3,3-dimethyl-2-butanol
(d) 3,3-dimethyl-1-butanol

33. Write the formula, and draw the structure for each of the following amines:
(a) ethylamine
(b) dipropylamine
(c) butyldimethylamine
(d) triethylamine

34. ■ Name the following amines:
(a) $CH_3CH_2CH_2NH_2$
(b) $(CH_3)_3N$
(c) $(CH_3)(C_2H_5)NH$
(d) $C_6H_{13}NH_2$

35. Draw structural formulas for all the alcohols with the formula $C_4H_{10}O$. Give the systematic name of each.

36. Draw structural formulas for all primary amines with the formula $C_4H_9NH_2$.

37. Complete and balance the following equations:
(a) $C_6H_5NH_2(\ell) + HCl(aq) \rightarrow$
(b) $(CH_3)_3N(aq) + H_2SO_4(aq) \rightarrow$

38. ■ Aldehydes and carboxylic acids are formed by oxidation of primary alcohols, and ketones are formed when secondary alcohols are oxidized. Give the name and formula for the alcohol that, when oxidized, gives the following products:
(a) $CH_3CH_2CH_2CHO$
(b) 2-hexanone

Compounds with a Carbonyl Group
(See Exercises 10.7–10.10 and ChemistryNow Screen 10.5.)

39. ■ Draw structural formulas for (a) 2-pentanone, (b) hexanal, and (c) pentanoic acid.

40. ■ Identify the class of each of the following compounds, and give the systematic name for each:
(a)

$$CH_3\overset{\overset{O}{\|}}{C}CH_3$$

(b)

$$CH_3CH_2CH_2\overset{\overset{O}{\|}}{C}H$$

(c)

$$CH_3\overset{\overset{O}{\|}}{C}CH_2CH_2CH_3$$

41. ■ Identify the class of each of the following compounds, and give the systematic name for each:
(a)

$$CH_3CH_2\underset{\underset{}{}}{\overset{\overset{CH_3}{|}}{C}}HCH_2CO_2H$$

(b)

$$CH_3CH_2\overset{\overset{O}{\|}}{C}OCH_3$$

(c)

$$CH_3\overset{\overset{O}{\|}}{C}OCH_2CH_2CH_2CH_3$$

(d)

Br—⟨benzene ring⟩—$\overset{\overset{O}{\|}}{C}OH$

42. Draw structural formulas for the following acids and esters:
(a) 2-methylhexanoic acid
(b) pentyl butanoate (which has the odor of apricots)
(c) octyl acetate (which has the odor of oranges)

▲ more challenging   ■ in OWL   Blue-numbered questions answered in Appendix O

43. ■ Give the structural formula and systematic name for the product, if any, from each of the following reactions:
(a) pentanal and $KMnO_4$
(b) pentanal and $LiAlH_4$
(c) 2-octanone and $LiAlH_4$
(d) 2-octanone and $KMnO_4$

44. Describe how to prepare 2-pentanol beginning with the appropriate ketone.

45. Describe how to prepare propyl propanoate beginning with 1-propanol as the only carbon-containing reagent.

46. ■ Give the name and structure of the product of the reaction of benzoic acid and 2-propanol.

47. Draw structural formulas, and give the names for the products of the following reaction:

$$\overset{\displaystyle O}{\overset{\|}{CH_3COCH_2CH_2CH_2CH_3}} + NaOH$$

48. Draw structural formulas, and give the names for the products of the following reaction:

49. ■ The Lewis structure of phenylalanine, one of the 20 amino acids that make up proteins, is drawn below (without lone pairs of electrons). The carbon atoms are numbered for the purpose of this question.
(a) What is the geometry of C_3?
(b) What is the O—C—O bond angle?
(c) Is this molecule chiral? If so, which carbon atom is chiral?
(d) Which hydrogen atom in this compound is acidic?

50. ■ The Lewis structure of vitamin C, whose chemical name is ascorbic acid, is drawn below (without lone pairs of electrons).

(a) What is the approximate value for the O—C—O bond angle?

(b) There are four OH groups in this structure. Estimate the C—O—H bond angles for these groups. Will they be the same value (more or less), or should there be significant differences in these bond angles?
(c) Is the molecule chiral? How many chiral carbon atoms can be identified in this structure?
(d) Identify the shortest bond in this molecule.
(e) What are the functional groups of the molecule?

Functional Groups
(See Example 10.7 and ChemistryNow Screen 10.5.)

51. ■ Identify the functional groups in the following molecules.
(a) $CH_3CH_2CH_2OH$
(b)
$$\overset{\displaystyle O}{\overset{\|}{H_3CCNHCH_3}}$$
(c)
$$\overset{\displaystyle O}{\overset{\|}{CH_3CH_2COH}}$$
(d)
$$\overset{\displaystyle O}{\overset{\|}{CH_3CH_2COCH_3}}$$

52. Consider the following molecules:
1.
$$\overset{\displaystyle O}{\overset{\|}{CH_3CH_2CCH_3}}$$
2.
$$\overset{\displaystyle O}{\overset{\|}{CH_3CH_2COH}}$$
3. $H_2C{=}CHCH_2OH$
4.
$$\overset{\displaystyle OH}{\overset{|}{CH_3CH_2CHCH_3}}$$

(a) What is the result of treating compound 1 with $NaBH_4$? What is the functional group in the product? Name the product.
(b) Draw the structure of the reaction product from compounds 2 and 4. What is the functional group in the product?
(c) What compound results from adding H_2 to compound 3? Name the reaction product.
(d) What compound results from adding NaOH to compound 2?

Polymers
(See Example 10.8, Exercise 10.10, and ChemistryNow Screens 10.9 and 10.10.)

53. Polyvinyl acetate is the binder in water-based paints.
(a) Write an equation for its formation from vinyl acetate.
(b) Show a portion of this polymer with three monomer units.
(c) Describe how to make polyvinyl alcohol from polyvinyl acetate.

54. Neoprene (polychloroprene, a kind of rubber) is a polymer formed from the chlorinated butadiene $H_2C = CHCCl = CH_2$.
  (a) Write an equation showing the formation of polychloroprene from the monomer.
  (b) Show a portion of this polymer with three monomer units.

55. Saran is a copolymer of 1,1-dichloroethene and chloroethene (vinyl chloride). Draw a possible structure for this polymer.

56. The structure of methyl methacrylate is given in Table 10.12. Draw the structure of a polymethyl methacrylate (PMMA) polymer that has four monomer units. (PMMA has excellent optical properties and is used to make hard contact lenses.)

General Questions on Organic Chemistry

These questions are not designated as to type or location in the chapter. They may combine several concepts.

57. Three different compounds with the formula $C_2H_2Cl_2$ are known.
  (a) Two of these compounds are geometric isomers. Draw their structures.
  (b) The third compound is a structural isomer of the other two. Draw its structure.

58. ■ Draw the structure of 2-butanol. Identify the chiral carbon atom in this compound. Draw the mirror image of the structure you first drew. Are the two molecules superimposable?

59. Draw Lewis structures, and name three structural isomers with the formula C_6H_{12}. Are any of these isomers chiral?

60. Draw structures, and name the four alkenes that have the formula C_4H_8.

61. Write equations for the reactions of *cis*-2-butene with the following reagents, representing the reactants and products using structural formulas.
  (a) H_2O
  (b) HBr
  (c) Cl_2

62. Draw the structure, and name the product formed if the following alcohols are oxidized. Assume an excess of the oxidizing agent is used. If the alcohol is not expected to react with a chemical oxidizing agent, write NR (no reaction).
  (a) $CH_3CH_2CH_2CH_2OH$
  (b) 2-butanol
  (c) 2-methyl-2-propanol
  (d) 2-methyl-1-propanol

63. Write equations for the following reactions, representing the reactants and products using structural formulas.
  (a) The reaction of acetic acid and sodium hydroxide
  (b) The reaction of methylamine with HCl

64. ■ Write equations for the following reactions, representing the reactants and products using structural formulas.
  (a) The formation of ethyl acetate from acetic acid and ethanol
  (b) The hydrolysis of glyceryl tristearate (the triester of glycerol with stearic acid, a fatty acid)

65. Write an equation for the formation of the following polymers.
  (a) Polystyrene, from styrene ($C_6H_5CH = CH_2$)
  (b) PET (polyethylene terephthalate), from ethylene glycol and terephthalic acid

66. Write equations for the following reactions, representing the reactants and products using structural formulas.
  (a) The hydrolysis of the amide $C_6H_5CONHCH_3$ to form benzoic acid and methylamine
  (b) The hydrolysis $\text{+CO(CH}_2\text{)}_4\text{CONH(CH}_2\text{)}_6\text{NH+}_n$, (nylon-6, 6, a polyamide) to give a carboxylic acid and an amine

67. ■ Draw the structure of each of the following compounds:
  (a) 2,2-dimethylpentane
  (b) 3,3-diethylpentane
  (c) 3-ethyl-2-methylpentane
  (d) 3-ethylhexane

68. ▲ Structural isomers.
  (a) Draw all of the isomers possible for C_3H_8O. Give the systematic name of each, and tell into which class of compound it fits.
  (b) Draw the structural formulas for an aldehyde and a ketone with the molecular formula C_4H_8O. Give the systematic name of each.

69. ▲ ■ Draw structural formulas for possible isomers of the dichlorinated propane, $C_3H_6Cl_2$. Name each compound.

70. ■ Draw structural formulas for possible isomers with the formula C_3H_6ClBr, and name each isomer.

71. Give structural formulas and systematic names for the three structural isomers of trimethylbenzene, $C_6H_3(CH_3)_3$.

72. Give structural formulas and systematic names for possible isomers of dichlorobenzene, $C_6H_4Cl_2$.

73. Voodoo lilies depend on carrion beetles for pollination. Carrion beetles are attracted to dead animals, and because dead and putrefying animals give off the horrible-smelling amine cadaverine, the lily likewise releases cadaverine (and the closely related compound putrescine) (page 466). A biological catalyst, an enzyme, converts the naturally occurring amino acid lysine to cadaverine.

$$H_2NCH_2CH_2CH_2CH_2 - \overset{\overset{\displaystyle H}{|}}{\underset{\underset{\displaystyle O}{\overset{\displaystyle |}{\overset{\displaystyle C}{\|}} - OH}}{C}} - NH_2$$

lysine

What group of atoms must be replaced in lysine to make cadaverine? (Lysine is essential to human nutrition but is not synthesized in the human body.)

74. Benzoic acid occurs in many berries. When humans eat berries, benzoic acid is converted to hippuric acid in the body by reaction with the amino acid glycine $H_2NCH_2CO_2H$. Draw the structure of hippuric acid, knowing it is an amide formed by reaction of the carboxylic acid group of benzoic acid and the amino group of glycine. Why is hippuric acid referred to as an acid?

75. ■ Consider the reaction of *cis*-2-butene with H_2 (in the presence of a catalyst).
(a) Draw the structure, and give the name of the reaction product. Is this reaction product chiral?
(b) Draw an isomer of the reaction product.

76. ■ Give the name of each compound below, and name the functional group involved.

(a)
$$\begin{array}{c} OH \\ | \\ H_3C-C-CH_2CH_2CH_3 \\ | \\ H \end{array}$$

(b)
$$\begin{array}{c} O \\ \| \\ H_3C-CCH_2CH_2CH_3 \end{array}$$

(c)
$$\begin{array}{c} H \quad O \\ | \quad \| \\ H_3C-C-C-H \\ | \\ CH_3 \end{array}$$

(d)
$$\begin{array}{c} O \\ \| \\ H_3CCH_2CH_2-C-OH \end{array}$$

77. Draw the structure of glyceryl trilaurate. When this triester is saponified, what are the products? (See page 476.)

78. ▲ A well-known company selling outdoor clothing has recently introduced jackets made of recycled polyethylene terephthalate (PET), the principal material in many soft drink bottles. Another company makes PET fibers by treating recycled bottles with methanol to give the diester dimethylterephthalate and ethylene glycol and then repolymerizes these compounds to give new PET. Write a chemical equation to show how the reaction of PET with methanol can give dimethylterephthalate and ethylene glycol.

79. ■ Identify the reaction products, and write an equation for the following reactions of $CH_2=CHCH_2OH$.
(a) H_2 (hydrogenation, in the presence of a catalyst)
(b) Oxidation (excess oxidizing agent)
(c) Addition polymerization
(d) Ester formation, using acetic acid

80. Write a chemical equation describing the reaction between glycerol and stearic acid to give glyceryl tristearate.

81. ■ The product of an addition reaction of an alkene is often predicted by Markovnikov's rule.
(a) Draw the structure of the product of adding HBr to propene, and give the name of the product.
(b) Draw the structure, and give the name of the compound that results from adding H_2O to 2-methyl-1-butene.
(c) If you add H_2O to 2-methyl-2-butene, is the product the same or different than the product from the reaction in part (b)?

82. An unknown colorless liquid has the formula $C_4H_{10}O$. Draw the structures for the four alcohol compounds that have this formula.

In the Laboratory

83. ■ Which of the following compounds produces acetic acid when treated with an oxidizing agent such as $KMnO_4$?

(a) H_3C-CH_3

(c)
$$\begin{array}{c} OH \\ | \\ H_3C-C-H \\ | \\ H \end{array}$$

(b)
$$\begin{array}{c} O \\ \| \\ H_3C-C-H \end{array}$$

(d)
$$\begin{array}{c} O \\ \| \\ H_3C-C-CH_3 \end{array}$$

84. ■ Consider the reactions of C_3H_7OH.

$$\begin{array}{c} H \\ | \\ H_3CCH_2-C-O-H \\ | \\ H \end{array} \xrightarrow[H_2SO_4]{Rxn\ A} \begin{array}{c} H\ \ H \\ | \ \ | \\ H_3C-C=C \\ | \\ H \end{array} + H_2O$$

$Rxn\ B \Big\downarrow + CH_3CO_2H$

$$\begin{array}{c} H \qquad O \\ | \qquad \| \\ H_3CCH_2-C-O-CCH_3 \\ | \\ H \end{array}$$

(a) Name the reactant C_3H_7OH.
(b) Draw a structural isomer of the reactant, and give its name.
(c) Name the product of reaction A.
(d) Name the product of reaction B.

85. You have a liquid that is either cyclohexene or benzene. When the liquid is exposed to dark-red bromine vapor, the vapor is immediately decolorized. What is the identity of the liquid? Write an equation for the chemical reaction that has occurred.

86. ▲ ■ Hydrolysis of an unknown ester of butanoic acid, $CH_3CH_2CH_2CO_2R$, produces an alcohol A and butanoic acid. Oxidation of this alcohol forms an acid B that is a structural isomer of butanoic acid. Give the names and structures for alcohol A and acid B.

87. ▲ You are asked to identify an unknown colorless, liquid carbonyl compound. Analysis has determined that the formula for this unknown is C_3H_6O. Only two compounds match this formula.
    (a) Draw structures for the two possible compounds.
    (b) To decide which of the two structures is correct, you react the compound with an oxidizing agent and isolate from that reaction a compound that is found to give an acidic solution in water. Use this result to identify the structure of the unknown.
    (c) Name the acid formed by oxidation of the unknown.

88. Describe a simple chemical test to tell the difference between $CH_3CH_2CH_2CH{=}CH_2$ and its isomer cyclopentane.

89. Describe a simple chemical test to tell the difference between 2-propanol and its isomer methyl ethyl ether.

90. ▲ ■ An unknown ester has the formula $C_4H_8O_2$. Hydrolysis gives methanol as one product. Identify the ester, and write an equation for the hydrolysis reaction.

91. ▲ ■ Addition of water to alkene X gives an alcohol Y. Oxidation of Y produces 3,3-dimethyl-2-pentanone. Identify X and Y, and write equations for the two reactions.

92. ■ 2-Iodobenzoic acid, a tan, crystalline solid, can be prepared from 2-aminobenzoic acid. Other required reagents are $NaNO_2$ and KI (as well as HCl).

2-aminobenzoic acid   2-iodobenzoic acid

(a) If you use 4.0 g of 2-aminobenzoic acid, 2.2 g of $NaNO_2$, and 5.3 g of KI, what is the theoretical yield of 2-iodobenzoic acid?
(b) Are other isomers of 2-iodobenzoic acid possible?
(c) To verify that you have isolated 2-iodobenzoic acid, you titrate it in water/ethanol. If you use 15.62 mL of 0.101 M NaOH to titrate 0.399 g of the product, what is its molar mass? Is it in reasonable agreement with the theoretical molar mass?

Summary and Conceptual Questions

The following questions may use concepts from this and previous chapters.

93. Carbon atoms appear in organic compounds in several different ways with single, double, and triple bonds combining to give an octet configuration. Describe the various ways that carbon can bond to reach an octet, and give the name, and draw the structure of a compound that illustrates that mode of bonding.

94. There is a high barrier to rotation around a carbon–carbon double bond, whereas the barrier to rotation around a carbon–carbon single bond is considerably smaller. Use the orbital overlap model of bonding (Chapter 9) to explain why there is restricted rotation around a double bond.

95. ■ What important properties do the following characteristics impart on an polymer?
    (a) Cross linking in polyethylene
    (b) The OH groups in polyvinyl alcohol
    (c) Hydrogen bonding in a polyamide like nylon

96. ■ One of the resonance structures for pyridine is illustrated here. Draw another resonance structure for the molecule. Comment on the similarity between this compound and benzene.

pyridine

97. ■ Write balanced equations for the combustion of ethane gas and liquid ethanol (to give gaseous products).
    (a) Calculate the enthalpy of combustion of each compound. Which has the more negative enthalpy change for combustion per gram?
    (b) If ethanol is assumed to be partially oxidized ethane, what effect does this have on the heat of combustion?

98. Plastics make up about 20% of the volume of landfills. There is, therefore, considerable interest in reusing or recycling these materials. To identify common plastics, a set of universal symbols is now used, five of which are illustrated here. They symbolize low- and high-density polyethylene, polyvinyl chloride, polypropylene, and polyethylene terephthalate.

PETE   HDPE   V

LDPE   PP

▲ more challenging   ■ in OWL   Blue-numbered questions answered in Appendix O

(a) Tell which symbol belongs to which type of plastic.

(b) Find an item in the grocery or drug store made from each of these plastics.

(c) Properties of several plastics are listed in the table. Based on this information, describe how to separate samples of these plastics from one another.

Plastic	Density (g/cm³)	Melting Point (°C)
Polypropylene	0.92	170
High-density polyethylene	0.97	135
Polyethylene terephthalate	1.34–1.39	245

99. ▲ Maleic acid is prepared by the catalytic oxidation of benzene. It is a dicarboxylic acid; that is, it has two carboxylic acid groups.

(a) Combustion of 0.125 g of the acid gives 0.190 g of CO_2 and 0.0388 g of H_2O. Calculate the empirical formula of the acid.

(b) A 0.261-g sample of the acid requires 34.60 mL of 0.130 M NaOH for complete titration (so that the H ions from both carboxylic acid groups are used). What is the molecular formula of the acid?

(c) Draw a Lewis structure for the acid.

(d) Describe the hybridization used by the C atoms.

(e) What are the bond angles around each C atom?

Let's Review | Chapters 6–10

Everyone enjoys a good fireworks display, and neon signs can be intriguing and even beautiful. Both owe their colorful display to the emission of light by various chemical substances, and these chapters have laid out some of the principles involved in this effect. When you have finished these chapters you will know more about how the colors of a fireworks display and the light emitted by neon signs are produced and what they have in common.

Charles D. Winters

THE PURPOSE OF *LET'S REVIEW*

- *Let's Review* provides additional questions for Chapters 6 through 10. Routine questions covering the concepts in a chapter are in the Study Questions at the end of that chapter and are usually identified by topic. In contrast, *Let's Review* questions combine several concepts from one or more chapters. Many come from the examinations given by the authors and others are based on actual experiments or processes in chemical research or in the chemical industries.

- *Let's Review* provides guidance for Chapters 6 through 10 as you prepare for an exam on these chapters. Although this is designated for Chapters 6 through 10 you may choose only material appropriate to the exam in your course.

- To direct your review, **Comprehensive Questions** are correlated with relevant chapter sections and with the OWL online homework system to which you may have purchased access. Some questions may include a screen shot from one of these tools so you see what resources are available to help you review.

Charles D. Winters

PREPARING FOR AN EXAMINATION ON CHAPTERS 6–10

1. Review **Go Chemistry** modules for these chapters. Go Chemistry modules are available at **www.cengage.com/chemistry/kotz** or **www.ichapters.com**.

2. Take the ChemistryNow **Pre-Test** and work through your **Personalized Learning Plan.** Work through ChemistryNow **Exercises, Guided Simulations,** and **Intelligent Tutors.**

3. **OWL** If you subscribe to OWL, use the **Tutorials** in that system.

4. Work on the questions below that are relevant to a particular chapter or chapters. See the solutions to those questions at the end of this section.

5. For background and help answering a question, use the Go Chemistry and OWL questions correlated with it.

KEY POINTS TO KNOW FOR CHAPTERS 6–10

Here are some of the key points you must know to be successful in Chapters 6–10.

- The properties of electromagnetic radiation.
- The origin of light from excited atoms.
- The quantum numbers and their relation to atomic structure.
- Electron configurations for the elements and common monatomic ions.
- Periodic trends in properties of the elements.
- Concepts of bonding: covalent bonds, octet rule, resonance
- Lewis structures for small molecules and ions.
- VSEPR theory to predict the shapes of simple molecules and ions and to understand the structures of more complex molecules.
- Electronegativity and its relation to bond and molecular polarity.
- Atom hybridization in molecules and ions.
- The principles of molecular orbital theory.
- Classification of organic molecules by functional group.
- Isomerism in organic molecules.
- Structures of common organic compounds
- Reactions of organic functional groups.
- Common polymers.

EXAMINATION PREPARATION QUESTIONS

▲ denotes more challenging questions.

Important information about the questions that follow:

- See the Study Questions in each chapter for questions on basic concepts.
- Some of these questions arise from recent research in chemistry and the other sciences. They often involve concepts from more than one chapter and may be more challenging than those in earlier chapters. Not all chapter goals or concepts are necessarily addressed in these questions.
- **Assessing Key Points** are short-answer questions covering the Key Points to Know on this page.
- **Comprehensive Questions** bring together concepts from multiple chapters and are correlated with text sections covering that topic, with Go Chemistry modules, and with questions in OWL that may provide additional background.
- The screens shots are largely taken from Go Chemistry modules available at **www.cengage.com/chemistry/kotz** or **www.ichapters.com.**

Assessing Key Points

1. Place the following types of radiation in order of increasing energy: (a) x-rays, (b) radio waves, (c) blue light, and (d) light with $\lambda = 520$ nm

2. Radiation called UVB (290–315 nm) is responsible for your sunburn at the beach. Another type of radiation [UVA (315-400 nm)] is also responsible for tissue dam-age (page 275). Which has the greater energy, UVA or UVB?

3. The quantum number n describes the _____ of an atomic orbital and the quantum number ℓ describes its _____.

4. For a $4d$ orbital, what are the values of n and ℓ? What is one possible value of m_ℓ?

5. What elements have these ground state electron configurations?
   (a) $[Kr]5s^1$ (b) $[Ar]3d^{10}4s^24p^4$

6. Which has the largest first ionization energy: N, P, or As?

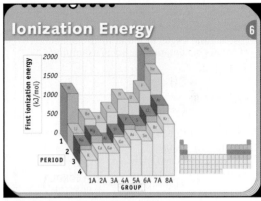

Screen from Go Chemistry module 11 on periodic trends

7. Which of the following is NOT a correct Lewis resonance structure for the N_2O molecule?

     (a) $\ddot{N}{=}N{=}\ddot{O}$ (b) $:\ddot{N}{-}N{\equiv}O:$

     (c) $:N{\equiv}N{-}\ddot{\underset{..}{O}}:$ (d) $:N{\equiv}N{=}\ddot{\underset{..}{O}}$

8. Consider the N_2O molecule in question 7.
   (a) Is the structure of the molecule bent or linear?
   (b) Is the N—O bond polar? Is the molecule polar?
   (c) What is the hybridization of the central N atom and what is its formal charge?

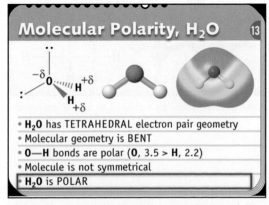

Screen from Go Chemistry module 13 on molecular polarity

9. If, in a molecule, three atomic orbitals combine, how many molecular orbitals will result?

10. To which class of organic molecules does each of these belong?

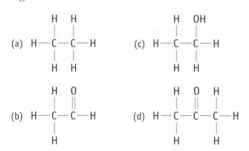

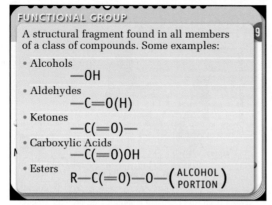

Screen from Go Chemistry module 15 on organic compounds

11. Name compound (d) in question 10 and draw an isomer of this compound.

12. Name the product of the oxidation with $KMnO_4$ of compound (c) in question 10.

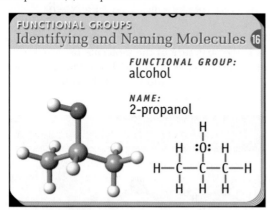

Screen from Go Chemistry module 15 on organic compounds

13. Which compound or compounds could be used to synthesize a polymer?

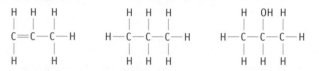

Comprehensive Questions

14. (Chapter 6) Blue light has a wavelength, λ, of 420. nm.
(a) What is the frequency of the light?
(b) If the total energy of a signal involving blue light is 2.50×10^{-14} J, how many photons reach your eyes?
Text Sections: 6.1 and 6.2
OWL Questions: 6.1e, 6.2d

15. (Chapters 6 and 7) Quantum numbers and electron configurations.
(a) When $n = 3$, $\ell = 1$, and $m_\ell = -1$, to what orbital does this refer? (Give the orbital label, such as $1s$.)
(b) For the $n = 5$ shell, there are _____ subshells and _____ orbitals. How many electrons can be accommodated in the $n = 5$ shell? _____
(c) What type of orbital is not possible based on quantum theory: $2p$, $3s$, $5g$, $3f$, $7d$?
(d) What is the maximum number of orbitals that can be associated with each of the following sets of quantum numbers? (One possible answer is "none.")
(i) $n = 3$
(ii) $n = 3$ and $\ell = 3$
(iii) $n = 2$, $\ell = 1$, and $m_\ell = 0$
(e) Which ion or ions are unlikely based on your knowledge of electron configurations and ionization energies? Ba^{3+}, Cr^{3+}, Al^{3+}, S^{3-}, Cu^+
(f) At what element is the $n = 3$ shell just completed?
Text Sections: 6.5, 6.7, and 7.2–7.4
OWL Questions: 6.5c, 7.4c

16. (Chapters 5 and 6) To prepare some tea, you want to heat 254 g of water from 12 °C to 90. °C in a microwave oven, which operates at a frequency of 2.45 Gigahertz ($\nu = 2.45 \times 10^9$ sec^{-1}).
(a) What is the wavelength of microwave radiation?
(b) Suppose a microwave oven is 48 cm wide. How many wavelengths of the given radiation are equivalent to 48 cm.
(c) How many moles of these microwave photons must be absorbed to heat your mug of water to 90. °C?
Text Sections: 5.2, 6.1, and 6.2
OWL Questions: 5.2e, 6.1e, 6.2d

17. (Chapters 5 and 6) Photosynthesis.

  (a) Calculate the enthalpy change for the production of one mole of glucose by the process of photosynthesis at 25 °C. $\Delta_f H°$[glucose(s)] = −1273.3 kJ/mol.

$$6\,CO_2(g) + 6\,H_2O(\ell) \rightarrow C_6H_{12}O_6(s) + 6\,O_2(g)$$

  (b) What is the enthalpy change involved in producing one molecule of glucose by this process?

  (c) Chlorophyll molecules absorb light of various wavelengths. One wavelength absorbed is 650. nm. Calculate the energy of a photon of light having this wavelength.

  (d) How many photons with a wavelength of 650. nm are required to produce one glucose molecule, assuming all of the light energy is converted to chemical energy?

Text Sections: 5.5, 5.7, 6.1, and 6.2
OWL Questions: 5.7d, 6.1e, 6.2d

18. (Chapter 6) The energy level diagram in Figure 6.8 (page 277) describes a H atom using the Bohr model.

  (a) What quantum levels are involved in the emission of UV, visible, and infrared light in the hydrogen spectrum?

  (b) What is the energy of the hydrogen atom's electron in its ground state?

  (c) What is the energy of an electron in the $n = 4$ state?

  (d) Calculate the energy of the transition from the $n = 2$ level to the $n = 1$ level.

  (e) Calculate the energy (in kJ/mol) required to ionize 1.0 mole of hydrogen atoms.

  (f) Calculate the wavelength of light required to cause ionization of an H atom. In what region of the electromagnetic spectrum is this radiation found?

Text Sections: 6.1–6.3
OWL Questions: 6.1b, 6.1e, 6.2d, 6.3c, 6.3e

19. (Chapter 7) Atom A has the ground state electron configuration $[Ne]3s^2 3p^5$. Atom B has the ground state electron configuration $[Ar]4s^2$. Identify A and B from their electron configurations; then identify the compound formed when these two elements react. Is this compound diamagnetic or paramagnetic? Write an equation for this reaction.

Text Sections: 6.7, 7.3, and 7.4
OWL Questions: 7.3g, 7.3h, 7.4c, 7.4e

20. (Chapter 7) Electron configurations and periodic trends.

  (a) What element has the ground state electron configuration $[Ar]3d^6 4s^2$?

  (b) What element has a 2+ ion with the ground state configuration $[Ar]3d^5$? Is the ion paramagnetic or diamagnetic?

  (c) How many unpaired electrons are there in a ground state Ni^{2+} ion?

  (d) The ground state configuration for an element is given here.

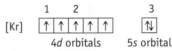

What is the identity of the element? Is an atom of the element paramagnetic or diamagnetic? How many unpaired electrons does a 3− ion of this element have?

  (e) What element has the following ground state electron configuration?

Is the element paramagnetic or diamagnetic? Write a complete set of quantum numbers for electrons labeled 1–3.

Electron	n	ℓ	m_ℓ	m_s
1	____	____	____	____
2	____	____	____	____
3	____	____	____	____

  (f) Answer the questions below about the elements A and B, which have the ground state electron configurations shown.

$$A = [Kr]5s^2 \qquad B = [Kr]4d^{10}5s^2 5p^5$$

Is element A a metal, nonmetal, or metalloid? Which element has the greater ionization energy? Which element has larger atoms? Which is more likely to form a cation? What is a likely formula for a compound formed between A and B?

Text Sections: 6.5, 6.7, and 7.3–7.5
OWL Questions: 6.5c, 7.3g, 7.3h, 7.4c, 7.4e, 7.5b, 7.5e

21. (Chapter 7) Periodic trends.

Part 1: General Periodic Trends

  (a) Of the elements S, Se, and Cl, which has the largest atomic radius?

  (b) Which has the larger radius, Br or Br^-?

  (c) Which should have the most negative electron affinity: N, O, S, or Cl?

  (d) Which has the largest first ionization energy: B, Al, or C?

  (e) Which of the following has the largest radius: O^{2-}, N^{3-}, or F^-?

Part 2: Consider the elements Al, C, Ca, Mg, K: Of these elements, _____ has the lowest ionization energy whereas _____ has the most negative electron affinity. The element with the largest radius is _____, and the element with the smallest radius is _____. The element with the largest difference between the first and second ionization energies is _____.

Text Section: 7.5
OWL Questions: 7.5b, 7.5e, 7.5i

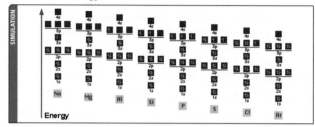

Screen from Go Chemistry module 11 on periodic trends

22. (Chapter 7) Electron configurations.

(a) Using the *spdf* notation [e.g., $1s^2 2s^2$], write ground state electron configurations for each of the following: arsenic, manganese, and plutonium. Use the noble gas notation for all cases.

(b) Using the orbital box notation, write electron configurations for the following atoms or ions: tin(II) ion, cobalt(III) ion, and oxide ion. Use the noble gas notation in all cases.

Text Sections: 7.3 and 7.4
OWL Questions: 7.3g, 7.3h, 7.4c

23. (Chapter 7) Ionization energies.

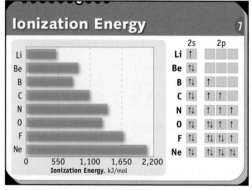

Screen from Go Chemistry module 11 on periodic trends

(a) Generally ionization energies increase on proceeding across a period, but this is not true for magnesium (738 kJ/mol) and aluminum (578 kJ/mol). Explain this observation.

(b) Explain why the ionization energy of phosphorus (1012 kJ/mol) is greater than that of sulfur (1000 kJ/mol) when the general trend in ionization energies in a period would predict the opposite.

Text Section: 7.5
OWL Question: 7.5e

Ionization Energy

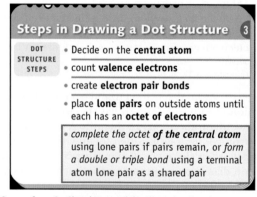

OWL Simulation 7.5d: This simulation illustrates the trend in orbital energies across the third period and allows us to understand trends in ionization energy and electron affinity.

24. (Chapters 8 and 9) Sketch the electron dot structure for each of the following, give the hybridization of the N atom, and arrange them in order of increasing N—O bond length: H_2NOH, NO_3^-, NO_2^-, NO^+.

Text Sections: 8.2, 8.4, 8.9, and 9.2
OWL Questions: 8.4b, 8.5d, 8.9a, 9.2f

Screen from Go Chemistry module 12 on drawing dot structures

25. (Chapters 5, 8, and 9) Brown NO_2 gas is a product of the reaction of copper with nitric acid. (See Figure 3.19, page 146, and Active Figure 3.19 on ChemistryNow.) Some NO_2 molecules form N_2O_4 where two NO_2 molecules are bonded through an N—N bond.

(a) Draw the Lewis electron dot structure of N_2O_4, specify the formal charges on each atom and the hybridization of the N atoms, indicate the N—O bond order, and give the bond angles.

(b) Is the reaction of NO_2 to form N_2O_4 endothermic or exothermic? (You can answer this by considering bond energies and could confirm it using enthalpies of formation.)

Text Sections: 5.7, 8.2, 8.3, 8.6, 8.9, and 9.2
OWL Questions: 5.7d, 8.3b, 8.5d, 8.6a, 8.6d, 8.6f, 8.9a, 8.9c, 9.2f, 9.2h

26. (Chapters 8 and 9) Sulfur can react with the sulfite ion to give the thiosulfate ion, $S_2O_3{}^{2-}$.

(a) Draw the Lewis electron dot structure for the sulfite ion, specify the formal charge on each atom and the S atom hybridization, and give the S—O bond order.

(b) Knowing that the thiosulfate ion is analogous with the sulfate ion, where a S atom has replaced an O atom, draw the electron dot structure for thiosulfate ion.

Text Sections: 8.2, 8.3, and 9.2
ChemistryNow Screens: 9.8–9.10, 10.4
OWL Questions: 8.3b, 8.5d, 8.6a, 8.6b, 8.6f, 8.9a, 9.2f, 9.2h

27. (Chapters 8 and 9) Chemistry of chlorine trifluoride.

(a) Sketch the Lewis electron dot structure for ClF_3 and indicate the hybridization of the central Cl atom.

(b) There are several geometries possible for ClF_3. Which is the most reasonable and why?

(c) Liquid ClF_3 is weakly conducting, a behavior attributed to the presence of $ClF_2{}^+$ and $ClF_4{}^-$ ions. Sketch the structures of these two ions and compare their geometries.

Text Sections: 8.2, 8.5, 8.6, and 9.2
OWL Questions: 8.5d, 8.6a, 8.6b, 8.6f, 9.2f, 9.2h

28. (Chapters 8 and 9) Nitrogen chemistry. Draw electron dot structures, and answer the accompanying questions, for nitryl chloride, hydroxylamine, and dinitrogen monoxide.

(a) Nitryl chloride, $ClNO_2$. (N is the central atom.)

(i) What is the electron pair geometry around the central N atom? Describe the molecular geometry of the molecule and specify the O—N—O and Cl—N—O bond angles.

(ii) What is the formal charge and hybridization of the N atom?

(iii) Is the molecule polar?

(b) Hydroxylamine, NH_2OH, is an ammonia derivative. (N is the central atom.)

(i) What is the electron pair geometry around the central N atom? Specify the H—O—N and H—N—H bond angles.

(ii) What is its formal charge and hybridization of the N atom?

(iii) Is the molecule polar?

(c) Dinitrogen monoxide, N_2O, can be obtained from oxidation of ammonia. Draw all the resonance structures for N_2O. Specify the geometry of the molecule, the N—N—O angle, and the formal charge on each atom in each resonance structure.

Text Sections: 8.2–8.8, and 9.2
OWL Questions: 8.3b, 8.4b, 8.6a, 8.6b, 8.6f, 8.8b, 9.2f, 9.2h

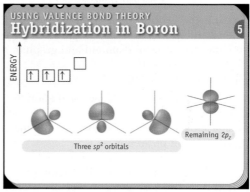

Screen from Go Chemistry module 12 on drawing dot structures

29. (Chapters 8–10) The Lewis structure of asparagine, one of the naturally occurring amino acids, is drawn below. The questions that follow are about this compound. The carbons are labeled with subscripts for the purpose of this question. Questions (a)–(e) refer to the letters accompanying the arrows in the figure.

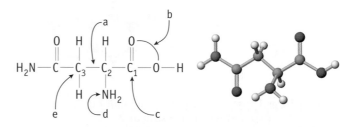

(a) What orbitals overlap to form bond (a)?

(b) What is the O—C—O bond angle labeled (b)?

(c) What hybridization is assigned to C_1?

(d) What is the molecular geometry around this N?

(e) What is this H—C_3—H bond angle?

(f) Identify any chiral carbon atom in this compound.

(g) How many lone pairs are missing in this drawing? Where should they be located?

(h) Name the three functional groups in the molecule.

Text Sections: 8.6, 9.2, 10.3, and 10.4
OWL Questions: 8.5d, 9.2f, 9.2g, 9.2h, 10.1d, 10.4c

30. (Chapters 9 and 10) Organic chemistry and hybridization.
  (a) Naphthalene is an aromatic hydrocarbon. What is the hybridization of the C atoms in naphthalene? How many resonance structures does naphthalene have?

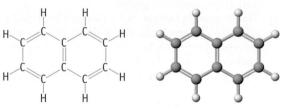

Naphthalene, $C_{10}H_8$

  (b) What is the hybridization of the C atoms in diamond and in graphite? (See Figure 2.7, page 64, for the structures of diamond and graphite.)
  Text Section: 8.4, 9.2, and 10.2
  OWL Questions: 8.4b, 9.2f, 9.2h

31. (Chapter 9) Experimental evidence for the ion Si_2^- was reported in 1996.
  (a) Using molecular orbital theory, predict the electron configuration of the ion.
  (b) What is the predicted bond order?
  (c) Is the ion paramagnetic or diamagnetic?
  (d) What is the highest energy molecular orbital that contains one or more electrons?
  Text Section: 9.3
  OWL Questions: 9.3d, 9.3f

32. (Chapters 8–10) The compound pictured below (anethole) is the substance that gives licorice its odor.

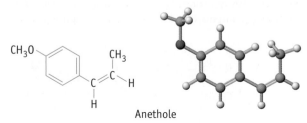

Anethole

  (a) Draw Lewis structures for the following:
    (1) a second resonance structure
    (2) any structural isomer of this compound
    (3) a geometric isomer of this compound
  (b) What orbitals overlap to form a C=C double bond in this compound?
  (c) Describe the π bonding in the C_6H_4 ring using molecular orbital theory.
  Text Sections: 8.2, 8.4, 9.2, and 10.1
  OWL Questions: 8.4b, 8.5d, 9.2o, 10.1c

33. (Chapters 2 and 8) Acetaminophen, which is sold under the tradename Tylenol, among others, has the structure shown here.

Acetaminophen

  (a) Which is the most polar bond?
  (b) Which is the strongest carbon-oxygen bond?
  (c) Give approximate values for the indicated bond angles in the molecule.
  (d) One Excedrin tablet contains 250 mg of acetaminophen. What amount (moles) of acetaminophen are you consuming in one tablet?
  (e) What is the weight percent of carbon in acetaminophen?
  Text Sections: 2.9, 2.10, 8.7, and 8.9
  OWL Questions: 2.9g, 2.9h, 2.10b, 8.6a, 8.6b, 8.6f, 8.7

34. (Chapters 8 and 9) Hydrazine, N_2H_4, is a useful commercial reducing agent.

Hydrazine, N_2H_4

  (a) Draw a Lewis electron dot structure for the molecule and specify the bond angles.
  (b) Specify the electron pair geometry around the N atoms and their hybridization.
  (c) Suppose hydrazine, N_2H_4, can be made from ammonia by the reaction

$$2\ NH_3(g) \rightarrow H_2N-NH_2(g) + H_2(g)$$

  Does the geometry around the N atom change in the course of the reaction of ammonia to produce hydrazine?
  (d) Use bond energies to calculate the enthalpy change for this reaction. Is it predicted to be endo- or exothermic?
  Text Sections: 8.2, 8.6, 8.9, and 9.2
  OWL Questions: 8.5d, 8.6a, 8.6b, 8.6f, 8.9c, 9.2f, 9.2h

35. (Chapters 8 and 9) Urea reacts with malonic acid to produce barbituric acid, a member of the class of compounds called phenobarbitals, which are widely prescribed as sedatives.

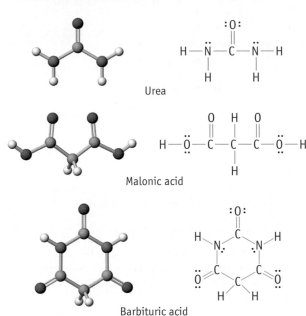

Urea

Malonic acid

Barbituric acid

(a) What bonds are broken and what bonds are made when malonic acid and urea combine to make barbituric acid? Is the reaction predicted to be exo- or endothermic?

(b) Write a balanced equation for the reaction.

(c) Specify the bond angles in malonic acid.

(d) Give the hybridization of the C atoms in barbituric acid.

(e) What is (are) the most polar bond(s) in barbituric acid?

(f) Is barbituric acid polar?

Text Sections: 8.6–8.9 and 9.2
OWL Questions: 8.6a, 8.6b, 8.6f, 8.7, 8.8b, 8.9c, 9.2f, 9.2h

36. (Chapter 10) The alkene *cis*-2-pentene reacts with hydrogen to produce another hydrocarbon.

(a) Draw the structures of the reactants and products.

(b) What type of reaction is illustrated here (addition, elimination, condensation, or esterification)?

(c) Name the product of the reaction.

(d) Sketch a geometric isomer of *cis*-2-pentene.

(e) Draw the structure and give the systematic name of each of the isomers of C_5H_{12}.

Text Section: 10.2
OWL Questions: 10.1c, 10.2a, 10.2c, 10.2e, 10.2g

37. (Chapters 8-10) In order to convert *cis*-2-butene to *trans*-2-butene, it is necessary to heat this compound to around 450 °C. Explain, in a short phrase or sentence, why it is necessary to supply so much energy to cause rotation around a carbon-carbon double bond.

Text Sections: 9.2 and 10.2
OWL Questions: 9.2o, 10.1c

38. (Chapters 8–10) The structure drawn below is for the molecule aspartame, one of several common artificial sweeteners.

(a) What is the approximate H—N—H bond angle (a)?

(b) What is the geometry of the indicated carbon atom (C_2) (b)?

(c) What is the hybridization of oxygen (c)?

(d) What is the electron pair geometry of carbon (C_7) (d)?

(e) Name the functional group enclosed in box (E).

(f) Name the functional group that contains the carbonyl group (F).

(g) Name the functional group enclosed in box (G).

(h) Name the functional group that contains the carbonyl group (H).

(i) Carbon atoms in this drawing (except those in the C_6H_5— group) are numbered 1–8. Which of these carbons is/are a chiral center?

(j) Hydrolysis of aspartame (reaction with water) will cleave this large molecule into three different compounds. Draw the structures of the products formed by this hydrolysis.

Text Sections: 8.6, 9.2, 10.1, 10.3, and 10.4
OWL Questions: 8.6a, 8.6b, 8.6f, 9.2f, 9.2h, 10.1d, 10.3h, 10.4c

39. (Chapter 10) You have two unlabeled flasks containing colorless liquids. One liquid is *cis*-2-pentene, the other cyclopentane, but you don't know which is which. To determine their identities you add bromine to each flask.

(a) What are the empirical and molecular formulas of *cis*-2-pentene and cyclopentane?

(b) Draw the structure of each compound.

(c) Describe what you observe when you add bromine to these compounds and indicate how the observation will allow you to tell the identity of the liquids in the flasks.

(d) Draw the structure of the product of the reaction with bromine, if any, for the two molecules.

Text Section: 10.2
OWL Questions: 10.2a, 10.2c, 10.2e, 10.2g

40. (Chapter 10) You have two beakers, one containing propanal and the other propanone (acetone). To tell which is which, you add a reagent, aqueous acidic $Na_2Cr_2O_7$.

(a) Draw the structures of propanal and propanone.

(b) Describe what you observe when you treat these compounds with aqueous acidic sodium dichromate and indicate how the observation will allow you to tell the identity of the liquids in the beakers.

(c) Draw the structure of the organic product of each reaction, if any, in each case.

Text Section: 10.4
OWL Questions: 10.4g, 10.4h

41. (Chapter 10) Consider the molecule illustrated below.

$$H-\underset{\underset{H}{|}}{\overset{\overset{H}{|}}{C}}-\underset{\underset{H}{|}}{\overset{\overset{H}{|}}{C}}-\overset{\overset{O}{||}}{C}-O-\underset{\underset{CH_3}{|}}{\overset{\overset{CH_3}{|}}{C}}-H$$

(a) To what class of organic compounds does this belong?

(b) Name the compound.

(c) Draw structures for and name the products that result when the compound reacts with aqueous sodium hydroxide followed by hydrochloric acid.

Text Section: 10.4
OWL Questions: 10.4k, 10.4m

42. (Chapter 10) Organic reactions.

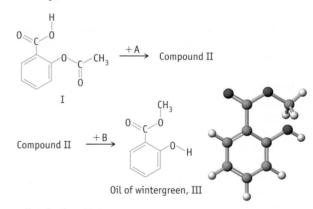

(a) Name compounds 1 and 2.

(b) Draw structures for the reaction products, compounds 3 and 4, and name each one.

Text Sections: 10.2, 10.3, and 10.4
OWL Questions: 10.2g, 10.3c, 10.4f, 10.4g

43. (Chapter 10) Compound I, aspirin, can be converted to compound III (oil of wintergreen) in two steps. Identify reactants A and B and draw the structure of compound II.

Text Section: 10.4
OWL Question: 10.4k

44. (Chapter 10) Give the structural formula for the product formed by polymerization of $H_2NCH_2CH_2CH_2CH_2CH_2CO_2H$. Is the product an addition polymer or a condensation polymer? Is it a polyester or a polyamide?

Text Section: 10.5
OWL Questions: 10.5c, 10.5d

45. (Chapter 10) The reaction of 1-octene, $C_6H_{13}CH{=}CH_2$, and water could, potentially, form two different isomeric products.

(a) Draw their structures and name the two possible isomeric products.

(b) In fact, only one product is formed in the water reaction. To identify the product, you first add a solution of $Na_2Cr_2O_7$ to this product and observe that a reaction occurs. Next you add aqueous NaOH to the product obtained from the dichromate reaction. There is no evidence of a reaction with NaOH (no heat was evolved and the organic product didn't dissolve in the aqueous solution). Based on these observations, which isomer was formed?

Text Sections: 10.2 and 10.4
OWL Questions: 10.3c, 10.4f, 10.4h

46. (Chapter 10) Draw structures and name the following:

(a) A chiral compound with the formula C_7H_{16}, in which the longest carbon chain contains 5 carbon atoms.

(b) An ester that is a structural isomer of butanoic acid.

(c) An aldehyde and a ketone with the formula C_4H_8O.

(d) An alkene, C_7H_{14}, in which the longest carbon chain is 5 carbons, and there is an ethyl group as a substituent.

Text Sections: 10.2 and 10.4
OWL Questions: 10.1d, 10.4c

47. (Chapter 10) In the lab, you have inadvertently spilled some 1.0 M NaOH(aq) on the sleeve of your polyester shirt. About a half an hour later, you notice a hole where the spill was. Explain why the NaOH caused this to happen.

Text Sections: 10.4 and 10.5
OWL Questions: 10.4k, 10.5c, 10.5d

48. (Chapter 10) Analysis of an unknown ester has determined that its formula is $C_4H_8O_2$. Hydrolysis of the ester, under acidic conditions, yields methanol. Draw the structure and give the name of the second product of hydrolysis and write a chemical equation for the hydrolysis reaction.

Text Section: 10.4
OWL Question: 10.k

49. (Chapter 10) When an acid reacts with an amine, an amide linkage is formed. (See equation on page 475.) Amino acids are characterized by having both a carboxylic acid and an amine functional group, so if an amino acid reacts with another amino acid of the same or different kind, an amide link is formed (and the product is called a peptide). (If many amino acids react, a polymer called a protein is formed.)

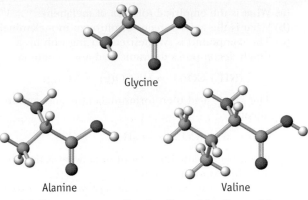

Glycine

Alanine   Valine

(a) Draw structures for the dipeptides formed by reacting glycine and alanine.

(b) How many tripeptides are possible when glycine, alanine, and valine react?

Text Sections: 10.4 and 10.5
OWL Questions: 10.4n, 10.5c, 10.5d

50. (Chapters 6 and 8) Fireworks and neon signs.

(a) As described on page 281 fireworks commonly use salts of sodium, strontium, barium, and copper, among other metals. Neon signs are filled with gases such as neon or a mixture of argon with minute particles of mercury. Based on the discussion of atomic spectra in Chapter 6, what do fireworks and neon signs have in common? How do they generate light?

(b) Chlorate and perchlorate salts are common ingredients in fireworks. After drawing the Lewis structures for these ions, describe their geometry.

(c) What are the formal charges on the atoms in the perchlorate ion?

Text Sections: 6.3, 8.2, 8.3, and 8.6
OWL Questions: 6.3c, 8.3b, 8.5d, 8.6a, 8.6b, 8.6f

51. (Chapters 2, 4, 5, 8, and 9) In 2007 and 2008 there were several international incidents when it was found that food imports from China contained high levels of melamine ($C_3H_6N_6$, 1,3,5-triazine-2,4,6-triamine). It was evidently added to foodstuffs to raise the apparent level of nitrogen, which normally comes from protein.

Melamine

(a) What is the empirical formula of melamine?

(b) What is the mass percent of nitrogen in melamine?

(c) The compound is synthesized starting with urea, which decomposes to cyanic acid and ammonia.

$$(NH_2)_2CO(s) \rightarrow HNCO(g) + NH_3(g)$$

The cyanic acid then forms melamine and carbon dioxide.

$$6\,HNCO(g) \rightarrow C_3H_6N_6 + 3\,CO_2$$

If you begin with 1.000 kg of urea, what is the theoretical yield of melamine?

(d) Is the first step in the synthesis of melamine exo- or endothermic?

Compound	$\Delta_f H°$ (kJ/mol)
$(NH_2)_2CO(s)$	-333.1
$HNCO(g)$	-101.67
$NH_3(g)$	-45.90

(e) Describe the hybridization of the C and N atoms of the melamine ring.

(f) What are the N—C—N and C—N—C bond angles in the melamine ring?

(g) Is melamine a polar molecule?

Text Sections: 2.10, 4.1, 5.7, 8.6, 8.8, 8.9, and 9.2
OWL Questions: 2.10b, 4.1c, 5.7d, 8.8b, 9.2f, 9.2h

Answers to Assessing Key Points Questions

1. See Figure 6.2: radio < 520 nm < blue light < x-rays

2. Energy UVB > energy UVA

3. n describes orbital size and energy and ℓ describes orbital shape. See pages 285–290.

4. For $n = 4$ and $\ell = 2$, m_ℓ could range from -2 to $+2$ including 0.

5. (a) Rb and (b) Se. See Table 7.3, page 310.

6. Nitrogen. See Active Figure 7.10, page 323.

7. (d) Too many electron pairs around the central N atom. The other structures are resonance structures of N_2O.

8. (a) Linear. (b) The N—O bond is polar, and the molecule is polar. (c) The central N atom is sp hybridized and has a $+1$ formal charge.

9. Three MOs. The number of MOs formed is always equal to the number of combining atomic orbitals. See pages 422–423.

10. (a) alkane (b) aldehyde (c) alcohol (d) ketone

11. (d) is 2-propanone, commonly called acetone. An isomer would be propanal, an aldehyde.

12. Oxidizing (c) (ethanol) first produces (b) in Question 10 (the aldehyde ethanal). Further oxidation gives acetic acid, CH_3CO_2H.

13. Only (a), an alkene, can be used to make a polymer, in this case polypropylene. See Table 10.12, page 481.

Solutions to Comprehensive Questions

14. (a) Convert the wavelength in nm to meters (1 nm = 1×10^{-9} m); then use the relation $\lambda \cdot \nu$ = velocity of light.

$$\text{Frequency} = \frac{\text{Velocity of light}}{\text{Wavelength}} = \frac{2.9979 \times 10^8 \text{ m·s}^{-1}}{4.20 \times 10^{-7} \text{ m}}$$
$$= 7.14 \times 10^{14} \text{ s}^{-1}$$

(b) Use Planck's equation to calculate the energy per photon, then find the number of photons.

E per photon $= h\nu = (6.626 \times 10^{-34} \text{ J·s})(7.14 \times 10^{14} \text{ s}^{-1})$
$E = 4.73 \times 10^{-19}$ J/photon
Number of photons
$= (2.50 \times 10^{-14} \text{ J})(1 \text{ photon}/4.73 \times 10^{-19} \text{ J})$
$= 5.29 \times 10^4$ photons

15. (a) One of the $3p$ orbitals

(b) There are 5 subshells and $n^2 = 25$ orbitals (one s, three p, five d, seven f, nine g). Number of electrons = $2 \times 25 = 50$.

(c) $3f$ orbitals are not possible: ℓ would be 3, and n and ℓ cannot be the same.

(d) (i) When $n = 3$ there can be 9 orbitals (one s, three p, five d). (ii) There are no orbitals for $n = 3$ and $\ell = 3$ (as explained in c above). (iii) This refers to one of the $2p$ orbitals.

(e) Barium has the configuration [Xe]$6s^2$, so only two electrons can be removed easily. A 3+ ion is not feasible. The S^{3-} ion is not likely because the S atom would need to acquire three electrons, whereas only two additional electrons can be accommodated in its $3s$ and $3p$ valence orbitals. (S has the ground state configuration [Ne]$3s^23p^4$.)

(f) The $n = 3$ shell is completed with copper.

16. (a) Use the relation $c = \lambda \cdot \nu$ to calculate wavelength from frequency.

$$\lambda = c/\nu = (2.998 \times 10^8 \text{ m}\cdot\text{s}^{-1})/(2.45 \times 10^9 \text{ s}^{-1}) = 0.122 \text{ m}$$

(b) Number of wavelengths = 0.48 m/0.122 m = 3.9

(c) We first need to know the energy per mole of photons and the heat needed to warm the water.

E per photon = $h\nu$ = $(6.626 \times 10^{-34} \text{ J}\cdot\text{s})(2.45 \times 10^9 \text{ s}^{-1})$
$\qquad$ = 1.62×10^{-24} J per photon

E per mol of photons =
$\qquad$ = $(1.62 \times 10^{-24} \text{ J/photon})(6.022 \times 10^{23} \text{ photons/mol})$
$\qquad$ = 0.978 J/mol of photons

Energy required = q = (254 g)(4.184 J/g·K)(363 K − 285 K)
$\qquad$ = 8.3×10^4 J

Now we can calculate the amount (mol) of photons required.

Amount of photons = $(8.3 \times 10^4 \text{ J})(1 \text{ mol photons}/0.978 \text{ J})$
$\qquad$ = 8.5×10^4 mol photons

17. (a) Use Hess's law, Equation 5.6 (page 237).

$$\Delta_r H^\circ = \Delta_f H^\circ [\text{glucose}] + 6\,\Delta_f H^\circ [O_2]$$
$$- \{6\,\Delta_f H^\circ [CO_2(g)] + 6\,\Delta_f H^\circ [H_2O(\ell)]\}$$

Recognizing $\Delta_f H^\circ [O_2] = 0$,

$\Delta_r H^\circ$ = (1 mol glucose/1 mol-rxn)(−1273.3 kJ/mol)
$\qquad$ − [(6 mol CO_2/1 mol-rxn)(−393.5 kJ/mol)
$\qquad$ + (6 mol H_2O/1 mol-rxn)(−285.83 kJ/mol)]
$\qquad$ = +2802.7 kJ/mol-rxn

Thus, $\Delta_r H^\circ$ = +2802.7 kJ per mol of glucose because 1 mol of glucose is consumed per mol of reaction.

(b) Energy per molecule =
$\qquad$ = (2802.7 kJ/mol)(1 mol/6.022 × 10^{23} molecules)
$\qquad$ = 4.654×10^{-21} kJ/molecule or 4.654
$\qquad\qquad\qquad\qquad\qquad\qquad$ × 10^{-18} J/molecule

(c) Using the approach in questions 14 and 16, we find light with a wavelength of 650. nm has an energy of 3.06×10^{-19} J/photon.

(d) More than 15 photons with λ = 650. nm are required to make one molecule of glucose.

$(4.654 \times 10^{-18} \text{ J/molecule})(1 \text{ photon}/3.06 \times 10^{-19} \text{ J})$
= 15.2 photons

18. (a) Emitting light in the UV region would require a transition from a higher level to $n = 1$. Visible light is emitted by transitions to $n = 2$ from higher energy levels. Infrared radiation arises from transitions to $n = 3$ from levels of higher energy. See Figure 6.10.

(b) -2.18×10^{-18} J/atom (Figures 6.8 and 6.10)

(c) E (for $n = 4$) = $-Rhc/n^2$
$\qquad\qquad\qquad$ = $-(2.18 \times 10^{-18} \text{ J/atom})/4^2$
$\qquad E = -1.362 \times 10^{-19}$ J/atom

(d) $\Delta E = E_2 - E_1 = (-5.45 \times 10^{-19} \text{ J})$
$\qquad\qquad\qquad\qquad\qquad - (-2.18 \times 10^{-18} \text{ J})$
$\qquad\qquad$ = -1.64×10^{-18} J
or $\Delta E = -(3/4)Rhc$

(e) The energy to ionize the H atom is $+2.18 \times 10^{-18}$ J/atom. Therefore, multiply by Avogadro's number to find the energy per mole (= 1312 kJ/mol).

(f) To ionize an H atom requires 2.18×10^{-18} J/atom. Use Planck's equation to calculate the frequency of radiation equivalent to this energy.

2.18×10^{-18} J = $(6.626 \times 10^{-34} \text{ J}\cdot\text{s})(\nu)$
$\nu = 3.29 \times 10^{15}$ s^{-1}
$\lambda = c/\nu = (2.998 \times 10^8 \text{ m}\cdot\text{s}^{-1})/(3.29 \times 10^{15} \text{ s}^{-1})$
$\qquad$ = 9.11×10^{-8} m (or 91.1 nm)

Radiation of this wavelength is found in the high energy UV region. See Active Figure 6.2.

19. Atom A is Cl and atom B is Ca. The two elements react to give $CaCl_2$, with Ca^{2+} and Cl^- ions. Neither of these ions has an unpaired electron and so both are diamagnetic.

$$Ca(s) + Cl_2(g) \rightarrow CaCl_2(s)$$

20. (a) Iron, Fe

(b) Manganese. The Mn^{2+} ion has 5 unpaired electrons and so is paramagnetic.

(c) Ni^{2+} has the electron configuration $[Ar]3d^8$ and has two unpaired electrons.

(d) The element is arsenic, As. It is paramagnetic but the 3− ion has no unpaired electrons $\{[Ar]3d^{10}4s^24p^6\}$.

(e) Tc, technetium. The element is paramagnetic.

Electron	n	ℓ	m_ℓ	m_s
1	4	2	−2	+1/2
2	4	2	0	+1/2
3	5	0	0	−1/2

Comment: The m_ℓ values for electrons 1 and 2 can have any value from −2 to +2 including 0. However, they cannot both have the same value. The m_ℓ value for electron 3, however, is fixed by the fact that $\ell = 0$. Also, m_s can be either ±1/2 for electrons 1 and 2, but they must have the same value. Finally, whatever the value of m_s for electrons 1 and 2, that for electron 3 must be the opposite because its spin is in the opposite direction.

(f) A is Sr, a metal, and B is I, a nonmetal. Iodine (B) has a higher ionization energy, and its atoms are smaller than those of Sr. (See App. F, page A-21, Table 7.5, and Figure 7.8.) Strontium, Sr, is a metal and so is likely to form cations (here Sr^{2+}). Iodine forms I^- ions, so A and B react to form SrI_2.

21. Part 1
(a) Se (Figure 7.8, page 320)
(b) Anions are always larger than the atoms from which are formed. See Figure 7.12, page 326.
(c) Cl (App. F, page A-21)
(d) C (Figure 7.10, page 323)
(e) These ions are isoelectronic; that is, they have the same number of electrons (here 10 electrons). For such a series, the ion with the largest negative charge and smallest nuclear charge will be the largest ion, here N^{3-}.

Part 2: K has the lowest ionization energy and C the most negative electron affinity. K has the largest radius and C has the smallest radius. K has the largest difference in 1st and 2nd ionization energy (because the 2nd electron comes from an inner shell). See Table 7.5.

22. (a) See Table 7.3 on page 310.

Arsenic: $[Ar]3d^{10}4s^24p^3$
Manganese: $[Ar]3d^54s^2$
Plutonium: $[Rn]4f^67s^2$

(b) Tin(II), Sn^{2+}

[Kr] ⇅ ⇅ ⇅ ⇅ ⇅   ⇅   ☐ ☐ ☐
    4d orbitals   5s orbital   5p orbitals

Cobalt(III), Co^{3+}

[Ar] ⇅ ↑ ↑ ↑ ↑   ☐
    3d orbitals   4s orbital

Oxide ion, O^{2-}. Its ground state electron configuration is isoelectronic with neon.

[He] ⇅   ⇅ ⇅ ⇅
    2s orbital   2p orbitals

23. (a) For Mg one electron is removed from a 3s orbital,

Mg, $1s^22s^22p^63s^2 \rightarrow Mg^+, 1s^22s^22p^63s^1$

whereas an Al atom loses an electron from a 3p orbital of slightly *higher* energy.

Al, $1s^22s^22p^63s^23p^1 \rightarrow Al^+, 1s^22s^22p^63s^2$

Comment: The orbital energies are graphically illustrated on the OWL Simulation 7.5d. This provides a clear explanation of the effect of orbital energies on ionization energies.

(b) This illustrates the effect on ionization energy of electron-electron repulsion in an electron pair. For S we have

[Ne]   ⇅   ⇅ ↑ ↑
    3s orbital   3p orbitals

The electron lost is one of the pair in the 3p orbitals. Removal of an electron is "assisted" by the loss of electron-electron repulsion when the electron is removed. Such pairing is not present in P.

24. Nitrogen-oxygen bond lengths in increasing order.

Increasing N—O bond length = decreasing bond order

Molecule	N Atom Hybridization
NO^+	sp
NO_2^-	sp^2
NO_3^-	sp^2
H_2NOH	sp^3

25. (a) Dot structure of N_2O_4

The N hybridization is sp^2 and the N—O bond order is 1.5.

(b) $\Delta_rH° = \Delta_fH°[N_2O_4(g)] - 2 \Delta_fH°[NO_2(g)]$
$= (1 \text{ mol}/1 \text{ mol-rxn})(9.08 \text{ kJ/mol})$
$\quad - (2 \text{ mol}/1 \text{ mol-rxn})(33.1 \text{ kJ/mol})$
$= -57.1 \text{ kJ/mol}$

The reaction involves only the formation of an N—N single bond, and, like the formation of any chemical bond, it is an exothermic process. N—N single bonds are often notably weak, and this is reflected in this value calculated from enthalpies of formation.

26. (a) Sulfite ion, SO_3^{2-}

The formal charge on each O atom is -1, whereas it is $+1$ on the central S. The SO bond order is 1, and S atom hybridization is sp^3.

(b) Thiosulfate ion, $S_2O_3^{2-}$

$$\left[\begin{array}{c} :\ddot{O}: \\ | \\ :\ddot{O}-S-\ddot{O}: \\ | \\ :\ddot{S}: \end{array}\right]^{2-}$$

27. (a) and (b) ClF_3 has trigonal pyramidal electron pair geometry with an sp^3d hybrid Cl atom. The most reasonable structure is T-shaped, adopted to minimize interactions between electron pairs. In the T-shape there are 4 lone pair-atom interactions at 90°. In an alternate structure, trigonal planar, there would be 6 such interactions. See Figure 8.8 and discussion, page 372.

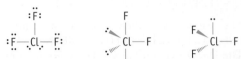

| Dot structure | Most likely structure | Possible alternate structure |

(c) The ClF_2^+ ion has a tetrahedral electron pair geometry and a bent molecular geometry. The ClF_4^- ion has an octahedral electron pair geometry and a square planar molecular geometry.

28. (a) Nitryl chloride has 24 valence electrons.

$$\ddot{O}=N-\ddot{C}\ddot{l}:$$
with $:\ddot{O}:$ above N

(i) The electron-pair geometry around N is trigonal planar with O—N—O and Cl—N—O bond angles of 120°.

(ii) The sp^2 hybridized N atom has a formal charge of +1. (The single-bonded O atom has a formal charge of −1 and the double bonded O has a formal charge of 0.)

(iii) The molecule is polar.

(b) The NH_2OH molecule has 14 valence electrons.

$$H-N-\ddot{O}-H$$
with H above N

(i) The electron-pair geometry around the N atom is tetrahedral, and the H—O—N and H—N—H angles are predicted to be about 109°.

(ii) The sp^3 hybridized N atom has a formal charge of 0.

(iii) The molecule is polar.

(c) N_2O has 16 valence electrons.

$$:N\equiv N-\ddot{O}: \longleftrightarrow \ddot{N}=N=\ddot{O} \longleftrightarrow :\ddot{N}-N\equiv O:$$
$$0 \;\; +1 \;\; -1 \qquad -1 \;\; +1 \;\; 0 \qquad -2 \;\; +1 \;\; +1$$

The molecule is linear (N—N—O bond angle 180°) with an sp hybridized N atom. Formal charges suggest that the resonance structure on the left above is predominant.

29. (a) sp^3 orbitals on each C atom overlap to form the C—C bond.

(b) 120°

(c) C_1 carbon is sp^2 hybridized.

(d) Trigonal pyramidal. The N atom is surrounded by two H atoms, a bond to C_2, and a lone pair.

(e) 109°, a tetrahedral angle

(f) C_2 is a chiral carbon. It is surrounded by four *different* groups.

(g) There are 8 lone pairs missing. Each O atom needs two lone pairs and each N atom needs one.

(h) At the left end of the molecule is an amide group ($-CONH_2$), at the right end there is a carboxylic acid group ($-CO_2H$), and the NH_2 on C_2 is an amine group.

30. (a) Naphthalene has sp^2 hybridized C atoms and three resonance structures.

(b) The C atoms of graphite are sp^2 hybridized (to account for the trigonal planar C atoms) and the tetrahedral C atoms of diamond are sp^3 hybridized.

31. (a) There are 9 valence electrons (4 for each Si plus 1 for the charge). Assuming that the MOs formed by the valence orbitals ($3s$ and $3p$) are identical to those formed by $2s$ and $2p$ in Figure 9.21, the configuration would be [core] $(\sigma_{3s})^2(\sigma^*_{3s})^2(\pi_{3p})^4(\sigma_{3p})^1$.

(b) The bond order is 1.5.

(c) Paramagnetic

(d) σ_{3p}

32. (a) Anethole alternate resonance structure and isomers

Resonance structure

Structural isomer

Geometric isomer

(b) See Figure 9.10. C=C bonds consist of one σ bond formed by direct overlap of hybridized sp^2 orbitals and one π bond formed by sideways overlap of unhybridized p orbitals.

(c) Six p orbitals, one from each of six C atoms, contribute to form 6 molecular orbitals (3 bonding and 3 antibonding). Six electrons, one from each of the C atoms, fill the bonding MOs to give three filled π MOs. See Figure 9.24.

33. (a) Most polar bond, O—H
(b) C=O bond is the strongest bond.
(c) 1 = 109.5°; 2 = 120°; 3 = 120°; 4 = 109.5°
(d) Molar mass of $C_8H_9NO_2$ is 151.165 g/mol. 250 mg is equivalent to 0.0017 mol.
(e) Weight percent C = 63.57%

34. (a) and (b) Electron dot structure of hydrazine

109° $\left(\ \begin{array}{c} H \quad\quad H \\ :N\!-\!N: \\ H \quad\quad H \end{array} \right.$ ← sp³ hybrid N with tetrahedral electron pair geometry

(c) N atom geometry does not change. It has a tetrahedral electron pair geometry (and trigonal pyramidal molecular geometry) in ammonia and hydrazine.
(d) Bonds broken on reaction = 2 NH

ΔH = 2 mol (391 kJ/mol) = 782 kJ
Bonds made = 1 NN + 1 HH
ΔH = 1 mol (163 kJ/mol) + 1 mol (436 kJ/mol)
     = 599 kJ
ΔH = +782 kJ − 599 kJ = +183 kJ

The reaction is endothermic.

35. (a) Two N—H bonds in urea and two C—O bonds and 2 O—H bonds in malonic acid are broken. Two N—C bonds are made in barbituric acid. Two molecules of water form, involving the formation of four O—H bonds.

ΔH for bond breaking
     = 2 NH bonds + 2 CO bonds + 2 OH bonds
     = 2 mol (391 kJ/mol) + 2 mol (358 kJ/mol)
          + 2 mol (463 kJ/mol)
     = 2424 kJ
ΔH for bond making
     = 2 NC bonds + 4 OH bonds
     = 2 mol (305 kJ/mol) + 4 mol (463 kJ/mol)
     = 2462 kJ
ΔH_{net} = +2424 kJ − 2462 kJ = −38 kJ

The reaction is predicted to be exothermic.
(b) $(NH_2)_2CO + CH_2(CO_2H)_2 \rightarrow C_4H_4N_2O_3 + 2\ H_2O$
(c) The H—O—C and H—C—H angles are 109°. The O—C—O and C—C—O angles are 120°.
(d) The CH_2 carbon atom is sp^3 hybridized, and the C atoms bonded to O are sp^2 hybridized.
(e) The CO bonds are the most polar (with a difference in electronegativity of C and O being 1.0).
(f) The molecule is polar.

36. (a) Hydrogenation reaction

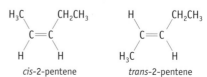

(b) Addition reaction (of H_2)
(c) Pentane
(d) See Example 10.3 on page 454.

cis-2-pentene   trans-2-pentene

(e) See the pentane isomers in the margin of page 449.

37. Energy must be supplied to break the C=C π bond to allow free rotation of one end of the molecule relative to the other. See page 420.

38. (a) 109°   (f) Amide
(b) Trigonal planar   (g) Carboxylic acid
(c) sp^3 (h) Ester
(d) Tetrahedral   (i) C_3 and C_6 are chiral centers
(e) Amine

(j) Reaction with water breaks the ester and amide links to give three products.

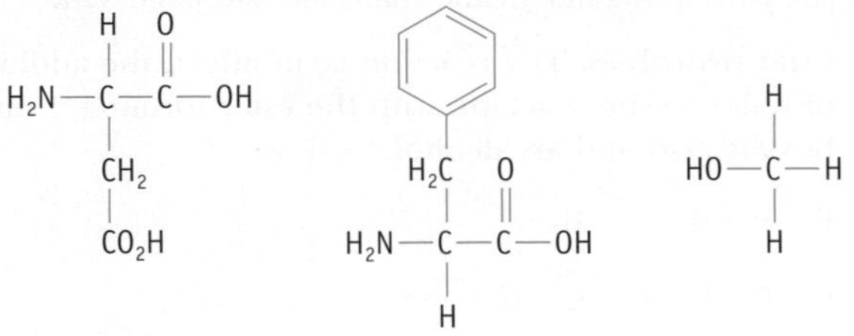

39. (a) Both have the same empirical (CH_2) and molecular formulas (C_5H_{10}).
(b) Structural isomers of C_5H_{10}

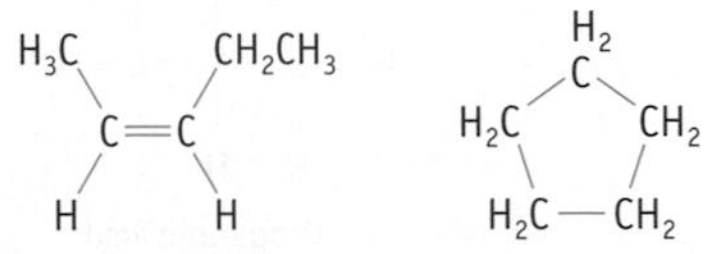

cis-2-pentene   cyclopentane

(c) The alkene, *cis*-2-pentene, will add bromine across the double bond to give 2,3-dibromopentane, and the color of Br_2 will disappear. (See Figure 10.7.) Cyclopentane will not react with bromine. The orange-red color of bromine will therefore remain.
(d) Adding Br_2 to an alkene

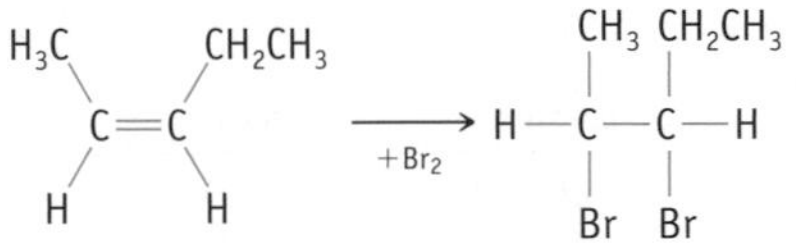

40. (a) and (c) Structures of propanone and propanal and reaction products.

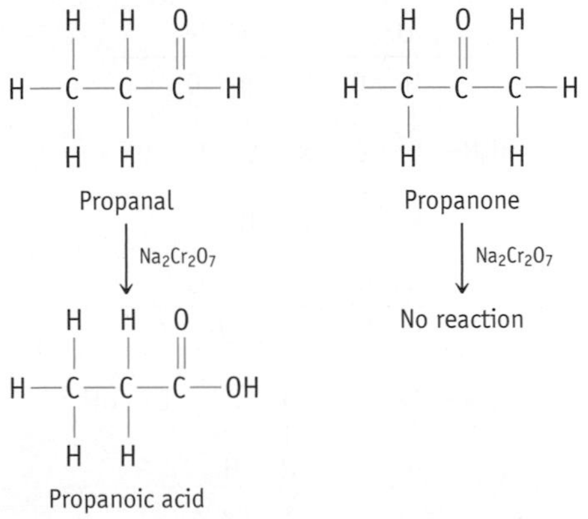

Propanal   Propanone

Propanoic acid

Of the isomers, only propanal reacts with the oxidizing agent in acid. The orange color of $Na_2Cr_2O_7$ fades and is replaced by the green color of Cr^{3+}.

41. (a) Ester
(b) 2-Propyl propanoate
(c) Products of reaction with NaOH followed by HCl.

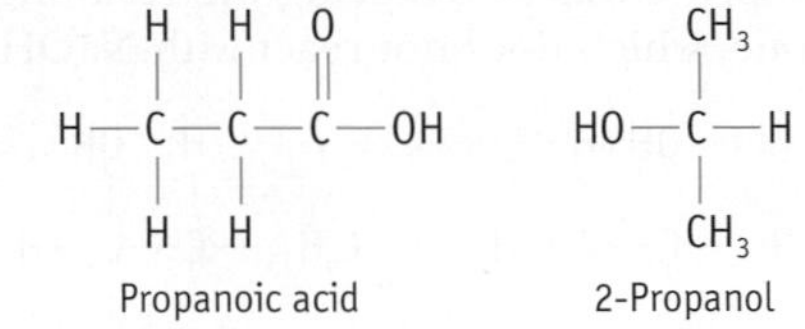

Propanoic acid   2-Propanol

42. (a) 1 is 1-Propanol and 2 is propene
(b) Compounds 3 and 4

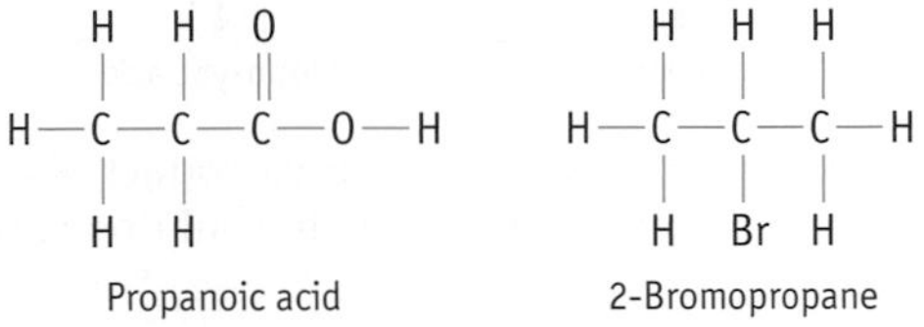

Propanoic acid   2-Bromopropane

Comment: When propene reacts with HBr, the HBr can add in two ways. The H atom could attach to the CH_2 carbon or to the CH carbon. The former is generally observed and is called a Markovnikov addition.

43. The group *ortho* to the carboxylic acid group is an ester. Therefore, first react aspirin with NaOH (followed by acid) to give compound II, 2-hydroxybenzoic acid (but better known as salicylic acid). Second, react II with methanol to give the desired ester (oil of wintergreen).

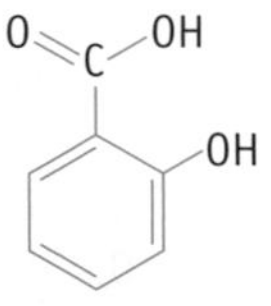

2-hydroxybenzoic acid
or
salicylic acid

44. The compound forms a polyamide, a condensation polymer. See Example 10.8 on page 486.

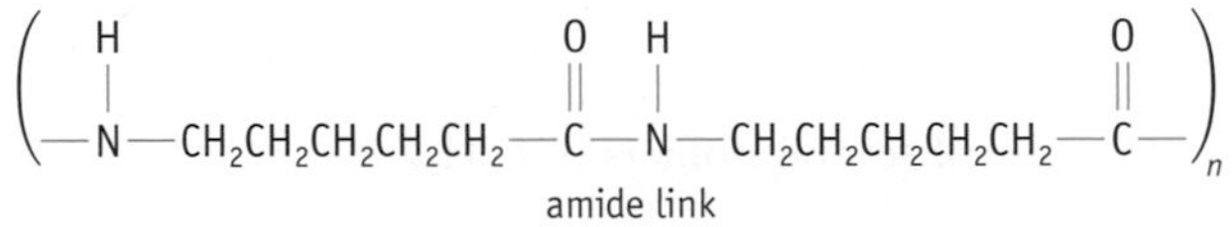

amide link

45. The two possible products from 1-octene with water arise because the OH of water can be found on C(1) or C(2) of the C_8 chain. The product here has OH on C(2). We prove this by oxidizing the resulting alcohol to a ketone, which does not react with NaOH.

$$
\begin{array}{cc}
\underset{\text{2-octanol}}{C_6H_{13}-\overset{\displaystyle OH}{\underset{\displaystyle H}{C}}-\overset{\displaystyle H}{\underset{\displaystyle H}{C}}-H}
&
\underset{\text{1-octanol}}{C_6H_{13}-\overset{\displaystyle H}{\underset{\displaystyle H}{C}}-\overset{\displaystyle OH}{\underset{\displaystyle H}{C}}-H}
\end{array}
$$

2-octanol $\xrightarrow{Na_2Cr_2O_7}$ Ketone

1-octanol $\xrightarrow{Na_2Cr_2O_7}$ Carboxylic acid

If the OH group was on C(1), the product of oxidation would be a carboxylic acid, which would react with NaOH.

46. (a) Chiral carbon is marked with *.

$$H-\overset{H}{\underset{H}{C}}-\overset{H}{\underset{H}{C}}-\overset{CH_3}{\underset{H}{\overset{*}{C}}}-\overset{CH_3}{\underset{H}{C}}-\overset{H}{\underset{H}{C}}-H$$

(b) Isomer of butanoic acid

$$H-\overset{H}{\underset{H}{C}}-\overset{H}{\underset{H}{C}}-\overset{O}{\overset{\|}{C}}-O-CH_3$$

methyl propanoate

(c) Aldehyde and ketone

$$\underset{\text{butanal}}{H-\overset{H}{\underset{H}{C}}-\overset{H}{\underset{H}{C}}-\overset{H}{\underset{H}{C}}-\overset{O}{\overset{\|}{C}}-H}
\qquad
\underset{\text{butanone}}{H-\overset{H}{\underset{H}{C}}-\overset{O}{\overset{\|}{C}}-\overset{H}{\underset{H}{C}}-\overset{H}{\underset{H}{C}}-H}$$

(d) One of several isomers of C_7H_{14}

$$\underset{\text{3-ethyl-1-pentene}}{C=\overset{H}{C}-\overset{H}{\underset{C_2H_5}{C}}-\overset{H}{\underset{H}{C}}-\overset{H}{\underset{H}{C}}-H}$$

47. An ester can react with NaOH to produce an alcohol and a carboxylic acid, so reaction with NaOH can destroy the polyester in the material. See page 474.

48. Ester hydrolysis. The reaction is, in effect, the addition of water to the reactant, with the ester forming a carboxylic acid and an alcohol.

$$\underset{\text{Methyl propanoate}}{H-\overset{H}{\underset{H}{C}}-\overset{H}{\underset{H}{C}}-\overset{O}{\overset{\|}{C}}-O-\overset{H}{\underset{H}{C}}-H} \xrightarrow{H_2O}$$

$$\underset{\text{Propanoic acid}}{H-\overset{H}{\underset{H}{C}}-\overset{H}{\underset{H}{C}}-\overset{O}{\overset{\|}{C}}-OH} + \underset{\text{Methanol}}{HO-\overset{H}{\underset{H}{C}}-H}$$

49. (a) Four peptides (2^2) are possible on reacting a mixture of two amino acids.

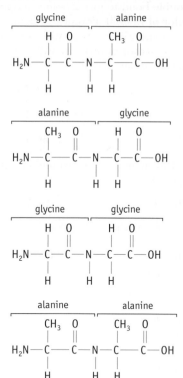

(b) 3^3 or 27 peptides are possible. One is illustrated here.

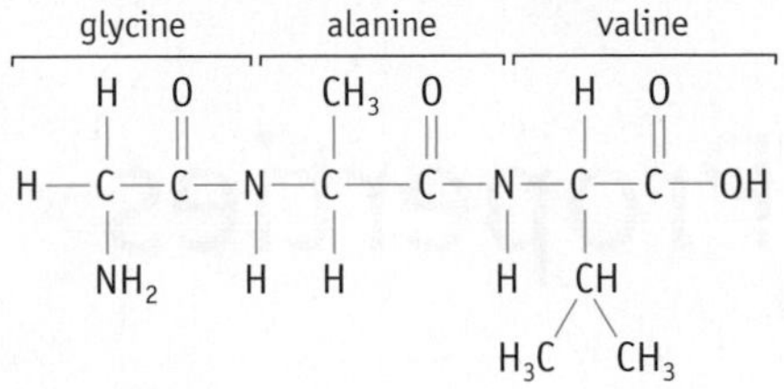

glycine   alanine   valine

50. (a) The colors of fireworks and neon signs arise the same way: from excited atoms, whether these are strontium atoms or neon atoms. As the atoms are excited by the input of energy, electrons move to higher quantum levels. Light is emitted as the electrons move back to lower quantum levels.

(b) Perchlorate and chlorate both have a tetrahedral electron pair geometry. The former has a tetrahedral shape, whereas the latter is trigonal pyramidal.

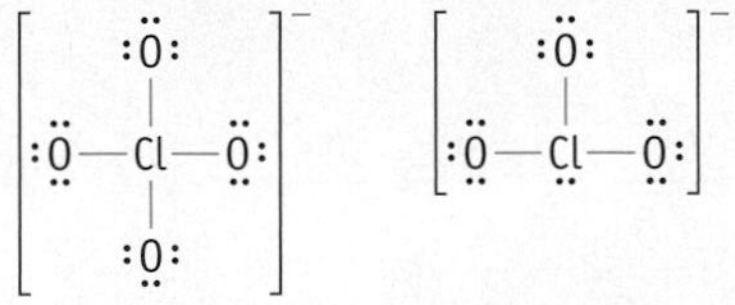

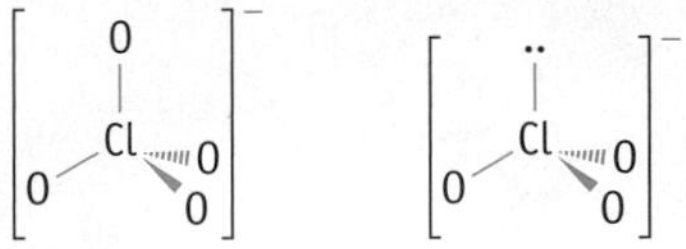

Perchlorate ion   Chlorate ion

(c) The formal charge on each O atom in ClO_4^- is -1, whereas it is $+3$ for Cl.

51. (a) Empirical formula = CH_2N_2

(b) Mass percent of N = 66.64%

$$\frac{\left[6 \text{ mol N} \left(\dfrac{14.0067 \text{ g}}{1 \text{ mol N}}\right)\right]}{126.12 \text{ g/mol } C_3H_6N_6} \times 100\% = 66.64\%$$

(c) Theoretical yield of melamine

$$1.000 \times 10^3 \text{ g urea} \left(\frac{1 \text{ mol}}{60.06 \text{ g urea}}\right) = 16.65 \text{ mol urea}$$

$$16.65 \text{ mol urea} \left(\frac{1 \text{ mol HNCO}}{1 \text{ mol urea}}\right)\left(\frac{1 \text{ mol } C_3H_6N_6}{6 \text{ mol HNCO}}\right)$$

$$= 2.775 \text{ mol } C_3H_6N_6$$

$$2.775 \text{ mol } C_3H_6N_6 \left(\frac{126.12 \text{ g}}{1 \text{ mol } C_3H_6N_6}\right) = 345.0 \text{ g } C_3H_6N_6$$

(d) $\Delta_r H° = \Delta_f H°[\text{HCNO(g)}] + \Delta_f H°[\text{NH}_3\text{(g)}]$
$\qquad\qquad\qquad - \Delta_f H°[(\text{NH}_2)_2\text{CO(s)}]$
$= (1 \text{ mol HNCO(g)}/1\text{mol-rxn})(-101.67 \text{ kJ/mol})$
$+ (1 \text{ mol NH}_3\text{(g)}/1 \text{ mol-rxn})(-45.90 \text{ kJ/mol})$
$- (1 \text{ mol } (\text{NH}_2)_2\text{CO(s)}/1 \text{ mol-rxn})(-333.1 \text{ kJ/mol})$
$\qquad = 185.5 \text{ kJ/mol-rxn}$

The reaction is endothermic.

(e) The C and N atoms in the melamine ring are sp^2 hybridized.

(f) The N—C—N and C—N—C bond angles in the ring are both 120°.

(g) The molecule is not polar.

11 | Gases and Their Properties

©Davis Barber/PhotoEdit

The Atmosphere and Altitude Sickness

Some of you may have dreamed of climbing to the summits of the world's tallest mountains, or you may be an avid skier and visit high-mountain ski areas. In either case, "acute mountain sickness" (AMS) is a possibility. AMS is common at higher altitudes and is characterized by a headache, nausea, insomnia, dizziness, lassitude, and fatigue. It can be prevented by a slow ascent, and its symptoms can be relieved by a mild pain reliever.

AMS and more serious forms of high altitude sickness are generally due to hypoxia or oxygen deprivation. The oxygen concentration in Earth's atmosphere is 21%. As you go higher into the atmosphere, the concentration remains 21%, but the atmospheric pressure drops. When you reach 3000 m (the altitude of some ski resorts), the barometric pressure is about 70% of that at sea level. At 5000 m, barometric pressure is only 50% of sea level, and on the summit of Mt. Everest, it is only 29% of the sea level pressure. At sea level, your blood is nearly saturated with oxygen, but as the partial pressure of oxygen drops, the percent saturation drops as well. At $P(O_2)$ of 50 mm Hg, hemoglobin in the red blood cells is about 80% saturated. Other saturation levels are given in the table (for a pH of 7.4).

$P(O_2)$ (mm Hg)	Approximate Percent Saturation
90	95%
80	92%
70	90%
60	85%
50	80%
40	72%

For more on the atmosphere, see page 534.

Questions:

1. Assume a sea level pressure of 1 atm (760 mm Hg). What are the O_2 partial pressures at a 3000-m ski resort and on Mt. Everest?
2. What are the approximate blood saturation levels under these conditions?

Answers to these questions are in Appendix Q.

M ountain climbers, hot air balloons, SCUBA diving, and automobile air bags (Figure 11.1) depend on the properties of gases. Aside from understanding how these work, there are at least three reasons for studying gases. First, some common elements and compounds (such as oxygen, nitrogen, and methane) exist in the gaseous state under normal conditions of pressure and temperature. Furthermore, many liquids such as water can be vaporized, and the physical properties of these vapors are important. Second, our gaseous atmosphere provides one means of transferring energy and material throughout the globe, and it is the source of life-sustaining chemicals.

The third reason for studying gases is also compelling. Of the three states of matter, gases are reasonably simple when viewed at the molecular level, and, as a result, gas behavior is well understood. It is possible to describe the properties of gases *qualitatively* in terms of the behavior of the molecules that make up the gas. Even more impressive, it is possible to describe the properties of gases *quantitatively* using simple mathematical models. One objective of scientists is to develop precise mathematical and conceptual models of natural phenomena, and a study of gas behavior will introduce you to this approach. To describe gases, chemists have learned that only four quantities are needed: the pressure (P), volume (V), and temperature (T, kelvins) of the gas, and amount (n, mol).

Chemistry⋅Now™

Throughout the text this icon introduces an opportunity for self-study or to explore interactive tutorials by signing in at **www.cengage.com/login**.

SAAB Car, USA, Inc.

FIGURE 11.1. Automobile air bags. Most automobiles are now equipped with airbags to protect the driver and passengers in the event of a head-on or side crash. Such bags are inflated with nitrogen gas, which is generated by the explosive decomposition of sodium azide:

$$2 \, NaN_3(s) \longrightarrow 2 \, Na(s) + 3 \, N_2(g)$$

The airbag is fully inflated in about 0.050 s. This is important because the typical automobile collision lasts about 0.125 s.

See ChemistryNow Screen 11.1 for questions about automobile air bags.

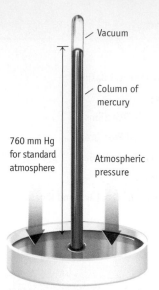

Vacuum

Column of
mercury

760 mm Hg
for standard
atmosphere

Atmospheric
pressure

FIGURE 11.2 A barometer. The pressure of the atmosphere on the surface of the mercury in the dish is balanced by the downward pressure exerted by the column of mercury. The barometer was invented in 1643 by Evangelista Torricelli (1608–1647). A unit of pressure called the torr in his honor is equivalent to 1 mm Hg.

■ **Hectopascals** Meteorologists have long measured atmospheric pressure in millibars. However, after the SI system of units became more widespread, they began to use the unit "hectopascal," which is equivalent to the millibar.
1 hectopascal (hPa) = 100 Pa = 1 mbar
1 kilopascal (kPa) = 1000 Pa = 10 hPa

11.1 Gas Pressure

Pressure is the force exerted on an object divided by the area over which it is exerted, and a barometer depends on this to measure atmospheric pressure. A barometer can be made by filling a tube with a liquid, often mercury, and inverting the tube in a dish containing the same liquid (Figure 11.2). If the air has been removed completely from the vertical tube, the liquid in the tube assumes a level such that the pressure exerted by the mass of the column of liquid in the tube is balanced by the pressure of the atmosphere pressing down on the surface of the liquid in the dish.

Pressure is often reported in units of **millimeters of mercury (mm Hg),** the height (in mm) of the mercury column in a mercury barometer above the surface of the mercury in the dish. At sea level, this height is about 760 mm. Pressures are also reported as **standard atmospheres (atm),** a unit defined as follows:

$$1 \text{ standard atmosphere (1 atm)} = 760 \text{ mm Hg (exactly)}$$

The SI unit of pressure is the **pascal (Pa).**

$$1 \text{ pascal (Pa)} = 1 \text{ newton/meter}^2$$

(The newton is the SI unit of force.) Because the pascal is a very small unit compared with ordinary pressures, the unit kilopascal (kPa) is more often used. Another unit used for gas pressures is the **bar,** where 1 bar = 100,000 Pa. To summarize, the units used in science for pressure are

$$1 \text{ atm} = 760 \text{ mm Hg (exactly)} = 101.325 \text{ kilopascals (kPa)} = 1.01325 \text{ bar}$$

or

$$1 \text{ bar} = 1 \times 10^5 \text{ Pa (exactly)} = 1 \times 10^2 \text{ kPa} = 0.9872 \text{ atm}$$

■ **EXAMPLE 11.1 Pressure Unit Conversions**

Problem Convert a pressure of 635 mm Hg into its corresponding value in units of atmospheres (atm), bars, and kilopascals (kPa).

Strategy Use the relationships between millimeters of Hg, atmospheres, bars, and pascals described earlier in the text.

Solution The relationship between millimeters of mercury and atmospheres is 1 atm = 760 mm Hg.

$$635 \text{ mm Hg} \times \frac{1 \text{ atm}}{760 \text{ mm Hg}} = \boxed{0.836 \text{ atm}}$$

The relationship between atmospheres and bars is 1 atm = 1.013 bar.

$$0.836 \text{ atm} \times \frac{1.013 \text{ bar}}{1 \text{ atm}} = \boxed{0.846 \text{ bar}}$$

The relationship between millimeters of mercury and kilopascals is 101.325 kPa = 760 mm Hg.

$$635 \text{ mm Hg} \times \frac{101.3 \text{ kPa}}{760 \text{ mm Hg}} = \boxed{84.6 \text{ kPa}}$$

Pressure is the force exerted on an object divided by the area over which the force is exerted:

Pressure = force/area

This book, for example, weighs more than 4 lb and has an area of 82 in², so it exerts a pressure of about 0.05 lb/in² when it lies flat on a surface. (In metric units, the pressure is about 3 g/cm².)

Now consider the pressure that the column of mercury exerts on the mercury in the dish in the barometer shown in Figure 11.2. This pressure exactly balances the pressure of the atmosphere. Thus, the pressure of the atmosphere (or of any other gas) can be measured by relating it to the height of the column of mercury (or any other liquid) the gas can support.

Mercury is the liquid of choice for barometers because of its high density. A barometer filled with water would be over 10 m in height. [The water column is about 13.6 times as high as a column of mercury because mercury's density (13.53 g/cm³) is 13.6 times that of water (density = 0.997 g/cm³, at 25 °C).]

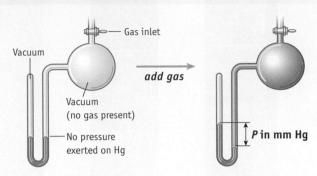

In the laboratory, we often use a U-tube manometer, which is a mercury-filled, U-shaped glass tube. The closed side of the tube has been evacuated so that no gas remains to exert pressure on the mercury on that side. The other side is open to the gas whose pressure we want to measure. When the gas presses on the mercury in the open side, the gas pressure is read directly (in mm Hg) as the difference in mercury levels on the closed and open sides.

You may have used a tire gauge to check the pressure in your car or bike tires. In the U.S., such gauges usually indicate the pressure in pounds per square inch (psi) where 1 atm = 14.7 psi. Some newer gauges give the pressure in kilopascals as well. Be sure to recognize that the reading on the scale refers to the pressure *in excess of atmospheric pressure*. (A flat tire is not a vacuum; it contains air at atmospheric pressure.) For example, if the gauge reads 35 psi (2.4 atm), the pressure in the tire is actually about 50 psi or 3.4 atm.

EXERCISE 11.1 Pressure Unit Conversions

Rank the following pressures in decreasing order of magnitude (from largest to smallest): 75 kPa, 250 mm Hg, 0.83 bar, and 0.63 atm.

11.2 Gas Laws: The Experimental Basis

Boyle's Law: The Compressibility of Gases

When you pump up the tires of your bicycle, the pump squeezes the air into a smaller volume (Figure 11.3). This property of a gas is called its **compressibility.** While studying the compressibility of gases, Robert Boyle (1627–1691) observed that the volume of a fixed amount of gas at a given temperature is inversely proportional to the pressure exerted by the gas. All gases behave in this manner, and we now refer to this relationship as **Boyle's law.**

Boyle's law can be demonstrated in many ways. In Figure 11.4, a hypodermic syringe is filled with air and sealed. When pressure is applied to the movable plunger of the syringe, the air inside is compressed. As the pressure (P) increases on the syringe, the gas volume in the syringe (V) decreases. When $1/V$ of the gas in the syringe is plotted as a function of P, a straight line results. This type of plot demonstrates that the pressure and volume of the gas are inversely proportional; that is, they change in opposite directions.

FIGURE 11.3 A bicycle pump— Boyle's law in action. This works by compressing air into a smaller volume. You experience Boyle's law because you can feel the increasing pressure of the gas as you press down on the plunger.

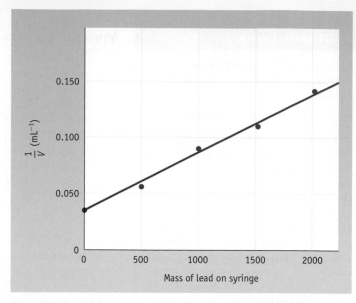

Active Figure 11.4 An experiment to demonstrate Boyle's law. A syringe filled with air was sealed. Pressure was applied by adding lead shot to the beaker on top of the syringe. As the mass of lead increased, the pressure on the air in the sealed syringe increased, and the gas was compressed. A plot of (1/volume of air in the syringe) versus *P* (as measured by the mass of lead) is a straight line.

Chemistry.Now™ Sign in at www.cengage.com/login and go to the Chapter Contents menu to explore an interactive version of this figure accompanied by an exercise.

Mathematically, we can write Boyle's law as:

$$P \propto \frac{1}{V} \quad \text{when } n \text{ and } T \text{ are constant}$$

where the symbol $\propto$ means "proportional to."

When two quantities are proportional to each other, they can be equated if a *proportionality constant*, here called C_B, is introduced.

$$P = C_B \times \frac{1}{V} \quad \text{or} \quad PV = C_B \quad \text{when } n \text{ and } T \text{ are constant}$$

This form of Boyle's law expresses the fact that *the product of the pressure and volume of a gas sample is a constant at a given temperature,* where the constant C_B is determined by the amount of gas (in moles) and its temperature (in kelvins). It follows from this that, if the pressure–volume product is known for a gas sample under one set of conditions (P_1 and V_1), then it is known for another set of conditions (P_2 and V_2). Under either set of conditions, the *PV* product is equal to C_B, so

$$P_1V_1 = P_2V_2 \quad \text{at constant } n \text{ and } T \tag{11.1}$$

This form of Boyle's law is useful when we want to know, for example, what happens to the volume of a given amount of gas when the pressure changes at a constant temperature.

■ EXAMPLE 11.2 Boyle's Law

Problem A sample of gaseous nitrogen in a 65.0-L automobile air bag has a pressure of 745 mm Hg. If this sample is transferred to a 25.0-L bag at the same temperature, what is the pressure of the gas in the 25.0-L bag?

Strategy Here, we use Boyle's law, Equation 11.1. The original pressure and volume (P_1 and V_1) and the new volume (V_2) are known.

Solution It is often useful to make a table of the information provided.

Initial Conditions	Final Conditions
$P_1 = 745$ mm Hg	$P_2 = ?$
$V_1 = 65.0$ L	$V_2 = 25.0$ L

You know that $P_1V_1 = P_2V_2$. Therefore,

$$P_2 = \frac{P_1V_1}{V_2} = \frac{(745 \text{ mm Hg})(65.0 \text{ L})}{25.0 \text{ L}} = \boxed{1940 \text{ mm Hg}}$$

Comment According to Boyle's law, P and V change in opposite directions. Because the volume has decreased, the new pressure (P_2) must be greater than the original pressure (P_1). A quick way to solve these problems takes advantage of this: if the volume decreases, the pressure must increase, and the original pressure must be multiplied by a volume fraction greater than 1.

$$P_2 = P_1 \left(\frac{65.0 \text{ L}}{25.0 \text{ L}} \right)$$

EXERCISE 11.2 Boyle's Law

A sample of CO_2 with a pressure of 55 mm Hg in a volume of 125 mL is compressed so that the new pressure of the gas is 78 mm Hg. What is the new volume of the gas? (Assume the temperature is constant.)

The Effect of Temperature on Gas Volume: Charles's Law

In 1787, the French scientist Jacques Charles (1746–1823) discovered that the volume of a fixed quantity of gas at constant pressure decreases with decreasing temperature (Figure 11.5).

Figure 11.6 illustrates how the volumes of two different gas samples change with temperature (at a constant pressure). When the plots of volume versus temperature

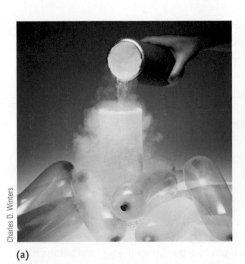
(a)

(b)

(c)

Charles D. Winters

FIGURE 11.5 A dramatic illustration of Charles's law. (a) Air-filled balloons are placed in liquid nitrogen (77 K). The volume of the gas in the balloons is dramatically reduced at this temperature. (b) After all of the balloons have been placed in the liquid nitrogen, (c) they are removed; as they warm to room temperature, they reinflate to their original volume.

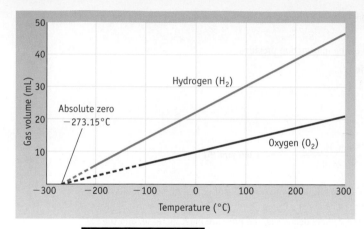

T (°C)	T (K)	Vol. H$_2$ (mL)	Vol. O$_2$ (mL)
300	573	47.0	21.1
200	473	38.8	17.5
100	373	30.6	13.8
0	273	22.4	10.1
−100	173	14.2	6.39
−200	73	6.00	—

Active Figure 11.6 | **Charles's law.** The solid lines represent the volumes of the samples of hydrogen and oxygen at different temperatures. The volumes decrease as the temperature is lowered (at constant pressure). These lines, if extended, intersect the temperature axis at approximately −273 °C.

Chemistry ⬡ Now™ Sign in at www.cengage.com/login and go to the Chapter Contents menu to explore an interactive version of this figure accompanied by an exercise.

■ **Boyle's and Charles's Laws** Neither Boyle's law nor Charles's law depends on the identity of the gas being studied. These laws describe the behavior of any gaseous substance, regardless of its identity.

are extended to lower temperatures, they all reach zero volume at the same temperature, −273.15 °C. (Of course, gases will not actually reach zero volume; they liquefy above that temperature.) This temperature is significant, however. William Thomson (1824–1907), also known as Lord Kelvin, proposed a temperature scale—now known as the Kelvin scale—for which the zero point is −273.15 °C (◀ page 27).

When Kelvin temperatures are used with volume measurements, the volume–temperature relationship is

$$V = C_c \times T$$

where C_c is a proportionality constant (which depends on the amount of gas and its pressure). This is **Charles's law,** which states that if a given quantity of gas is held at a constant pressure, its volume is directly proportional to the Kelvin temperature.

Writing Charles's law another way, we have $V/T = C_c$; that is, the volume of a gas divided by the temperature of the gas (in kelvins) is constant for a given sample of gas at a specified pressure. Therefore, if we know the volume and temperature of a given quantity of gas (V_1 and T_1), we can find the volume, V_2, at some other temperature, T_2, using the equation

$$\frac{V_1}{T_1} = \frac{V_2}{T_2} \quad \text{at constant } n \text{ and } P \tag{11.2}$$

Calculations using Charles's law are illustrated by the following example and exercise. Be sure to notice that the temperature T *must always be expressed in kelvins.*

■ **EXAMPLE 11.3 Charles's Law**

Problem A sample of CO$_2$ in a gas-tight syringe (as in Figure 11.4) has a volume of 25.0 mL at room temperature (20.0 °C). What is the final volume of the gas if you hold the syringe in your hand to raise its temperature to 37 °C?

Strategy Because a given quantity of gas is heated (at a constant pressure), Charles's law applies. Because we know the original V and T, and want to calculate a new volume at a new, but known, temperature, use Equation 11.2.

Solution Organize the information in a table. Remember the temperature must be converted to kelvins.

Initial Conditions

$V_1 = 25.0$ mL

$T_1 = 20.0 + 273.2 = 293.2$ K

Final Conditions

$V_2 = ?$

$T_2 = 37 + 273 = 310.$ K

Substitute the known quantities into Equation 11.2, and solve for V_2:

$$V_2 = T_2\left(\frac{V_1}{T_1}\right) = 310. \text{ K}\left(\frac{25.0 \text{ mL}}{293.2 \text{ K}}\right) = \boxed{26.5 \text{ mL}}$$

Comment As expected, the volume of the gas increased with a temperature increase. The new volume (V_2) must equal the original volume (V_1) multiplied by a temperature fraction that is greater than 1 to reflect the effect of the temperature increase. That is,

$$V_2 = V_1\left(\frac{310. \text{ K}}{293 \text{ K}}\right)$$

EXERCISE 11.3 Charles's Law

A balloon is inflated with helium to a volume of 45 L at room temperature (25 °C). If the balloon is cooled to −10 °C, what is the new volume of the balloon? Assume that the pressure does not change.

Combining Boyle's and Charles's Laws: The General Gas Law

The volume of a given amount of gas is inversely proportional to its pressure at constant temperature (Boyle's law) and directly proportional to the Kelvin temperature at constant pressure (Charles's law). But what if we need to know what happens to the gas when two of the three parameters (P, V, and T) change? For example, what would happen to the pressure of a sample of nitrogen in an automobile air bag if the same amount of gas were placed in a smaller bag and heated to a higher temperature? You can deal with this situation by combining the two equations that express Boyle's and Charles's laws.

$$\frac{P_1V_1}{T_1} = \frac{P_2V_2}{T_2} \quad \text{for a given amount of gas, } n \qquad \textbf{(11.3)}$$

This equation is sometimes called the **general gas law** or **combined gas law**. It applies specifically to situations in which the *amount of gas does not change*.

NASA/Science Source/Photo Researchers, Inc.

A weather balloon is filled with helium. As it ascends into the troposphere, does the volume increase or decrease?

■ **EXAMPLE 11.4 General Gas Law**

Problem Helium-filled balloons are used to carry scientific instruments high into the atmosphere. Suppose a balloon is launched when the temperature is 22.5 °C and the barometric pressure is 754 mm Hg. If the balloon's volume is 4.19×10^3 L (and no helium escapes from the balloon), what will the volume be at a height of 20 miles, where the pressure is 76.0 mm Hg and the temperature is −33.0 °C?

Strategy Here we know the initial volume, temperature, and pressure of the gas. We want to know the volume of the same amount of gas at a new pressure and temperature. It is most convenient to use Equation 11.3, the general gas law.

Solution Begin by setting out the information given in a table.

Initial Conditions

$V_1 = 4.19 \times 10^3$ L

$P_1 = 754$ mm Hg

$T_1 = 22.5$ °C (295.7 K)

Final Conditions

$V_2 = ?$ L

$P_2 = 76.0$ mm Hg

$T_2 = -33.0$ °C (240.2 K)

We can rearrange the general gas law to calculate the new volume V_2:

$$V_2 = \left(\frac{T_2}{P_2}\right) \times \left(\frac{P_1 V_1}{T_1}\right) = V_1 \times \frac{P_1}{P_2} \times \frac{T_2}{T_1}$$

$$= 4.19 \times 10^3 \text{ L} \left(\frac{754 \text{ mm Hg}}{76.0 \text{ mm Hg}}\right)\left(\frac{240.2 \text{ K}}{295.7 \text{ K}}\right)$$

$$= 3.38 \times 10^4 \text{ L}$$

Comment The pressure decreased by almost a factor of 10, which should lead to about a ten-fold volume increase. This increase is partly offset by a drop in temperature that leads to a volume decrease. On balance, the volume increases because the pressure has dropped so substantially.

Notice that the solution was to multiply the original volume (V_1) by a pressure factor larger than 1 (because the volume increases with a lower pressure) and a temperature factor smaller than 1 (because volume decreases with a decrease in temperature).

EXERCISE 11.4 The General Gas Law

You have a 22.-L cylinder of helium at a pressure of 150 atm and at 31 °C. How many balloons can you fill, each with a volume of 5.0 L, on a day when the atmospheric pressure is 755 mm Hg and the temperature is 22 °C?

The general gas law leads to other, useful predictions of gas behavior. For example, if a given amount of gas is held in a closed container, the pressure of the gas will increase with increasing temperature.

$$\frac{P_1}{T_1} = \frac{P_2}{T_2} \text{ when } V_1 = V_2 \text{ and so } P_2 = P_1 \times \frac{T_2}{T_1}$$

■ **Gay-Lussac's Law** Gay-Lussac's law states that, at constant volume, the pressure of a given mass of gas is proportional to the absolute temperature. In 1779 Joseph Lambert proposed a definition of absolute zero of temperature based on this relationship.

That is, when T_2 is greater than T_1, P_2 will be greater than P_1. In fact, this is the reason tire manufacturers recommend checking tire pressures when the tires are cold. After driving for some distance, friction warms a tire and increases the internal pressure. Filling a warm tire to the recommended pressure may lead to an underinflated tire.

Avogadro's Hypothesis

Front and side air bags are now common in automobiles. In the event of an accident, a bag is rapidly inflated with nitrogen gas generated by a chemical reaction. The air bag unit has a sensor that is sensitive to sudden deceleration of the vehicle and will send an electrical signal that will trigger the reaction (Figures 11.1 and 11.7). In many types of air bags, the explosion of sodium azide generates nitrogen gas.

$$2 \text{ NaN}_3(s) \rightarrow 2 \text{ Na}(s) + 3 \text{ N}_2(g)$$

Driver-side air bags inflate to a volume of about 35–70 L, and passenger air bags inflate to about 60–160 L. The final volume of the bag will depend on the amount of nitrogen gas generated.

The relationship between volume and amount of gas was first noted by Amedeo Avogadro. In 1811, he used work on gases by the chemist (and early experimenter with hot air balloons) Joseph Gay-Lussac (1778–1850) to propose that *equal volumes of gases under the same conditions of temperature and pressure have equal numbers of particles* (either molecules or atoms, depending on the composition of the gas.) This idea came to be known as **Avogadro's hypothesis.** Stated another way, the volume

When a car decelerates in a collision, an electrical contact is made in the sensor unit. The propellant (green solid) detonates, releasing nitrogen gas, and the folded nylon bag explodes out of the plastic housing.

Driver-side air bags inflate with 35–70 L of N_2 gas, whereas passenger air bags hold about 60–160 L.

The bag deflates within 0.2 s, the gas escaping through holes in the bottom of the bag.

FIGURE 11.7 Automobile air bags. See ChemistryNow Screen 11.1 for more on air bags.

of a gas at a given temperature and pressure is directly proportional to the amount of gas in moles:

$$V \propto n \text{ at constant } T \text{ and } P$$

Chemistry.ⷬ.Now™

Sign in at **www.cengage.com/login** and go to Chapter 11 Contents to see Screen 11.3 for exercises on **the three gas laws.**

■ **EXAMPLE 11.5 Avogadro's Hypothesis**

Problem Ammonia can be made directly from the elements:

$$N_2(g) + 3 H_2(g) \longrightarrow 2 NH_3(g)$$

If you begin with 15.0 L of $H_2(g)$, what volume of $N_2(g)$ is required for complete reaction (both gases being at the same T and P)? What is the theoretical yield of NH_3, in liters, under the same conditions?

Strategy From Avogadro's law, we know that gas volume is proportional to the amount of gas. Therefore, we can substitute gas volumes for moles in this stoichiometry problem.

Solution Calculate the volumes of N_2 required and NH_3 produced (in liters) by multiplying the volume of H_2 available by a stoichiometric factor (also in units of liters) obtained from the chemical equation:

$$V \text{ (}N_2 \text{ required)} = (15.0 \text{ L } H_2 \text{ available}) \left(\frac{1 \text{ L } N_2 \text{ required}}{3 \text{ L } H_2 \text{ available}} \right) = 5.00 \text{ L } N_2 \text{ required}$$

$$V \text{ (}NH_3 \text{ produced)} = (15.0 \text{ L } H_2 \text{ available}) \left(\frac{2 \text{ L } NH_3 \text{ produced}}{3 \text{ L } H_2 \text{ available}} \right) = 10.0 \text{ L } NH_3 \text{ produced}$$

EXERCISE 11.5 Avogadro's Hypothesis

Methane burns in oxygen to give CO_2 and H_2O, according to the balanced equation

$$CH_4(g) + 2 O_2(g) \longrightarrow CO_2(g) + 2 H_2O(g)$$

If 22.4 L of gaseous CH_4 is burned, what volume of O_2 is required for complete combustion? What volumes of CO_2 and H_2O are produced? Assume all gases have the same temperature and pressure.

11.3 The Ideal Gas Law

Four interrelated quantities can be used to describe a gas: pressure, volume, temperature, and amount (moles). We know from experiments that three gas laws can be used to describe the relationship of these properties (Section 11.2).

Boyle's Law	Charles's Law	Avogadro's Hypothesis
$V \propto (1/P)$	$V \propto T$	$V \propto n$
(constant T, n)	(constant P, n)	(constant T, P)

If all three laws are combined, the result is

$$V \propto \frac{nT}{P}$$

■ **Properties of an Ideal Gas** For ideal gases, it is assumed that there are no forces of attraction between molecules and that the molecules themselves occupy no volume.

This can be made into a mathematical equation by introducing a proportionality constant, now labeled **R**. This constant, called the **gas constant,** is a *universal constant,* a number you can use to interrelate the properties of any gas:

$$V = R\left(\frac{nT}{P}\right)$$

or   (11.4)

$$PV = nRT$$

The equation $PV = nRT$ is called the **ideal gas law.** It describes the behavior of a so-called ideal gas. As you will learn in Section 11.9, however, there is no such thing as an "ideal" gas. Nonetheless, real gases at pressures around one atmosphere or less and temperatures around room temperature usually behave close enough to the ideal that $PV = nRT$ adequately describes their behavior.

To use the equation $PV = nRT$, we need a value for R. This is readily determined experimentally. By carefully measuring P, V, n, and T for a sample of gas, we can calculate the value of R from these values using the ideal gas law equation. For example, under conditions of **standard temperature and pressure (STP)** (a gas temperature of 0 °C or 273.15 K and a pressure of 1 atm), 1 mol of gas occupies 22.414 L, a quantity called the **standard molar volume.** Substituting these values into the ideal gas law gives a value for R:

$$R = \frac{PV}{nT} = \frac{(1.0000 \text{ atm})(22.414 \text{ L})}{(1.0000 \text{ mol})(273.15)} = 0.082057 \frac{\text{L} \cdot \text{atm}}{\text{K} \cdot \text{mol}}$$

■ **STP—What Is It?** A gas is at STP, or standard temperature and pressure, when its temperature is 0 °C or 273.15 K and its pressure is 1 atm. Under these conditions, exactly 1 mol of a gas occupies 22.414 L.

With a value for R, we can now use the ideal gas law in calculations.

Chemistry ⚛ Now™

Sign in at **www.cengage.com/login** and go to Chapter 11 Contents to see Screen 11.4 for a simulation of the **ideal gas law.**

■ **EXAMPLE 11.6 Ideal Gas Law**

Problem The nitrogen gas in an automobile air bag, with a volume of 65 L, exerts a pressure of 829 mm Hg at 25 °C. What amount of N_2 gas (in moles) is in the air bag?

Strategy You are given P, V, and T and want to calculate the amount of gas (n). Use the ideal gas law, Equation 11.4.

Solution First, list the information provided.

$P = 829$ mm Hg $V = 65$ L $T = 25\ °C$ $n = ?$

To use the ideal gas law with R having units of (L · atm/K · mol), the pressure must be expressed in atmospheres and the temperature in kelvins. Therefore,

$$P = 829\ \cancel{\text{mm Hg}}\left(\frac{1\ \text{atm}}{760\ \cancel{\text{mm Hg}}}\right) = 1.09\ \text{atm}$$

$T = 25 + 273 = 298$ K

Now substitute the values of P, V, T, and R into the ideal gas law, and solve for the amount of gas, n:

$$n = \frac{PV}{RT} = \frac{(1.09\ \text{atm})(65\ \text{L})}{(0.082057\ \text{L} \cdot \text{atm/K} \cdot \text{mol})(298\ \text{K})} = \boxed{2.9\ \text{mol}}$$

Notice that units of atmospheres, liters, and kelvins cancel to leave the answer in units of moles.

EXERCISE 11.6 Ideal Gas Law

The balloon used by Jacques Charles in his historic balloon flight in 1783 (see page 533) was filled with about 1300 mol of H_2. If the temperature of the gas was 23 °C and its pressure was 750 mm Hg, what was the volume of the balloon?

The Density of Gases

The density of a gas at a given temperature and pressure (Figure 11.8) is a useful quantity. Because the amount (n, mol) of any compound is given by its mass (m) divided by its molar mass (M), we can substitute m/M for n in the ideal gas equation.

$$PV = \left(\frac{m}{M}\right)RT$$

Density (d) is defined as mass divided by volume (m/V). We can rearrange the form of the gas law above to give the following equation, which has the term (m/V) on the left. This is the density of the gas.

$$d = \frac{m}{V} = \frac{PM}{RT} \tag{11.5}$$

(a)

(b)

FIGURE 11.8 Gas density. (a) The balloons are filled with nearly equal amounts of gas at the same temperature and pressure. One yellow balloon contains helium, a low-density gas ($d = 0.179$ g/L at STP). The other balloons contain air, a higher density gas ($d = 1.2$ g/L at STP). (b) A hot-air balloon rises because the heated air has a lower density than the surrounding air.

FIGURE 11.9 Gas density. Because carbon dioxide from fire extinguishers is denser than air, it settles on top of a fire and smothers it. (When CO_2 gas is released from the tank, it expands and cools significantly. The white cloud is condensed moisture from the air.)

Gas density is directly proportional to the pressure and molar mass and inversely proportional to the temperature. Equation 11.5 is useful because gas density can be calculated from the molar mass, or the molar mass can be found from a measurement of gas density at a given pressure and temperature.

■ EXAMPLE 11.7 Density and Molar Mass

Problem Calculate the density of CO_2 at STP. Is CO_2 more or less dense than air?

Strategy Use Equation 11.5, the equation relating gas density and molar mass. Here, we know the molar mass (44.0 g/mol), the pressure ($P = 1.00$ atm), the temperature ($T = 273.15$ K), and the gas constant (R). Only the density (d) is unknown.

Solution The known values are substituted into Equation 11.5, which is then solved for molar mass (M):

$$d = \frac{PM}{RT} = \frac{(1.00 \text{ atm})(44.0 \text{ g/mol})}{(0.082057 \text{ L} \cdot \text{atm/K} \cdot \text{mol})(273 \text{ K})} = \boxed{1.96 \text{ g/L}}$$

The density of CO_2 is considerably greater than that of dry air at STP (1.2 g/L).

EXERCISE 11.7 Gas Density and Molar Mass

The density of an unknown gas is 5.02 g/L at 15.0 °C and 745 mm Hg. Calculate its molar mass.

Gas density has practical implications. From the equation $d = PM/RT$, we recognize that the density of a gas is directly proportional to its molar mass. Dry air, which has an average molar mass of about 29 g/mol, has a density of about 1.2 g/L at 1 atm and 25 °C. Gases or vapors with molar masses greater than 29 g/mol have densities larger than 1.2 g/L under these same conditions (1 atm and 25 °C). Gases such as CO_2, SO_2, and gasoline vapor settle along the ground if released into the atmosphere (Figure 11.9). Conversely, gases such as H_2, He, CO, CH_4 (methane), and NH_3 rise if released into the atmosphere.

The significance of gas density has been revealed in several tragic events. One occurred in the African country of Cameroon in 1984 when Lake Nyos expelled a huge bubble of CO_2 into the atmosphere. Because CO_2 is denser than air, the CO_2 cloud hugged the ground, killing 1700 people nearby (page 630).

Calculating the Molar Mass of a Gas from *P*, *V*, and *T* Data

When a new compound is isolated in the laboratory, one of the first things to be done is to determine its molar mass. If the compound is in the gas phase, a classical method of determining the molar mass is to measure the pressure and volume exerted by a given mass of the gas at a given temperature.

Chemistry₊⊙₊Now™

Sign in at **www.cengage.com/login** and go to Chapter 11 Contents to see:
• Screen 11.5 for an exercise on **gas density**
• Screen 11.6 for a tutorial on **using gas laws determining molar mass**

■ EXAMPLE 11.8 Calculating the Molar Mass of a Gas from *P, V,* and *T* Data

Problem You are trying to determine, by experiment, the formula of a gaseous compound to replace chlorofluorocarbons in air conditioners. You have determined the empirical formula is CHF_2, but now you want to know the molecular formula. To do this, you need the molar mass of the compound. You therefore do another experiment and find that a 0.100-g sample of the compound exerts a pressure of 70.5 mm Hg in a 256-mL container at 22.3 °C. What is the molar mass of the compound? What is its molecular formula?

526 Chapter 11 | Gases and Their Properties

Strategy Here, you know the mass of a gas in a given volume (V), so you can calculate its density, d. Then, knowing the gas pressure and temperature, you can use Equation 11.5 to calculate the molar mass.

Solution Begin by organizing the data:

$$m = \text{mass of gas} = 0.100\ g$$

$$P = 70.5\ \text{mm Hg, or } 0.0928\ \text{atm}$$

$$V = 256\ \text{mL, or } 0.256\ L$$

$$T = 22.3\ °C,\ \text{or } 295.5\ K$$

The density of the gas is the mass of the gas divided by the volume:

$$d = \frac{0.100\ g}{0.256\ L} = 0.391\ g/L$$

Use this value of density along with the values of pressure and temperature in Equation 11.5 ($d = PM/RT$), and solve for the molar mass (M).

$$M = \frac{dRT}{P} = \frac{(0.391\ g/L)(0.082057\ L \cdot atm/K \cdot mol)(295.5\ K)}{0.0928\ atm} = 102\ g/mol$$

With this result, you can compare the experimentally determined molar mass with the mass of a mole of gas having the empirical formula CHF_2.

$$\frac{\text{Experimental molar mass}}{\text{Mass of 1 mol } CHF_2} = \frac{102\ g/mol}{51.0\ g/\text{formula unit}} = 2\ \text{formula units of } CHF_2\ \text{per mol}$$

Therefore, the formula of the compound is $C_2H_2F_4$.

Comment Alternatively, you can use the ideal gas law. Here, you know the P and T of a gas in a given volume (V), so you can calculate the amount of gas (n).

$$n = \frac{PV}{RT} = \frac{(0.0928\ atm)(0.256\ L)}{(0.082057\ L \cdot atm/K \cdot mol)(295.5\ K)} = 9.80 \times 10^{-4}\ mol$$

You now know that 0.100 g of gas is equivalent to 9.80×10^{-4} mol. Therefore,

$$\text{Molar mass} = \frac{0.100\ g}{9.80 \times 10^{-4}\ mol} = 102\ g/mol$$

EXERCISE 11.8 Molar Mass from P, V, and T Data

A 0.105-g sample of a gaseous compound has a pressure of 561 mm Hg in a volume of 125 mL at 23.0 °C. What is its molar mass?

11.4 Gas Laws and Chemical Reactions

Many industrially important reactions involve gases. Two examples are the combination of nitrogen and hydrogen to produce ammonia,

$$N_2(g) + 3\ H_2(g) \longrightarrow 2\ NH_3(g)$$

and the electrolysis of aqueous NaCl to produce hydrogen and chlorine,

$$2\ NaCl(aq) + 2\ H_2O\ (\ell) \longrightarrow 2\ NaOH(aq) + H_2(g) + Cl_2(g)$$

If we want to understand the quantitative aspects of such reactions, we need to carry out stoichiometry calculations. The scheme in Figure 11.10 connects these calculations for gas reactions with the stoichiometry calculations in Chapter 4.

Chemistry｡੦｡Now™

Sign in at **www.cengage.com/login** and go to Chapter 11 Contents to see Screen 11.7 for a tutorial on **gas laws and chemical reactions: stoichiometry.**

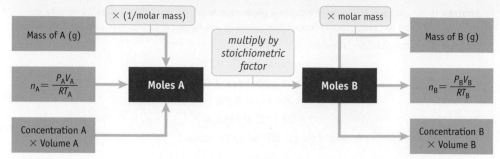

FIGURE 11.10 A scheme for stoichiometry calculations. Here, A and B may be either reactants or products. The amount of A (mol) can be calculated from its mass in grams and its molar mass, from the concentration and volume of a solution, or from P, V, and T data by using the ideal gas law. Once the amount of B is determined, this value can be converted to a mass or solution concentration or volume, or to a volume of gas at a given pressure and temperature.

■ EXAMPLE 11.9 Gas Laws and Stoichiometry

Problem You are asked to design an air bag for a car. You know that the bag should be filled with gas with a pressure higher than atmospheric pressure, say 829 mm Hg, at a temperature of 22.0 °C. The bag has a volume of 45.5 L. What quantity of sodium azide, NaN_3, should be used to generate the required quantity of gas? The gas-producing reaction is

$$2\ NaN_3(s) \longrightarrow 2\ Na(s) + 3\ N_2(g)$$

Strategy The general logic to be used here follows a pathway in Figure 11.10.

Use $PV = nRT$ with gas data $\longrightarrow$ Amount of N_2 required $\longrightarrow$ Use stoichiometric factor to calculate amount of NaN_3 required $\longrightarrow$ Use molar mass to calculate mass of NaN_3 required

Solution The first step is to find the amount (mol) of gas required so that this can be related to the quantity of sodium azide required:

$$P = 829\ \text{mm Hg}\ (1\ \text{atm}/760\ \text{mm Hg}) = 1.09\ \text{atm}$$

$$V = 45.5\ \text{L}$$

$$T = 22.0\ °\text{C, or } 295.2\ \text{K}$$

$$n = N_2\ \text{required (mol)} = \frac{PV}{RT}$$

$$n = \frac{(1.09\ \text{atm})(45.5\ \text{L})}{(0.082057\ \text{L} \cdot \text{atm/K} \cdot \text{mol})(295.2\ \text{K})} = 2.05\ \text{mol}\ N_2$$

Now that the required amount of nitrogen has been calculated, we can calculate the quantity of sodium azide that will produce 2.05 mol of N_2 gas.

$$\text{Mass of }NaN_3 = 2.05\ \text{mol}\ N_2 \left(\frac{2\ \text{mol}\ NaN_3}{3\ \text{mol}\ N_2}\right)\left(\frac{65.01\ \text{g}}{1\ \text{mol}\ NaN_3}\right) = \boxed{88.8\ \text{g}\ NaN_3}$$

■ EXAMPLE 11.10 Gas Laws and Stoichiometry

Problem You wish to prepare some deuterium gas, D_2, for use in an experiment. One way to do this is to react heavy water, D_2O, with an active metal such as lithium.

$$2\ Li(s) + 2\ D_2O(\ell) \longrightarrow 2\ LiOD(aq) + D_2(g)$$

What amount of D_2 (in moles) can be prepared from 0.125 g of Li metal in 15.0 mL of D_2O ($d = 1.11$ g/mL). If dry D_2 gas is captured in a 1450-mL flask at 22.0 °C, what is the pressure of the gas in mm Hg? (Deuterium has an atomic weight of 2.0147 g/mol.)

Strategy You are combining two reactants with no guarantee that they are in the correct stoichiometric ratio. This example must therefore be approached as a limiting reactant problem. You have to find the amount of each substance and then see if one of them is present in a limited amount. Once the limiting reactant is known, the amount of D_2 produced and its pressure under the conditions given can be calculated.

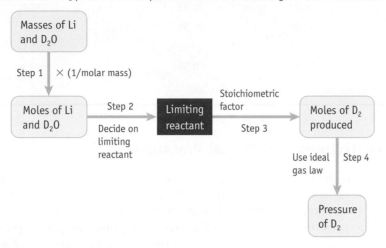

Lithium metal (in the spoon) reacts with drops of water, H_2O, to produce LiOH and hydrogen gas, H_2. If heavy water, D_2O, is used, deuterium gas, D_2, can be produced.

Solution

Step 1. *Calculate the amount (mol) of Li and of D_2O:*

$$0.125 \text{ g Li} \left(\frac{1 \text{ mol Li}}{6.941 \text{ g Li}} \right) = 0.0180 \text{ mol Li}$$

$$15.0 \text{ mL } D_2O \left(\frac{1.11 \text{ g } D_2O}{1 \text{ mL } D_2O} \right)\left(\frac{1 \text{ mol } D_2O}{20.03 \text{ g } D_2O} \right) = 0.831 \text{ mol } D_2O$$

Step 2. *Decide which reactant is the limiting reactant:*

$$\text{Ratio of moles of reactants available} = \frac{0.831 \text{ mol } D_2O}{0.0180 \text{ mol Li}} = \frac{46.2 \text{ mol } D_2O}{1 \text{ mol Li}}$$

The balanced equation shows that the ratio should be 1 mol of D_2O to 1 mol of Li. From the calculated values, we see that D_2O is in large excess, and so Li is the limiting reactant. Therefore, further calculations are based on the amount of Li available.

Step 3. *Use the limiting reactant to calculate the quantity of D_2 produced:*

$$0.0180 \text{ mol Li} \left(\frac{1 \text{ mol } D_2 \text{ produced}}{2 \text{ mol Li}} \right) = 0.00900 \text{ mol } D_2 \text{ produced}$$

Step 4. *Calculate the pressure of D_2:*

$P = ?$ $T = 22.0 \text{ °C, or } 295.2 \text{ K}$

$V = 1450 \text{ mL, or } 1.45 \text{ L}$ $n = 0.00900 \text{ mol } D_2$

$$P = \frac{nRT}{V} = \frac{(0.00900 \text{ mol})(0.082057 \text{ L} \cdot \text{atm/K} \cdot \text{mol})(295.2 \text{ K})}{1.45 \text{ L}} = \boxed{0.150 \text{ atm}}$$

EXERCISE 11.9 Gas Laws and Stoichiometry

Gaseous ammonia is synthesized by the reaction

$$N_2(g) + 3 H_2(g) \longrightarrow 2 NH_3(g)$$

Assume that 355 L of H_2 gas at 25.0 °C and 542 mm Hg is combined with excess N_2 gas. What amount of NH_3 gas, in moles, can be produced? If this amount of NH_3 gas is stored in a 125-L tank at 25.0 °C, what is the pressure of the gas?

TABLE 11.1 Components of Atmospheric Dry Air

Constituent	Molar Mass*	Mole Percent	Partial Pressure at STP (atm)
N_2	28.01	78.08	0.7808
O_2	32.00	20.95	0.2095
CO_2	44.01	0.0385	0.00033
Ar	39.95	0.934	0.00934

*The average molar mass of dry air = 28.960 g/mol.

11.5 Gas Mixtures and Partial Pressures

The air you breathe is a mixture of nitrogen, oxygen, argon, carbon dioxide, water vapor, and small amounts of other gases (Table 11.1). Each of these gases exerts its own pressure, and atmospheric pressure is the sum of the pressures exerted by each gas. The pressure of each gas in the mixture is called its **partial pressure.**

John Dalton (1766–1844) was the first to observe that the pressure of a mixture of ideal gases is the sum of the partial pressures of the different gases in the mixture. This observation is now known as **Dalton's law of partial pressures** (Figure 11.11). Mathematically, we can write Dalton's law of partial pressures as

$$P_{total} = P_1 + P_2 + P_3 \ldots \tag{11.6}$$

where P_1, P_2, and P_3 are the pressures of the different gases in a mixture, and P_{total} is the total pressure.

In a mixture of gases, each gas behaves independently of all others in the mixture. Therefore, we can consider the behavior of each gas in a mixture separately. As an example, let us take a mixture of three ideal gases, labeled A, B, and C. There are n_A moles of A, n_B moles of B, and n_C moles of C. Assume that the mixture ($n_{total} = n_A + n_B + n_C$) is contained in a given volume (V) at a given temperature (T). We can calculate the pressure exerted by each gas from the ideal gas law equation:

$$P_A V = n_A RT \qquad P_B V = n_B RT \qquad P_C V = n_C RT$$

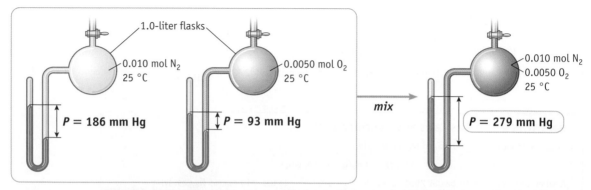

FIGURE 11.11 Dalton's law. In a 1.0-L flask at 25 °C, 0.010 mol of N_2 exerts a pressure of 186 mm Hg, and 0.0050 mol of O_2 in a 1.0-L flask at 25 °C exerts a pressure of 93 mm Hg (left and middle). The N_2 and O_2 samples are mixed in a 1.0-L flask at 25 °C (right). The total pressure, 279 mm Hg, is the sum of the pressures that each gas alone exerts in the flask.

where each gas (A, B, and C) is in the same volume V and is at the same temperature T. According to Dalton's law, the total pressure exerted by the mixture is the sum of the pressures exerted by each component:

$$P_{total} = P_A + P_B + P_C = n_A\left(\frac{RT}{V}\right) + n_B\left(\frac{RT}{V}\right) + n_C\left(\frac{RT}{V}\right)$$

$$P_{total} = (n_A + n_B + n_C)\left(\frac{RT}{V}\right)$$

$$P_{total} = (n_{total})\left(\frac{RT}{V}\right) \tag{11.7}$$

For mixtures of gases, it is convenient to introduce a quantity called the **mole fraction, X**, which is defined as the number of moles of a particular substance in a mixture divided by the total number of moles of all substances present. Mathematically, the mole fraction of a substance A in a mixture with B and C is expressed as

$$X_A = \frac{n_A}{n_A + n_B + n_C} = \frac{n_A}{n_{total}}$$

Now we can combine this equation (written as $n_{total} = n_A/X_A$) with the equations for P_A and P_{total}, and derive the equation

$$P_A = X_A P_{total} \tag{11.8}$$

This equation is useful because it tells us that *the pressure of a gas in a mixture of gases is the product of its mole fraction and the total pressure of the mixture.* For example, the mole fraction of N_2 in air is 0.78, so, at STP, its partial pressure is 0.78 atm or 590 mm Hg.

Chemistry⚛Now™

Sign in at **www.cengage.com/login** and go to Chapter 11 Contents to see Screen 11.8 for tutorials on **gas mixtures and partial pressures.**

■ EXAMPLE 11.11 Partial Pressures of Gases

Problem Halothane, $C_2HBrClF_3$, is a nonflammable, nonexplosive, and nonirritating gas that is commonly used as an inhalation anesthetic.

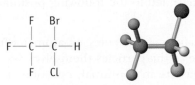

1,1,1-trifluorobromochloroethane, halothane

The total pressure of a mixture of 15.0 g of halothane vapor and 23.5 g of oxygen gas is 855 mm Hg. What is the partial pressure of each gas?

Strategy One way to solve this problem is to recognize that the partial pressure of a gas is given by the total pressure of the mixture multiplied by the mole fraction of the gas.

FIGURE 11.12 A molecular view of gases and liquids. The fact that a large volume of N_2 gas can be condensed to a small volume of liquid indicates that the distance between molecules in the gas phase is very large as compared with the distances between molecules in liquids.

Charles D. Winters

Solution Let us first calculate the mole fractions of halothane and of O_2.

Step 1. *Calculate mole fractions:*

$$\text{Amount of } C_2HBrClF_3 = 15.0 \text{ g} \left(\frac{1 \text{ mol}}{197.4 \text{ g}} \right) = 0.0760 \text{ mol}$$

$$\text{Amount of } O_2 = 23.5 \text{ g} \left(\frac{1 \text{ mol}}{32.00 \text{ g}} \right) = 0.734 \text{ mol}$$

$$\text{Total amount of gas} = 0.0760 \text{ mol } C_2HBrClF_2 + 0.734 \text{ mol } O_2 = 0.810 \text{ mol}$$

$$\text{Mole fraction of } C_2HBrClF_3 = \frac{0.0760 \text{ mol } C_2HBrClF_3}{0.810 \text{ total moles}} = 0.0938$$

Because the sum of the mole fraction of halothane and of O_2 must equal 1.0000, this means that the mole fraction of oxygen is 0.906.

$$X_{\text{halothane}} + X_{\text{oxygen}} = 1.0000$$

$$0.0938 + X_{\text{oxygen}} = 1.0000$$

$$X_{\text{oxygen}} = 0.906$$

Step 2. *Calculate partial pressures:*

$$\text{Partial pressure of halothane} = P_{\text{halothane}} = X_{\text{halothane}} \cdot P_{\text{total}}$$

$$P_{\text{halothane}} = 0.0938 \cdot P_{\text{total}} = 0.0938 \, (855 \text{ mm Hg})$$

$$P_{\text{halothane}} = \boxed{80.2 \text{ mm Hg}}$$

The total pressure of the mixture is the sum of the partial pressures of the gases in the mixture.

$$P_{\text{halothane}} + P_{\text{oxygen}} = 855 \text{ mm Hg}$$

and so

$$P_{\text{oxygen}} = 855 \text{ mm Hg} - P_{\text{halothane}}$$

$$P_{\text{oxygen}} = 855 \text{ mm Hg} - 80.2 \text{ mm Hg} = \boxed{775 \text{ mm Hg}}$$

EXERCISE 11.10 Partial Pressures

The halothane–oxygen mixture described in Example 11.11 is placed in a 5.00-L tank at 25.0 °C. What is the total pressure (in mm Hg) of the gas mixture in the tank? What are the partial pressures (in mm Hg) of the gases?

 Module 16

11.6 The Kinetic-Molecular Theory of Gases

So far, we have discussed the macroscopic properties of gases, properties such as pressure and volume that result from the behavior of a system with a large number of particles. Now we turn to the kinetic-molecular theory (◀ page 7) for a description of the behavior of matter at the molecular or atomic level. Hundreds of experimental observations have led to the following postulates regarding the behavior of gases.

- Gases consist of particles (molecules or atoms) whose separation is much greater than the size of the particles themselves (see Figure 11.12).
- The particles of a gas are in continual, random, and rapid motion. As they move, they collide with one another and with the walls of their container, but they do so without loss of energy.
- The average kinetic energy of gas particles is proportional to the gas temperature. *All gases, regardless of their molecular mass, have the same average kinetic energy at the same temperature.*

Let us discuss the behavior of gases from this point of view.

Robert Boyle (1627–1691) was born in Ireland as the 14th and last child of the first Earl of Cork. In his book *Uncle Tungsten*, Oliver Sacks tells us that "Chemistry as a true science made its first emergence with the work of Robert Boyle in the middle of the seventeenth century. Twenty years [Isaac] Newton's senior, Boyle was born at a time when the practice of alchemy still held sway, and he still maintained a variety of alchemical beliefs and practices, side by side with his scientific ones. He believed gold could be created, and that he had succeeded in creating it (Newton, also an alchemist, advised him to keep silent about this)."

Boyle examined crystals, explored color, devised an acid-base indicator from the syrup of violets, and provided the first modern definition of an element. He was also a physiologist, and was the first to show that the healthy human body has a constant

Robert Boyle (1627–1691).

Oesper Collection in the History of Chemistry, University of Cincinnati

temperature. Today, Boyle is best known for his studies of gases, which were described in his book *The Sceptical Chymist*, published in 1680.

The French chemist and inventor Jacques Alexandre César Charles began his career as a clerk in the finance ministry, but his real interest was science. He developed several inventions and was best known in his lifetime for inventing the hydrogen balloon. In August 1783, Charles exploited his recent studies on hydrogen gas by inflating a balloon with this gas. Because hydrogen would escape easily from a paper bag, he made a silk bag coated with rubber. Inflating the bag took several days and required nearly 225 kg of sulfuric acid and 450 kg of iron to produce the H_2 gas. The balloon stayed aloft for almost 45 minutes and traveled about 15 miles. When it landed in a village, however, the people were so terrified they tore it to

Jacques Alexandre César Charles (1746–1823).

Image Courtesy of Library of Congress

Smithsonian National Air & Space Museum

Jacques Charles and A. Roberts ascended over Paris on December 1, 1783, in a hydrogen-filled balloon.

shreds. Several months later, Charles and a passenger flew a new hydrogen-filled balloon some distance across the French countryside and ascended to the then-incredible altitude of 2 miles.

Molecular Speed and Kinetic Energy

If your friend walks into your room carrying a pizza, how do you know it? In scientific terms, we know that the odor-causing molecules of food enter the gas phase and drift through space until they reach the cells of your body that react to odors. The same thing happens in the laboratory when bottles of aqueous ammonia (NH_3) and hydrochloric acid (HCl) sit side by side (Figure 11.13). Molecules of the two compounds enter the gas phase and drift along until they encounter one another, at which time they react and form a cloud of tiny particles of solid ammonium chloride (NH_4Cl).

If you change the temperature of the environment of the containers in Figure 11.13 and measure the time needed for the cloud of ammonium chloride to form, you would find the time would be longer at lower temperatures. The reason for this is that the speed at which molecules move depends on the temperature. Let us expand on this idea.

The molecules in a gas sample do not all move at the same speed. Rather, as illustrated in Figure 11.14 for O_2 molecules, there is a distribution of speeds. Figure 11.14 shows the number of particles in a gas sample that are moving at certain speeds at a given temperature, and there are two important observations we can make. First, at a given temperature some molecules have high speeds, and others have low speeds. Most of the molecules, however, have some intermediate speed, and their most probable speed corresponds to the maximum in the curve. For oxygen gas at 25 °C, for example, most molecules have speeds in the range

Charles D. Winters

FIGURE 11.13 The movement of gas molecules. Open dishes of aqueous ammonia and hydrochloric acid are placed side by side. When molecules of NH_3 and HCl escape from solution to the atmosphere and encounter one another, a cloud of solid ammonium chloride, NH_4Cl is observed.

Chemical Perspectives

The Earth's Atmosphere

Earth's atmosphere is a fascinating mixture of gases in more or less distinct layers with widely differing temperatures.

Up to the troposphere, there is a gradual decline in temperature (and pressure) with altitude. The temperature climbs again in the stratosphere due to the absorption of energy from the sun by stratospheric ozone, O_3.

Above the stratosphere, the pressure declines because there are fewer molecules present. At still higher altitudes, we observe a dramatic increase in temperature in the thermosphere. This is an illustration of the difference between *temperature* and *thermal energy*. The temperature of a gas reflects the average kinetic energy of the molecules of the gas, whereas the thermal energy present in an object is the *total* kinetic energy of the molecules. In the thermosphere, the few molecules present have a very high temperature, but the thermal energy is exceedingly small because there are so few molecules.

Gases within the troposphere are well mixed by convection. Pollutants that are evolved on Earth's surface can rise into the stratosphere, but it is said that the stratosphere acts as a "thermal lid" on the troposphere and prevents significant mixing of polluting gases into the stratosphere and beyond.

The pressure of the atmosphere declines with altitude, and so the partial pressure of O_2 declines. The figure shows why climbers have a hard time breathing on Mt. Everest, where the altitude is 29,028 ft (8848 m) and the O_2 partial pressure is only 29% of the sea level partial pressure. With proper training, a climber could reach the summit without supplemental oxygen. However, this same feat would not be possible if Everest were farther north. Earth's atmosphere thins toward the poles, and so the O_2 partial pressure would be even less if Everest's summit were in North America, for example.

(See G. N. Eby, *Environmental Geochemistry,* Thomson/Brooks/Cole, 2004.)

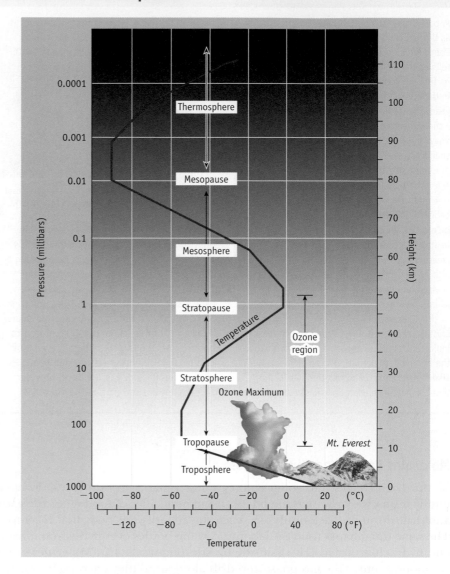

Average Composition of Earth's Atmosphere to a Height of 25 km

Gas	Volume %	Source
N_2	78.08	biologic
O_2	20.95	biologic
Ar	0.93	radioactivity
Ne	0.0018	Earth's interior
He	0.0005	radioactivity
H_2O	0 to 4	evaporation
CO_2	0.0385	biologic, industrial
CH_4	0.00017	biologic
N_2O	0.00003	biologic, industrial
O_3	0.000004	photochemical

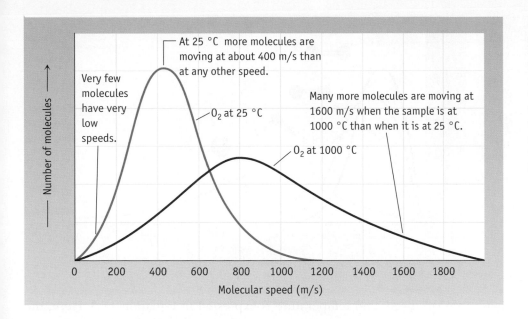

At 25 °C more molecules are moving at about 400 m/s than at any other speed.

Very few molecules have very low speeds.

O_2 at 25 °C

Many more molecules are moving at 1600 m/s when the sample is at 1000 °C than when it is at 25 °C.

O_2 at 1000 °C

Number of molecules

0   200   400   600   800   1000   1200   1400   1600   1800

Molecular speed (m/s)

FIGURE 11.14 The distribution of molecular speeds. A graph of the number of molecules with a given speed versus that speed shows the distribution of molecular speeds. The red curve shows the effect of increased temperature. Even though the curve for the higher temperature is "flatter" and broader than the one at a lower temperature, the areas under the curves are the same because the number of molecules in the sample is fixed.

from 200 m/s to 700 m/s, and their most probable speed is about 400 m/s. (These are very high speeds, indeed. A speed of 400 m/s corresponds to about 1000 miles per hour!)

A second observation regarding the distribution of speeds is that as the temperature increases the most probable speed increases, and the number of molecules traveling at very high speeds increases greatly.

The kinetic energy of a single molecule of mass m in a gas sample is given by the equation

$$KE = \frac{1}{2}(mass)(speed)^2 = \frac{1}{2} mu^2$$

where u is the speed of that molecule. We can calculate the kinetic energy of a single gas molecule from this equation but not of a collection of molecules because not all of the molecules in a gas sample are moving at the same speed. However, we can calculate the average kinetic energy of a collection of molecules by relating it to other averaged quantities of the system. In particular, the average kinetic energy is related to the average speed:

$$\overline{KE} = \frac{1}{2} m\overline{u^2}$$

(The horizontal bar over the symbols KE and u indicate an average value.) This equation states that the average kinetic energy of the molecules in a gas sample, $\overline{KE}$, is related to $\overline{u^2}$, the average of the squares of their speeds (called the "mean square speed").

Experiments also show that the average kinetic energy, $\overline{KE}$, of a sample of gas molecules is directly proportional to temperature with a proportionality constant of $\frac{3}{2}R$,

$$\overline{KE} = \frac{3}{2} RT$$

where R is the gas constant expressed in SI units (8.314472 J/K · mol).

Now, because $\overline{KE}$ is proportional to both $1/2\ m\overline{u^2}$ and T, temperature and $1/2\ m\overline{u^2}$ must also be proportional; that is, $1/2\ m\overline{u^2} \propto T$. This relation among

FIGURE 11.15 The effect of molecular mass on the distribution of speeds. At a given temperature, molecules with higher masses have lower speeds.

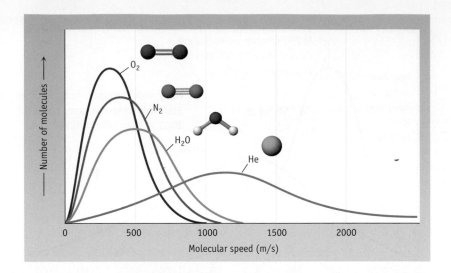

■ **Maxwell–Boltzmann Curves** Plots showing the relation between the number of molecules and their speed or energy (Figure 11.14) are often called Maxwell–Boltzmann distribution curves. They are named after James Clerk Maxwell (1831–1879) and Ludwig Boltzmann (1844–1906). The distribution of speeds (or kinetic energies) of molecules (as illustrated by Figures 11.14 and 11.15) is often used when explaining chemical phenomena.

mass, average speed, and temperature is expressed in Equation 11.9. Here, the square root of the mean square speed ($\sqrt{\overline{u^2}}$, called the **root-mean-square, or rms speed**), the temperature (T, in kelvins), and the molar mass (M) are related.

$$\sqrt{\overline{u^2}} = \sqrt{\frac{3RT}{M}} \qquad \text{(11.9)}$$

This equation, sometimes called *Maxwell's equation* after James Clerk Maxwell (Section 6.1), shows that the speeds of gas molecules are indeed related directly to the temperature (Figure 11.14). The rms speed is a useful quantity because of its direct relationship to the average kinetic energy and because it is very close to the true average speed for a sample. (The average speed is 92% of the rms speed.)

All gases have the same average kinetic energy at the same temperature. However, if you compare a sample of one gas with another, say compare O_2 and N_2, this does not mean the molecules have the same average speed (Figure 11.15). Instead, Maxwell's equation shows that the smaller the molar mass of the gas the greater the rms speed.

Chemistry꙰Now™

Sign in at **www.cengage.com/login** and go to Chapter 11 Contents to see:
- Screen 11.9 for a self-study module on **gases at different temperatures**
- Screen 11.11 for a tutorial on **Boltzmann distribution and calculation of distribution curves**

■ EXAMPLE 11.12 Molecular Speed

Problem Calculate the rms speed of oxygen molecules at 25 °C.

Strategy We must use Equation 11.9 with M in units of kg/mol. The reason for this is that R is in units of J/K · mol, and 1 J = 1 kg · m²/s².

Solution The molar mass of O_2 is 32.0 × 10⁻³ kg/mol.

$$\sqrt{\overline{u^2}} = \sqrt{\frac{3(8.3145 \text{ J/K} \cdot \text{mol})(298 \text{ K})}{32.0 \times 10^{-3} \text{ kg/mol}}} = \sqrt{2.32 \times 10^5 \text{ J/kg}}$$

To obtain the answer in meters per second, we use the relation $1\ J = 1\ kg \cdot m^2/s^2$. This means we have

$$\sqrt{\overline{u^2}} = \sqrt{2.32 \times 10^5\ kg \cdot m^2/(kg \cdot s^2)} = \sqrt{2.32 \times 10^5\ m^2/s^2} = \boxed{482\ m/s}$$

This speed is equivalent to about 1100 miles per hour!

EXERCISE 11.11 Molecular Speeds

Calculate the rms speeds of helium atoms and N_2 molecules at 25 °C.

Kinetic-Molecular Theory and the Gas Laws

The gas laws, which come from experiment, can be explained by the kinetic-molecular theory. The starting place is to describe how pressure arises from collisions of gas molecules with the walls of the container holding the gas (Figure 11.16). Remember that pressure is related to the force of the collisions (see Section 11.1).

$$\text{Gas pressure} = \frac{\text{force of collisions}}{\text{area}}$$

The force exerted by the collisions depends on the number of collisions and the average force per collision. When the temperature of a gas is increased, we know the average kinetic energy of the molecules increases. This causes the average force of the collisions with the walls to increase as well. (This is much like the difference in the force exerted by a car traveling at high speed versus one moving at only a few kilometers per hour.) Also, because the speed of gas molecules increases with temperature, more collisions occur per second. Thus, the collective force per square centimeter is greater, and the pressure increases. Mathematically, this is related to the direct proportionality between P and T when n and V are fixed, that is, $P = (nR/V)T$.

Increasing the number of molecules of a gas at a fixed temperature and volume does not change the average collision force, but it does increase the number of collisions occurring per second. Thus, the pressure increases, and we can say that P is proportional to n when V and T are constant, that is, $P = n(RT/V)$.

If the pressure is to remain constant when either the number of molecules of gas or the temperature is increased, then the volume of the container (and the area over which the collisions can take place) must increase. This is expressed by stating that V is proportional to nT when P is constant $[V = nT(R/P)]$, a statement that is a *combination of Avogadro's hypothesis and Charles's law*.

Finally, if the temperature is constant, the average impact force of molecules of a given mass with the container walls must be constant. If n is kept constant while the volume of the container is made smaller, the number of collisions with the container walls per second must increase. This means the pressure increases, and so P is proportional to $1/V$ when n and T are constant, as stated by *Boyle's law*, that is, $P = (1/V)(nRT)$.

Chemistry ⚛ Now™

Sign in at **www.cengage.com/login** and go to Chapter 11 Contents to see Screen 11.10 for simulations of **the gas laws at the molecular level.**

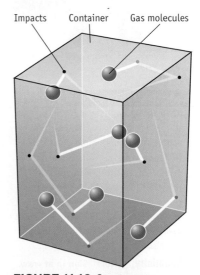

Impacts   Container   Gas molecules

FIGURE 11.16 Gas pressure.
According to the kinetic-molecular theory, gas pressure is caused by gas molecules bombarding the container walls.

FIGURE 11.17 Diffusion. (a) Liquid bromine, Br_2, was placed in a small flask inside a larger container. (b) The cork was removed from the flask, and, with time, bromine vapor diffused into the larger container. Bromine vapor is now distributed evenly in the containers.

(a)　　　　　　(b)

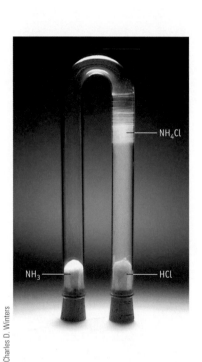

NH₄Cl

NH₃　　　HCl

Charles D. Winters

Active Figure 11.18 Gaseous diffusion. Here, HCl gas (from hydrochloric acid) and ammonia gas (from aqueous ammonia) diffuse from opposite ends of a glass U-tube. When they meet, they produce white, solid NH_4Cl. It is clear that the NH_4Cl is formed closer to the end from which the HCl gas begins because HCl molecules move slower on average than NH_3 molecules. See also Figure 11.13.

Chemistry ⚛ Now™ Sign in at www.cengage.com/login and go to the Chapter Contents menu to explore an interactive version of this figure accompanied by an exercise.

11.7 Diffusion and Effusion

When a pizza is brought into a room, the volatile aroma-causing molecules vaporize into the atmosphere, where they mix with the oxygen, nitrogen, carbon dioxide, water vapor, and other gases present. Even if there were no movement of the air in the room caused by fans or people moving about, the odor would eventually reach everywhere in the room. This mixing of molecules of two or more gases due to their random molecular motions is the result of **diffusion.** Given time, the molecules of one component in a gas mixture will thoroughly and completely mix with all other components of the mixture (Figure 11.17).

Diffusion is also illustrated by the experiment in Figure 11.18. Here, we have placed cotton moistened with hydrochloric acid at one end of a U-tube and cotton moistened with aqueous ammonia at the other end. Molecules of HCl and NH_3 diffuse into the tube, and, when they meet, they produce white, solid NH_4Cl (just as in Figure 11.13).

$$HCl(g) + NH_3(g) \longrightarrow NH_4Cl(s)$$

We find that the gases do not meet in the middle. Rather, because the heavier HCl molecules diffuse less rapidly than the lighter NH_3 molecules, the molecules meet closer to the HCl end of the U-tube.

Closely related to diffusion is **effusion,** which is the movement of gas through a tiny opening in a container into another container where the pressure is very low (Figure 11.19). Thomas Graham (1805–1869), a Scottish chemist, studied the effusion of gases and found that the rate of effusion of a gas—the amount of gas moving from one place to another in a given amount of time—is inversely proportional to the square root of its molar mass. Based on these experimental results, the rates of effusion of two gases can be compared:

$$\frac{\text{Rate of effusion of gas 1}}{\text{Rate of effusion of gas 2}} = \sqrt{\frac{\text{molar mass of gas 2}}{\text{molar mass of gas 1}}} \qquad (11.10)$$

The relationship in Equation 11.10—now known as **Graham's law**—is readily derived from Maxwell's equation by recognizing that the rate of effusion depends on

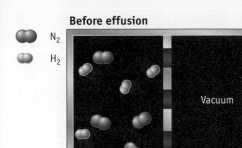

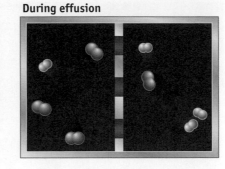

FIGURE 11.19 Effusion. H_2 and N_2 gas molecules effuse through the pores of a porous barrier. Lighter molecules (H_2) with higher average speeds strike the barrier more often and pass more often through it than heavier, slower molecules (N_2) at the same temperature. According to Graham's law, H_2 molecules effuse 3.72 times faster than N_2 molecules.

N₂

H₂

Vacuum

Porous barrier

the speed of the molecules. The ratio of the rms speeds is the same as the ratio of the effusion rates:

$$\frac{\text{Rate of effusion of gas 1}}{\text{Rate of effusion of gas 2}} = \frac{\sqrt{u^2 \text{ of gas 1}}}{\sqrt{u^2 \text{ of gas 2}}} = \frac{\sqrt{3RT/(M \text{ of gas 1})}}{\sqrt{3RT/(M \text{ of gas 2})}}$$

Canceling out like terms gives the expression in Equation 11.10.

Chemistry ⚛ Now™

Sign in at **www.cengage.com/login** and go to Chapter 11 Contents to see screen 11.12 for an exercise and tutorial on **diffusion.**

■ **EXAMPLE 11.13 Using Graham's Law of Effusion to Calculate a Molar Mass**

Problem Tetrafluoroethylene, C_2F_4, effuses through a barrier at a rate of 4.6×10^{-6} mol/h. An unknown gas, consisting only of boron and hydrogen, effuses at the rate of 5.8×10^{-6} mol/h under the same conditions. What is the molar mass of the unknown gas?

Strategy From Graham's law, we know that a light molecule will effuse more rapidly than a heavier one. Because the unknown gas effuses more rapidly than C_2F_4 ($M = 100.0$ g/mol), the unknown must have a molar mass less than 100 g/mol. Substitute the experimental data into Graham's law equation (Equation 11.10).

Solution

$$\frac{5.8 \times 10^{-6} \text{ mol/h}}{4.6 \times 10^{-6} \text{ mol/h}} = 1.3 = \sqrt{\frac{100.0 \text{ g/mol}}{M \text{ of unknown}}}$$

To solve for the unknown molar mass, square both sides of the equation and rearrange to find M for the unknown.

$$1.6 = \frac{100.0 \text{ g/mol}}{M \text{ of unknown}}$$

$$M = \boxed{63 \text{ g/mol}}$$

Comment A boron–hydrogen compound corresponding to this molar mass is B_5H_9, called pentaborane.

EXERCISE 11.12 Graham's Law

A sample of pure methane, CH_4, is found to effuse through a porous barrier in 1.50 min. Under the same conditions, an equal number of molecules of an unknown gas effuses through the barrier in 4.73 min. What is the molar mass of the unknown gas?

FIGURE 11.20 Isotope separation.
Separation of uranium isotopes for use in atomic weaponry or in nuclear power plants was originally done by gas effusion. (There are still plants in use in the U.S. at Piketon, Ohio, and Paducah, Kentucky.) The more modern approach is to use a gas centrifuge, and that is what is pictured here (left). (Right) UF_6 gas is injected into the centrifuge from a tube passing down through the center of a tall, spinning cylinder. The heavier $^{238}UF_6$ molecules experience more centrifugal force and move to the outer wall of the cylinder; the lighter $^{235}UF_6$ molecules stay closer to the center. A temperature difference inside the rotor causes the $^{235}UF_6$ molecules to move to the top of the cylinder and the $^{238}UF_6$ molecules to move to the bottom. (See the *New York Times*, page F1, March 23, 2004.)

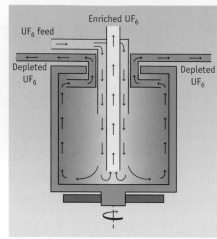

11.8 Some Applications of the Gas Laws and Kinetic-Molecular Theory

Separating Isotopes

The effusion process played a central role in the development of the atomic bomb in World War II and is still in use today to prepare fissionable uranium for nuclear power plants. Naturally occurring uranium exists primarily as two isotopes: ^{235}U (0.720% abundant) and ^{238}U (99.275% abundant). However, because only the lighter isotope, ^{235}U, is suitable as a fuel in reactors, uranium ore must be enriched in this isotope.

Gas effusion is one way to separate the ^{235}U and ^{238}U isotopes. To achieve this, a uranium oxide sample is first converted to uranium hexafluoride, UF_6. This solid fluoride sublimes readily; it has a vapor pressure of 760 mm Hg at 55.6 °C. When UF_6 vapor is placed is a chamber with porous walls, the lighter, more rapidly moving $^{235}UF_6$ molecules effuse through the walls at a greater rate than the heavier $^{238}UF_6$ molecules.

To assess the separation of uranium isotopes, let us compare the rates of effusion of $^{235}UF_6$ and $^{238}UF_6$. Using Graham's law,

$$\frac{\text{Rate of } ^{235}UF_6}{\text{Rate of } ^{238}UF_6} = \sqrt{\frac{238.051 + 6(18.998)}{235.044 + 6(18.998)}} = 1.0043$$

we find that $^{235}UF_6$ will pass through a porous barrier 1.0043 times faster than $^{238}UF_6$. In other words, if we sample the gas that passes through the barrier, the fraction of $^{235}UF_6$ molecules will be larger. If the process is carried out again on the sample now higher in $^{235}UF_6$ concentration, the fraction of $^{235}UF_6$ would again increase in the effused sample, and the separation factor is now 1.0043×1.0043. If the cycle is repeated over and over again, the separation factor is 1.0043^n, where n is the number of enrichment cycles. To achieve a separation of about 99%, hundreds of cycles are required!

Deep Sea Diving

Diving with a self-contained underwater breathing apparatus (SCUBA) is exciting. If you want to dive much beyond about 60 ft (18 m) or so, however, you need to take special precautions.

You Stink!

Do those dirty old sneakers in your closet stink? Did your friends ever tell you you have halitosis, the polite term for bad breath? Did your roommates ever experience flatulence (a malodorous gaseous emission, to say it politely) after eating too many beans? Or have you ever smelled the odor from a paper-making plant or from brackish water? The bad odors in all these cases can come from several gaseous, sulfur-containing compounds. Hydrogen sulfide (H_2S) and dimethylsulfide (CH_3SCH_3) are important contributors, but methyl mercaptan (CH_3SH) is the main culprit.

Methyl mercaptan, also called methanethiol, heads the list of things that smell bad. Sources say it smells like rotten cabbage, but you already know what it smells like even if you have not smelled rotten cabbage recently. It is a gas at room temperature, but can be condensed to a liquid in an ice bath.

Data for methyl mercaptan

Melting Point	−123 °C
Boiling point	+5.95 °C
Density (gas, 298 K, 1 atm)	1.966 g/L
$\Delta_f H°$	−22.3 kJ/mol

Current OSHA guidelines are that the compound should not exceed concentrations of 10 parts per million (ppm) in air (or about 20 mg/m³). Concentrations over 400 ppm have been known to cause death. However, humans can detect the odor of the compound at levels of a few parts per billion and so would leave the area if possible before concentrations became dangerous.

Bad breath comes from the formation of CH_3SH and similar compounds by the action of

enzymes in the mouth on sulfur-containing compounds. Two of these compounds are common amino acids, methionine and cysteine. Methyl mercaptan is also produced when you digest allicin, which is produced when garlic is chopped to put into your pizza or your salad.

How can you get rid of halitosis? One way is to use a mouthwash. This can wash away some sources of sulfur compounds and might mask the odor. A more suitable method, however, is to use a toothpaste that has anti-plaque agents such as zinc and tin salts. It is thought that these interfere with the enzymes that act on something like methionine to produce methyl mercaptan.

Methyl mercaptan is not just a source of bad odors. It is used industrially to make pes-

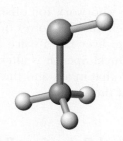

Methyl mercapatan or methanethiol.

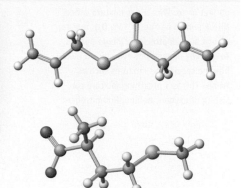

The digestion of allicin (top, from garlic) and methionine (bottom) is a source of CH_3SH in bad breath. Methionine is also made industrially using CH_3SH as one of the starting materials.

ticides, to regenerate catalysts in the petroleum industry, and to make methionine, which is used as a supplement in animal feed. Finally, mercaptans are added to natural gas and tanks of cooking gas. The three hydrocarbons in natural gas and cooking gas are odorless, so if you smell the unmistakable odor of a mercaptan you know there is a gas leak.

Questions:

1. *If an air sample contains CH_3SH with a concentration of 15 mg/m³, what is its partial pressure at 25 °C? How many molecules are there per cubic meter?*
2. *What are the bond angles in CH_3SH?*
3. *Is CH_3SH polar or nonpolar?*
4. *Do you expect CH_3SH gas to behave as an ideal gas? (See Section 11.9.)*
5. *Which gas diffuses most rapidly, CH_3SH, H_2S, or CH_3SCH_3?*

Answers to these questions are in Appendix Q.

When you breathe air from a SCUBA tank (Figure 11.21), the pressure of the gas in your lungs is equal to the pressure exerted on your body. When you are at the surface, atmospheric pressure is about 1 atm, and, because air has an oxygen concentration of 21%, the partial pressure of O_2 is about 0.21 atm. If you are at a depth of about 33 ft, the water pressure is 2 atm. This means the oxygen partial pressure is double the surface partial pressure, or about 0.4 atm. Similarly, the partial pressure of N_2, which is about 0.8 atm at the surface, doubles to about 1.6 atm at a depth of 33 ft. The solubility of gases in water (and in blood) is directly proportional to pressure. Therefore, more oxygen and nitrogen dissolve in blood under these conditions, and this can lead to several problems.

FIGURE 11.21 SCUBA diving.
Ordinary recreational dives can be made with compressed air to depths of about 60 feet or so. With a gas mixture called Nitrox (which has up to 36% O_2), one can stay at such depths for a longer period. To go even deeper, however, divers must breathe special gas mixtures such as Trimix. This is a breathing mixture consisting of oxygen, helium, and nitrogen.

OAR/National Undersea Research Program (NURP)

Nitrogen narcosis, also called "rapture of the deep" or the "martini effect," results from the toxic effect on nerve conduction of N_2 dissolved in blood. Its effect is comparable to drinking a martini on an empty stomach or taking laughing gas (nitrous oxide, N_2O) at the dentist; it makes you slightly giddy. In severe cases, it can impair a diver's judgment and even cause a diver to take the regulator out of his or her mouth and hand it to a fish! Some people can go as deep as 130 ft with no problem, but others experience nitrogen narcosis at 80 ft.

Another problem with breathing air at depths beyond 100 ft or so is oxygen toxicity. Our bodies are regulated for a partial pressure of O_2 of 0.21 atm. At a depth of 130 ft, the partial pressure of O_2 is comparable to breathing 100% oxygen at sea level. These higher partial pressures can harm the lungs and cause central nervous system damage. Oxygen toxicity is the reason deep dives are done not with compressed air but with gas mixtures with a much lower percentage of O_2, say about 10%.

Because of the risk of nitrogen narcosis, divers going beyond about 130 ft, such as those who work for offshore oil drilling companies, use a mixture of oxygen and helium. This solves the nitrogen narcosis problem, but it introduces another. If the diver has a voice link to the surface, the diver's speech sounds like Donald Duck! Speech is altered because the velocity of sound in helium is different from that in air, and the density of gas at several hundred feet is much higher than at the surface.

11.9 Nonideal Behavior: Real Gases

If you are working with a gas at approximately room temperature and a pressure of 1 atm or less, the ideal gas law is remarkably successful in relating the amount of gas and its pressure, volume, and temperature. At higher pressures or lower temperatures, however, deviations from the ideal gas law occur. The origin of these deviations is explained by the breakdown of the assumptions used when describing ideal gases, specifically the assumptions that the particles have no size and that there are no forces between them.

At standard temperature and pressure (STP), the volume occupied by a single molecule is *very* small relative to its share of the total gas volume. A helium atom with a radius of 31 pm has relatively about the same space to move about as a pea has inside a basketball. Now suppose the pressure is increased significantly, to 1000 atm. The volume available to each molecule is a sphere with a radius of only about 200 pm, which means the situation is now like that of a pea inside a sphere a bit larger than a Ping-Pong ball.

■ **Assumptions of the KMT—Revisited**
The assumptions of the kinetic molecular theory were given on page 532.
1. Gases consist of particles (molecules or atoms) whose separation is much greater than the size of the particles themselves.
2. The particles of a gas are in continual, random, and rapid motion. As they move, they collide with one another and with the walls of their container, but they do so without loss of energy.
3. The average kinetic energy of gas particles is proportional to the gas temperature. All gases, regardless of their molecular mass, have the same average kinetic energy at the same temperature.

The kinetic-molecular theory and the ideal gas law are concerned with the volume available to the molecules to move about, not the total volume of the container. The problem is that the volume occupied by gas molecules is not negligible at higher pressures. For example, suppose you have a flask marked with a volume of 500 mL. This does not mean the space available to molecules is 500 mL. Rather, the available volume is less than 500 mL, especially at high gas pressures, because the molecules themselves occupy some of the volume.

Another assumption of the kinetic-molecular theory is that the atoms or molecules of the gas never stick to one another by some type of intermolecular force. This is clearly not true as well. All gases can be liquefied—although some gases require a very low temperature (see Figure 11.12)—and the only way this can happen is if there are forces between the molecules. When a molecule is about to strike the wall of its container, other molecules in its vicinity exert a slight pull on the molecule and pull it away from the wall. The effect of the intermolecular forces is that molecules strike the wall with less force than in the absence of intermolecular attractive forces. Thus, because collisions between molecules in a real gas and the wall are softer, the observed gas pressure is less than that predicted by the ideal gas law. This effect can be particularly pronounced when the temperature is low.

The Dutch physicist Johannes van der Waals (1837–1923) studied the breakdown of the ideal gas law equation and developed an equation to correct for the errors arising from nonideality. This equation is known as the **van der Waals equation:**

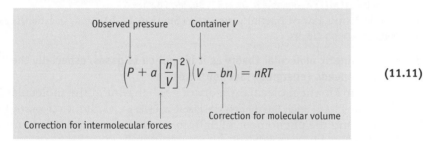

$$\left(P + a\left[\frac{n}{V}\right]^2\right)(V - bn) = nRT \qquad (11.11)$$

where a and b are experimentally determined constants (Table 11.2). Although Equation 11.11 might seem complicated at first glance, the terms in parentheses are those of the ideal gas law, each corrected for the effects discussed previously. The pressure correction term, $a(n/V)^2$, accounts for intermolecular forces. Owing to intermolecular forces, the observed gas pressure is lower than the ideal pressure ($P_{observed} < P_{ideal}$ where P_{ideal} is calculated using the equation $PV = nRT$). Therefore, the term $a(n/V)^2$ is added to the observed pressure. The constant a typically has values in the range 0.01 to 10 atm · L^2/mol^2. The actual volume available to the molecules is smaller than the volume of the container because the molecules themselves take up space. Therefore, an amount is subtracted from the container volume ($= bn$) to take this into account. Here, n is the number of moles of gas, and b is an experimental quantity that corrects for the molecular volume. Typical values of b range from 0.01 to 0.1 L/mol, roughly increasing with increasing molecular size.

As an example of the importance of these corrections, consider a sample of 4.00 mol of chlorine gas, Cl_2, in a 4.00-L tank at 100.0 °C. The ideal gas law would lead you to expect a pressure of 30.6 atm. A better estimate of the pressure, obtained from the van der Waals equation, is 26.0 atm, about 4.6 atm less than the ideal pressure!

EXERCISE 11.13 van der Waals's Equation

Using both the ideal gas law and van der Waals's equation, calculate the pressure expected for 10.0 mol of helium gas in a 1.00-L container at 25 °C.

TABLE 11.2. van der Waals Constants

Gas	a Values atm · L^2/mol^2	b Values L/mol
He	0.034	0.0237
Ar	1.34	0.0322
H$_2$	0.244	0.0266
N$_2$	1.39	0.0391
O$_2$	1.36	0.0318
CO$_2$	3.59	0.0427
Cl$_2$	6.49	0.0562
H$_2$O	5.46	0.0305

Chapter Goals Revisited

Now that you have studied this chapter, you should ask whether you have met the chapter goals. In particular, you should be able to:

Understand the basis of the gas laws and how to use those laws.

a. Describe how pressure measurements are made and the units of pressure, especially atmospheres (atm) and millimeters of mercury (mm Hg) (Section 11.1). Study Question(s) assignable in OWL: 1.

b. Understand the basis of the gas laws (Boyle's Law, Charles's Law, and Avogadro's Hypothesis) and how to apply them (Section 11.2). Study Question(s) assignable in OWL: 6, 8, 10, 12, 14.

Use the ideal gas law.

a. Understand the origin of the ideal gas law and how to use the equation (Section 11.3). Study Question(s) assignable in OWL: 18, 22, 24, 59, 63, 73, 81, 84, 88, 90, 96.

b. Calculate the molar mass of a compound from a knowledge of the pressure of a known quantity of a gas in a given volume at a known temperature (Section 11.3). Study Question(s) assignable in OWL: 26, 28, 30, 66, 85, 86, 92.

Apply the gas laws to stoichiometric calculations.

a. Apply the gas laws to a study of the stoichiometry of reactions (Section 11.4). Study Question(s) assignable in OWL: 32, 34, 65, 78.

b. Use Dalton's law of partial pressures (Section 11.5). Study Question(s) assignable in OWL: 39, 40, 70, 76, 83.

Understand kinetic molecular theory as it is applied to gases, especially the distribution of molecular speeds (energies) (Section 11.6).

a. Apply the kinetic-molecular theory of gas behavior at the molecular level (Section 11.6). Study Question(s) assignable in OWL: 41, 45, 101; Go Chemistry Module 16.

b. Understand the phenomena of diffusion and effusion and how to use Graham's law (Section 11.7). Study Question(s) assignable in OWL: 47.

Recognize why gases do not behave like ideal gases under some conditions.

a. Appreciate the fact that gases usually do not behave as ideal gases. Deviations from ideal behavior are largest at high pressure and low temperature (Section 11.9). Study Question(s) assignable in OWL: 51, 52.

KEY EQUATIONS

Equation 11.1 (page 518) Boyle's law (where P is the pressure and V is the volume)

$$P_1V_1 = P_2V_2$$

Equation 11.2 (page 520) Charles's law (where T is the Kelvin temperature)

$$\frac{V_1}{T_1} = \frac{V_2}{T_2} \quad \text{at constant } n \text{ and } P$$

Equation 11.3 (page 521)   General gas law (combined gas law)

$$\frac{P_1 V_1}{T_1} = \frac{P_2 V_2}{T_2} \quad \text{for a given amount of gas, } n$$

Equation 11.4 (page 524)   Ideal gas law (where n is the amount of gas (moles) and R is the universal gas constant, $0.082057 \; L \cdot atm/K \cdot mol$)

$$PV = nRT$$

Equation 11.5 (page 525)   Density of gases (where d is the gas density in g/L and M is the molar mass of the gas)

$$d = \frac{m}{V} = \frac{PM}{RT}$$

Equation 11.6 (page 530)   Dalton's law of partial pressures. The total pressure of a gas mixture is the sum of the partial pressures of the component gases (P_n).

$$P_{\text{total}} = P_1 + P_2 + P_3 + \ldots$$

Equation 11.7 (page 531)   The total pressure of a gas mixture is equal to the total number of moles of gases multiplied by (RT/V).

$$P_{\text{total}} = (n_{\text{total}}) \left(\frac{RT}{V} \right)$$

Equation 11.8 (page 531)   The pressure of a gas (A) in a mixture is the product of its mole fraction (X_A) and the total pressure of the mixture.

$$P_A = X_A P_{\text{total}}$$

Equation 11.9 (page 536)   Maxwell's equation relates the rms speed ($\sqrt{u^2}$) to the molar mass of a gas (M) and its temperature (T).

$$\sqrt{u^2} = \sqrt{\frac{3RT}{M}}$$

Equation 11.10 (page 538)   Graham's law. The rate of effusion of a gas—the amount of material moving from one place to another in a given time—is inversely proportional to the square root of its molar mass.

$$\frac{\text{Rate of effusion of gas 1}}{\text{Rate of effusion of gas 2}} = \sqrt{\frac{\text{molar mass of gas 2}}{\text{molar mass of gas 1}}}$$

Equation 11.11 (page 543)   The van der Waals equation: Relates pressure, volume, temperature, and amount of gas for a nonideal gas.

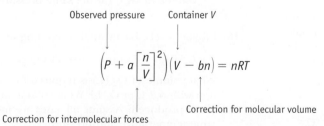

$$\left(P + a \left[\frac{n}{V} \right]^2 \right) (V - bn) = nRT$$

Observed pressure   Container V

Correction for intermolecular forces

Correction for molecular volume

STUDY QUESTIONS

OWL Online homework for this chapter may be assigned in OWL.

▲ denotes challenging questions.

■ denotes questions assignable in OWL.

Blue-numbered questions have answers in Appendix O and fully-worked solutions in the *Student Solutions Manual*.

PRACTICING SKILLS

Pressure
(See Example 11.1 and ChemistryNow Screen 11.2.)

1. ■ The pressure of a gas is 440 mm Hg. Express this pressure in units of (a) atmospheres, (b) bars, and (c) kilopascals.

2. The average barometric pressure at an altitude of 10 km is 210 mm Hg. Express this pressure in atmospheres, bars, and kilopascals.

3. Indicate which represents the higher pressure in each of the following pairs:
   (a) 534 mm Hg or 0.754 bar
   (b) 534 mm Hg or 650 kPa
   (c) 1.34 bar or 934 kPa

4. Put the following in order of increasing pressure: 363 mm Hg, 363 kPa, 0.256 atm, and 0.523 bar.

Boyle's Law and Charles's Law
(See Examples 11.2 and 11.3 and ChemistryNow Screen 11.3.)

5. A sample of nitrogen gas has a pressure of 67.5 mm Hg in a 500.-mL flask. What is the pressure of this gas sample when it is transferred to a 125-mL flask at the same temperature?

6. ■ A sample of CO_2 gas has a pressure of 56.5 mm Hg in a 125-mL flask. The sample is transferred to a new flask, where it has a pressure of 62.3 mm Hg at the same temperature. What is the volume of the new flask?

7. You have 3.5 L of NO at a temperature of 22.0 °C. What volume would the NO occupy at 37 °C? (Assume the pressure is constant.)

8. ■ A 5.0-mL sample of CO_2 gas is enclosed in a gas-tight syringe (see Figure 11.4) at 22 °C. If the syringe is immersed in an ice bath (0 °C), what is the new gas volume, assuming that the pressure is held constant?

The General Gas Law
(See Example 11.4.)

9. You have 3.6 L of H_2 gas at 380 mm Hg and 25 °C. What is the pressure of this gas if it is transferred to a 5.0-L flask at 0.0 °C?

10. ■ You have a sample of CO_2 in a flask A with a volume of 25.0 mL. At 20.5 °C, the pressure of the gas is 436.5 mm Hg. To find the volume of another flask, B, you move the CO_2 to that flask and find that its pressure is now 94.3 mm Hg at 24.5 °C. What is the volume of flask B?

11. You have a sample of gas in a flask with a volume of 250 mL. At 25.5 °C, the pressure of the gas is 360 mm Hg. If you decrease the temperature to −5.0 °C, what is the gas pressure at the lower temperature?

12. ■ A sample of gas occupies 135 mL at 22.5 °C; the pressure is 165 mm Hg. What is the pressure of the gas sample when it is placed in a 252-mL flask at a temperature of 0.0 °C?

13. One of the cylinders of an automobile engine has a volume of 400. cm^3. The engine takes in air at a pressure of 1.00 atm and a temperature of 15 °C and compresses the air to a volume of 50.0 cm^3 at 77 °C. What is the final pressure of the gas in the cylinder? (The ratio of before and after volumes—in this case, 400 : 50 or 8 : 1—is called the compression ratio.)

14. ■ A helium-filled balloon of the type used in long-distance flying contains 420,000 ft^3 (1.2×10^7 L) of helium. Suppose you fill the balloon with helium on the ground, where the pressure is 737 mm Hg and the temperature is 16.0 °C. When the balloon ascends to a height of 2 miles, where the pressure is only 600. mm Hg and the temperature is −33 °C, what volume is occupied by the helium gas? Assume the pressure inside the balloon matches the external pressure. Comment on the result.

Avogadro's Hypothesis
(See Example 11.5 and ChemistryNow Screen 11.3.)

15. Nitrogen monoxide reacts with oxygen to give nitrogen dioxide.

$$2\,NO(g) + O_2(g) \longrightarrow 2\,NO_2(g)$$

   (a) If you mix NO and O_2 in the correct stoichiometric ratio and NO has a volume of 150 mL, what volume of O_2 is required (at the same pressure and temperature)?
   (b) After reaction is complete between 150 mL of NO and the stoichiometric volume of O_2, what is the volume of NO_2 (at the same pressure and temperature)?

16. Ethane, C_2H_6, burns in air according to the equation

$$2\,C_2H_6(g) + 7\,O_2(g) \longrightarrow 4\,CO_2(g) + 6\,H_2O(g)$$

What volume of O_2 (L) is required for complete reaction with 5.2 L of C_2H_6? What volume of H_2O vapor (L) is produced? Assume all gases are measured at the same temperature and pressure.

Ideal Gaw Law
(See Example 11.6 and ChemistryNow Screen 11.4.)

17. A 1.25-g sample of CO_2 is contained in a 750.-mL flask at 22.5 °C. What is the pressure of the gas?

18. ■ A balloon holds 30.0 kg of helium. What is the volume of the balloon if the final pressure is 1.20 atm and the temperature is 22 °C?

19. A flask is first evacuated so that it contains no gas at all. Then, 2.2 g of CO_2 is introduced into the flask. On warming to 22 °C, the gas exerts a pressure of 318 mm Hg. What is the volume of the flask?

20. A steel cylinder holds 1.50 g of ethanol, C_2H_5OH. What is the pressure of the ethanol vapor if the cylinder has a volume of 251 cm^3 and the temperature is 250 °C? (Assume all of the ethanol is in the vapor phase at this temperature.)

21. A balloon for long-distance flying contains 1.2×10^7 L of helium. If the helium pressure is 737 mm Hg at 25 °C, what mass of helium (in grams) does the balloon contain? (See Study Question 14.)

22. ■ What mass of helium, in grams, is required to fill a 5.0-L balloon to a pressure of 1.1 atm at 25 °C?

Gas Density
(See Example 11.8 and ChemistryNow Screen 11.5.)

23. Forty miles above Earth's surface, the temperature is 250 K, and the pressure is only 0.20 mm Hg. What is the density of air (in grams per liter) at this altitude? (Assume the molar mass of air is 28.96 g/mol.)

24. ■ Diethyl ether, $(C_2H_5)_2O$, vaporizes easily at room temperature. If the vapor exerts a pressure of 233 mm Hg in a flask at 25 °C, what is the density of the vapor?

25. A gaseous organofluorine compound has a density of 0.355 g/L at 17 °C and 189 mm Hg. What is the molar mass of the compound?

26. ■ Chloroform is a common liquid used in the laboratory. It vaporizes readily. If the pressure of chloroform vapor in a flask is 195 mm Hg at 25.0 °C and the density of the vapor is 1.25 g/L, what is the molar mass of chloroform?

Ideal Gas Laws and Determining Molar Mass
(See Examples 11.7 and 11.8 and ChemistryNow Screen 11.6.)

27. A 1.007-g sample of an unknown gas exerts a pressure of 715 mm Hg in a 452-mL container at 23 °C. What is the molar mass of the gas?

28. ■ A 0.0125-g sample of a gas with an empirical formula of CHF_2 is placed in a 165-mL flask. It has a pressure of 13.7 mm Hg at 22.5 °C. What is the molecular formula of the compound?

29. A new boron hydride, B_xH_y, has been isolated. To find its molar mass, you measure the pressure of the gas in a known volume at a known temperature. The following experimental data are collected:

Mass of gas = 12.5 mg   Pressure of gas = 24.8 mm Hg

Temperature = 25 °C   Volume of flask = 125 mL

Which formula corresponds to the calculated molar mass?
(a) B_2H_6 (d) B_6H_{10}
(b) B_4H_{10} (e) $B_{10}H_{14}$
(c) B_5H_9

30. ■ Acetaldehyde is a common liquid compound that vaporizes readily. Determine the molar mass of acetaldehyde from the following data:

Sample mass = 0.107 g   Volume of gas = 125 mL

Temperature = 0.0 °C   Pressure = 331 mm Hg

Gas Laws and Stoichiometry
(See Examples 11.9 and 11.10 and ChemistryNow Screen 11.7.)

31. Iron reacts with hydrochloric acid to produce iron(II) chloride and hydrogen gas:

$$Fe(s) + 2\ HCl(aq) \rightarrow FeCl_2(aq) + H_2(g)$$

The H_2 gas from the reaction of 2.2 g of iron with excess acid is collected in a 10.0-L flask at 25 °C. What is the pressure of the H_2 gas in this flask?

32. ■ Silane, SiH_4, reacts with O_2 to give silicon dioxide and water:

$$SiH_4(g) + 2\ O_2(g) \rightarrow SiO_2(s) + 2\ H_2O(\ell)$$

A 5.20-L sample of SiH_4 gas at 356 mm Hg pressure and 25 °C is allowed to react with O_2 gas. What volume of O_2 gas, in liters, is required for complete reaction if the oxygen has a pressure of 425 mm Hg at 25 °C?

33. Sodium azide, the explosive compound in automobile air bags, decomposes according to the following equation:

$$2\ NaN_3(s) \rightarrow 2\ Na(s) + 3\ N_2(g)$$

What mass of sodium azide is required to provide the nitrogen needed to inflate a 75.0-L bag to a pressure of 1.3 atm at 25 °C?

34. ■ The hydrocarbon octane (C_8H_{18}) burns to give CO_2 and water vapor:

$$2\ C_8H_{18}(g) + 25\ O_2(g) \rightarrow 16\ CO_2(g) + 18\ H_2O(g)$$

If a 0.048-g sample of octane burns completely in O_2, what will be the pressure of water vapor in a 4.75-L flask at 30.0 °C? If the O_2 gas needed for complete combustion was contained in a 4.75-L flask at 22 °C, what would its pressure be?

35. Hydrazine reacts with O_2 according to the following equation:

$$N_2H_4(g) + O_2(g) \rightarrow N_2(g) + 2\ H_2O(\ell)$$

Assume the O_2 needed for the reaction is in a 450-L tank at 23 °C. What must the oxygen pressure be in the tank to have enough oxygen to consume 1.00 kg of hydrazine completely?

36. A self-contained underwater breathing apparatus uses canisters containing potassium superoxide. The superoxide consumes the CO_2 exhaled by a person and replaces it with oxygen.

$$4\ KO_2(s) + 2\ CO_2(g) \rightarrow 2\ K_2CO_3(s) + 3\ O_2(g)$$

What mass of KO_2, in grams, is required to react with 8.90 L of CO_2 at 22.0 °C and 767 mm Hg?

Gas Mixtures and Dalton's Law
(See Example 11.11 and ChemistryNow Screen 11.8.)

37. What is the total pressure in atmospheres of a gas mixture that contains 1.0 g of H_2 and 8.0 g of Ar in a 3.0-L container at 27 °C? What are the partial pressures of the two gases?

38. A cylinder of compressed gas is labeled "Composition (mole %): 4.5% H_2S, 3.0% CO_2, balance N_2." The pressure gauge attached to the cylinder reads 46 atm. Calculate the partial pressure of each gas, in atmospheres, in the cylinder.

39. ■ A halothane–oxygen mixture ($C_2HBrClF_3 + O_2$) can be used as an anesthetic. A tank containing such a mixture has the following partial pressures: P (halothane) = 170 mm Hg and P (O_2) = 570 mm Hg.
  (a) What is the ratio of the number of moles of halothane to the number of moles of O_2?
  (b) If the tank contains 160 g of O_2, what mass of $C_2HBrClF_3$ is present?

40. ■ A collapsed balloon is filled with He to a volume of 12.5 L at a pressure of 1.00 atm. Oxygen, O_2, is then added so that the final volume of the balloon is 26 L with a total pressure of 1.00 atm. The temperature, which remains constant throughout, is 21.5 °C.
  (a) What mass of He does the balloon contain?
  (b) What is the final partial pressure of He in the balloon?
  (c) What is the partial pressure of O_2 in the balloon?
  (d) What is the mole fraction of each gas?

Kinetic-Molecular Theory
(See Section 11.6, Example 11.12, and ChemistryNow Screens 11.9–11.12.)

41. ■ You have two flasks of equal volume. Flask A contains H_2 at 0 °C and 1 atm pressure. Flask B contains CO_2 gas at 25 °C and 2 atm pressure. Compare these two gases with respect to each of the following:
  (a) average kinetic energy per molecule
  (b) average molecular velocity
  (c) number of molecules
  (d) mass of gas

42. Equal masses of gaseous N_2 and Ar are placed in separate flasks of equal volume at the same temperature. Tell whether each of the following statements is true or false. Briefly explain your answer in each case.
  (a) There are more molecules of N_2 present than atoms of Ar.
  (b) The pressure is greater in the Ar flask.
  (c) The Ar atoms have a greater average speed than the N_2 molecules.
  (d) The N_2 molecules collide more frequently with the walls of the flask than do the Ar atoms.

43. If the speed of an oxygen molecule is 4.28×10^4 cm/s at 25 °C, what is the speed of a CO_2 molecule at the same temperature?

44. Calculate the rms speed for CO molecules at 25 °C. What is the ratio of this speed to that of Ar atoms at the same temperature?

45. ■ Place the following gases in order of increasing average molecular speed at 25 °C: Ar, CH_4, N_2, CH_2F_2.

46. The reaction of SO_2 with Cl_2 gives dichlorine oxide, which is used to bleach wood pulp and to treat wastewater:

$$SO_2(g) + 2\ Cl_2(g) \rightarrow OSCl_2(g) + Cl_2O(g)$$

All of the compounds involved in the reaction are gases. List them in order of increasing average speed.

Diffusion and Effusion
(See Example 11.13 and ChemistryNow Screen 11.12.)

47. ■ In each pair of gases below, tell which will effuse faster:
  (a) CO_2 or F_2
  (b) O_2 or N_2
  (c) C_2H_4 or C_2H_6
  (d) two chlorofluorocarbons: $CFCl_3$ or $C_2Cl_2F_4$

48. Argon gas is 10 times denser than helium gas at the same temperature and pressure. Which gas is predicted to effuse faster? How much faster?

49. A gas whose molar mass you wish to know effuses through an opening at a rate one third as fast as that of helium gas. What is the molar mass of the unknown gas?

50. ▲ A sample of uranium fluoride is found to effuse at the rate of 17.7 mg/h. Under comparable conditions, gaseous I_2 effuses at the rate of 15.0 mg/h. What is the molar mass of the uranium fluoride? (*Hint:* Rates must be converted to units of moles per time.)

Nonideal Gases
(See Section 11.9.)

51. ■ In the text, it is stated that the pressure of 4.00 mol of Cl_2 in a 4.00-L tank at 100.0 °C should be 26.0 atm if calculated using the van der Waals equation. Verify this result, and compare it with the pressure predicted by the ideal gas law.

▲ more challenging ■ in OWL Blue-numbered questions answered in Appendix O

52. ■ You want to store 165 g of CO_2 gas in a 12.5-L tank at room temperature (25 °C). Calculate the pressure the gas would have using (a) the ideal gas law and (b) the van der Waals equation. (For CO_2, $a = 3.59$ atm · L^2/mol^2 and $b = 0.0427$ L/mol.)

General Questions

These questions are not designated as to type or location in the chapter. They may combine several concepts.

53. Complete the following table:

	atm	mm Hg	kPa	bar
Standard atmosphere	____	____	____	____
Partial pressure of N_2 in the atmosphere	____	593	____	____
Tank of compressed H_2	____	____	____	133
Atmospheric pressure at the top of Mount Everest	____	____	33.7	____

54. On combustion, 1.0 L of a gaseous compound of hydrogen, carbon, and nitrogen gives 2.0 L of CO_2, 3.5 L of H_2O vapor, and 0.50 L of N_2 at STP. What is the empirical formula of the compound?

55. ▲ You have a sample of helium gas at −33 °C, and you want to increase the average speed of helium atoms by 10.0%. To what temperature should the gas be heated to accomplish this?

56. If 12.0 g of O_2 is required to inflate a balloon to a certain size at 27 °C, what mass of O_2 is required to inflate it to the same size (and pressure) at 5.0 °C?

57. Butyl mercaptan, C_4H_9SH, has a very bad odor and is among the compounds added to natural gas to help detect a leak of otherwise odorless natural gas. In an experiment, you burn 95.0 mg of C_4H_9SH and collect the product gases (SO_2, CO_2, and H_2O) in a 5.25 L flask at 25 °C. What is the total gas pressure in the flask, and what is the partial pressure of each of the product gases?

58. A bicycle tire has an internal volume of 1.52 L and contains 0.406 mol of air. The tire will burst if its internal pressure reaches 7.25 atm. To what temperature, in degrees Celsius, does the air in the tire need to be heated to cause a blowout?

59. ■ The temperature of the atmosphere on Mars can be as high as 27 °C at the equator at noon, and the atmospheric pressure is about 8 mm Hg. If a spacecraft could collect 10. m^3 of this atmosphere, compress it to a small volume, and send it back to Earth, how many moles would the sample contain?

60. If you place 2.25 g of solid silicon in a 6.56-L flask that contains CH_3Cl with a pressure of 585 mm Hg at

25 °C, what mass of dimethyldichlorosilane, $(CH_3)_2SiCl_2(g)$, can be formed?

$$Si(s) + 2\ CH_3Cl(g) \rightarrow (CH_3)_2SiCl_2(g)$$

What pressure of $(CH_3)_2SiCl_2(g)$ would you expect in this same flask at 95 °C on completion of the reaction? (Dimethyldichlorosilane is one starting material used to make silicones, polymeric substances used as lubricants, antistick agents, and water-proofing caulk.)

61. $Ni(CO)_4$ can be made by reacting finely divided nickel with gaseous CO. If you have CO in a 1.50-L flask at a pressure of 418 mm Hg at 25.0 °C, along with 0.450 g of Ni powder, what is the theoretical yield of $Ni(CO)_4$?

62. The gas B_2H_6 burns in air to give H_2O and B_2O_3.

$$B_2H_6(g) + 3\ O_2(g) \rightarrow B_2O_3(s) + 3\ H_2O(g)$$

(a) Three gases are involved in this reaction. Place them in order of increasing rms speed. (Assume all are at the same temperature.)
(b) A 3.26-L flask contains B_2H_6 at a pressure of 256 mm Hg and a temperature of 25 °C. Suppose O_2 gas is added to the flask until B_2H_6 and O_2 are in the correct stoichiometric ratio for the combustion reaction. At this point, what is the partial pressure of O_2?

63. ■ You have four gas samples:
1. 1.0 L of H_2 at STP
2. 1.0 L of Ar at STP
3. 1.0 L of H_2 at 27 °C and 760 mm Hg
4. 1.0 L of He at 0 °C and 900 mm Hg

(a) Which sample has the largest number of gas particles (atoms or molecules)?
(b) Which sample contains the smallest number of particles?
(c) Which sample represents the largest mass?

64. Propane reacts with oxygen to give carbon dioxide and water vapor.

$$C_3H_8(g) + 5\ O_2(g) \rightarrow 3\ CO_2(g) + 4\ H_2O(g)$$

If you mix C_3H_8 and O_2 in the correct stoichiometric ratio, and if the total pressure of the mixture is 288 mm Hg, what are the partial pressures of C_3H_8 and O_2? If the temperature and volume do not change, what is the pressure of the water vapor?

65. ■ Iron carbonyl can be made by the direct reaction of iron metal and carbon monoxide.

$$Fe(s) + 5\ CO(g) \rightarrow Fe(CO)_5(\ell)$$

What is the theoretical yield of $Fe(CO)_5$ if 3.52 g of iron is treated with CO gas having a pressure of 732 mm Hg in a 5.50-L flask at 23 °C?

66. ■ Analysis of a gaseous chlorofluorocarbon, CCl_xF_y, shows that it contains 11.79% C and 69.57% Cl. In another experiment, you find that 0.107 g of the compound fills a 458-mL flask at 25 °C with a pressure of 21.3 mm Hg. What is the molecular formula of the compound?

67. There are five compounds in the family of sulfur–fluorine compounds with the general formula S_xF_y. One of these compounds is 25.23% S. If you place 0.0955 g of the compound in a 89-mL flask at 45 °C, the pressure of the gas is 83.8 mm Hg. What is the molecular formula of S_xF_y?

68. A miniature volcano can be made in the laboratory with ammonium dichromate. When ignited, it decomposes in a fiery display.

$$(NH_4)_2Cr_2O_7(s) \rightarrow N_2(g) + 4\ H_2O(g) + Cr_2O_3(s)$$

If 0.95 g of ammonium dichromate is used and if the gases from this reaction are trapped in a 15.0-L flask at 23 °C, what is the total pressure of the gas in the flask? What are the partial pressures of N_2 and H_2O?

Thermal decomposition of $(NH_4)_2Cr_2O_7$.

69. The density of air 20 km above the earth's surface is 92 g/m³. The pressure of the atmosphere is 42 mm Hg, and the temperature is −63 °C.
   (a) What is the average molar mass of the atmosphere at this altitude?
   (b) If the atmosphere at this altitude consists of only O_2 and N_2, what is the mole fraction of each gas?

70. ■ A 3.0-L bulb containing He at 145 mm Hg is connected by a valve to a 2.0-L bulb containing Ar at 355 mm Hg. (See the accompanying figure.) Calculate the partial pressure of each gas and the total pressure after the valve between the flasks is opened.

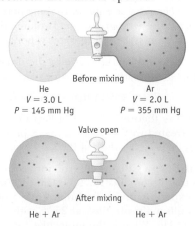

Before mixing

He
V = 3.0 L
P = 145 mm Hg

Ar
V = 2.0 L
P = 355 mm Hg

Valve open

After mixing

He + Ar

He + Ar

71. Chlorine dioxide, ClO_2, reacts with fluorine to give a new gas that contains Cl, O, and F. In an experiment, you find that 0.150 g of this new gas has a pressure of 17.2 mm Hg in a 1850-mL flask at 21 °C. What is the identity of the unknown gas?

72. A xenon fluoride can be prepared by heating a mixture of Xe and F_2 gases to a high temperature in a pressure-proof container. Assume that xenon gas was added to a 0.25-L container until its pressure reached 0.12 atm at 0.0 °C. Fluorine gas was then added until the total pressure reached 0.72 atm at 0.0 °C. After the reaction was complete, the xenon was consumed completely, and the pressure of the F_2 remaining in the container was 0.36 atm at 0.0 °C. What is the empirical formula of the xenon fluoride?

73. ■ A balloon at the circus is filled with helium gas to a gauge pressure of 22 mm Hg at 25 °C. The volume of the gas is 305 mL, and the barometric pressure is 755 mm Hg. What amount of helium is in the balloon? (Remember that gauge pressure = total pressure − barometric pressure. See page 517.)

74. If you have a sample of water in a closed container, some of the water will evaporate until the pressure of the water vapor, at 25 °C, is 23.8 mm Hg. How many molecules of water per cubic centimeter exist in the vapor phase?

75. You are given 1.56 g of a mixture of $KClO_3$ and KCl. When heated, the $KClO_3$ decomposes to KCl and O_2,

$$2\ KClO_3(s) \rightarrow 2\ KCl(s) + 3\ O_2(g)$$

and 327 mL of O_2 with a pressure of 735 mm Hg is collected at 19 °C. What is the weight percentage of $KClO_3$ in the sample?

76. ▲ ■ A study of climbers who reached the summit of Mount Everest without supplemental oxygen showed that the partial pressures of O_2 and CO_2 in their lungs were 35 mm Hg and 7.5 mm Hg, respectively. The barometric pressure at the summit was 253 mm Hg. Assume the lung gases are saturated with moisture at a body temperature of 37 °C [which means the partial pressure of water vapor in the lungs is $P\,(H_2O) = 47.1$ mm Hg]. If you assume the lung gases consist of only O_2, N_2, CO_2, and H_2O, what is the partial pressure of N_2?

77. Nitrogen monoxide reacts with oxygen to give nitrogen dioxide:

$$2\ NO(g) + O_2(g) \rightarrow 2\ NO_2(g)$$

   (a) Place the three gases in order of increasing rms speed at 298 K.
   (b) If you mix NO and O_2 in the correct stoichiometric ratio and NO has a partial pressure of 150 mm Hg, what is the partial pressure of O_2?
   (c) After reaction between NO and O_2 is complete, what is the pressure of NO_2 if the NO originally had a pressure of 150 mm Hg and O_2 was added in the correct stoichiometric amount?

▲ more challenging   ■ in OWL   Blue-numbered questions answered in Appendix O

78. ▲ ■ Ammonia gas is synthesized by combining hydrogen and nitrogen:

$$3 H_2(g) + N_2(g) \rightarrow 2 NH_3(g)$$

(a) If you want to produce 562 g of NH_3, what volume of H_2 gas, at 56 °C and 745 mm Hg, is required?

(b) To produce 562 g of NH_3, what volume of air (the source of N_2) is required if the air is introduced at 29 °C and 745 mm Hg? (Assume the air sample has 78.1 mole % N_2.)

79. Nitrogen trifluoride is prepared by the reaction of ammonia and fluorine.

$$4 NH_3(g) + 3 F_2(g) \rightarrow 3 NH_4F(s) + NF_3(g)$$

If you mix NH_3 with F_2 in the correct stoichiometric ratio, and if the total pressure of the mixture is 120 mm Hg, what are the partial pressures of NH_3 and F_2? When the reactants have been completely consumed, what is the total pressure in the flask? (Assume T is constant.)

80. Chlorine trifluoride, ClF_3, is a valuable reagent because it can be used to convert metal oxides to metal fluorides:

$$6 NiO(s) + 4 ClF_3(g) \rightarrow 6 NiF_2(s) + 2 Cl_2(g) + 3 O_2(g)$$

(a) What mass of NiO will react with ClF_3 gas if the gas has a pressure of 250 mm Hg at 20 °C in a 2.5-L flask?

(b) If the ClF_3 described in part (a) is completely consumed, what are the partial pressures of Cl_2 and of O_2 in the 2.5-L flask at 20 °C (in mm Hg)? What is the total pressure in the flask?

81. ▲ ■ Relative humidity is the ratio of the partial pressure of water in air at a given temperature to the vapor pressure of water at that temperature. Calculate the mass of water per liter of air under the following conditions:
(a) at 20 °C and 45% relative humidity
(b) at 0 °C and 95% relative humidity

Under which circumstances is the mass of H_2O per liter greater? (See Appendix G for the vapor pressure of water.)

82. ■ How much water vapor is present in a dormitory room when the relative humidity is 55% and the temperature is 23 °C? The dimensions of the room are 4.5 m^2 floor area and 3.5 m ceiling height. (See Study Question 81 for a definition of relative humidity and Appendix G for the vapor pressure of water.)

In the Laboratory

83. ▲ ■ You have a 550.-mL tank of gas with a pressure of 1.56 atm at 24 °C. You thought the gas was pure carbon monoxide gas, CO, but you later found it was contaminated by small quantities of gaseous CO_2 and O_2. Analysis shows that the tank pressure is 1.34 atm (at 24 °C) if the CO_2 is removed. Another experiment shows that 0.0870 g of O_2 can be removed chemically. What are the masses of CO and CO_2 in the tank, and what is the partial pressure of each of the three gases at 25 °C?

84. ▲ ■ Methane is burned in a laboratory Bunsen burner to give CO_2 and water vapor. Methane gas is supplied to the burner at the rate of 5.0 L/min (at a temperature of 28 °C and a pressure of 773 mm Hg). At what rate must oxygen be supplied to the burner (at a pressure of 742 mm Hg and a temperature of 26 °C)?

85. ▲ ■ Iron forms a series of compounds of the type $Fe_x(CO)_y$. In air, they are oxidized to Fe_2O_3 and CO_2 gas. After heating a 0.142-g sample of $Fe_x(CO)_y$ in air, you isolate the CO_2 in a 1.50-L flask at 25 °C. The pressure of the gas is 44.9 mm Hg. What is the empirical formula of $Fe_x(CO)_y$?

86. ▲ ■ Group 2A metal carbonates are decomposed to the metal oxide and CO_2 on heating:

$$MCO_3(s) \rightarrow MO(s) + CO_2(g)$$

You heat 0.158 g of a white, solid carbonate of a Group 2A metal (M) and find that the evolved CO_2 has a pressure of 69.8 mm Hg in a 285-mL flask at 25 °C. Identify M.

87. One way to synthesize diborane, B_2H_6, is the reaction

$$2 NaBH_4(s) + 2 H_3PO_4(aq) \rightarrow$$
$$B_2H_6(g) + 2 NaH_2PO_4(aq) + 2 H_2(g)$$

(a) If you have 0.136 g of $NaBH_4$ and excess H_3PO_4, and you collect the B_2H_6 in a 2.75 L flask at 25 °C, what is the pressure of the B_2H_6 in the flask?

(b) A by-product of the reaction is H_2 gas. If both B_2H_6 and H_2 gas come from this reaction, what is the *total* pressure in the 2.75-L flask (after reaction of 0.136 g of $NaBH_4$ with excess H_3PO_4) at 25 °C?

88. ■ You are given a solid mixture of $NaNO_2$ and NaCl and are asked to analyze it for the amount of $NaNO_2$ present. To do so, you allow the mixture to react with sulfamic acid, HSO_3NH_2, in water according to the equation

$$NaNO_2(aq) + HSO_3NH_2(aq) \rightarrow$$
$$NaHSO_4(aq) + H_2O(\ell) + N_2(g)$$

What is the weight percentage of $NaNO_2$ in 1.232 g of the solid mixture if reaction with sulfamic acid produces 295 mL of N_2 gas with a pressure of 713 mm Hg at 21.0 °C?

89. ▲ You have 1.249 g of a mixture of $NaHCO_3$ and Na_2CO_3. You find that 12.0 mL of 1.50 M HCl is required to convert the sample completely to NaCl, H_2O, and CO_2.

$$NaHCO_3(aq) + HCl(aq) \rightarrow$$
$$NaCl(aq) + H_2O(\ell) + CO_2(g)$$

$$Na_2CO_3(aq) + 2 HCl(aq) \rightarrow$$
$$2 NaCl(aq) + H_2O(\ell) + CO_2(g)$$

What volume of CO_2 is evolved at 745 mm Hg and 25 °C?

90. ▲ ■ A mixture of $NaHCO_3$ and Na_2CO_3 has a mass of 2.50 g. When treated with HCl(aq), 665 mL of CO_2 gas is liberated with a pressure of 735 mm Hg at 25 °C. What is the weight percent of $NaHCO_3$ and Na_2CO_3 in the mixture? (See Study Question 89 for the reactions that occur.)

91. ▲ Many nitrate salts can be decomposed by heating. For example, blue, anhydrous copper(II) nitrate produces nitrogen dioxide and oxygen when heated. In the laboratory, you find that a sample of this salt produced 0.195 g of mixture of NO_2 and O_2 with a pressure of 725 mm Hg at 35 °C in a 125-mL flask (and black, solid CuO was left as a residue). What is the average molar mass of the gas mixture? What are the mole fractions of NO_2 and O_2? What amount of each gas is in the mixture? Do these amounts reflect the relative amounts of NO_2 and O_2 expected based on the balanced equation? Is it possible that the fact that some NO_2 molecules combine to give N_2O_4 plays a role?

Charles D. Winters

Heating copper(II) nitrate produces nitrogen dioxide and oxygen gas and leaves a residue of copper(II) oxide.

92. ▲ ■ A compound containing C, H, N, and O is burned in excess oxygen. The gases produced by burning 0.1152 g are first treated to convert the nitrogen-containing product gases into N_2, and then the resulting mixture of CO_2, H_2O, N_2, and excess O_2 is passed through a bed of $CaCl_2$ to absorb the water. The $CaCl_2$ increases in mass by 0.09912 g. The remaining gases are bubbled into water to form H_2CO_3, and this solution is titrated with 0.3283 M NaOH; 28.81 mL is required to achieve the second equivalence point. The excess O_2 gas is removed by reaction with copper metal (to give CuO). Finally, the N_2 gas is collected in a 225.0-mL flask, where it has a pressure of 65.12 mm Hg at 25 °C. In a separate experiment, the unknown compound is found to have a molar mass of 150 g/mol. What are the empirical and molecular formulas of the unknown compound?

Summary and Conceptual Questions

The following questions may use concepts from the previous chapters.

93. A 1.0-L flask contains 10.0 g each of O_2 and CO_2 at 25 °C.
  (a) Which gas has the greater partial pressure, O_2 or CO_2, or are they the same?
  (b) Which molecules have the greater average speed, or are they the same?
  (c) Which molecules have the greater average kinetic energy, or are they the same?

94. If equal masses of O_2 and N_2 are placed in separate containers of equal volume at the same temperature, which of the following statements is true? If false, tell why it is false.
  (a) The pressure in the flask containing N_2 is greater than that in the flask containing O_2.
  (b) There are more molecules in the flask containing O_2 than in the flask containing N_2.

95. You have two pressure-proof steel cylinders of equal volume, one containing 1.0 kg of CO and the other containing 1.0 kg of acetylene, C_2H_2.
  (a) In which cylinder is the pressure greater at 25 °C?
  (b) Which cylinder contains the greater number of molecules?

96. ■ Two flasks, each with a volume of 1.00 L, contain O_2 gas with a pressure of 380 mm Hg. Flask A is at 25 °C, and flask B is at 0 °C. Which flask contains the greater number of O_2 molecules?

97. ▲ State whether each of the following samples of matter is a gas. If there is not enough information for you to decide, write "insufficient information."
  (a) A material is in a steel tank at 100 atm pressure. When the tank is opened to the atmosphere, the material suddenly expands, increasing its volume by 10%.
  (b) A 1.0-mL sample of material weighs 8.2 g.
  (c) The material is transparent and pale green in color.
  (d) One cubic meter of material contains as many molecules as 1.0 m³ of air at the same temperature and pressure.

98. Each of the four tires of a car is filled with a different gas. Each tire has the same volume, and each is filled to the same pressure, 3.0 atm, at 25 °C. One tire contains 116 g of air, another tire has 80.7 g of neon, another tire has 16.0 g of helium, and the fourth tire has 160. g of an unknown gas.
  (a) Do all four tires contain the same number of gas molecules? If not, which one has the greatest number of molecules?
  (b) How many times heavier is a molecule of the unknown gas than an atom of helium?
  (c) In which tire do the molecules have the largest kinetic energy? The highest average speed?

▲ more challenging ■ in OWL Blue-numbered questions answered in Appendix O

99. You have two gas-filled balloons, one containing He and the other containing H_2. The H_2 balloon is twice the size of the He balloon. The pressure of gas in the H_2 balloon is 1 atm, and that in the He balloon is 2 atm. The H_2 balloon is outside in the snow (-5 °C), and the He balloon is inside a warm building (23 °C).
    (a) Which balloon contains the greater number of molecules?
    (b) Which balloon contains the greater mass of gas?

100. The sodium azide required for automobile air bags is made by the reaction of sodium metal with dinitrogen oxide in liquid ammonia:

$$3 N_2O(g) + 4 Na(s) + NH_3(\ell) \rightarrow$$
$$NaN_3(s) + 3 NaOH(s) + 2 N_2(g)$$

    (a) You have 65.0 g of sodium and a 35.0-L flask containing N_2O gas with a pressure of 2.12 atm at 23 °C. What is the theoretical yield (in grams) of NaN_3?
    (b) Draw a Lewis structure for the azide ion. Include all possible resonance structures. Which resonance structure is most likely?
    (c) What is the shape of the azide ion?

101. ■ If the absolute temperature of a gas doubles, by how much does the average speed of the gaseous molecules increase? (See ChemistryNow Screen 11.9.)

102. ▲ Chlorine gas (Cl_2) is used as a disinfectant in municipal water supplies, although chlorine dioxide (ClO_2) and ozone are becoming more widely used. ClO_2 is a better choice than Cl_2 in this application because it leads to fewer chlorinated by-products, which are themselves pollutants.
    (a) How many valence electrons are in ClO_2?
    (b) The chlorite ion, ClO_2^-, is obtained by reducing ClO_2. Draw a possible electron dot structure for ClO_2^-. (Cl is the central atom.)
    (c) What is the hybridization of the central Cl atom in ClO_2^-? What is the shape of the ion?
    (d) Which species has the larger bond angle, O_3 or ClO_2^-? Explain briefly.
    (e) Chlorine dioxide, ClO_2, a yellow-green gas, can be made by the reaction of chlorine with sodium chlorite:

$$2 NaClO_2(s) + Cl_2(g) \rightarrow 2 NaCl(s) + 2 ClO_2(g)$$

Assume you react 15.6 g of $NaClO_2$ with chlorine gas, which has a pressure of 1050 mm Hg in a 1.45-L flask at 22 °C. What mass of ClO_2 can be produced?

12 | Intermolecular Forces and Liquids

John Kotz

Antarctica Scene—Icebergs, Penguins, Snow, Ice, and Fog

Antarctica is a place of unique wonder and beauty. Aside from the living creatures—many species of penguins, whales, and birds—one mostly thinks of ice and icebergs. Some icebergs are as large as a small state, while others are only the size of a football field. We all know ice floats on water, but what is the reason for this?

Questions:

1. Given the density of seawater ($d = 1.026$ g/mL) and of ice ($d = 0.917$ g/cm^3), is most of the volume of an iceberg above or below the waterline?
2. What volume is above or below the waterline?

Answers to these questions are in Appendix Q.

Hundreds of common compounds can exist in the liquid and vapor states at or near room temperature and under ordinary pressures, and the one that comes to mind immediately is water. Water molecules in the atmosphere can interact at lower temperatures and come together to form clouds or fog, and still larger clusters of molecules eventually can fall as rain drops. At only slightly lower temperatures, the molecules assemble into a crystalline lattice, which you see as snowflakes and ice.

The primary objectives of this chapter are to examine the intermolecular forces that allow molecules to interact and then to look at liquids, a result of such interactions. You will find this a useful chapter because it explains, among other things, why your body is cooled when you sweat and why ice can float on liquid water, a property shared by almost no other substance in its liquid and solid states.

12.1 States of Matter and Intermolecular Forces

The kinetic-molecular theory of gases (◀ Section 11.6) assumes that gas molecules or atoms are widely separated and that these particles can be considered to be independent of one another. Consequently, we can relate the properties of gases under most conditions by a simple mathematical equation, $PV = nRT$, known as the ideal gas law equation (Equation 11.4). In real gases, however, there are forces between molecules—intermolecular forces—and these require a more complex analysis of gas behavior (◀ page 543). If these intermolecular forces become strong enough, the substance can condense to a liquid and eventually to a solid. For liquids in particular, the existence of intermolecular forces makes the picture more complex, and it is not possible to create a simple "ideal liquid equation."

How different are the states of matter at the particulate level? We can get a sense of this by comparing the volumes occupied by equal numbers of molecules of a material in different states. Figure 12.1a shows a flask containing about 300 mL of liquid nitrogen. If all of the liquid were allowed to evaporate, the gaseous nitrogen, at 1 atm and room temperature, would fill a large balloon (more than 200 L). A great amount of space exists between molecules in a gas, whereas in liquids the molecules are close together.

The increase in volume when converting liquids to gases is strikingly large. In contrast, no dramatic change in volume occurs when a solid is converted to a liquid. Figure 12.1b shows the same amount of liquid and solid benzene, C_6H_6, side by side. As you see, they are not appreciably different in volume. This means that the atoms in the liquid are packed together about as tightly as the atoms in the solid phase.

Chemistry॰ꙮ॰Now™

Throughout the text this icon introduces an opportunity for self-study or to explore interactive tutorials by signing in at **www.cengage.com/login**.

John Kotz

Early morning fog over Lake Champlain in upstate New York.

■ **The Lotus Effect** The photograph on the cover of this book illustrates the importance of intermolecular forces. You can read about the lotus effect on the back of the title page and on the back cover of the book.

FIGURE 12.1 Contrasting gases, liquids, and solids. (a) When a 300-mL sample of liquid nitrogen evaporates, it will produce more than 200 L of gas at 25 °C and 1.0 atm. In the liquid phase, the molecules of N_2 are close together; in the gas phase, they are far apart. (b) The same volume of liquid benzene, C_6H_6, is placed in two test tubes, and one tube (right) is cooled, freezing the liquid. The solid and liquid states have almost the same volume, showing that the molecules are packed together almost as tightly in the liquid state as they are in the solid state.

Nitrogen gas

Liquid nitrogen

(a)

Liquid benzene   Solid benzene

(b)

Photos: Charles D. Winters

We know that gases can be compressed easily, a process that involves forcing the gas molecules much closer together. In contrast, the molecules, ions, or atoms in liquid or solid phases strongly resist forces that would push them even closer together. Lack of compressibility is a characteristic property of liquids and solids. For example, the volume of liquid water changes only by 0.005% per atmosphere of pressure applied.

Intermolecular forces influence chemistry in many ways:

- They are directly related to properties such as melting point, boiling point, and the energy needed to convert a solid to a liquid or a liquid to a vapor.
- They are important in determining the solubility of gases, liquids, and solids in various solvents.
- They are crucial in determining the structures of biologically important molecules such as DNA and proteins.

Bonding in ionic compounds depends on the electrostatic forces of attraction between oppositely charged ions. Similarly, the intermolecular forces attracting one molecule to another are electrostatic. By comparison, the attractive forces between the ions in ionic compounds are usually in the range of 700 to 1100 kJ/mol, and most covalent bond energies are in the range of 100 to 400 kJ/mol (Table 8.9). As a rough guideline, intermolecular forces are generally less than about 15% of the values of bond energies. Nonetheless, these interactions can have a profound effect on molecular properties and are the subject of this section.

The sections that follow are organized around the polarity of the molecules involved. We shall first describe forces involving polar molecules and then those involving nonpolar molecules. In Chapter 13, we shall describe ionic and metallic solids and the bonding in those substances.

Chemistry •☸• Now™

Sign in at **www.cengage.com/login** and go to Chapter 12 Contents to see:
- Screen 12.2 to view an animation of **gases, liquids, and solids at the molecular level**
- Screen 12.3 for an outline of **the important intermolecular forces**

12.2 Intermolecular Forces Involving Polar Molecules

Interactions Between Ions and Molecules with a Permanent Dipole

The distribution of bonding electrons in a molecule often results in a permanent dipole moment (◄ Section 8.7). Because polar molecules have positive and negative ends, if a polar molecule and an ionic compound are mixed, the negative end of the dipole will be attracted to a positive cation (Figure 12.2). Similarly, the positive end of the dipole will be attracted to a negative anion. Forces of attraction between a positive or negative ion and polar molecules—**ion–dipole forces**—are less than those for ion–ion attractions (which can be on the order of 500 kJ/mol), but they are greater than other types of forces between molecules, whether polar or nonpolar.

Ion–dipole attractions can be evaluated based on Coulomb's law (◄ Equation 2.3), which informs us that the force of attraction between two charged objects depends on the product of their charges divided by the square of the distance between them (◄ Section 2.7). Therefore, when a polar molecule encounters an ion, the attractive forces depend on three factors:

- The distance between the ion and the dipole. The closer the ion and dipole, the stronger the attraction.
- The charge on the ion. The higher the ion charge, the stronger the attraction.
- The magnitude of the dipole. The greater the magnitude of the dipole, the stronger the attraction.

The formation of hydrated ions in aqueous solution is one of the most important examples of the interaction between an ion and a polar molecule (Figure 12.3) The enthalpy change associated with the hydration of ions—which is generally called the **enthalpy of solvation** or, for ions in water, the **enthalpy of hydration**—is substantial. The solvation enthalpy for an individual ion cannot be measured directly, but values can be estimated. For example, the hydration of sodium ions is described by the following reaction:

$$Na^+(g) + x\,H_2O(\ell) \rightarrow [Na(H_2O)_x]^+(aq) \;\; (x \text{ probably} = 6) \qquad \Delta_rH° = -405 \text{ kJ/mol}$$

The enthalpy of hydration depends on $1/d$, where d is the distance between the center of the ion and the oppositely charged "pole" of the dipole.

As the ion radius becomes larger, d increases, and the enthalpy of hydration becomes less exothermic. This trend is illustrated by the enthalpies of hydration of the alkali metal cations (Table 12.1) and by those for Mg^{2+}, Li^+, and K^+ (Figure 12.3). It is interesting to compare these values with the enthalpy of hydration of the

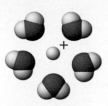

Water surrounding
a cation

Water surrounding
an anion

■ **Coulomb's Law** The **force** of attraction between oppositely charged particles depends directly on the product of their charges and inversely on the square of the distance (d) between the ions ($1/d^2$) (Equation 2.3, page 78). The **energy** of the attraction is also proportional to the charge product, but it is inversely proportional to the distance between them ($1/d$).

FIGURE 12.3 Enthalpy of hydration. The energy evolved when an ion is hydrated depends on the dipole moment of water, the ion charge, and the distance d between centers of the ion and the polar water molecule. The distance d increases as ion size increases.

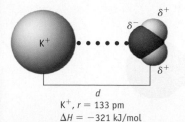

d

K^+, $r = 133$ pm
$\Delta H = -321$ kJ/mol

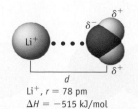

d
Li^+, $r = 78$ pm
$\Delta H = -515$ kJ/mol

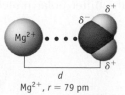

d
Mg^{2+}, $r = 79$ pm
$\Delta H = -1922$ kJ/mol

Increasing force of attraction; more exothermic enthalpy of hydration

TABLE 12.1 Radii and Enthalpies of Hydration of Alkali Metal Ions

Cation	Ion Radius (pm)	Enthalpy of Hydration (kJ/mol)
Li$^+$	78	−515
Na$^+$	98	−405
K$^+$	133	−321
Rb$^+$	149	−296
Cs$^+$	165	−263

H$^+$ ion, estimated to be −1090 kJ/mol. This extraordinarily large value is due to the tiny size of the H$^+$ ion.

Chemistry ⚛ Now™

Sign in at **www.cengage.com/login** and go to Chapter 12 Contents to see Screen 12.4 to view an animation of **ion–dipole forces.**

Strong attraction

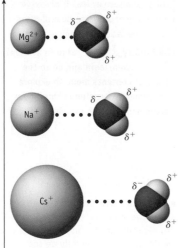

Weak attraction

■ **EXAMPLE 12.1** **Hydration Energy**

Problem Explain why the enthalpy of hydration of Na$^+$ (−405 kJ/mol) is somewhat more exothermic than that of Cs$^+$ (−263 kJ/mol), whereas that of Mg^{2+} is much more exothermic (−1922 kJ/mol) than that of either Na$^+$ or Cs$^+$.

Strategy The strength of ion–dipole attractions depends directly on the size of the ion charge and the magnitude of the dipole, and inversely on the distance between them. To judge the ion–dipole distance, we need ion sizes from Figure 7.12.

Solution The relevant ion sizes are Na$^+$ = 98 pm, Cs$^+$ = 165 pm, and Mg^{2+} = 79 pm. From these values, we can predict that the distances between the center of the positive charge on the metal ion and the negative side of the water dipole will vary in this order: Mg^{2+} < Na$^+$ < Cs$^+$. The hydration energy varies in the reverse order (with the hydration energy of Mg^{2+} being the most negative value). Notice also that Mg^{2+} has a 2+ charge, whereas the other ions are 1+. The greater charge on Mg^{2+} leads to a greater force of ion–dipole attraction than for the other two ions, which have only a 1+ charge. As a result, the hydration energy for Mg^{2+} is much more negative than for the other two ions.

EXERCISE 12.1 **Hydration Energy**

Which should have the more negative hydration energy, F$^-$ or Cl$^-$? Explain briefly.

Interactions Between Molecules with Permanent Dipoles

When a polar molecule encounters another polar molecule, of the same or a different kind, the positive end of one molecule is attracted to the negative end of the other polar molecule.

Many molecules have dipoles, and their interactions occur by **dipole–dipole attraction.**

Solid salts with waters of hydration are common. The formulas of these compounds are given by appending a specific number of water molecules to the end of the formula, as in $BaCl_2 \cdot 2\ H_2O$. Sometimes, the water molecules simply fill in empty spaces in a crystalline lattice, but often the cation in these salts is directly associated with water molecules. For example, the compound $CrCl_3 \cdot 6\ H_2O$ is better written as $[Cr(H_2O)_4Cl_2]Cl \cdot 2\ H_2O$. Four of the six water molecules are associated with the Cr^{3+} ion by ion–dipole attractive forces; the remaining two water molecules are in the lattice. Common examples of hydrated salts are listed in the table.

Compound	Common Name	Uses
$Na_2CO_3 \cdot 10\ H_2O$	Washing soda	Water softener
$Na_2S_2O_3 \cdot 5\ H_2O$	Hypo	Photography
$MgSO_4 \cdot 7\ H_2O$	Epsom salt	Cathartic, dyeing and tanning
$CaSO_4 \cdot 2\ H_2O$	Gypsum	Wallboard
$CuSO_4 \cdot 5\ H_2O$	Blue vitriol	Biocide

Photos: Charles D. Winters

Hydrated cobalt(II) chloride, $CoCl_2 \cdot 6\ H_2O$. In the solid state, the compound is best described by the formula $[Co(H_2O)_4Cl_2] \cdot 2\ H_2O$. The cobalt(II) ion is surrounded by four water molecules and two chloride ions in an octahedral arrangement. In water, the ion is completely hydrated, now being surrounded by six water molecules. Cobalt(II) ions and water molecules interact by ion–dipole forces. This is an example of a coordination compound, a class of compounds discussed in detail in Chapter 22.

For polar molecules, dipole–dipole attractions influence, among other things, the evaporation of a liquid and the condensation of a gas (Figure 12.4). An energy change occurs in both processes. Evaporation requires the input of energy, specifically the enthalpy of vaporization ($\Delta_{vap}H°$) [see Section 5.3 and Section 12.4]. The value for the enthalpy of vaporization has a positive sign, indicating that evaporation is an endothermic process. The enthalpy change for the condensation process—the reverse of evaporation—has a negative value.

The greater the forces of attraction between molecules in a liquid, the greater the energy that must be supplied to separate them. Thus, we expect polar compounds to have a higher value for their enthalpy of vaporization than nonpolar compounds with similar molar masses. For example, notice that $\Delta_{vap}H°$ for polar

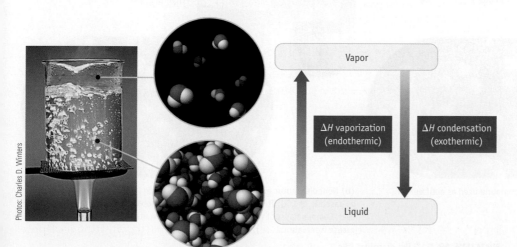

Photos: Charles D. Winters

Vapor

ΔH vaporization (endothermic)

ΔH condensation (exothermic)

Liquid

FIGURE 12.4 Evaporation at the molecular level. Energy must be supplied to separate molecules in the liquid state against intermolecular forces of attraction.

TABLE 12.2 Molar Masses, Boiling Points, and $\Delta_{vap}H°$ of Nonpolar and Polar Substances

	Nonpolar				Polar		
	M (g/mol)	BP (°C)	$\Delta_{vap}H°$ (kJ/mol)		M (g/mol)	BP (°C)	$\Delta_{vap}H°$ (kJ/mol)
N_2	28	−196	5.57	CO	28	−192	6.04
SiH_4	32	−112	12.10	PH_3	34	−88	14.06
GeH_4	77	−90	14.06	AsH_3	78	−62	16.69
Br_2	160	59	29.96	ICl	162	97	—

molecules is greater than for nonpolar molecules of approximately the same size and mass (Table 12.2).

The boiling point of a liquid also depends on intermolecular forces of attraction. As the temperature of a substance is raised, its molecules gain kinetic energy. Eventually, when the boiling point is reached, the molecules have sufficient kinetic energy to escape the forces of attraction of their neighbors. For molecules of similar molar mass, the greater the polarity, the higher the temperature required for the liquid to boil. In Table 12.2, you see that the boiling point for polar ICl is greater than that for nonpolar Br_2, for example.

Intermolecular forces also influence solubility. A qualitative observation on solubility is that "like dissolves like." In other words, polar molecules are likely to dissolve in a polar solvent, and nonpolar molecules are likely to dissolve in a nonpolar solvent (Figure 12.5) (◄ Chapter 8). The converse is also true; that is, it is unlikely that polar molecules will dissolve in nonpolar solvents or that nonpolar molecules will dissolve in polar solvents.

For example, water and ethanol (C_2H_5OH) can be mixed in any ratio to give a homogeneous mixture. In contrast, water does not dissolve in gasoline to an ap-

Ethylene glycol

(a) Ethylene glycol ($HOCH_2CH_2OH$), a polar compound used as antifreeze in automobiles, dissolves in water.

Hydrocarbon

(b) Nonpolar motor oil (a hydrocarbon) dissolves in nonpolar solvents such as gasoline or CCl_4. It will not dissolve in a polar solvent such as water, however. Commercial spot removers use nonpolar solvents to dissolve oil and grease from fabrics.

FIGURE 12.5 "Like dissolves like."

Photos: Charles D. Winters

preciable extent. The difference in these two situations is that ethanol and water are polar molecules, whereas the hydrocarbon molecules in gasoline (e.g., octane, C_8H_{18}) are nonpolar. The water–ethanol interactions are strong enough that the energy expended in pushing water molecules apart to make room for ethanol molecules is compensated for by the energy of attraction between the two kinds of polar molecules. In contrast, water–hydrocarbon attractions are weak. The hydrocarbon molecules cannot disrupt the stronger water–water attractions.

Chemistry. ☷. Now™

Sign in at **www.cengage.com/login** and go to Chapter 12 Contents to see Screen 12.4 to view an animation of **dipole–dipole forces.**

Hydrogen Bonding

Hydrogen fluoride, water, ammonia and many other compounds with O—H and N—H bonds have exceptional properties. Consider, for example, the boiling points for hydrogen compounds of elements in Groups 4A through 7A (Figure 12.6). Generally, the boiling points of related compounds increase with molar mass. This trend is seen in the boiling points of the hydrogen compounds of Group 4A elements, for example ($CH_4 < SiH_4 < GeH_4 < SnH_4$). The same effect is also operating for the heavier molecules of the hydrogen compounds of elements of Groups 5A, 6A, and 7A. The boiling points of NH_3, H_2O, and HF, however, deviate significantly from what might be expected based on molar mass alone. If we extrapolate the curve for the boiling points of H_2Te, H_2Se, and H_2S, the boiling point of water is predicted to be around $-90\ °C$. The boiling point of water is almost $200\ °C$ higher than this value! Similarly, the boiling points of NH_3 and HF are much higher than would be expected based on molar mass. Because the temperature at which a substance boils depends on the attractive forces between molecules, the extraordinarily high boiling points of H_2O, HF, and NH_3 indicate strong intermolecular attractions.

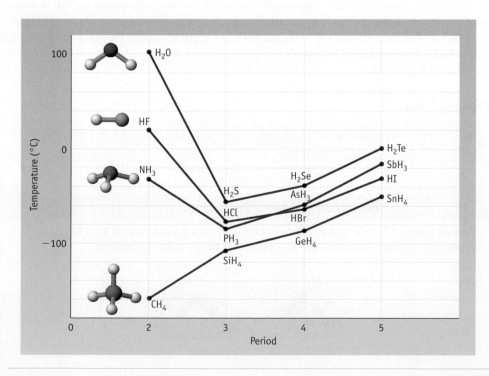

Active Figure 12.6 The boiling points of some simple hydrogen compounds. The effect of hydrogen bonding is apparent in the unusually high boiling points of H_2O, HF, and NH_3. (Also, notice that the boiling point of HCl is somewhat higher than expected based on the data for HBr and HI. It is apparent that some degree of hydrogen bonding also occurs in liquid HCl.)

Chemistry. ☷. Now™ Sign in at www.cengage.com/login and go to the Chapter Contents menu to explore an interactive version of this figure accompanied by an exercise.

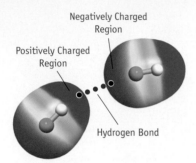

Negatively Charged Region

Positively Charged Region

Hydrogen Bond

Hydrogen bonding between HF molecules. The partially negative F atom of one HF molecule interacts through hydrogen bonding with a neighboring HF molecule. (Red regions of the molecule are negatively charged, whereas blue regions are positively charged. For more on electrostatic potential surfaces, see page 382.)

The electronegativities of N (3.0), O (3.5), and F (4.0) are among the highest of all the elements, whereas the electronegativity of hydrogen is much lower (2.2). This large difference in electronegativity means that N—H, O—H, and F—H bonds are very polar. In bonds between H and N, O, or F, the more electronegative element takes on a significant negative charge (see Figure 8.11), and the hydrogen atom acquires a significant positive charge.

There is an unusually strong attraction between an electronegative atom with a lone pair of electrons (most often, an N, O, or F atom in another molecule or even in the same molecule) and the hydrogen atom of the N—H, O—H, or F—H bond. This type of interaction is known as a **hydrogen bond.** Hydrogen bonds are an extreme form of dipole–dipole interaction where one atom involved is always H and the other atom is highly electronegative, most often O, N, or F. A hydrogen bond can be represented as

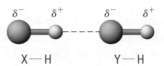

$$\delta^- \quad \delta^+ \qquad \delta^- \quad \delta^+$$
$$X—H \quad ----- \quad Y—H$$

The hydrogen atom becomes a bridge between the two electronegative atoms X and Y, and the dashed line represents the hydrogen bond. The most pronounced effects of hydrogen bonding occur where both X and Y are N, O, or F. Energies associated with most hydrogen bonds involving these elements are in the range of 5 to 30 kJ/mol.

Types of Hydrogen Bonds [X—H - - - :Y]

N—H - - - :N—	O—H - - - :N—	F—H - - - :N—
N—H - - - :O—	O—H - - - :O—	F—H - - - :O—
N—H - - - :F—	O—H - - - :F—	F—H - - - :F—

Hydrogen bonding has important implications for any property of a compound that is influenced by intermolecular forces of attraction. For example, hydrogen bonding affects the structures of molecular solids. In solid acetic acid, CH_3CO_2H, for example, two molecules are joined to one another by hydrogen bonding (Figure 12.7).

Chemistry Now™

Sign in at **www.cengage.com/login** and go to Chapter 12 Contents to see Screen 12.6 for a **description of hydrogen bonding.**

■ **EXAMPLE 12.2 The Effect of Hydrogen Bonding**

Problem Ethanol, CH_3CH_2OH, and dimethyl ether, CH_3OCH_3, have the same formula but a different arrangement of atoms. Predict which of these compounds has the higher boiling point.

Ethanol, CH_3CH_2OH

Dimethyl ether, CH_3OCH_3

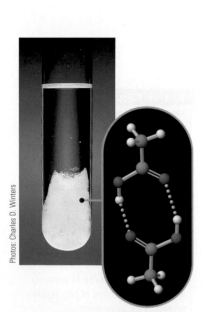

Photos: Charles D. Winters

FIGURE 12.7 Hydrogen bonding. Two acetic acid molecules can interact through hydrogen bonds. This photo shows partly solid glacial acetic acid. Notice that the solid is denser than the liquid, a property shared by virtually all substances, the notable exception being water.

562 Chapter 12 | Intermolecular Forces and Liquids

Strategy Inspect the structure of each molecule to decide whether each is polar and, if polar, whether hydrogen bonding is possible.

Solution Although these two compounds have identical masses, they have different structures. Ethanol possesses an O—H group, and an electrostatic potential surface in the margin shows it to be polar with a partially negative O atom and a partially negative H atom. The result is that hydrogen bonding between ethanol molecules is possible and makes an important contribution to its intermolecular forces.

$$CH_3CH_2 - \overset{\cdot\cdot}{\underset{|}{O}} : \cdots H - \overset{\cdot\cdot}{\underset{|}{O}} :$$
$$\qquad\qquad H \qquad\quad CH_2CH_3$$

hydrogen bonding in ethanol, CH_3CH_2OH

In contrast, dimethyl ether, although a polar molecule, presents no opportunity for hydrogen bonding because there is no O—H bond. The H atoms are attached to much less electronegative C atoms. We can predict, therefore, that intermolecular forces will be larger in ethanol than in dimethyl ether and that ethanol will have the higher boiling point. Indeed, ethanol boils at 78.3 °C, whereas dimethyl ether has a boiling point of −24.8 °C, more than 100 °C lower. Under standard conditions, dimethyl ether is a gas, whereas ethanol is a liquid.

EXERCISE 12.2 Hydrogen Bonding

Using structural formulas, describe the hydrogen bonding between methanol (CH_3OH) molecules. What physical properties of methanol are likely to be affected by hydrogen bonding?

Hydrogen Bonding and the Unusual Properties of Water

One of the most striking differences between our planet and others in our solar system is the presence of large amounts of water on Earth. Three fourths of the planet is covered by oceans; the polar regions are vast ice fields; and even soil and rocks hold large amounts of water. Although we tend to take water for granted, almost no other substance behaves in a similar manner. Water's unique features reflect the ability of H_2O molecules to cling tenaciously to one another by hydrogen bonding.

One reason for ice's unusual structure and water's unusual properties is that each hydrogen atom of a water molecule can form a hydrogen bond to a lone pair of electrons on the oxygen atom of an adjacent water molecule. In addition, because the oxygen atom in water has two lone pairs of electrons, it can form two more hydrogen bonds with hydrogen atoms from adjacent molecules (Figure 12.8a). The result, seen particularly in ice, is a tetrahedral arrangement for the hydrogen atoms around each oxygen, involving two covalently bonded hydrogen atoms and two hydrogen-bonded hydrogen atoms.

As a consequence of the regular arrangement of water molecules linked by hydrogen bonding, ice has an open-cage structure with lots of empty space (Figure 12.8b). The result is that ice has a density about 10% less than that of liquid water, which explains why ice floats. (In contrast, virtually all other solids sink in their liquid phase.) We can also see in this structure that the oxygen atoms are arranged at the corners of puckered, hexagonal rings. Snowflakes are always based on six-sided figures (◄ page 69), a reflection of this internal molecular structure of ice.

When ice melts at 0 °C, the regular structure imposed on the solid state by hydrogen bonding breaks down, and a relatively large increase in density occurs (Figure 12.9). Another surprising thing occurs when the temperature of liquid water is raised from 0 °C to 4 °C: The density of water increases. For almost every other substance known, density decreases as the temperature is raised. Once again, hydrogen bonding is the reason for water's seemingly odd behavior. At a tempera-

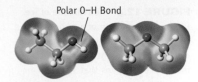

Polar O—H Bond

Electrostatic potential surfaces for ethanol (left) and dimethyl ether (right). The surface for ethanol clearly shows the polar O—H bond. The O atom in dimethyl ether has a partial negative charge, but there is no H atom attached. [Color coding: Red indicates a region of largest negative charge. Colors from yellow to green to turquoise indicate increasing positive charge (or decreasing negative charge). Blue indicates a region of partial positive charge.]

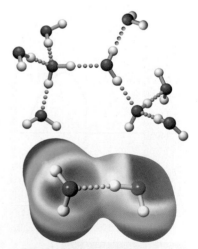

Hydrogen bonding in water. (above) Water readily forms hydrogen bonds. (below) An electrostatic potential surface for two water molecules shows the hydrogen bond involving the negatively charged O atom of one molecule and the positively charged H atom of a neighboring molecule.

FIGURE 12.8 The structure of ice.
(a) The oxygen atom of a water molecule attaches itself to two other water molecules by hydrogen bonds. Notice that the four groups that surround an oxygen atom are arranged as a distorted tetrahedron. Each oxygen atom is covalently bonded to two hydrogen atoms and hydrogen bonded to hydrogen atoms from two other molecules. The hydrogen bonds are longer than the covalent bonds. (b) In ice, the structural unit shown in part (a) is repeated in the crystalline lattice. This computer-generated structure shows a small portion of the extensive lattice. Notice the six-member, hexagonal rings. The corners of each hexagon are O atoms, and each side is composed of a normal O—H bond and a slightly longer hydrogen bond.

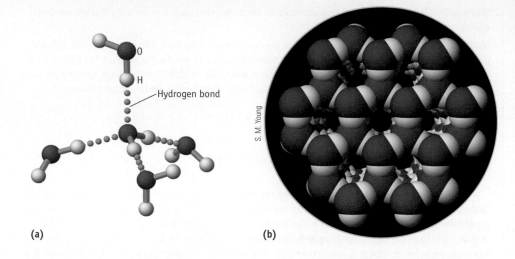

(a)   (b)

ture just above the melting point, some of the water molecules continue to cluster in ice-like arrangements, which require extra space. As the temperature is raised from 0 °C to 4 °C, the final vestiges of the ice structure disappear, and the volume contracts further, giving rise to the increase in density. Water's density reaches a maximum at about 4 °C. From this point, the density declines with increasing temperature in the normal fashion.

Because of the way that water's density changes as the temperature approaches the freezing point, lakes do not freeze solidly from the bottom up in the winter. When lake water cools with the approach of winter, its density increases, the cooler water sinks, and the warmer water rises. This "turn over" process continues until all the water reaches 4 °C, the maximum density. (This is the way oxygen-rich water moves to the lake bottom to restore the oxygen used during the summer and nutrients are brought to the top layers of the lake.) As the temperature decreases further, the colder water stays on the top of the lake, because water cooler than 4 °C is less dense than water at 4 °C. With further heat loss, ice can then begin to form on the surface, floating there and protecting the underlying water and aquatic life from further heat loss.

Extensive hydrogen bonding is also the origin of the extraordinarily high heat capacity of water. Although liquid water does not have the regular structure of ice, hydrogen bonding still occurs. With a rise in temperature, the extent of hydrogen bonding diminishes. Disrupting hydrogen bonds requires energy. The high heat capacity of water is, in large part, why oceans and lakes have such an enormous effect on weather. In autumn, when the temperature of the air is lower than the temperature of the ocean or lake, the water transfers energy as heat to the atmosphere, moderating the drop in air temperature. Furthermore, so much energy is available to be transferred for each degree drop in temperature that the decline in water temperature is gradual. For this reason, the temperature of the ocean or of a large lake is generally higher than the average air temperature until late in the autumn.

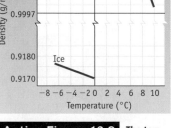

Active Figure 12.9 The temperature dependence of the densities of ice and water.

Chemistry ⚛ Now™ Sign in at www.cengage.com/login and go to the Chapter Contents menu to explore an interactive version of this figure accompanied by an exercise.

Chemistry ⚛ Now™

Sign in at **www.cengage.com/login** and go to Chapter 12 Contents to see Screen 12.7 to view an animation of **the transformation of ice to water** and for a table listing all of the **unusual properties of water.**

It is arguable that our world is what it is because of hydrogen bonding in water and in biochemical systems. Perhaps the most important occurrence is in DNA and RNA where the organic bases adenine, cytosine, guanine, and thymine (in DNA) or uracil (in RNA) are attached to sugar-phosphate chains (**Figure A**). The chains in DNA are joined by the pairing of bases, adenine with thymine and guanine with cytosine.

Figure B illustrates the hydrogen bonding between adenine and thymine. These models show that the molecules naturally fit together to form a six-sided ring, where two of the six sides involve hydrogen bonds. One side consists of a N $\cdots$ H—N grouping, and the other side is N—H $\cdots$ O. Here, the electrostatic potential surfaces show that the N atoms of adenine and the O atoms of thymine bear partial negative charges, and the H atoms of the N—H groups bear a positive charge. These charges and the geometry of the bases lead to these very specific interactions.

The fact that base pairing through hydrogen bonding leads to the joining of the sugar-phosphate chains of DNA, and to the double helical form of DNA, was first recognized by James Watson and Francis Crick on the basis of experimental work by Rosalind Franklin and Maurice Wilkins in the 1950s. It was this development that was so important in the molecular biology revolution in the last part of the 20th century. See page 392 for more on these scientists.

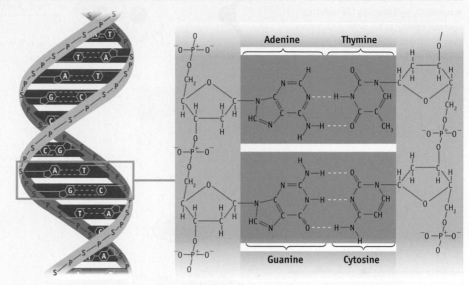

FIGURE A Hydrogen bonding in DNA. With the four bases in DNA, the usual pairings are adenine with thymine and guanine with cytosine. This pairing is promoted by hydrogen bonding.

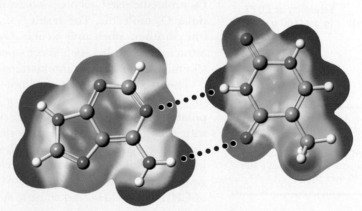

FIGURE B Hydrogen bonding between adenine and thymine. Electrostatic potential surfaces show that the polar N—H bond on one molecule can hydrogen bond to an electronegative N atom in a neighboring molecule.

12.3 Intermolecular Forces Involving Nonpolar Molecules

Many important molecules such as O_2, N_2, and the halogens are not polar. Why, then, does O_2 dissolve in polar water? Why can the N_2 of the atmosphere be liquefied (see Figure 12.1)? Some intermolecular forces must be acting between O_2 and water and between N_2 molecules, but what is their nature?

Dipole/Induced Dipole Forces

Polar molecules such as water can induce, or create, a dipole in molecules that do not have a permanent dipole. To see how this situation can occur, picture a polar water molecule approaching a nonpolar molecule such as O_2 (Figure 12.10). The

　Module 17

■ **Van der Waals Forces** The name "van der Waals forces" is a general term applied to attractive intermolecular interactions. (P. W. Atkins: *Quanta: A Handbook of Concepts,* 2nd ed., p. 187, Oxford, Oxford University Press, 2000.)

FIGURE 12.10 Dipole/induced dipole interaction. (a) A polar molecule such as water can induce a dipole in nonpolar O_2 by distorting the molecule's electron cloud. (b) Nonpolar I_2 dissolves in polar ethanol (C_2H_5OH). The intermolecular force involved is a dipole/induced dipole force.

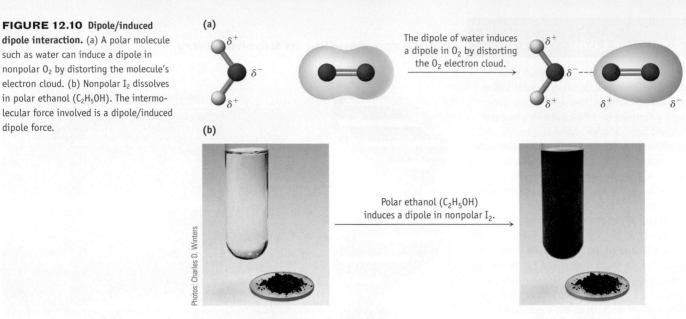

(a)

The dipole of water induces a dipole in O_2 by distorting the O_2 electron cloud.

(b)

Polar ethanol (C_2H_5OH) induces a dipole in nonpolar I_2.

Photos: Charles D. Winters

TABLE 12.3 The Solubility of Some Gases in Water*

	Molar Mass (g/mol)	Solubility at 20 °C (g gas/100 g water)†
H_2	2.01	0.000160
N_2	28.0	0.00190
O_2	32.0	0.00434

* Data taken from J. Dean: *Lange's Handbook of Chemistry.* 14th Ed., pp. 5.3–5.8, New York, McGraw-Hill, 1992.
† Measured under conditions where pressure of gas + pressure of water vapor = 760 mm Hg.

TABLE 12.4 Enthalpies of Vaporization and Boiling Points of Some Nonpolar Substances

	$\Delta_{vap}H°$ (kJ/mol)	Element/ Compound BP (°C)
N_2	5.57	−196
O_2	6.82	−183
CH_4 (methane)	8.2	−161.5
Br_2	29.96	+58.8
C_6H_6 (benzene)	30.7	+80.1
I_2	41.95	+185

---

electron cloud of an isolated (gaseous) O_2 molecule is symmetrically distributed between the two oxygen atoms. As the negative end of the polar H_2O molecule approaches, however, the O_2 electron cloud becomes distorted. In this process, the O_2 molecule itself becomes polar; that is, a dipole is *induced* in the otherwise nonpolar O_2 molecule. The result is that H_2O and O_2 molecules are now attracted to one another, albeit only weakly. Oxygen can dissolve in water because a force of attraction exists between water's permanent dipole and the induced dipole in O_2. Chemists refer to such interactions as **dipole/induced dipole interactions.**

The process of inducing a dipole is called **polarization,** and the degree to which the electron cloud of an atom or a molecule can be distorted depends on the **polarizability** of that atom or molecule. The electron cloud of an atom or molecule with a large, extended electron cloud, such as I_2, can be polarized more readily than the electron cloud in a much smaller atom or molecule, such as He or H_2, in which the valence electrons are close to the nucleus and more tightly held. In general, for an analogous series of substances, say the halogens or alkanes (such as CH_4, C_2H_6, C_3H_8, and so on), *the higher the molar mass, the greater the polarizability of the molecule.*

The solubilities of common gases in water illustrate the effect of interactions between a dipole and an induced dipole. In Table 12.3, you see a trend to higher solubility with increasing mass of the nonpolar gas. As the molar mass of the gas increases, the polarizability of the electron cloud increases and the strength of the dipole/induced dipole interaction increases.

London Dispersion Forces: Induced Dipole/Induced Dipole Forces

Iodine, I_2, is a solid and not a gas around room temperature and pressure, illustrating that nonpolar molecules must also experience intermolecular forces. An estimate of these forces is provided by the enthalpy of vaporization of the substance at its boiling point. The data in Table 12.4 suggest that these forces can range from very weak (N_2, O_2, and CH_4 with low enthalpies of vaporization and very low boiling points) to more substantial (I_2 and benzene).

To understand how two nonpolar molecules can attract each other, recall that the electrons in atoms or molecules are in a state of constant motion. When two

Two nonpolar atoms or molecules (depicted as having an electron cloud that has a time-averaged spherical shape).

Momentary attractions and repulsions between nuclei and electrons in neighboring molecules lead to induced dipoles.

Correlation of the electron motions between the two atoms or molecules (which are now dipolar) leads to a lower energy and stabilizes the system.

FIGURE 12.11 **Induced dipole interactions.** Momentary attractions and repulsions between nuclei and electrons create induced dipoles and lead to a net stabilization due to attractive forces.

atoms or nonpolar molecules approach each other, attractions or repulsions between their electrons and nuclei can lead to distortions in their electron clouds (Figure 12.11). That is, dipoles can be induced momentarily in neighboring atoms or molecules, and these induced dipoles lead to intermolecular attractions. The intermolecular force of attraction in liquids and solids composed of nonpolar molecules is an **induced dipole/induced dipole force**. Chemists often call them **London dispersion forces**. London dispersion forces actually arise between all molecules, both nonpolar and polar, but *London dispersion forces are the only intermolecular forces that allow nonpolar molecules to interact.*

A Closer Look

Hydrogen bonds involving water are also responsible for the structure and properties of one of the strangest substances on earth (Figure). When methane (CH_4) is mixed with water at high pressures and low temperatures, solid methane hydrate forms. Although the substance has been known for years, vast deposits of methane hydrate were only recently discovered deep within sediments on the floor of Earth's oceans. How these were formed is a mystery, but what is important is their size. It is estimated that global methane hydrate deposits contain approximately 10^{13} tons of carbon, or about twice the combined amount in all known reserves of coal, oil, and natural gas. Methane hydrate is also an efficient energy storehouse; a liter of methane hydrate releases about 160 liters of methane gas.

But of course there are problems to be solved. One significant problem is how to bring commercially useful quantities to the surface from deep in the ocean. Yet another is the possibility of a large, uncontrolled release of methane. Methane is a very effective greenhouse gas, so the release of a significant quantity into the atmosphere could damage the earth's climate.

Among the many sources of information is: E. Suess, G. Bohrmann, J. Greinert, and E. Lausch, *Scientific American*, November 1999, pp. 76–83.

Methane Hydrates: An Answer to World Fuel Supplies?

John Pinkston and Laura Stern/U.S. Geological Survey/*Science News*, 11-9-96

(a) Methane hydrate burns as methane gas escapes from the solid hydrate.

(b) Methane hydrate consists of a lattice of water molecules with methane molecules trapped in the cavity.

Methane hydrate. (a) When a sample is brought to the surface from the depths of the ocean, the methane oozes out of the solid, and the gas readily burns. (b) The structure of the solid methane hydrate consists of methane molecules trapped in a lattice of water molecules. Each point of the lattice shown here is an O atom of an H_2O molecule. The edges are O—H—O hydrogen bonds. Such structures are often called "clathrates." (For more on methane hydrates, see pages 259–260.)

Br₂   I₂

Induced dipole/induced dipole forces.
Br_2 (left) and I_2 (right) both consist of nonpolar molecules. They are a liquid and a solid, respectively, implying that there are forces between the molecules sufficient to cause them to be in a condensed phase. These forces between nonpolar substances are known as London dispersion forces or induced dipole/induced dipole forces.

Geckos use intermolecular forces! A little gecko can climb vertically 1 m up a polished glass surface in 1 s. Geckos have millions of tiny hairs or setae on their feet, and each setae ends in 1000 or more even tinier hairs at the tip. Recent research has found that geckos are unique in that they adhere to a surface through van der Waals forces of attraction between the hairs and the surface. (K. Autumn, "How gecko toes stick." *American Scientist* Vol. 94, pages 124–132, 2006.)

■ **EXAMPLE 12.3 Intermolecular Forces**

Problem Suppose you have a mixture of solid iodine, I_2, and the liquids water and carbon tetrachloride (CCl_4). What intermolecular forces exist between each possible pair of compounds? Describe what you might see when these compounds are mixed.

Strategy First, decide whether each substance is polar or nonpolar. Second, determine the types of intermolecular forces that could exist between the different pairs. Finally, use the "like dissolves like" guideline to decide whether iodine will dissolve in water or CCl_4 and whether CCl_4 will dissolve in water.

Solution Iodine, I_2, is nonpolar. As a molecule composed of large iodine atoms, it has an extensive electron cloud. Thus, the molecule is easily polarized, and iodine could interact with water, a polar molecule, by dipole/induced dipole forces.

Carbon tetrachloride, a tetrahedral molecule, is not polar (see Figure 8.15). As a consequence, it can interact with iodine only by dispersion forces. Water and CCl_4 could interact by dipole/induced dipole forces, but the interaction is expected to be weak.

The photo here shows the result of mixing these three compounds. Iodine does dissolve to a small extent in water to give a brown solution. When this brown solution is added to a test tube containing CCl_4, the liquid layers do not mix. (Polar water does not dissolve in nonpolar CCl_4.) (Notice the more dense CCl_4 layer [$d = 1.58$ g/mL] is underneath the less dense water layer.) When the test tube is shaken, however, nonpolar I_2 dissolves preferentially in nonpolar CCl_4, as evidenced by the disappearance of the color of I_2 in the water layer (top) and the appearance of the purple I_2 color in the CCl_4 layer (bottom).

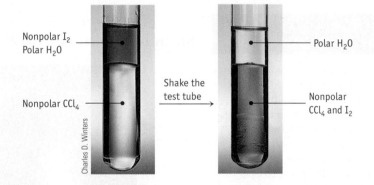

Nonpolar I_2
Polar H_2O

Nonpolar CCl_4

Shake the test tube

Polar H_2O

Nonpolar CCl_4 and I_2

EXERCISE 12.3 Intermolecular Forces

You mix water, CCl_4, and hexane ($CH_3CH_2CH_2CH_2CH_2CH_3$). What type of intermolecular forces can exist between each pair of these compounds?

Summary of Intermolecular Forces

Intermolecular forces involve molecules that are polar or those in which polarity can be induced (Table 12.5). Furthermore, several types of intermolecular forces can be at work in a single type of molecule (Figure 12.12). Also note in Figure 12.12 that while each individual induced dipole/induced dipole force is usually quite small, the sum of these forces over the entire structure of a molecule can actually be quite great, even in polar molecules.

Chemistry₊◌₊Now™

Sign in at **www.cengage.com/login** and go to Chapter 12 Contents to see Screen 12.5 to view an animation of **induced dipole forces** and for an exercise and tutorial on **intermolecular forces.**

TABLE 12.5 Summary of Intermolecular Forces

Type of Interaction	Factors Responsible for Interaction	Approximate Energy (kJ/mol)	Example
Ion–dipole	Ion change, magnitude of dipole	40–600	$Na^+ \ldots H_2O$
Dipole–dipole	Dipole moment (depends on atom electronegativities and molecular structure)	20–30	$H_2O \ldots CH_3OH$
Hydrogen bonding, X—H . . . :Y	Very polar X—H bond (where X = F, N, O) and atom Y with lone pair of electrons	5–30	$H_2O \ldots H_2O$
Dipole/induced dipole	Dipole moment of polar molecule and polarizability of nonpolar molecule	2–10	$H_2O \ldots I_2$
Induced dipole/induced dipole (London dispersion forces)	Polarizability	0.05–40	$I_2 \ldots I_2$

■ EXAMPLE 12.4 Intermolecular Forces

Problem Decide which are the most important intermolecular forces involved in each of the following, and place them in order of increasing strength of interaction: (a) liquid methane, CH_4; (b) a mixture of water and methanol (CH_3OH); and (c) a solution of bromine in water.

Strategy For each molecule, we consider its structure and decide whether it is polar. If polar, we consider the possibility of hydrogen bonding.

Solution (a) Methane is a covalently bonded molecule. Based on the Lewis structure, we can conclude that it must be a tetrahedral molecule and that it cannot be polar. The only way methane molecules can interact with one another is through induced dipole/induced dipole forces.

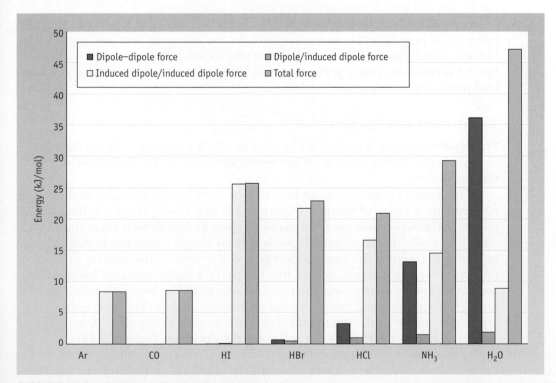

FIGURE 12.12 Energies associated with intermolecular forces.

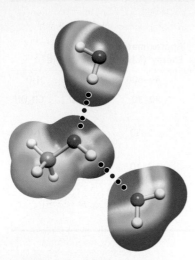

Hydrogen bonding involving methanol (CH₃OH) and water.

(b) Both water and methanol are covalently bonded molecules; both are polar; and both have an O—H bond. They therefore interact through the special dipole–dipole force called hydrogen bonding, as well as by dipole-dipole and London forces.

$$\underset{\delta^+ H}{\overset{\delta^+ H}{\diagdown}} \overset{\delta^-}{O} \cdots \overset{\delta^+}{H} - \overset{\delta^-}{O} \diagdown CH_3 \quad \text{and} \quad \underset{H_3C}{\overset{\delta^+ H}{\diagdown}} \overset{\delta^-}{O} \cdots \overset{\delta^+}{H} - \overset{\delta^-}{O} \diagdown H^{\delta^+}$$

(c) Nonpolar molecules of bromine, Br₂, interact by induced dipole forces, whereas water is a polar molecule. Therefore, dipole/induced dipole forces (and London forces) are involved when Br₂ molecules interact with water. (This is similar to the I₂–ethanol interaction in Figure 12.10.)

In order of increasing strength, the likely order of interactions is

$$\text{liquid } CH_4 < H_2O \text{ and } Br_2 < H_2O \text{ and } CH_3OH$$

EXERCISE 12.4 Intermolecular Forces

Decide which type of intermolecular force is involved in **(a)** liquid O₂; **(b)** liquid CH₃OH; and **(c)** N₂ dissolved in H₂O. Place the interactions in order of increasing strength.

12.4 Properties of Liquids

Of the three states of matter, liquids are the most difficult to describe precisely. The molecules in a gas under normal conditions are far apart and may be considered more or less independent of one another. The structures of solids can be described readily because the particles that make up solids—atoms, molecules, or ions—are close together and are usually in an orderly arrangement. The particles of a liquid interact with their neighbors, like the particles in a solid, but, unlike in solids, there is little long-range order in their arrangement.

In spite of a lack of precision in describing liquids, we can still consider the behavior of liquids at the molecular level. In the following sections, we will look further at the process of vaporization, at the vapor pressure of liquids, at their boiling points and critical properties, and at the behavior that results in their surface tension, capillary action, and viscosity.

Vaporization and Condensation

Vaporization or evaporation is the process in which a substance in the liquid state becomes a gas. In this process, molecules escape from the liquid surface and enter the gaseous state.

To understand evaporation, we have to look at molecular energies. Molecules in a liquid have a range of energies (Figure 12.13) that closely resembles the distribution of energies for molecules of a gas (see Figure 11.14). As with gases, the average energy for molecules in a liquid depends only on temperature: The higher the temperature, the higher the average energy and the greater the relative number of molecules with high kinetic energy. In a sample of a liquid, at least a few molecules have more kinetic energy than the potential energy of the intermolecular attractive forces holding the liquid molecules to one another. If these high-energy molecules are at the surface of the liquid and if they are moving in the right direction, they can break free of their neighbors and enter the gas phase (Figure 12.14).

Vaporization is an endothermic process because energy must be added to the system to overcome the intermolecular forces of attraction holding the molecules together. The energy required to vaporize a sample is often given as the standard

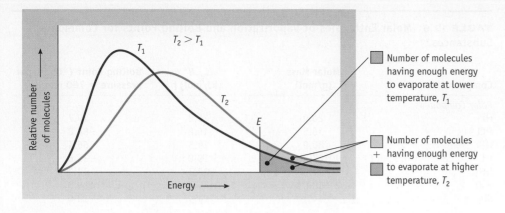

FIGURE 12.13 The distribution of energy among molecules in a liquid sample. T_2 is a higher temperature than T_1, and at the higher temperature, there are more molecules with an energy greater than E.

In the figure:
- $T_2 > T_1$
- Number of molecules having enough energy to evaporate at lower temperature, T_1
- + Number of molecules having enough energy to evaporate at higher temperature, T_2
- Axes: Relative number of molecules (vertical), Energy (horizontal)

molar enthalpy of vaporization, $\Delta_{vap}H°$ (in units of kilojoules per mole; see Tables 12.4 and 12.6 and Figure 12.4).

$$\text{Liquid} \xrightarrow[\substack{\text{heat energy absorbed} \\ \text{by liquid}}]{\text{vaporization}} \text{Vapor} \qquad \Delta_{vap}H° = \text{molar heat of vaporization}$$

A molecule in the gas phase can transfer some of its kinetic energy by colliding with slower gaseous molecules and solid objects. If this molecule loses sufficient energy and comes in contact with the surface of the liquid, it can reenter the liquid phase in the process called **condensation**.

$$\text{Vapor} \xrightarrow[\substack{\text{heat energy released} \\ \text{by vapor}}]{\text{condensation}} \text{Liquid}$$

Condensation is the reverse of vaporization. Condensation is exothermic, so energy is transferred to the surroundings. *The enthalpy change for condensation is equal but opposite in sign to the enthalpy of vaporization.* For example, the enthalpy change for the vaporization of 1.00 mol of water at 100 °C is +40.7 kJ. On condensing 1.00 mol of water vapor to liquid water at 100 °C, the enthalpy change is −40.7 kJ.

In the discussion of intermolecular forces, we pointed out the relationship between the $\Delta_{vap}H°$ values for various substances and the temperatures at which they boil (Table 12.6). Both properties reflect the attractive forces between particles in the liquid. The boiling points of nonpolar liquids (e.g., the hydrocarbons, atmospheric gases, and the halogens) increase with increasing atomic or molecular mass,

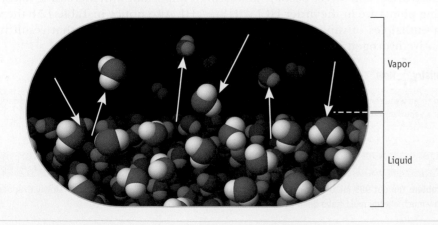

FIGURE 12.14 Evaporation. Some molecules at the surface of a liquid have enough energy to escape the attractions of their neighbors and enter the gaseous state. At the same time, some molecules in the gaseous state can reenter the liquid.

In the figure labels: Vapor, Liquid

TABLE 12.6 Molar Enthalpies of Vaporization and Boiling Points for Common Substances*

Compound	Molar Mass (g/mol)	$\Delta_{vap}H°$ (kJ/mol)†	Boiling Point (°C) (Vapor pressure = 760 mm Hg)
Polar Compounds			
HF	20.0	25.2	19.7
HCl	36.5	16.2	−84.8
HBr	80.9	19.3	−66.4
HI	127.9	19.8	−35.6
NH_3	17.0	23.3	−33.3
H_2O	18.0	40.7	100.0
SO_2	64.1	24.9	−10.0
Nonpolar Compounds			
CH_4 (methane)	16.0	8.2	−161.5
C_2H_6 (ethane)	30.1	14.7	−88.6
C_3H_8 (propane)	44.1	19.0	−42.1
C_4H_{10} (butane)	58.1	22.4	−0.5
Monatomic Elements			
He	4.0	0.08	−268.9
Ne	20.2	1.7	−246.1
Ar	39.9	6.4	−185.9
Xe	131.3	12.6	−108.0
Diatomic Elements			
H_2	2.0	0.90	−252.9
N_2	28.0	5.6	−195.8
O_2	32.0	6.8	−183.0
F_2	38.0	6.6	−188.1
Cl_2	70.9	20.4	−34.0
Br_2	159.8	30.0	58.8

*Data taken from D. R. Lide: *Basic Laboratory and Industrial Chemicals,* Boca Raton, FL, CRC Press, 1993.
†$\Delta_{vap}H°$ is measured at the normal boiling point of the liquid.

a reflection of increased intermolecular dispersion forces. The alkanes (such as methane) listed in Table 12.6 show this trend clearly. Similarly, the boiling points and enthalpies of vaporization of the heavier hydrogen halides (HX, where X = Cl, Br, and I) increase with increasing molecular mass. For these molecules, hydrogen bonding is not as important as it is in HF, so dispersion forces and ordinary dipole–dipole forces account for their intermolecular attractions (see Figure 12.12). Because dispersion forces become increasingly important with increasing mass, the boiling points are in the order HCl < HBr < HI. Also notice in Table 12.6 the very high enthalpies of vaporization of water and hydrogen fluoride that result from extensive hydrogen bonding.

Chemistry ⚛ Now™

Sign in at **www.cengage.com/login** and go to Chapter 12 Contents to see Screen 12.8 to view an animation of the **vaporization process** and for a table of $\Delta_{vap}H°$ values.

■ **EXAMPLE 12.5 Enthalpy of Vaporization**

Problem You put 925 mL of water (about 4 cupsful) in a pan at 100 °C, and the water slowly evaporates. How much energy must have been transferred as heat to vaporize the water?

Strategy Three pieces of information are needed to solve this problem:

1. $\Delta_{vap}H°$ for water = +40.7 kJ/mol at 100 °C.

2. The density of water at 100 °C = 0.958 g/cm³. (This is needed because $\Delta_{vap}H°$ has units of kilojoules per mole, so you first must find the mass of water and then the amount.)

3. Molar mass of water = 18.02 g/mol.

Solution A volume of 925 mL (or 9.25×10^2 cm³) is equivalent to 886 g, and this mass is in turn equivalent to 49.2 mol of water.

$$925 \text{ mL}\left(\frac{0.958 \text{ g}}{1 \text{ mL}}\right)\left(\frac{1 \text{ mol}}{18.02 \text{ g}}\right) = 49.2 \text{ mol H}_2\text{O}$$

Therefore, the amount of energy required is

$$49.2 \text{ mol H}_2\text{O}\left(\frac{40.7 \text{ kJ}}{\text{mol}}\right) = 2.00 \times 10^3 \text{ kJ}$$

2000 kJ is equivalent to about one quarter of the energy in your daily food intake.

EXERCISE 12.5 Enthalpy of Vaporization

The molar enthalpy of vaporization of methanol, CH_3OH, is 35.2 kJ/mol at 64.6 °C. How much energy is required to evaporate 1.00 kg of this alcohol at 64.6 °C?

Water is exceptional among the liquids listed in Table 12.6 in that an enormous amount of heat is required to convert liquid water to water vapor. This fact is important to your own physical well-being. When you exercise vigorously, your body responds by sweating to rid itself of the excess heat. Energy from your body is transferred to sweat in the process of evaporation, and your body is cooled.

Enthalpies of vaporization and condensation of water also play a role in weather (Figure 12.15). For example, if enough water condenses from the air to fall as an inch of rain on an acre of ground, the heat released exceeds 2.0×10^8 kJ! This is equivalent to about 50 tons of exploded dynamite, the energy released by a small bomb.

Vapor Pressure

If you put some water in an open beaker, it will eventually evaporate completely. Air movement and gas diffusion remove the water vapor from the vicinity of the liquid surface, so many water molecules are not able to return to the liquid.

If you put water in a sealed flask (Figure 12.16), however, the water vapor cannot escape, and some will recondense to form liquid water. Eventually, the masses of liquid and of vapor in the flask remain constant. This is another example of a **dynamic equilibrium** (◄ page 119).

$$\text{Liquid} \rightleftharpoons \text{Vapor}$$

Molecules still move continuously from the liquid phase to the vapor phase and from the vapor phase back to the liquid phase. The rate at which molecules move from liquid to vapor is the same as the rate at which they move from vapor to liquid; thus, there is no net change in the masses of the two phases.

When a liquid–vapor equilibrium has been established, the equilibrium vapor pressure (often just called the vapor pressure) can be measured. The **equilibrium vapor pressure** of a substance is the pressure exerted by the vapor in equilibrium with the liquid phase. Conceptually, the vapor pressure of a liquid is a measure of the tendency of its molecules to escape from the liquid phase and enter the vapor

The Image Bank/Getty Images

FIGURE 12.15 Rainstorms release an enormous quantity of energy. When water vapor condenses, energy is evolved to the surroundings. The enthalpy of condensation of water is large, so a large quantity of energy is released in a rainstorm.

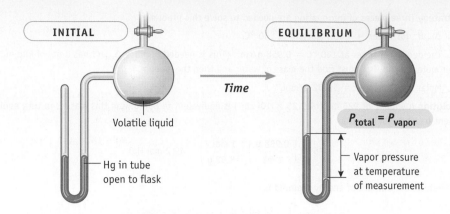

INITIAL

EQUILIBRIUM

Time

Volatile liquid

Hg in tube
open to flask

$P_{total} = P_{vapor}$

Vapor pressure
at temperature
of measurement

Active Figure 12.16 **Vapor pressure.** A volatile liquid is placed in an evacuated flask (left). At the beginning, no molecules of the liquid are in the vapor phase. After a short time, however, some of the liquid evaporates, and the molecules now in the vapor phase exert a pressure. The pressure of the vapor measured when the liquid and the vapor are in equilibrium is called the equilibrium vapor pressure (right).

Chemistry.⚬.Now™ Sign in at www.cengage.com/login and go to the Chapter Contents menu to explore an interactive version of this figure accompanied by an exercise.

■ **Equilibrium Vapor Pressure** At the conditions of *T* and *P* given by any point on a curve in Figure 12.17, the pure liquid and its vapor are in dynamic equilibrium. If *T* and *P* define a point not on the curve, the system is not at equilibrium. See Appendix G for the equilibrium vapor pressures of water at various temperatures.

phase at a given temperature. This tendency is referred to qualitatively as the **volatility** of the compound. The higher the equilibrium vapor pressure at a given temperature, the more volatile the substance.

As described previously (see Figure 12.13), the distribution of molecular energies in the liquid phase is a function of temperature. At a higher temperature, more molecules have sufficient energy to escape the surface of the liquid. The equilibrium vapor pressure must, therefore, increase with temperature.

It is useful to represent vapor pressure as a function of temperature. Figure 12.17 shows the vapor pressure curves for several liquids as a function of temperature. *All points along the vapor pressure versus temperature curves represent conditions of pressure and temperature at which liquid and vapor are in equilibrium.* For example, at 60 °C the vapor pressure of water is 149 mm Hg (Appendix G). If water is placed in an evacuated flask that is maintained at 60 °C, liquid water will evaporate until the pressure exerted by the water vapor is 149 mm Hg (assuming enough water is in the flask so that some liquid remains when equilibrium is reached).

Chemistry.⚬.Now™

Sign in at **www.cengage.com/login** and go to Chapter 12 Contents to see Screen 12.9 to view an animation on **equilibrium vapor pressure** and for a simulation of **vapor pressure curves.**

Active Figure 12.17 **Vapor pressure curves for diethyl ether [(C₂H₅)₂O], ethanol (C₂H₅OH), and water.** Each curve represents conditions of *T* and *P* at which the two phases, liquid and vapor, are in equilibrium. These compounds exist as liquids for temperatures and pressures to the left of the curve and as gases under conditions to the right of the curve.

Chemistry.⚬.Now™ Sign in at www.cengage.com/login and go to the Chapter Contents menu to explore an interactive version of this figure accompanied by an exercise.

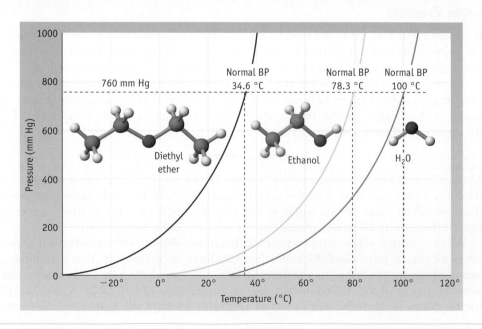

Problem You place 2.00 L of water in an open container in your dormitory room; the room has a volume of 4.25 × 10⁴ L. You seal the room and wait for the water to evaporate. Will all of the water evaporate at 25 °C? (At 25 °C the density of water is 0.997 g/mL, and its vapor pressure is 23.8 mm Hg.)

Strategy One approach to solving this problem is to calculate the quantity of water that must evaporate to exert a pressure of 23.8 mm Hg in a volume of 4.25 × 10⁴ L at 25 °C. We use the ideal gas law for this calculation.

Solution Calculate the amount and then mass and volume of water that fulfills the following conditions: P = 23.8 mm Hg, V = 4.25 × 10⁴ L, T = 25 °C (298 K).

$$P = 23.8 \text{ mm Hg} \left(\frac{1 \text{ atm}}{760 \text{ mm Hg}} \right) = 0.0313 \text{ atm}$$

$$n = \frac{PV}{RT} = \frac{(0.0313 \text{ atm})(4.25 \times 10^4 \text{ L})}{\left(0.082057 \dfrac{\text{L} \cdot \text{atm}}{\text{K} \cdot \text{mol}} \right)(298 \text{ K})} = 54.4 \text{ mol}$$

$$54.4 \text{ mol H}_2\text{O} \left(\frac{18.02 \text{ g}}{1 \text{ mol H}_2\text{O}} \right) = 980. \text{ g H}_2\text{O}$$

$$980. \text{ g H}_2\text{O} \left(\frac{1 \text{ mL}}{0.997 \text{ g H}_2\text{O}} \right) = 983 \text{ mL}$$

Only about half of the available water needs to evaporate to achieve the equilibrium water vapor pressure of 23.8 mm Hg at 25 °C.

EXERCISE 12.6 Vapor Pressure Curves

Examine the vapor pressure curve for ethanol in Figure 12.17.

(a) What is the approximate vapor pressure of ethanol at 40 °C?

(b) Are liquid and vapor in equilibrium when the temperature is 60 °C and the pressure is 600 mm Hg? If not, does liquid evaporate to form more vapor, or does vapor condense to form more liquid?

EXERCISE 12.7 Vapor Pressure

If 0.50 g of pure water is sealed in an evacuated 5.0-L flask and the whole assembly is heated to 60 °C, will the pressure be equal to or less than the equilibrium vapor pressure of water at this temperature? What if you use 2.0 g of water? Under either set of conditions, is any liquid water left in the flask, or does all of the water evaporate?

Vapor Pressure, Enthalpy of Vaporization, and the Clausius–Clapeyron Equation

Plotting the vapor pressure for a liquid at a series of temperatures results in a curved line (Figure 12.17). However, the German physicist R. Clausius (1822–1888) and the Frenchman B. P. E. Clapeyron (1799–1864) showed that, for a pure liquid, a linear relationship exists between the reciprocal of the Kelvin temperature $(1/T)$ and the natural logarithm of vapor pressure $(\ln P)$ (Figure 12.18).

$$\ln P = -(\Delta_{\text{vap}}H^\circ / RT) + C \qquad (12.1)$$

Here, $\Delta_{\text{vap}}H^\circ$ is the enthalpy of vaporization of the liquid; R is the ideal gas constant (8.314472 J/K · mol); and C is a constant characteristic of the liquid in question. This equation, now called the **Clausius-Clapeyron equation,** provides a method of obtaining values for $\Delta_{\text{vap}}H^\circ$. The equilibrium vapor pressure of a liquid can be measured at several different temperatures, and the logarithm of these pressures

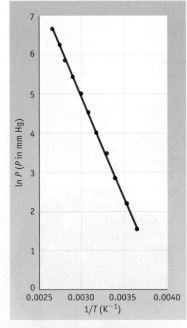

FIGURE 12.18 Clausius–Clapeyron equation. When the natural logarithm of the vapor pressure (ln P) of water at various temperatures (T) is plotted against $1/T$, a straight line is obtained. The slope of the line equals $-\Delta_{\text{vap}}H^\circ/R$. Values of T and P are from Appendix G.

is plotted versus $1/T$. The result is a straight line with a slope of $-\Delta_{vap}H^\circ/R$. For example, plotting data for water (Figure 12.18), we find the slope of the line is -4.90×10^3, which gives $\Delta_{vap}H^\circ = 40.7$ kJ/mol.

As an alternative to plotting $\ln P$ versus $1/T$, we can write the following equation that allows us to calculate $\Delta_{vap}H^\circ$ knowing the vapor pressure of a liquid at two different temperatures.

$$\ln P_2 - \ln P_1 = \left[\frac{-\Delta_{vap}H^\circ}{RT_2} + C \right] - \left[\frac{-\Delta_{vap}H^\circ}{RT_1} + C \right]$$

This can be simplified to

$$\ln \frac{P_2}{P_1} = -\frac{\Delta_{vap}H^\circ}{R} \left[\frac{1}{T_2} - \frac{1}{T_1} \right] \qquad (12.2)$$

For example, ethylene glycol has a vapor pressure of 14.9 mm Hg (P_1) at 373 K (T_1), and a vapor pressure of 49.1 mm Hg (P_2) at 398 K (T_2).

$$\ln \left(\frac{49.1 \text{ mm Hg}}{14.9 \text{ mm Hg}} \right) = -\frac{\Delta_{vap}H^\circ}{0.0083145 \text{ kJ/K} \cdot \text{mol}} \left[\frac{1}{398 \text{ K}} - \frac{1}{373 \text{ K}} \right]$$

$$1.192 = -\frac{\Delta_{vap}H^\circ}{0.0083145 \text{ kJ/K} \cdot \text{mol}} \left(-\frac{0.000168}{K} \right)$$

$$\Delta_{vap}H^\circ = 59.0 \text{ kJ/mol}$$

Chemistry ⚛ Now™

Sign in at **www.cengage.com/login** and go to Chapter 12 Contents to see Screen 12.9 for three tutorials on using the **Clausius–Clapeyron equation.**

EXERCISE 12.8 Clausius–Clapeyron Equation

Calculate the enthalpy of vaporization of diethyl ether, $(C_2H_5)_2O$ (see Figure 12.17). This compound has vapor pressures of 57.0 mm Hg and 534 mm Hg at -22.8 °C and 25.0 °C, respectively.

Boiling Point

If you have a beaker of water open to the atmosphere, the atmosphere presses down on the surface. If enough energy is added, a temperature is eventually reached at which the vapor pressure of the liquid equals the atmospheric pressure. At this temperature, bubbles of the liquid's vapor will not be crushed by the atmospheric pressure. The bubbles can rise to the surface, and the liquid boils (Figure 12.19).

The boiling point of a liquid is the temperature at which its vapor pressure is equal to the external pressure. If the external pressure is 760 mm Hg, this temperature is called the **normal boiling point.** This point is highlighted on the vapor pressure curves for the substances in Figure 12.17.

The normal boiling point of water is 100 °C, and in a great many places in the United States, water boils at or near this temperature. If you live at higher altitudes, however, such as in Salt Lake City, Utah, where the barometric pressure is about 650 mm Hg, water will boil at a noticeably lower temperature. The curve in Figure 12.19 shows that a pressure of 650 mm Hg corresponds to a boiling temperature of about 95 °C. Food, therefore, has to be cooked a little longer in Salt Lake City to achieve the same result as in New York City at sea level.

Charles D. Winters

FIGURE 12.19 Vapor pressure and boiling. When the vapor pressure of the liquid equals the atmospheric pressure, bubbles of vapor begin to form within the body of liquid, and the liquid boils.

Critical Temperature and Pressure

On first thought, it might seem that vapor pressure–temperature curves (such as shown in Figure 12.17) should continue upward without limit, but this is not so. Instead, when a specific temperature and pressure are reached, the interface between the liquid and the vapor disappears. This point is called the **critical point.** The temperature at which this phenomenon occurs is the **critical temperature, T_c,** and the corresponding pressure is the **critical pressure, P_c** (Figure 12.20). The substance that exists under these conditions is called a **supercritical fluid.** It is like a gas under such a high pressure that its density resembles that of a liquid, while its viscosity (ability to flow) remains close to that of a gas (▶ page 580).

Consider what the substance might look like at the molecular level under these conditions. The molecules have been forced almost as close together as they are in the liquid state, but each molecule has enough kinetic energy to exceed the forces holding molecules together. As a result, the supercritical fluid has a tightly packed molecular arrangement like a liquid, but the intermolecular forces of attraction that characterize the liquid state are less than the kinetic energy of the particles.

For most substances, the critical point is at a very high temperature and pressure (Table 12.7). Water, for instance, has a critical temperature of 374 °C and a critical pressure of 217.7 atm.

Supercritical fluids can have unexpected properties, such as the ability to dissolve normally insoluble materials. Supercritical CO_2 is especially useful. Carbon dioxide is widely available, essentially nontoxic, nonflammable, and inexpensive. It is relatively easy to reach its critical temperature of 30.99 °C and critical pressure of 72.8 atm. One use of supercritical CO_2 is to extract caffeine from coffee. The coffee beans are treated with steam to bring the caffeine to the surface. The beans are then immersed in supercritical CO_2, which selectively dissolves the caffeine but leaves intact the compounds that give flavor to coffee. (Decaffeinated coffee contains less than 3% of the original caffeine.) The solution of caffeine in supercritical CO_2 is poured off, and the CO_2 is evaporated, trapped, and reused.

TABLE 12.7 Critical Temperatures and Pressures for Common Compounds*

Compound	T_c (°C)	P_c (atm)
CH_4 (methane)	−82.6	45.4
C_2H_6 (ethane)	32.3	49.1
C_3H_8 (propane)	96.7	41.9
C_4H_{10} (butane)	152.0	37.3
CCl_2F_2 (CFC-12)	111.8	40.9
NH_3	132.4	112.0
H_2O	374.0	217.7
CO_2	30.99	72.8
SO_2	157.7	77.8

*Data taken from D. R. Lide: *Basic Laboratory and Industrial Chemicals,* Boca Raton, FL, CRC Press, 1993.

■ **Green Chemistry and Supercritical CO_2** It is not surprising that other uses are being sought for supercritical CO_2. One application being investigated is its use as a dry cleaning solvent. More than 10 billion kilograms of organic and halogenated solvents are used worldwide every year in cleaning applications. These cleaning agents can have deleterious effects on the environment, so it is hoped that many can be replaced by supercritical CO_2. (For more about supercritical CO_2 see page 609.)

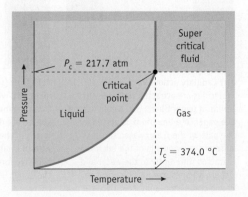

FIGURE 12.20 Critical temperature and pressure for water. The curve representing equilibrium conditions for liquid and gaseous water ends at the critical point; above that temperature and pressure, water becomes a supercritical fluid.

FIGURE 12.21 Intermolecular **forces in a liquid.** Forces acting on a molecule at the surface of a liquid are different than those acting on a molecule in the interior of a liquid.

Water molecules on the surface are not completely surrounded by other water molecules.

Water molecules under the surface are completely surrounded by other water molecules.

Surface Tension, Capillary Action, and Viscosity

Molecules in the interior of a liquid interact with molecules all around them (Figure 12.21). In contrast, molecules on the surface of a liquid are affected only by those molecules located at or below the surface layer. This leads to a net inward force of attraction on the surface molecules, contracting the surface area and making the liquid behave as though it had a skin. The toughness of this skin is measured by its **surface tension**—the energy required to break through the surface or to disrupt a liquid drop and spread the material out as a film. Surface tension causes water drops to be spheres and not little cubes, for example (Figure 12.22a), because a sphere has a smaller surface area than any other shape of the same volume.

Capillary action is closely related to surface tension. When a small-diameter glass tube is placed in water, the water rises in the tube, just as water rises in a piece of paper in water (Figure 12.22b). Because polar Si—O bonds are present on the

■ **Viscosity** Long chains of atoms, such as those present in oils, are floppy and become entangled with one another in the liquid; the longer the chain, the greater the tangling and the greater the viscosity.

FIGURE 12.22
Adhesive and cohesive forces.

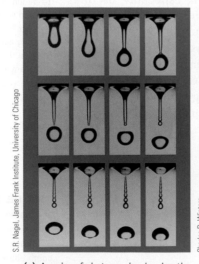

S.R. Nagel, James Frank Institute, University of Chicago

Charles D. Winters

Charles D. Winters

(a) A series of photographs showing the different stages when a water drop falls. The drop was illuminated by a strobe light of 5-ms duration. (The total time for this sequence was 0.05 s.) Water droplets take a spherical shape because of surface tension.

(b) Capillary action. Polar water molecules are attracted to the —OH bonds in paper fibers, and water rises in the paper. If a line of ink is placed in the path of the rising water, the different components of the ink are attracted differently to the water and paper and are separated in a process called chromatography.

(c) Water (top layer) forms a concave meniscus, while mercury (bottom layer) forms a convex meniscus. The different shapes are determined by the adhesive forces of the molecules of the liquid with the walls of the tube and the cohesive forces between molecules of the liquid.

The events of September 11, 2001, are etched in everyone's memory. The possibility of domestic terrorism, however, began almost two years before when a man was apprehended in late December 1999 at the Canadian border with bomb materials and a map of the Los Angeles International Airport. Although he claimed innocence, his fingerprints were on the bomb materials, and he was convicted of an attempt to bomb the airport.

Each of us has a unique fingerprint pattern, as first described by John Purkinji in 1823. Not long after, the English in India began using fingerprints on contracts because they believed it made the contract appear more binding. It was not until late in the 19th century, however, that fingerprinting was used as an identifier. Sir Francis Galton, a British anthropologist and cousin of Charles Darwin, established that a person's fingerprints do not change over the course of a lifetime and that no two prints are exactly the same. Fingerprinting has since become an accepted tool in forensic science.

In 1993 in Knoxville, Tennessee, detective Art Bohanan thought he could use it to solve the case of the kidnapping of a young girl. The girl had been taken from her home and driven away in a green car. The girl soon managed to escape from her attacker and was able to describe the car to the police. After four days, the police found the car and arrested its owner. But had the girl been in that car? Art Bohanan inspected the car for her fingerprints and even used the latest technique, fuming with superglue. No prints were found.

The abductor of the girl was eventually convicted on other evidence, but Bohanan wondered why he had never found her prints in the car. He decided to test the permanence of children's fingerprints compared with adults. To his amazement, he found that chil-

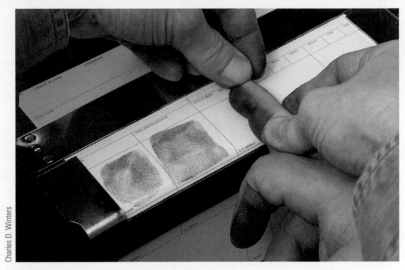

Charles D. Winters

Taking a fingerprint at the local police station.

dren's prints disappear in a few hours, whereas an adult's prints can last for days. Bohanan said, "It sounded like the compounds in children's fingerprints might simply be evaporating faster than adult's."

To answer this, you should know about the nature of fingerprints. The residue deposited by fingerprints is 99% water. The other 1% contains oils, fatty acids, esters, salts, urea [$(NH_2)_2CO$], and amino acids. An example of a fatty acid is myristic acid: $CH_3(CH_2)_{12}CO_2H$. An ester is the combination of an acid with an alcohol such as ethanol (CH_3CH_2OH), so an ester of myristic acid would be: $CH_3(CH_2)_{12}CO_2CH_2CH_3$

Scientists at Oak Ridge National Laboratory studied the fingerprints of 50 child and adult volunteers, identifying the compounds present by such techniques as mass spectrometry (◄ page 68). What they found clarified the mystery of the disappearing fingerprints.

Children's fingerprints contain more low–molecular-weight fatty acids than adult fin-

gerprints. In contrast, adult fingerprints contain esters of long-chain fatty acids with long-chain alcohols. These are waxes, semi-solid or solid organic compounds with high molecular weights. (Examples of waxes are lanolin, a component of wool, or carnauba wax used in furniture polish.)

Before puberty, children do not produce waxy compounds in their skin. However, sebaceous glands in adult skin produce sebum, a complex mixture of organic compounds (triglycerides, fatty acids, cholesterol, and waxes). There are only a few of these glands on the hands; most are on the mid-back, forehead, and chin. So, when you touch your face, this mixture of compounds is transferred to your fingers, and you can leave a fingerprint that is unique to you.

Question:

Why do children's fingerprints evaporate more readily than adult fingerprints?

Answer to this question is in Appendix Q.

---

surface of glass, polar water molecules are attracted by **adhesive forces** between the two different substances. These forces are strong enough that they can compete with the **cohesive forces** between the water molecules themselves. Thus, some water molecules can adhere to the walls; other water molecules are attracted to them and build a "bridge" back into the liquid. The surface tension of the water (from cohesive forces) is great enough to pull the liquid up the tube, so the water level rises in the tube. The rise will continue until the attractive forces—adhesion between water and glass, cohesion between water molecules—are balanced by the force of gravity pulling down on the water column. These forces lead to the characteristic concave, or downward-curving, meniscus seen with water in a test tube (Figure 12.22c).

In some liquids, cohesive forces (high surface tension) are much greater than adhesive forces with glass. Mercury is one example. Mercury does not climb the walls of a glass capillary. In fact, when it is in a glass tube, mercury will form a convex, or upward-curving, meniscus (Figure 12.22c).

One other important property of liquids in which intermolecular forces play a role is **viscosity,** the resistance of liquids to flow. When you turn over a glassful of water, it empties quickly. In contrast, it takes much more time to empty a glassful of olive oil or honey. Olive oil consists of molecules with long chains of carbon atoms, and it is about 70 times more viscous than ethanol, a small molecule with only two carbons and one oxygen. Longer chains have greater intermolecular forces because there are more atoms to attract one another, with each atom contributing to the total force. Honey (a concentrated aqueous solution of sugar molecules), however, is also a viscous liquid, even though the size of the molecules is fairly small. In this case, the sugar molecules have numerous —OH groups. These lead to greater forces of attraction due to hydrogen bonding.

Chemistry‧○‧Now™

Sign in at **www.cengage.com/login** and go to Chapter 12 Contents to see Screen 12.11 to watch videos on **surface tension, capillary action,** and **viscosity.**

Glycerol

EXERCISE 12.9 Viscosity

Glycerol ($HOCH_2CHOHCH_2OH$) is used in cosmetics. Do you expect its viscosity to be larger or smaller than the viscosity of ethanol, CH_3CH_2OH? Explain briefly.

Chapter Goals Revisited

Now that you have studied this chapter, you should ask whether you have met the chapter goals. In particular, you should be able to:

Describe intermolecular forces and their effects

a. Describe the various intermolecular forces found in liquids and solids (Sections 12.2 and 12.3). Study Question(s) assignable in OWL: 2, 4, 6, 7, 25–28, 30, 32, 39; Go Chemistry Module 17.

b. Tell when two molecules can interact through a dipole–dipole attraction and when hydrogen bonding may occur. The latter occurs most strongly when H is attached to O, N, or F (Section 12.2). Study Question(s) assignable in OWL: 7–10.

c. Identify instances in which molecules interact by induced dipoles (dispersion forces) (Section 12.3). Study Question(s) assignable in OWL: 7.

Understand the importance of hydrogen bonding

a. Explain how hydrogen bonding affects the properties of water (Section 12.2).

Understand the properties of liquids

a. Explain the processes of evaporation and condensation, and use the enthalpy of vaporization in calculations (Section 12.4). Study Question(s) assignable in OWL: 11, 12, 18, 31, 53.

b. Define the equilibrium vapor pressure of a liquid, and explain the relationship between the vapor pressure and boiling point of a liquid (Section 12.4). Study Question(s) assignable in OWL: 14, 15, 17, 19, 20, 29, 38, 50.

c. Describe the phenomena of the critical temperature, T_c, and critical pressure, P_c, of a substance (Section 12.4). Study Question(s) assignable in OWL: 23.

d. Describe how intermolecular interactions affect the cohesive forces between identical liquid molecules, the energy necessary to break through the surface of a liquid (surface tension), and the resistance to flow, or viscosity, of liquids (Section 12.4). Study Question(s) assignable in OWL: 41.

e. Use the Clausius–Clapeyron equation, which connects temperature, vapor pressure, and enthalpy of vaporization for liquids (Section 12.4). Study Question(s) assignable in OWL: 21, 22, 34.

For additional preparation for an examination on this chapter see the *Let's Review* section on pages 656–669.

KEY EQUATION

Equation 12.2 (page 576) The Clausius–Clapeyron equation relates the equilibrium vapor pressure, P, of a volatile liquid to the molar enthalpy of vaporization ($\Delta_{vap}H°$) at a given temperature, T. (R is the universal constant, 8.314472 J/K · mol.) Equation 12.2 allows you to calculate $\Delta_{vap}H°$ if you know the vapor pressures at two different temperatures. Alternatively, you may plot ln P versus $1/T$; the slope of the line is $-\Delta_{vap}H°/R$.

$$\ln\frac{P_2}{P_1} = -\frac{\Delta_{vap}H°}{R}\left[\frac{1}{T_2} - \frac{1}{T_1}\right]$$

STUDY QUESTIONS

OWL Online homework for this chapter may be assigned in OWL.

▲ denotes challenging questions.

■ denotes questions assignable in OWL.

Blue-numbered questions have answers in Appendix O and fully-worked solutions in the *Student Solutions Manual*.

Practicing Skills

Intermolecular Forces
(See Examples 12.1–12.4 and ChemistryNow Screens 12.3–12.7.)

1. What intermolecular force(s) must be overcome to
   (a) melt ice
   (b) sublime solid I_2
   (c) convert liquid NH_3 to NH_3 vapor

2. ■ What type of forces must be overcome within solid I_2 when I_2 dissolves in methanol, CH_3OH? What type of forces must be disrupted between CH_3OH molecules when I_2 dissolves? What type of forces exist between I_2 and CH_3OH molecules in solution?

3. What type of intermolecular forces must be overcome in converting each of the following from a liquid to a gas?
   (a) liquid O_2 (c) CH_3I (methyl iodide)
   (b) mercury   (d) CH_3CH_2OH (ethanol)

4. ■ What type of intermolecular forces must be overcome in converting each of the following from a liquid to a gas?
   (a) CO_2 (c) $CHCl_3$
   (b) NH_3 (d) CCl_4

5. Rank the following atoms or molecules in order of increasing strength of intermolecular forces in the pure substance. Which exists as a gas at 25 °C and 1 atm?
   (a) Ne   (c) CO
   (b) CH_4 (d) CCl_4

6. ■ Rank the following in order of increasing strength of intermolecular forces in the pure substances. Which exists as a gas at 25 °C and 1 atm?
(a) $CH_3CH_2CH_2CH_3$ (butane)
(b) CH_3OH (methanol)
(c) He

7. ■ Which of the following compounds would be expected to form intermolecular hydrogen bonds in the liquid state?
(a) CH_3OCH_3 (dimethyl ether)
(b) CH_4
(c) HF
(d) CH_3CO_2H (acetic acid)
(e) Br_2
(f) CH_3OH (methanol)

8. ■ Which of the following compounds would be expected to form intermolecular hydrogen bonds in the liquid state?
(a) H_2Se
(b) HCO_2H (formic acid)
(c) HI
(d) acetone (see structure below)

$$H_3C-\overset{\displaystyle O}{\overset{\displaystyle \|}{C}}-CH_3$$

9. ■ In each pair of ionic compounds, which is more likely to have the more negative enthalpy of hydration? Briefly explain your reasoning in each case.
(a) LiCl or CsCl
(b) $NaNO_3$ or $Mg(NO_3)_2$
(c) RbCl or $NiCl_2$

10. ■ When salts of Mg^{2+}, Na^+, and Cs^+ are placed in water, the positive ion is hydrated (as is the negative ion). Which of these three cations is most strongly hydrated? Which one is least strongly hydrated?

Liquids
(See Examples 12.5 and 12.6 and ChemistryNow Screens 12.8–12.11.)

11. ■ Ethanol, CH_3CH_2OH, has a vapor pressure of 59 mm Hg at 25 °C. What quantity of energy as heat is required to evaporate 125 mL of the alcohol at 25 °C? The enthalpy of vaporization of the alcohol at 25 °C is 42.32 kJ/mol. The density of the liquid is 0.7849 g/mL.

12. ■ The enthalpy of vaporization of liquid mercury is 59.11 kJ/mol. What quantity of energy as heat is required to vaporize 0.500 mL of mercury at 357 °C, its normal boiling point? The density of mercury is 13.6 g/mL.

13. Answer the following questions using Figure 12.17:
(a) What is the approximate equilibrium vapor pressure of water at 60 °C? Compare your answer with the data in Appendix G.
(b) At what temperature does water have an equilibrium vapor pressure of 600 mm Hg?
(c) Compare the equilibrium vapor pressures of water and ethanol at 70 °C. Which is higher?

14. ■ Answer the following questions using Figure 12.17:
(a) What is the equilibrium vapor pressure of diethyl ether at room temperature (approximately 20 °C)?
(b) Place the three compounds in Figure 12.17 in order of increasing intermolecular forces.
(c) If the pressure in a flask is 400 mm Hg and if the temperature is 40 °C, which of the three compounds (diethyl ether, ethanol, and water) are liquids, and which are gases?

15. ■ Assume you seal 1.0 g of diethyl ether (see Figure 12.17) in an evacuated 100.-mL flask. If the flask is held at 30 °C, what is the approximate gas pressure in the flask? If the flask is placed in an ice bath, does additional liquid ether evaporate, or does some ether condense to a liquid?

16. Refer to Figure 12.17 as an aid in answering these questions:
(a) You put some water at 60 °C in a plastic milk carton and seal the top very tightly so gas cannot enter or leave the carton. What happens when the water cools?
(b) If you put a few drops of liquid diethyl ether on your hand, does it evaporate completely or remain a liquid?

17. ■ Which member of each of the following pairs of compounds has the higher boiling point?
(a) O_2 or N_2 (c) HF or HI
(b) SO_2 or CO_2 (d) SiH_4 or GeH_4

18. ■ Place the following four compounds in order of increasing boiling point:
(a) SCl_2 (c) C_2H_6
(b) NH_3 (d) Ne

19. ■ Vapor pressure curves for CS_2 (carbon disulfide) and CH_3NO_2 (nitromethane) are drawn here.
(a) What are the approximate vapor pressures of CS_2 and CH_3NO_2 at 40 °C?
(b) What type of intermolecular forces exist in the liquid phase of each compound?
(c) What is the normal boiling point of CS_2? Of CH_3NO_2?
(d) At what temperature does CS_2 have a vapor pressure of 600 mm Hg?
(e) At what temperature does CH_3NO_2 have a vapor pressure of 60 mm Hg?

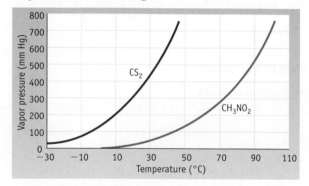

▲ more challenging   ■ in OWL   Blue-numbered questions answered in Appendix O

20. ■ Answer each of the following questions with *increases*, *decreases*, or *does not change*.

(a) If the intermolecular forces in a liquid increase, the normal boiling point of the liquid _____.

(b) If the intermolecular forces in a liquid decrease, the vapor pressure of the liquid _____.

(c) If the surface area of a liquid decreases, the vapor pressure _____.

(d) If the temperature of a liquid increases, the equilibrium vapor pressure _____.

21. ■ The following data are the equilibrium vapor pressure of benzene, C_6H_6, at various temperatures.

Temperature (°C)	Vapor Pressure (mm Hg)
7.6	40.
26.1	100.
60.6	400.
80.1	760.

(a) What is the normal boiling point of benzene?

(b) Plot these data so that you have a plot resembling the one in Figure 12.17. At what temperature does the liquid have an equilibrium vapor pressure of 250 mm Hg? At what temperature is it 650 mm Hg?

(c) Calculate the molar enthalpy of vaporization for benzene using the the Clausius–Clapeyron equation (Equation 12.2, page 576).

22. ■ Vapor pressure data are given here for octane, C_8H_{18}.

Temperature (°C)	Vapor Pressure (mm Hg)
25	13.6
50.	45.3
75	127.2
100.	310.8

Use the Clausius–Clapeyron equation (Equation 12.2, page 576) to calculate the molar enthalpy of vaporization of octane and its normal boiling point.

23. ■ Can carbon monoxide ($T_c = 132.9$ K; $P_c = 34.5$ atm) be liquefied at or above room temperature? Explain briefly.

24. Methane (CH_4) cannot be liquefied at room temperature, no matter how high the pressure. Propane (C_3H_8), another simple hydrocarbon, has a critical pressure of 42 atm and a critical temperature of 96.7 °C. Can this compound be liquefied at room temperature?

General Questions

These questions are not designated as to type or location in the chapter. They may combine several concepts.

25. ■ Rank the following substances in order of increasing strength of intermolecular forces: (a) Ar, (b) CH_3OH, and (c) CO_2.

26. ■ What types of intermolecular forces are important in the liquid phase of (a) C_2H_6 and (b) $(CH_3)_2CHOH$.

27. ■ Which of the following salts, Li_2SO_4 or Cs_2SO_4, is expected to have the more exothermic enthalpy of hydration?

28. ■ Select the substance in each of the following pairs that should have the higher boiling point:

(a) Br_2 or ICl

(b) neon or krypton

(c) CH_3CH_2OH (ethanol) or C_2H_4O (ethylene oxide, structure below)

$$H_2C - CH_2$$
$$\quad\ O$$

29. ■ Use the vapor pressure curves illustrated here to answer the questions that follow.

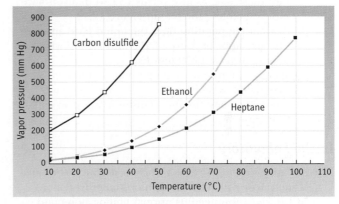

(a) What is the vapor pressure of ethanol, C_2H_5OH, at 60 °C?

(b) Considering only carbon disulfide (CS_2) and ethanol, which has the stronger intermolecular forces in the liquid state?

(c) At what temperature does heptane (C_7H_{16}) have a vapor pressure of 500 mm Hg?

(d) What are the approximate normal boiling points of each of the three substances?

(e) At a pressure of 400 mm Hg and a temperature of 70 °C, is each substance a liquid, a gas, or a mixture of liquid and gas?

30. ■ Which of the following salts will you most likely find as hydrated solids? Explain your reasoning.

(a) $Fe(NO_3)_3$ (c) NaCl

(b) $CoCl_2$ (d) $Al(NO_3)_3$

31. ■ Rank the following compounds in order of increasing molar enthalpy of vaporization: CH_3OH, C_2H_6, HCl.

32. ■ Rank the following molecules in order of increasing intermolecular forces: CH_3Cl, HCO_2H (formic acid), and CO_2.

33. Mercury and many of its compounds are dangerous poisons if breathed, swallowed, or even absorbed through the skin. The liquid metal has a vapor pressure of 0.00169 mm Hg at 24 °C. If the air in a small room is saturated with mercury vapor, how many atoms of mercury vapor occur per cubic meter?

34. ▲ ■ The following data are the equilibrium vapor pressure of limonene, $C_{10}H_{16}$, at various temperatures. (Limonene is used as a scent in commercial products.)

Temperature (°C)	Vapor Pressure (mm Hg)
14.0	1.0
53.8	10.
84.3	40.
108.3	100.
151.4	400.

(a) Plot these data as ln P versus $1/T$ so that you have plot resembling the one in Figure 12.18.
(b) At what temperature does the liquid have an equilibrium vapor pressure of 250 mm Hg? At what temperature is it 650 mm Hg?
(c) What is the normal boiling point of limonene?
(d) Calculate the molar enthalpy of vaporization for limonene using the the Clausius–Clapeyron equation (Equation 12.2).

In the Laboratory

35. You are going to prepare a silicone polymer, and one of the starting materials is dichlorodimethylsilane, $SiCl_2(CH_3)_2$. You need its normal boiling point and so measure equilibrium vapor pressures at various temperatures.

Temperature (°C)	Vapor Pressure (mm Hg)
−0.4	40.
+17.5	100.
51.9	400.
70.3	760.

(a) What is the normal boiling point of dichlorodimethylsilane?
(b) Plot these data as ln P versus $1/T$ so that you have a plot resembling the one in Figure 12.18. At what temperature does the liquid have an equilibrium vapor pressure of 250 mm Hg? At what temperature is it 650 mm Hg?
(c) Calculate the molar enthalpy of vaporization for dichlorodimethylsilane using the the Clausius–Clapeyron equation (Equation 12.2).

36. A "hand boiler" can be purchased in toy stores or at science supply companies. If you cup your hand around the bottom bulb, the volatile liquid in the boiler boils, and the liquid moves to the upper chamber. Using your knowledge of kinetic molecular theory and intermolecular forces, explain how the hand boiler works.

Charles D. Winters

37. ▲ The photos below illustrate an experiment you can do yourself. Place 10 mL of water in an empty soda can, and heat the water to boiling. Using tongs or pliers, turn the can over in a pan of cold water, making sure the opening in the can is below the water level in the pan.
(a) Describe what happens, and explain it in terms of the subject of this chapter.

Charles D. Winters

(a)   (b)

(b) Prepare a molecular level sketch of the situation inside the can before heating and after heating (but prior to inverting the can).

38. ■ If you place 1.0 L of ethanol (C_2H_5OH) in a room that is 3.0 m long, 2.5 m wide, and 2.5 m high, will all the alcohol evaporate? If some liquid remains, how much will there be? The vapor pressure of ethyl alcohol at 25 °C is 59 mm Hg, and the density of the liquid at this temperature is 0.785 g/cm³.

▲ more challenging   ■ in OWL   Blue-numbered questions answered in Appendix O

Summary and Conceptual Questions

The following questions may use concepts from this and previous chapters.

39. ■ Acetone, CH_3COCH_3, is a common laboratory solvent. It is usually contaminated with water, however. Why does acetone absorb water so readily? Draw molecular structures showing how water and acetone can interact. What intermolecular force(s) is (are) involved in the interaction?

$$H_3C-\overset{\overset{\displaystyle O}{\|}}{C}-CH_3$$

40. Cooking oil floats on top of water. From this observation, what conclusions can you draw regarding the polarity or hydrogen-bonding ability of molecules found in cooking oil?

41. ■ Liquid ethylene glycol, $HOCH_2CH_2OH$, is one of the main ingredients in commercial antifreeze. Do you predict its viscosity to be greater or less than that of ethanol, CH_3CH_2OH?

42. Liquid methanol, CH_3OH, is placed in a glass tube. Is the meniscus of the liquid concave or convex? Explain briefly.

43. Account for these facts:
    (a) Although ethanol (C_2H_5OH) (bp, 80 °C) has a higher molar mass than water (bp, 100 °C), the alcohol has a lower boiling point.
    (b) Mixing 50 mL of ethanol with 50 mL of water produces a solution with a volume slightly less than 100 mL.

44. Rationalize the observation that $CH_3CH_2CH_2OH$, 1-propanol, has a boiling point of 97.2 °C, whereas a compound with the same empirical formula, methyl ethyl ether ($CH_3CH_2OCH_3$), boils at 7.4 °C.

45. Cite two pieces of evidence to support the statement that water molecules in the liquid state exert considerable attractive force on one another.

46. During thunderstorms in the Midwest, very large hailstones can fall from the sky. (Some are the size of golf balls!) To preserve some of these stones, we put them in the freezer compartment of a frost-free refrigerator. Our friend, who is a chemistry student, tells us to use an older model that is not frost-free. Why?

47. Refer to Figure 12.12 to answer the following questions:
    (a) Of the three hydrogen halides (HX), which has the largest total intermolecular force?
    (b) Why are the dispersion forces greater for HI than for HCl?
    (c) Why are the dipole–dipole forces greater for HCl than for HI?
    (d) Of the seven molecules in Figure 12.12, which involves the largest dispersion forces? Explain why this is reasonable.

48. ▲ What quantity of energy is evolved (in joules) when 1.00 mol of liquid ammonia cools from −33.3 °C (its boiling point) to −43.3 °C? (The specific heat capacity of liquid NH_3 is 4.70 J/g · K.) Compare this with the quantity of heat evolved by 1.00 mol of liquid water cooling by exactly 10 °C. Which evolves more heat per mole on cooling 10 °C, liquid water or liquid ammonia? *(The underlying reason for the difference in heat evolved is scientifically illuminating and interesting. You can learn more by searching the Internet for specific heat capacity and its dependence on molecular properties.)*

49. A fluorocarbon, CF_4, has a critical temperature of −45.7 °C and a critical pressure of 37 atm. Are there any conditions under which this compound can be a liquid at room temperature? Explain briefly.

50. ▲ ■ The figure below is a plot of vapor pressure versus temperature for dichlorodifluoromethane, CCl_2F_2. The enthalpy of vaporization of the liquid is 165 kJ/g, and the specific heat capacity of the liquid is about 1.0 J/g · K.

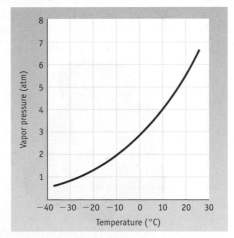

(a) What is the approximate normal boiling point of CCl_2F_2?
(b) A steel cylinder containing 25 kg of CCl_2F_2 in the form of liquid and vapor is set outdoors on a warm day (25 °C). What is the approximate pressure of the vapor in the cylinder?
(c) The cylinder valve is opened, and CCl_2F_2 vapor gushes out of the cylinder in a rapid flow. Soon, however, the flow becomes much slower, and the outside of the cylinder is coated with ice frost. When the valve is closed and the cylinder is reweighed, it is found that 20 kg of CCl_2F_2 is still in the cylinder. Why is the flow fast at first? Why does it slow down long before the cylinder is empty? Why does the outside become icy?
(d) Which of the following procedures would be effective in emptying the cylinder rapidly (and safely)? (1) Turn the cylinder upside down, and open the valve. (2) Cool the cylinder to −78 °C in dry ice, and open the valve. (3) Knock off the top of the cylinder, valve and all, with a sledge hammer.

51. Acetaminophen is used in analgesics. A model of the molecule is shown here with its electrostatic potential surface. Where are the most likely sites for hydrogen bonding?

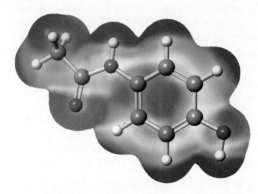

52. Shown here are models of two bases in DNA with the electrostatic potential surfaces: cytosine and guanine. What sites in these molecules are involved in hydrogen bonding with each other? Draw molecular structures showing how cytosine can hydrogen bond with guanine.

Cytosine

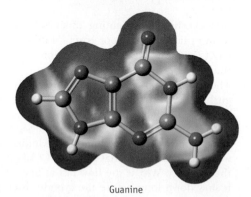

Guanine

53. List four properties of liquids that are directly determined by intermolecular forces.

54. List the following ions in order of hydration energies: Na^+, K^+, Mg^{2+}, Ca^{2+}. Explain how you determined this order.

55. Compare the boiling points of the various isomeric hydrocarbons shown in the table below. Notice the relationship between boiling point and structure; branched-chain hydrocarbons have lower boiling points than the unbranched isomer. Speculate on possible reasons for this trend. Why might the intermolecular forces be slightly different in these compounds?

Compound	Boiling point (°C)
Hexane	68.9
3-methylpentane	63.2
2-methylpentane	60.3
2,3-dimethylbutane	58.0
2,2-dimethylbutane	49.7

56. A 8.82 g sample of Br_2 is placed in an evacuated 1.00 L flask and heated to 58.8 °C, the normal boiling point of bromine. Describe the contents of the flask under these conditions.

57. Polarizability is defined as the extent to which the electron cloud surrounding an atom or molecule can be distorted by an external charge. Rank the halogens (F_2, Cl_2, Br_2, I_2) and the noble gases (He, Ne, Ar, Kr, Xe) in order of polarizability (from least polarizable to most polarizable). What properties of these substances could be used to determine this ranked order?

58. In which of the following organic molecules might we expect hydrogen bonding to occur?
(a) methyl acetate, $CH_3CO_2CH_3$
(b) acetaldehyde (ethanal), CH_3CHO
(c) acetone (2-propanone) (see Question 8)
(d) benzoic acid ($C_6H_5CO_2H$)
(e) acetamide (CH_3CONH_2 an amide formed from acetic acid and ammonia)
(f) N,N-dimethylacetamide [$CH_3CON(CH_3)_2$, an amide formed from acetic acid and dimethylamine]

59. A pressure cooker (a kitchen appliance) is a pot on which the top seals tightly, allowing pressure to build up inside. You put water in the pot and heat it to boiling. At the higher pressure, water boils at a higher temperature and this allows food to cook at a faster rate. Most pressure cookers have a setting of 15 psi, which means that the pressure in the pot is 15 psi above atmospheric pressure (1 atm = 14.70 psi). Use the Clausius-Clapeyron equation to calculate the temperature at which water boils in the pressure cooker.

▲ more challenging   ■ in OWL   Blue-numbered questions answered in Appendix O

60. Vapor pressures of $NH_3(\ell)$ at several temperatures are given in the table below. Use this information to calculate the enthalpy of vaporization of ammonia.

Temperature (°C)	Vapor Pressure (atm)
−68.4	0.132
−45.4	0.526
−33.6	1.000
−18.7	2.00
4.7	5.00
25.7	10.00
50.1	20.00

61. Chemists sometimes carry out reactions in liquid ammonia as a solvent. With adequate safety protection these reactions can be done above ammonia's boiling point in a sealed, thick-walled glass tube. If the reaction is being carried out at 20 °C, what is the pressure of ammonia inside the tube? (Use data from the previous question to answer this question.)

62. The data in the following table was used to create the graph shown below (vp = vapor pressure of ethanol (CH_3CH_2OH) expressed in mm Hg, T = kelvin temperature)

ln (vp)	1/T (K^{-1})
2.30	0.00369
3.69	0.00342
4.61	0.00325
5.99	0.00297
6.63	0.00285

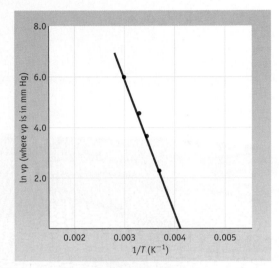

(a) Derive an equation for the straight line in this graph.
(b) Describe in words how to use the graph to determine the enthalpy of vaporization of ethanol.
(c) Calculate the vapor pressure of ethanol at 0.00 °C and at 100 °C.

13 | The Chemistry of Solids

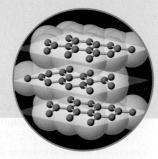

Graphite is composed of sheets of carbon atoms in six-member rings.

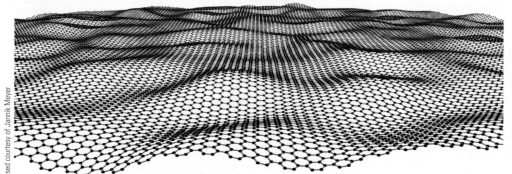

Graphene is a single sheet of six-member carbon rings. This latest material in the world of carbon chemistry has unusual electrical properties.

Used courtesy of Jannik Meyer

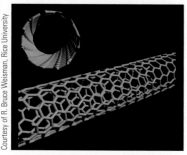

Courtesy of R. Bruce Weisman, Rice University

Carbon nanotubes are composed of six-member carbon rings.

Graphite to Graphene

One of the most interesting developments in chemistry in the last 20 years has been the discovery of new forms of carbon. First, there were buckyballs and then single-wall and multi-wall carbon nanotubes.

Common graphite, from which your pencil lead is made, consists of six-member rings of carbon atoms connected in sheets, and the sheets stack one on top of another like cards in a deck. But if carbon compounds are heated under the right conditions, the carbon atoms assemble into sheets, and the sheets close on themselves to form tubes. These are called **nanotubes** because the tubes are only a few nanometers in diameter. Sometimes they are single tubes, and other times there are tubes within tubes. Carbon nanotubes are at least 100 times stronger than steel but only one sixth as dense, and they conduct heat and electricity far better than copper. There has been enormous interest in their commercial applications, but there has also been difficulty in making them with consistent properties.

Now there is **graphene**, a single sheet of six-member carbon atoms. Researchers in England discovered them in a simple way: put a flake of graphite on Scotch tape, fold the tape over, and then pull it apart. The graphite layers come apart, and, if you do it enough times, only one layer—one C atom thick!—is left on the tape. This is clearly not the way to make graphene commercially, but methods have since been developed to make it in larger amounts. And now researchers are looking at ways to make graphene sheets in specific shapes, and to use them as transistors and other electronic devices.

Questions:

1. Based on a C—C distance of 139 pm, what is the side-to-side dimension of a planar, C_6 ring?
2. If a graphene sheet has a width of 1.0 micrometer, how many C_6 rings are joined across the sheet?
3. Estimate the thickness of a sheet of graphene (in pm). How did you determine this value?

Answers to these questions are in Appendix Q.

M any kinds of solids exist in the world around us (Figure 13.1 and Table 13.1). As the description of graphene shows, solid-state chemistry is one of the booming areas of science, especially because it relates to the development of interesting new materials. As we describe various kinds of solids, we hope to provide a glimpse of the reasons this area is exciting.

Chemistry.Now™

Throughout the text this icon introduces an opportunity for self-study or to explore interactive tutorials by signing in at **www.cengage.com/login**.

13.1 Crystal Lattices and Unit Cells

 Module 18

In both gases and liquids, molecules move continually and randomly, and they rotate and vibrate as well. Because of this movement, an orderly arrangement of molecules in the gaseous or liquid state is not possible. In solids, however, the molecules, atoms, or ions cannot change their relative positions (although they vibrate and occasionally rotate). Thus, a regular, repeating pattern of atoms or molecules within the structure—a long-range order—is a characteristic of most solids. The beautiful, external (macroscopic) regularity of a crystal of salt (Figure 13.1) suggests it has an internal symmetry.

TABLE 13.1 Structures and Properties of Various Types of Solid Substances

Type	Examples	Structural Units	Forces Holding Units Together	Typical Properties
Ionic	$NaCl$, K_2SO_4, $CaCl_2$, $(NH_4)_3PO_4$	Positive and negative ions; no discrete molecules	Ionic; attractions among charges on positive and negative ions	Hard; brittle; high melting point; poor electric conductivity as solid, good as liquid; often water-soluble
Metallic	Iron, silver, copper, other metals and alloys	Metal atoms (positive metal ions with delocalized electrons)	Metallic; electrostatic attraction among metal ions and electrons	Malleable; ductile; good electric conductivity in solid and liquid; good heat conductivity; wide range of hardness and melting points
Molecular	H_2, O_2, I_2, H_2O, CO_2, CH_4, CH_3OH, CH_3CO_2H	Molecules	Dispersion forces, dipole–dipole forces, hydrogen bonds	Low to moderate melting points and boiling points; soft; poor electric conductivity in solid and liquid
Network	Graphite, diamond, quartz, feldspars, mica	Atoms held in an infinite two- or three-dimensional network	Covalent; directional electron-pair bonds	Wide range of hardness and melting points (three-dimensional bonding > two-dimensional bonding); poor electric conductivity, with some exceptions
Amorphous	Glass, polyethylene, nylon	Covalently bonded networks with no long-range regularity	Covalent; directional electron-pair bonds	Noncrystalline; wide temperature range for melting; poor electric conductivity, with some exceptions

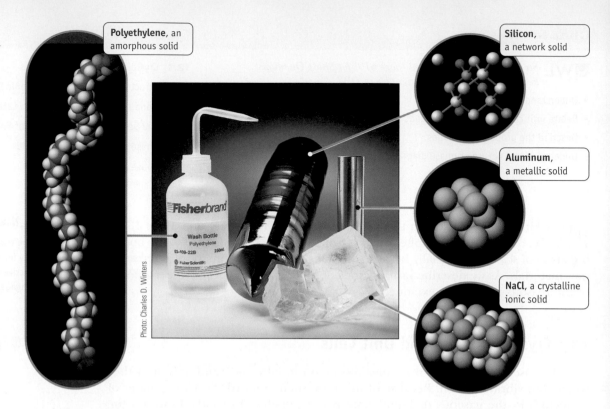

FIGURE 13.1
Some common solids.

Polyethylene, an amorphous solid

Silicon, a network solid

Aluminum, a metallic solid

NaCl, a crystalline ionic solid

Photo: Charles D. Winters

Structures of solids can be described as three-dimensional lattices of atoms, ions, or molecules. For a crystalline solid, we can identify the **unit cell**, the smallest repeating unit that has all of the symmetry characteristic of the way the atoms, ions, or molecules are arranged in the solid.

To understand unit cells, consider first a two-dimensional lattice model, the repeating pattern of circles shown in Figure 13.2. The yellow square at the left is a unit cell because the overall pattern can be created from a group of these cells by joining them edge to edge. It is also a requirement that unit cells reflect the stoichiometry of the solid. Here, the square unit cell at the left contains one smaller sphere and one fourth of each of the four larger circles, giving a total of one small and one large circle per two-dimensional unit cell.

You may recognize that it is possible to draw other unit cells for this two-dimensional lattice. One option is the square in the middle of Figure 13.2 that fully encloses a single large circle and parts of small circles that add up to one net small circle. Yet another possible unit cell is the parallelogram at the right. Other unit

FIGURE 13.2 Unit cells for a flat, two-dimensional solid made from circular "atoms." A lattice can be represented as being built from repeating unit cells. This two-dimensional lattice can be built by translating the unit cells throughout the plane of the figure. Each cell must move by the length of one side of the unit cell. In this figure, all unit cells contain a net of one large circle and one small circle. Be sure to notice that several unit cells are possible, with two of the most obvious being squares.

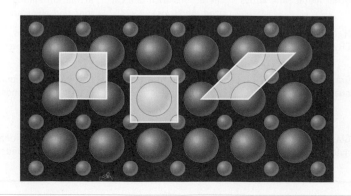

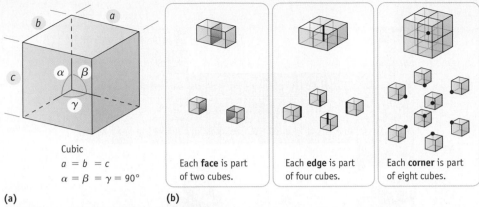

Cubic
$a = b = c$
$\alpha = \beta = \gamma = 90°$

(a)

Each **face** is part of two cubes.

Each **edge** is part of four cubes.

Each **corner** is part of eight cubes.

(b)

FIGURE 13.3 Cubic unit cells. (a) The cube is one of the seven basic unit cells that describe crystal systems. In a cube, all sides are of equal length, and all angles are 90°. In noncubic unit cells, the angles are not necessarily 90°, and the sides are not equal in length. (b) Stacking cubes to build a crystal lattice. Each crystal face is part of two cubes; each edge is part of four cubes; and each corner is part of eight cubes.

cells are possible, but it is conventional to draw unit cells in which atoms or ions are placed at the **lattice points;** that is, at the corners of the cube or other geometric object that constitutes the unit cell.

The three-dimensional lattices of solids can be built by assembling three-dimensional unit cells much like building blocks (Figure 13.3). The assemblage of these three-dimensional unit cells defines the **crystal lattice.**

To construct crystal lattices, nature uses seven three-dimensional unit cells. They differ from one another in that their sides have different relative lengths and their edges meet at different angles. The simplest of the seven crystal lattices is the **cubic unit cell,** a cell with edges of equal length that meet at 90° angles. We shall look in detail at just this structure, not only because cubic unit cells are easily visualized but also because they are commonly encountered.

Within the cubic class, three cell symmetries occur: **primitive cubic (pc), body-centered cubic (bcc),** and **face-centered cubic (fcc)** (Figure 13.4). All three have

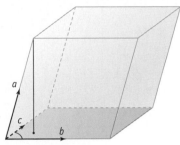

Unit cells. Of the possible unit cells, all are parallelpipeds (except for the hexagonal cell), figures in which opposite sides are parallel. In a cube, all angles (a-o-c, a-o-b, and c-o-b; where o is the origin) are 90°, and all sides are equal. In other cells, the angles and sides may be the same or different. For example, in a tetragonal cell, the angles are 90°, but $a = b \neq c$. In a triclinic cell, the sides have different lengths, the angles are different, and none equals 90°.

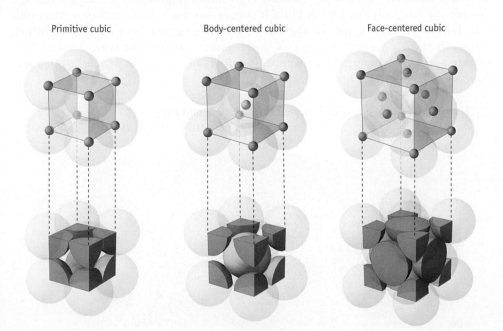

Primitive cubic   Body-centered cubic   Face-centered cubic

FIGURE 13.4 The three cubic unit cells. The top row shows the lattice points of the three cells, and the bottom row shows the same cells using space-filling spheres. The spheres in each figure represent identical atoms (or ions) centered on the lattice points. Because eight unit cells share a corner atom, only $\frac{1}{8}$ of each corner atom lies within a given unit cell; the remaining $\frac{7}{8}$ lies in seven other unit cells. Because each face of a fcc unit cell is shared with another unit cell, one half of each atom in the face of a face-centered cube lies in a given unit cell, and the other half lies in the adjoining cell.

FIGURE 13.5 Metals use four different unit cells. Three are based on the cube, and the fourth is the hexagonal unit cell (see page 595). (Many metals can crystallize in more than one structure.)

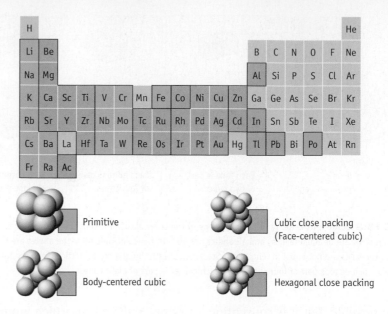

Primitive

Cubic close packing (Face-centered cubic)

Body-centered cubic

Hexagonal close packing

identical atoms, molecules, or ions at the corners of the cubic unit cell. The bcc and fcc arrangements, however, differ from the primitive cube in that they have additional particles at other locations. The bcc structure is called "body-centered" because it has an additional particle, of the same type as those at the corners, at the center of the cube. The fcc arrangement is called "face-centered" because it has a particle, of the same type as the corner atoms, in the center of each of the six faces of the cube. Examples of each structure are found among the crystal lattices of the metals (Figure 13.5). The alkali metals, for example, are body-centered cubic, whereas nickel, copper, and aluminum are face-centered cubic. Notice that only one metal, polonium, has a primitive cubic lattice.

When the cubes pack together to make a three-dimensional crystal of a metal, the atom at each corner is shared among eight cubes (Figures 13.3, 13.4, and 13.6a). Because of this, only one eighth of each corner atom is actually within a given unit cell. Furthermore, because a cube has eight corners, and because one eighth of the atom at each corner "belongs to" a particular unit cell, the corner atoms contribute a net of one atom to a given unit cell. Thus, *the primitive cubic arrangement has one net atom within the unit cell.*

(8 corners of a cube)(⅛ of each corner atom within a unit cell) =
1 net atom per unit cell for the primitive cubic unit cell

FIGURE 13.6 Atom sharing at cube corners and faces. (a) In any cubic lattice, each corner particle is shared equally among eight cubes, so one eighth of the particle is within a particular cubic unit cell. (b) In a face-centered lattice, each particle on a cube face is shared equally between two unit cells. One half of each particle of this type is within a given unit cell.

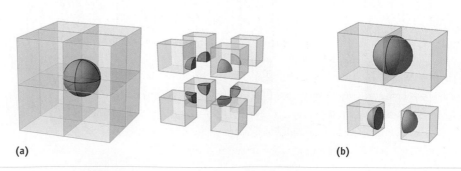

(a)

(b)

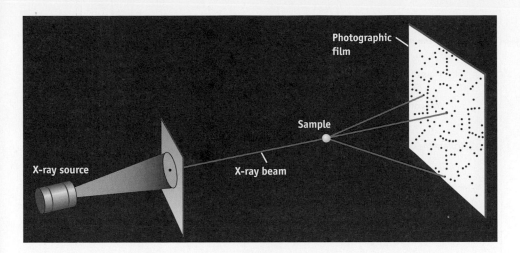

FIGURE 13.7 X-ray crystallography. In the x-ray diffraction experiment, a beam of x-rays is directed at a crystalline solid. The photons of the x-ray beam are scattered by the atoms of the solid. The scattered x-rays are detected by a photographic film or an electronic detector, and the pattern of scattered x-rays is related to the locations of the atoms or ions in the crystal.

In contrast to the primitive cubic lattice, a body-centered cube has an additional atom wholly within the unit cell at the cube's center. The center particle is present in addition to those at the cube corners, so *the body-centered cubic arrangement has a net of two atoms within the unit cell.*

In a face-centered cubic arrangement, there is an atom on each of the six faces of the cube in addition to those at the cube corners. One half of each atom on a face belongs to a given unit cell (Figure 13.6b). Three net particles are therefore contributed by the particles on the faces of the cube:

(6 faces of a cube)(½ of an atom within a unit cell) =
3 net face-centered atoms within a face-centered cubic unit cell

Thus, *the face-centered cubic arrangement has a net of four atoms within the unit cell,* one contributed by the corner atoms and another three contributed by the atoms centered in the six faces.

An experimental technique, x-ray crystallography, can be used to determine the structure of a crystalline substance (Figure 13.7). Once the structure is known, the information can be combined with other experimental information to calculate such useful parameters as the radius of an atom (Study Questions 13.7–13.10).

Chemistry Now™

Sign in at **www.cengage.com/login** and go to Chapter 13 Contents to see Screen 13.2 for a self-study module on **crystal lattices.**

EXAMPLE 13.1 Determining an Atom Radius from Lattice Dimensions

Problem Aluminum has a density of 2.699 g/cm³, and the atoms are packed in a face-centered cubic crystal lattice. What is the radius of an aluminum atom?

Strategy Our strategy for solving this problem is as follows:

1. Find the mass of a unit cell from the knowledge that it is face-centered cubic.

2. Combine the density of aluminum with the mass of the unit cell to find the cell volume.

3. Find the length of a side of the unit cell from its volume.

4. Calculate the atom radius from the edge dimension.

Aluminum metal. The metal has a face-centered cubic unit cell with a net of four Al atoms in each unit cell.

Charles D. Winters

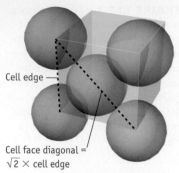

Cell edge

Cell face diagonal =
$\sqrt{2}$ × cell edge

One face of a face-centered cubic unit cell. This shows the cell face diagonal, $\sqrt{2}$ × edge, is equal to four times the radius of the atoms in the lattice.

Solution

1. Calculate the mass of the unit cell.

$$\text{Mass of 1 Al atom} = \left(\frac{26.98 \text{ g}}{1 \text{ mol}}\right)\left(\frac{1 \text{ mol}}{6.022 \times 10^{23} \text{ atoms}}\right) = 4.480 \times 10^{-23} \text{ g/atom}$$

$$\text{Mass of unit cell} = \left(\frac{4.480 \times 10^{-23} \text{ g}}{1 \text{ Al atom}}\right)\left(\frac{4 \text{ Al atoms}}{1 \text{ unit cell}}\right) = 1.792 \times 10^{-22} \text{ g/unit cell}$$

2. Calculate the volume of the unit cell.

$$\text{Volume of unit cell} = \left(\frac{1.792 \times 10^{-22} \text{ g}}{\text{unit cell}}\right)\left(\frac{1 \text{ cm}^3}{2.699 \text{ g}}\right) = 6.640 \times 10^{-23} \text{ cm}^3/\text{unit cell}$$

3. Calculate the length of a unit cell edge. The length of the unit cell edge is the cube root of the cell volume.

$$\text{Length of unit cell edge} = \sqrt[3]{6.640 \times 10^{-23} \text{ cm}^3} = 4.049 \times 10^{-8} \text{ cm}$$

4. Calculate the atom radius. Notice in the model of aluminum in the margin (and in Figure 13.4) that the Al atoms at the cell corners do not touch each other. Rather, the four corner atoms touch the face-centered atom. Thus, the diagonal distance across the face of the cell is equal to four times the Al atom radius.

$$\text{Cell face diagonal} = 4 \times (\text{Al atom radius})$$

The cell diagonal is the hypotenuse of a right isosceles triangle, so, using the Pythagorean theorem,

$$(\text{Diagonal distance})^2 = 2 \times (\text{edge})^2$$

Taking the square root of both sides, we have

$$\text{Diagonal distance} = \sqrt{2} \times (\text{cell edge})$$
$$= \sqrt{2} \times (4.049 \times 10^{-8} \text{ cm}) = 5.727 \times 10^{-8} \text{ cm}$$

We divide the diagonal distance by 4 to obtain the Al atom radius in cm.

$$\text{Al atom radius} = \frac{5.727 \times 10^{-8} \text{ cm}}{4} = 1.432 \times 10^{-8} \text{ cm}$$

Atomic dimensions are often expressed in picometers, so we convert the radius to that unit.

$$1.432 \times 10^{-8} \text{ cm}\left(\frac{1 \text{ m}}{100 \text{ cm}}\right)\left(\frac{1 \text{ pm}}{1 \times 10^{-12} \text{ m}}\right) = \boxed{143.2 \text{ pm}}$$

This is in excellent agree with the radius in Figure 7.8.

EXERCISE 13.1 Determining an Atom Radius from Lattice Dimensions

Gold has a face-centered unit cell, and its density is 19.32 g/cm³. Calculate the radius of a gold atom.

EXERCISE 13.2 The Structure of Solid Iron

Iron has a density of 7.8740 g/cm³, and the radius of an iron atom is 126 pm. Verify that solid iron has a body-centered cubic unit cell. (Be sure to note that the atoms in a body-centered cubic unit cell touch along the diagonal across the cell. They do not touch along the edges of the cell.) (Hint: the diagonal distance across the unit cell is edge × $\sqrt{3}$.)

It is a "rule" that nature does things as efficiently as possible. You know this if you have ever tried to stack some oranges into a pile that doesn't fall over and that takes up as little space as possible. How did you do it? Clearly, the pyramid arrangement below on the right works, whereas the cubic one on the left does not.

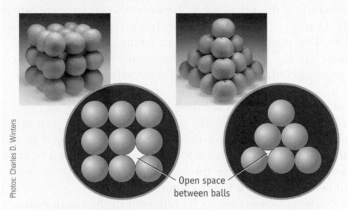

If you could look inside the pile, you would find that less open space is left in the pyramid stacking than in the cube stacking. Only 52% of the space is filled in the cubic packing arrangement. (If you could stack oranges as a body-centered cube, that would be slightly better; 68% of the space is used.) However, the best method is the pyramid stack, which is really a face-centered cubic arrangement. Oranges, atoms, or ions packed this way occupy 74% of the available space.

To fill three-dimensional space, the most efficient way to pack oranges or atoms is to begin with a hexagonal arrangement of spheres, as in this arrangement of marbles.

Succeeding layers of atoms or ions are then stacked one on top of the other in two different ways. Depending on the stacking pattern (Figure 1), you will get either a **cubic close-packed (ccp)** or **hexagonal close-packed (hcp)** arrangement.

In the hcp arrangement, additional layers of particles are placed above and below a given layer, fitting into the same depressions on either side of the middle layer. In a three-dimensional crystal, the lay-

ers repeat their pattern in the manner ABABAB. . . . Atoms in each A layer are directly above the ones in another A layer; the same holds true for the B layers.

In the ccp arrangement, the atoms of the "top" layer (A) rest in depressions in the middle layer (B), and those of the "bottom" layer (C) are oriented opposite to those in the top layer. In a crystal, the pattern is repeated ABCABCABC. . . . By turning the whole crystal, you can see that the ccp arrangement is the face-centered cubic structure (Figure 2).

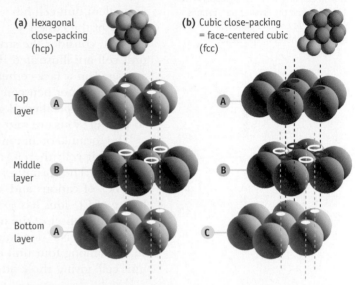

FIGURE 1 Efficient packing. The most efficient ways to pack atoms or ions in crystalline materials are hexagonal close-packing (hcp) and cubic close packing (ccp).

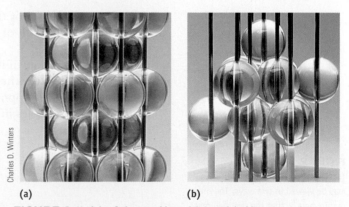

FIGURE 2 Models of close packing. (a) A model of hexagonal close-packing, where the layers repeat in the order ABABAB. . . . (b) A face-centered unit cell (cubic close-packing), where the layers repeat in the order ABCABC. . . . (A kit from which these models can be built is available from the Institute for Chemical Education at the University of Wisconsin at Madison.)

13.2 Structures and Formulas of Ionic Solids

The lattices of many ionic compounds are built by taking a primitive cubic or face-centered cubic lattice of ions of one type and placing ions of opposite charge in the holes within the lattice. This produces a three-dimensional lattice of regularly placed ions. The smallest repeating unit in these structures is, by definition, the unit cell for the ionic compound.

The choice of the lattice and the number and location of the holes that are filled are the keys to understanding the relationship between the lattice structure and the formula of a salt. Consider, for example, the ionic compound cesium chloride, CsCl (Figure 13.8). The structure of CsCl has a primitive cubic unit cell of chloride ions. The cesium ion fits into a hole in the center of the cube. (An equivalent unit cell has a primitive cubic unit cell of Cs^+ ions with a Cl^- ion in the center of the cube.)

Next, consider the structure for NaCl. An extended view of the lattice and one unit cell are illustrated in Figures 13.9a and 13.9b, respectively. The Cl^- ions are arranged in a face-centered cubic unit cell, and the Na^+ ions are arranged in a regular manner between these ions. Notice that each Na^+ ion is surrounded by six Cl^- ions. An octahedral geometry is assumed by the ions surrounding an Na^+ ion, so the Na^+ ions are said to be in **octahedral holes** (Figure 13.9c).

The formula of an ionic compound must always be reflected in the composition of its unit cell; therefore, the formula can always be derived from the unit cell structure. The formula for NaCl can be related to this structure by counting the number of cations and anions contained in one unit cell. A face-centered cubic lattice of Cl^- ions has a net of four Cl^- ions within the unit cell. There is one Na^+ ion in the center of the unit cell, contained totally within the unit cell. In addition, there are 12 Na^+ ions along the edges of the unit cell. Each of these Na^+ ions is shared among four unit cells, so each contributes one fourth of an Na^+ ion to the unit cell, giving three additional Na^+ ions within the unit cell.

(1 Na^+ ion in the center of the unit cell) + ($\frac{1}{4}$ of Na^+ ion in each edge $\times$ 12 edges)
= net of 4 Na^+ ions in NaCl unit cell

This accounts for all of the ions contained in the unit cell: four Cl^- and four Na^+ ions. Thus, a unit cell of NaCl has a 1:1 ratio of Na^+ and Cl^- ions, as the formula requires.

Another common unit cell again has ions of one type in a face-centered cubic unit cell. Ions of the other type are located in **tetrahedral holes**, wherein each ion is surrounded by four oppositely charged ions. As illustrated in Figure 13.10, there are eight tetrahedral holes in a face-centered unit cell. In ZnS (zinc blende), the sulfide

■ **Lattice Ions and Holes** Chemists usually think of ionic lattices as being built from the larger anions with the smaller cations located in the holes that remain. For NaCl, for example, an fcc lattice is built out of the Cl^- ions (radius = 181 pm), and the smaller Na^+ cations (radius = 98 pm) are placed in appropriate holes in the lattice.

FIGURE 13.8 Cesium chloride (CsCl) unit cell. The unit cell of CsCl may be viewed in two ways. The only requirement is that the unit cell must have a net of one Cs^+ ion and one Cl^- ion. Either way, it is a simple cubic unit cell of ions of one type (Cl^- on the left or Cs^+ on the right). Generally, ionic lattices are assembled by placing the larger ions (here Cl^-) at the lattice points and placing the smaller ions (here Cs^+) in the lattice holes.

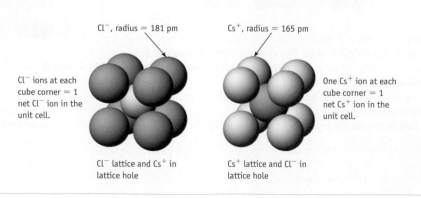

Cl^-, radius = 181 pm Cs^+, radius = 165 pm

Cl^- ions at each cube corner = 1 net Cl^- ion in the unit cell.

One Cs^+ ion at each cube corner = 1 net Cs^+ ion in the unit cell.

Cl^- lattice and Cs^+ in lattice hole

Cs^+ lattice and Cl^- in lattice hole

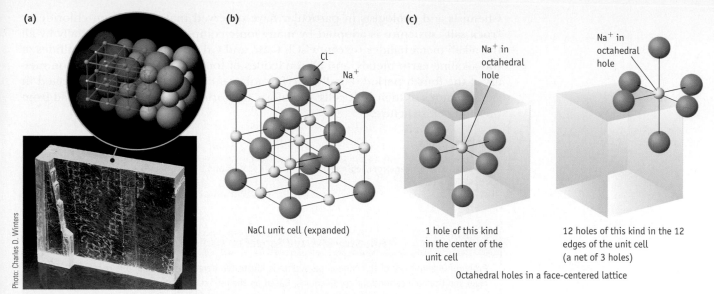

FIGURE 13.9 Sodium chloride. (a) Cubic NaCl is based on a face-centered cubic unit cell of Na^+ and Cl^- ions. (b) An expanded view of a sodium chloride lattice. (The lines represent the connections between lattice points.) The smaller Na^+ ions (silver) are packed into a face-centered cubic lattice of larger Cl^- ions (yellow). (c) A close-up view of the octahedral holes in the lattice.

ions (S^{2-}) form a face-centered cubic unit cell. The zinc ions (Zn^{2+}) then occupy one half of the tetrahedral holes, and each Zn^{2+} ion is surrounded by four S^{2-} ions. The unit cell consists of a net of four S^{2-} ions and four Zn^{2+} ions, which are contained wholly within the unit cell. This 1:1 ratio of the ions is reflected in the formula.

In summary, compounds with the formula MX commonly form one of three possible crystal structures:

1. M^{n+} ions occupying all the cubic holes of a primitive cubic X^{n-} lattice. Example, CsCl
2. M^{n+} ions in all the octahedral holes in a face-centered cubic X^{n-} lattice. Example, NaCl
3. M^{n+} ions occupying half of the tetrahedral holes in a face-centered cube lattice of X^{n-} ions. Example, ZnS

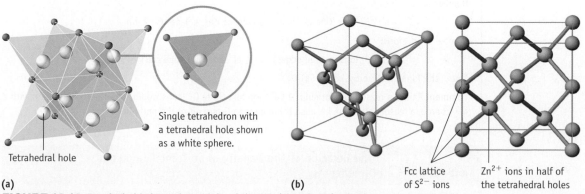

FIGURE 13.10 Tetrahedral holes and two views of the ZnS (zinc blende) unit cell. (a) The tetrahedral holes in a face-centered cubic lattice. (b) This unit cell is an example of a face-centered cubic lattice of ions of one type with ions of the opposite type in one half of the tetrahedral holes.

Chemists and geologists in particular have observed that the sodium chloride or "rock salt" structure is adopted by many ionic compounds, most especially by all the alkali metal halides (except CsCl, CsBr, and CsI), all the oxides and sulfides of the alkaline earth metals, and all the oxides of formula MO of the transition metals of the fourth period. Finally, the formulas of compounds must be reflected in the structures of their unit cells; therefore, the formula can always be derived from the unit cell structure.

Chemistry.ॢ.Now™

Sign in at **www.cengage.com/login** and go to Chapter 13 Contents to see Screen 13.3 to view an animation of **ionic unit cells.**

■ **EXAMPLE 13.2 Ionic Structure and Formula**

Problem One unit cell of the mineral perovskite is illustrated here. This compound is composed of calcium and titanium cations and oxide anions. Based on the unit cell, what is the formula of perovskite?

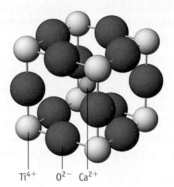

Ti⁴⁺   O²⁻   Ca²⁺

Strategy Identify the ions present in the unit cell and their locations within the unit cell. Decide on the net number of ions of each kind in the cell.

Solution The unit cell has Ti^{4+} ions at the corners of the cubic unit cell, a calcium ion in the center of the cell, and oxide ions along the edges.

Number of Ti^{4+} ions:

(8 Ti^{4+} ions at cube corners) × (⅛ of each ion inside unit cell) = 1 net Ti^{4+} ion

Number of Ca^{2+} ions:

One ion is in the cube center = 1 net Ca^{2+} ion

Number of O^{2-} ions:

(12 O^{2-} ions in cube edges) × (¼ of each ion inside cell) = 3 net O^{2-} ions

Thus, the formula of perovskite is $CaTiO_3$.

Comment This is a reasonable formula. A Ca^{2+} ion and three O^{2-} ions would require a titanium ion with a 4+ charge, a reasonable value because titanium is in Group 4B of the periodic table.

■ **EXAMPLE 13.3 The Relation of the Density of an Ionic Compound and its Unit Cell Dimensions**

Problem Magnesium oxide has a face-centered cubic unit cell of oxide ions with magnesium ions in octahedral holes. If the radius of Mg^{2+} is 79 pm and the density of MgO is 3.56 g/cm³, what is the radius of the oxide ion?

Strategy The unit cell contains 4 MgO units, so we can calculate the mass of the unit cell. Combining the unit cell mass and the density of the solid gives us the unit cell volume, from which we can find the length of one edge of the unit cell. The edge of the unit cell is twice the radius of a Mg^{2+} ion (2 times 79 pm) plus twice the radius of an O^{2-} ion (the unknown).

Solution

1. *Calculate the mass of the unit cell.* An ionic compound of formula MX and based on a face-centered cubic lattice of X^- ions with M^+ ions in the octahedral holes has 4 MX unit per unit cell.

$$\text{Unit cell mass} = \left(\frac{40.31\text{ g}}{1\text{ mol MgO}}\right)\left(\frac{1\text{ mol MgO}}{6.022 \times 10^{23}\text{ units of MgO}}\right)\left(\frac{4\text{ MgO units}}{1\text{ unit cell}}\right)$$
$$= 2.677 \times 10^{-22}\text{ g/unit cell}$$

2. *Calculate the volume of the unit cell from the mass and density.*

$$\text{Unit cell volume} = \left(\frac{2.667 \times 10^{-22}\text{ g}}{\text{unit cell}}\right)\left(\frac{1\text{ cm}^3}{3.56\text{ g}}\right) = 7.49 \times 10^{-23}\text{ cm}^3/\text{unit cell}$$

3. *Calculate the edge dimension of the unit cell in pm.*

$$\text{Unit cell edge} = (7.49 \times 10^{-23}\text{ cm}^3)^{1/3} = 4.22 \times 10^{-8}\text{ cm}$$

$$\text{Unit cell edge} = 4.22 \times 10^{-8}\text{ cm}\left(\frac{1\text{ m}}{100\text{ cm}}\right)\left(\frac{1 \times 10^{12}\text{ pm}}{1\text{ m}}\right) = 422\text{ pm}$$

4. *Calculate the oxide ion radius.*

One face of the MgO unit cell is shown in the margin. The O^{2-} ions define the lattice, and the Mg^{2+} and O^{2-} ions along the cell edge just touch one another. This means that one edge of the cell is equal to one O^{2-} radius (x) plus twice the Mg^{2+} radius plus one more O^{2-} radius.

$$\text{MgO unit cell edge} = x\text{ pm} + 2(79\text{ pm}) + x\text{ pm} = 422\text{ pm}$$

$$x = \boxed{\text{oxide ion radius} = 132\text{ pm}}$$

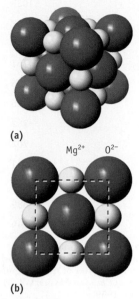

(a)

Mg^{2+} O^{2-}

(b)

Magnesium oxide. (a) A unit cell showing oxide ions in a face-centered cubic lattice with magnesium ions in the octahedral holes. (b) One face of the cell.

EXERCISE 13.3 Structure and Formula

If an ionic solid has an fcc lattice of anions (X) and all of the tetrahedral holes are occupied by metal cations (M), is the formula of the compound MX, MX_2, or M_2X?

EXERCISE 13.4 Density from Cell Dimensions

Potassium chloride has the same unit cell as NaCl. Using the ion sizes in Figure 7.12, calculate the density of KCl.

13.3 Bonding in Ionic Compounds: Lattice Energy

Ionic compounds typically have high melting points, an indication of the strength of the bonding in the ionic crystal lattice. A measure of that is the lattice energy, the main topic of this section.

Lattice Energy

Ionic compounds exist as solids under normal conditions. Their structures contain positive and negative ions arranged in a three-dimensional lattice (Figure 13.9). In an ionic crystal lattice, there are extensive attractions between ions of opposite charge and repulsions between ions of like charge. Each of these interactions is governed by an equation related to Coulomb's law (◄ page 78). For

$$U_{\text{ion pair}} = C(N_A)\left(\frac{(n^+e)(n^-e)}{d}\right)$$

The symbol C represents a constant; d is the distance between the ion centers; n^+ is the number of positive charges on the cation; n^- is the number of negative charges on the anion; and e is the charge on an electron; n^+e is assigned a positive value, and n^-e is assigned a negative value due to the respective charges of the ions. Including Avogadro's number, N_A, allows us to calculate the energy change for 1 mol of ion pairs. Be sure to notice that the energy depends directly on the charges on the ions and inversely on the distance between them.

In an extended ionic lattice, there are multiple cation–anion interactions. Let us take NaCl as an example (Figure 13.9). If we focus on an Na^+ ion in the center of the unit cell, we see it is surrounded by, and attracted to, six Cl^- ions. Just a bit farther away from this Na^+ ion, however, there are 12 other Na^+ ions, and there is a force of repulsion between the center Na^+ and these ions. (These are 12 Na^+ ions in the edges of the cube.) And if we still focus on the "center" Na^+ ion, we see there are eight more Cl^- ions, and these are attracted to the "center" Na^+ ion. If we were to take into account *all* of the interactions between the ions in a lattice, it would be possible to calculate the **lattice energy**, $\Delta_{\text{lattice}}U$, the energy of formation of one mole of a solid crystalline ionic compound when ions in the gas phase combine (see Table 13.2). For sodium chloride, this reaction would correspond to

$$Na^+(g) + Cl^-(g) \longrightarrow NaCl(s)$$

Lattice energy is a measure of the strength of ionic bonding. Often, however, chemists use **lattice enthalpy, $\Delta_{\text{lattice}}H$** rather than lattice energy because of the difficulty of estimating some energy quantities. The same trends are seen in both, though, and, because we are dealing with a condensed phase, the numerical values are nearly identical.

We shall focus here on the dependence of lattice enthalpy on ion charges and sizes. As given by Coulomb's law, the higher the ion charges, the greater the attraction between oppositely charged ions, and so $\Delta_{\text{lattice}}H$ has a larger negative value for more highly charged ions. This is illustrated by the lattice enthalpies of MgO and NaF. The value of $\Delta_{\text{lattice}}H$ for MgO (-4050 kJ/mol) is about four times more negative than the value for NaF (-926 kJ/mol) because the charges on the Mg^{2+} and O^{2-} ions [$(2+) \times (2-)$] are twice as large as those on Na^+ and F^- ions.

Because the attraction between ions is inversely proportional to the distance between them, the effect of ion size on lattice enthalpy is also predictable: A lattice built from smaller ions generally leads to a more negative value for the lattice enthalpy (Table 13.2 and Figure 13.11). For alkali metal halides, for example, the lattice enthalpy for lithium compounds is generally more negative than that for potassium compounds because the Li^+ ion is much smaller than the K^+ cation. Similarly, fluorides are more strongly bonded than are iodides with the same cation.

Calculating a Lattice Enthalpy from Thermodynamic Data

Lattice enthalpies can be calculated using a thermodynamic relationship known as a **Born–Haber cycle.** This calculation is an application of Hess's law (◄ page 233). Such a cycle is illustrated in Figure 13.12 for solid sodium chloride.

TABLE 13.2 Lattice Energies of Some Ionic Compounds

Compound	$\Delta_{\text{lattice}}U$ (kJ/mol)
LiF	−1037
LiCl	−852
LiBr	−815
LiI	−761
NaF	−926
NaCl	−786
NaBr	−752
NaI	−702
KF	−821
KCl	−717
KBr	−689
KI	−649

Source: D. Cubicciotti: Lattice energies of the alkali halides and electron affinities of the halogens. *Journal of Chemical Physics*, Vol. 31, p. 1646, 1959.

■ **Born–Haber Cycles** Calculation of lattice energies by this procedure is named for Max Born (1882–1970) and Fritz Haber (1868–1934), German scientists who played prominent roles in thermodynamic research.

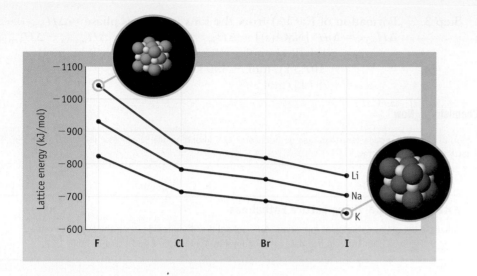

Steps 1 and 2 in Figure 13.12 involve formation of $Na^+(g)$ and $Cl^-(g)$ ions from the elements; the enthalpy change for each of these steps is known (Appendices F and L). Step 3 in Figure 13.12 gives the lattice enthalpy, $\Delta_{\text{lattice}}H$. $\Delta_f H°$ is the standard molar enthalpy of formation of NaCl(s) (Appendix L). The enthalpy values for each step are related by the following equation:

$$\Delta_f H° \text{ [NaCl(s)]} = \Delta H_{\text{Step 1a}} + \Delta H_{\text{Step 1b}} + \Delta H_{\text{Step 2a}} + \Delta H_{\text{Step 2b}} + \Delta H_{\text{Step 3}}$$

Because the values for all of these quantities are known except for $\Delta H_{\text{Step 3}}$ ($\Delta_{\text{lattice}}H$), the value for this step can be calculated.

Step 1a. Enthalpy of formation of Cl(g) $= +121.3$ kJ/mol (Appendix L)
Step 1b. ΔH for $Cl(g) + e^- \rightarrow Cl^-(g)$ $= -349$ kJ/mol (Appendix F)
Step 2a. Enthalpy of formation of Na(g) $= +107.3$ kJ/mol (Appendix L)
Step 2b. ΔH for $Na(g) \rightarrow Na^+(g) + e^-$ $= +496$ kJ/mol (Appendix F)

The standard enthalpy of formation of NaCl(s), $\Delta_f H°$, is -411.12 kJ/mol. Combining this with the known values of Steps 1 and 2, we can calculate ΔH_{step3}, which is the lattice enthalpy, $\Delta_{\text{lattice}}H$.

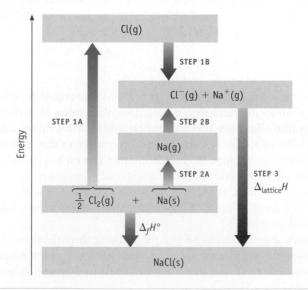

FIGURE 13.12 Born–Haber cycle for the formation of NaCl(s) from the elements. The calculation in the text uses enthalpy values, and the value obtained is the lattice enthalpy, $\Delta_{\text{lattice}}H$. The difference between $\Delta_{\text{lattice}}U$ and $\Delta_{\text{lattice}}H$ is generally not significant and can be corrected for, if desired. (Note that the energy diagram is not to scale.)

Step 3.   Formation of NaCl(s) from the ions in the gas phase = ΔH_{step3}

$$\Delta H_{step3} = \Delta_f H° \,[\text{NaCl(s)}] - \Delta H_{Step\,1a} - \Delta H_{Step\,1b} - \Delta H_{Step\,2a} - \Delta H_{Step\,2b}$$
$$= -411.12 \text{ kJ/mol} - 121.3 \text{ kJ/mol} - (-349 \text{ kJ/mol})$$
$$- 107.3 \text{ kJ/mol} - 496 \text{ kJ/mol}$$
$$= -787 \text{ kJ/mol}$$

Chemistry ⚛ Now™

Sign in at **www.cengage.com/login** and go to Chapter 13 Contents to see Screen 13.4 for an illustration of **lattice and lattice energy.**

EXERCISE 13.5 Using Lattice Enthalpies

Calculate the molar enthalpy of formation, $\Delta_f H°$, of solid sodium iodide using the approach outlined in Figure 13.12. The required data can be found in Appendices F and L and in Table 13.2.

13.4 The Solid State: Other Kinds of Solid Materials

So far, we have described the structures of metals and simple ionic solids. Now we will look briefly at the other categories of solids: molecular solids, network solids, and amorphous solids (Table 13.1).

Molecular Solids

Compounds such as H_2O and CO_2 exist as solids under appropriate conditions. In these cases, it is molecules, rather than atoms or ions, that pack in a regular fashion in a three-dimensional lattice. You have already seen one such structure, that of ice (Figure 12.8).

The way molecules are arranged in a crystalline lattice depends on the shape of the molecules and the types of intermolecular forces. Molecules tend to pack in the most efficient manner and to align in ways that maximize intermolecular forces of attraction. Thus, the water structure was established to gain the maximum intermolecular attraction through hydrogen bonding.

It is from structural studies on molecular solids that most of the information on molecular geometries, bond lengths, and bond angles discussed in Chapter 8 was assembled.

Network Solids

Network solids are composed entirely of a three-dimensional array of covalently bonded atoms. Common examples include two allotropes of carbon: graphite and diamond. Elemental silicon is also a network solid with a diamond-like structure.

Graphite consists of carbon atoms bonded together in flat sheets that cling only weakly to one another (Figure 2.7). Within the layers, each carbon atom is surrounded by three other carbon atoms in a trigonal planar arrangement. The layers can slip easily over another, which explains why graphite is soft, a good lubricant, and used in pencil lead. (Pencil "lead" is not the element lead, but rather a composite of clay and graphite.)

Diamonds have a low density ($d = 3.51$ g/cm³), but they are also the hardest material and the best conductor of heat known. They are transparent to visible light, as well as to infrared and ultraviolet radiation. Diamonds are electrically in-

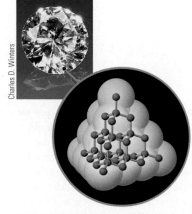

FIGURE 13.13 A diamond and the diamond lattice. The colors of diamonds may range from colorless to yellow, brown, or black. Poorer-quality diamonds are used extensively in industry, mainly for cutting or grinding tools. Industrial-quality diamonds are produced synthetically at present by heating graphite, along with a metal catalyst, to 1200–1500 °C and a pressure of 65–90 kilobars.

sulating but behave as semiconductors with some advantages over silicon. In addition to their use in jewelry, many diamonds are used as abrasives and in diamond-coated cutting tools. In the structure of diamond (Figure 13.13), each carbon atom is bonded to four other carbon atoms at the corners of a tetrahedron, and this pattern extends throughout the solid.

Silicates, compounds composed of silicon and oxygen, represent an enormous class of chemical compounds. You know them in the form of sand, quartz, talc, and mica, or as a major constituent of rocks such as granite. The structure of quartz is illustrated in Figure 13.14. It consists of tetrahedral silicon atoms covalently bonded to oxygen atoms in a giant three-dimensional lattice.

Most network solids are hard and rigid and are characterized by high melting and boiling points. These characteristics reflect the fact that a great deal of energy must be provided to break the covalent bonds in the lattice. For example, silicon dioxide melts at temperatures higher than 1600 °C.

Photo: Charles D. Winters

FIGURE 13.14 Silicon dioxide.
Common quartz, SiO$_2$, is a network solid consisting of silicon and oxygen atoms.

Amorphous Solids

A characteristic property of pure crystalline solids—whether metals, ionic solids, or molecular solids—is that they melt at a specific temperature. For example, water melts at 0 °C, aspirin at 135 °C, lead at 327.5 °C, and NaCl at 801 °C. Because they are specific and reproducible values, melting points are often used as a means of identifying chemical compounds.

Another property of crystalline solids is that they form well-defined crystals, with smooth, flat faces. When a sharp force is applied to a crystal, it will most often cleave to give smooth, flat faces. The resulting solid particles are smaller versions of the original crystal (Figure 13.15a).

Many common solids, including ones that we encounter every day, do not have these properties, however. Glass is a good example. When glass is heated, it softens over a wide temperature range, a property useful for artisans and craftsmen who can create beautiful and functional products for our enjoyment and use. Glass also possesses a property that we would rather it not have: When glass breaks, it leaves randomly shaped pieces. Other materials that behave similarly include common polymers such as polyethylene, nylon, and other plastics.

Charles D. Winters

(a) A salt crystal can be cleaved cleanly into smaller and smaller crystals that are duplicates of the larger crystal.

(b) Glass is an amorphous solid composed of silicon and oxygen atoms. It has, however, no long-range order as in crystalline quartz.

(c) Glass can be molded and shaped into beautiful forms and, by adding metal oxides, can take on wonderful colors.

FIGURE 13.15 Crystalline and amorphous solids.

The characteristics of these amorphous solids relate to their molecular structure. At the particulate level, amorphous solids do not have a regular structure. In fact, in many ways these substances look a lot like liquids. Unlike liquids, however, the forces of attraction are strong enough that movement of the molecules or ions is restricted.

Chemistry⚛Now™

Sign in at **www.cengage.com/login** and go to Chapter 13 Contents to see:
- Screen 13.5 for an exercise on **molecular solids**
- Screen 13.6 for a self-study module on **network solids**
- Screen 13.7 for a self-study module on **silicate minerals**

13.5 Phase Changes Involving Solids

The shape of a crystalline solid is a reflection of its internal structure. But what about physical properties of solids, such as the temperatures at which they melt? This and many other physical properties of solids are of interest to chemists, geologists, and engineers, among others.

Melting: Conversion of Solid into Liquid

The melting point of a solid is the temperature at which the lattice collapses and the solid is converted into a liquid. Like the liquid-to-vapor transformation, melting requires energy, called the enthalpy of fusion (given in kilojoules per mole) (◄ Chapter 5).

Energy absorbed as heat on melting = enthalpy of fusion = $\Delta_{fusion}H$ (kJ/mol)
Energy evolved as heat on freezing = enthalpy of crystallization = $-\Delta_{fusion}H$ (kJ/mol)

■ **Uncle Tungsten** *Uncle Tungsten* is the title of a book by Oliver Sacks (Alfred Knopf, New York, 2001). In it, he describes growing up with an uncle who had a light bulb factory and used tungsten. He also describes other "chemical adventures."

Enthalpies of fusion can range from just a few thousand joules per mole to many thousands of joules per mole (Table 13.3). A low melting temperature will certainly mean a low value for the enthalpy of fusion, whereas high melting points are associated with high enthalpies of fusion. Figure 13.16 shows the enthalpies of fusion for the metals of the fourth through the sixth periods. Based on this figure, we see that transition metals have high enthalpies of fusion, with many of those in the sixth period being extraordinarily high. This trend parallels the trend seen with the melting points for these elements. Tungsten, which has the highest melting point of all the known elements except for carbon, also has the highest enthalpy of fusion among the transition metals. For this reason, tungsten is used for the filaments in light bulbs; no other material has been found to work better since the invention of the light bulb in 1908.

Table 13.3 presents some data for several basic types of substances: metals, polar and nonpolar molecules, and ionic solids. In general, nonpolar substances that form molecular solids have low melting points. Melting points increase within a series of related molecules, however, as the size and molar mass increase. This happens because London dispersion forces are generally larger when the molar mass is larger. Thus, increasing amounts of energy are required to break down the intermolecular forces in the solid, a principle that is reflected in an increasing enthalpy of fusion.

The ionic compounds in Table 13.3 have higher melting points and higher enthalpies of fusion than the molecular solids. This trend is due to the strong ion–ion forces present in ionic solids, forces that are reflected in high lattice energies (page 599). Because ion–ion forces depend on ion size (as well as ion charge), there is a good correlation between lattice energy and the position of the metal or

TABLE 13.3 Melting Points and Enthalpies of Fusion of Some Elements and Compounds

Compound	Melting Point (°C)	Enthalpy of Fusion (kJ/mol)	Type of Interparticle Forces
Metals			
Hg	−39	2.29	Metal bonding; see pages 657–663.
Na	98	2.60	
Al	660	10.7	
Ti	1668	20.9	
W	3422	35.2	
Molecular Solids: Nonpolar Molecules			
O_2	−219	0.440	Dispersion forces only.
F_2	−220	0.510	
Cl_2	−102	6.41	
Br_2	−7.2	10.8	
Molecular Solids: Polar Molecules			
HCl	−114	1.99	All three HX molecules have dipole–dipole
HBr	−87	2.41	forces. Dispersion forces increase with size
HI	−51	2.87	and molar mass.
H_2O	0	6.01	Hydrogen bonding and dispersion forces
Ionic Solids			
NaF	996	33.4	All ionic solids have extended ion–ion inter-
NaCl	801	28.2	actions. Note the general trend is the same
NaBr	747	26.1	as for lattice energies (see Section 13.3 and
NaI	660	23.6	Figure 13.11).

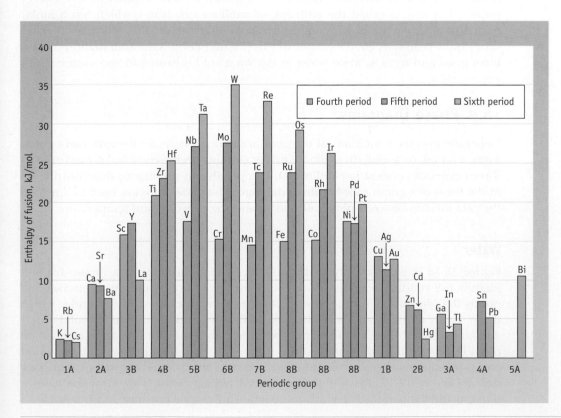

FIGURE 13.16 Enthalpy of fusion of fourth-, fifth-, and sixth-period metals. Enthalpies of fusion range from 2–5 kJ/mol for Group 1A elements to 35.2 kJ/mol for tungsten. Notice that enthalpies of fusion generally increase for group 4B–8B metals on descending the periodic table.

Iodine sublimes
when heated.

Charles D. Winters

halogen in the periodic table. For example, the data in Table 13.3 show a decrease
in melting point and enthalpy of fusion for sodium salts as the halide ion increases
in size. This parallels the decrease in lattice energy seen with increasing ion size.

Sublimation: Conversion of Solid into Vapor

Molecules can escape directly from the solid to the gas phase by sublimation
(Figure 13.17).

$$\text{Solid} \rightarrow \text{Gas} \qquad \text{Energy required as heat} = \Delta_{sublimation}H$$

Sublimation, like fusion and evaporation, is an endothermic process. The energy
required as heat is called the **enthalpy of sublimation.** Water, which has a molar
enthalpy of sublimation of 51 kJ/mol, can be converted from solid ice to water
vapor quite readily. A good example of this phenomenon is the sublimation of frost
from grass and trees as night turns to day on a cold morning in the winter.

13.6 Phase Diagrams

Depending on the conditions of temperature and pressure, a substance can exist as
a gas, a liquid, or a solid. In addition, under certain specific conditions, two (or even
three) states can coexist in equilibrium. It is possible to summarize this information
in the form of a graph called a **phase diagram.** Phase diagrams are used to illustrate
the relationship between phases of matter and the pressure and temperature.

Water

Figure 13.18 illustrates a phase diagram for water. The lines in a phase diagram
identify the conditions under which two phases exist at equilibrium. Conversely, all
points that do not fall on the lines in the figure represent conditions under which
there is only one state that is stable. Line A–B represents conditions for solid–vapor
equilibrium, and line A–C for liquid–solid equilibrium. The line from point A to
point D, representing the temperature and pressure combination at which the liquid
and vapor phases are in equilibrium, is the same curve plotted for water vapor pressure in Figure 12.17. Recall that the normal boiling point, 100 °C in the case of
water, is the temperature at which the equilibrium vapor pressure is 760 mm Hg.

Point A, appropriately called the **triple point**, indicates the conditions under which all three phases coexist in equilibrium. For water, the triple point is at $P = 4.6$ mm Hg and $T = 0.01$ °C.

The line A–C shows the conditions of pressure and temperature at which solid–liquid equilibrium exists. (Because no vapor pressure is involved here, the pressure referred to is the external pressure on the liquid.) For water, this line has a negative slope; the change for water is approximately -0.01 °C for each one-atmosphere increase in pressure. That is, the higher the external pressure, the lower the melting point.

The negative slope of the water solid–liquid equilibrium line can be explained from our knowledge of the structure of water and ice. When the pressure on an object increases, common sense tells us that the volume of the object will become

Case Study   The World's Lightest Solid

The *Guinness Book of Records* calls it the "world's lightest solid" and the "best thermal insulator." Even though it is 99.8% air and has a density of only about 1 mg/cm³, it is a light blue solid that, to the touch, feels much like Styrofoam chips that are used in packaging. It is also strong structurally, able to hold over 2000 times its weight (Figure A).

"It" is a silica aerogel, a low-density substance derived from a gel in which the liquid has been replaced by air (▶ page 666). There are aerogels based silicon and carbon as well as aluminum and other metals, but the silicon-based aerogel is the most thoroughly studied. This aerogel is made by polymerizing a compound like $Si(OC_2H_5)_4$ in alcohol. The resulting long-chain molecules form a gel that is

bathed in the alcohol. This substance is then placed in supercritical CO_2 (▶ page 609), which causes the alcohol in the nanopores in the gel to be replaced by CO_2. When the CO_2 is vented off as a gas, what remains is a highly porous aerogel with an incredibly low density.

Aerogels have been known for decades but have only recently received a lot of study. They do have amazing properties! Chief among them is their insulating ability, as illustrated in Figure B. Aerogels do not allow heat to be conducted through the lattice, and convective heat transfer is also poor because air cannot circulate throughout the lattice. One practical use for these aerogels is in insulating glass. However, before it can be truly useful for this purpose, researchers need to find a way to make completely transparent aerogel. (Silica aerogel is very light blue owing to Rayleigh scattering, the same process that makes the sky blue.) Aerogels are also biocompatible and have been studied as possible drug delivery systems.

Aerogel has been in the news in the past few years because it was used to catch comet dust in Project Stardust. A spacecraft was sent to intercept a comet in 2004 and returned to Earth in January 2006. On the spacecraft was an array holding blocks of aerogel. As the craft flew through the comet's tail, dust particles impacted the aerogel blocks and were "brought to a standstill as they tunneled through it without much heating or alteration, leaving carrot-shaped tracks." When the spacecraft was returned to Earth, scientists analyzed the particles and found that there were silicate minerals that seemed to have been formed in the inner regions of the solar

FIGURE B Aerogel as an insulator. http://stardust.jpl.nasa.gov/images/gallery/aerogelmatches.jpg

system. (See *Science*, Vol. 314, 15 December 2006.)

Questions:

1. *Assume the repeating unit in the aerogel polymer is $OSi(OC_2H_5)_2$. If the polymer is 99.8% air, how many silicon atoms are there in 1.0 cm³ of aerogel?*
2. *Suppose you wish to make a superinsulating window and so fill the gap between two sheets of glass with aerogel. What mass of aerogel is needed for a 180 cm × 150 cm window with a gap of 2.0 mm between the glass sheets?*

Answers to these questions are in Appendix Q.

FIGURE A Silica aerogel. A 2.5-kg brick is supported by a piece of silica aerogel weighing about 2 g. (http://stardust.jpl.nasa.gov/photo/aerogel.html)

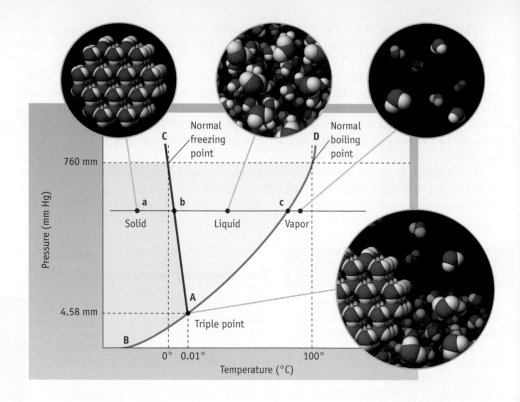

smaller, giving the substance a higher density. Because ice is less dense than liquid water (due to the open lattice structure of ice, Figure 12.8), ice and water in equilibrium respond to increased pressure (at constant T) by melting ice to form more water because the same mass of water requires less volume.

Phase Diagrams and Thermodynamics

Let us explore the water phase diagram further by correlating phase changes with thermodynamic data. Suppose we begin with ice at -10 °C and under a pressure of 500 mm Hg (point a on Figure 13.18). As ice is heated (at constant P), it absorbs about 2.1 J/g · K in warming from point a to point b at a temperature between 0 °C and 0.01 °C. At this point, the solid is in equilibrium with liquid water. Solid–liquid equilibrium is maintained until 333 J/g has been transferred to the sample and it has become liquid water at this temperature. If the liquid, still under a pressure of 500 mm Hg, now absorbs 4.184 J/g · K, it warms to point c. The temperature at point c is about 89 °C, and equilibrium is established between liquid water and water vapor. The equilibrium vapor pressure of the liquid water is 500 mm Hg. If 2260 J/g is transferred to the liquid–vapor sample, the equilibrium vapor pressure remains 500 mm Hg until the liquid is completely converted to vapor at 89 °C.

Carbon Dioxide

The features of the phase diagram for CO_2 (Figure 13.19) are generally the same as those for water but with some important differences.

In contrast to water, the CO_2 solid–liquid equilibrium line has a positive slope. Once again, increasing pressure on the solid in equilibrium with the liquid will shift the equilibrium to the more dense phase, but for CO_2 this will be the solid. Because solid CO_2 is denser than the liquid, the newly formed solid CO_2 sinks to the bottom in a container of liquid CO_2.

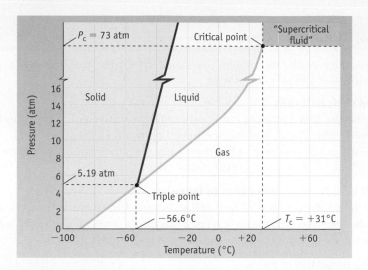

FIGURE 13.19 The phase diagram of CO_2. Notice in particular the positive slope of the solid–liquid equilibrium line. (For more on the critical point, see page 577.)

Another feature of the CO_2 phase diagram is the triple point that occurs at a pressure of 5.19 atm (3940 mm Hg) and 216.6 K (-56.6 °C). Carbon dioxide cannot be a liquid at pressures lower than this.

At pressures around normal atmospheric pressure, CO_2 will be either a solid or a gas, depending on the temperature. [At a pressure of 1 atm, solid CO_2 is in equilibrium with the gas at a temperature of 197.5 K (-78.7 °C).] As a result, as solid CO_2 warms above this temperature, it sublimes rather than melts. Carbon dioxide is called *dry ice* for this reason; it looks like water ice, but it does not melt.

From the CO_2 phase diagram, we can also learn that CO_2 gas can be converted to a liquid at room temperature (20–25 °C) by exerting a moderate pressure on the gas. In fact, CO_2 is regularly shipped in tanks as a liquid to laboratories and industrial companies.

Finally, the critical pressure and temperature for CO_2 are 73 atm and 31 °C, respectively. Because the critical temperature and pressure are easily attained in the laboratory, it is possible to observe the transformation to supercritical CO_2 (Figure 13.20).

Chemistry Now™

Sign in at **www.cengage.com/login** and go to Chapter 13 Contents to see Screen 13.8 to view animations of **phase changes** and to do an exercise on **phase diagrams.**

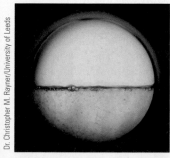

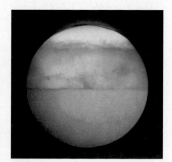

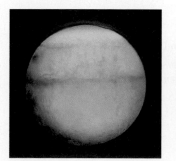

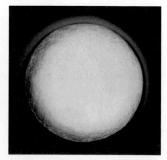

The separate phases of CO_2 are seen through the window in a high-pressure vessel.

As the sample warms and the pressure increases, the meniscus becomes less distinct.

As the temperature continues to increase, it is more difficult to distinguish the liquid and vapor phases.

Once the critical *T* and *P* are reached, distinct liquid and vapor phases are no longer in evidence. This homogeneous phase is "supercritical CO_2."

FIGURE 13.20 Transformation to supercritical CO_2.

Chapter Goals Revisited

Chemistry Now™ Sign in at **www. cengage.com/login** to:

- Assess your understanding with Study Questions in OWL keyed to each goal in the Goals and Homework menu for this chapter
- For quick review, download Go Chemistry mini-lecture flashcard modules (or purchase them at **www.ichapters.com**)
- Check your readiness for an exam by taking the Pre-Test and exploring the modules recommended in your Personalized Study plan.

Access **How Do I Solve It?** tutorials on how to approach problem solving using concepts in this chapter.

For additional preparation for an examination on this chapter see the *Let's Review* section on pages 656–669.

Now that you have studied this chapter, you should ask whether you have met the chapter goals. In particular, you should be able to:

Understand cubic unit cells

a. Describe the three types of cubic unit cells: primitive cubic (pc), body-centered cubic (bcc), and face-centered cubic (fcc) (Section 13.1).

b. Relate atom size and unit cell dimensions. Study Question(s) assignable in OWL: 7, 8, 10, 26, 29, 32, 34, 36, 43; Go Chemistry Module 18.

Relate unit cells for ionic compounds to formulas

a. Understand the relation of unit cell structure and formula for ionic compounds. (Section 13.2) Study Question(s) assignable in OWL: 4, 5, 6, 8; Go Chemistry Module 18.

Describe the properties of solids

a. Understand lattice energy and how it is calculated (Section 13.3). Study Question(s) assignable in OWL: 11, 13, 14, 16, 38.

b. Characterize different types of solids: metallic (e.g., copper), ionic (e.g., NaCl and CaF_2), molecular (e.g., water and I_2), network (e.g., diamond), and amorphous (e.g., glass and many synthetic polymers) (Table 13.1). Study Question(s) assignable in OWL: 17.

c. Define the processes of melting, freezing, and sublimation and their enthalpies (Sections 13.4 and 13.5). Study Question(s) assignable in OWL: 20.

Understand the nature of phase diagrams

a. Identify the different points (triple point, normal boiling point, freezing point) and regions (solid, liquid, vapor) of a phase diagram, and use the diagram to evaluate the vapor pressure of a liquid and the relative densities of a liquid and a solid (Section 13.5). Study Question(s) assignable in OWL: 21, 22, 23, 24.

STUDY QUESTIONS

OWL Online homework for this chapter may be assigned in OWL.

▲ denotes challenging questions.

■ denotes questions assignable in OWL.

Blue-numbered questions have answers in Appendix O and fully-worked solutions in the *Student Solutions Manual*.

Practicing Skills

Metallic and Ionic Solids
(See Examples 13.1–13.3 and ChemistryNow Screens 13.2 and 13.3.)

1. Outline a two-dimensional unit cell for the pattern shown here. If the black squares are labeled A and the white squares are B, what is the simplest formula for a "compound" based on this pattern?

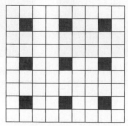

2. Outline a two-dimensional unit cell for the pattern shown here. If the black squares are labeled A and the white squares are B, what is the simplest formula for a "compound" based on this pattern?

3. One way of viewing the unit cell of perovskite was illustrated in Example 13.2. Another way is shown here. Prove that this view also leads to a formula of $CaTiO_3$.

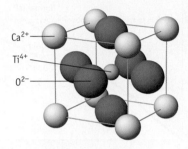

4. ■ Rutile, TiO_2, crystallizes in a structure characteristic of many other ionic compounds. How many formula units of TiO_2 are in the unit cell illustrated here? (The oxide ions marked by an *x* are wholly within the cell; the others are in the cell faces.)

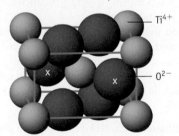

5. ■ Cuprite is a semiconductor. Oxide ions are at the cube corners and in the cube center. Copper ions are wholly within the unit cell.
   (a) What is the formula of cuprite?
   (b) What is the oxidation number of copper?

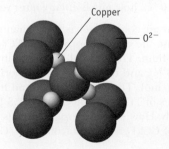

6. ■ The mineral fluorite, which is composed of calcium ions and fluoride ions, has the unit cell shown here.
   (a) What type of unit cell is described by the Ca^{2+} ions?
   (b) Where are the F^- ions located, in octahedral holes or tetrahedral holes?
   (c) Based on this unit cell, what is the formula of fluorite?

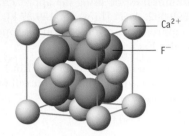

7. ■ Calcium metal crystallizes in a face-centered cubic unit cell. The density of the solid is 1.54 g/cm³. What is the radius of a calcium atom?

8. ■ The density of copper metal is 8.95 g/cm³. If the radius of a copper atom is 127.8 pm, is the copper unit cell primitive, body-centered cubic, or face-centered cubic?

9. Potassium iodide has a face-centered cubic unit cell of iodide ions with potassium ions in octahedral holes. The density of KI is 3.12 g/cm³. What is the length of one side of the unit cell? (Ion sizes are found in Table 7.12.)

10. ▲ ■ A unit cell of cesium chloride is shown on page 596. The density of the solid is 3.99 g/cm³, and the radius of the Cl^- ion is 181 pm. What is the radius of the Cs^+ ion in the center of the cell? (Assume that the Cs^+ ion touches all of the corner Cl^- ions.)

Ionic Bonding and Lattice Energy
(See ChemistryNow Screen 13.4.)

11. ■ List the following compounds in order of increasing lattice energy (from least negative to most negative): LiI, LiF, CaO, RbI.

12. Examine the trends in lattice energy in Table 13.2. The value of the lattice energy becomes somewhat more negative on going from NaI to NaBr to NaCl, and all are in the range of −700 to −800 kJ/mol. Suggest a reason for the observation that the lattice energy of NaF ($\Delta_{\text{lattice}}U = -926$ kJ/mol) is much more negative than those of the other sodium halides.

13. ■ To melt an ionic solid, energy must be supplied to disrupt the forces between ions so the regular array of ions collapses. If the distance between the anion and the cation in a crystalline solid decreases (but ion charges remain the same), should the melting point decrease or increase? Explain.

14. ■ Which compound in each of the following pairs should require the higher temperature to melt? (See Study Question 13.)
(a) NaCl or RbCl
(b) BaO or MgO
(c) NaCl or MgS

15. Calculate the molar enthalpy of formation, $\Delta_f H°$, of solid lithium fluoride using the approach outlined on pages 599-602. $\Delta_f H°$ [Li(g)] = 159.37 kJ/mol, and other required data can be found in Appendices F and L. (See also Exercise 13.5.)

16. ■ Calculate the lattice enthalpy for RbCl. In addition to data in Appendices F and L, you will need the following information:

$\Delta_f H°$ [Rb(g)] = 80.9 kJ/mol

$\Delta_f H°$ [RbCl(s)] = −435.4 kJ/mol

Other Types of Solids
(See ChemistryNow Screens 13.6 and 13.7.)

17. ■ A diamond unit cell is shown here.
(a) How many carbon atoms are in one unit cell?
(b) The unit cell can be considered as a cubic unit cell of C atoms with other C atoms in holes in the lattice. What type of unit cell is this (pc, bcc, fcc)? In what holes are other C atoms located, octahedral or tetrahedral holes?

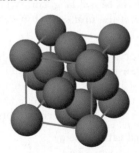

18. The structure of graphite is given in Figure 2.7.
(a) What type of intermolecular bonding forces exist between the layers of six-member carbon rings?
(b) Account for the lubricating ability of graphite. That is, why does graphite feel slippery? Why does pencil lead (which is really graphite in clay) leave black marks on paper?

Physical Properties of Solids

19. Benzene, C_6H_6, is an organic liquid that freezes at 5.5 °C (see Figure 12.1) to form beautiful, feather-like crystals. How much energy as heat is evolved when 15.5 g of benzene freezes at 5.5 °C? (The enthalpy of fusion of benzene is 9.95 kJ/mol.) If the 15.5-g sample is remelted, again at 5.5 °C, what quantity of energy as heat is required to convert it to a liquid?

20. ■ The specific heat capacity of silver is 0.235 J/g · K. Its melting point is 962 °C, and its enthalpy of fusion is 11.3 kJ/mol. What quantity of energy as heat, in joules, is required to change 5.00 g of silver from a solid at 25 °C to a liquid at 962 °C?

Phase Diagrams and Phase Changes
(See ChemistryNow Screen 13.8.)

21. ■ Consider the phase diagram of CO_2 in Figure 13.19.
(a) Is the density of liquid CO_2 greater or less than that of solid CO_2?
(b) In what phase do you find CO_2 at 5 atm and 0 °C?
(c) Can CO_2 be liquefied at 45 °C?

22. ■ Use the phase diagram given here to answer the following questions:

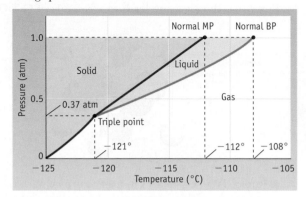

(a) In what phase is the substance found at room temperature and 1.0 atm pressure?
(b) If the pressure exerted on a sample is 0.75 atm and the temperature is −114 °C, in what phase does the substance exist?
(c) If you measure the vapor pressure of a liquid sample and find it to be 380 mm Hg, what is the temperature of the liquid phase?
(d) What is the vapor pressure of the solid at −122 °C?
(e) Which is the denser phase—solid or liquid? Explain briefly.

23. ■ Liquid ammonia, $NH_3(\ell)$, was once used in home refrigerators as the heat transfer fluid. The specific heat capacity of the liquid is 4.7 J/g · K and that of the vapor is 2.2 J/g · K. The enthalpy of vaporization is 23.33 kJ/mol at the boiling point. If you heat 12 kg of liquid ammonia from −50.0 °C to its boiling point of −33.3 °C, allow it to evaporate, and then continue warming to 0.0 °C, how much energy must you supply?

24. ■ If your air conditioner is more than several years old, it may use the chlorofluorocarbon CCl_2F_2 as the heat transfer fluid. The normal boiling point of CCl_2F_2 is −29.8 °C, and the enthalpy of vaporization is 20.11 kJ/mol. The gas and the liquid have specific heat capacities of 117.2 J/mol · K and 72.3 J/mol · K, respectively. How much energy as heat is evolved when 20.0 g of CCl_2F_2 is cooled from +40 °C to −40 °C?

General Questions

These questions are not designated as to type or location in the chapter. They may combine several concepts.

25. Construct a phase diagram for O_2 from the following information: normal boiling point, 90.18 K; normal melting point, 54.8 K; and triple point, 54.34 K at a pressure of 2 mm Hg. Very roughly estimate the vapor pressure of liquid O_2 at −196 °C, the lowest temperature easily reached in the laboratory. Is the density of liquid O_2 greater or less than that of solid O_2?

26. ▲ ■ Tungsten crystallizes in the unit cell shown here.

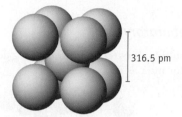

316.5 pm

(a) What type of unit cell is this?
(b) How many tungsten atoms occur per unit cell?
(c) If the edge of the unit cell is 316.5 pm, what is the radius of a tungsten atom? (*Hint:* The W atoms touch each other along the diagonal line from one corner of the unit cell to the opposite corner of the unit cell.)

27. Silver crystallizes in a face-centered cubic unit cell. Each side of the unit cell has a length of 409 pm. What is the radius of a silver atom?

28. ▲ ■ The unit cell shown here is for calcium carbide. How many calcium atoms and how many carbon atoms are in each unit cell? What is the formula of calcium carbide? (Calcium ions are silver in color and carbon atoms are gray.)

29. ■ The very dense metal iridium has a face-centered cubic unit cell and a density of 22.56 g/cm³. Use this information to calculate the radius of an atom of the element.

30. Vanadium metal has a density of 6.11 g/cm³. Assuming the vanadium atomic radius is 132 pm, is the vanadium unit cell primitive cubic, body-centered cubic, or face-centered cubic?

31. ▲ Calcium fluoride is the well-known mineral fluorite. It is known that each unit cell contains four Ca^{2+} ions and eight F^- ions and that the Ca^{2+} ions are arranged in an fcc lattice. The F^- ions fill all the tetrahedral holes in a face-centered cubic lattice of Ca^{2+} ions. The edge of the CaF_2 unit cell is 5.46295×10^{-8} cm in length. The density of the solid is 3.1805 g/cm³. Use this information to calculate Avogadro's number.

32. ▲ ■ Iron has a body-centered cubic unit cell with a cell dimension of 286.65 pm. The density of iron is 7.874 g/cm³. Use this information to calculate Avogadro's number.

33. ▲ You can get some idea of how efficiently spherical atoms or ions are packed in a three-dimensional solid by seeing how well circular atoms pack in two dimensions. Using the drawings shown here, prove that B is a more efficient way to pack circular atoms than A. A unit cell of A contains portions of four circles and one hole. In B, packing coverage can be calculated by looking at a triangle that contains portions of three circles and one hole. Show that A fills about 80% of the available space, whereas B fills closer to 90% of the available space.

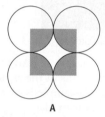 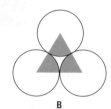

A   B

34. ▲ ■ Assuming that in a primitive cubic unit cell the spherical atoms or ions just touch along the cube's edges, calculate the percentage of empty space within the unit cell. (Recall that the volume of a sphere is $(4/3)\pi r^3$, where r is the radius of the sphere.)

35. ▲ The solid state structure of silicon is

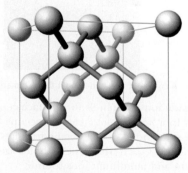

(a) Describe this crystal as pc, bcc, or fcc. What type of holes are occupied in the lattice?
(b) Calculate the density of silicon in g/cm³ (given that the cube edge has a length of 543.1 pm), and estimate the radius of the silicon atom. (Note: the Si atoms on the edges do not touch one another.)

36. ▲ ■ The solid state structure of silicon carbide, SiC, is shown below. Knowing that the Si—C bond length is 188.8 pm (and the Si—C—Si bond angle is 109.5°), calculate the density of SiC.

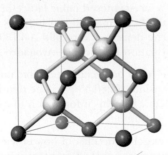

Unit cell of SiC.

Charles D. Winters

Sample of silicon carbide.

37. Spinels are solids with the general formula AB_2O_4 (where A^{2+} and B^{3+} are metal cations of the same or different metals. The best-known example is common magnetite, Fe_3O_4 [which you can formulate as $(Fe^{2+})(Fe^{3+})_2O_4$]. Another example is the mineral often referred to as spinel, $MgAl_2O_4$.

Charles D. Winters

A crystal of the spinel $MgAl_2O_4$ on a marble chip.

The oxide ions of spinels form a face-centered cubic lattice. In a *normal spinel*, cations occupy ⅛ of the tetrahedral sites and ½ of the octahedral sites.
(a) In $MgAl_2O_4$, in what type of holes are the magnesium and aluminum ions found?
(b) The mineral chromite has the formula $FeCr_2O_4$. What ions are involved, and in what type of holes are they found?

38. ■ Using the thermochemical data below, and an estimated value of -2481 kJ/mol for the lattice energy for Na_2O, calculate the value for the *second* electron affinity of oxygen [$O^-(g) + e^- \rightarrow O^{2-}(g)$].

Quantity	Numerical Value (kJ/mol)
Enthalpy of atomization of Na	107.3
Ionization Energy of Na	495.9
Enthalpy of formation of solid Na_2O	−418.0
Enthalpy of formation of $O(g)$ from O_2	249.1
First electron affinity of 0	−141.0

In the Laboratory

39. Lead sulfide, PbS (commonly called galena), has the same formula as ZnS.

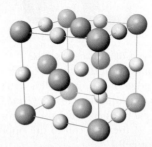

Unit cell of PbS.

Charles D. Winters

Sample of galena.

Does PbS have the same solid structure as ZnS? If different, how are they different? How is the unit cell of PbS related to its formula?

40. $CaTiO_3$, a perovskite, has the structure below.
  (a) If the density of the solid is 4.10 g/cm³, what is the length of a side of the unit cell?
  (b) Calculate the radius of the Ti^{4+} ion in the center of the unit cell. How well does your calculation agree with a literature value of 75 pm?

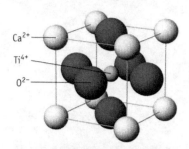

Ca²⁺
Ti⁴⁺
O²⁻

Unit cell of the perovskite CaTiO₃.

©DEA/C. Bevilacqua/Getty Images

A sample of perovskite CaTiO₃.

Summary and Conceptual Questions
The following questions may use concepts from this and previous chapters.

41. ▲ Boron phosphide, BP, is a semiconductor and a hard, abrasion-resistant material. It is made by reacting boron tribromide and phosphorus tribromide in a hydrogen atmosphere at high temperature (> 750 °C).
  (a) Write a balanced chemical equation for the synthesis of BP. *(Hint: Hydrogen is a reducing agent.)*
  (b) Boron phosphide crystallizes in a zinc blende structure, formed from boron atoms in a face-centered cubic lattice and phosphorus atoms in tetrahedral holes. How many tetrahedral holes are filled with P atoms in each unit cell?
  (c) The length of a unit cell of BP is 478 pm. What is the density of the solid in g/cm³.
  (d) Calculate the closest distance between a B and a P atom in the unit cell. (Assume the B atoms do not touch along the cell edge. The B atoms in the faces touch the B atoms at the corners of the unit cell. See page 594.)

42. ▲ Why is it not possible for a salt with the formula M_3X (Na_3PO_4, for example) to have a face-centered cubic lattice of X anions with M cations in octahedral holes?

43. ▲ ■ Two identical swimming pools are filled with uniform spheres of ice packed as closely as possible. The spheres in the first pool are the size of grains of sand; those in the second pool are the size of oranges. The ice in both pools melts. In which pool, if either, will the water level be higher? (Ignore any differences in filling space at the planes next to the walls and bottom.)

44. Spinels are described in Study Question 37. Consider two normal spinels, $CoAl_2O_4$ and $SnCo_2O_4$. What metal ions are involved in each? What are their electron configurations? Are the metal ions paramagnetic, and if so how many unpaired electrons are involved?

List of Appendices

A | Using Logarithms and the Quadratic Equation

An introductory chemistry course requires basic algebra plus a knowledge of (1) exponential (or scientific) notation, (2) logarithms, and (3) quadratic equations. The use of exponential notation was reviewed on pages 32–35, and this appendix reviews the last two topics.

A.1 Logarithms

Two types of logarithms are used in this text: (1) common logarithms (abbreviated log) whose base is 10 and (2) natural logarithms (abbreviated ln) whose base is e (= 2.71828):

$$\log x = n, \text{ where } x = 10^n$$
$$\ln x = m, \text{ where } x = e^m$$

Most equations in chemistry and physics were developed in natural, or base e, logarithms, and we follow this practice in this text. The relation between log and ln is

$$\ln x = 2.303 \log x$$

Despite the different bases of the two logarithms, they are used in the same manner. What follows is largely a description of the use of common logarithms.

A common logarithm is the power to which you must raise 10 to obtain the number. For example, the log of 100 is 2, since you must raise 10 to the second power to obtain 100. Other examples are

$$\log 1000 = \log (10^3) = 3$$
$$\log 10 = \log (10^1) = 1$$
$$\log 1 = \log (10^0) = 0$$
$$\log 0.1 = \log (10^{-1}) = -1$$
$$\log 0.0001 = \log (10^{-4}) = -4$$

To obtain the common logarithm of a number other than a simple power of 10, you must resort to a log table or an electronic calculator. For example,

$$\log 2.10 = 0.3222, \text{ which means that } 10^{0.3222} = 2.10$$
$$\log 5.16 = 0.7126, \text{ which means that } 10^{0.7126} = 5.16$$
$$\log 3.125 = 0.49485, \text{ which means that } 10^{0.49485} = 3.125$$

To check this on your calculator, enter the number, and then press the "log" key.

To obtain the natural logarithm ln of the numbers shown here, use a calculator having this function. Enter each number, and press "ln:"

$$\ln 2.10 = 0.7419, \text{ which means that } e^{0.7419} = 2.10$$
$$\ln 5.16 = 1.6409, \text{ which means that } e^{1.6409} = 5.16$$

To find the common logarithm of a number greater than 10 or less than 1 with a log table, first express the number in scientific notation. Then find the log of each part of the number and add the logs. For example,

$$\log 241 = \log (2.41 \times 10^2) = \log 2.41 + \log 10^2$$
$$= 0.382 + 2 = 2.382$$
$$\log 0.00573 = \log (5.73 \times 10^{-3}) = \log 5.73 + \log 10^{-3}$$
$$= 0.758 + (-3) = -2.242$$

Significant Figures and Logarithms

Notice that the mantissa has as many significant figures as the number whose log was found. (So that you could more clearly see the result obtained with a calculator or a table, this rule was not strictly followed until the last two examples.)

■ **Logarithms and Nomenclature**
The number to the left of the decimal in a logarithm is called the **characteristic**, and the number to the right of the decimal is the **mantissa**.

Obtaining Antilogarithms

If you are given the logarithm of a number, and find the number from it, you have obtained the "antilogarithm," or "antilog," of the number. Two common procedures used by electronic calculators to do this are:

Procedure A	Procedure B
1. Enter the log or ln.	1. Enter the log or ln.
2. Press 2ndF.	2. Press INV.
3. Press 10^x or e^x.	3. Press log or ln x.

Test one or the other of these procedures with the following examples:
1. Find the number whose log is 5.234:
   Recall that log $x = n$, where $x = 10^n$. In this case, $n = 5.234$. Enter that number in your calculator, and find the value of 10^n, the antilog. In this case,

$$10^{5.234} = 10^{0.234} \times 10^5 = 1.71 \times 10^5$$

   Notice that the characteristic (5) sets the decimal point; it is the power of 10 in the exponential form. The mantissa (0.234) gives the value of the number x.
2. Find the number whose log is -3.456:

$$10^{-3.456} = 10^{0.544} \times 10^{-4} = 3.50 \times 10^{-4}$$

   Notice here that -3.456 must be expressed as the sum of -4 and $+0.544$.

Mathematical Operations Using Logarithms

Because logarithms are exponents, operations involving them follow the same rules used for exponents. Thus, multiplying two numbers can be done by adding logarithms:

$$\log xy = \log x + \log y$$

For example, we multiply 563 by 125 by adding their logarithms and finding the antilogarithm of the result:

$$\log 563 = 2.751$$
$$\underline{\log 125 = 2.097}$$
$$\log xy = 4.848$$
$$xy = 10^{4.848} = 10^4 \times 10^{0.848} = 7.05 \times 10^4$$

One number (x) can be divided by another (y) by subtraction of their logarithms:

$$\log \frac{x}{y} = \log x - \log y$$

For example, to divide 125 by 742,

$$\log 125 = 2.097$$
$$\underline{-\log 742 = 2.870}$$
$$\log \frac{x}{y} = -0.773$$
$$\frac{x}{y} = 10^{-0.773} = 10^{0.227} \times 10^{-1} = 1.68 \times 10^{-1}$$

Similarly, powers and roots of numbers can be found using logarithms.

$$\log x^y = y(\log x)$$

$$\log \sqrt[y]{x} = \log x^{1/y} = \frac{1}{y} \log x$$

As an example, find the fourth power of 5.23. We first find the log of 5.23 and then multiply it by 4. The result, 2.874, is the log of the answer. Therefore, we find the antilog of 2.874:

$$(5.23)^4 = ?$$
$$\log (5.23)^4 = 4 \log 5.23 = 4(0.719) = 2.874$$
$$(5.23)^4 = 10^{2.874} = 748$$

As another example, find the fifth root of 1.89×10^{-9}:

$$\sqrt[5]{1.89 \times 10^{-9}} = (1.89 \times 10^{-9})^{1/5} = ?$$
$$\log (1.89 \times 10^{-9})^{1/5} = \frac{1}{5}\log(1.89 \times 10^{-9}) = \frac{1}{5}(-8.724) = -1.745$$

The answer is the antilog of -1.745:

$$(1.89 \times 10^{-9})^{1/5} = 10^{-1.745} = 1.8 \times 10^{-2}$$

A.2 Quadratic Equations

Algebraic equations of the form $ax^2 + bx + c = 0$ are called **quadratic equations.** The coefficients a, b, and c may be either positive or negative. The two roots of the equation may be found using the *quadratic formula:*

$$x = \frac{-b \pm \sqrt{b^2 - 4ac}}{2a}$$

As an example, solve the equation $5x^2 - 3x - 2 = 0$. Here $a = 5$, $b = -3$, and $c = -2$. Therefore,

$$x = \frac{3 \pm \sqrt{(-3)^2 - 4(5)(-2)}}{2(5)}$$

$$= \frac{3 \pm [2(5) / \sqrt{9 - (-40)}]}{10} = \frac{3 \pm \sqrt{49}}{10} = \frac{3 \pm 7}{10}$$

$$= 1 \text{ and } -0.4$$

How do you know which of the two roots is the correct answer? You have to decide in each case which root has physical significance. It is *usually* true in this course, however, that negative values are not significant.

When you have solved a quadratic expression, you should always check your values by substitution into the original equation. In the previous example, we find that $5(1)^2 - 3(1) - 2 = 0$ and that $5(-0.4)^2 - 3(-0.4) - 2 = 0$.

The most likely place you will encounter quadratic equations is in the chapters on chemical equilibria, particularly in Chapters 16 through 18. Here, you will often be faced with solving an equation such as

$$1.8 \times 10^{-4} = \frac{x^2}{0.0010 - x}$$

This equation can certainly be solved using the quadratic equation (to give $x = 3.4 \times 10^{-4}$). You may find the **method of successive approximations** to be especially convenient, however. Here we begin by making a reasonable approximation of x. This approximate value is substituted into the original equation, which is then solved to give what is hoped to be a more correct value of x. This process is repeated until the answer converges on a particular value of x—that is, until the value of x derived from two successive approximations is the same.

Step 1: First, assume that x is so small that $(0.0010 - x) \approx 0.0010$. This means that

$$x^2 = 1.8 \times 10^{-4} (0.0010)$$
$$x = 4.2 \times 10^{-4} \text{ (to 2 significant figures)}$$

Step 2: Substitute the value of x from Step 1 into the denominator of the original equation, and again solve for x:

$$x^2 = 1.8 \times 10^{-4}(0.0010 - 0.00042)$$
$$x = 3.2 \times 10^{-4}$$

Step 3: Repeat Step 2 using the value of x found in that step:

$$x = \sqrt{1.8 \times 10^{-4}(0.0010 - 0.00032)} = 3.5 \times 10^{-4}$$

Step 4: Continue repeating the calculation, using the value of x found in the previous step:

$$x = \sqrt{1.8 \times 10^{-4}(0.0010 - 0.00035)} = 3.4 \times 10^{-4}$$

Step 5: $\quad x = \sqrt{1.8 \times 10^{-4}(0.0010 - 0.00034)} = 3.4 \times 10^{-4}$

Here, we find that iterations after the fourth step give the same value for x, indicating that we have arrived at a valid answer (and the same one obtained from the quadratic formula).

Here are several final thoughts on using the method of successive approximations. First, in some cases the method does not work. Successive steps may give answers that are random or that diverge from the correct value. In Chapters 16 through 18, you confront quadratic equations of the form $K = x^2/(C - x)$. The method of approximations works as long as $K < 4C$ (assuming one begins with $x = 0$ as the first guess, that is, $K \approx x^2/C$). This is always going to be true for weak acids and bases (the topic of Chapters 17 and 18), but it may *not* be the case for problems involving gas phase equilibria (Chapter 16), where K can be quite large.

Second, values of K in the equation $K = x^2/(C - x)$ are usually known only to two significant figures. We are therefore justified in carrying out successive steps until two answers are the same to two significant figures.

Finally, we highly recommend this method of solving quadratic equations, especially those in Chapters 17 and 18. If your calculator has a memory function, successive approximations can be carried out easily and rapidly.

B* | Some Important Physical Concepts

B.1 Matter

The tendency to maintain a constant velocity is called inertia. Thus, unless acted on by an unbalanced force, a body at rest remains at rest, and a body in motion remains in motion with uniform velocity. Matter is anything that exhibits inertia; the quantity of matter is its mass.

B.2 Motion

Motion is the change of position or location in space. Objects can have the following classes of motion:

- Translation occurs when the center of mass of an object changes its location. Example: a car moving on the highway.
- Rotation occurs when each point of a moving object moves in a circle about an axis through the center of mass. Examples: a spinning top, a rotating molecule.
- Vibration is a periodic distortion of and then recovery of original shape. Examples: a struck tuning fork, a vibrating molecule.

B.3 Force and Weight

Force is that which changes the velocity of a body; it is defined as

$$\text{Force} = \text{mass} \times \text{acceleration}$$

The SI unit of force is the **newton,** N, whose dimensions are kilograms times meter per second squared ($kg \cdot m/s^2$). A newton is therefore the force needed to change the velocity of a mass of 1 kilogram by 1 meter per second in a time of 1 second.

*Adapted from F. Brescia, J. Arents, H. Meislich, et al.: *General Chemistry,* 5th ed. Philadelphia, Harcourt Brace, 1988.

Because the earth's gravity is not the same everywhere, the weight corresponding to a given mass is not a constant. At any given spot on earth, gravity is constant, however, and therefore weight is proportional to mass. When a balance tells us that a given sample (the "unknown") has the same weight as another sample (the "weights," as given by a scale reading or by a total of counterweights), it also tells us that the two masses are equal. The balance is therefore a valid instrument for measuring the mass of an object independently of slight variations in the force of gravity.

B.4 Pressure*

Pressure is force per unit area. The SI unit, called the pascal, Pa, is

$$1 \text{ pascal} = \frac{1 \text{ newton}}{m^2} = \frac{1 \text{ kg} \cdot m/s^2}{m^2} = \frac{1 \text{ kg}}{m \cdot s^2}$$

The International System of Units also recognizes the bar, which is 10^5 Pa and which is close to standard atmospheric pressure (Table 1).

TABLE 1 Pressure Conversions

From	To	Multiply By
atmosphere	mm Hg	760 mm Hg/atm (exactly)
atmosphere	lb/in²	14.6960 lb/(in² · atm)
atmosphere	kPa	101.325 kPa/atm
bar	Pa	10^5 Pa/bar (exactly)
bar	lb/in²	14.5038 lb/(in² · bar)
mm Hg	torr	1 torr/mm Hg (exactly)

Chemists also express pressure in terms of the heights of liquid columns, especially water and mercury. This usage is not completely satisfactory, because the pressure exerted by a given column of a given liquid is not a constant but depends on the temperature (which influences the density of the liquid) and the location (which influences gravity). Such units are therefore not part of the SI, and their use is now discouraged. The older units are still used in books and journals, however, and chemists must be familiar with them.

The pressure of a liquid or a gas depends only on the depth (or height) and is exerted equally in all directions. At sea level, the pressure exerted by the earth's atmosphere supports a column of mercury about 0.76 m (76 cm, or 760 mm) high.

One **standard atmosphere** (atm) is the pressure exerted by exactly 76 cm of mercury at 0 °C (density, 13.5951 g/cm³) and at standard gravity, 9.80665 m/s². The **bar** is equivalent to 0.9869 atm. One **torr** is the pressure exerted by exactly 1 mm of mercury at 0 °C and standard gravity.

B.5 Energy and Power

The SI unit of energy is the product of the units of force and distance, or kilograms times meter per second squared (kg · m/s²) times meters (× m), which is kg · m²/s²; this unit is called the **joule,** J. The joule is thus the work done when a force of 1 newton acts through a distance of 1 meter.

*See Section 11.1.

Work may also be done by moving an electric charge in an electric field. When the charge being moved is 1 coulomb (C), and the potential difference between its initial and final positions is 1 volt (V), the work is 1 joule. Thus,

$$1 \text{ joule} = 1 \text{ coulomb volt (CV)}$$

Another unit of electric work that is not part of the International System of Units but is still in use is the **electron volt,** eV, which is the work required to move an electron against a potential difference of 1 volt. (It is also the kinetic energy acquired by an electron when it is accelerated by a potential difference of 1 volt.) Because the charge on an electron is 1.602×10^{-19} C, we have

$$1 \text{ eV} = 1.602 \times 10^{-19} \text{ CV} \times \frac{1 \text{ J}}{1 \text{ CV}} = 1.602 \times 10^{-19} \text{ J}$$

If this value is multiplied by Avogadro's number, we obtain the energy involved in moving 1 mole of electron charges (1 faraday) in a field produced by a potential difference of 1 volt:

$$1 \frac{\text{eV}}{\text{particle}} = \frac{1.602 \times 10^{-19} \text{ J}}{\text{particle}} \times \frac{6.022 \times 10^{23} \text{particles}}{\text{mol}} \cdot \frac{1 \text{ kJ}}{1000 \text{ J}} = 96.49 \text{ kJ/mol}$$

Power is the amount of energy delivered per unit time. The SI unit is the watt, W, which is 1 joule per second. One kilowatt, kW, is 1000 W. Watt hours and kilowatt hours are therefore units of energy (Table 2). For example, 1000 watts, or 1 kilowatt, is

$$1.0 \times 10^3 \text{W} \times \frac{1 \text{ J}}{1 \text{ W} \cdot \text{s}} \cdot \frac{3.6 \times 10^3 \text{ s}}{1 \text{ h}} = 3.6 \times 10^6 \text{ J}$$

TABLE 2 Energy Conversions

From	To	Multiply By
calorie (cal)	joule	4.184 J/cal (exactly)
kilocalorie (kcal)	cal	10^3 cal/kcal (exactly)
kilocalorie	joule	4.184×10^3 J/kcal (exactly)
liter atmosphere (L · atm)	joule	101.325 J/L · atm
electron volt (eV)	joule	1.60218×10^{-19} J/eV
electron volt per particle	kilojoules per mole	96.485 kJ · particle/eV · mol
coulomb volt (CV)	joule	1 CV/J (exactly)
kilowatt hour (kWh)	kcal	860.4 kcal/kWh
kilowatt hour	joule	3.6×10^6 J/kWh (exactly)
British thermal unit (Btu)	calorie	252 cal/Btu

c | Abbreviations and Useful Conversion Factors

TABLE 3 Some Common Abbreviations and Standard Symbols

Term	Abbreviation	Term	Abbreviation
Activation energy	E_a	Entropy	S
Ampere	A	Standard entropy	$S°$
Aqueous Solution	aq	Entropy change for reaction	$\Delta_r S°$
Atmosphere, unit of pressure	atm	Equilibrium constant	K
Atomic mass unit	u	Concentration basis	K_c
Avogadro's constant	N_A	Pressure basis	K_p
Bar, unit of pressure	bar	Ionization weak acid	K_a
Body-centered cubic	bcc	Ionization weak base	K_b
Bohr radius	a_0	Solubility product	K_{sp}
Boiling point	bp	Formation constant	K_{form}
Celsius temperature, °C	T	Ethylenediamine	en
Charge number of an ion	z	Face-centered cubic	fcc
Coulomb, electric charge	C	Faraday constant	F
Curie, radioactivity	Ci	Gas constant	R
Cycles per second, hertz	Hz	Gibbs free energy	G
Debye, unit of electric dipole	D	Standard free energy	$G°$
Electron	e^-	Standard free energy of formation	$\Delta_f G°$
Electron volt	eV	Free energy change for reaction	$\Delta_r G°$
Electronegativity	χ	Half-life	$t_{1/2}$
Energy	E	Heat	q
Enthalpy	H	Hertz	Hz
Standard enthalpy	$H°$	Hour	h
Standard enthalpy of formation	$\Delta_f H°$	Joule	J
Standard enthalpy of reaction	$\Delta_r H°$	Kelvin	K

TABLE 3 Some Common Abbreviations and Standard Symbols (continued)

Term	Abbreviation	Term	Abbreviation
Kilocalorie	kcal	Pressure	
Liquid	ℓ	Pascal, unit of pressure	Pa
Logarithm, base 10	log	In atmospheres	atm
Logarithm, base e	ln	In millimeters of mercury	mm Hg
Minute	min	Proton number	Z
Molar	M	Rate constant	k
Molar mass	M	Primitive cubic (unit cell)	pc
Mole	mol	Standard temperature and pressure	STP
Osmotic pressure	Π	Volt	V
Planck's constant	h	Watt	W
Pound	lb	Wavelength	λ

C.1 Fundamental Units of the SI System

The metric system was begun by the French National Assembly in 1790 and has undergone many modifications. The International System of Units or *Système International* (SI), which represents an extension of the metric system, was adopted by the 11th General Conference of Weights and Measures in 1960. It is constructed from seven base units, each of which represents a particular physical quantity (Table 4).

TABLE 4 SI Fundamental Units

Physical Quantity	Name of Unit	Symbol
Length	meter	m
Mass	kilogram	kg
Time	second	s
Temperature	kelvin	K
Amount of substance	mole	mol
Electric current	ampere	A
Luminous intensity	candela	cd

The first five units listed in Table 4 are particularly useful in general chemistry and are defined as follows:

1. The *meter* was redefined in 1960 to be equal to 1,650,763.73 wavelengths of a certain line in the emission spectrum of krypton-86.
2. The *kilogram* represents the mass of a platinum–iridium block kept at the International Bureau of Weights and Measures at Sèvres, France.
3. The *second* was redefined in 1967 as the duration of 9,192,631,770 periods of a certain line in the microwave spectrum of cesium-133.

4. The *kelvin* is 1/273.15 of the temperature interval between absolute zero and the triple point of water.

5. The *mole* is the amount of substance that contains as many entities as there are atoms in exactly 0.012 kg of carbon-12 (12 g of ^{12}C atoms).

C.2 Prefixes Used with Traditional Metric Units and SI Units

Decimal fractions and multiples of metric and SI units are designated by using the prefixes listed in Table 5. Those most commonly used in general chemistry appear in italics.

C.3 Derived SI Units

In the International System of Units, all physical quantities are represented by appropriate combinations of the base units listed in Table 4. A list of the derived units frequently used in general chemistry is given in Table 6.

TABLE 5 Traditional Metric and SI Prefixes

Factor	Prefix	Symbol	Factor	Prefix	Symbol
10^{12}	tera	T	10^{-1}	*deci*	d
10^{9}	giga	G	10^{-2}	*centi*	c
10^{6}	mega	M	10^{-3}	*milli*	m
10^{3}	*kilo*	k	10^{-6}	micro	μ
10^{2}	hecto	h	10^{-9}	*nano*	n
10^{1}	deka	da	10^{-12}	*pico*	p
			10^{-15}	femto	f
			10^{-18}	atto	a

TABLE 6 Derived SI Units

Physical Quantity	Name of Unit	Symbol	Definition
Area	square meter	m^2	
Volume	cubic meter	m^3	
Density	kilogram per cubic meter	kg/m^3	
Force	newton	N	$kg \cdot m/s^2$
Pressure	pascal	Pa	N/m^2
Energy	joule	J	$kg \cdot m^2/s^2$
Electric charge	coulomb	C	$A \cdot s$
Electric potential difference	volt	V	$J/(A \cdot s)$

TABLE 7 Common Units of Mass and Weight

1 Pound = 453.39 Grams

1 kilogram = 1000 grams = 2.205 pounds

1 gram = 1000 milligrams

1 gram = 6.022×10^{23} atomic mass units

1 atomic mass unit = 1.6605×10^{-24} gram

1 short ton = 2000 pounds = 907.2 kilograms

1 long ton = 2240 pounds

1 metric tonne = 1000 kilograms = 2205 pounds

TABLE 8 Common Units of Length

1 inch = 2.54 centimeters (Exactly)

1 mile = 5280 feet = 1.609 kilometers

1 yard = 36 inches = 0.9144 meter

1 meter = 100 centimeters = 39.37 inches = 3.281 feet = 1.094 yards

1 kilometer = 1000 meters = 1094 yards = 0.6215 mile

1 Ångstrom = 1.0×10^{-8} centimeter = 0.10 nanometer = 100 picometers

$\qquad\quad = 1.0 \times 10^{-10}$ meter = 3.937×10^{-9} inch

TABLE 9 Common Units of Volume

1 quart = 0.9463 liter
1 liter = 1.0567 quarts

1 liter = 1 cubic decimeter = 1000 cubic centimeters = 0.001 cubic meter

1 milliliter = 1 cubic centimeter = 0.001 liter = 1.056×10^{-3} quart

1 cubic foot = 28.316 liters = 29.924 quarts = 7.481 gallons

D | Physical Constants

TABLE 10

Quantity	Symbol	Traditional Units	SI Units
Acceleration of gravity	g	980.6 cm/s	9.806 m/s
Atomic mass unit (1/12 the mass of ^{12}C atom)	u	1.6605×10^{-24} g	1.6605×10^{-27} kg
Avogadro's number	N	$6.02214179 \times 10^{23}$ particles/mol	$6.02214179 \times 10^{23}$ particles/mol
Bohr radius	a_0	0.052918 nm	5.2918×10^{-11} m
		5.2918×10^{-9} cm	
Boltzmann constant	k	1.3807×10^{-16} erg/K	1.3807×10^{-23} J/K
Charge-to-mass ratio of electron	e/m	1.7588×10^8 C/g	1.7588×10^{11} C/kg
Electronic charge	e	1.6022×10^{-19} C	1.6022×10^{-19} C
		4.8033×10^{-10} esu	
Electron rest mass	m_e	9.1094×10^{-28} g	9.1094×10^{-31} kg
		0.00054858 amu	
Faraday constant	F	96,485 C/mol e$^-$	96,485 C/mol e$^-$
		23.06 kcal/V · mol e$^-$	96,485 J/V · mol e$^-$
Gas constant	R	$0.082057 \dfrac{L \cdot atm}{mol \cdot K}$	$8.3145 \dfrac{Pa \cdot dm^3}{mol \cdot K}$
		$1.987 \dfrac{cal}{mol \cdot K}$	8.3145 J/mol · K
Molar volume (STP)	V_m	22.414 L/mol	22.414×10^{-3} m^3/mol
			22.414 dm^3/mol
Neutron rest mass	m_n	1.67493×10^{-24} g	1.67493×10^{-27} kg
		1.008665 amu	
Planck's constant	h	6.6261×10^{-27} erg · s	$6.6260693 \times 10^{-34}$ J · s

TABLE 10 (continued)

Quantity	Symbol	Traditional Units	SI Units
Proton rest mass	m_p	1.6726×10^{-24} g	1.6726×10^{-27} kg
		1.007276 amu	
Rydberg constant	R_a	3.289×10^{15} cycles/s	1.0974×10^7 m^{-1}
	Rhc		2.1799×10^{-18} J
Velocity of light (in a vacuum)	c	2.9979×10^{10} cm/s (186,282 miles/s)	2.9979×10^8 m/s

$\pi = 3.1416$

$e = 2.7183$

$\ln X = 2.303 \log X$

TABLE 11 Specific Heats and Heat Capacities for Some Common Substances at 25 °C

Substance	Specific Heat (J/g · K)	Molar Heat Capacity (J/mol · K)
Al(s)	0.897	24.2
Ca(s)	0.646	25.9
Cu(s)	0.385	24.5
Fe(s)	0.449	25.1
Hg(ℓ)	0.140	28.0
H_2O(s), ice	2.06	37.1
H_2O(ℓ), water	4.184	75.4
H_2O(g), steam	1.86	33.6
C_6H_6(ℓ), benzene	1.74	136
C_6H_6(g), benzene	1.06	82.4
C_2H_5OH(ℓ), ethanol	2.44	112.3
C_2H_5OH(g), ethanol	1.41	65.4
$(C_2H_5)_2O$(ℓ), diethyl ether	2.33	172.6
$(C_2H_5)_2O$(g), diethyl ether	1.61	119.5

TABLE 12 Heats of Transformation and Transformation Temperatures of Several Substances

Substance	MP (°C)	Heat of Fusion		BP (°C)	Heat of Vaporization	
		J/g	kJ/mol		J/g	kJ/mol
*Elements**						
Al	660	395	10.7	2518	12083	294
Ca	842	212	8.5	1484	3767	155
Cu	1085	209	13.3	2567	4720	300
Fe	1535	267	13.8	2861	6088	340
Hg	−38.8	11	2.29	357	295	59.1
Compounds						
H_2O	0.00	333	6.01	100.0	2260	40.7
CH_4	−182.5	58.6	0.94	−161.5	511	8.2
C_2H_5OH	−114	109	5.02	78.3	838	38.6
C_6H_6	5.48	127.4	9.95	80.0	393	30.7
$(C_2H_5)_2O$	−116.3	98.1	7.27	34.6	357	26.5

*Data for the elements are taken from J. A. Dean: *Lange's Handbook of Chemistry*, 15th Edition. New York, McGraw-Hill Publishers, 1999.

E | A Brief Guide to Naming Organic Compounds

It seems a daunting task—to devise a systematic procedure that gives each organic compound a unique name—but that is what has been done. A set of rules was developed to name organic compounds by the International Union of Pure and Applied Chemistry (IUPAC). The IUPAC nomenclature allows chemists to write a name for any compound based on its structure or to identify the formula and structure for a compound from its name. In this book, we have generally used the IUPAC nomenclature scheme when naming compounds.

In addition to the systematic names, many compounds have common names. The common names came into existence before the nomenclature rules were developed, and they have continued in use. For some compounds, these names are so well entrenched that they are used most of the time. One such compound is acetic acid, which is almost always referred to by that name and not by its systematic name, ethanoic acid.

The general procedure for systematic naming of organic compounds begins with the nomenclature for hydrocarbons. Other organic compounds are then named as derivatives of hydrocarbons. Nomenclature rules for simple organic compounds are given in the following section.

E.1 Hydrocarbons

Alkanes

The names of alkanes end in "-ane." When naming a specific alkane, the root of the name identifies the longest carbon chain in a compound. Specific substituent groups attached to this carbon chain are identified by name and position.

Alkanes with chains of from one to ten carbon atoms are given in Table 10.2. After the first four compounds, the names derive from Latin numbers—pentane, hexane, heptane, octane, nonane, decane—and this regular naming continues for higher alkanes. For substituted alkanes, the substituent groups on a hydrocarbon chain must be identified both by a name and by the position of substitution; this information precedes the root of the name. The position is indicated by a number that refers to the carbon atom to which the substituent is attached. (Numbering of the carbon atoms in a chain should begin at the end of the carbon chain that allows the substituent groups to have the lowest numbers.)

Names of hydrocarbon substituents are derived from the name of the hydrocarbon. The group —CH_3, derived by taking a hydrogen from methane, is called the methyl group; the C_2H_5 group is the ethyl group. The nomenclature scheme is easily extended to derivatives of hydrocarbons with other substituent groups such as —Cl (chloro), —NO_2 (nitro), —CN (cyano), —D (deuterio), and so on (Table 13). If two or more of the same substituent groups occur, the prefixes "di-," "tri-," and "tetra-" are added. When different substituent groups are present, they are generally listed in alphabetical order.

TABLE 13   Names of Common Substituent Groups

Formula	Name	Formula	Name
—CH_3	methyl	—D	deuterio
—C_2H_5	ethyl	—Cl	chloro
—$CH_2CH_2CH_3$	1-propyl (*n*-propyl)	—Br	bromo
—$CH(CH_3)_2$	2-propyl (isopropyl)	—F	fluoro
—$CH{=}CH_2$	ethenyl (vinyl)	—CN	cyano
—C_6H_5	phenyl	—NO_2	nitro
—OH	hydroxo		
—NH_2	amino		

Example:

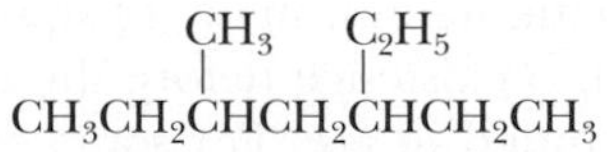

$$\underset{\displaystyle CH_3CH_2\overset{|}{C}HCH_2\overset{|}{C}HCH_2CH_3}{\overset{\displaystyle CH_3 \qquad C_2H_5}{}}$$

Step	Information to include	Contribution to name
1.	An alkane	name will end in "-ane"
2.	Longest chain is 7 carbons	name as a *heptane*
3.	—CH_3 group at carbon 3	3-*methyl*
4.	—C_2H_5 group at carbon 5	5-*ethyl*
Name:	5-ethyl-3-methylheptane	

Cycloalkanes are named based on the ring size and by adding the prefix "cyclo"; for example, the cycloalkane with a six-member ring of carbons is called cyclohexane.

Alkenes

Alkenes have names ending in "-ene." The name of an alkene must specify the length of the carbon chain and the position of the double bond (and when appropriate, the configuration, either *cis* or *trans*). As with alkanes, both identity and position of substituent groups must be given. The carbon chain is numbered from the end that gives the double bond the lowest number.

Compounds with two double bonds are called dienes, and they are named similarly—specifying the positions of the double bonds and the name and position of any substituent groups.

For example, the compound $H_2C{=}C(CH_3)CH(CH_3)CH_2CH_3$ has a five-carbon chain with a double bond between carbon atoms 1 and 2 and methyl groups on carbon atoms 2 and 3. Its name using IUPAC nomenclature is **2,3-dimethyl-1-pentene.** The compound $CH_3CH{=}CHCCl_3$ with a *cis* configuration around the double bond is named **1,1,1-trichloro-*cis*-2-butene.** The compound $H_2C{=}C(Cl)CH{=}CH_2$ is **2-chloro-1,3-butadiene.**

Alkynes

The naming of alkynes is similar to the naming of alkenes, except that *cis–trans* isomerism isn't a factor. The ending "-yne" on a name identifies a compound as an alkyne.

Benzene Derivatives

The carbon atoms in the six-member ring are numbered 1 through 6, and the name and position of substituent groups are given. The two examples shown here are **1-ethyl-3-methylbenzene** and **1,4-diaminobenzene.**

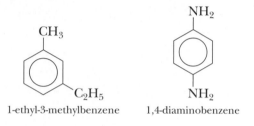

1-ethyl-3-methylbenzene   1,4-diaminobenzene

E.2 Derivatives of Hydrocarbons

The names for alcohols, aldehydes, ketones, and acids are based on the name of the hydrocarbon with an appropriate suffix to denote the class of compound, as follows:

- **Alcohols:** Substitute "-ol" for the final "-e" in the name of the hydrocarbon, and designate the position of the —OH group by the number of the carbon atom. For example, $CH_3CH_2CHOHCH_3$ is named as a derivative of the 4-carbon hydrocarbon butane. The —OH group is attached to the second carbon, so the name is 2-butanol.
- **Aldehydes:** Substitute "-al" for the final "-e" in the name of the hydrocarbon. The carbon atom of an aldehyde is, by definition, carbon-1 in the hydrocarbon chain. For example, the compound $CH_3CH(CH_3)CH_2CH_2CHO$ contains a 5-carbon chain with the aldehyde functional group being carbon-1 and the —CH_3 group at position 4; thus, the name is **4-methylpentanal.**
- **Ketones:** Substitute "-one" for the final "-e" in the name of the hydrocarbon. The position of the ketone functional group (the carbonyl group) is indicated by the number of the carbon atom. For example, the compound $CH_3COCH_2CH(C_2H_5)CH_2CH_3$ has the carbonyl group at the 2 position and an ethyl group at the 4 position of a 6-carbon chain; its name is **4-ethyl-2-hexanone.**
- **Carboxylic acids (organic acids):** Substitute "-oic" for the final "-e" in the name of the hydrocarbon. The carbon atoms in the longest chain are counted beginning with the carboxylic carbon atom. For example, *trans-*

$CH_3CH{=}CHCH_2CO_2H$ is named as a derivative of *trans*-3-pentene—that is, **trans-3-pentenoic acid.**

An **ester** is named as a derivative of the alcohol and acid from which it is made. The name of an ester is obtained by splitting the formula RCO_2R' into two parts, the RCO_2— portion and the —R' portion. The —R' portion comes from the alcohol and is identified by the hydrocarbon group name; derivatives of ethanol, for example, are called *ethyl* esters. The acid part of the compound is named by dropping the "-oic" ending for the acid and replacing it by "-oate." The compound $CH_3CH_2CO_2CH_3$ is named **methyl propanoate.**

Notice that an anion derived from a carboxylic acid by loss of the acidic proton is named the same way. Thus, $CH_3CH_2CO_2^-$ is the **propanoate anion,** and the sodium salt of this anion, $Na(CH_3CH_2CO_2)$, is **sodium propanoate.**

F | Values for the Ionization Energies and Electron Affinities of the Elements

1A (1)	2A (2)	3B (3)	4B (4)	5B (5)	6B (6)	7B (7)	8B (8,9,10)			1B (11)	2B (12)	3A (13)	4A (14)	5A (15)	6A (16)	7A (17)	8 (18)
H 1312																	He 2371
Li 520	Be 899											B 801	C 1086	N 1402	O 1314	F 1681	Ne 2081
Na 496	Mg 738											Al 578	Si 786	P 1012	S 1000	Cl 1251	Ar 1521
K 419	Ca 599	Sc 631	Ti 658	V 650	Cr 652	Mn 717	Fe 759	Co 758	Ni 757	Cu 745	Zn 906	Ga 579	Ge 762	As 947	Se 941	Br 1140	Kr 1351
Rb 403	Sr 550	Y 617	Zr 661	Nb 664	Mo 685	Tc 702	Ru 711	Rh 720	Pd 804	Ag 731	Cd 868	In 558	Sn 709	Sb 834	Te 869	I 1008	Xe 1170
Cs 377	Ba 503	La 538	Hf 681	Ta 761	W 770	Re 760	Os 840	Ir 880	Pt 870	Au 890	Hg 1007	Tl 589	Pb 715	Bi 703	Po 812	At 890	Rn 1037

TABLE 14 Electron Affinity Values for Some Elements (kJ/mol)*

H						
−72.77						

Li	Be	B	C	N	O	F
−59.63	0†	−26.7	−121.85	0	−140.98	−328.0
Na	**Mg**	**Al**	**Si**	**P**	**S**	**Cl**
−52.87	0	−42.6	−133.6	−72.07	−200.41	−349.0
K	**Ca**	**Ga**	**Ge**	**As**	**Se**	**Br**
−48.39	0	−30	−120	−78	−194.97	−324.7
Rb	**Sr**	**In**	**Sn**	**Sb**	**Te**	**I**
−46.89	0	−30	−120	−103	−190.16	−295.16
Cs	**Ba**	**Tl**	**Pb**	**Bi**	**Po**	**At**
−45.51	0	−20	−35.1	−91.3	−180	−270

*Data taken from H. Hotop and W. C. Lineberger: *Journal of Physical Chemistry, Reference Data*, Vol. 14, p. 731, 1985. (This paper also includes data for the transition metals.) Some values are known to more than two decimal places.
†Elements with an electron affinity of zero indicate that a stable anion A⁻ of the element does not exist in the gas phase.

G | Vapor Pressure of Water at Various Temperatures

TABLE 15 Vapor Pressure of Water at Various Temperatures

Temperature (°C)	Vapor Pressure (torr)	Temperature (°C)	Vapor Pressure (torr)	Temperature (°C)	Vapor Pressure (torr)	Temperature (°C)	Vapor Pressure (torr)
−10	2.1	21	18.7	51	97.2	81	369.7
−9	2.3	22	19.8	52	102.1	82	384.9
−8	2.5	23	21.1	53	107.2	83	400.6
−7	2.7	24	22.4	54	112.5	84	416.8
−6	2.9	25	23.8	55	118.0	85	433.6
−5	3.2	26	25.2	56	123.8	86	450.9
−4	3.4	27	26.7	57	129.8	87	468.7
−3	3.7	28	28.3	58	136.1	88	487.1
−2	4.0	29	30.0	59	142.6	89	506.1
−1	4.3	30	31.8	60	149.4	90	525.8
0	4.6	31	33.7	61	156.4	91	546.1
1	4.9	32	35.7	62	163.8	92	567.0
2	5.3	33	37.7	63	171.4	93	588.6
3	5.7	34	39.9	64	179.3	94	610.9
4	6.1	35	42.2	65	187.5	95	633.9
5	6.5	36	44.6	66	196.1	96	657.6
6	7.0	37	47.1	67	205.0	97	682.1
7	7.5	38	49.7	68	214.2	98	707.3
8	8.0	39	52.4	69	223.7	99	733.2
9	8.6	40	55.3	70	233.7	100	760.0
10	9.2	41	58.3	71	243.9	101	787.6
11	9.8	42	61.5	72	254.6	102	815.9
12	10.5	43	64.8	73	265.7	103	845.1
13	11.2	44	68.3	74	277.2	104	875.1
14	12.0	45	71.9	75	289.1	105	906.1
15	12.8	46	75.7	76	301.4	106	937.9
16	13.6	47	79.6	77	314.1	107	970.6
17	14.5	48	83.7	78	327.3	108	1004.4
18	15.5	49	88.0	79	341.0	109	1038.9
19	16.5	50	92.5	80	355.1	110	1074.6
20	17.5						

H | Ionization Constants for Weak Acids at 25 °C

TABLE 16 Ionization Constants for Weak Acids at 25 °C

Acid	Formula and Ionization Equation	K_a
Ascetic	$CH_3CO_2H \rightleftharpoons H^+ + CH_3CO_2^-$	1.8×10^{-5}
Arsenic	$H_3AsO_4 \rightleftharpoons H^+ + H_2AsO_4^-$	$K_1 = 2.5 \times 10^{-4}$
	$H_2AsO_4^- \rightleftharpoons H^+ + HAsO_4^{2-}$	$K_2 = 5.6 \times 10^{-3}$
	$HAsO_4^{2-} \rightleftharpoons H^+ + AsO_4^{3-}$	$K_3 = 3.0 \times 10^{-13}$
Arsenous	$H_3AsO_3 \rightleftharpoons H^+ + H_2AsO_3^-$	$K_1 = 6.0 \times 10^{-10}$
	$H_2AsO_3^- \rightleftharpoons H^+ + HAsO_3^{2-}$	$K_2 = 3.0 \times 10^{-14}$
Benzoic	$C_6H_5CO_2H \rightleftharpoons H^+ + C_6H_5CO_2^-$	6.3×10^{-5}
Boric	$H_3BO_3 \rightleftharpoons H^+ + H_2BO_3^-$	$K_1 = 7.3 \times 10^{-10}$
	$H_2BO_3 \rightleftharpoons H^+ + HBO_3^{2-}$	$K_2 = 1.8 \times 10^{-13}$
	$HBO_3^{2-} \rightleftharpoons H^+ + BO_3^{3-}$	$K_3 = 1.6 \times 10^{-14}$
Carbonic	$H_2CO_3 \rightleftharpoons H^+ + HCO_3^-$	$K_1 = 4.2 \times 10^{-7}$
	$HCO_3^- \rightleftharpoons H^+ + CO_3^{2-}$	$K_2 = 4.8 \times 10^{-11}$
Citric	$H_3C_6H_5O_7 \rightleftharpoons H^+ + H_2C_6H_5O_7^-$	$K_1 = 7.4 \times 10^{-3}$
	$H_2C_6H_5O_7^- \rightleftharpoons H^+ + HC_6H_5O_7^{2-}$	$K_2 = 1.7 \times 10^{-5}$
	$HC_6H_5O_7^{2-} \rightleftharpoons H^+ + C_6H_5O_7^{3-}$	$K_3 = 4.0 \times 10^{-7}$
Cyanic	$HOCN \rightleftharpoons H^+ + OCN^-$	3.5×10^{-4}
Formic	$HCO_2H \rightleftharpoons H^+ + HCO_2^-$	1.8×10^{-4}
Hydrazoic	$HN_3 \rightleftharpoons H^+ + N_3^-$	1.9×10^{-5}
Hydrocyanic	$HCN \rightleftharpoons H^+ + CN^-$	4.0×10^{-10}
Hydrofluoric	$HF \rightleftharpoons H^+ + F^-$	7.2×10^{-4}
Hydrogen peroxide	$H_2O_2 \rightleftharpoons H^+ + HO_2^-$	2.4×10^{-12}
Hydrosulfuric	$H_2S \rightleftharpoons H^+ + HS^-$	$K_1 = 1 \times 10^{-7}$
	$HS^- \rightleftharpoons H^+ + S^{2-}$	$K_2 = 1 \times 10^{-19}$
Hypobromous	$HOBr \rightleftharpoons H^+ + OBr^-$	2.5×10^{-9}

(continued)

TABLE 16 Ionization Constants for Weak Acids at 25 °C *(continued)*

Acid	Formula and Ionization Equation	K_a
Hypochlorous	$HOCl \rightleftharpoons H^+ + OCl^-$	3.5×10^{-8}
Nitrous	$HNO_2 \rightleftharpoons H^+ + NO_2^-$	4.5×10^{-4}
Oxalic	$H_2C_2O_4 \rightleftharpoons H^+ + HC_2O_4^-$	$K_1 = 5.9 \times 10^{-2}$
	$HC_2O_4^- \rightleftharpoons H^+ + C_2O_4^{2-}$	$K_2 = 6.4 \times 10^{-5}$
Phenol	$C_6H_5OH \rightleftharpoons H^+ + C_6H_5O^-$	1.3×10^{-10}
Phosphoric	$H_3PO_4 \rightleftharpoons H^+ + H_2PO_4^-$	$K_1 = 7.5 \times 10^{-3}$
	$H_2PO_4^- \rightleftharpoons H^+ + HPO_4^{2-}$	$K_2 = 6.2 \times 10^{-8}$
	$HPO_4^{2-} \rightleftharpoons H^+ + PO_4^{3-}$	$K_3 = 3.6 \times 10^{-13}$
Phosphorous	$H_3PO_3 \rightleftharpoons H^+ + H_2PO_3^-$	$K_1 = 1.6 \times 10^{-2}$
	$H_2PO_3^- \rightleftharpoons H^+ + HPO_3^{2-}$	$K_2 = 7.0 \times 10^{-7}$
Selenic	$H_2SeO_4 \rightleftharpoons H^+ + HSeO_4^-$	$K_1 = $ very large
	$HSeO_4^- \rightleftharpoons H^+ + SeO_4^{2-}$	$K_2 = 1.2 \times 10^{-2}$
Selenous	$HSeO_3 \rightleftharpoons H^+ + HSeO_3^-$	$K_1 = 2.7 \times 10^{-3}$
	$HSeO_3^- \rightleftharpoons H^+ + SeO_3^{2-}$	$K_2 = 2.5 \times 10^{-7}$
Sulfuric	$H_2SO_4 \rightleftharpoons H^+ + HSO_4^-$	$K_1 = $ very large
	$HSO_4^- \rightleftharpoons H^+ + SO_4^{2-}$	$K_2 = 1.2 \times 10^{-2}$
Sulfurous	$H_2SO_3 \rightleftharpoons H^+ + HSO_3^-$	$K_1 = 1.2 \times 10^{-2}$
	$HSO_3^- \rightleftharpoons H^+ + SO_3^{2-}$	$K_2 = 6.2 \times 10^{-8}$
Tellurous	$H_2TeO_3 \rightleftharpoons H^+ + HTeO_3^-$	$K_1 = 2 \times 10^{-3}$
	$HTeO_3^- \rightleftharpoons H^+ + TeO_3^{2-}$	$K_2 = 1 \times 10^{-8}$

I Ionization Constants for Weak Bases at 25 °C

TABLE 17 **Ionization Constants for Weak Bases at 25 °C**

Base	Formula and Ionization Equation	K_b
Ammonia	$NH_3 + H_2O \rightleftharpoons NH_4^+ + OH^-$	1.8×10^{-5}
Aniline	$C_6H_5NH_2 + H_2O \rightleftharpoons C_6H_5NH_3^+ + OH^-$	4.0×10^{-10}
Dimethylamine	$(CH_3)_2NH + H_2O \rightleftharpoons (CH_3)_2NH_2^+ + OH^-$	7.4×10^{-4}
Ethylenediamine	$H_2NCH_2CH_2NH_2 + H_2O \rightleftharpoons H_2NCH_2CH_2NH_3^+ \ OH^-$	$K_1 = 8.5 \times 10^{-5}$
	$H_2NCH_2CH_2NH_3^+ + H_2O \rightleftharpoons H_3NCH_2CH_2NH_3^{2+} \ OH^-$	$K_2 = 2.7 \times 10^{-8}$
Hydrazine	$N_2H_4 + H_2O \rightleftharpoons N_2H_5^+ + OH^-$	$K_1 = 8.5 \times 10^{-7}$
	$N_2H_5^+ + H_2O \rightleftharpoons N_2H_6^{2+} + OH^-$	$K_2 = 8.9 \times 10^{-16}$
Hydroxylamine	$NH_2OH + H_2O \rightleftharpoons NH_3OH^+ + OH^-$	6.6×10^{-9}
Methylamine	$CH_3NH_2 + H_2O \rightleftharpoons CH_3NH_3^+ + OH^-$	5.0×10^{-4}
Pyridine	$C_5H_5N + H_2O \rightleftharpoons C_5H_5NH^+ + OH^-$	1.5×10^{-9}
Trimethylamine	$(CH_3)_3N + H_2O \rightleftharpoons (CH_3)_3NH^+ + OH^-$	7.4×10^{-5}
Ethylamine	$C_2H_5NH_2 + H_2O \rightleftharpoons C_2H_5NH_3^+ + OH^-$	4.3×10^{-4}

J | Solubility Product Constants for Some Inorganic Compounds at 25 °C

TABLE 18A   Solubility Produce Constants (25 °C)

Cation	Compound	K_{sp}	Cation	Compound	K_{sp}
Ba^{2+}	*$BaCrO_4$	1.2×10^{-10}	Mg^{2+}	$MgCO_3$	6.8×10^{-6}
	$BaCO_3$	2.6×10^{-9}		MgF_2	5.2×10^{-11}
	BaF_2	1.8×10^{-7}		$Mg(OH)_2$	5.6×10^{-12}
	*$BaSO_4$	1.1×10^{-10}	Mn^{2+}	$MnCO_3$	2.3×10^{-11}
Ca^{2+}	$CaCO_3$ (calcite)	3.4×10^{-9}		*$Mn(OH)_2$	1.9×10^{-13}
	*CaF_2	5.3×10^{-11}	Hg_2^{2+}	*Hg_2Br_2	6.4×10^{-23}
	*$Ca(OH)_2$	5.5×10^{-5}		Hg_2Cl_2	1.4×10^{-18}
	$CaSO_4$	4.9×10^{-5}		*Hg_2I_2	2.9×10^{-29}
$Cu^{+,2+}$	$CuBr$	6.3×10^{-9}		Hg_2SO_4	6.5×10^{-7}
	CuI	1.3×10^{-12}	Ni^{2+}	$NiCO_3$	1.4×10^{-7}
	$Cu(OH)_2$	2.2×10^{-20}		$Ni(OH)_2$	5.5×10^{-16}
	$CuSCN$	1.8×10^{-13}	Ag^+	*$AgBr$	5.4×10^{-13}
Au^+	$AuCl$	2.0×10^{-13}		*$AgBrO_3$	5.4×10^{-5}
Fe^{2+}	$FeCO_3$	3.1×10^{-11}		$AgCH_3CO_2$	1.9×10^{-3}
	$Fe(OH)_2$	4.9×10^{-17}		$AgCN$	6.0×10^{-17}
Pb^{2+}	$PbBr_2$	6.6×10^{-6}		Ag_2CO_3	8.5×10^{-12}
	$PbCO_3$	7.4×10^{-14}		*$Ag_2C_2O_4$	5.4×10^{-12}
	$PbCl_2$	1.7×10^{-5}		*$AgCl$	1.8×10^{-10}
	$PbCrO_4$	2.8×10^{-13}		Ag_2CrO_4	1.1×10^{-12}
	PbF_2	3.3×10^{-8}		*AgI	8.5×10^{-17}
	PbI_2	9.8×10^{-9}		$AgSCN$	1.0×10^{-12}
	$Pb(OH)_2$	1.4×10^{-15}		*Ag_2SO_4	1.2×10^{-5}
	$PbSO_4$	2.5×10^{-8}			

(continued)

TABLE 18A Solubility Produce Constants (25 °C) *(continued)*

Cation	Compound	K_{sp}	Cation	Compound	K_{sp}
Sr^{2+}	$SrCO_3$	5.6×10^{-10}	Zn^{2+}	$Zn(OH)_2$	3×10^{-17}
	SrF_2	4.3×10^{-9}		$Zn(CN)_2$	8.0×10^{-12}
	$SrSO_4$	3.4×10^{-7}			
Tl^+	$TlBr$	3.7×10^{-6}			
	$TlCl$	1.9×10^{-4}			
	TlI	5.5×10^{-8}			

The values reported in this table were taken from J. A. Dean: *Lange's Handbook of Chemistry,* 15th Edition. New York, McGraw-Hill Publishers, 1999. Values have been rounded off to two significant figures.
*Calculated solubility from these K_{sp} values will match experimental solubility for this compound within a factor of 2. Experimental values for solubilities are given in R. W. Clark and J. M. Bonicamp: *Journal of Chemical Education,* Vol. 75, p. 1182, 1998.

TABLE 18B K_{spa} Values* for Some Metal Sulfides (25 °C)

Substance	K_{spa}
HgS (red)	4×10^{-54}
HgS (black)	2×10^{-53}
Ag_2S	6×10^{-51}
CuS	6×10^{-37}
PbS	3×10^{-28}
CdS	8×10^{-28}
SnS	1×10^{-26}
FeS	6×10^{-19}

*The equilibrium constant value K_{spa} for metal sulfides refers to the equilibrium $MS(s) + H_2O(\ell) \rightleftharpoons M^{2+}(aq) + OH^-(aq) + HS^-(aq)$; see R. J. Myers, *Journal of Chemical Education,* Vol. 63, p. 687, 1986.

K | Formation Constants for Some Complex Ions in Aqueous Solution

TABLE 19 Formation Constants for Some Complex Ions in Aqueous Solution*

Formation Equilibrium	K
$Ag^+ + 2\ Br^- \rightleftharpoons [AgBr_2]^-$	2.1×10^7
$Ag^+ + 2\ Cl^- \rightleftharpoons [AgCl_2]^-$	1.1×10^5
$Ag^+ + 2\ CN^- \rightleftharpoons [Ag(CN)_2]^-$	1.3×10^{21}
$Ag^+ + 2\ S_2O_3^{2-} \rightleftharpoons [Ag(S_2O_3)_2]^{3-}$	2.9×10^{13}
$Ag^+ + 2\ NH_3 \rightleftharpoons [Ag(NH_3)_2]^+$	1.1×10^7
$Al^{3+} + 6\ F^- \rightleftharpoons [AlF_6]^{3-}$	6.9×10^{19}
$Al^{3+} + 4\ OH^- \rightleftharpoons [Al(OH)_4]^-$	1.1×10^{33}
$Au^+ + 2\ CN^- \rightleftharpoons [Au(CN)_2]^-$	2.0×10^{38}
$Cd^{2+} + 4\ CN^- \rightleftharpoons [Cd(CN)_4]^{2-}$	6.0×10^{18}
$Cd^{2+} + 4\ NH_3 \rightleftharpoons [Cd(NH_3)_4]^{2+}$	1.3×10^7
$Co^{2+} + 6\ NH_3 \rightleftharpoons [Co(NH_3)_6]^{2+}$	1.3×10^5
$Cu^+ + 2\ CN^- \rightleftharpoons [Cu(CN)_2]^-$	1.0×10^{24}
$Cu^+ + 2\ Cl^- \rightleftharpoons [Cu(Cl)_2]^-$	3.2×10^5
$Cu^{2+} + 4\ NH_3 \rightleftharpoons [Cu(NH_3)_4]^{2+}$	2.1×10^{13}
$Fe^{2+} + 6\ CN^- \rightleftharpoons [Fe(CN)_6]^{4-}$	1.0×10^{35}
$Hg^{2+} + 4\ Cl^- \rightleftharpoons [HgCl_4]^{2-}$	1.2×10^{15}
$Ni^{2+} + 4\ CN^- \rightleftharpoons [Ni(CN)_4]^{2-}$	2.0×10^{31}
$Ni^{2+} + 6\ NH_3 \rightleftharpoons [Ni(NH_3)_6]^{2+}$	5.5×10^8
$Zn^{2+} + 4\ OH^- \rightleftharpoons [Zn(OH)_4]^{2-}$	4.6×10^{17}
$Zn^{2+} + 4\ NH_3 \rightleftharpoons [Zn(NH_3)_4]^{2+}$	2.9×10^9

*Data reported in this table are taken from J. A. Dean: *Lange's Handbook of Chemistry*, 15th Edition. New York, McGraw-Hill Publishers, 1999.

L Selected Thermodynamic Values

TABLE 20 Selected Thermodynamic Values*

Species	ΔH_f° (298.15 K) (kJ/mol)	S° (298.15 K) (J/K · mol)	ΔG_f° (298.15 K) (kJ/mol)
Aluminum			
Al(s)	0	28.3	0
AlCl$_3$(s)	−705.63	109.29	−630.0
Al$_2$O$_3$(s)	−1675.7	50.92	−1582.3
Barium			
BaCl$_2$(s)	−858.6	123.68	−810.4
BaCO$_3$(s)	−1213	112.1	−1134.41
BaO(s)	−548.1	72.05	−520.38
BaSO$_4$(s)	−1473.2	132.2	−1362.2
Beryllium			
Be(s)	0	9.5	0
Be(OH)$_2$(s)	−902.5	51.9	−815.0
Boron			
BCl$_3$(g)	−402.96	290.17	−387.95
Bromine			
Br(g)	111.884	175.022	82.396
Br$_2$(ℓ)	0	152.2	0
Br$_2$(g)	30.91	245.47	3.12
BrF$_3$(g)	−255.60	292.53	−229.43
HBr(g)	−36.29	198.70	−53.45

(continued)

*Most thermodynamic data are taken from the NIST Webbook at **http://webbook.nist.gov**.

TABLE 20 Selected Thermodynamic Values* *(continued)*

Species	ΔH_f° (298.15 K) (kJ/mol)	S° (298.15 K) (J/K · mol)	ΔG_f° (298.15 K) (kJ/mol)
Calcium			
Ca(s)	0	41.59	0
Ca(g)	178.2	158.884	144.3
Ca^{2+}(g)	1925.90	—	—
CaC$_2$(s)	−59.8	70.	−64.93
CaCO$_3$(s, calcite)	−1207.6	91.7	−1129.16
CaCl$_2$(s)	−795.8	104.6	−748.1
CaF$_2$(s)	−1219.6	68.87	−1167.3
CaH$_2$(s)	−186.2	42	−147.2
CaO(s)	−635.09	38.2	−603.42
CaS(s)	−482.4	56.5	−477.4
Ca(OH)$_2$(s)	−986.09	83.39	−898.43
Ca(OH)$_2$(aq)	−1002.82		−868.07
CaSO$_4$(s)	−1434.52	106.5	−1322.02
Carbon			
C(s, graphite)	0	5.6	0
C(s, diamond)	1.8	2.377	2.900
C(g)	716.67	158.1	671.2
CCl$_4$(ℓ)	−128.4	214.39	−57.63
CCl$_4$(g)	−95.98	309.65	−53.61
CHCl$_3$(ℓ)	−134.47	201.7	−73.66
CHCl$_3$(g)	−103.18	295.61	−70.4
CH$_4$(g, methane)	−74.87	186.26	−50.8
C$_2$H$_2$(g, ethyne)	226.73	200.94	209.20
C$_2$H$_4$(g, ethene)	52.47	219.36	68.35
C$_2$H$_6$(g, ethane)	−83.85	229.2	−31.89
C$_3$H$_8$(g, propane)	−104.7	270.3	−24.4
C$_6$H$_6$(ℓ, benzene)	48.95	173.26	124.21
CH$_3$OH(ℓ, methanol)	−238.4	127.19	−166.14
CH$_3$OH(g, methanol)	−201.0	239.7	−162.5
C$_2$H$_5$OH(ℓ, ethanol)	−277.0	160.7	−174.7
C$_2$H$_5$OH(g, ethanol)	−235.3	282.70	−168.49
CO(g)	−110.525	197.674	−137.168
CO$_2$(g)	−393.509	213.74	−394.359
CS$_2$(ℓ)	89.41	151	65.2
CS$_2$(g)	116.7	237.8	66.61
COCl$_2$(g)	−218.8	283.53	−204.6

(continued)

TABLE 20 Selected Thermodynamic Values* *(continued)*

Species	ΔH_f° (298.15 K) (kJ/mol)	S° (298.15 K) (J/K · mol)	ΔG_f° (298.15 K) (kJ/mol)
Cesium			
Cs(s)	0	85.23	0
Cs$^+$(g)	457.964	—	—
CsCl(s)	−443.04	101.17	−414.53
Chlorine			
Cl(g)	121.3	165.19	105.3
Cl$^-$(g)	−233.13	—	—
Cl$_2$(g)	0	223.08	0
HCl(g)	−92.31	186.2	−95.09
HCl(aq)	−167.159	56.5	−131.26
Chromium			
Cr(s)	0	23.62	0
Cr$_2$O$_3$(s)	−1134.7	80.65	−1052.95
CrCl$_3$(s)	−556.5	123.0	−486.1
Copper			
Cu(s)	0	33.17	0
CuO(s)	−156.06	42.59	−128.3
CuCl$_2$(s)	−220.1	108.07	−175.7
CuSO$_4$(s)	−769.98	109.05	−660.75
Fluorine			
F$_2$(g)	0	202.8	0
F(g)	78.99	158.754	61.91
F$^-$(g)	−255.39	—	—
F$^-$(aq)	−332.63		−278.79
HF(g)	−273.3	173.779	−273.2
HF(aq)	−332.63	88.7	−278.79
Hydrogen			
H$_2$(g)	0	130.7	0
H(g)	217.965	114.713	203.247
H$^+$(g)	1536.202	—	—
H$_2$O(ℓ)	−285.83	69.95	−237.15
H$_2$O(g)	−241.83	188.84	−228.59
H$_2$O$_2$(ℓ)	−187.78	109.6	−120.35
Iodine			
I$_2$(s)	0	116.135	0
I$_2$(g)	62.438	260.69	19.327
I(g)	106.838	180.791	70.250

(continued)

TABLE 20 Selected Thermodynamic Values* *(continued)*

Species	ΔH_f° (298.15 K) (kJ/mol)	S° (298.15 K) (J/K · mol)	ΔG_f° (298.15 K) (kJ/mol)
I⁻(g)	−197	—	—
ICl(g)	17.51	247.56	−5.73
Iron			
Fe(s)	0	27.78	0
FeO(s)	−272	—	—
Fe₂O₃(s, hematite)	−825.5	87.40	−742.2
Fe₃O₄(s, magnetite)	−1118.4	146.4	−1015.4
FeCl₂(s)	−341.79	117.95	−302.30
FeCl₃(s)	−399.49	142.3	−344.00
FeS₂(s, pyrite)	−178.2	52.93	−166.9
Fe(CO)₅(ℓ)	−774.0	338.1	−705.3
Lead			
Pb(s)	0	64.81	0
PbCl₂(s)	−359.41	136.0	−314.10
PbO(s, yellow)	−219	66.5	−196
PbO₂(s)	−277.4	68.6	−217.39
PbS(s)	−100.4	91.2	−98.7
Lithium			
Li(s)	0	29.12	0
Li⁺(g)	685.783	—	—
LiOH(s)	−484.93	42.81	−438.96
LiOH(aq)	−508.48	2.80	−450.58
LiCl(s)	−408.701	59.33	−384.37
Magnesium			
Mg(s)	0	32.67	0
MgCl₂(s)	−641.62	89.62	−592.09
MgCO₃(s)	−1111.69	65.84	−1028.2
MgO(s)	−601.24	26.85	−568.93
Mg(OH)₂(s)	−924.54	63.18	−833.51
MgS(s)	−346.0	50.33	−341.8
Mercury			
Hg(ℓ)	0	76.02	0
HgCl₂(s)	−224.3	146.0	−178.6
HgO(s, red)	−90.83	70.29	−58.539
HgS(s, red)	−58.2	82.4	−50.6

(continued)

TABLE 20 Selected Thermodynamic Values* *(continued)*

Species	ΔH_f° (298.15 K) (kJ/mol)	S° (298.15 K) (J/K · mol)	ΔG_f° (298.15 K) (kJ/mol)
Nickel			
Ni(s)	0	29.87	0
NiO(s)	−239.7	37.99	−211.7
NiCl$_2$(s)	−305.332	97.65	−259.032
Nitrogen			
N$_2$(g)	0	191.56	0
N(g)	472.704	153.298	455.563
NH$_3$(g)	−45.90	192.77	−16.37
N$_2$H$_4$(ℓ)	50.63	121.52	149.45
NH$_4$Cl(s)	−314.55	94.85	−203.08
NH$_4$Cl(aq)	−299.66	169.9	−210.57
NH$_4$NO$_3$(s)	−365.56	151.08	−183.84
NH$_4$NO$_3$(aq)	−339.87	259.8	−190.57
NO(g)	90.29	210.76	86.58
NO$_2$(g)	33.1	240.04	51.23
N$_2$O(g)	82.05	219.85	104.20
N$_2$O$_4$(g)	9.08	304.38	97.73
NOCl(g)	51.71	261.8	66.08
HNO$_3$(ℓ)	−174.10	155.60	−80.71
HNO$_3$(g)	−135.06	266.38	−74.72
HNO$_3$(aq)	−207.36	146.4	−111.25
Oxygen			
O$_2$(g)	0	205.07	0
O(g)	249.170	161.055	231.731
O$_3$(g)	142.67	238.92	163.2
Phosphorus			
P$_4$(s, white)	0	41.1	0
P$_4$(s, red)	−17.6	22.80	−12.1
P(g)	314.64	163.193	278.25
PH$_3$(g)	22.89	210.24	30.91
PCl$_3$(g)	−287.0	311.78	−267.8
P$_4$O$_{10}$(s)	−2984.0	228.86	−2697.7
H$_3$PO$_4$(ℓ)	−1279.0	110.5	−1119.1
Potassium			
K(s)	0	64.63	0
KCl(s)	−436.68	82.56	−408.77
KClO$_3$(s)	−397.73	143.1	−296.25
KI(s)	−327.90	106.32	−324.892

(continued)

TABLE 20 Selected Thermodynamic Values* *(continued)*

Species	ΔH_f° (298.15 K) (kJ/mol)	S° (298.15 K) (J/K · mol)	ΔG_f° (298.15 K) (kJ/mol)
KOH(s)	−424.72	78.9	−378.92
KOH(aq)	−482.37	91.6	−440.50
Silicon			
Si(s)	0	18.82	0
SiBr$_4$(ℓ)	−457.3	277.8	−443.9
SiC(s)	−65.3	16.61	−62.8
SiCl$_4$(g)	−662.75	330.86	−622.76
SiH$_4$(g)	34.31	204.65	56.84
SiF$_4$(g)	−1614.94	282.49	−1572.65
SiO$_2$(s, quartz)	−910.86	41.46	−856.97
Silver			
Ag(s)	0	42.55	0
Ag$_2$O(s)	−31.1	121.3	−11.32
AgCl(s)	−127.01	96.25	−109.76
AgNO$_3$(s)	−124.39	140.92	−33.41
Sodium			
Na(s)	0	51.21	0
Na(g)	107.3	153.765	76.83
Na$^+$(g)	609.358	—	—
NaBr(s)	−361.02	86.82	−348.983
NaCl(s)	−411.12	72.11	−384.04
NaCl(g)	−181.42	229.79	−201.33
NaCl(aq)	−407.27	115.5	−393.133
NaOH(s)	−425.93	64.46	−379.75
NaOH(aq)	−469.15	48.1	−418.09
Na$_2$CO$_3$(s)	−1130.77	134.79	−1048.08
Sulfur			
S(s, rhombic)	0	32.1	0
S(g)	278.98	167.83	236.51
S$_2$Cl$_2$(g)	−18.4	331.5	−31.8
SF$_6$(g)	−1209	291.82	−1105.3
H$_2$S(g)	−20.63	205.79	−33.56
SO$_2$(g)	−296.84	248.21	−300.13
SO$_3$(g)	−395.77	256.77	−371.04
SOCl$_2$(g)	−212.5	309.77	−198.3
H$_2$SO$_4$(ℓ)	−814	156.9	−689.96
H$_2$SO$_4$(aq)	−909.27	20.1	−744.53

(continued)

TABLE 20 Selected Thermodynamic Values* *(continued)*

Species	ΔH_f° (298.15 K) (kJ/mol)	S° (298.15 K) (J/K · mol)	ΔG_f° (298.15 K) (kJ/mol)
Tin			
Sn(s, white)	0	51.08	0
Sn(s, gray)	−2.09	44.14	0.13
SnCl$_4$(ℓ)	−511.3	258.6	−440.15
SnCl$_4$(g)	−471.5	365.8	−432.31
SnO$_2$(s)	−577.63	49.04	−515.88
Titanium			
Ti(s)	0	30.72	0
TiCl$_4$(ℓ)	−804.2	252.34	−737.2
TiCl$_4$(g)	−763.16	354.84	−726.7
TiO$_2$(s)	−939.7	49.92	−884.5
Zinc			
Zn(s)	0	41.63	0
ZnCl$_2$(s)	−415.05	111.46	−369.398
ZnO(s)	−348.28	43.64	−318.30
ZnS(s, sphalerite)	−205.98	57.7	−201.29

M | Standard Reduction Potentials in Aqueous Solution at 25 °C

TABLE 21 Standard Reduction Potentials in Aqueous Solution at 25 °C

Acidic Solution	Standard Reduction Potential $E°$ (volts)
$F_2(g) + 2\ e^- \longrightarrow 2\ F^-(aq)$	2.87
$Co^{3+}(aq) + e^- \longrightarrow Co^{2+}(aq)$	1.82
$Pb^{4+}(aq) + 2\ e^- \longrightarrow Pb^{2+}(aq)$	1.8
$H_2O_2(aq) + 2\ H^+(aq) + 2\ e^- \longrightarrow 2\ H_2O$	1.77
$NiO_2(s) + 4\ H^+(aq) + 2\ e^- \longrightarrow Ni^{2+}(aq) + 2\ H_2O$	1.7
$PbO_2(s) + SO_4{}^{2-}(aq) + 4\ H^+(aq) + 2\ e^- \longrightarrow PbSO_4(s) + 2\ H_2O$	1.685
$Au^+(aq) + e^- \longrightarrow Au(s)$	1.68
$2\ HClO(aq) + 2\ H^+(aq) + 2\ e^- \longrightarrow Cl_2(g) + 2\ H_2O$	1.63
$Ce^{4+}(aq) + e^- \longrightarrow Ce^{3+}(aq)$	1.61
$NaBiO_3(s) + 6\ H^+(aq) + 2\ e^- \longrightarrow Bi^{3+}(aq) + Na^+(aq) + 3\ H_2O$	≈ 1.6
$MnO_4{}^-(aq) + 8\ H^+(aq) + 5\ e^- \longrightarrow Mn^{2+}(aq) + 4\ H_2O$	1.51
$Au^{3+}(aq) + 3\ e^- \longrightarrow Au(s)$	1.50
$ClO_3{}^-(aq) + 6\ H^+(aq) + 5\ e^- \longrightarrow \frac{1}{2}\ Cl_2(g) + 3\ H_2O$	1.47
$BrO_3{}^-(aq) + 6\ H^+(aq) + 6\ e^- \longrightarrow Br^-(aq) + 3\ H_2O$	1.44
$Cl_2(g) + 2\ e^- \longrightarrow 2\ Cl^-(aq)$	1.36
$Cr_2O_7{}^{2-}(aq) + 14\ H^+(aq) + 6\ e^- \longrightarrow 2\ Cr^{3+}(aq) + 7\ H_2O$	1.33
$N_2H_5{}^+(aq) + 3\ H^+(aq) + 2\ e^- \longrightarrow 2\ NH_4{}^+(aq)$	1.24
$MnO_2(s) + 4\ H^+(aq) + 2\ e^- \longrightarrow Mn^{2+}(aq) + 2\ H_2O$	1.23
$O_2(g) + 4\ H^+(aq) + 4\ e^- \longrightarrow 2\ H_2O$	1.229
$Pt^{2+}(aq) + 2\ e^- \longrightarrow Pt(s)$	1.2
$IO_3{}^-(aq) + 6\ H^+(aq) + 5\ e^- \longrightarrow \frac{1}{2}\ I_2(aq) + 3\ H_2O$	1.195

(continued)

Acidic Solution	Standard Reduction Potential $E°$ (volts)
$ClO_4^-(aq) + 2\ H^+(aq) + 2\ e^- \longrightarrow ClO_3^-(aq) + H_2O$	1.19
$Br_2(\ell) + 2\ e^- \longrightarrow 2\ Br^-(aq)$	1.08
$AuCl_4^-(aq) + 3\ e^- \longrightarrow Au(s) + 4\ Cl^-(aq)$	1.00
$Pd^{2+}(aq) + 2\ e^- \longrightarrow Pd(s)$	0.987
$NO_3^-(aq) + 4\ H^+(aq) + 3\ e^- \longrightarrow NO(g) + 2\ H_2O$	0.96
$NO_3^-(aq) + 3\ H^+(aq) + 2\ e^- \longrightarrow HNO_2(aq) + H_2O$	0.94
$2\ Hg^+(aq) + 2\ e^- \longrightarrow Hg_2^{2+}(aq)$	0.920
$Hg^{2+}(aq) + 2\ e^- \longrightarrow Hg(\ell)$	0.855
$Ag^+(aq) + e^- \longrightarrow Ag(s)$	0.7994
$Hg_2^{2+}(aq) + 2\ e^- \longrightarrow 2\ Hg(\ell)$	0.789
$Fe^{3+}(aq) + e^- \longrightarrow Fe^{2+}(aq)$	0.771
$SbCl_6^-(aq) + 2\ e^- \longrightarrow SbCl_4^-(aq) + 2\ Cl^-(aq)$	0.75
$[PtCl_4]^{2+}(aq) + 2\ e^- \longrightarrow Pt(s) + 4\ Cl^-(aq)$	0.73
$O_2(g) + 2\ H^+(aq) + 2\ e^- \longrightarrow H_2O_2(aq)$	0.682
$[PtCl_6]^{2-}(aq) + 2\ e^- \longrightarrow [PtCl_4]^{2-}(aq) + 2\ Cl^-(aq)$	0.68
$I_2(aq) + 2\ e^- \longrightarrow 2\ I^-(aq)$	0.621
$H_3AsO_4(aq) + 2\ H^+(aq) + 2\ e^- \longrightarrow H_3AsO_3(aq) + H_2O$	0.58
$I_2(s) + 2\ e^- \longrightarrow 2\ I^-(aq)$	0.535
$TeO_2(s) + 4\ H^+(aq) + 4\ e^- \longrightarrow Te(s) + 2\ H_2O$	0.529
$Cu^+(aq) + e^- \longrightarrow Cu(s)$	0.521
$[RhCl_6]^{3-}(aq) + 3\ e^- \longrightarrow Rh(s) + 6\ Cl^-(aq)$	0.44
$Cu^{2+}(aq) + 2\ e^- \longrightarrow Cu(s)$	0.337
$Hg_2Cl_2(s) + 2\ e^- \longrightarrow 2\ Hg(\ell) + 2\ Cl^-(aq)$	0.27
$AgCl(s) + e^- \longrightarrow Ag(s) + Cl^-(aq)$	0.222
$SO_4^{2-}(aq) + 4\ H^+(aq) + 2\ e^- \longrightarrow SO_2(g) + 2\ H_2O$	0.20
$SO_4^{2-}(aq) + 4\ H^+(aq) + 2\ e^- \longrightarrow H_2SO_3(aq) + H_2O$	0.17
$Cu^{2+}(aq) + e^- \longrightarrow Cu^+(aq)$	0.153
$Sn^{4+}(aq) + 2\ e^- \longrightarrow Sn^{2+}(aq)$	0.15
$S(s) + 2\ H^+ + 2\ e^- \longrightarrow H_2S(aq)$	0.14
$AgBr(s) + e^- \longrightarrow Ag(s) + Br^-(aq)$	0.0713
$2\ H^+(aq) + 2\ e^- \longrightarrow H_2(g) \text{(reference electrode)}$	0.0000
$N_2O(g) + 6\ H^+(aq) + H_2O + 4\ e^- \longrightarrow 2\ NH_3OH^+(aq)$	−0.05
$Pb^{2+}(aq) + 2\ e^- \longrightarrow Pb(s)$	−0.126
$Sn^{2+}(aq) + 2\ e^- \longrightarrow Sn(s)$	−0.14
$AgI(s) + e^- \longrightarrow Ag(s) + I^-(aq)$	−0.15
$[SnF_6]^{2-}(aq) + 4\ e^- \longrightarrow Sn(s) + 6\ F^-(aq)$	−0.25
$Ni^{2+}(aq) + 2\ e^- \longrightarrow Ni(s)$	−0.25
$Co^{2+}(aq) + 2\ e^- \longrightarrow Co(s)$	−0.28

(continued)

TABLE 21 Standard Reduction Potentials in Aqueous Solution at 25 °C *(continued)*

Acidic Solution	Standard Reduction Potential $E°$ (volts)
$Tl^+(aq) + e^- \longrightarrow Tl(s)$	-0.34
$PbSO_4(s) + 2\ e^- \longrightarrow Pb(s) + SO_4^{2-}(aq)$	-0.356
$Se(s) + 2\ H^+(aq) + 2\ e^- \longrightarrow H_2Se(aq)$	-0.40
$Cd^{2+}(aq) + 2\ e^- \longrightarrow Cd(s)$	-0.403
$Cr^{3+}(aq) + e^- \longrightarrow Cr^{2+}(aq)$	-0.41
$Fe^{2+}(aq) + 2\ e^- \longrightarrow Fe(s)$	-0.44
$2\ CO_2(g) + 2\ H^+(aq) + 2\ e^- \longrightarrow H_2C_2O_4(aq)$	-0.49
$Ga^{3+}(aq) + 3\ e^- \longrightarrow Ga(s)$	-0.53
$HgS(s) + 2\ H^+(aq) + 2\ e^- \longrightarrow Hg(\ell) + H_2S(g)$	-0.72
$Cr^{3+}(aq) + 3\ e^- \longrightarrow Cr(s)$	-0.74
$Zn^{2+}(aq) + 2\ e^- \longrightarrow Zn(s)$	-0.763
$Cr^{2+}(aq) + 2\ e^- \longrightarrow Cr(s)$	-0.91
$FeS(s) + 2\ e^- \longrightarrow Fe(s) + S^{2-}(aq)$	-1.01
$Mn^{2+}(aq) + 2\ e^- \longrightarrow Mn(s)$	-1.18
$V^{2+}(aq) + 2\ e^- \longrightarrow V(s)$	-1.18
$CdS(s) + 2\ e^- \longrightarrow Cd(s) + S^{2-}(aq)$	-1.21
$ZnS(s) + 2\ e^- \longrightarrow Zn(s) + S^{2-}(aq)$	-1.44
$Zr^{4+}(aq) + 4\ e^- \longrightarrow Zr(s)$	-1.53
$Al^{3+}(aq) + 3\ e^- \longrightarrow Al(s)$	-1.66
$Mg^{2+}(aq) + 2\ e^- \longrightarrow Mg(s)$	-2.37
$Na^+(aq) + e^- \longrightarrow Na(s)$	-2.714
$Ca^{2+}(aq) + 2\ e^- \longrightarrow Ca(s)$	-2.87
$Sr^{2+}(aq) + 2\ e^- \longrightarrow Sr(s)$	-2.89
$Ba^{2+}(aq) + 2\ e^- \longrightarrow Ba(s)$	-2.90
$Rb^+(aq) + e^- \longrightarrow Rb(s)$	-2.925
$K^+(aq) + e^- \longrightarrow K(s)$	-2.925
$Li^+(aq) + e^- \longrightarrow Li(s)$	-3.045

Basic Solution	
$ClO^-(aq) + H_2O + 2\ e^- \longrightarrow Cl^-(aq) + 2\ OH^-(aq)$	0.89
$OOH^-(aq) + H_2O + 2\ e^- \longrightarrow 3\ OH^-(aq)$	0.88
$2\ NH_2OH(aq) + 2\ e^- \longrightarrow N_2H_4(aq) + 2\ OH^-(aq)$	0.74
$ClO_3^-(aq) + 3\ H_2O + 6\ e^- \longrightarrow Cl^-(aq) + 6\ OH^-(aq)$	0.62
$MnO_4^-(aq) + 2\ H_2O + 3\ e^- \longrightarrow MnO_2(s) + 4\ OH^-(aq)$	0.588
$MnO_4^-(aq) + e^- \longrightarrow MnO_4^{2-}(aq)$	0.564
$NiO_2(s) + 2\ H_2O + 2\ e^- \longrightarrow Ni(OH)_2(s) + 2\ OH^-(aq)$	0.49
$Ag_2CrO_4(s) + 2\ e^- \longrightarrow 2\ Ag(s) + CrO_4^{2-}(aq)$	0.446
$O_2(g) + 2\ H_2O + 4\ e^- \longrightarrow 4\ OH^-(aq)$	0.40

(continued)

Acidic Solution	Standard Reduction Potential $E°$ (volts)
$ClO_4^-(aq) + H_2O + 2\ e^- \longrightarrow ClO_3^-(aq) + 2\ OH^-(aq)$	0.36
$Ag_2O(s) + H_2O + 2\ e^- \longrightarrow 2\ Ag(s) + 2\ OH^-(aq)$	0.34
$2\ NO_2^-(aq) + 3\ H_2O + 4\ e^- \longrightarrow N_2O(g) + 6\ OH^-(aq)$	0.15
$N_2H_4(aq) + 2\ H_2O + 2\ e^- \longrightarrow 2\ NH_3(aq) + 2\ OH^-(aq)$	0.10
$[Co(NH_3)_6]^{3+}(aq) + e^- \longrightarrow [Co(NH_3)_6]^{2+}(aq)$	0.10
$HgO(s) + H_2O + 2\ e^- \longrightarrow Hg(\ell) + 2\ OH^-(aq)$	0.0984
$O_2(g) + H_2O + 2\ e^- \longrightarrow OOH^-(aq) + OH^-(aq)$	0.076
$NO_3^-(aq) + H_2O + 2\ e^- \longrightarrow NO_2^-(aq) + 2\ OH^-(aq)$	0.01
$MnO_2(s) + 2\ H_2O + 2\ e^- \longrightarrow Mn(OH)_2(s) + 2\ OH^-(aq)$	−0.05
$CrO_4^{2-}(aq) + 4\ H_2O + 3\ e^- \longrightarrow Cr(OH)_3(s) + 5\ OH^-(aq)$	−0.12
$Cu(OH)_2(s) + 2\ e^- \longrightarrow Cu(s) + 2\ OH^-(aq)$	−0.36
$S(s) + 2\ e^- \longrightarrow S^{2-}(aq)$	−0.48
$Fe(OH)_3(s) + e^- \longrightarrow Fe(OH)_2(s) + OH^-(aq)$	−0.56
$2\ H_2O + 2\ e^- \longrightarrow H_2(g) + 2\ OH^-(aq)$	−0.8277
$2\ NO_3^-(aq) + 2\ H_2O + 2\ e^- \longrightarrow N_2O_4(g) + 4\ OH^-(aq)$	−0.85
$Fe(OH)_2(s) + 2\ e^- \longrightarrow Fe(s) + 2\ OH^-(aq)$	−0.877
$SO_4^{2-}(aq) + H_2O + 2\ e^- \longrightarrow SO_3^{2-}(aq) + 2\ OH^-(aq)$	−0.93
$N_2(g) + 4\ H_2O + 4\ e^- \longrightarrow N_2H_4(aq) + 4\ OH^-(aq)$	−1.15
$[Zn(OH)_4]^{2-}(aq) + 2\ e^- \longrightarrow Zn(s) + 4\ OH^-(aq)$	−1.22
$Zn(OH)_2(s) + 2\ e^- \longrightarrow Zn(s) + 2\ OH^-(aq)$	−1.245
$[Zn(CN)_4]^{2-}(aq) + 2\ e^- \longrightarrow Zn(s) + 4\ CN^-(aq)$	−1.26
$Cr(OH)_3(s) + 3\ e^- \longrightarrow Cr(s) + 3\ OH^-(aq)$	−1.30
$SiO_3^{2-}(aq) + 3\ H_2O + 4\ e^- \longrightarrow Si(s) + 6\ OH^-(aq)$	−1.70

N | Answers to Exercises

Chapter 1

1.1 (a) Na = sodium; Cl = chlorine; Cr = chromium
(b) Zinc = Zn; nickel = Ni; potassium = K

1.2 (a) Iron: lustrous solid, metallic, good conductor of heat and electricity, malleable, ductile, attracted to a magnet
(b) Water: colorless liquid (at room temperature); melting point is 0 °C, and boiling point is 100 °C, density ~ 1 g/cm^2
(c) Table salt: solid, white crystals, soluble in water
(d) Oxygen: colorless gas (at room temperature), low solubility in water

1.3 Chemical changes: the fuel in the campfire burns in air (combustion). Physical changes: water boils. Energy evolved in combustion is transferred to the water, to the water container, and to the surrounding air.

Let's Review

LR 1 [77 K − 273.15 K] (1 °C/K) = −196 °C

LR 2 Convert thickness to cm: 0.25 mm(1 cm/ 10 mm) = 0.025 cm

Volume = length × width × thickness

V = (2.50 cm)(2.50 cm)(0.025 cm) = 0.16 cm^3 (answer has 2 significant figures.)

LR 3 (a) (750 mL)(1 L/1000 mL) = 0.75 L
(0.75 L)(10 dL/L) = 7.5 dL
(b) 2.0 qt = 0.50 gal
(0.50 gal)(3.786 L/gal) = 1.9 L
(1.9 L)(1 dm^3/1 L) = 1.9 dm^3

LR 4 (a) Mass in kilograms = (5.59 g)(1 kg/ 1000 g) = 0.00559 kg
Mass in milligrams = 5.59 g (10^3 mg/g) = 5.59 × 10^3 mg
(b) (0.02 μg/L)(1 g/10^6 μg) = 2 × 10^{-8} g/L

LR 5 Student A: average = −0.1 °C; average deviation = 0.2 °C; error = −0.1 °C. Student B: average = +0.01 °C; average deviation = 0.02 °C; error = +0.01 °C. Student B's values are more accurate and less precise.

LR 6 (a) 2.33 × 10^7 has three significant figures; 50.5 has three significant figures; 200 has one significant figure. (200. or 2.00 × 10^2 would express this number with three significant figures.)
(b) The product of 10.26 and 0.063 is 0.65, a number with two significant figures. (10.26 has four significant figures, whereas 0.063 has two.)
The sum of 10.26 and 0.063 is 10.32. The number 10.26 has only two numbers to the right of the decimal, so the sum must also have two numbers after the decimal.
(c) x = 3.9 × 10^6. The difference between 110.7 and 64 is 47. Dividing 47 by 0.056 and 0.00216 gives an answer with two significant figures.

LR 7 (a) (198 cm)(1 m/100 cm) = 1.98 m;
(198 cm)(1 ft/30.48 cm) = 6.50 ft
(b) (2.33 × 10^7 m^2)(1 km^2/10^6 m^2) = 23.3 km^2
(c) (19,320 kg/m^3)(10^3 g/1 kg)(1 m^3/10^6 cm^3) = 19.32 g/cm^3
(d) (9.0 × 10^3 pc)(206,265 AU/1 pc)(1.496 × 10^8 km/1 AU) = 2.8 × 10^{17} km

LR 8 Read from the graph, the mass of 50 beans is about 123 g.

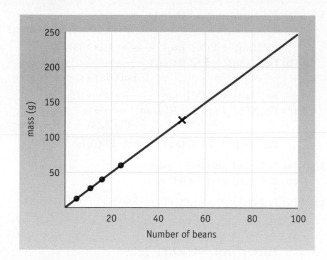

LR 9 Change all dimensions to centimeters: 7.6 m = 760 cm; 2.74 m = 274 cm; 0.13 mm = 0.013 cm.

Volume of paint = (760 cm)(274 cm)(0.013 cm) = 2.7×10^3 cm^3

Volume (L) = $(2.7 \times 10^3$ cm$^3)(1$ L$/10^3$ cm$^3) = 2.7$ L

Mass = $(2.7 \times 10^3$ cm$^3)(0.914$ g/cm$^3) = 2.5 \times 10^3$ g

Chapter 2

2.1 (a) Mass number with 26 protons and 30 neutrons is 56

(b) $(59.930788$ u$)(1.661 \times 10^{-24}$ g/u$) = 9.955 \times 10^{-23}$ g

(c) ^{64}Zn has 30 protons, 30 electrons, and $(64 - 30)$ = 34 neutrons.

(d) The mass of a ^{64}Zn atom is 63.929/12.0... or 5.3274 times the mass of a ^{12}C atom. (Note that mass of ^{12}C is defined as an exact value.)

2.2 The mass number of the second silver isotope is 109 $(62 + 47)$. Symbol: ^{109}Ag, abundance = 48.161%.

2.3 Use Equation 2.2 for the calculation.
Atomic mass = $(34.96885)(75.77/100) + (36.96590)$ $(24.23/100) = 35.45$. (Accuracy is limited by the value of the percent abundance to 4 significant figures.)

2.4 There are eight elements in the third period. Sodium (Na), magnesium (Mg), and aluminum (Al) are metals. Silicon (Si) is a metalloid. Phosphorus (P), sulfur (S), chlorine (Cl), and argon (Ar) are nonmetals.

2.5 The molecular formula is $C_3H_7NO_2S$. You will often see its formula written as $HSCH_2CH(N^+H_3)CO_2^-$ to better identify the molecule's structure.

2.6 (a) K^+ is formed if K loses one electron. K^+ has the same number of electrons as Ar.

(b) Se^{2-} is formed by adding two electrons to an atom of Se. It has the same number of electrons as Kr.

(c) Ba^{2+} is formed if Ba loses two electrons; Ba^{2+} has the same number of electrons as Xe.

(d) Cs^+ is formed if Cs loses one electron. It has the same number of electrons as Xe.

2.7 (a) (1) NaF: 1 Na^+ and 1 F^- ion. (2) $Cu(NO_3)_2$: 1 Cu^{2+} and 2 NO_3^- ions. (3) $NaCH_3CO_2$: 1 Na^+ and 1 $CH_3CO_2^-$ ion.

(b) $FeCl_2$, $FeCl_3$

(c) Na_2S, Na_3PO_4, BaS, $Ba_3(PO_4)_2$

2.8 (1) (a) NH_4NO_3; (b) $CoSO_4$; (c) $Ni(CN)_2$; (d) V_2O_3; (e) $Ba(CH_3CO_2)_2$; (f) $Ca(ClO)_2$

(2) (a) magnesium bromide; (b) lithium carbonate; (c) potassium hydrogen sulfite; (d) potassium permanganate; (e) ammonium sulfide; (f) copper(I) chloride and copper(II) chloride

2.9 The force of attraction between ions is proportional to the product of the ion charges (Coulomb's law). The force of attraction between Mg^{2+} and O^{2-} ions in MgO is approximately four times greater than the force of attraction between Na^+ and Cl^- ions in NaCl, so a much higher temperature is required to disrupt the orderly array of ions in crystalline MgO.

2.10 (1) (a) CO_2; (b) PI_3; (c) SCl_2; (d) BF_3; (e) O_2F_2; (f) XeO_3

(2) (a) dinitrogen tetrafluoride; (b) hydrogen bromide; (c) sulfur tetrafluoride; (d) boron trichloride; (e) tetraphosphorus decaoxide; (f) chlorine trifluoride

2.11 (a) $(1.5$ mol Si$)(28.1$ g/mol$) = 42$ g Si

(b) $(454$ g S$)(1.00$ mol S$/32.07$ g$) = 14.2$ mol S $(14.2$ mol S$)(6.022 \times 10^{23}$ atoms/mol$) = 8.53 \times 10^{24}$ atoms S

2.12 $(2.6 \times 10^{24}$ atoms$)(1.000$ mol$/6.022 \times 10^{23}$ atoms$)(197.0$ g Au$/1.000$ mol$) = 850$ g Au

Volume = $(850$ g Au$)(1.00$ cm$^3/19.32$ g$) = 44$ cm^3

Volume = 44 cm^3 = (thickness)(area) = (0.10 cm)(area)

Area = 440 cm^2

Length = width = $\sqrt{440 \text{ cm}^2} = 21$ cm

2.13 (a) Citric acid: 192.1 g/mol; magnesium carbonate: 84.3 g/mol

(b) 454 g citric acid $(1.000$ mol$/192.1$ g$) = 2.36$ mol citric acid

(c) 0.125 mol $MgCO_3$ $(84.3$ g/mol$) = 10.5$ g $MgCO_3$

2.14 (a) 1.00 mol $(NH_4)_2CO_3$ (molar mass 96.09 g/mol) has 28.0 g of N (29.2%), 8.06 g of H (8.39%), 12.0 g of C (12.5%), and 48.0 g of O (50.0%)

(b) 454 g C_8H_{18} (1 mol $C_8H_{18}/114.2$ g)(8 mol C/1 mol C_8H_{18})(12.01 g C/1 mol C) = 382 g C

2.15 (a) C_5H_4 (b) $C_2H_4O_2$

2.16 $(88.17$ g C$)(1$ mol C$/12.011$ g C$) = 7.341$ mol C

(11.83 g H)(1 mol H/1.008 g H) = 11.74 mol H

11.74 mol H/7.341 mol C = 1.6 mol H/1 mol C
= (8/5); (mol H/1 mol C) = 8 mol H/5 mol C

The empirical formula is C_5H_8. The molar mass, 68.11 g/mol, closely matches this formula, so C_5H_8 is also the molecular formula.

2.17 (78.90 g C)(1 mol C/12.011 g C) = 6.569 mol C
(10.59 g H)(1 mol H/1.008 g H) = 10.51 mol H
(10.51 g O)(1 mol O/16.00 g O) = 0.6569 mol O

10.51 mol H/0.6569 mol O = 16 mol H/1 mol O

6.569 mol C/0.6569 mol O = 10 mol C/1 mol O

The empirical formula is $C_{10}H_{16}O$.

2.18 (0.586 g K)(1 mol K/39.10 g K) = 0.0150 mol K
(0.480 g O)(1 mol O/16.00 g O) = 0.0300 mol O

The ratio of moles K to moles O atoms is 1 to 2; the empirical formula is KO_2.

2.19 Mass of water lost on heating is 0.235 g − 0.128 g = 0.107 g; 0.128 g $NiCl_2$ remain

(0.107 g H_2O)(1 mol H_2O/18.016 g H_2O)
= 0.00594 mol H_2O

(0.128 g $NiCl_2$)(1 mol $NiCl_2$/129.6 g $NiCl_2$)
= 0.000988 mol $NiCl_2$

Mole ratio = 0.00594 mol H_2O/0.000988 mol $NiCl_2$ = 6.01: Therefore x = 6

The formula for the hydrate is $NiCl_2 \cdot 6 H_2O$.

Chapter 3

3.1 (a) Stoichiometric coefficients: 2 for Al, 3 for Br_2, and 1 for Al_2Br_6
(b) 8000 atoms of Al requires (3/2)8000 = 12,000 molecules of Br_2

3.2 (a) 2 C_4H_{10}(g) + 13 O_2(g) ⟶
8 CO_2(g) + 10 H_2O(ℓ)
(b) 2 $Pb(C_2H_5)_4$(ℓ) + 27 O_2(g) ⟶
2 PbO(s) + 16 CO_2(g) + 20 H_2O(ℓ)

3.3 Epsom salt is an electrolyte, and methanol is a non-electrolyte.

3.4 (a) $LiNO_3$ is soluble and gives Li^+(aq) and NO_3^-(aq) ions.
(b) $CaCl_2$ is soluble and gives Ca^{2+}(aq) and Cl^-(aq) ions.
(c) CuO is not water-soluble.
(d) $NaCH_3CO_2$ is soluble and gives Na^+(aq) and $CH_3CO_2^-$(aq) ions.

3.5 (a) Na_2CO_3(aq) + $CuCl_2$(aq) ⟶
2 NaCl(aq) + $CuCO_3$(s)
(b) No reaction; no insoluble compound is produced.

(c) $NiCl_2$(aq) + 2 KOH(aq) ⟶
$Ni(OH)_2$(s) + 2 KCl(aq)

3.6 (a) $AlCl_3$(aq) + Na_3PO_4(aq) ⟶
$AlPO_4$(s) + 3 NaCl(aq)
Al^{3+}(aq) + PO_4^{3-}(aq) ⟶ $AlPO_4$(s)
(b) $FeCl_3$(aq) + 3 KOH(aq) ⟶
$Fe(OH)_3$(s) + 3 KCl(aq)
Fe^{3+}(aq) + 3 OH^-(aq) ⟶ $Fe(OH)_3$(s)
(c) $Pb(NO_3)_2$(aq) + 2 KCl(aq) ⟶
$PbCl_2$(s) + 2 KNO_3(aq)
Pb^{2+}(aq) + 2 Cl^-(aq) ⇌ $PbCl_2$(s)

3.7 (a) H_3O(aq) and NO_3^-(aq)
(b) Ba^{2+}(aq) and 2 OH^-(aq)

3.8 (a) H_3PO_4(aq) + H_2O(ℓ) ⇌
H_3O^+(aq) + $H_2PO_4^-$(aq)
(b) Acting as a base:
$H_2PO_4^-$(aq) + H_2O(ℓ) ⇌
H_3PO_4(aq) + OH^-(aq)

Acting as an acid:
$H_2PO_4^-$(aq) + H_2O(ℓ) ⇌
HPO_4^{2-}(aq) + H_3O^+(ℓ)

Because $H_2PO_4^-$(aq) can react as a Brønsted acid and as a base, it is said to be amphiprotic.
(c) CN^-(aq) + H_2O(ℓ) ⇌ HCN(aq) + OH^-(aq); cyanide ion is a Brønsted base.

3.9 $Mg(OH)_2$(s) + 2 HCl(aq) ⟶
$MgCl_2$(aq) + 2 H_2O(ℓ)

Net ionic equation: $Mg(OH)_2$(s) + 2 H^+(aq) ⟶
Mg^{2+}(aq) + 2 H_2O(ℓ)

3.10 Metals form basic oxides; nonmetals form acidic oxides.
(a) SeO_2 is an acidic oxide; (b) MgO is a basic oxide; and (c) P_4O_{10} is an acidic oxide.

3.11 (a) $BaCO_3$(s) + 2 HNO_3(aq) ⟶
$Ba(NO_3)_2$(aq) + CO_2(g) + H_2O(ℓ)

Barium carbonate and nitric acid produce barium nitrate, carbon dioxide, and water.
(b) $(NH_4)_2SO_4$(aq) + 2 NaOH(aq) ⟶
2 NH_3(g) + Na_2SO_4(aq) + 2 H_2O(ℓ)

3.12 (a) Fe in Fe_2O_3, +3; (b) S in H_2SO_4, +6;
(c) C in CO_3^{2-}, +4; (d) N in NO_2^+, +5

3.13 Dichromate ion is the oxidizing agent and is reduced. (Cr with a +6 oxidation number is reduced to Cr^{3+} with a +3 oxidation number.) Ethanol is the reducing agent and is oxidized. (The C atoms in ethanol have an oxidation number of −2. The oxidation number is 0 in acetic acid.)

3.14 (b) Cu is the reducing agent and Cl_2 is the oxidizing agent.
(d) $S_2O_3^{2-}$ is the reducing agent and I_2 is the oxidizing agent.

3.15 (a) Gas-forming reaction:

$$CuCO_3(s) + H_2SO_4(aq) \longrightarrow$$
$$CuSO_4(aq) + H_2O(\ell) + CO_2(g)$$

Net ionic equation:

$$CuCO_3(s) + 2\,H_3O(aq) \longrightarrow$$
$$Cu^{2+}(aq) + 3\,H_2O(\ell) + CO_2(g)$$

(b) Oxidation-reduction: $Ga(s) + O_2(g) \longrightarrow$
$$Ga_2O_3(s)$$

(c) Acid–base reaction:

$$Ba(OH)_2(s) + 2\,HNO_3(aq) \longrightarrow$$
$$Ba(NO_3)_2(aq) + 2\,H_2O(\ell)$$

Net ionic equation:

$$Ba(OH)_2(s) + 2\,H_3O(aq) \longrightarrow$$
$$Ba^{2+}(aq) + 4\,H_2O(\ell)$$

(d) Precipitation reaction:

$$CuCl_2(aq) + (NH_4)_2S(aq) \longrightarrow$$
$$CuS(s) + 2\,NH_4Cl(aq)$$

Net ionic equation:

$$Cu^{2+}(aq) + S^{2-}(aq) \longrightarrow CuS(s)$$

Chapter 4

4.1 $(454\ \text{g}\ C_3H_8)(1\ \text{mol}\ C_3H_8/44.10\ \text{g}\ C_3H_8)$
$= 10.3\ \text{mol}\ C_3H_8$

$10.3\ \text{mol}\ C_3H_8\ (5\ \text{mol}\ O_2/1\ \text{mol}\ C_3H_8)$
$(32.00\ \text{g}\ O_2/1\ \text{mol}\ O_2) = 1650\ \text{g}\ O_2$

$(10.3\ \text{mol}\ C_3H_8)(3\ \text{mol}\ CO_2/1\ \text{mol}\ C_3H_8)$
$(44.01\ \text{g}\ CO_2/1\ \text{mol}\ CO_2) = 1360\ \text{g}\ CO_2$

$(10.3\ \text{mol}\ C_3H_8)(4\ \text{mol}\ H_2O/1\ \text{mol}\ C_3H_8)$
$(18.02\ \text{g}\ H_2O/1\ \text{mol}\ H_2O) = 742\ \text{g}\ H_2O$

4.2 (a) Amount Al $= (50.0\ \text{g}\ Al)(1\ \text{mol}\ Al/26.98\ \text{g}\ Al)$
$= 1.85\ \text{mol}\ Al$

Amount $Fe_2O_3 = (50.0\ \text{g}\ Fe_2O_3)(1\ \text{mol}$
$Fe_2O_3/159.7\ \text{g}\ Fe_2O_3) = 0.313\ \text{mol}\ Fe_2O_3$

Mol Al/mol $Fe_2O_3 = 1.853/0.3131 = 5.92$

This is more than the 2:1 ratio required, so the limiting reactant is Fe_2O_3.

(b) Mass Fe $= (0.313\ \text{mol}\ Fe_2O_3)(2\ \text{mol}\ Fe/1\ \text{mol}$
$Fe_2O_3)(55.85\ \text{g}\ Fe/1\ \text{mol}\ Fe) = 35.0\ \text{g}\ Fe$

4.3 Theoretical yield $= 125\ \text{g}\ Al_4C_3(1\ \text{mol}\ Al_4C_3/143.95\ \text{g}$
$Al_4C_3)(3\ \text{mol}\ CH_4/1\ \text{mol}\ Al_4C_3)(16.04\ \text{g}\ CH_4/1\ \text{mol}$
$CH_4) = 41.8\ \text{g}\ CH_4$

Percent yield $= (13.6\ \text{g}/41.8\ \text{g})(100\%) = 33.0\%$

4.4 $(0.143\ \text{g}\ O_2)(1\ \text{mol}\ O_2/32.00\ \text{g}\ O_2)(3\ \text{mol}\ TiO_2/$
$3\ \text{mol}\ O_2)(79.88\ \text{g}\ TiO_2/1\ \text{mol}\ TiO_2) = 0.357\ \text{g}\ TiO_2$

Percent TiO_2 in sample $= (0.357\ \text{g}/2.367\ \text{g})(100\%)$
$= 15.1\%$

4.5 $(1.612\ \text{g}\ CO_2)(1\ \text{mol}\ CO_2/44.01\ \text{g}\ CO_2)(1\ \text{mol}\ C/$
$1\ \text{mol}\ CO_2) = 0.03663\ \text{mol}\ C$

$(0.7425\ \text{g}\ H_2O)(1\ \text{mol}\ H_2O/18.01\ \text{g}\ H_2O)(2\ \text{mol}\ H/$
$1\ \text{mol}\ H_2O) = 0.08243\ \text{mol}\ H$

$0.08243\ \text{mol}\ H/0.03663\ \text{mol} = 2.250\ H/1\ C = 9\ H/4\ C$

The empirical formula is C_4H_9, which has a molar mass of 57 g/mol. This is one half of the measured value of molar mass, so the molecular formula is C_8H_{18}.

4.6 $(0.240\ \text{g}\ CO_2)(1\ \text{mol}\ CO_2/44.01\ \text{g}\ CO_2)(1\ \text{mol}\ C/1$
$\text{mol}\ CO_2)(12.01\ \text{g}\ C/1\ \text{mol}\ C) = 0.06549\ \text{g}\ C$

$(0.0982\ \text{g}\ H_2O)(1\ \text{mol}\ H_2O/18.02\ \text{g}\ H_2O)(2\ \text{mol}\ H/1$
$\text{mol}\ H_2O)(1.008\ \text{g}\ H/1\ \text{mol}\ H) = 0.01099\ \text{g}\ H$

Mass O (by difference) $= 0.1342\ \text{g} - 0.06549\ \text{g} - 0.01099\ \text{g} = 0.05772\ \text{g}$

Amount C $= 0.06549\ \text{g}(1\ \text{mol}\ C/12.01\ \text{g}\ C) = 0.00545\ \text{mol}\ C$

Amount H $= 0.01099\ \text{g}\ H(1\ \text{mol}\ H/1.008\ \text{g}\ H) = 0.01090\ \text{mol}\ H$

Amount O $= 0.05772\ \text{g}\ O(1\ \text{mol}\ O/16.00\ \text{g}\ O) = 0.00361\ \text{mol}\ O$

To find a whole-number ratio, divide each value by 0.00361; this gives 1.51 mol C : 3.02 mol H : 1 mol O. Multiply each value by 2, and round off to 3 mol C : 6 mol H : 2 mol O. The empirical formula is $C_3H_6O_2$; given the molar mass of 74.1, this is also the molecular formula.

4.7 $(26.3\ \text{g})(1\ \text{mol}\ NaHCO_3/84.01\ \text{g}\ NaHCO_3) = 0.313$
$\text{mol}\ NaHCO_3$

$0.313\ \text{mol}\ NaHCO_3/0.200\ \text{L} = 1.57\ \text{M}$

Ion concentrations: $[Na^+] = [HCO_3^-] = 1.57\ \text{M}$

4.8 First, determine the mass of $AgNO_3$ required.

Amount of $AgNO_3$ required $= (0.0200\ \text{M})(0.250\ \text{L})$
$= 5.00 \times 10^{-3}\ \text{mol}$

Mass of $AgNO_3 = (5.00 \times 10^{-3}\ \text{mol})(169.9\ \text{g/mol})$
$= 0.850\ \text{g}\ AgNO_3$

Weigh out 0.850 g $AgNO_3$. Then, dissolve it in a small amount of water in the volumetric flask. After the solid is dissolved, fill the flask to the mark.

4.9 $(2.00\ \text{M})(V_{conc}) = (1.00\ \text{M})(0.250\ \text{L});\ V_{conc} = 0.125\ \text{L}$

To prepare the solution, measure accurately 125 mL of 2.00 M NaOH into a 250-mL volumetric flask, and add water to give a total volume of 250 mL.

4.10 (a) pH $= -\log\ (2.6 \times 10^{-2}) = 1.59$
(b) $-\log\ [H^+] = 3.80;\ [H^+] = 1.5 \times 10^{-4}\ \text{M}$

4.11 HCl is the limiting reagent.

$(0.350\ \text{mol}\ HCl/1\ \text{L})(0.0750\ \text{L})(1\ \text{mol}\ CO_2/$
$2\ \text{mol}\ HCl)(44.01\ \text{g}\ CO_2/1\ \text{mol}\ CO_2) = 0.578\ \text{g}\ CO_2$

4.12 $(0.953\ \text{mol}\ NaOH/1\ \text{L})(0.02833\ \text{L}\ NaOH) = 0.0270\ \text{mol}\ NaOH$

$(0.0270\ \text{mol}\ NaOH)(1\ \text{mol}\ CH_3CO_2H/1\ \text{mol}\ NaOH) = 0.0270\ \text{mol}\ CH_3CO_2H$

$(0.0270\ \text{mol}\ CH_3CO_2H)(60.05\ \text{g/mol}) = 1.62\ \text{g}$
CH_3CO_2H

$0.0270\ \text{mol}\ CH_3CO_2H/0.0250\ \text{L} = 1.08\ \text{M}$

4.13 $(0.100 \text{ mol HCl}/1 \text{ L})(0.02967 \text{ L}) = 0.00297 \text{ mol HCl}$

$(0.00297 \text{ mol HCl})(1 \text{ mol NaOH}/1 \text{ mol HCl}) = 0.00297 \text{ mol NaOH}$

$0.00297 \text{ mol NaOH}/0.0250 \text{ L} = 0.119 \text{ M NaOH}$

4.14 Mol acid = mol base = $(0.323 \text{ mol/L})(0.03008 \text{ L}) = 9.716 \times 10^{-3} \text{ mol}$

Molar mass = $0.856 \text{ g acid}/9.716 \times 10^{-3} \text{ mol}$
acid = 88.1 g/mol

4.15 $(0.196 \text{ mol Na}_2\text{S}_2\text{O}_3/1 \text{ L})(0.02030 \text{ L}) = 0.00398 \text{ mol Na}_2\text{S}_2\text{O}_3$

$(0.00398 \text{ mol Na}_2\text{S}_2\text{O}_3)(1 \text{ mol I}_2/2 \text{ mol Na}_2\text{S}_2\text{O}_3) = 0.00199 \text{ mol I}_2$

0.00199 mol I_2 is in excess, and was not used in the reaction with ascorbic acid.

I_2 originally added = $(0.0520 \text{ mol I}_2/1 \text{ L})(0.05000 \text{ L}) = 0.00260 \text{ mol I}_2$

I_2 used in reaction with ascorbic acid = $0.00260 \text{ mol} - 0.00199 \text{ mol} = 6.1 \times 10^{-4} \text{ mol I}_2$

$(6.1 \times 10^{-4} \text{ mol I}_2)(1 \text{ mol C}_6\text{H}_8\text{O}_6/1 \text{ mol I}_2)(176.1 \text{ g}/1 \text{ mol}) = 0.11 \text{ g C}_6\text{H}_8\text{O}_6$

Chapter 5

5.1 (a) $(3800 \text{ calories})(4.184 \text{ J/calorie}) = 1.6 \times 10^4 \text{ J}$
(b) $(250 \text{ calories})(1000 \text{ calories/calorie})(4.184 \text{ J/calorie})(1 \text{ kJ}/1000 \text{ J}) = 1.0 \times 10^3 \text{ kJ}$

5.2 $C = 59.8 \text{ J}/[(25.0 \text{ g})(1.00 \text{ K})] = 2.39 \text{ J/g} \cdot \text{K}$

5.3 $(15.5 \text{ g})(C_{\text{metal}})(18.9 \text{ °C} - 100.0 \text{ °C}) + (55.5 \text{ g})(4.184 \text{ J/g} \cdot \text{K})(18.9 \text{ °C} - 16.5 \text{ °C}) = 0$

$C_{\text{metal}} = 0.44 \text{ J/g} \cdot \text{K}$

5.4 Energy transferred as heat from tea + energy as heat expended to melt ice = 0

$(250 \text{ g})(4.2 \text{ J/g} \cdot \text{K})(273.2 \text{ K} - 291.4 \text{ K}) + x \text{ g } (333 \text{ J/g}) = 0$

$x = 57 \text{ g}$

57 g of ice melts with energy as heat supplied by cooling 250 g of tea from 18.2 °C (291.4 K) to 0 °C (273.2 K)

Mass of ice remaining = mass of ice initially − mass of ice melted

Mass of ice remaining = 75 g − 57 g = 18 g

5.5 $(15.0 \text{ g C}_2\text{H}_6)(1 \text{ mol C}_2\text{H}_6/30.07 \text{ g C}_2\text{H}_6) = 0.4988 \text{ mol C}_2\text{H}_6$

$\Delta_r H = 0.4988 \text{ mol C}_2\text{H}_6(1 \text{ mol-rxn}/2 \text{ mol C}_2\text{H}_6)(-2857.3 \text{ kJ/mol-rxn})$

$= -713 \text{ kJ}$

5.6 Mass of final solution = 400. g

$\Delta T = 27.78 \text{ °C} - 25.10 \text{ °C} = 2.68 \text{ °C} = 2.68 \text{ K}$

Amount of HCl used = amount of NaOH used = $C \times V = (0.400 \text{ mol/L}) \times 0.200 \text{ L} = 0.0800 \text{ mol}$

Energy transferred as heat by acid–base reaction + energy gained as heat to warm solution = 0

$q_{\text{rxn}} + (4.20 \text{ J/g} \cdot \text{K})(400. \text{ g})(2.68 \text{ K}) = 0$

$q_{\text{rxn}} = -4.50 \times 10^3 \text{ J}$

This represents the energy transferred as heat in the reaction of 0.0800 mol HCl.

Energy transferred as heat per mole = $\Delta_r H = -4.50 \text{ kJ}/0.0800 \text{ mol HCl} = -56.3 \text{ kJ/mol HCl}$

5.7 (a) Energy evolved as heat in reaction + energy as heat absorbed by H_2O + energy as heat absorbed by bomb = 0

$q_{\text{rxn}} + (1.50 \times 10^3 \text{ g})(4.20 \text{ J/g} \cdot \text{K})(27.32 \text{ °C} - 25.00 \text{ °C}) + (837 \text{ J/K})(27.32 \text{ K} - 25.00 \text{ K}) = 0$

$q_{\text{rxn}} = -16,600 \text{ J}$ (energy as heat evolved in burning 1.0 g sucrose)

(b) Energy evolved as heat per mole = $(-16.6 \text{ kJ/g sucrose})(342.2 \text{ g sucrose}/1 \text{ mol sucrose}) = -5650 \text{ kJ/mol sucrose}$

5.8 $C(s) + O_2(g) \longrightarrow CO_2(g) \qquad \Delta_r H_1° = -393.5 \text{ kJ}$

$2 [S(s) + O_2(g) \longrightarrow SO_2(g)]$
$\Delta_r H_2° = 2(-296.8) = -593.6 \text{ kJ}$

$CO_2(g) + 2 SO_2(g) \longrightarrow CS_2(g) + 3 O_2(g)$
$\Delta_r H_3° = +1103.9 \text{ kJ}$

Net: $C(s) + 2 S(s) \longrightarrow CS_2(g)$

$\Delta_r H°_{\text{net}} = \Delta_r H_1° + \Delta_r H_2° + \Delta_r H_3° = +116.8 \text{ kJ}$

5.9 $Fe(s) + {}^3\!/_2 Cl_2(g) \longrightarrow FeCl_3(s)$

$12 C(s, \text{graphite}) + 11 H_2(g) + {}^{11}\!/_2 O_2(g) \longrightarrow C_{12}H_{22}O_{11}(s)$

5.10 $\Delta_r H° = (6 \text{ mol/mol-rxn})\Delta_f H° [CO_2(g)] + (3 \text{ mol/mol-rxn})\Delta_f H°[H_2O(\ell)] - \{(1 \text{ mol}/1 \text{ mol-rxn})\Delta_f H° [C_6H_6(\ell)] + ({}^{15}\!/_2 \text{ mol/mol-rxn}) \Delta_f H° [O_2(g)]\} =$
$(6 \text{ mol/mol-rxn})(-393.5 \text{ kJ/mol}) + (3 \text{ mol/mol-rxn})(-285.8 \text{ J/mol}) - (1 \text{ mol/mol-rxn})(+49.0 \text{ kJ/mol}) - 0$
$= -3267.4 \text{ kJ/mol-rxn}$

Chapter 6

6.1 (a) Highest frequency, violet; lowest frequency, red
(b) The FM radio frequency, 91.7 MHz, is lower than the frequency of a microwave oven, 2.45 GHz.
(c) The wavelength of x-rays is shorter than the wavelength of ultraviolet light.

6.2 Orange light: 6.25×10^2 nm $= 6.25 \times 10^{-7}$ m

$\nu = (2.998 \times 10^8 \text{ m/s})/6.25 \times 10^{-7}$ m
$\quad = 4.80 \times 10^{14} \text{ s}^{-1}$

$E = (6.626 \times 10^{-34} \text{ J} \cdot \text{s/photon})(4.80 \times 10^{14} \text{ s}^{-1})$
$\qquad\qquad\qquad (6.022 \times 10^{23} \text{ photons/mol})$

$\quad = 1.92 \times 10^5 \text{ J/mol}$

Microwave: $E = (6.626 \times 10^{-34} \text{ J} \cdot \text{s/photon})$
$\qquad\qquad (2.45 \times 10^9 \text{ s}^{-1})(6.022 \times$
$\qquad\qquad 10^{23} \text{ photons/mol})$

$\qquad\qquad = 0.978 \text{ J/mol}$

Orange (625-nm) light is about 200,000 times more energetic than 2.45-GHz microwaves.

6.3 (a) E (per atom) $= -Rhc/n^2$
$\qquad\qquad\qquad = (-2.179 \times 10^{-18})/(3^2) \text{ J/atom}$
$\qquad\qquad\qquad = -2.421 \times 10^{-19} \text{ J/atom}$
(b) E (per mol) $= (-2.421 \times 10^{-19} \text{ J/atom})$
$\qquad\qquad\qquad (6.022 \times 10^{23} \text{ atoms/mol})$
$\qquad\qquad\qquad (1 \text{ kJ}/10^3 \text{ J})$
$\qquad\qquad\qquad = -145.8 \text{ kJ/mol}$

6.4 The least energetic line is from the electron transition from $n = 2$ to $n = 1$.

$\Delta E = -Rhc[1/1^2 - 1/2^2]$
$\quad = -(2.179 \times 10^{-18} \text{ J/atom})(3/4)$
$\quad = -1.634 \times 10^{-18} \text{ J/atom}$

$\nu = \Delta E/h$
$\quad = (-1.634 \times 10^{-18} \text{ J/atom})/(6.626 \times 10^{-34} \text{ J} \cdot \text{s})$
$\quad = 2.466 \times 10^{15} \text{ s}^{-1}$

$\lambda = c/\nu = (2.998 \times 10^8 \text{ m/s}^{-1})/(2.466 \times 10^{15} \text{ s}^{-1})$
$\quad = 1.216 \times 10^{-7}$ m (or 121.6 nm)

6.5 Energy per atom $= \Delta E = -Rhc[1/\infty^2 - 1/1^2]$
$\quad = 2.179 \times 10^{-18} \text{ J/atom}$

Energy per mole $= (2.179 \times 10^{-18} \text{ J/atom})(6.022 \times 10^{23} \text{ atoms/mol})$
$\quad = 1.312 \times 10^6 \text{ J/mol}$ ($= 1312 \text{ kJ/mol}$)

6.6 First, calculate the velocity of the neutron:

$\nu = [2E/m]^{1/2} = [2(6.21 \times 10^{-21} \text{ kg} \cdot \text{m}^2 \text{ s}^{-2})/(1.675 \times 10^{-27} \text{ kg})]^{1/2}$
$\quad = 2720 \text{ m} \cdot \text{s}^{-1}$

Use this value in the de Broglie equation:

$\lambda = h/m\nu = (6.626 \times 10^{-34} \text{ kg} \cdot \text{m}^2 \text{ s}^{-2})/$
$\qquad\qquad (1.675 \times 10^{-31} \text{ kg}) (2720 \text{ m s}^{-1})$
$\quad = 1.45 \times 10^{-6}$ m

6.7 (a) $\ell = 0$ or 1; (b) $m_\ell = -1$, 0, or +1, p subshell;
(c) d subshell; (d) $\ell = 0$ and $m_\ell = 0$; (e) 3 orbitals in the p subshell; (f) 7 values of m_ℓ and 7 orbitals

6.8 (a)

Orbital	n	ℓ
6s	6	0
4p	4	1
5d	5	2
4f	4	3

(b) A $4p$ orbital has one nodal plane; a $6d$ orbital has two nodal planes.

Chapter 7

7.1 (a) $4s$ ($n + \ell = 4$) filled before $4p$ ($n + \ell = 5$)
(b) $6s$ ($n + \ell = 6$) filled before $5d$ ($n + \ell = 7$)
(c) $5s$ ($n + \ell = 5$) filled before $4f$ ($n + \ell = 7$)

7.2 (a) chlorine (Cl)
(b) $1s^2 2s^2 2p^6 3s^2 3p^3$

$$[\text{Ne}] \overset{3s}{\boxed{\uparrow\downarrow}} \quad \overset{3p}{\boxed{\uparrow|\uparrow|\uparrow}}$$

(c) Calcium has two valence electrons in the 4s subshell. Quantum numbers for these two electrons are $n = 4$, $\ell = 0$, $m_\ell = 0$, and $m_s = \pm 1/2$

7.3 Obtain the answers from Table 7.3.

7.4

$$\text{V}^{2+} \quad [\text{Ar}] \overset{3d}{\boxed{\uparrow|\uparrow|\uparrow|\ |\ }} \quad \overset{4s}{\boxed{\ }}$$

$$\text{V}^{3+} \quad [\text{Ar}] \overset{3d}{\boxed{\uparrow|\uparrow|\ |\ |\ }} \quad \overset{4s}{\boxed{\ }}$$

$$\text{Co}^{3+} \quad [\text{Ar}] \overset{3d}{\boxed{\uparrow\downarrow|\uparrow|\uparrow|\uparrow|\uparrow}} \quad \overset{4s}{\boxed{\ }}$$

All three ions are paramagnetic with three, two, and four unpaired electrons, respectively.

7.5 Increasing atomic radius: C < Si < Al

7.6 (a) Increasing atomic radius: C < B < Al
(b) Increasing ionization energy: Al < B < C
(c) Carbon is predicted to have the most negative electron affinity.

7.7 Trend in ionic radii: $\text{S}^{2-} > \text{Cl}^- > \text{K}^+$. These ions are isoelectronic (they all have the Ar configuration). The size decreases with increased nuclear charge, the higher nuclear charge resulting in a greater force of attraction of the electrons by the nucleus.

7.8 $MgCl_3$, if it existed, would presumably contain one Mg^{3+} ion (and three Cl^- ions). The formation of Mg^{3+} is energetically unfavorable, with a huge input of energy being required to remove the third electron (a core electron).

Chapter 8

8.1

$$\left[\begin{array}{c} H \\ | \\ H-N-H \\ | \\ H \end{array} \right]^+ \quad :C\equiv O: \quad [:N\equiv O:]^+ \quad \left[\begin{array}{c} :\ddot{O}: \\ | \\ :\ddot{O}-S-\ddot{O}: \\ | \\ :\ddot{O}: \end{array} \right]^{2-}$$

8.2

$$\begin{array}{cc} \begin{array}{c} H \\ | \\ H-C-\ddot{O}-H \\ | \\ H \end{array} & \begin{array}{c} H-\ddot{N}-\ddot{O}-H \\ | \\ H \end{array} \\ \text{methanol} & \text{hydroxylamine} \end{array}$$

8.3

$$\left[\begin{array}{c} :\ddot{O}: \\ | \\ H-\ddot{O}-P-\ddot{O}-H \\ | \\ :\ddot{O}: \end{array} \right]^-$$

8.4　(a) The acetylide ion, C_2^{2-}, and the N_2 molecule have the same number of valence electrons (10) and identical electronic structures; that is, they are isoelectronic.

(b) Ozone, O_3, is isoelectronic with NO_2^-; hydroxide ion, OH^-, is isoelectronic with HF.

8.5　(a) CN^- : formal charge on C is -1; formal charge on N is 0.

(b) SO_3^{2-}: formal charge on S is $+2$; formal charge on each O is -1.

8.6 Resonance structures for the HCO_3^- ion:

$$\left[\begin{array}{c} \ddot{O}=C-\ddot{O}: \\ | \\ :\ddot{O}-H \end{array} \right]^- \longleftrightarrow \left[\begin{array}{c} :\ddot{O}-C=\ddot{O} \\ | \\ :\ddot{O}-H \end{array} \right]^-$$

(a) No. Three resonance structures are needed in the description of CO_3^{2-}; only two are needed to describe HCO_3^-.

(b) In each resonance structure, Carbon's formal charge is 0. The oxygen of the $-OH$ group and the double-bonded oxygen have a formal charge of zero; the singly bonded oxygen has a formal charge of -1. The average formal charge on the latter two oxygen atoms is $-\frac{1}{2}$. In the carbonate ion, the three oxygen atoms have an average formal charge of $-\frac{2}{3}$.

(c) H^+ would be expected to add to one of the oxygens with a negative formal charge; that is, one of the oxygens with formal charge of $-\frac{1}{2}$ in this structure.

8.7　$\left[:\ddot{F}-\ddot{Cl}-\ddot{F}: \right]^+$ ClF_2^+, 2 bond pairs and 2 lone pairs.

$\left[:\ddot{F}-\ddot{Cl}-\ddot{F}: \right]^-$ ClF_2^-, 2 bond pairs and 3 lone pairs.

8.8 Tetrahedral geometry around carbon. The Cl—C—Cl bond angle will be close to $109.5°$.

8.9 For each species, the electron-pair geometry and the molecular shape are the same. BF_3: trigonal planar; BF_4^-: tetrahedral. Adding F^- to BF_3 adds an electron pair to the central atom and changes the shape.

8.10 The electron-pair geometry around I is trigonal bipyramidal. The molecular geometry of the ion is linear.

$$\left[\begin{array}{c} :\ddot{Cl}: \\ | \\ :-I \\ | \\ :\ddot{Cl}: \end{array} \right]^-$$

8.11　(a) In PO_4^{3-}, there is tetrahedral electron-pair geometry. The molecular geometry is also tetrahedral.

$$\left[\begin{array}{c} :\ddot{O}: \\ | \\ :\ddot{O}-P-\ddot{O}: \\ | \\ :\ddot{O}: \end{array} \right]^{3-}$$

(b) In SO_3^{2-}, there is tetrahedral electron-pair geometry. The molecular geometry is trigonal pyramidal.

$$\left[\begin{array}{c} :\ddot{O}-S-\ddot{O}: \\ | \\ :\ddot{O}: \end{array} \right]^{2-}$$

(c) In IF_5, there is octahedral electron-pair geometry. The molecular geometry is square pyramidal.

$$\begin{array}{c} F \\ F_{\cdots}{\Large |}_{\cdots}F \\ I \\ F{\Large /}{\Large |}{\Large \backslash}F \\ \cdots \end{array}$$

8.12　(a) The H atom is positive in each case. H—F $(\Delta\chi = 1.8)$ is more polar than H—I $(\Delta\chi = 0.5)$.

(b) B—F $(\Delta\chi = 2.0)$ is more polar than B—C $(\Delta\chi = 0.5)$. In B—F, F is the negative pole, and B is the positive pole. In B—C, C is the negative pole, and B is the positive pole.

(c) C—Si $(\Delta\chi = 0.6)$ is more polar than C—S $(\Delta\chi = 0.1)$. In C—Si, C is the negative pole, and Si is the positive pole. In C—S, S is the negative pole, and C the positive pole.

8.13

$$\overset{-1}{:}\overset{+1}{\text{O}}\!-\!\overset{0}{\text{S}}\!=\!\overset{0}{\text{O}}: \longleftrightarrow \overset{0}{\text{O}}\!=\!\overset{+1}{\text{S}}\!-\!\overset{-1}{\text{O}}:$$

The S—O bonds are polar, with the negative end being the O atom. (The O atom is more electronegative than the S atom.) Formal charges show that these bonds are, in fact, polar, with the O atom being the more negative atom.

8.14 (a) $BFCl_2$, polar, negative side is the F atom because F is the most electronegative atom in the molecule.

(b) NH_2Cl, polar, negative side is the Cl atom.

(c) SCl_2, polar, Cl atoms are on the negative side.

8.15 (a)

Formal charges: S = +1, O = −1, Cl = 0

(Lewis structure of $SOCl_2$ with formal charges indicated)

(b) Geometry: trigonal pyramidal

(c) The molecule is polar. The positive charge is on sulfur, the negative charge on oxygen.

8.16 (a) C—N: bond order 1; C=N: bond order 2; C $\equiv$ N: bond order 3. Bond length: C—N > C=N > C $\equiv$ N

(b) $\left[:\!\overset{..}{\text{O}}\!-\!\overset{..}{\text{N}}\!=\!\overset{..}{\text{O}}:\right]^{-} \longleftrightarrow \left[\overset{..}{\text{O}}\!=\!\overset{..}{\text{N}}\!-\!\overset{..}{\text{O}}:\right]^{-}$

The N-O bond order in NO_2^- is 1.5. Therefore, the NO bond length (124 pm) should be between the length of a N—O single bond (136 pm) and a N=O double bond (115 pm).

8.17 $CH_4(g) + 2\ O_2(g) \longrightarrow CO_2(g) + 2\ H_2O(g)$

Break 4 C—H bonds and 2 O=O bonds:
(4 mol)(413 kJ/mol) + (2 mol)(498 kJ/mol) = 2648 kJ

Make 2 C=O bonds and 4 H—O bonds:
(2 mol)(745 kJ/mol) + (4 mol)(463 kJ/mol) = 3342 kJ

$\Delta_r H° = 2648\ \text{kJ} - 3342\ \text{kJ} = -694\ \text{kJ/mol-rxn}$
(value calculated using enthalpies of formation = −797 kJ/mol-rxn)

Chapter 9

9.1 The oxygen atom in H_3O^+ is sp^3 hybridized. The three O—H bonds are formed by overlap of oxygen sp^3 and hydrogen $1s$ orbitals. The fourth sp^3 orbital contains a lone pair of electrons.

The carbon and nitrogen atoms in CH_3NH_2 are sp^3 hybridized. The C—H bonds arise from overlap of carbon sp^3 orbitals and hydrogen $1s$ orbitals. The bond between C and N is formed by overlap of sp^3 orbitals from these atoms. Overlap of nitrogen sp^3 and hydrogen $1s$ orbitals gives the two N—H bonds, and there is a lone pair in the remaining sp^3 orbital on nitrogen.

9.2 (a) BH_4^-, tetrahedral electron-pair geometry, sp^3
(b) SF_5^-, octahedral electron-pair geometry, sp^3d^2
(c) SOF_4, trigonal-bipyramidal electron-pair geometry, sp^3d
(d) ClF_3, trigonal-bipyramidal electron-pair geometry, sp^3d
(e) BCl_3, trigonal-planar electron-pair geometry, sp^2
(f) XeO_6^{4-}, octahedral electron-pair geometry, sp^3d^2

9.3 The two CH_3 carbon atoms are sp^3 hybridized, and the center carbon atom is sp^2 hybridized. For each of the carbon atoms in the methyl groups, the sp^3 orbitals overlap with hydrogen $1s$ orbitals to form the three C—H bonds, and the fourth sp^3 orbital overlaps with an sp^2 orbital on the central carbon atom, forming a carbon–carbon sigma bond. Overlap of an sp^2 orbital on the central carbon and an oxygen sp^2 orbital gives the sigma bond between these elements. The pi bond between carbon and oxygen arises by overlap of a p orbital from each element.

9.4 A triple bond links the two nitrogen atoms, each of which also has one lone pair. Each nitrogen is sp hybridized. One sp orbital contains the lone pair; the other is used to form the sigma bond between the two atoms. Two pi bonds arise by overlap of p orbitals on the two atoms, perpendicular to the molecular axis.

9.5 Bond angles: H—C—H = 109.5°, H—C—C = 109.5°, C—C—N = 180°. Carbon in the CH_3 group is sp^3 hybridized; the central C and the N are sp hybridized. The three C—H bonds form by overlap of an H $1s$ orbital with one of the sp^3 orbitals of the CH_3 group; the fourth sp^3 orbital overlaps with an sp orbital on the central C to form a sigma bond. The triple bond between C and N is a combination of a sigma bond (the sp orbital on C overlaps with the sp orbital on N) and two pi bonds (overlap of two sets of p orbitals on these elements). The remaining sp orbital on N contains a lone pair.

9.6 H_2^+: $(\sigma_1 s)^1$ The ion has a bond order of ½ and is expected to exist. A bond order of ½ is predicted for He_2^+ and H_2^-, both of which are predicted to have electron configurations $(\sigma_1 s)^2 (\sigma^*_1 s)^1$.

9.7 Li_2^- is predicted to have an electron configuration $(\sigma_1 s)^2 (\sigma*_1 s)^2 (\sigma_2 s)^2 (\sigma*_2 s)^1$ and a bond order of $\frac{1}{2}$, the positive value implying that the ion might exist.

9.8 O_2^+: [core electrons] $(\sigma_2 s)^2 (\sigma*_2 s)^2 (\pi_2 p)^4 (\sigma_2 p)^2 (\pi*_2 p)^1$. The bond order is 2.5. The ion is paramagnetic with one unpaired electron.

Chapter 10

10.1 (a) Isomers of C_7H_{16}

CH₃CH₂CH₂CH₂CH₂CH₂CH₃   heptane

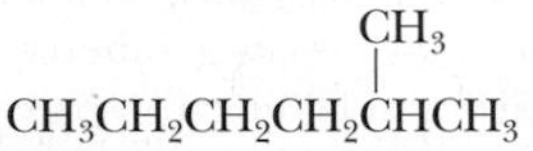

CH₃CH₂CH₂CH₂CHCH₃   2-methylhexane
                CH₃

CH₃CH₂CH₂CHCH₂CH₃   3-methylhexane
           CH₃

CH₃CH₂CHCHCH₃   2,3-dimethylpentane 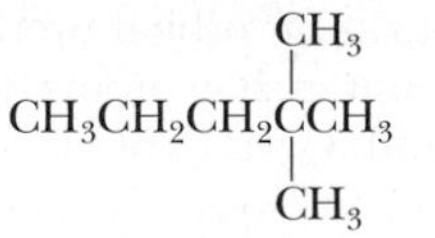
         CH₃   CH₃

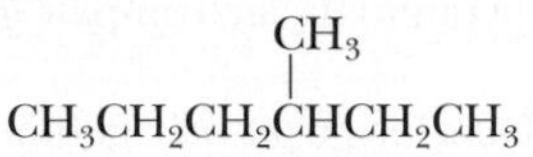

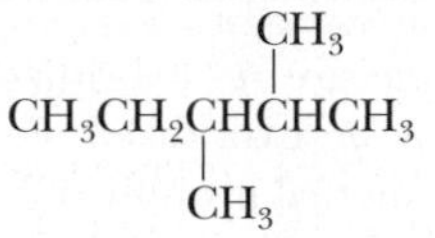

CH₃CH₂CH₂CCH₃   2,2-dimethylpentane 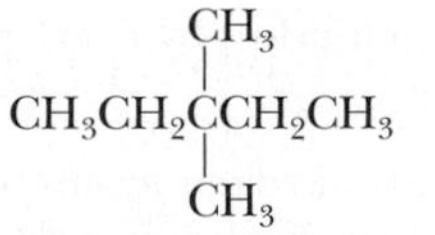
              CH₃

CH₃CH₂CCH₂CH₃   3,3-dimethylpentane 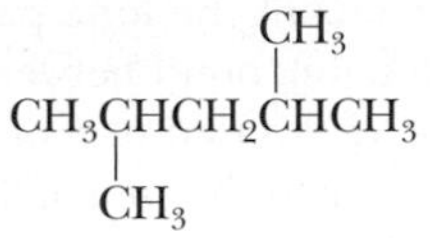
        CH₃

CH₃CHCH₂CHCH₃   2,4-dimethylpentane
    CH₃

2-Ethylpentane is pictured on page 450.

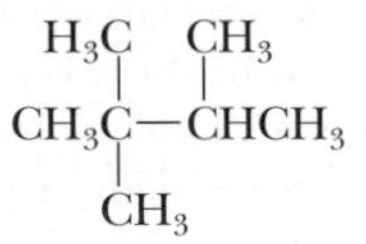

CH₃C—CHCH₃   2,2,3-trimethylbutane

(b) Two isomers, 3-methylhexane, and 2,3-dimethylpentane, are chiral.

10.2 The names accompany the structures in the answer to Exercise 10.1.

10.3 Isomers of C_6H_{12} in which the longest chain has six C atoms:

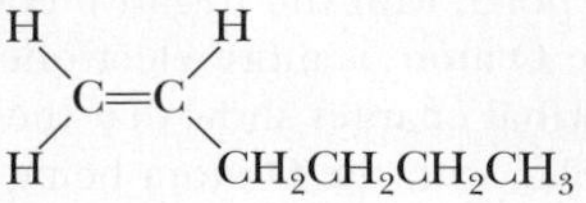

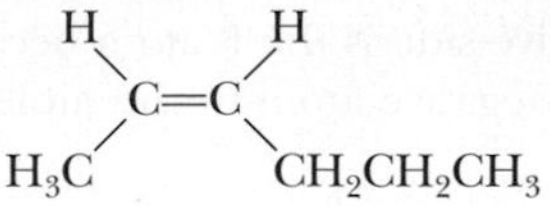

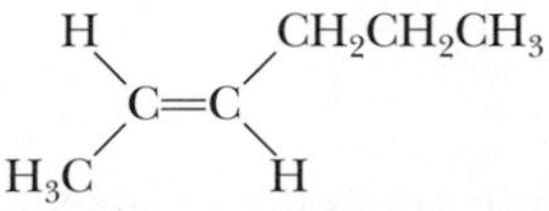

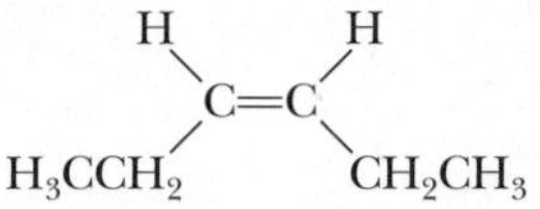

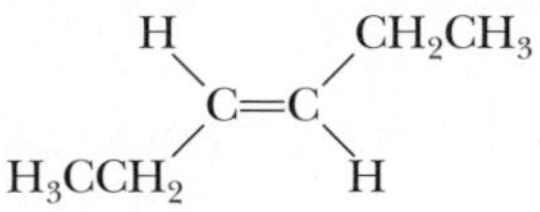

Names (in order, top to bottom): 1-hexene, *cis*-2-hexene, *trans*-2-hexene, *cis*-3-hexene, *trans*-3-hexene. None of these isomers is chiral.

10.4 (a)   (b)

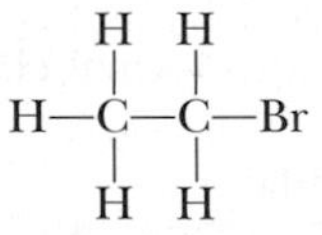

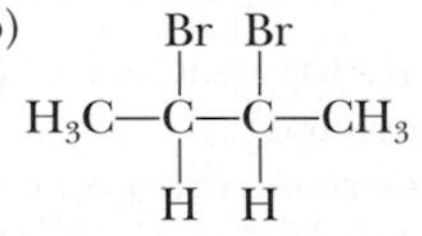

bromoethane   2,3-dibromobutane

10.5 1,4-diaminobenzene

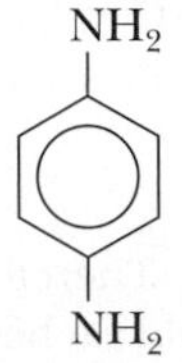

10.6 CH₃CH₂CH₂CH₂OH   1-butanol

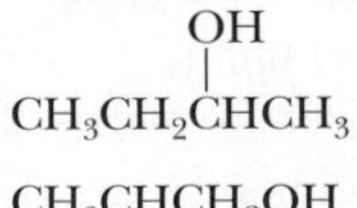

CH₃CH₂CHCH₃   2-butanol
  OH

CH₃CHCH₂OH   2-methyl-1-propanol 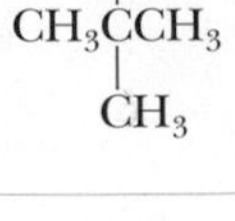
   CH₃

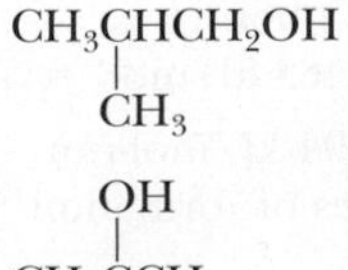

CH₃CCH₃   2-methyl-2-propanol
  CH₃ (OH)

10.7 (a)

$$CH_3CH_2CH_2\overset{\overset{\displaystyle O}{\|}}{C}CH_3 \quad \text{2-pentanone}$$

$$CH_3CH_2\overset{\overset{\displaystyle O}{\|}}{C}CH_2CH_3 \quad \text{3-pentanone}$$

$$CH_3CH_2CH_2CH_2\overset{\overset{\displaystyle O}{\|}}{C}H \quad \text{pentanal}$$

$$CH_3\underset{\underset{\displaystyle CH_3}{|}}{C}HCH_2\overset{\overset{\displaystyle O}{\|}}{C}H \quad \text{3-methylbutanal}$$

(b)

$$CH_3\underset{\underset{\displaystyle OH}{|}}{C}HCH_2CH_2CH_3, \quad \text{2-pentanol}$$

10.8 (a)

1-butanol gives butanal $\quad CH_3CH_2CH_2\overset{\overset{\displaystyle O}{\|}}{C}H$

(b)

2-butanol gives butanone $\quad CH_3CH_2\overset{\overset{\displaystyle O}{\|}}{C}CH_3$

(c) 2-methyl-1-propanol gives 2-methylpropanal

$$CH_3\underset{\underset{\displaystyle CH_3}{|}}{\overset{\overset{\displaystyle H}{|}}{C}}\overset{\overset{\displaystyle O}{\|}}{C}H$$

The oxidation products from these three reactions are structural isomers.

10.9 (a)

$$CH_3CH_2\overset{\overset{\displaystyle O}{\|}}{C}OCH_3 \quad \text{methyl propanoate}$$

(b)

$$CH_3CH_2CH_2\overset{\overset{\displaystyle O}{\|}}{C}OCH_2CH_2CH_2CH_3$$
$$\text{butyl butanoate}$$

(c)

$$CH_3CH_2CH_2CH_2CH_2\overset{\overset{\displaystyle O}{\|}}{C}OCH_2CH_3$$
$$\text{ethyl hexanoate}$$

10.10 (a) Propyl acetate is formed from acetic acid and propanol:

$$CH_3\overset{\overset{\displaystyle O}{\|}}{C}OH + CH_3CH_2CH_2OH$$

(b) 3-Methylpentyl benzoate is formed from benzoic acid and 3-methylpentanol:

(c) Ethyl salicylate is formed from salicylic acid and ethanol:

10.11 (a) $CH_3CH_2CH_2OH$: 1-propanol, has an alcohol (—OH) group

CH_3CO_2H: ethanoic acid (acetic acid), has a carboxylic acid (—CO_2H) group

$CH_3CH_2NH_2$: ethylamine, has an amino (—NH_2) group

(b) 1-propyl ethanoate (propyl acetate)

(c) Oxidation of this primary alcohol first gives propanal, CH_3CH_2CHO. Further oxidation gives propanoic acid, $CH_3CH_2CO_2H$.

(d) N-ethylacetamide, $CH_3CONHCH_2CH_3$

(e) The amine is protonated by hydrochloric acid, forming ethylammonium chloride, $[CH_3CH_2NH_3]Cl$.

10.12 Kevlar is a polyamide polymer, prepared by the reaction of terephthalic acid and 1,4-diaminobenzene.

$$n\,H_2NC_6H_4NH_2 + n\,HO_2CC_6H_4CO_2H \longrightarrow$$
$$\text{-(-HNC}_6\text{H}_4\text{NHCOC}_6\text{H}_4\text{CO-)}_n\text{- } + 2n\,H_2O$$

Chapter 11

11.1 0.83 bar (0.82 atm) > 75 kPa (0.74 atm) > 0.63 atm > 250 mm Hg (0.33 atm)

11.2 $P_1 = 55$ mm Hg and $V_1 = 125$ mL; $P_2 = 78$ mm Hg and $V_2 = ?$

$V_2 = V_1(P_1/P_2) = (125 \text{ mL})(55 \text{ mm Hg}/78 \text{ mm Hg})$
$= 88$ mL

11.3 $V_1 = 45$ L and $T_1 = 298$ K; $V_2 = ?$ and $T_2 = 263$ K

$V_2 = V_1(T_2/T_1) = (45 \text{ L})(263 \text{ K}/298 \text{ K}) = 40.$ L

11.4 $V_2 = V_1(P_1/P_2)(T_2/T_1)$

$= (22 \text{ L})(150 \text{ atm}/0.993 \text{ atm})(295 \text{ K}/304 \text{ K})$

$= 3200$ L

At 5.0 L per balloon, there is sufficient He to fill 640 balloons.

11.5 44.8 L of O_2 is required; 44.8 L of $H_2O(g)$ and 22.4 L $CO_2(g)$ are produced.

11.6 $PV = nRT$

$(750/760 \text{ atm})(V) =$
$(1300 \text{ mol})(0.08206 \text{ L} \cdot \text{atm/mol} \cdot \text{K})(296 \text{ K})$

$V = 3.2 \times 10^4$ L

11.7 $d = PM/RT$; $M = dRT/P$

$M = (5.02 \text{ g/L})(0.082057 \text{ L} \cdot \text{atm/mol} \cdot \text{K})$
$(288.2 \text{ K})/(745/760 \text{ atm}) = 121 \text{ g/mol}$

11.8 $PV = (m/M)RT$; $M = mRT/PV$

$M = (0.105 \text{ g})(0.082057 \text{ L} \cdot \text{atm/mol} \cdot \text{K})$
$(296.2 \text{ K})/[(561/760) \text{ atm } 0.125 \text{ L})] = 27.7 \text{ g/mol}$

11.9 $n(\text{H}_2) = PV/RT$

$= (542/760 \text{ atm})(355 \text{ L})/(0.08206 \text{ L} \cdot \text{atm/mol} \cdot \text{K})$
(298.2 K)

$n(\text{H}_2) = 10.3 \text{ mol}$

$n(\text{NH}_3) = (10.3 \text{ mol H}_2)(2 \text{ mol NH}_3/3 \text{ mol H}_2)$
$= 6.87 \text{ mol NH}_3$

$P (125 \text{ L}) = (6.87 \text{ mol})(0.082057 \text{ L} \cdot \text{atm/mol} \cdot \text{K})$
(298.2 K)

$P(\text{NH}_3) = 1.35 \text{ atm}$

11.10 $P_{\text{halothane}} (5.00 \text{ L})$
$= (0.0760 \text{ mol})(0.08206 \text{ L} \cdot \text{atm/mol} \cdot \text{K}) (298.2 \text{ K})$

$P_{\text{halothane}} = 0.372 \text{ atm}$ (or 283 mm Hg)

$P_{\text{oxygen}} (5.00 \text{ L})$
$= (0.734 \text{ mol})(0.08206 \text{ L} \cdot \text{atm/mol} \cdot \text{K})(298.2 \text{ K})$

$P_{\text{oxygen}} = 3.59 \text{ atm}$ (or 2730 mm Hg)

$P_{\text{total}} = P_{\text{halothane}} + P_{\text{oxygen}}$
$= 283 \text{ mm Hg} + 2730 \text{ mm Hg} = 3010 \text{ mm Hg}$

11.11 For He: Use Equation 11.9, with $M = 4.00 \times 10^{-3}$ kg/mol, $T = 298$ K, and $R = 8.314$ J/mol $\cdot$ K to calculate the rms speed of 1360 m/s. A similar calculation for N_2, with $M = 28.01 \times 10^{-3}$ kg/mol, gives an rms speed of 515 m/s.

11.12 The molar mass of CH_4 is 16.0 g/mol.

$$\frac{\text{Rate for CH}_4}{\text{Rate for unknown}} = \frac{n \text{ molecules/1.50 min}}{n \text{ molecules/4.73 min}} = \sqrt{\frac{M_{\text{unknown}}}{16.0}}$$

$M_{\text{unknown}} = 159 \text{ g/mol}$

11.13 $P(1.00 \text{ L})$
$= (10.0 \text{ mol})(0.082057 \text{ L} \cdot \text{atm/mol} \cdot \text{K}) (298 \text{ K})$

$P = 245 \text{ atm}$ (calculated by $PV = nRT$)

$P = 320 \text{ atm}$ (calculated by van der Waals equation)

Chapter 12

12.1 Because F^- is the smaller ion, water molecules can approach most closely and interact more strongly. Thus, F^- should have the more negative enthalpy of hydration.

12.2
$$\text{H}_3\text{C}-\overset{\overset{\displaystyle \text{H}}{\diagup}}{\text{O}} \ldots$$
$$\text{H}-\text{O}$$
$$\text{CH}_3$$

Hydrogen bonding in methanol entails the attraction of the hydrogen atom bearing a partial positive charge (δ^+) on one molecule to the oxygen atom bearing a partial negative charge (δ^-) on a second molecule. The strong attractive force of hydrogen bonding will cause the boiling point and the enthalpy of vaporization of methanol to be quite high.

12.3 Water is a polar solvent, while hexane and CCl_4 are nonpolar. London dispersion forces are the primary forces of attraction between all pairs of dissimilar solvents. For mixtures of water with the other solvents, dipole–induced dipole forces will also be important.

12.4 (a) O_2: induced dipole–induced dipole forces only.
(b) CH_3OH: strong hydrogen bonding (dipole–dipole forces) as well as induced dipole–induced dipole forces.
(c) Forces between water molecules: strong hydrogen bonding and induced dipole–induced dipole forces. Between N_2 and H_2O: dipole–induced dipole forces and induced dipole–induced dipole forces.

Relative strengths: a < forces between N_2 and H_2O in c < b < forces between water molecules in c.

12.5 $(1.00 \times 10^3 \text{ g})(1 \text{ mol}/32.04 \text{ g})(35.2 \text{ kJ/mol})$
$= 1.10 \times 10^3 \text{ kJ}$

12.6 (a) At 40 °C, the vapor pressure of ethanol is about 120 mm Hg.
(b) The equilibrium vapor pressure of ethanol at 60 °C is about 320 mm Hg. At 60 °C and 600 mm Hg, ethanol is a liquid. If vapor is present, it will condense to a liquid.

12.7 $PV = nRT$

$P = 0.50 \text{ g } (1 \text{ mol}/18.02 \text{ g})(0.0821 \text{ L} \cdot \text{atm/mol} \cdot \text{K})$
$(333 \text{ K})/5.0 \text{ L}$

$P = 0.15 \text{ atm.}$

Convert to mm Hg: $P = (0.15 \text{ atm})(760 \text{ mm Hg}/1 \text{ atm}) = 120 \text{ mm Hg}$. The vapor pressure of water at 60 °C is 149.4 mm Hg (Appendix G). The calculated pressure is lower than this, so all the water (0.50 g) evaporates. If 2.0 g of water is used, the calculated pressure, 460 mm Hg, exceeds the vapor pressure. In this case, only part of the water will evaporate.

12.8 Use the Clausius–Clapeyron equation, with $P_1 = 57.0$ mm Hg, $T_1 = 250.4$ K, $P_2 = 534$ mm Hg, and $T_2 = 298.2$ K.

$\ln [P_2/P_1] = \Delta_{\text{vap}}H/R \ [1/T_1 - 1/T_2]$
$= [\Delta_{\text{vap}}H/R][(T_2 - T_1)/T_1T_2]$

$\ln [534/57.0] = \Delta_{\text{vap}}H/(0.0083145 \text{ kJ/K} \cdot \text{mol})$
$[47.8/(250.4)(298.2)]$

$\Delta_{\text{vap}}H = 29.1 \text{ kJ/mol}$

12.9 Glycerol is predicted to have a higher viscosity than ethanol. It is a larger molecule than ethanol, and there are higher forces of attraction between molecules because each molecule has three OH groups that hydrogen-bond to other molecules.

Chapter 13

13.1 The strategy to solve this problem is given in Example 13.1.

Step 1. Mass of the unit cell

$= (197.0 \text{ g/mol})(1 \text{ mol}/6.022 \times 10^{23} \text{ atom/mol})(4 \text{ atoms/unit cell})$

$= 1.309 \times 10^{-21} \text{ g/unit cell}$

Step 2. Volume of unit cell

$= (1.309 \times 10^{-21} \text{ g/unit cell})(1 \text{ cm}^3/19.32 \text{ g})$

$= 6.773 \times 10^{-23} \text{ cm}^3/\text{unit cell}$

Step 3. Length of side of unit cell

$= [6.773 \times 10^{-23} \text{ cm}^3/\text{unit cell}]^{1/3} = 4.076 \times 10^{-8} \text{ cm}$

Step 4. Calculate the radius from the edge dimension.

Diagonal distance $= 4.076 \times 10^{-8} \text{ cm } (2^{1/2}) = 4 (r_{Au})$

$r_{Au} = 1.441 \times 10^{-8} \text{ cm } (= 144.1 \text{ pm})$

13.2 To verify a body centered cubic structure, calculate the mass contained in the unit cell. If the structure is bcc, then the mass will be the mass of 2 Fe atoms. (Other possibilities: fcc − mass of 4 Fe; primitive cubic − mass of 1 Fe atom). This calculation uses the four steps from the previous exercise in reverse order.

Step 1. Use radius of Fe to calculate cell dimensions. In a body-centered cube, atoms touch across the diagonal of the cube.

Diagonal distance = side dimension ($\sqrt{3}$) $= 4 r_{Fe}$

Side dimension of cube $= 4 (1.26 \times 10^{-8} \text{ cm})/(\sqrt{3}) = 2.910 \times 10^{-8} \text{ cm}$

Step 2. Calculate unit cell volume

Unit cell volume $= (2.910 \times 10^{-8} \text{ cm})^3 = 2.464 \times 10^{-23} \text{ cm}^3$

Step 3. Combine unit cell volume and density to find the mass of the unit cell.

Mass of unit cell $= 2.464 \times 10^{-23} \text{ cm}^3 (7.8740 \text{ g/cm}^3) = 1.940 \times 10^{-22} \text{ g}$

Step 4. Calculate the mass of 2 Fe atoms, and compare this to the answer from step 3.

Mass of 2 Fe atoms

$= 55.85 \text{ g/mol} (1 \text{ mol}/6.022 \times 10^{23} \text{ atoms})(2 \text{ atoms})$

$= 1.85 \times 10^{-22} \text{ g}).$

This is a fairly good match, and clearly much better than the two other possibilities, primitive and fcc.

13.3 M_2X; In a face-centered cubic unit cell, there are four anions and eight tetrahedral holes in which to place metal ions. All of the tetrahedral holes are inside the unit cell, so the ratio of atoms in the unit cell is 2 : 1.

13.4 We need to calculate the mass and volume of the unit cell from the information given. The density of KCl will then be mass/volume. Select units so the density is calculated as g/cm^3

Step 1. Mass: the unit cell contains 4 K^+ ions and 4 Cl^- ions

Unit cell mass $= (39.10 \text{ g/mol})(1 \text{ mol}/6.022 \times 10^{23} \text{ K}^+ \text{ ions})(4 \text{ K}^+ \text{ ions}) + (35.45 \text{ g/mol})(1 \text{ mol}/6.022 \times 10^{23} \text{ Cl}^- \text{ ions})(4 \text{ Cl}^- \text{ ions})$

$= 2.355 \times 10^{-22} \text{ g} + 2.597 \times 10^{-22} \text{ g} = 4.952 \times 10^{-22} \text{ g}$

Step 2. Volume: assuming K^+ and Cl^- ions touch along one edge of the cube, the side dimension $= 2 r_{K^+} + 2 r_{Cl^-}$. The volume of the cube is the cube of this value. (Convert the ionic radius from pm to cm.)

$V = [2(1.33 \times 10^{-8} \text{ cm}) + 2(1.81 \times 10^{-8} \text{ cm})]^3 = 2.477 \times 10^{-22} \text{ cm}^3$

Step 3: density = mass/volume $= 4.952 \times 10^{-22} \text{ g}/2.477 \times 10^{-22} \text{ cm}^3) = 2.00 \text{ g/cm}^3$

13.5 Use the Born–Haber cycle equation shown on pages 600–602. The unknown in this problem is the enthalpy of formation of NaI(s).

$\Delta_f H° \text{ [NaI(s)]} = \Delta H_{\text{Step 1a}} + \Delta H_{\text{Step 1b}} + \Delta H_{\text{Step 2a}} + \Delta H_{\text{Step 2b}} + \Delta_{\text{lattice}} H$

Step 1a. Enthalpy of formation of I(g) $= +106.8 \text{ kJ/mol}$ (Appendix L)

Step 1b. ΔH for $I(g) + e^- \rightarrow I^-(g) = -295 \text{ kJ/mol}$ (Appendix F)

Step 2a. Enthalpy of formation of Na(g) $= +107.3 \text{ kJ/mol}$ (Appendix L)

Step 2b. ΔH for $Na(g) \rightarrow Na^+(g) + e^- = +496 \text{ kJ/mol}$ (Appendix F)

Step 3 $= \Delta_{\text{lattice}} H = -702 \text{ kJ/mol}$ (Table 13.2)

$\Delta_f H° \text{ [NaI(s)]} = -287 \text{ kJ/mol}$

Chapter 14

14.1 (a) 10.0 g sucrose = 0.0292 mol; 250 g H_2O = 13.9 mol

$X_{\text{sucrose}} = (0.0292 \text{ mol})/(0.0292 \text{ mol} + 13.9 \text{ mol}) = 0.00210$

$c_{\text{sucrose}} = (0.0292 \text{ mol sucrose})/(0.250 \text{ kg solvent}) = 0.117 \text{ m}$

Weight % sucrose $= (10.0 \text{ g sucrose}/260 \text{ g soln})(100\%) = 3.85\%$

o | Answers to Selected Study Questions

CHAPTER 1

1.1 (a) C, carbon
(b) K, potassium
(c) Cl, chlorine
(d) P, phosphorus
(e) Mg, magnesium
(f) Ni, nickel

1.3 (a) Ba, barium
(b) Ti, titanium
(c) Cr, chromium
(d) Pb, lead
(e) As, arsenic
(f) Zn, zinc

1.5 (a) Na (element) and NaCl (compound)
(b) Sugar (compound) and carbon (element)
(c) Gold (element) and gold chloride (compound)

1.7 (a) Physical property
(b) Chemical property
(c) Chemical property
(d) Physical property
(e) Physical property
(f) Physical property

1.9 (a) Physical (colorless liquid) and chemical (burns in air)
(b) Physical (shiny metal, orange liquid) and chemical (reacts with bromine)

1.11 (a) Qualitative: blue-green color, solid physical state
Quantitative: density = 2.65 g/cm³ and mass = 2.5 g
(b) Density, physical state, and color are intensive properties, whereas mass is an extensive property.
(c) Volume = 0.94 cm³

1.13 Observations c, e, and f are chemical properties

1.15 calcium, Ca; fluorine, F

The crystals are cubic in shape because the atoms are arranged in cubic structures.

1.17 The macroscopic view is the photograph of NaCl, and the particulate view is the drawing of the ions in a cubic arrangement. The structure of the compound at the particulate level determines the properties that are observed at the macroscopic level.

1.19 The density of the plastic is less than that of CCl₄, so the plastic will float on the liquid CCl₄. Aluminum is more dense than CCl₄, so aluminum will sink when placed in CCl₄.

1.21 The three liquids will form three separate layers with hexane on the top, water in the middle, and perfluorohexane on the bottom. The HDPE will float at the interface of the hexane and water layers. The PVC will float at the interface of the water and perfluorohexane layers. The Teflon will sink to the bottom of the cylinder.

1.23 HDPE will float in ethylene glycol, water, acetic acid, and glycerol.

1.25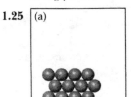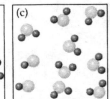

1.27 The sample's density and melting point could be compared to those of pure silver.

1.29 If too much sugar is excreted, the density of the urine would be higher than normal. If too much water is excreted, the density would be lower than normal.

1.31 (a) Solid potassium metal reacts with liquid water to produce gaseous hydrogen and a homogeneous mixture (solution) of potassium hydroxide in liquid water.

(b) The reaction is a chemical change.

(c) The reactants are potassium and water. The products are hydrogen gas and a water (aqueous) solution of potassium hydroxide. Heat and light are also evolved.

(d) Among the qualitative observations are (i) the reaction is violent, and (ii) heat and light (a purple flame) are produced.

1.33 (a) The water could be evaporated by heating the solution, leaving the salt behind.

(b) Use a magnet to attract the iron away from lead, which is not magnetic.

(c) Mixing the solids with water will dissolve only the sugar. Filtration would separate the solid sulfur from the sugar solution. Finally, the sugar could be separated from the water by evaporating the water.

1.35 Separate the iron from a weighed sample of cereal by passing a magnet through a mixture of the cereal and water after the flakes have become a gooey paste. Remove the iron flakes from the magnet and weigh them to determine the mass of iron in this mass of cereal.

1.37 Physical change

LET'S REVIEW: THE TOOLS OF QUANTITATIVE CHEMISTRY

1 298 K

3 (a) 289 K
(b) 97 °C
(c) 310 K (3.1×10^2 K)

5 42,195 m; 26.219 miles

7 5.3 cm^2; 5.3×10^{-4} m^2

9 250. cm^3; 0.250 L, 2.50×10^{-4} m^3; 0.250 dm^3

11 2.52×10^3 g

13 555 g

15 Choice (c), zinc

17 (a) Method A with all data included:
average = 2.4 g/cm^3

Method B with all data included:
average = 3.480 g/cm^3

For B, the 5.811 g/cm^3 data point can be excluded because it is more than twice as large as all other points for case Method B. Using only the first three points, average = 2.703 g/cm^3

(b) Method A: error = 0.3 g/cm^3 or about 10%

Method B: error = 0.001 g/cm^3 or about 0.04%

(c) Method A: standard deviation = 0.2 g/cm^3

Method B (including all data points):
st. dev. = 1.554 g/cm^3

Method B (excluding the 5.811 g/cm^3 data point):
st. dev. = 0.002 g/cm^3

(d) Method B's average value is both more precise and more accurate so long as the 5.811 g/cm^3 data point is excluded.

19 (a) 5.4×10^{-2} g, two significant figures
(b) 5.462×10^3 g, four significant figures
(c) 7.92×10^{-4} g, three significant figures
(d) 1.6×10^3 mL, two significant figures

21 (a) 9.44×10^{-3}
(b) 5694
(c) 11.9
(d) 0.122

23

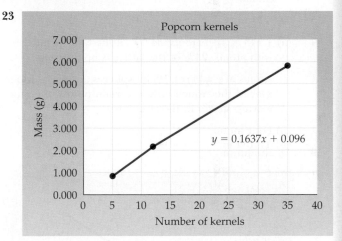

Slope: 0.1637 g/kernel

The slope represents the average mass of a popcorn kernel.

Mass of 20 popcorn kernels = 3.370 g

There are 127 kernels in a sample with a mass of 20.88 g.

25 (a) $y = -4.00x + 20.00$
(b) $y = -4.00$

27 $C = 0.0823$

29 $T = 295$

31 0.197 nm; 197 pm

33 (a) 7.5×10^{-6} m; (b) 7.5×10^3 nm; (c) 7.5×10^6 pm

35 50. mg procaine hydrochloride

37 The volume of the marbles is 99 mL − 61 mL = 38 mL. This yields a density of 2.5 g/cm^3.

39 (a) 0.178 nm^3; $1.78 \times 10^{-22} \text{ cm}^3$
(b) $3.86 \times 10^{-22} \text{ g}$
(c) $9.68 \times 10^{-23} \text{ g}$

41 Your normal body temperature (about 98.6 °F) is 37 °C. As this is higher than gallium's melting point, the metal will melt in your hand.

43 (a) 15%
(b) 3.63×10^3 kernels

45 8.0×10^4 kg of sodium fluoride per year

47 245 g sulfuric acid

49 (a) 272 mL ice
(b) The ice cannot be contained in the can.

51 7.99 g/cm^3

53 (a) 8.7 g/cm^3
(b) The metal is probably cadmium, but the calculated density is close to that of cobalt, nickel, and copper. Further testing should be done on the metal.

55 0.0927 cm

57 (a) 1.143×10^{21} atoms; 54.9% of the lattic is filled with atoms; 24% of the lattice is open space.

Atoms are spheres. When spheres are packed together, they touch only at certain points, therefore leaving spaces in the structure.

(b) Four atoms

59 Al, aluminum

61

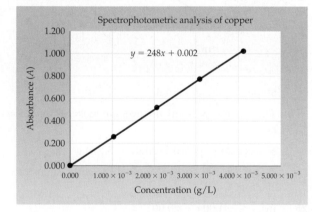

When absorbance = 0.635, concentration = $2.55 \times 10^{-3} \text{ g/L} = 2.55 \times 10^{-3} \text{ mg/mL}$

63

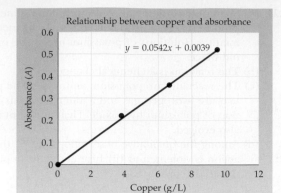

Slope = 0.054; y-intercept = 0.004; the absorbance for 5.00 g/L of copper is 0.27

CHAPTER 2

2.1 Atoms contain the following fundamental particles: protons (+1 charge), neutrons (zero charge), and electrons (−1 charge). Protons and neutrons are in the nucleus of an atom. Electrons are the least massive of the three particles.

2.3 (a) $^{27}_{12}\text{Mg}$
(b) $^{48}_{22}\text{Ti}$
(c) $^{62}_{30}\text{Zn}$

2.5

Element	Electrons	Protons	Neutrons
^{24}Mg	12	12	12
^{119}Sn	50	50	69
^{232}Th	90	90	142
^{13}C	6	6	7
^{63}Cu	29	29	34
^{205}Bi	83	83	122

2.7 $^{57}_{27}\text{Co}$, $^{58}_{27}\text{Co}$, $^{60}_{27}\text{Co}$

2.9 ^{205}Tl is more abundant than ^{203}Tl. The atomic mass of thallium is closer to 205 than to 203.

2.11 $(0.0750)(6.015121) + (0.9250)(7.016003) = 6.94$

2.13 (c), About 50%. Actual percent $^{107}\text{Ag} = 51.839\%$

2.15 ^{69}Ga, 60.12%; ^{71}Ga, 39.88%

2.17

	Symbol	Atomic No.	Atomic Mass	Group	Period	
Titanium	Ti	22	47.867	4B(IUPAC 4)	4	Metal
Thallium	Tl	81	204.3833	3A(IUPAC 13)	6	Metal

2.19 Eight elements: periods 2 and 3. 18 elements: periods 4 and 5. 32 elements: period 6.

2.21 (a) Nonmetals: C, Cl
(b) Main group elements: C, Ca, Cl, Cs
(c) Lanthanides: Ce
(d) Transition elements: Cr, Co, Cd, Ce, Cm, Cu, Cf
(e) Actinides: Cm, Cf
(f) Gases: Cl

2.23 Metals: Na, Ni, Np
Metalloids: None in this list
Nonmetals: N, Ne

2.25 Molecular Formula: H_2SO_4.
Structural Formula:

$$
\begin{array}{c}
\text{O} \\
\| \\
\text{O}-\text{S}-\text{O}-\text{H} \\
| \\
\text{O}-\text{H}
\end{array}
$$

The structure is not flat. The O atoms are arranged around the sulfur at the corners of a tetrahedron. The hydrogen atoms are connected to two of the oxygen atoms.

2.27 (a) Mg^{2+}
(b) Zn^{2+}
(c) Ni^{2+}
(d) Ga^{3+}

2.29 (a) Ba^{2+}
(b) Ti^{4+}
(c) PO_4^{3-}
(d) HCO_3^-
(e) S^{2-}
(f) ClO_4^-
(g) Co^{2+}
(h) SO_4^{2-}

2.31 K loses one electron per atom to form a K^+ ion. It has the same number of electrons as an Ar atom.

2.33 Ba^{2+} and Br^- ions. The compound's formula is $BaBr_2$.

2.35 (a) Two K^+ ions and one S^{2-} ion
(b) One Co^{2+} ion and one SO_4^{2-} ion
(c) One K^+ ion and one MnO_4^- ion
(d) Three NH_4^+ ions and one PO_4^{3-} ion
(e) One Ca^{2+} ion and two ClO^- ions
(f) One Na^+ ion and one $CH_3CO_2^-$ ion

2.37 Co^{2+} gives CoO and Co^{3+} gives Co_2O_3

2.39 (a) $AlCl_2$ should be $AlCl_3$ (based on an Al^{3+} ion and three Cl^- ions).
(b) KF_2 should be KF (based on a K^+ ion and an F^- ion).
(c) Ga_2O_3 is correct.
(d) MgS is correct.

2.41 (a) potassium sulfide
(b) cobalt(II) sulfate
(c) ammonium phosphate
(d) calcium hypochlorite

2.43 (a) $(NH_4)_2CO_3$
(b) CaI_2
(c) $CuBr_2$
(d) $AlPO_4$
(e) $AgCH_3CO_2$

2.45 Compounds with Na^+: Na_2CO_3 (sodium carbonate) and NaI (sodium iodide). Compounds with Ba^{2+}: $BaCO_3$ (barium carbonate) and BaI_2 (barium iodide).

2.47 The force of attraction is stronger in NaF than in NaI because the distance between ion centers is smaller in NaF (235 pm) than in NaI (322 pm).

2.49 (a) nitrogen trifluoride
(b) hydrogen iodide
(c) boron triiodide
(d) phosphorus pentafluoride

2.51 (a) SCl_2
(b) N_2O_5
(c) $SiCl_4$
(d) B_2O_3

2.53 (a) 67 g Al
(b) 0.0698 g Fe
(c) 0.60 g Ca
(d) 1.32×10^4 g Ne

2.55 (a) 1.9998 mol Cu
(b) 0.0017 mol Li
(c) 2.1×10^{-5} mol Am
(d) 0.250 mol Al

2.57 Of these elements, He has the smallest molar mass, and Fe has the largest molar mass. Therefore, 1.0 g of He has the largest number of atoms in these samples, and 1.0 g of Fe has the smallest number of atoms.

2.59 (a) 159.7 g/mol
(b) 117.2 g/mol
(c) 176.1 g/mol

2.61 (a) 290.8 g/mol
(b) 249.7 g/mol

2.63 (a) 1.53 g
(b) 4.60 g
(c) 4.60 g
(d) 1.48 g

2.65 Amount of SO_3 = 12.5 mol
Number of molecules = 7.52×10^{24} molecules
Number of S atoms = 7.52×10^{24} atoms
Number of O atoms = 2.26×10^{25} atoms

2.67 (a) 86.60% Pb and 13.40% S
(b) 81.71% C and 18.29% H
(c) 79.96% C, 9.394% H, and 10.65% O

2.69 66.46% copper in CuS. 15.0 g of CuS is needed to obtain 10.0 g of Cu.

2.71 $C_4H_6O_4$

2.73 (a) CH, 26.0 g/mol; C_2H_2
(b) CHO, 116.1 g/mol; $C_4H_4O_4$
(c) CH_2, 112.2 g/mol, C_8H_{16}

2.75 Empirical formula, CH; molecular formula, C_2H_2

2.77 Empirical formula, C_3H_4; molecular formula, C_9H_{12}

2.79 Empirical and molecular formulas are both $C_8H_8O_3$

2.81 XeF_2

2.83 ZnI_2

2.85

Symbol	^{58}Ni	^{33}S	^{20}Ne	^{55}Mn
Protons	28	16	10	25
Neutrons	30	17	10	30
Electrons	28	16	10	25
Name	nickel	sulfur	neon	manganese

2.87

S	N
B	I

2.89 (a) 1.0552×10^{-22} g for 1 Cu atom
(b) 6.286×10^{-22} dollars for 1 Cu atom

2.91 (a) strontium
(b) zirconium
(c) carbon
(d) arsenic
(e) iodine
(f) magnesium
(g) krypton
(h) sulfur
(i) germanium or arsenic

2.93 (a) 0.25 mol U
(b) 0.50 mol Na
(c) 10 atoms of Fe

2.95 40.2 g H_2 (b) < 103 g C   (c) < 182 g Al
(f) < 210 g Si   (d) < 212 g Na   (e) < 351 g Fe
(a) < 650 g $Cl_2(g)$

2.97 (a) Atomic mass of O = 15.873 u; Avogadro's
number = 5.9802×10^{23} particles per mole
(b) Atomic mass of H = 1.00798 u; Avogadro's number = 6.0279×10^{23} particles per mole

2.99 $(NH_4)_2CO_3$, $(NH_4)_2SO_4$, $NiCO_3$, $NiSO_4$

2.101 All of these compounds have one atom of some element plus three Cl atoms. The highest mass percent of chlorine will occur in the compound having the lightest central element. Here, that element is B, so BCl_3 should have the highest mass percent of Cl (90.77%).

2.103 The molar mass of adenine ($C_5H_5N_5$) is 135.13 g/mol. 3.0×10^{23} molecules represents 67 g. Thus, 3.0×10^{23} molecules of adenine has a larger mass than 40.0 g of the compound.

2.105 1.7×10^{21} molecules of water

2.107 245.75 g/mol. Mass percent: 25.86% Cu, 22.80% N, 5.742% H, 13.05% S, and 32.55% O. In 10.5 g of compound there are 2.72 g Cu and 0.770 g H_2O.

2.109 Empirical formula of malic acid: $C_4H_6O_5$

2.111 $Fe_2(CO)_9$

2.113 (a) $C_7H_5NO_3S$

(b) 6.82×10^{-4} mol saccarin
(c) 21.9 mg S

2.115 (a) NaClO, ionic
(b) BI_3
(c) $Al(ClO_4)_3$, ionic
(d) $Ca(CH_3CO_2)_2$, ionic
(e) $KMnO_4$, ionic
(f) $(NH_4)_2SO_3$, ionic
(g) KH_2PO_4, ionic
(h) S_2Cl_2
(i) ClF_3
(j) PF_3

2.117 (a) Empirical formula = molecular formula = CF_2O_2
(b) Empirical formula = C_5H_4; molecular formula = $C_{10}H_8$

2.119 Empirical formula and molecular formula = $C_5H_{14}N_2$

2.121 $C_9H_7MnO_3$

2.123 68.42% Cr; 1.2×10^3 kg Cr_2O_3

2.125 Empirical formula = ICl_3; molecular formula = I_2Cl_6

2.127 7.35 kg of iron

2.129 (d) Na_2MoO_4

2.131 5.52×10^{-4} mol $C_{21}H_{15}Bi_3O_{12}$; 0.346 g Bi

2.133 The molar mass of the compound is 154 g/mol. The unknown element is carbon.

2.135 $n = 19$.

2.137 (a) 2.3×10^{14} g/cm^3
(b) 3.34×10^{-3} g/cm^3
(c) The nucleus is much more dense than the space occupied by the electrons.

2.139 (a) 0.0130 mol Ni
(b) NiF_2
(c) nickel(II) fluoride

2.141 Formula is $MgSO_4 \cdot 7\,H_2O$

2.143 Volume = 3.0 cm^3; length of side = 1.4 cm

2.145 1.0028×10^{23} atoms C. If the accuracy is ± 0.0001 g, the maximum mass could be 2.0001 g, which also represents 1.0028×10^{23} atoms C.

2.147 Choice c. The calculated mole ratio is 0.78 mol H_2O per mol $CaCl_2$. The student should heat the crucible again and then reweigh it. More water might be driven off.

2.149 Required data: density of iron, molar mass of iron, Avogadro's number.

$$1.00\ cm^3 \left(\frac{7.87\ g}{1\ cm^3} \right) \left(\frac{1\ mol}{55.85\ g} \right) \left(\frac{6.02 \times 10^{23}\ atoms}{1\ mol} \right) =$$
$$8.49 \times 10^{22}\ atoms\ Fe$$

2.151 Barium would be more reactive than calcium, so a more vigorous evolution of hydrogen should occur. Reactivity increases on descending the periodic table, at least for Groups 1A and 2A.

2.153 When words are written with the pink, hydrated compound, the words are not visible. However, when heated, the hydrated salt loses water to form anhydrous $CoCl_2$, which is deep blue. The words are then visible.

CHAPTER 3

3.1 $C_5H_{12}(\ell) + 8\,O_2(g) \rightarrow 5\,CO_2(g) + 6\,H_2O(g)$

3.3 (a) $4\,Cr(s) + 3\,O_2(g) \rightarrow 2\,Cr_2O_3(s)$
(b) $Cu_2S(s) + O_2(g) \rightarrow 2\,Cu(s) + SO_2(g)$
(c) $C_6H_5CH_3(\ell) + 9\,O_2(g) \rightarrow 4\,H_2O(\ell) + 7\,CO_2(g)$

3.5 (a) $Fe_2O_3(s) + 3\,Mg(s) \rightarrow 3\,MgO(s) + 2\,Fe(s)$
Reactants = iron(III) oxide, magnesium
Products = magnesium oxide, iron
(b) $AlCl_3(s) + 3\,NaOH(aq) \rightarrow$
$$Al(OH)_3(s) + 3\,NaCl(aq)$$
Reactants = aluminum chloride, sodium hydroxide
Products = aluminum hydroxide, sodium chloride
(c) $2\,NaNO_3(s) + H_2SO_4(\ell) \rightarrow$
$$Na_2SO_4(s) + 2\,HNO_3(\ell)$$
Reactants = sodium nitrate, sulfuric acid
Products = sodium sulfate, nitric acid
(d) $NiCO_3(s) + 2\,HNO_3(aq) \rightarrow$
$$Ni(NO_3)_2(aq) + CO_2(g) + H_2O(\ell)$$
Reactants = nickel(II) carbonate, nitric acid
Products = nickel(II) nitrate, carbon dioxide, water

3.7 The reaction involving HCl is more product-favored at equilibrium.

3.9 Electrolytes are compounds whose aqueous solutions conduct electricity. Given an aqueous solution containing a strong electrolyte and another aqueous solution containing a weak electrolyte at the same concentration, the solution containing the strong electrolyte (such as NaCl) will conduct electricity much better than will be the one containing the weak electrolyte (such as acetic acid).

3.11 (a) $CuCl_2$
(b) $AgNO_3$
(c) All are water-soluble

3.13 (a) K^+ and OH^- ions
(b) K^+ and SO_4^{2-} ions
(c) Li^+ and NO_3^- ions
(d) NH_4^+ and SO_4^{2-} ions

3.15 (a) Soluble, Na^+ and CO_3^{2-} ions
(b) Soluble, Cu^{2+} and SO_4^{2-} ions
(c) Insoluble
(d) Soluble, Ba^{2+} and Br^- ions

3.17 $CdCl_2(aq) + 2\,NaOH(aq) \rightarrow$
$$Cd(OH)_2(s) + 2\,NaCl(aq)$$
$Cd^{2+}(aq) + 2\,OH^-(aq) \rightarrow Cd(OH)_2(s)$

3.19 (a) $NiCl_2(aq) + (NH_4)_2S(aq) \rightarrow NiS(s) + 2\,NH_4Cl(aq)$
$Ni^{2+}(aq) + S^{2-}(aq) \rightarrow NiS(s)$
(b) $3\,Mn(NO_3)_2(aq) + 2\,Na_3PO_4(aq) \rightarrow$
$$Mn_3(PO_4)_2(s) + 6\,NaNO_3(aq)$$
$3\,Mn^{2+}(aq) + 2\,PO_4^{3-}(aq) \rightarrow Mn_3(PO_4)_2(s)$

3.21 $HNO_3(aq) + H_2O(\ell) \rightarrow H_3O^+(aq) + NO_3^-(aq)$

3.23 $H_2C_2O_4(aq) + H_2O(\ell) \rightarrow H_3O^+(aq) + HC_2O_4^-(aq)$
$HC_2O_4^-(aq) + H_2O(\ell) \rightarrow H_3O^+(aq) + C_2O_4^{2-}(aq)$

3.25 $MgO(s) + H_2O(\ell) \rightarrow Mg(OH)_2(s)$

3.27 (a) Acetic acid reacts with magnesium hydroxide to give magnesium acetate and water.
$2\,CH_3CO_2H(aq) + Mg(OH)_2(s) \rightarrow$
$$Mg(CH_3CO_2)_2(aq) + 2\,H_2O(\ell)$$
Brønsted acid: acetic acid; Brønsted base: magnesium hydroxide
(b) Perchloric acid reacts with ammonia to give ammonium perchlorate
$HClO_4(aq) + NH_3(aq) \rightarrow NH_4ClO_4(aq)$
Brønsted acid: perchloric acid; Brønsted base: ammonia

3.29 $Ba(OH)_2(aq) + 2\,HNO_3(aq) \rightarrow$
$$Ba(NO_3)_2(aq) + 2\,H_2O(\ell)$$

3.31 Strong Brønsted acid examples: hydrochloric acid, nitric acid

Strong Brønsted base example: sodium hydroxide

3.33 (a) $(NH_4)_2CO_3(aq) + Cu(NO_3)_2(aq) \rightarrow$
$$CuCO_3(s) + 2\ NH_4NO_3(aq)$$

$$CO_3{}^{2-}(aq) + Cu^{2+}(aq) \rightarrow CuCO_3(s)$$

(b) $Pb(OH)_2(s) + 2\ HCl(aq) \rightarrow PbCl_2(s) + 2\ H_2O(\ell)$

$Pb(OH)_2(s) + 2\ H_3O^+(aq) + 2\ Cl^-(aq) \rightarrow$
$$PbCl_2(s) + 4\ H_2O(\ell)$$

(c) $BaCO_3(s) + 2\ HCl(aq) \rightarrow$
$$BaCl_2(aq) + H_2O(\ell) + CO_2(g)$$

$BaCO_3(s) + 2\ H_3O^+(aq) \rightarrow$
$$Ba^{2+}(aq) + 3\ H_2O(\ell) + CO_2(g)$$

(d) $2\ CH_3CO_2H(aq) + Ni(OH)_2(s) \rightarrow$
$$Ni(CH_3CO_2)_2(aq) + 2\ H_2O(\ell)$$

$2\ CH_3CO_2H(aq) + Ni(OH)_2(s) \rightarrow$
$$Ni^{2+}(aq) + 2\ CH_3CO_2{}^-(aq) + 2\ H_2O(\ell)$$

3.35 (a) $AgNO_3(aq) + KI(aq) \rightarrow AgI(s) + KNO_3(aq)$

$$Ag^+(aq) + I^-(aq) \rightarrow AgI(s)$$

(b) $Ba(OH)_2(aq) + 2\ HNO_3(aq) \rightarrow$
$$Ba(NO_3)_2(aq) + 2\ H_2O(\ell)$$

$$OH^-(aq) + H_3O^+(aq) \rightarrow 2\ H_2O(\ell)$$

(c) $2\ Na_3PO_4(aq) + 3\ Ni(NO_3)_2(aq) \rightarrow$
$$Ni_3(PO_4)_2(s) + 6\ NaNO_3(aq)$$

$$2\ PO_4{}^{3-}(aq) + 3\ Ni^{2+}(aq) \rightarrow Ni_3(PO_4)_2(s)$$

3.37 $FeCO_3(s) + 2\ HNO_3(aq) \rightarrow$
$$Fe(NO_3)_2(aq) + CO_2(g) + H_2O(\ell)$$

Iron(II) carbonate reacts with nitric acid to give iron(II) nitrate, carbon dioxide, and water.

3.39 $(NH_4)_2S(aq) + 2\ HBr(aq) \rightarrow 2\ NH_4Br(aq) + H_2S(g)$

Ammonium sulfide reacts with hydrobromic acid to give ammonium bromide and hydrogen sulfide.

3.41 (a) Br = +5 and O = −2
(b) C = +3 each and O = −2
(c) F = −1
(d) Ca = +2 and H = −1
(e) H = +1, Si = +4, and O = −2
(f) H = +1, S = +6, and O = −2

3.43 (a) Oxidation–reduction
Zn is oxidized from 0 to +2, and N in $NO_3{}^-$ is reduced from +5 to +4 in NO_2.
(b) Acid–base reaction
(c) Oxidation–reduction

Calcium is oxidized from 0 to +2 in $Ca(OH)_2$, and H is reduced from +1 in H_2O to 0 in H_2.

3.45 (a) O_2 is the oxidizing agent (as it always is) and so C_2H_4 is the reducing agent. In this process, C_2H_4 is oxidized, and O_2 is reduced.

(b) Si is oxidized from 0 in Si to +4 in $SiCl_4$. Cl_2 is reduced from 0 in Cl_2 to −1 in Cl^-. Si is the reducing agent, and Cl_2 is the oxidizing agent.

3.47 (a) Acid–base

$Ba(OH)_2(aq) + 2\ HCl(aq) \rightarrow$
$$BaCl_2(aq) + 2\ H_2O(\ell)$$

(b) Gas-forming

$2\ HNO_3(aq) + CoCO_3(s) \rightarrow$
$$Co(NO_3)_2(aq) + H_2O(\ell) + CO_2(g)$$

(c) Precipitation

$2\ Na_3PO_4(aq) + 3\ Cu(NO_3)_2(aq) \rightarrow$
$$Cu_3(PO_4)_2(s) + 6\ NaNO_3(aq)$$

3.49 a) Precipitation

$$MnCl_2(aq) + Na_2S(aq) \rightarrow MnS(s) + 2\ NaCl(aq)$$

$$Mn^{2+}(aq) + S^{2-}(aq) \rightarrow MnS(s)$$

(b) Precipitation

$$K_2CO_3(aq) + ZnCl_2(aq) \rightarrow ZnCO_3(s) + 2\ KCl(aq)$$

$$CO_3{}^{2-}(aq) + Zn^{2+}(aq) \rightarrow ZnCO_3(s)$$

3.51 (a) $CuCl_2(aq) + H_2S(aq) \rightarrow CuS(s) + 2\ HCl(aq)$
precipitation

(b) $H_3PO_4(aq) + 3\ KOH(aq) \rightarrow$
$$3\ H_2O(\ell) + K_3PO_4(aq)$$

acid–base

(c) $Ca(s) + 2\ HBr(aq) \rightarrow H_2(g) + CaBr_2(aq)$

oxidation–reduction and gas-forming

(d) $MgCl_2(aq) + 2\ H_2O(\ell) \rightarrow$
$$Mg(OH)_2(s) + 2\ HCl(aq)$$

precipitation

3.53 (a) $CO_2(g) + 2\ NH_3(g) \rightarrow NH_2CONH_2(s) + H_2O(\ell)$
(b) $UO_2(s) + 4\ HF(aq) \rightarrow UF_4(s) + 2\ H_2O(\ell)$

$$UF_4(s) + F_2(g) \rightarrow UF_6(s)$$

(c) $TiO_2(s) + 2\ Cl_2(g) + 2\ C(s) \rightarrow$
$$TiCl_4(\ell) + 2\ CO(g)$$

$$TiCl_4(\ell) + 2\ Mg(s) \rightarrow Ti(s) + 2\ MgCl_2(s)$$

3.55 (a) NaBr, KBr, or other alkali metal bromides; Group 2A bromides; other metal bromides except AgBr, Hg_2Br_2, and $PbBr_2$
(b) $Al(OH)_3$ and transition metal hydroxides
(c) Alkaline earth carbonates ($CaCO_3$) or transition metal carbonates ($NiCO_3$)
(d) Metal nitrates are generally water-soluble [e.g., $NaNO_3$, $Ni(NO_3)_2$].
(e) CH_3CO_2H, other acids containing the $-CO_2H$ group

3.57 Water soluble: $Cu(NO_3)_2$, $CuCl_2$. Water-insoluble: $CuCO_3$, $Cu_3(PO_4)_2$

3.59 Spectator ion, NO_3^-. Acid–base reaction.

$$2 H_3O^+(aq) + Mg(OH)_2(s) \rightarrow 4 H_2O(\ell) + Mg^{2+}(aq)$$

3.61 (a) Cl_2 is reduced (to Cl^-) and Br^- is oxidized (to Br_2).

(b) Cl_2 is the oxidizing agent and Br^- is the reducing agent.

3.63 (a) $MgCO_3(s) + 2 H_3O^+(aq) \rightarrow$
$$CO_2(g) + Mg^{2+}(aq) + 3 H_2O(\ell)$$

Chloride ion (Cl^-) is the spectator ion.

(b) Gas-forming reaction

3.65 (a) H_2O, NH_3, NH_4^+, and OH^- (and a trace of H_3O^+)

weak Brønsted base

(b) H_2O, CH_3CO_2H, $CH_3CO_2^-$, and H_3O^+ (and a trace of OH^-)

weak Brønsted acid

(c) H_2O, Na^+, and OH^- (and a trace of H_3O^+)

strong Brønsted base

(d) H_2O, H_3O^+, and Br^- (and a trace of OH^-)

strong Brønsted acid

3.67 (a) $K_2CO_3(aq) + 2 HClO_4(aq) \rightarrow$
$$2 KClO_4(aq) + CO_2(g) + H_2O(\ell)$$
gas-forming

Potassium carbonate and perchloric acid react to form potassium perchlorate, carbon dioxide, and water

$$CO_3^{2-}(aq) + 2 H_3O^+(aq) \rightarrow CO_2(g) + 3 H_2O(\ell)$$

(b) $FeCl_2(aq) + (NH_4)_2S(aq) \rightarrow$
$$FeS(s) + 2 NH_4Cl(aq)$$
precipitation

Iron(II) chloride and ammonium sulfide react to form iron(II) sulfide and ammonium chloride

$$Fe^{2+}(aq) + S^{2-}(aq) \rightarrow FeS(s)$$

(c) $Fe(NO_3)_2(aq) + Na_2CO_3(aq) \rightarrow$
$$FeCO_3(s) + 2 NaNO_3(aq)$$
precipitation

Iron(II) nitrate and sodium carbonate react to form iron(II) carbonate and sodium nitrate

$$Fe^{2+}(aq) + CO_3^{2-}(aq) \rightarrow FeCO_3(s)$$

(d) $3 NaOH(aq) + FeCl_3(aq) \rightarrow$
$$3 NaCl(aq) + Fe(OH)_3(s)$$
precipitation

Sodium hydroxide and iron(III) chloride react to form sodium chloride and iron(III) hydroxide

$$3 OH^-(aq) + Fe^{3+}(aq) \rightarrow Fe(OH)_3(s)$$

3.69 (a) Reactants: Na($+1$), I(-1), H($+1$), S($+6$), O(-2), Mn($+4$)

Products: Na($+1$), S($+6$), O(-2), Mn($+2$), I(0), H($+1$)

(b) The oxidizing agent is MnO_2, and NaI is oxidized. The reducing agent is NaI, and MnO_2 is reduced.

(c) Based on the picture, the reaction is product-favored.

(d) Sodium iodide, sulfuric acid, and manganese(IV) oxide react to form sodium sulfate, manganese(II) sulfate, and water.

3.71 Among the reactions that could be used are the following:

$$MgCO_3(s) + 2 HCl(aq) \rightarrow$$
$$MgCl_2(aq) + CO_2(g) + H_2O(\ell)$$

$$MgS(s) + 2 HCl(aq) \rightarrow MgCl_2(aq) + H_2S(g)$$

$$MgSO_3(s) + 2 HCl(aq) \rightarrow$$
$$MgCl_2(aq) + SO_2(g) + H_2O(\ell)$$

In each case, the resulting solution could be evaporated to obtain the desired magnesium chloride.

3.73 The Ag^+ was reduced (to silver metal), and the glucose was oxidized (to $C_6H_{12}O_7$). The Ag^+ is the oxidizing agent, and the glucose is the reducing agent.

3.75 Weak electrolyte test: Compare the conductivity of a solution of lactic acid and that of an equal concentration of a strong acid. The conductivity of the lactic acid solution should be significantly less.

Reversible reaction: The fact that lactic acid is an electrolyte indicates that the reaction proceeds in the forward direction. To test whether the ionization is reversible, one could prepare a solution containing as much lactic acid as it will hold and then add a strong acid (to provide H_3O^+). If the reaction proceeds in the reverse direction, this will cause some lactic acid to precipitate.

3.77 (a) Several precipitation reactions are possible:

i. $BaCl_2(aq) + H_2SO_4(aq) \rightarrow$
$$BaSO_4(s) + 2 HCl(aq)$$

ii. $BaCl_2(aq) + Na_2SO_4(aq) \rightarrow$
$$BaSO_4(s) + 2 NaCl(aq)$$

iii. $Ba(OH)_2(aq) + H_2SO_4(aq) \rightarrow$
$$BaSO_4(s) + 2 H_2O(\ell)$$

(b) Gas-forming reaction:

$$BaCO_3(s) + H_2SO_4(aq) \rightarrow$$
$$BaSO_4(s) + CO_2(g) + H_2O(\ell)$$

CHAPTER 4

4.1 4.5 mol O_2; 310 g Al_2O_3

4.3 22.7 g Br_2; 25.3 g Al_2Br_6

4.5 (a) CO_2, carbon dioxide, and H_2O, water
(b) $CH_4(g) + 2 O_2(g) \rightarrow CO_2(g) + 2 H_2O(\ell)$
(c) 102 g O_2
(d) 128 g products

4.7

Equation	2 PbS(s)	+ 3 O$_2$(g)	$\rightarrow$ 2 PbO(s)	+ 2 SO$_2$(g)
Initial (mol)	2.5	3.8	0	0
Change (mol)	−2.5	−³⁄₂(2.5) = −3.8	+²⁄₂(2.5) = +2.5	+²⁄₂(2.5) = +2.5
Final (mol)	0	0	2.5	2.5

The amounts table shows that 2.5 mol of PbS requires ³⁄₂(2.5) = 3.8 mol of O_2 and produces 2.5 mol of PbO and 2.5 mol of SO_2.

4.9 (a) Balanced equation: $4 Cr(s) + 3 O_2(g) \rightarrow 2 Cr_2O_3(s)$
(b) 0.175 g of Cr is equivalent to 0.00337 mol

Equation	4 Cr(s)	+ 3 O$_2$(g)	$\rightarrow$	2 Cr$_2$O$_3$(s)
Initial (mol)	0.00337	0.00252 mol		0
Change (mol)	−0.00337	−³⁄₄(0.00337) = −0.00252		²⁄₄(0.00337) = +0.00168
Final (mol)	0	0		0.00168

The 0.00168 mol Cr_2O_3 produced corresponds to 0.256 g Cr_2O_3.
(c) 0.081 g O_2

4.11 0.11 mol of Na_2SO_4 and 0.62 mol of C are mixed. Sodium sulfate is the limiting reactant. Therefore, 0.11 mol of Na_2S is formed, or 8.2 g.

4.13 F_2 is the limiting reactant.

4.15 (a) CH_4 is the limiting reactant.
(b) 375 g H_2
(c) Excess H_2O = 1390 g

4.17 (a) $2 C_6H_{14}(\ell) + 19 O_2(g) \rightarrow 12 CO_2(g) + 14 H_2O(g)$
(b) O_2 is the limiting reactant. Products are 187 g of CO_2 and 89.2 g of H_2O.
(c) 154 g of hexane remains
(d)

Equation	2 C$_6$H$_{14}$(ℓ)	+ 19 O$_2$(g)	$\rightarrow$ 12 CO$_2$(g)	+ 14 H$_2$O(g)
Initial (mol)	2.49	6.72	0	0
Change (mol)	−0.707	−6.72	+4.24	+4.95
Final (mol)	1.78	0	4.24	4.95

4.19 (332 g/407 g)100% = 81.6%

4.21 (a) 14.3 g $Cu(NH_3)_4SO_4$
(b) 88.3% yield

4.23 91.9% hydrate

4.25 84.3% $CaCO_3$

4.27 1.467% Tl_2SO_4

4.29 Empirical formula = CH

4.31 Empirical formula = CH_2; molecular formula = C_5H_{10}

4.33 Empirical formula = CH_3O; molecular formula = $C_2H_6O_2$

4.35 $Ni(CO)_4$

4.37 $[Na_2CO_3]$ = 0.254 M; $[Na^+]$ = 0.508 M; $[CO_3^{2-}]$ = 0.254 M

4.39 0.494 g $KMnO_4$

4.41 5.08×10^3 mL

4.43 (a) 0.50 M NH_4^+ and 0.25 M SO_4^{2-}
(b) 0.246 M Na^+ and 0.123 M CO_3^{2-}
(c) 0.056 M H^+ and 0.056 M NO_3^-

4.45 A mass of 1.06 g of Na_2CO_3 is required. After weighing out this quantity of Na_2CO_3, transfer it to a 500.-mL volumetric flask. Rinse any solid from the neck of the flask while filling the flask with distilled water. Dissolve the solute in water. Add water until the bottom of the meniscus of the water is at the top of the scribed mark on the neck of the flask. Thoroughly mix the solution.

4.47 0.0750 M

4.49 Method (a) is correct. Method (b) gives an acid concentration of 0.15 M.

4.51 0.00340 M

4.53 $[H_3O^+]$ = 10^{-pH} = 4.0×10^{-4} M; the solution is acidic.

4.55 HNO_3 is a strong acid, so $[H_3O^+]$ = 0.0013 M. pH = 2.89.

4.57

	pH	[H$_3$O$^+$]	Acidic/Basic
(a)	1.00	0.10 M	Acidic
(b)	10.50	3.2×10^{-11} M	Basic
(c)	4.89	1.3×10^{-5} M	Acidic
(d)	7.64	2.3×10^{-8} M	Basic

4.59 268 mL

4.61 210 g NaOH and 190 g Cl_2

4.63 174 mL of $Na_2S_2O_3$

4.65 1.50×10^3 mL of $Pb(NO_3)_2$

4.67 44.6 mL

4.69 1.052 M HCl

4.71 104 g/mol

4.73 12.8% Fe

4.75

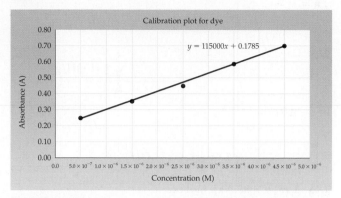

(a) slope = 1.2×10^5 M^{-1}; y-intercept = 0.18 M
(b) 3.0×10^{-6} M

4.77 (a) Products = $CO_2(g)$ and $H_2O(g)$
(b) $2\,C_6H_6(\ell) + 15\,O_2(g) \rightarrow 12\,CO_2(g) + 6\,H_2O(g)$
(c) 49.28 g O_2
(d) 65.32 g products (= sum of C_6H_6 mass and O_2 mass)

4.79 0.28 g arginine, 0.21 g ornithine

4.81 (a) titanium(IV) chloride, water, titanium(IV) oxide, hydrogen chloride
(b) 4.60 g H_2O
(c) 10.2 TiO_2, 18.6 g HCl

4.83 8.33 g NaN_3

4.85 Mass percent saccharin = 75.92%

4.87 SiH_4

4.89 C_3H_2O

4.91 1.85 kg H_2SO_4

4.93 The calculated molar mass of the metal is 1.2×10^2 g/mol. The metal is probably tin (118.67 g/mol).

4.95 479 kg Cl_2

4.97 66.5 kg CaO

4.99 1.29 g C_4H_8 (45.1%) and 1.57 g C_4H_{10} (54.9%)

4.101 62.2% Cu_2S and 26.8% CuS

4.103 (a) $MgCO_3(s) + 2\,H_3O^+(aq) \rightarrow$
$$CO_2(g) + Mg^{2+}(aq) + 2\,H_2O(\ell)$$
(b) Gas-forming reaction
(c) 0.15 g

4.105 15.0 g of $NaHCO_3$ require 1190 mL of 0.15 M acetic acid. Therefore, acetic acid is the limiting reactant. (Conversely, 125 mL of 0.15 M acetic acid requires only 1.58 g of $NaHCO_3$.) 1.54 g of $NaCH_3CO_2$ produced.

4.107 3.13 g $Na_2S_2O_3$, 96.8%

4.109 (a) pH = 0.979
(b) $[H_3O^+]$ = 0.0028 M; the solution is acidic.
(c) $[H_3O^+]$ = 2.1×10^{-10} M; the solution is basic.
(d) The new solution's concentration is 0.102 M HCl; the pH = 0.990

4.111 The concentration of hydrochloric acid is 2.92 M; the pH is -0.465

4.113 1.56 g of $CaCO_3$ required; 1.00 g $CaCO_3$ remain; 1.73 g $CaCl_2$ produced.

4.115 Volume of water in the pool = 7.6×10^4 L

4.117 (a) Au, gold, has been oxidized and is the reducing agent.

O$_2$, oxygen, has been reduced and is the oxidizing agent.

(b) 26 L NaCN solution

4.119 The concentration of Na_2CO_3 in the first solution prepared is 0.0275 M, in the second solution prepared the concentration of Na_2CO_3 is 0.00110 M.

4.121 (a) First reaction: oxidizing agent = Cu^{2+} and reducing agent = I^-

Second reaction: oxidizing agent = I_3^- and reducing agent = $S_2O_3^{2-}$

(b) 67.3% copper

4.123 x = 6; $Co(NH_3)_6Cl_3$.

4.125 11.48% 2,4-D

4.127 3.3 mol H_2O/mol $CaCl_2$

4.129 (a) Slope = 2.06×10^5; 0.024
(b) 1.20×10^{-4} g/L
(c) 0.413 mg PO_4^{3-}

4.131 The total mass of the beakers and products after reaction is equal to the total mass before the reaction (161.170 g) because no gases were produced in the reaction and there is conservation of mass in chemical reactions.

4.133 The balanced chemical equation indicates that the stoichiometric ratio of HCl to Zn is 2 mol HCl/1 mol Zn. In each reaction, there is 0.100 mol of HCl present. In reaction 1, there is 0.107 mol of Zn present. This gives a 0.93 mole HCl/mol Zn ratio, indicating that HCl is the limiting reactant. In reaction 2, there is 0.050 mol of Zn, giving a 2.0 mol HCl/mol Zn ratio. This indicates that the two reactants are present in exactly the correct stoichiometric ratio. In reaction 3, there is 0.020 mol of Zn, giving a 5.0 mol HCl/mol Zn ratio. This indicates that the HCl is present in excess and that the zinc is the limiting reactant.

4.135 If both students base their calculations on the amount of HCl solution pipeted into the flask (20 mL), then the second student's result will be (e), the same as the first student's. However, if the HCl concentration is calculated using the diluted solution volume, student 1 will use a volume of 40 mL, and student 2 will use a volume of 80 mL in the calculation. The second student's result will be (c), half that of the first student's.

4.137 150 mg/dL. Person is intoxicated.

CHAPTER 5

5.1 Mechanical energy is used to move the lever, which in turn moves gears. The device produces electrical energy and radiant energy.

5.3 5.0×10^6 J

5.5 170 kcal is equivalent to 710 kJ, considerably greater than 280 kJ.

5.7 0.140 J/g · K

5.9 2.44 kJ

5.11 32.8 °C

5.13 20.7 °C

5.15 47.8 °C

5.17 0.40 J/g · K

5.19 330 kJ

5.21 49.3 kJ

5.23 273 J

5.25 9.97×10^5 J

5.27 Reaction is exothermic because $\Delta_r H°$ is negative. The heat evolved is 2.38 kJ.

5.29 3.3×10^4 kJ

5.31 $\Delta H = -56$ kJ/mol CsOH

5.33 0.52 J/g · K

5.35 $\Delta_r H = +23$ kJ/mol-rxn

5.37 297 kJ/mol SO_2

5.39 3.09×10^3 kJ/mol $C_6H_5CO_2H$

5.41 0.236 J/g · K

5.43 (a) $\Delta_r H° = -126$ kJ/mol-rxn
(b)

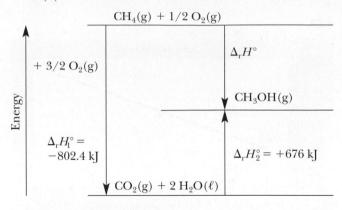

5.45 $\Delta_r H° = +90.3$ kJ/mol-rxn

5.47 $C(s) + 2 H_2(g) + 1/2 O_2(g) \rightarrow CH_3OH(\ell)$

$\Delta_f H° = -238.4$ kJ/mol

5.49 (a) $2 Cr(s) + 3/2 O_2(g) \rightarrow Cr_2O_3(s)$

$\Delta_f H° = -1134.7$ kJ/mol

(b) 2.4 g is equivalent to 0.046 mol of Cr. This will produce 26 kJ of energy transferred as heat.

5.51 (a) $\Delta H° = -24$ kJ for 1.0 g of phosphorus
(b) $\Delta H° = -18$ kJ for 0.2 mol NO
(c) $\Delta H° = -16.9$ kJ for the formation of 2.40 g of NaCl(s)
(d) $\Delta H° = -1.8 \times 10^3$ kJ for the oxidation of 250 g of iron

5.53 (a) $\Delta_r H° = -906.2$ kJ
(b) The heat evolved is 133 kJ for the oxidation of 10.0 g of NH_3

5.55 (a) $\Delta_r H° = +161.6$ kJ/mol-rxn; the reaction is endothermic.
(b)

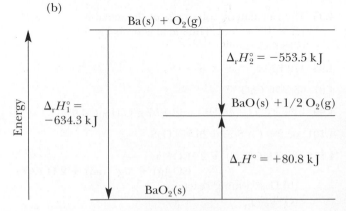

5.57 $\Delta_f H° = +77.7$ kJ/mol for naphthalene

5.59 (a) Exothermic: a process in which energy is transferred as heat from a system to its surroundings. (The combustion of methane is exothermic.)

Endothermic: a process in which energy is transferred as heat from the surroundings to the system. (Ice melting is endothermic.)

(b) System: the object or collection of objects being studied. (A chemical reaction—the system—taking place inside a calorimeter—the surroundings.)

Surroundings: everything outside the system that can exchange mass or energy with the system. (The calorimeter and everything outside the calorimeter comprise the surroundings.)

(c) Specific heat capacity: the quantity of energy that must be transferred as heat to raise the temperature of 1 gram of a substance 1 kelvin. (The specific heat capacity of water is 4.184 J/g · K).

(d) State function: a quantity that is characterized by changes that do not depend on the path chosen to go from the initial state to the final state. (Enthalpy and internal energy are state functions.)

(e) Standard state: the most stable form of a substance in the physical state that exists at a pressure of 1 bar and at a specified temperature. (The standard state of carbon at 25 °C is graphite.)

(f) Enthalpy change, ΔH: the energy transferred as heat at constant pressure. (The enthalpy change for melting ice at 0 °C is 6.00 kJ/mol.)

(g) Standard enthalpy of formation: the enthalpy change for the formation of 1 mol of a compound in its standard state directly from the component elements in their standard states. ($\Delta_f H°$ for liquid water is −285.83 kJ/mol)

5.61 (a) System: reaction between methane and oxygen

Surroundings: the furnace and the rest of the universe. Energy is transferred as heat from the system to the surroundings.

(b) System: water drops

Surroundings: skin and the rest of the universe

Energy is transferred as heat from the surroundings to the system

(c) System: water

Surroundings: freezer and the rest of the universe

Energy is transferred as heat from the system to the surroundings

(d) System: reaction of aluminum and iron(III) oxide

Surroundings: flask, laboratory bench, and rest of the universe

Energy is transferred as heat from the system to the surroundings.

5.63 Standard state of oxygen is gas, $O_2(g)$.

$O_2(g) \rightarrow 2\ O(g)$, $\Delta_r H° = +498.34$ kJ, endothermic

$3/2\ O_2(g) \rightarrow O_3(g)$, $\Delta_r H° = +142.67$ kJ

5.65

$SnBr_2(s) + TiCl_2(s) \rightarrow SnCl_2(s) + TiBr_2(s)$	$\Delta_r H° = -4.2$ kJ
$SnCl_2(s) + Cl_2(g) \rightarrow SnCl_4(\ell)$	$\Delta_r H° = -195$ kJ
$TiCl_4(\ell) \rightarrow TiCl_2(s) + Cl_2(g)$	$\Delta_r H° = +273$ kJ
$SnBr_2(s) + TiCl_4(\ell) \rightarrow SnCl_4(\ell) + TiBr_2(s)$	$\Delta_r H° = +74$ kJ

5.67 $C_{Ag} = 0.24$ J/g · K

5.69 Mass of ice melted = 75.4 g

5.71 Final temperature = 278 K (4.8 °C)

5.73 (a) When summed, the following equations give the balanced equation for the formation of $B_2H_6(g)$ from the elements.

$2\ B(s) + 3/2\ O_2(g) \rightarrow B_2O_3(s)$	$\Delta_r H° = -1271.9$ kJ
$3\ H_2(g) + 3/2\ O_2(g) \rightarrow 3\ H_2O(g)$	$\Delta_r H° = -725.4$ kJ
$B_2O_3(s) + 3\ H_2O(g) \rightarrow B_2H_6(g) + 3\ O_2(g)$	$\Delta_r H° = +2032.9$ kJ
$2\ B(s) + 3\ H_2(g) \rightarrow B_2H_6(g)$	$\Delta_r H° = +35.6$ kJ

(b) The enthalpy of formation of $B_2H_6(g)$ is +35.6 kJ/mol

(c)

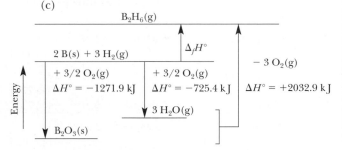

(d) The formation of $B_2H_6(g)$ is reactant-favored.

5.75 (a) $\Delta_r H° = +131.31$ kJ
(b) Reactant-favored
(c) 1.0932×10^7 kJ

5.77 Assuming $CO_2(g)$ and $H_2O(\ell)$ are the products of combustion:

$\Delta_r H°$ for isooctane is −5461.3 kJ/mol or −47.81 kJ per gram

$\Delta_r H°$ for liquid methanol is −726.77 kJ/mol or −22.682 kJ per gram

5.79 (a) Adding the equations as they are given in the question results in the desired equation for the formation of $SrCO_3(s)$. The calculated $\Delta_r H° = -1220.$ kJ/mol.

(b)

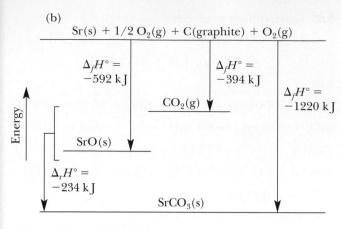

5.81 $\Delta_r H° = -305.3$ kJ

5.83 $C_{Pb} = 0.121$ J/g · K

5.85 $\Delta_r H = -69$ kJ/mol AgCl

5.87 36.0 kJ evolved per mol of NH_4NO_3

5.89 The standard enthalpy change, $\Delta_r H°$, is -352.88 kJ. The quantity of magnesium needed is 0.43 g.

5.91 (a) product-favored
(b) reactant-favored

5.93 The enthalpy change for each of the three reactions below is known or can be measured by calorimetry. The three equations sum to give the enthalpy of formation of $CaSO_4(s)$.

Ca(s) + 1/2 O_2(g)	→	CaO(s)	$\Delta_r H° = \Delta_f H°$ $= -635.09$ kJ
1/8 S_8(s) + 3/2 O_2(g)	→	SO_3(g)	$\Delta_r H° = \Delta_f H°$ $= -395.77$ kJ
CaO(s) + SO_3(g)	→	$CaSO_4$(s)	$\Delta_r H° = -402.7$ kJ
Ca(s) + 1/8 S_8(s) + 2 O_2(g)	→	$CaSO_4$(s)	$\Delta_r H° = \Delta_f H°$ $= -1433.6$ kJ

5.95

Metal	Molar Heat Capacity (J/mol · K)
Al	24.2
Fe	25.1
Cu	24.5
Au	25.4

All the metals have a molar heat capacity of 24.8 J/mol · K plus or minus 0.6 J/mol · K. Therefore, assuming the molar heat capacity of Ag is 24.8 J/mol · K, its specific heat capacity is 0.230 J/g · K. This is very close to the experimental value of 0.236 J/g · K.

5.97 120 g of CH_4 required (assuming H_2O(g) as product)

5.99 1.6×10^{11} kJ released to the surroundings. This is equivalent to 3.8×10^4 tons of dynamite.

5.101 (a)

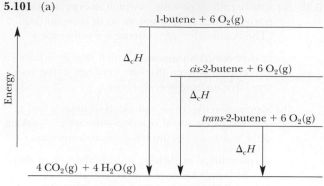

(b) *cis*-2-butene: $\Delta_f H° = 146.1$ kJ/mol

trans-2-butene: $\Delta_f H° = 142.8$ kJ/mol

1-butene: $\Delta_f H° = 155.3$ kJ/mol

(c)

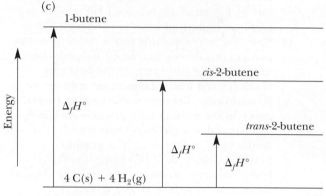

(d) -3.3 kJ/mol-rxn

5.103 (a) -726 kJ/mol Mg
(b) 25.0 °C

5.105 (a) Methane
(b) Methane
(c) -279 kJ
(d) CH_4(g) + 2 O_2(g) → $CH_3OH(\ell)$

5.107 (a) Metal Heated = 100.0 g of Al; Metal Cooled = 50.0 g of Au; Final Temperature = 26 °C
(b) Metal Heated = 50.0 g of Zn; Metal Cooled = 50.0 g of Al; Final Temperature = 21 °C

CHAPTER 6

6.1 (a) microwaves
(b) red light
(c) infrared

6.3 (a) Green light has a higher frequency than amber light
(b) 5.04×10^{14} s^{-1}

6.5 Frequency = 6.0×10^{14} s^{-1}; energy per photon = 4.0×10^{-19} J; energy per mol of photons = 2.4×10^5 J

6.7 Frequency = 7.5676×10^{14} s^{-1}; energy per photon = 5.0144×10^{-19} J; 302 kJ/mol of photons

6.9 In order of increasing energy: FM station < microwaves < yellow light < x-rays

6.11 Light with a wavelength as long as 600 nm would be sufficient. This is in the visible region.

6.13 (a) The light of shortest wavelength has a wavelength of 253.652 nm.
(b) Frequency = 1.18190×10^{15} s^{-1}. Energy per photon = 7.83139×10^{-19} J/photon.
(c) The lines at 404 (violet) and 436 nm (blue) are in the visible region of the spectrum.

6.15 The color is violet. $n_{initial} = 6$ and $n_{final} = 2$

6.17 (a) 10 lines possible
(b) Highest frequency (highest energy), $n = 5$ to $n = 1$
(c) Longest wavelength (lowest energy), $n = 5$ to $n = 4$

6.19 (a) $n = 3$ to $n = 2$
(b) $n = 4$ to $n = 1$; The energy levels are progressively closer at higher levels, so the energy difference from $n = 4$ to $n = 1$ is greater than from $n = 5$ to $n = 2$.

6.21 Wavelength = 102.6 nm and frequency = 2.923×10^{15} s^{-1}. Light with these properties is in the ultraviolet region.

6.23 Wavelength = 0.29 nm

6.25 The wavelength is 2.2×10^{-25} nm. (Calculated from $\lambda = h/m \cdot v$, where m is the ball's mass in kg and v is the velocity.) To have a wavelength of 5.6×10^{-3} nm, the ball would have to travel at 1.2×10^{-21} m/s.

6.27 (a) $n = 4$, $\ell = 0, 1, 2, 3$
(b) When $\ell = 2$, $m_\ell = -2, -1, 0, 1, 2$
(c) For a 4s orbital, $n = 4$, $\ell = 0$, and $m_\ell = 0$
(d) For a 4f orbital, $n = 4$, $\ell = 3$, and $m_\ell = -3, -2, -1, 0, 1, 2, 3$

6.29 Set 1: $n = 4$, $\ell = 1$, and $m_\ell = -1$

Set 2: $n = 4$, $\ell = 1$, and $m_\ell = 0$

Set 3: $n = 4$, $\ell = 1$, and $m_\ell = +1$

6.31 Four subshells. (The number of subshells in a shell is always equal to n.)

6.33 (a) ℓ must have a value no greater than $n - 1$.
(b) When $\ell = 0$, m_ℓ can only equal 0.
(c) When $\ell = 0$, m_ℓ can only equal 0.

6.35 (a) None. The quantum number set is not possible. When $\ell = 0$, m_ℓ can only equal 0.
(b) 3 orbitals
(c) 11 orbitals
(d) 1 orbital

6.37 (a) $m_s = 0$ is not possible. m_s may only have values of $\pm 1/2$.

One possible set of quantum numbers: $n = 4$, $\ell = 2$, $m_\ell = 0$, $m_s = +1/2$

(b) m_ℓ cannot equal -3 in this case. If $\ell = 1$, m_ℓ can only be -1, 0, or 1.

One possible set of quantum numbers: $n = 3$, $\ell = 1$, $m_\ell = -1$, $m_s = -1/2$

(c) $\ell = 3$ is not possible in this case. The maximum value of ℓ is $n - 1$.

One possible set of quantum numbers: $n = 3$, $\ell = 2$, $m_\ell = -1$, $m_s = +1/2$

6.39 2d and 3f orbitals cannot exist. The $n = 2$ shell consists only of s and p subshells. The $n = 3$ shell consists only of s, p, and d subshells.

6.41 (a) For 2p: $n = 2$, $\ell = 1$, and $m_\ell = -1$, 0, or $+1$
(b) For 3d: $n = 3$, $\ell = 2$, and $m_\ell = -2, -1, 0, +1$, or $+2$
(c) For 4f: $n = 4$, $\ell = 3$, and $m_\ell = -3, -2, -1, 0, +1, +2$, or $+3$

6.43 4d

6.45 (a) 2s has 0 nodal surfaces that pass through the nucleus ($\ell = 0$).
(b) 5d has 2 nodal surfaces that pass through the nucleus ($\ell = 2$).
(c) 5f has three nodal surfaces that pass through the nucleus ($\ell = 3$).

6.47 (a) Correct
(b) Incorrect. The intensity of a light beam is independent of frequency and is related to the number of photons of light with a certain energy.
(c) Correct

6.49 Considering only angular nodes (nodal surfaces that pass through the nucleus):

s orbital	0 nodal surfaces
p orbitals	1 nodal surface or plane passing through the nucleus
d orbitals	2 nodal surfaces or planes passing through the nucleus
f orbitals	3 nodal surfaces or planes passing through the nucleus

6.51

ℓ value	Orbital Type
3	f
0	s
1	p
2	d

6.53 Considering only angular nodes (nodal surfaces that pass through the nucleus):

Orbital Type	Number of Orbitals in a Given Subshell	Number of Nodal Surfaces
s	1	0
p	3	1
d	5	2
f	7	3

6.55 (a) Green light
(b) Red light has a wavelength of 680 nm, and green light has a wavelength of 500 nm.
(c) Green light has a higher frequency than red light.

6.57 (a) Wavelength = 0.35 m
(b) Energy = 0.34 J/mol
(c) Blue light (with λ = 420 nm) has an energy of 280 kJ/mol of photons.
(d) Blue light has an energy (per mol of photons) that is 840,000 times greater than a mole of photons from a cell phone.

6.59 The ionization energy for He^+ is 5248 kJ/mol. This is four times the ionization energy for the H atom.

6.61 $1s < 2s = 2p < 3s = 3p = 3d < 4s$

In the H atom orbitals in the same shell (e.g., $2s$ and $2p$) have the same energy.

6.63 Frequency = 2.836×10^{20} s^{-1} and wavelength = 1.057×10^{-12} m

6.65 260 s or 4.3 min

6.67 (a) size and energy
(b) ℓ
(c) more
(d) 7 (when ℓ = 3 these are f orbitals)
(e) one orbital
(f) (left to right) d, s, and p
(g) ℓ = 0, 1, 2, 3, 4
(h) 16 orbitals ($1s$, $3p$, $5d$, and $7f$) (= n^2)
(i) paramagnetic

6.69 (a) Drawing (a) is a ferromagnetic solid, (b) is a diamagnetic solid, and (c) is a paramagnetic solid.
(b) Substance (a) would be most strongly attracted to a magnet, whereas (b) would be least strongly attracted.

6.71 The pickle glows because it was made by soaking a cucumber in brine, a concentrated solution of NaCl. The sodium atoms in the pickle are excited by the electric current and release energy as yellow light as they return to the ground state. Excited sodium atoms are the source of the yellow light you see in fireworks and in certain kinds of street lighting.

6.73 (a) λ = 0.0005 cm = 5 μm
(b) The left side is the higher energy side, and the right side is the lower energy side.
(c) The interaction with O—H requires more energy.

6.75 (c)

6.77 An experiment can be done that shows that the electron can behave as a particle, and another experiment can be done to show that it has wave properties. (However, no single experiment shows both properties of the electron.) The modern view of atomic structure is based on the wave properties of the electron.

6.79 (a) and (b)

6.81 Radiation with a wavelength of 93.8 nm is sufficient to raise the electron to the n = 6 quantum level (see Figure 6.10). There should be 15 emission lines involving transitions from n = 6 to lower energy levels. (There are five lines for transitions from n = 6 to lower levels, four lines for n = 5 to lower levels, three for n = 4 to lower levels, two lines for n = 3 to lower levels, and one line for n = 2 to n = 1.) Wavelengths for many of the lines are given in Figure 6.10. For example, there will be an emission involving an electron moving from n = 6 to n = 2 with a wavelength of 410.2 nm.

6.83 (a) Group 7B (IUPAC Group 7); Period 5
(b) n = 5, ℓ = 0, m_ℓ = 0, m_s = +1/2
(c) λ = 8.79×10^{-12} m; ν = 3.41×10^{19} s^{-1}
(d) (i) $HTcO_4(aq) + NaOH(aq) \rightarrow$
$H_2O(\ell) + NaTcO_4(aq)$
(ii) 8.5×10^{-3} g $NaTcO_4$ produced; 1.8×10^{-3} g NaOH needed
(e) 0.28 mg $NaTcO_4$; 0.00015 M

6.85 Six emission lines are observed. More than one line is observed because the following changes in energy levels are possible: from n = 4 to n = 3, n = 2, and n = 1 (three lines), from n = 3 to n = 2 and n = 1 (2 lines), and from n = 2 to n = 1 (one line).

CHAPTER 7

7.1 (a) Phosphorus: $1s^2 2s^2 2p^6 3s^2 3p^3$

↑↓	↑↓	↑↓	↑↓	↑↓	↑↓	↑	↑	↑
1s	2s		2p		3s		3p	

The element is in the third period in Group 5A. Therefore, it has five electrons in the third shell.
(b) Chlorine: $1s^2 2s^2 2p^6 3s^2 3p^5$

↑↓	↑↓	↑↓	↑↓	↑↓	↑↓	↑↓	↑↓	↑
1s	2s		2p		3s		3p	

The element is in the third period and in Group 7A. Therefore, it has seven electrons in the third shell.

7.3 (a) Chromium: $1s^2 2s^2 2p^6 3s^2 3p^6 3d^5 4s^1$
(b) Iron: $1s^2 2s^2 2p^6 3s^2 3p^6 3d^6 4s^2$

7.5 (a) Arsenic: $1s^2 2s^2 2p^6 3s^2 3p^6 3d^{10} 4s^2 4p^3$;
$[Ar]3d^{10}4s^2 4p^3$
(b) Krypton: $1s^2 2s^2 2p^6 3s^2 3p^6 3d^{10} 4s^2 4p^6$;
$[Ar]3d^{10}4s^2 4p^6 = [Kr]$

7.7 (a) Tantalum: This is the third element in the transition series in the sixth period. Therefore, it has a core equivalent to Xe plus two $6s$ electrons, 14 $4f$ electrons, and three electrons in $5d$: $[Xe]4f^{14}5d^3 6s^2$
(b) Platinum: This is the eighth element in the transition series in the sixth period. Therefore, it is predicted to have a core equivalent to Xe plus two $6s$ electrons, 14 $4f$ electrons, and eight electrons in $5d$: $[Xe]4f^{14}5d^8 6s^2$. In reality, its actual configuration (Table 7.3) is $[Xe]4f^{14}5d^9 6s^1$.

7.9 Americium: $[Rn]5f^7 7s^2$ (see Table 7.3)

7.11 (a) 2
(b) 1
(c) none (because ℓ cannot equal n)

7.13 Magnesium: $1s^2 2s^2 2p^6 3s^2$

Quantum numbers for the two electrons in the $3s$ orbital:

$n = 3$, $\ell = 0$, $m_\ell = 0$, and $m_s = +1/2$

$n = 3$, $\ell = 0$, $m_\ell = 0$, and $m_s = -1/2$

7.15 Gallium: $1s^2 2s^2 2p^6 3s^2 3p^6 3d^{10} 4s^2 4p^1$

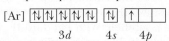

Quantum numbers for the 4p electron:

$n = 4$, $\ell = 1$, $m_\ell = -1$, 0, or $+1$, and $m_s = +\frac{1}{2}$ or $-\frac{1}{2}$

7.17 (a) Mg^{2+} ion

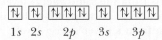

(b) K^+ ion

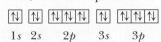

(c) Cl^- ion (Note that both Cl^- and K^+ have the same configuration; both are equivalent to Ar.)

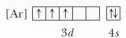

(d) O^{2-} ion

7.19 (a) V (paramagnetic; three unpaired electrons)

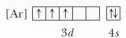

(b) V^{2+} ion (paramagnetic, three unpaired electrons)

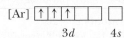

(c) V^{5+} ion. This ion has an electron configuration equivalent to argon, [Ar]. It is diamagnetic with no unpaired electrons.

7.21 (a) Manganese

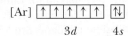

(b) Mn^{4+}

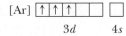

(c) The 4^+ ion is paramagnetic to the extent of three unpaired electrons.
(d) 3

7.23 Increasing size: C < B < Al < Na < K

7.25 (a) Cl^-
(b) Al
(c) In

7.27 (c)

7.29 (a) Largest radius, Na
(b) Most negative electron affinity: O
(c) Ionization energy: Na < Mg < P < O

7.31 (a) Increasing ionization energy: S < O < F. S is less than O because the IE decreases down a group. F is greater than O because IE generally increases across a period.
(b) Largest IE: O. IE decreases down a group.
(c) Most negative electron affinity: Cl. Electron affinity becomes more negative across the periodic table and on ascending a group.
(d) Largest Size: O^{2-}. Negative ions are larger than their corresponding neutral atoms. F^- is thus larger than F. O^{2-} and F^- are isoelectronic, but the O^{2-} ion has only eight protons in its nucleus to attract the 10 electrons, whereas the F^- has nine protons, making the O^{2-} ion larger.

7.33 Uranium configuration: $[Rn]5f^36d^17s^2$

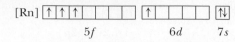

Uranium(IV) ion, U^{4+}: $[Rn]5f^2$

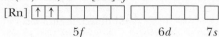

Both U and U^{4+} are paramagnetic.

7.35 (a) Atomic number = 20
(b) Total number of s electrons = 8
(c) Total number of p electrons = 12
(d) Total number of d electrons = 0
(e) The element is Ca, calcium, a metal.

7.37 (a) Valid. Possible elements are Li and Be.
(b) Not valid. The maximum value of ℓ is $(n-1)$.
(c) Valid. Possible elements are B through Ne.
(d) Valid. Possible elements are Y through Cd.

7.39 (a) Neodymium, Nd: $[Xe]4f^46s^2$ (Table 7.3)

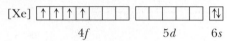

Iron, Fe: $[Ar]3d^64s^2$

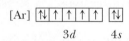

Boron, B: $[He]2s^22p^1$

(b) All three elements have unpaired electrons and so should be paramagnetic.
(c) Neodymium(III) ion, Nd^{3+}: $[Xe]4f^3$

Iron(III) ion, Fe^{3+}: $[Ar]3d^5$

Both neodymium(III) and iron(III) have unpaired electrons and are paramagnetic.

7.41 K < Ca < Si < P

7.43 (a) metal
(b) B
(c) A
(d) A
(e) Rb_2Se

7.45 In^{4+}: Indium has three outer shell electrons and so is unlikely to form a 4^+ ion.

Fe^{6+}: Although iron has eight electrons in its $3d$ and $4s$ orbitals, ions with a 6^+ charge are highly unlikely. The ionization energy is too large.

Sn^{5+}: Tin has four outer shell electrons and so is unlikely to form a 5^+ ion.

7.47 (a) Se
(b) Br^-
(c) Na
(d) N
(e) N^{3-}

7.49 (a) Na
(b) C
(c) Na < Al < B < C

7.51 (a) Cobalt
(b) Paramagnetic
(c) Four unpaired electrons

7.53 (a) 0.421 g
(b) paramagnetic; 2 unpaired electrons
(c) 99.8 mg; the nickel powder will stick to a magnet.

7.55 Li has three electrons ($1s^22s^1$) and Li^+ has only two electrons ($1s^2$). The ion is smaller than the atom because there are only two electrons to be held by three protons in the ion. Also, an electron in a larger orbital has been removed. Fluorine atoms have nine electrons and nine protons ($1s^22s^22p^5$). The anion, F^-, has one additional electron, which means that 10 electrons must be held by only nine protons, and the ion is larger than the atom.

7.57 Element 1 comes from Group 4A (IUPAC Group 14). The first two IEs correspond to removing electrons from a p subshell. With the third IE, there is a fairly large jump in IE corresponding to removing an electron from an s subshell. The fourth electron removed comes from the same s subshell and therefore does not increase the IE by as much. None of the IEs are large enough to correspond to removing an electron from a lower energy level.

Element 2 comes from Group 3A (IUPAC Group 13). There is a large change in IE between the third and fourth IEs. The first three IEs correspond to removing electrons from the same energy level. The large jump at the fourth IE corresponds to having to remove the electron from a lower energy level.

7.59 Most stable: (d) The two electrons are in separate orbitals, following Hund's rule, and are of the same spin.

Least stable: (a) In this case the electrons violate both Hund's rule and the Pauli exclusion principle.

7.61 $K\ (1s^22s^22p^63s^23p^64s^1) \rightarrow K^+\ (1s^22s^22p^63s^23p^6)$

$K^+\ (1s^22s^22p^63s^23p^6) \rightarrow K^{2+}\ (1s^22s^22p^63s^23p^5)$

The first ionization is for the removal of an electron from the valence shell of electrons. The second electron, however, is removed from the $3p$ subshell. This subshell is significantly lower in energy than the $4s$ subshell, and considerably more energy is required to remove this second electron.

7.63 (a) In going from one element to the next across the period, the effective nuclear charge increases slightly and the attraction between the nucleus and the electrons increases.

(b) The size of fourth period transition elements, for example, is a reflection of the size of the $4s$ orbital. As d electrons are added across the series, protons are added to the nucleus. Adding protons should lead to a decreased atom size, but the effect of the protons is balanced by repulsions of the $3d$ electrons and $4s$ electrons, and the atom size is changed little.

7.65 Among the arguments for a compound composed of Mg^{2+} and O^{2-} are:

(a) Chemical experience suggests that all Group 2A elements form $2+$ cations, and that oxygen is typically the O^{2-} ion in its compounds.

(b) Other alkaline earth elements form oxides such as BeO, CaO, and BaO.

A possible experiment is to measure the melting point of the compound. An ionic compound such as NaF (with ions having $1+$ and $1-$ charges) melts at 990 °C, whereas a compound analogous to MgO, CaO, melts at a much higher temperature (2580 °C).

7.67 (a) The effective nuclear charge increases, causing the valence orbital energies to become more negative on moving across the period.

(b) As the valence orbital energies become more negative, it is increasingly difficult to remove an electron from the atom, and the IE increases. Toward the end of the period, the orbital energies have become so negative that removing an electron requires significant energy. Instead, the effective nuclear charge has reached the point that it is energetically more favorable for the atom to gain an electron, corresponding to a more negative electron affinity.

(c) The valence orbital energies are in the order:

Li $(-520.7$ kJ$) <$ Be $(-899.3$ kJ$) >$ B $(-800.8$ kJ$)$ $<$ C $(-1029$ kJ$)$

This means it is more difficult to remove an electron from Be than from either Li or B. The energy is more negative for C than for B, so it is more difficult to remove an electron from C than from B.

7.69 The size declines across this series of elements while their mass increases. Thus, the mass per volume, the density, increases.

7.71 (a) Element 113: $[Rn]5f^{14}6d^{10}7s^27p^1$
Element 115: $[Rn]5f^{14}6d^{10}7s^27p^3$

(b) Element 113 is in Group 3A (with elements such as boron and aluminum), and element 115 is in Group 5A (with elements such as nitrogen and phosphorus).

(c) Americium $(Z = 95)$ + argon $(Z = 18)$ = element 113

7.73 (a) Sulfur electron configuration

$$\boxed{\uparrow\downarrow}\ \boxed{\uparrow\downarrow}\ \boxed{\uparrow\downarrow\,\uparrow\downarrow\,\uparrow\downarrow}\ \boxed{\uparrow\downarrow}\ \boxed{\uparrow\downarrow\,\uparrow\,\uparrow}$$
$$1s\quad 2s\quad\ \ 2p\quad\ \ 3s\quad\ \ 3p$$

(b) $n = 3$, $\ell = 1$, $m_\ell = 1$, and $m_s = +1/2$

(c) S has the smallest ionization energy and O has the smallest radius.

(d) S is smaller than S^{2-} ion

(e) 584 g SCl_2

(f) 10.0 g of SCl_2 is the limiting reactant, and 11.6 g of $SOCl_2$ can be produced.

(g) $\Delta_fH°[SCl_2(g)] = -17.6$ kJ/mol

7.75 (a) Z^* for F is 5.2; Z^* for Ne is 5.85. The effective nuclear charge increases from O to F to Ne. As the effective nuclear charge increases, the atomic radius decreases, and the first ionization energy increases.

(b) Z^* for a $3d$ electron in Mn is 13.7; for a $4s$ electron it is only 3.1. The effective nuclear charge experienced by a $4s$ electron is much smaller than that experienced by a $3d$ electron. A $4s$ electron in Mn is thus more easily removed.

CHAPTER 8

8.1. (a) Group 6A, six valence electrons
(b) Group 3A, three valence electrons
(c) Group 1A, one valence electron
(d) Group 2A, two valence electrons
(e) Group 7A, seven valence electrons
(f) Group 6A, six valence electrons

8.3 Group 3A, three bonds
Group 4A, four bonds
Group 5A, three bonds (for a neutral compound)
Group 6A, two bonds (for a neutral compound)
Group 7A, one (for a neutral compound)

8.5 (a) NF_3, 26 valence electrons

$$:\!\ddot{F}\!-\!\overset{\displaystyle .\,.}{N}\!-\!\ddot{F}\!:$$
$$\overset{\displaystyle |}{\underset{\displaystyle :\ddot{F}:}{}}$$

(b) ClO_3^-, 26 valence electrons

$$\left[:\overset{..}{\underset{..}{O}}-\overset{..}{Cl}-\overset{..}{\underset{..}{O}}: \atop :\overset{..}{\underset{..}{O}}: \right]^-$$

(c) HOBr, 14 valence electrons

$$H-\overset{..}{\underset{..}{O}}-\overset{..}{\underset{..}{Br}}:$$

(d) SO_3^{2-}, 26 valence electrons

$$\left[:\overset{..}{\underset{..}{O}}-\overset{..}{S}-\overset{..}{\underset{..}{O}}: \atop :\overset{..}{\underset{..}{O}}: \right]^{2-}$$

8.7 (a) $CHClF_2$, 26 valence electrons

$$\begin{array}{c} H \\ | \\ :\overset{..}{\underset{..}{Cl}}-\overset{}{\underset{}{C}}-\overset{..}{\underset{..}{F}}: \\ | \\ :\overset{..}{\underset{..}{F}}: \end{array}$$

(b) CH_3CO_2H, 24 valence electrons

$$\begin{array}{c} H \quad :\overset{..}{O} \\ | \quad\quad || \\ H-C-C-\overset{..}{\underset{..}{O}}-H \\ | \\ H \end{array}$$

(c) CH_3CN, 16 valence electrons

$$\begin{array}{c} H \\ | \\ H-C-C\equiv N: \\ | \\ H \end{array}$$

(d) H_2CCCH_2, 16 valence electrons

$$\begin{array}{c} H \quad\quad H \\ | \quad\quad\quad | \\ H-C=C=C-H \end{array}$$

8.9 (a) SO_2, 18 valence electrons

$$:\overset{..}{\underset{..}{O}}-\overset{..}{S}=\overset{..}{O} \longleftrightarrow \overset{..}{O}=\overset{..}{S}-\overset{..}{\underset{..}{O}}:$$

(b) HNO_2, 18 valence electrons

$$H-\overset{..}{\underset{..}{O}}-\overset{..}{N}=\overset{..}{O}$$

(c) SCN^-, 16 valence electrons

$$\left[\overset{..}{S}=C=\overset{..}{N}\right]^- \longleftrightarrow \left[:S\equiv C-\overset{..}{\underset{..}{N}}:\right]^- \longleftrightarrow \left[:\overset{..}{\underset{..}{S}}-C\equiv N:\right]^-$$

8.11 (a) BrF_3, 28 valence electrons

$$\begin{array}{c} :\overset{..}{\underset{..}{F}}: \\ | \\ :\overset{..}{Br}-\overset{..}{\underset{..}{F}}: \\ | \\ :\overset{..}{\underset{..}{F}}: \end{array}$$

(b) I_3^-, 22 valence electrons

$$\left[:\overset{..}{\underset{..}{I}}: \atop :\overset{..}{\underset{..}{I}}: \atop :\overset{..}{\underset{..}{I}}: \right]^-$$

(c) XeO_2F_2, 34 valence electrons

$$\begin{array}{c} :\overset{..}{\underset{..}{F}}: \\ | \\ :\overset{..}{\underset{..}{O}}-\overset{}{Xe}-\overset{..}{\underset{..}{O}}: \\ | \\ :\overset{..}{\underset{..}{F}}: \end{array}$$

(d) XeF_3^+, 28 valence electrons

$$\begin{array}{c} :\overset{..}{\underset{..}{F}}: \\ | \\ :\overset{..}{Xe}-\overset{..}{\underset{..}{F}}: \\ | \\ :\overset{..}{\underset{..}{F}}: \end{array}$$

8.13 (a) N = 0; H = 0
(b) P = +1; O = −1
(c) B = −1; H = 0
(d) All are zero.

8.15 (a) N = +1; O = 0
(b) The central N is 0. The singly bonded O atom is −1, and the doubly bonded O atom is 0.

$$\left[:\overset{..}{\underset{..}{O}}-\overset{..}{N}=\overset{..}{O}\right]^- \longleftrightarrow \left[\overset{..}{O}=\overset{..}{N}-\overset{..}{\underset{..}{O}}:\right]^-$$

(c) N and F are both 0.
(d) The central N atom is +1, one of the O atoms is −1, and the other two O atoms are both 0.

$$\overset{0}{H}-\overset{0}{\overset{..}{\underset{..}{O}}}-\overset{+1}{N}=\overset{0}{\overset{..}{O}} \atop \underset{-1}{:\overset{..}{\underset{.}{O}}:}$$

8.17 (a) Electron-pair geometry around N is tetrahedral. Molecular geometry is trigonal pyramidal.

$$\begin{array}{c} :\overset{..}{\underset{..}{Cl}}-\overset{..}{N}-H \\ | \\ H \end{array}$$

(b) Electron-pair geometry around O is tetrahedral. Molecular geometry is bent.

$$:\overset{..}{\underset{..}{Cl}}-\overset{..}{\underset{..}{O}}-\overset{..}{\underset{..}{Cl}}:$$

(c) Electron-pair geometry around C is linear. Molecular geometry is linear.

$$\left[\overset{..}{S}=C=\overset{..}{N}\right]^-$$

(d) Electron-pair geometry around O is tetrahedral. The molecular geometry is bent.

$$H-\overset{..}{\underset{..}{O}}-\overset{..}{\underset{..}{F}}:$$

8.19 (a) Electron-pair geometry around C is linear. Molecular geometry is linear.

$$\ddot{O}=C=\ddot{O}$$

(b) Electron-pair geometry around N is trigonal planar. Molecular geometry is bent.

$$\left[:\ddot{O}-\ddot{N}=\ddot{O} \right]^{-}$$

(c) Electron-pair geometry around O is trigonal planar. Molecular geometry is bent.

$$\ddot{O}=\ddot{O}-\ddot{O}:$$

(d) Electron-pair geometry around Cl atom is tetrahedral. Molecular geometry is bent.

$$\left[:\ddot{O}-\ddot{C}l-\ddot{O}: \right]^{-}$$

All have two atoms attached to the central atom. As the bond and lone pairs vary, the electron-pair geometries vary from linear to tetrahedral, and the molecular geometries vary from linear to bent.

8.21 (a) Electron-pair geometry around Cl is trigonal bipyramidal. Molecular geometry is linear.

$$\left[:\ddot{F}-\ddot{C}l-\ddot{F}: \right]^{-}$$

(b) Electron-pair geometry around Cl is trigonal bipyramidal. Molecular geometry is T-shaped.

$$\ddot{F}-\overset{\displaystyle .. }{Cl}-\ddot{F}:$$
$$|$$
$$:\ddot{F}:$$

(c) Electron-pair geometry around Cl is octahedral. Molecular geometry is square planar.

$$\left[\begin{array}{c} :\ddot{F}: \\ | \\ :\ddot{F}-Cl-\ddot{F}: \\ | \\ :\ddot{F}: \end{array} \right]^{-}$$

(d) Electron-pair geometry around Cl is octahedral. Molecular geometry is a square pyramid.

$$\begin{array}{c} :\ddot{F}: \\ :\ddot{F}\text{,,,}|\overset{\quad}{\quad}\ddot{F}: \\ Cl \\ :\ddot{F}\diagup\;\diagdown\ddot{F}: \end{array}$$

8.23 (a) Ideal O—S—O angle = 120°
(b) 120°
(c) 120°
(d) H—C—H = 109° and C—C—N angle = 180°

8.25 1 = 120°; 2 = 109°; 3 = 120°; 4 = 109°; 5 = 109°

The chain cannot be linear because the first two carbon atoms in the chain have bond angles of 109° and the final one has a bond angle of 120°. These bond angles do not lead to a linear chain.

8.27

$$\overset{\longrightarrow}{\underset{+\delta \quad -\delta}{C-O}} \qquad \overset{\longrightarrow}{\underset{+\delta \quad -\delta}{C-N}}$$

CO is more polar

$$\overset{\longrightarrow}{\underset{+\delta \quad -\delta}{P-Cl}} \qquad \overset{\longrightarrow}{\underset{+\delta \quad -\delta}{P-Br}}$$

PCl is more polar

$$\overset{\longrightarrow}{\underset{+\delta \quad -\delta}{B-O}} \qquad \overset{\longrightarrow}{\underset{+\delta \quad -\delta}{B-S}}$$

BO is more polar

$$\overset{\longrightarrow}{\underset{+\delta \quad -\delta}{B-F}} \qquad \overset{\longrightarrow}{\underset{+\delta \quad -\delta}{B-I}}$$

BF is more polar

8.29 (a) CH and CO bonds are polar.
(b) The CO bond is most polar, and O is the most negative atom.

8.31 (a) OH^-: The formal charge on O is −1 and on H it is 0.
(b) BH_4^-: Even though the formal charge on B is −1 and on H is 0, H is slightly more electronegative than B. The four H atoms are therefore more likely to bear the −1 charge of the ion. The BH bonds are polar with the H atom the negative end.
(c) The CH and CO bonds are all polar (but the C—C bond is not). The negative charge in the CO bonds lies on the O atoms.

8.33 Structure C is most reasonable. The charges are as small as possible and the negative charge resides on the more electronegative atom.

$$\underset{A}{\overset{-2 \;\; +1 \;\; +1}{:\ddot{N}-N\equiv O:}} \longleftrightarrow \underset{B}{\overset{-1 \;\; +1 \;\; 0}{:N=N=\ddot{O}}} \longleftrightarrow \underset{C}{\overset{0 \;\; +1 \;\; -1}{:N\equiv N-\ddot{O}:}}$$

8.35 (a)

$$\left[\overset{-1 \quad 0 \quad 0}{:\ddot{O}-\ddot{N}=\ddot{O}} \right]^{-} \longleftrightarrow \left[\overset{0 \quad 0 \quad -1}{\ddot{O}=\ddot{N}-\ddot{O}:} \right]^{-}$$

(b) If an H^+ ion were to attack NO_2^-, it would attach to an O atom because the O atoms bear the negative charge in this ion.

(c) $\qquad H-\ddot{O}-\ddot{N}=\ddot{O}: \longleftrightarrow :\ddot{O}-\ddot{N}=\ddot{O}-H$

The structure on the left is strongly favored because all of the atoms have zero formal charge, whereas the structure on the right has a −1 formal charge on one oxygen and a +1 formal charge on the other.

8.37 (i) The most polar bonds are in H_2O (because O and H have the largest difference in electronegativity).

(ii) Not polar: CO_2 and CCl_4

(iii) The F atom is more negatively charged.

8.39 (a) $BeCl_2$, nonpolar linear molecule

(b) HBF_2, polar trigonal planar molecule with F atoms the negative end of the dipole and the H atom the positive end.

(c) CH_3Cl, polar tetrahedral molecule. The Cl atom is the negative end of the dipole and the three H atoms are on the positive side of the molecule.

(d) SO_3, a nonpolar trigonal planar molecule

8.41 (a) Two C—H bonds, bond order is 1; 1 C=O bond, bond order is 2.

(b) Three S—O single bonds, bond order is 1.

(c) Two nitrogen–oxygen double bonds, bond order is 2.

(d) One N=O double bond, bond order is 2; one N—Cl bond, bond order is 1.

8.43 (a) B—Cl

(b) C—O

(c) P—O

(d) C=O

8.45 NO bond orders: 2 in NO_2^+, 1.5 in NO_2^-; 1.33 in NO_3^-. The NO bond is longest in NO_3^- and shortest in NO_2^+.

8.47 The CO bond in carbon monoxide is a triple bond, so it is both shorter and stronger than the CO double bond in H_2CO.

8.49 $\Delta_r H = -126$ kJ

8.51 O—F bond dissociation energy = 192 kJ/mol

8.53

Element	Valence Electrons
Li	1
Ti	4
Zn	2
Si	4
Cl	7

8.55 SeF_4, BrF_4^-, XeF_4

8.57

$$\left[\begin{array}{c} :O: \\ \| \\ H-C-O: \end{array} \right]^- \longleftrightarrow \left[\begin{array}{c} :O: \\ | \\ H-C=O \end{array} \right]^-$$

Bond order = 3/2

8.59 To estimate the enthalpy change, we need energies for the following bonds: O=O, H—H, and H—O.

Energy to break bonds = 498 kJ (for O=O) + 2 × 436 kJ (for H—H) = +1370 kJ.

Energy evolved when bonds are made = 4 × 463 kJ (for O—H) = −1852 kJ

Total energy = −482 kJ

8.61 All the species in the series have 16 valence electrons and all are linear.

(a) $\ddot{O}=C=\ddot{O} \longleftrightarrow :\ddot{O}-C\equiv O: \longleftrightarrow :O\equiv C-\ddot{O}:$

(b)

$$\left[\ddot{N}=N=\ddot{N} \right]^- \longleftrightarrow \left[:\ddot{N}-N\equiv N: \right]^- \longleftrightarrow \left[:N\equiv N-\ddot{N}: \right]^-$$

(c)

$$\left[\ddot{O}=C=\ddot{N} \right]^- \longleftrightarrow \left[:\ddot{O}-C\equiv N: \right]^- \longleftrightarrow \left[:O\equiv C-\ddot{N}: \right]^-$$

8.63 The N—O bonds in NO_2^- have a bond order of 1.5, whereas in NO_2^+ the bond order is 2. The shorter bonds (110 pm) are the NO bonds with the higher bond order (in NO_2^+), whereas the longer bonds (124 pm) in NO_2^- have a lower bond order.

8.65 The F—Cl—F bond angle in ClF_2^+, which has a tetrahedral electron-pair geometry, is approximately 109°.

$$\left[:\ddot{F}-\ddot{C}l-\ddot{F}: \right]^+$$

The ClF_2^- ion has a trigonal-bipyramidal electron-pair geometry with F atoms in the axial positions and the lone pairs in the equatorial positions. Therefore, the F—C—F angle is 180°.

$$\left[:\ddot{F}-\ddot{C}l-\ddot{F}: \right]^-$$

8.67 An H^+ ion will attach to an O atom of SO_3^{2-} and not to the S atom. The O atoms each have a formal charge of −1, whereas the S atom formal charge is +1.

$$\left[:\ddot{O}-\underset{\underset{:\ddot{O}:}{|}}{S}-\ddot{O}: \right]^{2-}$$

8.69 (a) Calculation from bond energies: $\Delta_r H° = -1070$ kJ/mol-rxn; $\Delta H° = -535$ kJ/mol CH_3OH

(b) Calculation from thermochemical data: $\Delta_r H° = -1352.3$ kJ/mol-rxn; $\Delta H° = -676$ kJ/mol CH_3OH

8.71 (a)

$$\left[:C\equiv N-\ddot{O}: \right]^- \longleftrightarrow \left[\ddot{C}=N=\ddot{O} \right]^- \longleftrightarrow \left[:\ddot{C}-N\equiv O: \right]^-$$
$$\quad {-1}\ {+1}\ {-1} \qquad\qquad {-2}\ {+1}\ {0} \qquad\qquad {-3}\ {+1}\ {+1}$$

(b) The first resonance structure is the most reasonable because oxygen, the most electronegative atom, has a negative formal charge, and the unfavorable negative charge on the least electronegative atom, carbon, is smallest.

(c) This species is so unstable because carbon, the least electronegative element in the ion, has a negative formal charge. In addition, all three resonance structures have an unfavorable charge distribution.

8.73

$$:-Xe \overset{\cdot\cdot}{\bigtriangledown}) 120° \qquad F-Cl \overset{\cdot\cdot}{\bigtriangledown}) 120°$$

(a) XeF_2 has three lone pairs around the Xe atom. The electron-pair geometry is trigonal bipyramidal. Because lone pairs require more space than bond pairs, it is better to place the lone pairs in the equator of the bipyramid where the angles between them are 120°.
(b) Like XeF_2, ClF_3 has a trigonal bipyramidal electron-pair geometry, but with only two lone pairs around the Cl. These are again placed in the equatorial plane where the angle between them is 120°.

8.75 (a) Angle 1 = 109°; angle 2 = 120°; angle 3 = 109°; angle 4 = 109°; and angle 5 = 109°.
(b) The O—H bond is the most polar bond.

8.77 $\Delta_r H = +146$ kJ = 2 $(\Delta H_{C-N}) + \Delta H_{C=O} - [\Delta H_{N-N} + \Delta H_{C\equiv O}]$

8.79 (a) Two C—H bonds and one O=O are broken and two O—C bonds and two H—O bonds are made in the reaction. $\Delta_r H = -318$ kJ. The reaction is exothermic.
(b) Acetone is polar.
(c) The O—H hydrogen atoms are the most positive in dihydroxyacetone.

8.81 (a) The C=C bond is stronger than the C—C bond.
(b) The C—C single bond is longer than the C=C double bond.
(c) Ethylene is nonpolar, whereas acrolein is polar.
(d) The reaction is exothermic ($\Delta_r H = -45$ kJ).

8.83 $\Delta_r H = -211$ kJ

8.85 Methanol is a polar solvent. Methanol contains two bonds of significant polarity, the C—O bond and the O—H bond. The C—O—H atoms are in a bent configuration, leading to a polar molecule. Toluene contains only carbon and hydrogen atoms, which have similar electronegativites and which are arranged in tetrahedral or trigonal planar geometries, leading to a molecule that is largely nonpolar.

8.87 (a)

$$H-\overset{\overset{\displaystyle H}{|}}{C}-S-\overset{\overset{\displaystyle H}{|}}{C}-H$$
$$\qquad \underset{H}{|} \qquad \underset{H}{|}$$

The bond angles are all approximately 109°.

(b) The sulfur atom should have a slight partial negative charge, and the carbons should have slight partial positive charges. The molecule has a bent shape and is polar.
(c) 1.6×10^{18} molecules

8.89 (a) Odd electron molecules: BrO (13 electrons)
(b) $Br_2(g) \rightarrow 2\ Br(g) \qquad \Delta_r H = +193$ kJ
$2\ Br(g) + O_2(g) \rightarrow 2\ BrO(g) \qquad \Delta_r H = +96$ kJ
$BrO(g) + H_2O(g) \rightarrow HOBr(g) + OH(g)$
$\qquad\qquad\qquad\qquad\qquad \Delta_r H = 0$ kJ
(c) ΔH of formation $[HOBr(g)] = -101$ kJ/mol
(d) The reactions in part (b) are endothermic (or thermal-neutral for the third reaction), and the enthalpy of formation in part (c) is exothermic.

8.91 (a) BF_3 is a nonpolar molecule, but replacing one or two F atoms with an H atom (HBF_2 and H_2BF) gives polar molecules.
(b) $BeCl_2$ is not polar, whereas replacing a Cl atom with a Br atom gives a polar molecule (BeClBr).

CHAPTER 9

9.1 The electron-pair and molecular geometry of $CHCl_3$ are both tetrahedral. Each C—Cl bond is formed by the overlap of an sp^3 hybrid orbital on the C atom with a $3p$ orbital on a Cl atom to form a sigma bond. A C—H sigma bond is formed by the overlap of an sp^3 hybrid orbital on the C atom with an H atom $1s$ orbital.

$$\overset{\overset{\displaystyle :\ddot{C}l:}{|}}{H-C-\ddot{C}l:}$$
$$\qquad \underset{:\ddot{C}l:}{|}$$

9.3

	Electron-Pair Geometry	Molecular Geometry	Hybrid Orbital Set
(a)	trigonal planar	trigonal planar	sp^2
(b)	linear	linear	sp
(c)	tetrahedral	tetrahedral	sp^3
(d)	trigonal planar	trigonal planar	sp^2

9.5 (a) C, sp^3; O, sp^3
(b) CH_3, sp^3; middle C, sp^2; CH_2, sp^2
(c) CH_2, sp^3; CO_2H, sp^2; N, sp^3

9.7 (a) Electron-pair geometry is octahedral. Molecular geometry is octahedral. S: sp^3d^2

$$\begin{bmatrix} & :\ddot{F}: & \\ :\ddot{F}\cdots & \overset{:\ddot{F}:}{|}\underset{|}{Si}\cdots & \ddot{F}: \\ :\ddot{F} & | & \ddot{F}: \\ & :\ddot{F}: & \end{bmatrix}^{2-}$$

(b) Electron-pair geometry is trigonal-bipyramidal. Molecular geometry is seesaw. Se: sp^3d

(c) Electron-pair geometry is trigonal-bipyramidal. Molecular geometry is linear. I: sp^3d

(d) Electron-pair geometry is octahedral. Molecular geometry is square-planar. Xe: sp^3d^2

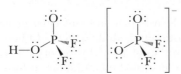

9.9 There are 32 valence electrons in both HPO_2F_2 and its anion. Both have a tetrahedral molecular geometry, and so the P atom in both is sp^3 hybridized.

9.11 The C atom is sp^2-hybridized. Two of the sp^2 hybrid orbitals are used to form C—Cl sigma bonds, and the third is used to form the C—O sigma bond. The p orbital not used in the C atom hybrid orbitals is used to form the CO pi bond.

9.13

$$\begin{array}{c} H_3C \qquad CH_3 \\ C{=}C \\ H \qquad H \end{array} \qquad \begin{array}{c} H \qquad CH_3 \\ C{=}C \\ Cl \qquad H \end{array}$$

cis isomer   *trans* isomer

9.15 H_2^+ ion: $(\sigma_{1s})^1$. Bond order is 0.5. The bond in H_2^+ is weaker than in H_2 (bond order =1).

9.17 MO diagram for C_2^{2-} ion

$$\begin{array}{l} \underline{\hspace{2cm}} \quad \sigma^*_{2p} \\[4pt] \underline{\hspace{1cm}}\;\underline{\hspace{1cm}} \quad \pi^*_{2p} \\[4pt] \underline{\uparrow\downarrow} \quad \sigma_{2p} \\[4pt] \underline{\uparrow\downarrow}\;\underline{\uparrow\downarrow} \quad \pi_{2p} \\[4pt] \underline{\uparrow\downarrow} \quad \sigma^*_{2s} \\[4pt] \underline{\uparrow\downarrow} \quad \sigma_{2s} \end{array}$$

The ion has 10 valence electrons (isoelectronic with N_2). There are one net sigma bond and two net pi bonds, for a bond order of 3. The bond order increases by 1 on going from C_2 to C_2^{2-}. The ion is not paramagnetic.

9.19 (a) CO has 10 valence electrons

$$[core] (\sigma_{2s})^2 (\sigma^*_{2s})^2 (\pi_{2p})^4 (\sigma_{2p})^2$$

(b) σ_{2p}

(c) Diamagnetic

(d) There are net 1 σ bond and 2 π bonds; bond order is 3.

9.21

$$\left[\begin{array}{c} :\ddot{F}: \\ | \\ :\ddot{F}{-}Al{-}\ddot{F}: \\ | \\ :\ddot{F}: \end{array} \right]^-$$

The electron pair and molecular geometries are both tetrahedral. The Al atom is sp^3 hybridized, and so the Al—F bonds are formed by overlap of an Al sp^3 orbital with a p orbital on each F atom. The formal charge on each of the fluorines is zero, and that on the Al is -1. This is not a reasonable charge distribution because the less electronegative atom, aluminum, has the negative charge.

9.23

Molecule/Ion	O—S—O Angle	Hybrid Orbitals
SO_2	120°	sp^2
SO_3	120°	sp^2
SO_3^{2-}	109°	sp^3
SO_4^{2-}	109°	sp^3

9.25
$$\left[:\ddot{O}{-}N{=}\ddot{O} \right]^- \longleftrightarrow \left[\ddot{O}{=}N{-}\ddot{O}: \right]^-$$

The electron-pair geometry is trigonal planar. The molecular geometry is bent (or angular). The O—N—O angle will be about 120°, the average N—O bond order is 3/2, and the N atom is sp^2 hybridized.

9.27 The resonance structures of N_2O, with formal charges, are shown here.

$$\overset{-2\;\;+1\;\;+1}{:\ddot{N}{-}N{\equiv}O:} \longleftrightarrow \overset{-1\;\;+1\;\;0}{\ddot{N}{=}N{=}\ddot{O}} \longleftrightarrow \overset{0\;\;+1\;\;-1}{:N{\equiv}N{-}\ddot{O}:}$$

A   B   C

The central N atom is sp hybridized in all structures. The two sp hybrid orbitals on the central N atom are used to form N—N and N—O σ bonds. The two p orbitals not used in the N atom hybridization are used to form the required π bonds.

9.29 (a) All three have the formula C_2H_4O. They are usually referred to as structural isomers.

(b) *Ethylene oxide:* Both C atoms are sp^3 hybridized.
Acetaldehyde: The CH_3 carbon atom has sp^3 hybridization, and the other C atom is sp^2 hybridized.
Vinyl alcohol: Both C atoms are sp^2 hybridized.

(c) *Ethylene oxide:* 109°.
Acetaldehyde: 109°
Vinyl alcohol: 120°.
(d) All are polar.
(e) Acetaldehyde has the strongest CO bond, and vinyl alcohol has the strongest C—C bond.

9.31 (a) CH_3 carbon atom: sp^3
C=N carbon atom: sp^2
N atom: sp^2
(b) C—N—O bond angle = 120°

9.33 (a) C(1) = sp^2; O(2) = sp^3; N(3) = sp^3; C(4) = sp^3;
P(5) = sp^3
(b) Angle A = 120°; angle B = 109°; angle C = 109°;
angle D = 109°
(c) The P—O and O—H bonds are most polar
($\Delta\chi$ = 1.3).

9.35 (a) C=O bond is most polar.
(b) 18 sigma bonds and five pi bonds
(c)

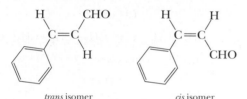

trans isomer   *cis* isomer

(d) All C atoms are sp^2 hybridized.
(e) All bond angles are 120°.

9.37 (a) The Sb in SbF_5 is sp^3d hybridized; whereas it is sp^3d^2 hybridized in SbF_6^-.
(b) The molecular geometry of the H_2F^+ ion is bent or angular, and the F atom is sp^3 hybridized.

$$\left[\; \ddot{\underset{\displaystyle H}{\overset{\displaystyle F}{|}}}\text{----} H \; \right]^+$$

9.39 (a) The peroxide ion has a bond order of 1.

$$\left[:\ddot{O}-\ddot{O}: \right]^{2-}$$

(b) [core electrons] $(\sigma_{2s})^2(\sigma^*_{2s})^2(\sigma_{2p})^2(\pi_{2p})^4(\pi^*_{2p})^4$

This configuration also leads to a bond order of 1.

(c) Both theories lead to a diamagnetic ion with a bond order of 1.

9.41 Paramagnetic diatomic molecules: B_2 and O_2

Bond order of 1: Li_2, B_2, F_2; Bond order of 2: C_2 and O_2; Highest bond order: N_2

9.43 CN has nine valence electrons
[core electrons] $(\sigma_{2s})^2(\sigma^*_{2s})^2(\pi_{2p})^4(\sigma_{2p})^1$
(a) HOMO, σ_{2p}
(b, c) Bond order = 2.5 (0.5 σ bond and 2 π bonds)
(d) Paramagnetic

9.45 (a) All C atoms are sp^3 hybridized
(b) About 109°
(c) Polar
(d) The six-membered ring cannot be planar, owing to the tetrahedral C atoms of the ring. The bond angles are all 109°.

9.47 (a) The geometry about the boron atom is trigonal planar in BF_3, but tetrahedral in $H_3N—BF_3$.
(b) Boron is sp^2 hybridized in BF_3 but sp^3 hybridized in $H_3N—BF_3$.
(c) Yes
(d) The ammonia molecule is polar with the N atom partially negative. While the BF_3 molecule is nonpolar overall, each of the B—F bonds is polarized such that the B has a partial positive charge. The partially negative N in NH_3 is attracted to the partially positive B in BF_3.
(e) One of the lone pairs on the oxygen of H_2O can form a coordinate covalent bond with the B in BF_3. The resulting compound would be (the lone pairs on the F's not shown):

$$H-\underset{\displaystyle H}{\overset{}{O}}-\underset{\displaystyle F}{\overset{\displaystyle F}{B}}-F$$

9.49 (a) NH_2^-: electron-pair geometry = tetrahedral, molecular geometry = bent, hybridization of N = sp^3

SO_3: electron-pair geometry = molecular geometry = trigonal planar, hybridization of S = sp^2

(b)

$$\left[\; \underset{\displaystyle H}{\overset{\displaystyle H}{}}N\text{-}\underset{\underset{\displaystyle :\ddot{O}:}{|}}{\overset{\overset{\displaystyle :\ddot{O}:}{|}}{S}}\text{----}\ddot{O}: \; \right]^-$$

The bond angles around the N and the S are all approximately 109°.
(c) The N does not undergo any change in its hybridication; the S changes from sp^2 to sp^3.
(d) The SO_3 is the acceptor of an electron pair in this reaction. The electrostatic potential map confirms this to be reasonable because the sulfur has a partial positive charge.

9.51 A C atom may form, at most, four hybrid orbitals (sp^3). The minimum number is two, for example, the sp hybrid orbitals used by carbon in CO. Carbon has only four valence orbitals, so it cannot form more than four hybrid orbitals.

9.53 (a) C, sp^2; N, sp^3

(b) The amide or peptide link has two resonance structures (shown here with formal charges on the O and N atoms). Structure B is less favorable, owing to the separation of charge.

$$\text{Structure A} \longleftrightarrow \text{Structure B}$$

A   B

(c) The fact that the amide link is planar indicates that structure B has some importance.

The principal sites of positive charge are the nitrogen in the amide linkage, and the hydrogen of the —O—H group. The principal regions of negative charge are oxygen atoms and the nitrogen of the free $-NH_2$ group.

9.55 MO theory is better to use when explaining or understanding the effect of adding energy to molecules. A molecule can absorb energy and an electron can thus be promoted to a higher level. Using MO theory, one can see how this can occur. Additionally, MO theory is a better model to use to predict whether a molecule is paramagnetic.

9.57 Lowest Energy = Orbital C < Orbital B < Orbital A = Highest Energy

9.59 (a) The attractive forces must be greater than the repulsive forces if a covalent bond is to form.

(b) As the atoms approach each other, the energy drops as the electron clouds overlap and electron density increases between the two nuclei. If the atoms approach still more closely, electrostatic repulsion of the nuclei for each other and of the electrons for each other increases dramatically.

(c) In neon, all of the orbitals in the $2s$ and $2p$ sublevels are filled with paired electrons; there is no orbital available that can overlap with another orbital on another atom. In the case of fluorine, there is an orbital on each atom that is not completely filled that can overlap with another orbital to form a bond.

9.61 (a) The molecule with the double bond requires a great deal more energy because the π bond must be broken in order for the ends of the molecules to rotate relative to each other.

(b) No. The carbon–carbon double bonds in the molecule prevent the CH_2 fragments from rotating.

CHAPTER 10

10.1 Heptane

10.3 $C_{14}H_{30}$ is an alkane and C_5H_{10} could be a cycloalkane.

10.5 2,3-dimethylbutane

10.7 (a) 2,3-Dimethylhexane

$$CH_3-CH-CH-CH_2-CH_2-CH_3$$
with CH_3 on second carbon and CH_3 on third carbon

(b) 2,3-Dimethyloctane

$$CH_3-CH-CH-CH_2-CH_2-CH_2-CH_2-CH_3$$
with CH_3 and CH_3 substituents

(c) 3-Ethylheptane

$$CH_3-CH_2-CH-CH_2-CH_2-CH_2-CH_3$$
with CH_2CH_3 substituent

(d) 3-Ethyl-2-methylhexane

$$CH_3-CH-CH-CH_2-CH_2-CH_3$$
with CH_2CH_3 and CH_3 substituents

10.9

$$H_3C-\overset{H}{\underset{CH_3}{C}}-CH_2CH_2CH_2CH_2CH_3 \quad \text{2-methylheptane}$$

$$CH_3CH_2CH_2-\overset{H}{\underset{CH_3}{C}}-CH_2CH_2CH_3 \quad \text{4-methylheptane}$$

$$CH_3CH_2-\overset{H}{\underset{CH_3}{\overset{*}{C}}}-CH_2CH_2CH_2CH_3 \quad \text{3-methylheptane. The C atom with an asterisk is chiral.}$$

10.11

$$CH_3CH_2CH_2-\overset{H}{\underset{CH_2CH_3}{C}}-CH_2CH_2CH_3 \quad \text{4-ethylheptane. The compound is not chiral.}$$

$$CH_3CH_2-\overset{H}{\underset{CH_2CH_3}{C}}-CH_2CH_2CH_2CH_3 \quad \text{3-ethylheptane. Not chiral.}$$

10.13 C_4H_{10}, butane: a low-molecular–weight fuel gas at room temperature and pressure. Slightly soluble in water.

$C_{12}H_{26}$, dodecane: a colorless liquid at room temperature. Expected to be insoluble in water but quite soluble in nonpolar solvents.

10.15

cis-4-methyl-2-hexene

trans-4-methyl-2-hexene

10.17 (a)

1-pentene

2-methyl-2-butene

2-methyl-1-butene

cis-2-pentene

3-methyl-1-butene

trans-2-pentene

(b)

cyclopentane

10.19 (a) 1,2-Dibromopropane, $CH_3CHBrCH_2Br$

(b) Pentane, C_5H_{12}

10.21 1-Butene, $CH_3CH_2CH=CH_2$, or 1-butene

10.23 Four isomers are possible.

cis-1-chloropropene

2-chloropropene

trans-1-chloropropene

3-chloro-1-propene

10.25

m-dichlorobenzene

o-bromotoluene

10.27

$CH_3CH_2Cl/AlCl_3$

ethylbenzene

10.29

$CH_3Cl/AlCl_3$

1,2,4-trimethylbenzene

10.31 (a) 1-Propanol, primary

(b) 1-Butanol, primary

(c) 2-Methyl-2-propanol, tertiary

(d) 2-Methyl-2-butanol, tertiary

10.33 (a) Ethylamine, $CH_3CH_2NH_2$

(b) Dipropylamine, $(CH_3CH_2CH_2)_2NH$

(c) Butyldimethylamine

(d) triethylamine

10.33 (a) 1-butanol, $CH_3CH_2CH_2CH_2OH$

(b) 2-butanol

(c) 2-methyl-1-propanol

(d) 2-methyl-2-propanol

10.37 (a) $C_6H_5NH_2(aq) + HCl(aq) \rightarrow (C_6H_5NH_3)Cl(aq)$

(b) $(CH_3)_3N(aq) + H_2SO_4(aq) \rightarrow$
$[(CH_3)_3NH]HSO_4(aq)$

10.39

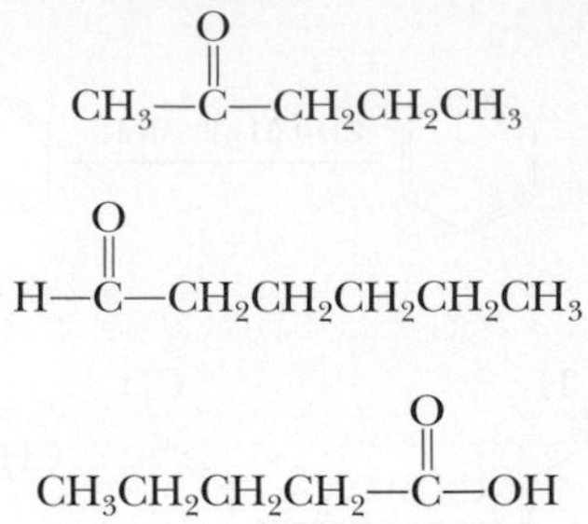

$$CH_3-\overset{\overset{\displaystyle O}{\|}}{C}-CH_2CH_2CH_3$$

$$H-\overset{\overset{\displaystyle O}{\|}}{C}-CH_2CH_2CH_2CH_2CH_3$$

$$CH_3CH_2CH_2CH_2-\overset{\overset{\displaystyle O}{\|}}{C}-OH$$

10.41 (a) Acid, 3-methylpentanoic acid
(b) Ester, methyl propanoate
(c) Ester, butyl acetate (or butyl ethanoate)
(d) Acid, *p*-bromobenzoic acid

10.43 (a) Pentanoic acid (see Question 39c)
(b) 1-Pentanol, $CH_3CH_2CH_2CH_2CH_2OH$

(c) $H_3C-\overset{\overset{\displaystyle OH}{|}}{\underset{\underset{\displaystyle H}{|}}{C}}-CH_2CH_2CH_2CH_2CH_2CH_3$

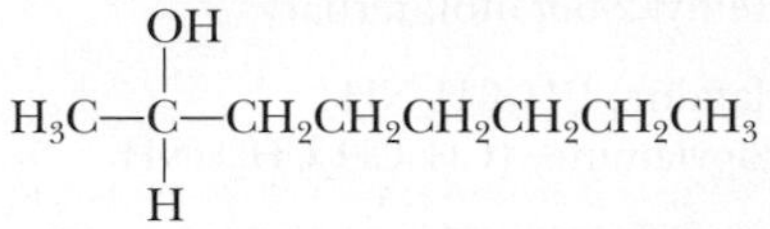

(d) No reaction. A ketone is not oxidized by $KMnO_4$.

10.45 Step 1: Oxidize 1-propanol to propanoic acid.

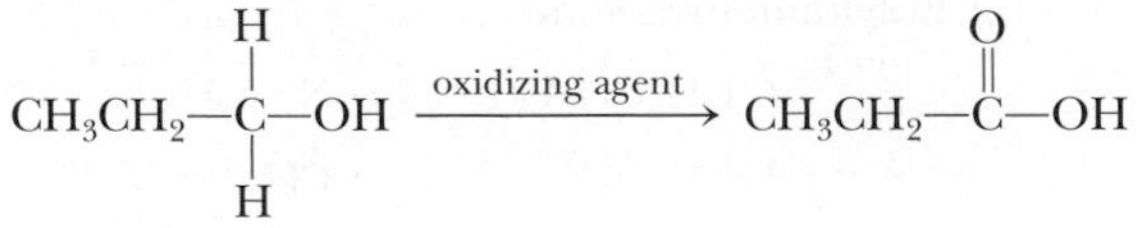

$$CH_3CH_2-\overset{\overset{\displaystyle H}{|}}{\underset{\underset{\displaystyle H}{|}}{C}}-OH \xrightarrow{\text{oxidizing agent}} CH_3CH_2-\overset{\overset{\displaystyle O}{\|}}{C}-OH$$

Step 2: Combine propanoic acid and 1-propanol.

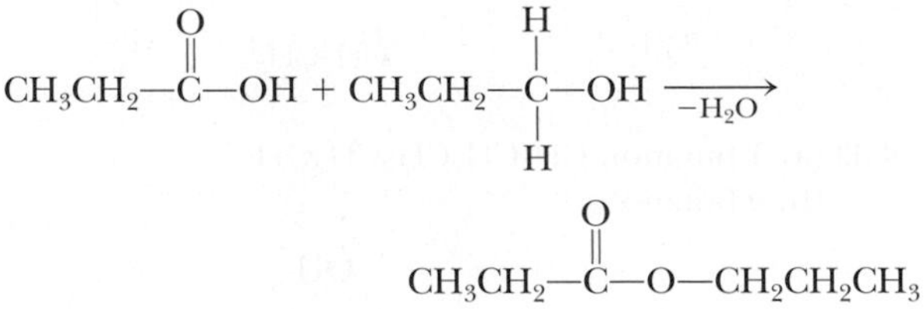

$$CH_3CH_2-\overset{\overset{\displaystyle O}{\|}}{C}-OH + CH_3CH_2-\overset{\overset{\displaystyle H}{|}}{\underset{\underset{\displaystyle H}{|}}{C}}-OH \xrightarrow{-H_2O}$$

$$CH_3CH_2-\overset{\overset{\displaystyle O}{\|}}{C}-O-CH_2CH_2CH_3$$

10.47 Sodium acetate, $NaCH_3CO_2$, and 1-butanol, $CH_3CH_2CH_2CH_2OH$

10.49 (a) Trigonal planar
(b) 120°
(c) The molecule is chiral. There are four different groups around the carbon atom marked 2.
(d) The acidic H atom is the H attached to the CO_2H (carboxyl) group.

10.51 (a) Alcohol (c) Acid
(b) Amide (d) Ester

10.53 (a) Prepare polyvinyl acetate (PVA) from vinylacetate.

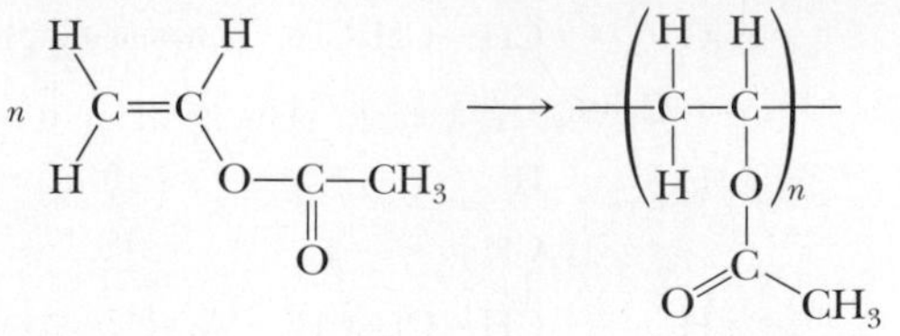

(b) The three units of PVA:

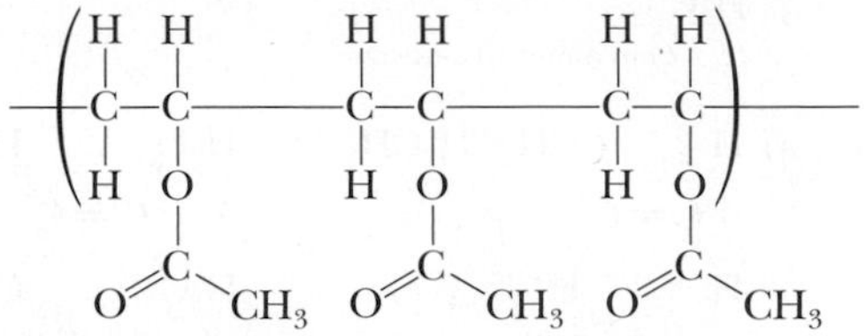

(c) Hydrolysis of polyvinyl alcohol

10.55 Illustrated here is a segment of a copolymer composed of two units of 1,1–dichloroethylene and two units of chloroethylene.

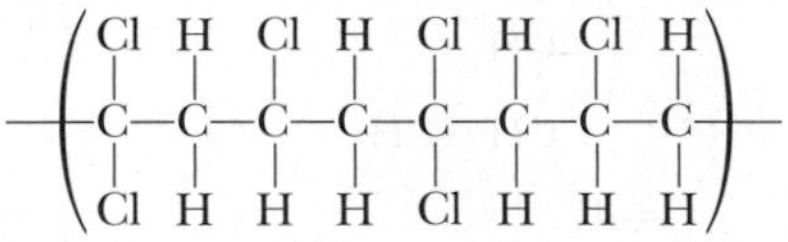

10.57

(a)

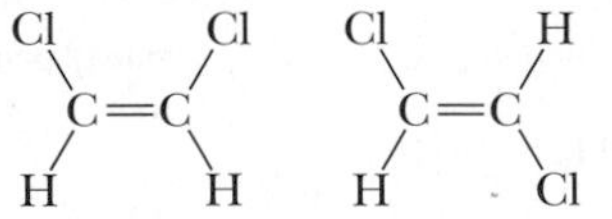

cis isomer   *trans* isomer

(b)

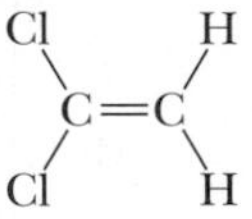

10.59

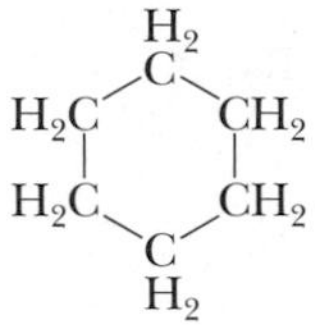

cyclohexane 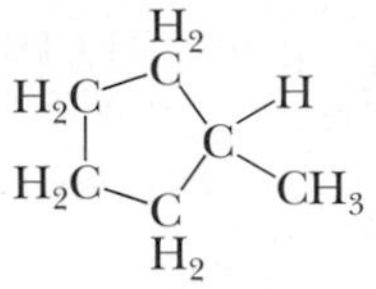   methylcyclopentane

$CH_3CH{=}CHCH_2CH_2C$
2-hexene
Other isomers are possible by moving the double bond and with a branched chain.

10.61

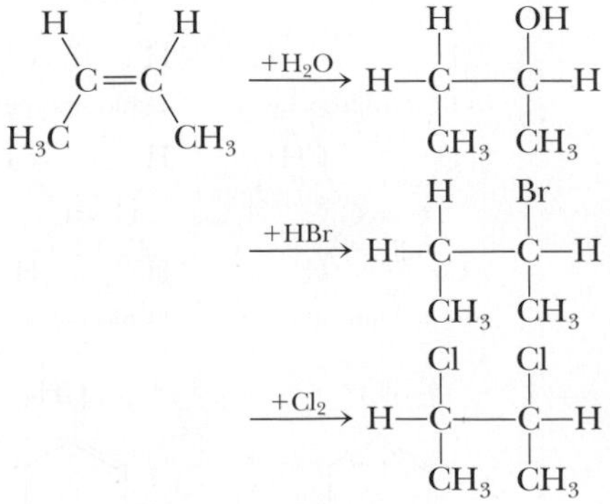

10.63 (a)

$$H_3C-\overset{\overset{\displaystyle O}{\|}}{C}-OH + NaOH \longrightarrow \left[H_3C-\overset{\overset{\displaystyle O}{\|}}{C}-O^- \right] Na^+ + H_2O$$

(b)

$$H_3C-\overset{\overset{\displaystyle H}{|}}{N}-H + HCl \longrightarrow CH_3NH_3^+ + Cl^-$$

10.65

$$n\,HOCH_2CH_2OH + n\,HO-\overset{\overset{\displaystyle O}{\|}}{C}-\underset{}{\bigcirc}-\overset{\overset{\displaystyle O}{\|}}{C}-OH \longrightarrow$$

$$\left(O-\overset{\overset{\displaystyle O}{\|}}{C}-\underset{}{\bigcirc}-\overset{\overset{\displaystyle O}{\|}}{C}-OCH_2CH_2O \right)_n + n\,H_2O$$

10.67 (a) 2, 3-Dimethylpentane

$$H_3C-\overset{\overset{\displaystyle CH_3}{|}}{\underset{\underset{\displaystyle CH_3}{|}}{C}}-CH_2CH_2CH_3$$

(b) 3, 3-Dimethylpentane

$$CH_3CH_2-\overset{\overset{\displaystyle CH_2CH_3}{|}}{\underset{\underset{\displaystyle CH_2CH_3}{|}}{C}}-CH_2CH_3$$

(c) 3-Ethyl-2-methylpentane

$$CH_3-\overset{\overset{\displaystyle H}{|}}{\underset{\underset{\displaystyle CH_3}{|}}{C}}-\overset{\overset{\displaystyle CH_2CH_3}{|}}{\underset{\underset{\displaystyle H}{|}}{C}}-CH_2CH_3$$

(d) 3-Ethylhexane

$$CH_3CH_2-\overset{\overset{\displaystyle CH_2CH_3}{|}}{\underset{\underset{\displaystyle H}{|}}{C}}-CH_2CH_2CH_3$$

10.69

1,1-Dichloropropane

$$H-\overset{\overset{\displaystyle Cl}{|}}{\underset{\underset{\displaystyle Cl}{|}}{C}}-CH_2CH_3$$

1,2-Dichloropropane

$$H-\overset{\overset{\displaystyle Cl}{|}}{\underset{\underset{\displaystyle H}{|}}{C}}-\overset{\overset{\displaystyle Cl}{|}}{\underset{\underset{\displaystyle H}{|}}{C}}-CH_3$$

1,3-Dichloropropane

$$H-\overset{\overset{\displaystyle Cl}{|}}{\underset{\underset{\displaystyle H}{|}}{C}}-\overset{\overset{\displaystyle H}{|}}{\underset{\underset{\displaystyle H}{|}}{C}}-\overset{\overset{\displaystyle Cl}{|}}{\underset{\underset{\displaystyle H}{|}}{C}}-H$$

2,2-Dichloropropane

$$H-\overset{\overset{\displaystyle H}{|}}{\underset{\underset{\displaystyle H}{|}}{C}}-\overset{\overset{\displaystyle Cl}{|}}{\underset{\underset{\displaystyle Cl}{|}}{C}}-\overset{\overset{\displaystyle H}{|}}{\underset{\underset{\displaystyle H}{|}}{C}}-H$$

10.71

1,2,3-trimethylbenzene   1,2,4-trimethylbenzene   1,3,5-trimethylbenzene

10.73 Replace the carboxylic acid group with an H atom.

10.75

butane (not chiral)

$$H-\overset{\overset{\displaystyle CH_3}{|}}{\underset{\underset{\displaystyle CH_3}{|}}{C}}-CH_3$$

10.77

glyceryl   glycerol   sodium laurate
trilaurate

10.79

add H₂ →

H—C—C—H (with H, CH₂OH on top, H, H below)

oxidize →

C=C (with H, CO₂H and H, H)

polymerize →

$\left(\begin{array}{c}\text{H CH}_2\text{OH H CH}_2\text{OH}\\ \text{C—C———C—C}\\ \text{H H H H}\end{array}\right)_n$

CH₃CO₂H →

$H_3C-\overset{O}{\overset{\|}{C}}-O-CH_2CH=CH_2$

10.81 (a)

H—C—C=C—H +HBr → H—C—C—C—H (with Br)

2-bromopropane

(b)

$H_3C-C-C=C-H \xrightarrow{+H_2O} H_3C-C-C-C-H$ (with CH₃, OH)

2-methyl-2-butanol

(c)

$H_3C-C=C-C-H \xrightarrow{+H_2O} H_3C-C-C-C-H$ (with CH₃, OH)

10.83 Compound (b), acetaldehyde, and (c), ethanol, produce acetic acid when oxidized.

10.85 Cyclohexene, a cyclic alkene, will add Br₂ readily (to give $C_6H_{12}Br_2$). Benzene, however, needs much more stringent conditions to react with bromine; then Br₂ will substitute for H atoms on benzene and not add to the ring.

10.87 (a) The compound is either propanone, a ketone, or propanal, an aldehyde.

propanone (a ketone) propanal (an aldehyde)

(b) The ketone will not undergo oxidation, but the aldehyde will be oxidized to the acid, $CH_3CH_2CO_2H$. Thus, the unknown is likely propanal.

(c) Propanoic acid

10.89 2-Propanol will react with an oxidizing agent such as KMnO₄ (to give the ketone), whereas methyl ethyl ether ($CH_3OC_2H_5$) will not react. In addition, the alcohol should be more soluble in water than the ether.

10.91

$H_2C=C-C-C-CH_3$ (with CH₃, H on top, H, CH₃, H below)

X = 3,3-dimethyl-1-pentene

↓ +H₂O

$H_3C-C-C-C-CH_3$ (with OH, CH₃, H on top, H, CH₃, H below)

Y = 3,3-dimethyl-2-pentanol

oxidizing agent →

$H_3C-\overset{O}{\overset{\|}{C}}-C-C-CH_3$ (with CH₃, H on top, CH₃, H below)

3,3-dimethyl-2-pentanone

10.93

H—C—H (methane)	methane	four single bonds
(formaldehyde, O double bond C, H H)	formaldehyde	one double bond and two single bonds
C=C=C (allene)	allene	two double bonds
H—C≡C—H (acetylene)	acetylene	one single bond and one triple bond

10.95 (a) Cross-linking makes the material very rigid and inflexible.

(b) The OH groups give the polymer a high affinity for water.

(c) Hydrogen bonding allows the chains to form coils and sheets with high tensile strength.

10.97 (a) Ethane heat of combustion = −47.51 kJ/g
Ethanol heat of combustion = −26.82 kJ/g

(b) The heat obtained from the combustion of ethanol is less negative than for ethane, so partially oxidizing ethane to form ethanol decreases the amount of energy per mole available from the combustion of the substance.

10.99 (a) Empirical formula, CHO

(b) Molecular formula, $C_4H_4O_4$

(c)

$HO-\overset{O}{\overset{\|}{C}}-C=C-\overset{O}{\overset{\|}{C}}-OH$ (with H H)

(d) All four C atoms are sp² hybridized.

(e) 120°

CHAPTER 11

11.1 (a) 0.58 atm
(b) 0.59 bar
(c) 59 kPa

11.3 (a) 0.754 bar
(b) 650 kPa
(c) 934 kPa

11.5 2.70×10^2 mm Hg

11.7 3.7 L

11.9 250 mm Hg

11.11 3.2×10^2 mm Hg

11.13 9.72 atm

11.15 (a) 75 mL O_2
(b) 150 mL NO_2

11.17 0.919 atm

11.19 $V = 2.9$ L

11.21 1.9×10^6 g He

11.23 3.7×10^{-4} g/L

11.25 34.0 g/mol

11.27 57.5 g/mol

11.29 Molar mass = 74.9 g/mol; B_6H_{10}

11.31 0.039 mol H_2; 0.096 atm; 73 mm Hg

11.33 170 g NaN_3

11.35 1.7 atm O_2

11.37 4.1 atm H_2; 1.6 atm Ar; total pressure = 5.7 atm

11.39 (a) 0.30 mol halothane/1 mol O_2
(b) 3.0×10^2 g halothane

11.41 (a) CO_2 has the higher kinetic energy.
(b) The average speed of the H_2 molecules is greater than the average speed of the CO_2 molecules.
(c) The number of CO_2 molecules is greater than the number of H_2 molecules [$n(CO_2) = 1.8n(H_2)$].
(d) The mass of CO_2 is greater than the mass of H_2.

11.43 Average speed of CO_2 molecule = 3.65×10^4 cm/s

11.45 Average speed increases (and molar mass decreases) in the order $CH_2F_2 < Ar < N_2 < CH_4$.

11.47 (a) F_2 (38 g/mol) effuses faster than CO_2 (44 g/mol).
(b) N_2 (28 g/mol) effuses faster than O_2 (32 g/mol).
(c) C_2H_4 (28.1 g/mol) effuses faster than C_2H_6 (30.1 g/mol).
(d) $CFCl_3$ (137 g/mol) effuses faster than $C_2Cl_2F_4$ (171 g/mol).

11.49 36 g/mol

11.51 *P* from the van der Waals equation = 26.0 atm

P from the ideal gas law = 30.6 atm

11.53 (a) Standard atmosphere: 1 atm; 760 mm Hg; 101.325 kPa; 1.013 bar.
(b) N_2 partial pressure: 0.780 atm; 593 mm Hg; 79.1 kPa; 0.791 bar
(c) H_2 pressure: 131 atm; 9.98×10^4 mm Hg; 1.33×10^4 kPa; 133 bar
(d) Air: 0.333 atm; 253 mm Hg; 33.7 kPa; 0.337 bar

11.55 $T = 290.$ K or 17 °C

11.57 $2 C_4H_9SH(g) + 15 O_2(g) \rightarrow$
$8 CO_2(g) + 10 H_2O(g) + 2 SO_2(g)$

Total pressure = 37.3 mm Hg. Partial pressures: CO_2 = 14.9 mm Hg, H_2O = 18.6 mm Hg, and SO_2 = 3.73 mm Hg.

11.59 4 mol

11.61 Ni is the limiting reactant; 1.31 g $Ni(CO)_4$

11.63 (a, b) Sample 4 (He) has the largest number of molecules and sample 3 (H_2 at 27 °C and 760 mm Hg) has the fewest number of molecules.
(c) Sample 2 (Ar)

11.65 8.54 g $Fe(CO)_5$

11.67 S_2F_{10}

11.69 (a) 28.7 g/mol $\simeq$ 29 g/mol
(b) *X* of O_2 = 0.17 and *X* of N_2 = 0.83

11.71 Molar mass = 86.4 g/mol. The gas is probably ClO_2F.

11.73 $n(He) = 0.0128$ mol

11.75 Weight percent $KClO_3$ = 69.1%

11.77 (a) $NO_2 < O_2 < NO$
(b) $P(O_2) = 75$ mm Hg
(c) $P(NO_2) = 150$ mm Hg

11.79 $P(NH_3) = 69$ mm Hg and $P(F_2) = 51$ mm Hg

Pressure after reaction = 17 mm Hg

11.81 At 20 °C, there is 7.8×10^{-3} g H_2O/L. At 0 °C, there is 4.6×10^{-3} g H_2O/L.

11.83 The mixture contains 0.22 g CO_2 and 0.77 g CO.

$P(CO_2) = 0.22$ atm; $P(O_2) = 0.12$ atm; $P(CO) = 1.22$ atm

11.85 The formula of the iron compound is $Fe(CO)_5$.

11.87 (a) $P(B_2H_6) = 0.0160$ atm
(b) $P(H_2) = 0.0320$ atm, so $P_{total} = 0.0480$ atm

11.89 Amount of Na_2CO_3 = 0.00424 mol
Amount of $NaHCO_3$ = 0.00951 mol
Amount of CO_2 produced = 0.0138 mol
Volume of CO_2 produced = 0.343 L

11.91 Decomposition of 1 mol of $Cu(NO_3)_2$ should give 2 mol NO_2 and ½ mol of O_2. Total actual amount = 4.72×10^{-3} mol of gas.
(a) Average molar mass = 41.3 g/mol.
(b) Mole fractions: $X(NO_2) = 0.666$ and $X(O_2) = 0.334$
(c) Amount of each gas: 3.13×10^{-3} mol NO_2 and 1.57×10^{-3} mol O_2
(d) If some NO_2 molecules combine to form N_2O_4, the apparent mole fraction of NO_2 would be smaller than expected (= 0.8). As this is the case, it is apparent that some N_2O_4 has been formed (as is observed in the experiment).

11.93 (a) 10.0 g of O_2 represents more molecules than 10.0 g of CO_2. Therefore, O_2 has the greater partial pressure.
(b) The average speed of the O_2 molecules is greater than the average speed of the CO_2 molecules.
(c) The gases are at the same temperature and so have the same average kinetic energy.

11.95 (a) $P(C_2H_2) > P(CO)$
(b) There are more molecules in the C_2H_2 container than in the CO container.

11.97 (a) Not a gas. A gas would expand to an infinite volume.
(b) Not a gas. A density of 8.2 g/mL is typical of a solid.
(c) Insufficient information
(d) Gas

11.99 (a) There are more molecules of H_2 than atoms of He.
(b) The mass of He is greater than the mass of H_2.

11.101 The speed of gas molecules is related to the square root of the absolute temperature, so a doubling of the temperature will lead to an increase of about $(2)^{1/2}$ or 1.4.

CHAPTER 12

12.1 (a) Dipole–dipole interactions (and hydrogen bonds)
(b) Induced dipole–induced dipole forces
(c) Dipole–dipole interactions (and hydrogen bonds)

12.3 (a) Induced dipole–induced dipole forces
(b) Induced dipole–induced dipole forces
(c) Dipole–dipole forces
(d) Dipole–dipole forces (and hydrogen bonding)

12.5 The predicted order of increasing strength is $Ne < CH_4 < CO < CCl_4$. In this case, prediction does not quite agree with reality. The boiling points are Ne (-246 °C) < CO (-192 °C) < CH_4 (-162 °C) < CCl_4 (77 °C).

12.7 (c) HF; (d) acetic acid; (f) CH_3OH

12.9 (a) LiCl. The Li^+ ion is smaller than Cs^+ (Figure 7.12), which makes the ion–ion forces of attraction stronger in LiCl.
(b) $Mg(NO_3)_2$. The Mg^{2+} ion is smaller than the Na^+ ion (Figure 7.12), and the magnesium ion has a 2+ charge (as opposed to 1+ for sodium). Both of these effects lead to stronger ion–ion forces of attraction in magnesium nitrate.
(c) $NiCl_2$. The nickel(II) ion has a larger charge than Rb^+ and is considerably smaller. Both effects mean that there are stronger ion–ion forces of attraction in nickel(II) chloride.

12.11 $q = +90.1$ kJ

12.13 (a) Water vapor pressure is about 150 mm Hg at 60 °C. (Appendix G gives a value of 149.4 mm Hg at 60 °C.)
(b) 600 mm Hg at about 93 °C
(c) At 70 °C, ethanol has a vapor pressure of about 520 mm Hg, whereas that of water is about 225 mm Hg.

12.15 At 30 °C, the vapor pressure of ether is about 590 mm Hg. (This pressure requires 0.23 g of ether in the vapor phase at the given conditions, so there is sufficient ether in the flask.) At 0 °C, the vapor pressure is about 160 mm Hg, so some ether condenses when the temperature declines.

12.17 (a) O_2 (-183 °C) (bp of $N_2 = -196$ °C)
(b) SO_2 (-10 °C) (CO_2 sublimes at -78 °C)
(c) HF ($+19.7$ °C) (HI, -35.6 °C)
(d) GeH_4 (-90.0 °C) (SiH_4, -111.8 °C)

12.19 (a) CS_2, about 620 mm Hg; CH_3NO_2, about 80 mm Hg

(b) CS_2, induced dipole–induced dipole forces; CH_3NO_2, dipole–dipole forces

(c) CS_2, about 46 °C; CH_3NO_2, about 100 °C

(d) About 39 °C

(e) About 34 °C

12.21 (a) 80.1 °C

(b) At about 48 °C, the liquid has a vapor pressure of 250 mm Hg.

The vapor pressure is 650 mm Hg at 75 °C.

(c) 33.5 kJ/mol (from slope of plot)

12.23 No, CO cannot be liquefied at room temperature because the critical temperature is lower than room temperature.

12.25 $Ar < CO_2 < CH_3OH$

12.27 Li^+ ions are smaller than Cs^+ ions (78 pm and 165 pm, respectively; see Figure 7.12). Thus, there will be a stronger attractive force between Li^+ ion and water molecules than between Cs^+ ions and water molecules.

12.29 (a) 350 mm Hg

(b) Ethanol (lower vapor pressure at every temperature)

(c) 84 °C

(d) CS_2, 46 °C; C_2H_5OH, 78 °C; C_7H_{16}, 99 °C

(e) CS_2, gas; C_2H_5OH, gas; C_7H_{16}, liquid

12.31 Molar enthalpy of vaporization increases with increasing intermolecular forces: C_2H_6 (14.69 kJ/mol; induced dipole) < HCl (16.15 kJ/mol; dipole) < CH_3OH (35.21 kJ/mol, hydrogen bonds). (The molar enthalpies of vaporization here are given at the boiling point of the liquid.)

12.33 5.49×10^{19} atoms/m^3

12.35 (a) 70.3 °C

(b)

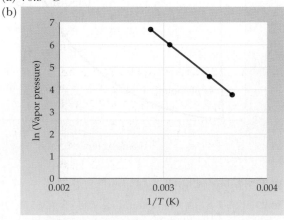

Using the equation for the straight line in the plot

$$\ln P = -3885\ (1/T) + 17.949$$

we calculate that $T = 312.6$ K (39.5 °C) when $P = 250$ mm Hg. When $P = 650$ mm Hg, $T = 338.7$ K (65.5 °C).

(c) Calculated $\Delta_{vap}H = 32.3$ kJ/mol

12.37 When the can is inverted in cold water, the water vapor pressure in the can, which was approximately 760 mm Hg, drops rapidly—say, to 9 mm Hg at 10 °C. This creates a partial vacuum in the can, and the can is crushed because of the difference in pressure inside the can and the pressure of the atmosphere pressing down on the outside of the can.

12.39 Acetone and water can interact by hydrogen bonding.

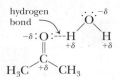

12.41 Glycol's viscosity will be greater than ethanol's, owing to the greater hydrogen-bonding capacity of glycol.

12.43 (a) Water has two OH bonds and two lone pairs, whereas the O atom of ethanol has only one OH bond (and two lone pairs). More extensive hydrogen bonding is likely for water.

(b) Water and ethanol interact extensively through hydrogen bonding, so the volume is expected to be slightly smaller than the sum of the two volumes.

12.45 Two pieces of evidence for $H_2O(\ell)$ having considerable intermolecular attractive forces:

(a) Based on the boiling points of the Group 6A hydrides (Figure 12.6), the boiling point of water should be approximately −80 °C. The actual boiling point of 100 °C reflects the significant hydrogen bonding that occurs.

(b) Liquid water has a specific heat capacity that is higher than almost any other liquid. This reflects the fact that a relatively larger amount of energy is necessary to overcome intermolecular forces and raise the temperature of the liquid.

12.47 (a) HI, hydrogen iodide

(b) The large iodine atom in HI leads to a significant polarizability for the molecule and thus to a large dispersion force.

(c) The dipole moment of HCl (1.07 D, Table 9.8) is larger than for HI (0.38 D).

(d) HI. See part (b).

12.49 A gas can be liquefied at or below its critical temperature. The critical temperature for CF_4 ($-45.7\ °C$) is below room temperature ($25\ °C$), so it cannot be liquefied at room temperature.

12.51 Hydrogen bonding is most likely at the O—H group at the "right" end of the molecule, and at the C=O and N—H groups in the amide group (—NH—CO—).

CHAPTER 13

13.1 Two possible unit cells are illustrated here. The simplest formula is AB_8.

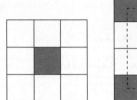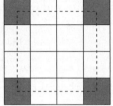

13.3 Ca^{2+} ions at eight corners = 1 net Ca^{2+} ion

O^{2-} ions in six faces = 3 net O^{2-} ions

Ti^{4+} ion in center of unit cell = 1 net Ti^{4+} ion

Formula = $CaTiO_3$

13.5 (a) There are eight O^{2-} ions at the corners and one in the center for a net of two O^{2-} ions per unit cell. There are four Cu ions in the interior in tetrahedral holes. The ratio of ions is Cu_2O.
   (b) The oxidation number of copper must be +1.

13.7 Calcium atom radius = 197 pm

13.9 There are three ways the edge dimensions can be calculated:
   (a) Calculate mass of unit cell ($= 1.103 \times 10^{-21}$ g/uc)

   Calculate volume of unit cell from mass ($= 3.53 \times 10^{-22}$ cm^3/uc)

   Calculate edge length from volume ($= 707$ pm)

   (b) Assume I$^-$ ions touch along the cell diagonal (see Exercise 13.2) and use I$^-$ radius to find the edge length. Radius I$^-$ = 220 pm

   Edge = $4(220\ \text{pm})/2^{1/2} = 622$ pm

   (c) Assume the I$^-$ and K$^+$ ions touch along the cell edge (page 599)

   Edge = $2 \times$ I$^-$ radius + $2 \times$ K$^+$ radius = 706 pm

   Methods (a) and (c) agree. It is apparent that the sizes of the ions are such that the I$^-$ ions cannot touch along the cell diagonal.

13.11 Increasing lattice energy: RbI < LiI < LiF < CaO

13.13 As the ion–ion distance decreases, the force of attraction between ions increases. This should make the lattice more stable, and more energy should be required to melt the compound.

13.15 $\Delta_f H° = -607$ kJ/mol

13.17 (a) Eight C atoms per unit cell. There are eight corners (= 1 net C atom), six faces (= 3 net C atoms), and four internal C atoms.
   (b) Face-centered cubic (fcc) with C atoms in the tetrahedral holes.

13.19 q (for fusion) = -1.97 kJ; q (for melting) = $+1.97$ kJ

13.21 (a) The density of liquid CO_2 is less than that of solid CO_2.
   (b) CO_2 is a gas at 5 atm and $0\ °C$.
   (c) Critical temperature = $31\ °C$, so CO_2 cannot be liquefied at $45\ °C$.

13.23 q (to heat the liquid) = 9.4×10^2 kJ

   q (to vaporize NH$_3$) = 1.6×10^4 kJ

   q (to heat the vapor) = 8.8×10^2 kJ

   $q_{\text{total}} = 1.83 \times 10^4$ kJ

13.25 O_2 phase diagram. (i) Note the slight positive slope of the solid–liquid equilibrium line. It indicates that the density of solid O_2 is greater than that of liquid O_2. (ii) Using the diagram here, the vapor pressure of O_2 at 77 K is between 150 mm Hg and 200 mm Hg.

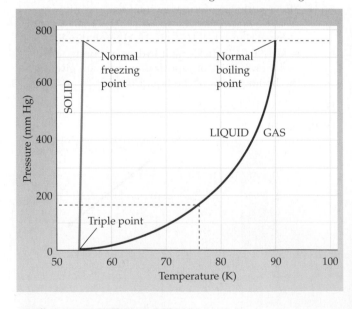

13.27 Radius of silver = 145 pm

13.29 1.356×10^{-8} cm (literature value is 1.357×10^{-8} cm)

13.31 Mass of 1 CaF_2 unit calculated from crystal data = 1.2963×10^{-22} g. Divide molar mass of CaF_2 (78.077 g/mol) by mass of 1 CaF_2 to obtain Avogadro's number. Calculated value = 6.0230×10^{23} CaF_2/mol.

13.33 Diagram A leads to a surface coverage of 78.5%. Diagram B leads to 90.7% coverage.

13.35 (a) The lattice can be described as an fcc lattice of Si atoms with Si atoms in one half of the tetrahedral holes.
(b) There are eight Si atoms in the unit cell.

Mass of unit cell = 3.731×10^{-22} g

Volume of unit cell = 1.602×10^{-22} cm^3

Density = 2.329 g/cm^3 (which is the same as the literature value)

In the Si unit cell we cannot assume the atoms touch along the edge or along the face diagonal. Instead, we know that the Si atoms in the tetrahedral holes are bonded to the Si atoms at the corner.

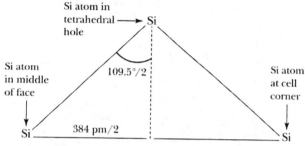

Distance = 1/2 (cell diagonal) = 384 pm

Distance across cell face diagonal = 768 pm

Sin (109.5°/2) = 0.817 = (768 pm/2)/(Si-Si distance)

Distance from Si in tetrahedral hole to face or corner Si = 235 pm

Si radius = 118 pm

Table 7.8 gives Si radius as 117 pm

13.37 (a) Mg^{2+} ions are in $\frac{1}{8}$ of the eight possible tetrahedral holes, and Al^{3+} ions are in $\frac{1}{2}$ of the four available octahedral holes.
(b) Fe^{2+} ions are in $\frac{1}{8}$ of the eight possible tetrahedral holes, and Cr^{3+} ions are in $\frac{1}{2}$ of the four available octahedral holes.

13.39 Lead sulfide has the same structure as sodium chloride, not the same structure as ZnS. There are four Pb^{2+} ions and four S^{2-} ions per unit cell, a 1:1 ratio that matches the compound formula.

13.41 (a) $BBr_3(g) + PBr_3(g) + 3 H_2(g) \longrightarrow$
$$BP(s) + 6 HBr(g)$$

(b) If B atoms are in an fcc lattice, then the P atoms must be in $\frac{1}{2}$ of the tetrahedral holes. (In this way it resembles Si in Question 13.35.)
(c) Unit cell volume = 1.092×10^{-22} cm^3
Unit cell mass = 2.775×10^{-22} g
Density = 2.54 g/cm^3
(d) The solution to this problem is identical to Question 13.35. In the BP lattice, the cell face diagonal is 676 pm. Therefore, the calculated BP distance is 207 pm.

13.43 Assuming the spheres are packed in an identical way, the water levels are the same. A face-centered cubic lattice, for example, uses 74% of the available space, regardless of the sphere size.

CHAPTER 14

14.1 (a) Concentration (m) = 0.0434 m
(b) Mole fraction of acid = 0.000781
(c) Weight percent of acid = 0.509%

14.3 NaI: 0.15 m; 2.2%; $X = 2.7 \times 10^{-3}$

CH_3CH_2OH: 1.1 m; 5.0%; $X = 0.020$

$C_{12}H_{22}O_{11}$: 0.15 m; 4.9%; $X = 2.7 \times 10^{-3}$

14.5 2.65 g Na_2CO_3; $X(Na_2CO_3) = 3.59 \times 10^{-3}$

14.7 220 g glycerol; 5.7 m

14.9 16.2 m; 37.1%

14.11 Molality = 2.6×10^{-5} m (assuming that 1 kg of seawater is equivalent to 1 kg of solvent)

14.13 (b) and (c)

14.15 $\Delta_{soln}H°$ for LiCl = -36.9 kJ/mol. This is an exothermic enthalpy of solution, as compared with the very slightly endothermic value for NaCl.

14.17 Above about 40 °C the solubility increases with temperature; therefore, add more NaCl and raise the temperature.

14.19 2×10^{-3} g O_2

14.21 1130 mm Hg or 1.49 bar

14.23 35.0 mm Hg

14.25 $X(H_2O) = 0.869$; 16.7 mol glycol; 1040 g glycol

14.27 Calculated boiling point = 84.2 °C

14.29 $\Delta T_{bp} = 0.808$ °C; solution boiling point = 62.51 °C

14.31 Molality = 8.60 m; 28.4%

14.33 Molality = 0.195 m; $\Delta T_{fp} = -0.362$ °C

14.35 Molar mass = 360 g/mol; $C_{20}H_{16}Fe_2$

14.37 Molar mass = 150 g/mol

P | Answers to Selected Interchapter Study Questions

THE CHEMISTRY OF FUELS AND ENERGY SOURCES

1. (a) From methane: $H_2O(g) + CH_4(g) \rightarrow$
$$3 H_2(g) + CO(g)$$

100. g CH_4(1 mol CH_4/16.043 g)
(3 mol H_2/mol CH_4)(2.016 g H_2/1 mol H_2)
= 37.7 g of H_2 produced

(b) From petroleum: $H_2O(g) + CH_2(\ell) \rightarrow$
$$2 H_2(g) + CO (g)$$

100. g CH_2(1 mol CH_2/14.026 g CH_2)
(2 mol H_2/1 mol CH_2)(2.016 g H_2/
1 mol H_2) = 28.7 g H_2 produced

(c) From coal: $H_2O(g) + C(s) \rightarrow$
$$H_2(g) + CO(g)$$

100. g C(1 mol C/12.011 g C)
(1 mol H_2/mole C)(2.016 g H_2/
1 mol H_2) = 16.8 g H_2 produced.

3. 70. lb(453.6 g/lb)(33 kJ/g) = 1.0×10^6 kJ

5. Assume burning oil produces 43 kJ/g (the value for crude petroleum in Table 2)

7.0 gal(3.785 L/gal)(1000 cm³/L)(0.8 g/cm³)
(43 kJ/g) = 0.9×10^6 kJ. Uncertainty in the numbers is one significant figure. This value is close to the value for the energy obtained by burning from 70 kg of coal (calculated in Q.3.)

7. Per gram: (5.45×10^3 kJ/mol)
(1 mol/114.26 g) = 47.7 kJ/g

Per liter: (47.7 kJ/g)(688 g/L) =
3.28×10^4 kJ/L

9. The factor for converting kW-h to kJ is
1 kW-h = 3600 kJ

(940 kW-h/yr)(3600 kJ/kW-h) =
3.4×10^6 kJ/yr

11. First, calculate $\Delta_r H°$ for the reaction
$CH_3OH(\ell) + 1.5 O_2(g) \rightarrow CO_2(g) + 2 H_2O(\ell)$,
using enthalpies of formation ($\Delta_r H° = 726.7$ kJ/mol-rxn). Use molar mass and density to calculate energy per L [-726.7 kJ/mol-rxn (1 mol-rxn/32.04 g)(787 g/ L) = 17.9×10^3 kJ/L]. Then use the kW-h to kJ conversion factor from Q. 9 to obtain the answer [(17.9×10^3 kJ/L)(1 kW-h/3600 kJ) = 4.96 kW-h/L].

13. Area of parking lot = 325 m $\times$ 50.0 m = 1.63×10^4 m²

2.6×10^7 J/m²(1.63×10^4 m²) = 4.3×10^{11} J

15. Amount of Pd = 1.0 cm³(12.0 g/cm³)
(1 mol/106.4 g) = 0.113 mol

amount of H = 0.084 g(1 mol/1.008 g) =
0.0833 mol

mol H per mol Pd = 0.083/0.113 = 0.74:
Simplest formula for this compound is $PdH_{0.74}$
(Because the compound is nonstoichiometric, we will not write a formula with a whole num-

we will not write a formula with a whole number ratio. For these compounds, it is common practice to set the amount of metal [Pd] to be an integer and H as a non-integer.)

17. Energy per gal. of gas = (48.0 kJ/g) $(0.737 \text{ g/cm}^3)(1000 \text{ cm}^3/\text{L})(3.785 \text{ L/gal})$ = $1.34 \times 10^5 \text{ kJ/gal}$

Energy to travel 1 mile = $(1.00 \text{ mile}/$ $55.0 \text{ gal/mile})(1.34 \times 10^5 \text{ kJ/gal}) = 2440 \text{ kJ}$

MILESTONES IN THE DEVELOPMENT OF CHEMISTRY AND THE MODERN VIEW OF ATOMS AND MOLECULES

1. Atoms are not solid, hard, or impenetrable. They have mass (an important aspect of Dalton's hypothesis), and we now know that atoms are in rapid motion at all temperatures above absolute zero (the kinetic-molecular theory).

3. mass e/mass p = 9.109383×10^{-28} g/1.672622×10^{-24} g = 5.446170×10^{-4}. (Mass of p and e obtained from Table 2.1, page 52.) The proton is 1,834 times more massive than an electron. Dalton's estimate was off by a factor of about 2.

THE CHEMISTRY OF LIFE: BIOCHEMISTRY

1. (a)

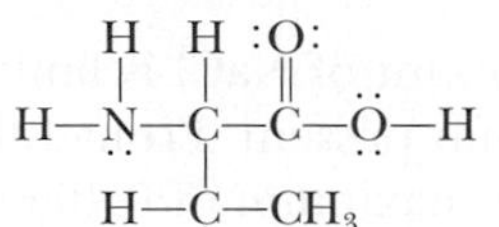

(b)

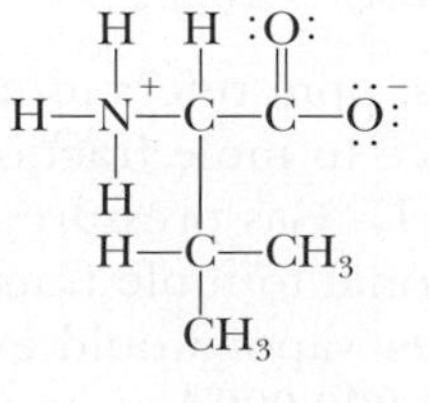

(c) The zwitterionic form is the predominant form at physiological pH.

3.

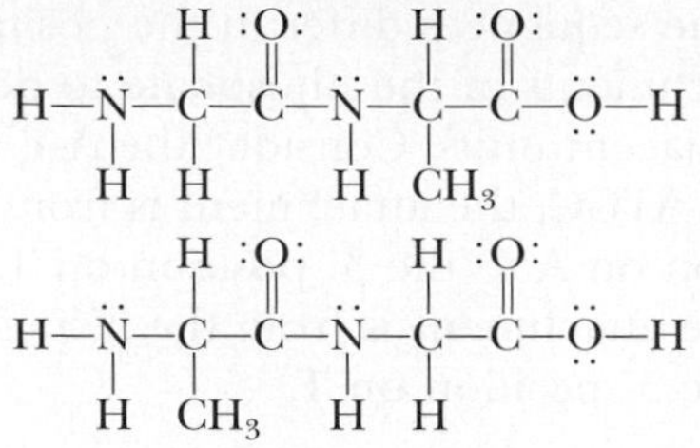

5.

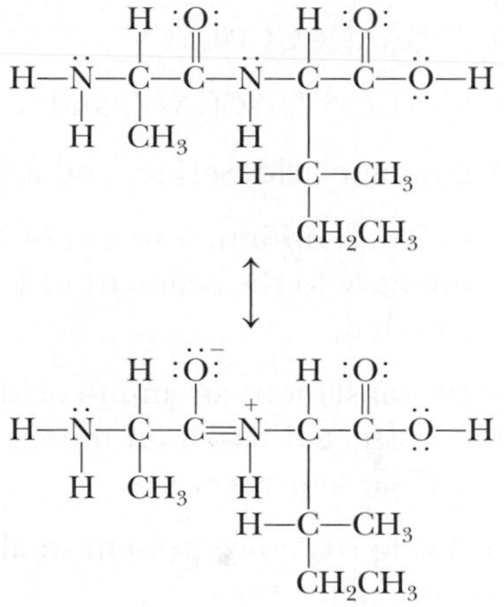

7. (a) The structure of ribose is given in Figure 13.

(b)

Adenosine

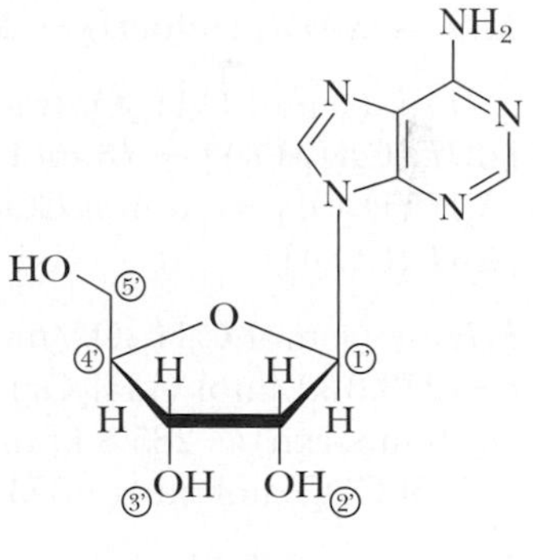

(c)

Adenosine-5'-monophosphate

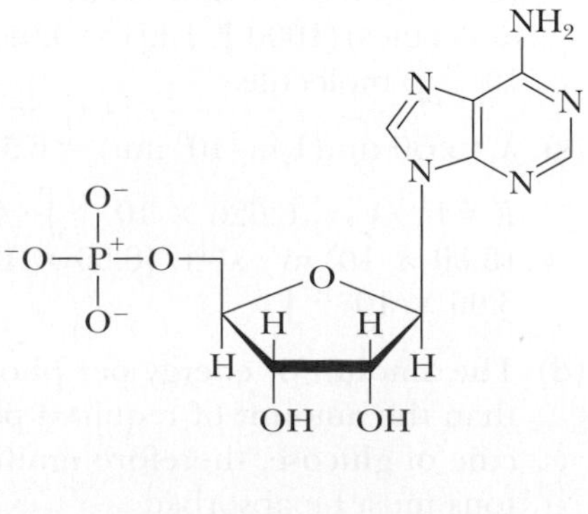

9. The sequences differ in the positions of attachments of the phosphate to deoxyribose on adjacent units. Consider the A-T attachments. In ATGC, the attachment is from the 5′ position on A to the 3′ position on T. In CGTA, the attachment is from the 3′ position on A to the 5′ position on T.

11. (a) 5′-GAATCGCGT-3′

   (b) 5′-GAAUCGCGU-3′

   (c) 5′-UUC-3′, 5′-CGA-3′, and 5′-ACG-3′

   (d) glutamic acid, serine, and arginine

13. (a) In transcription, a strand of RNA complementary to the segment of DNA is constructed.

   (b) In translation, an amino acid sequence is constructed based on the information in a mRNA sequence.

15. The 4-ring structure present in all steroids is given in Figure 18a.

17. (a) False (b) True (c) True (d) True

19. (a) $6\ CO_2(g) + 6\ H_2O(\ell) \rightarrow$
   $$C_6H_{12}O_6(s) + 6\ O_2(g)$$

   $\Delta_rH° = \Delta_fH°(\text{products}) - \Delta_fH°(\text{reactants})$

   $\Delta_rH° = (1\ \text{mol}\ C_6H_{12}O_6/\text{mol-rxn})$
   $[\Delta_fH°(C_6H_{12}O_6)] - (6\ \text{mol}\ H_2O/\text{mol-rxn})$
   $[\Delta_fH°(H_2O)] - (6\ \text{mol}\ CO_2/\text{mol-rxn})$
   $[\Delta_fH°(CO_2)]$

   $\Delta_rH° = (1\ \text{mol}\ C_6H_{12}O_6/\text{mol-rxn})$
   $(-1273.3\ \text{kJ/mol}\ C_6H_{12}O_6) - (6\ \text{mol}$
   $H_2O/\text{mol-rxn})(-285.8\ \text{kJ/mol}\ H_2O) -$
   $(6\ \text{mol}\ CO_2/\text{mol-rxn})(-393.5\ \text{kJ/mol}\ CO_2)$

   $\Delta_rH° = +2,803\ \text{kJ/mol-rxn}$

   (b) $(2803\ \text{kJ/mol})(1\ \text{mol}/6.022 \times 10^{23}$
   molecules$)(1000\ \text{J}/1\ \text{kJ}) = 4.655 \times$
   $10^{-18}\ \text{J/molecule}$

   (c) $\lambda = 650\ \text{nm}(1\ \text{m}/10^9\ \text{nm}) = 6.50 \times 10^{-7}\ \text{m}$

   $E = hc/\lambda = (6.626 \times 10^{-34}\ \text{J} \cdot \text{s})$
   $(3.00 \times 10^8\ \text{m} \cdot \text{s}^{-1})/(6.50 \times 10^{-7}\ \text{m}) =$
   $3.06 \times 10^{-19}\ \text{J}$

   (d) The amount of energy per photon is less than the amount of required per molecule of glucose, therefore multiple photons must be absorbed.

THE CHEMISTRY OF MODERN MATERIALS

1. The GaAs band gap is 140 kJ/mol. Use the equations $E = h\nu$ and $\lambda \times \nu = c$ to calculate a wavelength of 854 nm corresponding to this energy. Radiation of this wavelength is in the infrared portion of the spectrum.

3. The amount of light falling on a single solar cell = 925 W/m² $[(1\ \text{m}^2/10^4\ \text{cm}^2)$ $(1.0\ \text{cm}^2/\text{cell}) = 0.0925\ \text{W/cell}.]$ Using the conversion factor 1 W = 1 J/s, the energy incident on the cell is $(0.0925\ \text{W/cell})$ $(1\text{J/W} \cdot \text{s})(60\ \text{sec/min}) = 5.55\ \text{J}/(\text{min} \cdot \text{cell})$. At 25% efficiency, the energy absorbed for each cell is 1.39 J/min.

5. The density of dry air at 25 °C and 1.0 atm. is 1.2 g/L (see page 526), so the mass of air in aerogel is $0.99(1.2 \times 10^{-3}\ \text{g}) = 1.2 \times 10^{-3}\ \text{g}$. Add to this 0.023 g, the mass of 0.010 cm³ of SiO_2 (density of SiO_2, from web, is 2.3 g/cm³, mass of 0.010 cm³ is 0.023 g). Thus, the total mass is 0.0012 g + 0.023 g = 0.024 g, and the density of aerogel is 0.024 g/cm³.

ENVIRONMENTAL CHEMISTRY

1. $[Na^+] = 0.460\ \text{mol/L}$, $[Cl^-] = 0.550\ \text{mol/L}$; a larger amount of chloride than sodium ion is present in a sample of seawater.

3. The amount of NaCl is limited by the amount of sodium present. From 1.0 L sample of seawater, a maximum of 0.460 mol NaCl could be obtained. The mass of this amount of NaCl is 26.9 g $[(0.460\ \text{mol/L})(1.00\ \text{L})(58.43\ \text{g NaCl}/$ 1 mol NaCl$) = 26.9\ \text{g}].$

5. For gases, ppm refers to numbers of particles, and hence to mole fractions (see footnote to Table 1). Gas pressure exerted is directly proportional to mole fraction. Thus, 40,000 ppm water vapor would exert a pressure of 40,000/1,000,000th of one atmosphere, or 30.4 mm Hg (0.040 × 760 mm Hg). This would be the case at a little over 29 °C, at 100% humidity.

7. The concentration of Mg^{2+} in seawater is 52 mmol/L (Table 2). Assuming that all this is converted to Mg metal, one would expect to obtain 1.26 g from 1.0 L of seawater [0.052 mol(24.31 g/mol) = 1.26 g]. To obtain 100 kg of Mg, 79,000 L of seawater [100. kg(1000 g/kg)(1 L/1.26 g) = 7.9×10^4 L] would be needed.

9. (a) The volume occupied by 25 g of ice is 33 cm³ [25 g(1 cm³/0.92 g) = 33 cm³]. However, only 92% of the ice is submerged and the water displaced by ice (the volume of ice under the surface of water) is 25 cm³ (0.92 × 33 cm³ = 25 cm³). Thus, the liquid level in the graduated cylinder will be 125 mL.

(b) Melting 25 g of ice will produce 25 mL of liquid water. The water level will be 125 mL (the same as in (a), that is the water level won't rise as the ice melts).

Q Answers to Chapter Opening Puzzler and Case Study Questions

CHAPTER 1

Puzzler:

1. Sports drinks: colored, liquid, homogeneous, slightly more dense than pure water. (Dissolved salts raise the density of a solution: e.g., seawater is more dense than pure water.)

2. These drinks are often sold in 500-mL bottles. This is equivalent to 0.50 L or 5.0 dL.

Case Study: Ancient and Modern Hair Coloring

1. Lead (Pb); calcium (Ca)

2. $d = 11.35$ g/cm^3

3. S

4. Calcium hydroxide, known as slaked lime, is made by adding water (slaking) to lime, CaO

5. Sulfide ions (S^{2-}) are on the corners and faces of a cube; lead ions Pb^{2+} lie along each edge.

6. The overall structures are identical. The yellow spheres (S^{2-} in PbS, and Cl^- in NaCl) are at the corners and on the faces of a cube; the spheres representing Pb^{2+} and Na^+ lie along the cube's edges. The small difference in appearance is due to the relative sizes of the spheres.

LET'S REVIEW

Case Study: Out of Gas!

1. Fuel density in kg/L: (1.77 lb/L) (0.4536 kg/lb) = 0.803 kg/L

2. Mass of fuel already in tank: 7682 L (0.803 kg/L) = 6170 kg

   Mass of fuel needed: 22,300 kg − 6,170 kg = 16,100 kg (Answer has three significant figures.)

   Volume of fuel needed: 16,130 kg (1 L/0.803 kg) = 20,100 L

CHAPTER 2

Puzzler:

1. Eka-silicon is germanium. Its atomic weight is 72.61 (predicted 72), and its density is 5.32 g/cm^3 (predicted value 5.5 g/cm^3).

2. Other elements missing from Mendeleev's periodic table include Sc, Ga, the noble gases (He, Ne, Ar, Kr, Xe), and all of the radioactive elements except Th and U.

Case Study: Catching Cheaters with Isotopes

1. 7 neutrons

2. 8 neutrons

3. ^{14}C is formed in the upper atmosphere by a nuclear reaction initiated by cosmic radiation. The equation for its formation is $^{14}_{7}N + ^{1}_{0}n \rightarrow ^{14}_{6}C + ^{1}_{1}H$. (See discussion in Chapter 23 on equations for nuclear reactions.)

Case Study: What's in Those French Fries?

1. Acrylamide: C_3H_5NO, molar mass = 71.08; % N = (14.00/71.07)(100%) = 19.70 %.

   Asparagine, $C_4H_8O_3N_2$, molar mass = 132.12; % N = (28.00/132.12)(100%) = 21.20 %. Asparagine has the higher percent nitrogen.

2. Body mass in kg = 150 lb(0.4536 kg/1 lb) = 68.0 kg

   Total mass ingested = (0.0002 mg/kg body wt) (68.0 kg body wt) = 1.4×10^{-2} mg

   Number of molecules = 1.4×10^{-2} mg (1 g/1000 mg)(1 mol/71.08 g)(6.022×10^{23} molecules/mol) = 1×10^{17} molecules (1 significant figure)

CHAPTER 3

Puzzler:

$Fe^{2+}(aq) + H_2S(aq) \rightarrow FeS(s) + 2 H^+(aq)$
$2 Bi^{3+}(aq) + 3 H_2S(aq) \rightarrow Bi_2S_3(s) + 6 H^+(aq)$
$Ca^{2+}(aq) + SO_4^{2-}(aq) \rightarrow CaSO_4(s)$

Case Study: Killing Bacteria with Silver

1. 100×10^{15} Ag^+ ions(1 mol/6.022 x 10^{23} ions) = 2×10^{-7} mol Ag^+

2. 2×10^{-7} mol Ag^+(107.9 g Ag^+/1 mol Ag^+) = 2×10^{-5} g Ag^+ ions

CHAPTER 4

Puzzler:

1. Oxidation-reduction reactions.

2. Oxidation of Fe gives Fe_2O_3; oxidation of Al gives Al_2O_3.

3. The mass of Al_2O_3 formed by oxidation of 1.0 g Al = 1.0 g Al (1 mol Al/26.98 g Al) (1 mol Al_2O_3/2 mol Al)(102.0 g Al_2O_3/1 mol Al_2O_3) = 1.9 g Al_2O_3.

Case Study: How Much Salt Is There in Seawater?

1. Step 1: Calculate the amount of Cl^- in the diluted solution from titration data.

   Mol Cl^- in 50 mL of dilute solution = mol Ag^+ = (0.100 mol/L)(0.02625 L) = 2.63×10^{-3} mol Cl^-

   Step 2: Calculate the concentration of Cl^- in the dilute solution.

   Concentration of Cl^- in dilute solution = 2.63×10^{-3} mol/0.0500 L = 5.26×10^{-2} M

   Step 3: Calculate the concentration of Cl^- in seawater.

   Seawater was initially diluted to one hundredth its original concentration. Thus, the concentration of Cl^- in seawater (undiluted) = 5.25 M

Case Study: Forensic Chemistry: Titrations and Food Tampering

1. Step 1: Calculate the amount of I_2 in solution from titration data:

   Amount I_2 = (0.0425 mol $S_2O_3^{2-}$/L)(0.0253 L) (1 mol I_2/2 mol $S_2O_3^{2-}$) = 5.38×10^{-4} mol I_2

   Step 2: Calculate the amount of NaClO present based on the amount of I_2 formed, and from that value calculate the mass of NaClO.

   Mass NaClO = 5.38×10^{-4} mol I_2(1 mol HClO/1 mol I_2)(1 mol NaClO/1 mol HClO) (74.44 g NaClO/1 mol NaClO) = 0.0400 g NaClO

CHAPTER 5

Puzzler:

Step 1: Calculate mass of air in the balloon

Mass air = 1100 m^3(1,200 g/m^3) = 1.3×10^6 g

Step 2: Calculate energy as heat needed to raise the temperature of air in the balloon.

Energy as heat = $C \times m \times \Delta T$ = (1.01 J/g · K) (1.3 × 10^6 g)(383 K − 295 K) = 1.2 × 10^8 J (= 1.2 × 10^5 kJ)

Step 3: Calculate enthalpy change for the oxidation of 1.00 g propane from enthalpy of formation data. Assume formation of water vapor, $H_2O(g)$, in this reaction.

$C_3H_8(g) + 5\ O_2(g) \rightarrow 3\ CO_2(g) + 4\ H_2O(g)$

$\Delta_rH° = \Delta_fH°(\text{products}) - \Delta_fH°(\text{reactants})$ = (3 mol CO_2/mol-rxn)[$\Delta_fH°(CO_2)$] + (4 mol H_2O/mol-rxn) [$\Delta_fH°(H_2O)$] − (1 mol C_3H_8/mol-rxn)[$\Delta_fH°(C_3H_8)$]

$\Delta_rH°$ = (3 mol CO_2/mol-rxn)[−393.5 kJ/mol CO_2] + (4 mol H_2O/mol-rxn)[− 241.8 kJ/mol H_2O] − (1 mol C_3H_8/mol-rxn)[−104.7 kJ/mol C_3H_8)] = −2043 kJ/mol-rxn

q = −2043 kJ/mol-rxn(1 mol C_3H_8/mol-rxn) (1 mol C_3H_8/44.09 g C_3H_8) = −46.33 kJ/g C_3H_8

Step 4: Use answers from Steps 2 and 3 to calculate mass of propane needed to produce energy as heat needed.)

mass C_3H_8 = 1.2 × 10^5 kJ(1 g C_3H_8/46.33 kJ) = 2.5 × 10^3 g C_3H_8

(Answer has two significant figures.)

Case Study: Abba's Refrigerator

1. To evaporate 95 g H_2O: q = 44.0 kJ/mol (1 mol/18.02 g)(95 g) = 232 kJ (= 232,000 J)

   Temperature change if 750 g H_2O gives up 232 kJ of energy as heat:

   $Q = C \times m \times \Delta T$

   −232,000 J = (4.184 J/ g · K)(750 g)(ΔT); ΔT = −74 K

Case Study: The Fuel Controversy: Alcohol and Gasoline

In the following, we assume water vapor, $H_2O(g)$, is formed upon oxidation.

1. Burning ethanol: $C_2H_5OH(\ell) + 3\ O_2(g) \rightarrow 2\ CO_2(g) + 3\ H_2O(g)$

   $\Delta_rH°$ = (2 mol CO_2/mol-rxn)[$\Delta_fH°(CO_2)$] + (3 mol H_2O/mol-rxn)[$\Delta_fH°(H_2O)$] − (1 mol C_2H_5OH/mol-rxn)[$\Delta_fH°(C_2H_5OH)$]

$\Delta_rH°$ = (2 mol CO_2/mol-rxn)[−393.5 kJ/mol CO_2] + (3 mol H_2O/mol-rxn)[−241.8 kJ/mol H_2O] − (1 mol C_2H_5OH/mol-rxn)[−277.0 kJ/mol C_2H_5OH)] = −1235.4 kJ/mol-rxn

1 mol ethanol per 1 mol-rxn; therefore, q per mol is −1235.4 kJ/mol

q per gram: −1235.4 kJ/mol(1mol C_2H_5OH/ 46.07 g C_2H_5OH) = −26.80 kJ/g C_2H_5OH

Burning octane: $C_8H_{18}(\ell) + 12.5\ O_2(g) \rightarrow$ 8 $CO_2(g) + 9\ H_2O(g)$

$\Delta_rH°$ = (8 mol CO_2/mol-rxn)[$\Delta_fH°(CO_2)$] + (9 mol H_2O/mol-rxn)[$\Delta_fH°(H_2O)$] − (1 mol C_8H_{18}/mol-rxn)[$\Delta_fH°(C_8H_{18})$]

$\Delta_rH°$ = (8 mol CO_2/mol-rxn)[−393.5 kJ/mol CO_2] + (9 mol H_2O/mol-rxn)[−241.8 kJ/mol H_2O] − (1 mol C_8H_{18}/mol-rxn)[−250.1 kJ/mol C_8H_{18})] = −5070.1 kJ/mol-rxn

1 mol octane per mol-rxn; therefore, q per mol is −5070.1 kJ/mol

q per gram: −5070.1 kJ/1 mol C_8H_{18} (1 mol C_8H_{18}/114.2 g C_8H_{18}) = −44.40 kJ/g C_8H_{18}

2. For ethanol, per liter: q = −26.80 kJ/g (785 g/L) = −2.10 × 10^4 kJ/L

   For octane, per liter: q = −44.40 kJ/g (699 g/L) = 3.10 × 10^4 kJ/L

   Octane produces almost 50% more energy per liter of fuel.

3. Mass of CO_2 per liter of ethanol: = 1.000 L (785 g C_2H_5OH/L)(1 mol C_2H_5OH /46.07 g C_2H_5OH)(2 mol CO_2/1 mol C_2H_5OH)(44.01 g CO_2/1 mol CO_2) = 1.50 × 10^3 g CO_2

   Mass of CO_2 per liter of octane: = 1.000 L (699 g C_8H_{18}/L)(1 mol C_8H_{18} /114.2 g C_8H_{18})(8 mol CO_2/1 mol C_8H_{18})(44.01 g CO_2/1 mol CO_2) = 2.15 × 10^3 g CO_2

4. Volume of ethanol needed to obtain 3.10 × 10^4 kJ of energy from oxidation: 2.10 × 10^4 kJ/L C_2H_5OH)(x) = 3.10 × 10^4 kJ (x is volume of ethanol)

   Volume of ethanol = x = 1.48 L

   Mass of CO_2 produced by burning 1.48 L of ethanol = (1.50 × 10^3 g CO_2/L C_2H_5OH) (1.48 L C_2H_5OH) = 2.22 × 10^3 g CO_2

   To obtain the same amount of energy, slightly more CO_2 is produced by burning ethanol than for octane.

5. Your car will travel about 50% farther on a liter of octane, and it will produce slightly less CO_2 emissions, than if you burned 1.0 L of ethanol.

CHAPTER 6
Puzzler:

1. Red light has the longer wavelength.

2. Green light has the higher energy.

3. The energy of light emitted by atoms is determined by the energy levels of the electrons in an atom. See discussion in the text, page 275.

Case Study: What Makes the Colors in Fireworks?

1. Yellow light is from 589 and 590 nm emissions.

2. Primary emission for Sr is red: this has a longer wavelength than yellow light.

3. $4 \, Mg(s) + KClO_4(s) \rightarrow KCl(s) + 4 \, MgO(s)$

CHAPTER 7
Puzzler:

1. Cr: $[Ar]3d^5 4s^1$; Cr^{3+}: $[Ar]3d^3$; CrO_4^{2-} (chromium(VI)): $[Ar]$

2. Cr^{3+} is paramagnetic with three unpaired electrons.

3. Pb in $PbCrO_4$ is present as Pb^{2+}: $[Xe]4f^{14}5d^{10}6s^2$

Case Study: Metals in Biochemistry and Medicine

1. Fe^{2+}: $[Ar]3d^6$; Fe^{3+}: $[Ar]3d^5$

2. Both iron ions are paramagnetic.

3. Cu^+: $[Ar]3d^{10}$; Cu^{2+}: $[Ar]3d^9$; Cu^{2+} is paramagnetic; Cu^+ is diamagnetic.

4. The slightly larger size of Cu compared to Fe is related to greater electron–electron repulsions.

5. Fe^{2+} is larger than Fe^{3+} and will fit less well into the structure. As a result, some distortion of the ring structure from planarity occurs.

CHAPTER 8
Puzzler:

1. Carbon and phosphorus (in phosphate) achieve the noble gas configuration by forming four bonds.

2. In each instance, there are four bonds to the element; VSEPR predicts that these atoms will have tetrahedral geometry with 109.5° angles.

3. Bond angles in these rings are 120°. To achieve this preferred bond angle, the rings must be planar.

4. Thymine and cytosine are polar molecules.

Case Study: The Importance of an Odd Electron Molecule, NO

1. $\left[\ddot{\text{O}} = \text{N} - \ddot{\text{O}} - \ddot{\text{O}} : \right]^{-}$

2. There is a double bond between N and the terminal O.

3. Resonance structures are not needed to describe the bonding in this ion.

CHAPTER 9
Puzzler:

1. XeF_2 is linear. The electron pair geometry is trigonal bipyramidal. Three lone pairs are located in the equatorial plane, and the two F atoms are located in the axial positions. This symmetrical structure will not have a dipole.

2. The Xe atom is sp^3d hybridized. Xe-F bonds: overlap of Xe sp^3d orbitals with F 2p orbital. 3 lone pairs in Xe sp^3d orbitals.

3. This 36-electron molecule has a bent molecular structure.

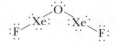

Case Study: Two Chemical Bonding Mysteries

1. Eight two-electron bonds, which would require 16 electrons, four more than the 12 available.

2. The compound has sp^3 hybridized B and N atoms and is polar. The B atom has a -1 formal charge and N has a $+1$ form charge. All bond angles are about $109°$.

3. $(54.3 \times 10^{-3} \text{ g AgBF}_4)(1 \text{ mol}/194.7 \text{ g}) = 2.79 \times 10^{-4}$ mol

The amount of $Ag(C_2H_4)_xBF_4$ that must have decomposed is 2.79×10^{-4} mol.

Molar mass of unknown $= (62.1 \times 10^{-3} \text{ g})/(2.79 \times 10^{-4} \text{ mol}) = 223$ g/mol

The compound $Ag(C_2H_4)BF_4$ where $x = 1$ has a molar mass of 223 g/mol.

CHAPTER 10

Puzzler:

1. (a) Trigonal planar, sp^2 hybridized. The other carbon atoms in this molecule have tetrahedral geometry and sp^3 hybridization.

(b) The non-planarity allows all of the atoms in the molecule to assume an unstrained geometry.

(c) Actually, there are two chiral centers, labeled with an asterisk (*) in the drawing below.

2. Camphor is a ketone.

Case Study: Biodiesel, a Fuel for the Future

1. $C_{12}H_{25}CO_2CH_3(\ell) + 20\ O_2(g) \rightarrow 14\ CO_2(g) + 14\ H_2O(g)$

2. $\Delta_r H° = (14 \text{ mol CO}_2/\text{mol-rxn})[\Delta_f H°(CO_2)] + (14 \text{ mol H}_2O/\text{mol-rxn})[\Delta_f H°(H_2O)] - (1 \text{ mol } C_{12}H_{25}CO_2CH_3/\text{mol-rxn})[\Delta_f H°(C_{12}H_{25}CO_2CH_3)]$

$\Delta_r H° = (14 \text{ mol CO}_2/\text{mol-rxn})[-393.5 \text{ kJ/mol CO}_2] + (14 \text{ mol H}_2O/\text{mol-rxn})[-241.8 \text{ kJ/mol H}_2O] - (1 \text{ mol } C_{12}H_{25}CO_2CH_3/\text{mol-rxn})[-771.0 \text{ kJ/mol } C_{12}H_{25}CO_2CH_3] = -8123.2$ kJ/mol-rxn

1 mol methyl myristate per mol-rxn, so q per mol $= -8123.2$ kJ/mol

3. Burning hexadecane: $C_{16}H_{34}(\ell) + 24.5\ O_2(g) \rightarrow 16\ CO_2(g) + 17\ H_2O(g)$

$\Delta_r H° = (16 \text{ mol CO}_2/\text{mol-rxn})[\Delta_f H°(CO_2)] + (17 \text{ mol H}_2O/\text{mol-rxn})[\Delta_f H°(H_2O)] - (1 \text{ mol } C_{16}H_{34}/\text{mol-rxn})[\Delta_f H°(C_{16}H_{34})]$

$\Delta_r H° = (16 \text{ mol CO}_2/\text{mol-rxn})[-393.5 \text{ kJ/mol CO}_2] + (17 \text{ mol H}_2O/\text{mol-rxn})[-241.8 \text{ kJ/mol H}_2O] - (1 \text{ mol } C_{16}H_{34}/\text{mol-rxn})[-456.1 \text{ kJ/mol } C_{16}H_{34}] = -9950.5 \text{ kJ/mol-rxn}$

1 mole hexadecane per mol-rxn, so q per mol: -9950.5 kJ/mol

For methyl myristate, q per liter $= (-8123.2 \text{ kJ/mol})(1 \text{ mol}/228.4 \text{ g})(0.86 \text{ g/L}) = -30.6$ kJ/L

For hexadecane, q per liter $= (-9950.5 \text{ kJ/mol})(1 \text{ mol}/226.43 \text{ g})(0.77 \text{ g/1 L}) = -33.8$ kJ/L

CHAPTER 11

Puzzler:

1. $P(O_2)$ at 3000 m is 70% of 0.21 atm, the value $P(O_2)$ at sea level, thus $P(O_2)$ at 3000 m $= 0.21 \text{ atm} \times 0.70 = 0.15$ atm (110 mm Hg). At the top of Everest, $P(O_2) = 0.21 \text{ atm} \times 0.29 = 0.061$ atm (46 mm Hg).

2. Blood saturation levels (estimated from table): at 3000 m, $>95\%$; at top of Everest, 75%.

Case Study: You Stink

1. To calculate $P(CH_3SH)$, use the ideal gas law:
$V = 1.00\ m^3(10^6\ cm^3/m^3)(1\ L/10^3\ cm^3) = 1.00 \times 10^3\ L$;

$n = 1.5 \times 10^{-3}\ g(1\ mol/48.11\ g) = 3.1 \times 10^{-5}\ mol$

$P = nRT/V = [3.1 \times 10^{-5}\ mol(0.08205\ L\ atm/mol \cdot K)(298\ K)]/1.0 \times 10^3\ L = 7.6 \times 10^{-7}$ atm. $(5.8 \times 10^{-4}\ mm\ Hg)$

Molecules per $m^3 = 3.1 \times 10^{-5}\ mol$ $(6.022 \times 10^{23}\ molecules/mol) = 1.9 \times 10^{19}$ molecules

2. Bond angles: H—C—H and H—C—S, 109.5°; C—S—H somewhat less than 109°.

3. Polar

4. It should behave as an ideal gas at moderate pressures and temperatures well above its boiling point.

5. H_2S (with the lowest molar mass) will diffuse fastest.

CHAPTER 12
Puzzler:

1. In ice, water molecules are not packed as closely as they are in liquid water. This structure results so that hydrogen bonding interactions between water molecules are maximized.

   A piece of ice floats at a level where it will displace its weight of seawater. Most of the volume of an iceberg is below the water line.

2. A 1000 cm³ piece of ice (mass = 917 g) would float with [0.917/1.026](100%) = 89.4% below the surface or 10.6% above the surface.

Case Study: The Mystery of the Disappearing Fingerprints

1. The chemical compounds in a child's fingerprints are more volatile because they have lower molecular weights than compounds in adults' fingerprints.

CHAPTER 13
Puzzler:

1. This geometry problem is solved using the numbers shown on the drawing.

   $x^2 + (69.5)^2 = (139)^2$

   Solving, $x = 120$ pm.

   The side-to-side distance is twice this value or 240. pm

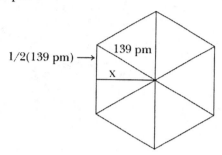

1/2(139 pm) → 139 pm x

2. $1.00\ \mu m = 1.00 \times 10^{-4}\ cm$ and $240\ pm = 2.4 \times 10^{-8}\ cm$.

   The number of C_6 rings spanning 1 μm is $1.00 \times 10^{-4}\ cm/2.40 \times 10^{-8}\ cm = 4.17 \times 10^3$ rings

3. Graphene is described as being one carbon atom thick so the thickness is twice the radius of a carbon atom or 154 pm.

Case Study: The World's Lightest Solid

1. The mass of 1.00 cm³ of aerogel is 1.00 mg $(1.00 \times 10^{-3}\ g)$ and 0.2% of this, $2.00 \times 10^{-6}\ g$, is the mass of the polymer. The number of silicon atoms in 1.00 cm³ $= 2.00 \times 10^{-6}\ g$ $(1\ mol\ (C_2H_5O)_2SiO/134.2\ g)(1\ mol\ Si/1\ mol$ $(C_2H_5O)_2SiO)(6.022 \times 10^{23}\ atoms\ Si/mol\ Si) = 9.0 \times 10^{15}\ atoms\ Si.$

2. Volume between glass panes = 150 cm × 180 cm × 0.2 cm = 5,400 cm³

   Density of aerogel = 1.00×10^{-3} g/cm³, so the mass of aerogel needed = 5400 cm³$(1.00 \times 10^{-3}$ g/cm³$) = 5.4$ g.

Index/Glossary

Italicized page numbers indicate pages containing illustrations, and those followed by "t" indicate tables. Glossary terms, printed in boldface, are defined here as well as in the text.

Abba, Mohammed Bah, 222
abbreviations, A-10
absolute temperature scale. *See* Kelvin temperature scale.
absolute zero The lowest possible temperature, equivalent to -273.15 °C, used as the zero point of the Kelvin scale, 27, 520
zero entropy at, 868
absorbance The negative logarithm of the transmittance, 191
absorption spectrum A plot of the intensity of light absorbed by a sample as a function of the wavelength of the light, 192, 1047
excited states and, *278*
absorptivity, molar, 192
abundance(s), of elements in Earth's crust, 63t, 963, 964t
of elements in solar system, *106*
of isotopes, 54, 56t
accuracy The agreement between the measured quantity and the accepted value, 30
acetaldehyde, 470t structure of, 435
acetaminophen, electrostatic potential surface of, 586 structure of, 477
acetate ion, buffer solution of, 815t
acetic acid, 472t
buffer solution of, 815t, 816
decomposition product of aspirin, 760
density of, 22
dimerization of, 756
formation of, 244
hydrogen bonding in, 562
ionization of, 811
orbital hybridization in, 418
production of, 469

quantitative analysis of, 169
reaction with ammonia, 780
reaction with ethanol, 735
reaction with sodium bicarbonate, 777
reaction with sodium hydroxide, 137, 472
structure of, 444, 468
titration with sodium hydroxide, 824, 826
in vinegar, 135
as weak acid, 771
as weak electrolyte, 121, 125
acetic anhydride, 168
acetoacetic acid, 201
acetone, 470t in diabetes, 201
hydrogenation of, 391
structure of, *419*, 468
acetonitrile, structure of, 396, *420*
acetylacetonate ion, as ligand, 1031
acetylacetone, enol and keto forms, 439
structure of, 397
acetylene, orbital hybridization in, 419
structure of, 444
acetylide ion, 435
acetylsalicylic acid. *See* aspirin.
acid(s) A substance that, when dissolved in pure water, increases the concentration of hydrogen ions, 131-139. *See also* Brønsted-Lowry acid(s), Lewis acid(s).
Arrhenius definition of, 132
bases and, 760-809. *See also* acid-base reaction(s).
Brønsted-Lowry definition, 133-136, 761
carboxylic. *See* carboxylic acid(s).
common, 132t
Lewis definition of, 789-793

reaction with bases, 136-138
strengths of, 769. *See also* strong acid, weak acid.
direction of reaction and, 776
acid-base adduct The product that occurs when a molecule or ion donates a pair of electrons to another molecule or ion in an acid-base reaction, 789
acid-base indicator(s), 830-832
acid-base pairs, conjugate, 764, 765t
acid-base reaction(s) An exchange reaction between an acid and a base producing a salt and water, 136-138, 149
characteristics of, 778t
equivalence point of, 185, 821
pH after, 786
titration using, 183-185, 821-832
acid ionization constant (K_a) The equilibrium constant for the ionization of an acid in aqueous solution, 769, 770t
relation to conjugate base ionization constant, 775
values of, A-23t
acid rain, 139
acidic oxide(s) An oxide of a nonmetal that acts as an acid, 139
acidic solution A solution in which the concentration of hydronium ions is greater than the concentration of hydroxide ion, 766
acidosis, 822
Acrilan, 481t
acrolein, formation of, 401
structure of, 397, 436
acrylamide, in foods, 96
acrylonitrile, electrostatic potential map of, 399

actinide(s) The series of elements between actinium and rutherfordium in the periodic table, 67, 315
activation energy (E_a) The minimum amount of energy that must be absorbed by a system to cause it to react, 694
experimental determination, 696-698
reduction by catalyst, 700
activity (A) A measure of the rate of nuclear decay, the number of disintegrations observed in a sample per unit time, 1073
actual yield The mass of material that is actually obtained from a chemical reaction in a laboratory or chemical plant, 168
addition polymer(s) A synthetic organic polymer formed by directly joining monomer units, 480-484
production from ethylene derivatives, 480
addition reaction(s) A reaction in which a molecule with the general formula X—Y adds across the carbon-carbon double bond, 456
adduct, acid-base, 789
adenine, 392
hydrogen bonding to thymine, 565
structure of, 107, *393*
adenosine 5'-triphosphate (ATP), structure of, 884
adhesive force A force of attraction between molecules of two different substances, 579
adhesives, 668
adipoyl chloride, 486
aerobic fermentation, 463
aerogel(s), 607
aerosol, 642t
air, components of, 530t
density of, 526
fractional distillation of, 1001

air bags, 515, 522, *523*
alanine, 498
  zwitterionic form, 808
albite, dissolved by rain
    water, 186
albumin, precipitation of, 719
alchemy, 339, 1061
alcohol(s) Any of a class of
    organic compounds charac-
    terized by the presence of a
    hydroxyl group bonded to a
    saturated carbon atom,
    461–465
  energy content of, 215
  naming of, A-19
  oxidation to carbonyl com-
    pounds, 468
  solubility in water, 465
aldehyde(s) Any of a class of
    organic compounds charac-
    terized by the presence of a
    carbonyl group, in which the
    carbon atom is bonded to at
    least one hydrogen atom,
    468–470
aldehydes, naming of, A-19
alkali metal(s) The metals in
    Group 1A of the periodic
    table, 62
  electron configuration of,
    311
  ions, enthalpy of hydra-
    tion, 557, 558t
  reaction with oxygen, 973
  reaction with water, 62, *63*,
    971, 973
  reduction potentials of,
    973
alkaline battery, 912
alkaline earth metal(s) The
    elements in Group 2A of the
    periodic table, 62, 975–979
  biological uses of, 977
  electron configuration of,
    311
alkalosis, 822
alkane(s) Any of a class of
    hydrocarbons in which each
    carbon atom is bonded to
    four other atoms, 448–452
  derivatives of, 462t
  general formula of, 447t
  naming of, A-17
  properties of, 452
  reaction with chlorine, 452
  reaction with oxygen, 452
  standard enthalpies of
    vaporization of, 572t
AlkA-Seltzer®, *149*, 760
  composition of, 104

alkene(s) Any of a class of
    hydrocarbons in which there
    is at least one carbon–car-
    bon double bond, 453–457
  general formula of, 447t
  hydrogenation of, 457
  naming of, A-18
alkyl groups Hydrocarbon sub-
    stituents, 451
alkylation, of benzene, 461
alkyne(s) Any of a class of
    hydrocarbons in which there
    is at least one carbon–car-
    bon triple bond, 456
  general formula of, 447t
  naming of, A-19
allene, structure of, 440, 444
allergy, to nickel, 896
allicin, 541
allotrope(s) Different forms of
    the same element that exist
    in the same physical state
    under the same conditions of
    temperature and pressure, 63
  boron, 981
  carbon, 63
  oxygen, 1001. *See also* ozone.
  phosphorus, 65, 992
  sulfur, 65, 1001
alloy(s),
  iron, 1027
  magnesium in, 976
  memory metal, 1018
alnico V, 1028
  ferromagnetism of, 292
alpha particle(s), 1061
  bombardment with, 1077
  predicting emission of,
    1068
alpha plot(s), 857
alpha radiation Radiation that
    is readily absorbed, 343
alpha-hydroxy acid(s), *787*
altitude sickness, 514
alum, formula of, 110
alumina, amphoterism of,
    1012
aluminosilicates, 989
  separation of, 982
aluminum, abundance of,
    63
  chemistry of, 985
  density of, 44
  production of, 981–982
  reaction with bromine, 67,
    207
  reaction with copper ions,
    900
  reaction with iron(III)
    oxide, 147

reaction with potassium
    hydroxide, 199
  reaction with sodium
    hydroxide, 970
  reaction with water, 904
  reduction by sodium, 972
aluminum bromide, dimer-
    ization of, 985
aluminum carbide, reaction
    with water, 169
aluminum chloride, prepa-
    ration of, 197
aluminum hydroxide,
    amphoterism of, 790,
    792
aluminum oxide, 982
  amphoterism of, 982
aluminum sulfate, 1012
amalgam, 925
americium, 1079
amide link, 486
amide(s) Any of a class of
    organic compounds charac-
    terized by the presence of an
    amino group, 468, 475–478
amine(s) A derivative of
    ammonia in which one or
    more of the hydrogen atoms
    are replaced by organic
    groups, 466
  as acids and bases, 798
α-amino acid(s) An amino acid
    in which the amine group
    and the carboxyl group are
    both attached to the same
    carbon atom.
  chirality of, 498
  zwitterionic form, 808
amino group A functional
    group related to ammonia,
    in which some or all of the
    hydrogen atoms are replaced
    by organic groups, 468,
    475
2-aminobenzoic acid, 494
ammonia, aqueous, equilib-
    rium constant expres-
    sion for, 728
  bond angles in, 370, *371*
  combustion of, balanced
    equation for, 118
  decomposition of, 679,
    689, 715
  as Lewis base, 793
  as ligand, 1031
  molecular polarity of, 383
  orbital hybridization in,
    411
  oxidation of, 163, *164*
  percent composition of, 89

pH of, 179
  production of, as equilib-
    rium process, 119
  by Haber process, 749
  equilibrium constant for,
    743
  spontaneity of, 875
  stoichiometry of, 527
  reaction with acetic acid,
    780
  reaction with boron triflu-
    oride, 364, 438
  reaction with copper sul-
    fate, 197
  reaction with hydrochloric
    acid, 779
  reaction with hydrogen
    chloride, 138, 533, 890
  reaction with nickel(II)
    nitrate and ethylenedi-
    amine, 758
  reaction with sodium hypo-
    chlorite, 993
  reaction with water, 136
  relation to amines, 466
  synthesis of, equilibrium
    constant, 885
  titration with hydrogen
    chloride, 828–830
  waste product of fish
    metabolism, 994
  as weak base, 771
ammonium carbamate, dis-
    sociation of, 756
ammonium chloride,
    decomposition of, 875
  in dry cell battery, 911
  reaction with calcium
    oxide, 196
ammonium cyanate, conver-
    sion to urea, 718
ammonium dichromate,
    decomposition of, 155,
    550
ammonium formate, solubil-
    ity of, 652
ammonium hydrogen sul-
    fide, decomposition of,
    754, 755
ammonium iodide, dissocia-
    tion of, 756
ammonium ion, 73
  in Lewis adduct, 790
ammonium nitrate, decom-
    position of, 250
  dissolution of, 862
  enthalpy of solution, 623
  in cold pack, 245
ammonium perchlorate, in
    rocket fuel, 1009, 1015

amorphous solid(s) A solid that lacks long-range regular structure and displays a melting range instead of a specific melting point, 603

amount, of pure substance, 82

amounts table, 159

ampere (A) The unit of electric current, 937

Ampère, André Marie, 1005

amphetamine, structure of, 437, 799

amphibole, 988

amphiprotic substance A substance that can behave as either a Brønsted acid or a Brønsted base, 136, 763, 790, 791t

amphoteric substance, aluminum oxide, 982

amplitude The maximum height of a wave, as measured from the axis of propagation, 270

analysis, chemical. See chemical analysis.
spectrophotometric, 192

Anderson, Carl, 1066

angstrom unit, 28

angular (azimuthal) momentum quantum number, 285
number of nodal surfaces and, 291

anhydrous compound The substance remaining after the water has been removed (usually by heating) from a hydrated compound, 97

aniline, as weak base, 771
reaction with sulfuric acid, 467
structure of, 459, 808

aniline hydrochloride, reaction with sodium hydroxide, 856

anilinium sulfate, 467

anion(s) An ion with a negative electric charge, 71
as Brønsted acids and bases, 762
as Brønsted bases, 798
effect on salt solubility, 840
as Lewis bases, 790
in living cells and sea water, 122t
naming, 76
noble gas electron configuration in, 330
sizes of, 326

anode rays, 343

anode The electrode of an electrochemical cell at which oxidation occurs, 905
in corrosion, 1023

anthracene, 650

antibonding molecular orbital A molecular orbital in which the energy of the electrons is higher than that of the parent orbital electrons, 423

anticodon A three-nucleotide sequence in tRNA, 505

antifreeze, 616, 634
ethylene glycol in, 619

antilogarithms, A-3

antimatter, 1066

antimony, isotopic abundance of, 57

antimony pentafluoride, reaction with hydrogen fluoride, 436

antineutrino, 1066

apatite(s), 977, 978

Appian Way, mortar in, 978

approximations, successive, method of, 739, A-5

aqua regia, 339, 996

aquarium, nitrogen cycle in, 994

aquation reaction, 720

aqueous solution A solution in which the solvent is water, 121
balancing redox equations in, 901–905
electrolysis in, 933
equilibrium constant expression for, 728

arginine, 201

argon, density of, 23

argyria, 148

Arnold, James R., 1077

aromatic compound(s) Any of a class of hydrocarbons characterized by the presence of a benzene ring or related structure, 421, 442, 458–461
general formula of, 447t
naming of, A-19

Arrhenius, Svante, 131

Arrhenius equation A mathematical expression that relates reaction rate to activation energy, collision frequency, molecular orientation, and temperature, 696

arsine, 997

asbestos, 976, 988

ascorbic acid, reaction with iodine, 676
structure of, 107, 491, 804
titration of, 189, 200

asparagine, structure of, 96

aspirin, absorption spectrum of, 302
history of, 760
melting point of, 17, 44
molar mass of, 86
preparation of, 197
structure of, 350, 436, 459
synthesis of, 168

astronomical unit, 33

atmosphere. See also air.
composition of, 534
pressure–temperature profile of, 533
standard. See standard atmosphere (atm).

atom(s) The smallest particle of an element that retains the characteristic chemical properties of that element, 13
ancient Greek ideas of, 339
Bohr model of, 276–278
composition of, 53
electron configurations. See electron configuration(s).
mass of, 52
quantization of energy in, 276, 284
size of, 52, 319. See also atomic radius.
structure of, 51

atomic bomb, 1080

atomic mass The average mass of an atom in a natural sample of the element, 55
Dalton and, 341

atomic mass unit (u) The unit of a scale of relative atomic masses of the elements; 1 u = 1/12 of the mass of a carbon atom with six protons and six neutrons, 52
equivalent in grams, 52

atomic number (Z) The number of protons in the nucleus of an atom of an element, 52, 344
chemical periodicity and, 60
even versus odd, and nuclear stability, 1067
in nuclear symbol, 1062

atomic orbital(s) The matter wave for an allowed energy state of an electron in an atom, 285–287
assignment of electrons to, 306–316
energies of, and electron assignments, 306–316, 336t
number of electrons in, 306t
order of energies in, 307
orientations of, 290
overlapping of, in valence bond theory, 406
quantum numbers of, 285
shapes of, 287–291

atomic radius, bond length and, 388
effective nuclear charge and, 320
periodicity, 319
transition elements, 1024

atomic reactor, 1080

atomic theory of matter A theory that describes the structure and behavior of substances in terms of ultimate chemical particles called atoms and molecules, 51

atomic weight. See atomic mass.

aurora borealis, 268

austenite, 1018

autoionization of water Interaction of two water molecules to produce a hydronium ion and a hydroxide ion by proton transfer, 765

automobile, hybrid gasoline-electric, 915

average reaction rate, 674

Avogadro, Amedeo, 83, 522

Avogadro's hypothesis Equal volumes of gases under the same conditions of temperature and pressure have equal numbers of particles, 522

Avogadro's law, kinetic-molecular theory and, 537

Avogadro's number The number of particles in one mole of any substance (6.022×10^{23}), 83

axial position, in cyclohexane structure, 453
in trigonal-bipyramidal molecular geometry, 372

azimuthal quantum number, 285

azomethane, decomposition of, 688, 690, 714

azurite, *21*, *1025*

background radiation, 1083

back-titration, 204

bacteria, copper production by, 1028

thermophilic, 16

bain-Marie, 339

baking powder, *780*, 1000

baking soda, 140, 974

reaction with vinegar, 777

balance, laboratory, precision of, *35*

balanced chemical equation A chemical equation showing the relative amounts of reactants and products, 116–118

enthalpy and, 227

equilibrium constant and, 741–744

ball-and-stick model(s) A diagram in which spheres represent atoms, and sticks represent the bonds holding them together, 70, 445

balloon, hot air, 208, *525*

hydrogen and helium, 968

models of electron pair geometries, 368

weather, *521*

Balmer, Johann, 276

Balmer series A series of spectral lines that have energies in the visible region, 276, 279

band of stability, nuclear, 1067

bar A unit of pressure; 1 bar = 100 kPa, 516, A-8

barium carbonate, decomposition of, 755

barium chloride, as strong electrolyte, 124

precipitation of, 845

reaction with sodium sulfate, 130

barium nitrate, in fireworks, 281

barium sulfate, as x-ray contrast agent, 977

precipitation of, 845

solubility of, 835

barometer An apparatus used to measure atmospheric pressure, 516

base(s) A substance that, when dissolved in pure water, increases the concentration of hydroxide ions, 131–139. *See also* Brønsted base(s), Lewis base(s).

acids and, 760–809. *See also* acid–base reaction(s).

Arrhenius definition of, 132

Brønsted definition, 761

Brønsted-Lowry definition, 133–136

common, 132t

Lewis definition of, 789–793

of logarithms, A-2

reaction with acids, 136–138

strengths of, 769. *See also* strong base, weak base.

direction of reaction and, 776

base ionization constant (K_b) The equilibrium constant for the ionization of a base in aqueous solution, 769, 770t

relation to conjugate acid ionization constant, 775

base units, SI, 25t, A-11

basic oxide(s) An oxide of a metal that acts as a base, 139

basic oxygen furnace, 1027

basic solution A solution in which the concentration of hydronium ions is less than the concentration of hydroxide ion, 766

battery A device consisting of two or more electrochemical cells, 911

energy per kilogram, 914t

bauxite, 982

Bayer process, 982

becquerel The SI unit of radioactivity, 1 decomposition per second, 1082

Becquerel, Henri, 342

Beer-Lambert law The absorbance of a sample is proportional to the path length and the concentration, 191

Beethoven, Ludwig van, 991

bends, 626

benzaldehyde, structure of, 469

benzene, boiling point elevation and freezing point depression constants for, 633t

bonding in, resonance structures in, 361, 421

derivatives of, 459, A-19

liquid and solid volumes, *556*

molecular orbital configuration of, 432

in organometallic compounds, 1051

reactions of, 461

structure of, 342, 459

vapor pressure of, 583, 632

benzenesulfonic acid, structure of, 805

benzoic acid, 471t

buffer solution of, 817

structure of, 245, 459, 653

benzonitrile, structure of, 444

benzyl acetate, 475

benzyl butanoate, 474t

beryllium dichloride, orbital hybridization in, 414

beta particle(s) An electron ejected at high speed from certain radioactive substances, 1061

predicting emission of, 1068

beta radiation Radiation of a penetrative character, 343

bicarbonate ion. *See also* hydrogen carbonate ion.

in biological buffer system, 822

bidentate ligands, 1031

bimolecular process A process that involves two molecules, 703

binary compound(s) A compound formed from two elements, 81

binding energy The energy required to separate a nucleus into individual protons and neutrons, 1069–1072

per nucleon, 1070

biochemistry, thermodynamics and, 884

biodiesel, 479

birefringence, *976*

bismuth subsalicylate, formula of, 109

in Pepto-Bismol, *128*

black powder, 281

black smokers, metal sulfides from, 112

black tongue, Pepto-Bismol and, *128*

blackbody radiation, 272

blast furnace, 1026

entropy and, 876

bleach, detection in food tampering, 188

hypochlorite ion in, 1009

sodium hypochlorite in, 619

blood, buffers in, 814, 822

oxygen saturation of, 514

pH of, 179, 822

blood alcohol level (BAL), 207

blue vitriol, 97

boat form, 453

body-centered cubic (bcc) unit cell, 591

Bohanan, Art, 579

Bohr, Christian, 1033

Bohr, Niels, 276, 346

Bohr effect, in hemoglobin, 1033

boiling point The temperature at which the vapor pressure of a liquid is equal to the external pressure on the liquid, 576

of common compounds, 572t

hydrogen bonding and, 561

intermolecular forces and, 560t

boiling point elevation, 632

boiling point elevation constant (K_{bp}), 633

Boltzmann, Ludwig, 536, 866

Boltzmann distribution curves. *See* Maxwell-Boltzmann distribution curves.

bomb calorimeter, 231, *232*

bombardier beetle, *677*

bond(s) An interaction between two or more atoms that holds them together by reducing the potential energy of their electrons, 349. *See also* bonding.

coordinate covalent, 364, 789, 1031

covalent, 349

formation of, 349

ionic, 349

multiple, 354

molecular geometry and, 373

polar, 375–379

properties of, 386–391

ferent substances, 18. *See also* reaction(s).

chemical compound(s). *See* compound(s).

chemical equation(s) A written representation of a chemical reaction, showing the reactants and products, their physical states, and the direction in which the reaction proceeds, 19, 113

balancing, 116–118, 899–905

manipulating, equilibrium constant and, 741–744

chemical equilibrium A condition in which the forward and reverse reaction rates in a chemical system are equal, 118–121, 724–759

factors affecting, 744–750

chemical formula. *See* formula(s).

chemical kinetics The study of the rates of chemical reactions under various conditions and of reaction mechanisms, 670–723

chemical potential energy, 210

chemical property An indication of whether and how readily a material undergoes a chemical change, 19

chemical reaction(s). *See* reaction(s).

chemistry, history of, 338–347

chemocline, 630

china clay, 989

chiral compound A molecule that is not superimposable on its mirror image, 445, 1038. *See also* enantiomers.

optical activity of, 342, 445

chlor-alkali industry, 974

chloramine, 958

chlorate ion, formal charges in, 360

Lewis structure of, 354

chlorine,

formation by aqueous electrolysis, 935

from sodium chloride electrolysis, 972

oxoacids of, 1008

production of, 1005

reaction with alkanes, 452

reaction with iron, 115

reaction with phosphorus, 113, 159

reaction with sodium, *4*, 146, 349, *350*

chlorine dioxide, as disinfectant, 553

chlorine oxide, in chlorine catalytic cycle, 722

chlorine trifluoride, reaction with nickel(II) oxide, 551

chlorobenzene, structure of, 459

chloroform, 452

boiling point elevation and freezing point depression constants of, 633t

enthalpy of formation, 250

chloromethane, 244

enthalpy of formation, 249

chlorophyll, magnesium in, 977

cholesterol, 1

chromate ion, water pollution by, 304

chromium(III) picolinate, 304

chymotrypsin, 721

cinnabar, 3, 810, 1001

cinnamaldehyde, structure of, 436, 469

cisplatin, atomic distances in, 45

discovery of, 1049

isomerization of, 892, 1037

preparation of, 204

rate of substitution reaction, 680

structure of, 102

cis-trans isomers, 420, 445, 699

cisplatin, 1049

in coordination compounds, 1037

citric acid, 471t

reaction with sodium hydrogen carbonate, 149

structure of, 772

Clapeyron, Émile, 575

clathrate, 567

Clausius, Rudolf, 575

Clausius-Clapeyron equation, 575

clay(s), 989

cleavage, of crystalline solids, 603

clock reaction, iodine, 676

close packing, in crystal lattice, 595

coagulation, of colloids, 644

coal tar, aromatic compounds from, 458t

cobalt, colors of complexes of, 1047t

cobalt-60, gamma rays from, 300

cobalt(II) chloride, reaction with hydrochloric acid, 724

cobalt(II) choride hexahydrate, 97, *559*

Cockcroft, J. D., 1078

coefficient(s), stoichiometric, 115, 728

coffee, decaffeination with supercritical carbon dioxide, 577

coffee-cup calorimeter, 230

cohesive force A force of attraction between molecules of a single substance, 579

coins, nickel in, 896

coke, in iron production, 1026

water gas from, 969

cold pack, 245

colligative properties The properties of a solution that depend only on the number of solute particles per solvent molecule and not on the nature of the solute or solvent, 617, 628–642

of solutions of ionic compounds, 639

collision theory A theory of reaction rates that assumes that molecules must collide in order to react, 692

colloid(s) A state of matter intermediate between a solution and a suspension, in which solute particles are large enough to scatter light but too small to settle out, 642–646

types of, 642t

color(s), fireworks, 281

of acid–base indicators, *832*

of coordination compounds, 1045–1048

neon signs, 303

of transition metal compounds, 1020

visible light, 270, 1045

combined gas law. *See* general gas law.

combustion analysis, determining empirical formula by, 171–173

combustion calorimeter, 231

combustion reaction The reaction of a compound with molecular oxygen to form products in which all elements are combined with oxygen; also called burning, 116, 117

common ion effect The limiting of acid (or base) ionization caused by addition of its conjugate base (or conjugate acid), 811–814

solubility and, 838

common logarithms, A-2

common names, 451

of binary compounds, 82

compact disc player, light energy in, 273

completion, reaction going to, 730

complex(es), 790. *See also* coordination compound(s).

formation constants of, 846, A-26t

in enzyme-catalyzed reaction, 702

solubility and, 846–848

composition diagram(s), 857

compound(s) Matter that is composed of two or more kinds of atoms chemically combined in definite proportions, 13

binary, naming, 81

coordination. *See* coordination compound(s).

covalent, 350

determining formulas of, 88–95

hydrated, 96, 1029

ionic, 70–80

ionization energies and, 330

molecular, 80–82

naming, 77

odd-electron, 366, 429

specific heat capacity of, 216t

standard molar enthalpy of formation of, 236

compressibility The change in volume with change in pressure, 517

concentration(s) The amount of solute dissolved in a given amount of solution, 174
absorbance and, 191
in collision theory, 693
effect on equilibrium of changing, 745
in equilibrium constant expressions, 726
graph of, determining reaction rate from, *672, 673*
of ions in solution, 174–179
known, preparation of, 177–179
partial pressures as, 729
rate of change, 671–675
reaction rate and, 676–683
units of, 618
concrete, aerated, 1013
condensation The movement of molecules from the gas to the liquid phase, 571
condensation polymer(s) A synthetic organic polymer formed by combining monomer units in such a way that a small molecule, usually water, is split out, 480, 484–487
silicone, 990
condensation reaction A chemical reaction in which two molecules react by splitting out, or eliminating, a small molecule, 484–487
condensed formula A variation of a molecular formula that shows groups of atoms, 68, 445
condition(s), standard. *See* standard state.
conjugate acid–base pair(s) A pair of compounds or ions that differ by the presence of one H$^+$ unit, 764, 765t
in buffer solutions, 814, 818
ionization constants of, 775
strengths of, 769
conservation, energy, 255
laws of, 114, 211
constant(s), acid and base ionization, 769, 770t
Boltzmann, 866
equilibrium. *See* equilibrium constant.
Faraday, 925, 937
formation, 846
gas. *See* gas constant.

Henry's law, 626t
physical, A-14t
Planck's, 272
radioactive decay, 1074
rate. *See* rate constant.
Rydberg, 276
significant figures in, 36
solubility product, 833
van der Waals, 543
water ionization, 766
contact dermatitis, 896
contact process, sulfuric acid production by, 1013
continuous spectrum The spectrum of white light emitted by a heated object, consisting of light of all wavelengths, 275
conversion factor(s) A multiplier that relates the desired unit to the starting unit, 26, 29, 38, A-10
in mass/mole problems, 83
coordinate covalent bond(s) Interatomic attraction resulting from the sharing of a lone pair of electrons from one atom with another atom, 364, 789, 1031
coordination complex(es), 790
coordination compound(s) A compound in which a metal ion or atom is bonded to one or more molecules or anions to define a structural unit, 1029–1035
bonding in, 1040–1044
colors of, 1045–1048
formulas of, 1032–1034
magnetic properties of, 1043
naming of, 1034
spectrochemical series of, 1046
structures of, 1036–1040
coordination isomers Two or more complexes in which a coordinated ligand and a noncoordinated ligand are exchanged, 1036
coordination number The number of ligands attached to the central metal ion in a coordination compound, 1031
geometry and, 1036
copolymer A polymer formed by combining two or more different monomers, 484

copper, 24
biochemistry of, 327
density of, 48
electrolytic refining, 1028
isotopes of, 101
ores of, *1025*
production of, 1028
radioactive isotope, half-life of, 714
reaction with nitric acid, 146
reaction with silver ions, 142, *143*, 897, 899
copper sulfate, reaction with ammonia, 197
copper(I) chloride, in fireworks, 281
copper(I) ion, disproportionation reaction, 946
copper(II) ion, complexes of, *790*
copper(II) nitrate, decomposition of, 552
copper(II) oxide, reduction by hydrogen, 892
copper(II) sulfate pentahydrate, 97
coral, calcium carbonate in, *132*
core electrons The electrons in an atom's completed set of shells, 311, 350
core electrons, molecular orbitals containing, 426
corrosion The deterioration of metals by oxidation–reduction reactions, 1021, 1023
corundum, 985
cosmic radiation, 1083
coulomb (C) The quantity of charge that passes a point in an electric circuit when a current of 1 ampere flows for 1 second, 915, 937, A-9
Coulomb's law The force of attraction between the oppositely charged ions of an ionic compound is directly proportional to their charges and inversely proportional to the square of the distance between them, 78, 557
lattice energy and, 599–600
covalent bond(s) An interatomic attraction resulting from the sharing of electrons between the atoms, 349
polar and nonpolar, 375–379

valence bond theory of, 405–422
covalent compound(s) A compound formed by atoms that are covalently bonded to each other, 350
covalent radius, 319
covellite, 1028
cracking, in petroleum refining, 461
Crick, Francis, 392, 503, 565
critical point The upper end of the curve of vapor pressure versus temperature, 577
critical pressure The pressure at the critical point, 577
critical temperature The temperature at the critical point; above this temperature the vapor cannot be liquefied at any pressure, 577
crocoite, 304
cross-linked polyethylene (CLPE), 482
cross-linking, in vulcanized rubber, 483
cryolite, 978
in fireworks, 281
in Hall-Heroult process, 983, 1008
crystal lattice A solid, regular array of positive and negative ions, 79, 591
cubic centimeter, 29
cubic close-packed (ccp) unit cell, 595
cubic unit cell A unit cell having eight identical points at the corners of a cube, 591
cuprite, unit cell of, 611
curie A unit of radioactivity
Marie and Pierre Curie, 65, 342, 1002, 1064, 1082
cyanate ion, resonance structures, 379
cycloalkanes Compounds constructed with tetrahedral carbon atoms joined together to form a ring, 452
general formula of, 447t
naming of, A-18
cycloalkenes, 455
cyclobutadiene, molecular orbitals in, 440
cyclobutane, decomposition of, 715
structure of, 453

dipole/induced dipole attraction The electrostatic force between two neutral molecules, one having a permanent dipole and the other having an induced dipole, 565

dipole moment (μ) The product of the magnitude of the partial charges in a molecule and the distance by which they are separated, 380, 381t

diprotic acid, 135

disaccharides, 473

dispersion(s), colloidal, 642

dispersion forces Intermolecular attractions involving induced dipoles, 567

disproportionation reaction, 932, 1009

distillation, in petroleum refining, 461

disulfur dichloride, preparation of, 196

DNA. *See* deoxyribonucleic acid.

dolomite, 156, 203, 976

domain, ferromagnetic, 292

dopamine, 205

double bond A bond formed by sharing two pairs of electrons, one pair in a sigma bond and the other in a pi bond, 354

in alkenes, 453

valence bond theory of, 416–419

Downs cell, for producing sodium, 972

dry cell battery, 911

dry ice, 222, *223*, 609

Duncanson, L. A., 430

dye(s), pH indicating, 181

rate of reaction with bleach, *672*, 675

synthetic, 467

dynamic equilibrium A reaction in which the forward and reverse processes are occurring, 119

molecular description of, 119, *120*

vapor pressure and, 573

dynamite, *464*

eagles, effect of DDT on, 7

earth, alchemical meaning of, 975

effective atomic number (EAN) rule. *See* eighteen-electron rule.

effective nuclear charge (Z^*) The nuclear charge experienced by an electron in a multielectron atom, as modified by the other electrons, 308, 309t

atomic radius and, 320

efficiency, of fuel cell, 947

effusion The movement of gas molecules through a membrane or other porous barrier by random molecular motion, 538

isotopic separation by, 540

eighteen-electron rule Organometallic compounds in which the number of metal valence electrons plus the number of electrons donated by the ligand groups totals 18 are likely to be stable, 1050, 1053

Einstein, Albert, 273, 1070

ekA-silicon, 59

elastic collision, 543

elastomer(s) A synthetic organic polymer with very high elasticity, 483

electric automobile, 915

electric current, unit of, 937

electric field, polar molecules aligned in, *380*

electrical energy, 210

electrochemical cell(s) A device that produces an electric current as a result of an electron transfer reaction, 905–909

commercial, 909–915

nonstandard conditions for, 925–928

notation for, 909

potential of, 915–924

work done by, 928

electrochemistry, 896–947

electrode(s) A device such as a metal plate or wire for conducting electrons into and out of solutions in electrochemical cells, 123, 905

hydrogen, 908

inert, 908

pH, 181-182

standard hydrogen, 916, 918

terminology for, 934t

electrolysis The use of electrical energy to produce chemical change, 898, 931–936

aluminum production by, 982

electrodes in, 934t

fluorine production by, 1005

hydrogen produced by, 969

of aqueous solutions, 933

of sodium chloride, 527, 932, *933*, 972

of water, *12*, 263, 1001

electrolyte(s) A substance that ionizes in water or on melting to form an electrically conducting solution, 123

electromagnetic radiation Radiation that consists of wave-like electric and magnetic fields, including light, microwaves, radio signals, and x-rays, 269–271

gamma rays as, 1062

electromotive force (emf) Difference in potential energy per electrical charge, 915, 918

electron(s) (e⁻) A negatively charged subatomic particle found in the space about the nucleus, 51

assignment to atomic orbitals, 306–316

as beta particle, 1061

bond pair, 352

configuration. *See* electron configuration(s)

core, 311, 350

molecular orbitals containing, 426

counting, 937

demonstration of, 342

diffraction of, 282

direction of flow in voltaic cells, 906

in electrochemical cell, direction of flow, 917

lone pair of, 352

measurement of charge of, 344, *345*

octet of, 351, 352

pairing, magnetic properties and, 292

quantization of potential energy, 276, 284

shells and subshells, 285, 306t, 306–309

spin. *See* electron spin

transfer in oxidation–reduction reactions, 142

valence, 311, 349–351. *See also* bond pair(s), lone pair(s).

of main group elements, 964

of main group elements, repulsions of, 368

wave properties of, 282

electron affinity The energy change occurring when an atom of the element in the gas phase gains an electron, 324

acid strength and, 794

electronegativity and, 378

values of, A-21t

electron capture A nuclear process in which an inner-shell electron is captured, 1066

predicting, 1069

electron cloud pictures, 287

electron configuration(s), in coordination compounds, 1041–1043

of elements, 309, 310t

of heteronuclear diatomic molecules, 429

of homonuclear diatomic molecules, 427–429

of ions, 316–318

Lewis notation for, 351

main group, 309

noble gas notation for, 311

orbital box notation for, 305, 309

spdf notation for, 309

of transition elements, 315, 317, 1021

electron density The probability of finding an atomic electron within a given region of space, related to the square of the electron's wave function, 285

electron spin, pairing of, 292, 306

quantization of, 293

electron spin magnetic quantum number, 291, 293, 306

electron transfer reaction(s). *See* oxidation-reduction reaction(s).

electron volt (eV) The energy of an electron that has been accelerated by a potential of 1 volt, 1063, A-9

extensive properties Physical properties that depend on the amount of matter present, 16

f-block elements Transition elements whose occurrence in the periodic table coincides with the filling of the f orbitals, 1020

f orbital(s). *See* atomic orbital(s).

face-centered cubic (fcc) unit cell, 591, 593–594

factor-label method. *See* dimensional analysis.

Fahrenheit temperature scale A scale defined by the freezing and boiling points of pure water, defined as 32 °F and 212 °F, 27

Falkenhagen, Hans, 347

family, in periodic table. *See* group(s).

Faraday, Michael, 458, 937

Faraday constant (F) The proportionality constant that relates standard free energy of reaction to standard potential; the charge carried by one mole of electrons, 925, 937

fat(s) A solid triester of a long-chain fatty acid with glycerol, 476

energy content of, 215

unsaturated, *457*

fatty acid(s) A carboxylic acid containing an unbranched chain of 10 to 20 C atoms, 476

common, 476t

feldspar, 989

Fermi, Enrico, 1078

ferrocene, 1052

ferromagnetism A form of paramagnetism, seen in some metals and their alloys, in which the magnetic effect is greatly enhanced, 292

filling order, of electron subshells in atoms, 307

film badge, radiation monitoring, 1084

filtration, *12*

fingerprints, components of, 579

fire extinguisher, carbon dioxide, *526*

fire retardant, boric acid as, 984

fireworks, 281

metals in, 158, *163*

first law of thermodynamics The total energy of the universe is constant, 211, 222–226, 862

first-order reaction, 679

half-life of, 690, *691*

integrated rate equation, 683

nuclear, 1074

fission The highly exothermic process by which very heavy nuclei split to form lighter nuclei, 1080

nuclear, 1060

fixed notation, 33

flotation, for ore treatment, 1028

fluid, 8

supercritical, 577, 609

fluorapatite, 978

fluorescence, 1005

fluoride ion, dietary sources of, 854

fluorine, bonding in, 352

compounds of, hydrogen bonding in, 561

with main group elements, 966t

molecular orbital configuration of, 428

production of, 1005

reaction with nitrogen dioxide, 706

sigma bond in, 407

fluorite, *21*, 810, *834*, *842*, 976

unit cell of, 611

fluorocarbonyl hypofluorite, 108

fluorspar, 1005

foam, 642t

food, energy content of, 215

food irradiation, 1088

food tampering, titration for detecting, 188

fool's gold. *See* iron pyrite.

force(s), A-7

intermolecular. *See* intermolecular forces.

formal charge The charge on an atom in a molecule or ion calculated by assuming equal sharing of the bonding electrons, 359

bond polarity and, 377

formaldehyde, 470t

Lewis structure of, 353

orbital hybridization in, 417, *418*

structure of, 468

formation, enthalpy change for, 236

standard molar free energy of, 879

formation constant An equilibrium constant for the formation of a complex ion, 846

values of, 846, A-28t

formic acid, *471*, 472t

as weak acid, 771

decomposition of, 717

in water, equilibrium constant expression for, 742

reaction with sodium hydroxide, 779

formula(s), chemical, 14

condensed, 445

empirical, 90-91, 171

general, of hydrocarbons, 447t

molecular. *See* molecular formula.

of ionic compounds, 74

structures and, 596–599

perspective, 445

predicting, 966–967

structural. *See* structural formula.

formula unit The simplest ratio of ions in an ionic compound, similar to the molecular formula of a molecular compound, 86

formula weight, 86

fractional abundance, 57

Franklin, Rosalind, 392, 565

Frasch, Herman, 1001

Frasch process, *135*

free available chlorine, 958

free energy. *See* Gibbs free energy.

free energy change (ΔG), 876

equilibrium constant and, 878–879, 885

free radical(s) A neutral atom or molecule containing an unpaired electron, 366

freezing point depression, 634

for ionic solutions, 640t

freezing point depression constant (K_{fp}), 634

frequency (n) The number of complete waves passing a point in a given amount of time, 269

relation to energy of radiation, 272

frequency factor, in Arrhenius equation, 696

Friedel–Crafts reaction, 791–792

Frisch, Otto, 1080

frontalin, 447

fuel, density of, 41

ethanol (E85), 240

fossil, 256–261

fuel cell A voltaic cell in which reactants are continuously added, 262, 914

automotive use, 915

efficiency of, 947

Fuller, R. Buckminster, 64

functional group A structural fragment found in all members of a class of compounds, 462

2-furylmethanethiol, structure of, 400

fusion The state change from solid to liquid, 219

enthalpy of, 604, 605t, A-16t

heat of, 219

fusion, nuclear The highly exothermic process by which comparatively light nuclei combine to form heavier nuclei, 1081

galena, 841, 1001

as pigment, 18

structure of, 614

gallium, *981*

isotopes of, 101

melting point of, 46

gallium citrate, radioactive isotope in, 1075

gallium oxide, formula of, 93

Galton, Sir Francis, 579

Galvani, Luigi, 898, 910

galvanic cell. *See* voltaic cell(s).

gamma radiation High-energy electromagnetic radiation, 270, 343, 1061

gangue A mixture of sand and clay in which a desired mineral is usually found, 1025

gas(es) The phase of matter in which a substance has no definite shape and a volume defined only by the size of its container, 8
  compressibility of, 517, 556
  density, calculation from ideal gas law, 525
  diffusion of, 538, 867
  dissolution in liquids, 626
  expansion as spontaneous process, 862
  ideal, 524
  in equilibrium constant expression, 729–730
  kinetic-molecular theory of, 532–537, 555
  laws governing, 517–523, 537
  mixtures of, partial pressures in, 530–532
  noble. *See* noble gas(es).
  nonideal, 542
  pressure of, 516
  properties of, 514–553
  solubility in water, 566t
  speeds of molecules in, 533
  standard molar volume, 524
  volume effects on equilibria of, 746
gas centrifuge, 540
gas chromatograph, 2
gas constant (*R*) The proportionality constant in the ideal gas law, 0.082057 L · atm/mol · K or 8.314510 J/mol · K, 524
  in Arrhenius equation, 696
  in kinetic energy–temperature relation, 535
  in Maxwell's equation, 536
  in Nernst equation, 925
  in nonequilibrium free energy change, 878
  in osmotic pressure equation, 637
gas-forming reaction(s), 139–141, 150
  energy per kilogram, 914t
Gay-Lussac, Joseph, 522
GC-MS. *See* gas chromatograph *and* mass spectrometers
Geber (Jabir ibn Hayyan), 339
gecko, *568*

Geiger, Hans, 344
Geiger-Müller counter, 1073
gel A colloidal dispersion with a structure that prevents it from flowing, 642t, 643
gems, solubility and, 810
general gas law An equation that allows calculation of pressure, temperature, and volume when a given amount of gas undergoes a change in conditions, 521
geometric isomers Isomers in which the atoms of the molecule are arranged in different geometric relationships, 445, 1037
  of alkenes, 453
germanium, as semiconductor, 661
  compounds of, 986
Germer, L. H., 282
gestrinone, 3
Gibbs, J. Willard, 876
Gibbs free energy (G) A thermodynamic state function relating enthalpy, temperature, and entropy, 876
  cell potential and, 928
  work and, 879
gigaton, 950
Gillespie, Ronald J., 368
Gimli Glider, 41
glass An amorphous solid material, 603, 664
  colors of, 1020
  etching by hydrogen fluoride, 1008
  structure of, 603
glass electrode, 927, *928*
glassware, laboratory, *17*, *29*, *37*
global warming, 954
glucose, combustion of, stoichiometry of, 161–162
  formation of, thermodynamics, 891
  oxidation of, 947
  reaction with silver ion, 157
  structure and isomers of, 473
glycerin, reaction with boric acid, 757
glycerol, 463t
  as byproduct of biodiesel production, 479
  density of, 22
  reaction with fatty acids, 476

structure of, 463
use in humidor, 652
glycinate ion, 1058
glycine, structure of, 798
glycoaldehyde, structure of, 401
glycolysis, 895
glycylglycine, electrostatic potential map of, 382
goethite, *842*
gold,
  density of, 16
  oxidation by fluorine, 924
  radioactive isotope, half-life of, 714
  reaction with sodium cyanide, 204
Goldstein, Eugene, 343
Goodyear, Charles, 483
gout, lead poisoning and, 991
  uric acid and, 789
Graham, Thomas, 538, 642
Graham's law, 538
gram (g), 29
graph(s), analysis of, 39
graphene, 588
graphite electrode, 908
  oxidation of, 935
graphite, conversion to diamond, 894
  structure of, 64, 588
gravitational energy, 210
gray The SI unit of radiation dosage, 1082
greenhouse effect, 260
ground state The state of an atom in which all electrons are in the lowest possible energy levels, 277
group(s) The vertical columns in the periodic table of the elements, 60
  similarities within, 964t
Group 1A elements, 62. *See also* alkali metal(s).
  chemistry of, 971–975
Group 2A elements, 62. *See also* alkaline earth metal(s).
  chemistry of, 975–979
Group 3A elements, 63
  chemistry of, 979–986
  reduction potentials of, 1017t
Group 4A elements, 63
  chemistry of, 986–991
  hydrogen compounds of, 561

Group 5A elements, 64
  chemistry of, 991–1000
Group 6A elements, 65
  chemistry of, 1001–1004
Group 7A elements, 65. *See also* halogens.
  chemistry of, 1005–1010
Group 8A elements, 66. *See also* noble gas(es).
guanine, 392
  electrostatic potential surface of, 586
  hydrogen bonding to cytosine, 565
guidelines, assigning oxidation numbers, 144
  solubility of ionic compounds in water, *125*
Gummi Bear, *229*
gunpowder, 975
gypsum, 96, 976, 1001

Haber, Fritz, 600, 749
Haber-Bosch process, 749
  thermodynamics of, 895
Hahn, Otto, 1080, 1095
hair coloring, history of, 18
half-cell A compartment of an electrochemical cell in which a half-reaction occurs, 905
half-life ($t_{1/2}$) The time required for the concentration of one of the reactants to reach half of its initial value, 690–692
  calculation of, 1095
  for radioactive decay, 1072
half-reactions The two chemical equations into which the equation for an oxidation–reduction reaction can be divided, one representing the oxidation process and the other the reduction process, 143, 899
  sign of standard reduction potential for, 919
  standard potentials for, 917, *919*
halide ions Anions of the Group 7A elements, 76
  compounds with aluminum, 985
halitosis, 541
Hall, Charles Martin, 982
Hall-Heroult process, aluminum production by, 982
halogenation, of benzene, 461

methanol *(Continued)*
  reaction with hydrogen bromide, 716
  spontaneity of formation reaction, 872
  synthesis of, 165, 890
methionine, 541
methyl acetate, reaction with sodium hydroxide, 680
methyl chloride, 452
  mass spectrum of, 110
  reaction with halide ions, 697
  reaction with silicon, 549
methyl ethyl ketone, 470t
methyl mercaptan, 541
methyl salicylate, 474, 638
N-methylacetamide, structure of, 402, 475
methylamine, as weak base, 771
  electrostatic potential map of, 382
methylamines, 466
2-methyl-1,3-butadiene. *See* isoprene.
3-methylbutyl acetate, 474t
methylcyclopentane, isomerization of, 753
methylene blue, 204
methylene chloride, 452
2-methylpentane, structure of, 449
2-methylpropene, reaction with hydrogen chloride, 457
  structure of, 444, 453
metric system A decimal system for recording and reporting scientific measurements, in which all units are expressed as powers of 10 times some basic unit, 25
mica, structure of, 989
Michaelis, Leonor, 702
microstates, 865
microwave radiation, 270
milk, coagulation of, 644
  freezing of, *22*
millerite, 170
Millikan, Robert, 344
milliliter (mL) A unit of volume equivalent to one thousandth of a liter; 1 mL = 1 cm3, 29
millimeter of mercury (mm Hg) A common unit of pressure, defined as the pressure that can support a 1-millimeter

column of mercury; 760 mm Hg = 1 atm, 516, A-8
mineral oil, density of, 42
minerals, analysis of, 169
  clay, 989
  silicate, 988
  solubility of, 810
miscible liquids Liquids that mix to an appreciable extent to form a solution, 621
mixture(s) A combination of two or more substances in which each substance retains its identity, 10–11, 14
  analysis of, 169–173
  gaseous, partial pressures in, 530–532
  models, molecular, 69
  moderator, nuclear, 1060
  Mohr method, 186
  Moisson, Henri, 1005
  molal boiling point elevation constant (K_{bp}), 633
molality (m) The number of moles of solute per kilogram of solvent, 618
  molar absorptivity, 192
  molar enthalpy of vaporization ($\Delta_{vap}H°$), relation to molar enthalpy of condensation, 571
  molar heat capacity, 216, A-15t
molar mass (M) The mass in grams of one mole of particles of any substance, 83
  from colligative properties, 637–638
  determination by titration, 187
  effusion rate and, 538
  from ideal gas law, 526
  molecular speed and, 536
  polarizability and, 566
  molar volume, standard, 524
molarity (M) The number of moles of solute per liter of solution, 174, 618
mole (mol) The SI base unit for amount of substance, 82, A-12
  conversion to mass units, 83
  of reaction, 167, 227
mole fraction (X) The ratio of the number of moles of one substance to the total number of moles in a mixture of substances, 531, 618

molecular compound(s) A compound formed by the combination of atoms without significant ionic character, 80–82. *See also* covalent compound(s).
  as Brønsted acids and bases, 762
  as Lewis acids, 791
  of main group elements, 966
  as nonelectrolytes, 124
molecular formula A written formula that expresses the number of atoms of each type within one molecule of a compound, 68
  determining, 88–95
  empirical formula and, 90
  relation to empirical formula, 91
molecular geometry The arrangement in space of the central atom and the atoms directly attached to it, 370
  hybrid orbitals and, *410*
  molecular polarity and, 380–386, 394t
  multiple bonds and, 373
  molecular models, 69
  molecular orbital(s), bonding and antibonding, 423
  from atomic *p* orbitals, 426
molecular orbital (MO) theory A model of bonding in which pure atomic orbitals combine to produce molecular orbitals that are delocalized over two or more atoms, 405, 422–432, 1040
  molecular orbital theory, for metals and semiconductors, 657
  resonance and, 431
  molecular polarity, 380–386, 394t
  intermolecular forces and, 557
  of lipids, 508
  miscibility and, 621
  of surfactants, 645
molecular solid(s) A solid formed by the condensation of covalently bonded molecules, 602
  solubilities of, 622

molecular structure, acid-base properties and, 793–799
  bonding and, 348–403
  entropy and, 869
  VSEPR model of, 367–375
molecular weight. *See* molar mass.
molecularity The number of particles colliding in an elementary step, 703
  reaction order and, 704
molecule(s) The smallest unit of a compound that retains the composition and properties of that compound, 14
  calculating mass of, 87
  collisions of, reaction rate and, 692
  early definition of, 341
  nonpolar, interactions of, 565–568
  polar, interactions of, 560
  shapes of, 367–375
  speeds in gases, 533
molybdenite, 1024
molybdenum, generation of technetium from, 1087
monatomic ion(s) An ion consisting of one atom bearing an electric charge, 72
  naming, 76
Mond, Ludwig, 1049
Mond process, 1050
monodentate ligand(s) A ligand that coordinates to the metal via a single Lewis base atom, 1031
monomer(s) The small units from which a polymer is constructed, 478
monoprotic acid A Brønsted acid that can donate one proton, 763
monosaccharides, 473
monounsaturated fatty acid, 476
moon, rock samples analyzed, 1088
moral issues in science, 7
mortar, lime in, 978, 979
Moseley, Henry G. J., 60, 344
mosquitos, DDT for killing, 7
Mulliken, Robert S., 404
multiple bonding, valence bond theory of, 416–421

multiple bonds, 354
  molecular geometry and, 373
  in resonance structures, 361
mutation, of retroviruses, 507
Mylar, 485
myoglobin, 1033
myristic acid, 579

naming, of alcohols, 463t, A-19
  of aldehydes and ketones, 470t, A-19
  of alkanes, 448t, 450, A-17
  of alkenes, 454, A-18
  of alkynes, 456t, A-19
  of anions and cations, 76
  of aromatic compounds, A-19
  of benzene derivatives, A-19
  of binary nonmetal compounds, 81
  of carboxylic acids, 471, A-19
  of coordination compounds, 1034
  of esters, 473, 474t, A-20
  of ionic compounds, 77
nanometer, 27
nanotubes, carbon, 588
naphthalene, enthalpy of formation, 247
  melting point, *17*
  solubility in benzene, 622
  structure of, 458
National Institute of Standards and Technology (NIST), 30, 175, 236
natural gas, 258
natural logarithms, A-2
neon, density of, 23
  line emission spectrum of, *276*
  mass spectrum of, *55*
neptunium, 1078
Nernst, Walther, 925
Nernst equation A mathematical expression that relates the potential of an electrochemical cell to the concentrations of the cell reactants and products, 925
net ionic equation(s) A chemical equation involving only those substances undergoing chemical changes in the

course of the reaction, 129–131
  of strong acid–strong base reactions, 137
network solid(s) A solid composed of a network of covalently bonded atoms, 602
  silicon dioxide, 987
  solubilities of, 623
neutral solution A solution in which the concentrations of hydronium ion and hydroxide ion are equal, 766
neutralization reaction(s) An acid–base reaction that produces a neutral solution of a salt and water, 137, 779
neutrino(s) A massless, chargeless particle emitted by some nuclear reactions, 1066
neutron(s) An electrically neutral subatomic particle found in the nucleus, 51
  bombardment with, 1078
  conversion to electron and proton, 1063
  demonstration of, 347
  in nuclear reactor, 1060
  nuclear stability and, 1067
neutron activation analysis, 1088
neutron capture reactions, 1078
newton (N) The SI unit of force, $1 N = 1 kg \cdot m/s^2$, A-7
Newton, Isaac, 340
Nicholson, William, 910
nickel, allergy to, 896
  in alnico V, 292
  coordination complex with ammonia, 1031
  density of, 44
  in memory metal, 1018
  reaction with oxygen, 892
nickel(II) carbonate, reaction with sulfuric acid, 141
nickel carbonyl, 1049
  decomposition of, temperature and spontaneity, 883
nickel(II) chloride hexahydrate, 98, 1029, *1030*
nickel(II) complexes, solubility of, *846*
nickel(II) formate, 335
nickel(II) ions, light absorption by, 190

nickel(II) nitrate, reaction with ammonia and ethylenediamine, 758
nickel(II) oxide, reaction with chlorine trifluoride, 551
nickel sulfide, quantitative analysis of, 170
nickel tetracarbonyl, substitution of, 721
nickel-cadmium (ni-cad) battery, 913
nicotine, structure of, 468, 798
nicotinic acid, structure of, 807
nitinol, 1018
nitramid, decomposition of, 720
nitrate ion, concentration in aquarium, 994
  molecular geometry of, 374
  resonance structures of, 362
  structure of, 357
nitration, of benzene, 461
nitric acid, 996
  as oxidizing agent, 146t
  pH of, 181
  production by Ostwald process, 996
  production from ammonia, 163
  reaction with copper, 146
  strength of, 794
  structure of, 357
nitric oxide. *See* nitrogen monoxide.
nitride(s), 992
nitrification, by bacteria, 994
nitrite ion, concentration in aquarium, 994
  linkage isomers containing, 1037
  molecular geometry of, 374
  resonance structures of, 363
nitrito complex, 1037
nitro complex, 1037
nitrogen, abundance of, 991
  bond order in, 386
  chemistry of, 991–996
  compounds of, hydrogen bonding in, 561
  compounds with hydrogen, 993

dissociation energy of triple bond, 992
  fixation of, 64, 951
  Henry's law constant, 626t
  liquid and gas volumes, *556*
  liquid, *519*, 992
  molecular orbital configuration of, 428
  oxidation states of, 992
  oxides of, 993, 995t
  reaction with hydrogen, 527
  reaction with oxygen, 740, 748
  transmutation to oxygen, 1077
nitrogen dioxide, 995t
  decomposition of, 714
  dimerization of, 367, *368*, 734, 748, 995
  free radical, 366
  reaction with carbon monoxide, 681, 707
  reaction with fluorine, 706
  reaction with water, 139
nitrogen fixation The process by which nitrogen gas is converted to useful nitrogen-containing compounds, such as ammonia, 64
nitrogen metabolism, urea and uric acid from, 789
nitrogen monoxide, 993, 995t
  biological roles of, 367
  free radical, 366
  molecular orbital configuration of, 429
  oxidation of, 244
  reaction with bromine, 701, 713
  reaction with oxygen, mechanism of, 708–710
nitrogen narcosis, 542
nitrogen oxide, enthalpy of formation, 246
nitrogen trifluoride, molecular polarity of, 384
  structure of, 356
nitrogenous base(s), pairing of, 565
nitroglycerin, *464*
  decomposition of, 238
nitromethane, vapor pressure of, 582
nitronium ion, Lewis structure of, 354
m-nitrophenol, structure of, 805

nitrosyl bromide, decomposition of, 754
formation of, 701, 713
nitrosyl ion, 435
nitrous acid, 996
strength of, 794
nitrous oxide. *See* dinitrogen oxide.
nitryl chloride, decomposition of, 710
electrostatic potential map of, 400
nitryl fluoride, 718
Nobel, Alfred, *464*
noble gas electron configuration, in ions, 330
noble gas(es) The elements in Group 8A of the periodic table, 66
compounds of, 365, 404
electron affinity of, 325
electron configuration of, 73, 313, 351, 964
noble gas notation An abbreviated form of spdf notation that replaces the completed electron shells with the symbol of the corresponding noble gas in brackets, 311
noble metals, 996
nodal surface A surface on which there is zero probability of finding an electron, 290, 291
node(s) A point of zero amplitude of a wave, 270, 284
nonbonding electrons. *See* lone pair(s).
nonelectrolyte A substance that dissolves in water to form an electrically nonconducting solution, 124
nonequilibrium conditions, reaction quotient at, 732, 925
nonideal gases, 542
nonideal solutions, 629
nonmetal(s) An element characterized by a lack of metallic properties, 60
anions formed by, 72
binary compounds of, 81
electron affinity of, 324
electronegativity of, 376
nonpolar covalent bond A covalent bond in which there is equal sharing of the bonding electron pair, 375
nonpolar molecules, 383
interactions of, 565–568

nonspontaneous reaction, 861. *See also* reactant-favored reaction(s).
normal boiling point The boiling point when the external pressure is 1 atm, 576
for common compounds, 572t
northern lights, 268
northwest–southeast rule A product-favored reaction involves a reducing agent below and to the right of the oxidizing agent in the table of standard reduction potentials, 921
novocaine, 805
nuclear binding energy The energy required to separate the nucleus of an atom into protons and neutrons, 1069–1072
nuclear charge, effective, 308, 309t
nuclear chemistry, 1060–1097
nuclear energy, 1081
nuclear fission A reaction in which a large nucleus splits into two or more smaller nuclei, 1080
nuclear fusion A reaction in which several small nuclei react to form a larger nucleus, 1081
nuclear magnetic resonance (NMR) spectrometer, *169*, 294
nuclear medicine, 1085
nuclear reaction(s) A reaction involving one or more atomic nuclei, resulting in a change in the identities of the isotopes, 1062–1067
artificial, 1077–1080
predicting types of, 1068
rates of, 1072–1077
nuclear reactor A container in which a controlled nuclear reaction occurs, 1080
breeder, 1094
natural, 1060, 1093
nuclear spin, quantization of, 294
nucleation, of gas bubbles, 641
nucleon A nuclear particle, either a neutron or a proton, 1070

nucleus The core of an atom, made up of protons and neutrons, 51
demonstration of, 344, *345*
stability of, 1067–1072
nutrition label, energy content on, 215
Nyholm, Ronald S., 368
nylon, 486

octahedral electron-pair geometry, orbital hybridization and, *410*, 414
octahedral holes, 596
octahedral molecular geometry, 369, 1036
octane, combustion of, 116
heat of combustion, 232
reaction with oxygen, 547
vapor pressure of, 583
octet A stable configuration of eight electrons surrounding an atomic nucleus, 351
octet rule When forming bonds, atoms of main group elements gain, lose, or share electrons to achieve a stable configuration having eight valence electrons, 352
exceptions to, 353, 364–367
odd-electron compounds, 366, 429, 995
odors, 541
oil(s) A liquid triester of a long-chain fatty acid with glycerol, 476
soaps and, 645
Oklo, natural nuclear rector at, 1060
oleic acid, 471t
olivine, 988
Olympic Analytical Laboratory, 1
optical isomers Isomers that are nonsuperimposable mirror images of each other, 445, 1038
orbital(s) The matter wave for an allowed energy state of an electron in an atom or molecule, 285
atomic. *See* atomic orbital(s).
molecular. *See* molecular orbital(s).
orbital box diagram A notation for the electron configuration of an atom in which each orbital is shown as a box and the number and

spin direction of the electrons are shown by arrows, 305, 309
orbital hybridization The combination of atomic orbitals to form a set of equivalent hybrid orbitals that minimize electron-pair repulsions, 408–416
orbital overlap Partial occupation of the same region of space by orbitals from two atoms, 406
order, bond. *See* bond order.
reaction. *See* reaction order.
ore(s) A sample of matter containing a desired mineral or element, usually with large quantities of impurities, 1025
insoluble salts in, 842
organic compounds, bonding in, 443–495
naming of, 448t, 450, A-17
organometallic chemistry, 1048–1053
orientation of reactants, effect on reaction rate, 695
Orlon, 481t
ornithine, 201
orpiment, 810
ortho position, 459
orthophosphoric acid, 999
orthorhombic sulfur, 1001
orthosilicates, 988
osmium, density of, 1020
osmosis The movement of solvent molecules through a semipermeable membrane from a region of lower solute concentration to a region of higher solute concentration, 635
osmotic pressure (Π) The pressure exerted by osmosis in a solution system at equilibrium, 636
Ostwald, Friedrich Wilhelm, 83
Ostwald process, 996
overlap, orbital, 406
overvoltage, 935
oxalate ion, as ligand, 1031
oxalic acid, 471t
as polyprotic acid, 763t
molar mass of, 87
titration of, 183, 827

petroleum, 259
  chemistry of, 461
  energy of combustion, 257t
pH The negative of the base-10 logarithm of the hydrogen ion concentration; a measure of acidity, 179–182, 767
  in aquarium, 994
  in buffer solutions, 814–821
  of blood, 822
  calculating equilibrium constant from, 780
  calculating from equilibrium constant, 782–787
  change in, during acid–base titration, 821
  common ion effect and, 811–814
pH meter, *181*, 927, *928*
phase change, as spontaneous process, 862
  condensation, 571
  heat transfer in, 220
  vaporization, 571
phase diagram A graph showing which phases of a substance exist at various temperatures and pressures, 606–609
phase transition temperature, 1018
phenanthroline, as ligand, 1031
phenol, structure of, 459
phenolphthalein, *830*
  structure of, 670
phenyl acetate, hydrolysis of, 713
phenylalanine, structure of, 397, 491
Philosopher's Stone, 340
phosgene, 398
  molecular polarity of, 381, *382*
phosphate ion, buffer solution of, 815t
  in biological buffer system, 822
  spectrophotometric analysis of, 205
phosphates, solubility in strong acids, 841
phosphine, 997
  decomposition of, 719
phosphines, in organometallic compounds, 1051
phosphoenolpyruvate (PEP), 884

phosphoric acid, 1000
  as polyprotic acid, 763t, 773
  structure of, 808
phosphorus, allotropes of, 65, 992
  chemistry of, 997–1000
  coordinate covalent bonds to, 365
  discovery of, 340, 997
  oxides of, 997
  reaction with chlorine, 113, 159
  reaction with oxygen, 116
  sulfides of, 998
phosphorus oxoacids, 999
phosphorus pentachloride, decomposition of, 738, 752, 755
phosphorus pentafluoride, orbital hybridization in, 414–415
phosphorus trichloride, enthalpy of formation, 246
phosphoserine, structure of, 436
photocell, *274*
photoelectric effect The ejection of electrons from a metal bombarded with light of at least a minimum frequency, 273
photon(s) A "particle" of electromagnetic radiation having zero mass and an energy given by Planck's law, 273
photosynthesis The process by which plants make sugar, 511
phthalic acid, buffer solution of, 815t
physical change(s) A change that involves only physical properties, 17
physical properties Properties of a substance that can be observed and measured without changing the composition of the substance, 14–16
  temperature dependence of, 15
pi (π) bond(s) The second (and third, if present) bond in a multiple bond; results from sideways overlap of p atomic orbitals, 417, 419
  in ozone and benzene, 431
  molecular orbital view of, 427

pickle, light from, 301
picometer, 27
pie filling, specific heat capacity of, 216
pig iron, 1026
pigment(s), 18
pile, voltaic, 910
Piria, Raffaele, 760
pitchblende, 342
pK_a The negative of the base-10 logarithm of the acid ionization constant, 775
  at midpoint of acid–base titration, 825
  pH of buffer solution and, 817
planar node. *See* atomic orbital(s) and nodal surface.
Planck, Max, 272, 346
Planck's constant (*h*) The proportionality constant that relates the frequency of radiation to its energy, 272
Planck's equation, 271–273
plasma A gas-like phase of matter that consists of charged particles, 1082
plaster of Paris, 97
plastic(s), recycling symbols, 494
plastic sulfur, 1001
plating, by electrolysis, 931
platinum, in cisplatin, 1049
  in oxidation of ammonia, 163, *164*
  in Zeise's salt, 430
platinum electrode, 908
platinum group metals, 1024
Plexiglas, 481t
plotting. *See* graph(s).
plutonium, 1078
plutonium-239, fission of, 1080
pOH The negative of the base-10 logarithm of the hydroxide ion concentration; a measure of basicity, 767
poisoning, carbon monoxide, 1033
  lead, 991
polar covalent bond A covalent bond in which there is unequal sharing of the bonding electron pair, 375
polarity, bond, 375–379
  molecular, 380–386, 394t
  intermolecular forces and, 557

solubility of alcohols and, 465
solubility of carboxylic acids and, 471
polarizability The extent to which the electron cloud of an atom or molecule can be distorted by an external electric charge, 566
polarized light, rotation by optically active compounds, 445, *446*
polonium, 65, 342, 1002
  from decay of uranium, 1064, 1065
polyacrylate polymer, in disposable diapers, 487
polyacrylonitrile, 481t
polyamide(s) A condensation polymer formed by elimination of water between two types of monomers, one with two carboxylic acid groups and the other with two amine groups, 485
polyatomic ion(s) An ion consisting of more than one atom, 73
  names and formulas of, 74t, 76
  oxidation numbers in, 145
polydentate ligand(s) A ligand that attaches to a metal with more than one donor atom, 1031
polydimethylsiloxane, 990
polyester(s) A condensation polymer formed by elimination of water between two types of monomers, one with two carboxylic acid groups and the other with two alcohol groups, 485
polyethylene, 480, 481t
  high density (HDPE), density of, 22
  in disposable diapers, 487
polyethylene terephthalate (PET), 485, 493
polyisoprene, 483
polymer(s) A large molecule composed of many smaller repeating units, usually arranged in a chain, 478–487
  addition, 480–484
  classification of, 480
  condensation, 480, 484–487
  silicone, 990

Project Stardust, 607
promethium, 1079
propane, as fuel, 249
  combustion of, balanced
      equation for, 117
  enthalpy of combustion,
      228
  percent composition of, 89
  structure of, 444
  use in hot air balloons, 208
1,2,3-propanetriol, 463t
propanoic acid, as weak
      acid, 771
propanol, 463t
propene, 453, 685
  hydrogenation of, 390
  reaction with bromine,
      457
propionic acid, 472t
proportionality constant,
      518, 535
proportionality symbol, 678
propyl alcohol, 463t
propyl propanoate, 478
propylene, 453
propylene glycol, 616
  as antifreeze, *465*
protein(s),
  as hydrophilic colloids, 644
  energy content of, 215
proton exchange membrane
      (PEM), 914
proton(s) A positively charged
      subatomic particle found in
      the nucleus, 51
  bombardment with, 1078
  demonstration of, 345
  donation by Brønsted acid,
      134, 761
  name of, 341
  nuclear stability and, 1067
Prout, William, 341
Prussian blue, 1020
purification, of mixtures, 11
Purkinji, John, 579
putrescine, 466
pyridine, resonance struc-
      tures of, 494
  structure of, 798
  substitutions on, 807
pyrite, iron, 13, *14*
pyrometallurgy Recovery of
      metals from their ores by
      high-temperature processes,
      1026
pyroxenes, structure of,
      988
pyruvate, production of
      lactate from, 895

quadratic equations, A-5
quadratic formula, use in
      concentration prob-
      lems, 738
qualitative information Non-
      numerical experimental
      observations, such as
      descriptive or comparative
      data, 5, 25
quantitative analysis, 169
quantitative information
      Numerical experimental
      data, such as measurements
      of changes in mass or vol-
      ume, 5, 25
quantity, of pure substance,
      82
quantization A situation in
      which only certain energies
      are allowed, 346
  of electron potential
      energy, 276, 284
  of electron spin, 293
  of nuclear spin, 294
  Planck's assumption of,
      272
quantum mechanics A general
      theoretical approach to
      atomic behavior that
      describes the electron in
      an atom as a matter wave,
      283–287
quantum number(s) A set of
      numbers with integer values
      that define the properties of
      an atomic orbital, 284–287,
      291
  allowed values of, 285
  angular momentum, 285
  in macroscopic system,
      867
  magnetic, 286
  Pauli exclusion principle
      and, 305
  principal, 277, 285
quartz, 987
  structure of, *603*
quinine, 103, 467

rad A unit of radiation dosage,
      1082
radial distribution plot,
      288
radiation, background,
      1083
  cancer treatment with,
      1086
  cosmic, 1083
  electromagnetic, 269–271

health effects of, 1082–
      1084
  safe exposure, 1084
  treatment of food with,
      1088
  units of, 1082
radiation absorbed dose
      (rad), 1082
radioactive decay series A
      series of nuclear reactions
      by which a radioactive iso-
      tope decays to form a stable
      isotope, 1063–1066
radioactivity, discovery of,
      342, *343*
radiochemical dating,
      1075
radium, 342
  from decay of uranium,
      1064
  radon, as environmental
      hazard, 1065
  from decay of uranium,
      1064
  radioactive half-life of, 691
Raoult, François M., 629
Raoult's law The vapor pressure
      of the solvent is propor-
      tional to the mole fraction of
      the solvent in a solution,
      629
rare gas(es). *See* noble
      gas(es).
Raschig reaction, 707, 993
rate. *See* reaction rate(s).
rate constant (k) The propor-
      tionality constant in the rate
      equation, 678–680
  Arrhenius equation for,
      696
  half-life and, 690
  units of, 680
rate constant, for radioactiv-
      ity, 1074
rate equation(s) The mathe-
      matical relationship between
      reactant concentration and
      reaction rate, 678
  determining, 680
  first-order, nuclear, 1074
  for elementary step, 704
  graphical determination
      of, 687–689
  integrated, 683–692
  integrated, for nuclear
      decay, 1074
  reaction mechanisms and,
      705–710
  reaction order and, 679

rate law. *See* rate
      equation(s).
rate-determining step The
      slowest elementary step of a
      reaction mechanism, 706
reactant(s) A starting sub-
      stance in a chemical reac-
      tion, 18, 114
  effect of adding or remov-
      ing, 745
  in equilibrium constant
      expression, 728
  heat as, 748
  rate of concentration
      change, 673
  reaction rate and,
      677–683
reactant-favored reaction(s)
      A system in which, when a
      reaction appears to stop,
      reactants predominate over
      products, 121
  equilibrium constant for,
      730
  predicting, 874, 878
reaction(s) A process in which
      substances are changed into
      other substances by rear-
      rangement, combination, or
      separation of atoms, 18. *See
      also* under element, com-
      pound, or chemical group of
      interest.
  (n, γ), 1078
  acid–base, 136–138, 149
  addition, 456
  aquation, 720
  in aqueous solution, 121
  stoichiometry of,
      182–189
  types of, 149
  autoionization, 765
  chain, 1080
  condensation, 484
  coupling of, 884
  direction of, acid–base
      strength and, 776
  reaction quotient and,
      732
  disproportionation, 1009
  electron transfer, 896–947.
      See also oxidation–
      reduction reaction(s).
  enthalpy change for,
      227–229
  esterification, 472
  exchange, 121, 149
  free energy change for,
      877

saltpeter, 971, 975
sandwich compounds, 1052
saponification The hydrolysis of an ester, 476
sapphire, 985
saturated compound(s) A hydrocarbon containing only single bonds, 448. *See also* alkanes.
saturated solution(s) A stable solution in which the maximum amount of solute has been dissolved, 620
reaction quotient in, 844
saturation, of fatty acids, 476
scanning electron microscopy (SEM), *27*
Scheele, Carl Wilhelm, 114, 1005, 1016
Schrödinger, Erwin, 283, 346
science, goals of, 6
methods of, 3–7
scientific notation A way of presenting very large or very small numbers in a compact and consistent form that simplifies calculations, 32–35, A-3
operations in, 34
Scott Couper, Archibald, 342
screening, of nuclear charge, 308
SCUBA diving, gas laws and, 542
Henry's law and 626
sea slug, sulfuric acid excreted by, *772*
sea water, density of, 39
ion concentrations in, 122t, 653t
magnesium in, 976
pH of, 181
salt concentration in, 186
sodium and potassium ions in, 971
Seaborg, Glenn T., 1078
sebum, 579
second, definition of, A-11
second law of thermodynamics The entropy of the universe increases in a spontaneous process, 863
secondary alcohols, 468
secondary battery A battery in which the reactions can be reversed, so the battery can be recharged, 911

second-order reaction, 679
half-life of, 690
integrated rate equation, 686
seesaw molecular geometry, 372
selenium, uses of, 1002
semimetals. *See* metalloid(s).
semipermeable membrane A thin sheet of material through which only certain types of molecules can pass, 635
shielding constant, effective nuclear charge and, 337
SI Abbreviation for Système International d'Unités, a uniform system of measurement units in which a single base unit is used for each measured physical quantity, 25, A-11
siderite, 154
sievert The SI unit of radiation dosage to biological tissue, 1082
sigma (s) bond(s) A bond formed by the overlap of orbitals head to head, and with bonding electron density concentrated along the axis of the bond, 407
sign conventions, for electron affinity, 325
for energy calculations, *217*, 224t, 226
for voltaic cells, 906
significant figure(s) The digits in a measured quantity that are known exactly, plus one digit that is inexact to the extent of ±1, 35–38
in atomic masses, 84
logarithms and, A-3
silicate ion, in minerals, 810
silane, comparison to methane, 962
reaction with oxygen, 547
silica, 987
silica aerogel, 607
silica gel, 988
silicates, minerals containing, 988
structure of, 603
silicon,
bond energy compared to carbon, 446
chemistry of, 986–990

purification of, 986
reaction with methyl chloride, 549
similarity to boron, 979
similarity to carbon, 962
unit cell of, 613
silicon carbide, 1014
unit cell of, 614
silicon dioxide, 987
comparison to carbon dioxide, 962
in gemstones, 810, 985
reaction with hydrogen fluoride, 1008
silicon tetrachloride, 986
molecular geometry, 369
silicone polymers, 990
Silly Putty, 990
silt, formation of, 644
silver, as bacteriocide, 148
density of, 44
isotopes of, 101
silver acetate, solubility of, 838
silver bromide, reaction with sodium thiosulfate, 198
solubility of, 832–833
silver chloride, free energy change of dissolution, 885
reaction with potassium nitrate, 122, 127, 129
solubility of, 837
in aqueous ammonia, 742, 847
silver chromate, 186
formation by precipitation, 129
solubility of, 837, 839
silver coulometer, 946
silver nitrate, reaction with potassium chloride, 122, 127, 129
silver(I) oxide, decomposition of, 892
silver oxide battery, 912
silver sulfide, reaction with aluminum, 156
silver-zinc battery, 945
simple cubic (sc) unit cell, 591
single bond A bond formed by sharing one pair of electrons; a sigma bond, 407
slag, in blast furnace, 1027
Slater's rules, 337
slime, 483
slope, of straight-line graph, 40, 687

Smalley, Richard, 255
smog, photochemical, 261
snot-tites, 1004
soap A salt produced by the hydrolysis of a fat or oil by a strong base, 476, 645
hard water and, 980
soapstone, 976
soda ash. *See* sodium carbonate.
soda-lime process, 974
Soddy, Frederick, 344, 1062
sodium, in fireworks, 281
preparation of, 971
reaction with chlorine, *4*, 146, 349, *350*
reaction with water, *5*
sodium acetate, calculating pH of aqueous solution, 785
in heat pack, 620
sodium azide, in air bags, *515*, 522, 528, 547
preparation of, 202, 553
sodium bicarbonate, 974. *See also* sodium hydrogen carbonate.
reaction with acetic acid, 777
sodium borohydride, 984, 1016
as reducing catalyst, 470
sodium carbonate, 177
calculating pH of aqueous solution, 787
industrial uses, 974
primary standard for acid–base titration, 187
sodium chloride, as strong electrolyte, 123
composition of, *4*, 13
crystal lattice of, 79
electrolysis of, 527, 932, *933*, 972
entropy of solution process, 873
ion charges in, 74
lattice enthalpy calculation for, 601
melting ice and, 639
standard enthalpy of formation of, 236
structure of, 596, *597*
sodium fluoride, 47
sodium hydrogen carbonate, reaction with citric acid, 149
reaction with tartaric acid, 140

standard molar enthalpy of formation ($\Delta_f H°$), enthalpy of solution from, 625
values of, A-29t

standard molar enthalpy of vaporization ($\Delta_{vap} H°$) The energy required to convert one mole of a substance from a liquid to a gas, 570, 572t

standard molar entropy (S°) The entropy of a substance in its most stable form at a pressure of 1 bar, 868, 869t
values of, A-29t

standard molar free energy of formation ($\Delta_f G°$) The free energy change for the formation of one mole of a compound from its elements, all in their standard states, 879
values of, A-29t

standard molar volume The volume occupied by one mole of gas at standard temperature and pressure; 22.414 L, 524

standard potential ($E°$cell) The potential of an electrochemical cell measured under standard conditions, 916
of alkali metals, 973
calculation of, 917, 921
equilibrium constant calculated from, 929

standard reaction enthalpy ($\Delta_r H°$) The enthalpy change of a reaction that occurs with all reactants and products in their standard states, 227
product-favored vs. reactant-favored reactions and, 239

standard reduction potential(s), 917, 920t
of halogens, 1006t
values of, A-36t

standard state The most stable form of an element or compound in the physical state in which it exists at 1 bar and the specified temperature, 227, 862

standard temperature and pressure (STP) A temperature of 0 °C and a pressure of exactly 1 atm, 524

standardization The accurate determination of the concentration of an acid, base, or other reagent for use in a titration, 186

standing wave A single-frequency wave having fixed points of zero amplitude, 284

starch, 473

starch-iodide paper, 188

stars, elements formed in, 51

state(s), ground and excited, 277
physical, changes of, 219
of matter, 7, 555
reaction enthalpy and, 228
standard. *See* standard state.

state function A quantity whose value is determined only by the state of the system, 226, 862

stearic acid, 471t

steel, production of, 1027

stem cell scandal, 6

stereoisomers Two or more compounds with the same molecular formula and the same atom-to-atom bonding, but with different arrangements of the atoms in space, 445

sterilization, by irradiation, 1088

steroids, 1

stibnite, 109, 810

stoichiometric coefficients The multiplying numbers assigned to the species in a chemical equation in order to balance the equation, 115
electrochemical cell potential and, 921
exponents in rate equation vs., 678
fractional, 227
in equilibrium constant expression, 728

stoichiometric factor(s) A conversion factor relating moles of one species in a reaction to

moles of another species in the same reaction, 160, 528
in solution stoichiometry, 182
in titrations, 185

stoichiometry The study of the quantitative relations between amounts of reactants and products, 115
ICE table and, 727
ideal gas law and, 527–530
integrated rate equation and, 684
mass relationships in, 159–162
of reactions in aqueous solution, 182–189
reaction rates and, 673, 674

storage battery, 911

STP. *See* standard temperature and pressure.

strained hydrocarbons Compounds in which an unfavorable geometry is imposed around carbon, 453

Strassman, Fritz, 1080

strategies, problem-solving, 42

strong acid(s) An acid that ionizes completely in aqueous solution, 133, 768
reaction with strong base, 778
reaction with weak base, 779
titration of, 822–824

strong base(s) A base that ionizes completely in aqueous solution, 133, 768

strong electrolyte A substance that dissolves in water to form a good conductor of electricity, 124

strontium, in fireworks, 281
isotopes of, 101

strontium-90, radioactive half-life, 1072

strontium carbonate, enthalpy of formation, 249

structural formula A variation of a molecular formula that expresses how the atoms in a compound are connected, 68, 445

structural isomers Two or more compounds with the same molecular formula but with

different atoms bonded to each other, 444, 1036
of alcohols, 464
of alkanes, 448
of alkenes, 453

styrene, enthalpy of formation, 247
structure of, 459

styrene-butadiene rubber (SBR), 484

Styrofoam, 481t

Styron, 481t

subatomic particles A collective term for protons, neutrons, and electrons, 51
properties of, 52t

sublimation The direct conversion of a solid to a gas, 223, 606

submicroscopic level Representations of chemical phenomena in terms of atoms and molecules; also called particulate level, 9

subshells, labels for, 285
number of electrons in, 306t
order of energies of, 307

substance(s), pure A form of matter that cannot be separated into two different species by any physical technique, and that has a unique set of properties, 10

substance(s), pure, amount of, 82

substituent groups, common, A-18t

substitution reaction(s), of aromatic compounds, 461

substrate, in enzyme-catalyzed reaction, 702

successive approximations, method of, 739, 783–784

successive equilibria, 846

sucrose, as nonelectrolyte, 125
enthalpy of combustion, 229
half-life of, 691
hydrolysis of, 714
rate of decomposition of, 675
structure of, 473

sugar, dietary Calories in, 229
reaction with silver ion, 157

sulfamate ion, structure of, 438

sulfamic acid, reaction with sodium nitrite, 551

sulfanilic acid, structure of, 808

sulfate ion, orbital hybridization in, 416

sulfide ion, in minerals, 810

sulfide(s), in black smokers, 112
 precipitation of, 128
 roasting of, 1003
 solubility of, 836

sulfur, allotropes of, 65, 1001
 chemistry of, 1003
 combustion of, 245, 728
 compounds with phosphorus, 998
 mining of, *135*
 natural deposits of, 1001

sulfur dioxide, 1003
 electrostatic potential map of, 399
 as Lewis acid, 791
 reaction with calcium carbonate, 891
 reaction with oxygen, 734
 reaction with water, 139

sulfur hexafluoride, 365
 orbital hybridization in, 414
 preparation of, 196

sulfur tetrafluoride, molecular polarity of, 384
 orbital hybridization in, 416

sulfur trioxide, 1003
 decomposition of, 891
 enthalpy of formation, 247

sulfuric acid, 1003
 dilution of, 178
 from sea slug, *772*
 in lead storage battery, 913
 as polyprotic acid, 763
 production of, 1013
  from elemental sulfur, 1004
 properties and uses of, 135
 reaction with hydrazine, 198
 reaction with nickel(II) carbonate, 141
 structure of, 102

sulfuryl chloride, decomposition of, 714, 757

sunscreens, *275*

supercritical fluid A substance at or above the critical temperature and pressure, 577, 609

superoxide ion, 435, 973
 molecular orbital configuration of, 428

superphosphate fertilizer, 155, 1004

supersaturated solution(s) A solution that temporarily contains more than the saturation amount of solute, 620
 reaction quotient in, 844

surface area, of colloid, 643
 reaction rate and, 677

surface density plot, *288*, *382*

surface tension The energy required to disrupt the surface of a liquid, 578
 detergents and, 645

surfactant(s) A substance that changes the properties of a surface, typically in a colloidal suspension, 645

surroundings Everything outside the system in a thermodynamic process, 212, 862
 entropy change for, 872

sweat, cooling by, 573

symbol(s), in chemistry, 10, 12–13

symmetry, molecular polarity and, 383

synthesis gas, 969

system The substance being evaluated for energy content in a thermodynamic process, 212, 862
 entropy change for, 872

systematic names, 451

Système International d'Unités, 25, A-11

talc, 976

tarnish, on silver, 156

tartaric acid, 471t
 as polyprotic acid, *763*
 reaction with sodium hydrogen carbonate, 140

technetium, 303, 1079

technetium-99m, 1085, 1087

Teflon, 481t
 density of, 22

temperature A physical property that determines the direction of heat flow in an object on contact with another object, 211
 change in, heat and, 215
 sign conventions for, 215
 in collision theory, 693, 695
 constant during phase change, 220
 critical, 577
 effect on solubility, 627
 effect on spontaneity of processes, 875
 electromagnetic radiation emission and, 271, *272*
 energy and, 211
 equilibrium constant and, 748
 equilibrium vapor pressure and, 574
 free energy and, 881–884
 gas, volume and, 520
 ionization constant for water and, 765t
 physical properties and, 15, *17*
 reaction rate and, 676
 scales for measuring, 26
 standard, 524

tempering, of steel, 1027

terephthalic acid, structure of, 485

termolecular process A process that involves three molecules, 703

tertiary alcohols, 468

Terylene, 485

testosterone, 1
 synthetic, 58

tetrachloromethane. *See* carbon tetrachloride.

tetrafluoroethylene, dimerization of, 717
 effusion of, 539

tetrahedral electron-pair geometry, orbital hybridization and, *410*, *411*

tetrahedral holes, 596

tetrahedral molecular geometry, 369, 1036
 in carbon compounds, 443–444
 in DNA backbone, 392

tetrahydrogestrinone (THG), 3

thallium, isotopes of, 101

thallium(I) sulfate, reaction with sodium iodide, 197

Thenard, Louis, *169*

thenardite, 169

theoretical yield The maximum amount of product that can be obtained from the given amounts of reactants in a chemical reaction, 168

theory A unifying principle that explains a body of facts and the laws based on them, 6
 atomic. *See* atomic theory of matter.
 kinetic-molecular, 8, 532–537, 555
 quantum. *See* quantum mechanics.

thermal energy, 210

thermal equilibrium A condition in which the system and its surroundings are at the same temperature and heat transfer stops, 213

thermite reaction, *147*, 166

thermodynamics The science of heat or energy flow in chemical reactions, 209, 862
 first law of, 211, 222–226, 862
 second law of, 863
 third law of, 868

thermometer, mercury, *211*

thermophilic bacteria, 16

thermoplastic polymer(s) A polymer that softens but is unaltered on heating, 478

thermosetting polymer(s) A polymer that degrades or decomposes on heating, 478

Thiobacillus ferrooxidans, 1028

thiocyanate ion, linkage isomers containing, 1037

thionyl chloride, 337

thioridazine, 205

third law of thermodynamics The entropy of a pure, perfectly formed crystal at 0 K is zero, 868

Thompson, Benjamin, Count Rumford, 213

Thomson, Joseph John, 51, 342

Thomson, William (Lord Kelvin), 27

thorium, radioactive decay of, 344

three-center bond, 984

thymine, 348, 392
 hydrogen bonding to adenine, 565

thyroid gland, imaging of, 1087
  treatment of hyperthyroidism, 1089
thyroxine, 1006, 1089
tin, density of, 44
tin(II) chloride, aqueous, electrolysis of, 935
tin iodide, formula of, 93
tin(IV) oxide, 1017
titanium, density of, 44
  in memory metal, 1018
titanium(IV) chloride, reaction with water, 201
  synthesis of, 155
titanium(IV) oxide, 1004
  as pigment, 1020
  quantitative analysis of, 171
  reaction with carbon, 892
titrant The substance being added during a titration, 823
titration A procedure for quantitative analysis of a substance by an essentially complete reaction in solution with a measured quantity of a reagent of known concentration, 183–185
  acid–base, 183, 821–832
  curves for, 823, 825
  oxidation–reduction, 188-189
Tollen's test, 157
toluene, structure of, 458
tonicity, 639
torr A unit of pressure equivalent to one millimeter of mercury, 516, A-8
Torricelli, Evangelista, 516
tracer, radioactive, 1086
trans-esterification reaction, 479
trans-fats, 476
transition, *d*-to-*d*, 1046
transition elements Some elements that lie in rows 4 to 7 of the periodic table, comprising scandium through zinc, yttrium through cadmium, and lanthanum through mercury, 66, 1018–1059
  atomic radii, 320, *321*
  cations formed by, 72
  commercial production of, 1025–1028
  electron configuration of, 315, 317, 1021

naming in ionic compounds, 77
  oxidation numbers of, 1021
  properties of, 1019–1025
transition state The arrangement of reacting molecules and atoms at the point of maximum potential energy, 694
translation, A-7
  of RNA, 506
transmittance (T) The ratio of the amount of light passing through the sample to the amount of light that initially fell on the sample, 190
transmutation, 1077. *See also* nuclear reaction(s).
transport proteins, 509
transuranium elements Elements with atomic numbers greater than 92, 1078
travertine, 16
trenbolone, 3
trichlorobenzene, isomers of, 460
trigonal-bipyramidal electron-pair geometry, orbital hybridization and, *410*, 414
trigonal-bipyramidal molecular geometry, 369
  axial and equatorial positions in, 372
trigonal-planar electron-pair geometry, orbital hybridization and, *410*, 413
trigonal-planar molecular geometry, 369
  in carbon compounds, 443
trigonal-pyramidal molecular geometry, 370
triiodide ion, orbital hybridization in, 416
trimethylamine, 789
  structure of, 798
trimethylborane, dissociation of, 757
triple bond A bond formed by sharing three pairs of electrons, one pair in a sigma bond and the other two in pi bonds, 354
  valence bond theory of, 419
triple point The temperature and pressure at which the

solid, liquid, and vapor phases of a substance are in equilibrium, 607
tritium, 54, 968, 1093
  fusion of, 1082
trona, 974
T-shaped molecular geometry, 372
tungsten, enthalpy of fusion of, 604
  melting point of, 1020
  unit cell of, 613
tungsten(IV) oxide, reaction with hydrogen, 155
turquoise, 810
  density of, 21
Tyndall effect The scattering of visible light caused by particles of a colloid that are relatively large and dispersed in a solvent, 643

U.S. Anti-Doping Agency (USADA), 1, 58
U.S. Environmental Protection Agency (EPA), 96
U.S. Food and Drug Administration (FDA), 188, 215
ultraviolet catastrophe, 272
ultraviolet radiation, 270
  skin damage and, *275*
uncertainty principle. *See* Heisenberg's uncertainty principle.
unimolecular process A process that involves one molecule, 703
unit cell(s) The smallest repeating unit in a crystal lattice, 590
  number of atoms in, 592
  shapes of, *591*
unit(s), of measurement, 25–29, 516
  SI, 25, A-11
universe, entropy change for, 872
  total energy of, 211
unpaired electrons, paramagnetism of, 292
unsaturated compound(s) A hydrocarbon containing double or triple carbon–carbon bonds, 456
unsaturated solution(s), reaction quotient in, 844
uracil, structure of, 402, 809

uranium(VI) fluoride, synthesis of, 155
uranium, fission reaction of, 1080
  isotopes of, 1060
  isotopic enrichment, 1080
  isotopic separation of, 540, 1008
  radioactive series from, 1064
uranium-235, fission of, 1080
uranium-238, radioactive half-life, 1072
uranium hexafluoride, 540, 1008, 1024
uranium(IV) oxide, 110
uranyl(IV) nitrate, 1059
urea, 789
  conversion to ammonium cyanate, 718
  production of, 201
  structure of, 397
  synthesis of, 155
uric acid, 789
urine, phosphorus distilled from, 997

valence bond (VB) theory A model of bonding in which a bond arises from the overlap of atomic orbitals on two atoms to give a bonding orbital with electrons localized between the atoms, 405–422
valence electron(s) The outermost and most reactive electrons of an atom, 311, 349–351
  Lewis symbols and, 351
  of main group elements, 964
valence shell electron pair repulsion (VSEPR) model A model for predicting the shapes of molecules in which structural electron pairs are arranged around each atom to maximize the angles between them, 368
valency, 341
valeric acid, 472t
van der Waals, Johannes, 543
van der Waals equation A mathematical expression that describes the behavior of nonideal gases, 543

PHYSICAL AND CHEMICAL CONSTANTS

Avogadro's number $N = 6.0221415 \times 10^{23}/mol$
Electronic charge $e = 1.60217653 \times 10^{-19}$ C
Faraday's constant $F = 9.6485338 \times 10^{4}$ C/mol electrons
Gas constant $R = 8.314472$ J/K $\cdot$ mol
  $= 0.082057$ L $\cdot$ atm/K $\cdot$ mol

π $\pi = 3.1415926536$
Planck's constant $h = 6.6260693 \times 10^{-34}$ J $\cdot$ sec
Speed of light $c = 2.99792458 \times 10^{8}$ m/sec
(in a vacuum)

USEFUL CONVERSION FACTORS AND RELATIONSHIPS

Length
SI unit: Meter (m)
1 kilometer = 1000 meters
  = 0.62137 mile
1 meter = 100 centimeters
1 centimeter = 10 millimeters
1 nanometer = 1.00×10^{-9} meter
1 picometer = 1.00×10^{-12} meter
1 inch = 2.54 centimeter (exactly)
1 Ångstrom = 1.00×10^{-10} meter

Mass
SI unit: Kilogram (kg)
1 kilogram = 1000 grams
1 gram = 1000 milligrams
1 pound = 453.59237 grams = 16 ounces
1 ton = 2000 pounds

Volume
SI unit: Cubic meter (m^3)
1 liter (L) = 1.00×10^{-3} m^3
  = 1000 cm^3
  = 1.056710 quarts
1 gallon = 4.00 quarts

Energy
SI unit: Joule (J)
1 joule = 1 kg $\cdot$ m^2/s^2
  = 0.23901 calorie
  = 1 C $\times$ 1 V
1 calorie = 4.184 joules

Pressure
SI unit: Pascal (Pa)
1 pascal = 1 N/m^2
  = 1 kg/m $\cdot$ s^2
1 atmosphere = 101.325 kilopascals
  = 760 mm Hg = 760 torr
  = 14.70 lb/in^2
  = 1.01325 bar
1 bar = 10^5 Pa (exactly)

Temperature
SI unit: kelvin (K)
0 K = -273.15 °C
K = °C + 273.15°C
? °C = (5 °C/9 °F)(°F $-$ 32 °F)
? °F = (9 °F/5 °C)(°C) + 32 °F

LOCATION OF USEFUL TABLES AND FIGURES

Atomic and Molecular Properties

Atomic electron configurations	Table 7.3
Atomic radii	Figures 7.8, 7.9
Bond dissociation enthalpies	Table 8.9
Bond lengths	Table 8.8
Electron affinity	Figure 7.11, Appendix F
Electronegativity	Figure 8.11
Elements and their unit cells	Figure 13.5
Hybrid orbitals	Figure 9.5
Ionic radii	Figure 7.12
Ionization energies	Figure 7.10, Table 7.5

Thermodynamic Properties

Enthalpy, free energy, entropy	Appendix L
Lattice energies	Table 13.2
Specific heat capacities	Appendix D

Acids, Bases and Salts

Common acids and bases	Table 3.2
Formation constants	Appendix K
Ionization constants for weak acids and bases	Table 17.3, Appendix H, I
Names and composition of polyatomic ions	Table 2.4
Solubility guidelines	Figure 3.10
Solubility constants	Appendix J

Miscellaneous

Charges on common monatomic cations and anions	Figure 2.18
Common polymers	Table 10.12
Oxidizing and reducing agents	Table 3.4
Selected alkanes	Table 10.2
Standard reduction potentials	Table 20.1, Appendix M